HANDBOOK OF PHOTOGRAPHY

HANDBOOK OF
PHOTOGRAPHY

Edited by

KEITH HENNEY
Editor, Photo Technique

and

BEVERLY DUDLEY
Managing Editor, Photo Technique

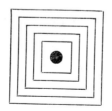

New York WHITTLESEY HOUSE *London*

McGRAW-HILL BOOK COMPANY, INC.

PUBLISHED BY WHITTLESEY HOUSE

A division of the McGraw-Hill Book Company, Inc.

Printed in the United States of America by The Maple Press Co., York, Pa.

PREFACE

The literature on photography abounds with books devoted to the elementary or purely artistic phases of the subject. Few books are devoted to the serious aspects of the technique of the photographic process or to the scientific basis underlying photography and its applications, and most of these treat only of some restricted branch of photography.

This "Handbook of Photography" was born of the desire of the editors to possess for their own use a comprehensive, authoritative reference work on photography and its technical and scientific applications—a reference text having the directness, rigor, and authority which might be found, for example, in the various engineering handbooks.

A number of workers in the photographic field, selected for their specialized knowledge, have cooperated in the preparation of material for this handbook. The work of the editors has been largely that of planning, organizing, and editing the individual manuscripts for each chapter, as well as of organizing the book as a whole.

The editors wish to express their appreciation to Richard S. Morse of the Eastman Kodak Co. and to Dr. Charles J. Smalley for the critical reviewing of several manuscripts included in this volume. Several of the illustrations are reproduced through the courtesy of the Bausch and Lomb Optical Co., the Eastman Kodak Co., and Julius Springer.

K. H.
B. D.

CONTENTS

LIST OF CONTRIBUTORS

Paul L. Anderson, E. E., photographer, writer, lecturer. East Orange, N. J. Special Printing Processes.

D. Burchan, Paper Testing Department, Agfa Ansco Corp., Binghamton, N. Y. Toning of Photographic Papers.

V. Bush, Eng. D., D. Sc., President, Carnegie Institution of Washington, Washington, D. C. Stereoscopic Photography.

O. O. Ceccarini, consulting engineer, Metro-Goldwyn-Mayer Pictures, Culver City, Calif. Color Photography.

Walter Clark, Ph. D., technical assistant to Vice-President in Charge of Research, Eastman Kodak Co., Rochester, N. Y. Infrared and Ultraviolet Photography.

R. F. Collins, A. B., A. M., Department of Geology, Smith College, Northampton, Mass. Geologic Photography.

Alan A. Cook, A. B., Scientific Bureau, Bausch and Lomb Optical Co., Rochester, N. Y. Shutters.

Ira B. Current, Paper Testing Department, Agfa Ansco Corp., Binghamton, N. Y. Toning of Photographic Papers.

Carl Dreher, B. S., Consulting Engineer, Hollywood, Calif. Motion-picture Photography.

Beverly Dudley, B. S., Managing Editor, *Photo Technique;* Associate Editor, *Electronics,* McGraw-Hill Publishing Company, Inc., New York. Outline of Photography; Photographic Sensitometry; Exposure and Exposure Meters; Light Filters; Fixing, Washing, and Drying; Defects in Negatives and Prints; Intensification and Reduction; Appendices.

Harold E. Edgerton, Sc. D., Department of Electrical Engineering, Massachusetts Institute of Technology, Cambridge, Mass. High-speed Photography.

Leon T. Eliel, Vice-President, Fairchild Aerial Surveys, Los Angeles, Calif. Aerial Photography.

George R. Harrison, Ph. D., Department of Physics, Massachusetts Institute of Technology, Cambridge, Mass. Spectroscopic Photography.

Keith Henney, M. A., Editor, *Photo Technique;* Editor, *Electronics,* McGraw-Hill Publishing Company, Inc., New York. Outline of Photography; Cameras; Printing Processes; Darkrooms and Darkroom Methods.

R. Kingslake, M. Sc., Associate Professor of Optics, University of Rochester, Rochester, N. Y. Optics of Photographic Lenses; The Photographic Objective.

F. F. Lucas, Hon. D. Sc., member of technical staff, Bell Telephone Laboratories, New York. Photomicrography and Technical Microscopy.

Haywood Parker, M. Sc., Service Department, Eastman Kodak Co., Rochester, N. Y. Photographic Materials.

John T. Rule, S. B., Division of Drawing, Massachusetts Institute of Technology, Cambridge, Mass. Stereoscopic Photography.

Harlan T. Stetson, M. Sc., Ph. D., cosmic terrestrial research, Massachusetts Institute of Technology, Cambridge, Mass. Astronomical Photography.

J. R. Weber, M. Sc., Ch. E., Du Pont Film Manufacturing Company, Parlin, N. J. Developers and Theory of Development; Technique of Development.

Deane R. White, Ph. D., Du Pont Film Manufacturing Company, Parlin, N. J. Developers and Theory of Development; Technique of Development.

A. T. Williams, Engineering Department, Weston Electrical Instrument Corp., Newark, N. J. Exposure and Exposure Meters.

Robert C. Woods, physicist, National Testing Laboratories, Inc., Rochester, N. Y. Radiography.

HANDBOOK OF PHOTOGRAPHY

CHAPTER I

OUTLINE OF PHOTOGRAPHY

By Keith Henney and Beverly Dudley

Present Status of Photography.—The fact that vision is the sense upon which we depend most in arriving at our ideas and conclusions of the exterior world is probably the reason why visual representations have always been so important in conveying intelligence between people. Crude drawings and sketches, for the purpose of imparting ideas, certainly antedate the written word and probably also the more refined elaborations of the spoken word, and they still find application. Orthographic projections, isometric perspective drawings, and symbolic or graphical representations, usually technical in character, are later developments of the first crude factual type of drawings. A totally different type of intelligence conveyance, in which aesthetics and the appreciation of the beautiful play a dominant part, has been developed in the various methods of painting, drawing, and the graphic arts. All these powerful methods of conveying intelligence—be it factual data or a desire to point out the beautiful in nature—depend for their success upon the interpretation of results through our visual sense. All of them make use of light as the common factor.

With the introduction of practical photographic processes beginning about 1837, a new, accurate, and relatively rapid means of portraying visual sensations became possible. At first these photographic processes were slow, cumbersome, and were infrequently employed, at least judged by present standards. But the results that could be obtained in the hands of skilled workers were quite remarkable. With the introduction of dry plates and roll film in the latter part of the nineteenth century, considerable impetus was given to photography. It became possible to use photographs to replace hand drawings for purposes of illustration in reading matter. Pictures could be made, relatively quickly, of many things for which a graphical record was desired. A new field of artistry became possible, although even now there are some who refuse to admit the artistic possibilities of photographic methods. The introduction of the film rather than the glass plate as a base for the photographic emulsion made possible the motion pictures and aided the adoption of photography as a hobby by a vast army of amateur photographers.

More recently, the introduction of high-speed film materials having good color sensitivity throughout most, if not all, of the visible spectrum and the wide acceptance of high precision cameras of miniature size produced a public "picture consciousness" which has been considerably strengthened in the last decade. This has resulted in, or perhaps it would be more precise to say that this has been associated with, considerable improvements in the graphic arts. Magazines, books, and newspapers are better illustrated than ever before, and there are more illustrations used in them. Since about 1935 or 1936 a number of publications have appeared which have been almost completely devoted to the pictorial representation of current events. Indeed

1

the effectiveness of pictures is so great that a large portion of newspaper readers, at least in the large metropolitan areas, form their opinions and biases through pictures rather than through the written word, and there is some doubt as to whether the users of such printed matter can truly be called "readers."

The universal appeal of pictorial representations, the wide applicability of photography to practically any and every activity directly or as an important adjunct, and the high quality and reliability of photographic equipment, together with its relative "foolproofness," have enabled even the youngest tyro to obtain recognizable pictures. Yet, in its more advanced forms, photography presents a challenge to the best artist, or scientific worker, or serious amateur. Because there is no field in which photography may not be used, it has an appeal which is perhaps more universal than any other hobby, so far as the amateur is concerned. The applications of modern photography are without number.

The most common field of photography is probably the motion-picture field. Each week millions of persons in the United States obtain entertainment, education, and emotion from motion pictures. The motion-picture industry is one of the largest in this country, and it affects the lives of all of us to such an extent that little further comment need be made on this subject.

Press photography is perhaps the next most important field affecting the greatest number of persons. Not only is it possible for the press photographer to supply his local paper with pictures of neighboring events but, because of the assistance which electrical science has rendered press photography, it is also possible to transmit photographs over a telephone circuit to any two points between which telephone communication exists. The publication of pictures of football games while the game is still in progress, even in cities far removed from that in which the game is played, has become so commonplace within the past several years as to occasion no particular comment. Indeed, one now looks for pictures of important events very shortly after they have transpired, and the large paper which does not supply this service is likely to be regarded as not being "up on its toes."

Although still employing other methods of pictorial presentation, modern advertising is using photography in increasing doses. Many examples of this type of commercial photography have high artistic merit and show much originality.

In other ways photography is used in science, engineering, medicine, law, education, and other professions and trades for establishing recorded data, for making observations and securing more or less quantitative data than would be possible through the use of the human eye only. X-ray photographs, for example, are of inestimable importance, not only in the medical sciences where they had their first appearance, but also in industrial analysis for the detection of flaws and other defects in metals. Infrared plates have permitted taking photographs of objects invisible to the human eye. High-speed photographs have apparently slowed down motion to enable studies to be made of fast-moving objects. In astronomy practically all present-day work is accomplished through the aid of photography, the astronomer seldom looking through the telescope for purposes of observation. Photographs taken in the stratosphere, with the aid of infrared plates, have shown the curvature of the earth. Through the aid of aerial mapping, photography is used to survey, quickly and accurately, large areas which might otherwise not be surveyed because of cost and inaccessibility. Photomicrography is important to the research worker in recording the microscopic, whether his field be foods, textiles, metallurgy, medicine, biology, chemistry, or what not.

Color photography is just beginning to make its appearance in practical form. Although color photography may be said to have had its origin in 1861 with the work of Maxwell, it is only within the past few years that high-quality color motion pictures have been available. Color photography for the amateur is gradually approaching, for already it is possible for him to purchase color film and make his own transparencies. Making prints in color from this color film or from color-separation negatives is still such a complicated and costly process that relatively few amateurs have attempted this field. But, in time, color processes will undoubtedly be developed into such a form that the average amateur can make complete use of color. Black-and-white prints may then be expected to be seen only in exceptional cases or where the utmost economy must be effected.

In practically every phase of industry, photography is employed at the present time. It is impossible to enumerate the various uses to which photography may be put, but perhaps enough has already been written to indicate its importance. What has been accomplished in the past provides a background by which we may make some type of estimate of the developments yet to come.

Elementary Photographic System in Monochrome.—All modern photographic processes depend for their operation upon the photochemical action which takes place when "light" strikes certain sensitized materials. In the vast majority of cases which are referred to as photographic processes, the photosensitized material consists of a thin layer or emulsion of a silver halide deposited on a transparent supporting base of glass, nitrocellulose gelatin, or paper. A photochemical change occurs in the silver halide grains which are exposed to light, although the exact nature of this alteration has not yet been entirely satisfactorily explained. Exposure of the grains of the silver halide produces a "latent image" of the object focused on the photographic material by a lens system. With the proper chemical processing operations, the exposed grains of silver salt are changed to metallic silver, and the unexposed grains are dissolved out of the emulsion. Since the silver grains are opaque when viewed by transmitted light, the light portions of the original image become dark, and the dark portions of the original object become more or less transparent. Thus the light and dark portions of the original object have been reversed, and for this reason the combination of the developed silver grains on their support of glass or gelatin is known as a negative.

If we now use this negative, in conjunction with a light source, as a new image and go through another similar photographic process, we can obtain on a glass plate, gelatin film, or, more usually, a paper base, another image. However, this second image will be reversed in intensity from that of the first negative; it will be a negative of a negative, and will therefore show bright and dark areas in monochrome in accordance with the original image.

This is the essence of the more common black-and-white photography. The details of the various operations will be dealt with in subsequent chapters of this book, but a brief introduction of the essential operations will be given in this chapter to provide a certain degree of unity and coherence which could not otherwise be obtained in a reference volume such as this handbook.

Light Source.—To actuate the photographic plate, the light source which is to be used must produce some radiation in the spectral region in which the sensitized plate is sensitive. All usual photographic materials are most sensitive in the blue end of the visible spectrum. Those photographic materials which are sensitive only to the blue end of the visible spectrum are usually known as "ordinary" or color-blind materials, indicating that their sensitiveness does not extend through the complete visual spectrum. Orthochromatic materials are sensitive in the blue, green, and, more or less, the yellow portions but are insensitive to the orange and red regions of the visible spectrum. Panchromatic materials are sensitive to all portions of the visible spectrum but still are more sensitive to the blue than red. Therefore, so far as the light source is concerned, almost any source of visible light can be used with panchromatic materials. Since incandescent light sources have the predominance of their energy in the red region, the exposure time required with such a source may be greater with orthochromatic materials than with panchromatic materials. With color-blind materials and incandescent lamps, the exposure time will be still further increased. When using orthonon emulsions it may be desirable to use a light source having a large portion of its energy in the blue end of the visible spectrum. This may be accomplished by using mercury-arc lamps.

Photography by Reflected Light.—Although the source of light provides the radiant energy which actuates the photosensitive material, it is not the image of the light source which it is usually desired to record photographically. It is almost the universal procedure, except in special branches of photography, to record the image of some object which is illuminated by the light source. The light reflected from the subject and falling on the photographic sensitized material produces the latent image. Since this is usually the case, the reflection characteristics of the subject to be photographed are just as important as the spectral characteristics of the light source or the photographic material.

All materials behave with respect to light in three distinct ways: they may reflect, absorb, or transmit light. There are no perfect absorbing, reflecting, or transmitting mediums, and, in general, all three characteristics take place at the same time and under the same conditions. A given medium, however, may show one of these three properties to a very large extent and the other properties to a very small extent. Consequently we refer to the medium in terms of the characteristic which it exhibits predominately.

The reflectance of a surface depends upon the nature of its surface as regards smoothness and polish, its color, and even the type and relative position of the light source with which it is used. A nonselective reflecting surface is one which changes the direction of the light rays of all wavelengths reaching it instead of absorbing them. A colored reflecting surface is one in which the amount of reflection is not uniform throughout the visible spectrum. A blue surface reflects blue light and shows more or less absorption in the other portions of the visible spectrum; a purple surface shows relatively high absorption in the yellow region and comparatively large reflection in the blue and red ends of the visible spectrum.

Lens and Focusing System.—In order that the illuminated subject may form a plane, two-dimensional image on the photographic film it is necessary that the outline, contrast, surface configurations, and other visual characteristics of the real subject be represented properly on the photosensitive material. This requires the use of a lens and focusing system of which the primary purpose is to focus the subject properly on the photosensitive material. The degree to which the latent image is produced is directly proportional to the amount of light falling upon the photosensitive material and the length of time of exposure. Therefore, if more light can be transmitted through the lens and can be made to fall on the plate, a shorter exposure will suffice to produce a given photographic effect.

The optical system of the camera depends to a large extent upon the type of photography which is to be accomplished. For astronomical photography, for example, the lens system would be a telescope; for spectroscopic photography a prism or grating forms an important part of the optical system; for photomicrography a microscope is essential; whereas for ordinary amateur photography, a single lens not highly corrected may suffice. For most types of photographic work, the lens system should have certain particular characteristics and attributes, which will be discussed in greater detail in Chap. II but which will be mentioned here.

In general, what is desired in most photographic applications is that the image on the photosensitive plate be an accurate two-dimensional reproduction of the three-dimensional subject as might be seen with one eye of the observer were it placed at the same position as the camera lens.

Briefly, it may be said that photographic lens systems differ from other lens systems in that they cover a wide angle of view. Telescopes, microscopes, and other objectives cover a field of view of perhaps 5 or 10°. A photographic lens system usually covers a field of view of 45 to 60°; in wide-angle photography the field of view may extend to 90 or 135°, and an extreme case has been recorded in which the field of view was as great as 180°. Throughout this large range of view, the lens system must be properly corrected for all forms of distortion, and all spectral colors must be in focus on the same plane simultaneously. Moreover, provision must be made for focusing the image on the photographic plate, although, in the simpler and less expensive cameras for amateur use, the lens is fixed once and for all to take pictures with reasonable sharpness of focus from infinity to some distance (usually between 6 and 20 ft.) near the camera.

Shutter.—The shutter in cameras consists of an aperture of some sort through which light from the image and lens passes on its way to the photographic plate. The function of the shutter is to act as a light chopper, *i.e.*, to open for a length of time sufficient to permit a definite quantity of light to fall upon the plate, thereby producing a latent image. The amount of time during which the shutter is open and permits the passage of light to the film depends upon the intrinsic brightness of the illuminated subject, the "speed" of the lens system, whether or not there is motion taking place in the subject being photographed, and, if so, the speed of the object, the distance of the object from the lens, and the direction of relative motion with respect to the lens, as well as upon the speed or sensitivity of the photosensitive material. The exposure is definitely associated with the "speed" of the lens, the intrinsic brightness of the illuminated subject, and the duration of time for which the open shutter permits light to pass through the lens to the photographic plate.

Various types of shutters are made at the present time, and each of these has its own peculiar characteristics, advantages, and disadvantages. There is no single shutter which, under all conditions, will provide ideal light-chopping conditions. Therefore, under certain circumstances, distortion of the photographed image will be apparent, or various portions of the photographic plate will not be uniformly exposed, thereby producing distortion by improper rendition of tone values.

Photographic Sensitive Materials.—The most important component of the entire photographic process, and the one which alone makes photography possible, is the sensitive plate or film; all other equipment, no matter how useful, is supplementary and of no avail without the photographically sensitive material. The characteristics of photographic sensitive materials will be discussed in greater detail in Chap. VI. If true tonal rendition is to be achieved in monochromatic photography, the amount of silver deposit on the negative should be exactly proportional to the intensity of illumination of the subject being photographed. The brightness range of most ordinary subjects is not usually greater than 100 to 1 and this range can generally be accommodated by average photographic negative materials. Where the silver deposit of the negative is not proportional to the illumination intensity of the subject being photographed, some tonal distortion will occur. Tonal distortion may also take place in printing the paper positive from the negative, so that for accurate tone reproduction both the negative and the print must have their exposure factors timed (other factors also enter into the matter but will be discussed in detail later) properly to produce a final result (print) having the same luminous visual intensity variations as the original subject.

Camera as an Integrated Unit.—The camera shown diagrammatically in Fig. 1 is the device which contains the various essential mechanical and optical elements for making the negative. Essentially it is a lighttight box holding the negative film or plates upon which the image is impressed. At the other end of the lighttight box is the lens and focusing system. The shutter may be before, behind, or between the elements of a complicated lens system, or in focal-plane shutters it may be immediately next to the photosensitive material. In addition to these essential elements, the camera is provided with a variety of semiessential and highly convenient features and adjustments. These include focusing rack and pinion arrangements; methods of aligning or misaligning the lens, with respect to the plate, for producing or eliminating certain distortions; a ground glass or optical focusing system; provisions for determining the angle of view to which the film will respond; methods for quickly changing from one plate to another; screwheads for attaching to tripod supports, view finders, range finders, etc.

The various types of work which are attempted make it desirable to put emphasis on certain features, perhaps at the expense of other features, for specialized branches of photography. For this reason a wide variety of cameras of different construction

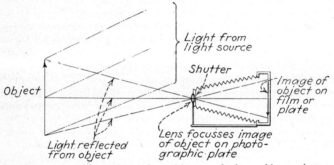

Fig. 1.—Diagram of camera focused on object, ready for making a photograph.

is available. Each of these has its own field of maximum utility, but no single type of camera is ideally suited to all types of photography. Large studio-type cameras with a wide variety of adjustments which can be made quickly and conveniently are frequently used when large prints of high detail are required. But these cameras are bulky. The miniature camera which has become so popular within the past decade is admirably adapted to rapid-fire picture taking, is eminently suited to candid photography. Its negatives are subject to deleterious effects of grain, scratches, and other negative imperfections, as the print must be enlarged to be useful. Miniature cameras do not have adjustments for eliminating angular or perspective distortion. For photography in which action plays a large part, the reflex type of camera is very popular since it enables the operator to view the subject up to the moment of taking the picture, and to center properly the most important action. The focal-plane shutters of these reflex cameras are sufficiently fast to stop motion where a between-the-lens shutter could not be used satisfactorily.

Developing and Fixing.—After the negative material has been exposed and the latent image is impressed on it, it becomes necessary to develop and fix the negative before it can be used to provide a print. The developing process is one in which the silver halide grains which were exposed to light are reduced to metallic silver, the process being carried on in the dark to prevent further exposure or fogging of the negative material. The fixing process dissolves out the undeveloped silver halide grains and leaves the metallic silver unaffected. The fixed negative must be washed to free it from the fixing solution, as otherwise the negative may turn yellow or brown with aging.

Printing.—The final operation is that of making the print by enlarging or contact printing. Like the negative, the exposed print must be developed, fixed, and washed.

Motion-picture Photography.—The differences between still- and motion-picture photography are differences of degree rather than differences of fundamental operation. The same fundamentals are necessary, *viz.*, illumination, lens, camera, sensitive material, and chemical operations of developing, fixing, and printing. One difference is that the individual pictures made are very small compared to those usually employed in still photography. But many miniature cameras make negatives which are only slightly larger than motion-picture frames. The chief difference between still- and motion-picture photography is that in motion-picture work numerous frames are exposed one after the other in rapid succession. One common practice is to make 24 exposures per second.

The prints, which are made on transparent film instead of on paper are viewed by projection upon a screen. When these frames are properly projected upon a screen in rapid succession the photographed subject appears to be in motion. Because of the physiological factor known as the persistance of vision, the human eye does not perceive each individual frame separately as such and is unaware that the motion picture is made up of many discrete frames, none of which record any appreciable motion. The film is projected intermittently, and flicker, due to the stop-start motion of the film through the projection camera, must be overcome. This is accomplished by projecting a fairly large number of frames per second (usually 24) and by projecting each frame twice by momentarily cutting off the light in the middle of the period for which an individual frame is in the light beam.

Amateur motion-pictures cameras employ 16- or 8-mm. film; professional machines use 35-mm. film. Some 8-mm. pictures are made by using 16-mm. film which is capable of recording two images side by side if the film is properly run through the camera twice. In processing this film the two halves are slit apart and the ends joined.

Photography in Colors.—In color photography, a subject is photographed, in effect, three times, each negative produced being made by exposure through a filter which passes approximately one-third of the visible spectrum. If positive prints from these three negatives are properly dyed or otherwise colored and are placed in superposition, a colored image will result. This print will closely resemble the original subject in form, contrast, and in color.

Red, green, and blue-violet filters are used to divide the visible spectrum into three parts for making the three negatives. The negative taken with the red filter contains densities which are proportional to the amount of red present in the original subject and which are passed by the red filter. Wavelengths corresponding to blue-violet and green are not passed by the red filter but are passed on to the negatives exposed behind the blue-violet and green filters, respectively. The process of making negatives from light corresponding to only a portion of the visible spectrum is known as "separation," and the negatives are known as separation negatives. It is quite likely that four or more divisions of the spectrum could be made with the possibility of greater fidelity in color of the final result, but this has not been found to be necessary.

At the present time there are two general methods of color photography, the additive and the subtractive methods. Both of them are based on the fundamental necessity of making color-separation negatives.

In the additive-color process the separation negatives may be made as outlined above. Black-and-white prints made from these negatives on transparent material (films or plates) may be placed in three projection lanterns and projected upon a screen, each image being accurately registered with the others. The positive print made from the red-filter negative is projected through the red filter; the positive made from the green-filter negative is projected through the green filter; and, finally, the blue-violet-filter positive is projected through the blue-violet filter.

Since the red-filter positive will be transparent where there was red in the subject, the red beam of the lantern will get through the positive and be projected upon the screen. Since, however, no green or blue-violet got through the red filter, these parts of the scene will be represented on the red-filter positive by dense deposits of silver, and none of the red lantern beam will get to the screen. Similarly, the green and blue-violet portions of the subject will be projected upon the screen by the appropriate lanterns.

Present-day color films and plates (except Kodachrome) are based on the additive principle. Between the support and the photosensitive material is placed a myriad of small blue, red, and green filters arranged in a regular or a heterogeneous pattern. The film or plate is exposed with the support side of the structure next to the lens, so that the rays of light reflected from the subject must go through the support and the myriad of filters. Light from a red portion of the subject will get through the red filters and expose the sensitive grains immediately behind the small red filters. Similarly the blue and green portions of the subject are recorded behind their corresponding filters. The material is now developed as a negative. The portions representing color in the original subject are deposits of silver and are more or less opaque. The negative is then bleached which removes these silver deposits and renders the negative transparent in the regions where there was light of the appropriate color in the subject. Next, the film is exposed to white light and developed again. In this process the silver halides, not exposed by the reflected light from the subject and representing portions of the subject which reflected no light, are rendered opaque.

If, therefore, there were no filters in the material, the plate or film would look like any other positive transparency. The small filters, however, are not destroyed by the processing, and light must pass through them before passing through the transparent portion of the positive which represent colored portions of the original subject.

In the subtractive process black-and-white positive prints are made from each of the separation negatives. The opacity of each part of these positives is inversely proportional to the light reflected from portions of the subject in which there was color of the wavelengths transmitted by the filter through which the corresponding negative was made. A heavy silver deposit on the red-filter positive represents a portion of the subject in which there was very little red. Looked at in another way, this heavy silver deposit represents a portion of the subject in which there was considerable nonred. Since white light minus red appears blue-green to the eye, the nonred portions of the positive are colored nonred (blue-green.) By any one of several processes, therefore, the silver deposits in the positives are dyed in colors complementary to those of the filters through which the negatives were made.

Thus the blue-violet-filter positive is colored yellow; the red-filter positive is colored blue-green (cyan); and the green-filter positive is colored magenta. When these three positives are superimposed and viewed by transmitted light or by light reflected from a white support placed under the three superposed positives (paper print), a colored image of the subject appears.

The essential difference between the additive and the subtractive processes is the use of colored light for viewing the additive positives (either from a lantern in projection or from the multitudinous filters which are part of the color material) and the use of white light for viewing the subtractive prints. In the additive processes the final result is made up by the addition of the individual contributions of the several colored images to an unilluminated screen. In the subtractive process, the purpose of the blue-green positive (made from the red-record negative) is to subtract from the white light, by which the result is viewed, the wavelengths that did not exist in the subject. Thus the blue-green positive subtracts blue-green or nonred from the white light. Since white light may be made up of blue-green and its complementary red, the result of subtracting blue-green from a white screen is the same as adding red to an unilluminated screen. Similarly the magenta positive subtracts nongreen from the white light; yellow subtracts nonblue-violet from the white light.

In the final subtractive print, red portions of the subject are represented by yellow and magenta superposed; blue is represented by blue-green and magenta; and green is represented by blue-green and yellow superposed. Where there was no color in the subject, there is no deposit of color on the final print and thus the white light by which the result is viewed passes through the positives unobstructed. Where there was black in the subject, all three colors are superposed in the final print and therefore the result is white light minus magenta, blue-green, and yellow. Since the wavelengths represented by these three colors cover the entire visible spectrum, all wavelengths to which the eye is sensitive are subtracted, and none of the white light is reflected or transmitted to the eye. This portion of the image appears black in consequence.

Since there is always some color in an additive picture but since there may be no color in portions of the subtractive print, the latter is brighter and more contrasty.

Unlike the additive material in which many small filters are a part of the material, Kodachrome is a color film in which the colors come about in another way. Kodachrome is a subtractive material. It is made up of three distinct layers of color material each substantially sensitive to only a portion of the spectrum. As a part of the processing of the film these layers are dyed in colors complementary to the colors they recorded when the exposure was made.

CHAPTER II

THE OPTICS OF PHOTOGRAPHIC LENSES

By R. Kingslake

The Nature and Properties of Light.—In spite of the enormous amount of theoretical and experimental work that has been done on light, its real nature still remains a mystery. The original corpuscular theory of Newton (1643–1727), in which light was supposed to consist of a hail of small discrete particles, was abandoned in favor of the wave theory of Huygens (1629–1695), Young (1773–1829), and Fresnel (1788–1827) because it did not adequately explain the phenomena of polarization, interference, and diffraction. The physical nature of the light waves postulated by Huygens was hotly debated during the nineteenth century, the matter reaching its climax in Maxwell's electromagnetic theory of light (1873). Even this elaborate and comprehensive theory could not explain certain aspects of the photoelectric effect or of the observed spectral distribution in the radiation from a hot body; an attempt to explain these phenomena led Planck (1900) to develop his quantum theory, which is a very elaborated form of corpuscular theory. At the present time, we have the two incompatible theories of light (electromagnetic waves and discrete quanta) in use together, the physicist choosing to adopt whichever theory best fits his experimental conditions.

Fig. 1.—Progress of a wave by means of wavelets.

Fortunately, in discussing lens action we need consider only the simple wave theory of light, without even inquiring into the nature of the hypothetical medium through which the waves are propagated. We call this medium the ether, and we adopt the simple Huygenian assumption that the wave front is propagated by means of wavelets which start from every point on a wave front, their common envelope constituting the new wave front. In Fig. 1 the full line W represents a wave front at any given instant, the wavelets starting out from a number of points are shown, together with the new wave front W' at a later time.

The velocity of light (c) is very high, being about 3×10^{10} cm. per sec. in vacuum, but light travels slower in passing through matter. The ratio of the velocity of light

TABLE I.—Some Typical Approximate Refractive Indices

Substance	Index	Substance	Index
Water	1.33	Fluorite	1.43
Alcohol	1.36	Quartz	1.54
Glycerin	1.46	Crown glass	1.46–1.53
Carbon disulphide	1.63	Flint glass	1.53–1.65
Monobromonaphthalene	1.66	Dense flint glass	1.65–1.92
Methylene iodide	1.74	Diamond	2.42

10

in vacuum to its velocity in a transparent material is called the "refractive index" of the material (see page 12). In practice, however, the refractive index is taken as being the ratio of the velocity of light in air to that in the material, since practically all lenses are used in air and the refractive index of the material relative to air is the really significant figure. The refractive index of air relative to vacuum is about 1.00028. Some other typical refractive indices are given in Table I.

Since light consists of waves of some kind, there must be a wavelength (λ), which is the distance from crest to crest measured along the direction in which the light is traveling; and there must be a definite frequency (ν) or number of waves passing a given point in a second. Furthermore, if c is the velocity of light, then these quantities are related by

$$c = \lambda\nu \tag{1}$$

It is found that the velocity c is about 3×10^{10} cm. per sec., or 186,000 miles per sec., for light of all colors in air, but it is also found that light of any one pure spectral color has a definite frequency ν and hence a definite wavelength λ in air. For light which is visible to the eye, these frequencies are very high, and the wavelengths are very short. Light waves too short to be seen are called ultraviolet and will affect a photographic emulsion or a photoelectric cell; light waves too long to be visible are called infrared, of which the shorter infrared waves up to $\lambda = 0.0012$ mm. can be photographed by means of special infrared-sensitive emulsions.

In Table II are given the approximate limits of the regions in the spectrum which appear to have the colors stated, but it should be remembered that color is a physiological or even a psychological phenomenon and that the colors of natural objects are never pure spectral colors but always more or less broad bands or mixtures of various pure colors. White light consists of a mixture of all the colors of the spectrum.

TABLE II.—APPROXIMATE WAVELENGTH AND FREQUENCY LIMITS OF COLORS IN THE VISIBLE SPECTRUM

Color in the spectrum	Frequency limits, per sec.	Wavelength limits (in air), microns
(Infrared)	Below 4.0×10^{14}	Greater than 0.75
Red	4.0–4.8	0.75–0.63
Orange	4.8–5.0	0.63–0.60
Yellow	5.0–5.2	0.60–0.58
Green	5.2–5.9	0.58–0.51
Blue	5.9–6.5	0.51–0.46
Violet	6.5–7.5	0.46–0.40
(Ultraviolet)	Over 7.5	Below 0.40

In the above table, the wavelength limits are given in microns. The micron (written μ) is equal to one-thousandth of a millimeter. Wavelengths are often expressed in terms of angstrom units ($1\text{Å} = 10^{-4}\ \mu = 10^{-7}$ mm.) or sometimes in millimicrons ($m\mu$). For example, the wavelength of monochromatic sodium light is 5893 Å. or 589.3 $m\mu$ or 0.5893 μ or 0.0005893 mm. This length is approximately 1/50,000 in.

Since the velocity of light is less in glass than in air, it follows that the light waves will become closer together in glass, as indicated schematically in Fig. 2, and hence the wavelength is reduced in glass to the same extent as the velocity. On emerging into air again, both the velocity and the wavelength resume their original values.

Polarized Light.—In ordinary light, the waves are vibrating in every direction, but it has been known for a long time that light reflected off the surface of glass at the correct angle[1] is vibrating in only one plane. Such a light is called polarized light, and has a number of interesting properties. For example, if polarized light vibrating in a horizontal plane is allowed to fall upon a vertical plate of glass at the polarizing angle, the whole of the light will be transmitted, and none of it will be reflected. This latter case is of great use in photography as a means of reducing the specular reflection or "glare" from polished surfaces.

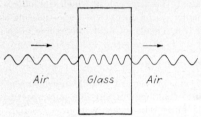

In practice, light is polarized by means of Nicol prisms made of calcite, or by "polaroid" filters. Polaroid is a sheet of plastic material containing certain submicroscopic crystals which transmit only those vibrations taking place in one direction.

Light Rays.—Since the new wave front formed by the Huygenian wavelets is parallel to the original wave front, the light will travel along lines which are everywhere perpendicular to the wave fronts themselves. These lines representing the

Fig. 2.—Passage of light waves through glass and air, showing change in wavelength in passing from one medium to another.

light paths are called "rays," and almost all our discussions of lens action will be on the basis of these rays, even though physically rays have no existence. Rays are the analogue of a railroad track, light quanta being the trains, with the difference that the quanta are in some unknown way accompanied by light waves which spread out on all sides of the ray and cause interference effects with the waves belonging to the neighboring rays. However, since the wavelength of the light is very small, these interference effects cause, in general, only an unimportant fine structure within the light distribution obtained on the assumption that each ray carries its proper share of the total amount of light in the beam. We may therefore say, in general, that where many rays cross there is likely to be a strong concentration of light.

The Law of Refraction.—When a train of light waves falls obliquely on the surface of separation between two different mediums in which the speed of light is different, the parts of the waves which cross the boundary will be accelerated or retarded, causing the waves to take up a new direction in the second medium (Fig. 3).

Considering now the ray path, we find that it is bent at the surface as shown dotted in Fig. 3, the whole phenomenon being known as "refrac-

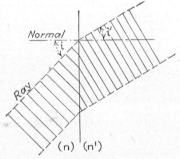

Fig. 3.—The refraction of light.

tion." If the angles between the ray and the normal[2] on left and right of the surface are, respectively, i and i' and if the refractive indices are similarly n and n', then it can be shown that these quantities are related by the equation

$$n \sin i = n' \sin i' \qquad (2)$$

which is the well-known "law of refraction." The two parts of the ray and the normal all lie in one plane called the "plane of incidence." It should be noted that, because

---

[1] This angle of incidence is such that its tangent is equal to the refractive index of the glass.

[2] The "normal" is a line drawn perpendicular to the refracting surface at the point where the ray strikes it.

of the symmetry of Eq. 2, the light may travel along a ray in either direction without changing the refraction conditions

The Action of a Lens.—The action of a lens is illustrated in Fig. 4. If expanding light waves start out from a point source *B* and travel toward a lens, presently one point of the wave will meet the lens, say at *a*. Then from *a* to *c* the light will travel slowly, while the light from *d*, which later reaches the rim of the lens, will continue at its original speed. All the intermediate parts of the wave will travel through some air and some glass, so that by the time the light inside the lens has reached *c*, the light from *d* will have reached *e*, and the emerging wave front will be *ec* as shown. This wave now proceeds onward, and, if the wave happens to be concave as shown, it will shrink to a "focus" at *B'*. We can imagine an ideal lens in which the emerging wave will be spherical, centered about a single point *B'*, but in practice, owing to the limitations imposed by the use of only spherical surfaces and by the limited availability of optical glass types, the emerging wave will generally not be spherical and there will

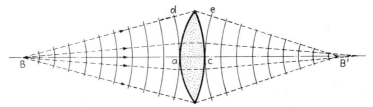

Fig. 4.—Refraction of light waves by means of a lens.

not be a perfect focus at *B'*. In such a case, we say that the lens has "aberrations," the nature of which will be discussed below.

We may, if we wish, discuss the action of this lens by the ray method by drawing the orthogonals (perpendicular lines) to the wave fronts as in Fig. 4. These rays are there shown dotted in, and it is seen at once that for our "ideal" lens all the rays emerging from it will cross at *B'*, whereas if the lens has aberrations, some of the rays will miss *B'* and cause a confused patch of light at *B'* instead of a sharp focus.

Lens Calculations.—For reasons connected with the manufacturing processes at present in use, only spherical or plane refracting surfaces are used in photographic lenses. Some attempts are being made to employ aspherical surfaces, but these are still entirely experimental. It is a comparatively simple matter to calculate the path of a light ray through a lens system, if the radii of curvature of the surfaces, the thicknesses of the successive lenses, and the refractive indices of the glasses are all given. The formulas by which these calculations are made assume a particularly simple form for the special case of a "paraxial" ray, which is a ray lying very close to the optical axis[1] of the lens. For such a ray, if *s*, *s'* are the distances of object and image, (*i.e.*, the crossing points of the ray with the axis) from a single refracting surface of radius *r* separating two mediums having refractive indices *n* and *n'*, then it can be proved that

$$\frac{n'}{s'} = \frac{n}{s} + \frac{n' - n}{r} \tag{3}$$

By applying this formula successively to all the surfaces in a lens, the position of the final image of a given object point can be determined.

The signs in this equation are correct if distances are measured outward from the pole of the surface as origin, and are regarded as positive or negative if to the right or left of the surface, respectively.

[1] The "axis" is defined as the line passing through the centers of curvature of all the lens surfaces.

Focal Length of a Lens.—The above process is a very laborious one, and to simplify it Gauss, about 1841, devised his system of principal and focal points. These are defined as follows: In Fig. 5 is shown a general lens system of any internal construction, such as a photographic objective, and a series of rays from a very distant axial object point is shown entering the left-hand end of the system. These will all emerge from the other end of the lens as a converging beam, as shown, and each ray will evidently possess an "equivalent refracting point" where the entering and emerging portions of the ray intersect. The surface which joins up all these equivalent

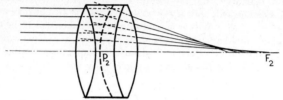

Fig. 5.—The equivalent refracting surface of a lens.

refracting points is called the "equivalent refracting surface" of the lens, and where this crosses the axis is the "second principal point" P_2 of the lens Also, the point at which the innermost rays lying close to the axis cross the axis is called the "second focal point" F_2, the distance from P_2 to F_2 being the focal length of the lens. If rays from a distant object point enter the lens at the right-hand end, there will be another principal point P_1 and another focal point F_1, the distance between them being another focal length. It can be proved that, in any lens whatever, these two focal lengths are equal.[1]

Combination of Two Lenses.—If two lenses of focal lengths f_1 and f_2 are used together in succession, the focal length F of the combination will be given by

$$\frac{1}{F} = \frac{1}{f_1} + \frac{1}{f_2} - \frac{d}{f_1 f_2} \tag{4}$$

where d is the distance between the second principal point of the first lens and the first principal point of the second lens (Fig. 6).

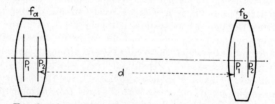

Fig. 6.—A system composed of two separated lenses.

It should be noted that if f_1 and f_2 are both positive, i.e., convex lenses, then increasing their separation will lengthen the combined focal length. On the other hand, if a positive and a negative lens are separated, the focal length of the combination is shortened. In the case when d is equal to f_1, the combined focal length is also f_1, and hence the presence of a second lens in the focal plane of the first lens does not affect the focal length of the first lens. In the limiting case when $d = f_1 + f_2$, the

[1] This statement is incorrect if the image and object happen to be situated in different mediums. The eye and the oil-immersion microscope objective are the only important systems in which this occurs.

power becomes zero and the focal length is infinite. This case represents the common telescope, or the so-called afocal system.

Distances of Object and Image.

1. *From the Principal Points.*—If p, p' are the distances of object and image, respectively, from the first and second principal points of a lens and if f is the focal length, then

$$\frac{1}{p'} = \frac{1}{p} + \frac{1}{f} \tag{5}$$

2. *From the Focal Points.*—If x, x' are the distances of object and image, respectively, from the first and second focal points of a lens, then

$$xx' = -f^2 \tag{6}$$

In both these equations, distances measured to the *left* of their respective focal or principal points must be regarded as negative and distances to the *right* as positive.

Calculation of the Focusing Scale for a Camera.—If the focal length of a camera lens is f, we may use the formula $xx' = -f^2$ to calculate the positions of the divisions on a focusing scale. For if x is the distance from the object to the first focal point of the lens, the distance of the object from the lens is $(f - x)$, and $x' = -\dfrac{f^2}{x}$ is the distance to be marked off from the ∞ mark on the focusing scale. Remember that the sign of x will be negative if the object is to the left of the lens, with the light going from left to right. This procedure applies only in the case of cameras in which the entire lens is moved back and forth to focus it. In some recent cameras only the front element of the lens is adjusted for focusing, and in these cases the correct focusing scale must be determined by computation or by direct trial and error. On account of the variation in the aberrations caused by this method of focusing, the trial-and-error method of constructing a focusing scale is probably the most satisfactory. The advantages of moving only the front lens are (1) greater rigidity is possible in the camera if no sliding front has to be provided and, (2) a very small longitudinal movement of the front lens often produces a very large movement of the final image on the plate.

The Thin Lens.—If a lens is extremely thin, its two principal points fall together within the lens, and we can then measure all our distances from the thin lens instead of from one or other of the principal points. This is often a great assistance in making approximate lens calculations or measurements.

Concave Lenses.—Concave lenses fit into the scheme outlined above for convex lenses, provided we remember that the focal points are interchanged in position (Fig.

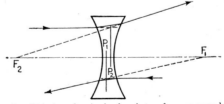

Fig. 7.—Focal and principal points of a concave lens.

7) as compared with a convex lens. This affects the use of the formula $xx' = -f^2$, connecting the distances of object and image from their respective focal points. To use this equation with a concave lens, if the light travels from left to right, x must mean the distance from the object to the first focal point (on the right) and x' is the distance

from the image to the second focal point (on the left). The two principal points fall within the lens as usual, and the focal length is now negative.

The Size of the Image.—The size of an image can be obtained at once if it is remembered that any ray entering toward the first principal point of a lens leaves from the second principal point at the same slope as it enters (Fig. 8). Thus, if an object subtends an angle θ at the first principal point of a lens, the image will subtend the same angle θ at the second principal point. Therefore, if p, p' represent the distances of the object and image from the two principal points, respectively, the magnification will be given by

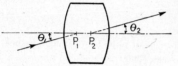

Fig. 8.—Equal slope property of the principal points. In this diagram $\theta_1 = \theta_2$.

$$m = \frac{\text{image size}}{\text{object size}} = \frac{\text{image distance}}{\text{object distance}} = \frac{p'}{p} \qquad (7)$$

If object and image distances are measured from the focal points (x, x'), then the magnification is given by

$$m = -\frac{x'}{f} = \frac{f}{x} \qquad (8)$$

(A negative magnification merely implies an inverted image.) If an object is very distant and subtends an angle θ at the lens, its image will lie in the focal plane and will also subtend an angle θ. Thus the linear size of the image in this case will be equal to $f \tan \theta$.

Telephoto Lenses.—A telephoto lens is a lens having a long focal length but a short "back focal distance," or distance from the rear lens surface to the focal point. The long focal length ensures a large-scale picture, but, since the image is close to the back of the lens, the over-all camera length is kept short. This result is achieved by using a positive front element and a negative rear element, usually of approximately equal focal length, separated by a finite distance. In such a combination (Fig. 9) the

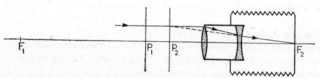

Fig. 9.—The telephoto lens.

two principal points fall in front of the convex element, giving the desired long focal length and short back focus. The focal length of the system can be altered by changing the separation. In the past, many "telenegative" lenses have been designed for use behind an ordinary photographic lens to convert it into a telephoto lens; it is now customary to use only complete telephoto lenses properly designed for the purpose. The ratio of focal length to back focal distance is called the "telephoto magnification."

Longitudinal Magnification.—If an object has a depth q along the lens axis, then its image will have a depth q' along the axis (Fig. 10), where A', B' are, respectively, the images of the object points A, B. Then the ratio q'/q is called the "longitudinal magnification" of the image. It can be shown that, *if q and q' are small*, the longitudinal magnification m' is equal to the square of the ordinary magnification m. Hence in any ordinary camera, where m is generally fairly small, m' is very small, and a considerable range of object distances appear equally in focus on the plate. On the other hand, in photomicrography where the magnification m is high, m' is very high, and only a very thin section of the object appears sharply in focus at a time. In this connection, it should be noted that for a fixed lens, if the object is moved to the right, *the image moves to the right also.*

Fig. 10.—Diagram illustrating longitudinal magnification.

Image of a Sloping Object.—It can be shown that a perfect lens will produce an undistorted image of a plane object set perpendicular to the axis, in a plane also perpendicular to the axis. If the object is plane but is inclined to the axis, then a perfect lens will produce an image on a plane which is also inclined to the axis, but the image will not be perfectly sharp all over. Thus when photographing a sloping object, it is necessary to stop down the lens if a sharp picture is desired. A good rule for the correct arrangement of object, lens, and plate is to ensure that object and image planes meet on the median plane of the lens (Fig. 11). The image will, of course, be badly distorted, but the distortion can be rectified by projection printing from a tilted negative, using a tilted easel to hold the bromide paper.

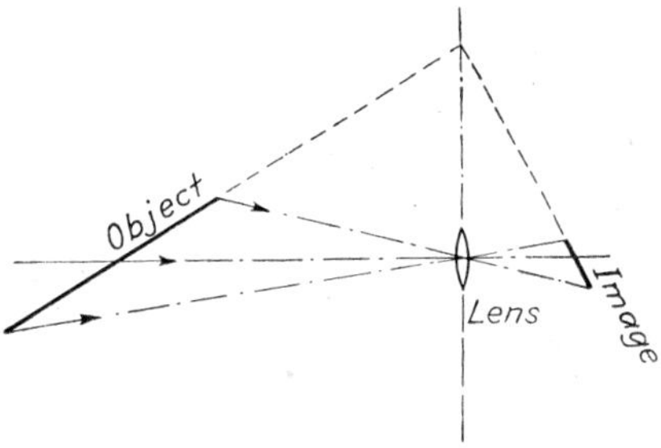

Fig. 11.—Photography of an oblique object.

Measurement of Focal Length of a Camera Lens.—The simplest method is to stand the camera flat upon a table covered with a sheet of paper and to turn it until the image of a distant object falls just at one edge of the picture. A pencil line x (Fig. 12) is then made along one side of the base of the camera, and the camera is rotated on the table until the same distant object just falls at the opposite edge of the picture. Another pencil line y is then drawn along the side of the camera base, and the two lines are produced until they intersect at P. The angle θ between them represents the angular field of the camera corresponding to the particular linear size of the picture used. Hence, by drawing a line across the previous two lines, of length equal to the linear picture dimension D, the focal length f can be at once read off.

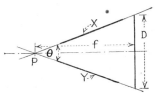

Fig. 12.—Determination of the focal length of a lens.

The focal length can also be measured by a "nodal slide" method. In this, the lens is mounted horizontally on a simple slide over a vertical axis of rotation. The image of a distant object is carefully observed while the lens is turned through a few degrees about the vertical axis, and the lens is then moved back and forth on its slide until no sideways motion of the image is seen during this small rotation. In this case the vertical axis passes through the second principal point of the lens, and the direct distance from the vertical axis to the image gives the focal length (Fig. 13). This follows from the equal-slope property of rays entering toward the first principal point of a lens and leaving from the second.

Limitation of the Beam of Light.—In every lens system, there is some material stop or diaphragm which actually limits the size of the beam of light passing through the system from a given object point. It may be a variable-iris diaphragm, as in a photographic lens, or it may be a lens cell as in a telescope or a projection lens or a microscope objective. By analogy with the eye, this stop is called the "iris" of the system. By further analogy with the eye, the image of the iris as seen from the entrance end of the system is called the "entrance pupil," this pupil being therefore

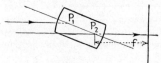

Fig. 13.—Diagram illustrating the nodal slide.

the common base of the cones of rays entering the system from various points in the object plane. Similarly, the image of the iris formed by that part of the lens system lying between the iris and the image is called the "exit pupil," which is thus the common base of all the cones of rays proceeding from the lens to various points in the image. The entrance and exit pupil are evidently images of each other, since they are both images of the iris.

The positions of the iris and the pupils in a symmetrical lens are indicated in Fig. 14, together with a typical beam of light passing through the system from a distant object to the image.

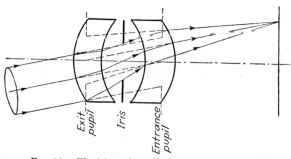

Fig. 14.—The iris and pupils of a symmetrical lens.

The Brightness of Optical Images.—In Fig. 15 is shown a lens represented merely by its two pupils. If the extreme entering ray from an axial object point has a slope θ

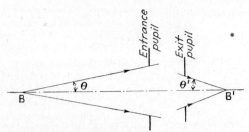

Fig. 15.—Passage of light through a lens.

and the emerging ray a slope θ', then the illumination E (foot-candles) on the photographic plate at B' is given by

$$E = k\pi B \sin^2 \theta' \qquad (9)$$

Here B is the intrinsic brightness of the object (in candles per square foot), and k is the transmission of the lens. "Transmission" is defined as the ratio of the amount of light leaving the lens to the amount entering it and is always less than unity; it will be discussed more fully on page 23.

It should be noted especially that this expression for E does not depend in any way on the distance of the object or on the slope θ of the entering ray but only on the intrinsic brightness of the object and the slope of the *emerging* ray. This is because there is a compensation here between the light-gathering power of the lens and the magnification. Suppose for example the distance of the object shown in Fig. 15 from the first focal point of the lens were reduced to half. The angle θ would be doubled, and the amount of light entering the lens from each little element of the object would become four times as great. But the image would now be twice as large as it was, and hence it would have four times its former area. Thus four times as much light would be spread over an image four times as large, and the resulting *illumination* on the plate would be unchanged.

Relation between Exposure and Aperture Ratio.—The relation between the aperture ratio of a lens and the illumination in the image can be deduced from the consideration that in a perfect lens the equivalent refracting surface ("principal plane") is a sphere centered about the focal point (Fig. 16). Hence, if h is the height of the incident ray above the lens axis, $\sin \theta'$ is approximately equal to (h/f). Now the diameter of the entering beam (the entrance-pupil diameter) is equal to $2h$, hence the "aperture number" or ratio of the focal length to the diameter of the entrance pupil is equal to $f/2h = 1/(2 \sin \theta')$. If this number is represented by A, e.g., $A = 4.5$ for an $f/4.5$ lens, we see that $\sin \theta' = 1/2A$, and hence the image illumination is given by $E = k\pi B/4A^2$ accurately for all apertures up to the very largest. Thus we reach the familiar result that the required exposure is proportional to the brightness of the object and inversely proportional to the square of the f-number and is independent of the distance of the object.

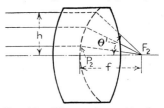

Fig. 16.—The aperture ratio of a perfect lens.

It is also interesting to see that the greatest possible aperture ratio[1] is $f/0.5$, for at this value $\theta' = 90°$ and the extreme ray would just graze the plate. Even this ratio is, strictly speaking, unattainable, for there must be some space between the back of the lens and the image plane.

If the bellows of a camera is extended to focus a near object, then the value of θ' becomes diminished in proportion to the ratio $\left(\dfrac{\text{original-image distance}}{\text{new-image distance}} \right)$, and the exposure required must be divided by the square of this ratio. Thus in changing from a distant object to equal conjugate distances (unit magnification), the aperture numbers must all be doubled, and the exposure made four times as great. If the magnification actually used is m, all marked f-numbers should be multiplied by $(1 + m)$, and exposures by $(1 + m)^2$.

The effect of a change of bellows length on exposure is very small except when the object is quite close to the lens, as may be seen from Table III.

The "Uniform Scale" (U. S.) system of designating the stops in a photographic lens is based on the area of the iris opening rather than its diameter. When it was introduced, $f/4$ was felt to be the limit of large apertures and was called "U. S. 1." Then the other apertures fell as shown in Table IV. This system is now practically obsolete.

---

[1] Bracey has designed a lens for astronomical purposes consisting of a reversed oil-immersion microscope objective, the photographic plate being attached by a layer of oil to the back (plane) surface of the lens. The aperture of this is given as $f/0.36$, such a speed being possible since for an immersion lens of this type, aperture number is defined by $f/2nh$ where n is the index of the oil, say 1.52. Bracey, *Astrophys. J.*, **83**, 179 (1936).

TABLE III.—EFFECT ON EXPOSURE, MAGNIFICATION, AND APERTURE, OF
EXTENDING BELLOWS

Distance between object and lens in multiples of the focal length, f	∞	$100f$	$50f$	$20f$	$10f$	$5f$	$3f$	$2f$	nf
Magnification, m	0	0.01	0.02	0.05	0.11	0.25	0.50	1.0	$\dfrac{1}{n-1} = m$
Multiply f-number by	1	1.01	1.02	1.05	1.11	1.25	1.50	2.0	$(1+m) = \dfrac{n}{n-1}$
Multiply exposure by	1	1.02	1.04	1.11	1.24	1.56	2.25	4.0	$(1+m)^2 = \dfrac{n^2}{(n-1)^2}$
Distance between lens and film, in multiples of focal length	f	$1.01f$	$1.02f$	$1.05f$	$1.11f$	$1.25f$	$1.50f$	$2.0f$	$\dfrac{nf}{n-1} = (1+m)f$
Bellows extension, from infinity position, in terms of focal length	0	$0.01f$	$0.02f$	$0.05f$	$0.11f$	$0.25f$	$0.50f$	$1.0f$	$mf = \dfrac{f}{n-1}$

TABLE IV.—COMPARISON OF METHODS OF SPECIFYING APERTURES

f-number	4	5.6	8	11	16	22
U. S. number	1	2	4	8	16	32

Measurement of Aperture Ratio.—As the aperture ratio is defined as $A = f/D$ where D is the diameter of the entrance pupil, it is necessary to measure f and D separately. The measurement of focal length is given on page 17. The entrance pupil can be measured by means of an ordinary traveling microscope equipped with an objective having a sufficiently long working distance to reach down into the lens as far as the entrance-pupil plane. Alternatively, the emerging parallel beam from a point of light at the focus may be allowed to fall on a piece of photographic printing paper, and the diameter of the disk of light so formed can be measured directly. If the experiment is performed while the lens is mounted upon a nodal slide, both f and D can be determined together.

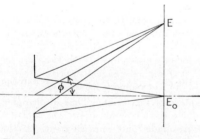

FIG. 17.—Oblique illumination in a camera.

Variation of Illumination over the Image.—The discussion of image illumination given on page 18 refers specifically to the center of the picture. At a field angle ϕ from the lens axis, the illumination will be reduced to $E_0 \cos^4 \phi$, where E_0 is its value on the axis. Two of these cosine terms appear because the oblique-image point is farther from the lens than

TABLE V.—VARIATION OF ILLUMINATION OF PHOTOGRAPHIC PLATE

Angle ϕ from Optical Axis, Degrees	Relative Light Intensity
0	1.000
5	0.984
10	0.941
15	0.870
20	0.780
25	0.675
40	0.344
60	0.062

the axial image point, one cosine is present because the aperture is projected as an ellipse in the outer parts of the field, and the fourth arises from the obliquity of the light as it falls on the plate (Fig. 17). Table V shows the variation in light intensity on the photographic plate for various angles off the optical axis.

The Vignetting Effect.—In addition to the loss of light caused by the $\cos^4 \phi$ law (Table V), in many lenses the mounts cut off oblique pencils more than axial pencils, causing the illumination in the outer parts of the picture to be still less (Fig. 18).

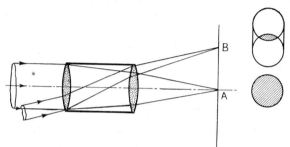

Fig. 18.—Diagram illustrating vignetting effect.

To an eye at A, the lens has a circular aperture, but viewed from B, the aperture is limited by the overlap of two ellipses, as shown at the right of Fig. 18. The combination of the $\cos^4 \phi$ relation with vignetting may produce such a diminution of light that the corners of the photographic print appear dark, and sometimes almost black. The vignetting effect can generally be reduced by stopping the lens down.

The magnitude of the vignetting effect can readily be determined by the arrangement shown in Fig. 19. In this diagram, S represents a lamp and G an opal-glass

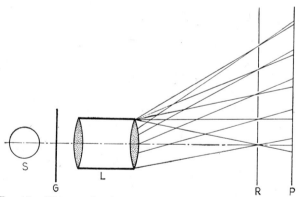

Fig. 19.—Diagram showing the measurement of vignetting effect.

plate before the lens L to be investigated. R is a row of pinholes in a metal screen placed in the focal plane of the lens and near a photographic plate P. Each pinhole in R will project on the plate a picture of the shape of the lens aperture corresponding to the particular point in the field occupied by the pinhole.

The Light Transmission of a Lens.—It might be thought that as a lens is made of glass, its light transmission would be determined only by the transparency of the glass itself. This is unfortunately very far from the case because a surface separating air from a medium of refractive index n reflects back a proportion $[(n - 1)/(n + 1)]^2$

of all light falling on it within 20 or 30° of the normal. This value ranges from 0.04 (4 per cent) for $n = 1.5$ up to 0.067 for $n = 1.7$. Consequently, taking a mean reflecting power of 0.05, the transmission of one glass-air surface is about 0.95, and if a lens has p glass-air surfaces, the over-all transmission will be $(0.95)^p$. Values of this are given in Table VI.

Now most of this reflected light emerges back again through the front of the lens, but 5 per cent of it is again reflected by each surface as the light passes through it, with the result that each double internal reflection causes about 0.25 per cent of the incident light to go back into the camera as unwanted light. If the theory is worked out fully including the effects of further multiple internal reflections, it is found that for light entering the lens along its axis, the total light transmitted is given by the fraction $(1 - r)/[1 + (p - 1)r]$ whereas it was seen above that the useful light is only $(1 - r)^p$. In these formulas r is the fraction reflected at each surface, and p is the number of surfaces. The difference between these two amounts represents the intensity of the unwanted light, which reaches alarming proportions in a lens containing five or six separate elements (see last column, Table VI) and explains why a picture taken by a simple landscape lens in a cheap camera is often much more contrasty than the same picture taken with a complex anastigmat. Each double internal reflection, of course, forms an image of the source somewhere, but as these ordinarily fall very far from the plate, they are recorded as general illumination and not as specific images. However, it does occasionally happen that one or more of these doubly reflected images falls on or nearly on the plate, where it forms a most annoying "ghost image." Ghosts of this type are most likely to occur when photographing a bright object such as the sun or an artificial source of light against a dark background. Occasionally a faint image of the iris itself is formed, after two internal reflections, on or almost on the plate, causing a "flare spot" to appear in the center of the picture.

TABLE VI.—STRAY LIGHT IN LENSES ($r = 0.05$)

Number of glass-air surfaces	Useful light transmitted, per cent	Total light transmitted, per cent	Difference (stray light), per cent	Ratio of unwanted to useful light, per cent
2	90.25	90.48	0.23	0.24
4	81.45	82.61	1.16	1.42
6	73.50	76.00	2.50	3.40
8	66.34	70.37	4.03	6.08
10	59.87	65.52	5.65	9.44
12	54.03	61.29	7.26	13.45

The true transmission of the glass itself sometimes becomes significant, especially in the near ultraviolet region of the spectrum, if extra-dense flint glasses have been included in the lens. This may become noticeable in enlargers used with ordinary developing papers which have a large portion of their sensitivity range in the near ultraviolet part of the spectrum. No fear need be entertained as to the infrared transmission of a lens, for optical glasses transmit to a wavelength of 2.5 μ whereas no photographic plate has yet been made which is sensitive beyond 1.2 μ in the infrared.

Bubbles and scratches in a lens generally act merely as direct obstructions to light and, unless of unusually serious magnitude, are insignificant. However, it should not be forgotten that enough light may be diffracted by a scratch to cause some softening of the contrast. Indeed, some "diffusion attachments" operate on this principle.

Optical Density.—While on the subject of light transmission, it is convenient to introduce the frequently occurring concept of optical density. "Light transmission" is defined as the ratio of the amount of light leaving the system to the amount entering it in the same time. This is a ratio which is rarely greater than 0.9, since that is the transmission of a single lens or plate of glass.

Since the transmissions of plates or other elements passed in succession by a beam of light must be *multiplied* together to yield the over-all transmission, it is more convenient to adopt a logarithmic unit which can be directly *added* for successive transmissions. Such a unit is "optical density," which is defined as log (1/transmission). Thus transmissions of 1, 10, and 50 per cent have densities, respectively, 2.0, 1.0, and 0.301. A transparent clear-glass plate transmitting 90 per cent of the light, has a density of 0.046.

The term "opacity" is sometimes used for the reciprocal of the transmission. Thus a transmission of 50 per cent has an opacity of 2 and a density of $\log_{10} 2$, or 0.301. If several plates are used in succession, their opacities must be multiplied together to get the over-all opacity.

Cleaning a Lens.—Dirt or finger marks on a lens act both as obstructions to light and as diffracting agents which soften definition and contrast. A lens should not be cleaned more than necessary as grit is likely to be harder than glass and indiscriminate wiping may scratch the lens surfaces. Clean chamois leather moistened with alcohol is a good cleanser, followed by the minimum of polishing with a dry chamois leather. Soft tissue paper or specially made lens paper may also be used. A lens should not be taken apart unless absolutely necessary as this will admit dust and dirt which will settle eventually on the inner lens surfaces. Slight decentration may also arise from casual disassembly of a lens.

If a lens has been dropped, it may be found that one of the balsam layers between the elements of a cemented component has started to break apart. In this case the lens should be returned to the makers to be recemented; this is not a job for the user to undertake himself.

Depth of Field.—We have so far supposed that the whole of our object lies in a plane at a fixed distance from the camera and that the image is sharply focused on the plate. If either of these conditions is not fulfilled, we shall, of course, obtain a blurred image. In practice it is found that a certain slight amount of blur is tolerable because it cannot be detected in the final picture, and thus we have a certain determinable "depth of field" for our camera, which is the range over which the object or the photographic plate may be moved along the axis of the lens before the consequent blurring of the picture becomes noticeable. To obtain a quantitative measure of this effect, we consider the passage of the beam of light from a single object point to the corresponding image point. If this image point is out of focus, a "circle of confusion" will be seen on the plate instead of a point of light, and if the diameter of this circle of confusion subtends an angle of a minute of arc or less at the observer's eye, he will be unable to say whether the image is in sharp focus or not.

Now a minute of arc is an angle of 1 in 3400, so that a circle of 0.1-mm. diameter should just be distinguishable as such when viewed at a distance of about 12 in. As this is the normal viewing distance for direct contact prints, a circle of confusion of 0.1-mm. diameter provides the limit of our depth of focus for such cases.

However, when the photographic picture is subsequently enlarged, as occurs in motion pictures for example, it is necessary to adopt a much more stringent criterion of sharpness than 0.1 mm.; indeed, the limit is then fixed by the coarseness of the grain structure in the photographic emulsion. The measured "resolving power" of emulsions runs from 30 lines per millimeter for fast negative emulsions down to 80 lines per millimeter for process plates and lantern plates. Thus we may expect that the minimum discernible circle of confusion over this range of emulsions will be similarly from 0.03 to 0.01 mm. On the average, it is commonly stated that, for the highest definition requirements, a circle of confusion of $\frac{1}{1000}$ in. (0.025 mm.) is permissible, while 0.1 mm. is satisfactory in making direct-contact prints.

Depth of Focus in the Image.—In Fig. 20 is shown the cone of rays from a lens in the neighborhood of an image point. Assuming that the lens is perfectly corrected, this

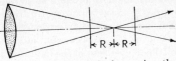

cone will shrink to a point at the best focus, and expand uniformly within and beyond this focus. Evidently, if the plate is situated anywhere in the range for which the expanded beam has a diameter less than that of the permissible circle of confusion c, the image will appear perfectly sharp, whereas outside this range some diffusion

Fig. 20.—Depth of focus in the image.

will be observed. If this range extends to a distance R to each side of the perfect focus, then $R = cA$, where A is the aperture number of the lens. The use of this relationship is chiefly found in determining the precision of focusing necessary in a camera, the permissible degree of nonflatness in films, etc.

Depth of Focus in the Object.—So far as the practical photographer is concerned, the important aspect of depth of focus is the range of distances in the object which will appear substantially in focus on the plate. This is more properly called "depth of field."

If the camera is focused accurately on a certain plane in the object, at a magnification m, then the distance *beyond* the focused plane corresponding to a circle of confusion c on the plate, is given by

$$R_1 = \frac{cs}{md - c} \tag{10}$$

where d is the diameter of the entrance pupil of the lens, and s is the longitudinal distance of the focused object plane from the entrance pupil. Similarly, the depth of focus *within* the focused plane is

$$R_2 = \frac{cs}{md + c} \tag{11}$$

If the object is fairly near the camera, md is large compared to c, and we can write approximately

$$R_1 = R_2 = \frac{cs}{md} \tag{12}$$

As an example in the use of these formulas, suppose we have an $f/4.5$ lens of focal length 100 mm. (4 in.). Then with an object at 10 ft. (3.28 m.) distance and assuming a permissible circle of confusion of 0.1 mm. on the film, we have

$$s = 3280 \text{ mm.}$$

$$d = \frac{100}{4.5} = 22.2 \text{ mm.}$$

$$c = 0.1 \text{ mm.}$$

$$m = \frac{f}{s - f} = \frac{1}{31.8}$$

$$md = 0.70$$

$$R_2 = \frac{328}{0.8} = 410 \text{ mm.} = 16.1 \text{ in.} = 1 \text{ ft. 4 in.}$$

$$R_1 = \frac{328}{0.6} = 546 \text{ mm.} = 21.5 \text{ in.} = 1 \text{ ft. 10 in.}$$

Hence the whole depth of acceptably sharp field would be from 8 ft. 8 in. to 11 ft. 10 in.

By the approximate formula (12) we have

$$R_1 = R_2 = 469 \text{ mm.} = 18.5 \text{ in.} = 1 \text{ ft. } 6 \text{ in.}$$

giving a range from 8 ft. 6 in. to 11 ft. 6 in.

Depth of Focus, Including Enlargement of the Print.—It can easily be shown that if we photograph the same object with two lenses of different focal lengths and diameters, if we subsequently enlarge the smaller picture to make it the same size as the larger picture, and if we insist on equally sharp definition in the two final equal-sized pictures, then the depths of focus of the two cameras will be proportional solely to the *diameters* of the two lenses. Thus an $f/2$ lens of 2-in. focus and an $f/4$ lens of 4-in. focus both have a diameter of 1 in. The 2-in. lens forms a picture half as large as the 4-in. lens, but after enlargement to make them equal in size, the depth of focus of each will turn out to be the same. This property constitutes the real advantage of the miniature camera, in that it permits the use of a fast lens without loss of depth of focus.

The Hyperfocal Distance.—In a fixed-focus hand camera, it is desirable to choose the focused plane so that the extreme end of the beyond-focus depth just reaches infinity. In this case, we write $R_1 = \infty$, whence $md = c$ from Eq. (10). Now since $m = f/x$ [Eq. (8), page 16], our focused distance in this case will be given by $x = fd/c$. This is called the "hyperfocal distance." It should be noted that in a camera correctly focused for this distance, the within-focus depth just reaches $x/2$. As an example, consider a camera lens of 100-mm. focal length and aperture $f/8$. The diameter of the pupil is $d = {}^{100}\!\!/_8 = 12.5$ mm., and the hyperfocal distance is given by $x = fd/c = (100 \times 12.5)/0.25 = 5.0$ m. (16 ft.), assuming the permissible circle of confusion on the plate corresponds to $c = 0.25$ mm. The range of object distances sensibly in focus then runs from ∞ up to 2.5 m. (8 ft.).

The Resolving Power of a Lens.—If we follow through all the implications of the Huygens wave theory of light, we find that the image of a point source formed by a perfect lens is not a true point, but a small disk of light surrounded by a series of very faint rings of light, called an "Airy disk." The practical diameter of the central circular patch is found to be $2\lambda f/d$, where λ is the wavelength of the light used (approximately 0.0005 mm.), f is the image distance from the lens, and d is the clear diameter of the lens. Hence two close point sources will be just "resolved" if their separation is equal to $\lambda f/d$ or λA, where A is the aperture number of the lens. This quantity is so small that it scarcely ever enters into photographic problems, for even at $f/16$, as might be used for copying work, the least resolvable separation of two adjacent star images is $16\lambda = 0.008$ mm., while the grain of even a process plate is at least twice as large as that and with ordinary plates it may reach ten or twenty times as large.

The Pinhole Camera.—A type of camera which should not be despised is the common pinhole camera, which is simply an ordinary camera having a pinhole in place of a lens. The size of the pinhole is of considerable importance, for if it is too large the picture will be blurred owing to the spreading of the cones of light from the various object points as they pass through the hole, but on the other hand if the pinhole is too small the light waves will spread out owing to diffraction effects, again causing a blurred picture. There is thus an optimum size of hole to be used with any given length of camera. It can be shown that the image of a single object point will be as small as possible, as a result of interference effects between light waves from the different parts of the hole, if the diameter of the hole A is given by the following formula:

$$A^2 = 0.00007f \tag{13}$$

where f is the length of the camera from pinhole to plate.   This formula leads to the values given in Table VII.

TABLE VII.—OPTIMUM SIZE OF PINHOLE

	3	4	6	10
f, in	3	4	6	10
A, in	0.014	0.017	0.020	0.026
Relative aperture	$f/210$	$f/230$	$f/300$	$f/380$
Size of image point, in	0.004	0.005	0.006	0.008

In the fourth line of Table VII is given the size of the spot of light falling on the plate from each separate object point for the stated values of f and A. It will be noticed that the image spots are in every case less than one-third as large as the pinhole itself and are not much greater than the normal sharpness requirement for ordinary photography. The relative apertures are very low (less than $f/200$) hence a long exposure is required, but, with a fast plate in bright sunlight, even this will amount to only a few seconds. The entire absence of distortion for any size of angular field is a very great advantage afforded by the pinhole camera, in addition to its evident cheapness and simplicity.

The variation in illumination over the field of a pinhole camera would be equal to that given by the $\cos^4 \phi$ law expressed in Table V, page 20, if the pinhole is pierced in a plane thin sheet of opaque material. If the edges of the pinhole have been raised by the insertion of the pin or if the sheet material has considerable thickness, then there will be some vignetting of the oblique beams, resulting in still less light at the corners of the picture. It is unlikely that a pinhole photograph would be satisfactory if a field much greater than about 90° were attempted.

Perspective Effects of Photography.—To understand the nature of photographic perspective, we need merely consider the tracks of rays from all parts of an extended scene into a simple pinhole camera. No change in the ray directions occurs at the pinhole, each ray continuing along its rectilinear path until intercepted by the photographic plate. The picture formed on the plate is then necessarily a "correct" representation of the three-dimensional object projected upon a two-dimensional plane surface. A pinhole is considered here instead of any real lens for simplicity and to be sure that distortion or other optical aberrations shall be absent.

However, such a picture although "correct" would not look pleasing unless it conformed to a number of long-established conventions. The first is that the plate plane shall be vertical. This corresponds to holding our eyes so that we look directly forward in a horizontal plane. If we tilt our head and look upward at a high building, we see the vertical sides of the building appearing to converge to a point in the sky, but we do not ordinarily realize that this is so, and we object strongly to a photograph taken on a nonvertical plate which shows this effect. On the other hand, a deliberate exaggeration of this appearance may be used to suggest great height in a building.

The second convention that must be observed is in the distance of the camera from the object. To look with our eyes at an automobile end-on from a distance of 3 or 4 ft. shows the near end disproportionately large and the far end relatively small. However, in a photograph, this disproportionate magnification of various parts of the picture can appear unpleasant or even absurd, and it should be avoided by always placing the camera as far as possible from the object to be photographed. To yield a picture of the required size, a lens of sufficiently long focal length must, of course, be used, and this is one of the chief objections to small hand cameras equipped with fixed short-focused lenses. A good rule is never to place the camera closer than 10 ft. from a person or other medium-sized object which it is desired to photograph.

The third point to notice is that for proper perspective the print must be viewed from the point originally occupied by the center of the lens. With amateur snapshots, this point is frequently too close to the print for the eye to accommodate, and a magnifier must be employed. The ideal magnifier is one having a focal length equal to that of the camera lens. If such a magnifier is used, the improvement in perspective is often amazing, and the whole scene takes on an impression of great reality. If the picture is enlarged, the viewing point is carried away from the print in proportion to the degree of enlargement, and for this reason alone enlargements of snapshots are frequently found to be much more "natural" and pleasing to the eye than the original contact prints. A good rule with miniature cameras is to enlarge by the ratio of 15 in. to the focal length of the camera lens, on the assumption that the enlargement will be viewed at approximately 15 in. distance.

A fourth factor which sometimes accounts for an unnatural picture is the size of the angular field of view covered by the photograph. Artists rarely show more than 30 or 40° in one picture, and photographs which include very much more than this are often deceptive. Almost all photographs taken with a wide-angle lens covering a field of 80 or 90° or even more are unsatisfactory, a typical example being a close view in a small steamship cabin which looks like a wide and spacious room in the print. The data in Table VIII may be useful, relating the focal length and size of angular field of lens with the size of picture produced by it.

TABLE VIII.—ANGULAR FIELD OF LENS

Camera	Length and width (In.)	Length and width (Mm.)	Diagonal, mm.	½ / 12.5 mm	1 / 25 mm	1⅜ / 35 mm	2 / 51 mm	3 / 76 mm	4 / 102 mm	5 / 127 mm	6 / 152 mm	7 / 178 mm	8 / 203 mm	10 in. / 254 mm
							Angular field of lens, degrees							
16-mm. cine	....	7.5 × 10	12.5	53	27	20	14	9.4	7	5.6	4.6	4	3.6	
35-mm. cine	....	18 × 24	30	100	61	47	33	22	17	13.4	11	9.5	8.4	
Leica	....	24 × 36	43.2	...	81	63	46	32	24	17.7	16	13.8	12	
Bantam	....	28 × 40	48.8	...	87	70	51	36	27	22	18	15.6	14	11
Vest pocket	....	45 × 60	75			94	73	53	41	33	28	23.8	21	16.3
Roll film	1⅝ × 2½	41 × 63	75.2											
Exakta	....	40 × 65	76.3											
Roll film	2¼ × 3¼	57 × 83	101				90	67	53	43	37	32	28	22
Film pack	....	60 × 90	107											24
Roll film	2½ × 3½	63 × 89	109				93	70	55	46	39	34	30	
Roll film	2½ × 4¼	63 × 108	125				102	79	63	52	45	39	34	27
Roll film	3¼ × 4¼	83 × 108	136					84	68	56	48	42	37	30
Roll film	2⅞ × 4⅞	73 × 124	144											
Film pack	....	90 × 120	150					89	73	61	52	46	41	33
	2¼ × 5½	57 × 140	151											
Studio or view	4 × 5	101 × 127	162					93	77	65	56	49	44	35
Studio or view	5 × 7	127 × 178	219						94	81	71	63	56	47
Studio or view	8 × 10	203 × 254	325							103	93	85	77	65

Choice of Focal Length for Various Purposes.—Under all circumstances a good rule to follow is that the focal length should be as long as possible, if good perspective representation is desired. In particular for portraiture, to form a head image, say, 3 in. high, a magnification of about one-third is required, and therefore if the subject is to be, for example, 9 ft. from the lens, the plate must be 3 ft. from the lens, requiring a focal length of 28 in. As this is very long, it is generally necessary to place the subject at less than 9 ft. from the camera, with consequent slight "distortion" of the perspective.

However, in spite of everything, small lenses are by far the most popular, mainly from considerations of portability and cheapness and because the depth of focus for a given f-aperture is considerably increased. Optically, also, small lenses are better because the aberrational defects in a particular type of lens shrink with the scale on which the lens is constructed, while the various aberration tolerances remain unchanged. Thus it is often possible to make an $f/1.5$ lens for 16-mm. motion pictures of a design which could not be made to exceed, say, $f/2.0$ when used with 35-mm. films, or perhaps $f/2.5$ for a miniature camera covering two frames of 35-mm. film.

Lens Defects.—We have discussed so far the properties of a perfect lens. In practice no lens is perfect and some slight knowledge of the kinds of defects likely to be encountered is useful to the practical photographer. The principal aberrations may be listed as follows:

1. Spherical aberration. A longitudinal variation of image position for different zones of the lens.

2. Coma. Variation of image size for different zones of the lens.

3. Chromatic aberration. Longitudinal variation of image position for different colors.

4. Chromatic difference of magnification, or transverse chromatic aberration. Variation of image size for different colors.

5. Distortion. Variation of magnification in different parts of the field.

6. Astigmatism. A longitudinal separation between the images of radial and tangential lines in the field.

7. Curvature of field. A curvature of the "field surfaces" obtained by joining up the radial and tangential astigmatic images over the entire field.

These will be considered separately.

Spherical Aberration.—In practically every lens of any kind it is found that rays from an object point on the lens axis, entering the lens at different distances out from the center, cross the axis again on the image side at different points. This is clearly a defect, since in a perfect lens all the rays from an axial object point cross the axis again together at the image point.

The situation for an entirely uncorrected simple convex lens is indicated in Fig. 21. The point P represents the "axial image point," which is the crossing point of rays passing through the lens near its center. The position of this image point is given by the formulas on page 15. Now in a simple lens, the other rays which pass through the outer parts of the lens fall short and cross the axis at points M, N, etc. The distance from P to M is called the spherical aberration of the lens for the particular ray concerned, usually the extreme marginal ray at full aperture. Evidently stopping down the diaphragm of such a lens will reduce the spherical aberration drastically. The dotted curve in Fig. 21 is a graph connecting the height of incidence of the ray with the position of its crossing point with the axis. This graph is approximately a parabola for an uncorrected lens because the aberration increases approximately as the square of the height of incidence; thus halving the lens diameter reduces the aberration to one-quarter of its previous amount.

In a spherically corrected lens, the aim is to make the extreme marginal ray cross the axis at the point P, which can be accomplished by a suitable choice of lens shape and construction. Then it generally happens that the intermediate rays do not cross the axis at this focus but fall a little short of it, giving the situation indicated in Fig. 22.

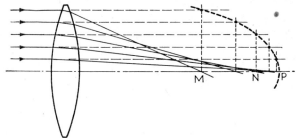

Fig. 21.—Diagram illustrating spherical aberration.

This small residual aberration for the intermediate zones of the lens is known as "zonal aberration" and is generally negligible, but it becomes of serious magnitude in microscope objectives and photographic lenses of over $f/3$ relative aperture. In large telescope objectives, zonal aberration would be so serious if spherical surfaces were

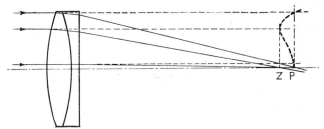

Fig. 22.—Diagram illustrating zonal aberration.

used that one or more of the lens surfaces is invariably made aspherical by judicious hand retouching, and consequently the quality of such a lens ultimately depends more on the skill of the retoucher than on the care of the designer.

The general effect of large spherical aberration in a lens is to produce an image of a point source consisting of a bright central point (the focus of the axial rays, represented by P in the ray diagrams) surrounded by a halo of light caused by the rays which miss the point P, as indicated in Fig. 23. With an extended object, of course, every point will be imaged as a patch of this sort, all the central bright spots serving to outline the image, and all the halos merging together to produce a general fog or haze over the picture. On stopping down the lens by means of its iris diaphragm, the halo becomes smaller, the central brightness remaining virtually unchanged until the entire halo has gone. Further stopping beyond that stage diminishes the central brightness also.

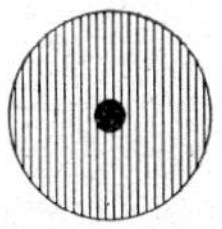

Fig. 23.—Image of a point source when spherical aberration is present.

The author once examined an $f/1.5$ lens which had a large residual of spherical aberration of this type. The outer halo could be completely removed by stopping the lens down to $f/2.9$, after which further stopping down merely diminished the brightness of the central spot. As far as extended objects are concerned, this lens would give its best image at $f/2.9$. Any enlargement of the aperture beyond $f/2.9$ would produce a haze over the whole picture resulting in bad loss of contrast, the effect being almost similar to admitting stray light into the camera by making holes in the bellows!

Spherical aberration can be immediately recognized in a lens by letting it form an image of a distant point source through a filter, to make the light reasonably monochromatic, and then examining the image with a strong magnifier or a low-power microscope.

Coma.—Coma is an aberration which does not exist in the center of the image (the lens axis) but increases steadily for images lying progressively farther out in the

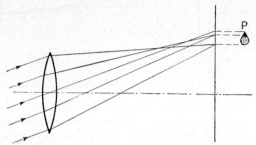

Fig. 24.—Image produced when coma is present.

field. It is essentially a difference in magnification, or distance of the image from the lens axis, for different zones of the lens. Each zone forms a minute ring image of an object point, all the various rings falling between two lines at 60° to one another as indicated in Fig. 24. The strongest concentration of light is, as for spherical aberration, where the rays through the middle of the lens form their focus, *viz.*, at P in Fig. 24. This comatic (cometlike) form of star image off the axis of the lens is very commonly found in an ordinary astronomical telescope having a slightly tilted objective. It is common too in photographic lenses, but there it is generally so

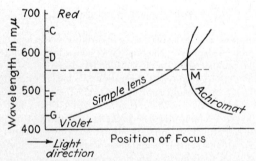

Fig. 25.—Curve relating wavelength with position of focus, for a simple lens and for an achromat.

mixed with astigmatism and other aberrations that few people have ever seen an image afflicted with pure coma and nothing else.

Chromatic Aberration.—This is characterized by a longitudinal displacement of the image plane for different wavelengths (colors). In an uncorrected positive lens the violet focus is the shortest and the red the longest, the other colors falling into their place between the two extremes. In an *achromatic* lens an attempt is made by combining two or more different kinds of glass to unite two colors at a common focus. When this is done, the intermediate colors fall closer to the lens than the united pair, and the extreme colors fall beyond, so that the curve connecting wavelength (λ) with image position becomes bent back on itself as shown in Fig. 25. This means that in the neighborhood of one wavelength the lens is substantially free from chromatic aberration, that being the "minimum focus wavelength" corresponding to the point m in Fig. 25. For lens systems to be used before the eye, this minimum-focus wavelength should fall at about 0.55 μ, which is the peak of the sensitivity curve of the eye, but for photographic work with ordinary plates, it should fall much lower, say at 0.45 μ or even less. For use with panchromatic materials having a very broad range of color sensitivity and sometimes even with two definite peaks of sensitivity at different wavelengths, the best position of the minimum-focus wavelength has not yet been decided. The only solution may be to make "apochromatic" lenses, *i.e.*, lenses in which the curve in Fig. 25 is practically flat or in which it has a double bend giving union of three colors at a common focus. Either of these conditions is hard to fulfill and is indeed almost impossible because of the necessity of correcting all the other aberrations at the same time. The longitudinal extent of the chromatic aberration of a lens is not diminished by stopping down, but its seriousness is reduced

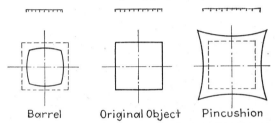

Barrel Original Object Pincushion

Fɪɢ. 26.—Outline of square images produced when distortion is present.

because the depth of focus becomes increased at smaller aperture and thereby absorbs more of the chromatic aberration.

Chromatic Difference of Magnification.—This exists in any lens in which the focal length is different in different colors; it should be carefully distinguished from ordinary chromatic aberration in which the position of the *focal point* varies in different colors. Chromatic difference of magnification produces colored fringes round the outer edges of the image, and in photography these are recorded as blurred outlines. The effect becomes worse if the image point lies farther from the center of the picture. It is especially serious in lenses to be used in color photography or in three-color process work, and it is not improved in any way by stopping down the lens.

In modern miniature cameras with good lenses, this defect is never likely to be large enough to be noticeable, even when taking pictures on Kodachrome film. Its effect in enlargers is liable to be much more serious, and is discussed under process and enlarging lenses below (on page 48 in Chap. III).

Distortion.—When distortion is present in a lens, the magnification is not constant all over the picture, but the outer parts may be magnified less or more than the central parts. These cases are illustrated in Fig. 26. In the upper part of that diagram are shown images of a uniformly divided scale taken with a lens having these two types of distortion, and in the lower part of the figure are shown the effects of these distortions on the image of a square. In the latter case, since the corners of the square are farther out than the sides, they are magnified relatively less or more than the sides, and hence the square is distorted into a barrel- or cushion-shaped figure. In each case, the perfect square-image is shown dotted. Distortion is unaffected by stopping down the lens, and is very serious in any lens where measurements are to be made on the plate, *e.g.*, in process lenses or lenses for map copying or aerial surveying. Lenses with a symmetrical construction are generally found to have very little if any distortion. Distortionless lenses are called "orthoscopic" or "rectilinear."

Astigmatism.—This aberration, like coma, does not exist on the axis of a well-centered lens but increases rapidly in the oblique pencils. It is characterized by a longitudinal difference in position between the images of radial lines in the field and

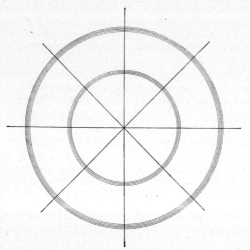

Fig. 27.—An astigmatic image.

tangential lines. Thus, if a wheel having a tangential rim and radial spokes is photographed the spokes may be in focus and the rim blurred, or vice versa (Fig. 27). In any oblique pencil through the lens from an extraaxial object point, the imaging beam nowhere contracts to a point when astigmatism is present (hence the name), but instead it shrinks to a pair of focal lines. Thus a series of sections across such a beam would appear as indicated in Fig. 28 if shown side by side. In this figure, the

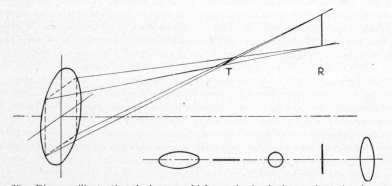

Fig. 28.—Diagram illustrating the images which are obtained when astigmatism is present.

focal line marked *R* points radially in toward the center of the picture, and hence radial lines in the picture would be imaged sharply there. The other focal line *T* is tangential to the picture, and tangential lines in the image are sharply defined there. Midway between the focal lines the beam has a circular section, which represents generally the position of best average definition.

Vignetting in a lens affects the astigmatism of very oblique pencils, because, when vignetting is present, the effective aperture of the lens is the intersection of two ellipses as shown in Fig. 28, and hence the lens aperture in the radial direction is smaller than in the tangential direction. This small radial aperture makes the radial focal line short, but it also gives great depth of focus to the tangential line; similarly, the large tangential aperture makes the tangential focal line long but gives the radial line very little depth of focus. Generally speaking, the result of this is that the radial lines have a definite focal position, whereas tangential lines are equally sharp over a considerable range of positions, and indeed often it is impossible to say where is the plane of best definition of tangential lines in the corners of the picture.

Curvature of Field.—If all the tangential focal lines in the image of a plane object are joined, they are found to lie on a surface called the "tangential field curve" of the lens; similarly the radial focal lines all lie on the "radial field curve" or, as it is more usually called, the "sagittal field curve" of the lens. These two field curves touch at the center of the field since the astigmatism always vanishes there, and in a well-corrected lens they both approximate reasonably to the plane of the plate. The field curves of a typical lens are shown in Fig. 29. Stopping down the lens does not

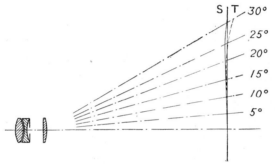

Fig. 29.—The field curves of a typical lens. The particular curves shown apply to the Cooke wide-angle *f*/8 lens.

affect the positions of these image curves, but it increases the depth of focus and shortens the focal lines themselves, so in practice it considerably reduces the effect of astigmatism on the image.

The Angular Field of a Lens.—This is limited by the state of correction of the lens aberrations, and generally the limits of the useful field of a lens become very evident in a photograph of some flat object (the front of a building, for instance) taken at full aperture on a large plate. The limit is usually expressed as the useful angular field measured outward from the axis before definition becomes too bad to be tolerated; this should strictly be called the "semifield." Sometimes the whole angular extent of the usable field is specified, and sometimes the field is indicated by stating the size of plate covered by a lens of given focal length. For ordinary lenses, a semifield of 22 or 25° is considered normal. For wide-angle lenses, 45° is a reasonable limit, *i.e.*, a 90° total field. Motion-picture lenses have smaller fields, for instance a lens of 1-in. (25.4-mm.) focal length for use with 16-mm. motion-picture film need only cover a semifield of 13°50', as each frame has the dimensions 7.5 by 10 mm., giving a diagonal length of 12.5 mm. The 35-mm. film has a frame of dimensions 18 by 24 mm., with a diagonal of 30 mm., and hence, when used with a lens of 2-in. focal length, the semifield is 16°30'. In the Leica and other miniature cameras covering two adjacent frames of 35-mm. film, the picture size is 24 by 36 mm., giving a diagonal of 43.2 mm., and hence with a 2-in. lens the semifield to be covered is 23°. With a

3-in. lens this drops to 15°48′. A common rule is that the diagonal of the field is about equal to the focal length of the lens; this rule implies a semifield of about 26° (see Table VIII for further illustrations).

Effect of Inserting a Parallel Plate into a Light Beam.—There is optically no effect whatever from the insertion of a plano-parallel plate of glass or other homogeneous transparent material into a parallel beam of light. Hence filters, prisms, etc., required for use with a lens focused on a distant object should be inserted into the beam before it enters the lens.

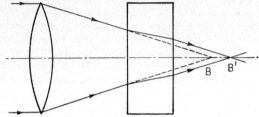

FIG. 30.—Passage of a converging beam through a parallel glass plate.

The situation is quite different if the parallel plate is inserted into a converging or diverging beam. If the beam is such that its central ray falls perpendicularly on the parallel glass slab, it is affected in the manner indicated in Fig. 30. Suppose the beam without the slab comes to a perfect focus at B, then when the slab is inserted the focus will be shifted away by about one-third of the slab thickness to B'. Moreover, the foci of rays at different slopes through the plate will be shifted by different amounts, resulting in the introduction of considerable spherical aberration.

But an oblique pencil is upset by the slab in a much more complicated fashion.

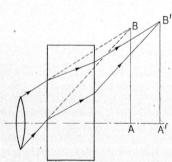

FIG. 31.—Passage of an oblique pencil of rays through a parallel plate.

In Fig. 31, if B is a perfect image point before inserting the slab, the image may go to a position B' after inserting the slab; but if $A'B'$ is greater or less than AB there will be distortion introduced, and moreover the image B' will in general suffer from spherical aberration, coma, astigmatism, and all the other aberrations due entirely to the passage of the rays through the slab. The amounts of these aberrations due to the parallel-sided slab are independent of the position of the slab but depend only on its thickness and refractive index. These remarks apply directly to filters inserted between the lens and the picture and to reflecting prisms of all kinds, which are optically equivalent to a parallel slab plus one or more plane mirrors.

The firm of Taylor-Hobson has designed special camera lenses for use in Technicolor, for in that process a beam-splitting prism must be inserted between the lens and the film; ordinary lenses would be useless here on account of the great thickness of the prism and the strong convergence of the rays passing through it.

Simple Lens Tests.—Undoubtedly the simplest test for a photographic lens is to photograph on a fine-grain film a distant vertical wall carrying on it sharp detail such as pieces of paper covered with printed matter of various sizes. The experiment should be done outdoors, but not in direct sunlight, so as to secure uniformity of illumination. In this way any nonuniformity of illumination over the field, due to a combination of vignetting and the $\cos^4 \phi$ law, will be made apparent, together with the quality and sharpness of definition over the whole field. To detect inequality of illumination most easily, the exposure should be on the short side, because then the underexposure produced by vignetting becomes exaggerated. Enlarger lenses should be tested with a cross-ruled glass screen in place of the negative, the image being caught on a sheet of bromide paper.

There have been many special lens-testing benches constructed which facilitate the testing of photographic lenses, but the direct photographic test, accompanied by tests for ghost images (see page 22), is likely to be as useful and as satisfactory as any other for the actual photographer to perform himself. A brief bibliography of lens tests is given at the end of this chapter.

Enlarging Lenses.—In general, the requirements to be satisfied by the lens on an enlarger are not essentially different from those of a camera lens. There are, however, a few minor points which should be emphasized. Strictly, enlarging lenses should be designed for the approximate magnification under which they will be used, as a change in object distance may seriously upset the corrections of a photographic lens. For instance, some good anastigmats which give a flat field with a distant object project an image when used in an enlarger which is backward curving, i.e., an image in which the corners are too far from the lens. Fortunately stopping down the enlarging lens will help all aberrations except distortion and transverse chromatic aberration. As regards these two defects, it can easily be shown that, if the lens is symmetrical about a central stop, they will be automatically removed when used at unit magni-

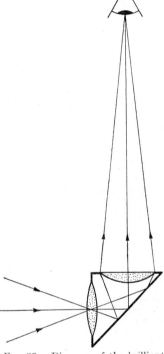

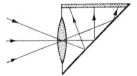

FIG. 32.—Diagram of a simple view finder.

FIG. 33.—Diagram of the brilliant view finder.

fication. Hence, if good correction of these aberrations is important, a lens of a symmetrical type is to be preferred for use on an enlarger. Incidentally, in three-color work with color-separation negatives, chromatic difference of magnification is a very serious defect and should be avoided wherever possible. For commercial color work, apochromatic process lenses are made in which this aberration is very well corrected for all colors of the spectrum.

View Finders.—The simplest view finder is really a small camera with a simple lens, a mirror, and a ground-glass screen (Fig. 32), and, since only a single mirror is used, the picture seen is reversed from left to right. However, as ground glass is very wasteful of light, it is more usual now to project the image into the plane of a viewing lens, which is so chosen as to project an image of the first lens into the plane of the observer's eyes (approximately) (Fig. 33). The observer then sees a brilliant picture in the plane of the viewing lens on which the effective outline of the field can be etched or marked in some suitable way.   The size of the etched frame bears the same relation to the camera picture as the focal length of the finder lens bears to that of the camera lens.

For cameras held close to the face, a direct-vision view finder may be used consisting of a plano-concave lens cut to a rectangular shape (Fig. 34).   The eye position is often indicated by a small view hole, and the field limits are marked on the lens at the position corresponding to a semifield ϕ projected outward from the point E', which is the virtual image of E formed by the concave lens.   In using this finder, the eye must be accommodated sufficiently to see the image of distant objects formed by the lens, and in a small compact camera this may be too close for convenient vision. In such a case, a convex lens may be mounted at E, having its focal plane coinciding with the image of distant objects formed by the concave lens, *i.e.*, with its posterior focal point.   The finder then becomes simply a reversed Galilean telescope.

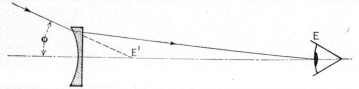

Fig. 34.—Diagram showing optical paths in a direct-vision view finder.

Parallax in View Finders.—Since the view-finder lens is necessarily displaced to one side of the camera lens, the picture seen in the view finder will be correct only for objects at one distance, usually infinity.   Some cameras therefore contain an arrangement which automatically causes the axes of finder and camera to converge correctly while adjusting the focus so as to intersect at the focused object, while others show a series of frames which outline the field seen at various distances, for instance, very distant, 6 ft. and 2 ft.

Bibliography

General geometrical optics:

HARDY and PERRIN: "The Principles of Optics," McGraw.
MARTIN, L. C.: "Applied Optics," Pitman.
GLEICHEN, A.: "Theory of Modern Optical Instruments," H.M.S.O.

Optics of photography:

TRAILL TAYLOR, J.: "The Optics of Photography and Photographic Lenses," Whitaker.
CONRADY, A. E.: "Photography as a Scientific Implement," Blackie & Son, Ltd.
LUMMER: "Contributions to Photographic Optics," Macmillan.
COLE, R. S.: "A Treatise on Photographic Optics," Low.
FOWLER, H. A., and L. E. VARDEN: Optical Glass in Photography, *Am. Phot.*, November, 1938.

Lens-testing methods:

RICHTER, MERTÉ, and VON ROHR: "Das photographische Objektiv," p. 367, Springer.
JEWELL, L. E.: *J. Optical Soc. Am.*, **2**, 51 (1919).
BENNETT, A. H.: *Nat. Bur. Standards (U. S.), Bull.*, **19**, 587 (1923); *Sci. Paper* 494.
————: *J. Optical Soc. Am.*, **14**, 235 (1927).
KINGSLAKE, R.: *J. Optical Soc. Am.*, **22**, 207 (1932).
GARDNER, I. C. and F. A. CASE: *J. Research Natl. Bur. Standards*, **18**, 449 (1937); *Res. paper* 984.
WILLIAMS, R. L.: Testing Sharpness of Photographic Lenses, *Am. Phot.*, June, 1935, 331.

CHAPTER III

THE DEVELOPMENT OF THE PHOTOGRAPHIC OBJECTIVE

By R. Kingslake

Landscape Lenses.—Historically, photographic lenses fall into two groups, the early period prior to 1886 and the anastigmat period since that time. In that year a revolution occurred in lens design as a result of the successful development of barium crown glass by Abbe and Schott, in Jena.

The earliest photographs were made by placing paper covered with a light-sensitive material in the focal plane of a camera obscura, the lenses used being first simple plano-convex lenses, and later simple meniscus "landscape" lenses as suggested by Wollaston in 1812 (Fig. 1). A suitably designed meniscus lens, with a stop in front of it on the concave side of the lens, will give good pictures at $f/11$ or $f/16$, covering with moderate definition a total field of about 45°. This lens is still universally adopted in low-priced cameras.

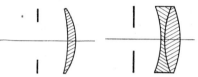

Fig. 1.—Meniscus landscape lens of Wollaston.

Fig. 2.—Achromatic landscape lens of Chevalier.

In addition to its cheapness, this lens has the advantage of possessing only two glass-air surfaces.

The lack of achromatism of this lens was soon found to be a disadvantage, even before the camera obscura became a photographic camera, and the achromatic landscape lens was introduced by Chevalier in 1821 (Fig. 2). The process of achromatization automatically removed both of the chromatic aberrations, thus improving the definition in a twofold manner.

The Petzval Portrait Lens.—The landscape lens at $f/11$ was successfully adopted in the early daguerreotype process, but exposures of half an hour or more were necessary even in sunlight. Consequently when daguerreotype portraiture was attempted, the need soon arose for a much faster lens. J. Petzval, of Vienna, solved the problem in 1841 by the design of his well-known portrait lens (Fig. 3), which is still popular although its regular manufacture has been abandoned in recent years since the introduction of anastigmats of equal or greater speed. The Petzval lens contained four single lenses and six glass-air surfaces and covered a field of 25° at an aperture of $f/3.4$. This general design was subsequently improved by Dallmeyer, Voigtländer, Zincke-Sommer, and Steinheil, reaching finally an aperture of $f/2.4$. It suffered from the disadvantage of astigmatic defects in the outer part of the field, which could not be removed so long as the designer was limited to the use of ordinary crown and flint glasses.

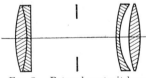

Fig. 3.—Petzval portrait lens.

Orthoscopic Lenses.—The processes of photography were at this time undergoing rapid improvement, and by 1858 the wet-collodion process had become generally adopted. Its relatively high speed made indoor and architectural photography a

practical possibility. At once the distortion of the landscape lens and the limited
field of the portrait lens became strongly noticeable and objectionable. In 1859,
J. T. Goddard attempted to remove the distortion of the landscape lens by introducing a cemented doublet between the lens and the diaphragm. Within the following
few years many other nondistorting or "orthoscopic" lenses were introduced, most of
which comprised two identical lenses placed symmetrically about a central stop, such
as Steinheil's "periscopic" lens of 1865 (Fig. 4). The argument here was that if the
lens is in front of the stop, pincushion distortion arises, whereas if the stop is in front
of the lens, the distortion is barrel-shaped. Thus, when both lenses are used together,
their distortions will neutralize each other. Some extremely wide-angle lenses were
made at this time, notably the Harrison and Schnitzer Globe lens, Sutton's panoramic

FIG. 4.—Steinheil's peri-   FIG. 5.—Busch Pantoskop
      scopic lens.   wide-angle lens.

lens containing water inside a hollow thick glass sphere, and the Busch Pantoskop lens.
This latter covered a field of 100° at $f/30$ (Fig. 5).

The Effects of Shifting the Stop.—The real advantages of the symmetrical construction were not at first realized. These follow from a consideration of the laws
governing the changes of aberrations as the stop is moved longitudinally along the
lens axis. These changes may be represented symbolically by the equations:

$$\left.\begin{aligned}
\text{Sph}^* &= \text{Sph} \\
\text{Coma}^* &= \text{Coma} + K \times \text{Sph} \\
\text{Ast}^* &= \text{Ast} + 2K \times \text{Coma} + K^2 \times \text{Sph}
\end{aligned}\right\} \tag{1}$$

The asterisk (*) indicates the value of each aberration after the stop has been shifted
by an amount represented by K. Thus, shifting the stop does not affect spherical
aberration at all, but it changes the coma if spherical aberration is present, and it
changes the astigmatism if either spherical aberration or coma or both are present.
In the landscape lens, the stop is placed at such a position that the coma is just neutralized by the $(K \times \text{Sph})$ term in the second equation above. Thus a landscape
lens must have spherical aberration if it is to be coma-free, and, of course, coma is a
much worse defect than spherical aberration since coma increases as the field increases,
whereas spherical aberration is constant over the entire
field. The field of a landscape lens must then be flattened
by a suitable choice of lens shape.

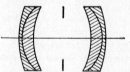

FIG. 6.—Rapid rectilinear
        lens.

The Rapid Rectilinear Lens.—In 1866, Dallmeyer and
Steinheil simultaneously and independently realized that,
if two identical lenses are mounted symmetrically about
a central stop, the three transverse aberrations-distortion,
chromatic difference of magnification, and coma, are
automatically removed (or drastically reduced), and hence each component of such
a symmetrical system need not be corrected for any of these three aberrations.
They therefore constructed a symmetrical lens, each half of which was corrected for
longitudinal chromatic and spherical aberration; the astigmatism was then removed
by placing the stop at the correct position relative to each component to make use of
the $(2K \times \text{Coma})$ term in the third equation above. In this way they produced the

well-known Rapid Rectilinear or Aplanat lens (Fig. 6), covering a field of 45° at $f/8$, and giving excellent definition at the center of the picture because of the good spherical correction.

The Petzval Theorem.—Actually, the astigmatism in the Rapid Rectilinear lens was deliberately not reduced to zero because that would give rather a badly curved field.   There is a simple theorem named after Petzval, which states that the radius of curvature of the central part of the astigmatism-free field of a lens is given by ρ in

$$\frac{1}{\rho} = \Sigma\left(\frac{n' - n}{nn' r}\right) \tag{2}$$

where r is the radius of curvature of a surface in the lens separating materials of refractive index n and n', the summation to be made for all the refracting surfaces in

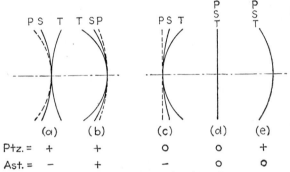

Fig. 7.—The Petzval surface and astigmatism curves.

the lens system.   This sum is independent of the object distance, the thicknesses and airspaces in the system, and the stop position.   It is therefore a very inflexible quantity which it is hard to vary or control.   The surface whose radius ρ is given by Eq. (2) is called the "Petzval surface" and represents the shape of the field if astigmatism is corrected.

If astigmatism is present, however, it is found that the longitudinal distances from this Petzval surface to the radial (sagittal) and tangential (meridional) focal lines, respectively, are in a ratio of 1:3, as indicated in the various cases illustrated in Fig. 7. In case a of this figure, it is clear that the introduction of a little negative (overcorrected) astigmatism has flattened the effective field, as compared with case e in which the astigmatism is zero.   The ideal case is, of course, zero Petzval sum and zero astigmatism; this condition is realized approximately in the modern "anastigmat" lenses (case d).

Attempts to Reduce the Petzval Sum.—It soon became apparent that a flat field free from astigmatism could only be obtained if the Petzval sum were drastically reduced in magnitude.   This could be done in three different ways: (1) A

Fig. 8.—Hypergon wide-angle lens.

single lens could be made to have a low sum by giving it a meniscus form with equal outside radii and considerable thickness.   This shape appears commonly in many types of anastigmat, reaching its limit in the nonachromatic Hypergon (Fig. 8) which is designed to cover a field of 140° at $f/22$.   (2) In an achromatic lens, if the crown and flint components are separated by a finite distance, the flint must be strengthened to compensate for its smaller effective diameter, and this will at once reduce the Petzval sum.   (3) To fulfill the Petzval sum and also the achromatic condition in a reasonably thin cemented doublet, the ratio of the V of each glass[1] to its refractive index n must be the same. Unfortunately in ordinary crown and flint glasses the n and V change in opposite directions, as indicated in Table I.

TABLE I.—INDEX AND DISPERSION OF OLD TYPES OF GLASS

Type	Index n	Constringence V	V/n
Hard crown	1.5175	60.5	39.9
Extra-light flint	1.5290	51.6	33.8
Light flint	1.5746	41.4	26.2
Dense flint	1.6041	37.8	23.5
Extra-dense flint	1.7402	28.4	16.3

However, by the use of barium glasses introduced by Schott and Abbe in 1886, it becomes possible to select pairs of glasses in which the values of V/n are the same (Table II).

TABLE II.—INDEX AND DISPERSION OF SOME "NEW" GLASS PAIRS

Type	Index n	Constringence V	V/n
Barium flint	1.6530	46.2	27.9
Light flint	1.5674	43.8	27.9
Dense barium crown	1.6098	53.3	33.1
Extra-light flint	1.5290	51.6	33.8
Dense barium crown	1.6016	59.9	37.3
Telescope flint	1.5151	56.4	37.2

The first lens to include these new glass pairs was the Ross Concentric (Fig. 9) designed by Schröder in 1888. This lens was a symmetrical system of two flat-field achromatic landscape lenses; not being spherically corrected, its aperture was limited to $f/16$, but it satisfactorily covered a wide field.

Now to correct the spherical aberration of a thin cemented doublet it is necessary that the convex element should have a lower index than the concave, as in the Rapid

 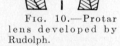 

Fig. 9.—Ross Concentric lens.   Fig. 10.—Protar lens developed by Rudolph.   Fig. 11.—Protar $f/4.5$ lens.

Rectilinear type, but in a new achromat combination the convex element must have a higher index than the concave. It is thus impossible to design a thin spherically corrected achromatic lens of the new glasses. Dr. Rudolph of the Zeiss Company realized this, and in 1890 produced his Protar lens (Fig. 10) consisting of an old-type achromat in front, and a new achromat behind. The front lens was given a very low or zero focal power, and it had enough overcorrected spherical aberration to com-

---

[1] The V-number of a glass is the reciprocal of its dispersive power, or $V = (n_D - 1)/(n_F - n_C)$. It is sometimes called the "constringence" or Abbe number of the glass.

pensate the inevitable spherical undercorrection of the new achromat rear element. Similarly, the glasses for the rear element were so chosen that the Petzval sum of the rear would compensate that of the front element. The shapes of the lenses were also chosen so as to correct the coma and astigmatism of the whole system.

The Protar lens, as first made, operated at $f/7.7$ or less. However, its aperture was subsequently raised to $f/4.5$ by changing the rear component into a triplet (Fig.

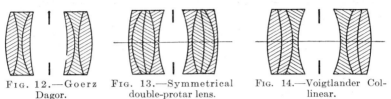

Fig. 12.—Goerz Dagor.   Fig. 13.—Symmetrical double-protar lens.   Fig. 14.—Voigtlander Collinear.

11) in which the positive barium crown element was divided into two parts placed one on each side of the light flint negative element.

In 1893, as a result of the simultaneous and independent activities of Rudolph at Zeiss and von Höegh at Goerz, the old and new achromat elements of the Protar were combined into one. The Zeiss Triple-Protar and the Goerz Dagor were practically identical designs, consisting of a symmetrical arrangement of two cemented triple elements (Fig. 12). Each element was in external form a thick meniscus lens, this

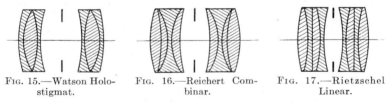

Fig. 15.—Watson Holostigmat.   Fig. 16.—Reichert Combinar.   Fig. 17.—Rietzschel Linear.

shape helping to reduce the Petzval sum in addition to flattening the field. The refractive indices were in the order high-medium-low while the V-numbers of the glasses were, respectively, high-low-high. Thus, if an imaginary line is drawn to bisect the middle lens of each element, the outside doublets are evidently new achromats and the inside doublets are old achromats.

In the same year, Rudolph designed the convertible double-protar lens (Fig. 13) in which the new and old achromats were directly cemented together forming quad-

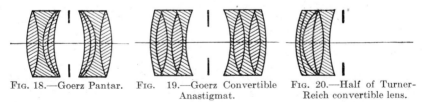

Fig. 18.—Goerz Pantar.   Fig. 19.—Goerz Convertible Anastigmat.   Fig. 20.—Half of Turner-Reich convertible lens.

ruple elements, which were then mounted symmetrically in pairs about a central stop. Because of the high degree of correction of these elements, they could be used separately as anastigmatic landscape lenses at $f/12$ or combined together in pairs to make a "set" of interchangeable lenses. Thus by having a "set" of three lenses of different foci, six possible focal lengths could be obtained. This design is still largely used by commercial photographers. Other variations of these symmetrical cemented anastigmats soon followed. Some typical examples are given in Table III:

TABLE III.—SYMMETRICAL ANASTIGMATS

Manufacturer	Lens System
Two Triplets	
Busch Leukar...	?
Goerz Dagor...	+ − + : (Fig. 12)
Gundlach Perigraphic....................................	?
Rodenstock Eikonar......................................	?
Schneider Angulon.......................................	− + − : (Fig. 15)
Schneider Symmar..	+ − + : (Fig. 12)
Steinheil Orthostigmat..................................	+ + − : (Fig. 14)
Voigtländer Collinear...................................	+ + − : (Fig. 14)
Watson Holostigmat......................................	− + − : (Fig. 15)
Zeiss Convertible Protar }	
Zeiss Ortho Protar }	− + − : (Fig. 15)
Zeiss Triple Protar.....................................	+ − + : (Fig. 12)
Two Quadruplets	
Beck Bystigmar..	− + + − : (Fig. 13)
Goerz Pantar..	+ − + + : (Fig. 18)
Reichert Combinar.......................................	+ + − + : (Fig. 16)
Rietzschel Linear.......................................	+ − + − : (Fig. 17)
Simon Octanar...	+ + − + : (Fig. 16)
Zeiss Double Protar.....................................	− + + − : (Fig. 13)
Two Quintuplets	
Goerz Convertible Anastigmat Series II..................	− + − + − : (Fig. 19)
Turner-Reich lens.......................................	− − + + − : (Fig. 20)

These completely cemented symmetrical lenses do not generally exceed $f/6.3$ in aperture, with some exceptions up to $f/4.5$, but they cover a wide field of as much as 90° in some cases. Some of the triplets are convertible but generally only at reduced aperture. In some cases a front lens of one type is convertible with a back lens of a different type such as the Polyplast of Dr. Stäble (Fig. 21).

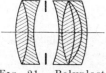 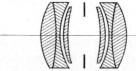

FIG. 21.—Polyplast   FIG. 22.—Meyer Plasmat, $f/4$.
convertible lens.

The convertible lens has largely disappeared from amateur use with the advent of fixed-lens hand cameras. To use a convertible lens adequately, a tripod and focusing screen are really necessary.

In recent years, considerable improvements have been made by separating one or more of the lenses in these symmetrical types, and in some cases departing from strict

 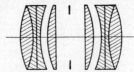 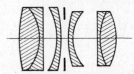

FIG. 23.—
Half of Taylor-
Hobson converti-
ble lens.

FIG. 24.—Schneider Ortho-
Angulon.

FIG. 25.—Meyer Kino-Plas-
mat, $f/1.5$.

symmetry. For example, in the Meyer Plasmat $f/4$ (Fig. 22), the two lenses nearest the stop in the Goerz Dagor have been detached, the same type of construction being adopted in the Ross $f/4$ wide-angle Xpres, the Schulze Euryplan $f/6$, the Busch

Stigmar $f/6.3$, the Bausch and Lomb Aero lenses, and the Zeiss distortionless Orthometar $f/4.5$. Some advantage has been gained by separating the old and new achromats in the double-protar type, for instance in the new Taylor-Hobson Series 15 convertible anastigmat $f/6.8$ (Fig. 23). The Schneider Ortho-Angulon contains two symmetrical quadruplets in which the inner elements have been detached (Fig. 24). The Meyer Kino-Plasmat $f/1.5$ is an extreme variant of these nearly symmetrical types (Fig. 25).

The Cooke Lens.—These recent developments represent the limit to which the wide-angle symmetrical "continental" type of lens has been carried. At the other end of the scale, we have the Petzval portrait lens and its variants, which have a large aperture (up to about $f/2.4$) but cover only a rather small field (20°). The limit along this line is the recent Zeiss R-Biotar for motion-picture photography of X-ray images on fluorescent screens, which has an aperture of $f/0.85$ and covers a field of only 14° (Fig. 26).

In order to provide a lens having intermediate properties between these "continental" and "Petzval" types, H. Dennis Taylor in 1893 and succeeding years devel-

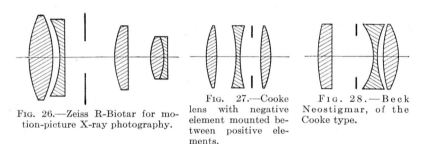

FIG. 26.—Zeiss R-Biotar for motion-picture X-ray photography.

FIG. 27.—Cooke lens with negative element mounted between positive elements.

FIG. 28.—Beck Neostigmar, of the Cooke type.

oped the well-known Cooke lens in which the Petzval sum is reduced by separating the constituents of an achromat.[1] A simple separated doublet would suffer from very bad distortion and transverse color; therefore, Taylor divided the positive element into two and mounted the negative element between them (Fig. 27). Although it is theoretically possible to design such a lens using old glasses, he shortened the system and made the corrections easier by using barium crown instead of ordinary crown for the convex elements. This type of lens can be made in apertures up to $f/3.5$, to cover a field of 55°, and has the great advantages of weak curves, few components, and no cemented surfaces. At the same time it has six glass-air surfaces, but if the iris is placed in the rear airspace no trouble from ghosts or flare spots is ordinarily encountered. The Cooke type of lens is made by many firms and has been regarded as the major real invention in lens design since the advent of the new glass types. The Beck Neostigmar is really of the Cooke type, with the diaphragm placed in the front airspace (Fig. 28).

The aperture of the Cooke lens was raised to $f/2.3$ in 1925 by Bielicke in the Astro Tachar lens (U. S. Pat. 1540752), and in 1926 by Lee in the Taylor-Hobson $f/2.5$ Speedic lens, by splitting the rear positive element into two closely spaced positive lenses (Fig. 29). Even the recent Zeiss Sonnar lens (Fig. 30) covering 45° at $f/1.5$ may be regarded as a development of the Cooke type in which both the middle negative lens and the rear positive lens have been made into cemented triplets, although, of course, it by no means follows that this design was actually arrived at by successive modifications from the original Cooke type.

[1] TAYLOR, H. D., Optical Designing as an Art, *Trans. Optical Soc. (London)*, **24,** 143 (1923).

Another modification of the Cooke lens is the Aldis lens (Fig. 31) designed in 1901 by H. L. Aldis, to cover 35° at $f/6$. In this type the front two lenses are thickened and cemented together to form a low-power negative system of such a shape as to correct the aberrations of the single positive lens forming the rear element.

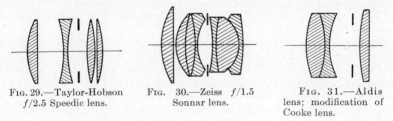

Fig. 29.—Taylor-Hobson   Fig. 30.—Zeiss $f/1.5$ Fig. 31.—Aldis
$f/2.5$ Speedic lens.   Sonnar lens.   lens; modification of
                                                        Cooke lens.

The Four-piece Lens.—In connection with the Cooke lens above, it was mentioned that the Petzval sum can be reduced by separating the positive and negative elements of an achromatic doublet.   If two such separated doublets are mounted symmetrically about a central stop, a lens is obtained which offers even more possibilities for a good design than does the Cooke lens.   Two independent series of designs based on this general principle have been developed, one in which the four lenses are all biconvex or biconcave and the other in which all four lenses are meniscus-shaped.   The first form is exemplified by the Goerz Celor $f/4.5$, designed by von Höegh in 1898 (Fig. 32).   Later modifications of this type are the Goerz Dogmar, the Steinheil Unofocal, and the Taylor-Hobson Aviar.   The second form may be said to have originated in the Alvan Clark lens of 1889 (U. S. Pat. 399499) in which two Gauss-type telescope objectives were combined together with their concave sides facing a central stop.

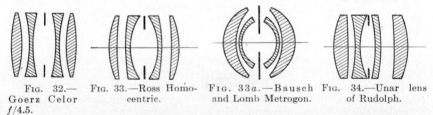

Fig. 32.—   Fig. 33.—Ross Homo-   Fig. 33a.—Bausch   Fig. 34.—Unar lens
Goerz Celor   centric.   and Lomb Metrogon.   of Rudolph.
$f/4.5$.

The Gauss telescope objective consists of a meniscus-shaped crown and flint elements in close contact and is characterized by being spherically corrected at two different wavelengths, thus having exceptionally good spherical correction throughout the whole spectrum.   One of the first anastigmats to embody this principle was the Ross Homocentric (Fig. 33) and the identical Meyer Aristostigmat designed by Kollmorgen in 1902.   The type is still being adopted for some purposes such as the $f/10$ process lens of Bausch and Lomb.   An extreme example of this form is the Richter lens (U.S. Pat. 2031792), the same type of construction being adopted in the Bausch and Lomb Metrogon (Fig. 33a).   The glass types employed in these symmetrical four-piece lenses are generally barium crown and light flint, but it is quite possible to satisfy the Petzval sum with old glasses as was shown by Martin in the Busch Omnar in 1902.   Rudolph tried mixing the Celor and Homocentric types by using the front half of the Celor with the rear of the Homocentric types in his Unar lens (Fig. 34), but it was not long manufactured.   The Wray Lustrar is also of this general type (Fig. 35).

Variations of the Celor type soon appeared.   For example, Goerz made the two negatives into cemented triplets in the Alethar process lens (Fig. 36), and Rudolph raised the aperture to $f/3.6$ with a 65° field in his symmetrical Planar lens (Fig. 37) by making both negatives into hyperchromatic negative doublets. This Planar type has provided the inspiration for a number of recent unsymmetrical lenses of extremely large aperture such as the Taylor-Hobson Opic $f/2$ (Fig. 38), the Zeiss Biotar $f/1.4$

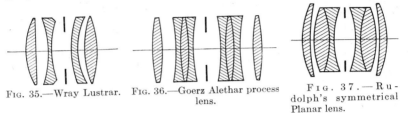

FIG. 35.—Wray Lustrar.   FIG. 36.—Goerz Alethar process lens.   FIG. 37.—Rudolph's symmetrical Planar lens.

(Fig. 39), the Schneider Xenon $f/2$, the Bausch and Lomb Raytar $f/2.3$, and the Kodak Ektar $f/2$. In extreme cases the rear positive lens is also doubled, either cemented or separated, as in the Xenon $f/1.3$. The Portrait Euryplan (Fig. 40) is really of the Planar type.

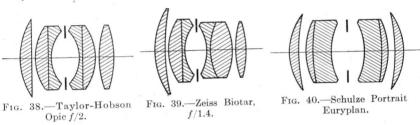

FIG. 38.—Taylor-Hobson Opic $f/2$.   FIG. 39.—Zeiss Biotar, $f/1.4$.   FIG. 40.—Schulze Portrait Euryplan.

The Ernostar lens $f/1.8$ (Fig. 41) designed in 1924 by Bertele is a four-piece lens in which the second negative has been made into a thick cemented triplet. The Meyer Primoplan $f/1.9$ is similar, but the second lens is a doublet of deep meniscus form (Fig. 42). In the Taylor-Hobson Super-speed Panchro $f/1.3$, the second lens is a doublet and the rear a triplet (Fig. 43).

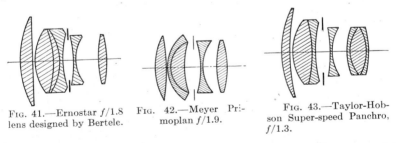

FIG. 41.—Ernostar $f/1.8$ lens designed by Bertele.   FIG. 42.—Meyer Primoplan $f/1.9$.   FIG. 43.—Taylor-Hobson Super-speed Panchro, $f/1.3$.

The Tessar Lens.—By cementing together the rear elements of an unsymmetrical Celor-type lens, Rudolph in 1902 produced the Tessar lens (Fig. 44), which is probably the best known and most generally used type of lens produced in recent times. The glasses are the familiar dense barium crown for the positives and light flint for the negatives, and the airspaces are adjusted to fulfill the Petzval sum. In a sense, the Tessar can be regarded as an extension of the Cooke three-lens type, but it is, perhaps, more accurate to regard it as a logical simplification of the four-lens type of construction. Another view is that the Tessar is a combination of the front half of a Cooke lens with the rear half of the original Protar lens. The Tessar lens has been made in apertures ranging from $f/15$ as an apochromatic process lens, down to $f/2.7$ for cine purposes. The field runs from 45 to 75°, depending on the aperture and focal length.

Modifications of the Tessar Type.—The first modification of the Tessar type of construction was the Voigtländer Heliar $f/4.5$ (Fig. 45) and Dynar $f/6$ (Fig. 46) designed by Harting in 1902, in which both the front and rear positive elements are made into cemented doublets. In a sense, these lenses are thus modifications of the

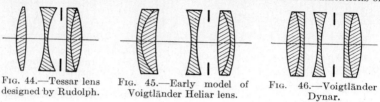

Fig. 44.—Tessar lens designed by Rudolph.   Fig. 45.—Early model of Voigtländer Heliar lens.   Fig. 46.—Voigtländer Dynar.

Cooke type. The Dallmeyer Pentac $f/2.9$, designed by Booth in 1919, is of the same general type as the Dynar. The modern Heliar lens is also of the Dynar type, the original Heliar type being no longer made. In 1903, Harting designed the Oxyn $f/9$ (Fig. 47) for process work, in which the front element of a Heliar was combined with the rear of a Dynar. This lens also is no longer made. In the Voigtländer Heliostigmat (Fig. 48), the front lens is doubled but the rear lens is a single positive element. This is a kind of inverted Tessar type.

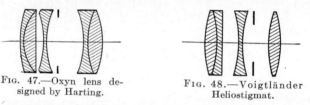

Fig. 47.—Oxyn lens designed by Harting.   Fig. 48.—Voigtländer Heliostigmat.

The Zeiss Biotessar $f/2.7$ (Fig. 49), designed by Merté in 1925, is really a Dynar in which an additional thin positive lens has been cemented to the front face of the rear doublet making it into a triplet.

Another modification of the Tessar is the Ross Xpres (1913) in which the rear lens is a triplet instead of a doublet (Fig. 50). This is made in apertures from $f/1.9$ to $f/4.5$, and covers a field of about 53°. The Gundlach Radar (Fig. 51) has also a triplet rear element.

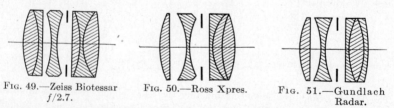

Fig. 49.—Zeiss Biotessar $f/2.7$.   Fig. 50.—Ross Xpres.   Fig. 51.—Gundlach Radar.

Telephoto Lenses.—A telephoto lens consists merely of a pair of widely spaced positive and negative elements. In such a system, the principal points are shifted out beyond the positive element so that, if this positive lens is turned toward the object, the true or equivalent focal length of the system will be much greater than the back focus. Hence a lens of long focal length, giving a large image, can be used on a small camera having a short bellows extension. The earliest telephoto lenses were merely small Galilean telescopes with the eyepiece racked out far enough to project a real image on the photographic plate. By 1891, optical manufacturers began making achromatic negative lenses in adaptors by which they could be mounted behind ordinary photographic lenses. Such "telenegative" lenses were rather unsuccessful on

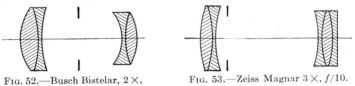

FIG. 52.—Busch Bistelar, 2 ×, *f*/7.   FIG. 53.—Zeiss Magnar 3 ×, *f*/10.

account of the low speed and poor correction of the whole system, but at *f*/11 or less they could be useful. By varying the separation of the telenegative lens from the positive lens, the over-all power of the system could be changed, such adjustable or Pancratic lenses giving a range of from 2 × to 8 × magnification.

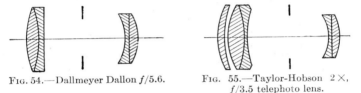

FIG. 54.—Dallmeyer Dallon *f*/5.6.   FIG. 55.—Taylor-Hobson 2 ×, *f*/3.5 telephoto lens.

However, it was soon realized that even a magnification 2 × is a very considerable advantage, and in 1898 Zeiss produced a complete telephoto lens of 2 × to 3 × power, at an aperture of *f*/6 to *f*/10. This was followed by other fixed-focus telephoto lenses, notably the Busch Bistelar 2 × *f*/7 (Fig. 52) designed by Martin in 1906, and the

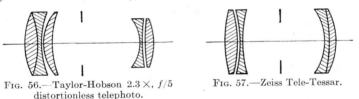

FIG. 56.—Taylor-Hobson 2.3 ×, *f*/5 distortionless telephoto.   FIG. 57.—Zeiss Tele-Tessar.

Zeiss Magnar 3 × (Fig. 53) *f*/10 by Rudolph and Wandersleb. Both these systems consisted of a cemented positive doublet in front and a cemented rear negative doublet. Most manufacturers have made telephoto types since 1900, of various constructions,

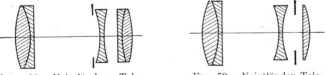

FIG. 58.—Voigtländer Tele-Dynar, *f*/6.3 lens.   FIG. 59.—Voigtländer Tele-Dynar *f*/4.5 lens.

but the aperture remained low until the Dallmeyer Dallon *f*/5.6 lens (Fig. 54) designed by Booth in 1919, and the Taylor-Hobson 2 × telephoto *f*/3.5 by Lee in 1925 (Fig. 55). The inevitable distortion of ordinary telephoto systems was finally overcome by Lee in the Taylor-Hobson distortionless telephoto *f*/5, 2.3 × (Fig. 56).

Other types of telephoto lens are the Zeiss Tele-Tessar (Fig. 57); the Voigtländer Tele-Dynar (Figs. 58, 59); the Ross Teleros (Fig. 60) and Telecentric (Fig. 61); the Stäble Neoplast (Fig. 62); the Plaubel Tele-Makinar (Fig. 63); the Schneider Tele-Xenar (Fig. 64); and the Goerz Telegor (Fig. 65).

The telephoto lens is now enjoying a new lease of life with the advent of miniature cameras and amateur motion pictures on 16-mm. film. It should be pointed out,

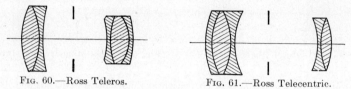

FIG. 60.—Ross Teleros.　　　　　FIG. 61.—Ross Telecentric.

however, that for these purposes some firms sell ordinary lenses of relatively long focus under the name of telephoto lenses, which are designed to give larger pictures than are obtained with the standard lens for that type of camera. This practice is justified by the much better definition and larger aperture obtainable with ordinary lenses than with real telephoto lenses.

Reversed Telephoto Systems.—In some cases, particularly with very short-focus lenses, the working distance (or back focus) is too short to accommodate auxiliary

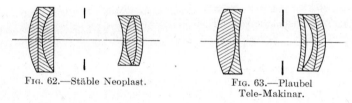

FIG. 62.—Stäble Neoplast.　　　　FIG. 63.—Plaubel
　　　　　　　　　　　　　　　　　Tele-Makinar.

apparatus such as the mirror in a reflex camera, the shutter in a cine camera, and in particular the beam-splitting prism of a Technicolor camera. In such cases there is a real advantage in placing a negative lens in front and a positive lens behind.

A notable example of this general construction is the Hill lens made by Beck (Fig. 66) to photograph the whole sky in a single picture.

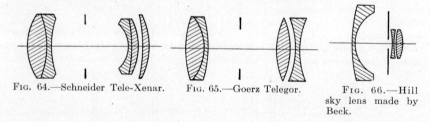

FIG. 64.—Schneider Tele-Xenar.　　FIG. 65.—Goerz Telegor.　　　FIG. 66.—Hill
　　　　　　　　　　　　　　　　　　　　　　　　　　　　　　　　　sky lens made by
　　　　　　　　　　　　　　　　　　　　　　　　　　　　　　　　　Beck.

Process Lenses.—Lenses for making half-tone and other printing blocks are designated "process lenses" and usually operate at approximately unit magnification and at low aperture (say $f/10$ to $f/30$). For these reasons a symmetrical type of construction is generally adopted, favorite types being the Celor or Homocentric forms containing four separated single lenses. Actually for photographing black lines on a white ground, the stray light due to internal reflection between eight glass-air surfaces is liable to cause loss of contrast, and it is likely that clearer reproduction might be obtained if a lens having fewer glass-air surfaces such as the Dagor were used.

It is clear that a high degree of freedom from distortion is most necessary in a process lens, especially in one used to copy maps or any other diagrams on which measurements are to be made. All aberrations other than distortion and transverse chromatic aberration can be eliminated by stopping the lens down to a small aperture, and the two latter aberrations will also vanish if the lens is symmetrical and used at unit magnification. However, in lenses suitably designed, these two aberrations can be made negligibly small even for magnifications other than unity.

For three-color process work, it is clearly essential to use a lens in which the transverse chromatic aberration is very highly corrected, since the size of picture produced must be identical in red, green, and blue light. Such a lens is called an "apochromatic process lens," and ordinarily requires very careful choice of glass in its design.

Enlarger Lenses.—In general, the requirements to be satisfied by an enlarging lens are not essentially different from those of a process lens. If an ordinary camera lens is used for enlarging, trouble may arise because such a lens has been designed for use with a distant object, and in an enlarger it operates at a magnification of one or two only. The effect of this may be that a lens having a well-corrected flat field when used on a camera has a curved field on an enlarger, and the definition may become worse still on account of coma and other aberrations which disappear when a distant object is used. Stopping the lens down will assist all these defects except distortion and transverse chromatic aberration, as was mentioned above under Process Lenses. Incidentally, for three-color separation work, an apochromatic objective is really necessary, for even the residual longitudinal chromatic aberration of an ordinary lens may give a blurred red image with perfectly sharp blue and green images.

Aero Lenses.—The lenses used in aerial photography fall into two groups, *viz.*, those for aerial surveying and those for military purposes. In the first group the aperture need not be high as aerial surveying is carried out only in perfect weather with bright sunlight, and it is doubtful if such photographs would be taken at an aperture greater than $f/8$ or $f/11$. On the other hand, distortion and to a lesser extent coma and transverse chromatic aberration must be corrected to a very high degree since extremely precise measurements are to be made on the photographs taken from the airplane. It goes without saying too that the definition over the whole picture must be very sharp. The achromatism should tend toward the green or yellow regions of the spectrum as a yellow haze-cutting filter is invariably used in surveying work.

For military purposes, however, a speed of at least $f/4.5$ is necessary since pictures must often be made in poor light, but distortion need not be quite so highly corrected as is necessary for map making. Nevertheless good distortion correction is valuable if it can be obtained, for then the same lens can be used for surveying if desired.

In all airplane work, a long focus is desirable to give a large-scale photograph when taken at a considerable altitude.

Lenses for Infrared Photography.—As was mentioned above under the description of chromatic aberration (page 30), when a lens is achromatized by the use of crown and flint glasses, there is one particular wavelength for which the focus falls closest to the lens. If a lens is intended to be used specifically in the infrared, *i.e.*, for wavelengths between 0.75 and 1.2 μ, the minimum focus should be at perhaps 0.9 or 1.0 μ, instead of being at 0.55 μ as in visual achromatism, or at 0.48 μ for photographic achromatism. Thus, lenses for infrared use must be heavily overcorrected chromatically.

Since a lens achromatized in this way would be virtually useless in blue light, an infrared filter is sometimes incorporated into the lens to prevent its use for other purposes.

Portrait Lenses.—Any lens of sufficient aperture may be used for portraiture. Moreover, as was mentioned on page 26, good perspective demands a long focus, consequently portrait lenses are usually somewhat large in size. The field to be covered in portraiture is usually very small, and consequently a lens of the Petzval type is really surprisingly satisfactory.

For artistic photography, there is a considerable demand for "soft-focus" or "diffusion" effects. These effects can be obtained by placing over the lens a diffusion

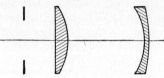

Fig. 67.—Dallmeyer-Bergheim diffuse portrait lens.

attachment, which is merely a glass disk carrying ridges or other means for diffracting a portion of the light. Some lenses are, however, specially designed to give a softness of contrast by deliberately leaving a suitable residual of spherical or chromatic aberration, or both, in the design. It is essential for this purpose that the definition itself shall be good, but there must be a softness or diffuseness of the light superposed on the image. In some lenses variable diffusion may be obtained by sliding one lens along the barrel. In other cases, the diffusion can be varied by stopping down the iris diaphragm. An interesting design for diffuse portraiture is the Dallmeyer-Bergheim lens, which consists of a telephoto combination of two simple lenses with variable separation to give variable sizes of pictures (Fig. 67).

Anamorphic Systems.—It is occasionally desired to have a lens which will give different magnifications in two directions.[1] This is possible by means of cylindrical lenses used in the manner indicated in Fig. 68. If the two lenses are equal in power and arranged with axes perpendicular to one another, the magnifications in the directions of the cylinder axes will be m and $1/m$, respec-

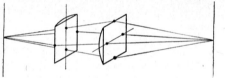

Fig. 68.—An anamorphic optical system.

tively. The value of m will become greater, the greater the separation between the lenses. The relative values of the magnifications can be altered by using two lenses of unequal focal length. If one cylindrical lens is rotated relative to the other, the image of a square becomes distorted into a rhomboid.

Supplementary Lenses.—These are lenses intended to be attached to the front of an existing lens to lengthen or shorten the focal length. They are generally simple

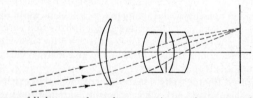

Fig. 69.—Passage of light rays through a portrait-attachment supplementary lens.

meniscus landscape lenses, designed to work with a stop situated at the entrance-pupil of the existing lens, as indicated in Fig. 69. If the supplementary lens is positive, the over-all focal length is shortened, and on a focusing camera the picture seen will be reduced in size. With a fixed-focus camera such as a cheap box camera, the addition of a positive lens in this way enables close objects to be photographed. The correct

[1] For a full discussion of the various means by which this may be attained, see Newcomer, U. S. Pat. 1932082 (1933); 1945950 and 1945951 (1934).

distance of the object is then marked on the lens mount, and the auxiliary lens becomes a "portrait attachment."

If a negative lens is added to an existing lens, the focal length is increased, and a larger picture results. The original Dallmeyer Adon lens was an interesting extreme case of a supplementary lens, for the Adon was a $2 \times$ Galilean telescope system; if the telescope were focused correctly for infinity, it would serve to double the size of the image of a distant object without upsetting the focus adjustment of the camera.

Astronomical Photographic Lenses.—At first, astronomical photography was done by merely placing a photographic plate in the focal plane of an ordinary telescope. However, in such a case the field of view is very small, being only about a degree in a refracting telescope and but a few minutes of arc in a reflector. Also, in a refractor the visual achromatism is entirely unsuited to photographic work, and a chromatically undercorrected zero-power "correcting lens" is commonly inserted in the telescope tube to improve the achromatism for photography.

As soon as photographic materials of a suitable character became available, toward the end of the last century, astronomical photography rapidly became more and more common. To cover a wide field of sky in a single exposure, large photographic lenses of the Celor or Cooke types were used. These have been constructed in focal lengths of several feet, at apertures up to $f/6$ and are very highly corrected systems.

In recent years, a number of interesting small lenses of great relative aperture have been developed for astronomical purposes. The first was Dennis Taylor's $f/2$ lens[1] consisting of two similar cemented triplet combinations, together with a strong concave lens placed very close to the focal plane (Fig. 70). This concave lens acts as a "field flattener," according to the plan suggested in 1866 by Piazzi-Smyth. By virtue of its position, the concave lens has practically no effect on

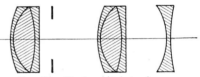

Fig. 70.—Taylor $f/2$ Astro lens.

the focal power or on the spherical aberration of the system, but it carries its full weight in reducing the Petzval sum. The Piazzi-Smyth lens has also been applied to large reflecting telescopes by Ross to improve their field of view.

In 1934, Rayton of the Bausch and Lomb Company constructed a high-speed spectrographic objective for Mount Wilson observatory, which consisted of a 4-mm. microscope objective enlarged eight times so as to give a focal length of 32 mm. The numerical aperture of the microscope objective was 0.85, giving an f-number of $1/(2 \times 0.85) = 0.59$. Even this very high speed was surpassed in 1936 by Bracey[2] who similarly enlarged an oil-immersion microscope objective having a numerical aperture of 1.4. This gives an equivalent f-number of $1/(2 \times 1.4) = 0.36$ and represents an increase in speed of 2.7 times over the Rayton lens. The objections to this lens are, however, the extreme smallness of the spectrum produced by it, since its focal length is only 16 mm., and also the necessity of oiling the plate to the back of the lens. Nevertheless, it represents the ultimate limit which has been achieved in the effort to obtain speed in a photographic lens.

The Principal Types of Photographic Lenses.—The following list includes most of the lenses made by some of the more prominent manufacturers in recent years. The data of current lenses have been derived from the makers' catalogues and advertisements in photographic journals, and from information supplied by them. The properties of obsolete lenses have been drawn largely from the bibliography given

[1] Brit. Pat. 127058.
[2] *Astrophys. J.*, **83**, 179 (1936).

below. While every effort has been made to secure accuracy, there may be some errors and omissions in the list. Also some firms have been omitted entirely as their catalogues were not available at the time of writing. It should be realized that the lens market is continually changing, old and unsatisfactory types being constantly

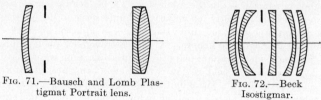

FIG. 71.—Bausch and Lomb Plastigmat Portrait lens.

FIG. 72.—Beck Isostigmar.

withdrawn from circulation and new designs substituted. Also, various firms have recently combined, thus eliminating a number of overlapping types of lens. Notable examples of this are the Zeiss-Ikon system, containing Zeiss, Goerz, Ernemann, Ica, and Contessa-Nettel, which was formed in 1926. The Agfa Company has recently

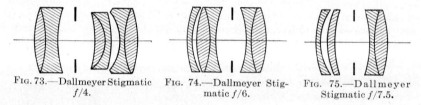

FIG. 73.—Dallmeyer Stigmatic $f/4$.

FIG. 74.—Dallmeyer Stigmatic $f/6$.

FIG. 75.—Dallmeyer Stigmatic $f/7.5$.

absorbed Rietzschel. Reichert has made no photographic lenses since the war, and Beck has recently given up all photographic lenses except the Hill sky lens. The Gundlach-Manhattan Optical Company ceased operations a few years ago. Many makers of cameras and enlarging equipment supply lenses, purchased from another

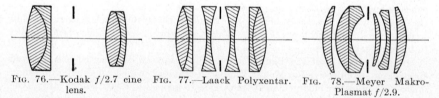

FIG. 76.—Kodak $f/2.7$ cine lens.

FIG. 77.—Laack Polyxentar.

FIG. 78.—Meyer Makro-Plasmat $f/2.9$.

manufacturer, which are sometimes engraved with the name of the maker of the apparatus. This accounts for a number of names which are not included in Table VI.

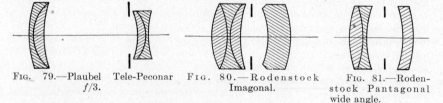

FIG. 79.—Plaubel Tele-Peconar $f/3$.

FIG. 80.—Rodenstock Imagonal.

FIG. 81.—Rodenstock Pantagonal wide angle.

In addition to the types in Table VI, many firms have made in the past lenses of the rapid-rectilinear, Petzval portrait and simple landscape types, all of which are now obsolete but are still to be found in common use. Lenses of the rapid-rectilinear type have been given various trade names, for example:

Beck: Biplanat, Symmetrical, Portrait Biplanat
Berthiot: Périgraphique
Busch: Rapid Symmetrical, Rapid Aplanat, Wide-angle Aplanat
Dallmeyer: Rapid Rectilinear
Fleury-Hermagis: Eidoskop
Goerz: Lynkeioskop and Paraplanat
Hartnack: Pantoskop
Ilex: Convertible Rapid Rectilinear
Meyer: Aristoplan and Aristoplanat
Rodenstock: Recti-aplanat, Wide-angle Aplanat
Schulze: Orthoskop and Sphäriskop
Steinheil: Aplanat
Suter: Aplanat
Voigtländer: Euryskop
Wollensak: Versar
Wray: Platystigmat

Also the very interesting series of Steinheil lenses, in which an attempt was made to reduce the Petzval sum by using old glasses, has been omitted. They are given in Table IV:

TABLE IV.—STEINHEIL LENSES

Lens	f-number	Field	Year
Group Aplanat	6	56°	1879
Group Antiplanet	6	62°	1881
Portrait Antiplanet	4	30°	1881
Rapid Antiplanet	6	60°	1893

Most manufacturers have made portrait lenses of the Petzval type or one of its modifications. These are now largely but not entirely obsolete. Table V gives a list of some of them:

TABLE V.—PORTRAIT LENSES

Maker	Lens	f-number	Field	Foci
Agfa	Ocellar	2.2	20°	35–65 mm.
Beck	Studio lens	3–6	37°	6–24 in.
Dallmeyer	Patent Portrait	3	36°	6–17 in.
Dallmeyer	Patent Portrait	4	36°	10–30 in.
Dallmeyer	Patent Portrait	6	41°	9–37 in.
Gundlach	Portrait A	5	60°	9–20 in.
Gundlach	Portrait B	4	60°	7½–24 in.
Rodenstock	Studio rapid lens	3.5	—	14–48 in.
Ross	Rapid Portrait	3.5	—	8¼–16 in.
Wollensak	Vesta	5	—	6–14 in.
Wollensak	Vitax	3.8	—	10–20 in.
Wray	Studio lens	4.5	—	10–12 in.

Principal Types of Anastigmat Lenses.—In Table VI, which follows, the lenses are given in alphabetical order under each manufacturer. A number immediately after

Table VI.—Photographic Objectives

Name	f-number	Field, degrees	Foci	Type and figure number	Remarks

Aldis Brothers, Sarehole Road, Sparkhill, Birmingham, England.

Name	f-number	Field, degrees	Foci	Type and figure number	Remarks
Aero	5.6	23	20 in.	—	Aero
Photomicro	3	—	0.9, 1.4 in.	—	Photomicrography
Photomicro	6.5	—	2, 3 in.	—	"
Series 0	3	40	2–12 in.	Cooke 27(?)	Portrait, general
Series 1	4.5	53	4–16 in.	Tessar 44(?)	
Series 2	6	53	4–6½ in.	31	
Series 2a	6.3	53	4–14 in.	Cooke 27(?)	
Series 3	7.7	52	5–11 in.	31	
Series 3a	7.7	100	5–11 in.	—	Wide angle

Agfa. I.G. Farbenindustrie, Frankfurt, Germany. (Agfa Ansco Company, Binghampton, N. Y.)

Name	f-number	Field, degrees	Foci	Type and figure number	Remarks
Apotar	4.5	60	85, 105 mm.	Cooke 27	Small cameras
Bilinar	11	60	100 mm.	Periscopic 4	" "
Igenar	8.8	60	75 mm.	Achr. men. 2	" "
Igestar	5.6	65	75, 100 mm.	Cooke 27	" "
Igestar	6.3	60	50–130 mm.	" "	" "
Igestar	7.7	65	100 mm.	" "	" "
Igestar	8.8	65	100 mm.	" "	" "
Kine anastigmat	2.8	35	12–20 mm.	" "	Cine 8, 16 mm.
Kine anastigmat	3.5	35	20–50 mm.	" "	Cine 16 mm.
Meniscus	13	—	75–100 mm.	Landscape 1	Box cameras
Ocellar	2.2	20	35–65 mm.	Petzval portrait 3	Cine 16 mm.
Prolinear	1.9	40	135 mm.	4-lens, mod. Cooke	Portrait
Solinar	3.5	55	50 mm.	4-lens, partly cem.	
Solinar	3.9	65	75 mm.		Small cameras
Solinar	4.5	65	50–135 mm.		
Symmetar	1.5	35	12, 20 mm.	5-lens, unsymm.	Cine 8, 16 mm.
Tele-ansatz	6.3	30	200 mm.	2 doublets	Tele
Tele-cine-anastigmat	3.5	9	80 mm.	4 lenses	" cine

Astro-Gesellschaft M.B.H., Berlin-Neukölln, Lahnstrasse 30, Germany.

Name	f-number	Field, degrees	Foci	Type and figure number	Remarks
Astan	3.5	—	—	—	Cine
Astrar	2.7	—	—	—	" min. cam.
Astro-kino	1.2	—	—	—	"
Pantachar	1.8	—	—	—	
Pantachar	2.3	—	—	—	
Portrait	2.3	—	75–100 mm.	—	Portrait. (Soft focus also made)
R.K. objective	1.25	—	—	—	X-ray cine
Tachar	1.5	—	—	—	Cine
Tacharette	1.5	—	—	—	"
Tacharette	1.8	—	—	—	"
Tachon	0.95	—	—	—	"
Telephoto	5	—	10–80 cm.	—	Tele

TABLE VI.—PHOTOGRAPHIC OBJECTIVES.—(*Continued*)

Name	*f*-number	Field, degrees	Foci	Type and figure number	Remarks
Bausch and Lomb Optical Company, Rochester, N. Y.					
Aero lens	4	62	8¼ in.	Plasmat 22	Aero
Aero lens	4.5	55	12 in.	" "	"
Aero lens	5	75	8¼ in.	" "	"
Aero lens	6	65	6 in.	" "	"
Aero lens	11	75	6½ in.	" "	"
Aero Tessar	6	27	24 in.	Radar 51	"
Aero Tessar	6	45	24 in.	" "	
Convertible Protar series 7a	6.3–7.7	63	4–23 in.	Double protar 13	Convertible
Extreme wide angle, series 5	18	90	3½–37 in.	Protar 10	Wide angle
Medium wide angle, series 4	12.5	70	2½–48 in.	" "	" "
Metrogon	6.3	90	5⅛, 6 in.	33a	Aero wide angle
Micro Tessar	4.5	—	16–72 mm.	Tessar 44	Photomicrography
Plastigmat	5.6	40	9–18 in.	71	Portrait
Process-anastigmat	10	35	13–25 in.	Homocentric 33	Process
Protar, series 7	12.5	56	7–39 in.	Half of protar 13	Landscape
Raytar	2.3	53	35–152 mm.	Biotar 39	Cine 35 mm.
Sigmar	4	44	16–22 in.	Cooke 27	Portrait
Tessar 1c	3.5	53	32–75 mm.	Tessar 44	Cine, min. cam.
Tessar	4.5	60	3½–19½ in.	" "	10 & 12 in. for aero
Tessar 2b	6.3	62	3½–23¼ in.	" "	General, photomicrography
Beck. R. and J. Beck, Ltd., 69 Mortimer St., London W.1., England.					
Bystigmar	6	60	4½–11 in.	13	Convertible
Cine lens	3.5	41	1.6–3 in.	—	Cine 35 mm.
Isostigmar 0	3.5	60	2–8 in.	72	
Isostigmar 1	4.5	60	3–12 in.	72	
Isostigmar 6	5.6	54	9½–17 in.	72	
Isostigmar 2	5.8	70	3–8 in.	72	
Isostigmar 4	6.3	90	3½–19 in.	72	
Isostigmar 1a	6.5	62	9–19 in.	72	
Isostigmar 3	7.7	65	4½–9 in.	72	
Isostigmar 5	11	—		72	Process
Neostigmar 1	4.5	60	5–8½ in.	28	
Neostigmar 2	6	70	5–8 in.	28	
Neostigmar 3	7.7	62	5–10½ in.	28	
Robin Hill lens	22	180	—	66	Sky lens
Boyer. Les Établissements Boyer, 25 Blvd. Arago, Paris (13e).					
Beryl	6.8	85	5–25 cm.	Dagor 12	Convertible
Opale	4.5	56	5–50 cm.	—	Portrait, soft
Perle	9	105	60–145 mm.	—	Wide angle
Rubis	3.5–4.5	30	30–70 cm.	Cooke 27	Portrait
Saphir	1.4	45	15–100 mm.	6 piece	Cine, min. cam.
Saphir	1.9	45	15–100 mm.	—	" " "

TABLE VI.—PHOTOGRAPHIC OBJECTIVES.—(*Continued*)

Name	f-number	Field, degrees	Foci	Type and figure number	Remarks
Boyer. Les Établissements Boyer, 25 Blvd. Arago, Paris (13e). (*Continued*)					
Saphir	2.3	45	15–100 mm.	—	Cine, min. cam
Saphir	3.5	62	15–170 mm.	Tessar 44	
Saphir	4.5	64	40–500 mm.	" "	
Saphir	6.3	62	54–500 mm.	" "	
Saphir-Aviation	4.5– 6.3	64	20–120 cm.	" "	Aero
Saphir Apo	9 –12.5	40	30–120 cm.	—	Process
Saphir B	4.5	—	85–210 mm.	Tessar 44	Enlarging
Topaz	2.9	52	2–18 cm.	Cooke 27	
Topaz	3.5	52	2–18 cm.	" "	
Topaz	4.5	58	75–135 mm.	" "	
Topaz	6.3	58	58–210 mm.	" "	
Busch. Emil Busch A.G., Optische Industrie, Rathenow bei Berlin, Germany.					
Bistelar	7	30	20–55 cm.	52	Tele
Glaukar	2.5	—	13 mm.	Cooke 27	Cine 8 mm.
Glaukar	2.8	35	20 mm.	" "	" 16 mm.
Glaukar	3.1	47	60–400 mm.	" "	
Glaukar	4.5	57	85–165 mm.	" "	
Glaukar	6.3	62	90–150 mm.	" "	
Glyptar	3.5	53	25–75 mm.	Tessar 44(?)	
Glyptar	4.5	53	55–400 mm.	" "	
Leukar	6.8	61	90–250 mm.	Two triples, symm.	
Leukar	7.7	61	330–450 mm.	" "	
Leukar	9	80	65–300 mm.	" "	
Omnar	4.5	75	13–25 cm.	Homocentric 33	
Omnar	5.5	75	9–45 cm.	" "	
Omnar	7.7	80	9–55 cm.	" "	
Perscheid	4.5	38	21–48 cm.	Special design	Artistic photography
Perscheid	5.5	38	60 cm.	" "	
Stigmar	6.3	—	—	Plasmat 22	Convertible
J. H. Dallmeyer, Ltd., Willesden, London N.W. 10., England. (Medo Photo Supply Co., 15 West 47th St., New York.)					
Adon	10–37	16–24	12–44 in. (var.)	Bistelar 52	Variable tele
Anastigmat	3.5	—	13–75 mm.	—	Cine, 8, 16 mm.
Dallmeyer-Banfield	6	33	18–30 in.	—	Portrait soft
Dallmeyer-Bergheim	6.5–15	—	12–55 in. (var.)	67	Var. tele, soft portrait
Dallon 6	5.6	30	4–30 in.	54	2× telephoto
Dallon 18	6.5	24	6–12 in.	54	" "
Dallon 17	6.8	20	15 in.	Bistelar 52	2½× "
Dallon 16	7.7	30	12–40 in.	54	2× "
Dalmac	3.5	50	2–15 in.	—	
Enlarging anastigmat	4.5	—	2–8½ in.	—	Enlarging
Grandac 1	10	12	25 in.	10 in., f/4 Petzval, with 4-in. neg. lens	Tele

TABLE VI.—PHOTOGRAPHIC OBJECTIVES.—(*Continued*)

Name	f-number	Field, degrees	Foci	Type and figure number	Remarks
J. H. Dallmeyer, Ltd., Willesden. London N.W. 10., England. (Medo Photo Supply Co., 15 West 47th St., New York.) (*Continued*)					
Grandac 2.	11	16	28 in.	Same with 5-in. neg. lens	Tele
Mutac.	4.5	48	6,9 in.	—	Conv. soft portrait
New Large Adon.	4.5	25	6–24 in.	Bistelar 52	Tele 2×
Pentac.	2.9	53	1–12 in.	Dynar 46	—
Perfac.	6.3	53	3–30 in.	—	"
Popular-telephoto.	6	25	9–12 in.	—	"
Portrait anastigmat.	3.5	46	9–15 in.	—	Portrait, var. soft
Portrait anastigmat. . . .	4.5	56	10–18 in.	—	
Portrait anastigmat. . . .	6	56	10–18 in.	—	
Serrac.	4.5	56	3–18 in.	—	
Soft-focus lens.	4.5	47	1–12 in	—	Portrait, general
Speed anastigmat.	1.5	45	15–76 mm.	—	Cine 16 mm.
Stigmatic 1.	4	40	6–12 in.	73	Portrait
Stigmatic 2.	6	70	4–15 in.	74	Convertible
Stigmatic 3.	7.5	75	3–16 in.	75	
Super-six.	1.9	48	1–6 in.	—	Cine, general
Triple anastigmat.	2.9	—	12–75 mm.	—	" 8, 16 mm.
Wide-angle anastigmat. .	11	100	3–9 in.	—	Wide angle
C. Friedrich, Munich, Germany.					
Biochron.	2	—	—	—	
Coronar.	4.5	—	50–360 mm.	4 uncem. lenses	
Corygon. . . . . : . .	2.9–6.3	—	25–135 mm.	Cooke 27	
C. P. Goerz, Berlin. (Now Part of Zeiss-Ikon.) (C. P. Goerz American Optical Company, 317 East 34th St., New York.)					
Alethar.	11	70	30–120 cm.	36	Process
Artar.	9–16	—	14–70 in.	Celor 32	Apo process
Celor.	3.5	—	—	32 unsymm.	
Celor.	4.5	70	6–48 cm.	32	
Celor.	6.3	70	9–27 cm.	32	
Cinegor.	1.2	—	25 mm.	—	Cine
Cinegor.	1.5				
Cinegor.	2	—	50–100 mm.	—	"
Cinegor.	2.5				
Convertible anastigmat series 2	—	—	—	19	Convertible
Dagor, series 3.	6.8	70–90	4–90 cm.	12	
Dagor, series 4.	11	90	30–120 cm.	12	Wide angle
Dogmar.	4.5	48	3–12 in.	Celor 32	
Dogmar.	5.5	48	12–16 in.	" "	
Gotar.	6.8–10	54	8–24 in.	" "	Process
Hypar.	3 –4.5	—	—	Cooke 27	
Hypergon.	22	140	6–12 cm.	8	Extreme wide angle
Kino Hypar.	2.7	—	15–100 mm.	—	Cine
Kino Hypar.	3	—	35–100 mm.	—	"
Pantar.	6.3	85	86–276 mm.	18	Convertible
Syntor.	6.8	64	12–21 cm.	Celor 32	
Telegor.	—	—	—	65	Tele
Telestar. . . :	4.5	38	6–13½ in.	—	"
Tenaxiar.	6.8	—	—	Cooke 27	

TABLE VI.—PHOTOGRAPHIC OBJECTIVES.—(*Continued*)

Name	f-number	Field, degrees	Foci	Type and figure number	Remarks
Gundlach-Manhattan Optical Company, Rochester, N. Y.					
Anastigmat, series 4....	6.3	60	5–16 in.	Celor 32	
Hyperion..............	4	52	7–18 in.	—	Portrait, soft
Perigraphic...........	5.6	56	6–16 in.	Two triples	Convertible
Radar....	4.5	62	3½–18 in.	51	
Turner-Reich.........	6.8	57	5–15 in.	20	"
Ultrastigmat..........	1.9	—	4, 5 cm.	—	Cine 35 mm.
Ilex Optical Company, Rochester, N. Y.					
Anastigmat series *D*....	7.5	61	3½–12 in.	—	
Cinemat..............	1.5	30	1, 2 in.	—	Cine 16, 35 mm.
Ilextigmat............	6.3	58	3½–23½ in.	—	Convertible
Medium wide-angle.....	16	80	5¼–12¾ in.	—	Wide angle
Paragon..............	4.5	53	32 mm., 3½–20 in.	—	Cine, general
Paragon-Cinemat.......	3.5	33	2, 3 in.	—	" 35 mm., min. cam.
Photoplastic..........	4.5	45	4½–21 in.	—	Portrait, var. soft
Portrait..............	3.5, 3.8	46	10–16 in.	—	"
Portrait..............	5	45	6½–21½ in.	—	"
Super-Cinemat........	2.6	46	35–75 mm.	—	Cine 35 mm.
Kern et Cie., A.G., Aarau, Switzerland. (Kern Company, 136 Liberty St., New York.)					
Kern lens.............	4.5	—	105–120 mm.	Celor 32	
Kern lens.............	6.3	—	85–480 mm.	" "	
Kernon...............	3.5	65	100, 150 mm.	Tessar 44	
Kernon...............	4.5	65	80–150 mm.	" "	
Kino-Aufnahme-Objektiv...........	1.8	—	30–75 mm.	Speedic 29	Cine
Kino-Aufnahme-Objektiv...........	2.5	—	25–75 mm.	Cooke 27	"
Kino-Aufnahme-Objektiv...........	3.5	—	25, 35 mm.	" "	"
Kino-Aufnahme-Objektiv...........	4.5	—	35 mm.	" "	"
Portrait.............	4.5	—	18–36 cm.	" "	Portrait
Spezial Objektiv.......	7.8	65	185 mm.	6-lens, symm.	Aero
Kodak. Eastman Kodak Company, Rochester, N. Y.					
Anastigmat...........	1.9	24	13, 25 mm.	Celor 32	Cine 16 mm.
Anastigmat...........	2.7	14	102 mm.	76	" " "
Anastigmat...........	2.7	40	13–15 mm.	Cooke 27	" " "
Anastigmat...........	3.5	36	56, 65 mm.	Celor 32	Enlarging
Anastigmat...........	3.5	36	12.7–50 mm.	Cooke 27	Cine 16 mm.
Anastigmat...........	4.5	19	38–152 mm.	Dallon 54	Cine tele
Anastigmat...........	4.5	52	3–12 in.	Tessar 44	
Anastigmat...........	5	46	1 in.	" "	Enlarging

TABLE VI.—PHOTOGRAPHIC OBJECTIVES.—(*Continued*)

Name	*f*-number	Field, degrees	Foci	Type and figure number	Remarks
Kodak.	Eastman Kodak Company, Rochester, N. Y.		(*Continued*)		
Anastigmat...........	6.3	52	53–128 mm.	Cooke 27	
Anastigmat...........	6.3	52	170 mm.	Celor 32	
Anastigmat...........	7.7	48	130 mm.	" "	Enlarging
Aviation..............	4.5	46	10 in.	Tessar 44	Aero
Aviation..............	5	46	12½ in.	" "	"
Aviation..............	6	24	24 in.	" "	"
Ektar................	2	54	45 mm.	Biotar 39	Min. cam.
Kodar................	7.9	52	98–173 mm.	Cooke 27	Enlarging
Photostat anastigmat...	10	50	13–21 in.	Celor 32	Photostat
Process anastigmat.....	8	50	10 in.	" "	Process
Process anastigmat.....	10	50	18 in.	Tessar 44	"
Laack.	Julius Laack Söhne, Curlandstrasse 60, Rathenow, Germany.				
Cine lens.............	2, 2.3	—	15–85 mm.	Petzval 3	Cine
Cine-Pololyt..........	2	27	25 mm.	Cooke 27	Cine 16 mm.
Cine-Polyxentar........	1.3, 1.5	—	12.5–25 mm.	77	Cine 8, 16 mm.
Dialytar.............	3.5	60	7.5–30 cm.	Celor 32	
Dialytar.............	4.5	65	7.5–36 cm.	" "	
Dialytar.............	6.3	85	7.5–21 cm.	Homocentric 33	General, wide angle
Dialytar *P*..........	3.5	55	30, 36 cm.	Cooke 27	Portrait
Dialytar *T*..........	2.7	50	15–165 mm.	Tessar 44	Min. cam.
Dialytar *T*..........	3.5	50	2–30 cm.	" "	
Dialytar *T*..........	4.5	60	2.5–40 cm.	" "	
Dialytar *T*..........	6.3	65	7.5–40 cm.	" "	
Dialytar wide-angle.....	8.7	100	7.5–25 cm.	Homocentric 33	Wide angle
Enlarging anastigmat...	3.5	—	2.5–12 cm.	Cooke, 27	Cheap enlarging lens
Enlarging anastigmat...	4.5	—	2.5–13.5 cm.	" "	" " "
Enlarging anastigmat...	6.3	—	5.5–13.5 cm.	" "	" " "
Pololyt...............	2.9	—	2–7.5 cm.	" "	
Pololyt...............	3.5	55	2–16.5 cm.	" "	
Pololyt...............	4.5	55	7.5–36 cm.	" "	
Pololyt...............	6.3	65	7.5–36 cm.	" "	
Polyxentar............	4.5	70	7.5–30 cm.	77	
Polyxentar............	6.8	70	18–36 cm.	77	
Regulyt..............	4.5	50	105 mm.	Cooke 27	Hand cameras, focusing by front lens only
Regulyt..............	6.3	60	105 mm.	" "	
Repro-Polyxentar......	9		13.5–36 cm.	77	Process
Teleanastigmat........	6.3	35	20–27 cm.	Two doublets	Tele
Texon................	3.5		2.5–21 cm.	Four lenses	Enlarging
Texon................	4.5		2.5–21 cm.	" "	"
	E. Leitz, Wetzlar, Germany. (750 Fifth Ave., New York.)				
Dygon................	2.8, 3.5	35	20 mm.	Cooke 27	Cine 16 mm.
Elmar................	3.5	65	35, 50 mm.	Tessar 44(?)	Min. cam.
Elmar................	4	27	90, 135 mm.	" "	" "
Elmar................	6.3	24	105 mm.	" "	" "
Hektor...............	1.9	34	73 mm.	6 comp, cem.	" "
Hektor...............	2.5	48	50 mm.	" " "	" "

TABLE VI.—PHOTOGRAPHIC OBJECTIVES.—(*Continued*)

Name	f-number	Field, degrees	Foci	Type and figure number	Remarks

E. Leitz, Wetzlar, Germany.   (750 Fifth Ave., New York.)   (*Continued*)

Name	f-number	Field, degrees	Foci	Type and figure number	Remarks
Hektor................	4.5	19	135 mm.	4 comp., middle cem.	Min. cam.
Hektor................	6.3	76	28 mm.	5 comp.	" " wide angle
Hektor rapid..........	1.4	27	25 mm.	7 comp. partly cem.	Cine 16 mm.
Hektor rapid..........	1.5	35	12 mm.	" " "	" 8, 9 mm.
Summar..............	2	48	50 mm.	Biotar 39	Min. cam.
Telyt.................	4.5	12	200 mm.	—	Min. cam. tele
Thambar.	2.2	27	90 mm.	4 comp., middle cem.	Portrait soft
Varob................	3.5	—	50 mm.	Tessar 44	Enlarging
Voort................	4	—	95 mm.	—	Enlarging

Hugo Meyer, Görlitz, Germany.   (245 West 55th St., New York.)

Name	f-number	Field, degrees	Foci	Type and figure number	Remarks
Aristostigmat..........	4.5	75	1½–20 in.	Homocentric 33	
Aristostigmat..........	6.3	90	1½–20 in.	" "	Wide angle
Double-Aristostigmat...	6.8	82	4–90 cm.	4 cem. lenses, symm.	Convertible
Double-anastigmat.....	6.8	62	1½–30 in.	Dagor 12	"
Double-Plasmat........	4	57	2–19 in.	22	"
Double-Plasmat........	5.5	57	2–19 in.	22	"
Helioplan.............	4.5	65	55–250 mm.	Celor 32	Enlarging
Euryplan.............	4.5	—	—	Plasmat 22	
Euryplan.............	6	85	2–24 in.	" "	Convertible
Kino-Plasmat..........	1.5	32	15–88 mm.	25	Cine
Kino-Plasmat..........	2	—	2–12 cm.	25	"
Makro-Plasmat.........	2.9	75	1–12 in.	78	
Portrait-Trioplan.......	3	40	3–19 in.	Cooke 27	Portrait
Primoplan............	1.5, 1.9	47	13–100 mm.	42	Min. cam.
Primotar.............	4.5	—	—	Tessar 44	
Process-Plasmat........	8	48	14–34 in.	Plasmat 22	Process
Tele-megor............	4	—	3–9 in.	Dallon 54	Tele
Trioplan.............	2.9	55	15–210 mm.	Cooke 27	
Trioplan	4.5	64	3–14 in.	" "	
Trioplan	6.3	64	2–14 in.	" "	
Veraplan.............	4.5, 6.8	—	—	6 element	Double anastigmat
Wide-angle Aristostigmat................	9	100	3–11 in.	Homocentric 33	Wide angle

O.I.P. Société Belge d'Optique et d'Instruments de Précision, Blvd. Albert 148, Ghent, Belgium.

Name	f-number	Field, degrees	Foci	Type and figure number	Remarks
Labor................	3.5, 4.5	40	45–440 mm.	Cooke 27	Portrait var. soft
Major................	4.5	60	135, 150 mm.	" "	
Major................	6.3	58	90–150 mm.	" "	
Miror................	4.5	58	50–210 mm.	Tessar 44	

TABLE VI.—PHOTOGRAPHIC OBJECTIVES.—(*Continued*)

Name	*f*-number	Field, degrees	Foci	Type and figure number	Remarks
Plaubel A.G., Königstrasse 66, Frankfurt a.M., Germany. (Photo Marketing Corp., 10 West 33rd St., New York.)					
Anticomar	2.9	—	75–180 mm.	Tessar 44	
Anticomar	4.5	—	30 cm.	" "	
Heliorthar	2	—	—	—	
Makinar	6.3	—	—	—	
Neocomar	1.8	—	—	—	
Rapid wide-angle Orthar	6.8	72	73 mm.	Homocentric 33	Wide angle
Supracomar	2	58	45 mm.	Biotar 39	
Telemakinar	6.3	—	21 cm.	Bistelar 52	Tele
Telemakinar	5.4	—	21 cm.	" "	"
Telemakinar *S*	4.8	—	19 cm.	63	"
Telemakinar *S*	6.3	—	19 cm.	63	"
Tele-Peconar	3	9 × 12 cm.	1–2 m.	79	Var. tele
C. Reichert, Optische Werke, Vienna XVII, Austria.					
Combinar	6.3	82	9–24 cm.	16	Convertible
Neukombinar	6.8	95	6–30 cm.	—	Wide-angle conv.
Polar	4	55	3–10 cm.	—	
Solar	6.8	61	12–21 cm.	Celor 32	
Rietzschel, Munich, Germany. (Now Part of Agfa Company.)					
Adjustable Telephoto	9	—	—	—	Tele
Linear *A*	4.5	75	6–42 cm.	17	Convertible
Linear *B*	5.5	75	6–60 cm.	17	"
Linear *C*	6.8	75	6–90 cm.	17	"
Reproduction Objective	11	—	30–120 cm.	—	Process
G. Rodenstock, Optische Werke, Munich 15, Germany.					
Apo-Process-Eurynar	—	—	—	—	Process
Eikonar	6.8	—	11–18 cm.	Two triples, symm.	Convertible
Eurygon	4.5	48	21–60 cm.	Cooke 27	
Eurynar	3.5	50	75–150 mm.	Celor 32	
Eurynar	4.5	56	50–300 mm.	" "	
Eurynar	6.5	60	105–480 mm.	" "	
Imagon	5.8	42	17–48 cm.	—	Portrait var. soft
Imagonal	6.8	60	6–150 cm.	80	
Lumar	—	—	—	Homocentric 33	
Pantagonal	18	125	8–75 cm.	81	Wide angle
Perigon	12	110	9–75 cm.	Protar 10	Wide angle
Tele-ansatz	—	—	—	—	Var. tele
Trinar	2.9	50	50–105 mm.	Cooke 27	
Trinar	4.5	55	50–300 mm.	" "	
Trinar	6.3	60	75–300 mm.	" "	
Ysar	3.5	52	50–105 mm.	Tessar 44	
Ysar	4.5	58	50–480 mm.	" "	

TABLE VI.—PHOTOGRAPHIC OBJECTIVES.—(*Continued*)

Name	*f*-number	Field, degrees	Foci	Type and figure number	Remarks
Ross, Ltd., Clapham Common, London S.W.4., England. (Medo Photo Supply Co., 15 West 47th St., New York.)					
Apo-Process-Xpres.....	9–16	60	13–48 in.	—	Process
Combinable...........	5.5	58	4–21 in.	—	Convertible
Compound-Homocentric	6.8	—	—	Two triples, symm.	
Concentric...........	16	—	—	9	Wide angle
Homocentric..........	5.6	56	12–24 in.	33	
Homocentric..........	6.3	56	5–15 in.	33	
Homocentric..........	6.8	56	4–12 in.	33	
Homocentric..........	8	56	7–24 in.	33	
Homocentric..........	8	—	—	—	Process
Process Xpres........	9–16	60	13–48 in.	—	Process
Telecentric..........	6.8	30	9–17 in.	61	2× tele
Teleros..............	5.5	30	6–22 in.	60	" "
Teleros..............	6.3	18	9–25 in.	—	3× "
Teleros..............	8	30	40 in.	60	2× "
Wide-angle...........	16	95	3–12 in.	—	Wide angle
Wide-angle-Xpres.....	4	80	4–20 in.	Plasmat 22	Aerial, infrared
Xpres...............	1.9	45	1–3 in.	—	Cine
Xpres...............	2.9	53	1–10 in.	50	
Xpres...............	3.5	53	1½–10 in.	50	
Xpres...............	4.5	53	3–21 in.	50	
H. R. Roussel, 3 Blvd. Richard Lenoir, Paris XIe, France.					
Kynor...............	3.5	—	20–100 mm.	—	Cine
Stylor...............	3.5	34	35–300 mm.	Tessar 44	
Stylor...............	4.5	53	50–400 mm.	" "	
Stylor...............	5.7	53	75–200 mm.	" "	
Stylor...............	6.3	53	54–500 mm.	" "	
Trylor...............	4.5	58	105–135 mm.	Cooke 27	
Trylor...............	6.3	58	54–270 mm.	" "	
Jos. Schneider and Co. Optische Werke, Bad Kreuznach, Germany. (Burleigh Brooks Inc., 127 West 42nd St., New York.)					
Aero Xenar...........	4.5	53	10–20 in.	Dynar 46	Aero
Angulon.............	6.8	105	3½–8¼ in.	Holostigmat 15	Wide-angle conv.
Componar...........	3.5	—	2–5¼ in.	—	Enlarging
Componar...........	4.5	—	2–5¼ in.	—	"
Dasykar.............	12.5	—	—	—	Wide angle
Isconar.............	4.5	60	—	Celor 32	
Kinoplan...........	2.7, 3, 3.5	—	—	Cooke 27	Cine
Kino-Xenon..........	1.5, 2	55	16–80 mm.	7 comp., 4 cem.	" 8, 16 mm.
Ortho-Angulon........	4.5	—	—	24	
Radionar............	2.9	56	2, 3 in.	Cooke 27	Focused by adj. front lens
Radionar............	3.5	53	2–3 in.	" "	" "
Radionar............	4.5	60	2–5 in.	" "	" "
Radionar............	6.3	56	3–12 in.	" "	" "

TABLE VI.—PHOTOGRAPHIC OBJECTIVES.—(*Continued*)

Name	*f*-number	Field, degrees	Foci	Type and figure number	Remarks

Jos. Schneider and Co., Optische Werke, Bad Kreuznach, Germany. (Burleigh Brooks Inc., 127 West 42nd St., New York.) (*Continued*)

Name	*f*-number	Field, degrees	Foci	Type and figure number	Remarks
Symmar	6.8	80	2–14 in.	Dagor 12	Convertible
Tele-Xenar	3.8	—	3, 4 in.	64	Distortionless tele cine 16 mm.
Tele-Xenar	4.5	35	5–9 in.	64	Tele
Tele-Xenar	5.5	48	7–14 in.	Dallon 54	" 2×
Xenar	2.8	53	1½–4 in.	Tessar 44	
Xenar	3.5	57	1½–12 in.	" "	
Xenar	4.5	57	2–19 in.	" "	
Xenar	5.5	57	3–12 in.	" "	
Xenon	1.3	27	1 in.	Like Biotar 39, With Double back lens	Cine 16 mm.
Xenon	1.5	33	2 in.	" " "	" 35 mm.
Xenon	2	55	20–80 mm.	Opic 38	" , min. cam.

Schulze; Later Schulze und Billerbeck, Potsdam, Germany.

Name	*f*-number	Field, degrees	Foci	Type and figure number	Remarks
Euryplan 1	4.5	80	9–32 cm.	40	Portrait
Euryplan 2	6	90	6–60 cm.	Plasmat 22	
Euryplan 3	7.7	82	6–60 cm.	" "	

G. Simon, Dresden, Germany.

Name	*f*-number	Field, degrees	Foci	Type and figure number	Remarks
Octanar	6.3	—	—	Combinar 16	
Tetranar	4.5–6.8	—	—	Homocentric 33	

Dr. Staeble G.M.B.H., Munich, Germany.

Name	*f*-number	Field, degrees	Foci	Type and figure number	Remarks
Choroplast	—	—	—	Homocentric 33	
Lineoplast	12.5	—	—	Protar 10	
Neoplast	—	—	—	62	Tele
Polyplast	5.9–12.5	—	8–43 cm.	21	Convertible

C. A. Steinheil Söhne, Munich, Germany.

Name	*f*-number	Field, degrees	Foci	Type and figure number	Remarks
Cassar	2.5–4.8	—	—	Cooke 27	
Orthostigmat *B*	6.8	85	5–60 cm.	Collinear 14	Convertible
Orthostigmat *D*	8	80	6–25 cm.	" "	"
Orthostigmat *F*	9	75	36–90 cm.	" "	Apo Process
Orthostigmat *D*	10	80	30–90 cm.	" "	Process
Orthostigmat *E*	12	100	7–25 cm.	" "	Wide angle
Triplar	2.8	—	—	—	
Unofocal 1	4.5	60	11–50 cm.	Celor 32	
Unofocal 2	6	70	6–30 cm.	" "	

Table VI.—Photographic Objectives.—(*Continued*)

Name	f-number	Field, degrees	Foci	Type and figure number	Remarks
Taylor, Taylor and Hobson Ltd., Leicester, England.　(Eastman Kodak Stores, Chicago.)					
Anglic, series 7*b*	6.5	90	3¼–12 in.	—	Wide angle
Apo, series 9	10, 16	62	13–48 in.	—	Process
Aviar, series 2	4.5	51	6–13½ in.	Celor 32	Aero, general
Aviar, series 3*b*	6	53	8½–15 in.	"　　"	"　　"
Cooke-anastigmat, series 14	6.3	53	13–21 in.	—	For color separation
Cooke-lens, series 2*a*	4.5	48	5–18 in.	27	
Cooke-lens, series 3*a*	6.5	62	5–18 in.	27	
Cooke-lens, series 4*a*	5.6	60	5–18 in.	27	
Cooke-lens, series 5*a*	8	65	5–18 in.	27	
Cooke-Convertible an-astigmat, series 15	6.8	53	12¼ in.	23 hemisymm	Convertible
Coric, series 13 Speedic 29	2.9	46	6¼ in.	—	
Distortionless Telephoto	5	—		56	Tele 2.3×
Eltic, series 8*b*	3.5	29	8–10½ in.	55	"　2×
Opic, series 0	2	50	1¼–5½ in.	38	
Panchro	2.5	—		29	Cine
Panfo	2.8	—	2, 3 in.	—	
Planital-Apo	12.5	—	16½–24 in.	—	Process
Portrait, series 14	6.3	—	13–21 in.	—	Portrait
Portrellic, series 2*e*	4.5	53	10½–18 in.	—	"　, var. soft
Portrellic, series 2*c*	4.5	48	10½–15 in.	—	Home portrait
Portric, series 2*d*	3.5	48	10½–15 in.	—	Portrait, var. soft
Portronic, series 6*a*	5.6	47	13–18 in.	—	"　　"　　"
Pressic, series 2*a*	3.5	47	6¼, 7½ in.	—	
Process, series 5*b*	8–16	65	9–36 in.	—	Process
Speedic series 10	2.5	45	6¼–9¼ in.	29	
Speed Panchro	2	64	24–108 mm.	Opic 38	Cine 35 mm.
Super-speed-Panchro	1.3	—	2¼ in.	43	"
Telic 8	5.6	30	8½–20 in.	Dallon 54	Tele 2×
Voigtländer und Sohn, Brunswick, Germany.　(Willoughby's, 110 West 32nd St., New York.)					
Apo-Collinear	9–12.5	66	8–40 in.	14	Process
Cine-Heliostigmat	2.5	35	1¼–4 in.	48	Cine
Collinear 2	6.3	62	3–20 in.	14	Convertible
Collinear 3	6.8	66	2–23 in.	14	"
Collinear 4	12.5	80	4–12 in.	14	Wide-angle conv.
Dynar	5.5	60	2¼–12 in.	46	
Heliar	3.5	45	¾–12 in.	46 (formerly 45)	
Heliar	4.5	60	1¼–24 in.	46　"　　"	
Heliostigmat	2.5	30	8¼, 13¼ in.	48	Portrait
Helomar	3.5	55	105 mm.	Cooke 27	
Oxyn	9	30	14–63 in.	47	Process
Skopar	3.5	58	5½–14 in.	Tessar 44	
Skopar	4.5	58	5½–14 in.	"　　"	
Teledynar	6.3	30	5½–12½ in.	58	Telephoto 2×
Teledynar (& Cine-tele anastigmat)	4.5	—	5¾–9¼ in.	59	Cine tele 2×
Universal-Heliar	4.5	45	12–19 in.	46	Portrait var. soft
Voigtar	3.5–7.7	—	75–105 mm.	Cooke 27	
W-Z soft-focus enlarging lens	—	—	7 in.	—	Enlarging

TABLE VI.—PHOTOGRAPHIC OBJECTIVES.—(*Continued*)

Name	*f*-number	Field, degrees	Foci	Type and figure number	Remarks
W. Watson and Sons Ltd., 313 High Holborn, London W.C., England.					
Holostigmat 1*a*	4.6	75	4¼–8¾ in.	15	Convertible
Holostigmat 1	6.1	70	4–14 in.	15	"
Holostigmat 3	9.5	61	11–26 in.	15	Process conv.
Holostigmat	11	110	3–9 in.	15	Wide angle
Testa	6.5	70	5¼, 6¼ in.	—	
Wollensak Optical Company, Rochester, N. Y.					
Anastigmat 5	7.5	—	3½–13 in.	—	
Cine-Velostigmat	1.5	25	25, 50 mm.	—	Cine 8, 16 mm.
Cine-Velostigmat	1.9	25	12 mm.	—	" " " "
Cine-Velostigmat	2.7	25	12–25 mm.	—	" " " "
Cine-Velostigmat	3.5	25	12, 25 mm.	—	" " " "
Cine-Telephoto	3.5–4.5	20	1½–6 in.	—	" 16 mm.
Cine Verito	3.5		1, 2 in.	—	" soft focus
Extreme wide angle	12.5	95	4½–13 in.	—	Wide angle
Varium	3.5	44	14–19 in.	—	Portrait soft
Velostigmat 1*a*	6.3	63	4½–17½ in.	—	Convertible
Velostigmat 2	4.5	53	3½–16 in.	—	
Velostigmat 3	9.5	90	4½–9 in.	—	Wide angle
Velostigmat 4	6.3	60	3½–12 in.	—	
Velostigmat Process	10	50	10¼–30 in.	—	Process
Verito	4	53	5–18 in.	—	Portrait, soft
Voltas	8	53	5–16 in.	—	
Wray Ltd., Optical Works, Bromley, Kent, England.					
Apo Lustrar	10	—	13–25 in.	—	Process
Diffused-image objective	4	—	6–10 in.	—	Portrait, soft
Lustrar	1.5	—	25, 50 mm.	—	Cine
Lustrar	2.5	—	¾–2 in.	35	" , general
Lustrar	2.8	—	3–8 in.	35	
Lustrar	3.5	—	20, 25 mm.	35	Cine
Lustrar	4.5	50	3–15 in.	Celor 32, un-symm.	
Lustrar	6.3	50	3½–15 in.	" "	
Plustrar	3.5	—	2–4 in.	Teleros 60	" tele
Plustrar	4.5	24	2–15 in.	" "	Tele
Plustrar	6.3	30	6–18 in.	" "	"
Process-Lustrar	10	64	13–25 in.	Lustrar 35	Process
Process-Lustrar	16	64	30, 36 in.	" "	"
Supar	3.5	46	2–5 in.	Cooke 27	
Supar	4.5	46	2–5 in.	" "	
Universal anastigmat	6.8	90	3½–7 in.	Dagor 12	Convertible
Wide-angle anastigmat	16	100	4–7 in.	Protar 10 back to front	Wide angle
Carl Zeiss, Jena, Germany. (485 Fifth Ave., New York.)					
Apo Planar	7.5–12.5	30–38	16–68 in.	37	Process
Apo Tessar	9–15	35–45	9½–72 in.	44	"
Biogon	2.8	63	35 mm.	6 comp. partly cem.	Min. cam.
Biotar	2	55	40–80 mm.	39	" "
Biotar	1.4	40	20–70 mm.	39	Cine, min. cam.
Biotessar	2.8	42	5¼, 6¼ in.	49	

TABLE VI.—PHOTOGRAPHIC OBJECTIVES.—(*Continued*)

Name	*f*-number	Field, degrees	Foci	Type and figure number	Remarks
Carl Zeiss, Jena, Germany. (485 Fifth Ave., New York.) (*Continued*)					
Convertible Protar 6a...	—	—	—	15	Convertible
Double Amatar........	6.8	—	—	—	"
Double Protar.........	6.3–7.7	45–75	4–16 in.	13	"
Kino-tele-Tessar.......	4	14	3–6 in.	—	Cine tele
Magnar...............	10	18	45 cm.	53	Tele 3×
Orthometar...........	4.5	64	35 mm., 210–250 mm.	Plasmat 22, un-symm.	Distortionless aero, min. cam.
Ortho-Protar.........	8	—	—	15	Distortionless, for photogrammetry
Planar...............	3.6–6.3	62–72	2–47 cm.	37	Process
Protar 1.............	4.5	—	—	11	
Protar 2.............	6.3	—	—	11	
Protar 2a............	8	75	9–43 cm.	11	
Protar 3.............	7.2	—	—	11	
Protar 3a............	9	97	7.5–41 cm.	10	
Protar 4.............	12.5	100	—	10	Wide angle
Protar 5.............	18	100	1½–10½ in.	10	Wide angle
Protar...............	12.5	45–50	7–27 in.	Half a double protar 13	Landscape
Quadruple-Protar 7.....	6.3	—	—	13	Predecessor to double protar
Quartz anastigmat.....	4.5	40	4¾, 10 in.	—	Achr. or nonachr. for ultraviolet
R-Biotar.............	0.85	14	45, 55 mm.	26	Cine for X-ray screens
Sonnar...............	1.4	27	25 mm.	30	Cine, min. cam.
Sonnar...............	1.5	45	50 mm.	30	" " "
Sonnar...............	2	27	10–85 mm.	—	" " "
Sonnar...............	2.8	30	50, 180 mm.	—	" " "
Sonnar...............	4	25	75, 135 mm.	4 comp. partly cem.	" " "
Tele-Tessar...........	6.3	26	18–40 cm.	57	Tele
Tessar...............	2.7	45	15–50 mm.	44	Cine
Tessar...............	2.8	50	2–3 in.	44	Min. cam.
Tessar...............	3.5	35–65	28–75 mm., 2–12 in.	44	Cine, general
Tessar...............	4.5	60	1½–20 in.	44	
Tessar...............	6.3	65	3–24 in.	44	
Tessar...............	5	27	20, 28 in.	44	
Tessar...............	8	75	28–55 mm.	44	Wide angle for min. cam.
Triotar..............	3.5, 4.5	52	5–12 cm.	Cooke 27	
Triotar..............	4	28	85 mm.	" "	Min. cam.
Triotar..............	5.6	25	105 mm.	" "	" "
Triple Protar........	5.6	—	—	Dagor 12	
Triplet..............	4.8	27	20–28 in.	Cooke 27	Portrait, aero
Unar.................	4.5–6.3	65	11–46 cm.	34	
Zeiss-Ikon, Dresden, Germany.					
Nettar...............	3.5–7.7	56	105–110 mm.	Cooke 27	Small cameras
Novar................	4.5	56	—	Tessar 44(?)	" "
Novar................	6.3	56	50–120 mm.	Cooke 27	" "

a name refers to the "series number" of that particular lens. In the second column is the *f*-number or range of *f*-numbers made, and in the third is the whole angular field covered by the lens. In column four the range of available focal lengths is stated. In the fifth column appears the diagram number illustrating the internal structure of the lens and also, in some cases, the name of a well known member of each type. This entry does not imply that the lens in question is a copy of the original type; it may be an entirely independent design using radically different glasses and radii of curvature, as has occurred, for example, in the Dynar and the Pentac, which appear alike in a diagram but which are really quite dissimilar designs.

In the last column appear remarks as to the purpose or uses of the various lenses. A dash (—) in any column implies that the particular information was not available.

Bibliography

Books:

Von Rohr, M.: "Theorie und Geschichte des photographischen Objektivs," Springer (1899).
Eder, J. M.: "Die photographischen Objektive," Knapp (1911).
Merté, W., R. Richter, and M. von Rohr: "Das photographische Objektiv," Springer (1932).
Fraprie, F. R.: "How to Choose and Use a Lens," Am. Photographic Pub. (1937).
Beck, C., and H. Andrews: "Photographic Lenses" (Beck; and Lund Humphries)
Traill-Taylor, J.: "The Optics of Photography and Photographic Lenses," Whitaker (London) (1898).
Lummer, O.: "Contributions to Photographic Optics," Macmillan (1900).
Gleichen, A.: "Theory of Modern Optical Instruments," H.M. Stationery Office.
Neblette, C. B.: "Photography," Van Nostrand.
Auerbach, F.: "The Zeiss Works," Foyle.
Encyclopaedia Britannica, 11th ed., Photography, by A. H. Hinton.

Periodicals:

Clay: R. S.: Traill-Taylor Memorial Lecture, *Phot. J.*, **46**, 458 (1922).
Kingslake, R.. The Development of the Photographic Objective, *J. Optical Soc. Am.*, **24**, 73 (1934).
Taylor, W., and H. W. Lee: The Development of the Photographic Lens, *Proc. Phys. Soc. (London)*, **47**, 502 (1935).
(See also a series of articles on current German lenses in *Photo Woche*, May to October, 1937.)

CHAPTER IV

CAMERAS

By Keith Henney

BASIC ELEMENTS

Any camera must have the following parts: a lens to form the image upon the sensitive material; a holder for the sensitive material; a lighttight enclosure (frequently a tube or bellows) to cover the space between the lens and the sensitive material; a shutter to open and close the lens aperture for the desired exposure time; a finder to show what is being photographed.

The simplest camera, *e.g.*, the popular box camera, has these elements in exceedingly simple form. The lens is fixed focus; the shutter is a simple flip-flap arrangement that makes an exposure with each push of the shutter lever whether up or down; the film runs over a pair of rollers as it is taken from the unexposed film spool and is wound up on the take-up spool.

To these basic elements other accessories and convenient adjustments may be added. The lens may have an adjustable diaphragm so that the amount of light admitted to the film or plate in unit time and the depth of focus may be controlled. The lighttight enclosure (the bellows) may be extensible so that the lens-film distance may be varied as required for focusing images at greater or lesser distances from the lens; the shutter may have various speeds so that exposure may be controlled independently of the aperture opening, and a spirit level may be added; the front board carrying the lens may be adjusted up or down and sideways or swing horizontally and vertically from some median position; the back which holds the film or plate may swing about a vertical or horizontal pivot; the bellows may have double or triple extension for photographing objects very near the lens and so on.

If the camera is to be focused, there must be a focusing scale or some other method must be provided for determining the correct distance of lens-to-film for a given object-to-lens distance.

Focusing is accomplished in several ways. The lens-film distance may be adjusted by extending or closing the bellows, or by screwing the lens and shutter into, or out of, a helical mount. The front lens only may be adjusted as to lens-film distance. Finally, the front lens may be removed completely for close-ups. The focal length of a camera lens may be increased or decreased by using either the back or front elements singly (if so designed) or by the use of accessory clip-on lenses.

A variable diaphragm opening may be provided by a simple series of holes in a metal slide which may be moved in front of the lens, or it may be continuously variable in diameter as in an iris.

The speeds at which the shutter may be opened and closed may be few or many; or the speed may be continuously variable over a wide range. Inexpensive hand cameras for amateur use seldom have shutter speeds slower than $\frac{1}{25}$ sec. because of the impossibility of getting snapshots at slower speeds without accompanying movement of the subject or camera during exposure. These cameras seldom have shutter speeds greater than $\frac{1}{100}$ sec. In cheap cameras the actual periods of time during which the shutter is open may vary widely from the marked speed. On the other

68

hand, more expensive shutters may have numerous speeds, and the actual periods of opening may correspond fairly closely with the markings placed on the shutter by the manufacturer.

The shutter may be an iris type or of the focal-plane type. These are described more fully in the section on shutters.

The enclosure between lens and film must be lighttight and in the focusing types of camera must be flexible. The simplest enclosure is that of a box camera. It is rugged and rigid and enables the lens to be maintained in a fixed position with respect to the sensitive material. In other types of camera the bellows is a molded or metal section into which another molded or metal section turns. With lenses of short focal length the variable lens-film distance is not very great, but the necessary accuracy of adjustment may be increasingly great.

The most common form of lighttight enclosure is the leather or composition bellows. If images are to be photographed natural size, the bellows must extend to a length equal to at least twice the focal length of the lens. When the bellows is not fully extended, it tends to sag and to cut off the edges of the picture. Therefore hooks are usually provided to hold up the center of the bellows when the lens is focused on distant objects, or when the camera is closed. These hooks engage with eyes on the camera frame automatically when the camera is closed and disengage when the bellows is extended beyond the point where support is needed.

The scene or object to be photographed is located in a view finder in the smaller cameras and upon a ground-glass screen placed in the focal plane in larger cameras. View finders are of several types as described on page 80.

CAMERA TYPES

Pinhole Camera.—The earliest, and simplest, form of camera uses a pinhole instead of a lens. Although it is capable of producing very beautiful landscapes of great softness, the pinhole camera is of academic interest only at the present time. A minute hole is punched in a sheet of metal or other opaque material and is placed in front of a lighttight enclosure at the rear of which is a screen on which the image is allowed to fall. The sensitive material may be placed upon this screen.

The pinhole has some advantages over the best of lenses. It suffers no distortion. It has infinite depth of field. It will cover a very wide angle, 125° compared to the 75 to 90° covered by a modern wide-angle lens. Photographs made with the pinhole have apparent depth that often compares most favorably with stereoscope camera pictures. Furthermore the pinhole camera is cheap!

The disadvantages are the excessively long exposures necessary and the fact that "wire sharpness" is not possible.

In Fig. 1 will be seen a side view through a pinhole camera. Point sources of light are not brought to a point focus as with a converging lens. A point source produces a cone of light, the dimensions of a cross section of the cone depending upon the size of the aperture. If the pinhole is circular, the cone will be circular; and if the hole is square, the point source will become a small square of light when it falls upon the screen. These circles (or squares) of confusion increase in size as the screen is moved away from the hole; but, since the image is enlarged at the same time and to the same degree as the enlargement of the circle of confusion, the relative sharpness of the image for a given pinhole is independent of the aperture-screen distance. The size of the image is increased by increasing the distance between pinhole and screen. The time of exposure will be directly proportional to the square of the distance between pinhole and screen.

Increasing the size of the hole will increase the illumination but will also increase the circles of confusion so that the sharpness of the picture will suffer. Decreasing the size of the hole will increase the sharpness—up to a certain point. As the size of the hole approaches one-half wavelength of the light being used (for example the blue Fraunhofer G line), the phenomenon of diffraction will cause the image of a point source to become a series of concentric circles of maximum and minimum brightness, thereby ruining the image.

For a given wavelength of light and a given screen-pinhole distance there is a best diameter of hole (see page 26.) For example at a screen distance of 6 in. the best diameter of hole is 0.02 in. This amounts to a working aperture of $f/300$ so that the pinhole in this case would have a speed $\frac{1}{2500}$ of that of an $f/6$ lens.

Pinhole Camera Construction.—Since this type of camera is occasionally used for pictorial work, the following data will outline the practical angles of pinhole-camera

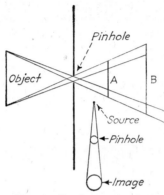

Fig. 1.—Fundamentals of pinhole camera. Image of point source is circular if pinhole is circular. Image at B is larger than image at A; as image becomes larger, definition becomes poorer.

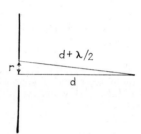

Fig. 2.—Relation of aperture and image size for best definition. The best radius of hole = $\sqrt{\lambda d}$ where λ = wavelength of light to be used and d = distance of screen from aperture.

construction. A thin sheet of copper or brass may be punctured by a needle and tacked to a larger piece of wood or other material. If the metal in which the hole is punched is comparatively small, there is greater likelihood that the piece will not be deformed during the puncturing process. The metal plate may be laid down on a piece of wood, the needle being forced through the center of the metal with a quick tap of a mallet. The hole should then be cleaned up by means of a small file, when the needle is again thrust through the hole. Now the metal sheet should be blackened by holding it over a smoky flame or by dipping it while hot into nitrate of silver. Several pinholes of different sizes may be mounted on a piece of cigar-box wood or other light material and arranged to be pushed in front of an aperture in the front of the camera. Since the exposure time is so long a shutter will not be needed. All that is necessary is to push the desired pinhole to the center of the aperture, and to push it away at the end of the exposure. Sufficient space must be allowed between the several pinholes so that the camera aperture is effectively closed when no pinhole is in position in front of this aperture.

Table I will be useful in determining needle size.

Clerc[1] notes that a 5-sec. exposure will suffice when using a very rapid modern plate for an open landscape at midday in fine weather with an aperture of 0.6 mm. with the plate at a distance of 8 in. from the pinhole.

[1] "Photography, Theory and Practice," 2d ed., Pitman (1937).

TABLE I.—PINHOLE CAMERA DATA

Pinhole diameter, in.	Nearest needle size	Pinhole to screen distance, in.
0.053	1	40
0.040	4	20
0.032	5	14
0.027	7	10
0.023	8	8
0.020	10	5

Box Cameras.—Many a photographer has started along his chosen path with a box camera. A tyro can make no better pictures with an expensive camera with many adjustments than he can with the simplest of all cameras—any more than a beginner at the piano can make better music on a $1000 instrument than he can on a secondhand battered piano. It is true, however, that the better cameras have greater potentialities in the hands of even the inexperienced amateur if he is willing to follow directions and to make haste slowly when it comes to trying out all the adjustments.

A box camera is distinctly a box with a lens at one end, and with some sort of negative carrier at the other end. The lens is of small aperture so that all objects between about 8 or 10 ft. and infinity have reasonable sharpness. The relative slowness of the lens ($f/11$ to $f/16$) is not such a handicap as it was before the advent of modern fast emulsions now in common use.

The box camera is cheap; prices vary from less than a dollar up to $5. Picture sizes vary from postage stamp size (Ulca) or less (Coronet uses 16-mm. film) to one-half vest-pocket and up to $3\frac{1}{4}$ by $5\frac{1}{2}$ in.

Some box cameras have masks in them making it possible to make pictures of two different sizes on a given size of film. Some cameras have built-in yellow filters; in others the front lens of a simple doublet is movable so that close-up pictures may be made. For example the Eastman Kodak Diway lens (Fig. 3) has a thin low-power negative lens in front of the diaphragm. This lens is removable by a lever, and the back component alone is focused for objects at $6\frac{1}{2}$ ft. The depth of field at this aperture ($f/12.5$) is from 5 to 10 ft. The front lens is normally in place and keeps dust out of the shutter.

Front lens removable

FIG. 3.—Kodak Diway lens.

The cheapest box cameras have ground-glass finders; better cameras of the box type have brilliant finders (see page 80 for description of finders.)

Some modern miniature cameras are little more than box cameras of advanced design, since the lens is practically fixed focus. Several 35-mm. cameras have $f/4.5$ lenses which are used at all distances from 18 ft. to infinity by merely pulling the lens out of the camera body to a stop position. For subjects closer than 18 ft. the lens is pulled out another notch, when all subjects between 6 and 18 ft. will be reasonably sharp.

Some so-called reflex cameras are merely box cameras with a large reflection type view finder.

The great virtues of the box camera are its simplicity and its cheapness. There are few adjustments. All that is required for good pictures is fair light, a steady hand,

and the ability to keep the subject from approaching too close to the lens.   The negatives will stand some enlargement, but not a great deal, naturally.

Folding Cameras.—Next above the box camera in complexity is the folding camera for roll film.   This group comprises cameras from the very cheapest to the most expensive.   The simplest camera of this type has a lens which snaps forward into fixed position when the front of the camera is opened.   It is used, therefore, exactly like a box camera with the advantage that it is more compact.   Its lens operates at about the same aperture as that in the box camera.

With lenses of larger aperture and consequently of smaller depth of focus, some means of focusing must be provided.   The lens as a whole may be moved along a track with a focusing scale in feet or meters placed alongside; or the lens may turn

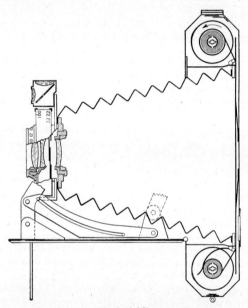

Fig. 4.—Single folding camera.

in a threaded mount, or only the front element of a doublet may turn, with the distance scale placed along a circular portion of the camera structure.

Folding roll-film cameras are seldom equipped with lenses of greater aperture than $f/6.3$ or $f/4.5$.   One reason is the cost of such lenses, and another is the shallow depth of field.   When the camera at large apertures is focused upon a near object and operated with the diaphragm wide open, the user must estimate the distance to the subject with accuracy greater than that possessed by the average person.   Since at any aperture the required accuracy of adjustment of the lens-film distance increases as the lens-subject distance decreases, cameras of the type being described are seldom equipped for working closer to a subject than 6 ft.   If, however, a short-focal-length lens is to be used, as in a miniature camera, the lens may have a larger aperture, and focusing may be possible up to within 3 ft. of the subject.

Thousands of miniature cameras with fairly large-aperture lenses but not equipped with coupled range finders find their way to the secondhand market because the purchaser cannot get sharp pictures—largely due to the lack of the necessary ability to estimate distance.   A purchaser of a miniature camera naturally expects enlargements.   An out-of-focus condition that will not mar a contact print, however, becomes excessively annoying when an enlargement of any reasonable magnification is made.

Folding roll-film cameras may be purchased in sizes from 35 mm. and half vest-pocket up to postcard (3½ by 5½ in).   Prices vary from a few dollars up to several hundred.

TABLE II.—FOCAL LENGTH OF LENSES USED ON ROLL-FILM CAMERAS

Picture Size, In. (Approximate)	Focal Length, In. (Approximate)
1 × 1½	2
1⅝ × 2½	3
2¼ × 3¼	4
2½ × 4¼	5
3¼ × 4¼	5⅛
3¼ × 5½	6¾

The better grades of roll-film cameras have rising and falling fronts (the extent of rise or fall may be about one-fourth the height of the picture) which make it possible to raise or lower the lens to include or exclude various portions of the foreground. The better cameras have superior general construction, are heavier, and are more sturdy.   They often have two finders, a brilliant type and a direct-vision type.

The folding type of camera possesses several advantages over the box type of camera.   It is more compact; better models have better lenses and more adjustments. Since the lens may be focused accurately upon the desired subject, enlargements of considerable magnification are possible.

Hand Cameras for Plates and Film Packs.—Approaching the professional view camera in complexity, sturdiness, and general utility are the hand cameras designed to use either film pack, plates, or cut film in plateholders.   Such cameras have been built in sizes as small as vest pocket, but the most popular sizes are the 6 by 9 cm., 9 by 12 cm. and 4 by 5 in.   They are generally fitted with a shutter of the Compur type; they carry well-corrected lenses of the anastigmat type with apertures of $f/4.5$, $f/3.5$, and sometimes $f/2.8$ and often have double extension bellows for making pictures approaching natural size.   They have fronts which can be raised or lowered or moved sideways, and some of the more versatile have removable lens boards, reversible backs, triple extension bellows and tilting backs.   Such cameras differ from a studio or view camera only in being more compact and less weighty.   The lens and bellows may be racked back into the camera frame and the front closed.   The camera then becomes very compact.   A few models are thin enough to be placed in a coat pocket.

Cameras of this general type are often fitted with focal plane shutters and are used for newspaper and sport photography.   The popular Speed Graphic is of this type. When equipped with a coupled range finder and a flash-bulb synchronizer, the graphic type of camera is an extremely versatile instrument.   They are available in sizes from 2¼ by 3¼ in. to 4 by 5 in.

View and Studio Cameras.—The chief difference between view or studio cameras and the better hand cameras lies in the compactness of the latter.   View and studio cameras fold up but not into such small space as the hand cameras.   View and studio cameras usually have frames of wood, hand cameras are usually built on metal frames.   View and studio cameras are made in sizes from 3¼ by 4¼ in. up.   The lenses of these cameras are removable.   Focusing from the back is possible.   This is of importance in close-up work (especially with wide-angle lenses) where the front of the camera might obtrude itself into the field of view.

The studio camera is heavier and bulkier than the view camera and is usually mounted on a support which can be rolled about the studio on wheels.

A typical 8- by 10-in. studio camera has the following characteristics: triple extension bellows (30 in.); back capable of being raised to form an angle of 45° with the camera bed or of being dropped through an arc of more than 70°; rising and falling front movement of 3¼ in. above center and ¾ in. below center; lateral movement of lens of 2 in. and a horizontal swing of 80°; weight, 9¾ lb.; dimensions folded, 4½ by 11½ by 11¾ in.

Reflex Cameras.—In the reflex camera it is possible to focus the image of the subject to be photographed until the instant of exposure. This important and useful feature is accomplished in the following manner.

A mirror at an angle of about 45° is placed between the lens and the ground-glass focusing screen which is placed, not directly behind the lens as in other cameras, but in the top of the camera and at 90° to the path of the rays from the lens to the sensitive material. The image, therefore, is seen right side up and full size (usually), although reversed from left to right. When the exposure is to be made, the mirror moves out of the way of the light rays. The mirror is pivoted about its upper end, and before the shutter is opened for the exposure, the mirror is urged upward by a spring to close the top of the camera so that no light through the ground glass can fog the film.

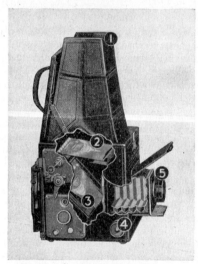

Fig. 5.—Graflex form of reflex camera. 1, hood; 2, ground glass; 3, mirror; 4, focusing knob; 5, lens.

The great advantage of the reflex camera is the fact that a moving object can be followed on the ground-glass screen and kept in continuous focus until the exposure is made. For this reason the reflex is the favored camera for action photography. The disadvantages of the reflex are: (1) bulk and weight; (2) to get sufficient light on the screen, it is necessary to focus with the lens wide open. If, then, the lens is to be stopped down before making the exposure, the time taken to adjust the stop and to recompose the picture may eliminate one of the reflex camera's great advantages.

The ground-glass screen is surrounded by a hood to keep light from it, except that coming from the lens. In small reflex cameras, focusing becomes more difficult because of stray light getting on the screen. Certain of the small reflex cameras have rather large hoods, which keep stray light from the screen and thereby aid the user to get sharp focus. Many small reflex cameras have built-in magnifying lenses located over the center of the screen so that still sharper focus is possible. The grain of the ground-glass screen may sometimes be too coarse to allow the accuracy of focusing necessary when the lens aperture is large.

One way to get around the difficulty of focusing the reflex camera at small lens apertures is to use two lenses, one for making the picture and one for focusing. These lenses are moved with the same focusing adjustment, so that, when the image is accurately focused upon the viewing screen, it is also in sharp focus on the sensitive material. The focusing lens may have longer focal length than the picture-taking lens, so that an enlarged image will be seen on the focusing screen. Because the depth of field of the focusing lens is shallower than that of the taking lens, the user will get sharper images than if the two lenses have the same focal length. One difficulty of the reflex camera is the fact that it is focused and adjusted at waist level. In a crowd it is desirable to use a camera which can be held at (or above) eye level; not all reflex cameras can be held upside down for such situations. Certain high-grade miniature reflex cameras are equipped with eye-level finders of the wire frame type.

Miniature Cameras.—Recent years have seen a remarkable sale of so-called miniature cameras. This increase in popularity of small cameras—which are not at all recent in origin or use—is due to several causes, not the least of which is that finishing plants catering to amateurs are now equipped to give good service on the small films used and can now deliver an enlargement of reasonable size which compares favorably in quality with a contact print of the same size and made from a larger negative.

From the user's standpoint the miniature camera has the following advantages: the camera is compact; it is cheap to operate; its short-focal-length lens has much greater depth of field[1] than the lenses on the larger amateur cameras; these lenses may have exceptionally large apertures without too great expense; small lenses are easier to correct for distortion so that the miniature camera will produce negatives which may be enlarged many diameters; high shutter speeds are possible with the small between-lens shutters used in small cameras. To these advantages of the camera and its accessories must be added those secured by modern high-speed and fine-grain films.

The disadvantages of the miniature camera are largely those which arise from the fact that the image is small and in general cannot be seen on a ground-glass screen as in larger cameras. The difficulty of composing a picture is increased on this account. Because of the small size of picture made with miniature cameras, it is practically necessary to enlarge all the pictures. In the enlargement process, some fineness of detail is inevitably lost, especially in large "blow ups." A print 8 by 10 in. made by contact from an 8- by 10-in. negative will have greater detail than one blown up from a 24- by 36-mm. negative. Therefore, in those situations where the maximum detail is required, the large camera must be used. This is the case where photoengravings are to be made with a fine screen for use on coated paper. The loss of detail will not be apparent, however, if engravings are made with coarse screens or are printed on anything but the better grades of coated paper.

The miniature camera of good construction and with coupled range finder comes the nearest to the "universal camera" of any yet devised. It will make pictures under light conditions which would preclude the possibility of any sort of success with large cameras having longer focal-length lenses of smaller aperture. The miniature will make pictures which can be enlarged many diameters and thus can compete with the larger cameras when a large print is desired—with the disadvantage that the detail in the enlargement will not be so great as in the contact print. The depth of field of the short focal-length lenses used on miniature cameras is a distinct advantage not possessed by lenses of larger focal length used on large cameras.

Portability is one of the small camera's great advantages.

Types of Miniature Cameras.—Cameras taking pictures $2\frac{1}{4}$ by $2\frac{1}{4}$ in. in size are usually classed as "miniatures" although no strict definition is possible. Cameras of this general class, therefore, may be grouped as follows: (1) small cameras not equipped with coupled range finders; (2) small cameras equipped with coupled range finder; (3) reflecting cameras.

In group 1 are found fixed-focus cameras or cameras which may be focused. The latter are equipped with focusing scales. With the latter camera the user must first estimate, or measure, the distance of the object from the lens and then set the camera

---

[1] When the lens is focused upon an object 4 ft. distant, the range of sharp focus for a 2-in. lens operating at $f/2$ is about 3 in; with a $5\frac{1}{4}$-in. lens the range of sharp focus at $f/4$ is about 1 in.

accordingly. The camera may make a single exposure, or it may carry enough film to make 36 exposures. The lenses are fairly well corrected. Some are equipped with masking devices so that, on a given film, two sizes of pictures may be made. Cameras of this type, equipped with large-aperture lenses, produce good results in the hands of those who can estimate or measure distance accurately. In general, however, the user cannot expect to enlarge his negatives as much as negatives made with cameras having coupled range finders and lenses with greater correction. These small guess-the-distance cameras are not comparable with the second group for the serious photographer.

In the second group are those cameras which represent the acme of manufacturing precision. In size of picture made, they range from the 24- by 36-mm. negative made on 35-mm. standard motion-picture film to $2\frac{1}{4}$ by $3\frac{1}{4}$ in. They utilize coupled range finders. They are fitted with lenses with very high correction, often arranged to be interchangeable with other lenses of shorter or longer focal length. In the Leica, Contax, Exakta, and similar types of cameras a focal-plane shutter operating at speeds up to $\frac{1}{1250}$ sec. is supplied. The accuracy of adjustment and the correction of the lenses is so great in these cameras that enlargements of 10 to 30 times are not out of the ordinary at all. In a few cameras, roll film, cut film, or plates may be used. Many accessories are available for cameras of this general class, which extends the possibilities of the camera. The user need not purchase anything but the camera and lens, however, to have a complete outfit. The additional lenses, and other accessories, will cost a great deal more than the camera itself and form desirable equipment which can be accumulated over a period of time—or never purchased at all. An important feature is the mechanical coupling between the shutter-cocking mechanism and the film-advance mechanism, making it impossible to make double exposures.

In the third group are the reflecting cameras. Some of them have a single lens; others have two lenses, one for focusing and one for making the exposure. In general these cameras do not have interchangeable lenses, although front lenses may be used to reduce or increase the focal length of the taking lens. Certain models, however, are equipped so that the lenses may be changed for others of longer or shorter focal length.

In the Contaflex of Zeiss Ikon the focusing lens brings the image, not to a ground-glass screen, but to a plano-convex lens of rectangular shape, the underside of which is matted. The image is "brilliant" to the corners. For critical focusing a magnifying lens can be swung into position over the image. This latter feature is characteristic of several of the miniature reflex cameras. In addition, the Contaflex has a built-in photoelectric exposure meter.

Certain two-lens cameras are not reflex types. The second lens is merely a view-finder lens and is not connected mechanically with the taking lens. The second lens makes it possible for the user to see an image of his scene full size and right-side up by means of a reflecting mirror. The finder lens is of fixed focus and is not connected with, or related to, the taking lens. The latter must be set to the correct focusing position after the user has estimated or measured the distance of the subject from the lens.

Optical and Mechanical Requirements for Miniature Cameras.—Speaking before the Photographic Society of America, Rochester, 1938, H. W. Zieler discussed the maximum inaccuracies that may exist in manufacture and alignment maintenance in a high-grade camera making a negative 1 by $1\frac{1}{4}$ in. in size. He stated that a 2-in. lens at $3\frac{1}{2}$ ft. at an aperture of $f/1.5$ must be focused with a maximum tolerance of 0.001 in. The focal length of the lens must be matched to the focusing mechanism to within 0.001 in. The total variation from all causes in the mechanical dimensions of the coupled range finder must not be over 0.001 in.

Fig. 6*A*.   Fig. 6*B*.

Fig. 6*A*.—Opaque screen projector recommended for continuous reference or reading 16-mm. film pictures. The projector is equipped with an advancing lever which advances documents one picture at a time. It also has a winding crank which enables the operator to move the film rapidly through the projector.

Fig. 6*B*.—Library-type projector for 35-mm. film records.

Fig. 6*C*.—Recordak check and document recorder.

All this shows the precision of manufacture, and the precision of maintenance required, if the small camera is to produce 8- by 10-in. prints (8× enlargements) that are satisfactory from the standpoint of detail.

Sequence Cameras.—Several miniatures have optional accessory rapid-film winders which shorten the time required to wind up a new film and to set the shutter. The Robot camera has a built-in device which makes the exposure when the release button is pushed, moves the film forward, and cocks the shutter when the release is allowed to return to its normal position. When a strong spring is wound up by the user, it is possible to make 24 exposures as fast as the release button can be pressed. A sequence of exposures made with this camera resembles a series of frames made with a motion-picture camera with the exception that each individual exposure may be made in $\frac{1}{500}$ sec. Interchangeable lenses are available for the camera.

Stereoscope Cameras.—Double-lens cameras for making stereoscopic exposures are described in the chapter on Stereoscopic Photography. These cameras range in price from $12 up to several hundred dollars. The simplest use ordinary roll film and make individual pictures $2\frac{1}{4}$ by $2\frac{1}{4}$ in. The higher priced units have reflex focusing, use plates or film, and come in several sizes, usually 45 by 107 mm. or 6 by 13 cm.

Identification Cameras.—These cameras are for use in schools, etc., where a large number of portraits are to be made for identification purposes. One type, listing at about $100, holds 100 ft. of negative film, unperforated, giving 500 exposures $1\frac{3}{8}$ in. wide. The camera is operated 4 ft. from the subject and is fitted with an $f/3.5$ lens. Another type holds 200 ft. of film, taking 1000 individual exposures, and is fitted with an $f/4.5$ lens of good correction. Printing machines are available for this type of camera.

Certain 35-mm. cameras are available which hold enough film for 250 exposures; these may be used for schools, etc., where a large number of negatives are to be made without the bother of frequent change of film.

Panorama Cameras.—Cameras of this type have means for revolving the camera on the tripod so that it covers a field of view wide in relation to its height. Thus the panorama camera is useful for covering large groups of people, as at conventions and gatherings, large estates, mountain vistas, geological surveys, etc. In the Folmer Graflex No. 10 Circuit panorama camera, speeds varying from $\frac{1}{2}$ to $\frac{1}{12}$ sec. are available; the lens is a triple convertible with focal lengths of 10, $15\frac{1}{2}$, and 20 in. and is equipped with a meter to indicate the amount of film used for any exposure, permitting the determination of the amount of film left in the container. Film in lengths up to 10 ft. and widths of 6, 8, and 10 in. is used.

Recording Cameras and Projectors.—A valuable extension of the use of photographic equipment lies in the recording of documents, such as bank checks, books, letters, etc. Devices for this purpose are really automatic cameras which make the exposures as fast as the documents are fed into a hopper at one end. The operator does not need to be an expert photographer. Banks may photograph up to 100 checks per minute with the Recordak. The microfilm Recordak uses 35-mm. fine-grain film and is adapted to the use of libraries, companies wishing to record blueprints, etc.

Projection machines are furnished for viewing the photographed records. Recordaks are supplied on a rental basis; library-type projectors are sold to the user.

CAMERA ADJUSTMENTS

With the exception of the fixed-focus cameras of exceeding simplicity, all cameras have certain adjustments which increase their versatility. These adjustments are listed below.

Focusing.—Usually focusing is accomplished by changing the lens-film distance by moving the entire lens. The lens may sometimes be screwed into a threaded mount instead of being moved by means of a bellows. In other cases only the front section of the lens may be moved. As already indicated, certain simple cameras have only two focusing positions of the lens, one for close-ups and one for distant scenes. In either of these positions the lens acts as a fixed-focus lens.

Rising Front.—The lens board may be raised above a median position so that less of the foreground and more of the upper part of a picture may be included without

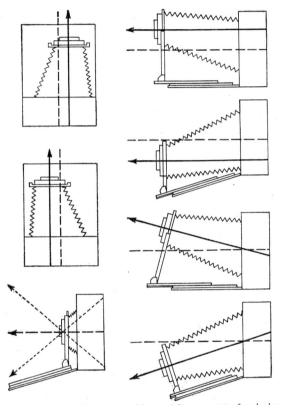

Fig. 7.—Typical adjustment of lens with respect to focal plane.

tilting the camera, a method which produces bad perspective. Tall buildings may be photographed in this manner, especially if the camera is equipped with a swing back.

Falling Front.—The lens board may be lowered so that more of the foreground may be included.

Side Movement of Lens.—When the camera is placed so that the picture is to be made the long way of the film, a rising and falling motion of the lens is made possible by another adjustment. This sideways movement (when the camera is vertical) can be employed to include more of the right or left of a picture without moving the position of the film.

Swing Back.—This adjustment permits the film to be tilted about a horizontal pivot through the center (or some other line) of the film. By this means the top (or bottom) may be moved closer to the lens. It is usually possible to make the same adjustment along a vertical axis.

If the camera is pointed upward to include in the picture the top of a building or other tall object and if the plate is not maintained parallel to the lines of the building, these lines will seem to converge near the top. This distortion is apparent and not real, because, if the eye is placed at the position of the lens, it will be seen that the lines of the building *do* converge. In a photograph, however, the viewer does not wish the actual truth but wishes to see the building as he would see it if viewed from a more distant point.

By combining the use of the rising front and the swing back the lines of the building can be kept parallel. The film should be maintained parallel to the lines of the building by means of the swing back, and the top of the building should be brought into the scene by using the rising front.

By making use of the swing back it is often possible to bring into sharp focus two objects located at different distances from the camera. If an object near the top of the picture is to be in focus at the same time an object near the bottom is in focus and if the two objects are at different distances from the lens, the edge of the film

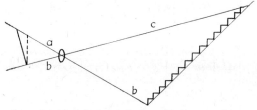

Fig. 8.—By tilting the swing back from vertical position, top and bottom of stairs can be more nearly focused at the same lens position.

that represents the more distant object should be moved closer to the lens than the edge on which the closer object is to be registered.

When the swing back and rising front are to be used, the lens of the camera should be able to cover sharply a larger area than the normal size of the sensitive material. In these cases the image at the edge of the film is of importance; therefore the lens must be well corrected and should be used at as small an aperture as the exposure time will permit.

Removable Lens Board.—View and studio cameras and some folding hand cameras have removable lens boards so that lenses of longer or shorter focal length may be used interchangeably.

Reversible Back.—Cameras used by advanced amateurs and by professionals have reversible backs so that the picture may be made either with the short or the long dimension of the plate as the bottom of the picture without turning the camera itself. Such cameras do not require a tripod hole on the long dimension of the camera body.

Other Adjustments.—Occasionally the bed of the camera may be tilted upward or downward; the back may be raised as well as tilted, etc. Such adjustments are useful when making exposures in cramped quarters or when using wide-angle lenses, but in general these adjustments are seldom used.

CAMERA ACCESSORIES

View Finders.—The majority of cameras are equipped with view finders by which the user can tell when he has included the required subjects in his scene. View and studio cameras do not usually have such finders. The picture is composed upon a ground-glass screen.

Simplest of the view finders is the direct-vision type. This consists of a wire frame, more or less the exact size of the film or plate to be used, and a peep sight. Usually the frame is situated at the lens position; the peep sight is usually at the focal plane. The camera is held at eye level; therefore the picture composed in this type of finder tends to be more natural than one composed in a type that must be held at waist level. (Photographers for fashion magazines usually choose a very low point of view to accentuate the vertical lines of the models and their clothes rather than the horizontal lines. A reflex type of camera is preferred for this purpose.)

The frame and the peep sight need not necessarily be located, respectively, at the lens and at the focal plane, but wherever they are located, their relative dimensions with respect to each other and the eye and to their respective locations must be such that the eye will see what the camera lens embraces. These finders generally fail to include the proper view when the camera is very close to the object and should not be relied upon for close-ups.

Reflecting-type Finders.—Cameras of the simplest types are usually equipped with a finder consisting of a lens, a mirror, and a ground glass upon which the lens

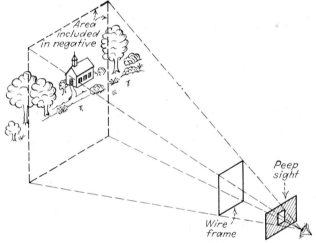

Fig. 9.—Direct-vision view finder.

focuses the image. The image is right side up but is reversed, right to left. The focal length of the finder lens is short enough (about 1 in.) so that a small image is produced and all objects within the range of the camera adjustment will be in focus. There is no relation between the focal lengths of the finder and the camera lenses.

A reflecting type of finder which is more efficient in its use of the light collected by the lens is commonly known as the "brilliant" type. The lens forms an image, not upon a ground-glass screen, but in a second lens which confines the light collected into a narrow cone and directs it to the user's eye. At a normal viewing distance of 12 in. above the finder, the cone of light is wide enough to include both eyes of the user. It is necessary that the user assume such a position that his eyes intercept the cone of light or he will not see the image of the scene he is to photograph. A hood is usually part of a brilliant finder. It shields the image from extraneous light.

In still another type of finder (direct-vision optical finder) a strong negative lens forms a virtual image in front of the lens and a weak positive lens projects this virtual image to a comfortable position with respect to the eye, *i.e.*, about 15 ft. away. The image in such an optical finder is erect and not reversed.

More elaborate finders are arranged to indicate to the photographer when his camera is properly focused as well as to show him the field of view that is being covered.

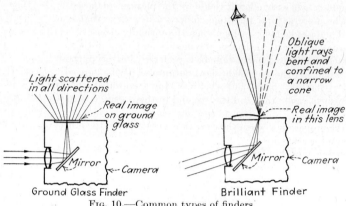

Fig. 10.—Common types of finders.

The field seen through the finder is often smaller than that actually covered by the lens, so that the user is certain of getting into his picture all that he sees in the finder. The fact that the lens of the camera and the lens of the finder do not view the subject from the same point is not a serious matter unless close-ups are made. Errors due to separation of the two lenses are minimized by placing the finder as close as possible to the camera lens and by making the finder axis and the camera axis intersect at about 15 ft. in front of the camera.

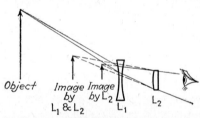

Fig. 11.—Use of negative lens to form virtual image in front of lens L_1 which is then projected to a comfortable position with respect to the eyes.

Parallax.—Certain view finders automatically compensate the error arising from parallax which causes the picture as actually registered on the sensitive material to be different from that seen in the view finder. As the camera is brought close to the object, the view is restricted by a mask which is mechanically connected with the coupled range-finder mechanism. In general, however, the photographer must be careful to include the desired object in the center of his composition when working up close to the object and when relying upon the view finder to determine what is actually being photographed. If the camera is equipped with a ground glass, it will be much safer to make the actual composition by this means than to rely upon the view finder.

Focusing Scale.—Cameras of the focusing type must use a focusing scale unless the operator is to focus his scene on a ground-glass screen each time he makes an exposure or unless he has an "automatic focus" type of coupled range finder. All but reflex, view, and studio cameras employ a focusing scale which may be used or not as the owner of the camera desires. With lenses of long focal length it is more important to estimate distance accurately than with short-focal-length lenses because of the shallower depth of field of the former. If the negatives made by the short-focal-length lens are to be enlarged to the same size as those produced by the longer lens, the accuracy of focusing must be the same.

The following formula may be used in marking out a focusing scale. First determine the setting of the lens for focusing upon a distant (infinity) object. Then the difference between the lens-film distance for this setting and that required to focus accurately upon a nearer object will be found from

$$D = \frac{f^2}{s - f}$$

where f = the focal length of the lens in inches;

s = the distance of object to lens in inches;

D = the distance, in inches, of the lens from the infinity position.

Example.—Design a focusing scale for a 5-in. lens. The lens focuses a distant object sharply when it is 5 in. from the film. An object 25 ft. from the lens will be sharply focused when the lens is moved away from the infinity setting by $f^2/(s - f)$ in. or $25 \div [(25 \times 12) - 5]$ or 0.085 in. If the object is only 6 ft. from the lens, the lens must be moved away from the infinity setting $25 \div (72 - 5)$ or 0.37 in. from its infinity setting.

With cameras having lenses of focal lengths of about 5 to 6 in. and having focusing scales parallel to the motion of the lens in focusing, the maximum error in estimating

 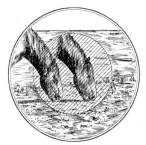 

Fig. 12*A*.—Range finder in focused position.	Fig. 12*B*.—Coupled range finder in unfocused position.	Fig. 12*C*.—Out-of-focus adjustment of range finder with horizontally split file.

distance is such that at $f/8$ the lens must be set to within $\frac{1}{32}$ in. of the position determined by accurately focusing on a ground glass. If the lens has a shorter focal length and correspondingly greater depth of field, then the error in estimating distance and setting the lens for the estimated distance may be greater. On vest-pocket size and somewhat larger cameras the maximum permissible error is of the order of the distance between the 25- and the 50-ft. marks on the focusing scale. For miniature cameras the error should not amount to more than the interval between the 13- and 20-ft. marks. Naturally the error may be greater if the camera lens is operated at a smaller aperture.

Range Finders.—A valuable accessory to any camera is a range finder by which the user is enabled to measure accurately the distance of the object from the lens. The photographer may then set the lens-film distance by means of the focusing scale, or, if the range finder is mechanically connected to the lens in some manner, the act of measuring the distance automatically sets the lens-film distance.

Range finders are of several types (described below) all depending upon the principle of presenting to the photographer two images of the object. When the range finder is properly adjusted, the two images merge, and the distance to the object is read from a scale attached. In some range finders the object or field of view is split so that one-half is displaced with respect to the other when the range finder is wrongly adjusted. In others two complete images are visible until the exact adjustment is secured.

Principle of Range Finders.—In Fig. 13 consider two rays of light from an object E so far distant that the rays from it are essentially parallel. Let these rays pass through apertures O and Q. The rays will also pass through A and B. Now consider another object situated on the ray passing through O. The ray from D passing through O will pass through B but, because of the closeness of D, a ray from it passing through Q will not pass through A but rather through some point such as C. The closer the object D, the further apart will B and C be. Thus the distance between B and C is a measure of the distance of the object D from the line OQ. If some means is provided at Q to bend the ray from D so that it goes through A, the amount of adjustment necessary will be a measure of the distance from O to D. A fixed point of comparison is provided

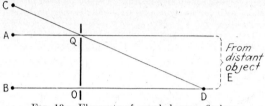

Fig. 13.—Elements of coupled range finder.

by reflecting the beam twice and moving B over to the original position of A. Thus B and C, when adjusted to C', are presented to the eye together, and any difference in their positions is readily seen (see Fig. 14).

The distance between O and Q is known as the base of the range finder. Increasing the base increases the accuracy of the distance determination but increases the difficulty of using the device. If too great a base distance is used, the two images may be so far apart that it will be difficult for the user to find them.

Kodak Pocket Range Finder.—In Fig. 15, with the eye at the indicated position, the field of view is divided horizontally by the edge of the mirror 1 so that one-half of the field comes straight to the eye while the other half is brought to the eye by

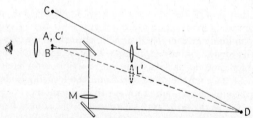

Fig. 14.—Mechanism of range finder by which point C is moved to C', the relative motion required being a function of the distance.

reflections from mirrors 1 and 2. These mirrors are approximately $1\frac{1}{2}$ inches apart. This distance constitutes the base of the range finder. When the mirrors are parallel to each other, the vertical lines of an object at infinity appear continuous in the two halves of the field. For objects closer to the range finder, mirror 1 must be moved so that it is not parallel to mirror 2 in order to make the two halves of the field merge. This is accomplished by turning the actuating cam which swings the lever bearing mirror 1. The spring urges the lever against the cam so that backlash in the cam is eliminated. Because of the definite relation which exists between the angle between the mirrors and the distance from the object as viewed in the range finder, it is possible to calculate a scale which indicates the distance directly when the two halves of the field coincide. This scale is mounted in the window of the actuating cam so that as the cam is rotated the scale rotates with it and a small index mark indicates the distance between image and range finder. A small lens is placed so that the scale is easily seen at one edge of the view.

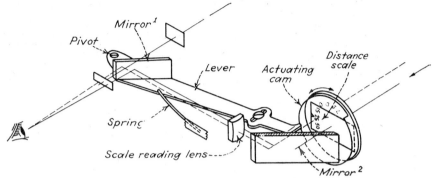

Fig. 15.—Kodak pocket range finder.

Kodak Coupled Range Finder.—Mechanically coupling the range finder to the lens of a camera enables the user to measure distance and set the lens of his camera with one motion. Thus the range finder becomes a focusing device rather than a distance indicator, although it will also measure the distance of the object to be photographed.

In the Kodak coupled range finder employed on certain miniature cameras, two images of the same object are created by two lenses. To make the two images coin-

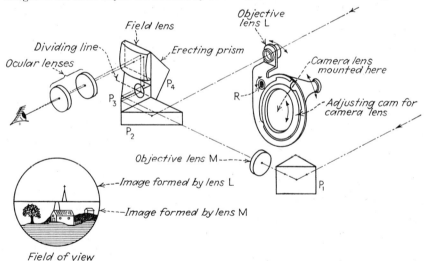

Fig. 16.—Kodak coupled range finder.

cide, one lens is moved with respect to the other. The objective lens of the range finder is carried on a movable support which is actuated by an adjusting cam which is turned by the focusing knob. Turning this knob moves the camera objective along its axis and thereby focuses it by means of a helical thread. This cam is so constructed that, when the range-finder objective is correctly placed for the given object, the camera objective is focused upon this object.

The two images presented to the eye of the user form a field divided into two halves. With the camera in normal position the lower half of the image as viewed in the eyepiece is the fixed portion of the image. When the camera lens is out of focus, the upper half of the image is displaced to the right or left. Focusing consists in bringing these two halves of the field into proper relationship so that a unified image results.

In Fig. 16 the two images created by L and M occur on the face of prism P_4 at the common boundary of prisms P_2 and P_3. The rays from M travel above prism P_2 while the rays from L travel inside the prism P_2 and are reflected at a point just below the other rays. Both rays are then deflected by prism P_3 back to form the split image. Prism P_4 is an erecting prism to present the image to the eye right side up. The field lens collects all the rays forming the image so that they are carried to the eye. The ocular lenses are provided so that the images, which are only a short distance from the eye, may be seen easily. The objectives and oculars actually amount to two small telescopes giving a magnification of $3\times$.

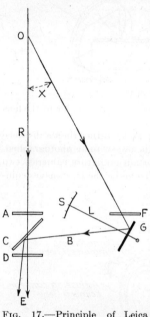

The eyepiece, which carries the ocular lenses, is adjustable along its axis to allow for variations in individual eyesight. The user is instructed to adjust the eyepiece for an object 8 ft. away, a setting which enables images for both distant and near objects to be accommodated by the eye.

Leica Coupled Range Finder.—The principle of the range finder fitted to Leica 35-mm. cameras may be seen from Fig. 17.

"A ray of light[1] from the object at O passes through the window A, through the glass sheet C, which is set at an angle of 45° to line $O A$, through the window D, and into the eye at E. Another ray of light from the same point on the object passes through window F, is reflected from mirror G, then from the glass sheet C, and finally passes through window D into the eye at E. Thus the eye at E will see two images, a direct one, such as that shown in the large circle in Fig. 12, and one reflected from the mirror G, which is the one shown in the small circle in

Fig. 17.—Principle of Leica range finder.

Fig. 12. The mirror G can be rotated about an axis H by means of lever L, and it is obvious that if this mirror G is rotated to the proper position the ray of light OGC will then emerge from window D along the line OE, and the two images will seem to have become one, or are coincident. Corresponding to this proper position of the mirror G, the end of the lever L indicates on the empirically calibrated scale S the distance OC, which is called the "range" of the object at O."

Figure 18 shows the range finder as fitted to the cameras. A collar, which is part of each lens available for the Leica camera, fits against a small roller which in turn actuates the prism of the range finder. The field seen in the range finder is enlarged about $1\frac{1}{2}$ times. A circular image is seen in the Leica range finder, the center of the image being brighter than the surrounding part of the field. Two complete images are seen in this center portion unless the range finder is properly focused for the desired object.

[1] CORNOG, I. CLYDE, The Autofocal Camera, *Am. Phot.*, January, 1937, p. 1.

An orange-red filter may be placed over one of the range-finder ports so that a deep color is imparted to one of the images, increasing the ease of accurate focusing by an increase in contrast between the two images.

The base of the Leica range finder is approximately 40 mm.

Zeiss Coupled Range Finder.—The principle of this type of finder is shown in Fig. 19.

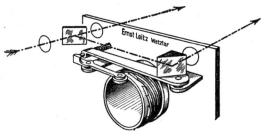

FIG. 18.—Leica range finder as fitted to camera.

"At *P'* there are two prisms of triangular cross section and very small angle. Viewed in the direction of the arrow these prisms would look like the inset in Fig. 19. In the figure these prisms are shown in such a position that a ray of light such as *OP* will pass through them without any change in direction, and the ray would go along the line *OE* into the eye at *E*; together they act here like a sheet of glass with parallel faces. These prisms are arranged so that they will rotate about the line *OPE* in opposite directions and at equal rates as the focusing device of the camera is adjusted. Having been turned for a little way, the pair no longer act like a sheet of plane parallel glass, but like a single prism, since now one side of the combination is thicker than the other. This can easily be demonstrated by using the pointed ends of two lead pencils to represent the prisms, holding the pencils perpendicular to the plane of Fig. 19, and rotating each towards the right-hand side of the figure, in opposite directions. The result is that the ray of light is caused to deviate from the path *OPE* to the path *OPE'*. In this case mirror *G* is fixed, as is the sheet of glass *C*, so that the ray *OGC* passes into the eye at *E'*. It is obvious that by rotating the prisms as described the two images can be brought into coincidence along the line *PE'*."

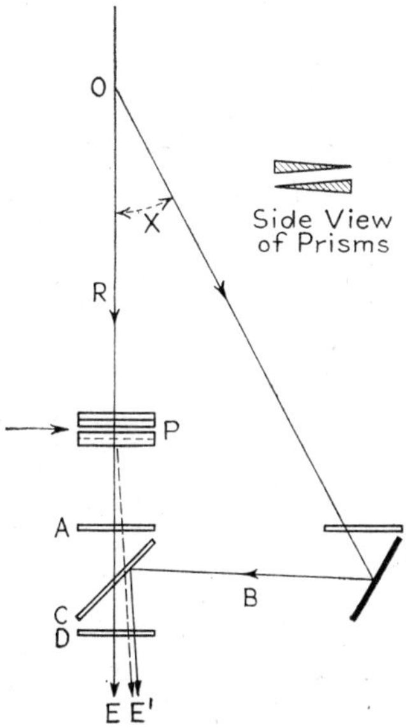

In the Zeiss range finder, use is made of the fact that the color of light passing through a very thin metallic layer is complementary to the color of the light reflected by the layer. The colors into which white light are split by a semitransparent gold coating are red and green which, when mixed, become white again.

FIG. 19.—Zeiss coupled range finder.

The image-dividing mirror is given a coating of gold so that the objects in the image will be seen in nearly their natural colors in the central field when the camera is properly focused because the green and the red portions of the image will be rejoined then. The mechanical details of the range finder are shown in Fig. 20.

The base of the Zeiss range finder is approximately 4 in.   The field of view of the red image is reduced in size so that only the part of the scene to be reproduced with maximum sharpness is visible.

The following notes on range finders are taken from the Zeiss Ikon bulletin "Contax Photography."

The simplest form of range finder comprises merely two mirrors, one fixed in position and the other variable (see Fig. 21).   Since "the full distance range between infinity and about 3 ft. only involves a movement of the movable mirror through some

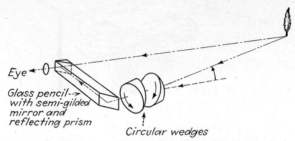

Fig. 20.—Rotating-wedge range finder.

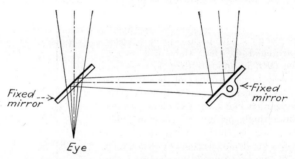

Fig. 21.—Simple two-mirror range finder.

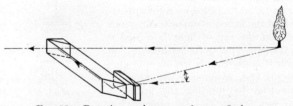

Fig. 22.—Rotating-wedge type of range finder.

3° which must be linked up with a movement of the focusing mount of the lens through 140°, . . . a small error in the mirror will involve a considerable error in the focusing.

"A very considerable advance on this construction is reached in the rotating-wedge distance meter.   In this instrument, a range of focusing distances between infinity and 3 feet involves a revolution of the two wedges through 90°, so that a gain in accuracy is reached, together with a comparative immunity from mechanical breakdown and damage through shock.

"A further gain which the wedge principle introduces is that the base distance can be made of a solid glass pencil, one end of which is semi-gilded.   This, though valuable, is not so important as the possibility of separating the wedges from the base prism. The wedges can be placed on the actual lens mounting, while the base prism and eye-piece remain in the camera body. In this way, those portions of the meter which are most sensitive to mechanical shock can be safely protected by the body, thus affording a very high degree of security from breakdown.

"A still further step in the development of the distance meter may be taken. The distance meter may work on the 'swing-wedge' method, and its field of view is arranged to agree with that of the camera lens. A combined distance meter and view finder thus results. The swing-wedge principle involves the use of two cylindrical lenses, their outer sides plane and their inner sides ground circular, placed in close contact. The front lens is concave, and remains stationary, while the rear lens, which is convex, swings from side to side. The combined distance-meter-view-finder makes it possible to increase the field of view through the distance meter that would otherwise only be possible with the rotating wedge distance meter by increasing considerably the size of the camera. Such combination is clearly useful from the point of view of ease in focusing, quickness of exposure after focusing, and certainty of sharp pictures, since there is only one eyepiece to be looked through instead of two."

Accuracy of Coupled Range Finders.—The following data are taken from a paper by Cornog.[1]

"The principle of the range finder may be discussed in connection with Fig. 17. The 'range' of the object is the distance CO, or R, measured from the center line connecting the two mirrors G and C, and the 'base' B of the instrument is the distance between the centers of these same mirrors. The base B subtends the angle X at the object, so that

$$\tan X = \frac{B}{R} \tag{1}$$

where X is expressed in radians and B and R in feet, or meters. This relation may be expressed in terms of the position of the lever arm on the scale S (Fig. 17), as in Eq. 2,

$$S = \frac{L}{2} \tan^{-1} \frac{B}{R} \tag{2}$$

"The range of the object is given, therefore, by the expression

$$R = \frac{B}{\tan X} \tag{3}$$

which may be called the 'law' of the range finder.

"Since the angle X is always very small, it is necessary that a range finder be well constructed if precise results are to be obtained: given a good instrument, the determining factor then becomes the adjustment for coincidence. In a reasonably well constructed instrument of the type of Fig. 17, such as may be found on a camera, the base length is about two inches, and with ordinary care in setting for coincidence an object twenty feet distant can be located within ± 4 inches, or within a length of 8 inches, while if the object is only three feet away its position can be located within ± 0.1 inch, or within a length of 0.2 inch."

A good lens operating at an aperture of $f/1.5$ focused on an object 20 ft. distant will have a depth of focus from 17 ft. 10 in. to 22 ft. 10 in.; focused on an object 4 ft. distant objects between 3 ft. 11 in. and 4 ft. 1½ in. will be in focus (circle of confusion ⅟₅₀₀ in.). Thus it may be seen that the accuracy of adjustment of the range finder is such that the depth of field of even the fastest lens will take care of minor errors in operating the range finder.

[1] *Ibid.*

Depth-of-field Indicator.—A useful accessory included on most miniature cameras and on many larger cameras is a depth-of-field, or depth-of-focus, table. Such a table shows the distance range which will be in sharp focus when the camera is focused upon a given distance and the lens is working at a given aperture. Often the depth-of-field table is in the form of an indicator which shows the user the depth as soon as he has focused the lens upon the desired distance. All such depth-of-field scales or indicators are based upon a certain value of the circle of confusion (see below); on miniature cameras in which the negatives are often enlarged considerably in making prints, the circle of confusion considered is much smaller than is used when large-size images are secured.

Illustrations of two types of depth-of-field indicators are shown.

Depth of Field.—If a lens is focused upon a given distance, objects in the plane at that distance will be sharply in focus. Objects near this plane will not be so sharply focused, but they will be sharper than objects at greater distances from this plane.

FIG. 23.—Depth-of-field indicator.

If the lens is stopped down, objects at considerable distance from the plane upon which the lens is focused may be relatively sharp, although not so sharp as objects in the plane upon which the lens is accurately focused.

The distance from the nearest to the farthest subjects which appear sharply focused is called the depth of field. But this distance range is subjective, depending upon the inability of the human eye to distinguish between a point and a small circle.

If the lens is focused accurately upon a given plane, then points of light in other planes will not produce points of light in the plane of the film but will produce circles which are cross sections of the pencils of light which come to a point focus in front of, or behind, the film plane. Therefore, the only points of light existing in the film plane are images of points of light in the plane upon which the lens is exactly focused. All other points in front of or behind this plane will be reproduced upon the film plane as circles, larger circles being produced by point sources existing at greater distances from the plane upon which the lens is focused than by points nearer the plane upon which the lens is focused. These circles are known as "circles of confusion."

It is generally assumed that, if a print is viewed from a distance of 12 in., circles of confusion $\frac{1}{100}$ in. in diameter or less will not be perceived as circles by the eye; they will look like points.

A depth-of-field table, can be calculated on the basis of a given circle of confusion. If a camera makes negatives which are not to be enlarged, then the depth-of-field table may be based upon a circle of confusion of $\frac{1}{250}$ in. If, however, negatives are to be enlarged so that the resultant print has circles of confusion no greater than $\frac{1}{250}$ in., the accuracy with which the camera is focused must be correspondingly greater. Depth-of-field tables used with miniature cameras are often based upon a circle of confusion as small as $\frac{1}{2000}$ in.

Depth-of-field Table.—Assuming a permissible circle of confusion, the distance from the lens of the nearest object which is in focus when the lens is focused upon infinity, is known as the *hyperfocal distance*. This varies with focal length, circle of confusion, and aperture. The hyperfocal distance, in feet, is

$$H = \frac{F^2}{(f \times C \times 12)} \tag{4}$$

where F = the focal length of the lens in inches;

f = the working aperture f/number;

C = the diameter of the circle of confusion in inches.

The hyperfocal distance is sometimes defined as the distance of the nearest object in focus when the lens is focused upon this object sharply and when objects very far away are acceptably sharp. The value of H is used in calculating depth of focus as outlined below.

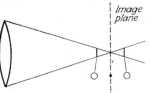

In making a depth-of-focus table the distances desired are the distance to which sharpness extends beyond and inside the distance upon which the lens is focused. Thus, if the lens is focused upon a plane 10 ft. from the camera, between what limits will other objects be focused? These distances may be obtained as follows:

Fig. 24.—Point source is focused to a point only in image plane. Elsewhere the point becomes a circle.

$$\text{Near distance} = \frac{H \times a}{H + a} = D_N \tag{5}$$

$$\text{Far distance} = \frac{H \times a}{H - a} = D_F \tag{6}$$

and for objects 6 ft. or less from the camera

$$\text{Near distance} = \frac{H \times a}{H + \left(a - \dfrac{f}{12}\right)} = D_N \tag{7}$$

$$\text{Far distance} = \frac{H \times a}{H - \left(a - \dfrac{f}{12}\right)} = D_F \tag{8}$$

where H = the hyperfocal distance in feet;

a = the distance in feet to which the camera is focused;

f = the focal length in inches.

Example.—Assume a lens of 5-in. focal length, aperture f/5, circle of confusion of $\frac{1}{400}$ in. diameter. What is the hyperfocal distance and what are the nearest and farthest objects in focus when the lens is focused on an object 25 ft. distant? Hyperfocal distance $H = F^2/(f \times C \times 12)$ ft.

$$H = \frac{5 \times 5 \times 400}{5 \times 12} = \frac{10,000}{60} = 167 \text{ ft.}$$

Therefore, if the lens is focused upon infinity, objects 167 ft. from the camera and beyond will be in focus.

$$\text{Near-object distance} = \frac{H \times a}{H + a} = \frac{167 \times 25}{167 + 25} = 21.7$$

$$\text{Far-object distance} = \frac{H \times a}{H - a} = \frac{167 \times 25}{167 - 25} = 27.4$$

Therefore objects within a range of 21.7 and 27.4 ft. will be in focus.

It will be noted that the depth in front of the plane upon which the lens is focused is shallower than the depth behind (farther from the camera) the image plane. At 25 ft., an object 3.2 ft. in front of the 25-ft. plane will be in focus; an object 4.4 ft. behind this plane will be in focus. If, therefore, it is desirable to make an object closer than 21 ft. be in focus at the same time an object 25 ft. distant is in focus, it will be necessary to focus the camera on a plane somewhat closer than 25 ft. for a given aperture.[1]

Universal Depth-of-field Table.—In the following table (Eastman Kodak) the data are figured for a circle of confusion such that the angle between two lines connecting the edges of the circle with the optical center of the lens is 2 min. of arc. This amounts to a circle whose diameter is approximately $\frac{1}{2000}$ of the focal length of the lens. In such a table the circles of confusion are large for large prints and small for small prints.

TABLE III.—UNIVERSAL DEPTH-OF-FIELD TABLE[1]

Aperture diameter, mm.	35	25	17.5	12.5	9.0	6.0	4.5	3.0	2.2	1.5
Distance focused upon, ft.					Depth of field, ft.					
Over 100	195 − ∞	140 − ∞	100 − ∞	71 − ∞	51 − ∞	34 − ∞	26 − ∞	17 − ∞	12 − ∞	8.5−∞
100	66.5−202	58.6−∞	50.0− ∞	41.5−∞	34.0−∞	25.5−∞	19.5−∞	14.5−∞	11.0−∞	8.0−∞
50	39.9− 66.9	37.0−77.4	31.0−101.0	29.3−∞	25.2−∞	20.2−∞	16.9−∞	12.6−∞	10.0−∞	7.5−∞
25	22.2− 28.6	21.2−30.4	19.9− 33.4	18.5−38.5	16.7−49.2	14.4−95.0	12.6−∞	10.0−∞	8.3−∞	6.3−∞
15	13.9− 16.2	13.6−16.8	13.0− 17.7	12.4−19.1	11.9−23.0	10.4−26.9	9.4−36.5	7.9−∞	6.8−∞	5.4−∞
10	9.5− 10.5	9.3−10.8	9.1− 11.1	8.8−11.7	8.4−12.4	7.7−14.2	7.2−16.5	6.3−21.0	5.5−51.5	4.6−∞
8	7.7− 8.3	7.6− 8.4	7.4− 8.7	7.2− 9.0	6.9− 9.5	6.5−10.5	6.1−11.6	5.4−15.1	4.9−22.2	4.1−∞
6	5.8− 6.2	5.8− 6.3	5.7− 6.4	5.5− 6.6	5.4− 6.8	5.1− 7.3	4.9− 7.9	4.4−10.0	4.1−11.7	3.5−21
5	4.8− 5.1	4.8− 5.2	4.8− 5.3	4.7− 5.4	4.5− 5.6	4.3− 5.9	4.2− 6.3	3.9− 7.9	3.5− 8.5	3.1−12.5
4	3.9− 4.1	3.9− 4.1	3.9− 4.2	3.8− 4.2	3.7− 4.3	3.6− 4.5	3.5− 4.7	3.3− 5.7	3.1− 5.8	2.8− 7.5
3.5	3.4− 3.6	3.4− 3.6	3.4− 3.6	3.3− 3.7	3.3− 3.8	3.2− 3.9	3.1− 4.1	2.9− 4.8	2.7− 4.9	2.5− 5.9
3	3.0− 3.0	3.0− 3.0	3.0− 3.0	2.9− 3.1	2.8− 3.2	2.8− 3.3	2.7− 3.4	2.6− 3.6	2.4− 3.9	2.2− 4.2
2.5	2.5− 2.5	2.5− 2.5	2.5− 2.5	2.4− 2.6	2.4− 2.6	2.3− 2.7	2.3− 2.8	2.2− 2.9	2.1− 3.1	1.9− 3.5

[1] Computed for critically sharp definition, for fine detail. Where fine detail is not concerned, as in portraiture, the depth is effectively greater. This table applies only to normal lens equipment, *not to wide-angle, long-focus, or telephoto lenses.*

The obvious use for a scale or indicator showing depth of focus is to determine the nearest and most distant planes which will be in focus when the lens is accurately focused upon a certain plane. But the indicator may be used in other ways. As an example suppose that it is desirable to bring both a near and a far object into focus. Which shall one focus upon, the near object or the far object?

Suppose an object is 15 ft. from a camera which has a lens of 2-in. focal length. At the same time, an object at infinity must be in focus. Such a lens, focused at 15 ft. and working at $f/9$, will focus all objects between $9\frac{1}{2}$ and 35 ft. with good sharpness. But the distant object is farther away and will not be ·sharp. If, however, the lens is focused upon a plane 26 ft. distant, all objects between infinity and 12.6 ft. will be in focus. Therefore the camera should not be focused upon either the near object or the distant object but somewhere between.

Other Accessories.—Discussion of filters, diffusion disks, accessory supplementary lenses, plates, and films will be found in several other chapters of this book.

Other accessories used by the well-equipped photographer include tripods, cut-film holders, film and plate adapters, etc.

[1] GORDON, ALFRED, Depth of Focus in a Nutshell, *Am. Phot.*, February, 1937, p. 112 (how to make scales and charts); and MARTIN, F. T., Scale for Indicating Exposures When Bellows is Extended, *Am. Phot.*, January, 1938, p. 38.

The tripod is a necessity in all except candid and sports photography. The tripod must be chosen for the function it is to perform. If it is to support a small camera for a single shot, it need not be so heavy or so stable as the tripod which must support a heavy camera such as that used for making color-separation negatives. For the small camera the metal folding tripods are suitable, those made in the Orient excepted. In nearly every case these Oriental tripods are "weak in the knees." They must be chosen with extreme care. A 9- by 12-cm. camera can be supported on a metal telescopic tripod for a single shot, but, if separation negatives are to be made, a sturdier support is needed. In this case where three exposures must be made from exactly the same point of view, a wooden tripod of heavy construction is recommended.

The tripod will tend to slip along the floor or surface less if its legs make a fairly large angle with the floor or ground. On the other hand, it will tend to move less when changing films, etc., if the angle with the ground or floor is small, *i.e.*, if the tripod legs are well spread out. Rubber feet are useful on floors; spokes are advisable when the tripod is to be used out of doors.

Hand cameras as purchased are usually supplied with three plateholders. These are metal single plateholders into which cut-film sheaths may be placed. Reducing sheaths are available for these metal plateholders. These sheaths fit into the slots where the plates ordinarily fit, and the sheaths themselves have grooves into which the cut film may be used. A film-pack adapter is merely a holder made of metal, usually, with an extension on the rear into which the film pack may be placed.

Folding roll-film cameras are seldom equipped with plateholders or detachable backs into which cut film, plates, or film-pack adapters may be placed. Studio or view cameras employ film or plateholders habitually. These are usually made of wood and are made in forms which will take either plates or films. In those which hold plates, film sheaths may be placed so that either plates or films may be employed. Therefore the plateholder is more universally useful than the holder adapted only for cut film.

Wooden plate or film holders tend to warp in damp places; metal holders tend to rust.

Synchronized flash guns are devices which enable the photographer to fire off a flash bulb at the same instant the shutter of his camera is opened. In principle they are all alike although the practical application of the several types may differ. When the shutter release is pushed to the point where the shutter is opened an electrical contact is made. Such devices are generally used with between-lens shutters and not with focal-plane shutters. In the latter type of shutter, the various portions of the film or plate are exposed in sequence as the shutter opening moves across the image plane. The photographer is likely to find on his negative only a portion of the expected picture when the focal-plane type of shutter is used, unless the synchronized device is properly engineered with this type of shutter in mind.

A lens shade is an accessory that is little used, but which should be in every photographer's kit. Many a photograph, taken slightly against the light, which has turned out to be rather hazy would have been sharp if a lens hood or shade had been used.

CAMERA-OBJECT RELATIONSHIPS

The material in this chapter, up to this point, deals with the physical equipment by which photographs are made. Good pictures, however, depend not only upon the equipment but upon the manner in which this equipment is used. Much depends upon where the camera was placed when the exposure was made, *e.g.*, how close to or how far from the object. It is here, and in other matters, that the photographer must use judgment; and, while this handbook is concerned almost exclusively with physical equipment, the following material in this chapter (and a few paragraphs in the chapter on Optics of Photographic Lenses) deals with the proper relations that must exist between the camera and the object to be photographed, if a pleasing result is to be secured from the photographer's efforts.

Perspective.—Most photographs are attempts to represent, on a two-dimensional plane, a three-dimensional scene or object. One of the photographer's most difficult problems is to give the viewer of the photograph some idea of the relations in space existing between the several parts of the scene or object. The appearance of the several objects of a scene in respect to their relative positions and dimensions is known as perspective. If a photograph shows these several objects to be in the same relative position and dimension as they would appear to the eye if placed at the position of the lens, the perspective of the photograph is natural. A good lens always does this: the photograph made with it is natural if the eye looks at the print from the proper viewpoint—but this is rarely the case.

When one looks down a long lane of trees, those trees in the receding distance seem to become shorter and shorter as the distance increases. If the photograph makes the

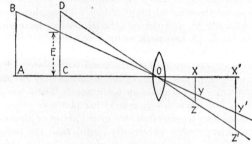

Fig. 25.—Two objects of same height (*AB* and *CD*) are focused at *X'Y'* and *X'Z'* by long-focus lens or at *XY* and *XZ* by short-focus lens.

nearer trees appear taller, when compared to the distant trees, than they would appear if the observer were actually looking at the scene, the perspective is exaggerated and is unnatural.

If certain conditions are fulfilled, the perspective of the photograph will be more natural than if these conditions are not carried out. It is often said that a long-focus lens produces better perspective than a short-focal-length lens. It is true that the focal length of the lens enters into the problem, but the essential condition to be fulfilled is that *the angle subtended by the print at the eye must be equal to the angle subtended by the object at the lens.* Under this condition the perspective of the print will be natural.

The angle subtended by the print at the eye depends upon the viewing distance. Since 10 in. is generally considered as normal viewing distance, when the print is held in one's hands, the lens to be used is one that will focus upon the sensitive material when placed 10 in. from that sensitive material—in other words, a 10-in. lens focused upon infinity.

All pictures made from the same viewpoint, no matter whether with a long-focal-length lens or a short-focal-length lens, will have the same perspective. The short-focal-length lens may include a wider field of view, and a given object will be smaller than when made with the long lens, but if the fields of view of the final prints are the same and if the relative heights of two objects in the two prints are measured, they will be found to be the same.

In Fig. 25, *AB* and *CD* are two images of equal height but one is closer to the camera lens than the other. A short-focal-length lens will focus these images in the plane *XYZ*. Object *AB* will have a height on the image plane of *XY*, and object

CD will have a height of *XZ*. The ratio of *XZ* to *XY* will be equal to the ratio of *BA* to *EC*. A long-focal-length lens will focus the two objects in the plane *X'Z'*, and the ratio of the two image heights will be *X'Z'/X'Y'*, which, by similar triangles, is

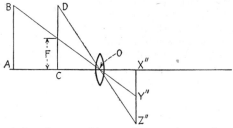

Fig. 26.—Effect of moving close to object to increase image size. Viewed at normal distance (10 in.) a print made under these conditions will appear distorted in perspective.

equal to *BA/EC*. Therefore the perspective will be exactly the same in the two cases. The images produced by the long-focal-length lens will be larger than the images produced by the short-focal-length lens, but the angle subtended at the lens by the two objects will be exactly the same in the two cases. The print made with the long-focus lens should be viewed at a distance *OX'*, while the print made with the lens of short focal length should be viewed at a distance of *OX*. If the image *XYZ* is enlarged so that it has the same dimensions as *X'Y'Z'*, then it may be viewed at the distance *OX'*, and so far as perspective is concerned there will be no difference between the two prints.

The objection to the lens of short focal length is the natural tendency of the user to move up close to the subject in order to get a large image. This is sure to produce an exaggerated perspective. In Fig. 26 the relative sizes of the two images on the final print will be *XZ/XY = X'Z'/X'Y' = AB/EC* when made with the two lenses from the same viewpoint. If the short-focal-length lens is moved closer to the image (Fig. 26), the ratio of the two images will be *X"Z"/X"Y" = AB/FC*, with the result that the nearer object will be larger, when compared to the farther object, than it appears in the print made from the longer focal-length lens.

Example.—The relation between image distance, object distance, and focal length of lens is

$$\frac{I}{O} = \frac{F}{d - F}$$

where O = size of object;
$\quad I$ = size of image;
$\quad d$ = distance of object from lens;
$\quad F$ = focal length of lens.

Assume two poles in the ground, 10 m. apart and 10 m. high. The camera is first placed 20 m. from the first pole. The focal length is 5 cm. (0.05 m.). On the print the nearest pole will have an image height determined by the above formula of 1000 cm./(L/O) = $^{1000}\!\!/_{400}$ = 2.5 cm. The pole farther away will have a height of 1.66 cm. These two images will have a ratio of 2.5:1.66 or 1.5. The image of the nearer pole will be 1.5 times as high as the one farther away.

Now move closer to the poles so that the negative is made at a distance of 10 m. from the nearer pole. In this case the two image heights will be, respectively, 5 cm. and 2.5 cm., or the nearer pole will be twice as high as the farther pole.

Proper Viewing Distance.—Prints must be viewed at the proper distance if the perspective is to be natural. Consider two prints, one made with a short-focal-length lens and the other with a long-focus lens. The short-focus lens was moved closer to the object when the exposure was made to secure an image more nearly equal in size to that of the other lens. If the print made with the short lens is held at the same distance as the print made with the longer lens, the perspective will not be natural, but if the smaller print is moved closer to the eyes, the perspective will seem more natural. The viewer may have to shut one eye so that he can approach close enough to the print to embrace all of it, but the perspective will be more nearly like that made with the long lens.

If a scene is photographed with a lens covering a very wide angle, it will be difficult to view the entire picture at once, so that the print will be moved away from the eyes. This distorts the perspective. On the other hand, if a telephoto lens is used which covers a very narrow angle, it will be natural for the user to move the print closer to the eyes so that the print fills the field of vision. This distorts the perspective in the other direction.

The important criterion is that the print is to be viewed at such a distance that the angle subtended at the eye is equal to the angle subtended at the lens by the object.

An enlargement from a negative made with a short-focal-length lens and viewed from the proper viewing distance will often have a better perspective than a print made by contact with a negative produced with a lens of longer (although improper) focal length for the viewing distance to be employed. A 5- by 7-in. print made with

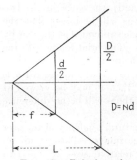

Fig. 27.—Relations between focal length of taking lens and proper viewing distance for print.

a 7-in. lens should be viewed at 7 in. viewing distance. If held at 10 in. the perspective will be somewhat unnatural. A negative made with a 2-in. lens and enlarged 5 times will produce a print when viewed at 10 in. which will have more natural perspective than the contact print of the same size made with the 7-in. lens. The difference in perspective, however, will be small.

If L is the viewing distance of the print, f is the focal length of the taking lens, and n is the linear magnification of the print compared with the negative, then[1]

$$L = nf \qquad (9)$$

from which the correct viewing distance or the best linear magnification may be found if the other two factors are known.

Example.—What is best degree of enlargement for a negative made with a 2-in. (5-cm.) lens when the print is to be viewed at 30 in.? (This figure approaches the distance at which salon prints are viewed.)

$$n = \frac{L}{f} = \frac{30}{2} = 15$$

Thus a print from a 35-mm. negative should be approximately 13 by 20 in.; or at a viewing distance of 10 in. the best size for a 35-mm. enlargement is 5 by 7 in.

Choice of Focal Length.—Since the eye includes an angle of about 50°, it is advisable to include only this angle in a print. Thus we have the rule that the focal length of the lens should be equal approximately to the diagonal of the plate or film to be covered. For example, a certain lens designed to cover a 4- by 5-in. plate has an equivalent focal length of $6\frac{13}{32}$ in. Focused upon an object at infinity, this lens subtends at the plate an angle of approximately 53°.

[1] This may be proved by Fig. 27. Let d be the diagonal of the plate to be covered by a lens of focal length f, and let D be the diagonal of the enlargement. The condition is that the print and the negative subtend equal angles at the eye of the observer and at the lens, respectively.

By similar triangles, $D/2 \div d/2 = L \div f = D \div d$.
But $D = nd$. Therefore

$$\frac{Nd}{d} = \frac{L}{f}$$

or

$$N = \frac{L}{f}$$

CHAPTER V

SHUTTERS

By Alan A. Cook

In the early days of photography shutters were seldom necessary. Photosensitive materials were slow and long exposures were required. Dry plates appeared in 1880, roll film in 1884, and the first Kodak in 1888. For successful amateur photography there was then a need for an exposing device to uncover the camera lens for a definite short period of time and then to close it again.

There were earlier shutters, many of them homemade. Some were built like a guillotine with a simple slide and a slit in it and a rubber band set of springs to snap the slide opening across the front of the lens—an early conception of the focal-plane shutter. Another type consisted of two blades sliding like double doors at right angles to the lens axis or pivoted above to swing out at the start of the exposure and back into an overlapping position at the center when the exposure ended. Such blades were of light thin material and could be located between the lens elements. The casing could serve as a holder for the lens mounts.

Interlens Shutters.—The principles of this early design were naturally carried into the development of the interlens shutter. This term will be used to describe shutters that open centrally and are located between or near the lens elements, as distinguished from focal-plane shutters which are located near the plane of the film or plate.

Single-blade Shutters.—The interlens shutter in its simplest form is an exposure mechanism with a single moving blade. Inexpensive box cameras are usually equipped with a device of this kind and Fig. 1 shows the details of construction of such a shutter from

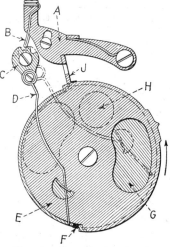

Fig. 1.—Construction details of Eastman single-blade automatic shutter (Julius Springer).

an Eastman camera. A is the release lever, and B is the release-lever spring, which has a double action according to the position of the double-action link C. The main spring D connects C with the shutter blade E. For alternate exposures this blade oscillates between the position shown in solid lines in Fig. 1 and the dotted-line position. At each pressure on the release lever the opening in the blade G revolves over the lens opening H to give an exposure of about $\frac{1}{25}$ sec. The lug F stops the rotation of the blade at the proper place after exposure. Note that both the link C and the main spring D have a double action for alternate exposures and that the actuating force on the blade is not the direct pressure of the release lever but the effect of the tension produced in the main spring D. J is a lug which holds the blade until the pressure on the D spring has developed maximum tension.

A more modern box-camera shutter is shown in Fig. 2. It consists of two moving parts and two springs. When the exposure trigger is depressed, shutter cover 14 moves from a position in contact with stud 15 (Fig. 2*A*) to stud 16. In so doing, cam edge 25 of the shutter cover contacts stud 18 on the shutter blade, moving it

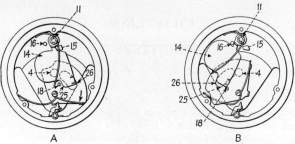

A   B

Fig. 2.—Shutter of modern box camera.

across the face of the camera so that the opening in the shutter blade, 26, comes opposite the opening 4, thereby exposing the film. When the trigger is released, spring 11 causes the cover to move from its position in *B* to its original position in *A*.

Another, more complex, single-blade shutter is shown in Fig. 3. *A* is a view of the individual parts of the No. 1 Kodo shutter of Eastman Kodak. *B* shows the assembled shutter.

Figure 4 shows how a disk diaphragm operates to provide four different sized openings for the lens to permit an adjustment for varying light conditions.

Before going on to shutters of more complicated design, it will be advisable to define more accurately the different parts of an interlens shutter and describe their

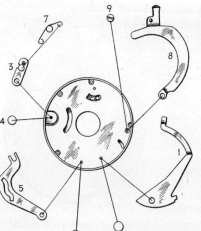

Fig. 3*A*.

Fig. 3*B*.

Fig. 3*A*.—Parts of No. 1. Kodo shutter for box camera. 1, speed pointer; 2, speed-pointer rivet; 3, opening lever; 4, opening-lever rivet; 5, blade controller; 6, blade-opener rivet; 7, trigger spring; 8, trigger assembly; 9, trigger screw.

Fig. 3*B*.—Modern box-camera shutter, completely assembled.

function. In general, an interlens shutter has a casing which serves as a lens holder and contains three separate units:

1. A diaphragming device to provide an adjustable aperture for the lens.

2. A blade mechanism to open and close for exposure.

3. A retarding device to slow down the action of the blades from maximum speed of action, thus providing a series of definite time intervals and a lever which can be set to operate the shutter at any one of these intervals.

Diaphragms are commonly of two types. The rotating disk shown in Fig. 4 is the cheapest, but it does not provide a continuous series of lens openings and is bulky if more than a few stops are to be used. The iris diaphragm consists of a number of ring sectors, usually made of thin metal, which will be called "diaphragm leaves." Figure 5 shows the action of a typical iris leaf. It has a pivot A at one end, the other end is provided with a stud or some similar

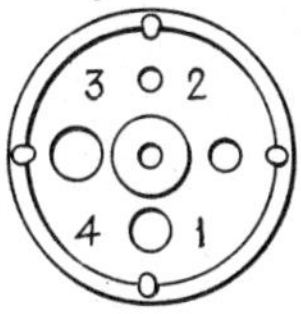

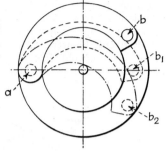

Fig. 4.

Fig. 5.

FIG. 4.—Disk diaphragm of simple Kodak shutter.

FIG. 5.—Action of a single diaphragm leaf (Julius Springer). a, fixed end of leaf on pivot; b, movable end of leaf at full opening; b_1, movable end of leaf at intermediate position; b_2, movable end of lead at smallest opening.

fastening which is fitted into a short slot in a rotatable ring. Three different positions of the single leaf are shown in Fig. 5. Figure 6 shows how a seven-leaved

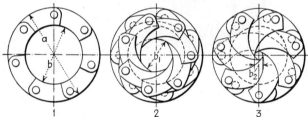

FIG. 6.—Action of seven-leaved iris diaphragm (Julius Springer). 1, full opening; 2, half closed; 3, smallest opening.

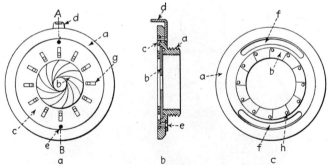

FIG. 7.—Complete iris-diaphragm assembly (Julius Springer). a, mounting plate, b, leaves, 12 in all; c, slotted ring; d, iris opening indicator; e, iris ring connected to d; f; slot to limit rotation of ring; g, slot in which movable end of leaf is carried; h, stud that pivots fixed end of leaf in mounting plate.

diaphragm operates in the same three positions. The central lens opening can be made larger or smaller by simple rotation of a slotted control ring in which the free ends of all the leaves are fitted.

Figure 7 is a complete iris-diaphragm assembly with 12 leaves to provide openings that are almost complete circles. This drawing shows the number of parts involved and gives an idea of the small space within which they can be fitted. This is an important point because the available space between the lenses in modern photographic objectives is very limited. In small short-focus lenses there is often only $\frac{1}{32}$ in. of space for diaphragm leaves.

Multiblade Shutters.—About 1900, single-blade shutters were found to be inadequate. Photography had to find means of "stopping" faster motion. Double-blade shutters, as shown in Fig. 8, were the first answer to this demand. *A, B,* and *C*

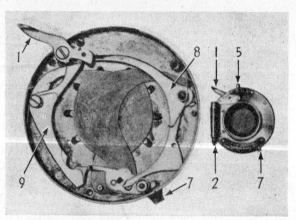

Fig. 8*A*.—FPK Automatic shutter made by Bausch & Lomb (from W. O. Hammer) 1, release lever; 2, pump for bulb release; 5, exposure indicator; 7, diaphragm adjustment and indicating lever; 8, lever operating blades; 9, levers operating for bulb and time exposure.

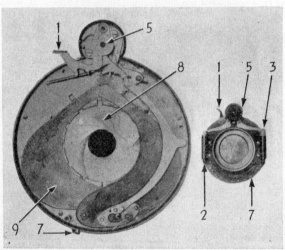

Fig. 8*B*.—Automatic shutter made by Bausch & Lomb (from W. O. Hammer). 1, release lever; 2, pump for bulb release; 3, pump for retarding device; 5, diaphragm indicator and adjusting cam; 7, diaphragm lever; 8, diaphragm leaves; 9, blades.

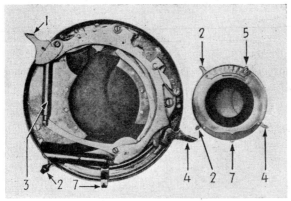

FIG. 8*C*.—Wollensak Regno setting shutter. 1, release lever; 2, pump for bulb release; 3, pump for retarding device; 4, setting lever; 5, exposure indicator; 7, diaphragm lever.

FIG. 9.—Blade action of double-blade shutters.

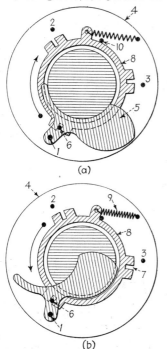

FIG. 10.—Blade action of three-blade shutter (Julius Springer). (*a*), blade open; (*b*), blade closed; 1, pivot of blade 5; 2–3, pivots of blades which have been removed for illustration (they are exactly similar to 5); 4, mounting plate; 5, blade; 6, stud to connect blade 5 with sector ring 8; 7, slot in sector ring; 8, sector ring; 9, spring; 10, stop stud fixed on plate 4.

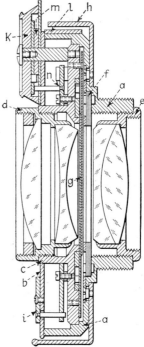

FIG. 11.—Compact shutter and lens assembly (Julius Springer). *a*, back case or housing; *b*, front cover plate; *c*, mechanism mounting plate; *d*, front lens mount; *e*, back lens mount; *f*, iris diaphragm leaves; *g*, shutter blades; *h*, diaphragm lever and indicator; *i*, disk for *t*, *b*, or *i* exposures; *k*, exposure indicating ring; *l*, diaphragm scale; *m-n*, levers to regulate the gear-retarding device.

Fig. 12.—Photograph showing the construction of the popular Compound shutter, made by Frederich Deckel, Munich. 1, finger release; 2, air pump for bulb release; 3, pump retarding device; 4, setting lever for motor spring; 5, exposure indicator (time, bulb, instantaneous); 6, speed-setting dial; 7, diaphragm adjusting and indicating lever; 8, adjusting cam under speed-setting dial; 9, pin to connect cam 8 with dial 6.

Fig. 13.—Retarding device of the Compound shutter (Julius Springer). a, air cylinder; b, speed-setting dial; c, speed-setting cam, pivoted at d; d, pivot for speed-setting cam; e, piston inside cylinder; f, retard-lever link; g, pivot for retard-lever link; h, retard lever; i, pin connecting dial and cam and regulating position of the link f.

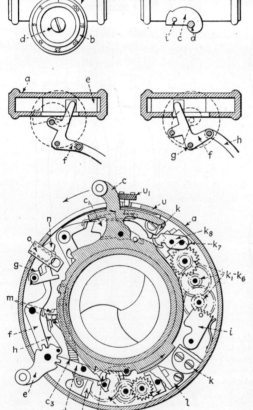

Fig. 14A.—Mechanism of modern Compur shutter, #0 (Julius Springer). a, backing case; c, setting lever, linked with leaves c_1 and c_2 and mainspring c_3; e, release lever, linked with levers d, f, and g; h, trigger for the sector ring, moved by e; i, k_1 to k_8, retarding device; e, e_1, mechanism of self-timer; m, projections of sector ring; n_1, knob for operating self-timer; o, cable-release bushing; p, stop for release lever e.

A

are different makes of shutters of this period. The blades are clearly shown—in the closed position in 8*A* and 8*C*, in the open position in Fig. 8*B*. Although these shutters were a great advance over previous models and were used all over the world on American-made cameras, they were merely one step in a long series of development. As increasing speed and accuracy became necessary, a different type of blade action was devised.

Figure 10 shows a three-blade shutter with blades 2 and 3 removed. In this illustration, 5 is a blade which is operated by rotation of the ring 8 through pressure

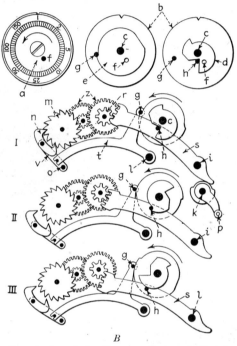

B

Fig. 14*B*.—Retarding device of the Compur shutter (Julius Springer). *I*, shutter set for slowest speeds to $\frac{1}{10}$ sec.; *II*, shutter set for medium speeds from $\frac{1}{10}$ to $\frac{1}{100}$ sec.; *III*, shutter set for fastest speeds.

The labeled parts are as follows: *a*, speed-indicating dial; *b*, fixed plate support for cam; *c*, pivot for dial and cam; *d*, *e*, speed-control cams working together; *f*, pin connecting the cams with dial *a*; *g*, *h*, pins regulating positions of two levers by cams; *i*, pivot of gear sector *s*; *k*, pivot or setting lever *p*; *l*, pivot of retard lever *t*; *m*, *n*, escapement mechanism which is thrown out of action at speeds of $\frac{1}{10}$ sec. and faster; *o*, pivot of escapement lever *v*; *p*, setting lever; *r*, gear retard, acting with *z* and *m* (these gears do not operate at maximum speed because the gear sector *s* is depressed to its lowest extent by pin *h* before lever *p* is operated); *s*, gear sector pivoted at *i*; *t*, retard lever; *z*, gear retard.

on stud 6 which is firmly attached to the blade. Note that only a few degrees of rotation of the ring 8 suffice to open the blade completely and that spring 9 acts to close it by pulling the ring back to position *b* where it is stopped by stud 10 which is fixed in the case. All this makes for rapid action when the parts are made of light, rigid material.

These are only typical of the principles of modern shutters because shape and number of blades as well as the method of operating them are all subject to wide variations in different commercial designs.   The question of blade action in relation to shutter efficiency will be discussed in a later paragraph.

There is one design of blade mechanism which is worth noting although shutters made to that pattern are no longer on the market.   This design is characterized by blades revolving in one continuous motion from closed position through open position to closed again.   The principle itself is interesting because blades that open and close in one motion are theoretically capable of higher speeds than the design actually used at present in which the blades open, come to rest, and then close again.

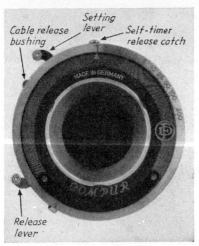

Fig. 15.—Photograph of modern Compur shutter.

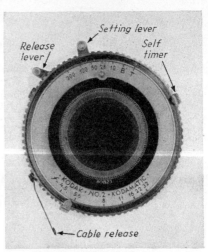

Fig. 16.—Illustration of Kodamatic shutter.

Fig. 17.—Mechanism of Wollensak Betax shutter.

Retarding Devices.—In the timing-control mechanism of a shutter there have been tried a number of different mechanical principles.   Among the first were adjustable spring tension on the main lever of the shutter (the one which operates the blades) and the application of a leather brake to a coil spring to slow down its action.   The air pump as a retarding device was mentioned in an American patent in 1885 and has

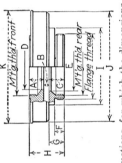

Deckel shutter constructions, for which the dimensions are given in Table I.

TABLE I.—DIMENSIONS OF DECKEL SHUTTERS

| Shutter | Mounting thread | | Flange thread | A | B | C | D | E | F | G | H | I | J | K | Diaphragm opening | |
	Front	Rear													Max.	Min.
No. 00 Compur	0.886 × 50	0.826 × 50	0.925 × 50	.308	.072	.250	0.630	0.800	.170	.230	0.630	1.105	1.732	1.771	0.660	.062
No. 0 Compur	1.161 × 50	1.066 × 50	1.180 × 50	.418	.049	.320	0.906	1.044	.242	.273	0.787	1.457	2.244	2.295	0.905	.078
No. 1 Compur	1.575 × 34	1.420 × 34	1.537 × 34	.400	.083	.304	1.141	1.382	.250	.310	0.787	1.925	2.675	2.718	1.141	.091
No. 1 Compound	1.230 × 50	1.230 × 50	1.330 × 40	.384	.083	.360	1.063	1.204	.303	.362	0.827	1.850	2.598	2.620	1.063	.091
No. 2 Compur	1.606 × 40	1.606 × 40	1.732 × 30	.355	.102	.370	1.378	1.378	.303	.374	0.827	2.303	3.071	3.090	1.378	.118
No. 3 Compound	2.192 × 40	2.192 × 40	2.362 × 30	.398	.110	.397	1.575	1.800	.331	.394	0.905	2.578	3.425	3.470	1.574	.118
No. 4 Compound	2.677 × 40	2.677 × 40	3.019 × 30	.425	.133	.426	2.052	2.052	.362	.440	0.984	3.280	4.173	4.200	2.047	.157
No. 5 Compound	3.259 × 40	3.259 × 40	3.547 × 26	.487	.147	.469	2.578	2.538	.406	.450	1.103	4.016	4.941	4.970	2.539	.197

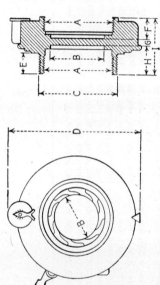

Ilex shutter construction, for which the dimensions are given in Table II.

TABLE II.—ILEX SHUTTER SPECIFICATIONS[1]

(Precise Nos. 00, 0, 1; Universal Nos. 0, 1, 2, 3, 4, 5; Acme Nos. 00, 0, 1, 2, 3, 4; General Nos. 0, 1, 2, 3, 4)

Shutter number	Inside diameter of inner barrel	Threads per in.	Maximum diaphragm aperture	Over-all diameter of shutter flange thread	Threads per in.	Maximum outside over-all	Length of back case flange thread	Threads per in.	Depth from front barrel lip to shutter blade plate	Total thickness of blades and diaphragm	Depth from back barrel lip to diaphragm leaf plate	Over-all length of shutter inner barrel
	A		B	C		D	E		F	G	H	I
No. 00 Precise	21.3 0.839	50	14.0 0.551	24.0 0.945	50	48.5 1.575	4.0 0.158	50	10.0 0.394	2.5 0.098	5.0 0.197	17.5 0.689
No. 00 Acme	22.5 0.886	50	17.4 0.685	25.3 0.996	50	64.0 2.520	4.5 0.177	50	7.2 0.284	3.5 0.138	6.3 0.248	17.0 0.669
No. 0 Prec., Univ., Acme, Gen.	26.9 1.059	50	19.0 0.748	29.7 1.169	40	64.0 2.520	5.5 0.217	40	9.2 0.362	3.5 0.138	7.3 0.287	20.0 0.787

[1] Ilex Optical Co., Rochester, N. Y.

NOTE: The upper numbers of the pairs are in millimeters. The lower numbers of the pairs are in inches.

TABLE II.—ILEX SHUTTER SPECIFICATIONS[1]—(*Continued*)

(Precise Nos. 00, 0, 1; Universal Nos. 0, 1, 2, 3, 4, 5; Acme Nos. 00, 0, 1, 2, 3, 4, 5; General Nos. 0, 1, 2, 3, 4)

Shutter number	Inside diameter of inner barrel	Threads per in.	Maximum diaphragm aperture	Over-all diameter of shutter flange thread	Threads per in.	Maximum outside over-all	Length of back case outside thread	Threads per in.	Depth from front barrel lip to shutter blade plate	Total thickness of blades and diaphragm	Depth from back barrel lip to diaphragm leaf plate	Over-all length of shutter inner barrel
	A		B	C		D	E		F	G	H	I
No. 1 Prec., Univ., Acme, Gen.	30.7 1.248	50	25.5 1.004	33.6 1.323	40	68.5 2.697	6.7 0.364	40	9.2 0.362	3.5 0.138	8.3 0.327	21.0 0.827
No. 2 Univ., Acme, Gen.	36.9 1.452	50	27.5 1.083	40.8 1.606	40	77.5 3.051	7.0 0.276	40	9.2 0.362	3.5 0.138	8.8 0.347	21.5 0.847
No. 3 Univ., Acme, Gen.	44.6 1.756	50	34.8 1.370	48.5 1.909	40	89.5 3.523	7.2 0.284	40	9.2 0.362	3.5 0.138	9.3 0.366	22.0 0.866
No. 4 Univ., Acme, Gen.	59.0 2.323	40	44.0 1.732	63.5 2.500	30	108.0 4.251	7.2 0.284	30	9.6 0.378	3.5 0.138	9.9 0.390	23.0 0.906
No. 5 Univ.	75.3 2.965	40	63.5 2.500	82.0 3.228	30	140.0 5.511	9.0 0.354	30	12.5 0.492	5.0 0.197	10.0 0.394	27.7 1.090

[1] Ilex Optical Co., Rochester, N. Y.

NOTE: The upper numbers of the pairs are in millimeters. The lower numbers of the pairs are in inches.

been used a great deal.   It is reliable so long as it can be kept clean, but this is hardly possible in a hand camera that is exposed to dust when in use.   A later method, first made practical in 1910, depends on the braking action of a train of gears or an escapement-wheel mechanism of some kind.   This gear and escapement retarding device is now considered the most accurate yet devised and is used on all modern interlens shutters.

With three separate mechanisms built into one small casing, it is not surprising that a photographic shutter is a complicated mechanism.   It has to be to fulfill the functions of diaphragm action and timing control.   Figure 11 is a drawing of the complete assembly with lenses attached.   The mechanical clearances are very small especially in the smaller outfits, and this is one reason why amateur repairs nearly always end up by ruining the shutter completely.   The remarkable fact about shutters is that designers have been able to put so much mechanism into a small space and that manufacturers have been able to make them perform reliably.

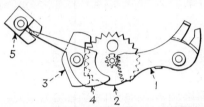

Fig. 18.—Retarding device for Wollensak Betax shutter. 1, lever engaging pinion on escapement; 2, escapement; 3, pallet whose number of oscillations are controlled by escapement 2; 4, pallet lever, offering resistance and providing smoothness of operation; 5, slot in escapement balance in which pallet lever rides.

Automatic Action.—There is one other point to be considered in this short outline; the difference between automatic shutters and those that have to be set for each exposure.   Early shutters were all the second type; there was a setting lever plus a release lever, and two operations were required to complete the exposure.   This is a disadvantage that was recognized at the beginning of shutter development.   Automatic shutters were attempted by designers as early as 1892.   The principle had already been demonstrated in the trigger action of automatic revolvers.   As applied to shutters, this trigger action consists of some mechanical arrangement of two springs on the main lever of a shutter in such a fashion that the shutter blades are closed by spring 1 after being forced by hand against the pressure of spring 2; *i.e.*, spring 2 opens the blades when released after tension is applied to it by hand.   After its action of opening the blades, it is disconnected from the lever by a slip catch (or some similar device) and spring 2 is then free to close the blades.

It is a simple device mechanically, and there are many ways to accomplish this automatic feature of shutter action.   But there is, as usual, a disadvantage.   In automatic shutters spring 2 must open the blades against the pressure of spring 1,

TABLE III.—WOLLENSAK SHUTTER DIMENSIONS

Number	0	1	2	3	4	5
Over-all length, in	0.710	0.808	0.827	0.946	1.024	1.024
Diameter case	1.521	1.970	2.345	2.940	3.705	4.660
Maximum diaphragm opening	0.552	0.710	1.024	1.380	1.761	2.233
Front lens opening	0.838	1.059	1.204	1.764	2.389	2.901
Threads, per in	50	50	50	40	40	40
Back lens opening	0.838	1.059	1.204	1.764	2.389	2.901
Threads, per in	50	50	50	40	40	40
Length flange hub, in	0.177	0.197	0.197	0.293	0.316	0.335
Diameter flange hub	0.953	1.185	1.325	1.997	2.623	3.128
Threads, per in	40	40	40	30	30	30

therefore it must be stronger than spring 1. From this it follows that an automatic shutter never closes so fast as it could if it did not have this double-spring feature. For this reason the fastest interlens shutters are not the automatics but are of the type that must be set by hand before each exposure.

TABLE IV.—DIMENSIONS—WOLLENSAK STUDIO SHUTTERS

No.	Outside diameter, in.	Light opening, in.	Lens opening, in.	Bulb attachment
1	$3\frac{1}{2}$	$2\,\frac{1}{16}$	$2^{13}\!/_{32}$	No. 4
2	$4\frac{1}{4}$	$2\,\frac{7}{16}$	$2^{15}\!/_{16}$	No. 5
3	$4\frac{7}{8}$	$2^{15}\!/_{16}$	$3^{13}\!/_{32}$	No. 5
4	$5\frac{7}{8}$	$3\,\frac{1}{2}$	$3^{29}\!/_{32}$	No. 6
5	$6\frac{7}{8}$	$4\,\frac{1}{8}$	$4\,\frac{1}{2}$	No. 6

Focal-plane Shutters.—Interlens shutters have certain disadvantages: (1) maximum speed at present is about $\frac{1}{500}$ sec.; (2) their efficiency at high speeds is low; (3) shutters of large size are always slower than small ones of the same design on account of the increased friction and the inertia of the parts that must be set in motion. This is a decided disadvantage with large-aperture lenses and has led to an almost universal use of focal-plane outfits for high-speed photography.

FIG. 19.—Curtain of Graflex shutter.

The focal-plane shutter is simply a black curtain, like a window shade, on two rollers with slits of different width cut across it. Figure 19 is the curtain which can be wound to use any one of four slits. (The square opening at the top is for time and bulb exposures.) The spring tension on the curtain is also variable and is controlled by a separate winding key. The results, expressed in reciprocals of 1 sec., are tabulated on the index plate, Fig. 20. The whole outfit, fitted in its frame and assembled on the back of a Graflex camera, is illustrated and described in Fig. 21. This is probably the simplest form of focal-plane shutter.

In the Leica camera the design has been changed to provide a slit of variable width instead of a number of slits, and the film-winding mechanism has been geared to the shutter-winding shaft so that both operations are performed with one motion. This shutter is now actually made up of two curtains. The separation of the ends

R.B.GRAFLEX-SERIES D
CURTAIN APERTURE

TENSION NUMBER	$\frac{1}{8}$	$\frac{3}{8}$	$\frac{3}{4}$	$1\frac{1}{2}$
1	350	110	40	10
2	440	135	50	15
3	550	160	65	20
4	680	195	75	25
5	825	235	80	30
6	1000	295	90	35

THE FOLMER GRAFLEX CORPORATION
ROCHESTER, N.Y., U.S.A.

FIG. 20.—Index plate for setting the speed of Graflex shutter.

is the slit of variable width. Slit width is adjusted to the proper value, in setting the shutter for exposure, by winding up the curtains on one roller. When released, spring pressure on two separate rollers at the other end of the camera draws the two curtains across the film aperture as a unit. The range of rated speeds on the latest Leica cameras is from 1 to $\frac{1}{1000}$ sec.

The shutter of the Contax camera uses a metal strip assembly instead of cloth as curtain material with an adjustable width of slit. This Contax shutter is rated at $\frac{1}{1250}$ sec. at its fastest speed.

The advantage in respect to speed that focal-plane shutters have over those of the interlens type is due to the fact that the focal-plane shutter does not expose the whole area of the film at once. The blades of an interlens shutter actually move much faster than a curtain at the focal plane; for example, assume a $\frac{1}{8}$-in. slit in a curtain shutter set for $\frac{1}{1000}$ sec. in a miniature camera, the film width being about $1\frac{3}{8}$ in. (*i.e.*, $1\frac{1}{8}$ in.), and the slit requires $1\frac{1}{1000}$ or 0.00909 sec. to complete the exposure. Compare this with an interlens shutter where at maximum speed the blades open and close completely within $\frac{1}{500}$ or 0.002 sec. in the fastest models.

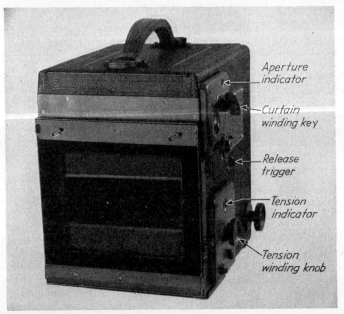

Fig. 21.—Back of Graflex camera showing focal-plane shutter construction.

A disadvantage accompanies the high speed of focal-plane shutters. The result is distortion, caused by the fact that a moving object is not completely "stopped" by a focal-plane shutter but changes its position during the time required for the slit to travel across the area of the film. The elliptical wheels of racing cars are a familiar example of this. This distortion makes the focal-plane shutter unsuitable for aerial mapping where complete freedom from distortion is desirable.

Shutters of Special Types.—There are few other kinds of shutters that need be mentioned. Those for studio use are generally made only in large sizes, to accommodate portrait lenses, and are limited to a bulb exposure. In these shutters one set of blades often serves for both diaphragm and shutter blades by the introduction of a stop ring which can be adjusted to prevent the blades from opening to their full extent when the release is operated. Exposures of about $\frac{1}{8}$ sec. are the fastest possible with these outfits, and longer exposures are secured by holding the release for the required length of time.

In a stereo shutter **two** separate blade assemblies are mounted at the proper distance in a single casing and connected by a long lever to operate from the standard mechanism of one of the shutters. Shutters of this type are never so fast as the standard models with one set of blades.

Another and different principle is found in the louver or Venetian-blind shutter. One model was designed for use in an aerial camera and was located midway between the lens and the plate. There have been few practical applications of this type.

Efficiency and Accuracy of Shutter Testing.—*Interlens Shutters.*—Efficiency may be defined as the ratio of light transmitted by a shutter during the exposure interval to the amount of light that would have gone through if the full aperture had been open during that interval. An efficient shutter is one whose blades open fast and close fast; the wide-open position should be held for as long a part of the prescribed exposure time as possible. Efficiency varies with the size of lens aperture that is employed.

The efficiency ratio may be expressed graphically when the constants of the shutter have been determined. A typical set of such diagrams are shown in Figs. 25, 26,

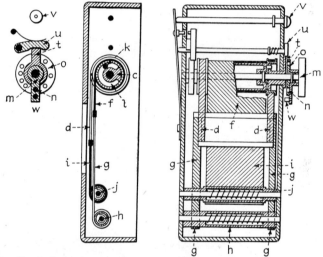

Fig. 22.—Focal-plane shutter of Leica camera. The parts labeled are as follows: *c*, roller for extension bands of lower curtain *i*; *f*, upper curtain; *g*, extension bands; *h*, spring roller for bands *g* of upper curtain; *i*, lower curtain; *j*, spring roller for lower curtain; *k*, pin connecting rollers *c* and *e*; *m*, winding knob; *n*, coupling pin connecting winding knob *m* with axle.

and **27.** In these the area DT (or $\frac{2}{5}\,DT$ for Fig. 27) represents ideal performance or full opening for the total interval at which the shutter is set to operate. The shaded area in each diagram represents the time the shutter is actually open, and the ratio of the two is the efficiency in percentage.

The determination of the constants of any particular shutter requires special equipment of a high order of precision. One really needs a slow-motion picture of the shutter blades in the act of opening and closing, and the separate pictures must be exactly timed. Such a set of pictures is presented in Fig. 28, and the time interval between pictures in this case is $\frac{1}{1000}$ sec. The timing accuracy of the shutter is shown also, being $1\frac{1}{1000}$ sec. for this particular exposure. Efficiency is here measurable by simply comparing the total open area of the blades in all exposures on the print and the ideal area of 11 pictures at the full circular aperture; in this case it is about **60** per cent.

The apparatus required to make such an analysis, as shown in Fig. 29, was designed by P. G. Nutting for use in the Kodak Laboratories. It consists of an arc lamp as light source, a constant-speed motor to drive a cylinder on the rim of which are 20 small flat mirrors, a holder for the shutter, a small lens to form an image of the blades, and a rotating drum to hold the film that is to record the separate images. The mirror cylinder must turn at exactly 50 r.p.s. (or 3000 r.p.m.) if its 20 mirrors

FIG. 23.—Mechanism of metal focal-plane shutter used in the Contax camera.

FIG. 24.—Linked metal bars (lower left) and assembly of bars in focal-plane shutter for Contax.

are to give exactly 1000 flashes per second on the shutter blades. It is impossible to make an accurate determination of efficiency without special apparatus like this. Photometric methods are accurate if properly carried out, but they involve considerable labor for a complete analysis.

Focal-plane Shutters.—In the case of focal-plane shutters, efficiency is more easily determined. All one needs to know is the essential lens and shutter dimensions given in Fig. 30. Examination of this drawing shows that the distance E between the shutter curtain and the film is the determining factor in efficiency. Only when

$E = 0$, *i.e.*, when the shutter is at the emulsion surface, is a focal-plane shutter 100 per cent efficient. The aperture ratio of the lens also enters into the calculation, so that a focal-plane shutter 80 per cent efficient for an $f/4.5$ lens may be totally

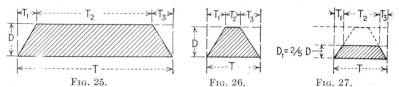

| Fig. 25. | Fig. 26. | Fig. 27. |

FIG. 25.—Efficiency diagram of interlens shutter. The total time of operation of the shutter is T; the time during which the leaves are entirely open is T_2. During the interval T_1 the shutter is opening, whereas during T_3 it is closing. D represents the diameter of the aperture. The efficiency is the ratio of the shaded area to the area of the entire rectangle, and may be expressed as

$$\eta = \frac{D(T_2 + \frac{1}{2}T_1 + \frac{1}{2}T_3)}{DT}$$

In this case, the efficiency is 86.5 per cent.

FIG. 26.—Efficiency diagram for interlens shutter. The efficiency of the shutter represented in this case is less than that of the shutter of Fig. 25 because the ratio of T_2/T is much less than in the former case. Efficiency is 61.1 per cent.

FIG. 27.—Efficiency diagram of interlens shutter, illustrating that for a given shutter speed, the shutter efficiency, η, increases as the diameter of the aperture, D, is decreased. Efficiency is 84.5 per cent.

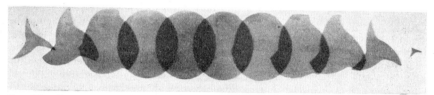

FIG. 28.—Shutter test strip. The single exposures are made with a time interval of $\frac{1}{1,000}$ sec. each. Shutter efficiency is about 60 per cent for this case.

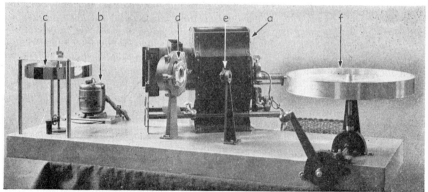

FIG. 29.—Shutter-testing outfit of P. G. Nutting. *a*, arc lamp; *b*, motor drive; *c*, mirror-wheel assembly; *d*, shutter holder; *e*, auxiliary lens; *f*, drum for film strip.

unsuitable when an $f/2.0$ lens is put on the same camera. In Fig. 31, slit width and efficiency are plotted for three different values of *e*, and typical efficiency curves are drawn to show how efficiency varies with lens aperture.

Shutter Tests.—To test the accuracy of a shutter one does not need the special equipment required to make a measurement of efficiency. Neon tubes operated on 60-cycle a.-c. line give 120 flashes per second, which is suitable for testing the slow range of shutter speeds. Such a test requires only a good tripod or a steady hand. The pictures must be taken at night. Pick out a neon sign in which one vertical line is well separated from the rest, take the picture from about 6 ft. distance and from a position such that other lights do not fog the film, and swing the camera steadily during the exposure so that the image of the neon tube moves steadily across the center of the field during the time the shutter is open. This will give one flash of light on the film for every $\frac{1}{120}$ sec. that the shutter was open, (for 60-cycle source), and by simply counting the number of lines the length of the exposure can be calculated.

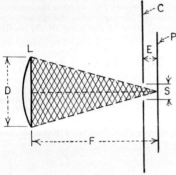

FIG. 30.—The essential lens and shutter dimensions required for determining the efficiency of focal-plane shutters. *C*, curtain of focal-plane shutter; *D*, diameter of the lens aperture; *E*, distance between shutter and photographic material; *F*, focal length of lens; *L*, camera lens; *P*, plane of photographic material; *S*, width of slit in shutter curtain. For focal-plane shutters, the efficiency is given by

$$\eta = \frac{1}{1 + \dfrac{ED}{SF}} = \frac{SF}{SF + ED}.$$

For faster exposures a rotating automobile tire is a suitable test object. The idea is to measure with the shutter the length of travel of a piece of white tape stuck on the wheel in a radial position to extend all the way from the outer rim of the tire, the point where it touches the road, to the center of the hub cap. In an open space where there is plenty of light, jack up one back wheel of the car. Use a long piece of white tape $\frac{1}{2}$ in. wide, mark it with two lines as shown in Fig. 32, and stick it firmly on the tire and hub. If the speedometer is correct and reads 15 m.p.h. when the picture is taken, the outer portion of the tire will then be rotating at 30 m.p.h., when one wheel only is rotating. This speed is 158,400 ft. per hr., 44 ft. per sec., or 528 in. per sec. (0.528 in. per $\frac{1}{1000}$ sec.) The photograph should be taken with the camera in line with the axle and at a distance such that the wheel and tire fill about half the film area. By measuring on the print and scaling from the 5.28-in. distance marked on the tape, the travel of the $\frac{1}{2}$-in. width of the tape during the shutter opening can be measured. One must remember that the tape is actually $\frac{1}{2}$ in. wide. It should appear $\frac{1}{2}$ plus 0.528 in., or 1.028 in. wide for a shutter exposure of exactly $\frac{1}{1000}$ sec. Furthermore, the travel of any point of the tape not on the outermost portion of the tire is proportional to its distance from the center of the hub, and its rate of travel can be easily determined. On a 16 by 5.50 tire, for example, the outside diameter is 27 in., radius 13.5 in. For a point 10 in. from the hub the speed ratio is 10 divided by 13.5 times 0.528 in.—which equals 0.391 in. in $\frac{1}{1000}$ sec.

The results of this method of testing will be found difficult to interpret in the case of focal-plane shutters, because of the distortion factor previously mentioned. It does give a true measure of the ability of a shutter to stop motion and to that extent is a reliable test of accuracy when carefully carried out.

Care of Shutters.—It is in order to list a few precautions for the user of photographic shutters of any type. A good shutter is built like a good watch and should be treated with the same consideration. It should not be oiled, greased, cleaned, or taken apart by anyone except an expert repairman. If the shutter fails to work properly, send it to the manufacturer for repair. Keep it as free from dust and dirt as possible and in a case of some kind when not in use. Cameras with focal-plane shutters made of cloth should not be left open in the sunlight; the sun's image is hot enough to burn holes in them. In fact, it is unwise to leave a camera open in the sunlight at any time. The reason for this is that the emulsions used on films have

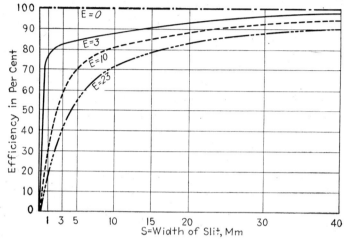

Fig. 31.—Efficiency of focal-plane shutter at different distances from the film plane to the shutter curtain, E. Curve $E = 0$ represents ideal case, impossible in practice; curve $E = 3$ is plotted for $f/4.5$ lens of 120-mm. focal length, curve $E = 10$ is plotted for $f/5.7$ lens of 260-mm. focal length; curve $E = 23$ is plotted for $f/5.7$ lens of 260-mm. focal length.

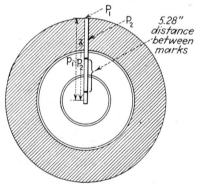

Fig. 32.—Automobile tire as a shutter test object. If P_1 is the angular velocity of the point p_1, and P_2 the angular velocity of p_2, then $P_2/P_1 = p_2/p_1$, and the shutter speeds may be determined by photographing the wheel while rotating at a known speed.

been enormously increased in speed during the past few years. Cameras and shutters have not yet caught up with them, from the point of view of being built to prevent fogging when the outfits are left in bright sunlight for a considerable length of time.

Bibliography

Yost, Lloyd: Testing Focal Plane Shutters, *Am. Phot.*, December, 1936, p. 808.
Clark, R. G.: Measuring Shutter Speeds, *Am. Phot.*, July, 1937, p. 498.
Holmes, L. S.: On Checking Relative Shutter Speeds, *Am. Phot.*, September, 1937, p. 626.
Wolcott, F. W.: Camera Shutter Speed Experiments, *Camera*, January, 1938, p. 17.
Greenlaw, D. S.: Accurate Method of Testing Shutter Speeds, *Am. Phot.* June, 1938, p. 400.
Waters, L. A.: Testing Shutter Shutters, *Camera*, November, 1938, p. 316.
Hay and Von Rohr: "Handbuch der Wissentshaftlichen und Angewandten Photographie," Vol. 2, in "Die Photographische Kamera und die Zeibehör," by Karl Pritschow, Springer, Berlin.

CHAPTER VI

PHOTOGRAPHIC MATERIALS

By Haywood Parker

Many substances are sensitive to light and thus can be used to form photographic images. The modern art and science of photography, however, is based almost exclusively on the use of the light-sensitive gelatino-silver halide emulsions. The use of various other materials, such as bichromated colloids, the ferroprussiate or blue-print papers, the diazotype materials, and even the collodion wet plate, is restricted to such specialized fields that they are not generally included in discussions of photographic materials.

In general, photographic materials are made up of two basic parts: the light-sensitive emulsion, in which the image is formed; and the base or mechanical support which maintains the emulsion in the correct geometrical form. In addition to these two essentials, practical materials often contain additional layers for various specialized purposes.

Photographic emulsions in general fall into two classes: negative emulsions, very sensitive to light and intended for use in the camera; and positive emulsions, much less sensitive and used for preparing prints from the camera negative. Although there is actually no sharp division between these two classes, in general their properties differ so greatly that they are usually considered separately.

The Emulsion.—The light-sensitive layer, or photographic emulsion, consists of a suspension of minute silver halide crystals in gelatin. Thus it is not a true emulsion in the colloid chemical sense but, by virtue of widespread and long continued use, the term has taken on this specialized meaning in photography, and there is little danger of confusion.

Preparation.—Negative emulsions are prepared by adding a solution of silver nitrate slowly to a solution of potassium bromide and gelatin, with continual stirring. By double decomposition this produces a precipitate of silver bromide which is kept dispersed and prevented from settling by the gelatin. Since free silver ions tend to react with gelatin, care is taken to keep the potassium bromide present in excess throughout the precipitation.

After precipitation is complete, the emulsion is digested, by boiling if it is acid, or at a moderate temperature if it is made alkaline with ammonia. During this treatment, the smallest crystals tend to go into solution and to precipitate on the larger crystals (Ostwald ripening); there is also a tendency for recrystallization through collisions and coalescence.[1]

When the ripening has been carried to the desired point, the emulsion is cooled to allow the gelatin to set. It is then shredded into small pieces and washed in cold water to remove the soluble potassium nitrate formed as a by-product of the precipitation reaction as well as the excess potassium bromide.

After washing, the emulsion is again melted, and more gelatin and various special agents such as hardeners, wetting agents, etc., are added. Next the emulsion is given a further ripening treatment and is then mixed thoroughly, filtered, and coated in a

---

[1] Sheppard, S. E., and R. H. Lambert, Grain Growth in Silver Halide Precipitates, "Colloid Symposium Monograph," vol. 6, p. 265, 1938.

thin uniform layer on the properly prepared support material. Here it is set by chilling and dried. The drying conditions must be carefully controlled to prevent any sudden changes in the rate of drying, which would cause variations in the sensitivity over the surface of the emulsion.

For most negative emulsions a small percentage of potassium iodide is mixed with the potassium bromide. This produces mixed crystals of silver bromoiodide which are more sensitive to light than the pure silver bromide. The ripening treatments also cause a great increase in sensitivity, partly because of the increase in grain size but largely due to a reaction with certain components of the gelatin.

Positive emulsions are prepared in a similar manner, except that chlorides or mixtures of chloride and bromide are normally used instead of bromide and iodide. Chloride emulsions for contact printing papers are often coated without washing to remove the soluble salts.

In actual practice, each of the above steps may involve several operations, and all the steps are mutually interdependent. They must all be carefully adjusted to one another in order to obtain the properties desired in the finished emulsion. While a great deal of research has been carried out by photographic manufacturers on the effects of variations in the different steps, very little of the information gained has found its way into the scientific literature. Actually this is of little importance since it is a knowledge of the properties of the finished materials, rather than the details of manufacture, which is of interest to the user of photographic materials.

Photographic Gelatin.—The unique importance of gelatin in photography is due to its desirable physical characteristics, combined with certain peculiar and very valuable chemical properties.

Physically, gelatin has the property of absorbing water and swelling. Below a certain temperature range (ordinarily 35 to 40°C.) this swelling is limited, and the gelatin remains in the semisolid gel form. Above this temperature the swollen gelatin melts to the sol form, or a colloidal solution, which will take up water without limit. When the sol is cooled, however, it will again set to a firm gel even in concentrations as low as 1 per cent. Thus the gelatin is particularly suited for use as the binder for the sensitive silver halide grains, since it can be made alternately liquid or solid as required in the various steps of manufacture, and after exposure of the finished material it will again swell to allow penetration of the developer chemicals to the exposed grains.

In addition to its action as a mechanical binder, it also acts as a protective colloid. If aqueous solutions of silver nitrate and potassium bromide are mixed, the resulting minute particles of insoluble silver bromide rapidly agglomerate into a curdy precipitate which settles out. Also, the particles are spontaneously developable, *i.e.*, a normal photographic developer solution will reduce all the silver bromide particles to metallic silver, even without exposure to light. However, if even a small quantity of gelatin is present, it prevents the agglomeration of the particles, and it also prevents any action by the developer until the grains have been rendered developable by exposure to light or by some chemical action.

An equally important property, however, is the effect of gelatin on the sensitivity of the grains. When the silver bromide is first precipitated, it is comparatively insensitive. During the digestion, however, the sensitivity may be increased from 100 to 1000 times, provided a suitable gelatin was used and the initial precipitation was made in the proper manner. This sensitizing action is partly due to the presence in the gelatin of minute quantities of certain types of organic compounds containing labile sulfur which, under the conditions of the digestion is capable of reacting to form specks of silver sulfide on the surface of the silver bromide grains.[1]

[1] SHEPPARD, S. E., Photographic Gelatin, *Phot. J.*, **65**, 380 (1925).
———, Some Factors in Photographic Sensitivity, *J. Soc. Motion Picture Engrs.*, **24**, 500 (1935).

Silver Halide Crystals.—The photographic properties of the emulsion are controlled chiefly by the composition, size, and condition of the silver halide crystals.

The slower positive emulsions are composed of silver chloride, silver bromide, or mixtures of the two in various proportions. The faster negative emulsions consist of pure silver bromide, or, more usually, silver bromide with a small proportion (3 to 5 per cent) of silver iodide.

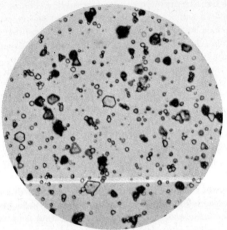

Fig. 1.—Grain structure of a medium-speed emulsion. (Magnification, about 1580 ×.

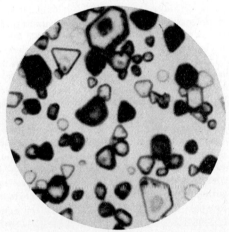

Fig. 2.—Grain structure of an ultrarapid emulsion, showing the hexagonal and triangular shape of many of the grains. (Magnification, about 3500 ×.)

The grains vary in size from submicroscopic up to as much, in exceptional cases, as 7 or 8 μ in diameter. The available evidence indicates that all the grains, even those below the limits of resolution of the microscope, are definitely crystalline. The larger grains show the form of flat hexagonal or triangular plates with rounded corners, though occasionally needle-shaped crystals and irregular lumps appear[1]

[1] Travelli, A. P. H., and S. E. Sheppard, "The Silver Bromide Grain of Photographic Emulsions," Van Nostrand, (1921).

(see Figs. 1, 2). Owing to the unidirectional shrinkage of the emulsion in drying, these flat crystals are oriented parallel to the plane of the emulsion.[1] Though the smaller grains appear only as round spots in photomicrographs, owing to limitations of the resolving power, it is reasonable to believe that they belong to the same crystal species as the larger grains.

In any one emulsion the large grains show, as a class, higher sensitivity than the smaller grains, though this difference is statistical and there are many individual exceptions.

In bromoiodide emulsions the large grains also contain a higher proportion of iodide; this may be a contributing factor in the greater sensitivity, but it is not the only factor since the grains in pure bromide emulsions show a similar increase in sensitivity with size.[2]

The sensitivity to light, or rather to developability, is not uniform over the surface of the grain but is concentrated at one or more sensitivity specks. It has been established that these sensitivity specks are caused by minute quantities of silver sulphide in the crystals. These impurities probably produce strains in the crystal lattice and tend to concentrate or orient the products of light action from the adjacent portions of the crystal in order to form developable nucleii.

Since the grains of different sizes differ in sensitivity, the characteristics of the emulsion depend to a considerable extent on the way in which its grains are distributed along the various sizes. The size relations of the grains are best shown by size-frequency curves in which the number of grains falling in each class size, expressed as a fraction of the total number of grains, is plotted against the class size. In general, emulsions containing very small grains are slow, and the sensitivity increases as the average grain size is increased. When the majority of the grains are in one size group, *i.e.*, when the size-frequency curve shows a high maximum with only low wings, the emulsion tends to be more contrasty; if the sizes are more widely distributed, the maximum contrast tends to be lower. These relations are only general and are modified by other factors affecting the grain sensitivity, such as the extent of formation and the distribution of sensitivity specks. The size-frequency curves for the grains in two typical emulsions are shown in Fig. 3. Curve *B* is for a slow lantern-slide emulsion that has comparatively low speed and high contrast; curve *A* is for a portrait-film emulsion which has comparatively high speed and low contrast.

The size distribution and the sensitivities of the grains are determined by the conditions of precipitation and ripening of the emulsion. The initial grain sizes are determined by such factors as the concentrations of the silver nitrate and potassium bromide solutions, the quantity of gelatin present, and the rate of mixing. The final size distribution is affected by the nature of the original precipitate and by the conditions of digestion. The presence of silver halide solvents such as excess potassium bromide or, in the case of alkaline digestion, of ammonia, seems to favor the production of larger grains through Ostwald ripening, by facilitating the solution of the smallest grains. The sensitivity specks of silver sulphide are also formed during the digestion, and their production is controlled by the conditions of the digestion and the nature of the gelatin.[3]

Other Emulsion Components.—In commercial practice, various substances in addition to the gelatin and silver halide are added to control the properties of the emulsion. Sensitizers to increase the light sensitivity may be either "chemical."

[1] SILBERSTEIN, L., The Orientation of Grains in a Dried Photographic Emulsion, *J. Optical Soc. Am.*, **5**, 171 (1921).

[2] SHEPPARD, S. E., and A. P. H. TRAVELLI, The Sensitivity of Silver Halide Grains in Relation to Size, *J. Franklin Inst.*, **203**, 829 (1927).

[3] CHIBISOFF, K. W., "Ripening of Photographic Emulsions," p. 405, IXth Cong. intern. phot., Paris (1935).

such as the various classes of sulphur compounds which apparently act by favoring the growth of sensitivity specks and which cause a general increase in sensitivity, or "optical," such as the dyes which extend the absorption bands of the dyed grains, thus extending the sensitivity to new regions of the spectrum.   Antifogging agents of various chemical types are added to restrain the formation of spontaneously developable fog grains and to allow the digestion process to be carried as far as possible.

The physical properties of the emulsion are modified by hardening agents that decrease the swelling and raise the melting point of the gelatin so that it can withstand higher temperatures in processing.   Chrome alum was originally widely used, though more recently organic tanning agents have been introduced.   Wetting agents which reduce the surface tension of the melted emulsion are added to facilitate the coating.

Printing-paper emulsions contain other addition agents, or doctors, of various types to control such properties as image color, contrast, surface texture, etc.

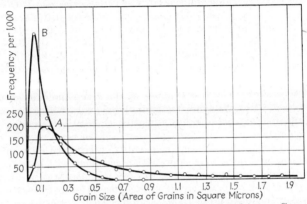

Fig. 3.—Size-frequency curves for the grains of two typical emulsions.   Curve B is for slow lantern-slide emulsions, while curve A is for portrait-film emulsion.

Physical Properties of the Emulsion.   *Thickness.*—Negative emulsions are usually coated comparatively thick, 0.0012 to 0.0016 in. (0.03 to 0.04 mm.) when dry, in order to obtain a long exposure scale (good exposure latitude).[1]   Positive emulsions are normally somewhat thinner, while emulsions designed for reversal processing are much thinner, so that in the first exposure the high-light areas are exposed practically completely, giving clean high lights in the positive.   With images viewed by reflected light, such as prints on paper, the maximum density is limited by reflections from the surface, rather than by total concentration of silver.   Therefore paper emulsions may be coated very thin to give conveniently rapid processing.

Because of the nature of the coating process, emulsions on continuous strips of support, such as paper or film base, can be coated with extremely uniform thickness, while with emulsions on plates there may be some variations in thickness, unless polished plate glass is used.

Melting Point.—Emulsions with plain unhardened gelatin usually melt in pure water at about 95°F.; however, most emulsions have at least some hardening, so that the average melting point is more nearly 105 to 110°F., and some special emulsions have much higher melting points.   The succession of processing solutions, at various pH values and with various salt concentrations causes a cycle of swelling and deswelling changes which may test the tenacity of the gelatin to the utmost.   Therefore,

[1] SHEPPARD, S. E., "Behavior of Gelatin in the Processing of Motion Picture Film," *Trans. Soc. Motion Picture Engrs.*, **11**, 707 (1927).

unless special precautions are taken, the safe processing temperature is at least 20°F. below the melting point in water. This would indicate that hardening might be desirable with all emulsions, but since the hardening reduces the swelling and thus the penetration of processing solutions, it may affect the developing characteristics unfavorably; consequently a high degree of hardening is given only where the conditions of use demand it, as with emulsions for use in tropical climates.

The melting point alone, however, is not the only measure of permissible processing temperatures, since thickly coated emulsions are more susceptible to mechanical damage when swollen than are thinly coated emulsions with similar melting points.

Optical Properties.—Since the silver grains reflect a certain amount of the incident light, the emulsion forms a turbid medium, in which the light is scattered to a certain extent around the point at which it enters the emulsion. This causes a small spreading of the developable image around the edges of the optical image; this spreading is called "irradiation." The amount of spread is proportional to the exposure, in any particular emulsion, but for most work the effect on the definition is not of importance except for very great exposures. When the negative image is to undergo considerable enlargement in printing, as in miniature-camera negatives, overexposure should be avoided to prevent loss of definition from irradiation. Also when precise measurements are to be made on the developed image, this spreading must be taken into account. The spreading is occasionally of practical value, as in the measurement of brightness in astronomy. Since a star image is practically a point, it is too small for a measurement of density. However, since the distance to which the irradiation is effective is proportional to the brightness, the diameter of the developed image gives a measure of the brightness of the star.[1]

Effects of Processing.—As has been mentioned, the gelatin swells to different extents in the various processing solutions, but so long as a critical temperature is not exceeded, it shrinks on drying to substantially its original form. The presence of a silver image does cause minute changes, however, so that, for instance, two adjacent point images tend to draw closer together during the processing, and, in extremely precise measurements of position, this factor must be considered. Also, since near the edges of a plate the strains are not evenly balanced, a slight distortion may occur. For this reason precise measurements are never attempted near the edges of a plate.

Supports.—The material used as a mechanical support for the emulsion must first of all be photographically inert, *i.e.*, it must have no deleterious action on the emulsion before exposure, on the latent image produced by the exposure, or on the final silver image produced by development, and it should not be affected by the solutions used in processing the exposed emulsion. The physical properties required vary considerably and are determined by the use to which the material will be put. Of the various materials which might be suitable, the only ones in common use are glass, cellulose ester films, and paper.

Glass.—For many years glass was the chief, and is still an important, base for negative emulsions and positive transparencies. It is practically completely inert and transparent, and it maintains its form without bending and without any shrinking or swelling during or after processing. However, it has the disadvantages of weight, bulk, fragility, and, for some applications, nonflexibility. Therefore it has been superseded for most purposes by the more convenient cellulosic films, though it is still used for those special applications where rigidity and absolute freedom from swelling or shrinking are important. Also, because of the possibility of coating single plates by hand or small batches of plates by machine, it is generally used for experimental emulsions which are used only in small quantities, such as the various specially sensitized emulsions used in spectroscopy and astronomy.

[1] Ross, F. E., "The Physics of the Developed Photographic Image," Van Nostrand (1924).

Glass for photographic use should be flat and free from any imperfections which affect the transparency, such as bubbles or striations, and it should preferably be practically colorless. For most purposes, specially selected cast or drawn glass is suitable, though for certain special cases, such as very large size plates used in photomechanical reproduction, ground and polished plate glass is used.

For the ordinary plate sizes, up to 8 by 10 in., glass approximately 0.05 to 0.06 in. thick is generally used. The larger sizes are usually coated on heavier glass, the thicknesses used for one type of plate being shown in Table I.

TABLE I.—THICKNESS OF GLASS USED IN PLATES FOR THE GRAPHIC ARTS

Plate Size	Thickness, In.
8 × 10	0.060
10 × 12	0.075
11 × 14	0.085
14 × 17	0.085
16 × 20 to 24 × 31	0.130 (⅛)
26 × 34 to 30 × 40	0.190 (³⁄₁₆)

Occasionally plates are supplied on specially thin glass that has a certain amount of flexibility, hence permitting the use of the plates in instruments, such as certain types of spectrographs, where the focal plane is slightly curved.

Since the emulsion will not stick to plain glass, plates are subbed with some material such as sodium silicate or hardened gelatin to which the film emulsion can adhere.

Film.—Photographic film base is normally composed of a cellulose derivative, usually cellulose nitrate or cellulose acetate, mixed with certain materials, called plasticizers, which keep the film flexible and transparent. Camphor is the usual plasticizer for nitrate film, while various high-boiling-point organic liquids, such as certain of the hydroxy-substituted amines or certain organic phthalates, are used with cellulose acetate.

Film is light in weight, flexible, strong, and transparent.

The flexibility allows it to be used in long strips that can be fed through the camera or other apparatus, slowly or rapidly as desired, by more or less simple mechanical means. The light weight and mechanical toughness also give film an advantage over glass by simplifying the problems of storage, handling, and transportation, particularly when any considerable quantities are involved. Film is not completely inert but swells slightly in the processing solutions, and shrinks on drying, but this is of importance only where the most extreme precision in reproduction of geometrical form is required, as in some astronomical work and in aerial mapping. Materials for these purposes are available on film base which has been specially treated so that the dimensional changes are practically zero.

Cellulose acetate film has the advantage of low imflammability, since it presents no greater hazard than an equal weight of newspaper. In the past, its physical and mechanical properties were not so desirable as those of nitrate film. In recent years these properties have been much improved, and acetate film is finding increasing use, particularly where the fire hazard offered by nitrate film is of consequence.

The thickness of film base varies according to the type of film and manner in which it will be used. Thus roll film must be sufficiently flexible to pass through the camera readily. Cut films, on the other hand, should be sufficiently stiff to remain flat in the film holder and to handle conveniently during and after processing. Motion-picture film must be sufficiently flexible to pass through the camera or projector, though the curves are not so sharp as in some roll-film cameras, and the film must be strong enough to withstand the strain imposed by the pull-down mechanism. Some representative values are shown in Table II.

TABLE II.—THICKNESS OF FILM BASE

	Thickness, Mμ.
Roll film	85
Motion-picture film	140
Cut film	200

The emulsion will not adhere directly to cellulose nitrate or acetate. Therefore, the surface of the film base must be specially prepared to ensure adhesion of the emulsion.[1] This is usually done by coating with a thin layer of substratum or "sub" containing an adhesive, such as gelatin, a solvent for the adhesive, and a solvent for the film base. Since the sub contains both solvents and nonsolvents for the gelatin as well as for the cellulose esters, the relative proportions of the constituents must be chosen with care.

Paper.—Paper is an ideal support for photographic prints since it is more or less flexible, opaque, economical, and durable. The requirements are rather rigid, since the paper must not affect the keeping properties of the emulsion or the permanence of the developed image and must be unaffected by the immersion in alkaline developers and acid-fixing baths. Photographic paper is made from specially pure stock, with particular attention to freedom from metallic impurities and any substances which might affect the emulsion or the silver image, either directly or through decomposition products. Originally rag stock was much used, but with the increasingly severe chemical treatments given cloth fibers in dyeing, cleaning, and stripping the dyes, particularly the use of chlorine bleaches, the rag fibers are often rather badly broken down; hence high-grade sulphite pulp has been found to produce more stable papers.

Papers for positive emulsions are made in both single weight and double weight and are provided with a coating of baryta in hardened gelatin to present a smooth surface for the emulsion, and to increase the reflecting power of the paper. The texture of the print surface is controlled largely by the composition and handling of this baryta coating.

For some applications, where very rapid processing and drying is important, the paper base is waterproofed by impregnation with a lacquer of cellulose nitrate or cellulose acetate.

Requirements for Special Cases.—While certain properties, such as inertness toward the emulsion or the processing solutions, are required of all support materials, certain particular properties may become of great importance in materials for specialized uses. Thus the motion pictures require a flexible base with considerable mechanical toughness, exhibiting little shrinkage during processing or on aging. Ordinary amateur photography, making use almost exclusively of roll film and film packs, is based on the use of a flexible film support, but factors such as toughness and low shrinkage are of less importance. Certain very precise fields on the other hand, such as astronomy and precision cartography, can tolerate no shrinkage or distortion; hence they utilize only emulsions on glass. In aerial mapping, where low shrinkage is important, the factors of weight and flexibility are also of great importance, so that specially prepared low-shrinkage film is used.

In most fields of photography, however, these refinements are of no significance, and the choice of support material can be made on the basis of greatest convenience in use, which in most cases means film.

Protective and Other Additional Coatings.—In addition to the base or mechanical support, and the sensitive emulsion, many commercial materials have other layers which improve the photographic or mechanical properties in various ways.

Gelatin Backing (Noncurling).—Since the gelatin emulsion swells on wetting and shrinks on drying, while the film base is substantially unaffected, strains are produced

[1] FUCHS, E., Preliminary Preparation of Photographic Layers, *Phot. Ind.*, **34**, 552 (1936).

which tend to cause the material to curl.   The early films, coated on a comparatively thin base, often curled into a tight roll no larger than a pencil.   In order to prevent this curling, most films are now coated on the back with a layer of hardened gelatin, which has practically the same shrinkage as the emulsion and so balances the strains.

Antihalation Backings.—When a beam of light enters the emulsion, it is scattered to some extent by successive reflections from the surfaces of the silver bromide grains, causing irradiation, as has been described.   At the brighter points in the image the emulsion cannot absorb all the light, and a considerable portion passes into the base. Of this light, the rays which strike the back of the support nearly normal to the surface pass out into the air and do no harm, provided the plateholder or pressure plate has a nonreflecting surface.   However, all rays striking the rear surface at less than a certain critical angle undergo total internal reflection and pass back through the base,

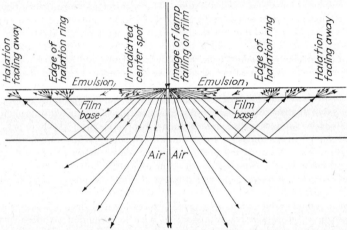

Fig. 4.—Diagram illustrating how halation is produced in ordinary emulsions by surface reflections.

reaching the emulsion at some distance from the original image.   Thus, around every bright point of the image, there is produced a circle or halo of light, with a diameter depending on the thickness of the base (hence it is smaller for film than for glass). This effect, called "halation," is illustrated in Fig. 4.   The halation can be prevented by placing some material between the emulsion and the rear air surface which will absorb the troublesome light.   Thus the base can be dyed a light gray, and, since the halation-producing light passes twice through the emulsion at a considerable angle, it is greatly reduced in intensity, while the printing light, which must pass only once, is only slightly affected.   With films which have a gelatin backing, however, it is more customary to color the backing with a dye, or a pigment, which is decolorized during treatment in one of the usual photographic solutions, such as developer or fixing bath.   Since it is only necessary to absorb light to which the emulsion is sensitive, orthochromatic materials are usually provided with a red backing which absorbs blue and green, while panchromatic materials are provided with a dark-green backing which absorbs chiefly red and blue but also some green.

Double Coating.—In order to increase the exposure latitude or the brightness range which they can record, some films (and plates) are coated with two thicknesses of emulsion.   The bottom emulsion is usually slower than the top emulsion, so that it is not affected until the exposure approaches the shoulder region for the top emulsion.

For this reason it greatly extends the straight-line portion of the characteristic curve for the combination.

The slow bottom emulsion also reduces the effect of halation to a considerable extent, because it absorbs part of the light that would otherwise get through to the base and also, being less sensitive, it is affected much less by the light which is reflected from the rear surface of the base.

Overcoating.—The grains of the emulsion can be made developable by mechanical action as well as by light action, so that scratches and abrasions show up as dark streaks after development. In order to prevent the formation of such defects during handling, films are often provided with a thin top coating or overcoating of clear gelatin. Film-pack emulsions are practically always overcoated, as are some roll films. Since the overcoating hinders diffusion of the processing solutions to some extent, an overcoated emulsion usually develops more slowly than a similar emulsion without the overcoat. This is why certain film packs require a longer time of development than the corresponding emulsions on roll film.

Paper emulsions are often particularly sensitive to abrasion, so that they are often given an overcoat or "antiabrasion" layer.

Stripping Film.—In certain special processes, particularly in the graphic arts, it is desirable to remove the emulsion from its original support and transfer it to a new support, either so that it can be trimmed as desired and combined with portions from other negatives or so that it can be reversed, right for left. Emulsions for this purpose are generally coated on a thin skin of hardened gelatin or cellulose nitrate or acetate, to give them sufficient mechanical strength for handling after stripping. This skin is cemented to the support by an adhesive which holds it in place until stripping is desired.

Characteristics of Photographic Materials.—The methods of measurement and the significance of the various relations between exposure, development, and density—*i.e.*, the sensitometric characteristics, such as emulsion speed, contrast, latitude, fog, etc.—are discussed in the chapter on Photographic Sensitometry, and some values are given below in the discussion of specific materials.

In addition to the speed, contrast, rate of development, etc., there are several other properties to be considered in the selection of materials for any particular purpose. Of these, the spectral sensitivity and the graininess and resolving power are probably the most important.

Spectral Sensitivity.—The normal human eye is sensitive to radiant energy over the wavelength range from approximately 400 to 760 mμ, or from violet to red, with the maximum of sensitivity to the yellow-green, at around 550 (Fig. 5).

The spectral sensitivity of the photographic emulsion, however, is quite different, beginning far in the ultraviolet and overlapping the visual sensitivity only in the blue. The different silver halides vary slightly, but all are practically completely insensitive to green, yellow, and red. Therefore ordinary emulsions are said to be color blind, because they reproduce colored objects in very different brightness relations than are seen by the eye.

This normal sensitivity of the silver halide can, however, be greatly extended by the use of certain sensitizing dyes. At first, commercial emulsions were sensitized only into the green. This gave a very noticeable improvement in the rendition of colored objects but hardly justified the name "orthochromatic" (true color) which was applied to distinguish these improved emulsions from the ordinary color-blind materials. Later, when really "true color" emulsions were produced, which were sensitive to the red as well as the blue and green, they were called "panchromatic" (all color). The first panchromatic emulsions had only low sensitivity to the green and red as compared to the normal blue sensitivity, but, as new and better sensitizing dyes became available, the sensitizing was improved to the extent that the present supersensitive type of panchromatic emulsions have very high red and green sensitivity.

The use of sensitizing dyes is not limited to the visible regions of the spectrum but has enabled the sensitivity to be pushed far into the infrared; hence now the photographic emulsion is much more versatile than the eye, and it is possible to take pictures with the completely invisible radiations on either side of the visible spectrum.

Types of Dyes.—In order to exert a sensitizing action, a dye must stain the silver halide; beyond this, however, the various sensitizers apparently have no common characteristics. Sensitizers are found in many chemical classes, but the majority of the most useful dyes seem to belong to either the cyanines, the xanthenes, the styryls, or the flavines.[1] As would be expected, the dyes, or rather the dyed silver halide, must absorb the wavelengths to which sensitivity is conferred. It has been found that this holds quantitatively and that for any single dye the spectral sensitivity curve

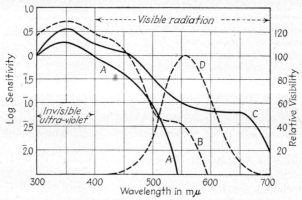

Fig. 5.—Spectral characteristic of eye sensitivity (curve *D*) compared with sensitivity of various types of photographic materials. Curve *A* is the characteristic for a typical noncolor sensitive film, curve *B* that for typical orthochromatic material, and curve *C* that for a representative panchromatic emulsion.

is practically exactly the same shape as the spectral absorption curve of the dyed grains.[2]

The amount of dye needed is very small, and in fact, if the concentration is increased above a certain optimum value, the sensitivity decreases sharply. In a few cases where measurements are available, this optimum seems to correspond approximately to a monomolecular layer of dye on the surface of the grains.[3]

Methods of Use.—Commercial emulsions are usually sensitized by adding the sensitizing dye directly to the emulsion before coating. Coated plates may also be sensitized by bathing in solutions of the dyes. The time of treatment, dye concentration, etc., vary with the different dyes.[4]

Bathing plates in sensitizing solutions was formerly practiced rather widely by experimenters in color photography and by scientific workers needing materials sensitized to special regions of the spectrum. The manipulation is rather difficult,

---

[1] Staud, C. J., J. A. Leermakers, and B. H. Carroll, Optical Sensitizing of Photographic Emulsions (paper presented at fall 1937 meeting of Am. Chem. Soc.).

[2] Leermakers, J. A., Quantitative Relationships Between Light Absorption and Spectral Sensitivity of Dye-sensitized Photographic Emulsions, *J. Chem. Phys.*, **5**, 889 (1937).

[3] Leermakers, J. A., B. H. Carroll, and C. J. Staud, Photographic Emulsions, *J. Chem. Phys.*, **5**, 893 (1937).

[4] Dundon, M. L., Color Sensitizing Photographic Plates by Bathing, *Am. Phot.*, **20**, 670 (1926).

however, and the degree of sensitizing is apt to vary, not only from plate to plate but even over the surface of one plate, therefore, with the wide variety of sensitizings now available in commercial emulsions and the possibility of obtaining any of a large number of other sensitizings on special order,[1] the need for sensitizing by bathing has practically disappeared.

Measurement and Specification of Spectral Sensitivity.—The spectral sensitivity of an emulsion can be measured by the ordinary sensitometric procedures by confining the exposing light to a single wavelength, as with a monochromator, or to limited regions of the spectrum, as with color filters. However, a quicker and more convenient method, which at the same time gives more readily comprehended pictorial presentation, is to expose the material in a spectrograph equipped with a neutral density wedge over the slit.[2]

In either case, the results show the spectral response of the material to the particular light employed. In order to obtain the absolute spectral sensitivity, it is necessary to take into account the spectral distribution of energy in the exposing light.

Spectrograms contain the more complete general information but require considerable care in interpretation. In particular, it is necessary to consider the spectral quality of the light used in the exposure. Spectrograms are usually made to "day-light," which is supposed to correspond to "mean noon sunlight," which is defined as having a color temperature of 5400°K., or to "tungsten" at a color temperature of 2360°K., which is comparatively poorer in blue and stronger in red than the "daylight." In either case, the short wavelength, or blue, end of the spectrogram is artificially restricted by absorption by the glass in the apparatus, so that the spectrogram is apt to give a false impression of the sensitivity to blue.

The wedge over the slit generally has a uniform density gradient, so that the exposure decreases logarithmically with the height above the base line.

Spectrograms for various types of negative materials are shown in Fig. 6.

A spectrogram is, essentially, a response curve for light of one particular quality. Equal-energy

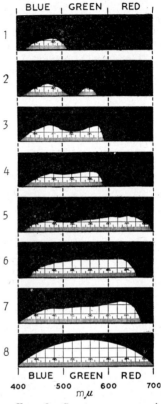

Fig. 6.—Spectrograms, made with tungsten illumination, and various color sensitizings, as follows: 1, ordinary unsensitized emulsion; 2, 3, and 4, various degrees of orthochromatic sensitizing; 5, type *A* panchromatic; 6, type *B* panchromatic; and 7, type *C* panchromatic. Curve 8 shows the spectral sensitivity of the human eye.

curves (Fig. 5) in which the absolute sensitivities are plotted against wavelengths give more quantitative information but are also much more difficult to construct. From the equal-energy curve, response curves can be obtained for any light whose spectral distribution is known, merely by multiplying the sensitivity at each wavelength by the relative energy in the light at that wavelength.

[1] MEES, C. E. K., Photographic Plates for Use of Spectroscopy and Astronomy, *J. Optical Soc. Am.*, **21**, 754 (1931); **22**, 204 (1932); **23**, 229 (1933).

[2] JONES, L. A., Photographic Sensitometry, *J. Soc. Motion Picture Engrs.*, **18**, 324 (1932).

Even ordinary spectrograms, however, are very useful, particularly in comparing various emulsions, since they present graphically the differences in spectral sensitivity. This is particularly true with emulsions used for certain scientific purposes where the sensitivity over a limited wavelength range may be very important.

Unfortunately, neither the spectrogram nor the equal-energy curve can be defined by a few numerical constants. For most practical applications, it is sufficient to know the integrated response over various spectral regions, and this can be expressed numerically.

In most practical applications, as for instance in color photography, this selection of definite spectral regions is accomplished by the use of color filters which transmit only the region desired. Therefore, the "filter factors," or the ratios between the sensitivity to the unfiltered light and the sensitivity to the portions of that light passed by the filters, often give the most useful quantitative information.

Obviously, the filter factor will depend on the quality of the light as well as the transmission of the filter and the color sensitivity of the emulsion. Thus the factors

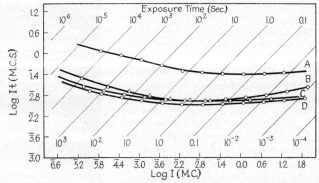

Fig. 7.—Curves for several typical photographic materials illustrating failure of the reciprocity law.

quoted by the manufacturer of an emulsion can be accurate for light of only one quality, and it will be necessary to make a correction when light of any other quality is used.

Reciprocity Failure.—In calculations of photographic exposures, validity is implicitly assumed for the reciprocity law of Bunsen and Roscoe, which states that the product of a photochemical reaction is proportional to the total energy involved, *i.e.*, the product of intensity and time, and is independent of the absolute value of either factor separately. It has long been known, however, that this rule does not hold for photographic emulsions and that for each emulsion there is an optimum intensity for which the exposure required to give a certain density is a minimum. This is shown for several commercial plates in Fig. 7, where the curves show the exposures required to produce a density of 0.6 for a wide range of intensities.

In most normal photographic practice this reciprocity law failure is not of great concern, since, as can be seen, most of the curves show very little slope over the range of exposure times ordinarily encountered. However, in any photometric work and in cases where the exposures are very long, as in astronomical photography, or extremely short, as in sound recording, the reciprocity failure must be taken into account.

Closely related to the reciprocity failure is the intermittency effect,[1] or failure of an exposure given in several installments to give the same density as a continuous

[1] Webb, J. H., The Relationship between Reciprocity Law Failure and the Intermittency Effect in Photographic Exposure, *J. Optical Soc. Am.*, **23**, 157 (1933).

exposure of equal total energy and at the same intensity. This effect, likewise, is of no concern in normal photographic practice.

The precautions which must be observed in photographic photometry to avoid errors from these and various other sources have been discussed by Harrison[1] and more recently by Jones.[2]

Graininess.—The photographic image is composed of discrete particles of silver, and thus under sufficiently high magnification the apparently smooth image presents a granular or mottled appearance. Since even the largest grains are only a few microns in diameter, very high magnification would be necessary to make the individual grains visible. Nevertheless, with negative emulsions particularly, the inhomogeneous appearance becomes noticeable at low magnification, in some cases at less than $5 \times$ linear enlargement. This inhomogeneous appearance, termed graininess, seems to be due to a clumping or grouping of the individual grains into more or less dense clusters, with areas of lower density between them. This graininess is of no concern when the image is to be viewed or printed in its original size but becomes very important when the image is to be enlarged greatly. Thus it is important in miniature-camera work, in motion pictures, and in certain scientific work, such as spectrography.

Graininess is determined chiefly by the nature of the emulsion, but with any particular emulsion it is affected by such things as the composition of the developer, the degree of development, the density, the nature of the enlarging optics, the contrast of the printing medium, and the sharpness and definition in the negative image. In general, graininess increases with gamma, increases with density, and is more noticeable if the negative image is not sharp. Graininess is also more apparent when there are any considerable areas of uniform density in the print. Thus, in any attempt to compare the graininess of two emulsions, all these factors must be held constant.

Since the nature of the emulsion is itself controlled by so many factors, it is impossible to make definite statements which hold without many exceptions. In general, however, it can be said that graininess tends to increase as the emulsion speed increases. Thus, when the image is to be enlarged to any extent, it is usually undesirable to employ a very high-speed emulsion unless the conditions of exposure demand it. However, since this relation holds in only a general manner, the emulsion speed should never be taken as more than a rough indication of the probable graininess.

The method of measuring graininess depends on the use to which the emulsion will be put. Thus graininess of miniature negatives should be judged from carefully prepared enlargements,[3] while graininess of motion-picture film should be judged under actual projection conditions.[4] For scientific work, such as spectroscopy, the relative graininess can be judged from microphotometer tracings of regions uniformly blackened to a density of 0.3.[5] Curves of this type for some typical commercial plates and for a group of special emulsions supplied for use in spectroscopy are shown in Fig. 8.

Methods of using microphotometer tracings to derive quantitative values for graininess have also been proposed.[6]

[1] HARRISON, G. R., Instruments and Methods Used for Measuring Spectral Light Intensities, *J. Optical Soc. Am.*, **19**, 267 (1929).

[2] FORSYTHE, W. E., editor, "Measurement of Radiant Energy." Reference is made especially to Chap. VIII, Measurements of Radiant Energy with Photographic Materials, by L. A. Jones.

[3] CRABTREE, J. I., and VITTUM, A New Ultra Fine Grain Developer, *Am. Phot.*, **30**, 188 (1936).

[4] CRABTREE, J. I., and C. H. SCHWINGEL, Duplication of Motion Picture Negatives, *J. Soc. Motion Picture Engrs.*, **19**, 891 (1932).

[5] MEES, C. E. K., "Photographic Plates for Use in Spectroscopy and Astronomy," Eastman Kodak Co.

[6] VAN KREVELD, A., Objective Measurements of Graininess of Photographic Materials, *J. Opt. Soc. Amer.*, **26**, 170 (1936).

GOETZ, A., and W. O. GOULD, The Objective Quantitative Determination of the Graininess of Photographic Emulsions, *J. Soc. Motion Picture Engrs.*, **29**, 510 (1937).

Resolving Power.—The ability of the emulsion to reproduce fine detail is limited by the inhomogeneity of the image and the spreading of light around the edges of the optical image.   The resolving power is conditioned by two factors, the turbidity and the contrast.[1]

The turbidity is dependent on the light-scattering power and the absorption of the emulsion.   Thus coarse-grain emulsions which show greater scattering tend to have lower resolving power, while emulsions which have been dyed to increase the absorption (so that the exposure is confined to the surface crystals) show an increase in resolving power.   In actual practice, the effective resolving power depends on a number of factors besides the emulsion properties, particularly the contrast of the optical image, the density of the image produced, and the spectral quality of the exposing radiation.

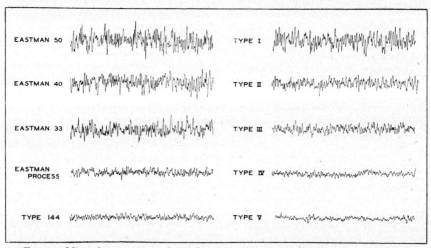

Fig. 8.—Microphotometer tracings of regions of uniformly blackened areas of various photographic films, showing relative graininess.   The Roman numerals refer to the basic emulsions supplied with various types of color sensitizing for spectrographic work.

Resolving power is measured by photographing a series of line gratings, the numerical value being equal to the number of equal-width black and white lines per millimeter that can be resolved.   Since the resolving power depends on so many external factors in exposure and development, the absolute value is of much less importance than the relative values for different emulsions.   The average resolving powers for a group of emulsions covering a considerable range of speed and contrast are shown in Table III.   These values were obtained with an optical image contrast of 20 and for the density showing maximum resolving power when development was carried to give $\gamma = 0.8 \, \gamma_\infty$.

Negative Emulsions.—Because of the extremely varied types of work which must be handled in the various fields of photography, negative emulsions with widely varying characteristics are needed and have become available.   The chief variations are in spectral sensitivity, speed, contrast, graininess, and resolving power.

Spectral Sensitivity.—As mentioned previously, ordinary emulsions are sensitive only to blue and ultraviolet light, orthochromatic emulsions are sensitive also to green, and panchromatic emulsions are sensitive to all colors of the visible spectrum.

[1] *Ibid.*

Ordinary emulsions are used for photoengraving line and half-tone work, for copying from various types of black-and-white originals, and, to a limited extent, for certain types of commercial work and some outdoor subjects.

Orthochromatic materials are widely used for general photography, particularly for exposures by daylight. With materials having a high green sensitivity, the rendering of colored objects is appreciably better than with ordinary materials, though reds are still rendered too dark and blues too light. Many workers, however, feel that this disadvantage is offset by the convenience of being able to handle the orthochromatic materials under red safe lights, which give considerable illumination in the darkroom.

TABLE III.—RESOLVING POWER TO WHITE LIGHT OF SEVERAL TYPES OF EMULSIONS

Material	Resolving Power
Eastman 50 Plates	38
Eastman 40 Plates	40
Eastman 33 Plates	60
Eastman Process Plates	80
Eastman Spectroscopic Plates, Type I	45
Eastman Spectroscopic Plates, Type II	50
Eastman Spectroscopic Plates, Type III	70
Eastman Spectroscopic Plates, Type IV	85
Eastman Spectroscopic Plates, Type 144	80
Eastman Spectroscopic Plates, Type V	160

The degree of orthochromatism, or the ratio of green to blue sensitivity varies considerably among the many materials available. Thus the filter factors for the various materials vary considerably, particularly with the heavier correction filters and the contrast filters.

Panchromatic materials are used in all cases where a reasonably true rendering of the tone values of colored objects is desired. They are also very useful for exposures by artificial light, which is rich in red and poor in blue light. Under such conditions the red sensitivity gives the panchromatic materials a much higher effective speed than either the orthochromatic or ordinary emulsions. Naturally, panchromatic emulsions are necessary for natural color photography, at least for the red-filter negative.

Panchromatic materials differ considerably among themselves in the relative sensitivities to the blue, green, and red regions of the spectrum. While there are a great many variations, panchromatic sensitizings can be grouped for convenience into three types, for which typical spectrograms are shown in Fig. 6.

Type A, or ordinary panchromatic, which was the only sensitizing available until a few years ago, has a comparatively high sensitivity to the blue, with much lower sensitivities to green and red. It is used in only a few materials at present.

Type B, or orthopanchromatic, has a high green and blue sensitivity and only slightly lower red sensitivity. It most nearly matches the color sensitivity of the eye, though blues are still rendered slightly too light. With daylight this can be compensated by the use of the light-yellow Wratten K2 filter, which holds back part of the blue light. With artificial light the reds and blues both are rendered slightly too light, and the correct rendering is obtained in combination with the light-green Wratten X1 filter.

Type C, or hyperpanchromatic, has fairly high green sensitivity but even higher red sensitivity. It is used principally when the highest possible speed is desired, particularly with artificial light. Emulsions with this sensitizing render both blues and reds somewhat too light and green and yellow-green too dark. However, a true tone rendering can be obtained by use, with daylight, of the light-green Wratten X1 filter, which holds back both blue and red slightly, and, with artificial light, by the darker Wratten X2 filter, which holds back more of the red.

Average filter factors for these three types of panchromatic sensitizings and for several degrees of orthochromatic sensitizing are given in Table IV. For most purposes these are sufficiently accurate; it is only necessary to know to which group any emulsion belongs. For very precise work, where very close matching of exposures is necessary, the exact filter factors for any particular material can be obtained from the manufacturer. However, since the filter factors depend on the spectral quality of the light as well as on the emulsion, the values will hold only for light of the quality specified. For light of any other quality they will serve only as a rough guide.

TABLE IV.—FILTER FACTORS FOR THE TYPES OF EMULSION SENSITIVITY ILLUSTRATED IN FIG. 6

Filter Name	No.	Ordinary Day	Ordinary Tung.	Ortho 2 Day	Ortho 2 Tung.	Ortho 3 Day	Ortho 3 Tung.	Ortho 4 Day	Ortho 4 Tung.	Pan A Day	Pan A Tung.	Pan B Day	Pan B Tung.	Pan C Day	Pan C Tung.
Aero 1..	3	4	3	3	2.5	2.5	2	2	1.5	2	....	1.5	....	1.5	
Aero 2..	5	18	14	8	5	4.5	2.5	2.5	2	2.5	....	2	....	2	
Kodak Color.	4	8	5	4	3	3	2	2	1.5	2	1.5	1.5	1.5	1.5	1.5
K1.....	6	4	3	3	2.5	2.5	2	2	1.5	2	1.5	1.5	1.5	1.5	1.5
K1½...	7	8	5	4	3	3	2	2	1.5	2	1.5	1.5	1.5	1.5	1.5
K2.....	8	12	9	5	4	3.5	2.5	2.5	2	2.5	2	2	2	2	1.5
K3.....	9	20	15	9	5	5	3	2.5	2	2.5	2	2	2	1.5	2
Minus Blue	12	..	....	15	9	7	5	3	2.5	3	2.5	2	1.5	2	1.2
G......	15	..	....	24	14	12	8	5	3	4.5	3	3	2	2.5	2
B......	58	..	....	24	15	16	9	8	4.5	12	9	6	6	7	6
A......	25	..	....	....	....	....	....	....	....	8	4	7	4	4	2
C4.....	49	6	8	7	10	8	11	9	12	10	5	12	24	12	24
C5.....	47	2	2.5	2.5	3	3	3.5	3	3.5	3	5	5	10	5	10
E......	23	..	....	....	....	....	....	....	....	7	3.5	5	3.5	3.5	2
F......	29	..	....	....	....	....	....	....	....	12	5	15	8	8	4
L......	50	..	....	....	....	....	....	....	....	20	30	24	40	24	40
N....:.	61	..	....	....	....	....	....	....	....	14	10	7	7	9	8
X1.....	11	..	....	....	....	....	....	....	....	....	....	....	3	5	
X2.....	13	..	....	....	....	....	....	....	....	....	....	....	....	....	5

Speed and Contrast.—The "emulsion speed" is a measure of the sensitivity of the emulsion and determines the exposure required to produce the desired image. The several methods of measuring speed differ greatly from one another; but, however determined, a practical speed rating should indicate the relative exposure required to produce a negative of good quality. For this, we do not need an absolute value but only relative values which will give the ratios between the exposures required by different films.

The relative speeds of the negative emulsions vary over a range of over 100 to 1 for daylight and even greater range for artificial light. Naturally, emulsions at the extremes of this range are used only for special purposes, while the great majority of materials in general use is grouped within a range of about 3 to 1, with the upper side of this range roughly one-fourth the speed of the extreme ultrafast emulsions and the lower side about six times the speed of the slow-process emulsions.

Except for a few extremely fine-grain special copying materials, the slowest negative materials are the so-called "process" emulsions used chiefly in the graphic arts. They have high resolving power, low graininess, high rate of development, and high contrast. Thus they are particularly suited for copying black-and-white and line originals and for half-tone work. The regular process materials have ordinary non-color sensitive emulsions, but panchromatized emulsions are also available with the general characteristics of the process materials, though with somewhat higher speed.

The "commercial" emulsions have from about four to eight times the speed of the ordinary process emulsions. They have fairly fine grain and high resolving power, and the contrast can usually be varied over a considerable range by proper choice of developer and developing time. They are useful for copying and for general commercial work, particularly in the studio in cases where very short exposures are not of particular importance. They are available with ordinary, orthochromatic, or panchromatic emulsions, the speed increasing in that order.

Above the so-called commercial emulsions there is a large group which makes up the majority of negative materials, including practically all the amateur roll films, as well as the films used for portrait work and for a large part of the general commercial work. The emulsions in this group are practically all either orthochromatic or panchromatic, and the speeds range from about equal to about three times that of the faster commercial emulsions. The contrast and development characteristics vary over a wide range, but in general the contrast is considerably lower than for the commercial emulsions. In general, the materials in this group offer the most practical compromise between the various desirable properties, such as ease of handling, reasonably high speed, considerable exposure latitude, graininess low enough for most uses, good keeping qualities, etc.

In addition to this large group of general-purpose materials there are a few ultra-speed emulsions with speeds ranging up to practically four times the upper limit of the general group. They are intended for use only in cases where extreme speed is essential, as in press photography where exposures are often made under very difficult conditions. They are available with both orthochromatic and panchromatic sensitizings.

Factors Influencing Choice of Negative Emulsions.—For the great majority of photographic work practically any of the fairly fast emulsions, those falling in the "portrait" group in the classification above, will serve quite satisfactorily. For some special types of work, however, certain other emulsions will be definitely superior. In selecting an emulsion for any particular purpose the various properties such as speed, color sensitivity, contrast, exposure latitude, graininess, and resolving power should be considered, but the choice should be determined by those characteristics which are of real importance in the work at hand.

Thus, while emulsion speed is undoubtedly very important, it will often be more desirable to consider how slow a material can be used, rather than to seek the fastest material available, since this allows much greater leeway in selection of other desirable characteristics.[1]

Somewhat connected with speed is the question of color sensitivity. Thus, for exposures with tungsten light, panchromatic emulsions are necessary, except in cases where long exposures can be given. Panchromatic materials are becoming increasingly popular for general work and are necessary where various colors must be rendered

[1] CASSIDY, E. H., Are Fast Films Worth the Price?, *Brit. J. Phot.*, **84**, 84 (1937).

in a reasonably true tonal relationship or where orange or red filters are used. They are particularly valuable in portrait photography since they avoid the exaggeration of skin defects given by blue-sensitive materials and thus minimize the need for retouching. In many cases, however, particularly for daylight exposures, orthochromatic or even ordinary materials will be quite satisfactory and may be desirable. Thus some landscape workers prefer these to panchromatic emulsions because the greater reproduction of blue atmospheric haze increases the apparent separation of planes and enhances the "aerial perspective."

The user often does not give much consideration to the contrast characteristics, probably because with many emulsions the contrast can be varied over a considerable range by proper control of exposure and development (Fig. 9) and because the range of contrasts obtainable in printing materials makes it possible to obtain acceptable prints from negatives of widely varying contrast. In some applications, however, the

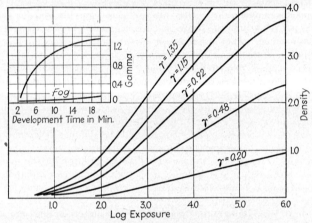

Fig. 9.—Graphs illustrating the fundamental characteristics of negative materials. The large curve shows the D-$\log_{10} E$ characteristic, sometimes referred to as the H and D curve. The smaller graph shows the manner in which fog and gamma increase with time of development.

contrast characteristics are very important. This is particularly true with the various processes of color photography, where a low-contrast negative which will not exceed the exposure range of the printing process is usually needed. Also in copying line originals the high contrast desirable to offset the inescapable losses from such sources as lens flare can only be obtained with some of the special high-contrast materials.

Exposure latitude is to a considerable extent dependent on contrast. Thus very high contrast materials can obviously have very little exposure latitude. Fortunately this is not serious as in practically all cases where very high contrast is needed the exposures are under precise control. For normal work, however, particularly with daylight exposures, a certain amount of latitude is very desirable. Fortunately, most of the modern double-coated emulsions have even more latitude than is often used.

Graininess and resolving power have become of considerable importance since the wide adoption of the miniature camera. Obviously, with any of the small negatives which require many times enlargement, the graininess is very important. With the larger sizes of negatives, however, which will be used only for contact printing or for a limited degree of enlargement, the graininess of most modern materials is so low that it can be disregarded, at least until all other desirable characteristics have been obtained.

Types of Negative Materials.—The various emulsions are supplied on plates, cut films, roll films, film packs, and the special modifications of these such as motion-picture films.

Plates and cut films, which are loaded into holders or special magazines in the darkroom, are most widely used commercially and are the only forms available in the larger sizes. Since they are handled in holders, they are particularly suited for use with the professional types of cameras using ground-glass focusing. Also, since each negative is a separate entity, it can be exposed and developed individually, which is often very desirable. Because of the wide variety of applications, most of the various emulsion types are available in this form. Most of the special emulsions, such as the spectroscopic materials which are coated on special order, are supplied only on plates.

Film packs have many of the desirable characteristics of cut films, such as use with ground-glass focusing and individual handling when necessary, but with the additional advantage that the films in the pack are protected from light, both before it is used and after the films have been exposed. Thus the film pack can be loaded into and removed from the holder or adapter in the light, and a darkroom is necessary only for development of the films. The films used in the packs must be flexible and so have a thinner base than cut films. The result is that the films are more difficult to hold flat; hence, while film packs serve excellently in the smaller sizes, up to about 4 by 5 in., they do not work particularly well in the large sizes. Only the more widely used emulsions are furnished in film packs.

Roll films consist of a long strip of film wound on a flanged wooden or metal spool with an opaque backing paper. This backing paper is sufficiently longer than the film to provide a leader for threading through the camera without exposing any film to the light. Because of their great convenience, roll films are most widely used by amateurs. Previously only one or two emulsions were available on roll films, but now a wide selection of medium and high-speed emulsions, with orthochromatic or panchromatic sensitizing, can be obtained.

A comparatively new development is the daylight-loading magazine containing a short length of 35-mm. film, with standard motion-picture negative perforation, for use in miniature cameras. In this case the film is wound on a spool inside a lighttight container, with the end of the film extending through a slit, light-locked with black plush. The end of the film which is threaded into the camera in the light is, of course, fogged, but after the camera is closed, fresh film is drawn from the magazine. When the whole strip has been exposed, it is wound back into the magazine and so can be removed from the camera in the light.

Aerial films can be considered as a special type of roll film, supplied in greater widths and in very much greater lengths than ordinary roll film. Instead of a full-length backing paper, which would add unnecessary bulk and weight, they are supplied with opaque leader strips cemented to the ends of the film and long enough to wrap several times around the roll, thus protecting it from light. Because of the large negative size, the film base is thicker than that for roll film and is often especially prepared to have very low shrinkage.

Motion-picture film consists of long narrow strips, having perforations along one or both sides to allow accurate positioning of successive small portions of the film in the exposure aperture of the camera. For commercial users the film is usually furnished wound on simple cores and requires a darkroom for loading into the camera magazine. The films supplied for amateur use, however, are wound on special reels with solid flanges which allow daylight loading. The 35-mm. films are usually available on either nitrate or safety (acetate) base, while 16-mm. films can be furnished only on safety base.

Negative papers are occasionally mentioned as being more economical than film. The grain of the paper, however, makes them unsuited for the regular photographic uses requiring contact printing or enlarging. Negative papers, or fast emulsions coated on paper base, are finding wide use in various types of recording instruments and for copying documents and drawings. A special waterproof paper base, coated with a thin emulsion suitable for reversal processing is used for the "direct positives" produced by the while-you-wait automatic portrait machines.

Standard Sizes.—In the course of the evolution of photography, cameras taking many and various sizes of films or plates have been introduced. While many of the odd sizes have become more or less obsolete, enough cameras remain in use to require the supplying of an unnecessarily large number of film and plate sizes. Thus one manufacturer lists 30 sizes of roll films, 13 sizes of film packs, 49 sizes of cut films, and 37 sizes of plates. Even this does not show the total number of negative sizes, since there are a number of cameras using one of the regular roll films but making an odd size negative in order to get more pictures per spool.

Fortunately, there seems to be a tendency for most new apparatus to use one of the more popular sizes listed in Table V. This is very desirable since the odd sizes are sometimes difficult to obtain, while the popular sizes are generally available and the rapid turnover insures reasonably fresh stock.

In connection with these sizes, it should be noted that the nominal dimensions for cut films and plates are the upper limit of the actual dimensions and the lower limit for interior dimensions of the film and plateholders. With roll films and film packs on the other hand, the listed sizes are the nominal sizes of the picture area and the actual film size may be somewhat greater.

In commercial photofinishing it is the usual practice to employ printing masks somewhat smaller than the actual negative image size in order to allow a slight tolerance in positioning the negative on the printer.

TABLE V.—MORE POPULAR NEGATIVE SIZES

Inches

$$
\begin{aligned}
&1 \ \ \times \ \ 1\tfrac{1}{2} \ (24 \times 36 \text{ mm.}) \\
&1\tfrac{5}{8} \times \ \ 2\tfrac{1}{2} \\
&2\tfrac{1}{4} \times \ \ 3\tfrac{1}{4} \\
&2\tfrac{1}{2} \times \ \ 3\tfrac{1}{2} \ (6.5 \times 9 \text{ cm.}) \\
&2\tfrac{1}{2} \times \ \ 4\tfrac{1}{4} \\
&3\tfrac{1}{4} \times \ \ 4\tfrac{1}{4} \\
&3\tfrac{1}{2} \times \ \ 4\tfrac{3}{4} \ (9 \times 12 \text{ cm.}) \\
&3\tfrac{1}{4} \times \ \ 5\tfrac{1}{2} \\
&4 \ \ \times \ \ 5 \\
&5 \ \ \times \ \ 7 \\
&8 \ \ \times \ 10 \\
&10 \ \ \times \ 12 \\
&11 \ \ \times \ 14
\end{aligned}
$$

In the case of motion-picture films the permissible variations are much smaller than with cut films or roll films. The various measurements and tolerances for the sizes which have been standardized in this country are shown in Fig. 10.

The 35-mm. film is standard for professional motion pictures. Most of the prints in this size are made on nitrate-base film, and in most localities there are strict safety regulations governing the showing of such prints. Prints on acetate film are not affected by such restrictions.

The 16-mm. film was originally introduced as an amateur film, though it is coming into more general use in educational, advertising, and other semiprofessional fields as well as in strictly amateur work. Films in this size are required by law to be on acetate "safety" base, which offers no more fire hazard than an equivalent weight of newsprint. Most 16-mm. films are put through a reversal process to obtain a positive image on the same film that was exposed in the camera. However, there are films available for the regular negative-positive processing. Emulsions of various speeds and with both orthochromatic and panchromatic sensitizings are available, as well as several direct-color films.

For sound recording on 16-mm. film, the perforations are omitted from one side, making this space available for the sound track without encroaching on the picture area. Thus the regular silent film can be run in sound projectors without any change in size or position of the projection aperture. Sound film cannot be used in silent projectors unless they are fitted with special sprockets and pulldown claws operating on only one side of the film.

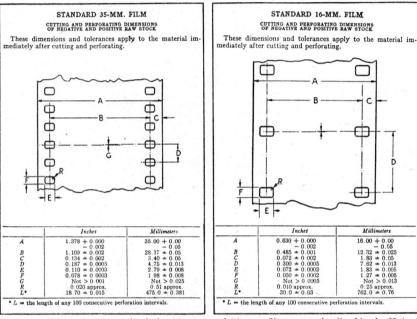

Fig. 10.—Dimensional standards for 35-mm. and 16-mm. film as standardized in the United States of America.

The 8-mm. film was derived from the 16-mm. size in an attempt to lower the film cost to amateurs. Since the picture area is only one-fourth that of the 16-mm. film, graininess and resolving power are very important, and it is necessary to use specially prepared and very thinly coated emulsions. There are two 8-mm. systems in use. In one case, the film is originally 16-mm. wide, and it is run twice through the camera, exposing one-half of the width on each passage. After processing, the film is slit to give two lengths of the 8-mm. width, with perforations on only one side. In the other case, the camera takes the film in the final 8-mm. width. The double-width film has less tendency to give trouble from stretching of the wet film during processing.

Identification of Cut Films.—Since it is often difficult to identify the emulsion surface of cut films for proper loading into the film holder, cut films are usually supplied with reference notches near one corner. When the notches are on the right side of the top edge, the emulsion side of the film faces the operator. In addition, the number, shapes, and arrangement of the notches are used to identify the type of emulsions as indicated in Fig. 11.   Each manufacturer uses a different notching code, so the user must take care not to confuse them.

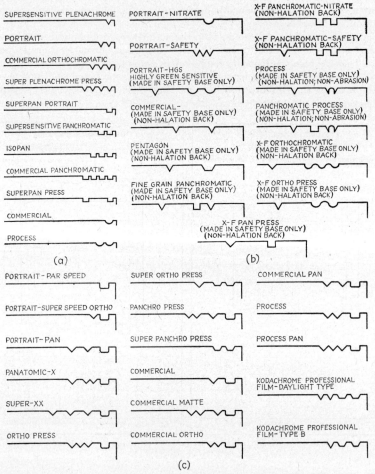

Fig. 11.—Reference notches cut into cut film for purposes of identification.   When the emulsion side faces the photographer, the notches are in the top-right corner.   (*a*) Agfa Ansco film.   (*b*) DuPont film.   (*c*) Eastman film.

Positive Materials.—The positive emulsions used for photographic prints differ considerably among themselves but, in general, have much finer grain and are much slower than the negative emulsions and have somewhat higher contrast.   Positives are made both on transparent supports for viewing by transmitted light, either directly or by projection, and on opaque supports for viewing by reflection.   The differences in the optical conditions in these two cases so change the apparent properties that it is necessary to consider them separately.

Transparencies.—The principal positive materials which are viewed by transmitted light are motion-picture positive films and lantern-slide plates, which are both normally used for projection of the image on a screen.

Motion-picture positive film is coated with a bromide emulsion which has approximately the speed of the slower process negative emulsions. It is not color sensitized, as it is always exposed to a negative in monochrome, and it is desirable to be able to handle it under bright orange or green safe lights. The maximum gamma is rather high, and the behavior during development differs somewhat from that of most negative emulsions in that, as the development time is increased, not only is the slope of the characteristic curve (gamma) increased but the curve is shifted to the left, as shown in Fig. 12. Thus the correct exposure depends very markedly on the degree of development to be given.

The toe portion of the curve is of more importance than in the case of negative materials, since it is desirable that the brightest high lights should have as low a density as possible, in order to allow a bright screen image. This introduces some distortion of tone values since the high-light tones, falling on the toe of the curve, will have a

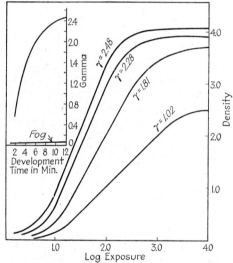

Fig. 12.—Characteristic curves for a typical motion-picture positive emulsion.

lower contrast than the middle tones and shadows. Thus the attempt is made to keep the toe of the curve as short as possible.

The graininess is much lower and the resolving power much higher than for the ordinary negative materials. For this reason and because reasonably high contrast is readily obtained, positive film is used to some extent in microcopying work.

Positive emulsions of extra-high contrast are available for special work.

Lantern-slide plates of the ordinary type have emulsions somewhat similar to that of positive film. They are available, however, in several degrees of contrast. As with other positive materials the more contrasty emulsions are somewhat slower. The normal tone of the developed image is a neutral black, but slightly warm or cold tone images can be obtained by proper modification of the developer.

A special type of lantern-slide plates, coated with a slower chlorobromide emulsion of very fine grain, allows a wide variation in image tone. By proper control of the development conditions, with corresponding variations in exposures, the image tone can be varied from a neutral black through a warm brown to a sepia, and in some cases even to a red.

Paper Prints.—The great majority of photographic prints are made on paper and are viewed by reflected light. This has two important effects. First, a certain fraction of the incident light is reflected by the emulsion surface and the grains near the surface; this reflected light definitely limits the maximum black that can be obtained. Thus, with some matte-surface papers where the diffuse reflection is considerable, the maximum black reflects as much as 6 per cent of the incident light, thus giving a total brightness range from high lights (represented by the clear paper base) to shadows of only 15 to 1 or a density range of 1.18. With certain glossy papers, on the other hand, where the diffuse reflection is low, the total density range may be as much as 1.7 or more. This effect definitely limits the tone range that can be reproduced by any particular paper. Fortunately, the brightness range, at least of the important parts, of normally lighted subjects is usually not greater than about 1 to 40 and so can be reproduced satisfactorily on paper. While the maximum density varies also with the particular type of emulsion, average values for the various surface finishes are as follows:

Glossy	1.5–1.7
Semimatte	About 1.4
Matte	About 1.2

The manner in which the light is reflected depends upon the state of the surface. With an optically smooth or "glossy" surface, the angle of reflection is equal to the angle of incidence, as with a mirror, and little or no light is scattered in other directions. With an optically rough surface, on the other hand, the reflected light is scattered in all directions. In the case of a photographic print, or any other picture on paper, it is the "diffuse" or scattered reflection which limits the maximum density, since the print can be turned so that the specular, or mirrorlike, reflection does not reach the eye. In measuring the diffuse reflection, in order to calculate the density, the paper is usually illuminated at an angle of 45° and viewed normal to the surface.

The second effect is that, in the high lights and middle tones, the light passes through the emulsion to the base and then is reflected back through the emulsion. Therefore each area of the silver deposit has twice the density it would have for transmitted light. Thus, since the maximum density is already limited by reflection, paper emulsions are coated very much thinner than emulsions of film or glass.

For papers, three types of emulsions are used, differing in the composition and grain size of the silver halide; bromide, for black tones; chloride, for black tones; and chlorobromide of very fine grain for warm tones on direct development.

Speed.—Paper emulsions cover a wide range of speeds, the ratio between the slowest and fastest paper emulsions being considerably greater than the ratio between fast papers and the fastest negative materials, as is shown by the approximate values in the table.

TABLE VI.—RELATIVE SENSITIVITY OF VARIOUS PHOTOGRAPHIC MATERIALS

Type of Emulsion	Relative Sensitivity
Positive emulsions (lantern slide, etc.)	1,000–3,000
Bromide papers	300–1,000
Chlorobromide papers, warm tones	100–200
Special warm-tone lantern slides, according to tone desired	1–25
Chloride papers	1–5

Bromide emulsions are comparatively fast, having speeds only slightly less than the positive films, and so are suitable for printing by projection. Chloride papers are very slow and so are normally suitable only for contact printing. The chlorobromide papers cover a considerable range in speed, depending on the composition. The slower ones, with speeds similar to the chloride papers, are suitable only for contact printing.

Others, with higher bromide content, may be used for either contact or projection printing while the fastest ones are suitable chiefly for projection.

In general, for any particular type of paper emulsion, the more contrasty grades are slower than the softer grades.

In connection with speed, the spectral sensitivity is important. The chloride emulsions and the very slow chlorobromide emulsions are sensitive to the violet and near ultraviolet but have very little sensitivity above 450 mμ. Thus they may be handled safely under a bright-yellow safe light with a cut between 500 and 550 mμ. The faster chlorobromide emulsions have additional sensitivity in the blue, extending

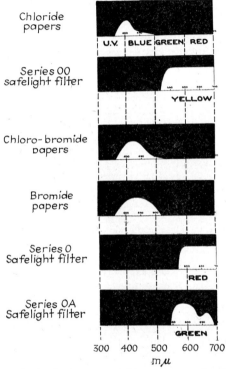

Fig. 13.—Spectrograms for various paper emulsions, compared with the spectral transmissions of suitable safe-light filters.

up to about 500 mμ, and the bromide emulsions are sensitive still further, up to about 520 mμ. Thus for safe handling these emulsions require safe lights which pass no light at wavelengths shorter than about 550 mμ (Fig. 13).

In all cases the maximum sensitivity is in the violet and near ultraviolet; consequently the tungsten light which is nearly always used for printing is really very inefficient, as only a very small percentage of the radiated energy is effective in printing. Mercury-vapor lamps and other sources of ultraviolet radiation are much more efficient so far as photographic action is concerned, but because of cost, inconvenience, or insufficient intensity, they are seldom used.

The so-called "high efficiency" tungsten lamps are sufficiently effective, and, since they are convenient to handle and are comparatively inexpensive, they are generally used for printing. However, it should be remembered that the proportion of light of the shorter wavelengths decreases rapidly as the voltage is lowered, so that fluctuations in line voltage may cause considerable changes in printing time, even though the visual brightness is not noticeably affected.

Contrast, Effect of Development.—Owing to the thinness of coating and the fine grain, paper emulsions develop rapidly. During the very first period of development the contrast increases with time as in the case of negative emulsions. During this period, however, the shadow density is low and the characteristic curve is badly distorted. As the shadow density approaches the maximum black, the curve is straightened out somewhat and then begins to move to the left, with no change in slope or contrast and with little or no further increase in shadow density. These effects vary slightly with the different types of emulsions, for instance, with some bromide and chlorobromide papers, the contrast does increase slightly on continuing development after the maximum black is reached.

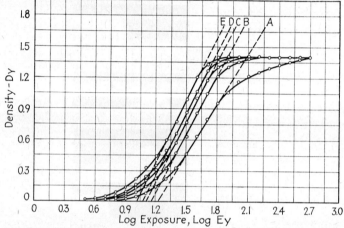

Fig. 14.—Typical D-$\log_{10} E$ curves for chloride paper. The lettered curves represent different times of development. These curves show that development affects the speed, but does not affect the gamma appreciably.

The effect of time of development on the characteristics of chloride, chlorobromide, and bromide types of papers is shown, respectively, in Figs. 14, 15, and 16. Time of development increases, for the various curves, in alphabetical order.

In general, however, since it is necessary to develop sufficiently to reach the maximum black in order to avoid uneven development, muddy shadows, and distorted tone rendering, the contrast cannot be controlled in development. On the other hand, since there is usually a period between the time when the maximum black is reached and when development fog appears, during which the densities continue to increase without changing contrast, it is possible to correct for slight variations in exposure by adjustment in development. This exposure-development latitude varies considerably between the different papers.

It has been suggested that the contrast of a particular paper could be varied by changing the developer formula. While in isolated cases this might be possible, it has been shown that the variations normally obtained are less than the differences between two adjacent contrast grades of the paper.[1]

Paper Contrast.—As little or no control of contrast is possible during development, many of the papers are supplied in several degrees of contrast. In the case of negative

[1] BENEDICT, H. C., Facts and Foibles in Photography, *Camera Craft*, **43**, 226 (1936).

emulsions the contrast can be expressed in terms of the slope of the characteristic curve or of the density difference obtained for a given range of exposure or range of object brightness. Because of the length of the straight-line portion of the curve, it is

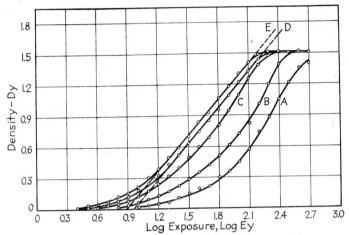

Fig. 15.—D-log$_{10}$ E characteristics for a typical chlorobromide paper.

not difficult to obtain theoretically correct tone reproduction in the negative. With papers, on the other hand, the straight-line portion of the characteristic curve is comparatively short, and, except when special effects are wanted, it is necessary to make use of the full density range, which is determined by the paper surface and type of emul-

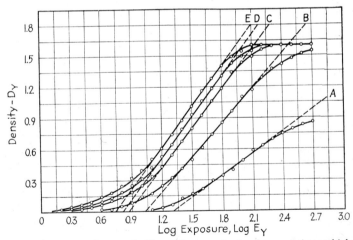

Fig. 16.—D-log$_{10}$ E curves for a typical bromide paper for development times which increase in alphabetical order. The characteristics resemble those of negative emulsions.

sion. Thus it is not possible to obtain perfect reproduction over the whole range of tones. However, if the extreme shadow tones are ignored, the negative exposure can be so chosen that, with the proper combination of materials, the curvature in the negative just balances the curvature in the positive, giving practically perfect reproduction over the greater part of the tone scale.[1]

The range of negative tones which can be reproduced in the print is determined by the paper-exposure scale, or the ratio between the exposure which will just produce a visible density and the least exposure which will produce the maximum black.

Since negatives made by amateurs are made under widely varying conditions of lighting, and consequently of subject brightness, and since development conditions are not always carefully controlled, amateur negatives vary widely in density range. Therefore printing papers for amateur use are usually supplied in a number of grades of contrast, with exposure scales varying from about 1:5 for the extra-contrast papers, to as much as 1:50 for the very soft papers. This range of contrasts is covered in five or six steps, so that it is possible to get acceptable prints from negatives having density ranges between 0.7 (opacity range of 5 to 1) and 1.7 (opacity range of 50 to 1) (Fig. 17).

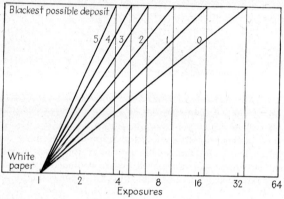

FIG. 17.—Relative contrast of six types of printing paper popuarly used in amateur photography. The slope of the curve is a measure of contrast, whereas the distance from unity to the projection on the abscissa is a measure of the relative exposure range obtainable.

The professional photographer's negatives are usually made with controlled lighting and controlled conditions of development, and so have a comparatively uniform density range. Therefore papers for professional use are often made in only one or two degrees of contrast, corresponding approximately to the "normal" grade of the amateur papers.

Although all the paper-emulsion types can be made in a range of contrasts, the chloride or gaslight papers tend in general to have the shortest exposure scales (most contrasty), and the bromide papers tend to have much longer exposure scales. The chlorobromide papers are, in general, intermediate.

Although paper contrast could be expressed by a numerical value, derived possibly from the exposure scale, photographers in general do not have the means for measuring the density ranges of their negatives in order to make use of such values. Therefore the various contrast grades have been designated by such descriptive terms as "soft," "medium," "normal," "hard," "vigorous," etc. This works fairly satisfactorily, though there is the disadvantage that, since the terms are only generally descriptive, different manufacturers may use one term for papers of considerably different exposure scale.

---

[1] JONES, L. A., The Evolution of Negative Film Speeds in Terms of Print Quality, J. Franklin Inst., **227**, 297 (March 1939).

The exposure scales for the three contrast grades of a typical enlarging paper are: normal, 32; medium, 16; and contrast, 11. The scales for the various contrast grades of a typical amateur contact-printing paper run from 45 for the softest to 4.5 for the most contrasty.

Image Tone (Color).—The chloride emulsions and the bromide emulsions usually tend to give images of neutral or cold black tones on normal development, and many of them will give definitely blue-black tones with very active developers. Slightly warm tones can sometimes be obtained with restrained or slow-acting developers, but the possibilities for control are normally rather limited.

The fine-grain chlorobromide emulsions tend to give warm-toned images on direct development, particularly with the slower types of papers. Even warmer tones, ranging to definite browns, can be obtained by the use of restrained developers.

Also, the colors given by the various aftertreatments depend very markedly on the size and condition of the grains in the original silver image. The effectiveness of the treatments also depend on the condition of the silver grains. Thus the direct sepia-toning solutions, such as the hypo-alum toner, work comparatively rapidly and give pleasing results with the naturally warm-toned images on chlorobromide papers, but work only very slowly, if at all, with the coarse-grained cold-tone images on bromide paper. On the other hand, the bleach and redevelop type of sepia toner which works satisfactorily with cold-tone images tends to give unpleasant yellow tones with the naturally warm-tone images.

In addition to the inherent color determined by the size and condition of the grains of the silver grains, the apparent-image tone is markedly affected by the color of the base, which is usually white or very slightly tinted cream or buff but is occasionally supplied with a comparatively strong color.

Sheen.—As has been mentioned, paper surfaces vary in sheen, or the ratio between specular and diffuse reflection, from the almost purely specular glossy surfaces to the almost purely diffuse matte. Although the degree of gloss probably could be expressed quantitatively, as by the percentage of specular reflection, this would be of little value to most users, and the descriptive terms such as glossy, luster, semimatte, matte, etc., are more generally understandable and useful.

While the choice of sheen is largely a matter of personal preference, some types of prints definitely call for specific surfaces. Thus small contact prints are generally made on glossy papers because of the greater density range and the sharper rendering of fine detail. For the same reasons the glossy surface is preferred, usually demanded, for pictures to be reproduced by any of the photomechanical processes. For portrait and pictorial prints on the other hand, the softer and less glaring surfaces, such as luster and semimatte, are usually preferred. The matte surfaces are easiest to work on with pencil or water or oil colors.

The sheen is controlled by incorporating in the emulsion various inert substances such as starch and by varying the composition and method of application of the baryta layer.

Texture.—In addition to the almost microscopic surface irregularities which control the sheen, the papers may have coarse irregularities giving various degrees of roughness to the surface. Smooth surfaces can be obtained with any sheen from glossy to absolute matte, but the rough surfaces cannot give a real gloss.

In addition to the various degrees of roughness, some special-purpose or novelty papers have a definite surface pattern such as the linen finish.

Smooth or fine-grain surfaces are preferable for small prints, while the rougher surfaces may be valuable for large prints and enlargements, either for suppressing an excess of fine detail or, with a high degree of enlargement, for concealing lack of fine detail and suppressing the apparent graininess.

The various degrees of roughness are usually controlled by varying the composition and coating conditions of the baryta layer; the pattern textures are produced on the baryta layer under pressure by embossed rollers.

Weight or Thickness.—Most papers which will be used for small-size prints are supplied on either single- or double-weight stock, while papers for large prints, such as the professional papers and enlarging papers, particularly those with rough surfaces, may be supplied only in double weight. Some papers, such as those for postcard prints, are supplied on a thin cardboard.

Papers having the usual baryta coating cannot be folded without cracking. Therefore a few papers, such as those used for document copying and for advertising illustrations which will be folded for mailing, are supplied on a special thin base without the baryta layer.

Special Emulsion Types.—In addition to the regular black-and-white negative and printing emulsions already described, there are a number of more or less specialized emulsions which, because of special requirements in the mode of use or in the method of preparation, differ in properties sufficiently to justify separate discussion.

Printing-out Papers.—At present the vast majority of photographic prints are made on developing-out papers, with which the latent image produced by exposure is converted to a visible silver image by the action of the developer solution. Printing-out papers (P O P), on which the visible image is produced by direct photochemical darkening, were formerly widely used but are now used only in special cases, such as the preparation of portrait proofs, and are losing ground even here.

While the normal developing-out emulsions are prepared with an excess of soluble halide, printing-out emulsions contain an excess of soluble silver salt, usually the tartrate or citrate, which acts as an acceptor for the halogen liberated by the photochemical action.

The sensitivity is naturally very low; the papers can be handled safely in artificial light or weak daylight, and for printing they require a light rich in ultraviolet, such as that from a carbon-arc or a mercury-vapor lamp or strong daylight. Even so, the exposures are a matter of minutes. The contrast is fairly low, the exposure scale being equal to that of the softer grades of bromide paper.

After exposure, the image can be fixed by removal of the unchanged silver salts with a solvent such as hypo. This leaves the image an unpleasant yellow color, which can be corrected by toning the image by precipitation of gold, to give red or reddish-purple tones, or precipitation of platinum, to give black tones. Even aside from the unpleasant color, the untoned image is rather impermanent because the very finely divided silver is rapidly attacked by any sulphur compounds in the paper or in the atmosphere. Toning can be done after fixing but gives more dependable and uniform results before fixing. Portrait proofs on P O P are seldom fixed or toned.

P O P emulsions may be in either gelatin or collodion. In Europe, printing-out papers supplied for amateur use sometimes have the toning agents incorporated in the emulsion (self-toning papers), so that prints can be made without a darkroom and can be processed merely by washing in water.

Because of the excess of soluble silver salts, printing-out-paper emulsions are rather unstable and tend to darken on aging if any moisture is present. This can be prevented by keeping the paper thoroughly desiccated.

Reversal Emulsions.—In some cases it is desirable or necessary that the final positive image be produced in the same emulsion as was used for the original exposure. At the completion of development, the emulsion contains two images, the negative image of silver and a complementary positive image of the unaffected silver halide which is normally removed by fixation. Thus, if the silver image is removed by treatment in a bleach bath which does not attack the silver halide, the residual silver halide can be blackened, by exposure and development or by chemical action, to give the desired positive.

In ordinary emulsions, there is much more silver bromide than is used in a normal negative image, and the highlights of the residual positive will be dense and fogged. Therefore emulsions intended for reversal processing are thinly coated so that the high lights of a normally exposed, negative image will use up practically all the silver halide.

There are always some very small insensitive grains which will not be affected by the first development, even in heavily exposed areas, and thus remain to fog the high lights of the positive. Therefore a silver halide solvent, such as ammonia or hypo, is often used in the developer or in a rinse bath after development, to dissolve out these small grains, thereby increasing the brilliance of the positive image.

When all the residual silver halide is utilized in the positive, there is no latitude for the original exposure, and any small local variations in thickness, which in ordinary work would be of no importance, have a marked effect. While some compensation for variations in negative exposure can be made by regulating the action of the silver halide solvent, the range of control is limited. A much greater degree of control can be exercised by taking advantage of the differential sensitivity of the residual silver halide grains and giving a controlled second exposure. Thus, where the negative exposure was heavy, there will be little silver halide left, and it is given a heavy exposure to render it all developable. On the other hand, where the original exposure was light, there will be a great deal of silver halide left and a slight second exposure is given, so that only part is rendered developable and the final positive is not too dense.

In this process, after removal of the negative image, the film is scanned by a photo-electric cell which controls the intensity of the second exposure. Where the negative image was heavy, there is less residual silver bromide, so that more radiation reaches the photocell, which in turn increases the second exposure. With a thin or under-exposed negative image, the reverse occurs. Thus the density of the positive image is compensated as described above, and positives of good quality are obtained with a wide range of camera exposures.

Reversal Materials.—Screen-plate color materials, such as the Lumière Autochrome plates and Dufaycolor films must be processed by reversal so that the positive image will be in register with the screen-filter elements. They are usually processed with an ammonia first developer and a strong second developer which completely blackens the residual positive image. There is little or no latitude in exposure.

Substandard motion-picture films, particularly for amateur use where only one positive is ordinarily needed, are processed by reversal in order to obtain better definition and lower graininess and to reduce the cost. Since exposures are made under widely varying light conditions, some type of compensating processing is practically a necessity. The Kodak automatically controlled second exposure was devised to compensate for varying exposures throughout a single length of film.

"Direct positive" paper for automatic portrait machines has a fairly fast fine-grain orthochromatic emulsion thinly coated on a waterproofed paper base and is processed by reversal in order to reduce the time between exposure and delivery of the finished print. Lighting and exposure are standardized, and the whole residual positive is darkened either by full exposure and redevelopment or, more generally, by conversion to silver sulphide.

In addition to the regular reversal process, there are other methods of securing the effect of a positive image directly. The so-called "tintype" made use of a collodion emulsion coated on a black support and developed to give a whitish silver deposit, which then appeared as a positive against the dark background.

Positive images can also be produced directly by making use of the solarization region of the characteristic curve. With ordinary emulsions this would require excessively great exposures, but special materials, on both film and paper, are now available which are sufficiently sensitive to be usable with projection pointers and enlargers. The whole emulsion is made developable by treatment during manufacture. Exposure to light reduces the developable density so that exposure to a negative image gives a negative, or to a positive, a positive.

X-ray Films.—Because of the very low absorption of X-rays by the silver halide of the emulsion, only a small portion of the incident radiation is effective in producing a developable density. In order to increase the absorption and thus the photographic effect, emulsions for use with X rays contain a high percentage of silver bromide and formerly were very thickly coated. Because of the difficulties encountered in developing and fixing these thick emulsions, X-ray films are now given emulsion coatings of normal thickness on both sides.

Even with emulsions very rich in silver bromide, when the more penetrating X rays are used, the direct action on the photographic emulsion is comparatively slight, and it is now customary to place the film between intensifying screens coated with a substance such as calcium tungstate, which fluoresces under the action of X rays. Thus the greater part of the exposure is due to visible light from the intensifying screens.

Since the radiographs are often needed in a hurry, particularly in emergency surgical cases, and since it is often not possible to keep the processing solutions down to the recommended temperature, X-ray emulsions are usually hardened to a greater degree than most negative films, in order to reduce the risk of trouble or damage from excessive swelling.

Emulsions for Color Photography.—Because of the great differences between the various systems of color photography, the characteristics required of the emulsions used also vary greatly.

Additive Processes.—The only additive processes of practical importance at the present are the integral screen-plate processes such as the Autóchrome plates and the Agfacolor and Dufaycolor films, which are processed by reversal, and the Finlay process which uses separate taking and viewing screens. The requirements of the reversal processes have been discussed. The Finlay process, which uses comparatively coarse mosaic screens, employs a regular fast panchromatic plate for the negative, the only requirement being that the color sensitivity be sufficiently uniform to remain properly matched to the taking screen and compensating filter. The plate exposed behind the taking screen in an ordinary camera is developed to a negative in the regular manner. Prints are made on positive plates, similar to lantern-slide plates, which are then bound in register with the viewing screen which has the same pattern as the taking screen. Thus as many positives as desired can be made from one negative, also there is a chance to control the contrast and to compensate for errors in exposure of the negative by controlling the exposure and development of the positive. This and other advantages claimed over the reversal processes are somewhat offset by the larger size of the individual screen elements.

Subtractive Processes.—The materials used in the various subtractive processes can be divided into negative, positive, and reversal. Color-separation negatives obtained by any of the taking systems can in most cases be used with any one of several printing systems, while the reversal system gives the color photograph directly, as with the additive processes.

Negative Materials.—The simplest system, from the viewpoint of demands on the emulsion, is the production of the three color-separation negatives by successive exposures in an ordinary camera. Practically any panchromatic emulsion could be used, provided its contrast characteristics were suitable for the subject and the printing process to be used. As a matter of convenience, however, it may be desirable to choose a material which has, as nearly as possible, equal filter factors for the three tricolor filters. For most lighting conditions, this will mean a material with a type *B* or orthopanchromatic sensitizing.

Since the making of three successive exposures is ordinarily practical only for still-life subjects and since satisfactorily accurate one-shot cameras are very expensive, various bipack and tripack films have been developed, to allow one exposure in an ordinary camera.

The tripack consists of three films placed in contact and exposed simultaneously, to make the three separation negatives. The first two films are placed with their emulsion surfaces in contact, so that the front film, which is blue sensitive, is exposed through the base. This emulsion is yellow-dyed, or carries a yellow-filter layer on its surface, to prevent any blue light from reaching the two rear films. The second film is orthochromatic and so makes the green-sensation record. It is on a thin support and is backed with a red-filter layer so that only red light reaches the rear panchromatic emulsion.

The two front emulsions must be as thin and transparent as possible, in order to avoid excessive absorption of light, which would increase the exposure required, and in order to reduce scattering of light which makes the rear image unsharp. The ratios between the speeds of the three emulsions must be correct to compensate for the absorption of light in the first and second emulsions, so that the one exposure will give three well-matched negatives. It is desirable, but not necessary, to have the development rates adjusted so that the three negatives can be developed together.

Because of the scattering of light in the first two emulsions, and the separation of the rear emulsion by the thickness of the film base, the loss of definition is such that tripack negatives usually do not give satisfactory enlargements and so are more suitable for use in the large sizes of studio and view cameras than in the smaller hand cameras and are more satisfactory for portraiture than for general commercial work.

To reduce this loss in definition, while still avoiding many of the complications of the double-mirror cameras, various bipacks have been devised. The bipack is essentially a tripack with the rear film removed and exposed directly to a second image supplied by some type of beam splitter, such as a semitransparent mirror. The front emulsion of the bipack, which is exposed through the base, makes the blue negative, while the back emulsion may make either the green or red negative, depending on the design of the pack. In the Technicolor and Eastman bipack systems, the red negative is made on the rear film of the bipack, and the green negative is made on a separate film.[1]

Positive Materials.—To obtain a color print from the three separation negatives, three positive images, in dyes or pigments of the respective complementary or minus colors, are superimposed in register. Thus a yellow positive, which absorbs blue, is made from the blue-filter negative, a magenta, which absorbs green, from the green-filter negative, and a blue-green (cyan), which absorbs red, from the red-filter negative (see chapter on Color Photography). These can be made by any of several processes. A number of these, such as the bichromated gelatin, or so-called carbon process, the gum-bichromate process, and their various modifications (particularly the widely used carbro process) do not directly involve the use of sensitive silver halide emulsions, and so they need not be described here. However, there are several methods in which silver images are used to form dye or pigment images of the proper color.

[1] BALL, J. A., The Technicolor Process of Three Color Cinematography, *J. Soc. Motion Picture Engrs.*, **25**, 127 (1935).

Toning Processes for Color Photography.—One obvious method of converting the black-and-white silver image into a color image is by toning, with either inorganic or dye tones. The emulsions carrying the three-color images are then superimposed bodily on a white base. Thus the three positives are separated by the thickness of the emulsions and their supports. In order to reduce the total thickness to a minimum, the Chromatone process makes use of stripping films, in which the special printing emulsion is coated on a very thin cellulose film which is cemented to a heavier film base with an adhesive soluble in warm water. Thus the heavy bases furnish protection during the development and toning processes and are discarded when the emulsions are transferred to the final support. This particular process is understood to use special inorganic toning solutions, in which the silver images are converted into colored inorganic compounds, but dye tones, with the silver image converted into a compound which could mordant the dyes, might also be used.

Pigmented Gelatin.—Rather than use the silver image as a base for the color image, it can be used to form a relief image in pigmented gelatin, similar to that obtained with the various "carbon" processes. In this case, pigment of the proper color is incorporated in the emulsion during manufacture. The emulsion is exposed through the transparent base, and the absorption of light by the pigment holds the image near the bottom of the emulsion. Thus, when the gelatin is hardened in the vicinity of the silver image, either during development or by means of a special silver bleach, and the unhardened gelatin removed with warm water, there is left a relief image with thickness proportional to the density of the silver print. The three partial color positives thus obtained are then transferred to the final support. In the carbro process, the differential hardening is caused by the action of the bleach on a silver image in contact with the layer of pigmented gelatin.

Imbibition Processes.—If, instead of making colored relief images which are cemented together, plain gelatin reliefs are made, they can be used as printing matrices by saturating them with dye solutions of the proper colors, and placing them, one at a time, in close contact with a gelatin layer containing a mordant to which the dyes will transfer.

Wash-off relief film has an unhardened positive emulsion containing a yellow dye to control the penetration of the printing light. The film is exposed through the base, and the silver image is developed to completion. It is then treated in an acid bichromate bleach which oxidizes the silver image and hardens the adjacent gelatin. Bathing in warm water removes the unhardened gelatin and develops the relief image, or matrix. After fixing, washing, and drying, the matrix is bathed in the proper dye solution. The three dyed matrices can be superimposed in register for inspection of color balance and contrast. Changes in contrast can be effected by controlling the acidity of the dye solutions, and slight inaccuracies in color balance can be corrected by washing out part of the excess colors. When the color balance is satisfactory, the matrices are squeegeed successively into close contact with a gelatin-coated paper containing an aluminum mordant. Thus in the final print the three dye images are contained in a single gelatin layer. Additional prints can be made merely by redyeing the matrices and transferring as before.

The Technicolor process uses this type of imbibition printing, transferring the successive dye images to a gelatin-coated final film.

Catalytic Bleach.—Another method of utilizing the silver image directly in the formation of the dye image makes use of the fact that certain reagents, which alone have no effect on the dye, destroy it wherever there is a silver image. Thus this is in effect a reversal process, giving a negative dye image from a negative, and a positive dye image from a positive. However, because of the absorption of light by the dye, the sensitivity is so low that it is suitable only for printing.

The Kodachrome Reversal Process.—This process uses an integral tripack, or mono-pack, with the three emulsions for making the color-separation negatives and their corresponding partial-color positives coated on one support.[1] Thus the difficulties of handling three separate films is avoided, and exposures can be made in any ordinary camera. The emulsion next the base is sensitized to red, the middle emulsion is sensitized to green, and the top emulsion is sensitive only to blue and carries a yellow dye to prevent blue light from reaching either of the lower layers. The different emulsions are separated by very thin layers of clear gelatin. Since the total residual positive method of reversal is used, the emulsions are very thin, and the total thickness of the three combined emulsions and two intermediate layers is no greater than the thickness of an ordinary negative emulsion.

The three partial-color positives are produced during the development of the silver positives by interaction between "coupling" compounds and development reaction products to form dye densities proportional to the silver densities. The formation of three different dye images in their appropriate layers requires a rather complicated processing procedure which can be handled satisfactorily only by properly controlled processing stations.

The three emulsion layers must not only be coated extremely uniformly but must be very accurately balanced for color sensitivity, speed, and contrast. This requires very rigid control in manufacture. The result, however, is that the user has no worry other than giving a reasonably correct exposure.

Bibliography

Periodicals:

SILBERSTEIN, L.: Orientation of Grains in Dried Photographic Emulsion, *J. Optical Soc. Am.*, **5,** 181 (1921).

SHEPPARD, S. E.: Photographic Gelatin, *Phot. J.*, **65,** 380 (1925).

DUNDON, M. L.: Color Sensitizing Photographic Plates by Bathing, *Am. Phot.*, **20,** 670 (1926).

SHEPPARD, S. E.: Behavior of Gelatin in the Processing of Motion Picture Film, *Trans. Soc. Motion Picture Engrs.*, **11,** 707 (1927).

———, and P. H. TRAVELLI: The Sensitivity of Silver Halide Grains in Relation to Size, *J. Franklin Inst.*, **203,** 829 (1927).

HARRISON, G. R.: Instruments and Methods Used for Measuring Spectral Light Intensities, *J. Optical Soc. Am.*, **19,** 267 (1929).

MEES, C. E. K.: Photographic Plates for Use in Spectroscopy and Astronomy, *J. Optical Soc. Am.*, **21,** 753 (1931); *J. Optical Soc. Am.*, **22,** 204 (1933); *J. Optical Soc. Am.*, **23,** 229 (1933).

JONES, L. A.: Photographic Sensitometry, *J. Soc. Motion Picture Engrs.*, **18,** 324 (1932).

CRABTREE, J. I., and C. H. SCHWINGEL: Duplication of Motion Picture Negatives, *J. Soc. Motion Picture Engrs.*, **19,** 891 (1932).

WEBB, J. H.: The Relationship between Reciprocity Failure and the Intermittent Effect in Photographic Exposure, *J. Optical Soc. Am.*, **23,** 157 (1933).

SHEPPARD, S. E.: Some Factors in Photographic Sensitometry, *J. Soc. Motion Picture Engrs.*, **24,** 500 (1935).

BALL, J. A.: The Technicolor Process of Three Color Cinematography, *J. Soc. Motion Picture Engrs.*, **25,** 127 (1935).

BENEDICT, H. C.: Facts and Foibles in Photography, *Camera Craft*, **43,** 226 (1936).

CRABTREE, J. I., and VITTUM: A New Fine Grain Developer, *Am. Phot.*, **30,** 188 (1936).

MANNES, L. D., and L. GODOWSKY, JR.: The Kodachrome Process for Amateur Cinematography in Natural Colors, *J. Soc. Motion Picture Engrs.*, **25,** 65 (1936).

FUCHS, E.: Preliminary Preparation of Photographic Layers, *Phot. Ind.*, **34,** 552 (1936).

BARTH, W.: A Film for Making Direct Duplicates in a Single Step, *J. Soc. Motion Picture Engrs.*, **27,** 419 (1936).

BAINES, H.: Private Life of Roll Film Spool, *Phot. J.*, **77,** 218 (1937).

CASSIDY, E. H.: Are Fast Films Worth While? *Brit. J. Phot.*, **84,** 84 (1937).

STAUD, C. J., J. A. LEERSMAKER, and B. H. CARROLL: Optical Sensitizing of Photographic Emulsions, Paper Presented before the fall 1938 meeting of the Amer. Chem. Soc.

[1] MANNES, L. D., and L. GODOWSKY, JR., The Kodachrome Process for Amateur Cinematography in Natural Colors, *J. Soc. Motion Picture Engrs.*, **25,** 65 (1935).

LEERSMAKER, J. A.: *J. Chem. Phys.*, **5,** 779 (1937).
——, B. H. CARROLL, and C. J. STAUD: *J. Phys. Chem.*, **5,** 893 (1937).
VARDEN, L. E., and J. N. HARMAN, JR.: New High Speed Emulsions, *Am. Phot.*, 18 (1938).
VARDEN, L. E.: Direct Copy Film, *Am. Phot.*, 236 (1938).
ARNOLD, P. H.: Sensitivity Tests with Ultraspeed Negative Films, *J. Soc. Motion Picture Engrs.*, **31,** 541 (1938).
ARMOR, A. E.: Manufacture of Motion Picture Film, *Phot. J.*, 459 (1938).
ALBERSHEIM, W. J.: Latent Image Theory, *J. Soc. Motion Picture Engrs.*, **32,** 73 (1939).

Books:

TRAVELLI, A. P. H., and S. E. SHEPPARD: "The Silver Bromide Grain in Photographic Emulsions," Van Nostrand (1921).
ROSS, F. E.: "Physics of the Developed Image," Van Nostrand (1924).
CHIBISOFF, K. W.: "Ripening of Photographic Emulsions," p. 405, IXth Cong. intern. de Phot., Paris (1936).
FORSYTHE, W. E., *et al.:* "Measurement of Radiant Energy," McGraw (1937).
SHEPPARD, S. E., and R. H. LAMBERT: "Grain Growth in Silver Halide Precipitates," Colloid Symposium Monograph, vol. 6, p. 265 (1938).
"New Kodak Films," Eastman Kodak Co. (1938).

CHAPTER VII

PHOTOGRAPHIC SENSITOMETRY

By Beverly Dudley

Introduction. *Meaning of Photographic Sensitometry.*—The term "photographic sensitometry" is frequently used in a restricted sense to specify the sensitivity of photographic materials to visible light or other radiations. A somewhat broader view will be taken here. We shall use the term photographic sensitometry to denote the quantitative determination of all the various characteristic responses of the photographic materials to radiant energy. By radiant energy we shall usually mean visible light.

According to this definition, photographic sensitometry deals with those characteristic responses which are produced by: (1) the intensity and spectral distribution of the source of radiant energy acting upon the photosensitive materials, (2) the total duration of time and the manner in which the photographic materials are exposed to radiant energy, and (3) the processing (developing, fixing, washing, drying, etc.) to which the photographic materials are subjected.

The characteristics of photographic materials which may be determined through sensitometry include: (1) the response to the intensity of the source of energy to which the material is exposed, usually specified in some "speed" or "sensitivity" rating; (2) the spectral sensitivity, or the relative response to energy at various wavelengths; (3) the response to exposure of continuous duration; (4) the effect of intermittent exposure, involving the manner in which photographic materials integrate the energy to which they are exposed; (5) the response of the photographic material to varying conditions of processing (especially development) for specified exposure; and (6) the graininess. According to our definition such matters as the resolving power of the photographic material and the distortions of the images which occur also properly belong to the province of photographic sensitometry. However, these matters are not of sufficient general importance and interest to be treated in this chapter, although they may be of considerable practical importance in certain branches of photography, such as astronomical photography or where images must be reproduced accurately to scale.

Photographic sensitometry may be used to determine the characteristics of photographic materials which reproduce colored images as well as those materials which, for want of a better name, may be termed monochrome, and which produce images in varying densities without any appreciable spectral selectivity. The sensitometry of materials for color photography is somewhat more involved, elaborate, and extensive than that required for monochrome photography, but the fundamental principles involved are identical in both cases.

In general, the procedure for the determination of sensitometric data is as follows: Test strips of the material under examination are given precisely known, graded exposures to a light source of specified intrinsic luminous intensity and spectral distribution. These strips are developed for specified lengths of time under known conditions of temperature, in a developer of known composition and concentration. The developer used depends upon the purpose for which the sensitometric measurements are made, but it is usually one which produces an unstained neutral-gray

153

deposit of silver. The test strips are then dried, after which the densities of the silver deposits for each exposure step on the same strip are measured. The values of density and the corresponding values of the logarithm of exposure are plotted for each strip. Similar plots are made for other strips having different times of development, so that a family of curves $D = \log_{10} E$ is obtained. This family of curves gives most of the essential information relating to the characteristics of photosensitive materials.

The determination of the sensitometric characteristics of photographic materials requires a knowledge and control of (but preferably standardization of) the following conditions and apparatus:

1. A light source emitting radiations of known spectral distribution and known intensity.

2. A means for producing a series of graded exposures of known magnitudes.

3. Standardized conditions of processing (especially with regard to development) the material under test.

4. A method of determining quantitatively the density, graininess, and other characteristics of the material after exposure and processing.

5. A method of properly interpreting quantitatively the results of sensitometric measurements.

From standardization of 1 and 2 it is possible to determine the magnitude and character of the stimulus (exposure) applied to the photographic material. Step 4 enables us to determine the characteristic responses of the photographic material to the various stimuli provided by steps 1 and 2. Step 5 not only enables us to correlate properly the stimuli and its response, but enables us to express the causal relations in such manner as to permit of optimum use of photographic materials, filters, light sources, and other accessories. An understanding of photographic sensitometry is also useful in recognizing and correcting faults of over- or underexposure, incorrect rendition of tone, incorrect rendition of colored objects in monochromatic or color photography, etc.

Application of Sensitometry.—Originally photographic sensitometry was used almost exclusively by manufacturers of film material for the determination of film characteristics and by a few scientific workers using photography. The first impetus toward extensive general uses of photographic sensitometry came from the motion-picture field with the introduction of sound pictures. While sensitometric methods and processes are not yet employed by the average photographer or serious amateur (nor are they likely to be used except in the simplest fundamental steps), a knowledge and understanding of sensitometric methods may not only be advisable in aiding the proper exposure and processing for portraits, pictorial, and other subjects but may be essential—or very nearly so—for motion-picture work, certain kinds of scientific photography, and color, aerial, and other branches of photography where exacting requirements must be met.

Light Sources for Photographic Sensitometry.—The first step in photographic sensitometry involves giving the photosensitive material a series of standard (or at least precisely known) exposures. The exposure of the material under accurately known conditions is accomplished by means of a sensitometer which consists, functionally, of (1) a standard source of light or other radiation and (2) some form of exposing device, such as an accurate shutter, which determines the quantity of light which is permitted to act on the photosensitive material.

We shall first give some consideration to the light sources and the exposure devices suitable for sensitometry. In a later section consideration will be given to sensitometers in which the light source and exposure device are combined.

Practical Light Sources.—The most important of a wide variety of light sources which have been used for photographic sensitometry include, in approximately chronological order: (1) sunlight, (2) the British Parliamentary candle, specifications for which were given as early as 1860; (3) a phosphorescent plate in which the radiation was provided by a layer of calcium sulphide activated by burning magnesium ribbon; (4) the Harcourt pentane lamp which burns a mixture of pentane vapor and air; (5) the Hefner lamp which burns pure amyl acetate (and which is still sometimes used as a standard light source); (6) acetylene flames of various types with completely specified burners; and (7) incandescent electric lamps. Unfortunately none of these standards is ideally suited to photographic sensitometry, principally because of lack of precision and reproducibility, but also in some cases because of unsuitable spectral distribution of energy.

The characteristics necessary in a light source for photographic sensitometry are:

1. Accurately known (preferably standardized) and appropriate spectral-energy distribution.

2. Adequate intensity of output so that exposures need not be too long.

3. Stability of characteristics throughout the useful life of the light source.

4. Reproducibility of characteristics between successive uses of the light source.

5. Convenience in use.

These requirements are fulfilled in the most desirable manner, for purposes of photographic sensitometry, by incandescent lamps which have been carefully standardized and which are operated under carefully controlled conditions.

Modern practical sources of light for photographic sensitometry may be made from:

1. Cylindrical acetylene flame devised by Fery and Sheppard and Mees, fitted with suitable filter (Wratten No. 79).

2. Tungsten lamps operating at a color temperature of 2360°K. fitted with a Davis and Gibson liquid filter.

This latter type of light source was standardized as a satisfactory light source for photographic purposes at the seventh International Congress of Photography which met in London in 1928.

Both the spectral-energy distribution of the radiation emitted from the luminous source as well as the intensity or magnitude of these radiations affect the density of the exposed and developed photographic material. Consequently these two characteristics of the luminous source must be accurately known if precise sensitometric results are to be obtained.

The spectral composition of a luminous source specifies the relative amounts of energy emitted at various wavelengths. Usually this relation is represented by means of a spectral-energy curve in which the abscissas are wavelength and the ordinates are relative energy. Figure 1 shows spectral-energy curves for one type of luminous source.

Effect of Spectral Distribution of Light Source.—It is important that the spectral-energy distribution or color composition of the radiations emitted by any source which is to be used as a standard of intensity in photographic sensitometry shall be known and appropriate because photographic materials do not have the same spectral sensitivity as does the human eye, which is used in the subjective evaluation of the characteristics of any light source. Furthermore, with respect to their spectral sensitivities, photographic materials differ enormously among themselves. Photographic materials are more sensitive at the blue and ultraviolet end of the visible spectrum than elsewhere. Consequently a denser silver deposit will result if the luminous source of given absolute intensity has most of its energy in the blue end of the spectrum rather than in some other region. In fact, the use of certain types of safe lights for photographic darkrooms depends upon so choosing the light source with respect to the film characteristics that the visible light occurs at that portion of the spectrum for which the film is relatively insensitive. A 15-watt red lamp used as a safe light for noncolor-sensitive emulsions may produce no appreciable exposure or fog, whereas a 15-watt blue lamp might badly expose the film under the same conditions.

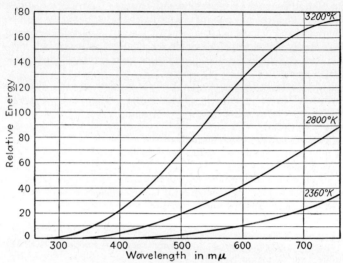

Fig. 1.—Curves of energy output plotted against wavelength for tungsten lamps operating at three different temperatures.

The sensitivity of the human eye to equally intense radiations of different wavelengths is termed the visibility curve. The visibility curve for the average human eye is given in Fig. 2. The net over-all response of the human eye to a light source con-

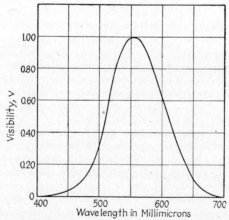

Fig. 2.—Spectral sensitivity of the normal human eye.

taining energy at many wavelengths depends upon the visibility curve of the human eye, as well as spectral-energy distribution of the light source, and is termed the luminosity. If a light of given intensity is yellow, the luminosity will be high, as the human eye is most sensitive to yellow; if the same amount of energy is used in a deep red or a blue light, the luminosity is small, as the eye is relatively insensitive to these colors.   If the energy is concentrated in the infrared or the ultraviolet portions of the spectrum, the luminosity is zero, for the eye is not sensitive to these radiations.

An exactly analogous situation exists with regard to photographic materials. Corresponding to the visibility curve of the human eye, the sensitivity of a photographic material to radiation of a given wavelength is known as its photobility.   The net or over-all response of a photographic material exposed to heterochromatic light is the product of the spectral-energy distribution of the light source and the photobility; it is termed the "photicity" of the material.   Photicity of photographic materials is analogous to the luminosity of the human eye (see Chap. X, Light Filters).

Although by no means a rigorous treatment of the subject, the previous paragraphs will indicate the necessity of maintaining known or standard conditions for precise sensitometric work.   It is also necessary to determine just what is a suitable or appropriate spectral-energy distribution for the light source used in sensitometry.

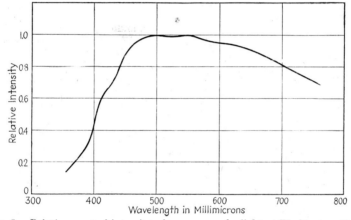

Fɪɢ. 3.—Relative spectral intensity of mean noon daylight at Washington, D. C.

Selecting a Standard Light Source.—In establishing standards for sensitometry, it is desirable that the standards be such as will give useful results in practice.   Since a very considerable portion of all photographic negatives are exposed with daylight illumination, there are certain practical advantages in choosing for the sensitometric light source one which will provide a spectral-energy distribution giving white light similar to that of daylight.   Because "daylight" varies considerably both according to time and geographical location, it is more practical to specify the characteristics of the white light of the sensitometric source in terms of the average daylight over a long period of time.   Measurements on mean daylight have been made over a number of years; the curve for mean noon daylight at Washington, D. C., is shown in Fig. 3. Once having established a suitable standard so far as regards spectral-energy distribution, the next step is to find a means of realizing this standard under controlled conditions.

None of the light sources which have been used produce a spectral-energy curve, of themselves, sufficiently like that of mean noon daylight to be suitable for photographic sensitometry.   The most suitable, convenient, and precise light sources (incandescent lamps) produce spectral-energy curves which are lacking in blue and excessive in red radiations.   However, the spectral-energy distribution of the tungsten lamp can be made to approximate that of mean noon daylight quite satisfactorily through the use of appropriate (Davis-Gibson) filters.

Effect of Voltage on Incandescent Lamps.—The spectral-energy distribution, as well as the intrinsic brightness, of incandescent lamps depends upon the temperature at which they are operated, and this in turn depends upon the filament voltage and current. Therefore, for precise standardized conditions, the filament voltage must be maintained constant. Maintaining constant voltage on the filament of the lamp likewise keeps the absolute magnitude of the emitted radiation constant, another essential requirement for sensitometry.

As the temperature of the tungsten lamp is raised, a larger portion of the total energy is shifted into the blue end of the spectrum so that the lamps tends to approach a more nearly white light source. But, even at the highest temperature at which tungsten lamps can be operated, a filter is required, for incandescent lamps are still entirely too deficient in blue radiation to produce a true white-light source. Furthermore, as the temperature of the lamp is raised, the life is considerably decreased and the characteristics change more rapidly with age. A temperature of about 2500°K. is the highest at which incandescent lamps may be operated if they are to give satisfactory characteristics so far as life, reproducibility, and precision are concerned.

The manner in which the life, radiant energy, and other characteristics of tungsten-filament lamps vary with the applied voltage has been studied at the National Bureau of Standards.[1] Some of the results of this investigation may be used to determine the effect on the light output of small variations in applied voltage. Suppose we let F represent the luminous output (lumens) of the lamp at voltage V, and F_0 the normal or rated luminous output of the lamp at its normal or rated voltage, V_0. Then we may use the approximate relation

$$F = F_0\left(\frac{V}{V_0}\right)^{B_2} \tag{1}$$

(where B_2 is an exponent which depends upon the size and type of the lamp) to compute the allowable variation in voltage for a specified small variation in luminous output. In order to make the most use of this equation, it is desirable to specify F and V in terms of the normal values F_0 and V_0, and the variations from these normal values, b and d, respectively. We may therefore write

$$F = F_0(1 \pm b) \tag{2}$$

and

$$V = V_0(1 \pm d) \tag{3}$$

where b represents the change in luminous output as a result of the voltage variation d. Substituting these last two equations into Eq. (1), we have

$$F = F_0(1 \pm b) = F_0\left[V_0\left(\frac{1 \pm d}{V_0}\right)\right]^{B_2} = F_0(1 \pm d)^{B_2} \tag{4}$$

from which

$$(1 \pm b) = (1 \pm d)^{B_2} \tag{5}$$

From Eq. (5) the maximum allowable voltage variation, $\pm d$ which may be tolerated for a specified fluctuation in luminous output $\pm b$ is then given by

$$\pm d = (1 \pm b)^{\frac{1}{B_2}} - 1 \tag{6}$$

In all these equations, the plus signs are to be used if the voltage (and hence the light output) increases, whereas the minus signs are to be used if they decrease. Figure 4

---

[1] BARROW, L. E., and J. FRANKLIN MEYER, "Characteristic Equations of Vacuum and Gas-filled Tungsten Lamps," *Bur. Standards J. Research,* **9,** 721 (1932).

shows the variation in light output for various types of incandescent lamps for small voltage fluctuations.

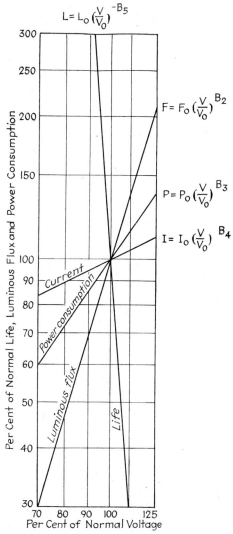

$$L = L_o \left(\frac{V}{V_o}\right)^{-B_5}$$

$$F = F_o \left(\frac{V}{V_o}\right)^{B_2}$$

$$P = P_o \left(\frac{V}{V_o}\right)^{B_3}$$

$$I = I_o \left(\frac{V}{V_o}\right)^{B_4}$$

Fig. 4.—Variations of life (L), light output (F), power consumption (P), and current consumption (I) of tungsten lamps in terms of normal filament voltage.

For simplicity in calculation without the use of tables, Eq. (6) may be expanded by means of the binomial-expansion theorem. The first three terms of this expansion are:

$$\pm d = \pm \frac{b}{B_2} + \frac{(1 - B_2)b^2}{2B_2} \pm \frac{(1 - B_2)(1 - 2B_2)b^3}{6B_2^3} \tag{7}$$

The expansion of Eq. (7) is only valid for small values of b, in which case the series converges rapidly and the third term will seldom be required. Values of B_2 for various types of incandescent lamps are given in Table I.

TABLE I.—VALUES OF B FOR VARIOUS INCANDESCENT LAMPS

Type of lamp	Power rating, watts	Value of			
		B_2	B_3	B_4	B_5
Vacuum lamp........................	15– 60	3.513	1.5805	0.5805	13.5
Gas-filled lamps.....................	40– 60	3.685	1.523	0.523	13.5
Gas-filled lamps.....................	60–150	3.613	1.523	0.523	13.5
Gas-filled lamps.....................	200–250	3.384	1.543	0.543	13.1

To illustrate the use of this equation, let us find the maximum permissible voltage variation d for a variation of 1 per cent of the light output, *i.e.*, $b = 0.01$, for a 100-watt lamp. For lamps between 60 and 150 watts, $B_2 = 3.613$, so that, substituting values for b and B_2 into Eq. (7), we obtain, for an increase in voltage,

$$+d = 0.0027678 + 0.00001001 = 0.002778 = 0.2778 \text{ per cent}$$

Thus, in order to maintain the light output constant to within 1 per cent, the voltage applied to the lamp must be maintained constant to within about $\frac{1}{4}$ per cent.

The plus signs in the above equations are to be used when d and b increase; the minus signs are used when they decrease. We therefore get two answers for a given voltage variation (depending upon whether the variation is an increase or a decrease). The above example was considered to be an increase in both b and d. If it had been considered a decrease, the result would have been -0.2758 per cent which, for practical purposes is the same thing.

The best types of commercial voltmeters are accurate to within 0.25 per cent; laboratory standards are available which are accurate to 0.1 per cent. Consequently, for precise sensitometric work the most accurate voltmeters are required to maintain the voltage constant, or recourse must be made to potentiometric methods of control.

Filters for Incandescent Sources of Luminous Intensity.—Since none of the light sources which are suitable for photographic sensitometry—from the standpoints of convenience, reproducibility and stability of characteristics, or adequate intensity— have spectral-energy-distribution curves approximating that of mean noon sunlight, it is necessary to select a source of light on other grounds and then to modify its spectral distribution through the medium of absorbing filters.

An acetylene flame, used in conjunction with a Wratten No. 79 filter has been used for some time as a suitable source of white light. Although the spectral distribution of this combination departs appreciably from that of mean noon sunlight, this departure is frequently of little practical importance. In fact Jones states that "speed values determined from this source-filter combination using materials differing widely in spectral sensitivity agree very well with speed values determined by using actual sunlight."

A liquid filter has been developed by Davis and Gibson[1] which, when used with an acetylene flame or incandescent electric lamp operated at 2360°K., produces a close approximation to mean noon sunlight. The filters are stable and easily reproducible. For use with an incandescent light source operating at 2360°K., the filter is made up of two solutions as follows:

[1] DAVIS, R., and K. GIBSON, *Trans. Soc. Motion Picture Engrs.*, **12** (May, 1928).

SOLUTION A

Copper sulphate.. 3.707 g.
Mannite... 3.707 g.
Pyradine.......................,................................... 30.0 cc.
Distilled water to make..'........ 1000.0 cc.

SOLUTION B

Cobalt ammonium sulphate.. 26.827 g.
Copper sulphate.. 27.180 g.
Sulphuric acid (sp. gr. 1.835) .... 10.00 cc.
Distilled water to make... 1000.0 cc.

Exposure Devices.—In making photographic sensitometric measurements, it is customary and convenient to subject several strips of the material to be tested to a series of graded exposures so that the developed test strip contains varying amounts of silver deposit from the minimum (represented by fog density) to the maximum possible for the type of material under test. Usually the test strips are exposed in a series of discrete or stepped exposures varying in geometrical ratio, and the developed test strip is sometimes spoken of as a scale of grays. To expose a test strip of this type some type of exposure modulator or graduated exposure-determining device is required. Furthermore it is essential to know the manner in which the density of the silver deposit builds up with the duration of the exposure time, as well as with the manner in which the photographic material is exposed.

Reciprocity Law and Intermittency Effects.—It is usually assumed that the photochemical reaction of photographic materials is directly proportional to the total energy affecting the material and that the exposure E is equal to the intensity of the radiations I impinging upon the plate and the time t during which these radiations act. As a result of this assumption, it is implicitly assumed that the photochemical effect is independent of the absolute value of either factor, I or t and, consequently, that the photographic materials properly integrate the effects of incident radiant energy. To a first approximation, this assumption is true. This is the reciprocity law.[1]

The assumption is not exactly true for photographic materials, however, and while the failure of the reciprocity law is usually insignificant for most applications of photography, it cannot be neglected where extremely long or extremely short exposures are given. The intermittency effect, by which is meant the failure of a photographic material to record the same density for a continuous exposure as for intermittent exposure of the same total energy, is closely related to the failure of the reciprocity law. Like the failure of the law of reciprocity, the intermittency law does not produce appreciable errors for the majority of applications to which photosensitive materials are used. However, neither effect can be neglected where precise results are desired, such as in photographic sensitometry, or where very short or very long exposures are involved.

Both of the effects mentioned above must be given consideration in photographic sensitometry since these factors affect the design and construction of suitable sensitometric exposure devices. An exposure device operating continuously does not produce the same effect as an intermittent exposure device which permits the same total energy to be impressed on the photographic materials. These two factors also affect the definition of exposure for sensitometric work, and the proper interpretation of sensitometric data.

Several formulas have been derived to express the response of the photosensitive material for those cases where intermittency effect and failure of the law of reciprocity need be considered. Of these, one of the simplest which agrees reasonably well with

---

[1] J. H. Webb has published a number of important papers on the reciprocity law in the *Journal of the Optical Society of America.*

experimentally observed facts, especially for low-intensity exposures, expresses the exposure[1] E in terms of the luminous intensity of specified distribution I and the total time of exposure t in the form

$$E = I^m t^n \tag{8}$$

where the exponents may have values greater than unity. Some investigators have found more complicated relations in which it was necessary to express the exposure in terms of the characteristics of the photographic material under investigation. Obviously this is an undesirable situation, and it is convenient to have the various factors involved as independent of one another as possible.

Since the failure of the law of reciprocity and the intermittency law do not produce appreciable errors for the ordinary range of luminous intensities and exposure times used in sensitometry (or in general photography, for that matter), the exposure has been defined to be

$$E = It \tag{9}$$

This is a simple relation for the exposure and is based on the assumption that the exposure is of continuous duration. This definition of exposure, which is used in sensitometry, has the additional advantage that effects of intermittency can be studied independently, using the continuous exposure, as employed in ordinary sensitometric methods, as a standard of comparison. In photographic sensitometry the exposure is expressed in meter-candle-seconds unless otherwise stated.

Methods of Making Exposure.—The adoption of the above definition of exposure makes it evident that the graduated exposure of sensitometric strips may be controlled in any one of three ways:

1. By keeping the intensity I constant and varying t.
2. By keeping t constant and varying the intensity I.
3. By varying both I and t.

In these three cases it is assumed that the spectral-energy distribution of the luminous source remains unchanged.

For simplicity in the construction and use of sensitometers, only the first two methods are in common use, and the first two classifications enumerated above give rise to the two classifications of sensitometers or exposure devices in common use. If the illumination is maintained constant and exposure is varied by altering the time throughout which exposure takes place, a time scale of exposure is obtained. A sensitometer operating on this exposure principle is termed a "time-scale sensitometer." On the other hand, if the time during which the exposure is made is kept constant and the exposure is varied by altering the intensity of illumination between successive steps, an intensity scale of exposure results. A sensitometer using this principle is commonly referred to as an intensity-scale instrument. Both the intensity-scale and the time-scale sensitometers may be made to produce a sensitometric strip which is either continuous or stepped in its density variation.

Following Jones,[2] we may classify exposure devices in the following manner:

Type I: Intensity-scale instruments
  I variable, t constant
  1. Continuously varying exposure
  2. Stepped exposure

---

[1] In this case, we use the term exposure (for want of a better name) to indicate the intensity-time product function, which will be integrated by the photographic material so as to give the same effect as if the law of reciprocity was exactly followed and the intermittency law was nonexistent.

[2] JONES, L. A., Photographic Sensitometry, *J. Soc. Motion Picture Engrs.*, **18**, 32 (1932).

Type II: Time-scale instruments
    I constant, t variable
        A. Exposure intermittent
            1. Continuously varying exposure
            2. Stepped exposure
        B. Exposure nonintermittent
            1. Continuously varying exposure
            2. Stepped exposure

Intensity-scale Exposure Devices.—Probably the first attempts at photographic sensitometry were made with plates or tablets having numerous areas of varying transmission (or density) which were placed in contact with the photographic material under test and then exposed to a suitable light source for a known length of time. The areas of varying density were numbered, and the faintest number which could be read, after exposure and development, indicated the speed or sensitivity of the material. A later modification of this general principle made use of tablets whose density varied continuously, rather than in steps.

Intensity-scale sensitometers have also been introduced which consist of a series of tubes or cells of equal length, at one end of which is placed the photographic plate, the other ends of the various tubes being closed by opaque plates containing apertures of variable areas. If these apertures and tubes are properly illuminated, the exposure of the film will be directly proportional to the area of the aperture.

A method of obtaining directly the H and D curve of a photographic material using a square neutral-gray wedge behind which the photographic material under test is exposed was suggested in 1910 by R. Luther. The resultant negative is preferably developed to a high contrast. After being rotated through 90° with respect to its original position, the negative is placed in register with the wedge through which the exposure was made, so that the lines of equal density on the negative are perpendicular to the lines of equal density on the tablet wedge of continuously graded density. By direct observation of this wedge-negative combination, the density-log E characteristic may be seen. By making a print through the wedge and the negative, preferably on high-contrast paper, a permanent record may be obtained. This method of determining the D-$\log_{10} E$ characteristics has advantages where a rapid means of testing is desired. It is not likely, however, that sufficient precision can be obtained for standardized sensitometric work.

It is generally agreed that an intensity-scale instrument represents the ideal form of sensitometer since photographic materials are almost always exposed under variable intensity conditions in practice. However, no really satisfactory sensitometer of the intensity-scale type giving the required reproducibility, intensity, and precision has been developed for commercial use.

None of the intensity-scale instruments is completely satisfactory for sensitometric work, primarily because such devices are inherently complicated and require the highest degree of mechanical and optical workmanship to obtain the necessary precision. The wedges (either stepped or of continuously varying density) which are required are difficult to produce accurately with nonselective absorption and proper density variation. They must be stable, reproducible, and permanent in their characteristics. Since they diffuse the light passing through them, the results obtained through their use will correspond only to the conditions under which the graduated density tablets were used. With the tube type of sensitometers, it is required that the illumination level be as uniform as possible; moreover the intensity range is limited.

Intensity-scale devices may be produced by:

1. Varying the distance between the light source and the sensitive material for the various exposures.

2. Using different areas of a uniformly lighted source.

3. Reducing the intensity of the light reaching the different portions of the sensitive material by means of screens of known absorbing power.

The last of these is the only method now in general use.

Time-scale Exposure Devices.—Although, in practice, photographs are taken with a shutter giving sensibly the same time of exposure to all parts of the negative, it is most convenient and accurate to use time-scale devices in photographic sensitometry. The reason lies in the greater simplicity, ease of construction, and inherent precision of time-scale exposure modulators as compared with intensity-scale modulators. Such time-scale devices make use of a constant source of illumination and vary the exposure by altering the time during which this light impinges on the photographic material. Consequently a simple light chopper will suffice for this system. Such a light chopper may take the form of: (1) a rotating wheel or drum with various segments cut out through which the light passes as the wheel is rotated, (2) a slotted plate falling under the influence of gravity or moved at some uniform velocity, or (3) a slotted tape which moves past the aperture through which the light passes to expose the photographic material. The slotted rotating disk or drum is usually the most convenient form of varying the exposure and can be made to give either intermittent or nonintermittent exposures. Nonintermittent exposure modulators may be made by rotating the disk sufficiently slowly that the required exposure is obtained with one complete revolution of the disk. Intermittent exposures result if the required exposure is built up through successive individual exposures obtained from several revolutions of the disk. The slots may be cut to give steps of varying exposure.

Differences between Intermittent and Continuous Exposure.—A distinction must be made between these two types of exposure devices, as it has been found that they do not give the same results. The reason behind this discrepancy lies in the fact that photographic materials have been found not to integrate an intermittent exposure correctly, except to a rough first approximation. For this reason the characteristics of the photographic material observed by intermittent exposure will depend upon the intermittency of exposure as well as the total time duration for which the exposure is made. As might be expected the magnitude and character of the intermittency effect varies with the character of the photographic material under consideration. Furthermore, whereas the speed is higher and the gamma lower[1] for nonintermittent exposures as compared with intermittent exposures for certain intensity levels, this condition may be reversed at other intensity levels at which the comparisons are made. For these reasons the effects obtained with intermittent and nonintermittent exposures cannot be compared. Since intermittent exposure is not encountered in practice, there is good reason for preferring the nonintermittent-exposure type of device in sensitometry.

Rotating disks, falling plates, and other time-varying exposure modulators can be made rather accurately, the precision being determined by the precision with which the slots are cut or the precision with which the shutter devices are moved past the film to give the necessary exposure. When rotating-disk exposure devices are used, the speed of rotation may be determined with precision by means of rotation counters. With a precisely cut disk properly driven, accurate results are easily obtainable.

Since the characteristic curves of photographic materials are customarily plotted in linear rectilinear coordinates with density D as the ordinates and $\log_{10} E$ as the abscissas, it is convenient to make the progressive exposure steps of the sensitometer bear a logarithmic ratio to one another. This may be accomplished by so cutting the disks that the angle of arc in successive steps bears a known ratio to one another. The disk used by Hurter and Driffield was based on this principle. It had nine apertures

---

[1] See p. 190 for definitions of speed and p. 179 for definition of gamma.

or slots decreasing in angle of arc from the center outward. The largest aperture was 180°, the second one was 90°, the third 45°, etc. The relation between the aperture, angle of arc of the aperture, and the relative exposure of their disk is given in Table II.

TABLE II.—EXPOSURE CHARACTERISTICS FOR SECTORED DISK

Aperture number	1	2	3	4	5	6	7	8	9
Arc angle, degrees	180	90	45	22.5	11.2	5.3	2.6	1.3	0
Relative exposure	256	128	64	32	16	8	4	2	1
$\log_{10} E_{REL}$	2.41	2.11	1.81	1.51	1.20	0.9	0.6	0.3	0

It will be seen that $\log_{10} E_{REL}$ is a uniform progression; the absolute value of the exposure of the nth step being twice that of the $(n - 1)$st step. At the present time successive steps are often made equal to $\sqrt{2}$ or $\sqrt[3]{2}$ times the next step in order that more steps and finer gradations may be obtained between successive steps.

Practical Sensitometers.—Practical sensitometers usually take the form of a rotating disk or cylinder in which slots of various widths are cut. Figure 5 shows the working

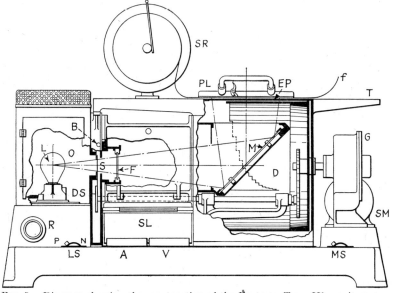

FIG. 5.—Diagram showing the construction of the Eastman Type IIb sensitometer.

essentials of the Eastman Type IIb sensitometer popularly employed in motion-picture work. A line switch LS turns on current to a standardized lamp L, whose intensity is controlled by adjustments of the rheostat R. The beam from the lamp travels in a cone until it strikes the mirror M, which reflects the beam upward to the motion-picture film f, held in position by the plate PL. A shutter is provided at S, and a filter may be used, if desired, at F. The exposure drum D is driven by the synchronous motor SM through the gear train G and is coupled to the shutter S in such a way that the shutter is opened for only one complete revolution of the drum D. Slots are cut in the drum in such a way that the exposure for each slot is $\sqrt{2}$ times that of the preceding slot. The total exposure range of the drum is 1024 to 1.

Development for Sensitometry.—The sensitometric strips are developed after exposure. Since the density of the silver deposit depends upon the developing conditions as well as upon the exposure, it is apparent that the developer and the conditions of development must be standardized for precise sensitometric work. The conditions which are chosen for standardization, however, cannot be established once and for all, for consideration must be given to the type of work being accomplished. The development conditions will obviously be different for research work on developers than for routine processing of a certain class of film.

The investigations of various workers have shown that the constitution of the developing solution affects such photographic characteristics of a given material as rate of development, contrast, density, fog, latitude, speed, etc. A paper by Clark[1] summarizes the effect of changes in the constitution of developers and may be consulted by those interested.

Developers for Sensitometry.—For a comparison of emulsion characteristics and for investigations in which the control of processing is not involved, standard developers and developing conditions may be established for photographic sensitometric work. A developer suitable for this class of work should have the following characteristics:

1. Good reproducibility
2. Low temperature coefficient
3. Low sensitivity to changes in concentration of bromide
4. Production of neutral density image free from stains and selective absorption.
5. Good keeping qualities.

For many years a pyro developer was used for sensitometric work. Such a developer was generally suitable since pyro developers were extensively used in practice. However, since some of the reaction products of pyro developers are definitely colored and are absorbed by the film, the developed negative has a yellowish stain which has considerable absorption to the blue, violet, and ultraviolet. The photographic and visual density are therefore likely to be quite different and corrections are required when converting one density into the other. Pyro developers have fallen somewhat into disuse during recent years, so that a pyro developer for sensitometric work does not have the merit it formerly possessed.

A developer suggested by Sheppard and Travelli,[2] suitable as a standard developer for scientific sensitometric work, consists of:

p-Aminophenol hydrochloride	7¼	g.
Sodium sulphite (anhydrous)	50	g.
Sodium carbonate (anhydrous)	50	g.
Water to make	1000	cc.

This developer produces a neutral-gray deposit, has desirable fog characteristics, contains no bromide, and is relatively insensitive to the presence of bromide so that the regression of inertia with increase in time of development and speed should be independent of development time. This developer has a relatively high temperature coefficient,[3] so that for precise sensitometric work the temperature must be controlled accurately during development.

[1] CLARK, W., *Phot. J.*, **65** (n.s. 49), 76 (1925).

[2] JONES, L. A., "Photographic Sensitometry," Eastman Kodak Co. (1934).

[3] The temperature coefficient for a particular developing agent is defined as the ratio of the velocity constants k for any two temperatures. The difference in temperatures for the two velocity constants is chosen as 10°C. Thus, if k_{20} is the velocity constant at 20°C., and k_{30} is the velocity constant at 30°C., the temperature coefficient τ of this developer between 20° and 30°C. will be

$$\tau = \frac{k_{30}}{k_{20}} \tag{10}$$

If sensitometry is being carried out for the control of photographic processing, it is desirable that the developer and the developing conditions be as nearly as possible like those under which the processed materials are being developed. Not only should the same type of developer be used, but the same developing solution should be used at the same time that processing is accomplished. The developer becomes exhausted upon use, and its effective composition changes. Consequently the action of the developer after some use may be considerably different from that when the developer was freshly compounded. To insure that the developed sensitometric strips will afford a precise index of the processing performance which it is desired to test, it is essential that the sensitometric strips be developed along with the material under test in such a way that both types of material receive identical processing.

Technique of Development.—In its broad aspects, the technique of development for sensitometry is no different from the development technique of other photographic materials. However, the particular problems involved in sensitometry often make it desirable to pay more than ordinary attention to such factors as (1) evenness of development, (2) temperature of the developer, (3) agitation of developing solutions, (4) prevention of bubbles, streaks, stains, etc.

Through the use of thermostatic control, it is easily possible to control the temperature of the developing solution to $\pm 0.1°C.$, and through more elaborate temperature-control baths still further control can be effected. Temperature variations of $0.1°C.$ will not cause serious errors in sensitometric work due to the temperature coefficient of developers. Where thermostatic control of the developing solutions is not possible or practicable, the temperature of the developing bath may be maintained reasonably constant by immersing the developing tank or tray in a large tank of water which is thoroughly agitated. After the developing solution is in temperature equilibrium with its surrounding bath, the thermal inertia of the water surrounding the developing tank will assist in preventing sudden or appreciable temperature variations of the developing bath.

In any case it is desirable to use a comparatively large volume of developing solution so that the reaction products may be considerably diluted, thereby influencing the effective concentration of the solution a minimum amount. The sensitometric strips should be agitated in the solution so that fresh solution is constantly presented to their surfaces. Rocking the trays or tanks has been found beneficial and produces fairly uniform results. Brushing the surface of the strip with a camel's-hair brush is another very effective means of removing exhausted developer from the surface of the strips but is probably not so reproducible as rocking the trays, since different workers handle the brush strokes differently.

Density Determinations.—With the test strips exposed to a series of known exposures and developed under specified and controlled conditions, it now remains to evaluate in some appropriate manner the response of the photographic material (the amount of silver deposit) to the stimulus (exposure). Visual inspection of the silver deposit is unsatisfactory. For quantitative work, the magnitude of the silver deposit corresponding to the various exposures on the strip is determined optically by the amount of light which the photographic material transmits or reflects. In the case of negatives, the transmission of the material may be used; for printing papers, the amount of reflected light determines the density.

Fundamental Definitions Used in Sensitometry.—Before we can discuss the determination of density properly, it is essential to establish certain definitions. To do this, let I_0 be the luminous flux incident upon the negative, I_t the luminous flux transmitted through the negative, T the transmission of the negative, O its opacity, and D its density. Then, by definition,

$$T = \frac{I_t}{I_0} \tag{11}$$

$$O = \frac{I_0}{I_t} \tag{12}$$

$$D = \log_{10} O = \log_{10} \frac{I_0}{I_t} = \log_{10} \frac{1}{T} = -\log_{10} T \tag{13}$$

To a first approximation, D is proportional to the amount of silver deposited per unit area.

Similar equations may be derived to apply to printing papers as well as to negatives. If I_0 is the luminous flux reflected by the white paper having no exposure and I_r is the light flux reflected from the paper having a deposit of silver whose density is D, then

$$D = \log_{10} \left(\frac{I_0}{I_r} \right) \tag{14}$$

There is nothing in the preceding equations which leads one to suspect that the application of these formulas would not give definite and precisely reproducible results.

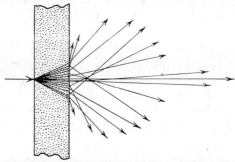

Fig. 6.—Polar diagram illustrating the scattering of light in passing through a photographic film.

That such is not the case depends upon the fact that in passing through the developed silver image of a negative, the light beam is scattered, as shown in Fig. 6, so that the determination of density and transmitted light flux depends upon the manner in which the transmitted light flux is measured.

Scattering of Light by Negative.—To study in greater detail the significance of the scattering of light, suppose I_0 in Fig. 7 represents a narrow pencil or beam of light incident upon the photographic negative to be measured for density. In passing through the negative, part of the beam is transmitted directly through the film A; part of the light is also scattered or diffused as it passes through the film, and emerges at some angle from normal. If we investigate the intensity of the transmitted rays as a function of the angle or direction from the point where the normal rays emerge, we find that we can construct a polar diagram as shown in Fig. 7. The lengths of the vectors represent the intensities of the light in that direction. Obviously, a three-dimensional vector plot is obtained, although, for simplicity, only a two-dimensional drawing is shown in the plane of the paper. The outline or envelope of these vectors shows the manner in which the emergent light is distributed as a result of partial diffusion of the normal ray I_0.

By means of this diagram it may be seen that the value of the transmitted light will depend upon the manner in which it is measured, and consequently several values of density can be obtained.

If we measure all the light transmitted through the negative, *i.e.*, if we determine all the light in the envelope (by means of an integrating sphere, for example), as shown in Fig. 8, we obtain what is known as diffuse density.

The light transmitted through a negative may be measured by means of an integrating sphere and radiant-energy detector. The integrating sphere consists of a hollow sphere whose inner surface is covered with some coat of diffusing and reflecting material. The film is placed in contact with a small aperture in the integrating sphere, the aperture being small compared with the dimensions of the sphere. Thus the film and aperture are sensibly a portion of the spherical surface of the integrating sphere.

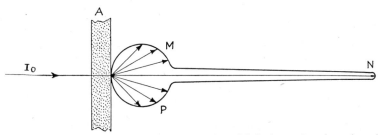

Fig. 7.—Polar diagram illustrating the scattering of light in passing through a photographic film. The relative intensity of the emerging beam in any direction is proportional to the length of the arrows in that direction.

The detector may be a phototube and associated electrical circuit, a thermocouple, bolometer, or similar device. Preferably a nonselective indicator should be used. Direct rays from the aperture are prevented from reaching the indicating device by means of a shield, and only that energy coming through the aperture which has been reflected by the spherical walls of the integrating sphere affects the indicating device or detector.

If now, the film is placed very close to the aperture, as in Fig. 8, so that it forms a portion of the wall of the integrating sphere, the transmitted rays normal to the film,

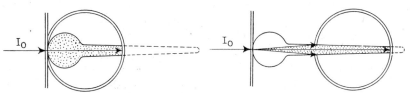

Fig. 8.—By measuring all the light passing through the negative, the diffuse density is determined.

Fig. 9.—By measuring only that portion of the light passing straight through the negative, specular density may be determined.

as well as the diffused rays coming through the negative, will be collected by the integrating sphere and will determine the reading of the indicating device.

Diffuse and Specular Density.—The value of the density computed from the incident and emergent light in this case is known as "diffuse density." It is based upon measurement of the total transmission of the negative (both normal or undeflected, as well as diffused light) and will give the smallest possible value of density. The measurements made on the basis of diffuse density are appropriate for contact prints, since contact prints use all the transmitted light.

If now the film is removed a considerable distance from the aperture, as in Fig. 9, so that the only rays passing through the aperture are those which are transmitted by the negative without diffusion, the value of density obtained from such measurements will be higher than the diffused density. The reason for this is that in this case not all the transmitted light is used to actuate the indicating device; the diffuse component does not affect the indicating device at all, or only slightly. Density determinations based on such measurements are known as specular-density measurements. The magnitude of the difference in determinations of diffuse and specular density will depend upon the size and shape of the grains in the emulsion, grain-size frequency distribution, thickness of the layer, number of developed grains per unit area of the layer, and similar characteristics of the film.

If the negative has some intermediate position from those mentioned above, some intermediate value of density will be determined. Density determinations made in some such manner as shown in Fig. 10, where the normal rays as well as some of the diffused rays are effective in actuating the indicating device, are known as intermediate densities. Obviously an indefinite number of intermediate densities may be determined, depending upon the relation of the film and the aperture of the integrating sphere.

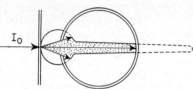

Fig. 10.—Intermediate density may be determined from measurements which make use of the specular as well as some of the diffused rays of light passing through the negative.

The relation between specular and diffuse density gives a measure of the discrepancies of the various methods of density determination. The ratio of the specular density, sometimes designated by $D\|$ to the diffuse density $D\text{⫲}$, has been designated as Q by A. Callier who first studied this subject. The quantity Q, which is defined to be

$$Q = \frac{D\|}{D\text{⫲}} \tag{15}$$

is known as Callier's factor coefficient or Q factor.

In general, Q may be expected to vary from 1.0 for grainless plates to 1.9 or more for fast plates with appreciable grain. The value of Q is not a constant for a given type of film or plate, however, but depends upon the density of the film or plate as

TABLE III.—MEASUREMENTS SHOWING RELATION BETWEEN Q AND DENSITY[1]

Diffuse density $D\text{⫲}$	Specular density $D\|$	Callier's factor Q
0.0641	0.108	1.68
0.110	0.180	1.64
0.223	0.332	1.49
0.335	0.509	1.41
0.460	0.650	1.41
0.550	0.770	1.40
0.640	0.891	1.39
0.790	1.07	1.36
1.08	1.44	1.37
1.31	1.75	1.34
1.58	2.00	1.27
1.89	2.40	1.25

[1] From L. A. Jones, "Photographic Sensitometry," Eastman Kodak Co. (1934).

well. Table III, taken from Jones,[1] shows the manner in which Q depends upon the density of the negative.

Effective Density of Printing.—Since the conditions under which contact printing is done make use of all the transmitted light, it is evident that the most useful density, or the effective value of density for contact printing is diffuse density. For all practical purposes the diffuse density may be used as the effective density values for contact printing.

Unfortunately, the effective density of a developed film or plate cannot be so readily specified for projection printing. The reason lies in the fact that projection printing corresponds more nearly, in its optical system, to some intermediate value of density which varies with the enlarging conditions. In some instances, however, the conditions for projection printing may closely approach the conditions for specular density. They are generally nearer to specular than to diffuse density. The effective density of a developed negative for projection printing depends upon the optical system used in the projection equipment.

Densitometers.—Having exposed the sensitometric strips in a known and predetermined manner and having developed them under standardized or known conditions, it is now necessary to determine quantitatively the effects produced by the exposure. This is done by measuring the amount of silver deposit per unit area or the density of the negative. Such a measurement is made most readily with a special form of photometer designed to measure the magnitude of the light transmitted by the silver deposit on the film. Such a form of specialized photometer is called a densitometer, or, if the area being measured may be limited to that of a small hole or slit, a microdensitometer or microphotometer.

There are various types of densitometers, operating on various principles. All of them, however, make use of determinations of the radiation incident on a detector, both without and with the negative—whose density is to be determined—in the path of the light beam.

All densitometers contain as fundamental features a source of light to provide the measuring beam passing through the negative, a means of limiting this beam to the desired area of the negative, and a means of comparing the brightness of this beam with that of another (or a part of the same beam) which has not been made to pass through any portion of the negative. The densitometer must, therefore, provide some means for measuring the intensity of the light without the negative in one of its beams I_0 and the intensity of the same or an equal light beam with a portion of the negative in its path I and must provide some means for comparing these two intensities. Thus, essentially, all density (or transmission) measurements may be regarded as determining the difference between two different conditions.

Some detecting or indicating device is required to compare the relationship of these two conditions. The comparison between the intensities of these two light beams, which should have the same spectral distribution, can be made by visual observation. In this case, accurate and reproducible results can be obtained only when the two light beams being compared can be placed side by side in an optical system and when provision has been made for diminishing the intensity of the stronger beam continuously, by known amounts and without changing its spectral distribution, until it matches the intensity of the weaker beam. In densitometers which make use of visual comparisons, a good balance can be obtained only if the two light beams are of the same color. Moreover, the judgment of the operator enters into the determination of the conditions of balance. Because of the vagaries of human judgment over a period of time, these subjective methods of measurement do not usually give such

---

[1] Jones, L. A., "Photographic Sensitometry," *J. Soc. Motion Picture Engrs.*, **18**, 324 (1932).

precise and reproducible results as measurements made with an objective detector such as a phototube or thermocouple. This is especially true when the eye is subject to fatigue. A very important advantage of subjective determinations of density, however, is the wide range of light values over which the eye is sensitive. Another advantage is that such systems may be less expensive than objective methods, since no indicator need be incorporated in the densitometer itself.

In the case of objective densitometers, the indicating instrument may be a phototube (either photovoltaic, photoconductive or photoemissive), a thermocouple, or similar radiant-energy-detecting device. These detecting indicators may be selectively sensitive to radiations of various wavelengths, as in the case of phototubes, or may respond uniformly to radiations over a wide range of wavelengths, as in the case of the thermocouple. In selecting an indicator for a densitometer, consideration must be given to the wavelength-response characteristic of the detecting device, as well as the frequency-energy characteristic of the luminous source, for the results obtained depend considerably upon these two factors.

Subjective-type Densitometers.—The subjective or eye-matching densitometers are usually modifications of some well-known type of photometer. Because of the simple optical means which it provides for matching two beams of light and because of the fairly high precision attendent with its use, the Lummer-Brodhun cube employed in photometry is most frequently used as the method of comparing the intensity of the two light beams. In order that variations in the brightness of the lamp may be eliminated, it is common practice to use a beam-splitting device which produces two optical beams from the same luminous source. The intensity of both beams will vary together if fluctuations occur in the intensity of the light source, but the ratio of the intensities of the two beams will remain unchanged. The principal variations in the design of photometers of this type occur in the means used to diminish the intensity of the stronger beam. Methods most commonly used for this purpose include absorbing filters or wedges, rotating sectors, polarizing plates whose axes may be varied with respect to one another, variable diaphragms, and variable distance between the detector or comparator and the lamp in order to make use of the inverse square law.

Objective-type Densitometers.—The objective (or physical) type of densitometer may be similar in many respects to the subjective type of densitometer. The two forms differ in one important respect, however, in that as a means of comparing the two light beams, the human eye is replaced by some sensitive element such as a photoelectrically sensitive device, a thermocouple, radiometer, or similar piece of physical apparatus. This sensitive element is connected directly or through appropriate amplifying systems to a deflecting device, such as a galvanometer, so that objective comparisons may be made between the two light beams. Two advantages result from the use of an objective indicator. In the first place, the results obtained are likely to be more precise and reliable, since they do not depend upon the judgment of the observer. Secondly, by making an appropriate choice in the selection of the sensitive element and light source, it is possible to make measurements in portions of the spectrum to which the eye is insensitive.

Objective densitometers may be made in three types: (1) null instruments, (2) deflection instruments, and (3) automatic-recording densitometers. The null type of instruments are in general similar to subjective instruments in that the measuring and comparison beams are balanced against one another. Their intensities are brought to equality by reducing the intensity of the stronger beam until they are matched, when the indicating device will read zero or some other reference value. Null instruments are among the most precise types of densitometers which have been constructed, since it is usually possible to balance out most, if not all, of the factors producing irregularities or systematic errors.

In the deflecting type of densitometer, the difference in intensity of the measuring and comparison light beams is measured directly by some deflection instrument, and no effort is made to create equality between the intensities of the two beams.

Automatic-recording densitometers are elaborations of the null or deflecting type of instruments. In place of the deflecting type of indicator, a recording pen is provided which makes a plot of the density as the position of the photosensitive material under measurement is changed.

A wide variety of densitometers and microdensitometers has been described in the literature for general photographic research and for such specialized branches of photography as radiography, astronomical photography, spectroscopy, etc. A few representative densitometers for general photographic work will be described, but for

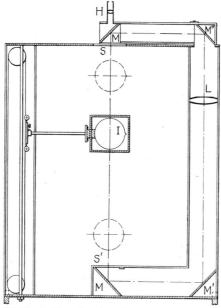

Fig. 11.—Diagrammatic illustration showing the essential design of the Capstaff-Green densitometer which makes use of the inverse-square law of illumination.

additional detailed information or for information on densitometers for specialized applications, the technical literature should be consulted.

Capstaff-Green Densitometer.—The Capstaff-Green densitometer is of the subjective type and depends upon the inverse-square law for its calibration and for its method of balancing the equality of the comparison and measuring light beams. A diagram showing the essential elements of construction is shown in Fig. 11. This densitometer consists of a light source which is split into two beams. One beam traverses the path from lamp I to the reflecting mirrors M, M', M'' and finally falls upon a partially reflecting mirror M in the eyepiece H. The other beam travels directly from the lamp I through a diffusing screen S, upon which the negative to be measured is placed, and thence to the partially reflecting mirror M. The lamp may be moved up and down on a suitable carriage. It is driven by a steel tape passing over pulleys, the tape being graduated to read density directly. The lamp is adjusted to its zero or reference position with the negative removed until both fields of the mirror in the eyepiece are equally illuminated. The negative is then inserted on the screen S and the lamp

again moved until a balance of intensity is obtained in the eyepiece, when density of
the negative may be read directly from the calibrations of the steel tape.   Calibration
of this tape involves the inverse-square law.

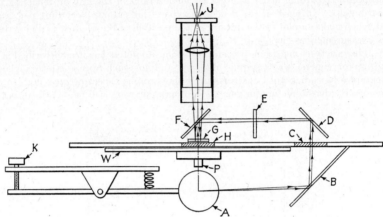

Fig. 12.—Optical system of the Capstaff-Purdy densitometer manufactured by the
Eastman Kodak Company.   The negative is placed on the stage, *H*, and light from the
lamp *A* is split into two beams.   One beam passes directly through the negative to the
eyepiece, *J*, whereas the other travels from the lamp to the mirrors *B*, *D*, and *F*, where it is
reflected onto a split mirror *G* and then is reflected to the eyepiece *J* where a split field is
observed.   When the wedge, *W*, is adjusted so that the two fields of the eyepiece match,
the density may be read off from the wedge calibration.   The knurled screw, *K*, is used in
making adjustments for the reference position of the wedge.

Capstaff-Purdy Densitometer.—The Capstaff-Purdy densitometer manufacturered
by the Eastman Kodak Company is an example of a subjective type of instrument
which depends for its indications upon a calibrated wedge.   Figure 12 shows a diagram

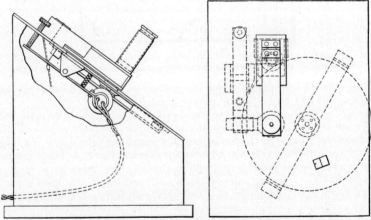

Fig. 13.—Side and panel views of the Capstaff-Purdy densitometer.

of the essential optical system of this densitometer, and Fig. 13 shows a schematic
diagram of the completed device.   Here again the light from the lamp *A* is split into
two beams.   One of these traverses from the lamp *A* through a diffusing glass *H* (over

which the negative is placed) and then passes through a field-forming photometer head. This latter consists of the partly reflecting, partly absorbing, mirror *F* and the mirror *G*, which has a circular disk from which the silver has been removed so that the direct rays from the lamp may pass through it. The other beam traverses the path from the lamp *A* to the mirror *B* through a graduated wedge *C*, a second mirror *D*, and finally impinges on the partially reflecting mirror *F*, where it is reflected to the mirror *G* and viewed together with the direct beam from *A*. Equality of the direct and reflected beams is obtained by rotating the calibrated wedge *W* until a portion of the wedge having suitable absorption intercepts the reflected light beam. The match of the two fields is made by looking through the eyepiece *J* and rotating the circular wedge. The initial adjustment for zero density (when the negative is removed from

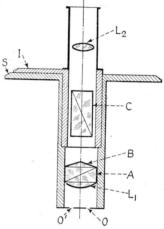

Fig. 14.

Fig. 15.

Fig. 14.—External view of Eastman transmission densitometer.

Fig. 15.—Optical parts as used in the Martens polarization photometer head. The essential parts are: *A*, Wollaston polarizing prism; *B*, biprism for splitting the field; *C*, analyzing Nicol prism; *I*, index pointer; L_1, field lens cemented to Wollaston prism; L_2, eyepiece lens; *O*, aperture for one field; *O′*, aperture for other field; *S*, scale.

the densitometer) is made by moving the position of the lamp slightly by means of the key *K*.

Figure 14 shows an external view of the completed instrument. The edge of the wedge projects beyond one side of the case and may be rotated by the finger. The wedge is made by copying on a photosensitive plate a circular wedge cast in gray-dyed gelatin. Each such wedge must be calibrated against a standard before the densitometer can be used to indicate density directly, and a suitable calibration scale must be affixed to the circular wedge. The scale is read through a small circular window.

Marten's Polarization Densitometer.—Another form of subjective densitometer is the Marten's densitometer, which makes use of the variation in absorption of two polarizing prisms as their axes are rotated with respect to one another. A polarizing plate or crystal, usually designated as a polarizer, is used for the production of a beam of plane-polarized light. Another polarizing device, called the analyzer, is placed in alignment with the polarizer. Through the relative rotation of the polarizer and analyzer, the intensity of the light transmitted by the combination may be controlled.

Figure 15 shows the schematic diagram of the optical parts of the Marten's polarization photometer head, and Fig. 16 shows the complete instrument, including the arrangement of split-beam illumination. In Fig. 15, "two beams of light enter the instrument through two circular apertures, O and O', each approximately 6 mm. in diameter. Both of these beams are polarized by means of the Wollaston prism A, which splits the light into two components, one of which is polarized in a plane perpendicular to that of the plane of polarization of the other. On the upper face of the Wollaston prism is cemented a Fresnel biprism which forms the photometric field. The analyzing prism C is of the Nicol type. The lens L_1 cemented to the lower face of the Wollaston prism is a field lens, while L_2 is the eyepiece lens. The analyzing prism C is supported so that it may be rotated about the optical axis of the instrument, its orientation being indicated by the index I reading on a scale S, which remains in a fixed position relative to the Wollaston prism A. The photometric field as seen by the eye placed at the exit pupil of the eyepiece is circular in shape, divided along a

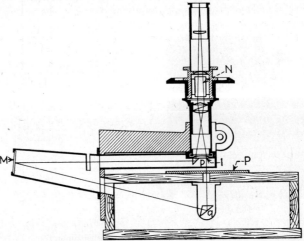

Fig. 16.—Section diagram showing construction of Martens polarization densitometer. The essential parts are: 1, lens for forming an image of subject, M at apex of biprism; M, light source diffusing plate; N, analyzing Nicol prism; P, photographic plate to be measured; p, prism for reflecting light from M to eyepiece; q, prism for reflecting light from M through photographic plate, P, to eyepiece.

diameter by an image of the apex of the biprism B. The field thus consists of two juxtaposed semicircular areas, the relative brightness of the two being controlled by a rotation of the analyzer C. One half of this photometric field is illuminated by light which enters the aperture O, while the other is illuminated by light which enters the aperture O'. If the densities of the two beams entering the instrument are equal, the two halves of the photometric field will be of identical brightness when the index I reads at 45 degrees on the scale S or at a similar position in each of the other three quadrants of the graduated scale S. If an absorbing material is placed over one of the apertures (either O or O') the two parts of the field will no longer be of equal brightness but by rotating the analyzer C the brightness can be restored. The relative brightness of the two parts of the photometric field for any specified angular relationship between the position of the analyzer and the polarizer may be computed by means of the tangent-square law. Hence for any setting which has been made to equalize the brightness of the two fields, after the insertion of the photographic density in one of the two beams, the magnitude of that density may be directly computed."[1]

[1] Jones, L. A., "Photographic Sensitometry," Eastman Kodak Co. (1934).

The instrument shown in Fig. 16 is usually referred to as the Marten's photometer head, and in order to construct a satisfactory instrument for the measurement of density, this must be associated with certain elements suitable for illuminating the photographic density to be measured and for providing the comparison beam. One arrangement for the provision of satisfactory illumination is shown in Fig. 16, in which M represents a ground-glass diffusing surface illuminated to a relatively high level by some external light source placed to the left of M in the figure. The total-reflecting prism p reflects light from M through one of the apertures in the nosepiece of the photometer head, thus serving to provide the comparison beam which illuminates one-half the photometric field. A lens l, mounted as shown just below the nosepiece of the photometer head, forms an image of M approximately in the plane occupied by the apex of the Fresnel biprism. A second total-reflecting prism g reflects light from M through the other aperture of the nosepiece, thus illuminating the other half of the photometer field. The photographic plate or film to be measured is placed in the position as indicated at P. In this arrangement of the Marten's polarization photometer, the illumination of the photographic deposit to be measured is by means of a semispecular beam of light; hence the value of density approaches that of specular density for the deposit in question. By placing a small disk of white pot-opal glass immediately below P, it will be possible to obtain readings of diffuse density. In this case, it will, of course, be necessary to balance the illumination by the insertion of a proper amount of absorbing material in the comparison beam reflected by the small prism p. Under such conditions, it is somewhat difficult to obtain sufficient illumination to read very high densities with precision. The ground glass M may, however, be removed, and by using a light source of high intrinsic brilliancy and a properly designed optical system, a high concentration of light flux may be obtained on the opal glass directly underneath P; in this way more satisfactory results may be obtained in reading high values of diffuse density.

Interpretation of Results.—It now remains to interpret the results of the exposure, development, and density-determining processes which we have gone through for our sensitometric determinations. There are a number of ways in which the results of the sensitometric process may be interpreted, but generally graphical methods of interpretation are most useful and direct.

H and D Characteristic.—The most important relation in photography, so far as concerns the characteristics of photosensitive materials, is that showing the relation between the exposure of the material and the resulting density of the silver deposit. This relation is shown in Fig. 17 by means of the familiar characteristic curve or H and D curves, named in honor of Hurter and Driffield—early research workers in the field of photographic sensitometry. This characteristic curve is obtained by giving the photographic-sensitive material a series of graded exposures, the exposure of one step bearing a known relation to that of the preceding and succeeding steps. The density of each step in the developed silver image is then measured and is plotted against the logarithms (to the base 10) of the corresponding exposures. Because of the scales used, these characteristic curves are sometimes referred to as the D-$\log_{10} E$ curves. One reason for using a logarithmic scale for exposure is because large ranges of exposure values are encountered, and this wide range could not be compressed conveniently into a linear scale. By plotting the density against the logarithm of the exposure, it is found that the characteristic curve begins by curving upward from the zero-density axis. An approximately linear region of the curve then usually follows, especially in the case of negative materials. The curve finally decreases in slope and, after reaching some maximum value, generally decreases in density for extremely large values of exposure. These five regions are commonly known, respectively, as the region of no exposure (AB), the region of under exposure (BC), the region of correct exposure[1] (CD) in which density is proportional to $\log_{10} E$, the region of overexposure (DE), and the region of reversal (EF), since in this last region density decreases rather than increases with increasing exposure.

In the case of many photographic materials, it has been found experimentally that a considerable portion of the H and D curve is represented satisfactorily, within the limits of experimental error, by a straight line. The linear relation between the logarithm of the exposure and the density is of utmost importance in the correct rendering of tone values in black-and-white photography and in the correct rendering of both tone and color in color photography. For the correct proportional rendering of the various object brightnesses in the negative, the camera exposure is usually adjusted so that the straight-line portion of the D-$\log_{10} E$ curve, *i.e.*, the region between C and D, is used. For the fulfillment of this condition the minimum density

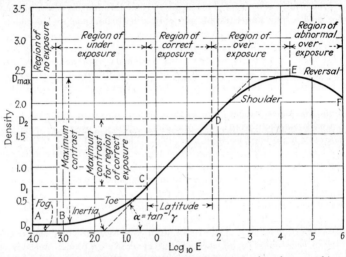

FIG. 17.—Typical D-$\log_{10} E$ or H and D characteristic curve for photographic materials, with important regions specified.

in the negative (corresponding to the deepest shadow in the object) must not be less than that of point B, and the maximum negative density (corresponding to the highest light in the object) must not exceed that of point E.

Latitude.—Projection of the points C and D on the two rectangular axes determines the range in density as well as the exposure range for which linearity between density and log E exists. The exposure range for which this linearity exists is called the latitude of the photographic material. Thus latitude is defined to be

$$L = \log_{10} E_2 - \log_{10} E_1 = \log_{10} \frac{E_2}{E_1} \quad \text{(in } \log_{10} E \text{ units)} \quad (16)$$

$$= \frac{E_2}{E_1} \quad \text{(in exposure units)} \quad (17)$$

[1] The linear portion of the D-$\log_{10} E$ curve is called the region of correct exposure because it is usually desired to have the opacity of the negative directly proportional to the exposure. Thus the usually desired condition is that for which $O = kE$. Since $D = A + \log_{10} O$, the usually desired condition requires that relation between density and exposure be

$$D = A + \log_{10} k + \log_{10} E = B + \log_{10} E$$

which condition is fulfilled by the linear region of the H and D curve.

Of course, it may sometimes be desired to introduce certain forms of distortion intentionally in order to attain artistic or other desired effects. In this case, the straight-line portion would not necessarily represent the region of correct exposure.

The latitude of a photographic material is closely related to the maximum contrast which may be recorded on that material without distortion of tone rendering. For proper tone rendering the maximum contrast C_{max} of a photographic material may be specified as the difference in densities between the extreme ends of the straight-line portion of the H and D curve. If D_2 is the maximum density corresponding to the point D on the straight portion and D_1 is the minimum density on the straight portion of the curve, the maximum contrast for correct tone rendition is

$$C_{max} = D_2 - D_1 \tag{18}$$

But $D_2 = A + \gamma \log_{10} E_2$, and $D_1 = A + \gamma \log_{10} E_1$. Consequently, the maximum contrast may be expressed in terms of the exposure range, and latitude may be expressed as

$$C_{max} = \gamma \log_{10} E_2 - \gamma \log_{10} E_1 = \gamma \log_{10} \frac{E_2}{E_1} \tag{19}$$

$$= \gamma L \tag{20}$$

where L is expressed in $\log_{10} E$ units. In these equations, γ is the slope of the straight-line portion of the D-$\log_{10} E$ characteristic. Attention should be directed to the fact that the L and γ for a given photographic material depend upon the characteristics of material as well as its development. For a given photographic material γ depends on development. The symbols C_{max}, L, and γ refer only to the straight-line portion or linear region of the D-$\log_{10} E$ curve; the extension and the application of these symbols to the curved portions of the characteristic is unwarranted.

Gradient and Gamma.—The gradient or slope of the H and D characteristic is another important factor in specifying the characteristics of photosensitive materials. The gradient of the D-$\log_{10} E$ characteristic is defined as the derivative

$$G = \frac{dD}{d(\log_{10} E)} = \tan \alpha \tag{21}$$

where, as usual, dD represents a differential increment of density, $d(\log_{10} E)$ represents a differential increment of $\log_{10} E$, and α represents the angle between the characteristic curve and the abscissa. In general the gradient is not constant. At the extreme left of the curve, the gradient may begin with a finite value, in the region of underexposure, but builds up to a maximum value in the region of correct exposure represented by the straight line. Beyond the point D the slope (gradient) continually decreases in the region of overexposure until at the point E, representing the maximum density to which the material may be processed, the gradient is zero. Beyond point E the gradient is negative in the region of reversal.

For the straight-line portion of the curve the gradient of any single characteristic curve is constant and is usually defined in terms of the angle α which the line CD makes with the abscissa. The slope of this straight line is designated as

$$G = G_{dc} = \frac{dD}{d(\log_{10} E)} = \tan \alpha = \gamma = \text{constant} \tag{22}$$

Since the region between D and C is constant, we may replace the differentials by finite differences and write

$$\gamma = \frac{\Delta D}{\Delta \log_{10} E}. \tag{23}$$

Thus, if D_2 and D_1 are the density differences corresponding to exposures of E_2 and E_1 (in meter-candle-seconds), then so long as these two points D_1-$\log_{10} E_1$ and D_2-$\log_{10}$

E_2 fall on the straight-line portion of the curve, γ can be calculated from the relation

$$\gamma = \frac{(D_2 - D_1)}{(\log_{10} E_2 - \log_{10} E_1)} \tag{24}$$

$$= \frac{D_2 - D_1}{\log_{10} E_2/E_1}. \tag{25}$$

Although γ is given as the tangent of the angle α, it should be realized that the true value of γ cannot be determined by measuring (by means of a protractor, for example) the slope of the curve. The reason for this is that the choice of the scales in the graphical plot affects the slope of the curve as plotted but does not affect the relation between the corresponding density and exposure values. From this last relation we are able to calculate, for the straight-line portion of the curve, differences in density produced by exposure increments, when γ is known. Thus

$$\Delta D = \gamma(\Delta \log_{10} E) = D_2 - D_1 = \gamma\left(\log_{10} \frac{E_2}{E_1}\right) \tag{26}$$

Inertia.—The extension of the straight line DC to the axis of 0 density defines the inertia of the photographic material. The inertia i thus represents the

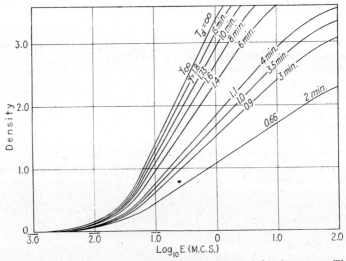

Fig. 18.—Family of D-$\log_{10} E$ curves for different times of development. The γ corresponding to the development time T is specified for each curve.

minimum exposure which produces a deposit of silver, under the assumption that the H and D characteristic is a straight line down to zero density.

So far we have been considering a single D-$\log_{10} E$ curve which, for purposes of simplicity, has been somewhat idealized. However, it has already been mentioned that the particular H and D curve for a given material depends, not only on the photographic material itself, but also on the processing conditions. Furthermore, certain of the idealized conditions which have been implicitly assumed do not always occur in practice, and the deviation from the ideal case requires further study.

To study the effects of nonidealized conditions and of processing on the characteristics of photographic sensitive materials, consider the family of H and D curves of Fig. 18. These curves represent a series of D-$\log_{10} E$ curves as might be obtained for some practical photographic material. The region of reversal is not included in these curves, as it is of no practical importance.

The various individual curves of the family of Fig. 18 have been plotted for varying times of development. The lowest curve is for a development time of 2 min., and the highest curve represents development time of 15 min.

The finite density for very low values of exposure represents density due to development and other types of fog. It is at once apparent, as might be expected, that the fog density increases with the time of development. Although fog occurs in all practical cases (it may be relatively low for certain types of emulsions), fog does not contribute anything useful to the image but merely provides a deposit of silver uniformly over the surface. For this reason the curves often published by manufacturers are "corrected for fog" by subtracting the amount of fog density—assumed constant for all values of exposure—from the measured density at any specified

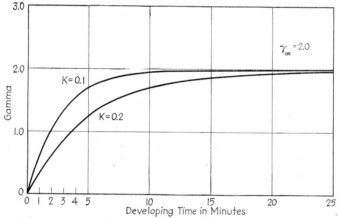

Fig. 19.—Time-gamma curves for typical photographic materials for two different values of development constant k.

exposure value. The effect of this fog correction is to shift all the curves somewhat lower on the density scale. For such fog-corrected characteristics the density indicated by the ordinates is, not the absolute value of density of the photographic material, but rather the density due to exposure in excess of the fog density. If the fog density is very small, as in the case of process or lantern-slide materials, the corrected and uncorrected family of curves may not differ appreciably. The difference between curves which are or are not corrected for fog will be much greater, however, in the case of many panchromatic materials which have inherently greater fog.

Time-gamma Curves.—It will be seen from Fig. 18 that the increase in gamma is not a linear function of the development time. Instead γ increases fairly rapidly with time for low values of development time, but as the development time increases, the increment in per unit of time decreases. Ultimately, the characteristic curves approach a definite value of gamma when the time of development is infinitely long. The value of the maximum gradient, or G_{max}, for infinitely long development time is known as "gamma infinity" and is represented by the symbol γ_∞. If we plot γ against the time of development T_d, the manner in which γ increases with developing time will become more evident. The γ-T_d curve of Fig. 19 shows this relationship, from which it is evident that, as T_d is prolonged, γ approaches a limiting value which is designated γ_∞ and commonly spoken of as gamma infinity. The value of gamma infinity is of considerable significance in both the practical and theoretical aspects of sensitometry.

The time-gamma curves are often useful in the processing of photographic materials. It has already been indicated that a desirable relation between the density of the silver deposit and the brightness of the image is attained for a value of gamma equal to unity. Therefore, if a time-gamma curve for a particular type of photosensitive material and developer is available, reference to the γ-T_d curve will indicate immediately the development time required to give this value of gamma. The time-gamma curves for the same photographic material for two values of k are given in Fig. 19. The ultimate value of gamma attained, however, γ_∞, is shown as being the same in both cases, although this is not always necessarily true.

If development proceeds in accordance with a simple law of physical chemistry, as it does for many materials, at least approximately, it can be shown that, theoretically, the time-gamma curve is related to the maximum value of gamma through the equation

$$\gamma = \gamma_\infty(1 - e^{-kt}) \tag{27}$$

where k = the constant of development;

t = the time of development;

γ_∞ = the maximum value of gamma to which the photographic material can be developed.

This equation holds for many types of materials, although the validity of these theoretical relationships in practice depends upon the degree to which the actual H and D curve conforms with the theoretical or ideal family of H and D curves.

From this last equation, the value of γ_∞ can be determined if we know the value of γ which is obtained for a development time t, when development has been carried on with a developer whose development constant is k. Thus

$$\gamma_\infty = \frac{\gamma}{1 - e^{-kt}} \tag{28}$$

Often, however, the value of the development constant is not known with sufficient precision to be useful in the above equation for the determination of gamma infinity. In such cases γ_∞ may be determined from the measurements made on two density strips, both of which have been processed together in the same solution, but for different lengths of time. For these conditions, we have, for the first sensitometric strips processed for time t_1,

$$\gamma_1 = \gamma_\infty(1 - e^{-kt_1}) \tag{29}$$

and for the second strip developed for time t_2,

$$\gamma_2 = \gamma_\infty(1 - e^{-kt_2}) \tag{30}$$

If we process the second strip twice as long as the first strip, then $t_2 = 2t_1$, and the equation for γ_2 becomes

$$\gamma_2 = \gamma_\infty(1 - e^{-2kt_1}) = \gamma_\infty[1 - (e^{-kt_1})^2] \tag{31}$$

Combining these two equations for γ_1 and γ_2, we obtain

$$\frac{\gamma_2 - \gamma_1}{\gamma_1} = e^{-kt_1} \tag{32}$$

from which the development constant is found to be,

$$k = \frac{1}{t_1} \log_e\left(\frac{\gamma}{\gamma_2 - \gamma_1}\right) \tag{33}$$

Certain development characteristics of any particular photographic material may be deduced from the values of γ and k. The following table is prepared from material on this subject by L. A. Jones.

TABLE IV.—EFFECT OF k AND γ ON NEGATIVE

k	γ	Effect on development	Effect on gamma
High	High	Starts quickly and proceeds at a high rate. Image may be built up to high contrast by continued development	Builds up to a high value (process plates typical example)
High	Low	Image flashes up quickly but does not build up to high densities	Builds up quickly but soon ceases to increase. Reaches relatively low limiting value
Low	High	Development starts slowly, but by continued development high densities may be obtained	Builds up gradually at low rate, but with extended development time high values of are obtained
Low	Low	Development starts slowly. Image does not build up to high contrast	Increases at a relatively low rate which soon decreases, approaching low value as limiting factor. Further development does not increase contrast

Time of Development for Required Gamma.—Sometimes it is required to know the development time to obtain a given value of γ. Provided the development constant is known [or can be calculated from Eq. (33)], the development time can be determined from the equation

$$\gamma = \gamma_\infty(1 - e^{-kt}) = \gamma_\infty - \gamma_\infty e^{-kt} \tag{34}$$

$$\frac{\gamma_\infty - \gamma}{\gamma_\infty} = e^{-kt} \tag{35}$$

Taking the natural logarithm of both sides, dividing by k, and making all values positive, we obtain

$$t = \frac{1}{k} \log_e \left(\frac{\gamma_\infty}{\gamma_\infty - \gamma}\right) \tag{36}$$

It is therefore seen that the time of development depends upon the value of γ to which the material is processed, as well as upon the maximum value of γ of the material. For purposes of preparing tables showing relative sensitometric characteristics of photographic materials, a value of gamma equal to unity is arbitrarily chosen. The time of development to attain unity gamma is expressed symbolically as $T_{\gamma=1}$ and is given by

$$T_{\gamma=1} = \frac{1}{k} \log_e \left(\frac{\gamma_\infty}{\gamma_\infty - 1}\right) \tag{37}$$

If γ_∞ is less than unity, this equation has no meaning, as evidenced by the fact that $T_{\gamma=1}$ will then be negative.

Spectral Sensitivity of Photographic Materials.—No treatment of the subject of photographic sensitometry would be complete without some mention of the spectral sensitivity of photographic materials or the relative sensitivity to radiations of various colors or wavelengths and the methods of determining spectral sensitivity. This is especially true since panchromatic materials have come into extensive use. The recent introduction of practical forms of color films also makes desirable a treatment of spectral sensitivity of photographic materials.

A knowledge of the way in which sensitivity of photographic materials is distributed throughout the spectrum is of importance from the practical as well as the theoretical points of view. In monochrome photography the spectral sensitivity of the negative material completely governs the monochrome brightness of the colors in the original image, although filters may be used to modify spectral characteristics of the negative. The rendition of color in color photographic processes is determined largely by the spectral sensitivity of the negative material. It is well known, for example, that in black-and-white photography fairly pure red, orange and yellow are rendered in about the same tone value as black with ordinary blue-sensitive materials. In the case of some panchromatic materials which have been rendered very sensitive to the longer wavelengths of visible radiations, these same colors may be rendered as almost white. The correct rendering of colored objects on the black-to-white tone scale, which represents the entire discrimination gamut of the photographic process, is conditioned almost entirely by the spectral sensitivity of the material. It is evident, therefore, that a knowledge of the spectral sensitivity characteristic of photographic materials which determines responses such as are mentioned above, is of great importance wherever monochrome or color rendering of colored objects is to be considered.

A brief outline of the historical development of the determination of spectral sensitivity is given by Jones.[1]

Methods of Determining Color Response.—All the available methods used for determining the spectral sensitivity or color response of photographic materials involve the isolation of more or less narrow spectral bands. These bands are then impressed on the photographic material under specified exposure conditions. The response produced when the photosensitive material is exposed to these more or less homogeneous radiations is then observed either qualitatively or quantitatively. For this observation a wide variety of spectral instruments has been devised. Suitable instruments include monochromatic sensitometers, spectrographs, tricolor tablets, ratiometers, color charts, and filter assemblies. The methods for producing the required spectral bands may be grouped into (1) dispersion radiation methods and (2) methods using filters and white light. The dispersion methods make use of some suitable dispersion element such as a prism or grating and may be roughly classified into two types, depending upon what proportion of the spectrum acts on the photographic material at a given time. In one classification, only a narrow band of the spectrum is exposed to the photosensitive material, and the type of instrument used to provide the necessary narrow band of radiant energy is a monochromatic sensitometer. In the other classification, which may make use of a spectrograph, the entire visible spectrum—or a fairly large part of the spectrum—may be used in exposing the photographic material. Since the method of operation is different and since the results in these two cases are expressible in different ways, it seems desirable to give some brief consideration to these two dispersion methods.

Dispersion Method Using Monochromatic Sensitometer.—In the dispersion method using a monochromatic sensitometer, radiation of high spectral purity—as obtained from a grating, prism, or double prism—is permitted to expose the photographic material for varying lengths of time, corresponding to varying exposures. The time of exposure is varied by some suitable mechanism, a satisfactory method being that in which a slotted sector disk provides varying exposures when it is rotated. A monochromatic sensitometer operating on this principle and described by Jones and Sand-

---

[1] JONES, L. A., "Photographic Sensitometry," Eastman Kodak Co. (1934).

vik[1], makes use of a disk so cut as to produce 12 exposures, each of which is twice the duration of the preceding one. The total range of exposures is 2048 to 1 for a complete rotation of this disk. The absolute values of exposure are determined by the velocity with which the disk rotates and the intensity of the energy impinging upon the plate. The radiant energy acting upon the photographic plate is measured by means of a thermopile placed in the same plane as that of the material being exposed.

Except for the radiation-dispersion system and the greater sensitivity and refinements necessary because monochromatic rather than heterochromatic radiations are being measured, the monochromatic sensitometer is similar to the ordinary sensitometer; the exposed test strips obtained are similar to those of the ordinary type of sensitometer. The exposed strip is developed under standardized conditions, and the densities corresponding to the various exposure conditions are determined in the manner already described. Where it is necessary to study the effects of developing conditions, a series of strips is made under identical exposure conditions, but the conditions of development are altered as may be required. With a series of such strips, representing various conditions of exposure and development at any given monochromatic radiation, the characteristics of the photographic material for that radiation may be determined. By making other observations at different wavelengths, the complete wavelength-exposure-density characteristics of the material may be determined. The results may be plotted in the usual manner as a family of D-$\log_{10} E$ characteristics or as gamma-development time curves except for the manner in which the radiant energy of exposure is specified.

In the ordinary methods of sensitometry, exposure values are given in terms of the meter-candle-second for a white light source. A white light source has no significance in monochromatic sensitometry, so that some other unit of measurement is needed. The unit of exposure which has been most widely adapted for this purpose is the erg. Since the photographic material integrates more or less perfectly the energy which falls upon it over a period of time, it is necessary, of course, to include the time factor, and in expressing photographic exposure in energy units it is necessary to multiply the rate at which energy falls upon the surface (radiant flux density) by the time during which the exposure persists. Exposure, therefore, must be expressed in terms of ergs (or other suitable energy units) per unit area.

The monochromatic sensitometric data may be plotted in the usual manner except that curves for each monochromatic radiation will be obtained instead of a single set of data corresponding to white light radiation. If several H and D curves are plotted for varying wavelengths of monochromatic radiation, it will be found that the D-$\log_{10} E$ curves vary, depending upon the wavelength at which measurements were determined. If families of D-$\log_{10} E$ curves are available, the characteristics of the photographic material may be plotted as a function of the wavelength of radiation. The curve of Fig. 20 shows the gamma versus wavelength plot for varying development conditions, whereas Fig. 21 shows a family of H and D curves, one curve being determined for each of several wavelengths of monochromatic radiation.

With a set of data available showing density and gamma as a function of exposure, developing conditions, and various monochromatic radiations, it is possible to determine the relative spectral sensitivity of the material. Several possible methods are available for expressing spectral sensitivity. We might, for example, compute spectral sensitivity in terms of the reciprocal inertia for various monochromatic radiation measurements in much the same way as sensitivity for a white light source is specified in the H and D system. We might define spectral sensitivity in terms of the energy required to give a specified value of density (say unity) for a fixed time of development,

· JONES, L. A., and O. SANDVIK, Spectral Distribution of Sensitivity of Photographic Materials, *J. Optical Soc. Am.*, **12**, 401, 484 (1926).

but the results in this case will not be directly comparable with those determined in the first instance.

For theoretical purposes there is considerable argument for defining spectral sensitivity in terms of the energy required to give a density of unity when development

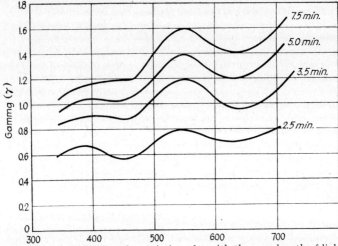

FIG. 20.—Typical curves showing the variation of γ with the wavelength of light, for the development times indicated. The wavelengths of light are measured in millimicrons.

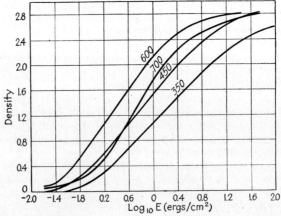

FIG. 21.—D-$\log_{10} E$ characteristics of typical negative material, measured at four different wavelengths, for identical processing conditions. In general the γ increases with the wavelength, and this fact has important practical considerations in color photography.

for all wavelengths is carried out to a gamma of unity. For practical purposes, however, it seems that the evaluation of spectral sensitivity in terms of a fixed development time is more suitable, and, in order to discount somewhat the misleading effects of gamma variation, it seems probable that the determination of the energy per unit area of the photosensitive material required to give a density of unity, for a fixed time of development, is most satisfactory as a mode of expressing spectral sensitivity. The most suitable development time is probably that which produces on a sensitometric strip exposed to white light a gamma approximately equal to that at which the material is usually developed in practice. In Fig. 20 is shown a spectral-sensitivity curve determined in this manner. This is for high-speed panchromatic motion-picture film, the development time used being that which gives a gamma of 0.7 on a white-light sensitometric strip.

"It should be borne in mind that the spectral sensitivity curve, when plotted in accordance with the specifications given in this section, represents the characteristics of the photographic material itself, quite apart from any consideration of the energy distribution in the light source used."[1] The curve of Fig. 20 shows the spectral sensitivity when used with a hypothetical light source emitting equal amounts of energy at all wavelengths, and corresponding, therefore, to ideal white light. If it is desired to determine the effective spectral response when used with some other light source in which the spectral-energy distribution deviated from this equal-energy distribution, it will be necessary to compute a new family of characteristic curves showing the effective spectral sensitivity of the photographic material when used with the desired light source. These effective spectral sensitivity curves may be computed

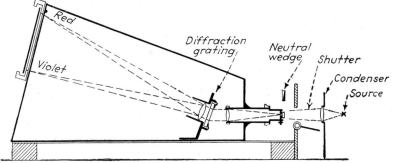

Fig. 22.—Optical system for wedge spectrograph for making determinations of spectral sensitivity of films when used with specified light source. This method does not determine absolute film characteristics, but relates them to the light source employed in making the measurements.

from the spectral sensitivity for curves of an ideal white light source and the curve of spectral-energy distribution of the light source actually used. The method of determining spectral sensitivity by means of monochromatic sensitometers, although precise, is tedious and time consuming.

Dispersion Methods Using Wedges with Spectroscopes.—More rapid, although less accurate, methods of determining the relative spectral response characteristics of photographic materials have been devised in which a spectrum, such as that from a prism or grating, is permitted to fall on a film after having passed through a neutral density wedge of constant gradient. The wedge is so placed with respect to the spectrum that it attenuates all portions of the spectrum equally well. This is accomplished by spreading out the spectrum in one direction and by placing the wedge so that its density contours are perpendicular to the wavelength scale. Figure 22 shows the essential elements in such a wedge spectrogram method of determining the spectral characteristics of emulsions.

The wedge spectrogram method has the advantage of speed and simplicity and gives in graphic form good indications of the relative spectral sensitivity of the photographic material. A typical wedge spectrogram is shown in Fig. 23.

[1] Jones, L. A., "Photographic Sensitometry," Eastman Kodak Co. (1934).

from which it will be seen that the transition edges are not sharply defined. By making a series of successive positive and negative prints of the original wedge spectrogram, using photographic materials and developers producing high contrast, it is possible to sharpen this edge to obtain a negative or positive in which this edge is rather clearly defined.   This procedure is seldom used, however, for it is customary to inspect the results directly from the original wedge spectrogram, determining from this visual inspection the relative sensitivity at various wavelengths.   In the original wedge spectrogram, the relative sensitivity will be indicated by the amount of silver deposit and the extent of blackening of the negative; the examples shown are prints made from original wedge-spectrogram negatives.

It should be noted that the results obtained in this case represent, not only the spectral-sensitivity characteristics of the photographic material, but the combined results of the photographic sensitivity and the spectral-energy distribution of the light source.   Thus, the wedge spectrogram represents the spectral photicity of the material for the given light source and provides curves which are at variance with those which may be obtained by methods using monochromatic sensitometers.

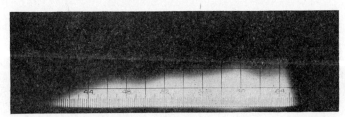

Fig. 23.—Typical wedge spectrogram for panchromatic material.

The wedge used over the slit in Fig. 22 has a linear and constant density gradient, and therefore the distribution of radiation along the slit increases logarithmically from one end of the slit to the other.   The resultant envelope curves are thus logarithmic in form and cannot be compared directly with the curves obtained by monochromatic sensitometric methods.   It should also be kept in mind that, if the wedge is not completely a neutral gray over the range of wavelengths for which the light source produces radiations and the photographic material is sensitive, then the overall wedge spectrograms will be affected by the selective absorption of the wedge.   For wavelengths below about 450 mμ wedges have appreciable selective absorption, so that the apparent decrease in sensitivity of photographic materials at the short visible wavelengths is partly due to selective absorption of the wedge.

Stepped wedges, rather than constant-gradient wedges, have also been used and have been found to be useful where it is desired to make density measurements directly from such spectrograms.   If the wedge is removed completely, the density of the silver deposit will give an indication of the spectral sensitivity of the photographic material when used with the given light source.   In this case, measurements of the amount of silver deposit at various wavelengths by means of a microdensitometer enable spectral-photicity curves to be obtained.

Selective Absorption Methods.—The spectral sensitivity of a photographic material as determined by the methods of monochromatic sensitometry and by the usual spectrographic technique is most conveniently and almost necessarily expressed graphically, the usual mode being a curve showing sensitivity as a function of wave length.   It is almost impossible to express the information relative to the spectral sensitivity as derived by these methods in brief numerical terms.   It is frequently desirable to sacrifice some of the precision of the methods already discussed for less precise methods in order to obtain a more simple specification expressible in a few numerical terms of the spectral sensitivity of the photographic material. A common numerical method of specifying the color sensitivity makes use of the relative sensitivity of the photographic material to a fairly wide range of wavelengths in a given region of the visible spectrum. In order to isolate the desired regions of the spectrum, selective filters are commonly employed.

Probably the most widely used and the most useful method of this type involves the use of three filters having such selective absorption characteristics as to divide the spectrum into three broad bands, each having approximately the same range of wavelengths. In the ideal case a set of tricolor filters for this type of work might have complete transmission between the ranges of 400 to 500 mμ, 500 to 600 mμ, and 600 to 700 mμ, respectively, with very sharp cutoffs and complete absorption outside the three transmission ranges. Such filters would not diminish the intensity of the light in their transmission band because of the ideal transmission characteristics which have been assumed. By exposing four test strips of a given photographic material to a given light source properly, a tricolor specification for the spectral photicity of the photographic material may be obtained. In order to do this, one of the test strips should be exposed through each of the three tricolor filters, while the fourth strip should be exposed directly to the light source without the use of any filter. The test strips are processed in the usual manner, and the density of silver deposit on the four strips is determined. The test strip for which no filter was provided will be the densest, since all the spectral energy of the light fell upon it. Let the density of this test strip be D_0. Let the density of the test strips be D_1, D_2, and D_3, for the green, blue, and red filters whose transmission bands are 400 to 500 mμ, 500 to 600 mμ, and 600 to 700 mμ, respectively. Then the tricolor sensitivity of the photographic material (when used with the given light source) may be determined as follows:

$$\frac{D_1}{D_0} = S_1 \tag{38}$$

$$\frac{D_2}{D_0} = S_2 \tag{39}$$

$$\frac{D_3}{D_0} = S_3 \tag{40}$$

In practice, of course, such ideal filters as have been assumed do not exist and do not transmit unabsorbed all wavelengths in their transmission bands. Because of the absorption in the transmission band, it is necessary to multiply the ideal factors or sensitivities, as given above, by multiplying factors K_1, K_2, and K_3 (each less than unity), which factors represent the mean transmission of the practical filter in the transmission region.

A typical set of filters for tricolor work, such as might be used for determining the tricolor sensitivity of photographic materials, are the Wratten No. 25, Wratten No. 58, and Wratten No. 49 filters. The approximate factors for these filters are, respectively, $K_1 = 0.8$, $K_2 = 0.3$, and $K_3 = 0.15$. Consequently, if these filters are used with the four test strips to give a specification of the tricolor sensitivity of photographic materials used with a given light source, the sensitivities may be expressed as

$$\frac{K_1 D_1}{D_0} = S_1 \tag{41}$$

$$\frac{K_2 D_2}{D_0} = S_2 \tag{42}$$

$$\frac{K_3 D_3}{D_0} = S_3 \tag{43}$$

Here, as with the case of the spectral sensitivity determined by means of the wedge spectrograph, the results obtained are the spectral photicity of the material, *i.e.*, the relative sensitivity evaluated according to the light source used in the measurements, rather than the absolute sensitivity of the photographic material. However, it is ordinarily the spectral photicity, rather than the absolute spectral sensitivity of the material, which is of greater practical importance.

The method of determining the tricolor sensitivity of a photographic material through the use of three filters which divide the spectrum into three approximately equal broad bands may be extended, if desired, so that the spectral response at more than three points may be determined. The procedure is the same as that already outlined, except that more filters (usually "monochromatic" filters) are used to determine the relative response at various wavelengths. Comparison with the test strip for which no filter was used will enable the relative sensitivity to be determined for the wavelength band which the filter transmits. The results obtained in this manner can be expressed numerically, but the method becomes laborious and time consuming and is not very precise.

A similar method of determining the relative spectral-response characteristic of photographic materials is available through the use of progressive cut filters, which may be used to isolate various regions of the spectrum for the determination of the relative spectral response in the transmission range. The disadvantages of this system are similar to those enumerated above. This method has been used where a monochromatic spectrophotometer or a wedge spectrograph is not available but otherwise has little practical use.

Speed or Sensitivity.—By speed or sensitivity of a photosensitive material is meant the amount of radiant energy required to produce a stipulated density or density difference. It has already been mentioned that the characteristics of the D-$\log_{10} E$ curve depend to a marked extent upon the processing to which the photographic material is subjected. For the complete specification of the H and D characteristics of a photographic material, a family of D-$\log_{10} E$ curves is required. Therefore it is evident that no single numeric or "figure of merit" can completely and adequately specify the characteristics of the material. Nevertheless, several different methods of expressing sensitivity or speed by means of a single quantity have been developed and are more or less widely used in this country as well as in Europe. Because of the fact that the true speed and sensitivity of the material depends upon the processing and because the processing conditions in actual use frequently differ widely from those for which the speed determinations were made, the absolute values of film speeds have little significance. Relative speeds, as determined by the same manufacturer for different types of emulsions of his manufacture, have somewhat greater significance. Speed ratings of one manufacturer may not be comparable with those of another.

It should be pointed out that the comparison of various types of photographic sensitive materials on a basis of speed or sensitivity is a problem which not only is difficult but which has not yet been completely and satisfactorily solved. Several methods of determining speed or sensitivity of photosensitive materials are available, and each system has its advantages and shortcomings. In most of the systems the speed rating is affected by conditions of processing, and this introduces complications of a practical nature, tending to mitigate against too wide dissemination of speed ratings by manufacturers who find themselves in a competitive field. Because of the lack of any generally accepted and recognized standard of speed, manufacturers are sometimes reluctant to give speed ratings of their photographic materials. Moreover, the various methods of rating speed do not give comparable results, and for this reason, the tables of film speeds which are published should be regarded merely as qualitative and approximate.

Several methods for assigning to every kind of emulsion an arbitrary number to serve as an index of its relative speed have been devised. In each system the number increases with the speed or sensitivity of the emulsion, but the different systems are rather inconsistent and do not produce results which are comparable with one another because of the different speed criteria used. The most widely used systems for determining sensitivity of emulsions are based on:

1. The threshold speed, which was the earliest method of specifying film or plate characteristics.

2. Inertia speed, a later method introduced by Hurter and Driffield.

3. Latitude-inertia speed, which is coming more and more into common use.

4. Minimum useful gradient speed.

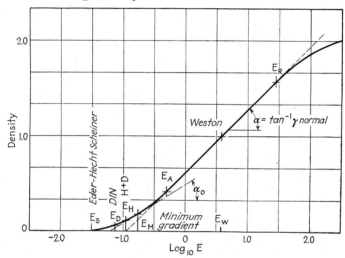

Fig. 24.—D-$\log_{10} E$ characteristic and the exposure values from which a number of well-known speed systems are determined. This curve is used only for purposes of illustration and does not represent the characteristic of any particular material.

Threshold-speed Ratings.—In methods of sensitometry which do not involve the measurement of the densities of the developed strip, the only possible means of determining speed is to note the exposure required to produce a density which is just perceptible. Actually fog density is always present to a greater or lesser extent and will contribute to the minimum perceptible density, so that what is usually determined is the minimum perceptible density difference due to exposure and fog. A further disadvantage of this method is that the minimum perceptible density depends greatly upon the conditions under which inspection is made. Consequently, unless the density determinations are made under carefully controlled and standardized conditions, the values of threshold speed obtained by different observers, from the same test strip, may differ widely.

The earliest method of determining the sensitivity or speed of photographic materials made use of the threshold sensitivity. By threshold sensitivity is meant the minimum exposure which will result in a detectable deposit of silver, as represented by the exposure E_s in Fig. 24. This method is based on the assumption that an emulsion having a low threshold exposure will be a relatively fast emulsion. The most familiar speed ratings based upon the threshold speed are the Scheiner ratings, the Eder-Hecht speeds, and the DIN numbers, of which the latter is a modification of the threshold-speed method.

The Scheiner ratings are derived from the Scheiner type of sensitometer which employs a sector wheel having a continuously graded, rather than a stepped, exposure variation. The aperture of the original Scheiner sensitometer was bounded by a continuous logarithmic curve arranged so that the maximum aperture was 100 times as large as the minimum. A linear scale, divided from 1 to 20 in equally spaced units, was placed along the slot aperture, so that the 20 sensitometric steps corresponded to a sensitivity or speed range of 100 to 1. This scale was placed between the rotating sector of the sensitometer and the photosensitive material, so that the images of reference cross lines, together with the Scheiner numbers, appeared on the plate after exposure and development of the sensitometric strip. Because of this arrangement the Scheiner speed scale consists of numbers in arithmetic progression from 1 to 20, corresponding to a speed or sensitivity range of from 1 to 100. In the Scheiner type of sensitometer the larger numbers represent denser deposits of silver produced during exposure. The speed or sensitivity of the material was expressed by the densest line or number which could be read. The relative sensitivity given by any specified number in the Scheiner rating is 1.27 times as great as the sensitivity represented by the next lower number in the Scheiner scale.

The Austrian Eder-Hecht speed is similar to the German Scheiner rating in that an arithmetic progression of the speed numbers represents a geometric progression of relative sensitivity or speed. The Eder-Hecht sensitometer consists of a continuously graduated density wedge, behind which the photosensitive material is placed for an exposure of specified intensity and duration. Across this wedge, lines representing density contours are ruled. The lines are numbered so that the greatest density of the Eder-Hecht wedge is represented by the largest numbers. The density gradient of the Eder-Hecht wedge is stated by Jones to be 0.4 density units per centimeter but the tablets are not very precise and discrepancies between wedge calibration is frequent. If it is assumed that the wedge has a uniform density gradient, an arithmetic progression of speed numbers represents a geometric progression of relative sensitivity or speed. In this respect, at least, the Scheiner and Eder-Hecht ratings are similar. However, the actual numbers used to designate the sensitivity of a particular film in the two systems are considerably at variance.

Although the method of sensitometry which makes use of the minimum detectable deposit of density is simple and requires no sensitometric measuring equipment, the system is not a very satisfactory one and has several inherent and serious disadvantages. The main objection to this system is that it is difficult to determine the exposure for which a "just detectable" density is produced. Even if it were not difficult to determine minimum detectable density, the shape of the D-$\log_{10} E$ curve is such that the point E_s of Fig. 24 cannot be determined accurately. Furthermore the speed rating is determined from the characteristics of the D-$\log_{10} E$ curve at the foot of the curve corresponding to underexposure. The ratings based on minimum detectable density differences consequently do not give any information for the region of correct exposure, nor do they give any information relating to the extreme upper portions of the H and D curve. It is perfectly possible, therefore, that the minimum detectable density may be due to fog rather than intentional exposure. It is also possible for two emulsions having widely varying D-$\log_{10} E$ curves to produce fog density at the same minimum exposure. Thus, whereas the two films might bear the same Scheiner or Eder-Hecht ratings, their D-$\log_{10} E$ characteristics could easily be quite dissimilar. The Scheiner rating system has found extensive use, especially in Europe, despite its obvious disadvantages.

A modification of the threshold-sensitivity method which overcomes the difficulty of determining the minimum detectable density is the Deutsche Industrial Normal rating system. This is usually referred to as the DIN system. According to the

DIN system, the reference value adopted is the exposure required to produce a density of 0.1, *i.e.*, an opacity of 1.26 or a transmission of 0.79, represented by the point E_D on the curve of Fig. 24 when the test strip is subjected to a specific development procedure. This criterion obviates the first objection to the Scheiner and Eder-Hecht systems, since it determines the index from a precise, definitely specified and measured density rather than from an estimation of barely perceptible fogging. In practice the emulsion is exposed through a step wedge, which is a plate in which successive steps differ in density by a constant amount. The various steps are numbered, and the number corresponding to the step which produces a density of 0.1 is the DIN number. Like the Scheiner and Eder-Hecht systems, however, the DIN system ignores the general form of the D-$\log_{10} E$ curve. The DIN rating is based upon data taken in the region of underexposure. The speed numbers are determined through the use of developing technique which gives the greatest film sensitivity.

Inertia-speed Ratings.—A considerable improvement over the threshold sensitivity of specifying emulsion speed was made by Hurter and Driffield, who suggested that the speed of a photographic material could be specified satisfactorily in terms of its inertia. Thus they adopted as their criterion of speed the exposure indicated by the extension of the straight-line portion of the D-$\log E$ curve to the axis of zero density, the corresponding exposure being the inertia of the photosensitive material. By so doing, they took into account the shape of the H and D curve in the region of correct exposure. The exposure E_h of Fig. 24, corresponding to the extension of the linear portion of the D-$\log E$ curve to the exposure axis, is called the "inertia" of the emulsion, and the inertia value is frequently referred to as i. Hurter and Driffield proposed to specify the speed or sensitivity S by the relation

$$S = \frac{k}{i} \qquad (44)$$

where i = the inertia of the photographic material E_h;

k = an arbitrarily determined constant.

Hurter and Driffield originally chose the value 34 for k since, at the time they made their researches, this figure gave speed values for practical materials which were convenient in magnitude. However, other values for k have been used, the number 10 being in common use.

Hurter and Driffield used the inertia as a measure of film speed since they took this point to be indicative of the beginning of the region of correct exposure and proper tone rendition. The H and D speed rating is, therefore, a system of numbers proportional to the inertia values through the factor k. An essential difference between the Hurter and Driffield system and the methods based on threshold speeds is that the inertia is determined from measurements at several points on the curve, while in the threshold or one-tenth-density systems, sensitivity is determined from a single observation. In this respect the H and D system is the more rational procedure since the Scheiner, Eder-Hecht, and DIN systems ignore the linear portion of the curve. However, the H and D system gives no indication of the latitude or exposure range of the photographic material.

Figure 25 shows how two emulsions could have the same threshold but different inertia. Thus, according to the Scheiner system, both would have the same speed, while, according to the H and D system, one emulsion would be much faster than the other. On the other hand, the H and D system ignores completely the foot of the curve. However, there are times when it is desirable to permit a portion of the image to extend into this region. In the H and D system the relation of speed to index number is linear, while in the Scheiner system it is not. Thus, 26° Scheiner indicates a speed twice that of the 23° Scheiner, while 1300 H and D is twice as fast as 650 H and D.

The Watkins speed scale, like the H and D, is based on the inertia of the photographic material but uses for k the number 68 instead of 34 chosen by Hurter and Driffield or the value 10 frequently used in the United States. However, L. A. Jones ("Photographic Sensitometry") reports that the Watkins constant, as determined from measurements on emulsions, is more nearly 50 than 68.

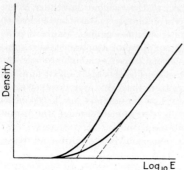

Fig. 25.—D-$\log_{10} E$ curves showing that two emulsions might have the same threshold speed (as determined by the point at which their curves reach the abscissa) but quite different inertia values. The differences are due to the curvature of the toe of the curves.

The Wynne system is another one of several in which plate speed is specified in terms of inertia and differs from the others in the units selected for the specification of film or plate speed. The numbers of the Wynne system are expressed in terms of lens aperture, as indicated by the symbol F which precedes the Wynne speed number. The Wynne ratings are proportional to the square root of the Watkins number multiplied by 6.4. Thus a Watkins speed of 64 corresponds to a Wynne speed of 51.2.

For many purposes and under many conditions, the expression of speed in terms of inertia is of great value. As long as all the straight-line portions of a family of D-$\log_{10} E$ curves pass through a common intersection point which lies on the $\log_{10} E$ axis, inertia and hence speed are independent of development time. Under such

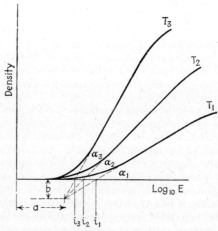

Fig. 26.—D-$\log_{10} E$ curves with depressed common intersection point, illustrating that the inertia speed of a film may depend upon the degree of development which it receives.

conditions the speed becomes a very significant constant for the photographic material. Unfortunately, the existence of a common intersection point lying upon the $\log_{10} E$ axis is frequently not found in practice. In most cases of normal development a common intersection point is found, provided that proper corrections have been made for fog. This intersection point very frequently lies below the $\log_{10} E$ axis and in relatively rare cases is located above that axis. Assuming for the moment that a common intersection point does exist, its coordinates may be represented by a and b as shown in Fig. 26, and it has been proposed to define the speed of the material in terms of the coordinates of this point. Under such conditions it is evident that the inertia is a function of gamma, and hence speed based upon inertia value will become a function of gamma. A speed value of this nature can only be significant provided the corresponding gamma value is specified. For the purpose of certain theoretical investigations into the nature of exposure and development, a knowledge of the coordinates of the intersection point, as shown in Fig. 26, may be of great value, but it does not appear to be very significant for the purpose of determining the practical speeds.

Another difficulty with this method of specifying emulsion speeds is that some photographic materials do not have a common point of intersection for the various D-$\log_{10} E$ curves, and some materials—especially some positive printing papers—do not have a very satisfactory straight-line relation between density and the logarithm of the exposure. There is also a wide divergence in the relative shape of the curve in the region of underexposure.

Latitude-inertia Method of Speed Determination.—A modification of the inertia-speed ratings, which is in reality another method of rating film speed, is the method in which the speed is specified in terms of the inertia as well as the latitude of the emulsion.

In the Weston system of film-speed rating, which has found wide acceptance in the United States, the speed is determined from the D-$\log_{10} E$ characteristic of the film, processed to the value of gamma most frequently encountered in practice for that particular type of film. As shown in Fig. 24, the Weston film-speed number S is given by

$$S = \frac{4}{E_w} \tag{45}$$

where $\log_{10} E_w$, determined from the characteristic curve, is chosen to be numerically equal to the gamma of the curve, *i.e.*, $\log_{10} E_w = \gamma$.

Minimum Useful Gradient Speed.—Another method of specifying speed or sensitivity is based on some minimum useful gradient or slope of the D-$\log_{10} E$ characteristic curve. When it is considered that the chief functions of a photographic negative material as used in practice is to reproduce as density differences the brightness differences existing in the object photographed, it seems logical to demand that the minimum useful exposure be determined by some specified gradient of the D-$\log_{10} E$ characteristic.

A system has been suggested that allows for the actual usefulness of the upper part of the region of strict underexposure as the Weston system does not and the H and D does only accidentally—but allowing for it in a manner that avoids the dangers of the Scheiner and DIN systems. In this realistic approach to the problem of speed rating, the measure of sufficient exposure would be that exposure for which the rate of increase of density with increasing $\log_{10} E$ first reaches a certain fraction of the rate found in the linear portion. This fraction would be the fraction of the proper contrast shown in the (strictly underexposed) deepest shadows, in an otherwise perfect negative exposed to the predetermined minimum useful gradient.

The difficulty with such a system is in the matter of deciding upon the value which is to be taken as representing the minimum useful gradient. According to Sheppard, the minimum useful gradient will in general depend not only upon the negative but also upon the positive aspect of tone reproduction, so that its fixation is not expressible by a unique function of the negative material itself.

Nevertheless, the Eastman Kodak Co. has recently adopted a method of film-speed rating based on minimum useful gradient.[1] This method involves drawing the characteristic curve, and selecting the exposures at which the slope (or gradient) of the curves is 0.3 that of the average gradient for a log exposure range of 1.5, the origin of this exposure range being taken at the threshold value.

Comparison of Speed Ratings in Common Use.—Before closing the subject of the speed or sensitivity ratings of photographic materials, it may be well to compare the ratings of the various methods in common use. Such a comparison between ratings based on various modes of determining speed has no justification, from theoretical considerations. But intercomparisons of the various film-speed ratings has some practical utility, in these days of elaborate exposure meters, when the film speed is given in one mode of rating and the exposure-determining device is based on some other system. The practical photographer is then faced with the problem of determining the method of transposing from one system to another.

Appendix B gives the comparative ratings of the more important film-speed ratings in use at the present time. The data in this table may be considered to represent average conditions fairly well. The characteristics of some particular emulsion in question may be such as to prohibit use of this Appendix B for comparisons with any degree of precision. Consequently, for any specific situation, the translation from one speed rating to another can be used only as a rough approximation or as a guide to the correct order of magnitude.

Some Practical Applications of Sensitometry.—In its scientific aspects, photographic sensitometry is of considerably more importance to the manufacturer of photographic materials, the motion-picture laboratory technician, the astronomer, the physicist, the color engraver, and the advanced worker in color photography than to the commercial or amateur photographer. Yet even the least scientifically inclined photographer makes some use of sensitometric principles when he makes a successful negative or print, and a complete understanding of the significance and technique of sensitometry will aid in making better photographs. It is the purpose of this section to discuss some of the more practical aspects of sensitometry and the application of sensitometric concepts to the making of photographs having proper monochrome rendition of tone.

Characteristics of Negatives.—It has been shown that the D-$\log_{10} E$ characteristic is one of the most important in specifying the stimulus-response relation of photographic materials, especially if we limit ourselves to a discussion of monochrome photography. This characteristic may be used in a qualitative sort of way, to detect defects in exposure or processing of negative materials. The methods for so doing may be applied by anyone who has a proper understanding of the philosophical significance of photographic sensitometry, even though he does not possess measuring equipment.

In exposing a negative, the relation between the brightness of the original subject being photographed and the brightness of the film when viewed by transmitted light has been reversed; it is for this reason that the film is called a negative. The brighter the original subject, the darker (the more dense) will be the resulting negative, for the same time of exposure. Similarly, the brighter portions of the subject will show up on the negative as denser or more opaque portions in the representation of the original subject. There is consequently some sort of correspondence between the brightness of the elementary areas of the original subject and the opacities of the corresponding areas as seen in the negative. In order that the negative may portray properly the original subject, it is necessary that the brightness of the elementary areas of the original subject be directly proportional to the opacity of the corresponding elementary areas as

[1] CLARK, WALTER, The Problem of Film Speeds, *Photo Technique*, **1**, 12 (1939).

photographed on the negative. If we designate by B_2 the brightness of the brightest part of the original image and by B_1 the brightness of the darkest elementary area of the original image and if we designate the opacities of the corresponding elementary areas by O_2 and O_1 and the transmission by T_2 and T_1, respectively, then we require that the condition of proper photographic reproduction be such that

$$B_2 = AO_2 = \frac{A}{T_2} \tag{46}$$

and

$$B_1 = AO_1 = \frac{A}{T_1} \tag{47}$$

where A is a proportionality constant. The brightness range of the original subject is $\Delta B = B_2 - B_1$, and the opacity range of the corresponding subject as photographed as $\Delta O = AO_2 - AO_1$. Therefore, the relation between the brightness range of the original image and the image as photographs is such that

$$\Delta B = A(\Delta O) \tag{48}$$

These relations show that for accurate rendition of tone values in monochrome, the brightness and the brightness range of the original image must be rendered on the negative as proportional opacities and opacity ranges, respectively.

If we plot a curve of the brightness and opacity of the original and photographed images on rectangular coordinates, as in Fig. 27, we obtain a straight line for the region of correct exposure. But the brightness of the original image determines the exposure which is given to the photographic material so that we might, if we chose, plot Fig. 27 with exposure as the abscissas rather than the brightness. We would then have a graph showing a straight-line relationship between the exposure of the original image and the opacity of the photographed image.

Let us go one step farther and, instead of plotting the exposure and the opacity, plot the

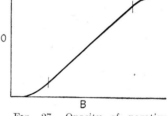

Fig. 27.—Opacity of negative material as a function of the brightness of the subject being photographed. The curve greatly resembles the typical D-$\log_{10} E$ characteristic.

logarithms of these values on cross-section paper. The resultant graph would then have as its ordinates $\log_{10} O$, which by definition is the density, and would have as its abscissas $\log_{10} E$. We find that this new plot is, consequently, merely the straight-line portion of the H and D characteristic, and we may immediately draw the conclusion that for properly rendering tone values the exposure and density relations must be such that the entire image is photographed on the straight-line portion of the H and D curve.

If the exposure is so chosen that all the brightness range of the original subject does not fall upon the straight-line portion of the curve, some distortion of tone values will occur. If too small an exposure is given, the less bright portions of the original image may be compressed in the density range required for accurate reproduction. This condition will be apparent to the photographer by the fact that the detail is lacking in the shadows of the original subject (the less dense portions of the negative). On the other hand, if too great an exposure is given, the brightest portions of the original subject may not be represented on the negative by their true proportional differences in density. In this case, the practical photographer makes use of sensitometric concepts by saying that the high lights of the original image (the most dense portions of the negative) lack detail. But if the exposure is correctly chosen and if the brightness range of the original subject is such that the entire brightness range can be photographed on the linear or portion of the D-$\log_{10} E$ characteristic, then all tones of the original image will be proportional to the density of the corresponding photographed image, and correct tone rendition occurs, so far as the negative is concerned.

We have now to investigate another characteristic of negatives. So far we have been concerned only with the fact that true tone rendition requires that the brightness of the elementary areas in the original image be reproduced on the negative by opacity values which are proportional to the brightness of the corresponding area photographed or by density values which are proportional to the logarithm of the brightness. We have not inquired into the absolute value of the proportionality constant A in the previous equations, which is a measure of the contrast of the negative.

Suppose, first of all, that the opacity-brightness relations (or the density-$\log_{10} E$ relations) are such that the brightness of an elementary area of a photographed image

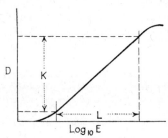

Fig. 28.—Characteristic curve of photographic materials. In considering true tone rendition by photographic methods, it is convenient to consider only the linear region for which the density difference K and latitude L apply.

is exactly equal to the brightness of the corresponding area of the original image, *i.e.*, that $A = 1$, in Eqs. (46) to (48). Then the contrast or density range of the negative will be exactly equal to the contrast of the original subject. If, however, the density range of the negative is less than this ideal value, the original brightness in the subject is compressed, and the tones in the negative are too "flat." On the other hand, if the density range in the negative is greater than the ideal case, the brightness of the original subject is exaggerated in the negative, and the negative is said to be "too contrasty."

The contrast in negatives is its density range, *i.e.*, the range from the minimum or fog density to its maximum density. If we wish to limit ourselves to a consideration of the portion of the D-$\log_{10} E$ curve for which correct tone rendition occurs, then the density range is that corresponding to the linear portion of the D-$\log_{10} E$ curve. For this region of the curve, we have from Fig. 17 the relation for contrast C:

$$C = \Delta D = D_2 - D_1 = \gamma(\log_{10} E_2 - \log_{10} E_1) = \gamma \log_{10}\left(\frac{E_2}{E_1}\right) \qquad (49)$$

This last relation shows that the contrast ΔD is proportional to the γ and to the exposure range. So long as we stay on the linear region of the D-$\log_{10} E$ curve, we may use γ as a measure of the contrast obtainable; the contrast actually obtained depends upon E_2 and E_1 as well as upon γ, however.

It has already been shown (see page 181) that for any given photographic negative material, the value of γ depends upon the processing conditions. Specifically, it has been shown that, for a given film and developer, γ depends upon the time and temperature of development. Therefore, for a given exposure range, we may control contrast by the manner in which the negative material is developed (or by the value of γ to which the material is processed).

The exposure and development conditions and their effects on the characteristics of negatives may be shown graphically as in Fig. 28. This curve enables us to bring out a third point not already mentioned. In Fig. 28, the exposure range for the straight-line portion of the curve is L. If $\log_{10} E_{\min}$ and $\log_{10} E_{\max}$ specify the minimum and maximum values of exposure for the straight-line portion of the curve, then

$$L = \log_{10} \frac{E_{max}}{E_{min}} \tag{50}$$

If now, the brightness range of the subject being photographed (ΔB) is greater than L, then no matter how accurately the exposure of the negative is timed, some portion of the brightness range of the original subject will fall on the curved portions of the H and D characteristic and cannot be precisely and accurately reproduced, so far as concerns tone value. Consequently, a third condition which must be fulfilled is that the brightness range of the original subject must be equal to, or less than, the exposure range R, corresponding to the straight-line portion of the negative.

On the other hand, if the actual exposure range or brightness range of the original subject is small compared to the linear region of the photographic material, appreciable variation in absolute exposure can be tolerated without loss of fidelity of tone rendering.

We may now summarize the essential conditions which must be fulfilled to obtain correct tone rendition of the original subject in the negative. Correct exposure is required in order that the straight-line portion of the characteristic curve may be utilized or in order that the density of all tones of the original image may be recorded on the negative proportional to the corresponding logarithm of the brightness of the original image. Furthermore, the brightness range of the original subject should not exceed the exposure range corresponding to the linear region of the D-$\log_{10} E$ characteristic. Finally, in order that all tones may be correctly rendered, it is essential that the negative be properly developed. Thus we can hope to obtain true tone rendering in a negative only by following three fundamental axioms: (1) the negative must have a linear exposure range equal to or greater than the brightness range of the subject it is desired to photograph in correct tone rendition; (2) the exposure must be correct, so that the image will be reproduced through the use of the straight portion of the D-$\log_{10} E$ curve; and (3) processing conditions must be such as to produce a negative whose γ is unity. In the last case, it is customary to say that correct tone rendition requires the negative to be developed to a gamma of unity, and such developing procedure is a sufficient condition. For making the final print, however, it is not a necessary condition, and so far as printing is concerned, this last requirement is unnecessarily severe. But as applied to the negative, as an end in itself, the above three conditions must be fulfilled if proper tone rendering in monochrome is to be attained.

Characteristics of Positive Materials.—In nearly all photographic applications, the negative is used merely as a means to an end. We are not accustomed to view pictures in which the brightness ranges are transposed into density ranges. The usual procedure is to make another reversal of the photographed image by making a positive or print. The process of making a positive (usually a print on paper) may be regarded merely as making a negative of an image in which the brightness areas have been reversed, *i.e.*, that of making a negative of a negative. Considered in this light, it is evident that the same type of arguments as have already been used for formulating the conditions of correct tone rendition in the case of the negative, apply equally well to the proper tone rendition in the case of positive prints. Largely due to inherent differences between the characteristics of negatives and the corresponding characteristics suitable for making positive reproductions, certain minor modifications may be required.

In discussing positive printing materials, it is desirable to differentiate between two types, so far as concerns the method by which the image is viewed. Certain positive materials, such as motion-picture films and lantern slides, are transparent and are consequently viewed by transmitted light.   Such materials require little comment at this time, since their characteristics resemble those negative materials which have already been discussed.   They differ from negative materials mainly in that their speeds are lower, and the maximum values of their gammas are usually higher than those of negatives.   Spectral sensitivity, latitude, grain, etc., of positive materials may also differ from those of negative materials.   The other classification of positive materials includes opaque materials, such as printing papers, which must be viewed by reflected light.   Their characteristics are sufficiently different from those of negative materials to warrant some consideration at this point.

Printing papers of the bromide type, designed for making enlarged prints from a negative, have emulsions which resemble those of negatives; consequently the D-$\log_{10} E$ characteristics are similar to those of negative materials.   The density range and sensitivity are somewhat more restricted than in the case of negatives, but, like negative materials, the gamma increases with the development time, although only to a small extent.

The characteristics of chloride papers, which are most frequently employed in contact printing, differ considerably from those of bromide papers.   The gamma of chloride papers is much less affected by the development time than the gamma of bromide papers, and development extended beyond the time required to produce gamma infinity acts so as to change the effective speed rather than the gamma of the chloride material.

The chief differences between the characteristics of negatives and the corresponding characteristics of printing papers are:

1. The printing paper is opaque, and consequently must be viewed by reflected light.

2. As a consequence of the above, the blackness of the silver deposit is measured by the reflection of light from the surface of the paper, rather than by passing light through this material, and this density is spoken of as the reflection density.

3. The density range of printing papers depends to a large degree upon the surface texture but is usually less than the density range of negative materials and is often between 1.5 and 2.0.

4. The D-$\log_{10} E$ characteristics of the printing-paper materials have a shorter straight-line region than that of many negative materials.   In some cases no linear region may exist.

5. The gamma infinity of printing papers, especially chloride papers, is determined largely by the characteristics of the emulsion coating of the paper and, to a relatively small extent, by the conditions of development.

6. As a result of (5), variations in contrast of printing are secured by the selection of a suitable grade of printing paper rather than through any conditions of processing of printing papers.

The density of printing papers is defined in a manner analogous to that used for negatives.   However, since we must deal with reflected rather than transmitted light, certain minor modifications are required in specifying the density of printing papers. If I_0 is the luminous flux reflected from a perfectly white surface (such as magnesium carbonate, which is frequently used as a reference) and if I_r is the light flux reflected from the paper having a black deposit of silver, then the amount of light reflected by the silver deposit or the reflecting power of the developed paper is

$$R = \frac{I_r}{I_0} \tag{51}$$

The density of the developed silver deposit is then defined as

$$D = \log_{10}\left(\frac{I_0}{I_r}\right) = \log_{10}\left(\frac{1}{R}\right) = -\log_{10} R$$

which, except for the necessary changes required by the fact that we are dealing with reflected light rather than transmitted light, is identical with the definition of density already given by Eq. (13).

Just as the scattering of light in passing through a negative produces values of density which depend somewhat on the conditions under which measurements are made, so does the scattering of light from the surface of the paper cause similar vagaries in the determination of the density of printing papers. The reflectance of printing papers partakes of the characteristics of both diffuse and specular effects. Therefore, the conditions under which density measurements are made, and especially the angles at which the light strikes and is reflected from the paper, should be specified. Furthermore, the surface texture of the particular grade of paper affects appreciably the reflection coefficient R. The result is that, although equal amounts of silver deposit per unit area should, theoretically, give the same density readings under ideal conditions, this condition is not encountered in practice.

There are two fundamental characteristics of printing materials (so far as concerns their sensitometric characteristics) which are of major importance in the making of a proper print.[1] These are: (1) the contrast or the density range and (2) the exposure range of the material.

The density range, by which is meant the range in density from the minimum (or zero) to the maximum of which the paper is capable, is termed the contrast of the paper.[2] Thus, if the maximum density of the paper is D_2 and the minimum density is D_1, then the contrast (or density range) of the printing material is [as has been shown in Eq. (18)]

$$C = \Delta D = D_2 - D_1 \tag{52}$$

The density range, or contrast, of the printing material determines the maximum and minimum blackness of the silver deposit on the print. For a given type of emulsion, on a paper surface of specified texture, the density is a function of the exposure, as given by the exposure-density characteristic of the printing material. But for a given type of emulsion and a given exposure, the density obtained is affected by the surface texture of the paper. The density range, or contrast, is important in that it determines the range in tones, from black to white, which are to appear in the final print.

The second important characteristic of printing materials is the exposure range E_r of the printing material. It is defined in much the same way as latitude for negative materials,

$$E_r = \log_{10} E_2 - \log_{10} E_1 \qquad (\log_{10} E \text{ units}) \tag{53}$$
$$= \frac{E_2}{E_1} \qquad (\text{exposure units}) \tag{54}$$

and defines the range of exposure (exposure is defined to be $E = It$) corresponding to the density range for which we may expect to obtain a deposit of silver when the print is exposed.

The exposure range is of practical importance in that it determines the minimum to maximum density range of the negative from which a satisfactory print may be made. If we consider the negative as the original subject and if we consider that we are "photographing" this negative (which we now consider as our original image),

[1] There are, of course, other factors which may be taken into account for aesthetic, psychological, or artistic reasons, but we are not concerned with these factors at this point.

[2] Perhaps it may be well to remind the reader that we are here concerned only with the sensitometric aspects of printing materials. The subjective evaluation of contrast, from the artistic, aesthetic, or psychological point of view may not always agree with the sensitometric definition. But we are not concerned here with subjective evaluations.

then the basic concepts which have already been discussed for the proper tone rendition on the negative apply equally well for the case of positive or printing materials. We have, of course, to transfer the term "brightness range of the original subject" into "opacity range of the negative," but otherwise the concepts are the same, and need not again be gone through at this point.

It is sufficient to call attention to the point that, in the ideal case, the exposure range of the printing material must equal or exceed the opacity range of the negative if we are to obtain a print which is an accurate, although reversed, reproduction of the negative. Another necessary condition for ideal reproduction is that throughout the exposure range a linear relation should exist between the logarithm of the exposure and the density; in other words, we desire to work on the straight-line portion of the D-$\log_{10} E$ curve of the print as well as the straight-line portion of the D-$\log_{10} E$ curve of the negative.

Unfortunately, this is not a practical solution because of the limited exposure and density range of printing materials. As a result of the short ranges of density and exposure, the toe and shoulder of the D-$\log_{10} E$ curve are employed in most printing applications; a print limited to the straight-line region of the characteristic curve would very likely be flat (lacking in contrast) and would be suitable only for subjects in which the brightness range (exposure range in the case of negatives) was decidedly limited.

Notwithstanding the fact that many papers have a very short linear region of the D-$\log_{10} E$ characteristics and certain papers may have no linear region, the concept of the gamma, or slope of the straight-line portion of the curve, is a useful one to apply in the case of printing or positive materials. To distinguish the characteristics of the positive or printing materials from that of negative materials, we shall use the symbol γ_p to designate the gamma of the positive material, and γ_n to designate the gamma of negative materials. This distinction between the slope of the characteristics of the two types of photographic materials will be especially useful when we come to consider the proper rendition of tone in the entire photographic process.

Because the D-$\log_{10} E$ curves of many printing papers have a relatively short linear region, the concept of γ_p is not so thoroughly intrenched as that of γ_n for negative materials. Manufacturers do not specify the limiting values of γ_p which may be expected to obtain upon prolonged development, nor do they specify the density range or the exposure range from which some conception of γ_p might be derived.

Printing papers are available having various values of exposure range and density range, and these factors do give in some measure an indication of the gamma of the printing material under consideration. However, papers are not specified by the manufacturers according to their sensitometric characteristics, except in a somewhat roundabout mystical manner in which vague terms are employed. With sufficient exposure, the density range of a printing material is determined, to a very considerable degree, by the texture of its surface. The exposure range of papers is usually specified by the manufacturers by such vague terms as "soft," "vigorous," or "hard," in decreasing values of exposure range, or by some numerical system. Such designations are hardly satisfactory from the sensitometric point of view. And yet the system has worked apparently quite well. There seems to be little inclination on the part of manufacturers to employ a more rigorous specification for their printing materials so long as the average photographer does not demand more specific data.

Even though we may not know the actual H and D characteristics of the printing material we are employing, the concept of the D-$\log_{10} E$ curve is a useful one. Through its use, we may prepare a chart of printing-paper characteristics, so far as this relates to the accurate reproduction of the "image" of the negative. Such a set of curves, as is shown in Fig. 29, is based on the assumption that we wish to reproduce,

	Underexposure	Correct exposure	Overexposure	Characteristics of negative materials	Characteristics of positive or printing materials
Insufficient contrast	Shadows lack detail / Other tones too flat 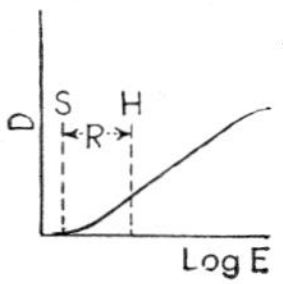 [graph, Log E]	Detail in all tones / All tones too flat 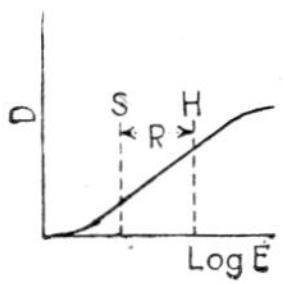 [graph, Log E]	High lights lack detail / Other tones too flat 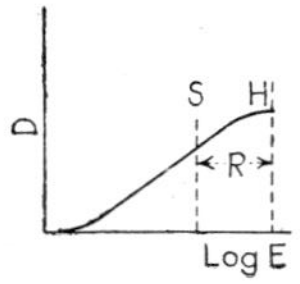 [graph, Log E]	Characteristic: Tones too flat and lacking in contrast. Cause: Underdevelopment. Too short development time. Developer solution too cold, or incorrectly compounded. Prevention: Correct development time and temperature. Developer solution properly compounded. Remedy: Contrast and density may be increased by intensifying negative. No remedy for faulty exposure	Characteristic: Tones too flat and lacking in contrast. Cause: Possibly underdevelopment. Printing paper too flat and lacking in contrast. Prevention: Use of correct grade of printing paper. Possibly correct development. Remedy: Make new print
Correct contrast	Shadows lack detail / Other tones correctly rendered 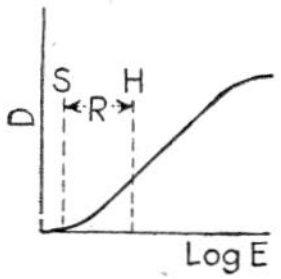 [graph, Log E]	Detail in all tones / All tones correctly rendered 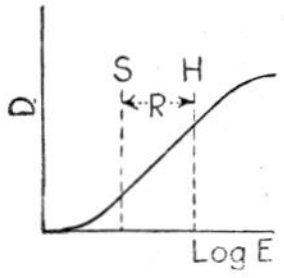 [graph, Log E]	High lights lack detail / Other tones correctly rendered 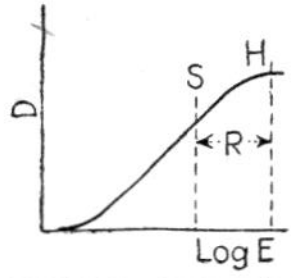 [graph, Log E]	Characteristic: All tones correctly rendered. Cause: Correct development. Prevention: None desired. Remedy: None required	Characteristic: All tones correctly rendered. Cause: Correct grade of contrast in printing paper. Possibly correct development. Prevention: None desired. Remedy: None required
Excessive contrast	Shadows lack detail / Other tones too contrasty 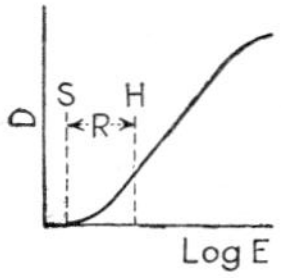 [graph, Log E]	Detail in all tones / All tones too contrasty 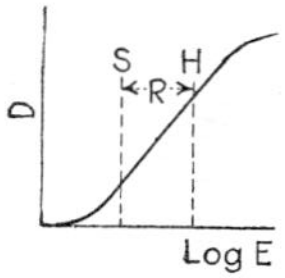 [graph, Log E]	High lights lack detail / Other tones too contrasty 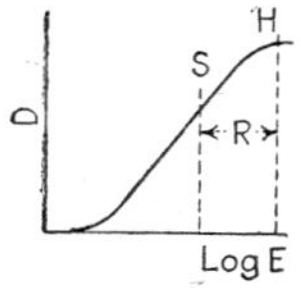 [graph, Log E]	Characteristic: Tones have excessive contrast. Cause: Overdevelopment. Too long development time. Developer solution too warm, or incorrectly compounded. Prevention: Correct development time and temperature; properly compounded developer solution. Remedy: Contrast and density may be decreased by reducing negative. No remedy for faulty exposure	Characteristic: Tones have excessive contrast. Cause: Possibly overdevelopment. Printing paper too contrasty for the negative. Prevention: Use of correct grade of contrast in printing paper. Remedy: Make new print
	Characteristic: Shadows lack detail. Cause: Underexposure. Prevention: Increased exposure. Remedy: None; make new negative or print	Characteristic: Detail in all tones. Cause: Correct exposure. Prevention: None required. Remedy: None required	Characteristic: High lights lack detail. Cause: Overexposure. Prevention: Reduced exposure. Remedy: None; make new negative or print		

FIG. 29.—*D*-log *E* characteristics of photographic materials correlated with conditions of exposure and development.

as faithfully as possible, the images of the negative, except that they will, of course, be reversed in tone. This diagram has been so prepared that by its use and by an analysis of the print the photographer may determine errors which may have been made, either in the exposure of the print or in selecting the type of paper for a given negative.

Tone Rendition.—In most applications of photography, the ultimate goal is a positive print, either a transparency or paper print, in which the brightnesses of the elementary areas of the original subject are to be reproduced in the positive print. For correct rendition of tones in monochrome photography, the brightness of these elementary areas in the final print must equal the brightness of the corresponding elementary areas of the original subject or image. The final print is the result of two reversal processes (the negative and the print), both of which have already been discussed in some detail.

Let B represent the brightness of the original subject, and B_p the brightness of the resultant print, the brightness varying with each elementary area from point to point. Then if for all elementary areas B_p is exactly equal to B, the monochrome rendition of the original subject in the print will equal the brightness of the original subject as evaluated by the human eye, and perfect rendition of tone results. Because of the limitations of photographic materials, this ideal condition is never completely realized, although it may be approached more or less closely.

The exposure range of the negative E_n is proportional to B, and the relationship between density and exposure ranges is then

$$D_n = \gamma_n(\log_{10} E_n - \log_{10} i_n) = \gamma_n \log_{10} \frac{E_n}{i_n} \tag{55}$$

where i_n is the inertia, or the exposure corresponding to the intersection of the straight-line portion of the D-$\log_{10} E$ curve, extended to the zero density axis. But the density range is also given in terms of the opacity range O_n, and the transmission range T_n is given in terms of the relation

$$D_n = \log_{10} O_n = \log_{10} \left(\frac{1}{T_n}\right) \tag{56}$$

so that

$$D_n = \log_{10} O_n = \log_{10} \left(\frac{1}{T_n}\right) = \gamma_n \log_{10} \frac{E_n}{i_n} \tag{57}$$

By taking the antilogarithms of both sides of the equation, we obtain

$$O_n = \left(\frac{1}{T_n}\right) = \left(\frac{E_n}{i_n}\right)^{\gamma_n} \tag{58}$$

If now, the negative is developed so that $\gamma = 1$, then the opacity range of the negative will be directly proportional to its exposure range.

In the printing process, the exposure range of the positive material E_p is inversely proportional to the opacity range of the negative O_n. The opacity range of the positive printing material is given by

$$O_p = \left(\frac{1}{T_n}\right) = \left(\frac{E_n}{i_p}\right)^{\gamma_p} \tag{59}$$

where the symbols have the same meaning as given above but refer to the positive printing material rather than to the negative, as indicated by the subscript p. If the positive material is printed in such a manner that $\gamma_p = 1$, either through proper development or by selection of the proper grade of paper, then the silver deposit on the print will have an opacity range which is proportional to its exposure range. Since the exposure range of the positive is obtained from the opacity range of the negative. the print will give accurate monochrome rendition of the original image. The condition that $\gamma_p = 1$ is a sufficient condition for the production of a print having proper tone rendition, but it is unnecessarily rigid.

The opacity range of the positive material O_p is

$$O_p = K\left(\frac{E_p}{i_p}\right)^{\gamma_p} \tag{60}$$

Similarly, the exposure range of the positive is a function of the opacity range of the negative, as shown by the relation

$$\left(\frac{E_p}{i_p}\right) = k\left(\frac{E_n}{i_n}\right)^{\gamma_n} \tag{61}$$

Consequently, by substituting $k(E_n/i_n)\gamma_n$ for E_p/i_p in the equation for O_p, the opacity range of the positive may be expressed as

$$O_p = K\left(\frac{E_p}{i_p}\right)^{\gamma_p} = Kk\left(\frac{E_n}{i_n}\right)^{\gamma_n\gamma_p} \tag{62}$$

Now the exposure range of the negative material E_n/i_n is in turn proportional to the brightness range of the original image or subject so that, if this brightness range is expressed by B_2/B_1, we have

$$\left(\frac{E_n}{i_n}\right) = M\left(\frac{B_2}{B_1}\right) \tag{63}$$

and finally

$$O_p = KkM\left(\frac{B_2}{B_1}\right)^{\gamma_p\gamma_n} = \left(\frac{B_2}{B_1}\right)^{\gamma_p\gamma_n} \tag{64}$$

This equation shows that the opacity range of the positive or print is proportional to the brightness range of the original image raised to some power which is the product of the gammas of the positive and negative materials. So long as the product of the gammas is unity, *i.e.*, $\gamma_n\gamma_p = 1$, the absolute values of the individual gammas is of little consequence. Therefore, if we have a negative in which the gamma is different from unity, we may still obtain accurate tone rendition by so selecting the printing medium that its gamma is such that the product will be unity. For example, if the negative is "flat" so that $\gamma_n = \frac{1}{2}$, then proper tone in the print may be obtained by using a "contrasty grade" of paper such that $\gamma_p = 2$. The product of the gammas will be $\gamma_p\gamma_n = \frac{1}{2} \times 2 = 1$ and we shall have established the condition of proper tone rendition.

Graphical Representation of Tone Rendition.—Up to the present time, it has been assumed that the straight-line regions of the D-$\log_{10} E$ curves of both negative and positive materials were the only portions used. This assumption does not conform to practice, and in extending the representation of tone rendering in monochrome, it is desirable to use graphical methods to show the effect of the various characteristics. Mathematical methods, which are both simple and accurate, can no longer be used when curvature of the characteristics enters into consideration.

A method of representing the entire and essential concepts in the proper tone rendition of the complete photographic process has been developed by Jones,[1] and that method is reproduced here. The method consists of using the second of four quadrants to represent the brightness and brightness range of the original subject (the resultant H and D characteristics of the negative exposed to the subject), the third

[1] Jones, L. A., *J. Optical Soc. Am.*, **5**, 232 (1921); *J. Franklin Inst.*, **190**, 39 (1920).

quadrant for the resultant D-$\log_{10} E$ characteristics of the developed positive material printed from the negative, the fourth quadrant for the variation of the eye response when viewing the subject and when viewing the positive-print reproduction, and the first quadrant to compare the resulting visual sensation when comparing the positive reproduction with that of the original subject. This diagram is shown in Fig. 30.

Starting from the scale of subject brightness ($\log_{10} B$ scale) which determines the exposure and exposure range, we find the H and D characteristics of the developed negative as given in the second quadrant. True tone rendition is obtained on the

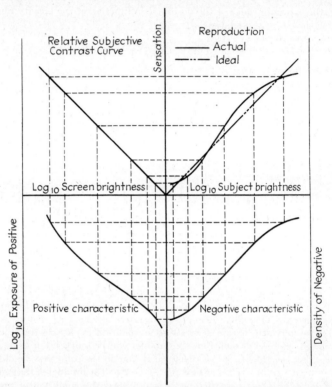

Fig. 30.—Four-quadrant diagram illustrating the method of determining correctness of tone reproduction. This diagram provides a method by which the final print can be compared with the original subject; it does not take into account tone variations which may be desired for aesthetic purposes.

straight-line portion of this curve. From the D-$\log_{10} E$ curve of the negative, we arrive at the same characteristic of the printing material (third quadrant) through the process of printing or making the positive. Here again, true tone rendition is obtained over the straight-line portion of the characteristic curve of the positive material. However, the curvature of the characteristics of the printing material are such as to exaggerate, rather than compensate, for tone distortions occurring in the negative. Finally, by viewing the positive or print by reflected light, we obtain the scene brightness through the brightness characteristic of the human eye which translates the scene brightness into visual sensations. By comparing the visual sensations thus produced, with the subject brightness, we obtain the curve in the first quadrant, which represents the distortion characteristics of the final print reproduction. If this characteristic is a straight line, the reproduction is free from distortion, whereas the degree of distortion is proportional to the curvature of this characteristic.

By studying the various steps represented in the four quadrants, we are able to determine what change in photographic technique and processing is required in order to minimize tone distortion.

Bibliography

Periodicals:

MEES, C. E. K., and S. E. SHEPPARD: Instruments for Sensitometric Investigations, *Phot. J.*, **44,** 200 (1904).

———— and ————: The Sensitometry of Photographic Plates, *Phot. J.*, **44,** 282 (1904). (Contains excellent bibliography.)

WALLACE, R. J.: On the Sensitiveness of Photographic Plates at Different Temperatures, *Astrophys. J.*, **28,** 39 (1908).

MEES, C. E. K.: Effect of Humidity on the Sensitiveness of Photographic Plates, *Astrophys. J.*, **40,** 236 (1914).

HARRISON, G. R.: Characteristics of Photographic Materials in the Ultraviolet, *J. Optical Soc. Am.*, **11,** 341 (1925).

JONES, L. A., and O. SANDVIK: Spectral Distribution of Sensitivity of Photographic Materials, *J. Optical Soc. Am.*, **12,** 401 (1926).

HARRISON, G. R.: Instruments and Methods used for Measuring Spectral Light Intensities by Photography, *J. Optical Soc. Am.*, **19,** 267 (1929).

TUTTLE, CLIFTON: A Recording Physical Densitometer, *J. Optical Soc. Am.*, **26,** 282 (1936).

ROBERTS, CREIGHTON: Photographic Determinations of Film Strip Exposures, *Am. Phot.*, 533 (1937).

PITT, F. G. H.: Measurement of Specular Density, *Phot. J.*, 486 (1938).

KOERNER, A. M., and CLIFTON TUTTLE: Standardization of Photographic Density, *Phot. J.*, 739 (1938). *J. Soc. Motion Picture Engrs.*, **19,** 739 (1937).

See also the many papers published in the *Journal of the Optical Society of America* and the *Journal of the Society of Motion Picture Engineers.*

Books:

HARDY, A. C., and F. H. PERRIN: "Principles of Optics," Chap. 11, McGraw (1932).

"Motion Picture Laboratory Practice," Eastman Kodak Co. (1937).

FORSYTHE, W. E.: "Measurement of Radiant Energy," Chap. 8, McGraw (1937). (Contains excellent bibliography.)

NEBLETTE, C. B.: "Photography Principles and Practice," 3d ed., Van Nostrand (1938).

CHAPTER VIII

EXPOSURE AND EXPOSURE DEVICES

By Beverly Dudley and A. T. Williams

Exposure. Theoretical Considerations.—Two fundamental steps are involved in the making of any picture by photographic processes which involve the use of silver salts. In the first of these a "negative" is produced on which is recorded, in reverse manner, the light and dark portions of the original subject. In the second step a positive print is made by using the negative as the original object, and reversing its tone shades so that the brightness of the various elementary areas of the print bear some direct or positive relation to the brightness of the corresponding elementary areas of the original object. In both steps, the process in which light falls upon the sensitized photographic material is an important step and is known as exposure of the photographic material.

In the final analysis, the positive print is the desired result. Any intermediate steps, such as those involving the making of the negative, must be regarded as a means to the desired end and, accordingly, should be treated in this light. Since the final print is produced from the negative, it is evident that the characteristics of the negative, which include its general or average density, its range of density, and its tone gradation, will influence the printing time, range of density, and tone gradation of the final print. For this reason it is essential to ascertain that the negative is properly prepared in all respects; in this chapter, however, we shall be primarily concerned with the proper exposure of the negative, leaving its subsequent processing to later chapters. The manner in which the negative and the positive print are exposed to light, the duration of the exposure time, the characteristics of the photographic material, the spectral characteristics and intensity of the light source, the characteristics of any filters which may be used, are all important factors to consider in arriving at the proper exposure which will produce the desired final results. This chapter will be devoted to a consideration of these factors.

Photochemical Action Occurring during Exposure.—The emulsions of photographic materials consist of a layer of silver halide deposited on a transparent substance such as gelatin or glass in the case of negative materials or on a paper base in the case of positive materials. It is characteristic of the silver halides that, when acted upon by light, they undergo some form of alteration so that the grains which have been exposed to light may be converted into black deposits of metallic silver in the process of development.[1]

A minimum amount of light, however, is required to effect the change in the grains of the silver halide. If less than this amount of light fails to reach the emulsion, the grains will not be affected, and consequently they cannot be changed into metallic silver during development. As the quantity of light impinging upon the emulsion increases beyond the minimum amount necessary to produce a minimum observable silver deposit, more and more layers of silver halide are exposed and are subject to sub-

---

[1] The exact physics underlying the production of the latent image in the emulsion need not concern us here. There is no universal agreement as to the mechanism by which the latent image is produced, and this point will not be discussed here.

sequent development. Consequently, the density of the silver deposit of the developed negative increases, at least within limits, as the amount of light falling upon the emulsion is increased. The relation between the quantity of light falling upon the sensitized material and the density of the silver deposit depends upon a number of factors but is expressed by means of the D-$\log_{10} E$ characteristic curve. The most important of these factors are discussed in the chapter on Photographic Sensitometry, which should be consulted for additional information on this subject.

Requirements for Correct Tone Reproduction.—A scientifically correct print is one in which the light intensities of the various portions of the print are proportional to[1] the light intensities of the corresponding elementary areas of the original object. Since the negative is a reversal of the light intensities of the original subject and also that of the print, it follows that the opacity of the elementary areas of a scientifically

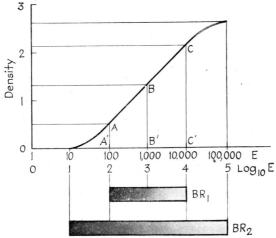

Fig. 1.—D-$\log_{10} E$ diagram illustrating correct tone rendition when the brightness range of the subject does not exceed that of the linear portion of the curve.

correct negative must be proportional to the light intensities of the corresponding areas of the original object. In order that this condition may be fulfilled, the range of light intensities of the original object must be so related to the characteristics of the film, through proper exposure, that it corresponds to the linear portion of the D-$\log_{10} E$ characteristic curve. A similar condition must be fulfilled in making the print.[2]

In addition to determining the exposure so that the linear portion of the D-$\log_{10} E$ characteristic curve is employed, it is essential that the photosensitive materials selected for use have sufficient latitude to accommodate the brightness range of the original object. Conversely, if the latitude of a given emulsion is small, then, for a scientifically correct negative, it is essential that this material not be used to photograph objects which have a large brightness range.

An example will help to make these statements more clear. Let the curve of Fig. 1 represent the characteristics of a film having a latitude of 100, *i.e.*, the ratio of the exposure at point C is 100 times that of point A, or the difference between $\log_{10} E$ at

[1] In the ideal case, which is not attainable where the print is viewed by reflected light, the intensities of the print would be exactly equal to the corresponding intensities of the corresponding areas of the object photographed.

[2] See page 205 for treatment of correct tone rendition from the viewpoint of the characteristics of photosensitive materials.

point C and $\log_{10} E$ at point A is 2. If now we have an object whose brightness range does not exceed 100 to 1, as indicated by the strip BR_1, then it will be possible to choose an exposure such that the densities of the negative will be directly proportional to the brightness intensities of elementary areas of the original subject. On the other hand, if we try to photograph on this same film a subject having a brightness range of 10,000 to 1 as indicated by the strip BR_2, it will only be possible to reproduce correctly the range from 100 to 10,000 units representing a range of 100 to 1. Greater light intensities than those represented by the point C will not produce densities in the negative proportional to the brightness of the object. Similarly for low values of brightness of the original subject, to the left of A, a correct relation between brightness of the original object and density of the negative will no longer be possible. The result is that between the points A and C we are able to obtain correct tone reproduction; beyond these points tone distortion results.

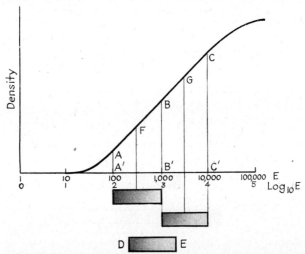

Fig. 2.—If the brightness range of the subject being photographed does not exceed the exposure range for which the D-$\log_{10} E$ characteristic is linear, several exposures are possible, all of which can give correct tone rendition.

The ratio of the latitude of the film to the brightness range of the object determines the necessary precision of the exposure. If, as shown in BR_1 of Fig. 1, the brightness range and the latitude are equal, then there is only one possible exposure for which correct tone rendition is possible, and this is represented as the mean exposure, given by the point B. If, on the other hand, the brightness range of the original subject is much less than the latitude of the film, several different exposures will be possible, each of which is capable of producing correct tone rendition. For example, if we are photographing a subject having a brightness range of 10 to 1 on a film having a latitude of 100 to 1, we may so determine the exposure that the brightness range occurs between A and B, between B and C, of Fig. 2, or anywhere between these extreme limits, *e.g.*, D and E. We may, therefore, select as the mean exposure any value between G and F and still obtain correct results. Since the exposure at G is 10 times that at F, it is possible to make a 10 to 1 error in exposure and still obtain a negative having correct tone rendition. In Fig. 1 such a range in exposure was not possible because the film latitude and brightness range of the object being photographed were of equal magnitude.

From this discussion, it is evident that the following conditions must be fulfilled in order that a scientifically correct negative may be produced:

1. The brightness range of the original object must not exceed the latitude of the photographic material; or, conversely,

2. The latitude of the photographic material must be at least equal to, and preferably should exceed, the brightness range of the object being photographed.

3. The more nearly equal are the brightness range of the object and the latitude of the photosensitive material, the more critical is the exposure which must be given to obtain correct tone rendition.

4. If the brightness range of the object exceeds the latitude of the film, only a portion of the scene will be reproduced with proper tone value; other portions of the object will have tone distortion.

5. If the brightness range of the object being photographed is less than the latitude of the film any one of several correct exposures may be used.

6. The greater the ratio of film latitude to brightness range of the object, the less critical need be the exposure of the film.

Definition of Exposure.—The altering of the silver halide grains by the photochemical action of the light in order to produce a latent image is called exposure. To a first approximation[1] it has been found that the photochemical action taking place during exposure obeys the reciprocity law of Bunsen and Roscoe. As an application of this law to photochemical reactions, the exposure E may be expressed as

$$E = It \tag{1}$$

where I = the intensity of the light acting upon the sensitized photographic material;
t = the time during which this illumination is permitted to act on the photographic material.

For exposure to white light, which represents the usual conditions, the exposure is measured in meter-candle-seconds. As indicated in the chapter on Photographic Sensitometry, the light source has a spectral distribution like that of mean noon sunlight, and the exposure time t is usually continuous rather than the integrated effect of intermittent or chopped exposures.[2] The equation shows that the exposure, and consequently the photographic effect as measured by the density of silver deposit, depends directly upon the intensity of the light source and increases the longer the material is subjected to light rays. Because the exposure depends upon the time during which the light acts on the film, the film is able to integrate the quantity of light falling upon it. A practical advantage of this effect is that through sufficiently long exposure it is possible to photograph objects which might otherwise not be sufficiently bright to produce a photographic image.

The exposure is not the only factor determining the photographic effect produced, although it is a very important factor in this connection. The photographic effect, by which is meant the density of the silver deposit, is determined by the characteristics of the sensitive material and by the processing conditions as well as by the exposure. These factors are related graphically by means of the D-$\log_{10} E$ characteristic and are discussed in the chapter on Photographic Sensitometry.

By means of the D-$\log_{10} E$ characteristic curves, it is possible to determine the density produced on a certain photosensitive material for given exposure and processing conditions. Such curves provide a clue to what might be expected, by way of

---

[1] Careful investigations show that the reciprocity law is not exactly obeyed by photographic materials. Failure of the reciprocity law is not of serious consequence in most branches of practical photography, and, for a first approximation, may be neglected.

[2] If the film is exposed intermittently, it is found that the photographic effects are not the same as when the film is exposed for the same time duration but continuously rather than intermittently.

photographic effect, when photographing an object with a camera and lens system. However, the D-$\log_{10} E$ characteristics are usually expressed in terms of density and meter-candle-seconds. The illumination of the object being photographed is not ordinarily determined in meter-candle-seconds, and even if this were possible, through the use of properly calibrated exposure or illumination meters, the intensity of illumination on the plate is vastly different from that of the original object because of the reduction in size, the effect of the aperture stop, the focal length, and other characteristics of the lens system. To make maximum use of the sensitometric concepts and to understand fully the various and numerous factors which enter into exposure, it is desirable to provide the connecting link which relates the exposure, as given in the sensitometric sense of the term, and the brightness of the object as this may be determined by measurements with an exposure or illumination meter. It is proposed to construct this connecting link based upon theoretical considerations for two reasons: (1) An

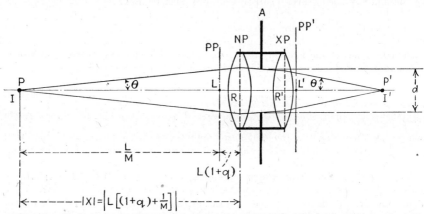

Fig. 3.—Optical system of a camera showing axial rays. The luminous intensity, I', of the point P' on the photographic plate can be expressed in terms of the luminous intensity, I, of the point on the subject, P, and the characteristics of the lens system.

understanding of the theory of exposure provides an excellent basis for understanding the practical treatment which is to follow; (2) the relations and equations which are derived from theoretical considerations are required for a full explanation of the use of exposure tables given in another section of this chapter.

Image Brightness as a Function of Optical System.—It is now necessary to establish the connecting link by which the brightness of the image on the photographic plate may be determined from the illumination of the original object being photographed. This link involves the optical system of the camera, which, so far as exposure is concerned, includes the iris diaphragm, the bellows extension, a filter (if one is used), and the shutter, as well as the lens system proper.

Let Fig. 3 represent the lens system of the camera, in which a point object P, whose luminous intensity is I, produces an image object of itself P' with luminous intensity I' on the photographic plate. The iris diaphragm or aperture is represented as being at A. The principal planes of the lens are represented as lying at PP and at PP', while the entrance and exit pupils are designated as being at NP and XP, respectively, and the principal focal lengths are L and L'.

The point P may be self-luminous or may be illuminated by reflected light. In either case it will illuminate the entrance pupil of the lens NP with an intensity inversely proportional to the square of the distance between P and R, the latter being in the plane of the entrance pupil, and directly proportional to its luminous intensity I. Let the distance between P and R be X. Then the intensity of light falling upon the entrance pupil will be proportional to I/X^2. The distance X may be considered as being made up of two components. One of these is the distance from P to the interior principal focal length L, which distance is given by $-L/M$ where M is the linear magnification produced by the lens system. The negative sign is required because of the inversion of the image. The second component of the distance X is the distance LR from the plane of the principal focus to the plane of the entrance pupil. Since the principal-focus and the entrance-pupil planes are never very far removed from one another, the distance LR may be expressed by $L(1 + q)$ where q is a small positive or negative decimal. Neglecting the negative sign required because of the image inversion, the distance from P to R may be expressed as

$$X = L\left[(1 + q) + \frac{1}{M}\right] \tag{2}$$

The intensity I' of the light at the point P' is proportional to the cone whose half angle is θ. The maximum diameter of this cone at the exit pupil is determined by the area of the aperture, which is given by

$$A = \frac{\pi d^2}{4} \tag{3}$$

where d = the diameter of the aperture.

The cone of light emerging from the exit pupil comes to a focus at P' and produces an image of P whose size is proportional to the linear magnification of the system M. The intensity of the image at P' is inversely proportional to the area of the image. But the area of this image is

$$a = \frac{\pi M^2}{4} \tag{4}$$

so that I' is proportional to $4/\pi M^2$.

Finally, the intensity of the image at P' is reduced by absorption and reflection by the separate elements of the lens system. Of the light incident upon the lens, some is absorbed, but a greater part is reflected from the lens surfaces, especially if these are uncemented. The quantity of the emerging light is always less than that incident upon the system and is proportional to the incident light and the transmission of the lens system T. Consequently I' is proportional to T.

Having discussed briefly the separate factors which influence the intensity of the image, we may now combine the separate effects. Thus, for an object P on, or very near to, the optical axis of the lens system, the intensity of the image is

$$I' = \frac{kIAT}{X^2a} \tag{5}$$

where k is a numerical constant depending upon the units of measurement. By substituting for A, X, and a, the values already determined, and by simplifying, the expression becomes

$$I' = I\left[\frac{kTd^2}{L^2[M(1 + q) + 1]^2}\right] \tag{6}$$

Since q is a small fraction, little error is introduced if it is neglected, and for practical purposes the above equation may be simplified to

$$I' = I\left[\frac{kTd^2}{L^2(M + 1)^2}\right] \tag{7}$$

This equation gives in the most general form the connecting link relating the intensity of the image and that of the original subject, so far as the lens system is concerned, provided that the object and image are not far removed from the optical axis of the lens. For objects considerably off the optical axis, and especially when the view angle is large, the intensity of the image at a corner of the plate may vary considerably from that given by Eq. (7).

By definition the f-number of a lens is the ratio of the focal length to the diameter of the aperture. Thus we may substitute f for L/d in the above equations, where f represents the f-number of the lens for a specified diameter of aperture d. When this substitution is made, we obtain

$$I' = \frac{IkT}{f^2(M + 1)^2} \tag{8}$$

which is, perhaps, in its simplest and most practical form. This equation states that the intensity of the image is proportional to the intensity of the original object, proportional to the transmission of the lens system, inversely proportional to the square of the f-number, and inversely proportional to the square of the linear magnification plus one.

Image Brightness as Function of Filter.—A filter is frequently employed in photography to increase contrast, to produce desirable pictorial effects, or to distinguish between tone rendition of various colors. The property inherent in all filters is absorption of a portion of the spectrum to which the photographic emulsion is sensitive, and it thereby decreases the effective intensity of illumination on the photographic material. Because of this reduction of luminous intensity, the exposure must be increased. The filter factor, for a particular filter, light source, and photographic emulsion, is a measure of the required increase in exposure and is also a measure of the extent to which it reduces the quantity of light reaching the photographic material.

If the filter factor is F, the intensity of the light passing through it[1] is inversely proportional to the filter factor or to $1/F$. We may consider the effect of the filter, as well as that of the lens system, in determining the intensity of the image for the filter and lens system

$$I' = \frac{IkT}{Ff^2(M + 1)^2} \tag{9}$$

Exposure Time and Film Speed.—The sensitivity or speed of a photographic material is an important factor in determining the exposure required to produce a given photographic effect. Various methods of determining and specifying the speed of photographic materials are in use and are described in the chapter on Photographic Sensitometry. It is sufficient to say that in all the common methods of specifying film speed, the larger numerical units indicate the faster or more sensitive emulsions, *i.e.*, those requiring the least exposure to produce an image of given density. This may be seen by comparing the speed numbers in the various systems with the relative exposure as given in column 1 of the table of film speeds, Appendix B.

The various film-speed systems are not based on the same fundamental use of the D-$\log_{10} E$ curve, and the film-speed numbers do not progress uniformly in the various systems; in some cases the speed numbers progress proportionately to the relative speed, in others they do not. It is possible, however, to devise a relationship between

[1] In speaking of the transmission of light through a filter it must be remembered that a true filter does not provide equal absorption for all wavelengths to which the photographic material is sensitive. Strictly speaking, it is therefore improper to deal with the intensity of light passing through the filter without considering the spectral distribution of the light and the spectral transmission of the filter. These factors are implicitly taken into account, however, in the determination of the filter factor.

the various film-speed numbers, as given in Appendix B, although such relations are to be regarded as being, at best, rough approximations. If S_a is some arbitrary or relative film-speed or film-sensitivity number (as given in column 1 of Appendix B) and S_n is the film speed or sensitivity in the n system of rating, then the various film-speed numbers will be related to the relative sensitivity by the equations given in Table I.

TABLE I.—EQUATIONS FOR VARIOUS FILM-SPEED RELATIONS

Film-speed system	Film-speed symbol	Film speed, related to relative film speed, S_A, of Appendix B	K_n
Weston	S_B	$S_B = 0.233 \, S_A$	0.233
American H and D ($k = 10$)	S_C	$S_C = 5.8 \, S_A$	5.8
European H and D	S_D	$S_D = 27 \, S_A$	27
Watkins	S_E	$S_E = 10.65 \, S_A$	10.65
Wynne	S_F	$S_F = 20.9 \sqrt{S_A}$	
Burroughs-Wellcome	S_G	$S_G = 2.83/S_A$	
American Scheiner	S_H	$S_H = (1 + 9.5 \log_{10} S_A)$	
European Scheiner	S_I	$S_I = (5 + 9.5 \log_{10} S_A)$	
Eder Hecht	S_J	$S_J = (43 + 24 \log_{10} S_A)$	
DIN	S_K	$S_K = [(10 \log_{10} S_A) - 7]/10$	
Eastman*	S_L	$S_L = 1.165 \, S_A$	1.165

* The film-speed values for the Eastman Kodak Co. minimum-gradient film-speed system are based on published data for only a few emulsions, from which it was determined that the Kodak numbers are approximately five times the Weston speed numbers for the same emulsion.

For those film-speed systems (designated by a K_n factor in the last column) for which the speed numbers are proportional to the relative film speed, the exposure and film speed bear a very simple and convenient relation to one another. To show this, suppose we photograph a very simple object without any detail whatsoever, such as a uniformly lighted sheet of paper. The exposed and developed negative will then have a uniform density, D_0, or a uniform opacity, O. Let the light intensity at which the photograph was made be I, the shutter speed be t_0, and the film speed be S_{n_0}; consequently the exposure is $E_0 = I_0 t_0$. Then, if the negative is properly exposed, the opacity will be

$$O = CS_{n_0}E_0 = CS_{n_0}I_0t_0 \qquad (10)$$

Suppose, now, that we change the film speed and desire the same opacity of the negative. It will then be necessary to alter the exposure, E, and if I_0 remains constant, t_0 will have to be changed to t. Thus, for a new film speed, S_n, we have

$$O = CS_nE = CS_nIt \qquad (11)$$

and since the opacity is the same in both cases we have that

$$S_{n_0}t_0 = S_nt \qquad (12)$$

and thus

$$t = \frac{S_{n_0}t_o}{S_n} \qquad (13)$$

which shows that for a given photographic effect, the shutter speed is inversely proportional to the film speed. As an example of the use of this equation, suppose we were to give an exposure of $\frac{1}{50}$ sec. to a film having a speed of Weston 12. This exposure will produce a negative of some definite opacity O. If we now desire to obtain this same opacity with another film having a speed of Weston 24, our equations show that, if the exposure time is the only variable, this must be reduced to $\frac{1}{100}$ sec. to produce the desired effect. If we had chosen the Wynne system instead of the Weston system in this example, the exposure time in the second case would have been $\frac{1}{200}$ sec., because in this system doubling the speed number quadruples the exposure or requires only one-fourth the exposure for the same photographic effect.

Correlation of Factors Affecting Exposure.—We are now in a position to correlate all the factors affecting the exposure of the film. The exposure given to the film in the camera is $E = I't$ where I' is given by Eq. (9). Therefore the exposure of the film in the camera is

$$E = I't' = \frac{IkTt}{Ff^2(M+1)^2} \tag{14}$$

which is now related to the exposure It in meter-candle-seconds as given by the H and D characteristic curves.

If we arbitrarily select some exposure E_0 for which we determine the values of exposure meters, exposure tables, or other exposure conditions in terms of other reference values of light intensity I_0, filter factor F_0, lens transmission T_0, aperture stop f_0, magnification M_0, exposure time t_0, and film speed S_0, the reference exposure is

$$E_0 = I_0't_0' = \frac{I_0kT_0t_0}{F_0f_0^2(M_0+1)^2} \tag{15}$$

In order that identical photographic effects may be obtained, it is necessary that $E = E_0$ so that

$$\frac{IkTt}{Ff^2(M+1)^2} = \frac{I_0kT_0t_0}{F_0f_0^2(M_0+1)^2} \tag{16}$$

From this relation we obtain, by dividing by the left-hand side of the equation and taking account of actual film speed S and reference film speed S_0

$$1 = \left(\frac{f^2}{f_0^2}\right)\left(\frac{t_0}{t}\right)\left(\frac{S_0}{S}\right)\left(\frac{F}{F_0}\right)\left(\frac{I_0}{I}\right)\left[\frac{(M+1)^2}{(M_0+1)^2}\right]\left(\frac{T_0}{T}\right) \tag{17}$$

This relation will be found invaluable for determining the exposure conditions for some unknown conditions when the exposure for other reference conditions are known. This equation can be especially helpful in extending the use of the exposure tables, given in a later section of this chapter, beyond the conditions for which they now apply. In practice $M_0 \ll 1$, $F_0 = 1$, and T_0/T is always 1 for the same lens system. Thus Eq. (17) may be reduced to the more practical form

$$1 = \left(\frac{f^2}{f_0^2}\right)\left(\frac{t_0}{t}\right)\left(\frac{S_0}{S}\right)F\left(\frac{I_0}{I}\right)(M+1)^2 \tag{18}$$

Since Eqs. (17) and (18) are in the form of ratios between known and unknown conditions, it does not make any difference in what units the factors are expressed, so long as both factors in the same parenthesis are expressed in the same system. Thus both S and S_0 must be expressed in the same speed system. This may be Weston, H and D, or Watkins. But the equations do not apply if S_0 is expressed in H and D and S in Weston figures.

The equations may be manipulated by simple algebra to determine any of the other factors which may be desired.

As a somewhat extreme but complete example of the application of these exposure equations, consider the following problem in which it is assumed that all the factors represented by letters having zero subscripts are known and the exposure is to be calculated for entirely different conditions.

Suppose we know from experience in copying a photograph full size ($M_0 = 1$), when the brightness is 100 candles per sq. ft. ($I_0 = 100$), the film speed is Weston 16 ($S_0 = 16$), and the aperture stop is $f/8$ ($f_0 = 8$), that the shutter speed is $\frac{1}{10}$ sec. ($t_0 = \frac{1}{10}$). No filter is used for the known conditions so that $F_0 = 1$. The transmission of the lens will not usually be known,[1] but for the sake of argument, assume a Tessar is used with a transmission of 85 per cent, so that $T_0 = 0.85$.

Now suppose we wish to determine the shutter speed when we use a film whose speed is Weston 20 ($S = 20$), an aperture stop of $f/5.6$ ($f = 5.6$), a filter whose factor is 4 ($F = 4$). Assume we use two identical lamps, instead of one as previously, so that $I = 2I_0 = 200$. Suppose we use a lens with more glass elements than before, so that the transmission may be taken as 68 per cent. Let us copy the photograph double size so that $M = 2$.

By multiplying Eq. (17) by t, we find the time exposure to be

$$t = t_0\left(\frac{f}{f_0}\right)^2\left(\frac{S_0}{S}\right)\left(\frac{F}{F_0}\right)\left(\frac{I_0}{I}\right)\left[\frac{(M+1)^2}{(M_0+1)^2}\right]\left(\frac{T_0}{T}\right) \tag{19}$$

Substituting the values given above, we find

$$t = \frac{1}{10} \times \left(\frac{5.6}{8}\right)^2 \times \left(\frac{16}{20}\right) \times 4 \times \left(\frac{100}{200}\right) \times \left[\frac{(2+1)^2}{(1+1)^2}\right] \times \frac{0.85}{0.68} = \frac{9}{40} \text{ sec.}$$

The value found is approximately 1/4.5 sec. so that $\frac{1}{4}$ sec. or $\frac{1}{5}$ sec. should be used, depending upon the shutter speed available.

Exposure. Practical Considerations.—In this section, it is proposed to discuss in some detail and from a practical rather than a theoretical point of view, the various factors which enter into and determine the exposure which must be given to the photographic material. Fundamentally, as we have seen from theoretical considerations, the important factors affecting exposure include: brightness of the object, aperture stop or f-number, filter factor, shutter speed, film speed or sensitivity, magnification of the image, and transmission of the lens system. From the practical point of view, however, a number of these factors frequently require simultaneous consideration in photographic practice. Thus, for example, the transmission of the lens system, as well as the magnification of the image, is involved when supplementary or telephoto lens are used or when only a single element of a doublet is used. Likewise the magnification of the image occurs in such practical matters as enlarging or reducing the size of the image or in copying to size. The intensity and quality of the illumination of the object is especially important when photographing outdoor subjects by daylight, as the time of day, condition of the sky, and type of subject being photographed influence the intrinsic brightness of the object.

Intensity and Quality of Light.—The intensity and quality of the light reaching the film from the object is undoubtedly the most important consideration in determining the photographic exposure. In comparatively few cases, as in astronomical photography, the objects being photographed are self-luminous. In this case only the intensity and spectral distribution of the luminous source need be considered. But where objects are illuminated by reflected light, as occurs in the great majority of instances of practical photography, the magnitude and spectral reflectance of the object must be considered as well as the intensity and quality of the light by which it is illuminated. For bright objects, for which the reflectance is high, more light will be produced at the camera lens from a given source of illumination than for those cases in which the objects are dark and the reflectance is small.

[1] See p. 226.

In considering the reflection of light from objects, attention should be directed not only to their reflection factor as determined by visual brightness but also to their reflection characteristics as related to the spectral sensitivity of the film and the spectral characteristics of the light source being used. A white light source has approximately equal energy in all parts of the visible spectrum and, for practical purposes, may also be considered to have equal energy in all parts of the spectrum to which the common photographic materials are sensitive. A white object photographed with white light will reflect much of the light into the lens, and the required exposure will be relatively short.

On the other hand a colored object will reflect that part of the white light corresponding to the color of the object and will absorb, more or less, colors of other portions of the spectrum. For objects having the same apparent brightness or reflection the photographic effect will be greatest for those colors to which the photographic material is most sensitive—in most cases, the blue end of the spectrum. Thus, for example, of a red and blue object illuminated by white light and appearing equally bright, the blue object will require the less exposure to produce a given density on the film. The reason for this is that the film is, most probably, more sensitive to blue than to red portions of the spectrum. This is certainly true in the case of "ordinary" or orthonon materials whose sensitivity lies almost entirely in the blue region of the spectrum; it is less true for orthochromatic materials which are sensitive to the blue, green, and yellow. While panchromatic emulsions are sensitive to all visible colors, maximum sensitivity is in the blue and green portions of the spectrum, although they have good sensitivity to the yellow, orange, and red. For practical purposes, the visual brightness of the subject may be used as an indication of the photographic effect, especially since the majority of scenes contain objects or areas of neutral colors, or colors having a wide range of spectral values. For fully panchromatic materials which are sensitive to all visible colors, the visual brightness of the object may be taken, for practical purposes, as an indication of the photographic effect.

The color of the light source must be considered in a similar way. A white object illuminated by a blue light can only reflect blue light to the film. The required exposure may be less than that of a white-light source of equal energy and of a white object. A blue object photographed by a blue light may produce approximately the same photographic effect as the white object illuminated by blue light of equal energy, because in each case the amount of blue light reflected is approximately the same. But a red object illuminated by blue light will absorb most of the light, reflecting little to the film, and in this case a comparatively long exposure must be given to produce a negative of specified density. It may happen that no matter how great an exposure is given, the object cannot be successfully photographed under these conditions. The rules by which the spectral characteristics of the film, light source, object, and filter (if one is used) affect exposure can be stated mathematically[1] but need not be considered in a practical treatment of the subject of exposure.

Broadly speaking, the more intense is the light by which an object is photographed, the greater will be the exposure and the resulting density, all other factors remaining unchanged. If a given or specified exposure is desired and the intensity of the light is increased, then the shutter speed will have to be increased, the aperture will have to be decreased (larger f-number), or some other factor will have to be altered in order to compensate for the increase in light. There are some exceptions to this general statement, however. A certain minimum amount of light must strike the film before the latent image is impressed on the emulsion; if less than this exposure is given, the grains of silver halide are not altered in the process of development. On the other hand, for

---

[1] Portions of this subject are treated in greater detail in the chapter on Light Filters.

very large exposures—much larger than are encountered in ordinary practice—the density of the silver deposit may no longer increase as the exposure is increased.

From Eq. (18) we may derive the following practical formula which indicates the light intensity required when various factors are changed. Thus

$$I = I_0\left(\frac{t_0}{t}\right)\left(\frac{f}{f_0}\right)^2\left(\frac{S_0}{S}\right)\left(\frac{T_0}{T}\right)F(M + 1)^2 \tag{20}$$

is the most general case likely to occur in practice. Equation (20) refers only to the intensity and not the spectral-energy distribution of the illuminant.

As an example of the application of this equation, suppose, as reference conditions, it is known that, for a light intensity of 100 units ($I_0 = 100$), an aperture stop of $f/8$ ($f_0 = 8$), and a film speed of Weston 20 ($S_0 = 20$), the required shutter speed is $\frac{1}{25}$ sec. ($t_0 = \frac{1}{25}$). When we are photographing a beach scene with a yellow filter having a factor of 5 ($F = 5$), it is desired to know what light intensity would be required for the same shutter speed ($t = \frac{1}{25}$) when the same film is used ($S = 20$) but when the aperture stop is $f/4$ ($f = 4$). For photographs of this type the magnification is so small that it may be neglected and we may consider that $M = 0$. Furthermore, since the same lens is used in both cases, $T_0 = T$, and consequently (T_0/T) becomes unity. Substituting these values into Eq. (20) the required illumination is found to be

$$I = 100\left(\frac{\frac{1}{25}}{\frac{1}{25}}\right)(\frac{4}{8})^2(\frac{20}{20}) \times 5 = 125 \tag{21}$$

so that the light required is not changed appreciably from its original value.

Aperture Stop or f-number.—The aperture stop or f-number is defined as the ratio of the principal focal length of a lens L to the diameter of its exit pupil d, or

$$f = \frac{L}{d} \tag{22}$$

For example, if a lens whose principal focal length is 8 in. has an aperture 1 in. in diameter, the f-number is $f/8$. For a given lens the f-number varies as the diameter of the iris diaphragm is changed. This diameter determines the amount of light reaching the film. By varying the f-number, the amount of light and consequently the exposure of the film may be controlled. It is customary to mark the lens system with a series of f-numbers each of which gives twice the exposure of the next highest number. Since the exposure is proportional to the square of the f-number, for the exposures to be doubled the f-numbers must progress in sequence according to $\sqrt{2}$.

TABLE II.—PROGRESSION OF ENGLISH AND CONTINENTAL APERTURE SYSTEMS

Continental System	English System
$f/1.6$	$f/1.4$
$f/2.3$	$f/2.0$
$f/3.2$	$f/2.8$
$f/4.5$	$f/4$
$f/6.3$	$f/5.6$
$f/9$	$f/8$
$f/12.5$	$f/11$
$f/18$	$f/16$
$f/25$	$f/22$
$f/36$	$f/32$
$f/50$	$f/45$
$f/72$	$f/64$

There are two methods of marking f-numbers in common use as shown in the Table II. In each case the exposure given by any stop is twice that of the next larger stop. The f-numbers engraved on a lens usually follow either the English or the Continental f-markings quite consistently, although some deviation from this practice frequently occurs for the largest aperture—the smallest f-number. For example, many lenses are marked in the English system but have a maximum aperture of $f/4.5$ rather than $f/4$.

From Eq. (18) we obtain, for the most general expression for the aperture stop, the expression,

$$f = f_0(M + 1)\sqrt{\left(\frac{t}{t_0}\right)\left(\frac{S}{S_0}\right)\left(\frac{I}{I_0}\right)\left(\frac{T}{T_0}\right)\left(\frac{1}{F}\right)} \tag{23}$$

As an example of the application of this relation, suppose exposure tables show that the proper exposure is $\frac{1}{25}$ sec. ($t_0 = \frac{1}{25}$) at an aperture stop of $f/8$ ($f_0 = 8$) if the film speed has a rating of Weston 16 ($S_0 = 16$). If we use a film having a speed of Weston 32 ($S = 32$), a filter having a factor of 4 ($F = 4$), and choose an exposure time $t = \frac{1}{5}$ sec. for identical conditions of illumination ($I_0 = I$), what will be the required aperture stop if the magnification may be neglected ($M = 0$)? Substituting values in Eq. (23), we find

$$f = 8 \times 1 \times \sqrt{\frac{\frac{1}{5}}{\frac{1}{25}} \times \frac{32}{16} \times 1 \times \frac{1}{4}} = 12.6 \tag{24}$$

If the lens is marked with an aperture of $f/12.5$, this should be used, otherwise an aperture of $f/11$ is likely to be nearest to the correct value. Intermediate f-number apertures can be obtained by setting the index of the iris diaphragm at a position intermediate between two markings. For all practical purposes $f/12.5$ would lie about one-third the distance from $f/11$ and $f/16$ and so on.

Filter Factor.—The purpose of filters is to absorb light of certain portions of the spectrum, thereby modifying the quality of the light reaching the negative. This modification of the quality of the light may be desired for technical or artistic reasons, but it always acts to reduce the amount of light reaching the film from that which would reach it if the filter were not used. In general, it may be said that the more dense a filter is, the more light it absorbs, and consequently the longer must be the exposure time—other conditions remaining unchanged—to produce a given film density.

But the color of a filter, or, more correctly, its spectral absorption, is also important in determining the increase in exposure occasioned by the use of the filter. The more light which a filter absorbs to which the film is sensitive, the greater will be the filter factor, and the greater will be the increase in exposure required as a result of using the filter. A filter absorbing blue light may appear yellow or orange to the eye and may seem to be, visually, as dense as a blue filter which has its principal absorption at the red end of the visual spectrum. But it is quite likely that the yellow filter will have the greater filter factor and consequently will require greater increase in exposure than the blue filter. The reason for this is that the film is usually more sensitive to blue than to red light, so that the yellow filter will cut out more effectively the light acting on the film than will the blue filter. It should be remembered that the filter factor is not a constant for a given filter but depends upon the spectral absorption of the filter (which is constant), the spectral sensitivity of the film, and the spectral-energy distribution of the light source used. Consequently the filter factor will change as the filter is used with different films or light sources.[1]

From Eq. (18) we can determine what effect the filter has on aperture stop, shutter speed, film sensitivity, or light intensity, etc. From this equation we find that

$$F = \left(\frac{t}{t_0}\right)\left(\frac{S}{S_0}\right)\left(\frac{f_0}{f}\right)^2\left(\frac{I}{I_0}\right)\left(\frac{T}{T_0}\right)(M + 1)^2 \tag{25}$$

---

[1] See chapter on Light Filters for further discussion of this point.

Ordinarily this equation is of little practical importance, although occasionally it may be found useful where a neutral-density filter is advantageous in cutting down the light without affecting the other quantities involved, as may sometimes be necessary when photographing bright sources of illumination.

For example, let the reference conditions be $S_0 = 16$, $t_0 = \frac{1}{10}$ sec., and $f_0 = 16$. It is desired to determine the filter factor for a neutral (gray) filter when the Weston film speed is $S = 40$, the aperture is $f = 4$, and the shutter speed is $t = \frac{1}{10}$ sec. The magnification, change in light, and transmission through the lens may be neglected. The required filter factor is then

$$F = \frac{\frac{1}{10}}{\frac{1}{10}} \times \frac{40}{16} \times \left(\frac{16}{4}\right)^2 = 40 \tag{26}$$

If a neutral-density filter is used, it should have a transmission of $\frac{1}{40}$ or a density of

$$D = \log_{10} \frac{1}{T} = \log_{10} 40 = 1.6 \tag{27}$$

This equation cannot be applied to filters having selective absorption unless the spectral characteristics of the filter are correlated with those of the light source and film in arriving at the desired result.

Shutter Speed.—The shutter speed may have two important functions in photography. Usually its most important function is to determine the quantity of light reaching the film by establishing the time during which the light passes through the lens to the photographic material. Its other function is to limit the time of exposure so that the relative motion between a moving object and its background does not produce a blur on the negative. These two functions of the shutter are entirely separate and distinct, although it may happen that the shutter speed for obtaining one of the desired conditions is also that for obtaining the other.

Since these two functions are distinct, it is necessary to determine them separately for the exposure and sharpness of image desired. It is then necessary to select the most suitable shutter speed and to adjust the aperture, if necessary, for the film speed and prevailing light conditions. If the shutter speed required to stop motion is longer than that required to give adequate exposure, the shutter speed determined for proper exposure should be given. On the other hand, if the shutter speed required to stop motion is less than that required to give proper exposure, the shutter speed should be used which will prevent blurring, and the f-number should be decreased to that value which will produce the desired exposure.

In order that the apparent motion of a moving object may be eliminated in a photograph, it is necessary that the shutter speed be sufficiently rapid that no appreciable motion of the object is apparent while the shutter is opened. The actual exposure time required to stop motion will depend upon the focal length of the lens, the distance between the camera and the moving object, and upon the speed of the moving object. It will also depend upon the direction of motion with respect to the camera, for a slightly longer exposure can be given, for a specified velocity of travel, if the object is coming toward or is receding from the camera rather than moving directly across the field of view.

Table III indicates the longest exposure times which may be regarded as being satisfactory to stop motion for the conditions stipulated. Faster shutter speeds may be given if unusually sharp negatives are desired, but light conditions, film, speed, aperture stop, and other matters affecting exposure must be taken into account to ascertain that the film is not underexposed. Slower shutter speeds should not be given unless some blurring of the image is tolerable.

TABLE III.—SHUTTER SPEEDS REQUIRED TO STOP MOTION ON THE PHOTOGRAPH

Relative motion between camera and object, m.p.h.	Distance between camera and object being photographed in multiples of the focal length of the lens system, F					
	$60F$	$100F$	$150F$	$250F$	$500F$	$1000F$
	Shutter speeds, fractions of a second					
0–1	$\frac{1}{30}$	$\frac{1}{20}$	$\frac{1}{12}$	$\frac{1}{6}$	$\frac{2}{5}$	$\frac{1}{2}$
2	$\frac{1}{60}$	$\frac{1}{30}$	$\frac{1}{25}$	$\frac{1}{15}$	$\frac{1}{8}$	$\frac{1}{3}$
3	$\frac{1}{100}$	$\frac{1}{60}$	$\frac{1}{40}$	$\frac{1}{25}$	$\frac{1}{12}$	$\frac{1}{6}$
4	$\frac{1}{125}$	$\frac{1}{75}$	$\frac{1}{50}$	$\frac{1}{30}$	$\frac{1}{15}$	$\frac{1}{8}$
6	$\frac{1}{200}$	$\frac{1}{100}$	$\frac{1}{75}$	$\frac{1}{50}$	$\frac{1}{25}$	$\frac{1}{10}$
8	$\frac{1}{250}$	$\frac{1}{150}$	$\frac{1}{100}$	$\frac{1}{60}$	$\frac{1}{30}$	$\frac{1}{15}$
10	$\frac{1}{300}$	$\frac{1}{200}$	$\frac{1}{125}$	$\frac{1}{75}$	$\frac{1}{40}$	$\frac{1}{20}$
15	$\frac{1}{500}$	$\frac{1}{300}$	$\frac{1}{200}$	$\frac{1}{125}$	$\frac{1}{60}$	$\frac{1}{30}$
20	$\frac{1}{600}$	$\frac{1}{400}$	$\frac{1}{250}$	$\frac{1}{150}$	$\frac{1}{75}$	$\frac{1}{40}$
30	$\frac{1}{1000}$	$\frac{1}{600}$	$\frac{1}{400}$	$\frac{1}{250}$	$\frac{1}{125}$	$\frac{1}{60}$
40	$\frac{1}{1200}$	$\frac{1}{750}$	$\frac{1}{500}$	$\frac{1}{300}$	$\frac{1}{150}$	$\frac{1}{75}$
60	$\frac{1}{2000}$	$\frac{1}{1000}$	$\frac{1}{750}$	$\frac{1}{500}$	$\frac{1}{250}$	$\frac{1}{100}$
80	$\frac{1}{2400}$	$\frac{1}{1500}$	$\frac{1}{1000}$	$\frac{1}{600}$	$\frac{1}{300}$	$\frac{1}{150}$
100	$\frac{1}{3000}$	$\frac{1}{2000}$	$\frac{1}{1250}$	$\frac{1}{750}$	$\frac{1}{400}$	$\frac{1}{200}$

The maximum shutter speed which is attainable with between-the-lens shutters is about $\frac{1}{500}$ sec. Faster shutter speeds may be obtained with focal-plane shutters. However, when a focal-plane shutter is used to photograph objects in rapid motion, distortion of the object is very likely to result. This is because the slit in the focal-plane shutter travels across the negative at a comparatively slow speed, while the image of the object travels across the plate. Depending upon the direction of the shutter motion relative to that of the moving object, focal plane distortion of this sort may result in foreshortened, lengthened, or tilted images. There is no remedy for this type of distortion, although it becomes less serious as the speed of the moving object is reduced and as the distance between the moving object and the camera is increased.

Changes in shutter speed which may be required when changes are made in aperture stop, film speed, intensity of light, or other factors may be found from the relation:

$$ t = t_0 F\left(\frac{S_0}{S}\right)\left(\frac{f}{f_0}\right)^2 (M+1)^2 \left(\frac{I_0}{I}\right)\left(\frac{T_0}{T}\right) \tag{28} $$

For example, suppose that the exposure table is calculated for reference Weston film speed of $S_0 = 16$, reference aperture $f_0 = 16$, and basic exposure time $t_o = \frac{1}{25}$ sec. and that it is desired to determine the exposure time for a film speed $S = 8$ at an aperture $f = 32$ with a filter factor $F = 1.5$ when the subject is so small that $M \to 0$. Using the above equation we find the new exposure time to be

$$ t = \frac{1}{25} \times 1.5 \times \frac{16}{8} \times \left(\frac{32}{16}\right)^2 \times 1^2 = \frac{12}{25} \cong \frac{1}{2} \tag{29} $$

Film Sensitivity or Speed.—The sensitivity or speed of negative materials is an important factor in determining the exposure required to produce a given deposit of silver. Various methods of determining the speed of photographic materials are in use; these methods are discussed in the chapter on Photographic Sensitometry and will not be treated here. It is sufficient to say that in all the common methods of specifying film speed, the larger numerics indicate the faster (more sensitive) materials, *i.e.*, those requiring less exposure to produce a given density on the negative. All other factors remaining constant, the quantity of light reaching the film may be reduced more and more, for a given density, the higher the speed of the film, provided the speed numbers are all in the same system of measurement. The speed numbers in the various systems do not progress in the same proportion as film speed increases, however.

So far as concerns the determination of exposure, the film-speed number has its principal value in connection with exposure meters which are calibrated in one of the various systems. It may be presumed, therefore, that, when a film and an exposure meter are both marked in the same system of film-speed units, the exposure conditions calibrated on the exposure meter will apply directly for the film marked in that system. Frequently it happens that an exposure meter is calibrated for one system of speed rating, whereas the film speed or sensitivity is given in another system. By means of the film-speed conversion table (see Appendix B), it is possible to determine approximately the equivalent speed of films in the various systems and, from the appropriate conversions, to make use of the dissimilar ratings of the film and meter calibration. In making such conversions, however, it must be remembered that the various speed systems may have been based on fundamentally different methods of measurement and that the equivalent conversions are determined empirically from measurements on a large number of films. Thus, while the conversion factors given represent average values, it is quite possible that some particular emulsion may not fit average conditions, and in such instances the conversion equivalents may be considerably in error.

The spectral sensitivity of the film has an important bearing on the exposure. Panchromatic materials are sensitive to all visible light but have maximum sensitivity to blue light and decreasing sensitivity throughout the rest of the visible spectrum. However, the sensitivity even to red light is sufficient that no difficulty will be encountered when objects of various colors are photographed or when lights of various colors are used for purposes of illumination. Orthochromatic materials, which are insensitive to the red and possibly orange portions of the visible spectrum, require longer exposures in yellow or orange light than panchromatic materials having the same daylight speed. Ordinary (or blue-sensitive) materials are sensitive only to the blue region of the visible spectrum, so that it may be quite impossible to make photographs with red or orange light, no matter how long an exposure is made. It is because of the change in spectral sensitivity that most films are now given two film speed ratings. One of these is a rating for light of daylight quality, having approximately equal energy in all portions of the visible spectrum. The other film speed is given for illumination by tungsten lamps operated at temperatures at about 2800 to 3000°K. For photoflash and photoflood illumination, in which the lamps operate at temperatures of 3200 to 3300°K., an appropriate film-speed rating will usually be somewhere between the daylight and the tungsten film-speed rating, although, if there is any doubt, the rating for tungsten lamps should be used.

If we know as reference conditions the aperture stop f_0, the shutter speed t_0, the film speed S_0, and the intensity of illumination I_0 for certain exposure conditions, we may determine new values of aperture stop f, shutter speed t, film speed, and intensity of illumination I for a properly exposed negative. From Eq. (18) we have

$$S = S_0 F\left(\frac{f}{f_0}\right)^2\left(\frac{t_0}{t}\right)\left(\frac{I_0}{I}\right)\left(\frac{T_0}{T}\right)(M + 1)^2 \tag{30}$$

As an example, suppose an aperture stop of $f/8$ is required for certain conditions when the film speed has a rating of Weston 8 and the shutter speed is $\frac{1}{20}$ sec. If the light is doubled, and a shutter speed of $\frac{1}{10}$ sec. is used with an aperture stop of $f/16$, what is the required film speed? The magnification and transmission factor may be neglected, and no filter is used. From these conditions we find that $S_0 = 8$, $F = 1$, $f_0 = 8$, $f = 16$, $t_0 = \frac{1}{20}$, $t = \frac{1}{10}$, and $I_0/I = 0.5$, since the final illumination I is twice the initial illumination I_0. From these values we obtain, from Eq. (30)

$$S = 8 \times 1 \times \left(\frac{16}{8}\right)^2 \times \left(\frac{\frac{1}{20}}{\frac{1}{10}}\right) \times \frac{1}{2} = 8 \tag{31}$$

so that a film of the same speed is suitable.

Exposure with Supplementary Lenses.—Sometimes supplementary lenses are used to increase or decrease the equivalent focal length of a lens. Since the addition of the supplementary lens does not change the engravings of the f-numbers, which are a measure of the diameter of the aperture, but does change the focal length of the lens, the supplementary lens changes the effective f-number of the combination so far as this is a measure of the light-collecting power of the lens system. Consequently the exposure is altered from that required when the supplementary lens is not used, at least so far as the engraved f-numbers may be taken as an indication of exposure.

The manner in which the actual exposure must be modified because of the change in focal length when a supplementary lens is used may be easily determined. Let E_0 be the exposure which is required for a given set of light conditions when the focal length of the lens is L_0 and the diameter of the aperture is d_0. Let E be the exposure required when the supplementary lens is used with the regular lens, so that the focal length of the combination is now L. The diameter of the aperture stop, as indicated by the engraved f-numbers remains unchanged and is therefore d_0. Then the engraved f-number will be

$$f_0 = \frac{L_0}{d_0} \tag{32}$$

whereas the true f-number of the combination will be

$$f = \frac{L}{d_0} \tag{33}$$

Thus for a given aperture the f-number is directly proportional to the focal length of the combination lens system. In terms of the exposure required without the supplementary lens, the exposure required when the supplementary lens is used will be

$$E = E_0\left(\frac{f}{f_0}\right)^2 = E_0\left(\frac{L}{L_0}\right)^2 \tag{34}$$

Sometimes the magnification which the supplementary lens produces will be given rather than its effect on the focal length. The f-number of the combination of this case will be

$$f = f_0(M + 1) \tag{35}$$

in terms of the engraved f-numbers and the magnification M, whereas the exposure will be

$$E = E_0(M + 1)^2 \tag{36}$$

in terms of the magnification and the exposure without the supplementary lens.

As an example, suppose we have a lens of 15-cm. focal length with a maximum f-number of 4.5. Then the maximum aperture will be $d_0 = L_0/f_0 = 15/4.5 = 3.33$ cm. If we use a supplementary lens which makes the combined focal length equal to

25 cm., then the maximum f-number will be $f = 25/3.33 = 7.5$. The exposure will then be

$$E = \left(\frac{25}{15}\right)^2 E_0 = 1.66^2 E_0 = 2.76 E_0 \tag{37}$$

or two and three-fourths that of the exposure without the supplementary lens. If a supplementary lens were used which decreased the focal length of the combination, the f-number would be reduced and the exposure with the supplementary lens would be less than that required without it.

In order to reduce to the minimum the mental labor involved in calculating exposures when making enlarged or reduced photographic images, Table IV has been prepared. This table shows the increase in exposure which is required for various magnifications from $\frac{1}{100}$ to 100 in column 2. In the third column, the ratio of the increase in exposure to that required for copying natural size is given.

Exposure with Single Elements of Lenses.—When a single element of a doublet is used rather than both elements (as in convertible lenses), the focal length of the single element is increased beyond that of the complete lens. So far as the exposure is concerned, the situation is very nearly the same as if a supplementary lens were used to increase the equivalent focal length. Consequently the remarks made under the paragraph above apply equally well here.

Exposure with Telephoto Lenses.—The function of a telephoto lens is to produce large images of distant objects with relatively short bellows extensions. A telephoto

TABLE IV.—RELATIVE EXPOSURE FOR ENLARGING OR REDUCING SIZE OF PHOTOGRAPH

M	$(1 + M)^2$	Relative exposure	M	$(1 + M)^2$	Relative exposure
$\frac{1}{100}$	1.02	0.25	10	121	30.25
$\frac{1}{90}$	1.02	0.25	11	144	36
$\frac{1}{80}$	1.03	0.26	12	169	42
$\frac{1}{70}$	1.03	0.26	13	196	49
$\frac{1}{60}$	1.03	0.26	14	225	56
$\frac{1}{50}$	1.04	0.26	15	256	64
$\frac{1}{40}$	1.05	0.26	16	289	72
$\frac{1}{30}$	1.07	0.27	17	324	81
$\frac{1}{20}$	1.10	0.28	18	361	90
$\frac{1}{10}$	1.21	0.30	19	400	100
$\frac{1}{9}$	1.24	0.31	20	441	110
$\frac{1}{8}$	1.27	0.32	22	529	132
$\frac{1}{7}$	1.31	0.326	24	625	156
$\frac{1}{6}$	1.36	0.34	26	729	182
$\frac{1}{5}$	1.44	0.36	28	841	210
$\frac{1}{4}$	1.56	0.39	30	961	240
$\frac{1}{3}$	1.78	0.45	35	1,296	324
$\frac{2}{5}$	1.96	0.49	40	1,681	420
$\frac{1}{2}$	2.25	0.56	45	2,116	529
$\frac{3}{5}$	2.56	0.64	50	2,601	650
$\frac{4}{5}$	3.24	0.81	55	3,136	784
1	4	1.00	60	3,721	930
2	9	2.25	65	4,356	1,089
3	16	4.00	70	5,041	1,260
4	25	6.25	75	5,776	1,444
5	36	9.00	80	6,561	1,640
6	49	12.25	85	7,396	1,849
7	64	16.00	90	8,281	2,070
8	18	20.25	95	9,126	2,304
9	100	25.00	100	10,201	2,550

lens consists of a positive doublet lens, such as are found in all good cameras, behind which is placed a compound negative lens at approximately half the distance of the focal length of the positive element. The telephoto lens may be constructed as a complete lens system, in which case fixed magnification is obtained, or it may be made by adding the negative element to the existing camera lens. In the latter case the size of the image is variable, since image size depends upon the separation between the two elements, which separation in turn is variable.

Fixed telephoto lenses are focused in the usual way, and no difficulty is encountered in determining the exposure. The procedure is the same as determining the exposure for any ordinary lens, since the equivalent focal length and aperture stops are specified by the manufacturer.

For telephoto lenses having variable focus, the determinations of exposure and magnification are not so simple as in the case of fixed-focus lenses. If L_p is the focal length of the positive lens element, L_n is the focal length of the negative lens element, M is the linear magnification obtained, and d is the bellows extension, the equivalent focal length of the combination is

$$L_f = ML_p \tag{38}$$

and the magnification obtained is

$$M = 1 + \frac{d}{L_n} \tag{39}$$

The equivalent aperture stop of the telephoto lens f_e in terms of the aperture stop marked for the positive lens element f_p is

$$f_e = Mf_p = f_p\left(1 + \frac{d}{L_n}\right) \tag{40}$$

It should be noted that for any given magnification the equivalent aperture of the telephoto lens is always M times the aperture stop of the positive element.

For example, if we have a 15-cm. positive lens with an aperture stop of $f/5.6$, a negative lens of 8 cm., and the bellows extension of 24 cms., the magnification is

$$M = 1 + {}^{24}\!/_8 = 1 + 3 = 4 \tag{41}$$

The focal length of the combination of lenses is

$$L_f = 4 \times 15 = 60 \text{ cm.} \tag{42}$$

and the maximum aperture

$$f_e = 4 \times 5.6 = 22.4 \tag{43}$$

When the equivalent aperture stop is determined, the telephoto lens may be used the same as any other lens and the exposure is determined with tables and exposure meters in the usual manner.

Absorption and Reflection in Lenses.—The amount of light transmitted through a lens depends not only upon the f-number and quantity of light incident upon it but also upon the amount absorbed in passing through the individual elements and that reflected from its various surfaces. The light transmission decreases as the number of elements of a lens increases, so that for a given aperture stop a simple lens may easily transmit more light than a more complicated and more highly corrected lens. Thus, so far as light transmission at a given aperture is concerned, a meniscus lens may transmit more light than a Tessar or Plasmat, and consequently may be a "faster" lens. Since the amount of light transmitted through the lens determines the exposure, it is apparent that all lenses do not produce the same exposure under identical light conditions and when used at the same aperture. It is, of course, true that the loss of light in a lens is not serious in the majority of cases arising in practical photography and that the latitude of film is sufficient to render absorption and reflection effects of a lens negligible in most cases.

On the other hand, the absorption and reflection of light which occurs in lenses is important for four practical reasons. Loss of light may be of considerable importance in those cases where very short exposures must be given under very unfavorable light conditions. Secondly, a lens of simple construction may actually transmit more light than a more elaborate lens of greater aperture (smaller f-number). Since the price of a lens is roughly proportional to its maximum aperture, it may actually happen that a simple, inexpensive lens having an f-number of $f/2$ is actually faster than a more complicated and expensive lens having an aperture stop of $f/1.5$. If speed is the only consideration, the less expensive lens may very easily be the better buy. In the third place, the fact that not all lenses have the same transmission at the same aperture stop gives support to the recommendation of exposure-meter manufacturers that the exposures determined from the meter may have to be altered in certain individual cases and that correction factors may have to be determined for each lens or camera. Finally, reflection of light from the surfaces of the individual glass components results in scattered light which decreases the contrast of the negative and may produce a dull print where a sparkling contrasty result was expected.

TABLE V.—ABSORPTION AND REFLECTION OF CEMENTED AND UNCEMENTED LENSES

Lens surface	Syntor lens		Dagor lens	
	Percentage of incident light	Percentage of transmitted light	Percentage of incident light	Percentage of transmitted light
First..............................	100.00	94.53	100.00	94.51
Second...........................	93.91	88.77	93.71	93.68
Third.............................	88.77	84.75	93.48	93.47
Fourth...........................	84.55	80.72	92.65	88.81
Fifth.............................	80.72	77.06	88.81	86.12
Sixth.............................	76.88	73.39	84.37	84.36
Seventh..........................	73.39	69.38	84.19	84.16
Eighth...........................	68.93	65.16	83.43	78.86

In general, as may be seen from Table V,[1] more light is lost by reflection from uncemented surfaces than is lost by transmission through a glass component. The loss of light at cemented surfaces due to reflection is generally negligible. It should be noted that the Dagor consists of four uncemented elements, whereas the Syntor consists of six cemented pieces of glass. Both lenses were marked as having a maximum aperture of $f/6.8$. But the Syntor transmits about 83 per cent as much light as the Dagor, and so far as light efficiency is concerned, the Syntor at $f/6.8$ is equivalent to the Dagor stopped down to $f/7.5$.

Exposure for Near-by Objects.—When the lens is extended beyond its infinity position for photographing objects near-by, the f-number engraved on the lens is no longer an accurate index of the light-gathering power of the lens, and consequently the indi-

[1] Compiled from data given on p. 81, Neblette, "Photography—Principles and Practice," 1st ed.

cated f-numbers lose their meaning in relation to the required exposure. The equivalent f-number and exposure under such conditions are given by Eqs. (35) and (36), respectively, in terms of magnification obtained. They may also be given in terms of the lens characteristics.

Let L_0 be the principal focal length of the lens, *i.e.*, the focal length for an object at infinity, and let L be the equivalent focal length when the bellows is extended for photographing near-by objects. Also let f_0 represent the aperture marked on the lens and f represent the actual f-number. Then the actual f-number when the bellows is extended, as for copying, is

$$f = f_0\left(\frac{L}{L_0}\right) = f_0(M + 1) \tag{44}$$

whereas the exposure required is

$$E = E_0\left(\frac{L}{L_0}\right)^2 = E_0(M + 1)^2 \tag{45}$$

where E_0 is the exposure required under the same conditions but with the lens at its infinity position.

For example, suppose we know that an exposure of $\frac{1}{25}$ sec. is required at aperture of $f/4.5$ when a lens of 15-cm. focal length is set at its infinity position. It is required to know the equivalent f-number and exposure when the lens-to-plate distance is increased to 30 cm. From the above equations involving focal lengths, we find the equivalent f-number to be

$$f = 4.5 \times {}^{30}\!/_{15} = f/9 \tag{46}$$

Methods of Determining Exposure.—There are three possible methods of determining photographic exposure: (1) estimating or guessing at it on the basis of past experience; (2) using exposure tables, calculators, or guides; and (3) using exposure meters. Estimating or guessing light values is extremely difficult because of the self-adjusting features of the human eye by which the iris automatically adapts the eye to light levels over a wide range. The use of exposure tables, calculators, or guides is of some assistance, but nevertheless experience is required to judge whether the light is intense, bright, or cloudy-bright. Furthermore, the eye cannot see "light" having wavelengths shorter than 400 mμ, and it is the wavelengths below those that the eye cannot see to which the photographic materials are usually most sensitive. Exposure meters are generally preferred to the previous methods outlined. There are three general types of exposure meters: (1) actinometers, based on the use of sensitive paper which darkens upon exposure to light, (2) visual exposure meters which measure reflected light through the medium of the human eye, and (3) photoelectric meters, capable of measuring either direct or reflected light by means of a photoelectric cell and a sensitive electric-current meter. The construction, use, advantages, and disadvantages of these various types of meters will be considered in greater detail in a later section of this chapter.

Relative Success Obtained with Various Exposure Aids.—The success which may be expected from the use of these various exposure devices depends upon their intelligent use and an understanding of their operation and limitations. It is reported[1] that Milbauer has found that the percentage of correct exposure given by these devices is as shown in Table VI. While these exact figures may not be supported by other observers, especially since the manner in which the results were obtained is not specified, it is safe to assume that the figures given by Milbauer are reasonable and at least approximately correct. Presumably these figures apply to amateur photog-

[1] *Fot. Rundschau,* **74** (No. 20), 348 (1937).

raphers, for professional photographers should certainly be able to determine exposure correctly, even without any aids, more than 45 per cent of the time.

Economic Justification for Exposure Meters.—If we adopt Milbauer's figures as given in Table VI, it is possible to arrive at some conclusions regarding the economic justification of photographic exposure aids.

TABLE VI.—CORRECT EXPOSURE OBTAINED WITH VARIOUS EXPOSURE AIDS

Exposure Device	Percentage of Correct Exposures
Exposure tables	45.0
Slide-rule devices, circular calculators, etc	47.2
Visual-type exposure meters, carefully used	87.8
Photoelectric exposure meters	97.3

By discarding exposure tables for exposure calculators of the slide-rule or disk type, it is possible to increase the number of properly exposed negatives from 45 to 47.2 per cent, a gain of 2.7 per cent. If a visual type of instrument is employed, the gain in correct exposures jumps from 45 to 87.8 per cent, representing an increase of 32.8 per cent. Good visual-type exposure meters are available in the United States for less than $3, and if their use assures that an additional 33 per cent of the negatives which are taken will be properly exposed, the meter will have paid for itself by the time $10 worth of film has been exposed.

On the basis just outlined, the use of a photoelectric exposure meter cannot be economically justified so easily because of the greater expense of these meters and the fact that the maximum possible improvement remaining is only 12.2 per cent. But the use of a photoelectric exposure meter will enable 52.3 per cent more films to be correctly exposed than exposure tables, and 10.5 per cent more than are correctly exposed with visual exposure meters. If $20 is assumed to be the price for a photoelectric exposure meter and that it will give an additional 52.3 per cent of correctly exposed film than exposure tables, it will take a film expenditure of $40 to pay for the meter. The 12.2 per cent improvement of the photoelectric type over the visual type of meter is attained with an expenditure for the meter of an additional $17. The sum will be amortized by a 12.2 per cent increase in properly exposed negatives after $139 worth of films have been exposed.

But an exposure meter merits consideration aside from the purely monetary aspect. The picture is the final result that is desired, and one picture may well be worth the cost of the meter in aesthetic value to the maker or commercially on the photographic market.

Exposure Devices. *Use of Exposure Tables.*—Undoubtedly the best method available for determining the proper exposure of photographic materials under most conditions (and for most branches of photography) is the proper use of the photoelectric type of exposure meter. Although the prices of these units have been reduced considerably in the past few years, they are still relatively expensive and are beyond the means of some photographers. In such cases recourse may be made to visual exposure meters or to exposure tables or calculators.

Reasonably extensive exposure tables are included in this chapter as an aid to the determination of the correct exposure. Such tables must be used with judicious discretion, and their use does not assure that proper exposure will always be attained. They can give only approximate exposure values which, on the basis of experience, have proved satisfactory for the conditions to which they apply. Unusual conditions encountered in practical photography may frequently require that the photographer deviate somewhat from the exposures indicates in the tables.

For convenience in use, the tables are divided into the following sections:

1. Black-and-white still photography. This section includes much basic data which is also applicable to other types of photography.

2. Color still photography.

3. Black-and-white motion-picture photography.

4. Color motion-picture photography.

Within each group will be found representative, or basic, exposure data which may be used as a guide for various lighting conditions including lighting by photoflood, Mazda, and photoflash lamps, as well as by daylight.

Conditions for Which Tables Are Determined.—The basic exposures given in the following tables are recommended as being approximately correct for the conditions stipulated in the title; additional conditions for which the tables apply will be found in the notes at the bottom of each table. In general, the tables are determined for those film speeds, apertures, shutter speeds, and lighting conditions which are believed to be most typical and consequently most frequently used. However, the exposure tables may be extended to apply to other conditions not listed but which the photographer may elect to use for some particular reason or another. The tables of basic exposure may be extended to apply to conditions other than the typical conditions by making the necessary alterations for various film-speed ratings, apertures, shutter speeds, and filters derived from Eq. (18).

In establishing the data for these exposure tables, it was desirable that some method be adopted to express the speed or sensitivity of the various types of emulsions which might be used in practice. Because of the soundness upon which the method is based, the excellent results which practical photographers have achieved using it, its rather extensive adoption in the photographic field, and the comparative ease with which the photographer can obtain speed ratings of a wide range of emulsions, the Weston film-speed rating has been chosen as the standard in the determination of the exposure tables.[1] The table of film-speed ratings given in Appendix B will assist the photographer in determining the speed of the film used.

Tables for Black-and-white Still Photography.—Listed among the tables giving basic exposure data for monochrome still photography are a number of tables which apply equally well to color or to motion-picture photography. They are included here since it is intended that this section give as much fundamental data on exposure as possible. The tables in other following sections of this chapter apply to those specialized cases where the specific type of photography demands a somewhat different treatment of exposure than can be given here.

Table VII gives the relation between the aperture (in both the f and the uniform systems—U. S.) and the relative exposure. The table may be used to convert an exposure with any given aperture to the exposure time required for an entirely different aperture, by forming a simple ratio. For example, suppose the tables of exposure indicate that the proper basic exposure is $t_0 = \frac{1}{10}$ sec. at an aperture $f_0 = 8$, but that we desire to find the exposure for an aperture $f = 5.6$. The relative exposure for $f = 8$ is 64, whereas for $f = 5.6$ it is 32. Since the aperture is increased in size, a smaller exposure time will be required and will in fact be $\frac{32}{64}$ times $\frac{1}{10}$ or $\frac{1}{20}$ sec.

The absolute values of numbers in the third column have no significance, and were chosen so that all figures would be greater than unity. The numbers have significance

---

[1] The photographer may make conversions to other methods of film speed, if he chooses, by means of the table of relative speed values given in Appendix B. However, it is recommended that the factors enumerated in Speed or Sensitivity, p. 190, be given careful and thoughtful consideration before the tables are converted to other film-speed ratings, as the systems by which film speed is determined vary widely. In any case the use of the Weston speed ratings is to be preferred to other speed ratings when using the exposure tables in this chapter.

only as indicating the relative exposures between the various apertures, as indicated in the example above.

Table VIII gives basic exposure data for the photography of outdoor subjects in daylight. For purposes of simplicity, this table has been reduced to the minimum amount of essential data which requires consideration and consequently should be used as a guide rather than as providing exact data. It is suitable, without correction, for clear days when the sun is shining unobscured and for films having speeds of Weston 24 to 48, and it applies for the larger part of the day. The table is supplemented with footnotes outlining the conditions for which the table applies and giving data on extending the range of the table.

TABLE VII.—RELATION BETWEEN APERTURES AND RELATIVE EXPOSURE

Aperture		Relative exposure	Aperture		Relative exposure
Number	U. S.		Number	U. S.	
$f/1.0$	0.063	1.00	$f/9$	5	81
$f/1.2$	0.088	1.44	$f/11.3$	8	128
$f/1.4$	0.125	2.00	$f/12.5$	9.8	156
$f/1.5$	0.141	2.25	$f/16$	16	256
$f/1.7$	0.18	2.88	$f/18$	20	324
$f/2.0$	0.25	4.00	$f/22.6$	32	512
$f/2.2$	0.30	4.84	$f/25$	40	625
$f/2.4$	0.36	5.76	$f/32$	64	1,024
$f/2.8$	0.50	8.00	$f/36$	80	1,296
$f/3.2$	0.64	10.24	$f/45.2$	128	2,048
$f/3.5$	0.77	12.25	$f/50$	156	2,500
$f/4.0$	1.0	16.0	$f/64$	256	4,096
$f/4.5$	1.26	20.25	$f/72$	324	5,184
$f/5.6$	2.0	32.0	$f/90.5$	512	8,192
$f/6.3$	2.5	39.7	$f/100$	625	10,000
$f/8$	4.0	64.0			

The exposure for outdoor subjects depends upon the quantity and quality of light which is available, and these in turn depend upon the time of day and the latitude as well as the state of the sky. Table IX shows the variation in light during the day for clear sky with sun shining unobstructed. The table is calculated for both the northern and southern hemispheres for latitudes as great as 65°. It may be used without correction for fully panchromatic materials to within an hour of sunrise and sunset. For orthochromatic materials, the exposures may be doubled or tripled within 2½ hr. of sunrise and sunset. The table does not show the exact exposure required for certain film speeds and apertures but merely indicates the manner in which the light varies throughout the day. If the correct exposure is known for a specified hour at a certain latitude and a given time of the year, the table may be used to indicate the correct exposure at other periods of the day and time of year, and even for other latitudes, within reason. For example, suppose the correct exposure for a clear day in New York City (latitude 42° N.) at 10 A.M., June (Eastern standard time or 11 A.M. day-light-saving time), is found to be ¹⁄₁₀ sec. Table IX shows that the relative light for this condition is 1.5. For the same film speed and aperture the exposure time may now be found for some other time of day. At 5 P.M., for example, the relative exposure due to decreased light is found to be 3. Thus the shutter speed should be increased by the factor $3/1.5 = 2$, so that for taking a picture in New York at 5 P.M. in June, the correct exposure time would be $\frac{1}{5}$ sec. if $\frac{1}{10}$ sec. were correct for the exposure at 10 A.M.

Table X gives basic exposure data for indoor photography using daylight only. Like Table VIII it has been reduced to the simplest possible form, and consequently should be regarded as being suggestive rather than providing exact data. It may be used for films having speeds of Weston 10 to 20 without correction. The tables are calculated for that part of the day in which the intensities of daylight are greatest. If desired, Table X may be corrected with the data provided by Table IX.

TABLE VIII.—EXPOSURES FOR BLACK-AND-WHITE STILL PHOTOGRAPHY IN DAYLIGHT
(Weston Rating—24 to 48)

Subject	Aperture	Sky conditions				
		Intensely bright day	Direct sun on bright day	Slightly cloudy, bright day	Dull day, sky overcast	Very dull day
		Shutter speed, sec.				
A. Clouds; open snow and glacier scenes; open sea; snow "against the light"	f/32	1/30	1/15	1/8	1/4	1/2
	f/16	1/125	1/60	1/30	1/15	1/8
	f/8	1/500	1/250	1/125	1/60	1/30
	f/4	1/2000	1/1000	1/500	1/250	1/125
	f/2	1/8000	1/4000	1/2000	1/1000	1/500
B. Sport scenes in snow or glacier; open landscape or beach; sport scenes in open; landscapes with light foreground	f/32	1/12	1/5	1/2	1	2
	f/16	1/50	1/25	1/12	1/5	1/2
	f/8	1/200	1/100	1/50	1/25	1/12
	f/4	1/800	1/400	1/200	1/100	1/50
	f/2	1/3200	1/1600	1/800	1/400	1/200
C. Wide streets and squares; light buildings; woods and landscapes with dark foregrounds; figures and groups in open, or at edge of woods	f/32	1/2	1	2	4	8
	f/16	1/8	1/4	1/2	1	2
	f/8	1/30	1/15	1/8	1/4	1/2
	f/4	1/125	1/60	1/30	1/15	1/8
	f/2	1/500	1/250	1/125	1/60	1/30
D. Buildings and rocks dark or against the light; persons and groups in shade of trees; persons and objects at windows in scene; narrow streets; light woodlands	f/32	2	4	8	16	32
	f/16	1/2	1	2	4	8
	f/8	1/8	1/4	1/2	1	2
	f/4	1/30	1/15	1/8	1/4	1/2
	f/2	1/125	1/60	1/30	1/15	1/8

This table shows recommended exposures for four different types of subjects and five different sky conditions which are typical of conditions likely to be encountered.

1. Light Values.—The light values are calculated for those conditions for which the light value in Table IX is unity (1). For other light values, multiply the shutter speed by the factor given in Table IX. The corrections for sky conditions are in addition to those given in Table IX for various latitudes and times of day.

2. Film Speed.—Tables are based on daylight film-speed rating of Weston 24 to 48. For other Weston film ratings, the shutter speed is inversely proportional to the Weston speed.

3. Time of Day.—Table applies to within 1 hr. of sunrise and sunset for panchromatic materials or within $2\frac{1}{2}$ hr. of sunrise and sunset for orthochromatic materials for all latitudes up to about 55°. For greater latitudes the tables cannot be used so close to sunrise or sunset without additional exposure.

4. Aperture.—Recommended exposures for five standard apertures are given. For converting to other apertures, see Eq. 23.

TABLE IX.—SHOWING VARIATION OF EXPOSURE DUE TO CHANGES OF LIGHT DURING THE DAY

Latitude	Month (northern hemisphere)	Local standard time									Month (southern hemisphere)
		12 M. 12 M.	11 A.M. 1 P.M.	10 A.M. 2 P.M.	9 A.M. 3 P.M.	8 A.M. 4 P.M.	7 A.M. 5 P.M.	6 A.M. 6 P.M.	5 A.M. 7 P.M.	4 A.M. 8 P.M.	
0–20°	June	1	1	1	1½	2	3				Dec.
	May, July	1	1	1	1½	2	3				Jan., Nov.
	Apr., Aug.	1	1	1	1½	2	3				Feb., Oct.
	Mar., Sept.	1	1	1	1½	2	3				Mar., Sept.
	Feb., Oct.	1	1	1	1½	2	3				Apr., Aug.
	Jan., Nov.	1	1	1½	2	3	4				May, July
	Dec.	1½	1½	1½	2	3	4				June
20–35°	June	1	1	1	1½	2	3	4			Dec.
	May, July	1	1	1½	1½	2	3	6			Jan., Nov.
	Apr., Aug.	1	1½	1½	2	3	4				Feb., Oct.
	Mar., Sept.	1½	1½	1½	2	3	6				Mar., Sept.
	Feb., Oct.	1½	1½	2	3	4	8				Apr., Aug.
	Jan., Nov.	2	2	2	3	4	8				May, July
	Dec.	2	2	3	4	6					June
35–45°	June	1	1	1½	1½	2	3	4			Dec.
	May, July	1	1½	1½	1½	2	3	4			Jan., Nov.
	Apr., Aug.	1½	1½	1½	2	3	4	6			Feb., Oct.
	Mar., Sept.	1½	1½	2	2	3	6				Mar., Sept.
	Feb., Oct.	2	2	3	3	4	6				Apr., Aug.
	Jan., Nov.	2	2	3	4	4	6				May, July
	Dec.	3	3	4	6	6					June
45–55°	June	1	1	1	1½	2	3	4	6		Dec.
	May, July	1½	1½	1½	2	3	4	6	8		Jan., Nov.
	Apr., Aug.	1½	1½	2	2	3	4	6	8		Feb., Oct.
	Mar., Sept.	2	2	2	3	4	6	8			Mar., Sept.
	Feb., Oct.	2	2	3	4	6	8				Apr., Aug.
	Jan., Nov.	3	3	4	6	8					May, July
	Dec.	4	4	6	8						June
55–60°	June	1	1	1	1½	2	3	4	6	8	Dec.
	May, July	1½	1½	1½	2	3	4	6	8		Jan., Nov.
	Apr., Aug.	1½	1½	2	2	3	4	6	8		Feb., Oct.
	Mar., Sept.	2	2	2	3	4	6	8			Mar., Sept.
	Feb., Oct.	3	3	3	4	6	8				Apr., Aug.
	Jan., Nov.	4	4	4	6	8					May, July
	Dec.	4	4	6	8						June
60–65°	June	1	1	1	1½	2	3	4	6	8	Dec.
	May, July	1½	1½	1½	2	3	4	6	8	11	Jan., Nov.
	Apr., Aug.	2	2	2	3	4	6	8	11		Feb., Oct.
	Mar., Sept.	3	3	3	4	6	8	11			Mar., Sept.
	Feb., Oct.	4	4	6	8	11					Apr., Aug.
	Jan., Nov.	6	6	8	11						May, July
	Dec.	8	8	11							June

This table gives the variation in exposure time which is required for various portions of the day and year, and for various latitudes from 65°N. to 65°S. The table may be used in conjunction with Table II for determining recommended exposures for outdoor subjects, or subjects lighted from daylight rather than artificial light.

The table is calculated for local standard time. If daylight-saving time is in effect, correct the actual time to standard time by subtracting 1 hr. before using the tables. Daylight-saving time is one hour earlier than standard time.

The table is calculated on the basis of clear sky, unobstructed by clouds.

TABLE X.—BASIC EXPOSURES FOR BLACK-AND-WHITE STILL PHOTOGRAPHY,
INDOORS: DAYLIGHT
(Weston Ratings—10 to 20)

	Aperture	Sky conditions				
		Intensely bright day	Direct sun on bright day	Slightly cloudy day	Dull day, sky overcast	Very dull day
		Exposure time				
A. White walls, and more than one window	f/32	20 s	40 s	1½ m	3 m	5 m
	f/16	5 s	10 s	20 s	40 s	1⅓ m
	f/8	1 s	2 s	4 s	8 s	15 s
	f/4	⅕ s	½ s	1 s	2 s	4 s
B. White walls, only one window	f/32	30 s	1 m	2 m	4 m	15 m
	f/16	7 s	15 s	30 s	1 m	4 m
	f/8	2 s	4 s	8 s	15 s	30 s
	f/4	½ s	1 s	2 s	4 s	8 s
C. Medium-colored walls and furnishings, more than one window	f/32	40 s	1⅓ m	2½ m	5 m	10 m
	f/16	10 s	20 s	40 s	1⅓ m	3 m
	f/8	2½ s	5 s	10 s	20 s	40 s
	f/4	1 s	2 s	4 s	8 s	15 s
D. Medium-colored walls and furnishings, one window	f/32	1 m	2 m	4 m	8 m	15 m
	f/16	15 s	30 s	1 m	2 m	4 m
	f/8	4 s	8 s	15 s	30 s	1 m
	f/4	1 s	2 s	4 s	8 s	15 s
E. Dark-colored walls and furnishings, more than one window	f/32	1½ m	3 m	6 m	12 m	25 m
	f/16	20 s	40 s	1½ m	3 m	5 m
	f/8	5 s	10 s	20 s	40 s	1½ m
	f/4	1 s	2 s	4 s	8 s	15 s
F. Dark-colored walls and furnishings, only one window	f/32	3 m	6 m	12 m	25 m	50 m
	f/16	40 s	1½ m	3 m	6 m	12 m
	f/8	10 s	20 s	40 s	1½ m	3 m
	f/4	2½ s	5 s	10 s	20 s	40 s

　　Table X gives the recommended exposure for indoor subjects lighted by daylight. Because indoor photography is subject to widely differing light conditions, some judgment will have to be exercised in using this table.

　　1. Light Values.—The table is based on light values of unity (1) as given in Table IX. If other conditions apply, the exposure time given in Table X should be multiplied by the factors in Table IX which are appropriate. Table X applies to conditions where the room being photographed has free access to full daylight. If tall buildings in the immediate surroundings block off much of the daylight, the exposure times given may have to be increased considerably.

　　2. Film Speed.—Table X is based on film speeds having a daylight rating of Weston 10 to 20. For other film speeds, exposure time is inversely proportional to the Weston rating.

　　3. Time of Day.—The time of day for which Table X applies is to within 1 hr. of sunrise and sunset for panchromatic material or to within 2½ hr. of sunrise and sunset for orthochromatic materials if the room has free access to full daylight. If tall buildings cut off available daylight, the exposures may have to be increased considerably during the early morning or late afternoon.

　　4. Aperture.—Exposures for four standard apertures are given. For converting to other apertures see Eq. (23).

Table XI gives the exposure data for photoflood lamps, having various types of reflectors, for various distances between lamp and the subject. The table is devised for only one photoflood lamp; if two, three, or four lamps are used in the same reflector, the exposure times may be reduced to one-half, one-third, or one-fourth of the time specified for the single lamp.

TABLE XI.—TABLE OF BASIC EXPOSURE FOR BLACK-AND-WHITE STILL PHOTOGRAPHY
USING PHOTOFLOOD LAMP
(Weston Ratings—10 to 20)

Reflector	Distance, lamps to subject, ft.	No. 1 lamp Aperture				No. 2 lamp Aperture				No. 4 lamp Aperture			
		f/4	f/8	f/16	f/32	f/4	f/8	f/16	f/32	f/4	f/8	f/16	f/32
		Shutter speed, sec.											
None	2	1/60	1/15	1/4	1	1/125	1/30	1/8	1/2	1/500	1/125	1/30	1/8
	3	1/30	1/8	1/2	2	1/60	1/15	1/4	1	1/250	1/60	1/15	1/4
	4	1/20	1/5	1	4	1/30	1/8	1/2	2	1/125	1/30	1/8	1/2
	6	1/8	1/2	2	8	1/15	1/4	1	4	1/30	1/8	1/2	2
	8	1/5	3/4	3	12	1/10	2/5	1 1/2	6	1/20	1/5	3/4	3
	10	1/4	1	4	15	1/8	1/2	2	8	1/15	1/4	1	4
	15	1/2	2	8	30	1/4	1	4	15	1/8	1/2	2	8
	20	3/4	3	12	45	2/5	1 1/2	6	25	1/5	3/4	3	12
White paper (Exposure values depend to large extent on angle over which light is directed)	2	1/250	1/60	1/15	1/4	1/500	1/125	1/30	1/8	1/1000	1/250	1/60	1/15
	3	1/125	1/30	1/8	1/2	1/250	1/60	1/15	1/4	1/500	1/125	1/30	1/8
	4	1/80	1/20	1/5	1	1/150	1/40	1/10	1/2	1/300	1/80	1/20	1/5
	6	1/30	1/8	1/2	2	1/60	1/15	1/4	1	1/125	1/30	1/8	1/2
	8	1/20	1/5	3/4	3	1/40	1/10	2/5	1 1/2	1/80	1/20	1/5	4/5
	10	1/20	1/4	1	4	1/30	1/8	1/2	2	1/60	1/15	1/4	1
	15	1/8	1/2	2	8	1/15	1/4	1	4	1/30	1/8	1/2	2
	20	1/5	3/4	3	12	1/10	2/5	1 1/2	6	1/20	1/5	3/4	3
Polished metal (Exposure values depend to large extent on angle over which light is directed)	2	1/600	1/150	1/40	1/10	1/1200	1/300	1/60	1/20	1/2400	1/600	1/150	1/40
	3	1/300	1/80	1/20	1/5	1/600	1/150	1/40	1/10	1/1200	1/300	1/80	1/20
	4	1/150	1/40	1/10	2/5	1/300	1/80	1/20	1/5	1/600	1/150	1/40	1/10
	6	1/80	1/20	1/5	4/5	1/150	1/40	1/10	2/5	1/300	1/80	1/20	1/5
	8	1/45	1/10	2/5	1/2	1/80	1/20	1/5	4/5	1/150	1/40	1/10	2/5
	10	1/60	1/8	1/2	2	1/60	1/15	1/4	1	1/30	1/8	1/2	2
	15	1/10	2/5	1 1/2	6	1/20	1/5	4/5	3	1/60	1/12	1/3	1 1/3
	20	1/15	1/2	2	8	1/15	1/4	1	4	1/30	1/8	1/2	2

Table XI gives the recommended exposures for subjects lighted by photoflood lamps of various sizes and for different distances between the lamp and the subject.

1. Film Speed.—Table XI is based on the use of film having a tungsten speed rating of Weston 10 to 20. For other film speeds the exposure time required is inversely proportional to the Weston rating.

2. Aperture.—Exposures for four standard apertures are given. For converting data of Table XI for other apertures, see Eq. (23).

3. Number of Lamps.—Only one lamp of the type specified is assumed. If n similar lamps are used at the same distance from the subject, divide the exposure times by n. It should be noted that two No. 1 lamps are equivalent to one No. 2 lamps, and two No. 2 lamps are equivalent to one No. 4 photoflood lamp.

4. Distance between Lamp and Subject.—If lamps are used at varying distances from the subject, the exposure time for each lamp, separately, should be determined. The resultant exposure may then be calculated by determining the reciprocal of the sum of the reciprocals of the separate exposures. For example, if one No. 1 lamp is 4 ft. from the subject, and one No. 2 lamp is 6 ft. from the subject, the exposures at $f/16$ are $\frac{1}{5}$ and $\frac{1}{4}$ sec., respectively. The resultant exposure time is then

$$t = \frac{t_1 t_2}{t_1 + t_2} = \frac{\frac{1}{5} \times \frac{1}{4}}{\frac{1}{5} + \frac{1}{4}} = \frac{\frac{1}{20}}{\frac{9}{20}} = \frac{1}{9} \text{ sec.}$$

It should be noted that the resultant exposure time will always be less than the shortest exposure for any given single lamp.

5. Reflectors.—No very specific data can be given for those cases in which reflectors are used, because the shape and surface of the reflector have large effects on the light beam which cannot be determined unless the reflecting system is fairly completely specified. In such cases it is best to determine the proper exposure by means of an exposure meter. However, as a rough and approximate guide, the exposures given in Table XI may be considered as being approximately correct for the types of reflectors ordinarily used. This statement is based on experience and empirical relations rather than scientific facts and applies to the majority of reflectors for photographic use. It does not apply to spotlight reflectors where the rays are collimated into a very narrow beam, in which case a shorter exposure may be appropriate.

TABLE XII.—EXPOSURE FOR BLACK-AND-WHITE STILL PHOTOGRAPHY, 100-WATT MAZDA LAMPS
(Weston Ratings—10 to 20)

Reflectors	Distance, lamps to subject, ft.	Aperture										
		$f/1.4$	$f/2.0$	$f/2.8$	$f/4.0$	$f/5.6$	$f/8$	$f/11$	$f/16$	$f/22$	$f/32$	$f/45$
		Shutter speed										
None	2	$\frac{1}{8}$	$\frac{1}{4}$	$\frac{1}{2}$	1	2	4	8	15	30	1 m	2 m
	3	$\frac{2}{5}$	$\frac{1}{2}$	1	$2\frac{1}{2}$	$4\frac{1}{2}$	9	18	35	$1\frac{1}{4}$ m	$2\frac{1}{2}$ m	$4\frac{1}{2}$ m
	4	$\frac{1}{2}$	1	2	4	8	15	30	1 m	2 m	4 m	8 m
	6	1	2	4	9	18	36	$1\frac{1}{4}$ m	$2\frac{1}{2}$ m	5 m	10 m	20 m
	8	2	4	8	15	30	1 m	2 m	4 m	8 m	15 m	30 m
	10	3	6	12	25	45	$1\frac{1}{2}$ m	3 m	6 m	12 m	25 m	45 m
	15	8	16	30	1 m	2 m	4 m	8 m	15 m	30 m	1 h	2 h
	20	12	22	45	$1\frac{1}{2}$ m	3 m	6 m	12 m	25 m	45 m	$1\frac{1}{2}$ h	3 h
White paper (exposure values depend to large extent on angle over which light is directed)	2	$\frac{1}{15}$	$\frac{1}{8}$	$\frac{1}{4}$	$\frac{1}{2}$	1	2	4	8	15	30	1 m
	3	$\frac{1}{8}$	$\frac{1}{4}$	$\frac{1}{2}$	$1\frac{1}{4}$	$2\frac{1}{4}$	$4\frac{1}{2}$	9	18	36	$1\frac{1}{4}$ m	$2\frac{1}{2}$ m
	4	$\frac{1}{4}$	$\frac{1}{2}$	1	2	4	8	15	30	1 m	2 m	4 m
	6	$\frac{1}{2}$	1	2	$4\frac{1}{2}$	9	18	36	$1\frac{1}{4}$ m	$2\frac{1}{2}$ m	5 m	10 m
	8	1	2	4	8	15	30	1 m	2 m	4 m	8 m	15 m
	10	$1\frac{1}{2}$	3	6	12	25	45	$1\frac{1}{2}$ m	3 m	6 m	12 m	25 m
	15	4	8	15	30	1 m	2 m	4 m	8 m	15 m	30 m	1 h
	20	6	12	22	45	$1\frac{1}{2}$ m	3 m	6 m	12 m	25 m	45 m	$1\frac{1}{2}$ h
Polished metal (exposure values depend to large extent on angle over which light is directed)	2	$\frac{1}{30}$	$\frac{1}{15}$	$\frac{1}{8}$	$\frac{1}{4}$	$\frac{1}{2}$	1	2	4	8	15	30
	3	$\frac{1}{15}$	$\frac{1}{8}$	$\frac{1}{4}$	$\frac{1}{2}$	1	2	4	8	15	30	1 m
	4	$\frac{1}{8}$	$\frac{1}{4}$	$\frac{1}{2}$	1	2	4	8	15	30	1 m	2 m
	6	$\frac{1}{4}$	$\frac{1}{2}$	1	2	4	8	15	30	1 m	2 m	4 m
	8	$\frac{1}{2}$	1	2	4	8	15	30	1 m	2 m	4 m	8 m
	10	$\frac{3}{4}$	$1\frac{1}{2}$	3	6	12	25	45	$1\frac{1}{2}$ m	3 m	6 m	12 m
	15	2	4	8	15	30	1 m	2 m	4 m	8 m	15 m	30 m
	20	3	6	12	25	45	$1\frac{1}{2}$ m	3 m	6 m	12 m	25 m	45 m

Table XII gives recommended exposures for artificially lighted subjects for various apertures, types of reflectors, and distances between lamp and subject.

1. Film Speed.—Table XII is based on an assumed film speed for tungsten of Weston 10 to 20. For other film speeds the required exposure time is inversely proportional to the Weston rating of this film.

2. Aperture.—The exposures for various apertures are given, but conversion may be made for other apertures, if this is desirable, by Eq. (23).

3. Number of Lamps.—Table XII is based on the assumption that one 100-watt lamp is used, having a clear or white-frosted, rather than daylight, bulb. If daylight bulbs are used, the exposures will have to be increased for the same lamp rating, because of the filtering action of the bulb. For lamps of other power ratings than 100 watts, the exposures given should be multiplied by $100/W$, where W is the power consumption of the lamp used, in watts.

If several lamps at varying distances from the subject are used, the resultant exposure may be found from the individual exposures required for each lamp. If the exposure time required for one lamp is t_1, and that required by another lamp, t_2, the net or resultant exposure is given by

$$t = \frac{t_1 t_2}{t_1 + t_2}$$

4. Subject.—Table XII is based on average- or medium-colored subjects. If dark subjects are photographed, the exposure should be increased. The exposure may be decreased if light-colored objects are being photographed.

5. Reflectors.—No very specific data can be given for those cases in which reflectors are used, because the shape and surface of the reflector have large effects on the light beam which cannot be determined unless the reflecting system is specified. The values given may be regarded as correct for average conditions, however.

TABLE XIII.—EXPOSURES FOR STILL BLACK-AND-WHITE PHOTOGRAPHY WITH
PHOTOFLASH LAMPS
(Weston Ratings—10 to 20)

Photoflash	No. 10 lamp			No. 20 lamp			No. 75 lamp		
Type of reflector	None	Paper*	Metal*	None	Paper*	Metal*	None	Paper*	Metal*
Distance, lamp to subject, ft.	Aperture			Aperture			Aperture		
3	$f/25$	$f/36$	$f/50$	$f/35$	....	....	$f/50$		
4	$f/19$	$f/27$	$f/38$	$f/27$	$f/38$	$f/54$	$f/38$	$f/54$	
5	$f/15$	$f/21$	$f/30$	$f/21$	$f/30$	$f/42$	$f/30$	$f/42$	
6	$f/12.5$	$f/18$	$f/25$	$f/17.5$	$f/25$	$f/35$	$f/25$	$f/35$	$f/50$
8	$f/9$	$f/12.6$	$f/18$	$f/14$	$f/20$	$f/28$	$f/19$	$f/27$	$f.32$
10	$f/7.5$	$f/10.5$	$f/15$	$f/11$	$f/16$	$f/22$	$f/16$	$f/22$	$f.32$
15	$f/5$	$f/7$	$f/10$	$f/7$	$f/10$	$f/14$	$f/10$	$f/14$	$f/20$
20	$f/4$	$f/5.6$	$f/8$	$f/5.6$	$f/8$	$f/11$	$f/8$	$f/11$	$f/16$
30	$f/2.5$	$f/3.6$	$f/5.0$	$f/3.5$	$f/5.0$	$f/7.0$	$f/5$	$f/7.0$	$f/10$
50	$f/1.5$	$f/2.1$	$f/3.0$	$f/2.1$	$f/3.0$	$f/4.2$	$f/3.0$	$f/4.2$	$f/6.0$

* See note 3.

Table XIII gives suggested exposures for black-and-white photography with photoflash lamps with various types of reflectors for various distances between lamp and subject.

1. Film Speed.—The table is based on a tungsten film speed of Weston 10 to 20. For other film speeds, the required f-number is directly proportional to the Weston rating.

2. Number of Lamps.—Table XIII is calculated for one photoflash lamp in each reflector. If n similar lamps are used in the same reflector, the f-number given should be multiplied by n. For example, if four No. 10 lamps 10 ft. from the subject are used in a polished-metal reflector, the aperture would be $4 \times 7.5 = f/30$.

3. Reflectors.—Where reflectors are used, the data are to be regarded as approximate because the manner in which the reflector directs the light modifies the exposure considerably.

Table XII shows basic exposure data for ordinary incandescent lamps operated at normal voltages which result in a lamp life of approximately 1000 hr. The use of clear or frosted lamps, rather than blue "daylight" lamps, is assumed. The table is calculated for a lamp having a power-consumption rating of 100 watts, but the correct exposure for lamps of other power rating W may be determined by multiplying by $100/W$. The table applies to portraits and light-colored interiors. For darker subject matter the exposures should be increased; exposure should be decreased for lighter than average subjects.

Table XIII gives the proper aperture when photoflash lamps are used at a specified distance from the subject. The table is based on the assumption that the shutter will be opened throughout the duration of the flash; if synchronized flashes are used, one stop larger than is indicated should be used.

Exposure data for flashlight powders is given in Table XIV, although photoflash lamps have almost entirely superseded the use of flashlight powders. The table gives the basic amount of flashlight or magnesium powder suitable for use with a film having a speed or sensitivity rating of Weston 24 to 48.

TABLE XIV.—EXPOSURE WITH FLASHLIGHT POWDERS
(Weston Ratings—24 to 48)

Distance between subject and flashlight, ft.	Aperture at which photograph is made				
	$f/4$	$f/5.6$	$f/8$	$f/11$	$f/16$
	Basic amount of flashlight powder required, gr.				
1	0.37	0.75	1.5	3	6
2	0.87	1.75	3.5	7	14
5	2.87	5.75	11.5	23	46
7	4.62	9.25	18.5	37	74
10	7.5	15	30	60	120
15	13.75	27.5	55	110	220
20	20	40	80	160	320
30	37.5	75	150	300	600
50	75	150	300	600	1200
70	120	240	480	960	1920
100	200	400	800	1600	3200

The tables are based on film sensitivity of Weston 24 to 48. For other speeds,

	multiply apertures by 6	for Weston speeds between	0.6 and	1.2
"	"	" 4 " " "	" 1.5 "	3.5
"	"	" 2.5 " " "	" 4 "	8
"	"	" 1.4 " " "	" 10 "	20
"	"	" 1 " " "	" 24 "	48
"	"	" 0.6 " " "	" 64 "	128

The method of calculating exposure through the use of closing the diaphragm until the detail which it is desired to record just disappears may be explained as follows: Cover the camera and head with focusing cloth, and focus the subject at the full lens aperture. After the eyes have been accustomed to the luminous intensity of the ground-glass screen, stop down the lens aperture slowly until the detail in the deepest shadow it is desired to record has just disappeared. Detail in the deepest shadow would be faintly, but distinctly, observable when the eyes are directly opposite that portion of the ground glass on which the shadows occur. Note this aperture stop

f_0. The exposure for any film having a Weston speed of 24 to 48 will be found in Table XV for the aperture f at which the photograph is made. This table is suitable for use with black-and-white or color photography so long as proper correction is made for film speed and the light employed is suitable for color photography.

TABLE XV.—USE OF DIAPHRAGM APERTURE IN DETERMINING EXPOSURE
(Weston Rating—24 to 48)

Aperture used in making the exposure	Aperture at which desired detail can just be seen, f_0									
	$f/2.8$	$f/4.0$	$f/5.6$	$f/8$	$f/11$	$f/16$	$f/22$	$f/32$	$f/45$	$f/64$
	Required exposure for film having Weston speed of 24 to 48									
$f/2$	1¼ m	40 s	20 s	10 s	5 s	2½ s	1 s	½ s	¼ s	⅛ s
$f/2.8$	2½ m	1¼ m	40 s	20 s	10 s	5 s	2½ s	1 s	½ s	¼ s
$f/4$	5 m	2½ m	1¼ m	40 s	20 s	10 s	5 s	2½ s	1 s	½ s
$f/5.6$	10 m	5 m	2½ m	1¼ m	40 s	20 s	10 s	5 s	2½ s	1 s
$f/8$	20 m	10 m	5 m	2½ m	1¼ m	40 s	20 s	10 s	5 s	2½ s
$f/11$	40 m	20 m	10 m	5 m	2½ m	1¼ m	40 s	20 s	10 s	5 s
$f/16$	1 h 20 m	40 m	20 m	10 m	5 m	2½ m	1¼ m	40 s	20 s	10 s
$f/22$		1 h 20 m	40 m	20 m	10 m	5 m	2½ m	1¼ m	40 s	20 s
$f/32$			1 h 20 m	40 m	20 m	10 m	5 m	2½ m	1¼ m	40 s
$f/45$				1 h 20 m	40 m	20 m	10 m	5 m	2½ m	1¼ m
$f/64$					1 h 20 m	40 m	20 m	10 m	5 m	2½ m

The tables are calculated for films having a speed of Weston 24 to 48. For films having other speeds

multiply exposure time by 40	for speeds between	0.6 and	1.2
" " " " 16	" " "	1.5 "	3
" " " " 6	" " "	4 "	8
" " " " 2.5	" " "	10 "	20
" " " " 1	" " "	24 "	48
" " " " 0.4	" " "	64 "	128

Exposures for outdoor photography at night are given in Table XVI. The table is based on a film having a speed of Weston 8 and applies for various types of subjects. Values of exposure are given for apertures of from $f/2$ to $f/32$, but data for other apertures may be determined by interpolation, or by means of Eq. (23).

Table XVII gives the maximum exposures for moving objects which will "stop motion" in the photograph when a lens of 5- or 2-in. focal length is used. Corrections for other focal lengths may be made in the manner indicated at the bottom of the table. The shutter speeds given are based on the relative apparent speed of the object across the camera field and do not bear any relation to the shutter speed which may be required for proper exposure. The shutter speed required for exposure may be determined from other tables or by exposure meters, but Table XVII gives the limiting shutter speeds if sharp outlines are desired for moving objects.

This table should be used in conjunction with exposure tables when photographing moving objects. It is, perhaps, best to determine the shutter speed from Table XVII for the type of moving subject being photographed, after which the aperture and film speed for this shutter speed may be determined. For example, if we are photographing a small boat moving 10 m.p.h. (approximately 9 knots) obliquely across the field when it is 25 ft. from the camera, the shutter speed required for a 5-in. lens will be ⅟₂₀₀ sec. By reference to Table VIII, we find that the subject matter falls into group A. If the sky is slightly cloudy an exposure of $\frac{1}{30}$ sec. at $f/16$ is required. But, since the permissible shutter speed is $\frac{1}{200}$ sec., we shall have to increase the aperture to obtain correct exposure at $\frac{1}{200}$ sec. If we are using a film having a speed

TABLE XVI.—EXPOSURE FOR OUTDOOR PHOTOGRAPHY AT NIGHT
(Weston Ratings—10 to 20)

Subject	Aperture								
	$f/2$	$f/2.8$	$f/4.0$	$f/5.6$	$f/8$	$f/11$	$f/16$	$f/22$	$f/32$
	Exposure time								
Shop fronts, brightly lighted	4 s	8 s	15 s	30 s	1 m	2 m	4 m	8 m	15 m
Illuminated grounds, or buildings with interior illumination	8 s	15 s	30 s	1 m	2 m	4 m	8 m	15 m	30 m
Open street scenes, without near dark objects	15 s	30 s	1 m	2 m	4 m	8 m	15 m	30 m	1 h
Open street scenes, without dark near objects, snow-covered ground or wet pavements	10 s	20 s	40 s	$1\frac{1}{4}$ m	$2\frac{1}{2}$ m	5 m	10 m	20 m	40 m
Street scenes with near dark objects	30 s	1 m	2 m	4 m	8 m	15 m	30 m	1 h	2 h
Street scenes with near dark objects, snow-covered ground or wet pavement	20 s	40 s	$1\frac{1}{4}$ m	$2\frac{1}{2}$ m	5 m	10 m	20 m	40 m	$1\frac{1}{3}$ h
Buildings with floodlight illumination only	30 s	1 m	2 m	4 m	8 m	15 m	30 m	1 h	2 h
Floodlighted open street scenes without near dark objects	1 m	2 m	4 m	8 m	15 m	30 m	1 h	2 h	4 h
Floodlighted street scenes, with near dark objects	2 m	4 m	8 m	15 m	30 m	1 h	2 h	4 h	8 h

Table XVI gives suggested exposures for various subjects for outdoor night photography. The wide range of conditions which are actually encountered requires that Table XVI be used as a guide in determining suitable exposures, rather than to provide fixed and unvarying data.

1. Film Speed.—Table XVI is based on a film speed having a tungsten rating of Weston 10 to 20. For converting the given exposures with films having other speeds,

multiply exposure time by 16 for speeds between 0.6 and 1.2
    "   "   "   " 6   "   "   "   1.5 "   3
    "   "   "   " 2.5 "   "   "   4   "   8
    "   "   "   " 1.0 "   "   "   10 " 20
    "   "   "   " 0.4 "   "   "   24 " 48
    "   "   "   " 0.15 "   "   "   64 " 128

2. Aperture.—Table XVI shows exposures for nine apertures. For converting to other apertures, see Eq. (23).

of Weston 20 for which Table VIII applies, we can then determine the requisite aperture by using the expression

$$f = f_0 \sqrt{\frac{t}{t_0}} \tag{47}$$

Thus the correct aperture for our example will be

$$= 16\sqrt{\frac{\frac{1}{200}}{\frac{1}{30}}} = 6.2 \tag{48}$$

An aperture of $f/6.3$ would be correct.

TABLE XVII.—EXPOSURE FOR MOVING OBJECTS

Speed, m.p.h.	Typical subjects	2-in.-focal-length lens			5-in.-focal-length lens		
		Objects moving directly toward camera	Objects moving obliquely across field of view	Objects moving across field of view	Objects moving directly toward camera	Objects moving obliquely across field of view	Objects moving across field of view
		Exposure time, sec.					
0–1	Landscapes, sea scapes, street groups	$\frac{1}{4}$	$\frac{1}{8}$	$\frac{1}{12}$	$\frac{1}{10}$	$\frac{1}{20}$	$\frac{1}{30}$
2	Slow-walking pedestrians	$\frac{1}{8}$	$\frac{1}{150}$	$\frac{1}{25}$	$\frac{1}{20}$	$\frac{1}{40}$	$\frac{1}{60}$
3	Walking pedestrians	$\frac{1}{12}$	$\frac{1}{25}$	$\frac{1}{40}$	$\frac{1}{30}$	$\frac{1}{60}$	$\frac{1}{100}$
4	Fast-walking pedestrians	$\frac{1}{15}$	$\frac{1}{25}$	$\frac{1}{50}$	$\frac{1}{40}$	$\frac{1}{75}$	$\frac{1}{125}$
6	Slow cyclists	$\frac{1}{25}$	$\frac{1}{50}$	$\frac{1}{75}$	$\frac{1}{60}$	$\frac{1}{100}$	$\frac{1}{200}$
8	Slow vehicles in heavy traffic	$\frac{1}{30}$	$\frac{1}{60}$	$\frac{1}{100}$	$\frac{1}{80}$	$\frac{1}{150}$	$\frac{1}{250}$
10	Cyclists, trotting horses	$\frac{1}{40}$	$\frac{1}{75}$	$\frac{1}{125}$	$\frac{1}{100}$	$\frac{1}{200}$	$\frac{1}{300}$
15	Slow street traffic	$\frac{1}{60}$	$\frac{1}{100}$	$\frac{1}{200}$	$\frac{1}{150}$	$\frac{1}{250}$	$\frac{1}{500}$
20	Automobiles (city traffic)	$\frac{1}{60}$	$\frac{1}{150}$	$\frac{1}{250}$	$\frac{1}{200}$	$\frac{1}{400}$	$\frac{1}{600}$
30	Automobiles	$\frac{1}{125}$	$\frac{1}{250}$	$\frac{1}{400}$	$\frac{1}{300}$	$\frac{1}{600}$	$\frac{1}{1000}$
40	Automobiles	$\frac{1}{150}$	$\frac{1}{250}$	$\frac{1}{500}$	$\frac{1}{400}$	$\frac{1}{750}$	$\frac{1}{1200}$
60	Trains, automobiles	$\frac{1}{250}$	$\frac{1}{500}$	$\frac{1}{750}$	$\frac{1}{600}$	$\frac{1}{1000}$	$\frac{1}{2000}$
80	Fast trains	$\frac{1}{300}$	$\frac{1}{600}$	$\frac{1}{1000}$	$\frac{1}{800}$	$\frac{1}{1500}$	$\frac{1}{2400}$
100	Airplanes	$\frac{1}{400}$	$\frac{1}{750}$	$\frac{1}{1250}$	$\frac{1}{1000}$	$\frac{1}{2000}$	$\frac{1}{3000}$

Table XVII gives the maximum exposures which may be given, if sharp images are desired, for two lenses of different focal length, and for various speeds of moving objects. The table is based on an assumed distance of 25 ft. between the camera and the moving object, but conversions may be made for other conditions. For example, let S_0 be the shutter speed given for the 5-in. lens. Then the shutter speed S for other distances between camera and subject d and for lenses of focal length l is

$$S = S_0\left(\frac{5}{l}\right)\left(\frac{d}{25}\right)$$

The distance d is in feet, whereas l is in inches. Thus, for fast trains at 100 ft. with a 2-in. lens, the longest permissible exposure is

$$S = \frac{1}{2400} \times \left(\frac{5}{2}\right) \times \left(\frac{100}{25}\right) = \frac{10}{2400} = \frac{1}{240}\text{ sec.}$$

if the train is traveling across the field of view.

Table XVII bears no connection to the shutter speeds required by light conditions to give the necessary exposure to the film; it simply gives the longest exposure permissible which may be expected to "stop motion." Table XVII should then be used with other tables to determine the aperture and shutter speeds required to give the proper exposure to the film for existing light conditions.

Tables for Still Color Photography.—So long as the reduced speed and additional color sensitivity of color films are properly taken into account, the tables for black-and-white still photography could be used for still color photography. However, it is convenient to have tables which automatically take these factors into account.

Table XVIII gives basic exposure data for still color photography in somewhat the same way that Table VIII gives similar data for black-and-white photography. For shutter speeds or apertures which are not given, extensions to the table may be made in the manner already described. The table is based on film speed of Weston 4 to 8 which applies to the present Kodachrome and Dufaycolor film in daylight.

TABLE XVIII.—EXPOSURES FOR STILL COLOR PHOTOGRAPHY IN DAYLIGHT
(Weston Ratings—4 to 8)

Subject	Aperture	Sky conditions				
		Intensely bright day	Direct sun on bright day	Slightly cloudy bright day	Dull day, sky overcast	Very dull day
		Exposure time, sec.				
A. Clouds; open snow and glacier scenes; open sea; snow scenes "against the light"	f/32	1/10	1/5	1/2	3/4	1½
	f/16	1/40	1/20	1/10	1/5	1/2
	f/8	1/150	1/75	1/40	1/20	1/8
	f/4	1/500	1/300	1/150	1/75	1/30
	f/2	1/2000	1/1000	1/500	1/300	1/125
B. Sport scenes in snow or glacier; open landscapes or beach; sport scenes in open; landscapes with light foreground	f/32	1/4	3/5	1	2	4
	f/16	1/15	1/8	1/4	1/2	1
	f/8	1/60	1/30	1/15	1/8	1/4
	f/4	1/250	1/125	1/60	1/30	1/15
	f/2	1/1000	1/500	1/250	1/125	1/60
C. Wide streets and squares; light buildings; woods and landscapes with dark foregrounds; figures and groups in open or at edge of woods	f/32	1½	3	6	12	24
	f/16	1/2	3/4	1½	3	6
	f/8	1/10	1/5	1/2	1	2
	f/4	1/40	1/20	1/8	1/4	1/2
	f/2	1/150	1/75	1/30	1/15	1/8
D. Buildings and rocks, dark or against the light; persons and groups in shade of trees; persons and objects at windows; narrow streets; light woodlands	f/32	6	12	24	45	1½ min.
	f/16	1½	3	6	12	24
	f/8	1/2	1	2	3	6
	f/4	1/8	1/4	1/2	3/4	1½
	f/2	1/30	1/15	1/8	1/5	1/2

Table XII gives the exposures for still color photography in daylight. If possible, an exposure meter should be used when exposing color film because of its small latitude; otherwise Table XII may be used as a guide for suggested exposure.

1. Film Speed.—The table is calculated for a film speed having a daylight rating of Weston 4.0 to 8.0. For conversion to other film speeds, shutter speed is inversely proportional to the Weston rating.

2. Aperture.—Suggested exposures for five different standard apertures are given. For conversion to other apertures see Eq. (23).

3. Time of Day.—For use up to within $2\frac{1}{2}$ hr. of sunrise and sunset except when taking sunrise and sunset scenes.

4. Subject: for Average Subjects.—Average subjects combine dark and light objects in approximately equal proportions. When in doubt, use exposures given.

Light-colored subjects include snow and beach scenes, light-colored flowers, subjects with blond complexions, light-colored buildings, and other subjects of similar character. In such cases the exposure may be reduced from that given in the table.

Dark-colored subjects include dark foliage, deep-colored flowers, dark animals, buildings, and similar objects. For such cases the exposures given in the table may be increased.

The exposure table may be used both for close-ups and distant views, but attention must be given as to whether the subjects are of average brightness, light, or dark.

5. Filters.—The exposures are based on the use of film without filters. If a filter is used, the time of exposure will have to be multiplied by the filter factor.

Table XIX shows the apertures and shutter speeds for giving the proper exposures with color film having a speed of Weston 4 to 8 when used with the various sizes of photoflood lamps now on the market.

TABLE XIX.—BASIC EXPOSURE FOR COLOR PHOTOGRAPHY WITH PHOTOFLOOD LAMPS
(Weston Ratings—4 to 8)

Distance between light and subject, ft.	Aperture									
	$f/1.4$	$f/2.0$	$f/2.8$	$f/4.0$	$f/5.6$	$f/8$	$f/11$	$f/16$	$f/22$	$f/32$
	Shutter speed, sec.									
	8,650 lumens—No. 1 photoflood									
2	$\frac{1}{32}$	$\frac{1}{15}$	$\frac{1}{8}$	$\frac{1}{4}$	$\frac{1}{2}$	1	2	4	8	15
3	$\frac{1}{15}$	$\frac{1}{8}$	$\frac{1}{4}$	$\frac{1}{2}$	1	2	5	10	18	35
4	$\frac{1}{8}$	$\frac{1}{4}$	$\frac{1}{2}$	1	2	4	8	15	30	1 m
6	$\frac{1}{4}$	$\frac{1}{2}$	1	2	5	10	20	40	$1\frac{1}{3}$ m	$2\frac{2}{3}$ m
8	$\frac{1}{2}$	1	2	4	8	15	30	1 m	2 m	4 m
10	$\frac{2}{5}$	$1\frac{1}{2}$	3	6	12	25	50	$1\frac{1}{2}$ m	$3\frac{1}{3}$ m	7 m
15	1	2	4	8	15	30	1 m	2 m	4 m	8 m
20	3	6	12	25	50	$1\frac{2}{3}$ m	$3\frac{1}{3}$ m	6 m	12 m	25 m
	17,000 lumens—No. 2 photoflood									
2	$\frac{1}{64}$	$\frac{1}{32}$	$\frac{1}{15}$	$\frac{1}{8}$	$\frac{1}{4}$	$\frac{1}{2}$	1	2	4	8
3	$\frac{1}{32}$	$\frac{1}{15}$	$\frac{1}{8}$	$\frac{1}{4}$	$\frac{1}{2}$	1	2	5	10	18
4	$\frac{1}{15}$	$\frac{1}{8}$	$\frac{1}{4}$	$\frac{1}{2}$	1	2	4	8	15	30
6	$\frac{1}{8}$	$\frac{1}{4}$	$\frac{1}{2}$	1	2	5	10	20	40	$1\frac{1}{3}$ m
8	$\frac{1}{4}$	$\frac{1}{2}$	1	2	4	8	15	30	1 m	2 m
10	$\frac{2}{5}$	$\frac{4}{5}$	$1\frac{1}{2}$	3	6	12	25	50	$1\frac{1}{2}$ m	$3\frac{1}{3}$ m
15	$\frac{1}{2}$	1	2	4	8	15	30	1 m	2 m	4 m
20	$1\frac{1}{2}$	3	6	12	25	50	$1\frac{2}{3}$ m	$3\frac{1}{3}$ m	6 m	12 m
	33,500 lumens—No. 4 photoflood									
2	$\frac{1}{125}$	$\frac{1}{64}$	$\frac{1}{32}$	$\frac{1}{15}$	$\frac{1}{8}$	$\frac{1}{4}$	$\frac{1}{2}$	1	2	4
3	$\frac{1}{64}$	$\frac{1}{32}$	$\frac{1}{15}$	$\frac{1}{8}$	$\frac{1}{4}$	$\frac{1}{2}$	1	2	5	10
4	$\frac{1}{32}$	$\frac{1}{15}$	$\frac{1}{8}$	$\frac{1}{4}$	$\frac{1}{2}$	1	2	4	8	15
6	$\frac{1}{15}$	$\frac{1}{8}$	$\frac{1}{4}$	$\frac{1}{2}$	1	2	5	10	20	40
8	$\frac{1}{8}$	$\frac{1}{4}$	$\frac{1}{2}$	1	2	4	8	15	30	1 m
10	$\frac{1}{5}$	$\frac{2}{5}$	$\frac{4}{5}$	$1\frac{1}{2}$	3	6	12	25	50	$1\frac{1}{2}$ m
15	$\frac{1}{4}$	$\frac{1}{2}$	1	2	4	8	15	30	1 m	2 m
20	$\frac{3}{4}$	$1\frac{1}{2}$	3	6	12	25	50	$1\frac{2}{3}$ m	$3\frac{1}{3}$ m	6 m

Table XIX is based on the following conditions:

1. Film Speed.—Suitable for color film having a tungsten rating of Weston 4 to 8, such as Dufaycolor or Kodachrome film. For films having other speeds, the shutter speed is inversely proportional to the Weston speed rating.

2. Apertures.—Table XIX gives the exposure for 10 apertures. Conversion may be made for other apertures by the method given by Eq. (23).

3. Lamps.—Exposures are given for photoflood lamps operation at 33.5 lumens per watt in polished metal reflectors. If white paper reflectors are used, multiply the exposure time by 2; if no reflectors are used, multiply exposure time by 4.

It is assumed that only one lamp is used. If n lamps are used, all the same distance from the subject, divide the shutter speed by n for proper exposure.

The apertures suitable for photography with photoflash lamps when the shutter is opened during the flash is given in Table XX.   If synchronized flashes are used, the next larger aperture (next smaller f-number) should be used.

TABLE XX.—EXPOSURE FOR COLOR PHOTOGRAPHY WITH PHOTOFLASH LAMPS
(Weston Rating—4 to 8)

| Distance, lamp to subject, ft. | No. 10 lamp | | | No. 20 lamp | | | No. 75 lamp | | |
| | Type of reflector | | | Type of reflector | | | Type of reflector | | |
	None	White paper*	Polished metal*	None	White paper*	Polished metal*	None	White paper*	Polished metal*
					Aperture				
2	$f/16$	$f/22$	$f/32$	$f/22$	$f/32$	$f/45$	$f/32$	$f/45$	$f/64$
3	$f/11$	$f/16$	$f/22$	$f/16$	$f/22$	$f/32$	$f/22$	$f/32$	$f/45$
4	$f/8$	$f/11$	$f/16$	$f/11$	$f/16$	$f/22$	$f/18$	$f/25$	$f/36$
6	$f/4.5$	$f/6.3$	$f/9$	$f/8$	$f/11$	$f/16$	$f/11$	$f/16$	$f/22$
8	$f/4.0$	$f/5.6$	$f/8$	$f/5.6$	$f/8$	$f/11$	$f/9$	$f/12.5$	$f/18$
10	$f/3.2$	$f/4.5$	$f/6.3$	$f/4.5$	$f/6.3$	$f/9$	$f/6.3$	$f/9$	$f/12.5$
15	$f/2.0$	$f/2.8$	$f/4.0$	$f/2.8$	$f/4.0$	$f/5.6$	$f/4.5$	$f/6.3$	$f/9.0$
20	$f/1.5$	$f/2.2$	$f/3.2$	$f/2.2$	$f/3.2$	$f/4.5$	$f/3.5$	$f/4.5$	$f/6.3$
30	$f/1.0$	$f/1.5$	$f/2.0$	$f/1.5$	$f/2.0$	$f/3.2$	$f/2.2$	$f/3.2$	$f/4.0$

* See note 3.

Table XX gives the suggested exposures for still color photography with photoflash lamps with various reflectors and for various distances between the subject and the lamp.

1. Film Speed.—Table XX is based on the use of film having a tungsten speed rating of Weston 4 to 8, such as Dufaycolor or Kodachrome.   For other film speed,

multiply f-number by	2.5	for Weston speeds between	0.6	and	1.2
" " " "	1.6	" " "	"	1.5	"	3
" " " "	1	" " "	"	4	"	8
" " " "	0.6	" " "	"	10	"	20
" " " "	0.4	" " "	"	24	"	28

2. Lamps.—It is assumed that only one lamp is used.   If n lamps are used in the same distance from the subject, multiply the apertures given by $\sqrt{n}$.   For example, if four No. 10 lamps without reflectors are used 8 ft. from the subject, the required aperture will be $f/4 \times \sqrt{4} = f/8$.

3. Reflectors.—When reflectors are used, exposure depends to a large extent on the angle over which the light is distributed.   Consequently, the values given should be regarded merely as suggestive for average conditions.

Tables for Black-and-white Motion-picture Photography.—Fundamentally the same laws of exposure apply to motion-picture as to still photography with the exception that a sufficient number of pictures must be taken per second to reduce flicker to a minimum and give a sense of motion when the individual frames are projected.   In practice, this means that about 16 to 24 frames per second must be made, so that it is manifestly impossible to give an exposure time longer than from $1/16$ to $1/24$ sec., and usually in practice the actual exposure is more likely to be between $1/30$ and $1/50$ at 16 frames per sec.   Since the shutter speed is, furthermore, fixed or adjustable in wide steps, it is necessary to make changes in the exposure by means of varying the aperture.

Table XXI gives basic exposure for motion-picture photography in black and white with daylight illumination.

Table XXII gives basic exposures when the illumination is from photoflood lamps.

Tables for Color Motion-picture Photography.—Table XXIII gives basic exposure data for color motion-picture photography in daylight, whereas Table XXIV gives similar data for photoflood illumination.

TABLE XXI.—EXPOSURES FOR BLACK-AND-WHITE MOTION-PICTURE PHOTOGRAPHY IN DAYLIGHT
(Weston Rating—24 to 48)

Subject	Shutter speed, sec.	Sky conditions				
		Intensely bright day	Direct sun or bright sky	Slightly cloudy bright day	Dull day, sky overcast	Very dull day
		Aperture				
A. Clouds; open snow and glacier scenes; open sea; snow "against the light"	1/20	*f*/40	*f*/27	*f*/20	*f*/14	*f*/10
	1/30	*f*/32	*f*/22	*f*/16	*f*/11	*f*/8
	1/40	*f*/27	*f*/18	*f*/14	*f*/10	*f*/7
	1/50	*f*/22	*f*/16	*f*/11	*f*/8	*f*/5.6
	1/60	*f*/18	*f*/12.5	*f*/9	*f*/6.3	*f*/4.5
B. Sport scenes in snow or glacier; open landscapes or beach; sport scenes in open; landscapes with light foreground	1/20	*f*/27	*f*/20	*f*/14	*f*/10	*f*/7
	1/30	*f*/22	*f*/16	*f*/11	*f*/8	*f*/5.6
	1/40	*f*/19	*f*/14	*f*/10	*f*/7	*f*/5.0
	1/50	*f*/16	*f*/11	*f*/8	*f*/5.6	*f*/4
	1/60	*f*/12.5	*f*/9	*f*/6.3	*f*/4.5	*f*/3.2
C. Wide streets and squares; light buildings; woods and landscapes with dark foregrounds; figures and groups in open, or at edge of woods	1/20	*f*/10	*f*/7	*f*/5.0	*f*/3.5	*f*/2.4
	1/30	*f*/8	*f*/5.6	*f*/4	*f*/2.8	*f*/2.0
	1/40	*f*/7.0	*f*/5.0	*f*/3.5	*f*/2.4	*f*/1.7
	1/50	*f*/5.6	*f*/4	*f*/2.8	*f*/2	*f*/1.4
	1/60	*f*/4.5	*f*/3.2	*f*/2.3	*f*/1.6	*f*/1.0
D. Buildings and rocks, dark or against the light; persons and groups in shade of trees; persons and objects at windows in sun; narrow streets; light woodlands	1/20	*f*/4.5	*f*/3.5	*f*/2.4	*f*/1.7	*f*/1.2
	1/30	*f*/4.0	*f*/2.8	*f*/2.0	*f*/1.4	*f*/1.0
	1/40	*f*/3.5	*f*/2.4	*f*/1.7	*f*/1.2	
	1/50	*f*/3.0	*f*/2.2	*f*/1.5	*f*/1.0	
	1/60	*f*/2.4	*f*/1.4	*f*/1.0		

Table XXI gives suggested exposures for black-and-white motion-picture photography using daylight illumination. It is calculated for the following conditions:

1. Light Values.—For unity (1) light values as given in Table IX. For latitudes and times of the day and year for which the light value is not unity, multiply the aperture given in Table XXI by the square root of the light values given in Table IX.

2. Film Speed.—Calculated for films having a daylight speed of Weston 24 to 48. For conversion for other film speeds,

multiply *f*-number by 0.15 for Weston speeds between 0.6 and 1.2
" " " 0.25 " " " " 1.5 " 3.5
" " " 0.4 " " " " 4 " 8
" " " 0.6 " " " " 10 " 20
" " " 1 " " " " 24 " 48
" " " 1.5 " " " " 64 " 128
" " " 2.5 " " " " 150 " 320.

3. Time of Day.—To within 1 hr. of sunrise and sunset for panchromatic materials; to within 2½ hr. of sunrise and sunset for orthochromatic materials.

Exposure Devices. *Exposure Calculators.*—Exposure calculators in the form of sliding scales or disks which may be rotated with respect to other marked scales, usually cover a wide range of light conditions, film speeds, aperture, shutter speeds, and sometimes give additional factors affecting exposure such as filter factors.

TABLE XXII.—BASIC EXPOSURE FOR BLACK-AND-WHITE MOTION-PICTURE
PHOTOGRAPHY, PHOTOFLOOD ILLUMINATION
(Weston Ratings—10 to 20)

Lamp	Distance, lamp to subject, ft.	Shutter speed, sec.				
		$\frac{1}{20}$	$\frac{1}{30}$	$\frac{1}{40}$	$\frac{1}{50}$	$\frac{1}{60}$
		Aperture				
8,650 lumens, one No. 1 lamp	2	f/10	f/8	f/7	f/6.3	f/4.5
	3	f/7	f/5.6	f/5	f/4.5	f/3.5
	4	f/5	f/4.0	f/3.5	f/3.0	f/2.4
	6	f/3.5	f/2.8	f/2.4	f/2.2	f/1.7
	8	f/2.4	f/2.0	f/1.7 ·	f/1.5	f/1.2
	10	f/1.9	f/1.5	f/1.3	f/1.2	
	15	f/1.2	f/1.1	f/1.0		
17,000 lumens, one No. 2 lamp or two No. 1 lamps	2	f/12.5	f/11	f/10	f/9	f/6.3
	3	f/10	f/8	f/7	f/5.6	f/4.5
	4	f/7	f/5.6	f/4.5	f/4.5	f/3.5
	6	f/4.5	f/4.0	f/3.5	f/2.7	f/2.4
	8	f/3.5	f/2.8	f/2.4	f/2.1	f/1.7
	10	f/2.4	f/2.2	f/1.8	f/1.7	f/1.3
	15	f/1.9	f/1.5	f/1.3	f/1.2	
	20	f/1.3	f/1.1			
33,500 lumens, one No. 4 lamp or two No. 2 lamps or four No. 1 lamps	2	f/20	f/16	f/14	f/12.5	f/10
	3	f/14	f/11	f/10	f/9	f/6.8
	4	f/10	f/8	f/7	f/6.3	f/4.8
	6	f/7	f/5.6	f/4.5	f/4.5	f/3.5
	8	f/4.5	f/4.0	f/3.5	f/3.1 ·	f/2.4
	10	f/3.8	f/3.0	f/2.6	f/2.3	f/1.2
	15	f/2.4	f/2.0	f/1.7	f/1.5	
	20	f/1.5	f/1.2			

Table XXII gives the suggested exposure for black-and-white motion-picture photography using photoflood illumination. It is based on the following conditions:

1. Film Speed.—Calculated for films having a tungsten speed rating of Weston 10 to 20. For converting to other film speeds,

multiply aperture by 0.25 for Weston speeds between　0.6 and　1.2
　　　"　　　　"　　"0.4　　"　　"　　　　"　　　"　　1.5　"　　3
　　　"　　　　"　　"0.6　　"　　"　　　　"　　　"　　4　"　　8
　　　"　　　　"　　"1　　"　　"　　　　"　　　"　　10　"　　20
　　　"　　　　"　　"1.5　　"　　"　　　　"　　　"　　24　"　　48
　　　"　　　　"　　"2.5　　"　　"　　　　"　　　"　　64　"　　128
　　　"　　　　"　　"4.0　　"　　"　　　　"　　　"　　160　"　　320

2. Lamps.—Number of lamps as indicated. It is assumed that polished-metal reflectors are used.
3. Subject Matter.—It is assumed that subjects of average brightness are being photographed. If light subjects are photographed, the exposure may be reduced somewhat, whereas if dark subjects are being photographed, the exposures should be increased.
4. Shutter Speed.—As indicated. For standard speed of 16 to 24 frames per second.

These calculators are usually designed for daylight and cannot be used for artificial light unless special scales for artificial illumination are provided. The scales are designed to take into account the various light conditions of the sky, type of subject, film speed, time of day, time of year, and even geographic latitude.

For a given amount of information, calculators are usually somewhat more compact than tables and, since a particular series of settings may be obtained for a given specific

TABLE XXIII.—EXPOSURES FOR COLOR MOTION-PICTURE PHOTOGRAPHY IN DAYLIGHT
(Weston Ratings—10 to 20)

Subject	Shutter speed, sec.	Sky conditions				
		Intensely bright day	Direct sun on bright day	Slightly cloudy bright day	Dull day, sky overcast	Very dull day
		Apertures				
A. Clouds; open snow and glacier scenes, open sea; snow "against the light"	1/20	f/20	f/14	f/10	f/7	f/5
	1/30	f/16	f/11	f/8	f/5.6	f/4
	1/40	f/14	f/10	f/7	f/4.5	f/3.5
	1/50	f/11	f/8	f/5.6	f/4	f/2.8
	1/90	f/9	f/6.3	f/4.5	f/3.2	f/2.4
B. Sport scenes in snow or glacier; open landscapes or beach; sport scenes in open; landscapes with light foreground	1/20	f/14	f/10	f/7	f/5	f/3.5
	1/30	f/11	f/8	f/5.6	f/4.0	f/2.8
	1/40	f/10	f/7	f/4.5	f/3.5	f/2.6
	1/50	f/8	f/5.6	f/4.0	f/2.8	f/2.0
	1/90	f/6.3	f/4.5	f/3.2	f/2.4	f/1.6
C. Wide streets and squares; light buildings, woods, and landscapes with dark foregrounds; figures and groups in open or at edge of woods	1/20	f/5	f/3.5	f/2.5	f/1.8	f/1.2
	1/30	f/4	f/2.8	f/2.0	f/1.4	f/1.0
	1/40	f/3.5	f/2.5	f/1.8	f/1.2	
	1/50	f/2.8	f/2.0	f/1.4	f/1.0	
	1/90	f/2.4	f/1.6	f/1.2		
D. Buildings and rocks; dark against the light; persons and groups in shade of trees; persons and objects at windows in sun; narrow streets; light woodlands	1/20	f/2.5	f/1.8	f/1.2		
	1/30	f/2.0	f/1.4	f/1.0		
	1/40	f/1.8	f/1.2			
	1/50	f/1.4	f/1.0			
	1/90	f/1.2				

Table XXIII gives suggested exposures for color motion-picture photography in daylight. It is calculated for the following conditions:

1. *Light Values.*—For unity (1) light values as given in Table IX. If other light values apply, multiply exposure apertures of Table XXIII by the square root of the appropriate light values given in Table IX.

2. *Film Speed.*—For films having a daylight speed rating of Weston 5 to 10. For other film speeds,

multiply f-number by 0.25 for Weston speeds between 0.6 and 1.2
" " " " 0.4 " " " " 1.5 " 3
" " " " 0.6 " " " " 4 " 8
" " " " 1 " " " " 10 " 20
" " " " 1.5 " " " " 24 " 48

3. *Time of Day.*—To within 1 hr. of sunrise and sunset, unless sunrise or sunset photographs are being made.

TABLE XXIV.—BASIC EXPOSURE FOR COLOR MOTION-PICTURE PHOTOGRAPHY,
PHOTOFLOOD LAMPS
(Weston Ratings—10 to 20)

Lamp	Distance, subject to lamp, ft.	Shutter speed, sec.				
		1/20	1/30	1/40	1/50	1/90
		Aperture				
8,650 lumens, one No. 1 Lamp	2	f/4.5	f/3.5	f/3.0	f/2.7	f/1.9
	3	f/3	f/2.4	f/2.2	f/2.0	f/1.5
	4	f/2.2	f/1.7	f/1.5	f/1.3	f/1.0
	6	f/1.5	f/1.2	f/1.0		
	8	f/1.0				
17,000 lumens, one No. 2 lamp or two No. 1 lamps	2	f/5.6	f/4.8	f/4.5	f/4.0	f/2.7
	3	f/4.5	f/3.5	f/3.0	f/2.5	f/2.0
	4	f/3.0	f/2.4	f/2.0	f/2.0	f/1.5
	6	f/2.0	f/1.7	f/1.5	f/1.2	
	8	f/1.5	f/1.2	f/1.0		
	10	f/1.0				
33,500 lumens, one No. 4 lamp or two No. 2 lamps or four No. 2 lamps	2	f/9	f/7	f/6.3	f/5.6	f/4.5
	3	f/6.3	f/4.5	f/4.5	f/4.0	f/3.0
	4	f/4.5	f/3.5	f/3.0	f/2.8	f/2.0
	6	f/3.0	f/2.5	f/2.0	f/2.0	f/1.5
	8	f/2.0	f/1.7	f/1.5	f/1.4	f/1.0
	10	f/1.6	f/1.3	f/1.1		
	15	f/1.0				

Table XXIV gives suggested exposure for color motion-picture photography using photoflood illumination. The table is calculated for the following conditions:

1. Film Speeds.—Based on films having a tungsten rating of Weston 10 to 20. For conversion for films having other speed ratings,

multiply f-number by 0.35 for Weston speeds between 0.6 and 1.2
    "   "   "   " 0.5   "   "   "   1.5 " 3
    "   "   "   " 0.7   "   "   "   4 " 8
    "   "   "   " 1   "   "   "   10 " 20
    "   "   "   " 1.4   "   "   "   24 " 48
    "   "   "   " 2.0   "   "   "   64 " 128
    "   "   "   " 2.8   "   "   "   160 " 320

2. Lamps.—It is assumed that only one lamp is used in each reflector. If n lamps are used at the same distance from the subject, divide the apertures (f-numbers) given by $\sqrt{n}$.

condition for which the exposure is to be made, are usually more convenient and flexible than tables. The use of such slide-rule or circular calculators requires, as do also the tables which have been given, that the photographer estimate the light conditions for each particular case. This necessity, of course, introduces possible errors due to mistakes or errors of judgment. But tests indicate that the errors from this cause are smaller than might be expected and that the proper use of calculators enables even inexperienced persons to obtain well-exposed negatives.

Many types of exposure calculators are on the market and may usually be purchased for about 10 to 50 cents. Some of the calculators are quite elaborate and complicated; the simpler types are, perhaps, more useful for the beginner.

Actinometers.—Of historical interest, although seldom used any more, are actinometers which determine the "actinic value" of the light by determining the time required for a piece of photographic printing-out paper to darken to a standard tint. Most P O P materials are insensitive to the yellow, orange, and red portions of the spectrum and are therefore more suitable for use with "ordinary" negative materials than with orthochromatic or panchromatic materials.

When using an actinometer, it should be held in the shadiest area of the scene where full details are desired. It should be directed toward the light, and the time for the incident light (that which falls upon the object or scene) to darken the sensitive paper to a standard tint should be measured.

The Watkins and Wynne actinometers are made in watch form, and by means of scales the time required for the sensitive paper to darken can be translated into exposure values. While many actinometers have appeared on the market, the Watkins and Wynne have been accepted as standards of this type. Since they measure the light falling upon the scene, certain corrections are necessary for scenes of abnormal reflectance. These corrections, which are furnished with the meters, vary from $\frac{1}{10}$ to $1\frac{1}{2}$ times the indicated exposure. Actinometers have an advantage of being small and inexpensive. It is sometimes difficult to determine when the photographic paper is exactly the same tint as the comparison standard, but the proper tinting time can usually be determined with an error of less than 100 per cent, and such error can be tolerated in black-and-white photography because of the wide film latitude which is available in modern films. A disadvantage is that under low light conditions an appreciable time is required for the sensitive paper to reach the same tint as the standard, thus requiring considerable time to obtain exposure data.

Visual-type Exposure Meters.—Visual types of exposure meters may be divided into three broad classes: (1) photometer devices by which the brightness of a scene is determined from a comparison with a calibrated incandescent lamp whose brilliance may be measured or estimated in some manner, (2) wedge-extinction types in which the exposure is determined by varying a graduated neutral-density wedge until shadow detail disappears, and (3) stepped-wedge devices whose steps are lettered or numbered, the dimmest letter which can be discerned being taken as an indication of the integrated light intensity of the scene. The wedge is usually a piece of celluloid or glass coated with a gelatin dye of varying density so that it varies approximately from transparency to opaqueness. When using visual-exposure meters, care and sufficient time must be taken to allow the eye to accommodate itself properly in order to obtain correct meter settings or readings. Unlike the actinometer, visual exposure meters measure reflected light.

Photometer devices operate essentially on the same principle as that of an optical pyrometer. The brilliance of a lamp filament is matched with the brightness of the scene as seen through an optical finder. To make the indications dependent only upon the intensity of the lamp filament and not on its color, both scene and filament are usually viewed through filters which transmit a narrow band of wavelengths. The temperature of the filament may be estimated by determining the power taken by the lamp from a small filament lighting battery. The lamp temperature is usually adjustable by means of a variable resistance in series with the lamp. Several years ago the Bell and Howell Company manufactured such a photometer exposure device, but this instrument has been superseded by photoelectric exposure meters. The Bell and Howell photometer contains a small electric bulb and dry cell connected together through a self-contained rheostat. The meter is directed at the object or scene, and the rheostat set so that the lamp filament can be clearly seen. The rheostat is then turned, slowly dimming the filament, stopping just at the point where it blends with the subject so that the filament cannot be seen. By means of scales on the photometer the correct exposure can be determined for various types of films and plates.

The Zeiss Diaphot exposure disk is an example of the wedge-extinction type of meter. It consists of a rotating disk carrying a continuously variable optical wedge, together with a window for observing shutter speeds. The scales of shutter speeds are contained on a fixed disk which also contains a small eyepiece traveling over the circular wedge. The eyepiece contains a blue filter to destroy sense of color and give visual indication of light intensity only. In operation the photographer looks through the eyepiece to the subject. The wedge is rotated until shadow detail just disappears, when the correct exposure is indicated in the window of the rotating number.

Fig. 4.   Fig. 5.

Fig. 4.—Leudi visual exposure meter. A series of partially opaque numbers is seen through the slot shown on the upper edge. The exposure is determined in terms of the dimmest number which can be distinguished.

Fig. 5.—The Instoscope visual exposure meter with focusing eyepiece.

In the Justaphot and Cinephot visual exposure meters the necessity of measuring the details in the shadow areas is overcome by observing when a translucent figure is just discernible. The figures correspond to exposure time and the light striking them is varied by means of a diaphragm. In operation the figures, corresponding to the desired exposure time, are set in the line of vision in the instrument. The diaphragm is then fully closed and the meter placed in the correct eye position and aimed at the object or scene to be photographed. The diaphragm is then opened until the translucent number is just discernible. By means of scales on the meter the correct f-stops for the various films and plates can be determined.

At the present time the stepped-wedge exposure meters are the most common of the visual type. Many modifications have been produced, but usually this type consists of two concentric telescoping tubes. At the end of one of these tubes is a focusing lens and eyepiece which exclude extraneous light when the instrument is held to the light. Near one end of the other tube are several areas of graded density, each of which is either lettered or numbered. The photographer looks through the eyepiece toward the scene to be photographed and sees various graded patches each with its corresponding numeral or letter. The dimmest figure which can be read is taken as the appropriate "light value" for the conditions under consideration. The outer telescoping tube is usually provided with a series of scales which relate the light values as seen through the instrument, the film speed, the shutter speed, the aperture, and, sometimes, filter factors. The proper exposure may usually be determined with a simple setting of a ring which may be turned or slid relative to the fixed scales attached to the main tube.

Since the operation of this type of instrument depends upon a subjective estimate of the dimmest figure which can be read, it is necessary that the sliding tubes be adjusted for proper focus and that the eye become accommodated to the light at which readings are taken. It is usually recommended that no readings be taken until the operator has looked through the exposure device for at least 5 sec., allowing this time for eye accommodation.

These visual exposure devices are simple, inexpensive, small, convenient in operation, and robust. They are usually superior to photoelectric devices for low values of light intensity where the ordinary photoelectric devices are insensitive. A properly made and calibrated and intelligently used visual exposure meter will find use in almost any photographic activity. The principal disadvantages of these instruments are that they are subjective in operation, thereby introducing human errors, are relatively slow in affording a reading, and some types are improperly calibrated.

The relative calibration of several visual exposure meters was determined from the calibrations attached to the meter, and it was found that at least some of these visual meters are poorly or carelessly designed. A light value as determined by the meter might give a correct exposure for one aperture and shutter speed, but the same light value might be off several hundred per cent when used with different apertures or shutter speeds. This error occurs in the printed scales attached to the instrument and is in addition to any errors of absolute exposure which may result from incorrect manufacture of the stepped wedges. It may be expected that some error will occur when fractions of a

Fig. 6.—Bewi Sr. visual exposure meter with focusing eyepiece. This meter has a blue filter and viewing screen covering the average field of view, which enables the photographer to obtain a good idea of what his photograph will look like and at the same time enables him to determine exposure.

second or minute are rounded off to simple rather than awkward values. Such errors should not exceed 25 per cent, however, and a 25 per cent error is negligible for most photographic purposes.

Table XXV shows the values of relative exposure for various apertures and the exposures for these apertures as indicated by several popular types of visual exposure meters. It was arbitrarily assumed that the exposures were correct for an aperture of $f/2.8$. This was the largest aperture common to all instruments, but any other aperture might be considered as "par"; the only effect would be to shift the errors to some other aperture. Assuming the exposure for the $f/2.8$ aperture to be correct, the exposure time for other apertures was calculated and compared with that indicated by the meters, as shown in the table. The errors were also tabulated.

It will be observed that for the first type of meter, a very small and simple vest-pocket type, the errors become cumulative because of the manner in which the progression of apertures was chosen relative to that of the exposure time. The second exposure meter reaches a constant error for small apertures but also results in relative errors for large apertures, also because of the manner in which the progression of apertures was chosen. The third instrument was designed so that the apertures and shutter speeds progressed in proper sequence, and the result is that nowhere does it produce any serious errors due to this cause. Errors of 50 per cent might be expected from inexpensive instruments of this type and would probably produce no great harm for amateur work.

TABLE XXV.—COMPARISON OF SOME VISUAL EXPOSURE METERS

Aperture	Correct relative exposure	Leudi		Instoscope		Bewi Jr. Model II		Bewi Sr.	
		Marked exposure	Error, per cent	Marked exposure	Error, per cent	Marked exposure	Error, per cent	Marked exposure	Error, per cent
f/1.0	0.25	0.20	− 25						
f/1.4	0.50	0.50	0	...	....	...	.....	0.50	0.0
f/2.0	1	1	0	1	0	...	.....	1	0.0
f/2.8	2.0	2	0	2	0	2	0	2	0.0
f/3.5	3.1	5	+ 61.3	4	+ 29	3	−3.2	3	− 3.2
f/4.0	4.0	....	....	8	+100	4	0	4	0.0
f/4.5	5.0	10	+100	...	....	...	.....	6	+20.0
f/5.6	8.0	....	....	15	+ 87.5	8	0	8	0.0
f/6.3	10.1	25	+147	...	....	...	.....	12	+18.8
f/8.0	16.0	60	+275	30	+ 87.5	15	−6.3	15	− 6.3
f/9.0	20.2	....	....	...	....	...	.....	25	+23.8
f/11.0	33.0	120	+375	60	+ 87.5	30	−6.3	30	− 6.3
f/12.5	41.5	....	....	...	....	...	.....	45	+ 8.45
f/16	64.0	300	+369	120	+ 87.5	60	−6.3	60	− 6.3
f/18	81.0	....	....	...	....	...	.....	90	+11.1
f/22	128.0	600	+369	240	+ 87.5	120	−6.3	120	− 6.3
f/25	164.0	....	....	...	....	...	.....	180	+ 9.75
f/32	256.0	1500	+485	...	....	240	−6.3	240	− 6.3
f/36	324.0	....	....	...	....	...	.....	360	+11.1
Lens aperture..........		f/1–f/32		f/2–f/22		f/2.8–f/32		f/1.2–f/36	
Scheiner rating........		17–29°		17–31°		16–26°		1–32°	
Exposure time........		1/1000 s–25 m		1/1000 s–25 m		1/400 s–2 h		1/3000 s–3 h	

The range of film speeds, apertures, shutter speeds, filter factors, and light conditions which visual exposure meters include in their operation, of course, varies with the instrument. Usually, however, they may be expected to have from 10 to 20 graded areas for determining the light value. The film speeds, which are usually marked in Scheiner speeds (since most of these devices are made in Europe), range from Scheiner 16 or 18 minimum up to Scheiner 30 or 32 maximum, although with the introduction of faster films, the upper range may be expected to be extended in the future. Shutter speeds usually vary from 1/1000 or 1/500 sec. minimum to about 30 min. to 2 hr. for the maximum exposure time. Filter factors up to 16 may be expected to be taken into account on some of the better designed devices, although in many of the less expensive models no provision is made for taking into account the filter factors. Table XXV shows the range of aperture stop, film speed, and exposure time for several well-known makes of devices.

Photoelectric Exposure Meters.—The photoelectric type of exposure meter, when properly used, is the most precise type of exposure device available. It gives an indication of light conditions on a scale and is devoid of subjective estimates which introduce additional human errors. It is not well suited to use where the light intensity is low, largely because of the low output of the photoelectric cell, and it is the most expensive type of exposure instrument generally available. When properly used and within the range of light intensities for which it gives a positive indication, it is unusually satisfactory.

The photoelectric type of instrument consists essentially of a barrier-layer type of photoelectric cell and a sensitive direct-current measuring instrument. The barrier cell may consist of disks of copper and copper oxide in contact, or of iron and selenium. When such a combination of elements is exposed to light, electrons are released resulting in a current flow both in the photoelectric cell and the external circuit. This current will flow so long as light falls upon the sensitive surface. If this external circuit consists of a galvanometer or a sensitive d.-c. meter a deflection of the meter will be obtained and the meter can be calibrated to indicate the amount of light falling on the photoelectric cell, or the scale can be calibrated in exposure values. The current flowing depends upon the type of materials used in the photoelectric cell, but

Fig. 7.—The General Electric exposure meter using the Weston film-speed system and calibrated in foot-candles.

for any given cell the current is approximately proportional to the area of the cell and to the amount of light falling upon its sensitive surface. Consequently, for a given cell, the meter may be calibrated in terms of some convenient illumina-

Fig. 8.—Weston Model 650 exposure meter, calibrated in candles per square foot.

tion units. A peculiarity of the barrier type of cell is that it converts, directly and without the assistance of batteries, luminous flux into an electric current. Consequently, since no batteries are required, such photoelectric exposure meters may be made quite small and compact. Moreover, so far as is known, there is no deterioration of the barrier-layer type of photoelectric cell, so that the life of a photoelectric exposure meter appears to be limited only by physical damage. By means of a calculator or tables the meter readings can be translated into exposure values. When a photo-electric exposure meter is directed at a scene its indication depends upon the average brightness of the area taken in by the meter. The angle subtended by the diameter of this area, having its apex at the exposure meter, corresponds to the view angle of a camera and is usually referred to as the acceptance angle of the exposure meter. This acceptance angle is governed by the location of the cell with respect to the case or by the use of baffles over the photoelectric cell.

Operation of Photoelectric Exposure Meters.—It is a characteristic of photoelectric exposure meters, as well as of other types of exposure devices, that the integrated or "average" illumination upon the subject is the quantity which is determined by the instrument. But from the photographic aspect the subject is composed of areas of different color and luminous intensity, and it is these differences in intensity (and in color photography, the differences in color) which it is desired to record on the photo-graphic plate. Since the subject may consist of varying areas of dark and light sub-jects, it becomes evident that the integrated light may not result in the best exposure value. This may be made more clear by means of an example.

Suppose we have a checkerboard of alternate white and black squares which we wish to photograph in such a manner as to reproduce most nearly the original image. From the discussion on page 204 of the chapter on Photographic Sensitometry, it is evident that the exposure should be such that light reflected from the white areas should provide an exposure for the negative falling on the straight-line portion of the D-$\log_{10} E$ curve. Similarly the light reflected from the black squares should be such as to produce an exposure which will fall upon the straight-line portion of this same characteristic. When an exposure meter is used to determine the exposure, the meter will read a value of illumination (as a result of light reflected from the checkerboard) which is the integrated sum of the white and black areas. A single reading rather than two (one for the black squares and one for the white squares) is obtained, much the same as if the entire cardboard were gray in tone. Of course, this integrated meter reading serves some purpose since it tends to prevent gross over- or under-exposure, but the method of measuring average light or obtaining an average exposure value is not always a certain method of obtaining correct exposure data (see page 257 which explains methods of using exposure meters).

Two inherent difficulties have been encountered in the above example, and each may be overcome with intelligent use of the exposure meter. These have to do with: (1) the angle of view throughout which the photoelectric exposure meter is effective, and (2) the fact that the indication of the meter is due to the average brightness of the object or scene included within the acceptance angle of the meter.

The acceptance angles of most photoelectric exposure meters on the market at the present time are too large, as many of them exceed the angle of view of the typical camera lens, which is approximately 60°. This means that all the light within a cone whose angle is 60° ($\pm$30° from the axis) has an effect upon the photoelectric cell, but because of reflectance of light by the glass over the cell and the surface of the cell, the loss of light at oblique angles is appreciable. Therefore all exposure meters tend to be quite selective to the center part of the scene. Consequently, if it is desired to obtain readings of light or dark areas independently of the integrated light value of the entire scene, it is necessary to make the readings with the exposure meter sufficiently close to the subject so that the desired area to be measured, but no other area, falls within the 60° cone. For example, if the light intensity of a person's face is to be determined, the exposure meter should be pointed at the face and should be not more than about a foot from the face when the reading is taken. The reading obtained will indicate the average value of the light reflected from the face, which may be quite different from that reflected from a dark suit.

The acceptance angle of the majority of meters on the market today is entirely too large, so that the meter indications are affected by light from areas which are considerably outside the picture area. Large acceptance angles are therefore objectionable from the viewpoint of the photographer since the meter must be more carefully used to prevent erroneous readings. The manufacturing cost of a photoelectric exposure meter is governed quite largely by the acceptance angle, as large angles permit the use of considerably cheaper galvanometers because more current is available from the photoelectric cell resulting from the increased area from which the light is accepted.

Methods of Limiting the Acceptance Angle.—The acceptance angle of an exposure meter may be controlled by any method which will restrict or prevent oblique light from reaching the photoelectric cell. One method is to locate the photoelectric cell deep into the meter case so that the case itself acts as a baffle. This method is used to a large extent in the meters made in Europe but, owing to lack of space within the meter case, the amount of baffling obtained is so small that the resulting acceptance angle is entirely too large. Some meters such as the Mini-Photoscop exposure meter mount the photoelectric cell on an angle (approximately 45° from the vertical plane) and also utilize a mirror mounted so that the cell and mirror form an angle of 45°. This method quite definitely limits the acceptance in the vertical plane but is not very effective in the horizontal plane, the theory being that the elimination of excessive sky and foreground light is adequate. Other meters such as the Weston, Metrovick, Helios, etc., utilize a mechanical baffle over the photoelectric cell. These mechanical baffles usually consist of either thin plates latticed together or solid or laminated thin plates containing a number of holes, the ratio of the width to the depth of the individual holes being the factor which governs the acceptance angle. The General Electric exposure meter utilizes a mechanical baffle but is different in actual construction from the above meters. Instead of using a relatively thin plate containing a number of holes, this meter has a sliding baffle of appreciable depth (1.4 in.) and contains a single hole (1.53 by 0.74 in.) for the light to enter. This baffle when not in use forms a protective cover for the entire meter.

Polar diagrams (Fig. 9) show the acceptance angles of a number of exposure meters. It will be seen that while all the meters are more selective to light at normal incidence, many of them are affected too much by oblique light which would be far outside of the view angle of most cameras.

Scale Calibrations.—Meters having scales calibrated to be direct reading in either *f*-stops or shutter speeds are quite convenient to use provided the same type of film or plate is always used and also if the same *f*-stop or shutter speed is used at all times. It should be obvious that, if a scale is calibrated in *f*-numbers, it can be direct reading only for definite combinations of shutter speeds and film speeds; or if the scale is calibrated in shutter speeds, it can be direct reading only for certain combinations of *f*-stops and film speeds. Also, while the combination of *f*-stop and shutter speed indicated may be correct as far as exposure is concerned, it may not be a usable combination, since the *f*-stop may be incorrect in order to obtain sufficient depth of focus, or the shutter speed may be too slow to arrest motion.

Because of these limitations the trend in exposure meters now is toward using scales with either arbitrary scales, as on the Weston Junior and Cine Meters, Mini-Photoscop, etc., or with scales calibrated in fundamental units, such as the General Electric meter which is calibrated in foot-candles or the Weston Universal which is calibrated in candles per square foot. These meters are extremely flexible tools as the scale calibrations are independent of film speeds, *f*-stops, or shutter speeds. By means of a calculator which is an integral part of these meters the scale readings can easily be translated into a series of exposure values, the choice of any combination depending upon whether the shutter speed must be fast enough to stop motion or whether considerable depth of focus is desired.

TABLE XXVI.—CHARACTERISTICS OF POPULAR PHOTOELECTRIC METERS ON THE AMERICAN MARKET

Trade name	Country of manufacture	Acceptance angle,[1] degrees Horizontal plane	Vertical plane	Scale length, in.	Scale deflection for a brightness of 1 candle per sq. ft., in.	Film speeds Range covered	System used[2]	No. of speeds on meter	f-stops Range covered	No. of values on meter	Value per division	Shutter speeds, sec. Range covered	No. of values on meter	Exposure difference per division, per cent	Scale calibration
Avo	England	Note A	..	1.66	.....	200-5000	H & D	17	1-32	11	1	1/2000-60	18	26-150	None (coincident pointer)
Bewi	Germany	88	88	1.62	0.032	17-29	Scheiner	5	1.4-36	10	1	1/2000-3600	24	100-150	Arbitrary units
DeJur-Amsco	United States	162	124	1.44	0.012	0.3-200	Weston	19	1-32	20	½	1/1000-60	33	41	Arbitrary units
General Electric	United States	90	50	1.84 0.084	0.010	3-60	Weston	13	1-45	70	⅓-½	1/1000-60	43	26-100	Foot-candles
Helios	Germany	92	92	Note B	0.012	14-32	Scheiner	7	1.4-16	8	1	1/1000-4	12	100-150	Note D
Metrovick	England	126	94	1.5	0.024	18-29	Scheiner	9	1.5-32	19	½	1/1000-96	32	41	Shutter speeds, sec.
Mini-Photoscop	Germany	136	94	1.25	0.026	14-26	Scheiner	5	1.4-32	14	⅓-1	1/2000-60	17	100-150	Arbitrary units
Photar	United States	150	135	1.90	0.0059	5-160	Weston	7	1.5-32	13	½-1	1/1000-100	23	41-150	Arbitrary units
Rhamstine	United States	156	129	1.28	0.0064	11-29 17-32	Scheiner Scheiner	19	1.4-32	12	½-1	1/1000-4	12	100-150	f-stops
Sixtus	Germany	122	102	1.14	0.240	9/10-3⅗/10	DIN	6	1.4-45	11	1	1/100-240	18	100-150	Shutter speeds, sec.
Weston 650 } Universal	United States	60	60	1.33	0.032	1-250	Weston	25	1.5-32	27	⅓	1/200-100	52	26	Candles per sq. ft.
Weston 850	United States	89	89	1.33	0.015	2-500	Weston	17	2-32	17	½	1/1000-64	33	41	Arbitrary units
Weston 819 Cine	United States	30	30	1.33	0.005	1.5-250	Weston	16	1-22	19	½	6-64 frames per sec.	Note C	41	Arbitrary units

[1] The acceptance angle values tabulated are the results of actual tests all made in exactly the same manner. Data were obtained by measuring the response of the meter to a uniform source of brightness for different angular displacements of the meter with respect to the source of light. These data were plotted on rectangular coordinate paper by plotting angular deviation from normal incidence as abscissas and per cent response as ordinate. The tangents of the curve obtained were projected to intersect the abscissas and the total included angle was interpreted as being the acceptance angle of the meter. The same values would be obtained if the data were plotted upon polar coordinate paper, although it would be a little more difficult to obtain actual numerical values because of the difficulty in determining the point at which to project a tangential line.

[2] The majority of the instruction books furnished with exposure meters do not state whether the film speed values are in European or American Scheiner degrees.

Note A: The Avo meter is calibrated to measure incident light and not reflected light, and therefore the acceptance angle is not important.

Note B: The Helios meter is equipped with a lens over the scale so that the scale is magnified about 3× to 4×.

Note C: The Weston 819 Cine meter calculator is calibrated in frames per second. It is direct reading for cine cameras having nominal shutter angles of 110° and 170°.

Note D: The Helios meter has a self-contained rheostat to adjust the pointer to a definite mark. For low light values where it is impossible to obtain sufficient deflection to reach the mark the rheostat is cut out and multiplying factors read from the scale. The calculator exposure values must be multiplied by the factor obtained.

Characteristics of Photoelectric Exposure Meters.—Table XXVI gives the essential operating characteristics of the more important photoelectric exposure meters available in the United States.[1]

Desirable characteristics of exposure meters of this type include: (1) approximate equality of horizontal and vertical acceptance angles, (2) long scale, (3) high sensitivity, (4) accommodation to wide range of f-numbers, (5) accommodation to wide range of film speeds, (6) accommodation to wide range of shutter speeds, and (7) scale calibrated in arbitrary units which are proportional to light intensity or, preferably, in terms of photometric units.

The polar-sensitivity characteristics of a number of photoelectric exposure meters are shown in Fig. 9.

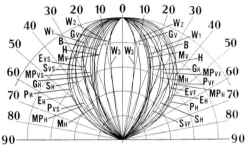

Fig. 9.—Polar diagram showing the relative sensitivity of a number of photoelectric exposure meters for light coming from the angles indicated. The zero angle is, of course, the optical axis of the meter. The letters refer to the various exposure meters as follows:

B, Bewi; *E*, Electrophot (Rhamstine); *G*, General Electric; *H*, Helios; *M*, Meltrovick; *MP*, Mini-Photoscop; *P*, Photar; *S*, Sixtus; W_1, Weston Universal 650; W_2, Weston Junior 850; W_3, Weston Cine 819.

The significance of the subscripts is given as follows:

h, horizontal plane; vf, vertical plane, foreground; vs, vertical plane, sky.

Methods of Using Photoelectric Exposure Meters. *Brightness-range Method.*—Fundamentally we desire to expose the negative, so that the light intensities from the various areas of the scene being photographed will make use of the straight-line portion of the D-$\log_{10} E$ characteristic. This means that the exposure of both the brightest part as well as the darkest part of the scene will fall on the linear region of the D-$\log_{10} E$ curve. The range between the lightest and darkest light values of the scene is termed the brightness range, and if this does not exceed about 125 (*i.e.*, if the brightest area is not more than 125 times as bright as the darkest area), it is usually possible to make an exposure on modern films so that the straight-line portion of the curve is used. The method by which this is accomplished is known as the brightness-range method.

To use this method, the readings of the meter should be numerically proportional to the light intensity reaching the meter, rather than in f-stops or arbitrary letters or figures. The light reflected from the brightest portion of the scene as well as that from the darkest portion of the scene is independently measured. The ratio of these two readings determines the brightness range of the scene being photographed. The geometric mean of these two readings is then taken as the light reading for which the exposure should be made. An example will make this clear.

[1] A more complete table of characteristics of photoelectric exposure meters appears in *Photo Technique*, **1**, No. 1, June, 1939.

Suppose the brightest part of the scene measures 500 candles per sq. ft. and the darkest part measures 5 candles per sq. ft. The geometric mean of these readings is the square root of their product, or $\sqrt{5 \times 500} = \sqrt{2500} = 50$. Thus the reading 50 should be taken as the most suitable light value for which to determine the exposure time for the given aperture and film. On some meters the geometric mean of the two readings may be determined by properly marked scales and limiting marks, as in the Weston Model 650 Universal exposure meter.

Darkest Object Method.—Since the range of scene brightness does not often exceed about 128 (which particular figure is chosen because only an approximate value is required and this one is a power of 2), it is often quite satisfactory to measure the brightness of the darkest object or the darkest shadow in which detail is desired, if these can be approached sufficiently closely to be measured and are not below the sensitivity of the exposure meter. This light reading may then be multiplied by 10, and this reading can be taken as the best compromise for determining the proper exposure for the entire scene.

For example, suppose that the darkest shadow measured 5 candles per sq. ft. as before. The proper exposure for the entire scene, according to the darkest object method would be $5 \times 10 = 50$, which should be used for determining the shutter speed or aperture from the calibration of the meter.

Brightest Object Method.—Sometimes the sensitivity of exposure meters is not sufficiently great to permit an accurate reading to be obtained by the "darkest object method." In such cases the brightest object method may be used, which is similar to that just described. In the brightest object method, the brightest object in the scene is measured. The reading thus obtained is divided by 10 to obtain the best meter reading for which to determine the exposure.

Suppose, for example, that a sheet of paper happens to be the brightest part in the scene being photographed, and that the meter reading is 650 foot-candles. The meter reading of 65 may then be taken as that most suitable for determining the camera adjustments by means of the tables attached to the meter.

Both the brightest object and the darkest object methods depend upon the assumption—which is usually true—that the brightness ratio of the scene does not greatly exceed about 100 to 1. If the brightness range is much greater than this, the latitude of the film may be inadequate to permit exposure of both the bright and the dark objects simultaneously on the linear region of the H and D curve. In such cases a compromise must be made if correct exposure is to be obtained. It is then expedient to determine which portion of the scene (light or dark) is of greater interest and to ascertain that the more important part is properly exposed, at the expense of the less important portions. Thus, for example, if a bright sheet of paper is the dominant subject in the entire scene, the brightest object method would ordinarily be the preferred method of the two. If a dark suit is to be properly photographed in the scene, the darkest object method is to be preferred.

Average-brightness Method.—Where it is inconvenient or impossible to measure the light value of the darkest object directly, then the average values of the entire scene can be measured by directing the meter toward the center of the scene. In this measurement it is preferable to have as little sky included as possible. For example, if buildings with reasonable foreground are to be photographed with open sky overhead, then the meter should be directed slightly downward, so that the imaginary 60° cone area covered by the electric eye does not extend into the sky area.

Substitution Method.—When the brightness of a dark-colored object in the shade is very low so that it cannot be measured with accuracy on the instrument, or possibly not at all, its approximate value may often be determined by the following substitution method. The method is especially suitable for auxiliary use with the darkest-object method.

Make a measurement of the same or similar object in the sunlight or other bright location where a readable indication can be obtained on the meter. Then replace this object with a sheet of white paper or white handkerchief and make a second reading on this. The ratio of these two readings will give the ratio of the reflectance of the paper to that of the object. Remove the paper, and place it in the position of the object whose reading is desired (and which is below the reading of the meter) and make a measurement from the paper. Divide this reading by the ratio previously formed to obtain the light value of the desired object.

For example, suppose the reading obtained on a similar object in a brighter location is 2 and the reading on the paper or handkerchief in the same location is 20. The ratio of these readings is 20:2 or 10. If now we obtain a reading of 1 from the sheet of paper placed upon the subject whose light value is desired, the reading from the desired subject will be $\frac{1}{10}$. It should be realized that this method is in certain cases a convenient approximation. It is most successful where no appreciable differences of color between the two objects being measured are incurred. For example, if the light is to be determined for dark-green foliage, it is best to make the ratio test between the paper and brightly lighted foliage, rather than between the paper and, let us say, red flowers.

Incidentally, these methods of using the photoelectric exposure meter are equally applicable for those cases in which a visual exposure meter is employed.

Coordination of cameras and meters is of considerable importance in order to obtain correct exposure. No meter or camera is perfect, and the calibration errors in both will probably bear an inverse ratio to the purchase price. This statement is based upon tests made on many meters and cameras. Unfortunately it is not as simple to test and readjust an exposure meter or camera as it is to test and readjust a watch, however, if with a particular meter or camera you obtain consistent underexposure or overexposure, the effect whether due to the camera or meter can be corrected by changing the film-speed setting. For example if consistent underexposure is obtained when using a film or plate rated at 23 Scheiner or 24 Weston then the rating should be decreased to, perhaps, 20 or 21 Scheiner or 16 or 20 Weston depending upon the extent of underexposure. This method of correction does not necessarily mean that the film or plate is incorrectly rated, but the method of changing the speed ratings merely offers a simple way to correct for incorrect exposures which may be due to incorrectly timed shutters, incorrectly calibrated diaphragms, or for the type of developer used, etc.

The actual aperture value depends upon whether the diaphragm is being opened or closed. For example, tests on many cameras showed that the f-stops not only varied in actual calibration but were dependent on whether the f-stop desired was approached from a smaller or larger opening. For example, if the diaphragm was moved from $f/3.5$ to $f/8$, the aperture would be larger than if the diaphragm was moved from $f/16$ to $f/8$. These errors are larger on short-focal-length cameras such as miniature and cine cameras than on the long-focal-length cameras because of the much smaller actual aperture. It was also found that these errors were considerably greater in the low-priced cameras. It is therefore recommended always to set the f-stop from the same direction, which will result in the same aperture at all times for the same f-stop calibration.

When using an exposure meter, it should be appreciated that it is a photographic tool and like any tool the more knowledge of it and the more experience you have with it, the better it will serve you. There has been and probably will continue to be much data published regarding the use of exposure meters for special applications. The majority of these data can be summarized as follows:

1. Measure the brightness of the principal area in the scene, the face for portraiture work, the principal building if taking a street scene, etc. Convert this reading into exposure values according to the instructions furnished with the meter. If the particular scene is extremely contrasty and details in the shadow and high-light areas are desired, then measurements should be taken of these two areas and a geometric mean value of exposure chosen.

2. For highly specialized work where special lighting and certain types of pictures are required, it may be necessary to develop a special technique in reading and interpreting the meter readings into photographic exposure. For example, on a certain type of setup it may be noticed that either over- or underexposure is consistently obtained. This may be due to any number of things such as the quality of the light being considerably different than that used in determining the film-speed value, camera calibration or meter calibration may be incorrect, etc., but, by considering the exposure meter, not as an infallible tool, but as a useful practical tool, corrections can be artificially made by altering the rated film speed value to correct for consistent over- or underexposure.

Bibliography

GOODWIN, W. N., JR.: The Photronic Photographic Exposure Meter, *J. Soc. Motion Picture Engrs.*, **20,** 95 (1933).

LAKSY, M., and B. RUBIN: A Practical Method and Photometer for Controlling Exposures in Photography, *J. Soc. Motion Picture Engrs.*, **21,** 155 (1933).

HARRISON, G. B.: Photoelectric Exposure Meters, *Phot. J.*, **74,** 169 (1934).

McKAY, H. C.: Making the Most of Exposure, *Am. Ann. Phot.*, 1935.

GOODWIN, W. N., JR.: Weston Speed Ratings and How Obtained, *Am. Phot.*, **32,** 538 (1938).

CHAPTER IX

PHOTOGRAPHIC LIGHT SOURCES

By Beverly Dudley

Definition of Light.—The various ways in which the term light is used make it desirable to formulate definitions so that a common basis for discussion may be provided.

Scientific Definition.—Because of the manner in which the term light is associated with subjective stimuli, it is extremely difficult, if not impossible, to frame an entirely satisfactory and scientific definition of this term. We may, however, devise a reasonably satisfactory definition which will be useful for many purposes. Thus light may be defined as the radiant energy having wavelengths of from 400 to 700 mμ.[1] These limits are approximately those for which the human eye is sensitive, so that the definition given above includes only those radiations which may be expected to produce, in the normal person, a visual sensation.

Physiological Definitions.—Physiologically, light may be defined as that radiant energy which, impinging upon the eye, travels through the cornea, aqueous humor, crystalline lens, and vitreous humor, successively, ultimately falling on, and passing through, the retina until it reaches the sensitive rods and cones where, in normal eyes, a photochemical reaction is set up leading to the excitation of the nerve endings.

Psychological Definition.—Psychologically, light may be defined as the stimulus to the eye which, in a normal person, results in sensations in the brain, permitting the perception of visual form, intensity, color, perspective, and size.

Photographic Definition.—In a broad sense "actinic" light, *i.e.*, that light which is capable of affecting photographic materials, may be defined as the radiant energy of such wavelengths as are capable of producing a latent image on a photographically sensitized film, plate, or emulsion. It is evident that the range of wavelengths of "actinic" light will depend upon the spectral-sensitivity characteristics of the photographic material. For panchromatic materials the range of wavelengths may be considered to be from about 350 to 700 mμ which corresponds fairly well to the range for which the human eye is sensitive. For orthochromatic materials, the upper limit may be taken at about 600 mμ, whereas for orthonon or noncolor-sensitive materials, the upper limit may be approximately 540 mμ. For special purposes, photographic materials may be sensitized to other wavelength ranges; "actinic light" for such materials will, necessarily, have wavelength limits different from those listed above.

Nature and Characteristics of Light.—At the present time there are two theories concerning the nature of light, coexisting side by side. These are the wave-motion theory, which is useful in explaining such phenomena as reflection, interference, refraction, diffraction, and polarization; and the quantum theory, which explains the more recent advances in X rays, radiation, and photoelectricity. The fact that two theories are required adequately to express the characteristics of electromagnetic radiation results from the inability of the human mind to conceive of more than two methods by which energy can be transferred. One of these is by the actual transfer of matter

---

[1] Millimicron is abbreviated mμ. For other units used in measuring and specifying light wavelength, see Chap. II, page 11, and Chap. X, page 293.

itself, and the other is through the medium of wave motion.   When our knowledge and insight into the physical nature of light are more highly developed, it is reasonable to believe that a single theory of light shall be developed which will embrace the experimental evidence and theoretical considerations which are now included, separately, in the wave motion and the quantum theories.

According to the wave theory, light may be regarded as an electromagnetic disturbance propagated in a hypothetical medium (called the ether) as a transverse wave[1] with a velocity of $c = 2.99796 \times 10^{10}$ cm. per sec. or approximately 186,300 miles per sec.

In any wave motion, the relation between the velocity of propagation c, the frequency (or number of alternations or vibrations per unit time) ν, and the wavelength (or distance from a point on one wave to the corresponding point on the next adjacent waves) λ, is $c = \lambda\nu$.   Light in the visible region extends from wavelengths of from

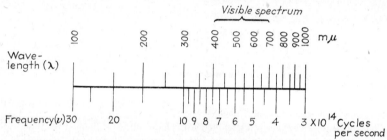

Fig. 1.—Wavelength-frequency relationship for the visible and adjacent spectrums for light traveling in free space.

400 to about 700 mμ, so that the frequency of visible light may be expected to occur within the range of approximately 7.5×10^{14} to 4.3×10^{14} cycles per sec. as shown in Fig. 1.   The color of a given light depends upon the frequencies or wavelengths of which it is composed, as well as the magnitude of the energy at these frequencies or wavelengths.

Light of only one frequency or a very small range of frequencies is said to be monochromatic and results in a sensation of a single pure or spectral color.   When more than one frequency is present, the light is said to be heterochromatic, but the unaided and untrained eye does not usually distinguish between monochromatic and heterochromatic radiations in the visible spectrum.   Pure monochromatic light of a single frequency does not exist, although it may be very closely approached.   White light consists of approximately equal intensities of all frequencies within the visible spectrum.   Consequently, by properly combining colored lights, it is possible to produce white light.

By permitting light to fall upon a smooth surface, the direction of propagation of the light may be altered, and the light is reflected from the surface.   If the reflecting surface is highly polished and smooth, the reflection taking place is regular or specular and is sharply defined.   In this case the angle of incidence of the light to the perpendicular of the surface always equals the angle of reflection.   If the reflecting surface is rough or coarse in comparison to the wavelength of light, the angles of incidence and reflection for the beam as a whole may not be equal or may be only approximately equal.   This type of reflection is called "diffuse reflection," and the beams are not sharply defined as in specular reflection.   Diagrams illustrating specular and diffuse reflection are shown in Fig. 2.

[1] A transverse wave is one in which the displacement occurs perpendicular to the direction of propagation.

Light impinging upon a medium is dispersed in three ways as shown in Fig. 3. Part of the light may be reflected, as already explained, or, if the medium is transparent, much of the light may be transmitted through it. The rest is absorbed in passing through the medium and is dissipated, ultimately making its appearance in the form of heat.

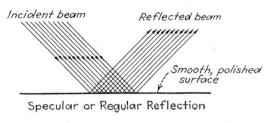

Specular or Regular Reflection

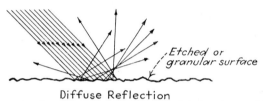

Diffuse Reflection

Fig. 2.—Diagrams illustrating specular reflection from polished surface and diffuse reflection from surface which is irregular compared with dimensions of light waves.

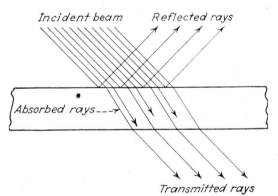

Fig. 3.—In passing through a transparent medium, some of the light rays are reflected, some are absorbed, and the rest are transmitted through the medium. The rays are bent in passing from two mediums having different indices of refraction.

The velocity of light in any material medium is less than the velocity in free space. Therefore, if light which is traveling through a vacuum is made to pass through a transparent medium, its velocity will be decreased. If the incidence is perpendicular or normal to the surface of the medium, the only effect will be a slowing down of the velocity of light while passing through the denser medium. However, if light impinges on the denser medium at some other angle, the relative change in velocity of propagation through the denser medium will result in a bending of the beam. At the surface of the two mediums the direction of the beam will change, and the light is diffracted.

In passing out of the denser transparent medium into free space again, the velocity of propagation will be increased. Consequently, the light wave will again be refracted but in a direction opposite to that of the first refraction.

Ordinarily natural light vibrates in all possible directions perpendicular to its direction of propagation. However, it is possible to restrict to a single plane the transverse displacement of the wave, and light vibrating in this manner is plane polarized.

Like sound or water waves, light waves curl around obstacles in their path, but because of the tremendous size of any physical object which we can observe compared to the wavelength of light, this effect is so very slight as to be practically nonexistent. Therefore we customarily regard light as being rectilinearly propagated, *i.e.*, as traveling in straight lines.

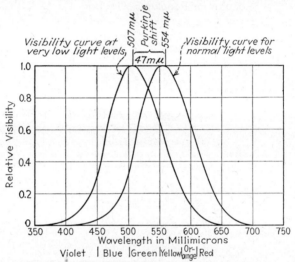

Fig. 4.—Relative visibility of the normal human eye at normal and greatly reduced light levels, showing the Purkinje shift.

According to the quantum theory, electromagnetic radiation (of which light is an example and forms a small portion of the total range of possible and available electromagnetic radiation) is always emitted and absorbed in discrete quantities. The unit of radiation is the quantum or photon. When one of these quanta is absorbed, the energy of the quanta manifests itself as radiant energy or waves which may have their wavelength in the visible region so as to produce light. The subject of quantum theory is beyond the scope of this book and is not essential for an elementary understanding of photographic principles.

The eye is not uniformly sensitive to all wavelengths (colors) within the visible spectrum, which extends from about 400 to 700 mμ. For a given amount of energy (light intensity) at the red end of the spectrum, the eye is relatively insensitive. The sensitivity of the eye increases as the wavelength is shifted from the red, through the red-orange, orange, orange-yellow, yellow, and for moderate light intensities finally reaches a maximum for the average human eye in the yellow-green region. Beyond this point of maximum sensitivity, the sensitivity of the eye decreases as we progress through the green, blue-green, blue, blue-violet, and trails off in the violet region. It is safe to say that probably no two human eyes are exactly alike in their sensitivity or response to colors, but for the average normal human eye, the relative sensitivity as a function of wavelength (color) is given by the curve of Fig. 4. The maximum sensitivity of the eye is seen to occur at 554 mμ at normal levels of illumination.

When the luminosity of an observed object is considerably reduced beyond that ordinarily used, there is a gradual shift in the visibility curve toward the shorter wavelengths, and the shape of the visibility curve undergoes minor modifications. For extremely low levels of illumination, the maximum sensitivity of the eye occurs at 507 mμ in the green portion of the spectrum, instead of at 554 mμ in the yellow-green part of the spectrum. Practical application is made of this Purkinje shift of the visibility curve with variation in illumination, in selecting safe lights which are employed when dealing with sensitive panchromatic materials. Since the eye is most sensitive to green light at low illumination levels, the safe light is made green so that

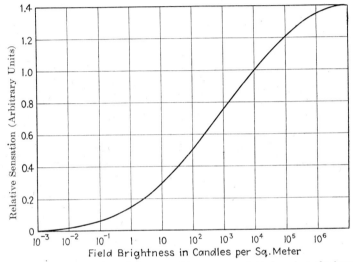

Fig. 5.—Relative sensation of the normal human eye plotted against the logarithm of the stimulus (field brightness). If the Weber-Fechner law were obeyed, this curve would be a sloping straight line instead of being s-shaped.

less light can be employed and thereby lessen the chance of fogging the photographic material.

Two other characteristics of the eye are important in photography, especially in motion-picture photography. These are the sensitivity of the eye to flicker and the persistence of vision.

The eye does not respond instantly to a sensation stimulus; when the stimulus is removed, the eye does not respond immediately. The eye will require about 0.01 sec. to perceive the stimulus and will retain the sensation of light for about 0.05 sec. after its cessation. The values given depend upon the general level of illumination and the flicker rate but are approximately correct for average conditions encountered in practical motion-picture photography.

If flicker at constant frequency occurs in a light source or in the level of illumination, it may be quite annoying. The flicker frequency which is least objectionable varies with the general level of illumination and the least perceptible difference in brightness between the bright and dark images. However, flicker is usually most objectionable between about 3 and 10 cycles per sec. If the flicker is such as to cut off the light entirely (as in the case of motion-picture projection), the highest frequency at which flicker is just apparent is called the "critical frequency." For a field brightness of 1 candle per sq. m., the critical frequency is 30 cycles; it is about 38 cycles at 10 candles per sq. m., 22 cycles at 0.1 candles per sq. m., 15 cycles at 0.01 candles per sq. m. and about 12 cycles at 0.001 candles per sq. m. These figures illustrate the importance of taking into consideration the general brightness of the image on the screen in determining optimum shutter speed.

The eye has a wide adaption to light stimulus and is sensitive over a wide range. When the relative sensation of the eye is plotted against the logarithm of the stimulus (logarithm of field brightness in candles per square meter) as independent ordinate, an s-shaped curve results, covering the tremendously large range of from 0.001 to 10^6 candles per sq. m. as shown in Fig. 5. The fact that relatively little change in sensation results from a large change in stimulus (when static conditions are assumed) indicates how unsuited the eye is as a substitute for objective types of instruments in determining light values.

Production of Light.—Visible light may be produced on a practical scale in two ways: (1) by increasing the temperature of the source until it is incandescent, *i.e.*, until some of the energy radiated falls within the visible region of wavelengths; and (2) by conduction of electricity through gases. The first of these methods is represented by the familiar tungsten filament lamp. Mercury-vapor lamps, neon signs, and sodium-vapor lamps are among the more common examples of the production of light by means of gaseous conduction.

In incandescent sources, light is produced by passing current through a fine wire contained in a glass enclosure which is either evacuated as completely as possible of the residual gases or is thoroughly evacuated after which an inert gas at low pressure is introduced into the enclosure. The purpose of the inactive gas is to increase the life of the lamp and to prevent the blackening of the enclosing bulb.

Other incandescent sources include the flames of candles, kerosene lamps, Welsbach mantles, gas burners, etc. In a popular sense a flame is a gas burning in air. The production of the flame is, however, not confined to a gas burning in air but is a phenomenon observed when any two gases undergo combustion accompanied by the evolution of light and heat, as when hydrogen burns in chlorine to produce hydrogen chloride. The luminosity of flames depends, in a complex manner, on a number of factors. In general, however, it may be said that: (1) the luminosity of a flame is dependent upon, or is influenced by, the glowing of solid matter, such as carbon, heated to incandescence; (2) the luminosity is increased by increasing the pressure of the burning gas; and (3) the luminosity is increased by raising the temperature of the burning gas.

In producing visible light through the use of gaseous conduction, the most common method is to fill, with a gas or vapor, a glass tube having metallic electrodes at its ends and applying a voltage between these electrodes. The voltage must be sufficiently high to break down the gas molecules and produce ionization together with radiation in the visible spectrum. Radiations outside of the visible region are also usually produced as well but are of no importance for purposes of illumination.

Light Spectra.—If the white light from the sun is analyzed, as by passing it through a prism or reflecting it from a finely ruled grating, it will be found to be composed of a continuous band of all the visible colors: red, orange, yellow, green, blue, and violet. Light from an incandescent lamp will also form a continuous band of colors when analyzed, but since this form of light is yellow rather than white, the colors from an incandescent lamp (operated at temperature which will result in a useful life of the lamp of about 1000 hr.) will be weaker in the green, blue, and violet regions than is the case with the white light from the sun. If we pass the light from a mercury-vapor or neon lamp through a prism, it will be found that the light produced is analyzed into its component parts but that the color distribution obtained is not at all continuous; in fact, only a few colored lines will be observed.

The spreading out of a complex light into a range of spectral colors is known as analyzing the light, and the range of colors is known as the spectrum. When the range of colors is continuous, as in the case of analyzed sunlight, the spectrum is continuous. When only certain lines appear, as when gaseous-conduction light sources are analyzed, the spectrum is discontinuous. The spectrum shows what colors (or light wavelengths) are present in the original light source. If the intensity of the energy at the various wavelengths is measured, a spectroradiometric curve can be plotted which shows in graphical form the relative or absolute intensity of the energy of which the beam is composed, as a function of wavelength. Such spectroradiometric curves are

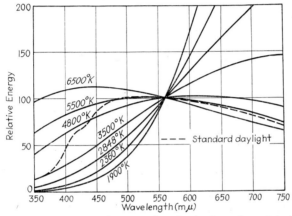

Fig. 6.—Relative energy at various wavelengths for incandescent bodies at various temperatures. The spectral-energy curve for daylight is shown by the dashed line, and is closely approximated, over most of the visual region, by a body having a color temperature of 5500° K.

of considerable importance, scientifically, in the investigation of the characteristics of light sources.

In a continuous spectrum all wavelengths within a given spectrum band are present to some extent, and the relation between the wavelength and the energy of the light source at that wavelength may be indicated by means of a continuous curve. Figure 6 shows the spectroradiometric curve for daylight at the earth's surface as well as for tungsten lamps operated at various temperatures.

In a discontinuous spectrum, energy may not be present for all wavelengths within the limits of the spectrum band, lack of certain wavelength lines being made apparent by a dark field. Such a spectrum is known as a "line spectrum," as compared with the continuous spectrum of the sun or incandescent lamps, for instance. In the curve of a line spectrum the presence of energy of a given wavelength is indicated by a vertical line whose length represents the relative or absolute intensity of the energy at this given wavelength. Figure 7 shows a line spectrum for a hot-cathode neon lamp.

Sometimes we may have a combination of the continuous as well as the line spectra, as when light from a mercury-vapor lamp and an incandescent lamp are analyzed simultaneously. Such a spectral curve unites the properties of both the continuous and the discontinuous spectra.

The radiometric curves for various types of light sources are of importance in the scientific and technical aspects of photography since the density of the image on the negative depends not only upon the characteristics of the film or plate, together with a filter, if this is used, but also to a very marked extent upon the characteristics of the light source employed in making the exposure. This subject will be treated at greater length in following sections in this chapter.

Photographic Effects of Light.—The fundamental action of light impinging upon a photographically sensitized material is to produce, after the necessary processing, a deposit of finely divided metallic silver which appears black by either transmitted or reflected light. The blackness or opaqueness of this silver deposit is termed the density of the photographic material. The density of the silver deposit depends, in a

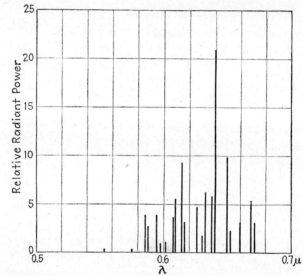

Fig. 7.—Line spectrum showing the relative intensity of the various lines in the spectrum for a neon lamp. Practically all of the energy is in the red and orange part of the visible band.

rather complicated manner, on several factors, among the most important of which may be mentioned:

1. The intensity of the light source to which the photographic material is exposed.
2. The spectral-energy distribution of the light source.
3. The sensitivity or speed of the photographic material exposed to white light.
4. The spectral sensitivity of the photographic material.
5. The manner in which the exposure is made, *i.e.*, whether the exposure is made continuously or intermittently.
6. The total duration of the time of exposure.
7. The processing conditions which the photographic material undergoes subsequent to exposure.

The effects of most of these factors upon the density of the photographic material have been discussed in the chapter on Photographic Sensitometry. In this chapter it is proposed to discuss, briefly, the first four factors listed above, since they are intimately associated with light sources, and a knowledge of their effects will facilitate a further discussion of the characteristics of light sources suitable for photography.

Density Dependent upon Light Intensity.—Suppose we have an optical bench upon which is mounted, at one end, a photographic plate behind a shutter which is arranged to let light through to the plate for a given amount of time, *e.g.*, *t* sec., but shuts off all light from reaching the film except when it is open. Let a convenient light source, such as an incandescent lamp, be arranged before the shutter in such a way that the distance between the film and the light source may be varied at will. It is assumed that the light source is maintained constant in intensity and spectral-energy distribution.[1] This may be accomplished by operating the lamp at sufficiently low temperatures (not more than 2400°K.) and by maintaining the temperature of the lamp constant. The most convenient way of maintaining constancy of the luminous output is to maintain the voltage across its terminals constant.

Under the conditions assumed, exposure of the photographic plate will only take place during the time the shutter is open, and during this time the illumination on the plate will depend upon the intrinsic brightness of the lamp with its associated filter as well as the distance between the lamp and the photographic plate. If the lamp is rated at *k* candle power and the distance between the lamp and photographic plate is *D*, then the light intensity on the photographic plate will be

$$I = \frac{k}{D^2} \qquad (1)$$

If *t* is the time during which the shutter is open, the exposure of the plate may then be defined as

$$E = It = \frac{kt}{D^2} \qquad (2)$$

By keeping *k* and *t* constant, the exposure given to the photographic plate may now be made to depend only upon the intensity of light falling upon the photographic plate *I*.

If we give different sections of the photographic plate different exposures by varying the distance *D* for each successive exposure and then determine the density of the silver deposit

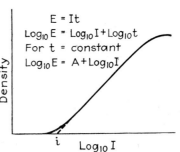

$E = It$
$\mathrm{Log_{10}} E = \mathrm{Log_{10}} I + \mathrm{Log_{10}} t$
For t = constant
$\mathrm{Log_{10}} E = A + \mathrm{Log_{10}} I$

Fig. 8.—Characteristic of typical negative materials, showing the manner in which the density depends upon the intensity of illumination for constant exposure time (constant shutter speeds).

after the film is properly processed, we may determine the manner in which the density depends upon the intensity of the light source to which it was exposed. If such a series of exposures is made, the densities are measured and plotted against intensity *I*, the results will give the typical characteristic curve shown in Fig. 8. From this curve it will be seen that: (1) for extremely low values of illumination, only a small silver deposit occurs corresponding to the fog density of the material; (2) for increasing values of illumination, additional deposits of silver occur; (3) for a considerable range, the density is proportional to the logarithm of the illumination; (4) this proportionality fails but reaches a maximum density after which (5) the density decreases for extremely large values of light intensity. In practice, this last region, corresponding to extremely large values of exposure, is of no practical use; the most important part of this characteristic is the linear region for which the density is proportional to the logarithm of the light intensity, so long as the shutter speed is maintained invariable.

Effect of Sensitivity of Photographic Material.—The sensitivity of a photographic plate may be, and is, expressed in a rather wide variety of ways.[2] Because of the

---

[1] For simplicity and consistency with sensitometric practice, let it be assumed that the spectral radiation of the lamp is modified by means of filters so that it closely approximates that of mean noon sunlight.

[2] See p. 190, Chapter on Photographic Sensitometry.

dissimilarity of the methods employed to express the sensitivity characteristics of photographic materials as well as the dissimilar numerical units employed, it is difficult to make any quantitive statements concerning the relation between the density of the silver deposit and the sensitivity or speed of the photographic material. In several common methods of expressing film characteristics the sensitivity or speed is a measure of the minimum exposure which would just produce a deposit of silver if the D-$\log_{10} E$ characteristic (as shown in Fig. 8) were a straight line.   All the methods of determining the speed or sensitivity of photographic plates are alike in that the higher numerics of any given system of speed notation represent the more sensitive or the faster emulsions.   Consequently, it may be said that, for a given light source, the density of the deposit will tend to increase as the speed number in any given system of the photographic materials is increased.   But it is not possible to determine, from speed ratings alone, what the ratio of the densities will be for two films exposed in a given manner but whose speeds are given in different methods of rating.   Thus it may be assumed that, for a given light source exposed to a plate for a given time, a denser deposit of silver will be obtained for a photographic material having a speed of 500 H and D than for one having a speed of 100 H and D.   Conversely, a denser deposit for identical exposure and processing conditions will be obtained for material having a rating of 26° Scheiner than for one having a rating of 18° Scheiner.   We cannot, however, make any statements as to the density due to a given exposure between films of 500 H and D and 26° Scheiner or of 100 H and D and 18° Scheiner without making measurements on the processed films.

Effect of Spectral Characteristics of Film and Light Source.—In color photography and in monochrome photography where colored objects must be photographed so that the final print shows the image in black, white, and shades of gray which are proportional to the luminosities of the various portions of the original subject, the spectral characteristics of the light source and of the photographic material are of considerable importance.

The spectral-sensitivity characteristics of the photographic material must be studied together with the spectral-energy distribution of the light source, for both characteristics enter into the correct tone rendition of the colored image.   It is possible to study the spectral characteristics of either the film or the light source alone, if we maintain constant the characteristic of the other factor.   But in any event it is essential that the spectral characteristics of both of these two factors be known.

Let the spectral distribution of energy intensity in a light source be represented by the symbol J_λ, and let the spectral sensitivity of the photographic material be designated by the symbol S_λ, where both J_λ and S_λ are continuous functions between their upper and lower wavelength limits, which theoretically are zero and infinity.   Then the photographic intensity of the light source, whose characteristics are specified by J_λ, when used with a photographic material whose spectral characteristics are specified by S_λ, is given by

$$I_p = \int_0^\infty J_\lambda\, S_\lambda\, d\lambda \tag{3}$$

The equation for the photographic intensity may be represented by the area under a curve whose boundary is determined by the boundaries of the curves representing the spectral characteristics of the film and the light source.

For those who may not be mathematically minded, the following illustrative examples may be more enlightening than the above equation.   Let Fig. 9 represent the relative spectral sensitivity of several photographic materials, as indicated, and let Fig. 10 represent the relative spectral-intensity distribution of three common light sources employed in photography.   Since we shall be concerned only with the relative spectral characteristics, all the light sources have been plotted with their intensity at 560 mμ taken as unity.

Knowing the characteristics of the light source and the film, it is now possible to determine the relative photographic effects of the light sources on a film of specified

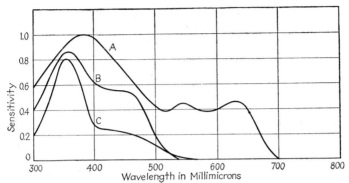

Fɪɢ. 9.—Relative spectral sensitivity of typical photographic materials. Curve *A* represents the sensitivity of panchromatic material; curve *B*, orthochromatic materials; and curve *C*, noncolor-sensitive materials.

characteristics when a definite exposure is given. This photographic effect is known as "photicity" and is analogous to luminosity in visual effects. The preceding equations indicate that we are to multiply, wavelength by wavelength, the sensitivity of the film by the spectral-energy distribution of the light source; the area under the

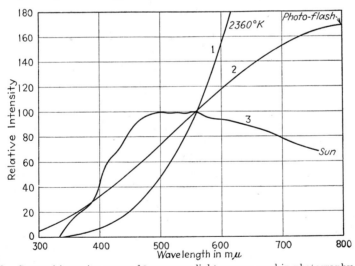

Fɪɢ. 10.—Spectral-intensity curves for common light sources used in photography plotted relative to the energy at 560 millimicrons, which is assumed to be unity or 100 per cent.

new curve is then proportional to the photographic intensity of the light source in question when used with the film exposure time. In Fig. 11 are shown the resulting curves for three types of photographic materials (ordinary, orthochromatic, and panchromatic) when used with sunlight as a source of light. Since, for a given time of exposure to sunlight, the density of the negative is proportional to the area under these curves, it is apparent that the panchromatic material is, in effect, considerably more sensitive than the other two photographic materials.   The peaks of sensitivity

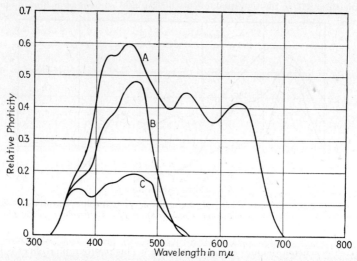

Fig. 11.—Relative sensitivity of panchromatic (*A*), orthochromatic (*B*) and noncolor-sensitive (*C*) photographic materials when used with sunlight illumination.   These curves are obtained by multiplying, wavelength by wavelength, the appropriate curves of Fig. 9 with the sunlight curve of Fig. 10.

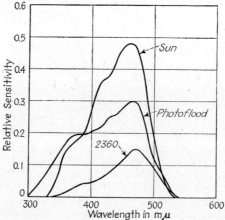

Fig. 12.—Relative-sensitivity curves for orthochromatic materials when used with various light sources.   These curves are obtained by multiplying, wavelength by wavelength, the orthochromatic curve of Fig. 9 with the appropriate curves of the light sources of Fig. 10.

as shown in Fig. 9 do not vary by more than 20 per cent, but the relative photicity as shown in Fig. 11 is about 1.00 for the orthonon material, as against 1.75 for the orthochromatic and 4.92 for the panchromatic materials.   The increased photicity results from the fact that the orthochromatic and panchromatic films are sensitive to a wider range of wavelengths than the orthonon or noncolor-sensitive films; to only a small extent is the increased photicity due to increased sensitivity of the peaks of their spectral curves.

Figure 12 shows curves plotted for the orthochromatic material whose characteristics are given in Fig. 9, but when used with three different light sources. The curve of smallest area is that obtained when a tungsten lamp at a temperature of 2360°K. is used to expose the film. The intermediate curve is that obtained with a photoflood tungsten-filament lamp, whereas the curve with the highest peak is that for sunlight. These curves show that, for a photographic material whose spectral sensitivity is that given by S_λ of Fig. 9, the sun produces the greatest photicity; while photoflood lamps are next. Tungsten-filament lamps at 2360°K. (a temperature commonly used in photographic sensitometric work) produces the least photographic effect for the photographic material selected. The resultant photicity curves would be different for photographic materials having other spectral-sensitivity curves. From an examination of the film and light-source curves, it would appear that the photographic effect of the sun and of the photoflood lamps would be about equal for the panchromatic materials, although a curve would have to be plotted to test the accuracy of this statement. It should be pointed out that Figs. 9 and 10 are plotted in terms of relative spectral sensitivity, and relative spectral-energy distribution, respectively. Consequently the photicity curves are relative and are to be used only for comparisons between two or more materials plotted in the same figure. The curves could, of course, be plotted in some definitely established units, but this is not necessary for illustrative purposes.

Classification of Light Sources.—Light sources for photographic purposes may be divided into two convenient classifications: (1) natural light sources whose inherent characteristics of intensity, time of occurrence, time of duration, and spectral characteristics are entirely out of the control of human beings; and (2) artificial light sources whose characteristics are very largely under human control and are, consequently, much more convenient and flexible than natural light sources.

Natural Light Sources.—Natural light sources may be divided into the following groups:

1. Astronomical:
    a. The sun
    b. The moon
    c. The stars and planets
2. Meteorological:
    a. Daylight, resulting from sun shining on the earth's atmosphere
    b. Lightning
    c. Aurora
3. Luminescent materials

Of these natural light sources, only sunlight and daylight (which results from the sun) are of sufficient importance to be generally used for ordinary photographic purposes. For special purposes, especially scientific work, some of the other sources may be used, but their use is relatively infrequent.

The Sun.—The spectrum of the sun is continuous. Light from the sun is closely approached by that of an incandescent source operating at about 5600°K. The spectrum of the sun as received at the earth's surface, is modified by the scattering and absorption of the earth's atmosphere. Absorption and scattering produced by particles in the atmosphere are the principle causes for this modification. Scattering and absorption increase as the sun approaches the horizon, since for this condition, the rays reaching the earth travel through a much longer atmospheric path than when the sun is at the zenith. The intensity of the sun's rays reaching the earth depends not only upon the time of day but also upon the time of year and the latitude of the observer. Changes in the spectral distribution of the light of the sun are easily observable throughout the day, the apparent reddening of the spectrum near sunrise or sunset being caused by the absorption of the shorter wavelengths as the rays pass through longer paths of the earth's atmosphere.   Because of the wide ranges which take place in the intensity and spectral distribution of the sun's rays as they reach the earth, it is evident that it is impossible to speak of "sunlight" (for any given particular condition) as representing a suitable standard of luminous intensity.

Although the radiant energy from the sun, at any given time, cannot be used as a standard, it does provide, however, one of the most convenient and practical of lumin-

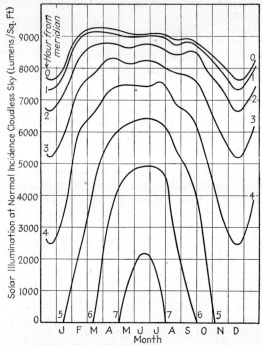

Fig. 13.—Solar illumination for each month of the year, and for various periods of the day, as determined from measurements made at Washington, D. C.

ous light sources.   Numerous measurements on the spectral distribution and intensity of the sun's rays which reach the earth have been made, and the mean or average value of these measurements are well known, do not vary, and consequently may be used to specify "mean noon sunlight."   Thus, mean noon sunlight as measured at Washington, D. C., is often used as a standard and as a comparison for other light sources.

Mean noon sunlight illumination for various times of the year and day at the surface of the earth at Washington, D. C., is given in Table I.   This table represents measurements made with the sun shining unobscured on a cloudless day.   The solar illumination is shown graphically in Fig. 13.   The curves are plotted in terms of hours from noon, instead of in terms of local standard time.   Thus the curve marked 2 applies for conditions at 10 A.M. or 2 P.M. standard time while the 0 curve represents noon data.

The manner in which the relative luminous energy from the sun varies throughout the day is shown in Fig. 14.   These curves are plotted on a relative basis, with noon sunlight for each month taken as 100 per cent, but, as 100 per cent for the various curves represents different values of absolute radiant energy, Fig. 14 should not be used in such a manner that data from one curve is transferred to or compared with data of another curve. These sets of curves show, for example, that at 9 A.M. (or 3 P.M.) the light from the sun in October (or February) is about 82 per cent of its value at noon for the same months, and therefore gives some indication of the increase in exposure which should be allowed if photographs are made several hours before or after noon. It is not correct to interpret these charts to indicate, for example, that the light from the sun at 4 P.M. (or 8 A.M.) in June will be equal to that at 9 A.M. in October because

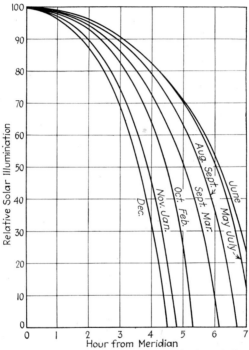

Fig. 14.—Diagram illustrating the manner in which the relative solar illumination varies throughout the day. The curves are plotted with noon illumination for each particular month as 100 per cent.

both happen to have values which are 82 per cent of their maximum value at noon, for the noon sunlight in June is greater than that in October. It should be noted that these curves are plotted for Washington, D. C. The use of this table at latitudes much different than that of Washington would require correction.

The spectral-energy distribution of the sun is an important consideration when photographic work is done by daylight. Early in the morning and late in the afternoon, the radiation of the sun contains relatively much more red and orange than it does at noon. For panchromatic materials little or no increase in exposure may be required in consequence of this fact. However, for orthochromatic materials, it may be necessary to increase the exposure late in the afternoon or early in the morning several times that required for panchromatic materials, simply because there is relatively less blue radiation in the sunlight (to which the orthochromatic material is sensitive) and relatively much more red (to which the orthochromatic materials are insensitive). For orthonon or noncolor-sensitive materials which have a peak of sensitivity at the blue end of the spectrum, it may be impossible to make photographs early in the morning or late in the afternoon except by means of excessively long exposure.

Moonlight.—Since the light from the moon comes to the earth as light reflected from the sun, it follows that the intensity of moonlight is very much weaker than that of sunlight. Moonlight varies cyclically every 28 days, as well as throughout the night and during the year. As a source of luminous intensity for photographic pur-

TABLE I.—SOLAR ILLUMINATION AT NORMAL INCIDENCE. LATITUDE 42°N. EAST OF MISSISSIPPI RIVER. CLOUDLESS SKY[1]

		Hour angle of sun from the meridian							
		0	1	2	3	4	5	6	7
		Solar illumination, lumens per sq. ft.							
Winter	Dec. 21	7600	7300	6640	5190	2460			
	Jan. 21	8120	7890	7290	6040	3760			
	Feb. 21	9140	9040	8440	7450	6140	2460		
Spring	Mar. 21	9270	9110	8710	7910	6700	4650	720	
	Apr. 21	9230	9060	8800	8300	7350	5860	3600	
	May 21	9070	8990	8630	8140	7480	6260	4700	1200
	June 21	9080	9000	8740	8220	7430	6420	4880	2160
Summer	July 21	9070	8990	8670	8140	7550	6330	4830	1200
	Aug. 21	8810	8710	8390	7830	6880	5460	2990	
	Sept. 21	8910	8760	8510	7710	6500	4590	720	
Fall	Oct. 21	8510	8420	7960	6910	5220	2100		
	Nov. 21	8120	7890	7290	5960	3390			
	Dec. 21								
		Time of day (local standard time)							
		12	11	10	9	8	7	6	5
			1	2	3	4	5	6	7

[1] From H. H. Kimball, *Trans. Illum. Eng. Soc.* (*N. Y.*), **18**, 457 (1923).

poses, the moon is not very effective. Approximately 150,000 times as long an exposure must be given for photographs taken in full moonlight on a clear night as would be required for the same scene by full, direct sunlight. This approximate rule varies with conditions, of course, but a simple practical rule to follow is to expose 25 min. by full moonlight for every $\frac{1}{100}$ sec. exposure which would be required for the same scene in full sunlight. If the moon is in one of its increasing or decreasing phases instead of being full, the exposure must be still further increased. Of course, if the moon itself is to be photographed, shorter exposures should be given.

Light from Stars and Planets.—The stars and planets provide so little light as to be suitable only for astronomical photographs, and even here the exposure is usually of the order of minutes, rather than small fractions of a second. The actual exposure time required for astronomical photography depends to a large extent upon the telescope used. For further data, reference should be made to the chapter on Astronomic Photography.

Meterological Light Sources.—Of the meterological sources of light, skylight or daylight is by far the most important for photographic purposes. Approximately one-fifth of the total illumination on a clear day is due to light from the sky (which, of course, results from the scattering of sunlight in the earth's atmosphere), rather than direct sunlight itself. For a cloudy, overcast sky in which the sun is not visible, the illumination on a vertical surface is almost independent of the direction of this surface and that of the sun. For a clear day, however, the illumination varies considerably with the angle between the sun and the vertical surface, for in this case direct sunlight enters into the consideration of the total or net illumination.

Table II shows the illumination from daylight for various conditions, whereas Table I shows the illumination due to direct sunlight. The total illumination may be estimated from these tables. For a clear day the net illumination is the sum of these two illuminations. On cloudy days with the sun obscured, the net illumination is that due to daylight and is given in Table II. For other conditions, some suitable proportion of the two components of the net illumination should be used.

Artificial Light Sources.—Artificial light sources may be classified for convenience according to the type of spectra they produce, or the purity of the emitted spectra. For special types of photographic work (especially in scientific photography) such classifications may be useful. However, for ordinary photography a somewhat arbitrary classification, based largely upon the apparatus employed to produce the light, appears to be generally more useful and will be employed in this section.

TABLE II.—ILLUMINATION FROM SKY LIGHT, LUMENS PER SQ. FT.[1]

Solar altitude, θ	On horizontal surface	On vertical surface, whose angle with sun is φ							Zenith luminosity
		$\varphi = 0°$	$\varphi = 45°$	$\varphi = 70°$	$\varphi = 90°$	$\varphi = 135°$	$\varphi = 180°$	Mean	
Cloudy Day									
0°	15.2	5.6	5.8	...	6.4	6.7	7.1	6.3	14.7
20°	726	298	280	...	273	273	272	279	919
41°	1505	614	608	...	615	622	606	613	1860
61°	2150	881	941	...	977	932	929	932	3340
71°	2950	1142	1103	...	1118	1122	1203	1138	4500
Clear Sky, Summer									
0°									
20°	840	1252	1038	803	526	316	293	704	370
40°	1340	1454	1325	932	686	417	358	754	745
60°	1600	1420	1255	923	751	559	486	....	1530
70°	1600	1291	1074	903	754	542	475	....	2140
Clear Sky, Winter									
0°	67.8	64.6	63.7	...	30.6	30.2	31.5	....	25.2
20°	683	1042	873	562	393	265	257	....	261
40°	977	1121	936	690	505	325	295	....	505

[1] From H. H. Kimball, *Trans. Illum. Eng. Soc.* (*N. Y.*), **18**, 457 (1923).

Light sources for practical photographic work may, accordingly, be classified as follows:

1. Incandescent sources (electric lamps and flames)
2. Arcs
3. Gaseous-discharge devices
4. Transient light sources

Incandescent Electric Lamps.—At the present time, incandescent electric lamps are probably the most important and most frequently used of all sources of artificial light. This is largely due to their convenience and cleanliness in operation, the production of a continuous spectrum of desirable energy distribution, their stability and relative constancy in use, the convenient methods of control of modeling and lighting which they permit, and, finally, the reasonable cost of installation, maintenance, and operation. Compared to gaseous-discharge lamps, incandescent electric lamps are inefficient producers of light, but for most purposes this relative inefficiency is overbalanced by the desirable spectral characteristics, the low cost, and especially the convenience of the incandescent lamps.

The radiant energy emitted from an incandescent source (whether incandescent lamp or flame) produces a continuous spectrum. The total radiant flux, as well as the spectral-energy distribution, is dependent upon the temperature of the incandescent body. Consequently, the temperature of incandescent bodies has an appreciable photographic effect, and for precise sensitometric or photometric work, must be maintained within narrow limits. In the case of incandescent electric lamps, the temperature may be most conveniently determined by controlling the voltage across the lamp terminals or the current flowing through the filament.

Types of Incandescent Lamps.—Incandescent lamps may be classified according to the type of material out of which the filament is constructed, such as carbon, tantalum, or tungsten. According to this classification, tungsten-filament lamps are by far in greater general use than any of the others. According to their evacuation, incandescent lamps may be classified as vacuum lamps or gas filled. In the vacuum lamps, the air and absorbed gases have been removed, and a high degree of vacuum is required, whereas in the gas-filled lamps a small amount of inert gas is admitted after the lamp has been thoroughly evacuated. The inert gas, which is usually nitrogen, is introduced to reduce evaporation from the filament. Reducing evaporation lengthens the life of the lamp and reduces the blackening of the bulb. Small lamps are still of the vacuum type, but practically all 110-volt lamps of 50 watts or high-power rating are now gas filled.[1]

Characteristics of Incandescent Lamps.—The resistance characteristics of carbon-filament and metallic-filament lamps differ markedly. As the voltage is increased, the resistance of the carbon-filament lamps, which was initially high, decreases; for the metallic-filament lamps, the initial resistance is low and increases as the voltage is raised.

The life of most incandescent lamps is rated at 1000 hr., although for particular purposes the life may be either increased or decreased. The life of the lamp depends upon the diameter of the filament and the temperature at which it is operated. Slight increases in operating voltage above the normal value result in substantial increases in the operating temperature and considerable reduction in life. On the other hand, reduction of the operating voltage below the normal value increases the life but reduces the operating temperature and the luminous output. The spectral-energy distribution is also changed as the voltage is varied, more of the energy being in the red when the voltage is reduced and tending toward the blue as the voltage is increased.

---

[1] A good summary of the characteristics of incandescent electric lamps is given in the "Standard Handbook for Electrical Engineers," McGraw.

While in general a life of 1000 hr. may usually be expected for well-made American lamps intended for general illumination,[1] the lamps for motion-picture production service have a rating of from 15 to 500 hr.; lamps for projection and stereopticon service are rated at either 25 or 50 hr., and those for spotlight or floodlight service are rated at 80 hr. or, more usually, at 200 hr. of life in the 110- to 120-volt sizes. Photoflood lamps for photographic service are operated at much higher temperatures than lamps intended for general illumination and have a rated life of from 2 to 15 hr.

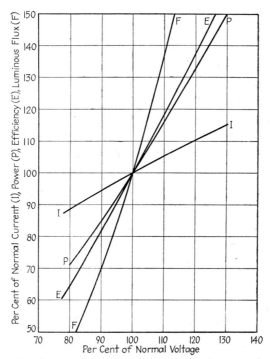

Fig. 15.—Operating characteristics of incandescent lamps in terms of per cent of normal operating voltage. The curves are designated as follows: *I*, current consumption; *P*, power consumption; *E*, efficiency; and *F*, light output.

The essential characteristics of operation of incandescent lamps are: (1) the efficiency or lumens per watt, (2) the light output in lumens, (3) the power consumption in watts, and (4) the current consumption in amperes; all of which are functions of the voltage at which the lamp is operated. The average characteristics and proper voltage of operation may be obtained from the manufacturer, but these characteristics will change as the operating voltage is varied. The manner in which the characteristics of incandescent lamps depend upon the operating voltage has been studied by Barrow and Meyer[2] at the National Bureau of Standards, and the following data are summarized from their paper.

---

[1] Cheap incandescent lamps of Japanese manufacture which have been on the American market are frequently found to have short life, relatively low luminous output, and higher power consumption than the equivalent American product. While it may be difficult to determine definitely the cause for these characteristics, it is not unlikely that these result from inadequate exhaust procedure.

[2] BARROW and MEYER, Characteristic Equations of Vacuum and Gas-filled Tungsten Filament Lamps, Research Paper 502, *Bur. Standards J. Research*, vol. 9 (1932).

Let E be the efficiency, F the light output, P the power consumption, and I the current consumption for any voltage V at which the lamps are operated. Also, let E_0, F_0, P_0, and I_0 be symbols representing the same concepts when the lamp is operated at the recommended voltage V_0, which is assumed to be the normal voltage. The characteristics of lamps operated at a voltage V, in terms of the known characteristics when the lamp is operated at normal, rated voltage V_0 are given by the following equations:

$$\log\left(\frac{E}{E_0}\right) = A_1\left(\log\left(\frac{V}{V_0}\right)\right)^2 + B_1\left(\log\left(\frac{V}{V_0}\right)\right) + C \tag{4}$$

$$\log\left(\frac{F}{F_0}\right) = A_2\left(\log\left(\frac{V}{V_0}\right)\right)^2 + B_2\left(\log\left(\frac{V}{V_0}\right)\right) \tag{5}$$

$$\log\left(\frac{P}{P_0}\right) = A_3\left(\log\left(\frac{V}{V_0}\right)\right)^2 + B_3\left(\log\left(\frac{V}{V_0}\right)\right) \tag{6}$$

$$\log\left(\frac{I}{I_0}\right) = A_4\left(\log\left(\frac{V}{V_0}\right)\right)^2 + B_4\left(\log\left(\frac{V}{V_0}\right)\right) \tag{7}$$

The values of the coefficients A_n, B_n, and C_1 differ for various sizes of lamps as may be seen from Table III. These operating characteristics are shown graphically in Fig. 15 for voltage ranges which are likely to be encountered in practice.

TABLE III.—COEFFICIENTS FOR DETERMINING CHARACTERISTICS OF OPERATION OF TUNGSTEN LAMPS

	Size and type of lamp				
	15–60-watt vacuum	40–50-watt	60–150-watt gas-filled lamps	200–500-watt	
Coefficient					Used to compute ratio of
	Normal lumens per watt				
	10.0	12.5	12.5	16.0	
A_1	−0.918	−1.482	−1.726	−1.690	Lumen per watt
B_1	1.932	2.162	2.090	1.841	" " "
C_1	1.000	1.09691	1.09691	1.20412	" " "
A_2	−0.946	−1.425	−1.669	−1.607	Light output, lumens
B_2	3.513	3.685	3.613	3.384	" "
A_3	−0.028	0.057	0.057	0.083	Power consumption
B_3	1.5805	1.523	1.523	1.543	" "
A_4	−0.028	0.057	0.057	0.083	Current
B_4	0.5805	0.523	0.523	0.543	"
B_5	13.5	13.5	13.5	13.1	Life
$(B_2 - B_3)$	1.9325	2.162	2.090	1.841	Most economical voltage
$(B_5 - B_2)$	9.99	9.82	9.89	9.72	" " "
$(B_2 - B_3)/(B_5 - B_2)$	0.1932	0.2202	0.2113	0.1883	" " "
$(B_5 - B_3)$	11.92	11.98	11.98	11.56	" " "
$1/(B_5 - B_3)$	0.0839	0.0835	0.0835	0.0865	" " "

Simpler forms of the above equations which may be used between 77 and 130 per cent of the normal rated voltage V_0 with an error not exceeding approximately 5 per cent have been derived by Moon,[1] who also gives the life of a lamp L operated at

[1] MOON, PARRY, "Scientific Basis of Illumination Engineering," McGraw-Hill.

Table IV.—Characteristics of Lamps for Photographic Purposes

Type	Power rating, watts	Operating voltage	Bulb size	Type of bulb	Base	Light output, lumens	Initial color temp., °K.	Life, hr.
For General Lighting—In or out of Studio								
Photoflash No. 10	....	3–125	A-19	Clear	Med. screw	......	....	One flash
Photoflash No. 20	....	3–125	A-23	Clear	Med. screw	...,..	....	" "
Photoflash No. 75	....	3–125	A-23	Clear	Med. screw	......	....	" "
Photoflood No. 1.	250	105–120	A-21	Inside frosted	Med. screw	8,650	....	2
Photoflood No. 2.	500	105–120	A-25	Inside frosted	Med. screw	17,000	....	6
Photoflood No. 4.	1000	105–120	PS-35	Inside frosted	Mogul screw	33,500	....	10
Movieflood......	2000	105–120	PS-52	Clear	Mogul screw	65,000	....	15
For General Lighting in Studio								
	500	110–120	A-25	....	Med. screw	......	3200	
	500	110–120	PS-40	Clear	Mogul screw	......		
	500	110–120	PS-40	Photo blue, inside frosted	Mogul screw			
	1000	115	G-40	....	Mogul screw	......	3200	
	1000	115	PS-52	....	Mogul screw	......	3200	
	1000	110–120	PS-52	Clear	Mogul screw			
	1000	110–120	PS-52	Photo blue, inside frosted	Mogul screw			
	1500	115	PS-52	....	Mogul screw	......	3200	
	1500	110–120	PS-52	Clear	Mogul screw			
	1500	110–120	PS-52	Photo blue, inside frosted	Mogul screw			
	2000	115	G-48	....	Mogul bipost	......	3200	
	5000	115	G-64	....	Mogul bipost	......	3200	
For Spotlights								
	400	110–120	G-30	Clear	Med. screw or Med. prefocus			
	400	110–120	G-30	Photo blue	Med. screw			
Enlarging Lamps								
	75	105–120	A-21	....	Med. screw			
	150	105–120	A-21	....	Med. screw			
	250	105–120	A-21	Inside frosted, outside coated white	Med. screw	......	....	2
	250	110–120	PS-30	Clear	Med. screw			
	400	110–120	PS-35	Clear or frosted	Med. skirted			
	1000	110–120	PS-52	Clear	Mogul			

Note: The letters indicate the shape of the bulb as follows: A—pear shape with short glass stem. G—globular (spherical). PS—pear-shaped. The numbers indicate the maximum diameter in eighths of an inch. Thus the number 40 indicates a bulb whose diameter is $4\frac{9}{8}$ or 5 in. maximum. As an example, a G-48 bulb would be globular or spherical in shape, and would have a maximum diameter of 6 in.

voltage V in terms of its rated life L_0 when operated at its rated voltage V_0. This equation for the life of the lamp is

$$\frac{L}{L_0} = \left(\frac{V}{V_0}\right)^{-B_5} \tag{8}$$

For the large user of illuminating incandescent lamps, power consumption and the cost of power may be an important economic factor. If the cost of power as well as the cost of the lamp plus its installation charge is known, the most economical operating voltage can be determined. Let c be the cost of one lamp plus its installation charge, in cents, and let b be the cost of power in cents per kilowatt-hour. Then[1] the most economical operating voltage V_e for a lamp of rated power P_0 and rated voltage V_0 is

$$V_e = V_0 \left[\frac{bP_0(B_2 - B_3)}{c(B_5 - B_2)}\right]^{\frac{1}{B_5 - B_1}} \tag{9}$$

where the values of B_n are those given in Table III. In general, the most economical operation will usually be found to be obtained at a voltage slightly above rather than at or below the rated voltage. Of course, if the lamp is operated at some voltage other than its rated voltage, its life, luminous output, and other characteristics will be affected in accordance with the equations given above from the paper by Barrow and Meyer.

Photoflood Lamps.—Incandescent lamps may be operated at considerably higher than their normal voltage for 1000-hr. operation. The main effects of this overvoltage operation are: (1) considerably greater light output is obtained, (2) together with a shift in spectral distribution toward the blue end of the visible spectrum (both factors of which are advantageous from the photographic standpoint), (3) the normal life of the lamp is greatly reduced, and (4) the temperature of the filament and the containing glass bulb is raised, sometimes to such an extent that the use of such lamps may require unusual methods of handling, ventilation, and fire protection. The photoflood lamps commercially available for photographic purposes are of this overvoltage type. If used in such a manner as to have a life of 1000 hr., their rated voltage would be 64 instead of 110 volts. The filaments of such bulbs must be heavier than the filaments for bulbs operating at normal temperatures in order to insure a life of even a few hours.

TABLE V.—CHARACTERISTICS OF PHOTOFLOOD LAMPS

Type of lamp	Operating voltage	Watts	Current, amp.	Lumens output	Lumens per watt	Rated average life, hr.	Max. temp., °K.
1	115–120	250	2.2	8,375	33.5	2	3490
2	115–120	500	4.35	16,750	33.5	6	3490
4	115–120	1000	8.7	33,500	33.5	10	3410

The reason why photoflood lamps are more efficient for photographic purposes than ordinary electric lamps of the same power rating is because they are operated at considerably higher temperature. Operation at temperatures of about 3400 to 3500°K. instead of the usual 2700 to 3000°K. for general service increases the efficiency, measured in lumens per watt. At the same time it produces relatively more blue than red radiation (compared with lamps for general service lighting), both of which effects

[1] *Ibid.*, p. 165–166.

are advantageous from the photographic standpoint.   These advantages are obtained only at a considerable loss of life, however.

Because of the short life of photoflood lamps, it is economical to operate them at their full rated luminous output only during the time exposures are made, and to make focusing and other camera and light adjustments with the lights operated at reduced voltage.   Three methods of accomplishing this result are shown in Fig. 16.   At (*A*) a resistance *R* is placed in series with the lamp, and a switch is connected across *R*. While making preliminary adjustments, the switch is opened, which reduces the current flowing through the lamp, and consequently requires that it operate at lower temperature and at lower light output.   When the switch is closed, the lamp operates at its full luminous output.   It is convenient to have the lamp operate at one-half of

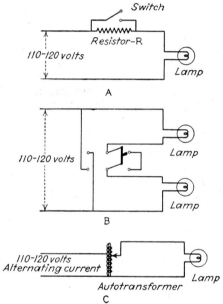

Fig. 16.—Three circuit diagrams illustrating methods which may be used to reduce the voltage across photoflood lamps when not required for making exposure, thereby increasing the life of these lamps.   *A* and *B* may be used with a.-c. or d.-c. circuits, but *C* can only be employed with a.-c. circuits.

its normal operating voltage, and, in order that this may be accomplished, it is necessary that *R* be of the proper resistance and have the proper power rating to carry the current taken by the lamp when operated at reduced output.

Because the resistance of incandescent lamps is not constant but varies with the type of filament and its temperature, it is not possible to use the simple application of Ohm's law for computing the resistance *R*.   The manner in which Ohm's law may be applied to this and similar problems, in which varying resistances are involved, is outside of the scope of this book but may be found in any good text on electrical engineering.   We prefer merely to give the results; Table VI shows the resistance and power rating which will be required for one of each of the three commonly available photoflood lamps.   If *n* lamps are used in parallel instead of only one, the resistance given in the table should be divided by *n* and the power rating should be multiplied by *n*, in order that the resistor may meet the electrical requirements of the circuit.

The power rating given for R is the minimum safe value. Some resistors, especially the vitreous enameled type, operate at high temperature at their rated power. In such cases using a resistor of two or three times the power rating specified (but of the same resistance) will fulfill the electrical-circuit requirements and permit the resistor to operate with smaller temperature rises.

The circuit shown in Fig. 16B is useful where two identical lamps are used. The double-pole double-throw switch puts the lamps in series for operation at low light intensities and places them in parallel when full light output is obtained. The current taken from the line when the lamps are used at full output is the sum of their individual currents at full output, *i.e.*, if two No. 2 lamps are used, the total current drawn from the line will be 8.7 amp. When the lamps are in series, the current taken from the line is about two-thirds of the rated output for any one lamp, or about 3 amp. for the two No. 2 lamps in series. The switch, wiring, and fuses must, therefore, be able to carry at least twice the current of each lamp used, or at least 9 amp. in the case used for purposes of illustration.

A method[1] of controlling the light output of lamps (ordinary Mazda as well as photoflood lamps) over a wide range of light intensities when alternating current is used is shown in Fig. 16c. An autotransformer[2] is used to vary the voltage applied to the lamp. The line is connected to the two fixed terminals of the autotransformer, while the lamp is connected between one fixed terminal and the varying arm. In commercially available autotransformers, the voltage across the lamp may be adjusted smoothly from zero to its full value so that the light output also varies smoothly. In certain models these autotransformers also act as voltage-step-up transformers and supply voltages in excess of the line voltage. This is frequently a valuable feature where ordinary Mazda lamps are used, since it enables greater than normal light output to be obtained, but with a decrease in life. It is not recommended that photoflood lamps be operated above their rated voltage as the increase in light output would be obtained by a considerable decrease in life, which is already quite short.

Several sizes of photoflood lamps are available commercially. Their electrical characteristics are given in Table VI.

The high temperature at which the filaments of these lamps operate causes the glass bulb to become hot enough to scorch paper or cloth which may come in contact

TABLE VI.—ELECTRICAL CHARACTERISTICS OF PHOTOFLOOD LAMPS OPERATING AT NORMAL AND HALF-NORMAL VOLTAGE

Photo-flood, num-ber	Photoflood, normal operation			Photoflood, reduced operation			Resistor	
	Voltage	Current, amp.	Resist-ance, ohms	Voltage	Current, amp.	Resist-ance, ohms	Resist-ance, ohms	Power rating, watts
1	115	2.2	52.3	57	1.46	39.0	40	85
2	115	4.35	26.4	57	2.88	19.8	20	170
4	115	8.7	13.3	57	5.7	10.0	10	330

with it. Consequently, these bulbs should be used in metal rather than paper reflectors. These bulbs consume considerably more power than most lamps used for home

[1] The autotransformer method cannot be used on direct-current circuits. Attempt to do so may result in blown fuses or burned or damaged autotransformer.

[2] Suitable autotransformers are made by: General Radio Co., Cambridge, Mass.; American Transformer Co., Newark, N. J.; United Transformer Co., New York, N. Y.

lighting, and care should be taken to ascertain that the wiring is adequate to carry the current required by the lamps. House circuits are usually wired and fused to carry currents not in excess of 15 amp. Consequently if this current is to be exceeded, it will be necessary that several lamps be operated from separate circuits so that the safe rating of any circuit is not exceeded.

Carbon Arcs.—The carbon arc is still used as a source of luminous radiation for photographic purposes, but the convenience of incandescent lamps and gaseous-discharge lamps, together with their more quiet operation, are responsible for the fact that incandescent lamps are displacing carbon arcs.

The electrical characteristics of the carbon arc are quite different from those of incandescent lamps. The resistance of the arc decreases as the current increases, which in turn further decreases the resistance. In order to prevent a disruptive

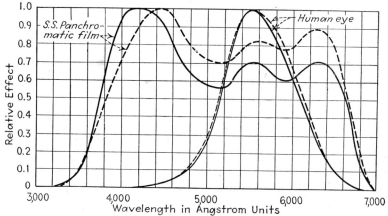

Fig. 17.—Visual and photographic effects (when using panchromatic emulsions) of daylight and carbon-arc illumination. The solid curves are for the arc.

discharge from taking place, a ballast resistance or other current-limiting device must be used in series with the arc to maintain stability of operation. The voltage across the arc is about 40 to 80 volts, depending upon the spacing between the electrodes, the voltage being proportional to the spacing. Increasing the current through the arc increases the size of the arc crater but does not materially affect the luminous output.

The spectrum produced by the arc is the continuous spectrum produced by the incandescent carbons, upon which are superimposed line and band spectra from the vapors of the arc. In the ordinary arc with untreated carbons most of the light is supplied by the positive crater. This crater operates at a color temperature of about 3700°K. and produces a brightness of about 13,000 candles per sq. cm. The arc produces a light which is more deficient in the long visible wavelengths and produces greater radiation in the shorter visible wavelengths than incandescent lamps.

The high-intensity carbon arc increases its efficiency over the ordinary carbon arc by diminishing the diameter of the electrodes with a given current (which is the usual method) or by increasing the current for a given diameter of carbon electrodes. The high-intensity carbon arc produces a gain in efficiency and a light which is more nearly white and steadier than that of the ordinary enclosed carbon arc. In one high-intensity carbon arc consuming 150 amp., the positive carbon is 16 mm. in diameter.

The spectrum produced by carbon arcs is intermediate between that of mean noon sunlight and that of incandescent electric lamps operated at temperatures in the region of 2700 to 3000°K. In spectral distribution, the carbon arc resembles the photoflood lamp. Since the light is a closer approach to white than that produced by incandescent lamps, no filters are required unless they are also required with a source of sunlight. The photographic effects of carbon arcs are similar to those of sunlight as shown in Fig. 17.

In order to modify their spectral characteristics, the carbons are frequently drilled lengthwise and are subsequently filled with a core of inorganic salts. Thus the white-flame arc used for photographic purposes has a core of rare-earth fluorides. Because this core material modifies the spectral radiation of the arc and increases the intensity of the line and band spectra as compared with the continuous spectra due to incandescence, it is difficult to make any definite statements as to the photographic effectiveness of various types of carbon arcs. Spectra produced by specially processed carbon electrodes may usually be obtained from the manufacturer.[1]

Enclosed Metallic Arc.—Enclosed arc lamps with metallic electrodes and known as Pointolite or Tungsarc are commercially available and are suitable for photographic

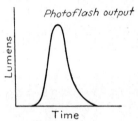

Fig. 18.—Light output of typical photoflash lamp as a function of time. The total duration of the flash is of the order of about $\frac{1}{20}$ sec.

purposes. The lamp consists of tungsten electrodes in an evacuated bulb containing a pool of metallic mercury vapor. A filament bridges the tungsten electrodes, and, when the voltage of about 40 volts is applied to the tube, the filament becomes incandescent, thereby vaporizing the mercury so that within a few seconds an arc forms between the two tungsten electrodes and the current rises to about 30 amp. The characteristic of the transformer supplying the lamp must be such that as the arc current is established the voltage across the lamp will fall to about 10 volts. This voltage is sufficiently low as to practically extinguish the filament. The spectrum produced is continuous and is largely that of the incandescence of the tungsten electrodes, but a discontinuous spectrum of mercury is also present.

Transient Light Sources.—Under the heading of transient light sources are included those devices which are intended to provide an intense flash of light for short duration for making photographic snapshots. Usually these transient light sources can be used only once, but experimental work is in progress to provide a "flash-flood" lamp which may be flashed as often as desired. The most common of these transient light sources for general photography are photoflash lamps and flashlight powders, although for special purposes, especially scientific photography, luminous gaseous-discharge lamps and spark discharges are also of interest.

Photoflash Lamps.—A very convenient and effective source of luminous intensity for making photographs with an exposure of about $\frac{1}{25}$ sec. is the photoflash lamp, which is available in several sizes. These lamps consist of a glass bulb containing a filament, metallic aluminum, and oxygen. The metallic aluminum may be in the form of thin (0.00004 cm.) foil or fine ribbons or wires, crumpled inside the glass envelope. The lamps have a standard Edison screw base, and operate at a voltage from 3 to 115 volts. Thus the lamps may be used in the ordinary house lighting circuit or may be flashed by means of several dry cells. When the current is turned on, the filament becomes incandescent and ignites the aluminum in the oxygen, producing a quick, brilliant flash lasting from about 0.03 to 0.06 sec. The characteristics of the luminous output as a function of time are shown in Fig. 18. The temperature of the flash is approximately 3500°K., although at the peak this temperature may be

[1] The spectral characteristics of various carbon arcs have been given in the National Bureau of Standards Scientific Paper 539.

exceeded. Table VII shows the relative photographic effects, in various portions of the visible spectrum, of daylight and photoflash illumination.

TABLE VII.—RELATIVE PHOTOGRAPHIC EFFECTS FOR VARIOUS EMULSIONS AND LIGHT SOURCES

| Plate | Relative photographic effect[1] | | | | | | | |
| | Photoflash lamp | | | | Daylight | | | |
	Red	Yellow	Green	Blue	Red	Yellow	Green	Blue
Blue-sensitive plate....................	30	15	30	160	30	10	25	180
Isochromatic plate.....................	30	30	30	160	30	20	30	180
Orthochromatic plate..................	30	20	30	180	30	15	30	180
Panchromatic plate I..................	180	80	30	100	90	40	30	180
Panchromatic plate II.................	70	60	50	120	60	40	40	140
Panchromatic plate III................	90	50	40	120	60	30	30	160

[1] From *Philips Tech. Rev.*, vol. 1, no. 10, (1936).

The light output of photoflash lamps is given in Table VIII. One of these lamps produces a maximum intensity of about 360,000 candles, which is about twice that of a 50-kw. tungsten lamp whose luminous intensity is about 166,000 candles, measured perpendicular to the plane of the filament. The spectrum is largely continuous although some superimposed lines of aluminum are present.

The photoflash lamp is quiet in operation and does not produce any smoke or objectionable odors, vapors, or gases since the combustion is confined entirely to the interior of the glass bulb. Of course, when once used, the aluminum is changed to aluminum oxides and the filament is usually burned out, so that the lamp can no longer be used.

It is sometimes found that photoflash bulbs operated at low voltage (3 volts is common) fail to flash. This is probably due to lack of contact between the filament and the crumpled aluminum. Such bulbs may be used on high-voltage circuits, however, and will then perform satisfactorily. It has been found that when several photoflash bulbs are used in the same reflector, igniting one lamp will serve to set off the other lamps. For this reason, it has sometimes been suggested that only one lamp in a group need be connected to the source of current. Such a procedure may be entirely satisfactory for portraiture or similar types of photography where the subject is relatively motionless and the shutter is opened during the entire duration of the flash. However, the practice of flashing several bulbs by contact is not to be recommended in those cases where the shutter is synchronized with the photoflash lamps, as the bulbs do not all flash at the same time. Consequently, the shutter may be closing before the "contact flashed" lamps actually ignite.

Bulbs have been known to explode while being flashed. The resulting shattering of glass can be dangerous. To safeguard against exploding lamps, photoflash lamps have recently been manufactured with a disk of colored salt painted on the bulb or the stem. These disks have one color in an absolutely dry atmosphere of oxygen but change their color in the presence of the moisture of the atmosphere. If any cracks or air leaks occur in the bulb, this salt changes color and indicates that the lamp is defective and may explode. Such lamps should not be used.

Photoflash lamps cannot, of course, be tested on line voltage or on batteries which pass sufficient current to heat the filament to incandescence.   By passing very small current through the lamp, insufficient to produce incandescence, a sensitive micro-ammeter or milliammeter in series with the filament will show a deflection if the filament circuit is continuous and the bulb is suitable for use.   Another method which has been used is to use a battery circuit with a high resistance relay in series with the lamp filament.   The relay contacts can be made to operate a lamp in another circuit if the filament of the photoflash lamp is intact.

When using photoflash lamps, the camera shutter may be opened temporarily while the lamps are flashed, after which the shutter is closed.   A much more convenient arrangement, and one which may be used where the general level of illumina-

TABLE VIII.—CHARACTERISTICS OF GENERAL ELECTRIC PHOTOFLASH LAMPS[1]

Lamp, number	Total light output, lumen-sec.	Max. output, million lumens	Time, sec., from closing circuit to		
			Start of flash	Peak of flash	End of flash
10	24,600	2.8	0.012	0.020	0.080
20 blue	6,200	1.0	0.013	0.025	0.080
20	52,900	6.1	0.013	0.025	0.080
75	171,000	8.8	0.020	0.041	0.160

[1] FORSYTHE, W. F. and M. A. EASLEY, Characteristics of General Electric Photoflash Lamps, *J. Optical Soc. Am.*, **21**, 685 (1934).

tion might fog the photographic plate, is to synchronize the action of the shutter with the switch or flashing mechanism of the photoflash lamp.   Several such synchronizing devices are available commercially.   In using such synchronizing devices, it is important that the peak of illumination of the photoflash lamp occur when the shutter is completely open.   Because photoflash lamps require about 0.020 to 0.040 sec. to reach their peak of illumination after current is turned on, a shutter speed of about $\frac{1}{25}$ sec. is usually used.   The synchronizer is usually designed so that the shutter action may be adjusted to the characteristics of the photoflash lamps for optimum performance.   It should be noted that the time of travel of focal-plane shutters across the film area is slow compared with the duration of the flash.   For this reason photoflash lamps operate most satisfactorily with between-the-lens shutters.

Flashlight Powders.—Rapid oxidization of metals such as magnesium and aluminum was formerly used to provide an intense source of light of short duration, but these flashlight powders have been almost entirely replaced by photoflash lamps.   Flashlight powders usually consist of a mixture of magnesium powder and an oxidizing material like potassium chlorate.   Since these mixtures oxidize rapidly with almost explosive violence, they must be handled with care.   They may be ignited by means of an open flame, a fuse, or an electrically heated wire.

Special Light Sources.—Sometimes special or unusual light sources are required for some particular purpose.   These may frequently be of considerable importance for certain applications of photography but are not of sufficient general interest to warrant extensive description.   For further details on such light sources, reference should be made to the literature.[1]

[1] FORSYTHE, W. E. editor, "Measurement of Radiant Energy," McGraw (1937), Chap. II, gives a good summary of the various light sources which are useful for scientific purposes, as well as a good bibliographical reference to the technical literature.

Reflectors.—The light produced from light sources may frequently be used much more effectively if a reflector is used with it. The reflector does not produce any more light than is generated by the light source, but directs it to the desired position where it may be used more advantageously. Reflectors may be used at the light source, in which case they are most efficient, or may be used near the subject being photographed, where their use gives flexible control over modeling and light contrast. Where sharp shadows are desired or are at least not objectionable, smooth, polished reflectors of the specular type may be used, but where "soft" diffused lighting is desired, etched, hammered, or diffuse reflectors are more suitable. The degree of

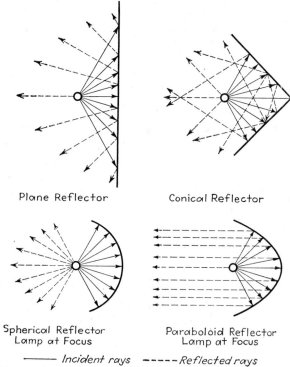

Plane Reflector   Conical Reflector

Spherical Reflector   Paraboloid Reflector
Lamp at Focus   Lamp at Focus

——— *Incident rays* ----- *Reflected rays*

Fig. 19.—Incident and reflected rays for various shapes of specular reflectors, showing approximately how the reflected beams are spread.

diffusion may be increased by placing diffusion screens of tissue paper, linen tracing paper, ground glass, opal glass, or similar material in the path of the light rays.

The effectiveness of a reflector used in conjunction with a light source depends upon: (1) the shape of the reflector, (2) the material out of which the reflector is made, and (3) the surface treatment of the reflector. Figure 19 shows a diagrammatic representation of a light source used with polished specular reflectors of certain common forms, together with the net light beams produced. From this diagram it is evident that the flat plane reflector is most suitable for producing a well-diffused source, whereas the parabolic reflector produces a sharply defined beam. Other forms of reflectors shown produce intermediate effects between these two extremes.

The material out of which the reflector is made as well as the polish of the surface determine the amount of incident light which is reflected from its surface. Table IX gives the reflection factors as a function of wavelength for several polished materials from which reflectors are constructed. The figures in this table represent the fraction of incident light which is reflected with unity as the ideal limiting figure. It is desirable that the reflection factors for a given material be as near unity as possible and that they do not vary with wavelength. The nearer the reflection factor approaches unity, the more efficient is the reflector. Constancy of reflection factor throughout a wide range of wavelengths is desirable in order that selective reflection may be avoided and so that reflected beam has the same spectral distribution ("color") as the light incident upon its surface.

Table X gives the reflection characteristics of several materials suitable for use as diffuse reflectors. Included in this table for purposes of comparison are the characteristics of black velvet (frequently used as an excellent light-absorbing medium) and black carbon in oil.

The effectiveness of commercially available reflectors for photographic purposes depends greatly upon their shape and the materials out of which they are constructed. As a rough approximation, however, it may be said that with conical reflectors made of white paper, the exposure need be only one-half of that required when no reflector is

TABLE IX.—REFLECTION FACTORS FOR COMMON REFLECTING MATERIALS

Wavelength, mμ	Metals							Mirrors	
	Aluminum	Chromium	Nickel	Monel metal	Silver	Steel	Zinc	Silver	Mercury
200	0.35	0.36	0.45	....	0.27	....	0.22		
250	0.53	0.32	0.40	....	0.33	0.38	0.39		
300	0.65	0.38	0.46	....	0.20	0.37	0.48		
350	0.71	0.41	0.49	....	0.66	0.45	0.51		
400	0.71	....	0.53	....	0.84	0.49			
450	....	....	0.59	0.57	0.88	0.54	0.54	0.86	0.73
500	....	0.55	0.61	0.58	0.90	0.55	0.55	0.87	0.71
550	....	....	0.63	0.59	0.91	0.55	0.56	0.88	0.71
600	....	....	0.65	0.60	0.92	0.55	0.58	0.88	0.70
650	....	....	0.66	0.62	0.93	0.56	0.60	0.89	0.71
700	....	0.56	0.69	0.64	0.94	0.58	0.61	0.90	0.73
800	....	....	0.70	0.67	0.95	0.58	0.62		
1,000	0.73	0.57	0.74	0.72	0.96	0.63	0.49		

TABLE X.—REFLECTION COEFFICIENTS

Substance	Wavelength, mμ			
	400	500	600	700
Magnesium carbonate............................	0.93	0.98	0.98	0.98
Magnesium oxide................................	0.97	0.98	0.98	0.98
Paper, white bond..............................	....	....	0.75	
Paper, white blotting..........................	0.64	0.72	0.79	0.70
Paper, newsprint stock.........................	0.38	0.61	0.63	0.78
White porcelain enamel.........................	0.77	0.73	0.72	0.70
Black carbon in oil............................	0.003	0.003	0.003	0.003
Black velvet...................................	....	....	0.0175	

used.   When polished metal reflectors are used, the exposure may be reduced to about one-fourth of that required when the same light source is used without a reflector.

Bibliography

Periodicals:

LANGMUIR, I.: Tungsten Lamps at High Efficiency, *Trans. Am. Inst. Elec. Engrs.*, **32**, 1913 (1913).

BATES, F.: A New Cadmium Vapor Arc Lamp, *Bur. Standards Scientific Paper* 371, 1920.

NUTTING, P. G.: The Design of Large Incandescent Lamps, *J. Optical Soc. Am.*, **7**, 399 (1923).

FORSYTHE W. E., and A. G. WORTHING: Properties of Tungsten, *Astrophys. J.*, **61**, 146 (1925).

JONES, H. A., and I. LANGMUIR: The Characteristics of Tungsten Filaments as Function of Temperature, *Gen. Elec. Rev.*, **30**, 310 (1927).

FOULKE, T. E.: Transmission of Visible Radiation through the Atmosphere, *Trans. Illum. Eng. Soc.* (*N. Y.*), **24**, 384 (1929).

HARRISON, G. R.: Instruments and Methods for Measuring Spectral Light Intensities by Photography, *J. Optical Soc. Am.*, **19**, 267 (1929).

MILLAR, P. S.: Safeguarding the Quality of Incandescent Lamps, *Trans. Illum. Eng. Soc.* (*N. Y.*), **26**, 948 (1931).

BARROW, and MEYER: Characteristic Equations of Vacuum and Gas-filled Tungsten Filament Lamps, *Bur. Standards J. Research*, **9**, 721 (1932).

WHITTAKER, J. D.: Silver Processed Incandescent Lamps, *Trans. Illum. Eng. Soc.* (*N. Y.*), **28**, 418 (1933).

FORSYTHE, W. E.: Tungsten Lamp Characteristics as Function of Applied Voltage, *Gen. Elec. Rev.*, **37**, 191 (1934).

HARRISON, G. R.: Current Advances in Photographic Photometry, *J. Optical Soc. Am.*, **24**, 59, (1934).

FORSYTHE, W. E., and M. A. EASLEY: Time-intensity Relation and Spectral Distribution of Radiation of the Photoflash Lamps, *J. Optical Soc. Am.*, **24**, 195 (1934).

SPANNER, H. J.: The High Pressure Mercury-cadmium Vapor Lamp, *Trans. Illum. Eng. Soc.* (*N. Y.*), **30**, 178 (1935).

HARRISON, W.: Applications of the New Gaseous Conduction Lamps, *Trans. Illum. Eng. Soc.* (*N. Y.*), **30**, 190 (1935).

BARNES, B. T., Spectral Distribution of Radiation from Three Reflector Units, *J. Optical Soc. Am.*, **25**, 167 (1935).

DAVIES, L. J.: Practical Electric Discharge Lamps, *Trans. Illum. Eng. Soc.*, (*London*), **1**, 49 (1936).

TEELE, R. T.: Photometry and Brightness Measurements, *J. Brit. Inst. Cinematography*, **4**, 9 (1936).

FORSYTHE, W. E., and M. A. EASLEY: Photographic Effectiveness of the Radiation from a Number of Photographic Sources, *J. Optical Soc. Am.*, **24**, 310 (1936).

PFUND, A. H.: Electric Welsbach Lamp, *J. Optical Soc. Am.*, **26**, 439 (1936).

HUFF, M. O.: Gaseous Discharge Tubes for Enlarging and Printing, *Camera* (*Phila.*), **53**, 361 (1936).

MACRAE, F. G. H.: Measuring Intensities of Colored Light, *Ideal Kinemat.*, **5** (no. 54), 13 (1937).

Sources of Artificial Daylight, *Instruments*, **10**, 150 (1937).

GEOGHAN, C.: Lighting for Color Photography, *Proc. Engravers' Monthly*, **44**, 279 (1937).

VAN LIEMPT, J. A. M., and J. R. DE VRIEND: Adjustment of Synchronization for the "Photoflux" Photoflash Bulb, *Philips Tech. Rev.*, **2**, 334 (1937).

STULL, W.: How to Improve Lighting of Homes for Cine Films, *Am. Cinematography*, **18**, 474 (1937).

BOYLE, S.: How Long Is a Flash? *Miniature Camera Mag.*, **1**, 744 (1937).

MERRILL, G. S.: Economics of Light Production with Incandescent Electric Lamps with Particular Reference to Their Operating Voltage, *Trans. Illum. Eng. Soc.* (*N. Y.*), **32**, 1077 (1937).

JAMES, D. A.: Testing Photoflash Bulbs, *Amateur Phot.*, **83**, 293 (1938).

SMETHURST, P. C.: Linking Contrast with Camera Exposure in Artificial Light, *Amateur Cine World*, **3**, 439 (1937); *Amateur Cine World*, **4**, 518 (1938).

DUSHMAN, S.: Recent Developments in Gaseous Discharge Lamps, *J. Soc. Motion Picture Engrs.*, **30**, 58 (1938).

MILI, GJON: Light Control in Photography, *J. Soc. Motion Picture Engrs.*, **30**, 388 (1938).

HARRIS, N. L.: Electrical Discharge Lamps and Their Application to Photography, *Phot. J.*, 401 (1938).

NOEL, E. B., and R. E. FARNHAM: Water Cooled Mercury Quartz Arc, *J. Soc. Motion Picture Engrs.*, **30**, 221 (1938).

Books:

LIBESSART, P.: Photographic Pyrometry of Short Light Flashes, pp. 762–767, IXth Congr. intern. de Phot., Paris (1935).

HARDY, A. C., and F. H. PERRIN: "Principles of Optics," McGraw.

LUCKIESH, M.: "Artificial Sunlight," Van Nostrand.

CHAPTER X

LIGHT FILTERS

By Beverly Dudley

THEORY OF FILTERS

As used in photography, filters are employed to alter the manner in which radiant energy (usually visible light) affects photosensitive materials. This alteration may be desired for artistic effects, to reduce the amount of necessary retouching, to increase contrast, or for registering photographically certain radiations at the exclusion of other radiations. The effects obtained by the use of filters depend, not only on the characteristics of the filter, but also on those of the photosensitive material and the source of energy affecting the photographic film.

Effects of Radiation.—Most forms of radiant energy occur as electromagnetic waves in which the vibrations are transverse or perpendicular to the direction of propagation of the wave. Figure 1 is intended to represent electromagnetic waves, such as those of light. The direction of propagation is indicated by the horizontal

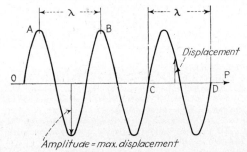

Fig. 1.—Diagram illustrating the properties of light waves.

arrow, the displacement of a particle due to wave motion is indicated by the vertical arrow, the displacement being zero when the wave crosses the zero axis OP. The amplitude of the wave is the maximum displacement from the reference axis OP. A complete wave is one vibration, such as AB or CD, and is measured from any point to the next successive corresponding point moving in the same direction and having the same displacement from the reference or zero axis OP. The distance between successive corresponding points in one complete vibration, such as AB or CD, is one wavelength and is usually measured in meters or submultiple portions of the meter. It is often symbolically designated as λ.

Radiant energy produces different chemical, physical, physiological, psychological, and photographic effects depending upon two wave characteristics. One of these characteristics is the amplitude or intensity of the radiated electromagnetic waves; in general the degree or extent of an effect produced is directly proportional to this amplitude or intensity. The other characteristic responsible for the different types of effects produced is the wavelength or frequency of the radiant energy. Wavelength is the length of one complete wave, measured from the corresponding portions of two successive waves; frequency is the number of complete waves passing a given point in a given time, the second being usually taken as the standard time interval. If c is the velocity at which electromagnetic waves travel, the relation between the wavelength λ and the frequency f is given by

$$c = f\lambda \tag{1}$$

from which

$$f = \frac{c}{\lambda} \tag{2}$$

and

$$\lambda = \frac{c}{f} \tag{3}$$

The velocity of light in vacuum has been measured by Michelson to be 2.99796×10^{10} cm. per sec. or 186,284 miles per sec. with a probable error of about 1 part in 95,000. For ordinary precision c can be taken to be 3×10^{10} cm. per sec.

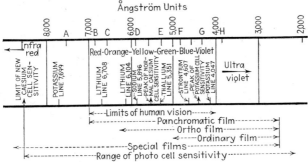

Fig. 2.—Wavelength chart, illustrating the range of sensitivity of the human eye, and various types of film emulsions.

Figure 2 shows the values of wavelength and frequency for various types of radiant energy. For visual and photographic effects the most important range of radiations are those lying between 400 and 700 mμ* in wavelength, since this range forms the visible spectrum. Wavelengths of from 200 to as much as 1200 mμ can be recorded on photographic plates commercially available, although the range of useful sensitivity of most photographic materials is from about 380 to 540 mμ for ordinary noncolorsensitive or orthonon materials, 380 to 600 mμ for orthochromatic materials, and 380 to 700 mμ for panchromatic materials. Radiations between 275 and 315 mμ produce sunburn; the X-ray region extends from 30 to 0.01 mμ, and radio waves may have a wavelength of from less than 1 cm. to 25,000 m.

Since any device producing radiant energy nearly always produces radiations of several wavelengths or a band of wavelengths rather than at a single isolated wave-

* The wavelength of electromagnetic radiations is usually measured in meters (m) or submultiples of the meter. For radio work the meter is the standard wavelength unit although with recent advances in very short waves the centimeter (0.01 m.) is sometimes employed. For shorter waves, still smaller units are employed.

The micron, which is one-millionth part of a meter (10^{-6} m.), is sometimes used for the unit of wavelength, although this is still too large a unit to give convenient numerical figures when dealing with wavelengths of visible light. For visible light, a common wavelength unit is the millimicron, which is one-thousandth of a micron, or one one-thousandth-millionth part of a meter (10^{-9} m.). Another unit often used in the visible spectrum is the angstrom unit (10^{-10} m.) which is equal to 0.1 mμ.

The symbol for a micron is μ; for a millimicron, mμ; for a centimeter, cm; for a meter, m; and for an angstrom unit Å. Therefore, $1\mu = 1000$ m$\mu = 10,000$ Å. $= 10^{-4}$ cm. $= 10^{-6}$ m.

length or frequency, energy sources frequently produce spurious or undesired frequencies as well as those which are desired. For example, sunlight is responsible for the highly desirable phenomenon of daylight, but because at the earth's surface sunlight also contains radiations as short as 290 mμ, it produces undesirable sunburn.

A group of waves constitutes a spectrum. If waves of all possible wavelengths between two limits are present the spectrum between these limits is said to be continuous; if some of the possible waves between the wavelength limits of the spectrum are absent, the spectrum is said to be discontinuous or may be referred to as a line or

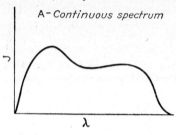

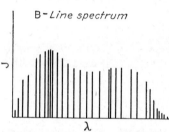

FIG. 3.—Continuous (A) and line (B) spectrums for two hypothetical light sources giving very nearly the same visual and photographic effects. The intensity, J, is plotted against wavelength, λ, in arbitrary units.

band spectrum. The energy-wavelength characteristics of a spectrum may be represented graphically by means of a spectroradiometric diagram in which the wavelength (or frequency) of the waves is represented by the abscissas and the energy is represented by the ordinates in rectangular coordinates. The spectroradiometric diagram for a continuous spectrum is a continuous curve (Fig. 3A) whereas that for a discontinuous or line spectrum is a series of lines, each of which represents the energy at the corresponding wavelength (Fig. 3B). The energy-wavelength (or spectroradiometric) characteristic of radiated energy is of primary importance in studying the effect of light and other radiations upon photographically sensitive materials and the characteristics of filters.

The alteration of the characteristics of the light emitted by a light source before it impinges upon a photographically sensitive material can be accomplished by means of reflecting or transmitting filters. A reflecting filter is one which reflects the radiant energy falling upon it, the change in the spectroradiometric characteristics of the light occurring during reflection and being due to selective reflection of this type of filter.

A transmitting filter is one in which the spectral-energy distribution of the light is altered by passing light through the filter, which must obviously be transparent although it may be (and usually is) colored.

In this connection it may be useful to distinguish color mediums having different properties. For convenience, these mediums may be grouped into pigments, dyes, and colored glass. Although differing considerably in their physical form, the two latter mediums are optically similar and consequently may be considered together. The pigments are opaque to light and materials containing pigments can only act as filters through the use of reflected light. Dyes and colored glasses, on the other hand, are partially or largely transparent for a substantial part of the visible spectrum and may therefore be used as filters by transmitting light through them. Thus the pigments act because of selective reflection, whereas dyes and colored glasses make use of their property of selective transmission; both have selective absorption.

All filters, whether operating by reflected or transmitted light, are effective because of selective absorption, i.e., the manner in which energy of some wavelengths is more greatly absorbed than energy of other wavelengths, the portion of the energy not absorbed being reflected by, or transmitted through, the filter. Thus selective absorption might be said to be the fundamental characteristic of all filters. However, since practically all filters are transmitting filters and operate by altering the spectral energy of the light passing through them, we may, for all practical purposes, consider selective transmission to be as fundamentally important as selective absorption. This is especially true when we consider that for transmitting filters, selective transmission and selective absorption are merely two different aspects of the same physical operation of energy absorption.

Properties of Filters.—We shall be concerned almost exclusively with filters operating by virtue of their property of selective transmission, and, unless otherwise stated, the term filter will refer to a transmitting, rather than a reflecting, type of material.

The inherent characteristic of such light filters is that, throughout the spectral region for which they are effective, the absorption (or transmission) of the radiant energy through them in this spectral region varies with the wavelength (or the frequency) in some nonuniform manner. For some wavelengths most of the radiation passes through the filter with little absorption or surface reflections; for other wavelengths most of the radiation (or light) is absorbed in the filter itself with comparatively little reflection or transmission. Some reflection always takes place at the polished surfaces of a light filter; likewise some absorption is always present for all wavelengths. For these reasons, no light filter can be theoretically perfect. However, in well-constructed filters the losses due to reflection and absorption (except in the region where absorption is desired) can be made sufficiently small (about 10 per cent in the best cases) as to be of little practical importance. This is especially true at the red end of the visible spectrum; blue filters are generally much less efficient.

The selective transmission characteristics of filters indicate that there are some wavelengths within the spectral region for which the filter is effective, or for which the absorption or attenuation of the energy is small. For these wavelengths, the emergent energy will be a large portion of the incident energy. For other ranges of wavelength, the transmission of the filter will be small (the absorption or attenuation will be high), and the emergent radiation will be greatly diminished in its intensity or amplitude from that incident upon the filter. For this range of wavelengths, the filter absorbs energy. The transition from the transmission range to the absorption range is more or less gradual.

In speaking of the selective transmission of filters, it is, perhaps, worth while to call attention to a common misconception, *i.e.*, the assumption that a colored material transmits only a narrow range of wavelengths in the immediate vicinity of the dominant color. This is seldom true.

The wavelength at which the filter fails to transmit the incident radiation is known as the cutoff wavelength. Since the cutoff wavelength is determined from the measurements of the incident and the emergent radiation intensities, the cutoff wavelength will depend upon the sensitivity with which the incident and emergent energy is determined. For this reason the cutoff wavelength is sometimes difficult to determine precisely, especially if the cutoff characteristic (the transmission in the region near the cutoff wavelength) is not sharp or abrupt.

The radiant energy which is incident upon but not transmitted by the filter is reflected to a comparatively small extent, and absorbed to a much larger extent, the absorbed energy reappearing as heat. The energy absorbed by the filter, as well as that reflected, cannot be utilized effectively for photographic purposes and is consequently wasted. The use of a filter is therefore inherently wasteful of the light available for photographic purposes. A corollary of this statement is that, from the physical standpoint, filters are inherently inefficient devices, although they may be highly effective in carrying out the intended alteration of the spectral distribution of light striking the photosensitive material. Fortunately, filter efficiency, per se, is seldom of importance and can usually be neglected for practical purposes if longer exposure time for a given aperture is not objectionable.

For certain applications in which the filter is used in connection with and in close proximity to the light source, as in some forms of colored stage lighting, the filter may be required to dissipate a considerable amount of heat. The intensity of the radiant energy is sometimes very high in such applications, and if any considerable portion of the spectral region must be blocked by the filter, thereby appearing as heat, the physical and optical characteristics of the filter may easily change with aging. The transmission characteristics may be altered, the filter may become brittle and break easily if a gelatin filter is used, or the filter may even be scorched. Fortunately, where filters are used for the more common photographic purposes, these extreme considerations of power dissipation are seldom important.

Since the essential property of a light filter is its transmission as a function of wavelength, it is apparent that the effectiveness of the filter can be evaluated only by a spectral analysis of the filter-transmission characteristic. Such spectroradiometric characteristics are determined experimentally by measurement and are expressed, usually, by means of a table or graph. Figure 4 shows the energy incident upon, and that emergent from, a certain filter for the light produced by an incandescent lamp. The ratio of the energy curves of the incident to the emergent radiation results in the curve $T\lambda$, or the transmission characteristic of the filter.

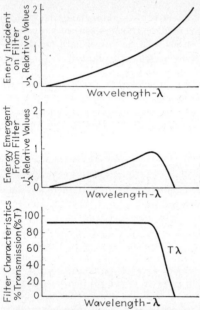

Fig. 4.—Effect of filter on light source. The top curve represents the spectral characteristic of a light source such as that of an incandescent lamp, while the bottom curve represents the transmission of hypothetical filter. The manner in which the filter alters the characteristics of the incandescent light is shown in the middle curve.

Effect of Thickness of Filter.—Although for photographic purposes light filters are nearly always made from gelatin or glass, the thickness of which is not determined, or susceptible to change, by the user, it can be shown that the filter-transmission characteristics depend considerably upon the thickness of the filter. For certain scientific branches of photography, *e.g.*, metallography, liquid filters are often employed in which the light passes through a glass tank or cell containing a colored or selective absorbing liquid which alters the spectral characteristics of the light. When such filters are used, the user has a fairly wide latitude in which to select the thickness of the filter medium and can, therefore, alter the characteristics of the filter by controlling the thickness of the filter cell or tank. In such cases it is necessary to know the manner in which the filter characteristics change with the thickness of the filter medium.

According to Beer's law, the ratio of the radiant energy transmitted through the filter to the incident radiant energy for radiation transmitted through a homogeneous medium is an exponential function of the thickness of the filter. This means simply that for equal increments of increase in the thickness of the filter, the transmission is cut down by the same ratio or the same percentage rather than by the same definite amount.

Another term for the transmission of an object is its transparency; other terms must now also be introduced. The opacity O_λ is the reciprocal of the transparency or transmission T_λ, or

$$O_\lambda = \frac{1}{T_\lambda} \tag{4}$$

The optical density is defined to be the common logarithm of the opacity, or from the relation between opacity and transparency, density is the common logarithm of the reciprocal of the transparency. Thus

$$D_\lambda = \log_{10} O_\lambda = \log_{10} \frac{1}{T_\lambda} = -\log_{10} T_\lambda \tag{5}$$

The apparent cutoff and the transparency or transmission curves change with variations in thickness of the filter. In specifying the transmission characteristics for filters, it is therefore evident that the thickness of the selective absorbing medium must be given before the complete filter characteristics are specified.

It should be noticed that no attention has been paid to the reflection losses at the surface of the filter. Such reflection losses depend upon the quality of polish of the filter surfaces, the angle of incidence of the light, and the index of refraction of the filter medium. They are usually small enough to be neglected without appreciable error.

Use of Several Filters.—Sometimes a filter transmission characteristic is desired which cannot be accurately or adequately fulfilled by any known dyed gelatin, colored glasses, or liquids. In such cases it is sometimes possible to obtain a close approach to the desired transmission characteristic by using two or more filters simultaneously, one in back of the other so that the light must pass through all filters in succession. The transmission of this combination of filters, τ_λ, is the product of the transmission characteristics of the separate individual filters T'_λ, T''_λ, etc. If we have three filters in use at the same time, the transmission characteristic of this combination in terms of the separate filter transmission characteristics will be,

$$\tau_\lambda = T'_\lambda T''_\lambda T'''_\lambda \tag{6}$$

The transmission characteristics of the individual filters are usually expressed graphically or by means of a table from which a transmission curve may be constructed. If the curves for the three filters are available, the above equation gives the over-all transmission for the three filters, used one behind the other simultaneously. It is evident that the over-all transmission characteristic is obtained by multiplying the transmission of the individual filters, wavelength by wavelength. Since the transmission of any filter can never be greater than unity (and can be unity only in the case of an absolutely perfect filter having zero losses), it follows that the use of several filters behind one another will give an over-all or net transmission for the filter system which will be successively smaller the greater the number of filters employed. For this reason the light available for photographic work is effectively diminished and a longer exposure required; so it is desirable not to use more filters than are necessary to produce the desired spectral transmission characteristic. In practice this number seldom if ever exceeds two. Other objections to the use of more filters than are absolutely essential result from multiple reflections from the surfaces of the filter and dimunition of optical quality as the number of filters is increased. Exception to this statement may be made for optically prepared filters intended for uses of this type, but the average photographer seldom encounters such cases.

Filter Factor.—The filter factor is not an inherent property of the filter alone which can be specified once and for all. Instead, the filter factor depends upon its spectral-transmission characteristics, the spectral characteristics of the source of radiant energy with which the filter is to be used, and also upon the spectral sensitiveness of the film upon which the modified light acts. Of these factors the only one which is inherently a property of the filter itself is spectral transmission of the filter. As the two other factors vary, the filter factor will change.

Graphical Construction Showing Action of Filters.—Before interpreting the theory of filters, it will be well to consider some fundamental principles relating to radiation, filter transmission, and the spectral sensitivity of the photosensitive material.

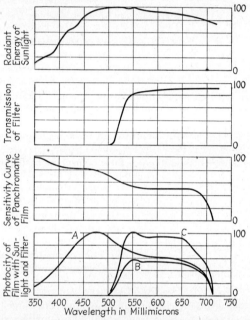

Fig. 5.—Spectral curves of sunlight (top), a yellow filter (second) and panchromatic material (third). The effect of exposing the panchromatic film to light of daylight quality is shown in curve *A* (bottom graph), whereas if a yellow filter is used, the effect is represented by curve *B*. The area under curve *A*, compared with the area under *B* gives an indication of the filter factor required. If the exposure with the filter is increased by the filter factor, curve *C* results.

In the spectral-distribution curves of Fig. 5, the top curve represents the spectral distribution of the light source (mean noon sunlight, in this case), the second curve represents the transmission characteristics of the filter (Wratten No. 15 or G filter), and the third curve represents the sensitivity of a typical panchromatic film. The bottom set of curves represents the net relative sensitivity of the panchromatic film when used with the sunlight source (curve *A*), as well as the net effect of the photographic film when used with the same sunlight source but with the G filter which cuts out all light below a wavelength of 500 mμ (curve *B*). The filter factor *F* is given by the ratio of the area below the curve *B* to the area below the curve *A*, whereas the exposure factor for the G filter (for mean noon sunlight and the panchromatic material indicated) is given by the ratio of the area under curve *A* to the area under curve *B*. If we increase the exposure by the proper filter factor, the results for the case in which the filter is used will be somewhat as indicated by curve *C*, which is the same as curve *B* except that its ordinates have all been multiplied by the "filter factor." By using the G filter and increasing the exposure by the proper filter factor, we have actually increased the density of the silver deposit on the film between 565 mμ (where the *C* curve crosses the *A* curve) and have decreased the density below 565 mμ.

The photographic operations taking place and illustrated graphically in Fig. 5 can, perhaps, be better understood if we consider the effect on the density of a developed panchromatic material having the characteristics given by the third curve when a photograph is made of a white or gray (nonselective absorbing) surface which is illuminated by mean noon sunlight. For an exposure such that the linear region of the H and D curve is employed, the density of the negative (as a function of wavelength) will be given by curve *A* when no filter is employed. Since we are not here concerned with color separation, this exposure will result in a uniformly dense negative whose density we shall call D_1. If we make another photograph of the same subject with the filter but with the same exposure as in the original case, the density of the second negative will be less than that of the first negative because those wavelengths below 550 mμ are considerably attenuated or entirely blocked from affecting the photographic negative. In this case the density of the second negative will be designated as D_2. However, if we make a third photograph of the nonselective surface through the filter but this time multiply the exposure by the exposure factor of the filter, the developed negative will have the same density D_1 as the original photograph. It is assumed that the processing conditions are the same in all cases.

It is therefore evident that the use of a filter changes the density of the developed negative as a function of wavelength or color, as is immediately evident by comparing curves *A* and *B* of the bottom graph of Fig. 5. From the explanation in the preceding paragraph it will be seen that the exposure factor for the filter is effective in tending to keep the density of the developed negative independent of the manner in which the filter alters the spectral distribution of density deposit, thereby making more certain that the straight-line region of the H and D characteristic is utilized. It may therefore be said that, in a general way, the filter alters the spectral response of the negative to the stimulus of the light source and object being photographed whereas the filter exposure factor represents an increase in the exposure which is required in order that the region of correct exposure of the H and D curve be maintained when some of the light is removed by the filter.[1]

Curve *A* at the bottom of the chart is determined by multiplying together for each wavelength from $\alpha = 350$ mμ to $\beta = 712$ mμ the relative intensity of the sunlight J_λ and the sensitivity of the photosensitive material R_λ. Curve *B* is determined for the same wavelength limits by multiplying together J_λ from the top curve, the filter transmission T_λ of the middle curve, and the spectral characteristics of the panchromatic material R_λ of the bottom curve. Thus we have illustrated graphically, the essential operations involved in determining filter factors for a given set of conditions. Since the middle curve (representing filter-transmission characteristic) will be the only one of the top three curves which will remain constant for a given filter and either the top curve will change for a different light source or the third curve will change for a different film emulsion, it is apparent that there is no single "filter exposure factor" which applies under all conditions for a given filter; this filter

---

[1] In this discussion it has been assumed that an ideal uniform nonselective absorbing medium has been photographed. In practice this is seldom, if ever, the case. The photography of images of varying colors and tone depths will produce an imaged (rather than a uniformly dense) negative. In such cases the results are not so simple as outlined above, and the effects of selective absorption of the filter and that of the filter exposure factor cannot be considered independently of one another. Yet the general conclusions given above hold true with secondary modifications.

exposure factor also depends upon the light source and the film. For this reason two filter exposure factors are usually given for the most common light sources, one for daylight and one for tungsten illumination.

Having worked out a graphical explanation for filter exposure factors, we now propose to reinterpret the preceding section in less technical terms more familiar to the average photographer.

When a light filter is used in combination with a given light source and photographic film, the time of exposure must be increased if the film is sensitized for rays corresponding to those colors which the filter absorbs. (In this, as well as the preceding discussion, no account is taken of loss of light by reflection from the surfaces of the filter or of absorption by the glass plates, cement, etc., except as these factors enter into the over-all transmission characteristic of the completed filter.) This increase in exposure is most necessary when the colors (wavelengths) absorbed by the filter are those for which the photosensitive material is most sensitive. The magnitude of the increase in the exposure which is necessary when a filter is used, may be said to depend upon the transmission characteristics of the filter. In a broader and less accurate manner, it may also be said that the filter exposure factor depends upon the color of a filter, for the color is entirely dependent (in the visible spectrum, of course) upon the absorption of the filter.

Items Affecting Filter Exposure Factor.—The increase in exposure required when a filter is used depends upon the density of color of the filter, since this determines the amount of absorption for a given color (wavelength). Thus, for example, although all yellow filters absorb blue light, a dense- or deep-yellow filter absorbs more blue than a light-yellow filter if both filters have spectral-transmission characteristics of the same shape but different magnitude. Consequently the deep-yellow filter would have a greater filter exposure factor than the pale-yellow filter. (This effect is not shown on the set of curves, but might easily be indicated by means of another filter-transmission curve having less transmission at all wavelengths than the G filter—representing a deeper or darker filter).

Another factor influencing the exposure through a given filter is the sensitiveness of a film for particular colors. If, for example, a film is relatively sensitive to all visible colors, as panchromatic films are, the filter exposure factor for a yellow filter which absorbs only the blue will be much less than if the film were of the ordinary (noncolor-sensitive or orthonon) variety and sensitive almost entirely to the blue rays. Thus, when used with a daylight source of light, the Wratten No. 8 or K2 filter has an exposure factor of 12 for ordinary or orthonon materials but a factor of 2.5 for orthochromatic and of only 2 for fully panchromatic materials.

A practical consideration in photography is the time of day in which outdoor scenes are taken. As daylight contains more blue-violet at noon than in the morning or later afternoon, the *increase* of the exposure time will be greater at noon than in the morning or the afternoon for a yellow filter. This statement refers only to the increase in exposure due to the filter factor; in practice the luminous intensity at noon is much greater than in the morning or afternoon, so that the absolute exposure is likely to be less than in the morning or afternoon. Similar fluctuations in spectral (color) distribution are caused by the seasons, as well as by the time of day, and by atmospheric conditions also. In general, where yellow filters are used, a good principle to follow is to increase the filter exposure factor the more blue the light source is and the less the film is sensitive to colors other than blue.

It is, therefore, impossible to state the correct increase of exposure time for every light condition or even for every filter, and when attempts are made to indicate filter factors, it should be understood that these factors are approximate and may require some deviations, depending upon the characteristics of the light source and film.

Unless otherwise stated, it may be understood that filter factors are given for white light of the quality of mean noon sunlight.

The medium in which the dye is contained (in gelatin filters) also has an influence on the filter factor. The more transparent this medium is, the less will be the increase in exposure attributable only to the use of the filter for a given degree of spectral correction. Thick gelatin films, as well as films made of celluloid (improperly or insufficiently purified gelatin), may require a much greater increase in exposure time than properly prepared gelatin, cemented gelatin, or glass filters. In the case of glass filters, or gelatin filters cemented between glass, the absorption of the glass and some-times of the cement will affect the filter exposure factor. The glass from which filters are made should be perfectly transparent and without the green tint which is fre-quently seen when the edges of glass plates are viewed. Nor is it sufficient that the edges of the glass plates be transparent rather than green, for, by adding compensating color ingredients, the glass may be made to appear white; however, the added ingred-ients provide additional absorption, so that, while presenting a neutral appearance and a neutral absorption at all visible wavelengths, the glass is not so transparent and efficient as might be desired. For cemented filters the increase in exposure can be reduced through the use of purest dyes and gelatin, colorless glass, and the clearest and most highly refined cement. Similar requirements are imposed on glass filters. For these reasons it is best to purchase filters properly made by a reputable manufacturer where the highest quality of work is being done.

TYPES OF FILTERS

Although the subject of this section is, properly, that type of device which modifies the spectral-energy distribution of the radiant energy affecting the photosensitive material, there are other optical accessories in photography which do not have as their main purpose the modification of the spectral distribution of energy. Nevertheless, the use and construction of some of these optical accessories are so closely related to the use and construction of real filters that they will be considered here. Therefore, it will be found that this chapter embraces: (1) filters, for changing the spectral-energy distribution of the light reaching the photographic material; (2) polarizing plates, for modifying the polarization of the light transmitted through the lens and only inci-dentally modifying its spectral-energy distribution; and (3) "special effects" plates, such as diffusion disks and supplementary lens attachments, whose purpose is to modify the optical system of the camera without appreciably affecting the spectral-energy distribution curve of the incident light.

Types of Filters by Construction.—In practice, the substances that are used for filters (or color mediums) are of five kinds: glasses, gelatins, colored liquids, dips and varnishes, and sprays. However, only the first three of these color mediums are of importance in photography, and of these three, colored liquids are seldom used except in certain scientific work.

But these various mediums are made up for practical use in several forms and may, therefore, be classified by construction as:

1. Dyed gelatin sheets.
2. Dyed gelatin sheets cemented between glass plates or disks.
3. Glasses, whose absorption is determined in the mix by metallic salts.
4. Colored liquids in transparent containers.

Each of these forms has its own inherent advantages and disadvantages, and all are used to some extent in photography.

Dyed gelatin filters are obtainable in a wide range of colors or spectral-transmission characteristics. As supplied commercially for photographic purposes, the dyed-gelatin sheets are available in thickness of a few thousands of an inch, and up to

10 by 14 in.   They are the least expensive type of filter but often fade, particularly when exposed to high temperatures.   After some use they become hard and brittle and are then easily broken.   Gelatin filters are easily marked with dirt or grease from the hands and are difficult to clean, especially, since because of their softness, rubbing their surface is likely to scratch them.   They are sufficiently thin that, when used alone, filter gelatins do not appreciably alter the focus of the photographic lens system. For temporary work, they are highly satisfactory, principally because of their low cost and wide range of available transmission characteristics, although they are unsatisfactory in a humid atmosphere.

The dyed gelatins cemented between glass have the advantage over colored glass in that the gelatin makes available a wide range of spectral-transmission characteristics. Furthermore, the filters are not so fragile as the gelatin sheets alone and can be more easily handled and cleaned.   The price for cemented filters is considerably higher than that for the gelatin sheets and is comparable with the price for colored-glass filters.

Glass filters are by far the most permanent in their spectral-transmission characteristics when once made.   But colored-glass filters are not yet available with such a wide variety of spectral-transmission curves as dyed gelatin; the colors desired are often difficult to control in the glass melts, and the final filter characteristics depend to a considerable extent upon the processing of the glass.   They are practically unaffected by temperature, within reasonable limits.   They are much more robust than dyed-gelatin sheets but are considerably heavier and are, of course, subject to cracking and breaking.

Colored liquids in transparent containers are useful in scientific work where the photographic equipment does not require portability.   A wide range of dyes in solution can be obtained, and by varying the thickness of the dye-containing cell, the density of the filter can be controlled quite easily.   Such liquid-cell filters are heavy and bulky and are difficult to keep clean; there is also the danger of spilling the liquid.   But where these disadvantages are of no serious consequence, the liquid-cell filters, particularly because of their flexibility have much to recommend them.   The spectral-transmission characteristics for substances in solution for the construction of liquid filters are listed for a wide variety of substances in the International Critical Tables, and also in Spectroradiometric Investigations of the Transmission of Various Substances, by W. W. Coblentz, National Bureau of Standards, Scientific Paper 418.

Types of Filters by Optical Excellence.—Light filters are usually available in not more than three different types or grades, so far as optical excellence is concerned; in many cases, the manufacturer provides only one grade.   The best filters are made of heavy glass, ground and polished optically plane with both surfaces parallel, or are made of thick glass plates cemented to dyed gelatin, the cemented filter likewise being ground and polished with optically flat, plane surfaces.   They are expensive but are finished with the same care as are high-quality lenses and are suitable for the most exacting requirements.

Light filters of very good commercial quality, perfectly suitable for amateur and even commercial work (except that of the most exacting requirements), are available in thinner glass or cemented gelatin and glass.   These filters are not so highly surfaced as the optical flats and are not recommended for use with lenses having a focal length greater than about 10 in., especially if a large aperture is used.   The majority of filters for amateur work and the less exacting commercial work are in this grade of excellence.

A third quality of light filter, available from at least one manufacturer, is made of colorless glass optically imperfect with gelatin cemented between the plates.   While not recommended for use in photography where the filter is in the direct path of the image rays, this grade of filter is suitable for visual work on such scientific applications as photomicrography or spectroscopy where the filter is placed in the path of a dispersed beam of light. The essential feature of filters for this service is their spectral-transmission characteristics and not their excellence from the optical standpoint.

Graduated Color Filters.—Most photographic filters are uniform in color or have the same spectral-transmission characteristic in each and every part of the filter. With such filters the light reaching all portions of the film is modified in its spectral characteristics in its passage through the filter.

Sometimes, however, it is desired to modify the spectral characteristics of the light reaching only a portion of the photographic film and to leave unchanged the spectral characteristics of the radiant energy reaching the other portions of the film. In such cases graduated filters are employed in which the density varies in some systematic manner. The most common types of graduated filters are the sky filters in which one portion of the filter is colorless—or, perhaps, has a slight amount of coloring—whereas another portion of the filter is fairly heavily colored yellow (for orthochromatic materials) or green (for panchromatic materials). The transition between the colored and colorless sections is usually gradual, and the colored portion of the filter may be of one density or may increase in density as one leaves the colorless portion. Some filters of this type are continuously graded from a pale to a deep hue at opposite ends of the filter.

Such graduated filters are true filters in the sense that at least a portion of the filter provides selective absorption, although another portion may not. Such filters are often known as "sky filters" or "cloud filters" since they are used extensively to absorb blue, thereby permitting greater contrast to be obtained between blue sky and the white clouds. These sky filters must be used either before or behind the lens system in the camera; if placed between the lens components where the rays converge to a point in passing through the filter, only a small spot on the filter is used, and instead of varying the spectral absorption for the image rays striking various portions of the film, the filter is likely to act as a neutral-density filter, merely increasing the exposure time without providing the desired tonal correction.

When graduated filters are used, care must be taken to ascertain that the filter is properly orientated with respect to the original subject and the image on the film in order to produce the desired effect. Some sky filters are marked by the manufacturer to indicate which is the top of the filter. In sky or cloud filters, the blue rays are to be absorbed by the filter, and since the blue rays come from the sky (top of the camera) and produce an image on the bottom of the film (image on film is upside down), the yellow portion of the sky filter should be at the top of the lens board.

In the case of graduated filters, (especially those which may be adjusted by the photographer) it is difficult, if not actually impossible to give suitable "filter exposure factors" since these factors depend not only upon the spectral characteristics of the light source, film and filter, but also upon what portion of the filter is used, and the manner in which color gradation appears in the filter. In many cases, no increase in exposure is required for a sky or cloud filter; in other cases the exposure must be increased several times. It is best to determine these filter exposure factors from experience, using the data provided by the manufacturer as a guide.

Polarizing Agents as Filters.—Although strictly speaking, polarizing agents are not light filters, except possibly accidentally or incidentally, recent progress in the manufacture of large-size polarizing gelatin screens (which are usually cemented between glass plates and surfaced and polished the same as filters) has led to the use of polarizing agents in photography in much the same manner as light or color filters. The use of these polarizing agents for controlling or modifying some of the properties of light makes them more nearly allied in their use and construction to filters than to any other piece of auxiliary equipment.

Before considering the use of polarizing agents as modifiers of the image rays affecting the photosensitive material, it is well to obtain some idea of the nature of light-wave motion, and the action of polarizing agents in general.[1]

Light may be considered an electromagnetic wave motion, in which the vibratory motion occurs at right angles to the direction of propagation. Such waves are called transverse waves. Figure 1 represents a transverse wave in which the displacement of the wave motion takes place only in the plane of the paper. When the wave motion takes place in a single plane, as in Fig. 1, the wave motion is said to be plane polarized. Ordinary light is considered to be composed of beams of plane-polarized light in which the vibrations occur in all possible directions perpendicular to the direction of propagation. That is to say, for ordinary light, the vibrations of a transverse wave occur in all possible directions in the plane perpendicular to the direction in which the light beam travels. It is, of course, difficult to represent, diagrammatically, the

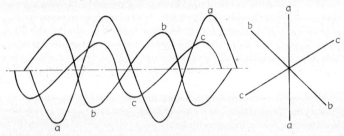

Fig. 6.—Three light waves, vibrating in different directions. The left-hand diagram illustrates how these waves might look as they pass the observer, while the right-hand diagram illustrates how they would look when viewed "head on." Through the use of polarizing plates, with optical axes aligned, only one of these vibrations, such as a-a could be transmitted.

precise state of affairs which theory and experiment indicate takes place at any one particular instant of time. The best explanation of ordinary nonpolarized light is to consider it to be composed of a great number of polarized waves which follow one another in such rapid succession that, over any interval of time for which light effects can be recorded, vibrations in all directions perpendicular to the direction of travel are equally represented. Figure 6 will indicate in an elementary and simplified manner the type of process which occurs. For simplicity a ray of ordinary light will be considered to be composed of three plane-polarized light rays, a, b, and c, the plane of polarization of each of these rays being different from that of the others. For simplicity it will be assumed that the amplitudes of the three plane-polarized waves are all equal. Then, if we looked at the composite light wave as it passed by us and were able to see the wave motion of the separate individual plane-polarized waves, the effect would be somewhat as indicated by the left diagram. On the other hand, if we could see the vibrations of the three plane-polarized beams as they come directly to us (or, e.g., as evaluated by a photographic plate) separately and individually, the effect of the three plane-polarized waves would be somewhat as indicated at the right which is an end projection. Actually, of course, ordinary light is composed of many more plane-polarized waves and the net picture is much more complicated than is indicated here, although the same fundamental principles apply.

In Fig. 6, the horizontal line is the zero axis and the waves are assumed to be traveling from left to right. The distance from this zero axis represents the wave displacement. The waves b and c appear to have less amplitude than wave a because

[1] A fairly extensive treatment of this subject may be found in Chap. 29 of "The Principles of Optics," by A. C. Hardy and F. H. Perrin, McGraw.

we are looking at them at an angle rather than perpendicularly. In the right hand part of Fig. 6, the lines represent the amplitudes of the three individual plane-polarized waves and all are of equal length.

A polarizing agent has the property of transmitting through it transverse waves vibrating in only one plane; all other transverse vibrations are partially or completely absorbed by the polarizing device. Therefore, if a polarizing device is placed in the path of a beam of light which has transverse vibrations in all directions, the light emerging after passing through the polarizing agent will be found to vibrate in only one direction normal to the plane of propagation. The property of polarizing agents to transmit light vibrating in one transverse direction but not in others is due to the proper orientation of many minute crystals in these polarizing devices.

The action of polarizing plates can be explained by analogy by considering the polarizing plates to be constructed in the form of a grating of parallel bars. Wave motion in such a direction as to be parallel with the bars will suffer no obstruction and will readily pass through them. On the other hand wave motion perpendicular to the bars will be effectively blocked.

Many surfaces produce a greater or lesser degree of plane polarization by reflection, rather than by transmission. Light, as from the sun, which is polarized in all directions perpendicular to its direction of travel, is more or less plane polarized after being reflected from the surfaces of insulators, such as glass, wood, linoleum, etc. The extent of this plane polarization which occurs in such surfaces depends upon the angle of the light incident upon the surface and is a maximum for many surfaces when the incident light strikes the reflecting surface at angles between 30 and 40°. The plane-polarized light reflected from such surfaces is largely responsible for objectionable glare. If the extent of the plane-polarized light can be reduced, the objectionable glare or reflections can likewise be reduced or eliminated.

If two polarizing plates are used one behind the other, the amount of light transmitted through them will depend upon the relation of the optical axes of the two plates. If the two polarizing agents are so aligned that their optical axes and the direction of the polarizing crystals are in the same direction, maximum light will be transmitted through the combination. The first crystal will, of course, cut out those rays which are polarized in directions other than that corresponding to its own polarizing structure. However, since both crystals are aligned so that their crystals are oriented in the same direction, the second crystal will act only in such a manner as to polarize light which already comes to it plane polarized; its affect on the light passing through it will therefore be simply that of absorption, as shown in Fig. 7.

However, if the second crystal or polarizing agent has its optical axis rotated with respect to that of the first crystal, the amount of light passing through the combination will depend upon the angles between the optical axes of the two crystals. If this angle is zero, maximum light is transmitted; if this angle is 90°, no light will be transmitted in the case of perfect polarizing agents. For intermediate angles, intermediate amounts of light will be passed. Therefore, by using two polarizing agents, one of which may be rotated with respect to the other, we have a means of controlling the total amount of light passing through the combination; we have also provided a means of limiting the directions in which the transmitted rays are capable of vibrating.

Use of Polarizing Plates in Photography.—In photography, polarizing crystals or plates are usually used singly for the purpose of reducing glare or reflections of the desired image. In most cases, elimination or reduction of reflections results in a more pleasing photograph and often permits effects to be obtained which would otherwise be very difficult or even impossible. The polarizing material is mounted in circular cells which slip on over the lens mount. These cells are arranged so that they may be rotated about the central axis of the camera in such a manner as to reduce the plane-polarized light (from flooring, windows, etc.) causing undesirable glare or reflections. Although the use of polarizing plates in front of the camera lens is often effective in reducing some undesirable reflections, it is most effective for glare and reflections within a fairly narrow angle around 35° from the central axis of the camera. It is not a cure-all for all reflection and glare troubles.

The commercially available polarizing disks give an appearance of being a fairly dark-gray color. These disks cut down the amount of light being transmitted through them. For this reason the exposure time must be increased when these disks are used. The exposure will probably be two to five times that required when no polarizing filter is used, although the factor provided by the manufacturer of such devices should be used in determining the increase in exposure.

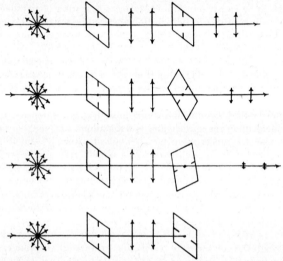

Fig. 7.—Unpolarized light, coming from the extreme left, is polarized to vibrate in a vertical plane after passing through the first polarizing plate. When the polarizing axis of the second plate is rotated with respect to that of the first, more or less light is permitted to pass. When the axes of the two plates are at right angles, no light passes through the second plate.

With cameras having ground-glass screens, the polarizing filter is placed over the lens and rotated about its own axis until the desired effect is obtained. In the case of reflex cameras having a taking as well as a viewing lens, the effect of the polarizing filter can be seen by placing this on the viewing lens, and rotating until the proper effect is obtained. The polarizing filter is then transferred to the taking lens without changing its angular rotation, and the exposure is made in the usual way, except for increase in exposure. For cameras having an eye-level or reflecting type of view finder, the lens can be held up to the eye and rotated about its own axis until the desired reflections are reduced to a minimum. The filter is then placed over the lens, without rotating it, and the exposure made. Polarizing filters for photographic use are provided with marks indicating the direction in which the crystals of the polarizing material are aligned; the relative position of these marks may be used to indicate whether the polarizing filter has been turned or not. For those cameras in which focusing is accomplished by rotating the front lens component, the focusing must obviously be completed before the polarizing filter is attached to the lens. Depending upon the type of camera and view finder, one of the methods outlined above can be used in applying the polarizing filter.

Neutral-tint Density Filters.—Although not filters in the sense that they alter the spectral-energy distribution of the light passing through them, neutral density disks or plates are similar to filters in their general use and construction. These devices are gray in appearance since they are made to have as nearly as possible the same absorption for all wavelengths in the visible spectrum. For this reason, neutral density filters show no selective absorption in the visible spectrum, which is the characteristic of all true filters. The purpose of these devices is to absorb all colors equally well, and they may be obtained in various densities. They are used to cut down the amount of light when it is not desirable to use a smaller aperture which would increase the depth of focus. Neutral density filters are also sometimes used with tricolor filters to cut down the amount of light when certain filters are used, so that all three of the color filters may have the same exposure factors. They are also frequently used for extending the useful range of optical pyrometers and for other optical systems where the intensity but not the spectral distribution of the light must be altered.

Neutral density filters may be made by dyeing gelatin with several dyes to produce equal absorption throughout the entire visible spectrum. Sometimes neutral density "filters" are made by depositing a thin film of metal (by a sputtering or sintering process) on a plate of glass. Silver, platinum, and aluminum are frequently used for this purpose. For rough work, satisfactory neutral density filters may easily be made by cementing a piece of uniformly exposed and developed negative between plates of glass. Such a filter scatters the light much more than a dyed gelatin filter; moreover, it is difficult or impossible to obtain uniform absorption over any appreciable area of exposed and developed photographic film. A further source of trouble is that the developed film or plate may not be a neutral density filter; if it becomes stained during development or fixing, it is likely to show selective absorption.[1] In spite of these difficulties, such simple developed-film neutral density filters are often quite suitable for certain classes of work.

In photographic work, neutral density filters are used, like true filters, before (or behind) the lens system of the camera. When used for spectroscopic and other uses where the purpose is merely to cut down the intensity of the light, these filters may be placed at any suitable point in the path of the light beam. Neutral density filters may be obtained in a wide variety of sizes, either square or round and mounted or unmounted. The Wratten dyed-gelatin neutral density filters are available in several density values, and complete sets may be obtained in which the density of the filters progresses in decimal, logarithmic, or percentage laws of transmission.

Neutral-tint Wedges.—Similar to the neutral-tint density filters described above are the neutral-tint wedges, which may be of the stepped or continuously variable types. In the former case the wedge is divided into several sections, each of which is uniform over its entire area, but each area of which has a value of transmission different from adjacent areas. These stepped wedges are usually constructed so that successive steps in the wedge represent equal increments of density or equal steps in transmission or absorption. In the continuously variable type of wedge, the transmission at one end is high, whereas at the other end it is low; the transition from one to the other usually taking place gradually, and uniformly.

[1] A nonselective absorbing deposit of a developed negative may be obtained by using a developer suggested by Sheppard and Travelli, at the VIIth International Congress of Photography, and consisting of

p-Aminophenol hydrochloride	7¼	g.
Sodium sulphite (anhydrous)	50	g.
Sodium carbonate (anhydrous)	50	g.
Water to make	1000	cc.

Supplementary Lens Attachments.—Ordinary supplementary lens attachments are not filters at all, although their construction and mechanical use makes it desirable to consider them along with filters, since they are used in the same manner as filters. Such supplementary lenses usually fall into two classes: (1) those intended to increase the effective focal length of the lens system thereby, at the same time narrowing the field of view; and (2) those which decrease the focal length and increase the angle of view. The first class of supplementary lenses reduces the speed of the lens system since the focal length is increased for any given aperture. Conversely, the second class of supplementary lenses increases the speed of the lens.

Supplementary lenses which increase the focal length of the lens system are sometimes called portrait lenses; those which decrease the focal length are sometimes referred to as wide-angle, copying, or reproduction lenses. A set of supplementary lenses usually costs but a small fraction of the cost of the lens system in a camera, and their use provides a lens system having several focal lengths and angles of view.

These supplementary lenses are usually mounted in metal cells which slip over the camera lens, or are held on the camera lens by means of a metal-spring holder.

Special-effects Equipment.—A wide variety of lens accessories is available under this name including diffusion disks for giving a soft diffused effect without making the image out of focus; fog plates for making negatives possessing the appearance of being taken in heavy fog; duplicator disks, in which one-half of the disk is opaque and the other transparent and permitting (by rotation of the disk) exposures of half of the film at a time for trick effects, etc.

CARE, MOUNTING, AND CEMENTING OF FILTERS

Care of Filters.—When properly constructed, surfaced, and polished, filters are of as high quality as optical lenses, and should be given the same careful consideration accorded to a good lens. When not in use, the filters should be kept in a substantial case or other suitable container which will keep the individual plates separated from one another and in their proper place. By keeping filters in their proper container, the chance of getting them dirty, scratching the surfaces, or otherwise marring their optical properties will be minimized, and the plates will always be ready for use. Filters should be kept in a dry place at normal room temperatures and should be protected from strong light, ultraviolet, infrared, heat, and similar radiations. Although colored-glass filters are not ordinarily harmed by these radiations, the above precautions are especially necessary for certain gelatin and cemented gelatin filters which are subject to change in their transmission characteristics with aging and which are frequently unstable to heat and strong light. Excessive heat is likely to soften the Canada balsam in cemented filters, and, if this occurs, the definition of the filter will most probably be ruined. Plain gelatin films, without protective glass, should be kept flat by placing the films in a clean white envelope or between sheets of soft paper and pressing between parallel surfaces, as the leaves of a book.

Cleanliness is necessary in handling filters as well as in handling lenses, and this is especially true in the case of gelatin films because of the difficulty of cleaning the surfaces should they become soiled. Filters not mounted in cells should be handled only by holding them by their edges or corners; they should not be grasped with the fingers covering a portion of their surface. Some filters are protected at their edges with binding tape, and this provides a satisfactory, if somewhat narrow, means of holding the plates.

Cleaning Filters.—Like lenses, filters should be cleaned by brushing their surfaces with light, fine tissue paper, lens tissue, or a camel's-hair brush. If the filters become so dirty that brushing does not suffice to clean them, they may be moistened slightly by breathing upon them and rubbing the surfaces with lens tissue, after making certain that all the grit has been removed from the surfaces. Solid glass filters can be cleaned by rubbing the surface with lens tissue dampened with denatured alcohol. This procedure is not recommended for cemented filters as alcohol is a solvent for Canada balsam; moreover the alcohol may cause the gelatin to swell if it reaches the cemented edges, thereby destroying the desirable optical properties of the filter. Under no circumstances should cemented gelatin filters or gelatin films be washed in water, alcohol, or other liquid. Gelatin films may be cleaned by laying one surface down on a clean sheet of paper placed on a hard flat surface and rubbing the upper surface with a soft material, such as flannel or preferably lens tissue. The surfaces of gelatin film scratch very easily, and there is, therefore, a limit to the amount of cleaning which may be done by this method. Should it be necessary to cut gelatin film, the film should be protected by placing it between two sheets of thin paper, and the three thicknesses should be cut simultaneously with sharp scissors or a sharp edge such as a razor blade. If dull scissors are used, the gelatin may chip and flake, especially if it is brittle from age.

Mounting of Filters.—Filters can be used in several positions on the camera, the position determining the method of mounting. They may be used before the lens, behind the lens, or immediately in front of the film. Although filters of mediocre quality can be used if placed in this last position, this form of mounting has the disadvantages of requiring a filter as large as the film on which the latent image is formed, and defects in the surface of the filter or specks of dust on its surface show up on the negative. Filters behind the lens do not have these disadvantages but are inaccessible. Before-the-lens filters are accessible for change and need be only slightly larger than the lens barrel diameter. This form of mounting is almost universally used at the present time.

The position of the filter affects the focusing of the lens on the film, and this fact must be taken into consideration where sharp negatives are required. If the filter is placed before the lens, the plane of sharp focus will be slightly moved back from where it is without the filter. For many cases, such as landscape photography, this change in focus is not important, especially if the filter is very thin, as a gelatin film. But where the sharpest images are required, as in copying line drawings, focusing should be done with the filter in place. Since filters always cut down the amount of light and since it is often difficult to focus with colored light, the use of "dummy" filters is frequently resorted to. Dummy filters have no appreciable selective absorption, but alter the image rays through the camera in the same way the usual filter does. Therefore focusing can be done with such a dummy with ease, and the desired filter can replace it when the photograph is being made.

When the filter is placed on the back combination of the lens, the plane of sharp focus with the filter in place is moved forward by about one-third the thickness of the filter, so that focusing must be done with the filter in place. If the filter is placed immediately in front of the photographic plate, the shift in focus will be negligible when a gelatin film is used. But if a thick glass or cemented filter is used in a holder in front of the plate, the bellows extension must be shortened by the thickness of the filter. If this is not done, the image will be properly in focus on the filter and not on the photographic plate.

Filters may be mounted on the camera lens in two general methods. A very convenient way, especially for the amateur photographer having a small number of filters of the same size, is to have the filters mounted in circular metal cells which slip on the camera lens. However, when a filter is to be used with several lenses of different size, it is usually more satisfactory to use square filter plates and to support these in a frame or holder fitting over, or held just in front of, the lens. Circular cells, as well as other filter holders, should be designed to hold the filters against the lens securely but without pressure.

Cementing Filters.—It is impossible for the average photographer having no optical measuring devices and but little technical knowledge of the design of optical parts to construct high-quality filters for photographic purposes; such filters had best be purchased. Certain instances do arise, however (for instance, that in which a filter is to be used in the path of a beam of dispersed light, as in photomicrography), where the optical quality of the filter is secondary to its spectral-transmission characteristics, and for such cases cemented filters can be made which will answer the purpose satisfactorily.

Such cemented filters use, as their main optical apparatus, the gelatin films, such as are available from the Eastman Kodak Co. and known as Wratten gelatin films. These are available in about a hundred different spectral-transmission characteristics and densities and will be an adequate selection for almost any photographic purpose.

It is also essential that good-quality cover plates be used. Plate glass of selected quality, free from striae, bubbles, or other defects, is generally used for protecting the gelatin film. Glass which, when viewed along the edges with white-light illumination, has green color is not suitable for good-quality filters, as this glass has appreciable absorption at both ends of the visible spectrum. Normal white glass (as distinguished from glass which is made to appear white by adding decolorizers) should be used, as the decolorizers merely introduce additional absorption in the green portion of the spectrum, thereby making the entire glass approximately neutral. Glass which has been made white by the addition of decolorizers might be used, but the efficiency of the filter and the filter exposure factor will be affected.

Canada balsam is the most common cement for optical parts. This is a mixture of turpentine and resins and is used in its natural condition. Canada balsam is a thick, viscous, yellow fluid, having much the appearance of honey. A good grade of filtered balsam will be required for cementing optical parts.

All cementing operations should be carried out in a dust-free room. The Wratten gelatin film will be found to be clean when purchased, but the glass plates, which should be the same size as the gelatin film or slightly larger, should be thoroughly cleaned by washing in potassium permanganate to rid them of grease and then washing in clean hot water. The plates may be dried by evaporation or may be dried with a soft cloth, if care is taken to remove all lint before beginning the cementing operation.

The Canada balsam may be used at ordinary temperatures; it may also be thinned by adding turpentine or alcohol. However, a much more satisfactory method is to use the balsam without the addition of other ingredients, thinning the cement by heating the balsam slightly in a hot water bath. When the balsam is thinned sufficiently by the application of heat, a drop is placed in the center of one of the glass plates by means of a stirring rod, and the gelatin film is placed on top of this spot of cement. The gelatin should then be flattened down, making sure that no bubbles are left between it and the glass plate. Provided they are clean, the fingers may be used to flatten the gelatin to the glass plate, especially if protected by lens tissue. A drop of cement is then placed on top of the gelatin and the top plate is pressed down, making sure that all air bubbles are excluded. It is important to use sufficient cement so that some will flow out on all edges; too little balsam will ruin the job as more cannot be added. Not a little technique and skill are required to perform these operations satisfactorily, and good results cannot be obtained consistently; there is bound to be some spoilage if any quantity of work is undertaken.

When this sandwich has been prepared, it should be pressed together. There will probably be a decided tendency for the plates to slide upon one another. This may be counteracted by holding the edges in place and binding the sandwich of glass-gelatin-glass with thread. After being bound in this manner, the filter is set away, under pressure, to dry at ordinary temperatures for about 2 weeks. When the filter is thoroughly dry, the pressure and then the thread are removed. Any Canada balsam which may have hardened on the surface of the plates can be removed by rubbing the surface of the plates with a cloth dampened with alcohol, but no alcohol must be allowed to get at the cemented edges. The edges of the filter should be protected to prevent the entry of liquids which might injure the cemented joint.

FILTERS IN PHOTOGRAPHY

In selecting filters for photographic use, several factors should be considered. Among these are: (1) optical excellence required, (2) spectral sensitivity of the film used, (3) distribution of spectral energy in illuminant, (4) effect desired in the finished photograph, (5) service for which filter is to be used, and (6) cost. The first and fifth of these items will determine, to a very large extent, the cost of the filter. For commercial work where the filter must be of the highest grade and where it will probably be used frequently, the matter of cost is relatively unimportant, and a glass or cemented gelatin filter of the highest optical quality will be required. For practically all amateur work, a good-quality glass or cemented gelatin filter will be quite satisfactory. For experimental or temporary work, or where the filter is used infrequently, the plain uncemented gelatin often meets the optical requirements quite well, although structurally gelatins leave much to be desired.

As has already been mentioned, the over-all characteristics of the photographic image will depend, in its tone or color value, upon the spectral characteristics of the film, the light source, and the filters, and proper consideration must be given to these factors when selecting filters for a given purpose. For example, when reproducing colors in their correct monochromatic tonal value, a yellow filter for orthochromatic and a green filter for panchromatic films will usually prove to be as good a selection as any for most common light sources. On the other hand, for certain types of color film exposed by light from incandescent lamps, a photometric bluish filter is required. For other types of work and for special effects, such specialized booklets as "Photography of Colored Objects" and "Wratten Light Filters," published by Eastman Kodak Co., should be consulted, especially with respect to the spectral-transmission characteristics of commercially available filters.

Classification of Photographic Filters.—While it is not possible to cover in detail the use and application of the several hundred filters commercially available, those filters which have photographic importance may be divided, according to their spectral-transmission characteristics, into several well-defined groups. The filters falling into any single group perform the same general function, the various groups representing different functional attributes. These groups may be classified as follows:

Compensation or Equalizing Filters.—These filters provide partial absorption in parts of the visible and near-visible spectrum for the purpose of providing a certain compensation or equalization of all colors in their effect on the photographic film. Because most photographic materials have their greatest sensitivity in the ultraviolet and blue end of the visible spectrum, compensation filters often have their greatest absorption in this region. Most yellow filters for black-and-white photography are compensation, equalizing, or correction filters.

Contrast Filters.—Contrast filters provide virtually complete absorption for certain colors in the object being photographed.

Selective or Separation Filters.—Selective or separation filters, in indirect color photography using color-separation films or negatives, are used to decompose the visible spectrum into the three colors (the primary red, green, and blue or their complementary colors) for making the three separation or partial images.

Monochromatic Filters.—Monochromatic filters transmit only a narrow band of wavelengths, completely or nearly completely absorbing the remainder. Consequently, when viewed by transmitted light, they usually appear as a pure color. Monochromatic filters are used in scientific photography (especially in spectroscopic photography) but ordinarily are not used in general photography.

Safe Lights.—Light filters used for darkroom illumination are known as safe lights. A characteristic of safe-light filters is that they provide total or large absorption for that portion of the spectrum for which the photosensitive material being processed is sensitive, transmitting the rest of the spectrum for the darkroom illumination. For panchromatic materials (which are sensitive to practically all the visible spectrum), the best compromise is to use a safe-light filter transmitting radiations at the green portion of the spectrum. Of course, the green light transmitted by such a safe light will affect the panchromatic film, since it is sensitive to green light. The advantage of using this green filter is that the eye is most sensitive to green light when the luminous intensity is low, so that for a given visual effect less light can be used if it is green than if it is of some other color.

It will be noted that the classification given above is based upon the shape of the spectral-transmission curve with reference to the material or purpose for which the filter is to be used. This is quite logical, for it is the spectral transmission as given by the shape of this curve which is of primary importance in the use and application of a filter. There are, of course, other methods of classifying filters, as, for instance, according to their apparent color when white light is transmitted through them or according to their use, based on their position in the optical circuit (*e.g.*, as taking filters and safe lights) rather than in their function as varying the spectral-energy distribution.

Compensation or Equalizing Filters.—Perhaps the most common types of filters in photographic work are those filters which are intended to alter the spectral-energy distribution of the light source in such a manner as to give a monochrome print (in black-and-white photography) in which the various shades in the print are proportional to the visible luminous effect produced by the colored original image. To accomplish this effect, it is necessary that the brightness of the colors in the original image be reproduced in accordance with their effect on the human eye, as indicated in the standard visibility curve.

It is evident that only panchromatic materials can give results in which the black, gray, and white tones are accurately proportional to the visibility of the original subject; other types of film emulsions are deficient in their sensitivity at the red, orange, or yellow parts of the spectrum, so that these colors are rendered too dark in the final print.

Certain green filters (such as the Wratten X1 and X2) are compensating filters intended to provide as accurate tone correction as is possible in monochrome photography. Yellow filters, such as the K1 or K2, are also compensation filters which provide an approximation to proper tone values, when used with orthochromatic types of materials, by cutting down the effective sensitivity of the film to the blue end of the spectrum.

Other examples of compensation filters are those used in photometric work. With the greater general use of color films, such photometric filters are also sometimes recommended to enable a film intended for use with one type of light source, *e.g.*, mean noon sunlight, to be used with another type of light source (such as incandescent electric lamps).

Contrast Filters.—If two colors which produce very nearly the same luminous effect to the eye are photographed on a panchromatic negative and a black-and-white print is made, it will be found that these colors have nearly the same tone value.

While these colors were easily distinguished in the original because of their difference in predominant wavelength, the result in the final print is unsatisfactory because, since we cannot reproduce in color, we must depend simply on shades of gray to indicate proper tone values. To indicate the difference in color which we see in the original, it is necessary to produce a contrast between these two colors in the black-and-white print. When this is done, the accurate tone rendition of the original image, as evaluated by the visibility curve of the human eye, is, of course, destroyed, but the effect obtained is usually much more desirable, notwithstanding.

To produce monochrome contrast between colors, it is necessary to photograph the image so that one of the colors will produce a darker print (or lighter negative) than the other. When it becomes necessary to make use of that form of distortion known as increasing the color contrast, it is usually customary to reproduce the red and orange colors lighter than the corresponding green and blue colors of the same visibility. To accomplish this contrast in photography, we may make use of the practical rule which states that to photograph a color in black and white so that the print of it appears lighter than the original image, a filter should be used which is of the same color as the image. Conversely, to reproduce a color in the final print darker than it appears in the original, use a filter complementary to that color. The filter should absorb light of the color to be rendered dark.

The following table will give an idea of the colors of the filters which may be used to render certain colors lighter or darker. For purposes of illustration Wratten filters suitable for the purpose are also listed.

TABLE I.—FILTERS FOR PRODUCING COLORS LIGHTER OR DARKER

Color of subject	To render subject lighter, use		To render subject darker, use	
	Color	Example[1]	Color	Example[1]
Red	Red	29, 25, 15	Blue green	47, 58
Orange	Orange	15, 25	Blue	47
Yellow	Yellow	15, 25	Indigo blue	47
Yellow-green	Yellow-green	11	Violet	35, 36
Green	Green	58, 15, 13	Red	27, 25
Blue-green	Blue-green	47, 58	Red-orange	29, 25
Blue	Blue	47	Orange-yellow	29, 25
Purple	Purple	47	Green	58
Magenta; pink	Magenta	29, 25	Green	58

[1] Numbers refer to Wratten filters.

As examples of the use of contrast filters may be mentioned the use of a red filter (Wratten No. 25 or No. 29) for photographing blue prints, which without such a filter would give a gray and white result lacking in detail and contrast. The red Wratten No. 25 filter also finds application in photographing furniture where it is desirable to show the wood grain; the Wratten No. 15 filter is also useful in this application.

Selective or Separation Filters.—In accordance with the theories of Wunsch, Young, and Helmholtz and first demonstrated by Maxwell, three-color photography is based upon the fact that a colored image may be constructed by superimposing in register three partial (or separation) images, each of which is colored one of the three primary colors, red, green, and blue. The partial images are made by splitting the color of the original image into three groups of primary colors by means of filters.

Two methods of three-color photography are possible, and both are in common use: the additive process and the subtractive process.

In both processes the purpose of the taking filters is to split up the light reflected by the colored image into the three-component primary colors. If the final color print or transparency is to be an accurate reproduction of the original colored image, any filters suitable for making the partial-image negatives must fulfill certain require- ments, both as regards optical requirements and spectral characteristics.

Optically, the three separation filters which are to be used together for color- separation photography must be accurately surfaced and polished and for the highest quality work must be matched as a set. This requirement is essential to insure that the partial negatives are all exactly the same size, so that they will permit trans- parencies or prints to be made which will register accurately when superimposed upon one another in the final result. If precise color-separation work is to be undertaken, it is probably desirable to purchase the separation filters as a set rather than to pur- chase the filters separately and individually at various times. Unless experimental work is in progress, it is unwise to use tricolor separation filters together which are not recommended by the manufacturer to be used as a complete set. It is also desirable that all three filters in a tricolor filter set be of the same manufacture unless the user is sufficiently conversant with color-separation work as to be willing to accept the risk and expense of mistaken judgment.

The spectral-transmission curves for separation filters for three-color photography should have low and uniform absorption in the transmission range, complete absorp- tion outside the transmission range, and cutoff characteristics as sharp and abrupt as possible. The spectral-transmission characteristics of the three filters should overlap only slightly or not at all; the spectral characteristics of some filter sets recom- mended for color-separation work show definite gaps in which certain wavelengths in the visible spectrum are not transmitted by any of the three filters.

By making the absorption low in the transmission region, the exposure factor for the filters will be reduced to a minimum. Uniform absorption in the transmission region assures that no discrimination will be given to any of the spectral colors passed by the filter. Tricolor filters should have abrupt cutoff characteristics to assure that the color of the final result will be as nearly as possible independent of the abso- lute exposure, although depending upon the relative exposure through the three tri- color filters. The matter can be comprehended more clearly by reference to Fig. 7.

Assume that a set of ideal tricolor taking filters have spectral-transmission charac- teristics as shown in Fig. 7*A*. The blue filter will then pass wavelengths between 400 and 500 mμ without absorption but will be completely absorbing for wavelengths outside this region. Similarly, let the transmission range for the green filter be from 500 to 600 mμ and that for the blue filter be from 600 to 700 mμ. Then negatives made through the use of these ideal taking filters will show the three primary colors sharply differentiated, each primary color being passed by its corresponding taking filter, and only by this filter.

If instead of the theoretically ideal taking filters of Fig. 7*A*, we have a set of tri- color filters as shown in Fig. 7*B*, the situation is quite different. In the latter case light from the colored image is not split into three well-defined primary colors. Because of the gradual cutoff characteristics, any one filter may transmit more than one primary color. As was true also in the case of Fig. 7*A*, the relative exposures through these three filters must be proportional to the relative exposure factors of the three filters. But because any filter of Fig. 7*B* transmits primary colors outside its own primary color region, a proper color balance in the final result will be obtained only for one definite exposure; for other exposures of the partial negatives, the fidelity of color reproduction in the final result will be inaccurate even though the proper relative relation between exposure and filter exposure factors is maintained. In other words with filters having transmission curves such as shown in Fig. 8*B*, the color of the final result depends, not only upon the proper relative exposures and filter exposure factors, but also upon the absolute exposures given to the three partial negatives. The difficulties of obtaining satisfactory practical results are considerably greater in the latter case than in the former.

One point concerning sharp cutting filters should be noted in passing. Ideal filters, such as are indicated in Fig. 7*A*, fail to distinguish between monochromatic hues lying within the transmission band of a given filter. If, for example, we had two monochromatic sources of equal energy, one at 420 mμ and the other at 480 mμ, both would be passed equally well by the tricolor blue filter, and, if the photosensitive

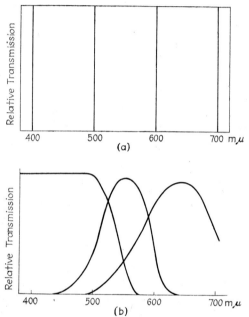

Fig. 7.—Wavelength-transmission characteristics of ideal (*a*) and actual (*b*) filters as used in three-color photography.

material were equally sensitive to radiations of 420 and 480 mμ, it would be impossible to distinguish between these two monochromatic colors in the final color picture. This condition is seldom of appreciable practical importance in photography because no colors in dyes or pigments with which we deal are purely monochromatic; pure monochromatic colors are seldom obtained, and then usually with inconvenience or difficulty. Another, but less important reason why this state of affairs is not of much practical concern is that practical taking filters do not approach the ideal characteristics of Fig. 7*A* very closely.

Monochromatic Filters.—These are sharp cutting filters which are usually used with gaseous-discharge luminous sources. The transmission band of these filters is usually sharp so that, when used with certain gas-discharge devices producing a discontinuous spectrum, certain desired lines will be transmitted, whereas other lines will be absorbed. Such monochromatic filters are not of importance for general photographic work but are useful in certain scientific applications of photography.

Sometimes sharp-cutting monochromatic filters are employed to indicate by visual examination the tone reproduction which will occur in black-and-white photography. For this application, the filter must be sufficiently sharp so that colors in the original subject are practically indistinguishable. The transmission region may lie anywhere in the visible spectrum, although there is some advantage in putting it near the yellow, where the eye is most sensitive. The Wratten No. 90 viewing filter is intended for this use, and while it is possible to distinguish between reds and greens, these colors are so dulled as to give sensibly a yellow visual image of varying luminosity.

Safe Lights.—Optical requirements on safe lights are practically nil except that the safe-light filter should transmit as much of the visible spectrum as possible, provided the photographic sensitive material is not sensitive to radiations of these wavelengths. In practice, the manufacturer of photographic materials usually specifies the type of filter and gives some indication as to the intensity of illumination which can be used with the various types of film and paper emulsions.

Filters for Commercial Work.—Where commercial work is being done, the selection of filters should be that which will provide maximum utility and flexibility with a minimum investment. Practically all subjects encountered in commercial photography can be treated adequately with modern photosensitive materials with less than a dozen filters. Those filters which have been found to be most useful are the Wratten (or equivalent) K1, K2, X1, X2, F, G, E, A, B, and C5, or Nos. 6, 8, 11, 13, 29, 15, 23, 25, 58, and 47, respectively. For those who do not care to obtain a full set of photographic filters, the A, G, and K2 filters will probably prove most satisfactory for general work.

The K1 filter is a light-yellow filter which gives some color correction with orthochromatic materials without increasing the exposure time unduly. It is useful where some color correction must be obtained with the least increase in exposure time. The K2 is a stronger yellow filter and gives better correction but requires a longer exposure than the K1. Like the K1, the K2 filter is intended for use with orthochromatic materials.

The X1 gives correction with panchromatic materials when used with daylight whereas the X2 is suitable for panchromatic materials used with incandescent luminous sources. They are not recommended for orthochromatic materials.

The F is a strong red filter for contrast work, copying blueprints, screen-plate analysis, or for haze cutting or infrared photography.

The G filter is a strong yellow-orange filter with sharp cutoff for contrast work, strong accentuation of clouds, telephotography, furniture, copying yellow faded matter, and general landscape photography.

The E filter is a general contrast red filter.

The A, B, and C5 are used in color-reproduction work. The A is a red, the B a green, and the C5 a blue-violet filter.

The spectral-transmission characteristics of these and other filters are shown in "Wratten Light Filters," published by the Eastman Kodak Co.

Filter Characteristics Summarized.—In this chapter we have discussed some of the more important characteristics of filters and have mentioned some of the uses of various kinds of filters. Considerably more might easily be written concerning the uses, and particularly the artistic uses, of light filters in photography. But there are many articles available in the literature on this subject, and, where artistic considerations are involved, it is impossible for a technical reference book to be of much value.

A table of filter factors for various makes of emulsions and filters will be found in Appendix D. While every effort has been made to make this list as accurate as possible, such a listing can be taken only as a guide. The results given in Appendix D are to be used with proper judgment of the factors already enumerated in this chapter.

Bibliography

COBLENTZ, W. W.: Light Filters Which Absorb All of the Infrared, *Bur. Standards Bull.* 9 (1913).

BRADY, E. J.: The Development of Daylight Glass, *Trans. Illum. Eng. Soc. (N. Y.)*, **9**, 937 (1914).

COBLENTZ, W. W.: Spectroradiometric Investigations of the Transmission of Various Substances, *Scientific Paper* 418, *Bur. Standards J. Research*, **16**, 267 (1921).

JONES, L. A.: Light Filters for the Isolation of Narrow Spectral Regions, *J. Optical Soc. Am.*, **16**, 259 (1928).

HOBBIE, E. H.: Glass for Protection from Infrared Radiation, *Trans. Illum. Eng Soc. (N. Y.)*, **28**, 658 (1933).

RAWLINGS, S. O.: Color Filters with Special Reference to Their Use in Photography, *Phot. J.*, **84**, 295 (1934).

TAYLOR, A. H.: Spectral Distribution of Mercury in Common Illuminants, *Gen. Elec. Rev.*, **37**, 414 (1934).

GIBSON, K. S.: A Filter for Obtaining Light at Wavelength 560 mμ, *J. Optical Soc. Am.*, **25**, 131 (1935).

Filter Factors for Zeiss Ikon and Carl Zeiss Filters, *Zeiss Mag.*, June, 1937, p. 114.

GAGE, H. P.: Glass Color Filters for Special Applications, *J. Optical Soc. Am.*, **27**, 159 (1938).

BACKSTROM, H., and A. BOSTROM: Polarized Illumination with Polarizing Screens in Front of Lenses, *Am. Phot.*, **32**, 153 (1938).

Books:

"Wratten Light Filters," Eastman Kodak Co. (1938).

HARDY, A. C., and F. H. PERRIN: "Principles of Optics," McGraw.

"Photographic Filters and How to Use Them," Ver Hahn Pub. Co., Hollywood, Calif.

"Jena Colored Optical Filter Glasses for Scientific and Technical Purposes," Jena Glass Works, Jena, Germany.

"Lifa Light Filter Handbook," Lifa Light Filter Works, Ausburg, Germany.

"Photography by Polarized Light," Eastman Kodak Co.

CHAPTER XI

DEVELOPERS AND THEORY OF DEVELOPMENT

BY D. R. WHITE AND J. R. WEBER

The development of the latent photographic image is a necessary and important step in current practical photography. The origin of photography antedates the knowledge of developers and processes of development, but the original methods have been practically completely supplanted by procedures using development as a step on account of the greatly increased photographic efficiency so obtained. A few photographic materials are still used without developers, notably printing-out papers, which, as their name suggests, are exposed until the image is visible. The reactions involved are directly induced by the action of the exposing light. Greater photographic efficiency results, in general, from smaller exposures, designed to produce only a latent image, itself invisible, with subsequent development and fixation to transform it into a permanent visible image.

There has been much speculation concerning the nature of the latent image, but experimental work to determine its nature is very difficult, and no theory yet advanced has secured unopposed acceptance. Study of development has had to proceed in spite of this lack of knowledge of the latent image developed. Much empirical data have been obtained and some theoretical relationships have resulted from years of experimental work devoted to this study.

Two classes of procedures have resulted and are recognized under the names "chemical" and "physical" development. The final images produced are not chemically distinguishable, but the course followed is primarily different in the source of the silver finally deposited as the image. In chemical development, the more important method, the silver halide of the emulsion supplies the silver for the final image. This is probably through an initial solution of the halide by the developing solution, followed at once by reduction and deposit of the silver on nucleuses forming the latent image. In physical development, the developing solution itself contains a soluble silver salt which deposits or plates out, as reduced by the developing agent, with the nucleuses from the latent image guiding the location and magnitude of the deposit. This type of development can be carried on even after fixation, though it is quite obvious that chemical development is impossible then.

With either type of development, the fundamental problem is to obtain a differential deposit of silver in such manner that at each point it is at least approximately proportional to the intensity of the latent image at that point. If this were achieved, there would be no deposit where there had been no exposure. In practice this clear-cut case is not attained, as there is in general an over-all veil or fog not accounted for by the exposure given. Developers differ much in their differential action. Only those developing agents and formulas are of general importance which are capable of a high degree of discrimination in their action.

In addition to the basic role of development just discussed, *i.e.*, the production of a visible image from the latent image, developing solutions are sometimes used which produce other effects at the same time. For some purposes it is desired to harden the gelatin of the emulsion locally where the silver is deposited. This has been accomplished commercially by the use of pyro developers with little or no sulphite. The resulting differentially hardened, gelatin layers have been used for various purposes, probably the most important of which is the production of relief images used as matrices for printing by dye-imbibition processes. A second supplementary effect sometimes sought and of growing importance is the deposit of a colored compound along with the silver image. Special developer formulas are in general required, but the resulting silver and dye images can be used for many purposes, and such dye images, with the silver removed, are of rapidly increasing importance in the processes of color photography.

CHEMICAL DEVELOPMENT

Inorganic Developers.—The history of photographic development has shown the use of a few inorganic chemical agents as developers. Prior to, and for a number of years after, 1851, ferrous oxalate was the common developer. This developer was prepared at the time of use, by adding one part of a 25 per cent solution of ferrous sulphate to three parts of a 25 per cent solution of neutral potassium oxalate, with constant stirring. The reddish mixture produced can be used without bromide as a developer.

Other inorganic agents suggested as developers include solutions of sulphurous acid which develop weakly and produce much fog. Copper ammonia oxalate and sodium, potassium, and hydrogen peroxides in alkaline solution have also been suggested.

An energetic inorganic developer which works without much fog, unless development is prolonged, is sodium hydrosulphite. A developing formula using such an agent has been recommended as follows:

Sodium hydrosulphite...	20 g.
Sodium bisulphite..	30 g.
Potassium bromide...	7 g.
Water to...	1 l.

Development time should not exceed 3 min.

While ferrous oxalate was still in use at the turn of the century, organic developing agents were fast replacing it, and today the use of inorganic compounds as photographic developers has practically disappeared.

Developers with Organic Reducers.—Experience has lead to a very definite basic pattern for developing formulas in common use. Following this pattern, modern developers consist of

Organic reducing agent or agents
Preservative
Accelerator
Restrainer

Compounds are also added for special purposes which do not fit in the four classifications given, and at times one compound functions in a dual role resulting in less compounds than the four classes listed. Instances of both types of variation will appear in the subsequent pages.

Organic Reducing Agents.—Chemically speaking, all developing agents are reducers, *i.e.*, they are themselves readily oxidized and hence tend to reduce compounds with which they come in contact. Considered without complete analysis of detail, the development process takes into solution the halide from the original silver halide and furnishes an electron to the positively charged silver ion, resulting in the deposit of metallic silver. The reactions in the solution which permit and complete the chain of changes eventuate in the oxidation of the developing agent and the accumulation of a halogen compound. Thus used developer contains oxidation products of the reducing agent and greater halide content than fresh solutions.

Not all reducing agents are developers. Many such compounds lack the power to discriminate between exposed and unexposed silver halide and thus lack that prime requisite of a photographic developer—the ability to transform a latent to a visible image.

While considering differentiations of this type, the role of the gelatin or other carrier of the silver halide should be mentioned. Silver halide precipitated from aqueous solution can be reduced by ordinary developers, independent of light exposure of any kind. Thus the characteristics normally associated with the latent image do not control such reactions even with reducers which are developing agents in the generally accepted sense of that term. It appears, therefore, that the gelatin or other carrier of the silver halide is of basic importance and plays a cooperative role in providing the conditions favorable to development of the latent image to a visible image, as distinct from indiscriminate reduction of the entire silver halide present.

In many cases, this differential action is primarily a rate or time effect. If permitted to act long enough, virtually all the silver halide will eventually be reduced. Normal developing conditions are designed to avoid such effects, but even within these regions there is a marked difference between the rate of development of fog and density resulting from exposure. Commonly the increase of exposure density with time is less rapid as development progresses. On the other hand, it is quite generally true that fog builds up more and more rapidly within corresponding limits of development times.

From these considerations, the developer appears in its true role as a differential reducer, acting preferentially to produce a visible image from an original latent image before the entire pattern is lost in fog.

In 1851 pyrogallol, or pyro, was discovered to be capable of developing the latent image. In 1880 the second organic compound to have developing action was discovered in hydroquinone. From then on the developing action of a large number of organic compounds has been recorded.

Generally speaking, it was observed that photographic developers were, to a large degree, the colorless or reduced forms of dyes or dye intermediates. A compound which would oxidize these compounds to their colored state would itself be reduced. Thus silver halide would oxidize pyrogallol to its yellow-brown oxidation product, and the silver halide would at the same time be reduced to metallic silver.

Almost without exception up to very recent times, all organic photographic developers have contained benzene as the nuclear structure. The structure of benzene is thought to be the ring

which is represented as

for the sake of simplicity.

By removing some of the hydrogen atoms, chemical radicals and groups can be substituted into the benezene nucleus. Thus phenol represents the substitution of one hydrogen in the ring by means of a hydroxyl (OH) group:

Phenol

This is also known as hydroxybenzene. Aniline represents the substitution of an amino (NH_2) group in the ring forming:

NH₂

Aminobenzene

All the organic developing agents in use today are derivatives of one of the above two basic agents.

The substitution of two hydrogen atoms by means of the hydroxyl group produces

1:4-Dihydroxybenzene (hydroquinone)

and the substitution of three hydrogen atoms of benzene by hydroxyl group produces

OH
OH
OH

1:2:3-Trihydroxybenzene (pyrogallol)

The relative positioning of the substituent groups and the kind of substituent has a decided influence on the relative activity of the agent as a photographic developer. Thus

OH
OH

1:3-Dihydroxybenzene (resorcinol)

is not a developer, while

OH
OH

1:2-Dihydroxybenzene (pyrocatechol or catechin)

is an energetic developer.

Developing agents belonging to the class in which the hydrogens of the benzene nucleus have been substituted by hydroxyl groups are known as "polyphenols."

One or two chlorine or bromine groups may also be substituted in the hydroquinone structure, yielding

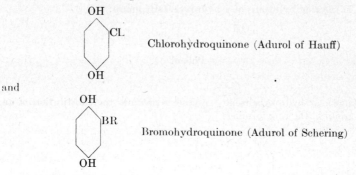

Chlorohydroquinone (Adurol of Hauff)

and

Bromohydroquinone (Adurol of Schering)

Another, and by far the largest, group of photographic developers are the "aminophenols" formed by substituting both hydroxyl (OH) and amino (NH₂) radicals into the benzene nucleus. The simplest and one of the oldest developers of this group is

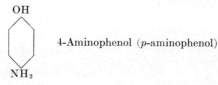

4-Aminophenol (*p*-aminophenol)

Since both hydrogens of the amino group and of the benzene nucleus of the aminophenols may be further substituted, a large number of derivatives of this basic member of the group are possible, thus

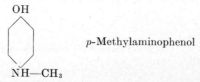

p-Methylaminophenol

is the base for metol which is usually sold in the form of sulphate salt.

One of the hydrogens of the amino group of *p*-aminophenol[1] may be substituted by the carboxymethyl group (—CH₂COOH) with the production of

---

[1] In organic chemistry the prefix letters *o*, *m*, and *p*, are used respectively for ortho-, meta-, and para- compounds. These prefixes indicate the position of the substituted atoms. The numbers from 1 to 6, in clockwise rotation beginning at the top are also used to indicate the position of the substitute atoms, groups, or side chains. Thus, when the substitution products of benzene have the substituent atoms, groups, or chains on adjacent carbon atoms, they are called "ortho-compounds," and the substituent atoms, or groups are said to be in the ortho or 1:2 position. When the substituent atoms or groups occupy the 1:3 position, the chain is called a "meta-compound." When the substituent atoms or groups occupy the 1:4 position, the chain is called a "para-compound." The following diagrams give the names, structures, and positions of xylene which was chosen for illustrative purposes.

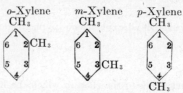

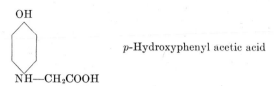

p-Hydroxyphenyl acetic acid

This developer is also known as *p*-hydroxyphenyl glycine, or shortened to "glycine."

Substitution of an amino and a hydroxyl group, para to each other, into benzyl alcohol or hydroxymethyl benzene, produces

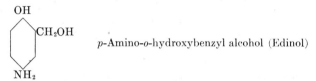

p-Amino-*o*-hydroxybenzyl alcohol (Edinol)

By substituting a methyl group in the benzene nucleus, methyl benzene or toluene is formed:

Further substitution by hydroxyl and amino groups produces

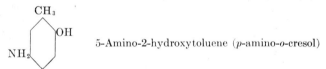

5-Amino-2-hydroxytoluene (*p*-amino-*o*-cresol)

This agent is credited as being the Monomet developing agent and also as one of the original metols.

The substitution of a single amino group in the benzene nucleus produces

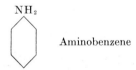

Aminobenzene

which is not a developer. While the substitution of a second amino group yields diaminobenzene, in which, if the substituted amino groups are opposite (para) to each other, the now well-known fine-grain developing agent

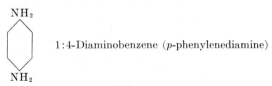

1:4-Diaminobenzene (*p*-phenylenediamine)

is produced. If the amino groups are located adjacent (ortho) to each other, the lesser known fine-grain developer

$$NH_2$$

NH_2   1:2-Diaminobenzene (*o*-phenylenediamine)

is formed.

Two amino and one hydroxyl group may be substituted into the benzene nucleus with the formation of

OH

NH_2   2:4-Diaminophenol

NH_2

which is marketed in the form of the hydrochloride salt as Amidol.

By substituting another benzene ring for one of the amino hydrogens of *p*-aminophenol, the *p*-hydroxydiphenylamine developers are formed:

H
|
—N—   OH

which were marketed as developers under the trade name of Duratol.

The product resulting from the substitution of a hydroxyphenyl group for one of the amino hydrogens of *p*-aminophenol, which is designated as

H
|
HO   —N—   OH   4:4'-Dihydroxydiphenylamine

appeared in the photographic developer market as Pyramidol.

Another class of developing agents is found in hydroxy-substituted benzidine or

H_2N   NH_2   4:4'-Diamino-*o*-hydroxydiphenyl

OH

which appears to be the Diphenal developer of prewar days.

Instead of the amino group, ring structures may be substituted for a nuclear hydrogen of phenol or aniline. Examples of these ring compounds include

H_2 H_2
C—C
O   NH   Morpholine
C—C
H_2 H_2

H_2 H_2
C—C
H_2C   NH   Piperidine
C—C
H_2 H_2

$$
\begin{array}{c}
\text{H}_2\ \text{H}_2 \\
\text{C}-\text{C} \\
\text{HN} \qquad\qquad \text{NH} \\
\text{C}-\text{C} \\
\text{H}_2\ \text{H}_2
\end{array}
\qquad \text{Piperazine}
$$

which yield the following developers:

$$
\begin{array}{c}
\text{H}_2\ \text{H}_2 \\
\text{C}-\text{C} \\
\text{O} \qquad\qquad \text{N}- \\
\text{C}-\text{C} \\
\text{H}_2\ \text{H}_2
\end{array}
\!\!\!\!\!\!\!\!\bigcirc\!\!-\text{OH}
\qquad \textit{p}\text{-Hydroxy-N-phenyl morpholine}
$$

$$
\begin{array}{c}
\text{H}_2\ \text{H}_2 \\
\text{C}-\text{C} \\
\text{H}_2\text{C} \qquad\qquad \text{N}- \\
\text{C}-\text{C} \\
\text{H}_2\ \text{H}_2
\end{array}
\!\!\!\!\!\!\!\!\bigcirc\!\!-\text{OH}
\qquad \textit{p}\text{-Hydroxy-N-phenyl piperidine}
$$

$$
\begin{array}{c}
\text{H}_2\ \text{H}_2 \\
\text{C}-\text{C} \\
\text{HN} \qquad\qquad \text{N}- \\
\text{C}-\text{C} \\
\text{H}_2\ \text{H}_2
\end{array}
\!\!\!\!\!\!\!\!\bigcirc\!\!-\text{OH}
\qquad \textit{p}\text{-Hydroxy-N-phenyl piperazine}
$$

With aniline, the corresponding *p*-amino-N-phenyl substitution products are formed, *viz.*,

$$
\begin{array}{c}
\text{H}_2\ \text{H}_2 \\
\text{C}-\text{C} \\
\text{O} \qquad\qquad \text{N}- \\
\text{C}-\text{C} \\
\text{H}_2\ \text{H}_2
\end{array}
\!\!\!\!\!\!\!\!\bigcirc\!\!-\text{NH}_2
\qquad \textit{p}\text{-Amino-N-phenyl morpholine, etc.}
$$

Instead of benzene as the nuclear ring, the naphthalene or double ring

may also be used as the basic nucleus, substitution into which yields another large class of developing agents.

As in the case of the benzene series, two hydrogen atoms must be substituted for by either hydroxyl or amino groups to make the substituted derivative a developing agent. Thus

α-naphthol

is not a developing agent, while

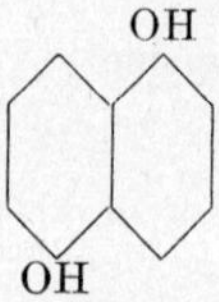

OH

1:5-Dihydroxynaphthalene

OH

is in the class of slow developing agents.

To increase their solubility, the sulphonic acid group, HSO_3 is introduced into the naphthalene structure.   Thus

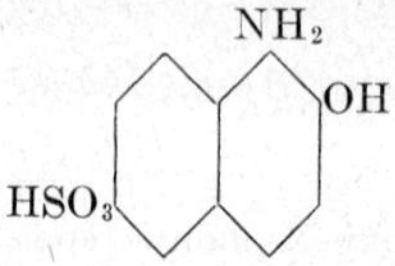

NH_2

OH

HSO_3 1-Amino-2-naphthol-6-sulphonic acid

is the well-known Eikonogen whose developing action is quite similar to pyrogallol while having the additional advantage of longer life than pyro.

The introduction of two amino groups, in conjunction with a solubilizing sulphonic acid group, into the naphthalene ring produces

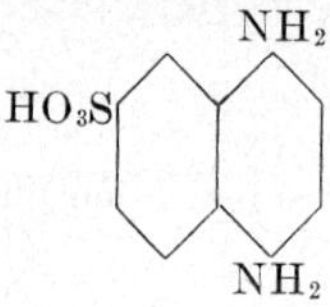

NH_2

HO_3S

1:4-Naphthalenediamine-7-sulphonic acid

NH_2

whose developing action is somewhat similar to the analogous p-phenylenediamine.

When one —CH— group of naphthalene is replaced by nitrogen, quinoline or its isomer, isoquinoline, is formed:

Quinoline   Isoquinoline
N   N

Further substitution of nuclear hydrogens of quinoline by hydroxyl or amino groups, or both, yields another class of photographic developing agents.   Thus

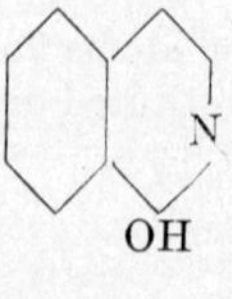

OH

N   1:4-Dihydroxyisoquinoline

OH

develops exposed silver halides to produce both metallic silver and the leuco form of an orange-red dye which can be converted to the colored form by mild oxidizing agents.

The developing action of the tetrahydroquinolines has long been known. An example of the earlier developers of this class is

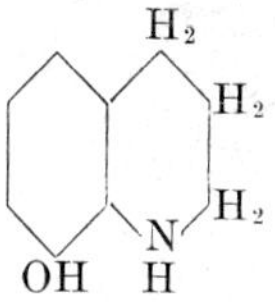

1,2,3,4-Tetrahydro-8-hydroxyquinoline

while recently the amino derivative

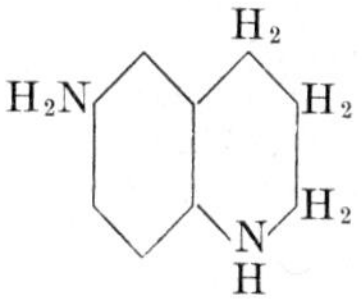

6 Amino-1,2,3,4-tetrahydroquinoline

has been suggested as a fine-grain developing agent.

Combinations of Developing Agents.—Various phenols, aminophenols and phenylenediamines have been combined to produce, for instance,

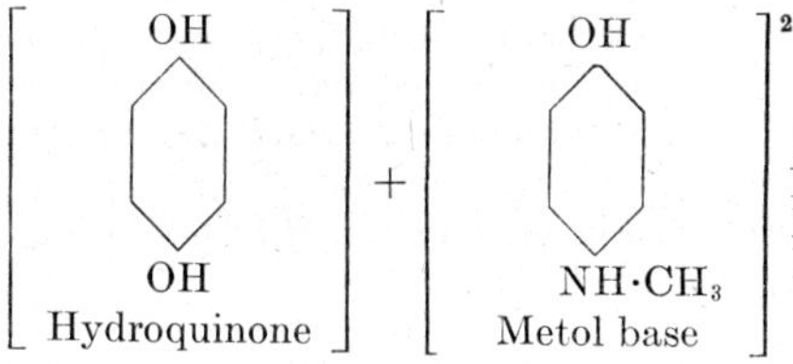

Metoquinone
Lumière and Seyewetz
F. P. 325,385, (1902)
B. P. 7163 (1903)

The combination of 1 mole of chlorohydroquinone with 2 moles of the base of metol

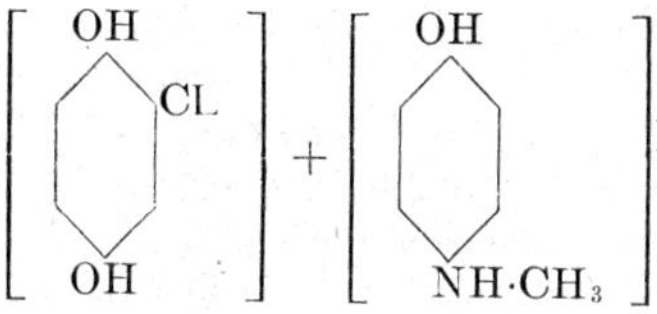

Lumiere and Jugla
B. P. 1795 (1914)

was known as Chloranol.

The product resulting from the combination of 1 mole each of *p*-phenylenediamine base and hydroquinone

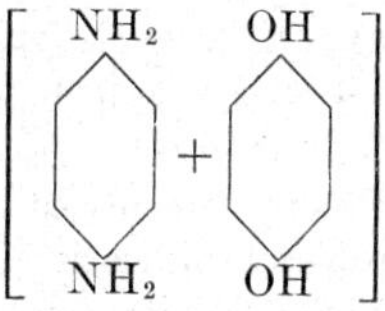

Hauff
B. P. 11,306 (1896)
Starnes
B. P. 466,626

appeared as the developing agent Hydramine.

Recently the combination of apparently pyrocatechol, 1 mole, and 1 mole of *p*-phenylenediamine base

$$\left[\overset{OH}{\underset{}{\bigcirc}}\!\!OH \;+\; \overset{NH_2}{\underset{NH_2}{\bigcirc}} \right] \begin{array}{l} \text{Hauff} \\ \text{B. P. 11,306 (1896)} \\ \text{Starnes} \\ \text{B. P. 466,626} \end{array}$$

has been introduced as the fine-grain developer Meritol.

One of the most popular developing agents of this type is the combination of 1 mole of hydroquinone with 2 moles of the sulphate salt of *o*-aminophenol:

$$\left[\underset{OH}{\overset{OH}{\bigcirc}} \;+\; \overset{OH}{\bigcirc}\!\!\underset{\dfrac{H_2SO_4}{2}}{\overset{NH\cdot CH_3}{+}} \right]^2 \begin{array}{l} \text{Hauff} \\ \text{B. P. 27,931} \\ \text{(1896)} \end{array}$$

which is marketed as Ortol.

Table I presents a number of the organic compounds which have been suggested as photographic developers. This list, while representative, is by no means complete.

While the tabulation indicates the large number of organic compounds which have at least been suggested as photographic developers, only a small percentage of these have been commercialized to the point of being given a trade name. Of the two or three dozen different agents which have appeared at one time or another on the photographic market, less than a dozen different developing agents are in common use today.

Of these agents which have remained in common use, it is interesting to note that two of them are the oldest of organic developers.

Pyrogallol.—The developing action of 1:2:3-trihydroxybenzene or pyrogallol (pyro), the oldest of organic developing agents, was observed in 1851 independently by V. Regnault and S. Archer. In its fresh state, it appears as a fine white crystalline powder and is extremely light. Owing to its tendency to float in the air at the slightest movement of air, the crystallized form is available which is more dense and causes less trouble in mixing than the older crystalline variety. The crystalline variety is also more stable against oxidation by the air. Pyro has a characteristic odor and is very soluble in alcohol, ether, water, and slightly soluble in warm benzene. The solubility in water and 10 per cent sodium sulphite solution, both at 15°C., is about 56 per cent.

Pyro is a soft working developer and, unless caustic hydroxides are used as the alkali, is slow acting. In addition to the metallic silver image produced by development with pyro, a secondary yellow-stain image comprising the oxidation products of pyro is produced *in situ* with the silver image. The combination of black silver with the yellow stain produces the brownish image associated with pyro development. Owing to the presence of the blue-absorbing yellow-image portion, pyro images are known to print somewhat more dense than they appear visually. Increasing the concentration of sulphite inhibits the formation of the stain image, and the developed image is neutral to blue-black in appearance.

To reduce the time of development and increase contrast, both metol and hydroquinone are used with pyro, particularly for deep tank work where the combination of pyro with metol only is ofttimes adopted. The keeping qualities of pyro developers are generally poor, being classed as 1 in which, to the same scale, metol is rated as 10 or highest. Crystallized pyro has appeared under the trade name Piral.

Hydroquinone.—In 1880, W. Abney discovered the developing action of the second oldest developer, hydroquinone, which is used to a greater extent than any of the other

TABLE I.—ORGANIC COMPOUNDS SUGGESTED FOR PHOTOGRAPHIC DEVELOPMENT

Compound	Discoverer	Date
Polyphenols		
Pyrogallol	von Regnault & S. Archer	1851
Hydroquinone	W. Abney (Eder, *Aus. Hndbh.*, 1903, 322)	1880
Pyrocatechol	Eder & Toth, *Phot. Korr.*, 1880, 191	1880
Chlorohydroquinone	Hauff, *Phot. Korr.*, 1897, 396	1897
Bromohydroquinone	Schering, D.R.P. 117,798	1897
2:3-Dichlorohydroquinone	Schering, D.R.P. 117,798	1897
2:3-Dibromohydroquinone	Schering, D.R.P. 117,798	1897
Toluhydroquinone		
Ethyl gallate	Lumière & Seyewetz, *B.J. Phot.*, 1897, 665	1897
1:4-Dihydroxy-2-acetophenone	Lumière & Seyewetz, *B.J. Phot.*, 1897, 665	1897
1:2:3-Trihydroxy-4-acetophenone	Lumière & Seyewetz, *B.J. Phot.*, 1897, 665	1897
1:2:6-Trihydroxy-4-benzophenone	Lumière & Seyewetz, *B.J. Phot.*, 1897, 665	1897
2:3:4-Trihydroxy-acetophenone	Lumière & Seyewetz, *B.J. Phot.*, 1897, 665	1897
1:2:6-Trihydroxyphenyl-4-phenyl-ketone	Lumière & Seyewetz, *B.J. Phot.*, 1897, 665	1897
Pyrogallol-dimethylaniline	Bayer, B.P. 10,721	1901
Pyrogallol-piperazine	Bayer, B.P. 10,721	1901
Pyrogallol-quinoline	Bayer, B.P. 10,721	1901
Pyrocatechol-dimethylamine	Bayer, B.P. 10,721	1901
Hydroquinone-triacetoamine	Bayer, B.P. 10,721	1901
Pyrogallol-methylether-monoglycollic acid	A.G.F.A., D.R.P. 155,568	1903
Pyrogallol-dimethylether-monoglycollic acid	A.G.F.A., D.R.P. 155,568	1903
Pyrogallol-1-monomethylether	Schultes, U.S.P. 2,017,295	1933
Pyrogallol-1-monoethylether	Schultes, U.S.P. 2,017,295	1933
Monethyl-pyrogallol	Stockelbach, U.S.P. 2,037,742	1934
Diethyl-pyrogallol	Stockelbach, U.S.P. 2,037,742	1934
Mono-tertiary butyl-pyrogallol	Stockelbach, U.S.P. 2,037,742	1934
2:5-Dimethyl-hydroquinone	K. & L. Schinzel, *Das Lichtbild*, Aus. 12/XI, 1936, 173	1936
2:5-Diethyl-hydroquinone	K. & L. Schinzel, *Das Lichtbild*, Aus. 12/XI, 1936, 173	1936
2:5-Diphenoxy-hydroquinone	K. & L. Schinzel, *Das Lichtbild*, Aus. 12/XI, 1936, 173	1936
2:5-Di-*p*-phenethyl-hydroquinone	K. & L. Schinzel, *Das Lichtbild*, Aus. 12/XI, 1936, 173	1936
2:5-Dibenzoylamino-hydroquinone	K. & L. Schinzel, *Das Lichtbild*, Aus. 12/XI, 1936, 173	1936
1:3-Dimethoxy-2-phenol	K. & L. Schinzel, *Das Lichtbild*, Aus. 12/XI, 1936, 173	1936
2:4:6-Trimethyl-1:3:5-Trihydroxybenzene	K. & L. Schinzel, *Das Lichtbild*, Aus. 12/XI, 1936, 173	1936
2:5-Diphenyl-3:6-dibenzyl-hydroquinone	Kodak-Schinzel, B.P. 498,869	1939
2:5-Diacetamino-hydroquinone	Kodak-Schinzel, B.P. 498,869	1939
Aminophenols		
4-Aminophenol	Andresen, *Farben-Industrie*, 1888, 187	1888
5-Amino-2-hydroxy toluene	Andresen, B.P. 1,736	1891
2:4-Diaminophenol	Andresen, D.R.P. 60,174	1891

TABLE I.—ORGANIC COMPOUNDS SUGGESTED FOR PHOTOGRAPHIC DEVELOPMENT
(*Continued*)

Compound	Discoverer	Date
Aminophenols.—(Continued)		
1:3-Diamino-4:6-dihydroxybenzene	Andresen, D.R.P. 60,174	1891
4-Methylaminophenol	Hauff, B.P. 15,434	1891
4-Dimethylaminophenol	Hauff, B.P. 15,434	1891
2-Amino-3-hydroxytoluene	Hauff, B.P. 15,434	1891
3-Amino-2-hydroxytoluene	Hauff, B.P. 15,434	1891
2-Hydroxy-3-amino-1:4-dimethyl benzene	Hauff, B.P. 15,434	1891
6-Methylamino-3-hydroxytoluene	Andresen, D.R.P. 60,174	1891
4-Hydroxyphenyl-amino-acetic acid	Bogisch, D.R.P. 75,505	1891
2-Hydroxyphenyl-amino-acetic acid	Hauff, B.P. 15,434	1891
2-Methylamino-3-hydroxytoluene	Hauff, B.P. 15,434	1891
3-Methylamino-2-hydroxytoluene	Hauff, B.P. 15,434	1891
3-Methylamino-2-hydroxybenzoic acid	Hauff, B.P. 15,434	1891
5-Amino-2-hydroxybenzyl alcohol	Hauff, B.P. 15,434	1891
4-Hydroxydiphenylamine	Hauff, B.P. 20,690	1891
3:5-Diamino-2-hydroxytoluene	Hauff, D.R.P. 74,842	1892
2-Aminophenol	Hauff, B.P. 27,931	1896
2-Methylaminophenol	Hauff, B.P. 27,931	1896
5-Chloro-2-methylaminophenol	Hauff, B.P. 27,931	1896
4-Chloro-2-methylaminophenol	Hauff, B.P. 27,931	1896
1-Hydroxy-4-phenylamino-acetamide	A.G.F.A., B.P. 9,537	1905
2-Hydroxy-3-amino-benzylamine	Einthorn, D.R.P. 167,572	1905
2-Benzyl-4-aminophenol	Schering, F.P. 382,367	1907
4:4'-Dihydroxydiphenylamine	Schering, F.P. 382,367	1907
2:4:6-Trimethyl-3-aminophenol	Homolka, *Phot. Korr.*, 1914, 256–8	1914
4-Aminocarvacrol	Lubs, *J. Ind. Eng. Chem.*, 1919, 455–6	1919
4-Toluolsulphonylaminophenol	Bucherer, D.R.P. 364,391	1922
4-Hydroxyethylamino-1-phenol	Reddelein & Müller, U.S.P. 1,758,892	1930
2-Hydroxyethylamino-1-phenol	Reddelein & Müller, U.S.P. 1,758,892	1930
3-Methyl-4-hydroxyethylamino-1-phenol	Reddelein & Müller, U.S.P. 1,799,568	1931
2-Chloro-4-hydroxyethylamino-1-phenol	Reddelein & Müller, U.S.P. 1,799,568	1931
4-Hydroxyethylamino-2amino-1-phenol	Reddelein & Müller, U.S.P. 1,853,455	1932
2-Dihydroxyethylamino-4amino-1-phenol	Reddelein & Müller, U.S.P. 1,853,455	1932
4-Hydroxyethylamino-2-acetamino-1-phenol	Reddelein & Müller, U.S.P. 1,853,455	1932
4-Hydroxy-N-phenyl morpholine	Reed, U.S.P. 1,937,844	1933
2-Hydroxy-N-phenyl morpholine	Reed, U.S.P. 1,937,844	1933
3-Methyl-4-hydroxy-N-phenyl morpholine	Reed, U.S.P. 1,937,844	1933
3-Methoxy-4-hydroxy-N-phenyl morpholine	Reed, U.S.P. 1,937,844	1933
3:4-Dihydroxy-N-phenyl morpholine	Reed, U.S.P. 1,937,844	1933
3-Amino-4-hydroxy-N-phenyl morpholine	Reed, U.S.P. 1,937,844	1933
1:4-Phenylene dimorpholine	Reed, U.S.P. 1,937,844	1933
4-Hydroxy-N-phenyl pyrrole	Reed, U.S.P. 1,937,844	1933
4-Hydroxy-N-phenyl tetrahydro pyrrole	Reed, U.S.P. 1,937,844	1933
4-Amino-N-phenyl morpholine	Reed, U.S.P. 1,937,844	1933
4-Amino-2-chlorophenol	Christiansen, *Jour. Am. Chem. Soc.* 45 (1923) 2193	1923
4-Hydroxy-N-phenyl thiomorpholine	Reed, U.S.P. 1,937,844	1933
4-Hydroxyphenyl-4'-toluidine	Trumbull, U.S.P. 1,969,243	1934
4-Hydroxyphenyl-2'-toluidine	Trumbull, U.S.P. 1,969,243	1934
4-Hydroxyphenyl-amisidine	Trumbull, U.S.P. 1,969,243	1934
4-Hydroxyphenyl-phenetidine	Trumbull, U.S.P. 1,969,243	1934
4-Chloro-2-methylamino-phenol	Schneider & Wilmanns, U.S.P. 2,060,594	1936
5-Chloro-2-methylamino-phenol	Schneider & Wilmanns, U.S.P. 2,060,594	1936

TABLE I.—ORGANIC COMPOUNDS SUGGESTED FOR PHOTOGRAPHIC DEVELOPMENT
(Continued)

Compound	Discoverer	Date
Aminophenols.—(Continued)		
4:6-Dichloro-2-methylaminophenol	Schneider & Wilmanns, U.S.P. 2,060,594	1936
4-Methyl-2-methylaminophenol	Schneider & Wilmanns, U.S.P. 2,060,595	1936
5-Methoxy-2-methylaminophenol	Schneider & Wilmanns, U.S.P. 2,060,595	1936
5-Dimethylamino-2-methylaminophenol	Schneider & Wilmanns, U.S.P. 2,060,596	1936
4-Amino-6-methyl-2-methylaminophenol	Schneider & Wilmanns, U.S.P. 2,060,596	1936
6-Amino-4-methyl-2-methylaminophenol	Schneider & Wilmanns, U.S.P. 2,060,596	1936
Polyamines		
1:4-Diaminobenzene	Andresen, D.R.P. 46,945	1888
2:5-Diaminotoluene	Andresen, D.R.P. 46,945	1888
4-Aminomethylaniline	Hauff, B.P. 15,434	1891
4-Aminodimethylaniline	Hauff, B.P. 15,434	1891
4-Aminoethylaniline	Hauff, B.P. 15,434	1891
4-Aminodiethylaniline	Hauff, B.P. 15,434	1891
4-Aminobutylaniline	Hauff, B.P. 15,434	1891
4-Amino-2-methyl-diethylaniline	Hauff, B.P. 15,434	1891
1:4-Dimethyl-2:5-diaminobenzene	Hauff, B.P. 15,434	1891
4-Amino-tetramethylaniline	Hauff, B.P. 15,434	1891
1:2:4-Triaminobenzene	A.G.F.A., B.P. 11,872	1893
1-Hydroxy-4:4'-diphenylamine	Cassela & Co., *Phot. Korr.*, 1897, 587	1897
1-Aminodimethyl-4-phenyl-aminoacetic acid	Hauff, B.P. 28,596	1897
1-Aminodiethyl-4-phenyl-aminoacetic acid	Hauff, B.P. 28,596	1897
1-Amino-4-phenyl-aminoacetic acid	Meister, Lucius & Bruning, (Eder, *Aus. Hndbh.*, 1903, 318)	1902
1:2-Diaminobenzene	Lumière & Seyewetz, *B.J. Phot.*, 1904, 866	1904
2:4-Diamino-diphenylamine	Schering, B.P. 20,050	1907
4:4'-Dihydroxy-diphenylamine	Schering, F.P. 382,367	1907
4:2':4'-Triamino-diphenylamine	Schering, F.P. 429,380	1910
4-Amino-4'-hydroxy-diphenylamine	Schering, F.P. 429,380	1910
4-Amino-4'-hydroxy-diphenylamine-2-sulphonic acid	Schering, F.P. 444,639	1911
4-Amino-dipropylaniline	Fischer, U.S.P. 1,102,028	1914
4-Amino-N-phenyl piperidine	Fischer, U.S.P. 1,102,028	1914
4-Amino-N-phenyl piperazine	Fischer, U.S.P. 1,102,028	1914
4-Amino-3-methyl-diethylaniline	Fischer U.S.P. 1,102,028	1914
3:4-Diamino-N-phenyl morpholine	Reed, U.S.P. 1,937,844	1933
1:4-Phenylene-dimorpholine	Reed, U.S.P. 1,937,844	1933
4-Amino-N-phenyl morpholine	Reed, U.S.P. 1,937,844	1933
3:4-Diamino-N-phenyl morpholine	Reed, U.S.P. 1,937,844	1933
2-Methyl-3:4-diamino-N-phenyl morpholine	Reed, U.S.P. 1,937,844	1933
4-Hydroxy-4'-dimethylaminodiphenylamine	Trumbull, U.S.P. 1,969,243	1934
2-Aminodiethylaniline	Kodak-Pathe, F.P. 804,472	1936
3-Bromo-4-aminodiethylaniline	Kodak-Pathe, F.P. 804,472	1936
2:5-Diamino-anisole	Kodak-Pathe, F.P. 804,472	1936
2-Amino-5-diethylamino-phenetole	Kodak-Pathe, F.P. 804,472	1936
N-Hydroxymethyl-4-aminoaniline	I.G. Farb., B.P. 460,580	1937

TABLE I.—ORGANIC COMPOUNDS SUGGESTED FOR PHOTOGRAPHIC DEVELOPMENT
(*Continued*)

Compound	Discoverer	Date
Polyamines.—(*Continued*)		
4-Amino-N-methylaniline-ω-sulphonic acid..........	I.G. Farb., B.P. 460,580	1937
4-Amino-N-ethylaniline-ω-sulphonic acid...........	I.G. Farb., B.P. 460,580	1937
4-Amino-N-benzylaniline-4′-sulphonic acid.........	I.G. Farb., B.P. 460,580	1937
4-Amino-N-diglycocoll-aniline....................	Taylor, B.P. 481,681	1938
Naphthalenes		
1-Amino-2-naphthol-6-sulphonic acid..............	Medola, *J. Chem. Soc.*, 1881, 39, 47.	1881
4-Amino-1-naphthol............................	Andresen, B.P. 5,207	1889
1:4-Dihydroxynaphthalene......................	Andresen, B.P. 5,207	1889
1:5-Dihydroxynaphthalene......................	Andresen, B.P. 5,207	1889
1:5-Dihydroxynaphthalene-6-sulphonic acid........	Andresen, B.P. 5,207	1889
1:2-Naphthalenediamine........................	Andresen, B.P. 5,207	1889
1:4-Naphthalenediamine-2-sulphonic acid..........	Andresen, B.P. 5,207	1889
1-Amino-2-naphthol-4-sulphonic acid..............	Andresen, B.P. 5,207	1889
1-Amino-2-naphthol-3:6-disulphonic acid..........	Andresen, B.P. 5,207	1889
2-Amino-1-naphthol-4-sulphonic acid.............	Andresen, B.P. 5,207	1889
3-Amino-2-naphthol-7-sulphonic acid..............	Andresen, B.P. 5,207	1889
2:3-Naphthylenediamine..	Andresen, B.P. 5,207	1889
1:4-Naphthylenediamine-7-sulphonic acid..........	Andresen, B.P. 5,207	1889
1:2-Diamino-8-naphthol-3:6-disulphonic acid.......	Andresen, B.P. 5,207	1889
1-Amino-methyl-4-naphthalenediamine............	Hauff, B.P. 15,434	1891
1-Diethyl-4-naphthalenediamine..................	Hauff, B.P. 15,434	1891
4-Methylamino-1-naphthol-6-sulphonic acid........	Hauff, B.P. 15,434	1891
1-Methylamino-4-hydroxy-2-naphthoic acid.........	Hauff, B.P. 15,434	1891
1-Amino-4-hydroxy-2-naphthoic acid..............	Hauff, B.P. 15,434	1891
1-Amino-2-hydroxy-3-naphthoic-4-sulphonic acid.....	Hauff, B.P. 15,434	1891
2:8-Diamino-1-naphthol-3:6-disulphonic acid.......	A.G.F.A., B.P. 21,595	1898
2:8-Diamino-1-naphthol-3:5-disulphonic acid.......	A.G.F.A., B.P. 21,595	1898
2:8-Diamino-1-naphthol-5-sulphonic acid...........	A.G.F.A., B.P. 21,595	1898
4-Methoxy-1-naphthol..........................	Homolka, D.R.P. 283,149	1914
4-Ethoxy-1-naphthol...........................	Homolka, D.R.P. 283,149	1914
4-Hydroxy-N-naphthyl morpholine...............	Reed, U.S.P. 1,937,844	1933
4-Hydroxyphenyl-1-naphthylamine...............	Trumbull, U.S.P. 1,969,243	1934
4-Hydroxyphenyl-2-naphthylamine...............	Trumbull, U.S.P. 1,969,243	1934
3-Phenylamino-1-naphthol........	Trumbull, U.S.P. 1,969,243	1934
4-Phenylamino-1-naphthol.......................	Trumbull, U.S.P. 1,969,243	1934
2-Phenyl-1:4-dihydroxynaphthalene...............	K. & L. Schinzel, *Das Lichtbild*, Aus. 12/XI, 1936, 173	1936
4-Benzoylamino-1:-4-dihydroxynaphthalene.........	K. & L. Schinzel, *Das Lichtbild*, Aus. 12/XI, 1936, 173	1936
4-Acetamino-1:2-dihydroxynaphthalene........... .	Kodak-Schinzel, B.P. 498,869	1939
2-Acetamino-3-chlor-1:4-dihydroxynaphthalene......	Kodak-Schinzel, B.P. 498,869	1939
2:8-Diacetamino-1:4-dihydroxynaphthalene.........	Kodak-Schinzel, B.P. 498,869	1939
Anthracenes		
1:2-Dihydroxyanthracene.......................	Kodak-Schinzel, Can. Pat. 380,527	1939
1:4-Dihydroxyanthracene.......................	Kodak-Schinzel, Can. Pat. 380,527	1939
1:2-Dihydroxyanthracene-monomethyl ether........	Kodak-Schinzel, Can. Pat. 380,527	1939
1:4-Dihydroxyanthracene-monoethyl ether..........	Kodak-Schinzel, Can. Pat. 380,537	1939

TABLE I.—ORGANIC COMPOUNDS SUGGESTED FOR PHOTOGRAPHIC DEVELOPMENT
(*Continued*)

Compound	Discoverer	Date
Heterocyclics		
o-Dihydroxyquinoline	Lumière & Seyewetz, (Eder, *Jahrbuch,* 1892, 93)	1892
p-Dihydroxyquinoline	Lumière & Seyewetz, (Eder, *Jahrbuch,* 1892, 93)	1892
o-Diaminoquinoline	Lumière & Seyewetz, (Eder, *Jahrbuch,* 1892, 93)	1892
p-Diaminoquinoline	Lumière & Seyewetz, (Eder, *Jahrbuch,* 1892, 93)	1892
o-Hydroxyhydromethyl-quinoline	Lembach & Schleicher, D.R.P. 89,181	1895
o-Hydroxyhydropropyl-quinoline	Lembach & Schleicher, D.R.P. 89,181	1895
o-Hydroxyhydroethyl-quinoline	Lembach & Schleicher, D.R.P. 89,181	1895
o-Hydroxyhydrobutyl-quinoline	Lembach & Schleicher, D.R.P. 89,181	1895
Tetrahydro-dihydroxyquinoline	A.G.F.A., B.P. 371	1896
Tetrahydro-ana-amino-*o*-hydroquinoline	A.G.F.A., B.P. 371	1896
Tetrahydro-*o*-hydroxyl-quinoline-ana-sulphonic acid.	A.G.F.A., B.P. 371	1896
o-Hydroxy-trihydromethyl-quinoline	A.G.F.A., B.P. 371	1896
o-Hydroxy-trihydroethyl-quinoline	A.G.F.A., B.P. 371	1896
o-Hydroxy-trihydropropyl-quinoline	A.G.F.A., B.P. 371	1896
o-Hydroxy-trihydrobenzyl-quinoline	A.G.F.A., B.P. 371	1896
o-Hydroxy-trihydrophenyl-quinoline	A.G.F.A., B.P. 371	1896
o-Hydroxy-trihydroacetyl-quinoline	A.G.F.A., B.P. 371	1896
o-Hydroxy-trihydrobenzoyl-quinoline	A.G.F.A., B.P. 371	1896
o-Hydroxy-trihydromethyl-quinoline carboxylic acid.	A.G.F.A., B.P. 371	1896
1-Phenyl-2:3-dimethyl-4-sulphamino-5-pyrazolone	Scheitlin, U.S.P. 930,091	1909
1-Ascorbinic acid (Vitamin C)	Mauer & Zapf, *Phot. Ind.,* 1935, 5, 90	1935
d-Ascorbinic acid (Isovitamin C)	Mauer & Zapf, *Phot. Ind.,* 1935, 5, 90	1935
1-Phenyl-3-methyl-4-amino-5-pyrazolone	I.G. Farb., B.P. 459,665	1937
1-*p*-Chlorophenyl-3-methyl-4-amino-5-pyrazolone	I.G. Farb., B.P. 459,665	1937
3-Amino-4-oxo-2-imino-tetrahydrothiophene	I.G. Farb., B.P. 459,665	1937
4:5-Diamino-2:6-dihydroxy-pyrimidine	I.G. Farb., B.P. 479,446	1938
6-Hydroxy-2:4:5-triamino-pyrimidine	I.G. Farb., B.P. 479,446	1938
2:4:5:6-Tetramino-pyrimidine	I.G. Farb., B.P. 479,446	1938
2:5-Diamino-4-methyl-pyrimidine	I.G. Farb., B.P. 479,446	1938
2:4:5-Trihydroxy-6-amino-pyrimidine	I.G. Farb., B.P. 479,446	1938
6-Amino-8-methoxy-1:2:3:4-tetrahydro-quinoline	I.G. Farb., B.P. 478,345	1938
Tetrahydro-quinoxaline	I.G. Farb., B.P. 478,345	1938
6-Amino-1:2:3:4-tetrahydro-quinaldine	I.G. Farb., B.P. 478,345	1938
6-Amino-8-methoxy-1:2:3:4-tetrahydro-quinaldine	I.G. Farb., B.P. 478,345	1938
5-Aminodihydro-2-methyl-indole	I.G. Farb., B.P. 478,345	1938
6-Amino-benzothiazoline	I.G. Farb., B.P. 478,345	1938
Aliphatic		
d-Aminoacetoacetic acid ethyl ester	I.G. Farb., U.S.P. 2,163,781	1937

photographic developers. Hydroquinone, as a devĕloper, is more understood than any other agent, but there still remains much doubt as to the exact nature of the reaction products of development caused when even this much-examined agent is used in a developer along with alkali, sulphite, and bromide.

1:4-Dihydroxybenzene, or hydroquinone (hydrochinone or quinol), is slightly soluble in cold water, very soluble in hot water, ether, and alcohol, and insoluble in benzene. Developing solutions of hydroquinone are practically inert at temperatures below 55°F.　The keeping quality is 3 or about one-third that of metol, according to Strauss.

In developing action hydroquinone is slow but tends to build strong contrasts. However, a minute trace of metol will accelerate the action of hydroquinone.　The dye safranine has also been observed to act as a catalytic agent in starting hydroquinone to develop.　On the other hand, hydroquinone is exceedingly sensitive to soluble bromides, producing high transparency in the slightly exposed areas, and for this reason is an excellent developer for line copy work where pure black and white are required.

Generally hydroquinone is used in combination with more active developing agents, usually metol.　When hydroquinone develops gelatino-silver halide emulsions, particularly if the sulphite concentration is a minimum, the oxidation products of the hydroquinone locally harden the gelatin wherever silver is produced.　Use has been made of this action to produce relief images which, being subsequently dyed, are used to transfer dye images in color photography.

p-Aminophenol.—In 1888 Andresen recommended *p*-aminophenol as a developing agent and thus opened the way to the largest class of developers, the aminophenols. A legion of derivatives of this basic agent have been suggested inasmuch as one of the amino hydrogens can be readily substituted by alkyl, aryl, and heterocyclic groups.

The free base of *p*-aminophenol is only sparingly soluble in water, soluble in alcohol, and insoluble in ether, while its sulphate, hydrochloride, oxalate, and tartrate salts are readily soluble in water.　The hydrochloride salt is soluble to the extent of 3 per cent in cold water (60°F.), but this solubility is reduced to 0.3 per cent in a 5 per cent sodium sulphite solution at the same temperature.　The stability of a *p*-aminophenol developer is 9, or almost as great as that of metol, according to the Strauss scale.　The various salts of *p*-aminophenol have appeared under the trade names: Citol, Diutall, Kodelen, Energol, Freedol, Indianol, Kathol, Para, and Unal.　The free base of *p*-aminophenol forms the active ingredient in the Rodinal type of developers.　Relatively large amounts of the salt dissolve in strong alkali, *e.g.*, sodium hydroxide, to form *p*-amino-sodium phenolate, which is the active developing ingredient of the *p*-aminophenol developers.　However, this compound is not very stable, so a small amount of the base itself is allowed to remain in the developer, thus acting as a preservative.　The following is typical of various methods suggested for the preparation of the Rodinal type of developer:

Dissolve 1 g. of potassium metabisulphite in 250 cc. of boiling hot water.　When dissolved, add 20 g. of *p*-aminophenol hydrochloride with constant stirring, and finally add 60 g. of potassium metabisulphite.　The mixture is stirred until all the metabisulphite has dissolved.　Then add, with constant stirring, 40 per cent sodium hydroxide solution until the mixture gradually becomes clear.　The addition of sodium hydroxide must be stopped just *before* the last trace of the cloudy precipitate disappears.　The solution is then made up to 400 cc. and stored in rubber-stoppered bottles.　For use the stock solution is diluted with 20 to 30 parts of water.　The high concentration of the stock solution is an advantage under some working conditions and, in fact, is the major advantage of this type of developer.　It has appeared also under the trade name of Azol, Activol, Artinal, and Paranol.

p-Aminophenol develops rapidly but does not build up great contrast and tends to produce less fog than most other rapid developers when development is carried out with warm solutions; for this reason, *p*-aminophenol is largely recommended for use in tropical countries or for warm weather use.

Metol.—In 1891, Bogisch observed the developing action of methylated-*p*-aminophenol and in that same year Hauff introduced metol as a developing agent.　The exact structural formula of the early metol is not certain and there is evidence to indicate that the first metol was *p*-methyl-amino-*m*-cresol. For a number of years now, however, metol has been considered to indicate the sulphate salt of *p*-methyl-aminophenol. This particular aminophenol salt has probably appeared under the guise of more different trade names than any other developing agent; a few of these trade names being Rhodol, Enol, Elon, Viterol, Scalol, Genol, and Satrapol.

Metol is soluble in water at 60°F. up to a concentration of 4.8 per cent and soluble to almost the same degree in 5 per cent sodium sulphite solution. It is insoluble in ether and alcohol, thus establishing one test of differentiation between it and *p*-aminophenol. The stability of metol, as a developer, is 10, the highest rating according to Strauss. Like *p*-aminophenol, metol is a soft-working developer but the combination with hydroquinone yields a developer which acts strongly on the weakly exposed portions and also builds strong contrasts. Thus, by varying the concentrations of these two agents, the metol working energetically even on the underexposed areas, with hydroquinone which favors the more exposed areas, developers can be compounded to take care of a wide range of desired results.

Metol will tolerate relatively large amounts of soluble bromide, in fact, metol developers tend to produce fog unless some bromide is included in the solution.

Glycine.—Instead of methylating one of the amino hydrogens of *p*-aminophenol, Bogisch, in 1891, substituted one of the amino hydrogens, by means of methyl carboxyl ($-CH_2COOH$), to form *p*-hydroxyphenyl aminoacetic acid or glycine.

Glycine is practically insoluble in water, alcohol, and ether; thus it is distinguished from the other commonly used developing agents. However, in a 5 per cent sodium sulphite solution at 60°F., glycine will dissolve to a concentration of almost 13 per cent by weight. As a developer it is slow acting but rather powerful. Its action resembles in many respects the characteristics of some metol-hydroquinone (MQ) developers. Even in the absence of soluble bromides glycine produces practically no fog. It yields fine-grained silver images and has been recommended for this type of development, either alone or in combinations, particularly with *p*-phenylenediamine. Glycine, above all other developers in use today, offers more resistance to oxidation by the air and thus is highly recommended for deep tank work. *p*-Hydroxyphenylglycine has also been marketed as Iconyl.

Amidol.—In the year 1891, Andresen introduced 2:4-diaminophenol as a developer, under the name Amidol. Amidol belongs to a rather small class of developing agents which can develop in the absence of alkalies; in fact, Amidol will develop in weak acidic solutions, but such development requires prolonged time. Amidol is soluble to concentrations of almost 16 per cent in water at 60°F., but only to 10 per cent in 5 per cent sodium sulphite solution at the same temperature. It is very slightly soluble in alcohol and insoluble in ether.

Amidol is the most energetic working developer in common use and is next to pyrogallol in its instability. It builds contrast slowly and tends to produce heavy fog when used in alkaline solutions. It will develop feebly in plain aqueous solution. Generally the alkalinity supplied by aqueous sodium sulphite is sufficient to cause Amidol to develop energetically, and the usual developers of this agent contain only Amidol and sodium sulphite and usually a small amount of potassium metabisulphite. It has sometimes been called the "teaspoon" developer since a teaspoon and a mixing vessel are the only measuring means required to mix the developing solution; the relative proportions of the developer being 1 part potassium metabisulphite, 4 parts sodium sulphite, 1 part Amidol, and 200 parts of water. Because of its instability, various agents have been recommended as preservatives, these include boric acid, glycollic acid, lactic acid, and tin chloride.

In 1888 Andresen described the developing action of *p*-diaminobenzene or *p*-phenylenediamine. Andresen found it necessary to use caustic alkali to obtain sufficient

TABLE II.—METHOD FOR IDENTIFICATION OF DEVELOPING AGENTS[1]

Developing agent	Water Solub.	Water Insolb.	Alcohol Solub.	Alcohol Insolb.	Ether Solub.	Ether Insolb.	Test 1 sodium carbonate	Test 2 Ammonium vanadate	Test 3 Potassium hydroxide	Test 4 Potassium ferricyanide + sodium carbonate	Confirmatory test
Glycine		+									
Hydroquinone	+		+		+		Yellow, changing to brown	O	Yellow, changing to brown	Gold-yellow, then brown	With test 7: dark green
Adurol	+		+		+		Yellow, changing to brown	O	Yellow, changing to brown	Green, then red-brown	With test 7: reddish brown
Pyrogallol	+		+		+		Yellow, changing to brown	Blue	Yellow, changing to brown	Brown	With 6: blue. Adding 1 there to: blue violet
Pyrocatechol	+		+		+		O	Violet	Green-brown	Green, then green-brown	With 6: green. Adding 1 there to red-violet
p-Aminophenol hydrochloride	+		+				O	Blue-green	Violet	Decolorized	With test 4 decolorized
Amidol	+		Slight				Blue	Red	Yellow-brown	With test 5 turns red	With test 5: red
Ortol	+		Slight				O	Brownish olive	Yellow	Red	With test 4: red.
Neol	Slight		Slight				Gray-white	Red-brown	O	Brown	With test 7: red
Metol	+			+		+	Yellow, changing to brown	Olive-green turning violet	Yellow-brown	Yellow-brown, then dark red-brown	With test 7: pale red
Edinol	+			+		+	O	Gradually violet	Yellow-brown	Bright-green, then blue-green	With test 7: violet.
Eikonogen	+			+		+	Yellow-green	Brown-red	Yellow-brown	Decolorized	With test 7: yellow.
p-Phenylenediamine-hydrochloride	+			+		+	O	Bright-green then olive-green	O	Green	With test 7: deep green

O. Indicates no change.

Test Legend

[1] H. PLAUMANN, *Phot. Ind.,* **34,** 341–342, April, 1931.
1. A few drops of 20 per cent sodium carbonate solution are added to the solution of developing agent.
2. The solution of developing agent is treated with one to two drops of 5 per cent ammonia vanadate solution.
3. A few drops of 5 per cent potassium hydroxide are added to agent.
4. The developing agent solution is first treated with 10 per cent potassium ferricyanide and then treated as in 1.
5. The developing agent solution is treated with only 10 per cent potassium ferricyanide.
6. 10 per cent ferrous sulphate added.
7. 2 per cent ferric chloride added.
NOTE: The developing-agent test solution comprises 50 cc. of 5 per cent aqueous solution of the agent.

gradation with *p*-phenylenediamine developers. In 1904 Lumière and Seyewetz recommended this agent as a substitute for physical development to produce fine-grain images particularly suitable for lantern slides because of the fineness of the deposit and the pleasing tone of the image.

p-Phenylenediamine base is slightly soluble in cold water and fairly soluble in 5 per cent sodium sulphite solution. The hydrochloride salt is soluble in water and insoluble in ether and alcohol. The dry developer exerts a rather toxic action on the human skin, particularly so in the case of persons who are allergic to its constituents.

The fine-grain characteristics of *p*-phenylenediamine developers, noted as early as 1904, have been widely applied in recent years for the development of miniature films. This particular characteristic is due, in part, to the fact that the developing energy of *p*-phenylenediamine is the least of those developing agents thus far evaluated by the reduction-potential method. The second probable cause for the fine-grain developing action of this developer is the solvent action exerted by the diamine on silver halides.

Owing to its weak developing energy, developing agents of more energetic action have been combined with *p*-phenylenediamine, either in the dry form or in the developing solution. These "booster" agents include: metol, Amidol, glycine, hydroquinone, and pyro.

Early in 1900, *p*-phenylenediamine was marketed in this country under the name of Metacarbol.

Method for Identification of Developing Agents.—The above developing agents and a number of those mentioned previously are included in the scheme for their identification, which was arranged by Plauman and given in Table II.

Reduction Potential and Velocity Constant.—The many compounds which have been found to be developers differ rather widely in their activity and power. It has proved difficult to compare them completely, since some will develop under conditions of temperature and alkalinity in which others are essentially inert, yet with change of conditions, the relative activity may change considerably. To bring a measure of order out of the complex situation, the concept of "reduction potential" has been introduced as one measure of developing power or activity. Reduction potential is measured by the ability of the reducer to overcome the restraining action of potassium bromide. With some developers, those of low reduction potential, there is produced a considerable reduction in density by the addition of a small standard quantity of bromide. With others of high reduction potential there is less density depression by a similar bromide addition. For purposes of numerical comparison, hydroquinone is assigned a value of 1 in the reduction-potential scale.

Table III gives the reduction potentials found for a number of developing agents.

Another property which seems closely allied to, but not identical with the reduction potential, is the rate of development, as represented by the "velocity constant" (see section on Development Quantitatively Considered). In general, reducers having high reduction potential also have high velocity constant, and, similarly, reducers of low reduction potential have low velocity constants. In spite of this, as a general trend, the literature indicates that small differences of reduction potential may not be represented by corresponding differences in velocity constant.

Preservative.—Reducers of the type described are readily oxidized by the air and provision must be made in the compounding and use of developing solutions to guard against deterioration through such aerial oxidation. The organic compounds in common use keep reasonably well in the dry state, but when damp or actually in solution, deterioration may become very rapid. Pyro shows the greatest rate of deterioration of the common reducers and consequently requires the greatest care, but suitable storage and mixing procedures must be provided for all the reducers.

Glass bottles tightly stoppered are suitable for storage of the dry powers when the quantities involved are suitable. Tin cans, lined with good-grade clean paper and taped to hinder the access of air and moisture, are also frequently used. Larger quantities of some reducers, e.g., hydroquinone, may be stored in strong cardboard containers where conditions are dry enough. The small user, wishing to preserve relatively small amounts will probably find the storage bottle best, and the large user will be guided by the shipping containers provided by the manufacturers.

TABLE III.—REDUCTION-POTENTIAL SERIES
(Nietz-Tschibissoff)

Ferrous oxalate	0.3
p-Phenylenediamine hydrochloride, no alkali	0.3
p-Phenylenediamine hydrochloride, plus alkali	0.4
Methyl-p-phenylenediamine hydrochloride, no alkali	0.7
Phenylhydrazine	<1.0
Hydroquinone	1.0
2-Hydroxyhydroquinone	>1.0
p-Hydroxyphenyl glycine (glycin)	1.6
Hydroxylamine	2.0
Toluhydroquinone	2.2
Methyl-p-phenylenediamine hydrochloride, plus alkali	3.5
Benzyl-p-aminophenol	<5.0
Dimethyl-p-phenylenediamine hydrochloride	5.0
p-Hydroxydiphenylamine	<6.0
p-Aminophenol	6.0
Chlorohydroquinone (Adurol-Hauff)	6.0–7.0
p-Amino-o-cresol	7.0
Dibromohydroquinone	8.0
p-Amino-m-cresol	9.0
Dimethyl-p-aminophenol sulphate	10.0
Dichlorohydroquinone	11.0
Pyrogallol	16.0
Methyl-p-aminophenol sulphate (metol)	20.0
Bromohydroquinone (Adurol-Schering)	21.0
p-Methylamino-o-cresol	23.0
2:4-Diaminophenol (Amidol) plus alkali	30–40
Thiocarbamide (Thiourea)	50.0

All developing formulas make provision for the preservation of the reducers, in solution, by presence of a compound or compounds as preservative. The most common and most universally used preservative is sodium sulphite. It also has other effects in the developer which will be noted later. The theoretical description of the action of sulphite as a preservative is not complete and unambiguous, but the fact of its activity remains. From an elementary point of view its activity is probably sufficient to consider it as a substance which itself may be oxidized to sodium sulphate and is preferentially oxidized with consequent preservation of the reducer. In most formulas the sulphite is present in three to ten times the concentration of the reducers, and this is probably vital to the prolonged life of the solution, but even small quantities of sulphite make relatively large differences to the initial rate of aerial oxidation of reducers.

In some formulas bisulphite or metabisulphite is used instead of the sulphite itself, but in alkaline solution the result is essentially the same.

The simple description just suggested of the preservative action of sulphite does not cover adequately all the facts, as hydroquinone, a developing agent, itself preserves a sulphite solution.

Experience has shown that the presence of two reducers in a developing formula frequently decreases the susceptibility of a developer to aerial oxidation. Metol preserves Amidol when used together in suitable formulas. Hydroquinone preserves metol particularly in metol-hydroquinone-borax formulas. Hydroquinone represents one of the most popular current cases of the preservative effect of the second reducer. Experiments have shown that the primary function of the hydroquinone in the formulas commonly compounded is that of preservative. Freshly mixed developer, lacking the hydroquinone, shows relatively little difference in its activity from the complete formula, but it is almost impossible to store it any length of time without a decrease in its activity, whereas the complete formulas keep reasonably well.

A few other preservatives have been suggested and tested but are far less important than sulphite. They include: acetone bisulphite; formaldehyde sodium sulphoxylate (known as Rongalite C); Mannitol; Sorbitol; lactic acid; stannous chloride; and glycollic acid. In a number of these cases, sulphite has been present also.

Other Effects of Sulphite Preservative.—While considered usually as a preservative, sulphite contributes greatly to the action of a developer in other ways. The usual photographic developing agents do not act so rapidly and energetically in the absence of sulphite as in its presence. Thus in spite of the fact that, as a reducing agent alone, sulphite cannot develop a photographic emulsion, it plays an important part in that development. In the brief description of the process of development given under Organic Reducing Agents, mention was made of the fact that one over-all effect of the development process is the increase of the halide content of the developing solution. That does not take place simply as an increase in the ion content of the solution and the sulphite is usually considered as the "halogen acceptor" which acts in the cooperative way required to balance the system. It has also been suggested that the sulphite itself can regenerate the original reducing agents from their oxidation products, while it is itself oxidized to the sulphate. With some reducers, the sulphite may form compounds which are more active as developers than the parent substances.

A second action of sulphite in a developing solution is its behavior as a silver halide solvent. It is relatively simple to demonstrate the existence of this effect by analytical means, though the action is not rapid and large like the solvent action of hypo. This solvent action has been suggested as a contributing cause of such fine-grain characteristics as the usual metol-hydroquinone-borax negative developers possess. The mechanism suggested for this action is this: The surface of the silver halide grains is dissolved by the relatively high sulphite content of these developers thus increasing slightly their separation and decreasing the chance of clumping during development. With the emulsions used on many printing papers, the sulphite content of the developer is of importance as it influences the tonal quality of the final print. The size of the particles making up the image is influenced by the solvent action of the sulphite, and the resultant deposit may be "cold" and blue-black in tone or "warm" and brown-black in tone.

Accelerator.—Experience has shown that developing agents increase in activity as the alkalinity increases. Thus the alkali in the developer has been termed the "accelerator." A considerable range of alkalies has been used in different photographic developing formulas. Their primary difference lies in the alkalinity produced, and there is little or no evidence of other or specific effect on the developer itself. Such specific action has been sought in the attempt to determine whether or not one alkali is better than another in results produced. Considering the complex nature of the reactions occuring, the possibility of such specific effects cannot be ruled out on theoretical grounds but must be the subject of careful experiments. As the result of such tests, the consensus is that the pH or alkalinity produced in the solution is the prime control factor affected by the alkali.

This statement is not to be construed to mean that the choice of alkali is of no significance, for there are various secondary effects of considerable importance. One of these is the stability of the solution. If a low alkalinity is desired, (pH but slightly greater than 7.0) it would be unwise to secure it by use of a small quantity of strong alkali such as sodium or potassium hydroxide because relatively small quantities of other chemicals, such as carbon dioxide from the air, could react with the hydroxide and change the pH considerably. It is better to secure the low alkalinity by higher concentration of weaker alkali. Of course, where high alkalinity, high pH, is desired, the stronger alkalies must be used, but sufficient concentration is then used to avoid rapid changes from introduction of small quantities of other agents. In some formulas the solutions are actually buffered in the chemical sense of that term, to insure maintenance of constant pH in the face of any factors which otherwise might normally be expected to affect it. In many other cases true buffering action is not obtained, but a concentration of alkali sufficient to prevent pH change from minor influences is used.

Ammonia is used as a developer alkali sometimes but its volatility militates against its use where stability in solution is necessary. Ammonia is a solvent for silver halides, particularly silver chloride, and this factor also limits its utility as an alkali. Its use in developers is not widespread, though occasionally special advantages have been claimed from it.

A second factor sometimes determining the choice of alkali is the effect of its introduction into the fixing bath. Sodium carbonate is the alkali most frequently used in developing formulas, but at times blisters are produced in emulsions when transferred from the alkaline developer to the acid fixer. This blistering is most apt to occur when the processing is being conducted at adversely high temperatures and is due to the formation of carbon dioxide bubbles from the reaction of the carbonate with the acid of the hypo. Borates, phosphates, and compounds of that nature do not form gaseous compounds under similar conditions and hence do not cause blistering. Boron compounds, particularly in the form of borate ions, have been used as additions to fixing baths to reduce sludging tendencies and increase the hardening life of the bath. Accordingly, the choice of borates as alkalies for developers is a particularly happy one, where suitable alkalinity can be obtained with them, not because of any specific effect of borates on development per se, but as an advantage to the fixing bath.

One specific combination used in so-called "buffered borax" formulas should be mentioned. That is the use of both borax and boric acid to secure the desired alkalinity. The pH of the bath can then be varied by varying the ratio of the two, giving good control of developer activity without resorting to low concentration for low pH. As borax alone does not give a very high pH, this combination cannot be used to secure rapid-acting contrasty formulas but is available for the slower softer ones frequently needed in development of negatives.

Sodium sulphite itself is weakly alkaline, and hence a developing formula as simple as sulphite and metol has been used upon occasion. It develops film but is rather quickly exhausted.

In addition to the direct effect on reducer activity, the pH of the solution markedly influences the swelling of the gelatin. Excessively high pH softens and swells the gelatin to the point of damaging it. Specially hardened emulsions are required where processing necessitates the use of the most extremely alkaline formulas. With ordinary emulsions this softening sets a limit to the alkalinity which may practically be used.

The pH of developing formulas cannot be judged accurately from the kind and quantity of alkali alone, but as a guide to the alkalinity which can be obtained with various alkalies, the following table has been prepared. Some of the compounds listed are not alkalies in the chemical definition of the term, but in solution with the other compounds, particularly sulphite, reactions take place producing the necessary alkalinity.

The dates given are those of the earliest literature reference found for this compound in photographic developers.

There are some other organic compounds representing addition products between other aldehydes and bisulphites which have been mentioned to produce the alkalinity needed in developers.

Before leaving the subject of alkalinity, one other specific effect should be mentioned, as it appears to have lead to some confusion. This is the effect on pH of the organic reducing agents themselves. Some of these compounds as handled commercially are in the form of salts which hydrolize in solution with resultant acid reaction on the solution as a whole. Metol is one particularly common example. If metol is added in increasing quantity to a typical borax developer formula, a point of

TABLE IV.—ALKALINE AGENTS FOR DEVELOPMENT

	Approximate pH for Typical Working Conditions
Sodium hydroxide	13.0
Potassium hydroxide	
Trisodium phosphate (1898)	12.0
Sodium carbonate	11.6
Ammonium hydroxide	10.7
Borax (1902)	9.2
Triethanolamine (1932)	10.1
Calgon (sodium hexametaphosphate and sodium phosphate (1936)	8.5
Acetone (1902)	
Acetone-bisulphite or sulphite (1902)	
Acetone-formaldehyde (1902)	
Lithium hydroxide	10.5
Sodium aminoacetate (Pinakol Salt) (1903)	
Sodium silicate (1902)	
Formaldehyde (1890)	
p-Formaldehyde (1890) or trioxymethylene	
Hexamethylenetetramine (1890)	
Formaldehyde-bisulphite compound (1890)	
Trimethylamine (1898)	10.0
Lithium carbamide (1904)	9.0
Sodium metasilicate (Metso) (1935)	8.5

maximum activity is quickly reached such that higher concentrations show less activity than the lower ones. When studied from the view of concentration alone, this behavior is anomalous, but when pH's are determined, it is found that the pH has dropped at the higher concentration, more than offsetting the increase of development rate to be expected from concentration. If now the same experiment is performed with the additional provision that the alkali be changed sufficiently to maintain constant pH, the result shows the typical increase of activity with concentration so frequently associated with chemical reactions.

Restrainer.—In an earlier paragraph it was emphasized that the ability of a reducer to reduce exposed silver halide as distinct from unexposed halide is of primary importance. This differential action is not alone a function of the reducer but is also affected by the other ingredients of the solution and by the conditions surrounding development as well as by the nature of the emulsion being developed. Of these various factors, the last-named, *i.e.*, the nature of the emulsion, is not within the scope of this chapter, but the other two (developer constitution and procedure) are here considered.

Experience shows that in the majority of formulas greater development differential is produced between exposed and unexposed silver halide when a restrainer is used. The most common chemical for this purpose is potassium bromide and, less commonly, chloride or iodide. A simple picture may be painted of the action of bromine ions as restrainers of development of a silver bromide emulsion. In this simple case it appears probable that the bromine ions in solution from the potassium bromide depresses the ionization of the minute quantities of silver bromide dissolving from the emulsion grains, thus reducing the rate of reaction, *i.e.*, the rate of production of photographic density. This simple picture gives no key to the magnitude of the effect nor does it give a basis upon which to predict whether or not development of image would be more or less affected than development of fog. Experience shows that in the majority of cases fog is restrained more effectually than image, thus increasing the differential nature of development.

A more complex situation exists in many practical cases as numerous emulsions consist of mixtures of at least two silver halides. Thus mixtures of silver bromide and iodide and of silver chloride and bromide are frequently encountered. In all such cases the chloride or the bromide predominates, as the iodide is never used commercially to a large extent. The simple picture presented in the previous paragraph is not adequate to describe completely the phenomenon, but the same sort of effects is produced, *i.e.*, fog is restrained more than image development.

When potassium iodide is used in the developer formula as a restrainer, the restraining effect is somewhat increased, as silver iodide is much less soluble than either silver bromide or chloride. Accordingly, when potassium iodide is used in a developer, smaller concentrations are used than of bromide.

Sometimes a combination of bromide and iodide is used in a developer, and some results of special interest have been achieved by properly proportioning the two compounds. When the developer is fresh, its action is restrained predominantly by the iodide and secondarily by the bromide. As the developer is used repeatedly, the iodide tends to replace the bromide in the emulsion passing through, owing to the extremely low solubility of the former. Thus the iodide content of the developer is reduced, while the bromide content is concurrently built up, and the reducers become less active through use. When correctly proportioned, the tendency to increase in activity owing to reduction of iodide content may be balanced against the decrease of activity due to accumulation of bromide and exhaustion of the reducers, with a resultant evening of developer activity throughout its life. In one such formula, designed for positive motion-picture film, the iodide was present only to the extent of $\frac{1}{40}$ g. per l., but this small quantity modified markedly the exhaustion characteristics of the bath in the manner indicated.

Little has been said of sodium or potassium chloride as a restrainer, for, while they have restraining properties, neither has received the sanction of widespread continued use accorded potassium bromide.

Restrainers of the type discussed are primarily intended to decrease inherent chemical or emulsion fog, *i.e.*, the fog developed spontaneously. When development is carried on under conditions such that the emulsion is permitted to come in contact with the air while wet with developer, a fog is sometimes caused which is known as "aerial" fog. This appears to be connected with the aerial oxidation of the developer chemicals. Many desensitizers tend to prevent its formation. Because of this, the suggestion has been made that this fog is due to chemiluminescence accompanying the oxidation of the reducing agent by the oxygen of the air. In most photographic processing an attempt is made to reduce to a minimum the exposure to the air of the emulsion while wet with developer. This is usually the simplest and cheapest way of avoiding such fog troubles. When this procedure is not sufficient, desensitizers may be used either in the developer or as a preliminary bath. A number of such compounds are known of which the most important are pinakryptol green, pinakryptol yellow, and phenosafranine.

Only small concentrations of these compounds are required, typical concentrations lying in the range from 1 part per 10,000 to 1 part per 100,000.

In addition to the inorganic restrainers and the organic desensitizers used for their respective effects in the control of fog, a number of organic antifogging compounds have been discovered. These compounds are not yet in common use in developers. They include

ANTIFOGGING COMPOUNDS
2-Mercaptobenziminazole
5-Nitrobenziminazole
6-Nitrobenziminazole
5-Chlorobenziminazole
6-Chlorobenziminazole
Aminobenzene
Thioacetanilide
Thioacetnaphthalide
Cysteine hydrochloride
Tetrazole
2,4-Thioketothiazolidine

These compounds are used in concentrations of 1 part in 10,000 to 1 part in 100,000. In general they delay the initial appearance of the image and prolong the development required.

Other Compounds Added to the Solution.—In addition to the four components typically found in developing solutions, many other substances have been added to secure special results. Some of these additional compounds will be considered here.

Methanol.—Methanol has been added to some solutions particularly those where a high concentration of reducer is desired, as it is frequently possible to maintain a higher concentration in solution with both methanol and water present than with water alone. The gelatin of the emulsion swells less when methanol is present in sufficient concentration than it does in the simple aqueous solution.

Sugar.—Sugar has been used to reduce the rate of diffusion of the developing solutions into the emulsion. Lower gamma may be obtained, and some have also felt that finer grain resulted from its use. There is little evidence that the grain is finer than would result from the lower gamma, *i.e.*, developed to the same gamma. There is little difference in graininess from the use of the sugar in the solution.

Citric Acid.—Citric acid is used as a clarifier. It tends to prevent precipitation of insoluble compounds from some types of hard water. Being an acid, its presence tends to reduce the pH, and hence it tends to reduce the rapidity of development. This requires its use in small amounts only.

Hardeners.—Various additions for developers have been suggested with a view to hardening the gelatin during development. These suggestions have included chrome alum, formaldehyde, and **para**-formaldehyde. Some success has been attained, but there is a definite general preference to separate the permanent hardening of gelatin from the developing bath. Very frequently this permanent hardening is provided by a hardening fixing bath. At other times it is provided by a hardening stop bath between development and fixation. Less commonly, it is obtained by use of a pre-bath before development. For such use, dilute formaldehyde solution may be used, but some workers have found undesirable fogging tendencies. This difficulty is by no means universal, and the method is applicable to some emulsions at least.

It is sometimes desirable to keep the swelling of the gelatin to a minimum during development, particularly when its permanent hardening is produced by either a stop or fixing bath. This need most frequently arises in processing emulsions under adversely high temperature conditions, and accordingly the term "tropical developer" is frequently used to designate a formula in which particular provision is made to avoid dangerous swelling even when processing at temperatures of 85°F. or over. Sodium sulphate is the usual addition to accomplish this result, as it reduces the swelling of the gelatin when present in relatively high concentration, 100 g. per l. or above. It tends to slow development somewhat, perhaps due to reduction of diffusion rate, but that is a rather small price to pay for the additional safety from damage by warm solutions. The sulphite of the developer itself has a similar tendency to restrain swelling of the gelatin, though it appears less marked. However, the quantity of sulphate required is less in the presence of high sulphite than with low sulphite concentrations. The protection afforded the emulsion by sulphate-sulphite combinations is not permanent, hence hardening baths designed to impart permanent hardening to the emulsion should be used after these "tropical developers."

Silver Halide Solvents.—The use of silver halide solvents has been proposed for a number of purposes, the most extreme of which is combined development and fixation. To secure this action a rather vigorous developer is required, as development must proceed in spite of the simultaneous fixation. In concentrated fixing solutions, fixation is often complete in 1 to 3 min. Such times are too short for development under these conditions, so low hypo concentrations are used to permit sufficient time for development. These methods, while possible, have not supplanted the use of developer and fixer separately and are rather rarely used.

When less drastic effects are sought weaker solvents may be used. The effect of the solvent action of sulphite was mentioned in the discussion of that chemical. Attempts have been made to secure fine grain by the addition of other weak silver halide solvents such as ammonium chloride and potassium thiocyanate. These have met with some success, but the presence of a silver halide solvent does not by itself insure fine-grain development.

Sometimes these silver halide solvents are used to modify the tone characteristics of the final image. This image is normally made up of finely divided silver which does not have any inherent color of its own but appears in tones of nearly neutral gray, as usually viewed. However, there is frequently a residual tone which depends upon the particle sizes from which the image is built up. Fine-grain deposits usually tend to show greater departures from neutral grays than coarser deposits, but the color of the deposit has not proved an accurate measure of graininess for coarse grains may be mixed with others fine enough to give a tone to the deposit. This discussion of image tone is given to suggest the probable mechanism of the action of silver halide solvents in affecting image tone. The image tone is not primarily important in negatives, though it has an effect there, as colored deposits frequently print as of greater contrast than their visual appearance or densities would indicate. It is primarily important in positives, paper prints, lantern slides, motion-picture prints, and the like.

In reversal work it is usually necessary to secure a pleasing tone in the final image, and silver halide solvents are sometimes used to improve the tone quality by changing it from a brownish-black to a neutral or blue-black quality. When used in the first developer of a reversal process, the solvent probably dissolves the extremely fine grains first. These grains are usually slow photographically and would otherwise remain to form part of the final image, thus giving foggy or plugged high lights and a brownish tone.

Blue-black Agents.—Other compounds have been found which affect the tone quality of the final image. Presumably this is through an effect on the aggregation of the silver of which the deposit is made.

"Blue-black" Agents
Quinine hydrochloride
Quinoline
Formocystine
5-Nitrobenziminazole
2, 4, 6-Trimethylphridine
Triazole
Benzotriazole
Iminazole
2-Methylbenzoxazole
2-Methylnaphthothiazole
Pseudo-thiohydantoin
Diphenyliodonium nitrate
Iodophenyl-phenyliodonium chloride

These blue-black agents are used in developers at concentrations around 1 part in 1000 to 1 part in 10,000. Like the antifogging agents, even a slight addition of these agents retards the initial appearance of the image and generally prolongs the time for complete development.

Additions for Fine-grain Development.—In the effort to secure fine grain many other compounds have been added to developers. Work of this kind is particularly difficult, as there is no universally accepted way of measuring graininess, and hours of painstaking work must go into the evaluation of any change. It is not surprising therefore to find disagreements between workers and even contradictory results in repeated tests under supposedly similar conditions.

Opposed to the careful and painstaking work done by some, there are many evidences of mysticism and wishful thinking in this phase of the literature of photography. To illustrate the wide range of additions which have been tried, the following list was prepared, covering additions suggested for *p*-phenylenediamine developers. This list is presented without any attempt at judgment of the value of the suggestion but only to show the range of materials.

Additions Suggested for Paraphenylenediamine Developers

Other reducing agents:

Metol
Hydroquinone
Pyrogallol
p-Aminophenol
Pyrocatechol
Rubinol (alkyl-substituted pyrogallol)
Resorcinol
Glycine

Alkali agents recommended:

Sodium carbonate
Lithium hydroxide
Disodium hydrogen phosphate
Trisodium phosphate
Ammonium hydroxide
Ammonium carbonate
Potassium carbonate

Sodium metaborate
Acetone

Miscellaneous agents recommended:

Sodium sulphate
Sodium bisulphite
Sodium nitrite
Sugar
Nickel chloride
Nickel ammonium sulphate
Benzoic acid
Boric acid
Salicylic acid
Tannic acid
Potassium bromide
Pinakryptol green
Isopropyl alcohol

Two-solution Development Processes.—In the discussion just concluded, developing formulas mixed as a single solution have been tacitly assumed. It is not necessary to so compound a developer, as the ingredients may be divided into two portions. In general the same compounds are used, and they fill the same roles in the development process, but the reducer and preservative may be used as one bath with the alkali as the other. When the bath is so divided, the emulsion is first soaked in one portion, then transferred to the other for actual development. Thus, if the emulsion is soaked in the reducer solution and then transferred to the alkali, only a limited amount of development is to be expected because of the limited quantity of reducer present in the emulsion. Successive transfers back and forth from one part to the other have also been suggested to secure and control the desired contrast, but none of these two-solution methods have yet been widely used. Adequate control of single solution baths has proved simpler.

Change Produced by Development.—Macroscopically the change produced by development is the formation of a visible silver image proportional, at least approximately, to the original latent image. Microscopically this consists of the reduction, *i.e.*, development, of silver halide grains. In general, except for fog, only those grains develop which have been rendered developable by exposure. Exceptions to this have been noted in the case of some grain clumps, where the whole group has developed from an original exposure of some one grain. The silver grains produced by development bear a general resemblance to the parent halide grain, but there is no longer the sharply crystalline structure of the original halide. Development appears to take place by the deposit of silver at one or more centers or nucleuses, spreading from these until the entire grain is developed.

Closely adjacent grains frequently appear to fuse and form clumps much larger than the individual grains in size. This clumping is one of the most important factors in the graininess of the final developed image, and it is through control of this factor that control of graininess is frequently sought. The use of sulphite and silver halide solvents in the reduction of graininess by separation of the individual graininess has already been mentioned in the discussion of their functions in developers. The specific effect of different reducing agents will be considered in the next section discussing fine-grain developers. In present-day emulsions, the largest grains have dimensions of only a few ten-thousandths of an inch, and if no element larger than this existed in the finished image, graininess would rarely be a trouble with current practices.

The distribution of developed grains within an emulsion layer is frequently far from uniform, though the layer is usually 0.001 in. or less in thickness. Variation of exposure with depth is one factor affecting this distribution, and variation of development with depth is another. This latter effect is probably less than the former, with formulas in common use, but separation of the two is difficult.

The thickness of the final dry developed emulsion layer often varies because of the removal of the bulk of the original silver halide in regions of low density and the retention of the silver grains in regions of high density. Thus the final surface may show a relief pattern due to the volume differences introduced by processing.

Fine-grain Developers.—The various efforts to produce fine-grain images center primarily around control of grain clumping during processing. This is not the only aspect of graininess, as three general phases are qualitatively recognized, though rarely quantitatively separated. In ascending order of unit size, they are:

1. The effect of the individual silver grains. These are usually but slightly larger than the elementary silver halide grains from which they were produced and consequently become visible only at the higher magnifications.

2. The effect of clumping of the particles. Some of the factors affecting this very important aspect of graininess have been mentioned, but they will be reviewed here to bring them together.

3. The effect of nonuniform distribution of clumps. This is, perhaps, the least definite of the effects.

Such separation into classes as has been practically attempted appears to be based upon some measure of magnification at which graininess disappears, or appears to match a standard graininess. At different levels of magnification the various effects become apparent. It is the second effect, clumping of grains, which appears as of greatest importance in current procedures.

In the discussions of sulphite and silver halide solvents in developers, it was pointed out that an effect on graininess was sought through solvent action on the surfaces of the grains which would tend to keep them separate and prevent clumping. This effect is suggested as the primary mode of action of the common borax developer formulas as fine-grain developers.

Much work has been done in the attempt to discover any specific fine-grain characteristics which may inhere in various reducers. These attempts have been quite generally unsuccessful, and no reducer has received wide credit as having fine-grain characteristics except paraphenylenediamine. This has been recognized for many years as having specific fine-grain characteristics. Two disadvantages have been found to its use. It produces a dermatitis on some skins, but this is not a very serious objection, since it is readily possible to avoid contact with the powder or the solution by careful handling and use of gloves if needed. The second is more serious. Paraphenylenediamine, used alone under conditions to produce minimum grain, does not produce such high effective emulsion speeds as some other developers, *e.g.*, the borax-type developers. Development times are rather long, and attempts have been made to obviate both disadvantages by use of additional compounds in the developer. The greatest success appears to have been obtained by the addition of glycine as a second reducer with the paraphenylenediamine. The rate of development is increased and the effective emulsion speed is higher with practically no change in graininess.

The extremely wide range of additions which have been tried with paraphenylenediamine was noted in an earlier paragraph.

Some success has attended the efforts to secure fine-grain results with other reducers. Various means of prolonging development have been tried. These have included dilution of developer and reductions of pH and in a few cases, finer grain has resulted. Greater success appears to have been obtained by the addition to developers of ammonium chloride in relatively high concentration. This was suggested in 1904[1] with concentrations of 150 to 200 g. per l. mentioned. The U. S. Pat. 2053515, issued in 1936, covers a fine-grain photographic developer comprising metol-hydroquinone as developing agent and ammonium chloride in amount sufficient to produce a fine-grain image.

In all attempts at fine-grain development, full advantage should be taken of all conditions tending toward that end. Some workers have concluded that fine grain is nothing but low gamma. This appears an oversimplification, but it is very generally true that low contrasts contribute to fine grain. Similarly, overexposure usually tends to increase graininess. Thus for minimum graininess negatives should be developed to as low a gamma as consistent with the work, and the exposure should be the minimum necessary to give the detail required.

Development Quantitatively Considered.—Quantitative studies of development have been made to establish a basis for its theoretical consideration and for the very practical purpose of control of processing. In using any new emulsion or developing formula, it is necessary to choose a developing time which, under the conditions of use, will give the contrast desired. Thus the quantitative study of development is of basic theoretical and practical interest. This study may be carried out through measurements of growth of either gamma or density as development proceeds.

When the study is based upon gamma, the attempt is made to determine the relationship between gamma and time of development. It is usually possible to express this relationship approximately through an expression of the form

$$\gamma = \gamma_\infty (1 - e^{-Kt}) \tag{1}$$

where γ = the gamma produced in the time t;

γ_∞ = the maximum gamma produced on prolonged development;

K = the velocity constant, so called.

Figure 1 shows this type of equation, represented by the solid line, plotted to approximate actual experimental data shown by 0's and the dotted line. It is at once evident that this does not fit exactly and, in general, regardless of values of γ_∞ and K chosen, only two points can be fitted. A noticeable difference between the two curves always occurs at low values of t as the equation shows finite values of γ at times shorter than that actually producing any measurable effects.

The period before any measurable development occurs is called the "induction period." It has no counterpart in the equation above, but a second, slightly different, equation takes account of it. The equation

$$\gamma = \gamma_\infty [1 - e^{-K(t-t_0)}] \tag{2}$$

may be made to fit three points of the experimental data and specifically allows for an induction period through the term t_0. This insures better fit than with the first equation; but it should be considered as only an empirical representation.

The equations just given approximate the relationship between γ and time of development. If, instead of γ, the progress of development of density for a given exposure is determined, the growth of density is found to be quite similar to the increase in gamma. In many cases, the family of sensitometric curves representing the results of different development times have straight-line portions which, when extrapolated, intersect in a point, called the tie point, which may be on or below but rarely is above the $D = 0$ axis. For the cases where a tie point exists and lies on the $D = 0$ axis, the growth of density of a point on the straight-line portion of the curve may be represented by equations of the same form as those used for the growth of

[1] Lumière, A., L. Lumière, and A. Seyewetz, *Brit. J. Phot.*, **51**, 866–867 (1904).

γ. Thus there are two equations,

$$D = D_{\infty}(1 - e^{-Kt})$$ (3)

and

$$D = D_{\infty}[1 - e^{-K(t-t_0)}]$$ (4)

corresponding to the two similar equations for γ.

Where a tie point exists but is depressed below the $D = 0$ axis, the equations may be written in the form

$$D = D_{\infty} - (D_{\infty} + D_0)e^{-Kt}$$ (5)

and

$$D = D_{\infty} - (D_{\infty} + D_0)e^{-K(t-t_0)}$$ (6)

where D_0 is the magnitude of the depression of the tie point, and, as usual, the consideration is limited to points on the straight-line portion of the sensitometric curve.

These equations are empirical in nature and difficulty will often be experienced in trying to apply them to too wide a range of developing conditions, particularly if emphasis is placed upon the very early stages of development.

In many cases the existence of a tie point is doubtful or definitely disproved. Under each conditions the similarity here apparent between γ and D equations will no longer remain.

The practical value of any of these equations lies in the ability to use them to interpolate or extrapolate from existing tests to other conditions. Thus, if we wish to develop a negative to $\gamma = 0.9$ and have tests showing the times required for, say, $\gamma = 0.7$ and $\gamma = 1.0$, interpolation is necessary to determine the correct time and may be done by the evaluation of the first γ equation. Of course, a worker who frequently meets such problems as this relatively simple case will very quickly learn to estimate correct times much more quickly than they can be calculated through the use of the equations. The importance of the mathematical methods increases as processing conditions are controlled more and more accurately, but for many amateur and commercial procedures, high precision in interpolations of the type indicated is nullified by poor technique and lack of the extreme care necessary to obtain reproducible results.

Considerable effort has been spent in the attempt to learn the true nature of the development process and to identify the various stages with corresponding constants in the equations. Thus the time of penetration of the developer into the emulsion, the invasion phase or induction period, is considered the counterpart of the t_0 of the equations.

Diffusion of the developer in, and of products of development out of, the emulsion must play an important part, and some efforts have been made to trace the course of development through these processes.

Adsorption theories of development have been advanced also, but none of these attempts to study the development process has yet supplanted the much simpler empirical relationships given above for practical interpretation of rate of development data.

A brief mathematical study of sensitometric curves and development data has recently been published,[1] based upon approximations designed to represent statistically emulsion conditions and development processes. The results obtained show unusually good agreement between calculated and observed values. The mathematical forms used depend upon many simplifying assumptions of a type which seem reasonable but for which little direct experimental evidence exists. Hence the final fit may be viewed

[1] ALBERSHEIM, W. J., *J. Soc. Motion Picture Engrs.*, **29**, 417–455 (1937).

either as evidence of the qualitative correctness of the assumptions or as the happy choice of equations having reasonably correct form and enough constants to permit a fit.

Bibliography

MATTHEWS, J. H., and F. E. BARMEIER: The Electro-potentials of Certain Photographic Developers and a Possible Explanation of Photographic Development, *Brit. J. Phot.*, **59,** 897 (1912).

SHEPPARD, S. E., and C. E. K. MEES: Some Points in Modern Chemical Theory and Their Bearing on Development, *Phot. J.*, **45,** 241 (1915).

HOMOLKA, B.: The Latent Image and Development, *Brit. J. Phot.*, **64,** 81 (1917).

NIETZ, A. H.: Theory of Development, *Phot. J.*, **60,** 280 (1920).

ERMEN, W. F. A.: Rodinal Type Developers, *Brit. J. Phot.*, **67,** 611 (1920).

SHEPPARD, S. E.: The Electrochemistry of Development, *Trans. Electrochem. Soc.*, **39,** 429 (1921).

DRUCE, J. G. F.: Stabilizing Solutions of Amidol, *Brit. J. Phot.*, **69,** 81 (1922).

WALL, E. J.: The Alkalis in Development, *Am. Phot.*, **16,** 481 (1922); *Brit. J. Phot.*, **69,** 634 (1922).

CRABTREE, J. I.: Photographic Methods of Testing Developers, *Am. Ann. Phot.*, p. 184 (1922).

SHEPPARD, S. E., and F. A. ELLIOTT: On the Theory of Development, *Trans. Faraday Soc.*, **19,** 355 (1923).

DUNDON, M., and J. I. CRABTREE: Fogging Properties of Developers, *Brit. J. Phot.*, **71,** 701, 719 (1924).

SHEPPARD, S. E., and F. A. ANDERSON: Equivalence of Sodium and Potassium Carbonates in Developers, *Brit. J. Phot.*, **72,** 232 (1925).

DAVIDSON, L. F.: Conditions Governing the Behavior of Silver Bromide Grain during Development, *Phot. J.*, **66,** 230 (1926).

VON HÜBL, Metol: Quinol Developer, *Phot. Rund.*, **63,** 481 (1926).

RABINOWITSCH, A. J.: The Mechanism of Development, *J. Phys.*, **5,** 232 (1934).

REINDERS, W., and M. C. F. BEUKERS: Metol-Hydroquinone Development, *Phot. J.*, **74,** 78 (1934).

WEINLAND, C. E.: Paraphenylenediamine—The Chemical, Camera (Phila), **49,** 145 (1934).

PANDALAI: Mechanism of Photographic Development, *J. Soc. Chem. Ind.*, **54,** 169T (1935).

LEHMANN, E., and E. TAUSCH: Chemistry of Metal-Quinol Development, *Phot. Korr.*, **71,** 17, 35 (1935).

DE LANGHE, J. E.: Theory of Photographic Developability, *Z. wiss. Phot.*, **35,** 201 (1936).

WILLCOCK, R. B.: Concentrated Phenolate Developers, *Brit. J. Phot.*, **83,** 256 (1936).

EVANS, R. M., and W. T. HANSON, JR.: Photographic Development and the Latent Image, *Phot. J.*, **77,** 497 (1937).

MURRAY, H. D.: A Theory of Photographic Development, *Phot. J.*, **77,** 388 (1937).

EVANS, R. M., and W. T. HANSON, JR.: Reduction Potential and Photographic Developers; The Effect of Sulphite in Developer Solutions, *J. Phys. Chem.*, **41,** 509 (1937).

CHAPTER XII

TECHNIQUE OF DEVELOPMENT

By D. R. White and J. R. Weber

The two most important physical factors which influence the rate and course of development are the temperature and the agitation of the solution. In addition to these principal factors there are others also, each of which plays its part, having a secondary influence on development. They include such factors as the position of the emulsion layer in the developing solution and the effect of adjacent areas.

Most of the mechanisms introduced in photographic development have for their object adequate control of temperature and agitation. Even when no special mechanical aids are used, it is still necessary to adequately control them to secure the results desired.

Control of Temperature and Effect of Variations.—In common with so many other chemical reactions, an increase of temperature increases the rate of development. The rate of increase of activity with increase of temperature is different for different developing agents. A characteristic, named the "temperature coefficient," has been used as the quantitative measure of the change of activity. This is defined as the ratio of the development times required to produce equal density at two temperatures differing by 10°C., which is, of course, a difference of 18°F. The values obtained range from 1.3 for metol alone, through 1.9 for pyro and metol-hydroquinone combinations, to 2.5 for glycine. In many charts and guides in practical use, the results are not expressed in the form of the temperature coefficient. Most frequently the tabulations are in the form of specific developing times for specific temperatures. In some cases, the subject is covered more broadly by giving developing time ratios or percentages such that, if correct time of development is known for one temperature, it may be calculated for other temperatures. These values do not always agree with the ones which may be calculated from the temperature coefficients given. This may indicate that the temperature coefficient is a function, not of the reducer alone, but of a specific formula. If this is true, the differences may be true ones, each applying to its own specific case. On the other hand, the practical tables rarely cover as wide a range as 18°F. (10°C.), and hence the differences found may be only differences in the precision of determination of the effect of temperature.

Table I gives the ratio of the developing time for temperature t to that at temperature 65°F., calculated on the basis of a temperature coefficient of 2.2.

These values, of course, cannot be in exact agreement with all the specific recommendations for specific formulas, but they are a fair approximation of the general trend of the recommendations for metol-hydroquinone and p-phenylenediamine developers and may therefore be used in varying times to compensate for temperature changes of such developers with reasonable certainty that the result will be satisfactory for practical purposes. If the work is extremely exacting, temperature variations should be avoided, or, if unavoidable, values fitting the specific conditions should be determined.

It is not universally agreed that change of time can compensate for all the changes introduced by change of temperature. This point is particularly strong in the con-

351

sideration of developers having more than one reducing agent, which will, in general, have unequal temperature coefficients. Here it appears probable that one reducing agent will be affected more than the other with consequent variation in the final result. For small variations from standard temperature, time compensation for temperature change may be used even in this case, though it may be impossible for large variations.

In view of all these factors, it is the best policy to hold developing temperatures to standard values where good reproducibility and uniform high quality are required. Many mechanisms and devices have been suggested to secure this desirable result under the extremely wide range of conditions and equipment encountered.

TABLE I.—DEVELOPING TIME AT VARIOUS TEMPERATURES

t	Time at temperature t / Time at temperature 65°F.
62	1.15
63	1.10
64	1.05
65	1.00
66	0.95
67	0.91
68	0.87
69	0.83
70	0.80
71	0.77
72	0.74
73	0.71
74	0.68

The most common device in use is a water bath. In small or improvised dark-rooms this may take the simple form of a large tray or tank filled with water of the desired temperature in which the developing tray or dish is set in such manner as to be as completely surrounded as possible. In more elaborate installations the same principle is used, but frequently the water in the bath is itself circulated, agitated, and thermostatically controlled to uniformly maintain the correct temperature.

In other systems, coils are used to secure the heat transfer from developer to thermostatically controlled systems as required to maintain uniform temperatures. This is most common in the largest installations, such as the motion-picture processing laboratories where jacketed tanks having the required capacity of several hundred gallons would be unnecessarily expensive.

The most common requirement of these systems is ability to cool the solution, for the desired developing temperature is often 65 or 68°F., either of which is below usual room temperatures in the common installations. Surprising as it may seem, members of the second Byrd Antarctic Expedition report that this cooling of developer was one of their difficult photographic problems while staying at Little America. Their water supply was melted snow, and, after melting and passing through the pipes in the rooms warmed for their habitation, cool water was at a premium. Where a supply of cool water is available, the simplest procedure is to cool the bath with a stream of it, as needed to maintain the desired temperature. The ability to use this means is seasonal in many places, and hence more elaborate means are often required, particularly under summer conditions.

With present-day perfection of small units of mechanical refrigeration, they have been quite generally introduced for the control of medium- to large-sized installations. The general scheme of control has to be fitted to the specific equipment, and accordingly the details will differ. Temperature changes during processing and washing are undesirable; hence it is usually desirable when making an installation of this type to provide for the control of all the processing baths and the wash water as well as of the developer itself.

Many professionals and most amateurs must work with less elaborate installations. The refinements of properly connected refrigeration with thermostatic control are things to dream about but not to use. Ice cubes from the refrigerator take the place of heat interchangers and thermostats. When cooling solution by such means, a water bath should be used, with the ice in the bath, not in the developer. Of course, it is somewhat quicker to cool with ice directly in the solution, but the dilution produced by the ice as it melts is an uncertain and undesirable quantity.

Water baths are occasionally cooled by the cooling effect of dissolving crystalline hypo. This is a hazardous method for photographic processes, as accidental splashes of the hypo solution can spoil the developer or make clear spots in the emulsion.

Influence of Agitation of Developing Solution.—The influence of agitation on the course of development can most readily be visualized by consideration of the development process as it actually takes place. The silver halide grains are embedded in a binding agent, usually gelatin, which hinders diffusion of chemicals to and from the solution. Thus, as development proceeds, there is a tendency for development products to collect locally and hinder development. At the surface of the gelatin layer in a region of high density there is a corresponding increase in concentration of development products due to diffusion from the layer when the body of the fluid is undisturbed. At a low-density region there is low concentration of these products as there has been little development. If now the solution is agitated, the development products adjacent to the gelatin layers will be washed away and evenly distributed through the body of the solution. This facilitates diffusion of fresh solution into the layer and development products out of the layer. In the region of high density a considerable increase of development is the result, but at the low density little change results. This nets an increase in γ, for agitated development.

Practically, it requires great care to secure reproducible agitation. Completely stagnant development is practically impossible due to the mechanical requirements of placing the film or plate in solution. Violent agitation is the other extreme, and it has proved more practical to secure uniformity of development through agitation than through either complete stagnation or specified intermediate agitation. This is probably due to the fact that development does not increase indefinitely as the rate of agitation increases but reaches a maximum or constant value, beyond which further increase in rate of stirring is no longer effective. A few cases have been noted where the most violent agitation tested even resulted in a decrease of development. No entirely satisfactory explanation of such a decrease of development with high agitation has yet been found, but the initial increase of development with rate of agitation is probably due to the difference in rapidity of removal of development products from the surface of the layer into the body of the liquid. The limit for this effect would appear to be that which would result from continuously supplying fresh developer to the emulsion surface.

One factor influencing results under conditions of low agitation is this: The products of development are usually of greater density than the developing solution and hence tend to sink under the influence of gravity. Accordingly it has sometimes been suggested that plates or films should be supported face down in the developing solution to secure optimum conditions for development; some mechanical devices have been made to do this, and at the same time create high-circulation velocities close to the emulsion surface. This procedure, carried to the limit by proper agitation, probably produces the maximum development which can be obtained from a given developer formula and film at any one temperature, since it appears that advantage is fully taken of all the physical factors affecting the result. This system is rarely used, as adequate results can usually be obtained by simpler means, a number of which are discussed on pages 354–357.

Stagnant Development.—As pointed out before, stagnant development is a limit rarely if ever attained, but in many practical cases agitation is so slight that it contributes little to the final result. Many classes of photographic materials are frequently developed by these methods. They include roll and cut films, radiographs, plates, and motion-picture film when handled on racks. Only the simplest mechanisms are required as the emulsion is merely supported, at rest, within the bath. The virtue of simplicity is marred by the fact that small residual effects interfere with the uniformity of the results. Unless the bath has just been thoroughly stirred, there are apt to be small thermal currents moving the developer enough to cause streaks. If the film or plate is put in quietly and smoothly, air bells are apt to be formed and cling to the emulsion, resulting in round white spots in exposed areas. Again, with such careful introduction of the film into the developer, clips and hangers are apt to leave marks from swirls and eddies which they cause in the solution. The introduction of a second film near one already partly developed may cause streaks on that for similar reasons. Vibrations of developing trays or tanks caused by machinery not associated with the processing at all may set up enough developer agitation to produce streaks and uneven development, particularly near holes in hangers or near clips holding films.

The best practice, when this general type of development is to be used, includes:

1. Thorough preliminary stirring of the developer to secure uniform conditions.

2. Thorough agitation of the film or plate when first introduced to dislodge air bells.

3. Avoidance of all conditions leading to local streaming or agitations of the developer.

Tray Developments. *Hand Agitation.*—Many systems and procedures have been devised to secure agitated development in the shallow trays used for so much photographic work. They range from the simple turning or moving of prints to elaborate, accurately timed rocking and brushing cycles.

In the simpler schemes the agitation is secured by more or less random handling of the films or prints. At times this is a definite program of moving the units from one place in the tray to another. Sometimes this is combined with tray tipping to secure greater agitation. With paper prints this is particularly practical, as the development is usually carried out by inspection, and minor variation in the time taken to come to the desired quality is not usually very serious.

This simple system is not adequate where accurately reproducible results are required. Accurate sensitometric testing necessitates the highest possible precision, and hence great efforts at development control have been made in sensitometric laboratories. Three classes of systems have been introduced to meet the requirements, differing in their mode of agitation. The three depend upon (1) rocked trays, (2) brushes, and (3) squeegees and agitator blades.

Rocked Trays.—In using rocked-tray development for sensitometric purposes, a definite, timed routine of rocking is usually set up. The trays used are customarily deeper than the usual developing trays to permit steeper angles and thus secure more violent washing effects as the developer sweeps across the emulsion surface. The films or plates, as needed, are laid or fastened in the tray to hold them mechanically. A typical cycle consists of tipping the tray to an angle of 30 to 45° in each of the four possible directions, completed three times each minute, thus giving very complete agitation, and renewal of the developer in contact with the emulsion surface. Attempts have been made to substitute mechanical rocking, for the hand system, but these have been unsuccessful owing to the rather peculiar difficulty that they were too regular. Certain preferred paths tended to appear, with resultant systematic streaking or unevenness. The slight irregularities of even the best hand systems appear to be enough to eliminate these, and hence net a better result.

The complete timed system is rarely applied to practical pictorial photography, but it is approximated in varying degrees. Tray rocking is sometimes accomplished by a shelf tipping with attached pendulum as driver, and sometimes by direct manual effort, but these are rarely carried to the extent frequently used for sensitometric testing.

Brushed Development and Roller Squeegees.—A second method for thorough and complete agitation of developer during tray development substitutes the brushing of the emulsion surface for the washing effect obtained by the tray-rocking procedures. For purposes of reproducibility this also requires a timed routine of operations. The brushing of the emulsion surface also introduces new hazards to the development. The brush must be soft to avoid scratching the emulsion. It may introduce foreign chemicals into the developer, as it is difficult to keep it thoroughly clean. These troubles are not insurmountable and brushed development is one of the best methods for securing uniform development within one development group. There is little or no evidence that the final comparisons between successive developments will be better than can be obtained by other means as that depends so greatly on other factors, such as the precision of timing, correctness of temperature, similarity of batches of developer used, condition of fixer, temperature of wash water, and drying conditions.

This method of developer agitation is little used except in work where greatest uniformity is required. This is much more commonly needed in scientific and sensitometric work than in pictorial work.

Allied to the brushing method is the use of velvet-covered roller squeegee, rolled over the emulsion surface. This replaces the sliding contact of the soft brush by the rolling contact of the soft squeegee. The hazards are very similar, and its use similarly limited.

Blade Squeegees. Windshield-wiper Methods.—Functionally the purposes of any of these agitation methods is to secure frequent and rapid change of the developer in contact with the emulsion. With this in mind, squeegees shaped like windshield-wiper blades have been used with the blade nearly, but not quite, in contact with the emulsion. As the blade is moved vigorously along, high turbulence is produced at the emulsion surface giving the uniform high agitation desired. In some cases the velocity of the moving blade has been made higher than the velocity of a wave in the tray of developer. The result was very uniform development, but the technique was hard on the surroundings, owing to splashing and slopping of the developer.

Mechanically, the guiding has been sometimes accomplished by setting the plate or film in a recess in the bottom of the tray and then using a solid blade, rolling or sliding over the recess which is made of such depth as to give small uniform clearance between the blade and the emulsion surface.

This system is also confined to work requiring a higher degree of development uniformity than usually needed for pictorial purposes.

Mechanical Agitation and Circulation Systems in Tank Development.—Aside from mechanical devices primarily intended to mechanize the systems just described, there have been many systems introduced to provide mechanically the agitation and circulation necessary for agitated development. The details depend upon the type of work being done, but in general they involve only a few basic elements. These are: (1) motion of the emulsion and its support through the developer; (2) low-velocity circulation, such as frequently associated with temperature-control systems; (3) high-velocity jets and circulation; (4) squeegees. These systems have been brought to their greatest technical perfection for work in and associated with the motion-picture industry, and consequently the details given primarily describe methods and practices found there. If the expense is warranted, these methods can be adapted to other photographic products, but the large amount of film processed, which is handled in long lengths, has resulted in specialized processing machinery not encountered in the other branches of photography.

Moving Film.—In mechanical handling of motion-picture film, one of the simplest and most obvious procedures is to secure agitation by the progress of the film through the solution. In fact, this agitation can only be avoided by rack and tank or various of the reel methods of developing film and is always present in any continuous developing machine. The development produced has its own peculiar characteristics when no other agitation is used. It is particularly subject to streaks, as unequal relative velocities are often set up with resultant nonuniform agitation across the film width. Development products tend to sweep back along the film, producing nonuniformity of development. This is particularly marked in the case of sensitometric tests, where the exposures progress systematically from one area to the next. In this case relatively large differences can exist depending upon the placing of the exposure on the film, low density or high density first. This sort of effect has lead to tacit standardization in developing sensitometric exposures in this type of equipment. By common consent the low density end is to lead in passing through the machine. With the random distribution of densities in pictures, this effect rarely takes that form, but sometimes there are trails of high or low density back of low- or high-density areas, respectively.

This limitation of the quality produced by the method is closely allied to the too regular agitation noted for mechanically rocked trays. Greater turbulence is usually required.

Low-velocity Circulation.—In addition to the agitation produced by the motion of film through the developer bath, it is well-nigh universal practice to add a circulation system which pumps the developer around through a feed or storage tank as well as through the developing tank proper. The velocities produced by this system are usually rather low, as its main purposes are control of temperature and use of a relatively large bulk of developer to insure uniform quality. In designing such systems, it is desirable to make the most of the agitation so set up and to adjust the system to try to break up the tendency to produce streaks due to the film motion itself.

High-velocity Jets.—The low-velocity circulation is better than none but cannot always be relied upon to eliminate streaks. As an extension of this basic idea, high-velocity jets have been introduced to scour the surface of the film and break up the streamline currents formed by the film motion. These jets are operated under the surface of the solution to avoid aerial oxidation, and in general must be close to the emulsion surface to secure the desired effect.

A variation of this idea, designed to develop plates or cut films uniformly has also been suggested and tested. The bottom of the developing tray can be made double, with small holes closely spaced drilled through the upper piece. A plate to be developed can be placed face down, supported a little above the tray bottom. Sufficient developer is used to adequately cover the plate and a pump is employed to make each hole direct a stream of developer against the emulsion surface. With some motion of the plate to avoid areas of high development corresponding to each jet, very uniform results were reported.

This, in conjunction with general circulation and film motion, is probably capable of the most uniform results commercially obtainable today.

Squeegees.—Various designs of squeegees have been tested in the attempt to produce uniform development under developing-machine conditions. Fixed soft squeegees may be placed directly or obliquely across the line of film travel in contact or nearly in contact with the emulsion surface. Thus they act as barriers to the developer set in motion by the film itself and reduce the tendency to streaked nonuniform development.

Good results have been reported with this system, but it has not been used commercially to the extent of the other systems mentioned.

Other Agitation Systems. *For Laboratory Use.*—In search for uniform reproducible development for test purposes a few other specialized devices have been developed. One of these for which the best results are claimed utilizes a relatively slow circulation for temperature control and a violent turbulence at the emulsion surface produced by blades moving close to, but not in contact with the emulsion surface. This mechanism is primarily designed for film, and arrangements are provided to hold the test strips rigidly and accurately to provide uniform clearance between the emulsion and the agitator blade. This blade is driven by a reciprocating mechanism, and the entire assembly is mounted in a thermostatically controlled bath. The film strips are vertical and the capacity is limited by practical rather than theoretical considerations.

The high degree of uniformity reported for an extended series of tests cannot be entirely due to this machine but must also be due to precision control of procedures at all other points in the test system.

In some test equipments the object is not entirely the attainment of highest theoretical perfection but is the simulation of commercial procedures, which, while they may be known to be lacking in some respects, may be the controlling objectives from a business viewpoint. Laboratory equipment designed to closely approximate commercial machine equipment (in which the chief agitation is due to film motion) has been designed, built, and used successfully. To bring this to a laboratory scale of size and yet not limit the linear speeds which can be used, the film is formed in a loop and driven around and around at any desired linear speed; no excessive bulks of solution are required, and the equipment can duplicate reasonably well many trade practices, yet be subject to the refinement of control needed for laboratory work.

Producing and Reproducing Results.—In a broad sense, there is no one standard universally applicable by which to judge correct development. In an artistic sense that development is right which gives the desired result regardless of custom, habits, and normal criteria. In technical or scientific work there are usually rather narrow limits within which results are accurate and satisfactory. In commercial operations there are often photographic steps which must be controlled within narrow practical tolerances to fit the photographic results to the needs of the other phases of the work. The motion-picture industry is the greatest commercial user of photographic materials, and great care must be exercised to maintain uniformity of development in order to permit the full artistry of the director, the cameraman, the actors, and the actresses to come through to the theater for the enjoyment of the public.

The final criterion of the success of all photographic development is the suitability of the resultant image for its intended purpose. The logical extension of this statement leads to the conclusion that the same emulsion may need to be developed different ways for different purposes. As a corollary, no development can be judged completely for its correctness without knowledge of the purpose which is to be served. When stated explicitly, these appear truisms, but failure to consider them in their logical relationships is rather common. The question "Is this developed correctly?" has no answer unsupported by other circumstance and condition. However, we live in a world such that few of us are pioneers, and, fortunately, it is not often necessary to start into uncharted seas of "correct" and "incorrect" development. In the early stages of any photographic experience criteria by which to judge correct development for the purposes involved are learned by necessity, to greater or less degree. This initial information is usually imparted along with some specific test or method by which to judge future developments.

Such methods may be divided into classes:

1. Inspection methods, with or without desensitization.
    a. Image nearly developed.
    b. Initial image appearance (Watkins factor).
2. Time-temperature methods (thermal system).
3. Sensitometric and test exposure control.

Inspection Methods.—Judging development by visual inspection of the image as it progresses and grows is one of the oldest procedures of the art of photography. It was particularly necessary with the handicaps of emulsion variations and nonuniformity under which the photographers of an earlier day labored. It is still an important method for practical work, though the burden of processing control is shared by other methods in many laboratories, particularly those using photography for scientific purposes and those handling large amounts of bulk work. Progress in manufacturing control of emulsion uniformity has been an extremely important factor in influencing this trend.

Two separate lines of attack have been pursued in the use of inspection methods for development control. In one system, known as the Watkins factorial method, development is based upon the experimental observation that for one emulsion and developer there is a constant ratio between the time to reach a given contrast and the time of appearance of the image. This may be restated in the form

$$\text{Time of development} = \text{time of appearance} \times \text{constant}$$

where the time of development refers to the development time for some contrast selected as suitable for the work and the time of appearance is the time between immersion of the emulsion in the developer and first appearance of the image. The constant is known as the Watkins factor and varies from emulsion to emulsion and from developer to developer. To operate this system adequately, the time of appearance of the developed image must be carefully determined. This is relatively easy with slow, noncolor-sensitized emulsions but becomes more difficult as the emulsion speed is increased. This fact tends to direct the use of the method toward the slower emulsions, such as the paper, lantern-slide, and slower negative emulsions.

The second and older line of inspection control is based upon judgment of the image as it approaches the density desired. It is subject to many of the limitations encountered in the Watkins system but has many exponents. Experience is required when changing from emulsion to emulsion, as the darkroom appearance of images depends upon the emulsion used and not upon its contrast and density alone. It is most readily applied to the slower emulsions where illumination levels may be higher than with high-speed emulsions. It is most valuable in the hands of a thoroughly experienced worker, where compensation in development is tolerable, and may lead to better final results than absolute uniformity of treatment.

Desensitization Methods.—Both of the methods enumerated above may be modified by the use of desensitizers with color-sensitized emulsions to permit more illumination in the darkroom and hence better inspection facilities. Many compounds have been found which have desensitizing action, but not all are suitable. Some produce fog and others leave the latent image in such condition as to be particularly subject to bleaching by darkroom lights used. Phenosafranine, pinakryptol green, and pinakryptol yellow are the most common desensitizers. They are not directly interchangeable, but any of them may be used in a separate bath prior to development. Some difficulty has been experienced in producing a stable developer with phenosafranine and hydroquinone in the same solution. No such trouble has been found with pinakryptol green, and this compound appears as the one of the three most available for use directly in the developer, as its presence was not found to influence the exhaustion life of the developer. Pinakryptol yellow is not suited to this use, as it is affected by the sulphite of the developer. A wide range of concentration has been used in the various experiments conducted. A concentration of 1 part in 20,000 is intermediate in this range and may be considered fairly representative. The action of a desensitizer is by no means instantaneous, and a minute or so must be allowed for its effect to occur.

The tests reported in the literature do not show clearly whether or not a desensitizer has a specific action on development. No large effects on contrast or emulsion speed are noted, where care has been exercised to avoid bleaching of the latent image by bright inspection lights.

The action of desensitizers is presented as destruction of color sensitivity of color-sensitized plates, and hence they are considered valueless with noncolor-sensitized emulsions. The literature of desensitizers is not increasing so rapidly as it did a few years ago, and this fact probably indicates a trend away from inspection methods of development control. Actually negative emulsion speeds have increased markedly and still appear to be on the increase as new products are manufactured and offered to the trade.

Time-temperature Methods.—The time-temperature method of development control, also known as the "thermal" system, is now widely recommended and used. Its success depends upon uniformity of emulsions and developer chemicals available to the photographer. Both factors are met through the present reliability and control in chemical industries. Basically the method is built on the thesis that, starting with a given emulsion and developer, control of the time factor will adequately govern development, and, accordingly, successive exposures may be developed to the same gamma by giving equal time of development. In many cases, compensation of development time is introduced to allow for variation of the developer temperature and for exhaustion and aging effects through repeated use. This, of course, requires considerable preliminary information and rather complete study of developer and development characteristics under practical conditions. Of course, it is not practical for any one organization to try to cover all the variations of amateur and commercial practice with all the widely different formulas available, but all the manufacturers in the United States are recognizing and encouraging the time-temperature system of development control by the development recommendation normally given, which takes the form of a recommended time at a certain temperature in a specified formula.

Of course, this method of development control is not the panacea of all the ills and troubles of development. In the discussion of agitation of developers, it was pointed out that even reproducible agitation is difficult to attain, and, correspondingly, specification of time and temperature alone is not complete. Some indication of agitation must be included to be complete. No adequate description of agitation is always possible, so the more exact phrasings of development recommendations usually include something to the effect that exact times for a given contrast would have to be determined by trials under the actual conditions to be used. For many purposes this exactness is unnecessary, and the recommendation may be followed directly with entirely satisfactory results.

Sensitometric and Test-exposure Control Methods.—In that section of the photographic industry where the greatest bulks are handled, the motion-picture laboratories, the development control is based upon standard test exposures of various kinds. Frequently the standard is a sensitometric exposure, and the development is controlled to produce a chosen gamma with the film going through at the time. Sometimes a picture, produced in standard manner is used instead of the sensitometric exposure. In this case the judgment is visual, to hold the picture quality to a satisfactory match of a more or less permanently fixed standard. In either case, development control is based upon the results with these standard exposures. In these large laboratories the customary procedure with developers for positive film is to maintain the developing bath at an essentially uniform level of activity by the use of buck-up or replacement solution as needed. The main bulk of developer is rarely changed. As temperatures are held uniform, there are two ways of varying development, variation of time and change of the rate of addition of make-up solution and overflow of spent developer.

With baths for processing the original negatives, the situation is somewhat different, as the developers are much less active and are more readily exhausted. The same basic methods, sensitometric tests and standard pictures may be used, but the baths are changed much more frequently. In general the footage of negative is much lower than that of positive, so the developing systems are not so large, and this procedure is more practical than it would be with positive film.

Such methods are applied much less frequently when photographic materials are processed in smaller quantities. The equipment to produce adequately standardized exposures tends to be rather expensive, and the methods previously outlined usually are relatively more attractive. On the other hand sensitometric study of development is almost necessary in the study of developing agents and formulas and in many of the scientific applications of photography, regardless of quantity of material handled.

Control Methods Chosen in Special Fields.—It will be of some value to consider the control methods chosen in some of the broad fields of photography, with some of the reasons for the specific choice.

Prints and Enlargements.—Prints and enlargements are typically developed on an inspection basis. The amount of inspecting done will depend somewhat upon the quantity and quality of work being done, being rather little in the cheaper amateur-finishing stations and much more in the careful printing done for exhibit work. Often, gross errors in printing exposure may be detected, when they occur, by watching the time of appearance of the image, as any large deviation from the normal will show at once an exposure error greater than tolerable for the quality of work being done.

Roll Films.—With multiple-exposure units, such as roll films, no development control of individual exposures has proved practical. Accordingly, either development based upon inspection of the entire roll, to try to get the best for the entire group, or time-temperature methods are most applicable. In many of the aids devised for handling the 35-mm. film used in miniature cameras, no provision is made for inspection, and hence time-temperature methods or, in the extreme case, trial exposures are practically forced upon the users.

Cut Films and Plates.—Cut films and plates are primarily single-exposure units and hence may be treated individually if necessary. Accordingly practices vary widely from place to place. Inspection methods are frequently used where suitable illumination is provided. The United States manufacturers of such products normally give their development recommendations in terms of formula and time-temperature processing, as that is about the only language by which to transfer development information from one place to another without sensitometric controls. Accordingly, many places handle their development on this basis. Sensitometric control of this work is rare.

Radiographs.—To the roentgenologist the photographic side of the process is only a tool to be used to his final ends. He is not interested primarily in the photographic side of the process, but needs uniform results from day to day. The darkrooms available are often lacking in space and conveniences necessary to an independent control of development uniformity. Hence, time-temperature methods and developer-exhaustion compensation charts find a wide use. Carefully carried out, these methods appear to give greater uniformity of results than inspection methods, though these are also widely used. Some difference of opinion exists as to the best method, and perhaps there is no general answer. After all is said and done, there is the question of retakes. and it may be best to make a fair quality radiograph by minor development compensation for an exposure variation, rather than to insist on hewing to the line of complete uniformity of development, let the retakes be what they may. This is not written in the spirit of condoning careless work, for pressure for quality is a continuous necessity. No major changes of development time from standard can be tolerated without being reflected in poor quality of some of the radiographs.

Motion-picture Film.—The commercial methods of control are largely based upon sensitometric and test-exposure control, as indicated before. Inspection methods are in use in some of the smaller units. If many scenes are on one roll, individual development treatment is manifestly impossible, but the roll may be treated as a unit to give the best average as judged by the experience of the worker.

Defects in Development.—Many defects in the final pictures are traceable to development difficulties. Some of these are similar to defects from other causes and accordingly both will be mentioned with an indication of some of the distinguishing characteristics.

White spots are produced by several different causes in processing, and, in addition to these troubles, they may be caused by lint or dirt on the original emulsion surface which frequently leaves enough of a shadow outline to be suggestive of the nature of the particle causing the difficulty. White spots in a print caused by black spots in the negative are usually readily identified by careful inspection of the negative.

Of the group traceable to processing, primarily development, the following are the most common:

Air Bells.—Air bells are often formed as the plate, film, or paper is placed in the developer. They take the form of small bubbles clinging to the emulsion surface and may stay throughout the entire time of development unless dislodged by mechanical means. They are more common in stagnant or weakly agitated developments, as thorough agitation supplies the forces necessary to dislodge them. When motion-picture film is developed by the rack and tank system, air bubbles are almost always formed on the lower bar of the rack and are very apt to remain there for it requires special care in agitating the rack to dislodge them. However, they may occur under many other conditions of development.

When the air bell is not dislodged, the developer can penetrate under it only by the relatively long path through the surrounding emulsion, thus effectively hindering development in a small usually circular area under the bubble. The bubble is usually dislodged in the fixer, and hence a small round clear area or white spot is formed.

Spots from Hypo Dust and Drops.—If a film is touched by splashes of hypo or by small particles of dry hypo clinging to the emulsion, local fixation can occur before development, with resultant clear areas. When the trouble is from a splash of hypo solution, the drop shape is often outlined by the fixed area. The area affected by this means may be large or small. Hypo dust settling on the emulsion surface may remain there to cause local fixation in its neighborhood. The cure is, of course, to prevent hypo reaching the emulsion surfaces. Some of the common practices leading to this sort of trouble include:

1. Carelessness in handling emulsions wet with fixer.
2. Carelessness in cleanliness of hands after contact with fixer.
3. Permitting drops of hypo to dry on tables or tank edges with subsequent possible transmission to the emulsion surface by direct contact or by draughts of air.
4. Permitting powder remaining from handling hypo at time of mixing fixer to reach the film.

Oil Spots.—When heavy enough, oil or grease deposits on the surface of the emulsion will prevent both development and fixation. Sometimes with lighter deposits, only development is effectively prevented but fixation occurs, leaving a clear spot in the emulsion layer. Under still other conditions, there may be a central, unfixed area outlined by a clear line where fixation but not development took place.

Of course, no one intends to let oil or grease come in contact with the emulsion surface, but it has been known to happen in many different cameras and darkrooms.

Spots from Desensitizing Particles.—Occasionally there are white spots due to desensitizing dust particles reaching the emulsion surface during manufacture. These are relatively much less frequent in occurrence than those from the causes noted.

Many black spots in prints and enlargements can be traced to white spots in the negative used. Black spots from other causes are not so common as white spots.

Pinhole Fog Areas.—Protecting paper covers, supposed to be light proof, sometimes have pinholes which produce local high fog areas. The cure is care in selecting material for such protecting covers, even when they may be considered only temporary.

Static Marks.—When handled rapidly, particularly under dry conditions, discharges of static electricity are sometimes produced which may leave many different types of marks. Some marks are easily recognized as branching or tree static, and some are less distinctive as more or less sharply defined black dots. In these cases, it is often difficult to distinguish these markings definitely from other possible causes of black spots.

Emulsion Aging.—Black spots are sometimes produced by aging of emulsions, particularly when in contact with paper and stored under conditions of high temperature and humidity.

Chemical Dust.—Many chemicals have been found which produce black spots in the final picture. All unnecessary contacts with dust, dirt, and chemical powders are to be avoided because of the danger from such contacts.

These causes of black spots are not all associated directly with development.

As distinct from spots, with their many sources, other than processing, streaks rarely have other cause than some processing irregularity, and most frequently this lies in development.

The retarding effect of products of development act in several different ways to cause streaks and irregularities of development.

Eberhard Effect or Mackie Line.—If a dark area is adjacent to one of less density, the products of development of the dense area diffuse out into the neighboring area and retard development more there than at points more distant from the high density. Thus the high-density area outlines itself with a line or band of reduced density. This effect is modified somewhat by the position of the emulsion layer during development. Thus, if the emulsion layer is horizontal in stagnant developer, a uniform effect all around the dense area is expected. On the other hand, if the emulsion layer is vertical, the effect may be more pronounced below dense areas than above, as the products of development are, in general, heavier than the original solution and hence tend to settle, affecting areas below the dense area more than above it. This may be traced as a streak an inch or so long under some conditions of development.

The effect of uniform motion of an emulsion layer, such as that produced in many motion-picture developing machines, has an effect very similar to that just outlined, except for the fact that in this case it is not gravity but the motion of the film through the viscous developer that tends to sweep development products back along the film and thus modify the development. For regularly arranged exposures, such as sensitometric test strips, this effect has been studied considerably, and considerable difference found at times. As a result, sensitometric exposures used in motion-picture laboratories are usually developed with the toe or low-density end leading.

These effects are most noticeable under conditions such that there is a large density difference between one area and its neighbor. They are less and less noticeable as the density difference diminishes and as the developer agitation is increased. The agitation evens out the development and makes it less subject to these local effects.

Irregularities of Agitation.—Uneven and irregular agitation can be produced in many ways. When the developer is nearly stagnant, small temperature differences may set up thermal currents sufficiently great to produce streaks.

As the agitation increases, disturbance due to this cause is less important, but regular lines of rapid and slow flow may be set up with resulting uneven development agitation. Holes in films and film hangers are a frequent contributing cause of streaks due to systematic differences in agitation. Such holes may produce local turbulence and agitation increasing development locally. An extreme case of this occurred when some motion-picture film was being developed in a "Stineman tank." This tank held the film in a spiral, wound on a form in a horizontal plane. The developer tray was set in a water bath for temperature control, and this bath was agitated by a stream of compressed air to insure uniformity of its own temperature. The resultant vibration of the developer in the tray was enough to cause streaks from each sprocket hole. These disappeared when the water bath was left completely stagnant during development or when sufficient agitation was introduced by rotating the reel holding the film to smooth out the unevenness due to the sprocket holes. Similarly, streaks on cut films, developed in one of the common styles of developing hanger, can sometimes be traced to the holes put in to lighten the frame and permit drainage of the solutions.

Reticulation.—At times under unfavorable conditions of processing, the gelatin, when it finally dries, is no longer smooth and even but is rough and presents an orange-peel type of surface and, in the more extreme cases, a cracked appearance. This condition is known as reticulation. It is usually caused by (1) solutions used at too high a temperature, (2) too sudden changes in temperature going from solution to solution, (3) too great changes of pH in going from solution to solution with consequent rapid change in swelling of gelatin, or (4) unsuitably warm and humid drying conditions. Care in selecting the working conditions and formulas to avoid the hazards noted and to secure favorable conditions should result in avoidance of this difficulty.

Formulas.—The choice of a suitable developing formula is an essential part of successful photographic work. Many different formulas may be found in the literature recommended for very similar uses, with few comprehensive comparative tests by which to judge their relative value. In the commercial field, when large bulks of chemicals are to be handled, it is often necessary to consider the initial cost and useful life more critically than necessary where the quantities in use are small. All these factors make the evaluation and complete comparison of all possible formulas much too broad and complex for fully detailed discussion. Accordingly, as a compromise between uncritical listing of all formulas suggested and too broad generalizations, the data are presented in the form of a limited number of typical formulas and tables indicating the range of concentrations of the various developer ingredients representative of developers of the specific type under discussion. Of necessity there has been a certain amount of arbitrariness in the selection of the individual formula listed as typical. This should not be construed as meaning that other formula are not good, but a complete presentation is, of course, impossible.

Developers for the Motion-picture Industry. *Borax Negative Developers.*—Borax developers are used quite generally in the motion-picture industry for development of picture negatives and variable-density sound-track negatives. The formula chosen depends upon the emulsion type, the contrast desired, the degree of agitation used, and the developing time considered desirable. The more concentrated and active

	No. 1		No. 2		No. 3		No. 4		Ranges	
	Metric	Avoirdupois	Metric	Avoirdupois	Metric	Avoirdupois	Metric	Avoirdupois	Metric	Avoirdupois
Sodium sulphite, anhydrous	90.0 g.	12 oz.	75.0 g.	10 oz.	100.0 g.	13 oz. 145 gr.	50.0 g.	6 oz. 290 gr.	60 –105 g.	8– 14 oz.
Rhodol (metol or Elon)	0.8 g.	47 gr.	2.5 g.	145 gr.	2.0 g.	115 gr.	0.40 g.	23 gr.	0.50– 3 g.	29 oz.–175 gr.
Hydroquinone	1.0 g.	58 gr.	3.0 g.	175 gr.	5.0 g.	290 gr.	2.25 g.	131 gr.	0.75– 5 g.	44–290 gr.
Borax	3.0 g.	174 gr.	5.0 g.	290 gr.	8.0 g.	1 oz. 29 gr.	1.25 g.	73 gr.	1.0 – 12 g.	58 gr.– 1.6 oz.
Boric acid					8.0 g.	1 oz. 29 gr.			0 – 12 g.	0– 1.6 oz.
Potassium bromide	0.1 g.	6 gr.							0 – 0.5 g.	0– 29 gr.
Citric acid							0.40 g.	23 gr.	0 – 0.5 g.	0– 29 gr.
Water to	1.0 l.	1 gal.	1.0 l.	1 gal.	1.0 l.	1 gal.	1.0 l.	1 gal.	1 l.	1 gal.

TABLE II.—BORAX NEGATIVE DEVELOPERS

formulas are used with stocks originally tending to low contrast and under conditions of low agitation. With greater agitation the activity is often reduced by reduction in concentration or alkalinity. The developer activity may be still further reduced when very low contrasts are desired with emulsions of high-contrast type. The typical example of this is the development of variable-density sound tracks recorded on positive motion-picture film.

The effective life of these formulas is usually rather short, as their activity drops rather rapidly with use from exhaustion of the reducers and accumulation of products of development.

This type of formula has also been applied to the development of other kinds of negatives and such developers have become generally used in both commercial and amateur negative developments. Several typical borax negative developers are given in Table II.

Developer 1 is a low-concentration borax type particularly applicable to agitated machine development for work in which low contrast is desired.

Developer 2 is more concentrated and consequently more active than 1. It may be used in machines where shorter developing times are desired. It may also be used with commercial and amateur negatives, particularly when nearly stagnant development is used.

Developer 3, as listed, has about the same activity as No. 2. If greater activity is desired, more borax and less boric acid may be used, keeping the total amount constant, and correspondingly, for less activity, the boric acid should be increased and the borax decreased.

Developer 4 is the least active of the group cited. It is used when lowest contrasts are desired, as in the case of variable-density sound tracks from records originally on motion-picture positive. This formula has the peculiar property of increasing in power to give contrast, as it stands after mixing and before use.

Carbonate Developers for High Contrast. *Positive.*—In the development of prints and variable-area sound-track records, developers are used which are much more active than the borax developers just listed. This activity is secured by greater concentration and higher alkalinity. The latter is probably the more important of the two factors.

Many considerations enter in the selection and use of such a formula. They include:

1. Ability to give desired gamma in an economically short time.
2. Freedom from fog and veiling tendency.
3. Suitability of formula for prolonged maintenance of constant developer activity by additions of buck-up solutions.
4. Freedom from tendency to stain.
5. Ability to produce pleasing tone quality in the prints.
6. Economy under conditions of use.

These limitations are more drastic than in the case of negative developers, as the bulk development in the industry is the development of the positive prints, and economy and uniformity of work are very necessary characteristics of the processing procedures.

In this case, as in other cases, greater activity, when desired, is secured by increase in alkalinity or in concentration or by decrease in bromide content. This last procedure is not completely independent from a control point of view, since bromide goes into the developer as a product of development, and hence developers which are used, as these are of necessity, have appreciable bromide content; adding solution or buck up is often mixed without bromide to keep the concentration down.

The alkalinity of the bath changes very little with use; consequently, most of the aging effects are due to the exhaustion of the reducer and accumulation of products of development.

Some silver in solution is usually found after the bath is old. This does not do direct harm so long as it stays in solution, but sometimes it appears to contribute to dichroic fog or stain.

Formulas producing the highest contrast are used for title work where extreme contrast is desired between the letter and the background. Economy often leads to developing such films in the same solution as the picture prints, but when a difference is made, it is in the direction indicated.

From elementary theory, variable-area sound records should also be developed to a maximum difference in density between exposed and unexposed areas. However, the advantage to be gained is often considered insufficient to warrant separate developing tanks and equipment.

Typical carbonate developers as used in this motion-picture industry are given in Table III.

Developer No. 5 is typical of the positive formulas in use in the motion-picture industry. Modifications are in use in some laboratories.

Developer No. 6 is more active than No. 5 and gives a higher contrast for the same developing time.

Replenishing solutions are usually made with the same concentration as the original but with all or part of the restrainer omitted, depending upon the balance sought under actual operating conditions.

Portrait and Commercial Work.—Through long years of work by many widely separated individuals there has grown up a wide range of favorite formulas in this class of work. It will not be possible to cover all the variations in this discussion.

Pyro-soda developers have been used for many years. They are most frequently prepared by making three stock solutions, mixing and diluting them as needed for use. The final developer oxidizes rapidly from contact with air and must be prepared just before use for best results. Contrast characteristics of the final solution may be controlled by the balance of the amounts of the three stock solutions used in the individual batch and by the dilution of the combination. Negatives with such developers usually have a characteristic pyro stain, tending to give them a distinct brownish tone. In extreme conditions this tone may be made heavy so that it will still remain after the silver is bleached out. Under ordinary conditions it is much less apparent, though it still plays a part in printing, tending to increase the effective printing contrast due to its brownish color more than it increases the visual appearance of contrast. One accustomed to using this type of negative is apt to be disappointed in results from a negative of similar visual quality made with developers not leaving this stain image, as the prints from the latter tend to be less contrasty. The difference is not such that it is possible to say that one is fundamentally better than the other type of negative as both yield good results in the hands of experienced users.

TABLE III.—CARBONATE DEVELOPERS: POSITIVE MOTION-PICTURE TYPE

	No. 5		No. 6		Range	
	Metric	Avoirdupois	Metric	Avoirdupois	Metric	Avoirdupois
Sodium sulphite (anhydrous)...........	40.0 g.	5 oz.145 gr.	60.0 g.	8.0 oz.	30 −75 g.	4 − 10 oz.
Rhodol (metol or Elon)............	0.31 g.	18 gr.	1.40 g.	88 gr.	0.30− 2.0 g.	18 −115 gr.
Hydroquinone........	6.00 g.	350 gr.	6.20 g.	390 gr.	4.0 − 7.5 g.	235 gr.− 1 oz.
Sodium carbonate (monohydrated)...	22.5 g.	3 oz.	56.0 g.	7 oz. 200 gr.	15 −60 g.	2 − 8 oz.
Potassium bromide...	0.86 g.	50 gr.	1.80 g.	112 gr.	0.50− 2.0 g.	29 −115 gr.
Potassium iodide....	......	....	......	....	0 − 0.025 g.	0 − 15 gr.
Citric acid..........	0.68 g.	40 gr.	......	....	0 − 1.0 g.	0 − 58 gr.
Potassium metabisulphite..........	1.50 g.	87 gr.	......	....	0 − 2.0 g.	0 −115 gr.
Water to...........	1 l.	1 gal.	1 l.	1 gal.	1 l.	1 gal.

No. 7 PYRO-SODA ABC FORMULA

STOCK SOLUTION A

Sodium bisulphite(or potassium metabisulphite)............	9.80 g.	1 oz. 130 gr.
Pyro...	60.0 g.	8 oz.
Potassium bromide.................................	1.10 g.	64 gr.
Water to make.....................................	1 l.	1 gal.

STOCK SOLUTION B

Sodium sulphite (anhydrous).........................	105 g.	13 oz.
Water to make......................................	1 l.	1 gal.

STOCK SOLUTION C

Sodium carbonate (monohydrated).....................	85 g.	10 oz.
Water to make......................................	1 l.	1 gal.

The dilutions and proportions usually recommended are 1 part each of solutions A, B, and C with 7 parts of water for tray development and 11 parts water for tank work. With many negative materials the developing times at 65°F. will then lie between 6 and 8 min. for the tray development and between 9 and 12 min. for the tank concentration.

The three-solution pyro-soda developer has been a favorite for years, but its instability after mixing is a marked disadvantage. A metol-pyro formula has been proposed to secure much greater stability. This also is prepared as three stock solutions.

No. 8 Metol-pyro Developer
Stock Solution, A

Metol..........	7.5 g.	1 oz.
Sodium bisulphite..........	7.5 g.	1 oz.
Pyro..........	30.0 g.	4 oz.
Potassium bromide..........	4.2 g.	245 gr.
Water to..........	1.0 l.	1 gal.

Stock Solution B

Sodium sulphite (anhydrous)..........	150 g.	20 oz.
Water to..........	1 l.	1 gal.

Stock Solution C

Sodium carbonate (monohydrated)..........	90.0 g.	12 oz.
Water to..........	1.0 l.	1 gal.

Control of the development characteristics may be exercised through the dilution used in making the developer from these stock solutions. One part of each, *A*, *B*, and *C* diluted with 8 parts of water for tray development and with 13 parts of water for tank development has been recommended. Developing times with normal negative materials will often lie between 7 to 9 min. at 65°F. for the tray developments and between 9 and 12 min. at 65°F. at the tank dilution.

Borax developers used in portrait and commercial work are the same type as the more concentrated of the formulas used for motion-picture negatives. The more dilute formulas may also be used, but under the conditions of low agitation usually encountered in this type of work the developing times become too long to be practical.

Metol, hydroquinone, carbonate developers are also used for these types of work. Great control of contrast characteristics can be obtained with these basic ingredients. Usually the rather soft working formulas are desired. These are obtained by using dilute formulas or lowering the pH by reduction in the carbonate or use of bisulphite as part of the preservative. The latter method is sometimes preferred when long life is desired, as the desired contrast characteristics can be thus combined with sufficient concentration to give good life.

Table IV.—Metol, Hydroquinone, Carbonate Developers

	No. 9		No. 10		Range	
	Metric	Avoir-dupois	Metric	Avoirdupois	Metric	Avoirdupois
Rhodol (metol or Elon)....	1.5 g.	88 gr.	1.0 g.	58 gr.	0.75– 1.5 g.	44 – 88 gr.
Sodium sulphite (anhydrous)...............	45.0 g.	6 oz.	15.0 g.	2 oz.	15.0 –45.0 g.	2 – 6 oz.
Sodium bisulphite..........	1.0 g.	58 gr.	......	....	0 – 4.0 g.	0 –232 gr.
Hydroquinone..........	3.0 g.	176 gr.	4.0 g.	232 gr.	1.0 – 4.0 g.	58 –232 gr.
Sodium carbonate (monohydrated).............	6.0 g.	350 gr.	26.5 g.	3 oz. 232 gr.	6.0 –30 g.	350 gr.– 4 oz.
Potassium bromide........	0.80 g.	47 gr.	0.60 g.	35 gr.	0.5 – 1.5 g.	29 – 87 gr.
Water to make..........	1.0 l.	1 gal.	1.0 l.	1 gal.	1 l.	1 gal.

Number 9 will give negatives of normal contrast on many negative emulsions in 5 to 7 min. at 65°F. for tray development. For tank use, this may be diluted with an equal quantity of water to obtain longer developing time, of the order of 14 min. at 65°F. If desired, this developer may be mixed double the indicated strength and diluted appropriately at the time of actual use.

Number 10 is a more active developer than No. 9. Developing times may be expected to be 4 to 6 min. at 65°F., tray development. The developer may be mixed double or triple strength as stock solution and diluted appropriately for use.

Formulas with glycine as the reducing agent are also proposed for some classes of work. They are not so commonly used as the others. One typical formula is

No. 11 Glycine Developer

Sodium sulphite, anhyd.	25 g.	3 oz. 145 gr.
Potassium carbonate.	50 g.	6 oz. 290 gr.
Glycine.	10 g.	1 oz. 145 gr.
Water to make.	1 l.	1 gal.

Number 11 may be expected to give normal development in 5 to 10 min. at 65°F. tray development. For slower tank development it may be diluted one part of developer and two parts water which will result in a development time of the order of 20 min. If desired, this developer may be mixed as stock solution at greater concentration, up to five times the concentration indicated, and then diluted appropriately before use.

Process Work.—In copying line drawings or printed matter an extremely high contrast between the lines and the background is desired. The emulsions made particularly for this work are of contrasty type, but, to make full use of them, contrasty developing formulas are usually required. This high-contrast characteristic is secured with metol-hydroquinone developers by using good concentrations of reducers and high enough alkalinity to secure rapid development. A relatively high potassium bromide content is common also, to secure freedom from fog with development times sufficient to come close to maximum possible contrasts.

Table V.—Process Developers

	No. 12		Range	
	Metric	Avoirdupois	Metric	Avoirdupois
Rhodol (metol or Elon)	1.0 g.	58 gr.	1.0– 5 g.	58–290 gr.
Sodium sulphite (anhydrous)	75.0 g.	10 oz.	37.5–75 g.	5–10 oz.
Hydroquinone	9.0 g.	1 oz. 87 gr.	6.0–10 g.	350 gr.–1 oz. 145 gr.
Sodium carbonate (monohydrated)	30.0 g.	4 oz.	22.5–45 g.	33–6 oz.
Potassium bromide	5.0 g.	290 gr.	3.0–12 g.	175 gr.–1 oz. 260 gr.
Water to	1. l.	1 gal.	1 l.	1 gal.

Number 12 may be expected to produce good contrast in 4 to 6 min. at 65°F. If less contrast is desired, one part of developer may be diluted with an equal quantity of water.

Where still greater developer activity is required to give maximum contrast in minimum time, carbonate is no longer used for the alkali, but soda is used in its place. High concentrations of both hydroquinone and bromide are typical.

The developer is usually prepared as two stock solutions, as it does not keep well after mixing. A typical formula is:

No. 13 High-contrast Process Developer

Solution A

Hydroquinone	22.5 g.	3 oz.
Sodium bisulphite	22.5 g.	3 oz.
Potassium bromide	22.5 g.	3 oz.
Water to make	1 l.	1 gal.

Solution B

Sodium hydroxide	52.5 g.	7 oz.
Water to make	1 l.	1 gal.

Solution A is usually made by taking 750 cc. (3 qt.) of warm water and dissolving the chemicals therein in the order given, then bringing to the volume indicated by the addition of cold water. Care must be exercised in making solution B, which should be mixed using cold water, as the solution of the hydroxide generates heat. For use, take equal volumes of the two solutions, and mix them just before use. The developing time is usually about 2 min. at 65°F.

Litho Developers.—The maximum contrast requirements are encountered in lithographic work where it is necessary to secure the maximum contrast between exposed and unexposed areas. This is necessary both for line and half-tone work. Special emulsions, formulas, and procedures are used to meet these needs, and some of the developing formulas used are quite different than those encountered elsewhere in photographic work. Both single-solution formulas and those mixed as two stock solutions are recommended.

TABLE VI.—LITHOGRAPHIC DEVELOPER

	No. 14		No. 15		Range	
	Metric	Avoirdupois	Metric	Avoirdupois	Metric	Avoirdupois
Hydroquinone..	30 g.	4 oz.	35.0 g.	4 oz. 290 gr.	6.0–37.5 g.	350 gr.– 5 oz.
Sodium sulphite (anhydrous)..	60 g.	8 oz.	55.0 g.	7 oz. 145 gr.	37.5–60 g.	5–8 oz.
Sodium hydroxide..........	25 g.	3 oz. 145 gr.	....	....	0 –25 g.	0– 3 oz. 145 gr.
Carbonate (monohydrated)	....	....	80.0 g.	10 oz. 290 gr.	0 –80 g.	0–10 oz. 290 gr.
Citric acid.....	....	....	5.5 g.	320 gr.	0 – 5.5 g.	0–320 gr.
Potassium bromide........	20 g.	2 oz. 290 gr.	10.0 g.	1 oz. 145 gr.	10 –20 g.	1 oz. 145 gr.– 2 oz. 290 gr.
Water to.......	1 l.	1 gal.	1 l.	1 gal.	1 l.	1 gal.

Number 14 is indicated as more active than No. 15. Development is expected to take about 1 min. at 70°F. for the former and toward $2\frac{1}{2}$ min. with the latter. The lower dilutions indicated under the "range" heading may be expected to produce less density.

One basic formula is recommended for preparation as two-stock solutions. Two different manufacturers recommend essentially the same formulas except that one suggests the addition of 20 cc. of phenosafranine solution (1:1000) to solution A.

No. 16 PARAFORMALDEHYDE DEVELOPER

SOLUTION A

Sodium sulphite (anhydrous).............................	1.0 g.	58 gr.
Paraformaldehyde.......................................	30.0 g.	4 oz.
Potassium metabisulphite................................	10.5 g.	1 oz. 175 gr.
Water to...	1 l.	1 gal.

SOLUTION B

Sodium sulphite (anhydrous)................................	120 g.	1 lb.
Boric acid (crystals)	30 g.	
Hydroquinone..	90 g.	12 oz.
Potassium bromide.......................................	6 g.	350 gr.
Water to..	3 l.	3 gal.

For use, mix one part of solution A and three parts of solution B. Development times of $1\frac{1}{2}$ to 3 min. may be expected at 65 to 70°F.

Commercial Development of Roll Films and Film Packs.—Under the conditions generally obtained in the commercial handling of amateur roll films, little individual attention can be given, particularly as the range of exposures on any one film is often so great that no one compensation of development could possibly be beneficial to all the pictures. Accordingly, there is a considerable tendency to use developer and development that will produce a good average out of the entire range of exposures. For very obvious commercial reasons, the development time should be moderate, as too short times would lead to difficulties in the control necessary for uniform quality, and prolonged development reduces the output. A long useful life is also necessary for satisfactory commercial work. A typical formula is:

No. 17 Roll Film Developer

Rhodol (metol or Elon)	0.75 g.		44 gr.
Sodium sulphite (anhydrous)	9.00 g.	1 oz.	87 gr.
Sodium bisulphite	9.00 g.	1 oz.	87 gr.
Hydroquinone	3.00 g.		175 gr.
Pyro	0.75 g.		44 gr
Sodium carbonate (monohydrated)	22.5 g.	3 oz.	
Water to	1 l.		1 gal.

With this formula, No. 17, normal development will take 7 to 14 min. at 65°F., depending upon the contrast desired and the films developed. The formula may be made somewhat more active by increasing the concentration of reducers.

Developers for Papers.—In choosing a developer for a printing paper, contrast and life characteristics are important, but attention must also be paid to the general tone of the final image. This tone can often be varied from cold tones, blacks and blue-blacks, to warm tones, brown-blacks, by choice of developer formula. The same formula frequently gives different tone quality on different papers. Hence no general rules for selection of developer formula can be laid down here. In general any factor which affects the grain-size distribution in the developed image will have an effect on its tone. Sometimes the addition of special compounds is suggested to give particular tone characteristics. These are presumably effective through an effect on the state of division of the silver particles making up the image.

The formulas recommended for different papers vary rather widely both in ratios of original constituents and in dilution. Most commonly they are metol, hydroquinone, carbonate developers. In many cases they are originally mixed as concentrated stock solutions, then diluted and used as needed.

Table VII.—Developers for Printing Papers

	No. 18		Range	
	Metric	Avoirdupois	Metric	Avoirdupois
Rhodol (metol or Elon)	1.2 g.	70 gr.	0.6– 1.5 g.	35– 87 gr.
Sodium sulphite (anhydrous)	19.0 g.	2 oz. 232 gr.	7.5–22.5 g.	1– 3 oz.
Hydroquinone	4.0 g.	232 gr.	2.0– 6.0 g.	115–350 gr
Sodium carbonate	26.0 g.	3 oz. 200 gr.	7.5–30.0 g.	1– 4 oz.
Potassium bromide	0.40 g.	23 gr.	0.3– 1.5 g.	17– 87 gr.
Water to make	1 l.	1 gal.	1 l.	1 gal.

It is strongly recommended that papers be developed in the formulas suggested by the manufacturers, as good print tone and contrast depend upon the use of a formula suited to the paper.

Fine-grain Developers.—Borax developers of the type discussed and listed for motion-picture negatives are considered fine-grain developers. The grain is not so fine as that which can be produced with some other types of formulas. As noted in the general discussion of fine-grain development, a wide range of additions to various basic types has been attempted, so much so that no attempt will be made to cover the entire range of constituents and concentrations. Another limitation to completeness in this case is the fact that for commercial reasons the formulas of some of the successful fine-grain developers have not been published.

The fact should be reiterated that overexposure and high values of gamma both tend, within normal limits of work, to increase graininess of the final result. Much of the value of fine-grain technique can be lost by inattention to such details of exposure and processing.

Paraphenylenediamine is the reducer around which has centered many of the attempts to produce particularly fine-grain images. Used with no other reducer in weakly alkaline solution, such as that produced by sulphite, the graininess is equal to or better than any other yet demonstrated. The effective emulsion speed is lower than with more active developers of the borax type. This speed loss has been obviated or reduced by the addition of a second reducer. Glycine has been used in this role in one series of formulas.

TABLE VIII.—PARAPHENYLENEDIAMINE DEVELOPERS

	No. 19		Range	
	Metric	Avoirdupois	Metric	Avoirdupois
Sodium sulphite (anhydrous)	90 g.	12 oz.	45–90 g.	6–12 oz.
p-Phenylenediamine (base)	10 g.	1 oz. 145 gr.	6–12 g.	350 gr.–1 oz. 260 gr.
Glycine	2 g.	115 gr.	0–12 g.	0–1 oz. 260 gr.
Water to	1 l.	1 gal.	1 l.	1 gal.

Developers for X Rays.—For normal development of X-ray films an active contrasty developer is desired. A rather concentrated developer is usually used to obtain the needed long-life characteristics, and this is accompanied with relatively high bromide content to keep fog down.

On occasion, X-ray developer has been used as a nearly universal developer in some laboratories, where it is the one developer always on hand. This practice is not to be

TABLE IX.—DEVELOPER FOR X-RAY FILM

	No. 20		Range	
	Metric	Avoirdupois	Metric	Avoirdupois
Rhodol (metol or Elon)	5.0 g.	290 gr.	2.0– 5.0 g.	117–290 gr.
Sodium sulphite (anhydrous)	60.0 g.	8 oz.	45.0–105 g.	6– 13 oz.
Hydroquinone	7.5 g.	1 oz.	7.5–10 g.	1– 1 oz. 145 gr.
Sodium carbonate (monohydrated)	50.0 g.	6 oz. 290 gr.	45 – 60 g.	6– 8 oz.
Potassium bromide	4.5 g.	260 gr.	4.0– 6.0 g.	232–350 gr.
Water to make	1 l.	1 gal.	1 l.	1 gal.

recommended as leading to best results, but the formulas are probably as near general applicability as any.

High-temperature Processing.—When processing is to be done under conditions such that it is impossible to keep the solutions from becoming warm, 80°F. or above, it is usually necessary to take special precautions to keep the gelatin from softening too much. Hardening agents may be used as prebath; ½ per cent formaldehyde solution may be used for this purpose.

A second method of meeting the situation is to use the developer loaded with chemicals which tend to reduce the swelling of gelatin. Sodium sulphate is most frequently used, though the sodium sulphite of the developer also tends to reduce swelling. Sodium sulphite concentrations in from 100 to 200 g. per l. protect the gelatin greatly in warm solutions. Developing times should be kept as short as possible, and development should be followed immediately by a hardening stop bath and good fixing bath with the shortest wash which will eliminate the hypo.

No. 21 For High Temperatures

Sodium sulphite (anhydrous)	50 g.	6 oz. 290 gr.
p-Aminophenol hydrochloride	7 g.	405 gr.
Sodium carbonate (monohydrated)	60 g.	8 oz.
Sodium sulphate (crystals)	100–200 g.	13.3–.26.6 oz.
Water to	1 l.	1 gal.

Development can be carried out up to 95°F. The development time varies with the sulphate concentration. Times of the order of 1½ min. may be expected with the lower concentration and of the order of 3 min. with the higher concentration indicated.

Reversal Development.—In reversal processing several special formulas have been worked out. The requirements are somewhat different than in direct development for other purposes. The first development of a reversal process must develop essentially all the silver which was rendered developable by the first exposure. In some cases a fog is intentionally developed to secure the desired characteristics from the emulsion in use. The characteristics above are often secured from the normal developer constituents, but in addition to these, weak silver halide solvents are sometimes introduced to (1) insure clear high lights or (2) reduce the tendency to brown tones. In both cases, the effectiveness of the procedure is at least in part due to the fact that the solubility of small grains is greater than of large. These small grains are in general slow, so they would be the ones least affected by first exposure and therefore most likely to remain to veil high lights on second development. These small grains are also the ones which would be expected to impart a brown tone to the final image. These effects are not large and startling and probably differ in importance with different emulsions, but the use of silver halide solvents in reversal development has been important in some cases. The silver halide solvents used vary from hypo itself as a very active solvent to potassium thiocyanate as a weak solvent.

No. 22 Reversal First Developer

Sodium sulphite (anhydrous)	50 g.	6 oz. 290 gr.
Rhodol (metol or Elon)	1 g.	58 gr.
Hydroquinone	8 g.	1 oz. 29 gr.
Sodium carbonate (monohydrated)	35 g.	4 oz. 290 gr.
Potassium bromide	5 g.	290 gr.
Potassium thiocyanate	9 g.	1 oz. 115 gr.
Water to	1 l.	1 gal.

Development times may be expected to lie in the range from 5 to 8 min. at 65°F. All steps of exposure and reversal processing have to fit together closely to form a complete reversal system designed to conform to the individual stock processed, hence no very exact figures can be given in this rather general discussion.

Rapid Processing.—All the formulas considered so far for materials other than papers have been designed for developing times of a number of minutes. In some cases, it is very desirable to develop the emulsions in much less time and various formulas have been worked out to reduce developing times to a minimum. Needless to say, such rapid processing methods can rarely be worked out to give the extreme activity with as good quality and control as the more usual formulas. Use is made of accelerating action of high alkalinity and concentration, so these formulas are not particularly economical, but they find a place where rapidity of development is of paramount importance.

One formula is given below:

No. 23 Rapid Developer

Sodium sulphite (anhydrous)	187.0 g.	1 lb. 9 oz.
Rhodol (metol or Elon)	21.5 g.	2 oz. 375 gr.
Hydroquinone	43.0 g.	5 oz. 315 gr.
Sodium hydroxide	43.0 g.	5 oz. 315 gr.
Water to	1 l.	1 gal.

The developing time is usually of the order of $1\frac{1}{2}$ min. at 65°F. After development a 5 per cent acetic acid stop bath should be used, followed by fixation in hypo with good hardening action.

Physical Development.—The primary distinction between chemical and physical development is the source of the silver. In chemical development the silver deposit is essentially produced by reduction *in situ* of the original halide. In physical development the silver is originally in the developer itself and deposits out on nucleuses to form the final image. The distinction becomes somewhat arbitrary and hard to define for a limiting case such that the first action of the developer is to dissolve silver halide, thus charging the developer with a soluble silver salt, then subsequent deposit from the solution on the nuclei. Probably ordinary development partakes at least to some extent of this nature, though the action of depositing silver is probably very local in nature and the body of the solution never contains any great quantity of silver salts.

Physical development is of interest for two reasons, as it gives an additional tool for the study of the nature of the latent image and as it produces images of unusually fine grain under the best conditions.

Physical development can be carried out after fixation, thus proving that the "latent image" is in reality of quite different nature than the silver halide itself. Fixation in a neutral or alkaline hypo solution is more favorable for this effect than the use of an acid fixing bath. This may be connected with the fact that acid fixing baths tend to attack or dissolve the silver of the developed image. Possibly there is a similar solvent action on the minute quantities of whatever material composes the "latent image." The probability of this connection is enhanced by the fact that there is other evidence which also indicates that the latent image is silver deposited in submicroscopic quantities in the gelatin.

In handling physical developers difficulty is often experienced, as they tend to deposit silver on other surfaces, such as the sides of the dish in which the development is taking place. The developing formulas are closely related to baths such as are used in silvering mirrors. The difficulties of the process and the very low effective emulsion speeds obtained, coupled with the small advantages to be gained, have kept physical development in a minor role in photographic processing.

Some attempts have been made to secure the fine grain rather generally credited to physical development without all its attendant disadvantages and uncertainties. Some success has been reported, but some others have failed in their attempts to obtain similar favorable results. The reasons for these diverse and opposing views have not been established.   A procedure recently recommended for physical development before fixation involves the following steps:

1. Treatment with potassium iodide bath.
2. Rinse.
3. Development in silver-salt bearing physical developer.
4. Fixation.
5. Washing and drying.

The baths suggested are:

For Step 1:

Potassium iodide	10 g.	1 oz. 145 gr.
Sodium sulphite (anhydrous)	25 g.	3 oz. 145 gr.
Water to	1 l.	1 gal.

For Step 3:

No. 24
STOCK SILVER SOLUTION

Sodium thiosulphate (hypo) (crystal)	160 g.	1 lb. 5 oz. 145 gr.
Sodium sulphite (anhydrous)	60 g.	8 oz.
Silver nitrate (crystal)	16 g.	2 oz. 58 gr.
Water to	1 l.	1 gal.

For use, add 1 part stock silver solution to 4 parts water, and add reducing agent as directed below.

To make up this stock silver solution, dissolve the sodium sulphite in 300 cc. (40 oz.) of water, then dissolve the silver nitrate in 100 cc. (16 oz.) of water and add to the sulphite solution, stirring until the white curdy precipitate dissolves.   Dilute the whole to 950 cc. (120 oz.) with water, add the thiosulphate, and stir until complete solution is obtained, after which the volume of the solution should be 1 l. (1 gal.). Filter through cotton.   The solution is fairly stable and keeps well.

At the time of use of the developer, for each liter of diluted solution add 1.7 g. of Amidol, or for each 15 oz. of diluted solution add 12 gr. of Amidol, and stir until completely dissolved.   The Amidol should not be added to the solution more than 10 min. before the development is to start.

With tray development, 35 min. to 1 hr. has been recommended.   Metals other than stainless steel or chromium plate are to be avoided and hard rubber or bakelite is preferred.

The special silver-bearing developer just described may be used for physical development after fixation if that is attempted.   Greatly increased exposures are required over those needed with ordinary chemical development.   Fixation should be carried on in the dark, with rather dilute neutral or alkaline hypo, such as represented by the formula below:

Sodium thiosulphate (hypo) (crystal)	45 g.	6 oz.
Ammonium hydroxide (sp. gr. 0.90)	2 cc.	2 fl. dram.
Water to	1 l.	1 gal.

The plate is to be removed from the hypo as soon as cleared and washed very thoroughly in water after which it may be developed immediately or dried and developed later.

Developers with Special Properties.—During the years of study of developers and development, various special effects have been discovered beyond the basic process of development.

Low-sulphite Pyro.—Pyro developers containing little sulphite produce two effects aside from the actual development, *i.e.*, the reduction of the exposed halide of the emulsion to silver.   They harden the gelatin locally, in the region where the silver deposit occurs, and they leave an insoluble oxidation product of the pyro along with the silver image. The existence and extent of this image may be shown by removal of the silver after such development. When weak, this is merely the familiar "pyro stain," but conditions may be chosen which make this quite a strong brownish image.

The first of these effects has been used to produce relief images of the type sometimes used in imbibition printing processes, particularly those used in color processes. When the original exposure is made through the transparent emulsion support, images can be produced close to that support and differing in thickness, depending upon the exposure received. This latter effect, difference in thickness of deposit with exposure, is enhanced by using an exposing light to which the emulsion is strongly absorbent, thus using the absorption characteristics of the emulsion itself to secure relief characteristics for the image; or, alternatively, to use a dyed gelatin to enhance the inherent optical absorption of the emulsion and thus enhance the image depth-exposure relationship. In either case, after development in the pyro developer without sulphite, the soft gelatin above the image which is hardened locally by development is washed off by warm water. A relief image thus results, which can be used for imbibition transfers and printing.

Several articles have been written concerning this subject. These formulas are taken from a summary in "The New Photo Miniature," old series, #207, new series #2, July 1935, by A. F. Odell.

A formula proposed for this hardening effect is:

No. 25 HARDENING PYRO DEVELOPER

Pyro	8.2 g.	1 oz.	40 gr.
Citric acid	0.2 g.		12 gr.
Potassium bromide	4.0 g.		235 gr.
Sodium hydroxide	3.4 g.		200 gr.
Ammonium chloride	1.7 g.		100 gr.
Water to	1 l.		1 gal.

A 2-min. development at 65° has been suggested, followed by a wash at 110 to 130°F. to remove the soft gelatin. The exposures for this work are made through the emulsion support.

Less practical use has been made of the colored image resulting from the deposit of the insoluble oxidation product of pyro along with the silver image. The fact that pyro-developed images tend to produce higher printing contrast than more nearly neutral-toned images of similar appearance was mentioned before. Some attempts have been made to use this color image as a yellow or minus-blue image in color photography, but it is not a good yellow, and its use has not been satisfactory.

Color-forming Developers.—A method for producing colored images by color-forming developers has been known for many years but has not been used to any extent until some of the recent work on color photography. In 1912 some procedures were described which resulted in the deposit of a colored compound along with the developed silver. In addition to the insoluble pyro oxidation product noted above, a wide range of colors can be produced by the use of "color formers" and color-forming developers. The colored deposit is the result of coupling the oxidation product of the reducing agent of the developer with a compound which may be in the developer solution or in the photographic emulsion itself to form *in situ* a new insoluble colored compound. This compound is little in evidence while the silver image is present but is very evident upon removing the silver by bleaching, and a very wide range of colors may be produced.

Only a few of the wide range of photographic developing agents lend themselves to this work, but a wide range of color formers is known for addition to the developer to produce many different shades. The developing agents are:

p-Phenylenediamine
Ethyl p-phenylenediamine
Diethyl p-phenylenediamine
Methyl p-phenylenediamine
Dimethyl p-phenylenediamine
These are sometimes supplied as the hydrochloride.

The methyl compounds are toxic to most people, the mono-compounds frequently give poor colors, as does the p-phenylenediamine itself leaving the diethyl p-phenylenediamine, usually supplied as the hydrochloride, as the most important agent for this special field. When this is used as the color-forming developer, a large number of compounds can be used to produce colors. A few are listed below:

For yellows:

Acetoacet-2,5-dichloranilide
Acetoacetanilide
Acetoacet-o-chloroanilide

For magenta:

p-Nitrophenylacetonitrile
1-Phenyl-3-methyl-5-pyrazolone

For blue to blue-green:

Alpha-naphthol
o-Hydroxydiphenyl
4-Chlorophenylphenol

In case commercial use of color formers is contemplated, the patent situation should be thoroughly investigated, as many are covered by patents, though the patents expired some years ago on the compounds used in the earlier work in this field.

Color can be produced by the direct development of the latent image, but the reducers and formulas used are rather weak as developers; it is somewhat simpler to develop and fix the emulsion as usual, then bleach and redevelop in the appropriate formula. This redevelopment again deposits the silver image which must be removed in turn by additional bleaching and fixation or equivalent steps.

A typical procedure for producing a colored image in positive motion-picture film for example is:

1. Expose and develop as for any ordinary print.
2. Rinse, fix, wash, and dry (if desired).
3. Bleach to silver ferrocyanide in:

Potassium ferricyanide	37.5 g.	5 oz.
Ammonia (concentrated)	5.0 cc.	5 fl. dr.
Water to	1 l.	1 gal.

4. Wash thoroughly
5. Redevelop in:

Diethyl p-phenylenediamine hydrochloride	3 g.	175 gr.
Sodium sulphite (anhydrous)	5 g.	290 gr.
Sodium carbonate (monohydrated)	35 g.	4 oz. 290 gr.
Water to	1 l.	1 gal.

to which the following solution has been added just before use:

Color former	¼–2 g.	15–120 gr.
Alcohol	100 cc.	12½ fl. oz.

The solution of diethyl *p*-phenylenediamine hydrochloride does not keep well, hence it should be made up only a short time before use.

6. Wash

7. Bleach in the same formula as used for step 3

8. Wash

9. Fix in a hypo solution free from acids and sulphites as they bleach many of the colors formed. A plain hypo bath of 20 to 30 per cent strength is suitable.

10. Wash, and dry as usual.

Extensions and variations of this process are used at present in experimental color processes. Accordingly, there is considerable activity in this field and new color formers, formulas, and processing methods appear imminent.

Bibliography

MEES, C. E. K., and S. H. WRATTEN: Development by Time, *Brit. J. Phot.*, **57,** 376 (1910); *Phot. J.*, **50,** 403 (1910).

WATKINS, A.: Testing the Developing Speed of Plates, *Brit. J. Phot.*, **68,** 383 (1921).

NEITZ, A. H., and A. WHITAKER: Effects of Dilution and Stirring of a Photographic Developer, *Brit. J. Phot.*, **73,** 630, 645, 660 (1926).

CRABTREE, J. I.: Graininess of Motion Picture Film, *J. Soc. Motion Picture Engrs.*, **27,** 77 (1927).

CARLTON, H. C., and J. I. CRABTREE: Some Properties of Fine Grain Developers for Motion Picture Films, *J. Soc. Motion Picture Engrs.*, **38,** 406 (1929).

CRABTREE, J. I.: Directional Effects in Continuous Film Processing, *J. Soc. Motion Picture Engrs.*, **19,** 207 (1932).

SEASE, V. B.: Some Notes on Fine Grain Negatives, *Camera*, **47,** 1 (1933).

AREY, LESLIE, B.: Ultra-Fine Grain by Modified Development, *Am. Phot.*, November, 1934, p. 682.

CRABTREE, J. I.: Uniformity in Photographic Development, *J. Soc. Motion Picture Engrs.*, **25,** 512 (1935).

FARTHING, J. W.: Processing Films at High Temperatures, *Am. Phot.*, December, 1935, p. 729.

PARKER, H., and J. I. CRABTREE: Rapid Processing Methods, Communication 577, Eastman Research Laboratories. See also *Am. Phot.*, March, 1936, p. 142; February, 1936, p. 67.

ENGLISH, F. L.: Some Factors Affecting Grain Size, *Am. Phot.*, May, 1937, p. 305.

MURRAY, H. D., and D. A. SPENCER: The Addition of Silver Iron, Reactants to Organic Developing Solutions, *Phot. J.*, July, 1937, p. 458.

EVANS, R. M., and W. T. HANSON JR.: Photographic Development and the Latent Image, *Phot. J.*, August, 1937, p. 497. See also *Communication* 615 from the Eastman Research Laboratories.

CRABTREE, J. I.: Maintenance of Negative Quality, *Am. Phot.*, November, 1937, p. 800.

SMETHURST, P. C.: Developer Agitation in Plate Tanks, *Brit. J. Phot.*, **84,** 664 (1937).

REINDERS, W., and M. C. F. BEUKERS: Fine Grain Developers and a Method of Determining Grain Size, *Phot. J.*, April, 1938, p. 192.

EVANS, R. M., and W. T. HANSON JR.: Reduction Potential and Composition of MQ Developers, *J. Soc. Motion Picture Engrs.*, May, 1938, p. 559.

STEVENS, G. W. W., and R. G. W. NORRISH: Mechanism of Photographic Reversal, *Phot. J.*, August, 1938, p. 513.

EVANS, R. M.: Maintenance of a Developer by Continuous Replenishment, *J. Soc. Motion Picture Engrs.*, September, 1938, p. 273.

CRABTREE, J. I., and R. W. HENN: A New Fine Grain Developer, *Camera*, January, 1939, p. 40.

CHAPTER XIII

FIXING, WASHING, AND DRYING

By Beverly Dudley

In general, the processing of photographic materials subsequent to that of development includes: (1) rinsing the negatives in a short-stop bath to stop development and to make the materials acid in order to prevent alkalinization of the fixing bath; (2) fixing the material so that the developed latent image may be permanent; (3) washing the material to rid it of the fixing solution which, in time, would otherwise stain it; and (4) drying. Sometimes one or more of these processes may be omitted. For example, short-stop baths are frequently dispensed with by the amateur who processes a relatively small quantity of material, and where the element of time is of importance, as it is in newspaper work, negatives may be used while they are still wet. But the normal procedure follows the processes enumerated above, and these will be dealt with in this chapter.

Short-stop Baths. *Function of the Short-stop Bath.*—The short-stop bath has two important functions. Its main purpose is to arrest development of the latent image after the photographic material is removed from the developer. If some short-stop bath is not employed, the film of developer solution adhering to the negative or print continues to develop the latent image much the same as if the photographic material were permitted to remain in the developing solution. The second purpose of the short-stop bath is to prevent the photographic material from carrying alkaline solutions from the developer into the fixing bath where an excess of alkali renders the fixing solution useless. The alkaline solutions which adhere to the film from the developer may be partially removed by washing the film thoroughly in water before fixing, but removal of the alkali is made much more effective by placing the photographic material in a short-stop bath or acid solution before fixing. The use of short-stop baths aids in the prevention of fog and developer stains and helps to prevent sludging of the fixing bath. If the acid short-stop bath contains hardening ingredients, it is possible to eliminate the hardening agents in the fixing bath.

Desirable Properties of Short-stop Baths.—The desirable properties of short-stop baths have been summarized by Crabtree and Russell[1] in the following manner:

1. The bath must be distinctly acid and to be efficient must remain acid during the life of the fixing bath. Although the stop bath must be sufficiently acid to insure long life, when the film leaves the bath, it is more or less acid and will therefore increase the free-acid content of the fixing bath which in turn will increase the tendency of the latter to sulphurize. The choice of acids therefore depends upon the propensity of the acid to precipitate sulphur in a hypo solution.

2. A stop bath should not be sufficiently acid to cause blisters, and the limit of acidity in this case is much less than in the case of a fixing bath because the alkalinity of the film is much greater when removed from the developer than after a slight rinse and previous to the immersion in the fixing bath.

[1] Crabtree, J. I., and H. D. Russell, Some Properties of Chrome Alum Stop Baths and Fixing Baths, *J. Soc. Motion Picture Engrs.*, **14** (No. 5), 483–512 (1930).

3. A hardening stop bath should have properties similar to those of a plain acid stop bath and in addition should produce satisfactory hardening throughout its life. Since the hardening produced by alum mixtures varies with the quantity of developer or alkali added, it is apparent that an acid hardening stop bath will not produce uniform hardening except for a limited time unless it is suitably revived.

Composition of Stop Baths.—The composition of a number of suitable stop baths is given in Table I. The chemicals should be mixed in the order in which they are given.

The 28 per cent acetic acid required for one of these stop baths may be made from glacial acetic acid by diluting 3 parts of glacial acetic acid with 8 parts of water.

TABLE I.—COMPOSITION OF STOP BATHS

Constituents	Nonhardening				Hardening	
	1	2	3	4	5[1]	6
Recommended for	Lantern slides	Plates	Bromide prints		Films and plates	
Sodium sulphate, g	192					
Sulphuric acid, cc	83.5					
Chrome alum, g	....	....	....	....	20	
Sodium bisulphite, g	....	....	....	....	20	
Acetic acid (28 per cent), cc	....	....	48	38.5		
Potassium metabisulphite, g	....	50				
Potassium chrome alum, g	....	....	....	....	....	30
Water to make, l	1.0	1.0	1.0	1.0	1.0	1.0

[1] Does not keep well.

With the acetic acid stop bath, negatives or prints should be immersed in the stop bath for about 5 sec. before fixing.

The potassium chrome alum stop bath is especially suitable for use in hot weather. When immersed in this hardening stop bath the negatives should be agitated for the first 30 or 40 sec. They should remain in this bath for 3 min. Agitation of the film assists in the prevention of blisters due to the decomposition of carbonate in the developer by the chrome alum and prevents stains due to the precipitation of chromium hydroxide by the alkali of the developer. This bath may require frequent renewal.

Processing Conditions.—To reduce to a minimum all tendency toward reticulation or uneven swelling of the gelatin, it is desirable that all processing solutions be maintained at the same temperatures. Since the temperature at which the processing solutions are used is usually determined by the temperature of satisfactory operation of the developer, which is usually between 65 to 70°F., it is desirable that the stop baths be used in this temperature range. The potassium chrome alum stop bath, however, may be used at temperatures considerably above this if it becomes necessary to operate with warmer solutions.

It is advisable to agitate the photographic materials immediately upon immersion in the stop bath.

The stop bath should be discarded when a sludge forms either in the bath or on the films or, in the case of hardening baths, when the bath fails to harden the gelatin emulsion. Some revival of baths may be accomplished by adding sufficient acid to maintain the original acidity. In many cases however, it will be more satisfactory to replace the exhausted solution with a new one, rather than to attempt to replenish it by the addition of acid.

Most developers contain carbonates which may be decomposed by the acid in the stop bath with the liberation of carbon dioxide. The evolution of carbon dioxide is prone to cause the emulsion to blister, especially if the materials are not agitated upon immersion in the stop bath. It may, therefore, be good practice to rinse the films or prints for a few seconds in clear water before placing them in the stop bath in order to remove as much of the developer as possible. This procedure will, however, dilute the stop bath.

Since the stop bath prevents development, no harm will be done if the films or prints are left in the stop bath until it is convenient to transfer them to the fixing solution. This procedure may be convenient where a small quantity of work is being done, since it permits the operator to prevent contamination of the developer with hypo which might be picked up on the fingers from the fixing solution.

Fixing. *Purpose of Fixing.*—After development of the photosensitive material (either film, plate, or paper) the emulsion contains the metallic silver image which has been reduced from a silver halide during the process of development; it also contains grains of silver halide which have not been acted upon by light during exposure and which, consequently, have not been changed to metallic silver during development. This remaining silver salt is still sensitive to light, even if the photosensitive material is desensitized, and the salt will therefore ultimately become dark and mask the image.

To prevent this action from taking place and to assure that the image will remain permanent, a fixing bath is employed. Permanance of the image may be accomplished either by (1) rendering the unexposed silver salt as permanent as the metallic silver and preventing its subsequent exposure or by (2) dissolving away the salt from the metallic silver image. In practice the latter method is universally employed.

The silver salts for which the fixing bath must be solvent are silver chloride, silver bromide, and silver iodide. Silver bromide is the most common, although all three may be present. All three of these halides are soluble in potassium cyanide (KCN), ammonium hydroxide (NH_4OH), and sodium thiosulphite ($Na_2S_2O_3$), but not all these solvents are suitable for ordinary photographic work. Potassium cyanide, for example, is highly poisonous, has a softening effect on the gelatin and is also a solvent for metallic silver. Ammonium hydroxide produces the objectionable and pungent odor of ammonia (NH_3). Sodium thiosulphite, commonly known as "hypo" from its other chemical name, sodium hyposulphite, is the only other alternative of the commonly available materials and is used almost exclusively in photographic fixing baths.

Chemistry of Fixing.—The chemistry of fixation, like practically all photographic chemistry, is rather involved and highly complicated, especially since many chemical compounds may be formed during the fixing process. No attempt will be made to indicate in any detail the possible chemical reactions which are thought to take place; an equation or two indicating the rationale of the essential operations may not, however, be entirely out of order.

The exposed and developed, but unfixed, photographic material contains deposits of metallic silver (Ag) as well as of silver halide which we may designate as AgY, if we understand the symbol Y to represent the appropriate halogen, usually bromide. Thus the developed film contains the compounds $Ag + AgY$, and it is desired to remove the halide leaving only the metallic silver. If the developed film is immersed in a solution of sodium thiosulphate $Na_2S_2O_3$, the chemical reactions may be described as

$$3Ag + 3AgY + XNa_2S_2O_3 = 3Ag + 3NaY + Na_5Ag_3(S_2O_3)_4 +$$
$$(X - 4)Na_2S_2O_3 \quad (1)$$

The first term on the right side of the equation represents the metallic silver which remains on the photographic film and is unaffected (for the most part[1]) by the sodium thiosulphate. The two middle terms represent compounds in solution in the hypo bath, while the last term shows how much hypo remains. Several silver-sodium thiosulphate compounds beside that shown are possible, and it is probable that a number of different ones coexist in equilibrium in the solution. Which particular compounds are present depends upon the concentration of silver or upon the exhaustion of the solution. A highly exhausted hypo bath may contain an appreciable quantity of $NaAgS_2O_3$, which is only slightly soluble and somewhat unstable. Because of the low solubility, this compound will be difficult to wash out from the film. It is also unstable and may break down to form silver sulphide (Ag_2S), which produces stains. It is important to observe that the amount of fresh hypo solution has been reduced from $XNa_2S_2O_8$ to $(X - 4)Na_2S_2O_3$, so that it will be less effective in subsequent fixations than in the original bath.

If only metallic silver and silver halide were brought over into the fixing solution, as indicated in the equation above, sodium thiosulphate would be a satisfactory solvent for the halide and would be a suitable fixing solution. However, the film carries over into the fixing solution a certain amount of the developer solution. The developer solution in the hypo oxidizes, and the oxidation products produce stains. This situation may be prevented through the use of a stop bath or, if this is not convenient, by adding to the fixing bath some substance which prevents the oxidation of the developer solution in the fixing bath, as well as an acid to neutralize the alkalinity of the developer. The addition of the acid (which is usually sodium sulphite) in the fixing bath also aids in preventing oxidation of the developing agent.

While fixing baths containing the silver halide solvent (hypo), an oxidation preventive (sodium sulphite) and an acid or acid sulphite (such as acetic acid or sodium bisulphite) produce a suitable fixing solution, a hardening agent is also usually added. This is desirable because the hardened film is not so easily damaged in handling and in subsequent operations as a nonhardened film. The three most important gelatin hardeners are: (1) potassium alum $[K_2SO_4 \cdot Al(SO_4)_3 \cdot 24H_2O]$; (2) chrome alum $[K_2SO_4 \cdot Cr_2(SO_4)_3 \cdot 24H_2O]$; and (3) formalin, which is a 40 per cent solution of formaldehyde ($HCHO$) in water.

Unless a stop bath is employed, free acid in a fixing bath is a necessity to prevent stains due to oxidation of the developer in the fixing bath. So far as the neutralization of the alkalinity of the developer is concerned, any acid might be used. Practically, however, the use of a strong acid results in the liberation of sulphur which in turn reacts with metallic silver to produce stains of silver sulphide, according to the equations:

$$Na_2S_2O_3 + 2HCl = 2NaCl + H_2SO_3 + S \tag{2}$$

$$2Ag + S = Ag_2S \tag{3}$$

Mechanism of Fixing.—In a given period of time and with active agitation of a fresh fixing bath whose volume is large compared to that of the material being fixed, a certain portion of the silver bromide originally present in the photosensitive material will be dissolved. In the next unit of time the same fraction of the silver which remains after the end of the first time interval will be dissolved, and so on. In time intervals of the same duration the same fraction of the remaining silver will be dissolved. The amount of silver dissolved in each time interval will decrease with time. The dissolving of the silver bromide is therefore a geometric or exponential process

[1] See RUSSELL, H. D., and J. I. CRABTREE, The Reducing Action of Fixing Baths on the Silver Image, *J. Soc. Motion Picture Engrs.*, **18** (No. 3), 371–397 (1932), for a study of deviations from this general statement.

rather than an arithmetic one. Since a certain fraction rather than a certain amount of the silver bromide is dissolved in each time interval, it is theoretically impossible for all the bromide to become dissolved, although the amount remaining undissolved may be made as small as may be desired by leaving the photographic material immersed in the fixing bath for a sufficiently long period of time.

Quantitatively, the amount of silver bromide left in the negative at any time can be computed in terms of the original amount of silver bromide when the law expressing the rate of dissolution is known. If the temperature and concentration of the fixing bath are maintained constant, the rate at which the silver bromide dissolves is (at least for a first approximation) proportional to the original amount of the salt and is also proportional to $(1 - k)$ where k is the fraction of the bromide dissolved in unit time. If S is the amount of the salt (silver bromide) remaining after any time t, the rate at which the silver bromide dissolves is expressed by the equation

$$\frac{dS}{dt} = -AS(1 - k) \tag{4}$$

where A is a constant which depends upon the units used and is to be determined experimentally. By separating the variables, integrating, and transforming from the logarithmic to the exponential form, the amount of undissolved salt S at any time t is given by the expression

$$S = e^{-A(1-k)t} \tag{5}$$

The factor k is termed the velocity constant of fixation and depends upon the temperature and concentration of the fixing bath. It is dependent upon the amount of silver bromide and the condition of the gelatin, although, for a given set of conditions, k is larger for chloride than for bromide emulsions, so that the latter would require a somewhat longer time for the same proportion of bromide to become dissolved.

From a theoretical point of view, an infinitely long time would be required to dissolve out completely all the bromide in a negative or plate. However, it is desirable to know at least approximately what length of time will be required to fix the photographic materials satisfactorily from a practical point of view. From the formulas which have already been developed, it can be shown that the time of fixing is

$$t = \frac{-1}{A(1 - k)} \log_e \left(\frac{S_2}{S_1}\right) \tag{6}$$

where S_2 = the amount of bromide left undissolved at the end of the fixing time;
S_1 = the amount of bromide originally present.
Since this equation involves the ratio of S_2 to S_1, we may determine the time of fixing for the bromide to be reduced to any fraction of its original value. A common practice in photography is to determine the "time of clearing" of a negative and to use this as the minimum time of fixation. The clearing time is that required for the negative to become free from its opalescence. It is claimed by Warwick[1] that from 5 to 12.5 per cent of the bromide remains undissolved when the negative is just cleared of its opalescence. If we use a value of 10 per cent as representing an average value, then $S_2/S_1 = 0.1$ and $\log_e (S_2/S_1) = -2.3026$. Thus the time of clearing is

$$t = \frac{2.3026}{A(1 - k)} \tag{7}$$

The equations developed may be regarded as giving some insight into the mechanism of operation of the fixing bath. As a general rule, the temperature and concen-

[1] WARWICK, W. A., The Laws of Fixation, *Am. Phot.*, November, 1918.

tration of the fixing baths used in practice vary so widely throughout their life that an evaluation of the constants is likely to be merely of academic interest.

So far as the physical action and effects taking place are concerned, the rate of fixation is determined largely by the penetration of the sodium thiosulphate through the film, because the chemical action takes place rapidly compared with the rate of penetration of the hypo. Of course, the rate of fixing depends upon the agitation of the fixing solution over the photosensitive material, as well as the freshness of the fixing solution. If agitation is lacking, the rate of fixing will be less than that which might otherwise be expected. In an unagitated fixing bath the chemical reactions take place only at the surface of the material, and any additional removal of silver halide then becomes dependent upon the relatively slow process of diffusion rather than upon mere solubility.

Requirements of a Fixing Bath.—To be perfectly satisfactory, a fixing bath should fulfill the following six requirements:

1. Throughout its life, the fixing bath should dissolve the silver halide from the emulsion without staining the photographic material.

2. The fixing bath should not precipitate sulphur, even when used at fairly high temperatures.

3. Throughout its useful life, the fixing bath should not precipitate aluminum sulphate.

4. The bath should not produce blisters in the gelatin coating of the film.

5. The fixing bath should provide a satisfactory degree of hardening.

6. The fixing bath should be economical, *i.e.*, its cost in terms of the amount of material fixed should be as low as possible.

Uneven stains are objectionable because of the denser image they produce in the final print. Uniform, colored stains may not be injurious in a negative from which positive prints are to be made. They may be objectionable in positive motion-picture film or in paper prints.

If the second requirement is not met, more or less colloidal sulphur will be precipitated in the gelatin of the film. The precipitated sulphur cannot be removed by washing, since sulphur is insoluble in water; it will, however, combine with the silver of the fixed negative, ultimately causing silver sulphide stains and fading of the image.

A precipitate of aluminum sulphite forms when the fixing bath becomes neutralized by the alkaline of the developer which is carried over into the fixing bath. The aluminum sulphite occurs as a reaction of the alum hardening agent with the alkaline sulphite preservative.

Blisters are usually produced in the fixing bath by the too rapid formation of carbon dioxide gas. Bubbles or gas pockets of carbon dioxide may then form within the gelatin layer which may finally break. The carbon dioxide is formed by the carbonate of the developer carried over into the fixing bath reacting with the acid of the acid hardening fixing solution.

Hardening is useful primarily to retard the swelling of the gelatin coating so that the film may be dried more rapidly than if it is not hardened. In unswollen and hardened film a minimum of water is present, and consequently drying may proceed rapidly. Hardened films may also be dried at higher temperature than unhardened film without the potential danger of softening or melting the gelatin coating. Hardening may not be required if the gelatin does not swell so much during the processing that the film may be handled and dried satisfactorily. However, the hardening agent may be conveniently added to the fixing bath so easily that it is worth while to employ the hardener as a safeguard.

Classification of Fixing Baths.—Several types of fixing baths are in common use and may be classified as follows:

1. Nonhardening fixing baths
    a. Plain hypo baths
    b. Acid hypo baths
2. Acid hardening fixing baths

The purpose of the plain hypo fixing bath is simply to dissolve the silver halide from the emulsion so that the sensitized grains will not be subject to exposure after development and thereby ultimately stain the photographic material. Acid fixing baths fulfill the same purpose, but, in addition, the acid neutralizes the alkali which is carried over from the developer into the fixing bath so that the fixing bath may be used over a longer period of time. The purpose of the acid hardening fixing bath, which is probably the most convenient and frequently used form of bath, is (1) to dissolve the silver halide, (2) to neutralize the alkali carried over from the developer into the fixing bath by the photographic material, and (3) to harden the emulsion so that it is easier to manipulate without danger of damaging it. A definite quantity of acid hardener is added to a specified amount of plain hypo solution to prevent troubles which might otherwise arise during the process of fixation.

After the negative or positive has been developed the desired length of time, it is necessary to stop development promptly. One method of accomplishing this is to remove the photographic material from the developing solution and rinse it in clear water which dilutes the developer clinging to the photographic material and consequently removes most of the adhering developing solution. However, this rinsing is never sufficiently complete to stop development entirely as some of the developer remains in the pores of the gelatin coating. If the photographic material is rinsed in an acid bath instead of in clear water, the acid will neutralize the alkali of the developer so that development can no longer continue. The immediate stopping of development eliminates stains which might otherwise appear on negatives and prints if only a plain solution of sodium thiosulphate were used in the fixing bath.

The alkali in the developer, which is added to energize the developing agent, softens the gelatin of the emulsion, thereby rendering the photographic material more susceptible to damage. The acid hardener is consequently added to counteract this effect by hardening the emulsion. White or potassium alum is frequently used as a hardening agent. It has, however, a limited hardening effect on the gelatin which, under certain conditions, is not sufficient to prevent softening of the gelatin at moderately high temperatures. Where greater hardening action is required, chrome alum is employed. Formalin or formaldehyde has even greater hardening effect than chrome alum. Consequently chrome alum or formalin hardeners are employed where considerable hardening is required or where the amount of hardening provided by potassium alum is insufficient.

To keep down the amount of oxidation which occurs during the fixing process, a preservative is added to the acid hardener. The purpose of this preservative is to inhibit the formation of sulphur, thereby eliminating (or at least reducing) the tendency for the formation of silver sulphide which turns brown and stains the negatives or prints. The preservative usually added is sodium sulphite. The preservative action is greater when the fixing bath is maintained slightly acid.

Plain Fixing Baths.—A plain solution of sodium thiosulphite will dissolve the silver halide grains in the developed emulsion and will, consequently, accomplish fixing, provided little or none of the developing solution is carried over into the fixing bath by the photographic materials. If a plain fixing bath is used, it is desirable, either to wash the film thoroughly between development and fixing in a bath of clear water, or to neutralize the alkali of the developer through the use of an acid stop bath or rinse between development and fixing. When the latter procedure is employed, some sodium sulphite must be added to the fixing bath in order to prevent sulphurization of the hypo bath by the acid carried from the stop bath into the fixing bath. If these precautions are not taken and the photographic materials are delivered to the fixing bath directly from the developer solution, the fixing bath soon becomes discolored from the oxidized developer, and these oxidized products stain the negatives and prints. With a warm fixing bath a tendency exists for the gelatin to swell and to become soft, which may easily result in frilling, reticulation, melting of the emulsion from the gelatin base or other difficulties.

The only problem likely to arise in the determination of the composition of a plain fixing bath is that of determining optimum concentration. Various investigations indicate that the maximum speed of fixing occurs when the hypo concentration is about 30 to 40 per cent.

Acid Hardening Fixing Baths.—A good summary of the properties and characteristics of acid hardening fixing baths has been given by Crabtree and Hartt[1] from which the following material is taken.

An acid hardening fixing bath contains the following ingredients: (1) a silver halide solvent, (2) an antistaining agent, (3) a preservative or sulphurization inhibitor, and (4) a hardening agent.

Although many solvents of silver halides are available, the most satisfactory for fixing purposes are sodium and ammonium thiosulphates. A solution of ammonium thiosulphate of given concentration fixes more rapidly than a corresponding solution of sodium thiosulphate, but ammonium thiosulphate is more expensive, and commercial grades are apt to contain free sulphur. For most purposes sodium thiosulphate fixes sufficiently rapidly and is entirely satisfactory.

Practically any acid will function as an antistaining agent because it has merely to neutralize the alkali in the developer carried over by the films and thereby retard oxidation of the developing agent. Organic acids are more suitable than inorganic acids because they are less dissociated and therefore have a correspondingly smaller tendency to precipitate sulphur from the fixing solution. Acetic acid has been found to be the most generally efficient for use in fixing baths, but much is still desired, from the standpoint of a perfect acid, for this purpose.

It is imperative, when compounding an acid fixing bath, to have a quantity of free acid present to prevent discoloration of the bath by developer oxidation products and to prevent the precipitation of the hardening agents by the alkali in the developer. This free acid tends to cause precipitation of sulphur from the hypo especially at temperatures above 70°F. It is therefore necessary to add some substance which will prevent the precipitation of sulphur without impairing the antistaining properties of the acid.

Two types of substances act in this manner. The first of these consists of the alkaline sulphites of which sodium sulphite is the most common. Since hypo decomposes in the presence of acid to form sodium sulphite and sulphur, it is considered that the addition of sulphite to an acid fixing bath retards the decomposition of the hypo because it tends to reverse the action by virtue of its mass action.

The second type of preservative consists of the alkali salts of organic acids which are commonly referred to as buffer salts; sodium acetate is a typical example. The effect of this type of substance is to buffer or reduce the hydrogen-ion concentration of the acid employed below the limits at which sulphur is precipitated from hypo by acids.

The hardening of gelatin may be either temporary or permanent. Temporary hardening agents raise the melting point and prevent the swelling of the gelatin only while the gelatin is in contact with the hardening solution. A concentrated solution

[1] CRABTREE, J. I., and H. A. HARTT, Some Properties of Fixing Baths, *J. Soc. Motion Picture Engrs.*, **13** (No. 38), 364–405 (1929).

of sodium sulphate is a typical temporary hardener. The hardening produced by such substances is reversible, *i.e.*, gelatin will subsequently absorb water and swell.

Permanent hardening is characterized by a reduced absorption of water (swelling) by the gelatin during subsequent washing. Various materials may be used for permanently hardening gelatin, such as formalin, quinone, tannin, organic developer oxidation products, and certain inorganic compounds. Formalin, quinone, and developer oxidation products harden gelatin only in alkaline or neutral solutions, and their application is therefore limited to use in developers or to hardening of completely washed film.

Of the inorganic compounds, the salts of iron, chromium, and aluminum exert the most powerful hardening action on the gelatin. Salts of aluminum are, perhaps, the most satisfactory hardeners because they are colorless, are readily soluble in water, and do not form colored compounds with the common developing agents, either in acid or alkaline solutions, but they give satisfactory hardening provided the wash water is not above 75 to 80°F. Sodium and potassium alum are equally efficient, but with the ammonium alum an evolution of ammonia takes place after the fixing bath becomes alkaline, and this tends to produce dichroic fog.

Composition of Fixing Baths.—By way of summary it may be stated that (1) plain fixing baths contain only a solvent for the unexposed silver halide grains, (2) acid nonhardening fixing baths contain the silver halide solvent as well as an acid antistaining agent and preservative or sulphurization inhibitor, while (3) acid hardening baths contain a gelatin hardening agent in addition to the ingredients already enumerated for (2).

The following tabulation shows some of the materials which have been used in fixing baths of the various types enumerated:

1. Silver solvent:
   Sodium thiosulphate (or "hypo")
   Ammonium thiosulphate
2. Antistaining agent. Practically any acid may be used, although organic acids are preferred because they show less dissociation. Suitable antistaining agents are:
   Acetic acid
   Citric acid
   Tartaric acid
   Oxalic acid
   Lactic acid
   Malic acid
   Maleic acid
   Sodium sulphite
   Sulphuric acid
   Sodium bisulphite ⎫ acid salts
   Potassium metabisulphite ⎭
3. Preservative or sulphurization inhibitor
   Alkaline sulphites (sodium sulphite, for example)
   Alkaline salts (sodium acetate, for example)
4. Gelatin-hardening agents
   Potassium alum
   Chrome alum
   Sodium sulphate (temporary hardener)
   Formalin (formaldehyde) ⎫
   Quinone ⎬ in alkaline or neutral solutions only
   Tannin ⎭

TABLE II.—COMPOSITION OF FIXING BATHS

Type of fixing bath	Plain		Acid nonhardening									Acid hardening																
	General purpose		General purpose				Films		Slides	Prints		General purpose			Motion picture							Prints		High temperature			Fast fixing	
Constituent	1	2	3	4	5	6	7	8	9	10	11	12	13	14	15	16	17	18	19	20	21	22	23	24	25	26	27	28
Sodium thiosulphate, g	250	400	228	275	230	240	250	475	185	240	145	174	240	240	300	300	300	300	300	300	300	250		230	210	270	250	150
Sodium sulphite (desiccated), g					16	10	10		4.25			24	15	7	15	37.5	15	15	17.5	5	15	15		46	40	54	15	
Acetic acid (glacial), cc												39	14	11	13	13	5			10		12.5			2.7			
Sulphuric acid (concentrated), cc																		2	2		2							
Potassium alum, g													15		15		15	15										
Potassium chrome alum, g						25	25									6			32			30						
Sodium bisulphite, g			42														6			10	20							
Borax, g												7.5										7.5					25	
Boric acid, g													7.5							5								
Potassium metabisulphate, g				22.5				60		15	24																	
Citric acid, g					14.5																					135		
Formalin, cc																								125				
Chrome alum, g																									84			
Ammonium chloride, g																											15	50
Hydrochloric acid, cc									3																			37.5
Water to make, l	1.0	1.0	1.0	1.0	1.0	1.0	1.0	1.0	1.0	1.0	1.0	1.0	1.0	1.0	1.0	1.0	1.0	1.0	1.0	1.0	1.0	1.0	1.0	1.0	1.0	1.0	1.0	1.0

The composition of fixing baths recommended for various purposes is given in Table II. No effort has been made to include all the fixing baths which have been published from time to time, but the solutions given are representative of current practice. The baths are divided into three main groups, according to whether they are plain fixing baths, acid nonhardening fixing baths, or acid fixing baths. Under these main groupings, the baths are further classified according to the use or special property for which they are recommended.

The plain fixing baths, 1 and 2, are simple nonhardening baths. They are suitable for use where the films are washed in a stop bath or in fresh water between development and fixing. The baths differ only in concentration of hypo, and the two concentrations given represent approximately the extreme concentrations encountered in practice for baths of this type.

Baths 3 to 6 inclusive are acid nonhardening baths which are suitable for plates, films, or prints.

Baths 7 and 8 are recommended for films, while bath 9 has been suggested as being especially suitable for slides. The sodium sulphite is first dissolved in about 50 cc. and the hydrochloric acid is added. The hypo is dissolved in about 900 cc. of water, and, when it has completely dissolved, the first solution is added to the hypo solution and the volume brought up to 1 l.

Baths 10 and 11 have been recommended for prints where a nonhardening bath is suitable.

Acid hardening fixing baths (12 and beyond) are the most suitable for general use as the processes of fixing and hardening are combined in a single bath operation. The first three baths under this classification are suitable for films, plates, or papers. Bath 12 is a potassium alum bath. Bath 17 keeps indefinitely before using and therefore can be made up in advance of use; it can also be used repeatedly. Since it becomes gradually alkaline with the addition of developer to the fixing solution, the bath should be discarded when it becomes frothy. One pint should fix fifty 4- by 5-in. prints.

Although listed here as especially suitable for motion-picture work, No. 15 is an acid hardening bath suitable for all professional films and plates. Bath 16 has the advantage of having the lowest effect on reduction of the silver image of a wide number of fixing solutions investigated by Russell and Crabtree (see page 378). Bath 18 is a chrome alum fixing bath for professional plates and films, as well as for motion-picture work. Since chrome alum baths often lose their hardening properties within a few days after their preparation, either with use or without, a fresh bath should be prepared immediately before using. There is a tendency for scum to form in old baths, but this scum may be removed by swabbing the surface of the film with cotton. For bath 20 the hypo should be dissolved in one-half the required volume of water. The sodium sulphite, acetic acid, boric acid, and potassium alum should then be added in the order given here, after which the volume of solution is brought up to 1 l. by adding the proper amount of water. This bath contains a minimum amount of sulphite, so that sulphurization will not occur within a period of 3 or 4 weeks when the temperature is 70°F. If the bath temperature rises above 70°F., double the amount of sulphite indicated may be used. Bath 21 is a suitable chrome alum fixing bath for motion-picture work. It does not harden the film excessively but maintains its hardening properties on keeping. The bath does not sludge with the addition of a relatively large amount of developing solution and, if the temperature does not exceed 70°F., will not sulphurize in less than 4 weeks.

Bath 22, suitable for paper prints, has an exceedingly long hardening sludge life, and produces considerable hardening of paper prints. This borax bath has been found to have a hardening life approximately four times that of bath 17 and a sludge life five times as long.

Fixing solutions suitable for tropical processing, or where the temperature of the solutions cannot be reduced to 70°F., are given in baths 24 to 26 inclusive. Bath 24 has considerable hardening action and will keep a week at 100°F., although it has not the keeping properties of the ordinary acid fixing and hardening baths. Bath 25 is a chrome alum fixing bath recommended for tropical processing where the temperature does not exceed 95°F. Bath 26 is a formalin solution for tropical development. The hypo should be dissolved in about half the required volume of water. The sodium sulphite and formalin should be added in that order, and the solution made up to 1 l. by the addition of the proper amount of water. The bath keeps well, although a harmless milky precipitate may form. The fumes of the formalin (40 per cent formaldehyde) are irritating, and for this reason formalin should be kept in closed containers as much as possible.

A fixing bath for prints or film, which, it is claimed, will completely fix in 2 min., is given as bath 27. The bath should be kept at 70°F. and should be made just prior to use as it does not keep well.

Another fixing bath suitable for rapid fixing is bath 28.

Practical Considerations in Fixing.—The rate at which photographic materials are fixed depends upon (1) the nature of the emulsion, (2) the concentration and composition of the fixing bath, (3) the degree of exhaustion or the extent to which the fixing solution has been used, (4) the rate of agitation of the photographic material in the rinse and fixing baths, and (5) the temperature of the solution.

In general, coarse-grained emulsions are fixed more slowly than those whose emulsions contain fine grains of silver halide. Likewise a film having a thin emulsion coating fixes more rapidly than one having a heavy, thick coating. Negative materials, particularly fast plates and films, contain some silver iodide which dissolves more slowly than the bromide, and this is another contributing factor to the relatively slow fixing of fast coarse-grained emulsions. In practice, the maximum time required to completely clear the film of its opalescence is about 10 to 15 min.; if the film takes more than this time to clear, it is usually economical to prepare a fresh fixing solution, even though the fixing solution may not be completely exhausted and would still be capable of fixing the material in 20 to 30 min. For negative materials, the time of fixing is often taken as twice the time required for the film to become completely cleared of its opalescence.

Printing papers may be completely fixed in about 1 min., provided the paper is thoroughly agitated in a fresh fixing solution and the free flow of the fixing bath around the print is not inhibited by the presence of other prints. In actual practice, however, the prints are not usually very well agitated in the fixing bath, and it is difficult to prevent two or more prints from adhering together. For this reason a longer time of fixation is required.

For a given emulsion and temperature, the time of fixation of a fresh hypo solution depends upon the concentration of the sodium thiosulphate, as shown in Fig. 1. From these curves, which are also representative of those obtained for other emulsions, it is seen that the optimum concentration is not extremely critical. Negative film fixes most rapidly when the concentration is 400 g. of hypo per liter, so that 40 per cent is the optimum solution. The motion-picture positive film is fixed most quickly in a 30 per cent solution. Most of the fixing baths are made with a concentration varying from 200 to 400 g. of hypo per liter of solution. Unless rapid fixation is required for some particular purpose, a 30 per cent solution will be found satisfactory for practically all purposes.

As the same fixing bath is used repeatedly, the rate of fixation continually decreases. The falling off of fixation rate is due to (1) dilution of the bath as a result of the addition of developer or rinse water, as well as the removal of hypo to the wash water when the films are changed from one solution to another; (2) the removal of thiosulphate ions by virtue of the formation of complex silver thiosulphate ions as mentioned on page 380; and (3) the accumulation of sodium iodide resulting from the conversion of the silver iodide of the emulsion to silver thiosulphate. It is, of course, possible to revive the bath by the addition of hypo, but, as stated above, it is usually good economy to replace the fixing bath with fresh solution when negatives require more than 10 to 15 min. to clear.

The rate of agitation of the photographic material in the fixing solution has an important bearing on the speed with which photographic materials are fixed. Experiments by Crabtree and Hartt[1] indicate that if the time of fixing films without agitation is taken as 100 per cent, the time of fixation when agitation is made every 30 sec. may

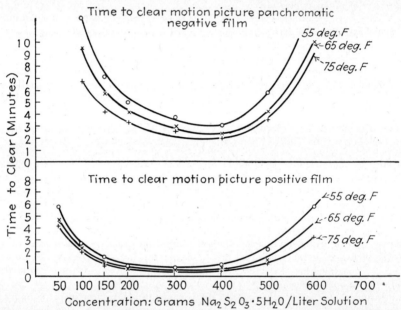

Fig. 1.—Clearing time of plain fixing bath for various temperatures and concentrations.

reduce this time to 80 per cent. The time of fixation may be reduced to from 88 to 60 per cent with continuous agitation, whereas, when brush treatment is used, the fixing time may be from 75 to 50 per cent of the time required without agitation, depending upon the emulsion and the solution employed.

Figure 1 also shows the effect of temperature upon the fixing time. For motion-picture negative film, Fig. 1 shows that with a 30 per cent solution the fixing time is decreased from about 3.75 to approximately 2 min. as the temperature is raised from 55 to 75°F. For a 40 per cent solution, the fixing time is decreased from 3 to 2 min. for the same temperature change. For positive film, an increase in temperature of from 55 to 75°F. reduces the fixing time from 50 to 30 sec. for a 30 per cent fixing solution. From the shape of the curves it is evident that the fixing time is approximately inversely proportional to the temperature of the bath for the range of temperatures normally encountered. For minimum fixing time, it is therefore advisable not to use the fixing solution too cold. At elevated temperatures, however, the

[1] CRABTREE, J. I., and H. A. HARTT, Some Properties of Fixing Baths, *Trans. Soc. Motion Picture Engrs.*, **13** (No. 38), 364–405 (1929).

gelatin may become softened, and other undesirable effects may take place. It is a good rule to keep the fixing bath between 65 and 70°F. The fixing bath should not be colder than 60°F.

A practical problem in the use of fixing baths is the determination of their exhaustion point. As the hypo bath is used, two important changes take place. First of all, the sodium thiosulphate is gradually used up in dissolving the unexposed grains of silver halide from the developed emulsion. With the decreasing amount of thiosulphate available for dissolving the silver salt, the time of fixing grows longer until finally the point is reached where the time of fixation exceeds the practical limit for efficient or economic fixing. The second change which occurs is a gradual diminution of the acidity of the fixing bath as a result of alkali being introduced into the bath from the developer. The hardening properties of the bath usually decrease fairly rapidly, and, when the acidity is below a certain point (usually near the neutral point), the bath is rendered useless by the formation of a sludge of aluminum sulphite which destroys the hardening properties of the bath. Consequently the bath should be discarded when the time of fixation becomes excessive, the practical limit usually being set at 10 to 15 min., or upon the formation of a precipitate of aluminum sulphite. The bath should also be discarded if it becomes dark or discolored and stains the negatives or prints, if it becomes frothy, or if the bath sulphurizes.

A simple method of determining whether or not a fixing bath has been exhausted is to immerse a test strip of film in the fixing solution until cleared of opalescence. The strip is then washed thoroughly in running water, after which it is immersed in a 1 to 3 per cent solution of sodium sulphide. If the test strip remains clear, the fixing bath may be regarded as satisfactory. However, if the test strip becomes colored brown or yellow, this discoloration is an indication that the soluble halides have not been entirely dissolved in the fixing bath, and consequently a new solution should be prepared. Slight changes in discoloration may be observed if only one-half of the test strip is treated in this manner; the untreated portion then acts as a control.

For purposes of economy and rapidity in fixation, the practice followed by some commercial firms, of using two fixing baths in cascade, has much to recommend it.

The film or print is placed first in a partially exhausted fixing bath where it is permitted to remain about 5 min., after which it is removed to a fresh fixing solution. When the first bath is exhausted, it is replaced by the second, and the second bath is, of course, replaced by a freshly compounded solution. The use of two baths insures more rapid fixing of the film than can be accomplished through the use of only one bath. Moreover, in being transferred to the second bath, the films do not carry over any alkali from the developer, but only the partially exhausted fixing solution. Consequently, the life of the second bath is longer than if the first or buffer bath were not employed. Another advantage of the use of two fixing baths is that, if the hardening properties of the first bath are impaired, the second bath may be used to provide the necessary amount of hardening.

Precautions should be taken to see that the first fixing bath does not produce dichroic fog, stains, or discolorations, since these will not be removed in the second bath. Both fixing baths should be maintained acid and should be discarded when any of the troubles mentioned above occur. The films should be agitated when being immersed in the fixing solution. This is especially true with respect to immersion in the first fixing bath.

Completion of Fixation.—A question of importance is the determination of completeness of fixation. Warwick[1] states that the clearing of the negative is a sign, not that the action between the silver bromide and the sodium thiosulphate is complete, but only that the opalescent layer of silver bromide has become so tenuous as to be

[1] WARWICK, A. W., The Laws of Fixation, *Am. Phot.*, November, 1918.

invisible　According to this view, from 5 to 12.5 per cent of the original bromide remains unattacked.　This view seems to have gained some support, for a practical rule frequently observed is to permit the film to remain in the fixing bath for a length of time double that required for the film to become clear.　On the other hand, experiments by Bullock, by Lumière and Seyewetz, and later by Crabtree and Hartt[1] indicate that a film which is cleared of its opalescence is completely fixed.　This statement applies, however, to fresh fixing solutions and not to partially exhausted baths. If the bath contains more than about 2 per cent, *i.e.*, 20 g. per l., of the silver halide which has been dissolved from fixed plates, all the removable silver salts are not removed from the plates.　Prolonged immersion in a partially exhausted fixing bath will not dissolve the remaining salt, but the residual salt may be removed by transferring the film to a fresh solution.　If any doubt exists as to the degree of fixation of a plate, it is common practice to permit the material to remain in the fixing bath for a length of time equal to twice the clearing time.　The use of two fixing baths in cascade is a much better solution to the problem, however.

Reducing Action of Fixing Baths.—Prolonged immersion of the film in a fixing bath has been found to reduce the density of the silver image.　For many applications of photography, this is not important.　In other applications, such as sensitometry, photographic photometry, or processing of sound motion pictures, this may be a point of practical importance.　The results of the reducing action of fixing baths have been studied by Russell and Crabtree,[2] and the following is summarized from their paper, which should be consulted for additional data, especially of a quantitative nature.

The rate of reduction of the density of the silver image in a given fixing bath is found to be greater for fine-grain than for coarse-grain emulsions.　The fixing bath having the lowest rate of reduction of density is given as formula 16 in the compilation of fixing baths.　The highest rates of reduction were obtained with fixing baths containing relatively high concentrations of sulphite and acid.

Acidity was the factor which affected the rate of reduction to the greatest extent in ordinary fixing baths.　Ammonium chloride, potassium bromide, and potassium iodide increased the rate of reduction.　Ammonium sulphite, sodium chloride, sodium sulphate, glycerin, and sugar decreased the reduction rate.　Oxygen and oxidizing agents such as peroxides have no apparent effect on the reduction rate in highly acid baths, but the presence of oxygen increases the rate of reduction in fixing baths containing low concentration of sulphite and acid.

It was found that the rate of reduction was also increased by an increase in temperature of the fixing bath.

Troubles with Fixing Baths.—The troubles which may be reasonably expected to occur from time to time when using fixing baths are tabulated for convenience and ready reference use.

Blisters.

1. *Distinguishing Characteristic.*—Blisters form on the surface of the photographic material, resembling blisters on the body.　On dry film, blisters appear as craterlike depressions when examined by reflected light.

2. *Cause.*—Blisters are caused by the evolution of carbon dioxide gas when sodium carbonate of the developer is neutralized by the acid of the fixing bath. Blisters are especially likely to occur if the gelatin is soft and is incapable of with-

---

[1] CRABTREE, J. I., and H. A. HARTT, Some Properties of Fixing Baths, *Trans. Soc. Motion Picture Engrs.*, November, 1929, pp. 364–305.

[2] RUSSELL, H. D., and J. I. CRABTREE, The Reducing Action of Fixing Baths on the Silver Image, *J. Soc. Motion Picture Engrs.*, **25**, (No. 3), 371–397 (1932).

standing the disruptive action of the evolved gas. Blisters are also likely to occur (*a*) if the fixing bath contains an excess of acid and the films are not rinsed thoroughly, (*b*) if a strongly acid rinse bath is used, or (*c*) especially during hot weather.

According to Crabtree and Hartt, the tendency of the fixing bath to produce blisters is governed by (*a*) the quantity of sulphite and carbonate contained in the film when immersed in the fixing bath, (*b*) the rate of agitation of the film when immersed in the fixing bath, (*c*) the nature and thickness of the gelatin film, (*d*) the duration of the rinse or wash used between development and fixing, (*e*) the degree of swelling of the gelatin when first placed in the fixing bath, and (*f*) the acidity of the fixing bath.

3. *Prevention.*—Rinsing the film in plain water after development but prior to fixing will remove developer alkali and reduce the amount of carbon dioxide formed. The films may then be hardened, if necessary, before fixing. The fixing bath should not contain an excess of acid. Strongly acid rinse baths should be avoided. Fixing should be carried out, if possible, at temperatures not exceeding 70°F., and the film should be agitated while immersed in the fixing bath.

4. *Remedy.*—None.

Dichroic Fog.

1. *Distinguishing Characteristic.*—Yellowish-pink stain when film is viewed by reflected light.

2. *Cause.*—Dichroic fog may be caused (*a*) by old or exhausted fixing bath containing an excess of dissolved silver salt or (*b*) by a fixing bath which does not contain acid.

3. *Prevention.*—Dichroic fog does not occur in fresh fixing baths. Replace fixing bath with a fresh solution, and use a fixing bath containing acid. Rinse film in water between development and fixing. Keep the fixing bath between 65 and 70°F.

4. *Remedy.*—See Chap. XVII, Defects in Negatives and Prints, page 518.

Failure to Harden.

1. *Distinguishing Characteristic.*—Film is soft rather than solidly hard.

2. *Cause.*—Insufficient hardening may be the result (*a*) of insufficient or impure alum, or impure alum which does not contain the correct proportion of aluminum sulphate; (*b*) of the fact that the bath is alkaline or neutral rather than acid; or (*c*) of the presence of too much acid or sulphate.

3. *Prevention.*—Depending upon the cause, prevention may be (*a*) use of sufficient amount of alum containing the proper proportion of aluminum sulphate. The hardening action of the alum is due to the aluminum sulphate. Since some grades of alum do not contain the proper proportion of aluminum sulphate, a larger portion of alum must be used with the deficient grades in order to prepare a bath of the adequate sulphate concentration. The hardening increases as the quantity of alum is increased. (*b*) The hardening bath should always be maintained acid, but excess of acid should be avoided. For a given amount of alum, the hardening increases as the quantity of acetic acid is increased until a maximum is reached, after which increasing the acetic acid content decreases the degree of hardening. In order to produce a fixing bath of long life before aluminum sulphite precipitates, a certain minimum quantity of acetic acid must be added to the fixing solution. However, the amount of acid required for this purpose is usually greater than that required to produce maximum hardening. (*c*) Reduce the amount of acid or sulphate, or increase the amount of alum relative to other ingredients if the failure of the bath to harden the film is attributed to cause (*c*) above.

4. *Remedy.*—The film may be hardened by immersing it in a hardening solution containing potassium alum, chrome alum, or formalin.

Milkiness or Sludging.

1*A. Distinguishing Characteristic.*—Formation of milky precipitate which is pale yellow and settles very slowly when the bath is standing, or yellow deposit of sulphur precipitated on the gelatin which may later cause fading of the image.

2*A. Cause.*—Such milkiness may be caused by (*a*) excess of acid in the hardener; (*b*) too little sulphite, or sulphite of impure quality when compounding the bath solution. Some loss of sulphite occurs through oxidation, especially if the fixing bath is stored in open tanks, but this loss can be prevented or minimized by covering the tank or by placing a floating cover on the solution. (*c*) High temperature of the fixing bath.

3*A. Prevention.*—Depending upon the cause enumerated above, milkiness may be prevented by (*a*) using less acid in the fixing bath; (*b*) use of the proper amount of sulphite, or sulphite of pure quality; or (*c*) keeping the fixing solutions, whenever possible, between 65 and 70°F.

4*A. Remedy.*—None, except to prepare a fresh fixing bath.

1*B. Distinguishing Characteristic.*—White precipitate which disappears on standing for several hours. A white gelatinous sludge of aluminum sulphate may also settle out.

2*B. Cause.*—This milky sludge may be caused by (*a*) too little acid in the hardener, (*b*) too little hardener in the fixing bath, or (*c*) exhausted fixing bath containing alum and sulphite but no acid.

3*B. Prevention.*—According to the cause enumerated above, milkiness may be prevented by the following methods: (*a*) The use of the correct amount of acid in compounding the fixing solution. Care should be taken, not only to observe that the proper amounts of acid are used, but to use either glacial or 28 per cent acetic acid, as called for in the formula. If 28 per cent acetic acid is used instead of the same amount of glacial acetic acid, the solution will contain less than one-third of the required amount of acid. (*b*) More hardener solution should be added to the fixing bath. (*c*) Acid may be added to the bath from time to time to prevent sludging.

4*B. Remedy.*—It is usually best to make up a fresh fixing bath.

1*C. Distinguishing Characteristic.*—Greenish gelatinous precipitate sometimes forming upon the film.

2*C. Cause.*—The sludge consists of chromium hydroxide and is caused by an excess of developer in the fixing solution.

3*C. Prevention.*—Milkiness due to this cause may be prevented by rinsing the film in water before fixing, by the use of an acid stop bath before fixing, or by the revival of the bath with the addition of acid. Frequently the formation of the green sludge may be prevented from forming on the film by agitating the film thoroughly when it is first immersed in the fixing bath.

4*C. Remedy.*—If the sludge is discovered while the film is still wet, it may frequently be removed by swabbing with soft cotton.

Scum.

1*A. Distinguishing Characteristic.*—Metallic appearing scum deposit on the surface of the fixing bath.

2*A. Cause.*—The scum consists of silver sulphide formed by the reaction of silver thiosulphate in the partially exhausted or infrequently used fixing solution, with the hydrogen sulphide gas present in the air.

3*A. Prevention.*—Protect the unused fixing baths from contact with the air by means of a cover on the container.

4*A*. *Remedy.*—The scum may be removed from the surface of the bath by drawing the edge of blotting paper or a piece of cheese cloth over the surface of the bath.

1*B*. *Distinguishing Characteristic.*—Greenish white scum, often precipitated on the surface of the film when chrome alum fixing baths are employed.

2*B*. *Cause.*—The scum consists of basic chromium sulphite or chromium hydroxide.

3*B*. *Prevention.*—To remove chromium scum, films which have been treated with a chrome alum fixing or hardening bath should be wiped or squeegeed carefully between the washing and drying operations. If this scum is not completely removed, the scum which remains will leave a stain on the negative and, after the film has dried, the scum will be difficult to remove. The scum may be removed from the wet film by swabbing the negative with moist absorbent cotton. Formation of the scum may often be prevented by (*a*) agitating the film thoroughly when first immersing it in the stop bath and (*b*) using a developer containing as little alkali as possible and by reviving the fixing bath at intervals with acid.

4*B*. *Remedy.*—None.

Sludging.—(See Milkiness.)

Stains.

1*A*. *Distinguishing Characteristic.*—Green stain (when using chrome alum baths) imparting to the gelatin an appearance as if colored by green dye.

2*A*. *Cause.*—According to Crabtree and Russell, the intensity of the stain is influenced by the relative proportions of carbonate and sulphite in the developer. An excess of carbonate increases the intensity of the stain, whereas an excess of sulphite decreases the stain intensity. The intensity of the stain is also materially increased at high temperatures (80 to 90°F.)

3*A*. *Prevention.*—Increasing the carbonate content of the hardening bath will reduce or eliminate the stain.

4*A*. *Remedy.*—By treating the film with a 5 per cent solution of sodium citrate or a 50 per cent solution of potassium hydroxide, the stain can usually be removed. This treatment destroys the hardening of the gelatin, however. Provided the stain is uniform over the entire film, a stain is not ordinarily objectionable from the photographic standpoint. If the stain is not uniform, prints will show the presence of the stain.[1]

1*B*. *Distinguishing Characteristic.*—Yellowish-white opalescent stain on film.

2*B*. *Cause.*—This stain is caused by the precipitation of sulphur on the gelatin. It may be due to (*a*) the use of an improperly compounded fixing bath which contains too little sulphite or a relative excess of acid or (*b*) a fixing bath which is too warm. When either of these conditions are encountered, colloidal or finely divided sulphur may be formed, which deposits on the gelatin.

3*B*. *Prevention.*—According to the cause listed above, the stain may be prevented by (*a*) properly compounding the fixing bath or (*b*) by maintaining the solution at temperatures between 65 and 70°F.

4*B*. *Remedy.*—These stains may be removed by first hardening the film in an alkaline solution of formalin, after which the film is bathed in a 10 per cent solution of sodium sulphite at a temperature of about 100 to 120°F. These stains cannot be removed by water or acid baths.

1*C*. *Distinguishing Characteristic.*—White powdery stains of aluminum sulphite.

2*C*. *Cause.*—Owing to insufficient acidity of the fixing bath. This may occur as a result of incorrect compounding or partial exhaustion of the bath.

---

[1] For other stains, see S. E. Sheppard and A. Ballard, Chemistry of the Acid Fixing and Hardening Bath, *J. Franklin Inst.*, **200**, 537 (1925).

3C. *Prevention.*—The following steps are recommended to prolong the life of the fixing bath and prevent formation of aluminum sulphite. (*a*) Developers containing an excess of alkali should be avoided. (*b*) Rinse the film between the developing and fixing, to remove as much developer as possible. The rinse may be made using clear water or an acid stop bath. Stop baths should be used with discretion, however, as an excess of acid may be carried over to the fixing bath, thereby causing sulphurization of the latter.

4C. *Remedy.*—The stains of aluminum sulphite may be removed by hardening the film in an alkaline solution of formalin, after which the film is bathed for a few minutes in a 5 per cent solution of sodium carbonate. The film should finally be thoroughly washed.

1D. *Distinguishing Characteristic.*—Fairly opaque stains on the film, having a dirty yellow color.

2D. *Cause.*—Such stains are produced when silver compounds are left in the film as a result of incomplete fixation. They may be due to (*a*) Insufficient agitation when immersing the film initially in the fixing bath. In such cases the developing solution, coming into contact with the film, reduces the silver halide (dissolved out by the sodium thiosulphate) back again to yellow metallic silver. (*b*) Use of old or exhausted fixing solution containing excess silver in solution. Some of this silver salt remains on the film if it is not thoroughly washed. Originally this compound is colorless, but upon exposure to the air a yellow stain results from the formation of silver sulphide.

3D. *Prevention.*—(*a*) Agitating the film when it is first immersed in the fixing bath will aid in preventing stains. In this case, the tendency to form a stain is greatest when strongly alkaline developing solutions are used and when the fixing baths are neutral or alkaline instead of being acid. Consequently the fixing baths should be acid and a developer having low alkaline content should be used, or the film should be rinsed in water between development and fixing. (*b*) Use only a fresh acid fixing solution.

4D. *Remedy.*—The following methods are frequently helpful in removing silver stains:

a. Wash the film thoroughly to remove any traces of sodium thiosulphate, and then bathe in a 1 per cent solution of potassium cyanide. (*Caution.* Cyanide is a deadly poison. In solution with water, cyanide produces deadly fumes of hydrocyanic acid. Consequently, this material must be carefully handled in well-ventilated rooms.) The cyanide will dissolve away the silver thiosulphate and some of the silver sulphide. Cyanide is also a solvent for metallic silver. Therefore, as soon as any signs of reduction of the silver image appear, the film should be removed from the cyanide bath and washed thoroughly in clear water.

b. Treatment with a weak solution of permanganate acid, followed by a thorough wash in clear water and then immersing the film in cyanide will often be useful in removing stains from old negatives.

c. In those cases in which the silver stain cannot be completely removed, it may be possible to make a new negative, free from stains, by copying the negative or print through a yellow filter, such as the Wratten G filter.

Water Supply.—Water is so frequently used in photographic processing that it is advisable to pay considerable attention to the purity and adequacy of the supply. For photographic purposes water may be used as a constituent of most processing solutions, or it may be used merely as a solvent or wash. In either case impurities in the water may result in imparting undesirable characteristics to the processing solutions, to the formation of deposits on the photographic materials, or to other undesirable effects. As a general rule water which is suitable for human consumption will also be satisfactory for photographic purposes. The filtered water obtained from public sources of supply may contain colloidal matter and dissolved salts which are not removed by filtration, and certain municipalities intentionally add chlorine or other substances as public health protective measures. These constituents of water may or may not be objectionable from the photographic standpoint, although they are not desirable.

Wherever possible, and certainly when any doubt exists concerning the suitability of the water supply for photographic purposes, photographic solutions and especially developing solutions should be prepared with distilled water. If this is impracticable, the solutions can be prepared with water which has been boiled.

Solutions are usually made by adding chemicals to a quantity of water called for by the formula. In some cases, however, water is added to a solution to obtain a given concentration or volume of solution, and in this case the final volume should be that called for in the formula.

Chemical analysis of the water supply may be useful in determining the amount of oxalate or lime which is to be added to coagulate slimes, to remove dissolved calcium salts, or in determining which of several water supplies is most likely to be free from dissolved or colloidal material. The greater the quantity of undesired products found in the water supply, the greater may be the difficulty expected from drying marks, and the less certain one can be of the purity of compounded solutions. Water supplies containing iron, metallic sulphides, or hydrogen sulphide should be avoided. But chemical analysis does not usually reveal much information as to the suitability of a water supply for photographic purposes, and trial tests with sample solutions and actual photographic materials are the only reliable means of determining the suitability of a certain water supply for photographic purposes. Two solutions should be prepared, one with distilled water and one with the water supply under consideration. Samples of the film are then processed in the two solutions, the one made with distilled water being used as a control. Comparisons of the processed films will then show what, if any, undesirable effects may be expected from the water supply under consideration. Another simple test which indicates the extent of the trouble which might be anticipated due to residual scum may be made by permitting a large drop of water to dry on a film; water suitable for photographic use should leave no scum or stain.

Water exists in various states of impurity, and while any source of water may be purified, purification is a time-consuming and expensive process which may not be economically justified if the original source is reasonably satisfactory for photographic purposes. Provided the distillation is carried out properly and with clean apparatus, distilled water is the purest form of water supply. Next, in order of purity, may be mentioned: (a) rain water collected on a clean surface and stored in clean containers, (b) melted snow and hail, (c) spring and well water, (d) water from flowing rivers, streams, and brooks, and (e) sea water.

The impurities which may be present in the various kinds of water are dissolved salts, such as bicarbonates, chlorides, and sulphates of calcium, magnesium, and potassium. If iron is present to any considerable degree, the water should not be used for photographic purposes. The water may also contain solid impurities, such as silt, and, while these are not usually so injurious as iron or various salts, they may be readily filtered out. Suspended matter, such as iron rust, dirt, or silt, should be removed by filtration, as otherwise these particles may settle and cause spots on negatives or prints processed in solutions made with such water. The water may also contain clay, slime, or colloidal animal or vegetable matter which is not removed by filtration. If such water is used in the preparation of photographic solutions, the undesired particles may gradually coagulate and settle as a sludge. Dissolved gases are sometimes encountered in water supplies. Hydrogen sulphide is objectionable in that it causes chemical fog, but it may be removed by boiling the water. Sea water contains about 3.5 per cent of soluble salts, mostly halides, which retard action of photographic solution. Consequently sea water should be avoided.

Effect of Impurities in Development. —If a developing solution is compounded with water containing calcium salts, a white precipitate of calcium sulphite may form on standing. If the developer contains sodium bisulphide or potassium metabisulphite, fine, needlelike calcium sulphite crystals may be precipitated as a sludge. In either case this sludge is harmless if it is permitted to settle, after which the clear solution may be decanted from the sludge. The developer is, nevertheless robbed of the sulphite to the extent of the sludge which has formed, but the effect is negligible except in the case of developers of low alkalinity. Borax developers are sensitive to small changes in alkalinity, however, so that it may be necessary to make allowance for the reduction of sulphite when such developers are prepared with calcium salts. If the developer is agitated, the sludge may become precipitated on the photographic material.

Sodium or potassium sulphide in the water used for preparing developing solutions will produce objectionable chemical fog, even though only very small quantities of sulphides are present. Removal of sulphides may be accomplished by treating the water with lead acetate to produce insoluble lead sulphide. Copper sulphate is sometimes added to water supplies for the purpose of killing vegetable and bacteriological matter. The amount of copper sulphate added is not usually sufficient to be harmful, although it may cause aerial fog.

The presence of chlorides or bromides in the water supply used in compounding developers exerts a restraining action on the developer which may, however, be compensated by properly adjusting the amounts of the other ingredients. Unless present in excess, magnesium salts will not be precipitated. Other salts have little or no effect upon the action of the developer.

The presence of sulphur in water from which developers are made will produce fog, as a result of the formation of sodium sulphide from the interaction of the sulphur with the carbonate of the developer. By boiling the water, the sulphur can usually be made to coagulate, after which it may be removed by filtration.

Animal matter in the water from which developers are compounded usually precipitates when the developer is mixed. Certain types of bacteria form growths which act on the sulphite to form sodium sulphite which fogs photographic materials.

Effect of Impurities in Fixation.—Calcium and magnesium sulphite are soluble in acetic acid and therefore are not precipitated in the fixing bath. Other dissolved salts, such as bicarbonates, chlorides, and sulphates, are harmless. Suspended matter in the form of dirt, iron rust, and certain types of vegetable and animal matter usually coagulates and settles out in the fixing bath if allowed to stand. While most suspended substances have practically no effect on the photographic properties of the fixing baths, the particles may settle on the film, retarding fixing action locally, and causing spots and stains. Extracts from vegetable matter or dissolved gases do not affect the photographic properties of a fixing bath but may cause blisters or stains.

Effect of Impurities on Washing.[1]—Dissolved salts of magnesium, calcium, or potassium in the water used for washing often cause trouble by crystallizing on the film in drying and, while not always visible, may detract from the transparency of the image. Water which is free of dissolved salts will also cause markings on the film if it is allowed to remain in droplets on either side of the film during drying. It is important, therefore, to remove all excess water from the film before drying.

Suspended mineral, vegetable, and animal matter generally leaves a scum on the film unless the gelatin surface is wiped previous to drying. If the water used for the

[1] This section taken from "Motion Picture Laboratory Practice," Eastman Kodak Co.

washing is run into a large settling tank or if it is properly filtered before use, most of the suspended matter will be removed.

Dissolved gases will sometimes produce blisters if the water is warm, or if the film is not sufficiently hardened in the fixing bath. When present in sufficient quantity, dissolved extracts sometimes produce stains which are very difficult to remove.

So far as is known, small traces of impurities which may be left in the gelatin coating of motion-picture negatives or positive film are not liable to impair the properties of the film seriously over a period of 4 or 5 years. However, as an added precaution, valuable film should be washed finally in distilled water.

Water Purification.—Water may be brought to various states of purification by: (1) distillation, (2) boiling, (3) filtration, and (4) chemical treatment. Distillation produces the purest water, but stills of adequate capacity are expensive, especially where large quantities of water are required, and the distilling process is slow. Whenever it can be readily obtained, it is advisable to use distilled water for the mixing of photographic solutions. It is not necessary that films be washed throughout the entirety of the washing process in distilled water, however. Removal of soluble materials may be accomplished by washing the films in ordinary tap water, as a general rule. For those cases in which complete washing with pure water is necessary, these preliminary washes may be followed with one or two baths using distilled water.

Except in those cases in which the water contains an excess quantity of dissolved salts, sufficient purification can usually be obtained by boiling the water and permitting this to stand while cooling. The boiling process coagulates most of the colloidal vegetable and animal matter, changes certain lime salts into an insoluble condition in which they settle out, and drives out dissolved gases which may be present, such as hydrogen sulphide, air, etc. Dissolved substances are, of course, not removed in this process. After the water has settled, it may be filtered through paper filters or fine-mesh cloth. A more rapid method of separating the settled particles from the supernatant liquid is to decant or siphon off the latter.

Filtration of the water supply may be used to remove suspended or undissolved particles, but the dissolved gases and colloidal matter cannot be removed by this process, unless the water has been boiled or otherwise treated to drive off dissolved gas and coagulate colloidal particles. Where only very small quantities of water are required, the ordinary paper filter or fine-mesh cloth fitted into a funnel may be employed. Where larger quantities of water are required, a barrel filled with sand, charcoal, or other filtering agents may be used. Many types of filters are available commercially.

If large quantities of water are required, chemical treatment is the most practical method of water purification. Coagulation of slime, which carries down suspended particles, may be effected by adding potassium alum in the proportions of 0.25 g. per l., or 15 gr. per gal. This method clears the solution quickly but does not remove dissolved salts. The addition of this small quantity of alum has been found to produce no harmful effects when such chemically treated water is used in the preparation of developing or fixing baths.

Solutions of sodium oxalate, sodium phosphate, or sodium sulphite may be used to coagulate slime and precipitate calcium and magnesium salts. These solutions are added to the water supply until no further precipitate is formed. This method does not remove dissolved salts.

Washing. *Purpose of Washing.*—The purpose of washing is to remove from the negatives or prints all or a part of the soluble chemicals or solutions which adhere to them in processing. Although in most cases negatives or prints are washed to remove from them the chemicals of the fixing bath, this is not always the case. Sometimes, for instance, the photosensitive materials are washed after development but prior to fixing. The general principles of washing are the same, however, no matter in which stage of processing washing takes place.

General Remarks on Washing.—The washing process is simply one of diluting or dissolving the material and carrying away the diluted products with the disposal of the wash water. No chemical action takes place during washing, or, at least, those chemical actions which may take place are accidental and undesired.

So far as concerns the removal of the product to be eliminated, the washing of photographic materials is largely independent of the temperature of the wash water. Most substances are more soluble in hot than in cold water, so that it might be expected that they would diffuse from the gelatin more rapidly in warm than in cold water. Any attempt to wash photographic materials more thoroughly or more quickly by elevating the temperature of the water is counteracted by the swelling of the gelatin at the increased temperature. This swelling tends to inhibit diffusion. Both of these counteracting effects occur at about the same rate with a rise in temperature, so that the rate of washing is largely independent of the temperature, at least within the range of temperatures usually employed for photographic work. At elevated temperatures the gelatin may become soft, and reticulation may take place. For this reason it is advisable that the temperature of the wash water be kept sufficiently low as not to soften the gelatin. Temperatures of 60 to 70°F. are usually satisfactory.

Hardening of the gelatin has little effect on the rate at which photosensitive materials may be washed, unless the material has been dried between the time of hardening and that of washing. If the gelatin has been hardened and dried before washing, it will not expand much when subsequently soaked in water, so that diffusion through it will be difficult. Before the gelatin has dried, hardening does not affect the diffusion through the gelatin.

The completeness of washing does depend upon the length of washing time and upon the agitation of the photographic materials in the wash water. It also depends upon the method of washing. As a first approximation, it may be stated that in general the longer the photographic material is washed, the more completely are the adhering chemicals removed. The removal of chemicals progresses geometrically rather than arithmetically; *i.e.*, in a given time interval, a certain percentage (rather than a certain amount) of the remaining chemicals are removed. By washing for a sufficiently long period of time, any desired degree of removal may be attained. The more actively the photographic materials are agitated in the wash solution the more quickly the chemicals are removed, as a general rule.

The most fundamental requirement in washing, however, is to provide an adequate supply of wash water. This may be done by immersing the photographic materials in running water, or by successively removing the photographic materials from one bath to a fresh bath.

Mechanism of Washing.—Two methods of washing are in extensive use: (1) the continuous-flow method and (2) the multiple-bath method. Both methods are capable of yielding satisfactory and thorough washing of the photographic material. but the physics of the essential operations is slightly different in these two cases. An understanding of the mechanism of washing is useful in obtaining the most complete washing for a given amount of water and in a given length of time.

In the continuous-flow system, fresh clean water is made to flow steadily over the negative or print. So long as fresh water is supplied, washing continues indefinitely; the prints are more or less continuously agitated with respect to the water flow, and the operation is carried out automatically. All continuous-flow methods may not be equally effective, however, and care should be taken to see that the method employed in continuous-flow washing is such as to actually fulfill the requirements given above.

An excellent example of this method of washing is that in which a thin film of fresh water is made to flow continuously over both sides of a film hanging vertically. The water dripping from the film is discarded. A much less satisfactory example of the continuous-flow method is represented by a tank in which the inlet and outlet pipes are close to one another and at the same end of the tank. In this case it is possible for a large part of the incoming fresh water to circulate immediately to the outlet drain without becoming effective in washing the film which remains in the central portion of the tank in relatively stagnant water. A better system for tank washing is to have the inlet at the bottom of one end of the tank, and the outlet at the top and opposite end of the tank. Any water which is discharged from such a system must have passed across the tank and, in so doing, washed the film. Moreover the tank is always filled with water so long as any water discharge takes place.

In the multiple-bath method, the negatives or prints are placed in a tank or tray with a fixed amount of water which is usually not changed so long as the photosensitive materials remain in them. During the time the photosensitive materials remain in any given tank or tray, the negatives should be thoroughly agitated; after a lapse of some time, the negatives are removed to another tank of fresh water. In so doing, they will carry over into the fresh bath some of the solution from the bath from which they were removed. While it is unavoidable that some of the solution be carried over, much more thorough and rapid washing can be effected if as much of the solution as possible is removed from the film before immersing into the succeeding wash. The transferring of the prints from one tank of water to another containing fresh water is continued until the prints are thoroughly washed. Usually six washes of about 5 min. each are sufficient to produce satisfactory washing.

Continuous Washing.—Experiments indicate that with thorough agitation of the photographic material in the wash water, the sodium thiosulphate diffuses exponentially, so that in equal time intervals, equal percentages of hypo are removed. With an exponential law representing the diffusion in the washing process it is theoretically impossible to remove all the undesired product. Practically, however, we may remove as much of the hypo as we desire by washing for a sufficiently long period of time.

To derive a quantitative expression for this method of washing, let M_0 be the amount of material, *e.g.*, hypo, originally present on the film, and let M be the amount washed out in time t. (The values of M_0 and M may be expressed as initial and final concentrations of the solution or as initial and final masses of material.) Then the net change in the amount of material on the film, dM, during a given time interval dt will be

$$dM = -k(M_0 - M)dt \qquad (8)$$

where k is a proportionality factor (sometimes called the constant of elimination) which depends upon the degree of agitation and the type of emulsion and usually varies between 0.1 and 0.15 for negatives, according to Warwick. It can be shown that the solution of this equation is

$$kt = \log_e \frac{M_0}{M_0 - M} = 2.30259 \log_{10} \frac{M_0}{(M_0 - M)} \qquad (9)$$

from which the time required to obtain any desired degree of washing becomes

$$t = \left(\frac{1}{k}\right) \log_e \frac{M_0}{M_0 - M} = \frac{2.30259}{0.1} \log_{10} \frac{M_0}{(M_0 - M)} \qquad (10)$$

In this equation, M_0 indicates the initial amount (or concentration) and $(M_0 - M)$ indicates the final amount or concentration of the material which remains.

To illustrate the use of this equation, suppose we wish to reduce the amount of hypo to 1/50,000 of its initial value before stopping washing. Then $(M_0 - M)$ is 1/50,000 of M_0, so that $(M_0)/(M_0 - M) = 50,000$. If we choose $k = 0.1$, then the time, in minutes, required for washing will be

$$t = 23.0259 \times 4.6990 = 108 \text{ min.} \tag{11}$$

Similarly, if a given negative has 1 g. of hypo on it initially, and we wish to carry out washing until the amount of hypo finally remaining is 0.0001, then

$$t = 23.0259 \log_{10}\left(\frac{1}{0.0001}\right) = 23.0259 \log_{10} 10,000 = 23.0259 \times 4 = 92 \text{ min.} \tag{12}$$

It should be realized that the results given by these equations depend upon the assumptions that the rate of diffusion is an exponential function of time and that the photosensitive material is thoroughly agitated in the continuously flowing wash water. The first assumption is generally well fulfilled in practice, so that the degree to which the above expressions represent actual conditions depends upon the degree to which the second assumption (which is under the control of the photographer) is fulfilled. For practical applications it may be said that the above equations represent favorable limiting conditions and that in any practical case the wash time may be increased advantageously over that given in the above equations.

Multiple-bath Washing.—In the multiple-bath system of washing, the removal of sodium thiosulphate (or other solute) is a slightly more complicated process. In any given wash, the amount of solute is removed continuously with agitation of the negative in the wash water until the final limiting value is reached. This limiting value is that for which the amount of solute in the wash water is in equilibrium with that remaining in the negative, *i.e.*, the concentration of solute in the negative is equal to the concentration of the wash water. The negative is then removed to another bath where the amount of solute removed progresses continuously until another equilibrium of lesser concentration is reached. Except for the instant when the film is initially introduced into a fresh wash bath, it is always immersed in a bath which is contaminated with hypo which this bath has removed from the film. Because the film is immersed in water containing hypo, only that amount of solute (hypo in this case) can be removed which will bring to equilibrium the solute in the gelatin with that of the wash water. There is no possibility of removing more solute from the film after the equilibrium condition has been reached no matter how long the material is washed beyond this point. For each bath, therefore, a time is reached beyond which the bath is no longer effective in the removal of solute, and further washing can be attained only by removal of the film to a fresh bath.

Following the method of the previous section, equations may be developed for the effect of each of a number of baths, as well as the over-all or net effect of several baths. The essential feature in multiple-bath washing is the number of baths required to reduce the original concentration of the solute to some definite and small fraction of its original value. This case has been treated by Warwick.[1] If n is the number of wash baths, all of which are similar, $1/A$ is the fraction of the solute left after n washings, V is the volume of the wash water in each bath, and v is the volume of solution on the surface of the film and carried over into one bath as a contamination from the preceding bath, then the number of baths required is given by

$$n = m\left(\frac{\log_{10} A}{\log_{10}\left(\frac{1 + V}{v}\right)}\right) \tag{13}$$

---

[1] Warwick, A. W., Scientific Washing of Negatives and Prints, *Am. Phot.*, **11** (No. 6), 317–327 (1917).

where m is a constant depending upon the type of material being washed. For plates and films washed in tanks, $m = 1$, whereas when washing is done in shallow trays, $m = 1.25$. For washing prints in trays, $m = 2$. Equation (13) gives the number of baths required (for specified values of A and V/v), under the assumption that the film is washed thoroughly in each bath.

Washing with Limited Water Supply.—It sometimes happens that the amount of water available for washing is limited so that the question arises as to the most effective use of the available supply. Under such restrictions it can be shown that the best utilization of a given water supply is that in which the total amount of water is divided into as many separate baths as possible so long as the amount of water in each bath is sufficient to cover the entire negative or print. Between wash baths the surface water from the negatives should be removed. The removal of the surface water is very effective in obtaining completeness of washing but is a point which is frequently neglected.

The conditions outlined above for the optimum use of a limited water supply are such that the reduction of hypo concentration per individual bath is not likely to be very high. Consequently a large number of baths is desirable. We may summarize the conditions for optimum use of a limited wash-water supply as follows: (1) wash the negatives or prints in the minimum amount of water in each bath which will completely cover all the surface area, (2) remove the surface water between baths by sponging the photographic material with a viscose sponge or lintless cloth, and (3) wash in as many baths as possible since each bath does not produce very much reduction in hypo concentration.

Importance of Adequate Water Supply.—In any wash bath, the most fundamental rule is to use plenty of water. For multiple-bath washing this general statement may be modified slightly, as in this case it is more important that the ratio of the volume of water in the bath be large compared to the volume of water carried over from one bath to another by the film. Plenty of water is one answer to this situation; a better answer, especially when the water supply is limited, is to make the ratio V/v as large as possible. A very effective way of increasing V/v is to remove as much of the surface water as possible between wash baths.

Washing Several Negatives in the Same Bath.—To save time in washing, it is common practice to place several negatives or prints in the same wash baths at the same time. So long as each sheet of material is always kept separated from all others, the general principles outlined for multiple wash baths hold.

On the other hand, if the sheets of photographic material are not agitated and especially if they are permitted to pile upon one another so that one sheet protects another from being washed by fresh water, hypo will not be effectively removed from the protected areas. Therefore such washing may not remove any appreciable percentage of hypo from the protected areas.

Even if the separate sheets are kept separated, it is still possible, if they are not thoroughly agitated, that some of the negatives or prints will sink to the bottom of the tank or tray, whereas others may remain at a higher level of wash water in the bath. Since the hypo solution is more dense than the fresh, uncontaminated water, it will tend to settle at the bottom of the tank. Thus the sheets at the bottom of the tank will receive less effective washing than those at the top.

Contamination of Partly Washed Materials.—The addition of negatives or prints fresh from the hypo bath into a bath of partially washed prints or negatives may easily undo all the effects of previous washing, so that it may be necessary to start washing all over again if complete washing is to be attained. The reason for this is that the materials having the higher concentration of hypo add considerable hypo to the wash water, so that the introduction of the hypo-laden materials may raise the hypo concentration of the partly washed materials. The same effect occurs if hypo-contaminated fingers are placed in the wash bath. In this case, to obtain a given degree of hypo elimination, washing will be prolonged beyond that time required if the bath is not contaminated.

A practical means of reducing to a minimum contamination from either of the causes mentioned above is to wash the photographic materials in cascade. Two methods are possible. In one of these the wash water remains constant for each bath, the baths being cascaded; in the other the water from one bath overflows into the next bath and all baths have their water changed periodically. The second method is to be preferred unless the amount of wash water is limited. The material to be washed is placed in the first or bottom tank and is removed, in due time, to higher tanks in which the water is successively less contaminated with hypo. Should it become necessary to add more negatives during the washing process, the partly washed negatives can be removed to a higher tray, whereas those fresh from the hypo bath are placed in the bottom tray. Thus the partly washed negatives or prints receive fresh water, whereas those fresh from the hypo bath receive water which is only slightly contaminated by hypo from the materials in the preceeding bath.

Completeness of Washing Negatives.—It is of practical importance to know when negatives are sufficiently thoroughly washed as to prevent hypo staining. Washing longer than is necessary is time consuming and accomplishes no essentially useful service. There are three methods in common use for determining the washing time. The first depends upon experience. The other methods depend upon chemical or electrolytic conductivity tests for traces of hypo or other solute.

The washing of negatives in trays is time consuming but is practical where only a small amount of work is being done. A common general rule, based on experience, is that a negative or print should pass through 6 to 12 changes, remaining in each bath for 5 min. In warm weather this method may be productive of frilling because of the frequent handling of the negatives which this process requires.

Where negatives or prints are washed in trays or tanks of running water the required time of washing may be determined from the time which it takes for a colored solution in the tank to become completely replaced by clear, colorless water. To this time should be added the minimum washing time for the material under consideration, as given in Table III. For example, if it takes 10 min. for the colored

TABLE III.—MINIMUM WASHING TIME FOR VARIOUS PHOTOGRAPHIC MATERIALS

Material	Washing Time Min.
Lantern-slide plates	3
Other plates	5
Film negatives of all kinds	7
Single-weight bromide papers	20–25
Double-weight bromide papers	35–60

solution to be replaced by clear water running into the tray, then film negatives should be washed at least 17 min., single-weight bromide papers should be washed 30 to 35 min., and lantern slides should be washed 13 min. Any colored solution or dye may be used to determine the length of time for the tank to become cleared, but it is desirable that this solution be one which has no deleterious effects on the negatives or prints.

A test solution for hypo may also be used. This solution is made by dissolving the chemicals in the following formula.

Potassium permanganate	0.3 g.	4 gr.
Sodium hydroxide	0.6 g.	8 gr.
Distilled water to make	250 cc.	8 oz.

To make a test solution add 1 cc. ($\frac{1}{4}$ dram) of the above solution to 250 cc. (8 oz.) of water in a clear glass container. Allow the wash water from several negatives or prints to drip into the test solution. If the color of the solution remains unchanged the photographic materials may be considered to be completely washed. The violet color of the test solution will turn to orange in about 30 sec. if a small amount of hypo from the drippings of the wash water is added. With larger amounts of hypo added to the test solution, the color will turn to a greenish yellow. Change of color of the test solution indicates incomplete washing.

The success of this test depends upon the water being free from oxidizable organic matter, for, if it is not, the organic matter will react the same as the hypo. To ascertain that the water is free from organic matter, it may be tested in the following manner. Prepare two samples of the permanganate-soda test solution using distilled water. To one of these samples, add a known volume of drippings from the wash water, then add an equal amount of tap water to the second test solution which is to serve as a control. If the sample to which the tap water has been added remains violet, the absence of organic matter is indicated. If the color of the solution is changed slightly by the addition of tap water, the presence of organic matter is indicated. In this case, the amount of hypo present in in the first solution will be indicated by the relative color change of the two samples. If both samples turn the same color, no appreciable amount of hypo is indicated as being present in the first solution. If the sample to which tap water was added turns pink, whereas the sample to which hypo was added turned yellow, the presence of hypo would be indicated in the water in which the prints were being washed.

Electrical methods of measuring conductivity of solutions may be used to determine the presence of hypo. The simplest of these methods, which is not so sensitive as some of the chemical tests, makes use of an ohmmeter such as is used in radio-set test equipment. The ohmmeter consists of a d'Arsonval or similar type of d-c measuring instrument, a small dry battery, and a variable resistance for adjusting the meter to its initial or zero setting, all connected in series with two terminals which are insulated from one another. In use, the terminals of the instrument are placed in clear water, and the rheostat is adjusted to the zero reading of the meter. When it is desired to test a solution for the presence of hypo, the terminals are immersed in the wash water, and the meter reading is observed. If the meter reads zero, the absence of hypo is indicated. If the meter reads some value greater than zero, the amount of hypo present is roughly proportional to the meter reading.

In order that such a device may be independent of the extent to which its electrodes are immersed, it is essential that the same area of the electrodes always be immersed when making measurements. Usually, in most commercial instruments, the electrodes are exposed a given amount, the remaining area being protected by insulation. The device will then give significant readings so long as the exposed portions of the electrodes are completely immersed in the liquid. The success of such a device depends to a large extent upon the sensitivity of the meter, upon the area of the exposed electrodes, and upon the separation between the electrodes.

Washing of Prints.—Hickman and Spencer in the *Photographic Journal*, 1925, vol. 63, page 443, showed that prints required a greater washing time than plates or film. While the larger part of the hypo is removed from the emulsion in a comparatively short time, a certain amount is tenaciously retained by the fibers of the paper support and is difficult to remove. For this reason much longer times of washing are required for prints than for plates or film. Prints on good paper should be washed at least 30 min. in a running stream of water while the simple double-weight paper should receive a 1- to $1\frac{1}{2}$-hr. washing. Increasing the velocity of the water or the flow of water over the print does not decrease the time of washing correspondingly as is the case with plates. The removal of hypo retained by the paper base appears to be a matter of time and not of the amount of water or the velocity employed.

In general the conditions applying to the washing of negatives apply equally well to the washing of prints, at least qualitatively. On the assumption that hypo would diffuse from both sides of the print instead of from only one side, it has sometimes been presumed that prints may be washed more rapidly than an equal number and size of film. It has also been stated that prints require a longer time of washing than an equivalent quantity of negatives on the basis that the fibrous texture of the paper holds hypo more tenaciously than do negatives, so that complete washing is not so readily accomplished.

Experiments by Hickman and Spencer[1] indicate that both points of view are correct within limits. A large percentage of the total hypo may be removed from prints within a comparatively short time, but considerably greater washing of prints than of negatives is required to remove the last traces of hypo. Consequently, for complete removal of hypo, prints should be washed in running water for a longer time than negatives or should be washed in more baths than an equivalent amount of negative material.

When prints are washed in running water, Warwick[2] gives as a practical rule the formula

$$t = K \log_{10} A \tag{14}$$

where t = the washing time, in minutes, required for satisfactory washing;

A = reciprocal of the fraction of hypo concentration which it is desired to obtain, *i.e.*, for attaining a final hypo concentration which is $1/50,000$ of the original hypo concentration, $A = 50,000$;

K = a constant to be determined experimentally, but which is approximately 15.5 for common practical cases of operation.

If, for example, we take $K = 16$, and $A = 100,000$, the washing time is

$$t = 16 \log_{10} 100,000 = 16 \times 5 = 80 \text{ min.} \tag{15}$$

whereas if we take $A = 10,000$, the washing time becomes

$$t = 16 \log_{10} 10,000 = 16 \times 4 = 64 \text{ min.} \tag{16}$$

Effect of Container on Washing.[3]—While the amount of water which is changed is of importance in the washing of photographic materials, Hickman and Spencer have determined that the elimination of hypo is sometimes affected by the characteristics of the wash water container in such a manner as to prolong the washing time much beyond that required for a complete change of water in the washing device. For example, these authors report that plates placed in a trough, through which a constant amount of water was flowing, were found to be washed free of hypo more rapidly if the trough was slightly inclined than if it was horizontal. The effectiveness of tank washing devices were found to vary considerably. The inclined trough was found to be the most effective, as well as one of the most simple, of washing devices.

It has been assumed (although not explicitly stated) that the material out of which the container is made had no appreciable effect on the time of washing of prints or negatives. This is a desirable condition and is realized to a very close approximation where the washing vessels are made of glass, enameled metal, glazed earthenware,

[1] Hickman, K. C. D., and D. A. Spencer, Washing of Photographic Products, *Phot. J.*, **65**, 443 (1925).

[2] Warwick, W. A., Scientific Washing of Negatives and Prints, *Am. Phot.*, **11** (No. 6), 317–327 (1917).

[3] A comprehensive study of the effectiveness of washing devices has been reported by Hickman and Spencer, *Phot. J.*, **62**, 225 (1922).

stainless steel, or other nonporous material. If, however, the vessels are made of unglazed earthenware, wood, or other semiporous or cellular materials, some of the wash solution will be absorbed by the porous material and will not be given up so readily as in the case of a nonporous material. In the case of a porous container, the fresh wash water will be required to wash out the solution from the pores as well as from the negatives and prints. The law of washing the container is similar to that of washing photographic negatives and prints, although the containers may wash more slowly than photographic products.

Temperature of the Wash Water.—So far as removal of hypo is concerned, the temperature of the wash water is not of great importance. But the temperature of the water has secondary effects which may be quite damaging, and it is best to keep the temperature of the wash water within certain limits, if this is at all possible.

As gelatin is warmed, it swells and finally, at sufficiently high temperatures, flows off its support. For this reason, the temperature should not become excessively high. A good general rule to follow is to keep the wash water between 60 and 70°F. whenever this is possible. For those cases in which it is not possible to keep the temperature of the wash water down to these limits, damage of the film may often be prevented by hardening the gelatin in a hardening bath. Sudden changes in the temperature of the gelatin are likely to cause wrinkles or reticulation. For this reason it may be advisable to keep the temperature of the wash water as near the temperature of other solutions as possible.

Hypo Eliminators.—To reduce the washing time required to eliminate hypo from negatives and prints, it has been suggested that the hypo be converted into some substance which can be more easily washed from the gelatin. There appears to be little advantage in using such hypo eliminators, however, for then the "hypo eliminator" must be removed from the gelatin, and the removal of this substance may take as long as the removal of the original hypo.

Drying.—Ordinarily the drying of photographic negatives and prints is not given serious consideration. In spite of the fact that comparatively little, if any, physical action takes place which may harm the materials during drying, certain practices are to be preferred to others.

Mechanism of Drying.—Although drying is often treated as an operation involving only a single step, two distinct phases of drying take place. The first of these is concerned with the removal of excess surface water; the second phase is one of evaporation of the remaining water much of which has been absorbed by the gelatin. In the second phase, evaporation takes place normally, or it may be accelerated through the use of forced-draft air blasts. Washes in alcohol or other liquids of low vapor pressure, and consequently having rapid evaporation, also result in accelerated drying.

Removal of the excess surface water is desirable for two reasons. In the first place it speeds up the total time required for drying by removing large drops or pools which would otherwise be required to evaporate. In the second place the tendency of the unremoved water to form water spots resulting in certain forms of spots or stains is greatly removed. The excess water may be removed from negatives and prints by blotting them with a soft but lintless cloth or absorbent material. In this case the cloth should be free from woven pattern, as otherwise the pattern may be impressed on the soft gelatin. Another very satisfactory way of removing excess surface water is to blot or rub off the water with viscose sponges. In this case care must be used, especially with miniature films, to see that small particles of the sponge do not become loose and deposit themselves on the film, where they might remain to produce spots on the final print.

After the surface water has been removed, the negatives or prints may be hung up to dry by evaporation. Drying may take place through the normal evaporation, although quicker drying can be obtained by playing a draft of air over the materials to be dried. If the air is heated, drying will be more rapid, but the temperature should not exceed 90°F.

While drying by forced air flow may sometimes be advantageous, this method tends to stir up the air more completely than normal drying and, in so doing, also stirs up dust and dirt which may be deposited upon the film. The deposit of dust particles on the film is particularly serious in the case of small negatives from which enlarged prints are made. One means of minimizing this contamination by foreign particles is to place the material to be dried in a wooden or metal frame or box which is covered with a cloth of very fine mesh; sufficiently fine so as not to permit dust particles to pass through it. The air may then be blown over this box. While the use of the fine mesh cloth will reduce the air circulation somewhat and thereby prolong the drying time, none of the particles outside of the frame can be deposited upon the film. By making the frame small enough to hold only the required number of negatives, the amount of dust inside the frame can be minimized.

Certain liquids having low vapor pressure so that they evaporate readily may be used to assist in rapid drying. Of these materials the most common and useful is alcohol. After washing has been completed, the surface water is drained off, and the negatives are immersed in alcohol.[1] The negatives are allowed to remain in the alcohol bath for a sufficiently long time for the alcohol to permeate the gelatin coating, thereby replacing as much of the remaining water as possible. Ordinarily from 3 to 5 min. should be sufficient for this purpose, after which the negatives may be removed, drained of their surface alcohol, and hung up to dry. If desired, much of the surface alcohol may be removed by blotting with a soft cloth or viscose sponge, but in this case care should be taken that lint deposits do not adhere to the negative.

The rapidity with which such an alcohol-treated negative will dry depends upon the degree to which air is circulated over the negative, the temperature and humidity of the air, and the percentage of water in the alcohol. Water and alcohol are miscible in all proportions, and as water is brought over to the alcohol bath from the final water wash bath, the alcohol becomes more and more diluted and loses some of its effectiveness as a rapid drying agent.

Sometimes it is found that a faint opalescent deposit appears on the negative which has been rinsed in alcohol. This is likely to occur if poor grades of alcohol (such as rubbing alcohol) are used but may usually be removed by rubbing the surface of the dried negative with a soft cloth or lens tissue. If a negative has not been sufficiently fixed, it will assume a white opaloid or white appearance when immersed in the alcohol bath. The removal of this opalescence may be accomplished by washing the negative in clear water and then returning it to the fixing bath for more thorough and complete fixation.

As alcohol is a solvent for the support sometimes used for certain films, it should not be employed with cellulose nitrate films. In this case drying may be hastened by immersing the film in a 40 per cent solution of formalin or formaldehyde for 5 min. following the final wash in clear water, after which the negative should be dried in a current of air at as high a temperature as is consistent with prevention of injury to the supporting base. Such procedure has considerable potentialities of damage to the negative, especially if attempted by the inexperienced worker and is recommended for use only in emergencies.

Quick drying can also be carried out by using ether instead of alcohol as the final wash bath. Ether and its fumes are highly inflammable and operations with this

[1] The use of an alcohol bath is suitable for glass plates and film materials made of cellulose acetate, as well as printing papers. Cellulose nitrate films are soluble in alcohol so that such negatives cannot be washed in alcohol. From 10 to 20 per cent water should be added to alcohol for this bath.

chemical should be carried out in open space or a well-ventilated room. Fumes of ether should not be breathed as it is an anesthetic.

Plates and films are usually dried vertically by placing them in racks or hanging them by clips from some convenient support. In this case evaporation may take place from both sides of the material. On the other hand, prints are often dried by placing them on a horizontal surface or by squeegeeing them to ferrotype plates, in which case effective evaporation can take place only from one surface of the print. Another common method of drying prints is to place them between white lintless blotters or alternate layers of blotting paper and waxed sheets. Pressure may be applied to a pile of such prints to reduce the tendency of curling.

Water spots on negatives result from the accumulation of water particles into drops. In drying, the gelatin swells at the edge of the drop and forms a crater around the perimeter of the drop, which remains after the drop has completely evaporated. The additional thickness of gelatin at the edge of the crater shows up later in the print as a slightly dark ring or stain. It is sometimes possible to remove such water spots by soaking the negative again in water and drying as uniformly as possible. Removal of the excess surface water will assist in minimizing stains due to water drops. Another method of removing drying marks is to completely bleach the film in a solution of

Potassium bromide	10 gr.
Potassium ferricyanide	10 gr.
Water	1 oz.

After bleaching, the negative is washed and then fully developed in a nonstaining developer.

Drying of Prints.—After a print has been washed thoroughly, the surface moisture may be removed by swabbing with a piece of wet absorbent cotton and the print placed in a rack, in a print dryer, or on a flat surface to dry. If the hardener in the fixing bath has hardened the emulsion side sufficiently, the print may be blotted by means of a moistened viscose sponge, or the excess water may be removed by a squeegee or print roller. The print is placed emulsion side against a clean flat surface, such as the polished surface of a ferrotype plate, and the surplus water is removed by running a rubber straightedged squeegee or a print roller over the back of the print. The print may be left on the ferrotype plate, if one is used, until it is thoroughly dry, when it will peel off easily.

The print may also be placed upon a drying stretcher, which consists of a frame of wooden strips, across which have been stretched sheets of thin porous cloth such as cheesecloth. Such a frame may be used in the open, or it may be placed in a warmed drying oven. In either case it is desirable to turn the prints over occasionally so that the tendency toward curling may be reduced.

The time required for a print to dry will depend upon the degree to which the emulsion has been hardened in the fixing bath, the extent to which the surplus water has been removed from the print, the temperature and humidity of the drying atmosphere, and the weight or thickness of the print paper.

Curling of Prints.—Prints frequently have a tendency toward curling. This is especially true in the case of prints dried on a drying stretcher and in the case of prints having a glossy rather than a dull or matte surface. If a slightly excessive amount of hardener was used in the fixing bath, and if, moreover, the temperature was above the ordinary room temperature and the humidity low, the crispness will be present to the extent of brittleness, with an inclination to crack, making it easy to injure the print in ordinary handling. Such an objectional condition in which a print dries when this method is followed requires use of expedients to produce a flat flexible print. These expedients are as follows:

The use of a glycerin bath.

Sponging and the use of blotters.

Coating the back of the print with gelatin.

Straightening the print.

To give flexibility to the print and overcome brittleness, as well as some of the tendency to curl, a glycerin bath may be used after completion of the final washing. The bath is composed of 1 part of glycerin to from 5 to 10 parts of water. The print should be allowed to remain in this bath until the solution has thoroughly permeated the gelatin coating, which usually requires at least 5 min., and then, without further washing, the print is placed upon the drying screen.

Whether a glycerin bath has been used or not, it is always advisable, while the prints are on the stretchers and before they are thoroughly dry, to sponge the backs of them lightly with water or alcohol and to lay a blotter on them. Even when the glycerin bath has not been used, this sponging, combined with the use of blotters, will aid greatly in drying the prints flat.

The serviceability of the blotters used extensively in print finishing is greatly increased by keeping them as dry as possible. After each time they are wetted, they should be spread out to dry before they are again used. Commercial blotters are ordinarily unsuitable for photographic purposes as they invariably contain chemicals that have a bleaching action on the print. Colored blotters are likewise unsuitable because of the likelihood of the color being transferred to the print. A white, chemically pure blotter is available for photographic purposes.

The curl of a print may be removed by the scraping effect of a straightedged ruler, the procedure being to lay the print face down on a hard clean surface and to draw it between the surface and the straightedge while it is held in close contact with the surface.

Ferrotyping.—Glazing or ferrotyping a print is a process for increasing the luster of a glossy-surfaced print so as to increase its contrast. To impart this gloss, ferrotype plates, *i.e.* thin iron sheets coated with a hard, smooth, glossy enamel, or chromium-metal plates, are used. Prints to be ferrotyped should be hardened in the fixing bath and allowed to remain in the final wash for the normal length of time. Upon completion of the final washing, dip the clean ferrotype plate in water to remove dust specks and lint. Then lay the print, face down, on the ferrotype plate, applying one corner first, and gradually bringing down the other corners until the print lies smooth and flat on the plate. Squeegee the surplus water from the print by means of a print roller or squeegee, making sure that the print is in firm, intimate contact with the plate and that all small air pockets are eliminated. In rolling or squeegeeing, work from the center toward the edges of the print. Instead of squeegeeing, the print and ferrotype plate may be passed through a wringer; this is effective where much work is being done. After squeegeeing or passing through the wringer, the prints are set away to dry.

If the ferrotype plate was clean and the directions given have been followed, the prints will fall away from the ferrotype tin after they have become completely dry. If they do not separate readily, the prints may be removed by prying loose one corner and slipping a thin piece of film between the tin and the print, using this film as a wedge to separate other parts of the print from the tin.

The prints should be trimmed immediately upon their removal from the ferrotype plates and should then be placed under pressure to minimize the tendency to curl. Tendency toward curling may be reduced by dampening the back of the prints occasionally with alcohol.

If a reasonable amount of care is exercised in handling ferrotype plates, and they are clean and well polished, little difficulty should be experienced. Occasionally the prints will stick, and the remedy in this case is to use an antisticking solution. This solution consists of ¼ oz. prepared ox gall, 2 drams of formalin, and 20 oz. of water. The prints are soaked in this solution for at least 3 min. after the final washing and are then transferred to the ferrotype tin without additional washing.

A common cause for the prints sticking to the ferrotype tins is insufficient hardening in the fixing bath, washing in water that was too warm, washing for too long a period of time, applying too much heat to the ferrotype prints in an effort to hasten drying, or failure to lubricate the plates properly. The lubrication polish for ferrotype plates is made as follows:

Benzol, gasoline, or benzine... 15 oz.
Paraffin.. 150 gr.

Polish the tin with a soft cloth dipped in this solution. Rub dry with clean cloth, and polish with a soft dry cloth until all traces of the solution have disappeared.

Use of Alcohol.—Alcohol may be used to hasten the drying of prints in the same manner as its use in the case of negatives. After the final wash in clear water, the print should be immersed in alcohol from 2 to 5 min. (depending upon the amount of water in the alcohol) and left until the print becomes translucent, *i.e.*, until the outline of the image may be seen through the back of the print. The surplus alcohol is then drained off, and the print is dried in the usual manner.

Alcohol-burning Method.—When alcohol is used to hasten the drying of the print, it can be burned from the surface more quickly than it will evaporate normally. The prints are washed in water and then in alcohol, as already explained. The surplus alcohol is drained off. With the wet print safely removed from inflammable materials, the print is held by one corner and an open flame is applied, enabling the inflammable alcohol to burn and in so doing to dry the print. Care must be exercised that the print is not scorched or that the fingers are not burned. If the print is allowed to remain too long in the alcohol bath, the alcohol will penetrate the paper fibers, and the entire print may be burned. The method is not recommended, except as an emergency measure.

Bibliography

Periodicals:

SHEPPARD, S. E., and C. E. K. MEES: Theory of Fixation, *Phot. J.*, **46,** 235 (1906).
PIPER, C. WELBORNE: The Rate of Fixing, *Brit. J. Phot.*, **61,** 437, 458, 511 (1914).
————: Further Experiments in Fixing, *Brit. J. Phot.*, **62,** 364 (1915).
WARWICK, A. W.: The Laws of Fixation, *Am. Phot.*, **11,** 585 (1917).
————: The Fixation of Prints, *Am. Phot.*, **11,** 639 (1917).
ELSDEN: The Theory and Practice of Washing, *Phot. J.*, **57,** 90 (1917); *Brit. J. Phot.*, **64,** 120 (1917).
HICKMAN, K. C. D., and D. A. SPENCER: The Washing of Photographic Products, *Phot. J.*, May, 1922; *Phot. J.*, May, 1923; *Phot. J.*, November, 1924.
LUMIÈRE, A., L. LUMIÈRE, and A. SEYEWETZ: When Are Plates Fixed? *Brit. J. Phot.*, **71,** 172 (1924).
————, ————, ————: The Time of Fixing Development Papers, *Brit. J. Phot.*, **71,** 108 (1924).
SHEPPARD, S. E., ELLIOTT, and SWEET: The Chemistry of Acid Fixing Bath, *J. Franlkin Inst.*, **196,** 45 (1923).

Books:

SHEPPARD: and C. E. K. MEES: "Theory of the Photographic Process," Longmans (1907).
————: "Gelatin in Photography," Van Nostrand.
ROSS, F. E.: "Physics of the Developed Image," Van Nostrand.
NEBLETTE, C. B.: "Photography, Principles and Practice," Van Nostrand.

CHAPTER XIV

PRINTING PROCESSES

By Keith Henney

The photographic process culminates in the making of a positive print, either on a transparent base for viewing by transmitted light or on a paper base for viewing by reflected light. The negative is only an incidental and intermediate (although extremely important) step in this process. The print is the final result, and by the print the photographer's efforts are judged as successes or failures.

General Printing Processes. *The Printing Method.*—When the negative is made, a tone reversal takes place, the bright portions of the object being reproduced in the negative as dark portions and the shadows or dark parts of the object becoming light or transparent portions of the negative. The reason for this reversal of tone is the fundamental basis of present-day photography. Light so affects the negative material that a metallic silver deposit of varying thickness represents the image in the processed negative. The high lights or brighter portions of the object are represented by denser deposits of silver which absorb more transmitted light than the less dense portions representing shadows of the object.

When the print is made, the tone values of the negative are reversed so that the dark portions, representing the high lights, become light portions in the print; and the transparent parts of the negative, representing the shadows of the original, become dark portions in the print.

If the negative and positive have been correctly exposed and processed, the relations between the brightness of the brightest, the least bright, and the intermediate portions of the original scene will be correctly reproduced in the final print. In the ideal case the actual values of these brightnesses will be reproduced as well as the relations between them, but in general all that is expected of the print is that two portions of the original, bearing a certain brightness ratio, will be represented in the print by that same brightness ratio. Thus, if two portions of the original scene have a brightness ratio of 3:1, these portions of the print should reflect light to the eye in a 3:1 ratio.

Types of Printing Processes, and Their Characteristics.—Prints may be made, in general, by two methods: they may be placed in contact with the negative, when a print having the same dimensions as the negative will result, or the positive material may have the image projected on it from the negative so that the print may be smaller or larger than the original, as well as the same size. If the print is to be reduced or enlarged in size, compared to the size of the negative, the print must be made by projection.

Printing processes may also be classified as to the medium used for the print, *viz.*, paper sensitized with silver salts or paper sensitized with salts of other metals, or as to whether the final print is in color or in monochrome, etc. In this chapter we are concerned with monochrome printing on materials sensitized with salts of silver.

The result usually desired is accuracy in portraying the original scene, not only in perspective, but in tone values as well, considering that colors in the original are reduced to black, white, and shades of gray, in the final print. But artistically the

412

desired print may depart widely from being an accurate representation of the original, not only in tone value, but in the component parts which make up the scene. In the hands of an artist, a print may have very little in common with the original scene, since the artist has means of removing from the print any objectionable portion of the original, or lacking a desirable element in the original, the artist may add this element to the print. The tone values are frequently distorted for artistic purposes.

Color photography, however, is as yet a realistic medium, in which the effort is made to make an accurate representation of the original. In time it is probable that photographers will learn how to make use of certain distortions in color photography as they have in monochrome—all with the aim of producing a work of art rather than an accurate representation of the original subject.

The Printing Problem.—If the aim is to produce an accurate reproduction of the original scene, the photographer must consider the following factors, which are considered in greater detail in the chapter on Photographic Sensitometry.

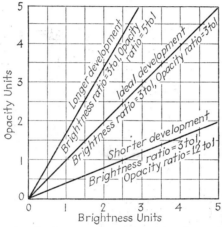

Fig. 1.—Effect of negative development on compressing or increasing opacity range with respect to scene brightness range.

The original subject reflects light in varying degrees depending upon the nature of the illumination, and upon the color and reflectance of the component parts. It is desired to have the final print show these differences in reflecting ability. It is possible in processing the negative to compress the scale or brightness range of the original, to expand it, or to make the negative show accurately the brightness differences of the original. Thus, if the ratio between the maximum and minimum brightness of the original is 20:1, the opacity of the negative representing these portions of the original may show a ratio of less than, equal to, or greater than 20:1.

If the scale is compressed, *i.e.*, if this brightness ratio is reduced, the negative is flat, whereas, if the opacity range is expanded, the negative is contrasty compared to the original. If it is desired to make the print an accurate reproduction of the tone values of the original, some compensation must be made for the fact that a flat or contrasty negative does not accurately portray the original.

Practically, the photographer performs these compensations by using a paper which has less or more contrast. With the flat negative, in which the brightness range of the original has been compressed, a contrasty paper should be used; conversely, a "soft" paper, lacking in contrast, should be used with the contrasty negative, the degree of softness or contrast depending upon the degree of compensation required.

If the negative has been processed so that the brightness range of the original is correctly reproduced in opacity range, then a normal paper would be used. Prints obtained in these three cases will all look alike, if the photographer has processed and used his materials correctly.

The photographer may make use of this ability to compensate for errors occurring in the making of a negative or print. For example, the scientifically minded photographer knows the brightness range which may be expected from paper of certain contrast. If he must photograph a scene in which the brightness range is greater than this paper will reproduce, he will intentionally make a "soft" negative in which the brightness range of the original has been compressed into the scale which can be reproduced by the paper. On the other hand if certain negatives are flat because of some error in processing, the photographer may select a grade of paper which compensates for this error.

Printing Materials and Their Characteristics. *Types of Silver Salt Materials.*—Printing papers are generally known as chloride, bromide, and chlorobromide papers, these names indicating in a general way the chief ingredient in their emulsions. Chloride papers are the slowest and are used for contact printing; bromide papers, the fastest of all printing papers, are roughly 100 times more sensitive than the chloride papers. They are used for projection printing. Intermediate in speed are the chlorobromides; roughly one-twentieth as sensitive as the bromides.

The chlorobromide papers are used when the operator wants the maximum control over print color and contrast by variations of development procedure, and when the simplest types of afterdevelopment toning are to be employed.

Chlorobromides vary considerably in speed. Some are almost as slow as the chlorides; others are almost as fast as the bromides; some may even be slower than papers used for contact printing. These papers are usually not made in the wide range of contrasts available in both chlorides and bromides, but a wide range of control in warmth of tone is possible with them. They have deeper blacks, and give a more faithful rendering of shadows than chlorides or bromides.

Characteristics of Printing Materials.—Curves representing the relation between exposure and opacity (usually plotted as the logarithm of the exposure against the density which is the logarithm of the opacity) of positive materials are similar to those of negative materials. In general the straight or linear portions of these curves are much shorter than those of negative materials. The effect of varying the processing is markedly different for printing papers than for negative materials, as illustrated in the chapter on Photographic Materials.

Printing papers are sensitive only to the shorter wavelengths, *viz.*, blue, and can be processed in yellow or red light. Negative materials, on the other hand, may be sensitive to the entire visible spectrum and even beyond.

Even to the light to which the paper is sensitive, printing papers are much less sensitive than negative materials.

Another difference between positive and negative materials lies in the manner in which varying contrast is secured. If the photographer prolongs the development of a film or plate, the contrast increases. By variations in development procedure, contrast in negative materials may be controlled. But contrast is varied only to a small extent by development variations when positive printing papers are processed. Contrast effects are obtained through proper choice of paper, rather than by methods of processing. If a contrasty result is desired from a negative having normal gradation, a contrast paper will be used. This contrast paper used with a soft negative will produce a normal print having normal gradation. Similarly a soft print may be obtained from a normal negative by the use of soft paper, and a normal result will be obtained by using a soft paper with a contrasty negative.

These effects may be summarized as follows:

TABLE I.—PRINT CHARACTERISTICS

Negative	Paper grade	Print
Soft	Soft Normal Contrast	Excessively flat Soft or flat Normal
Normal	Soft Normal Contrast	Soft or flat Normal Contrasty
Contrasty	Soft Normal Contrast	Normal Contrasty Excessively contrasty

Tone and Exposure Range.—Printing papers have two general characteristics. One is opacity (or density) or tone range; the other is exposure range. By tone range is meant the ratio of the light reflected from the brightest high light of the paper to the light reflected by the deepest shadow. All papers will print black if exposed long enough. All reflect white light if unexposed and if the base is untinted. The texture of the surface has a marked effect upon the tone range. A matte surface will reflect more light from a black portion of the picture than will a glossy paper. Therefore the black of a matte print will not be so black as that of a glossy print.

The exposure range is the ratio between the exposure required to give the deepest black and the exposure required to give a silver deposit which is just perceptible. The exposure range is usually much less than the opacity range of negative materials.

A contrast paper may have an exposure range of 5 to 1; a soft paper may have an exposure range as great as 50 to 1. Papers or other degrees of contrast will have exposure ranges between these values. With this degree of contrast control available by selecting the most suitable paper, the photographer can make prints having accurate tone reproduction from negatives having opacity ranges of 5 to 1 (density range of 0.7) up to 50 to 1 (density range of 1.7).[1]

The photographer who aims at prints for salons will choose meticulously the paper which has the tone and exposure range necessary to show what he considers will get favorable attention from the salon judges. For truest reproduction, a paper of proper exposure range must be chosen to be used with a given negative. But prize-winning results are often attained by deliberately (or accidentally) disregarding this rule.

If the photographer makes a single kind of negative, portraits for instance, under accurately controlled conditions of exposure and development, he will need to use but a single grade of printing paper. The amateur and the commercial finisher, however, must have at hand several grades of paper, some hard and some soft, because they must print from negatives made under all sorts of conditions, and often processed under conditions which may produce opacity ratios which are not like the subject brightness ratios. Most photographers compromise by using a normal or medium grade for most work and sacrificing some accurateness in printing negatives which are not exactly suited to these grades. Harder or softer papers are used for these negatives which are patently out of the normal or average class.

[1] With carbon and platinum processes much longer exposure scales are possible, platinum making possible a range of 100 to 1.

Matte vs. Glossy Prints.—On the question of tone range of matte compared to glossy prints, a communication from Rowland S. Potter, in *The Camera*, April, 1936, is interesting. Sensitometric curves were made of normal grade Velour Black, a chlorobromide enlarging paper. Successive exposures differed by $\sqrt{2}$. The maximum reflection density of glossy paper is clearly greater (see Fig. 2) than that of a matte paper. If the matte print is waxed, its maximum density lies somewhere between that

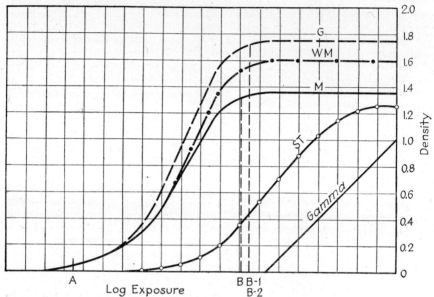

Fig. 2.—Effect of waxing matte print *WM* in increasing maximum density, approaching that of a glossy print *G*.

of the glossy and the fully matted print. The table below gives the pertinent data from this investigation.

TABLE II.—EFFECT OF VARIOUS TYPES OF SURFACES ON PRINTING PAPERS

Paper surface	Maximum density	Relative range in opacity	% increase in opacity over matte	Gamma	Exposure range	Relative range in exposure	% increase in exposure range over matte surface
Matte............	1.36	1.00	——	1.83	18.84	1.00	
Waxed matte......	1.6	1.73	73	2.20	22.13	1.175	17.5
Glossy...........	1.75	2.45	145	2.28	22.13	1.175	17.5

It will be noted that the darkest black of the glossy print is nearly $2\frac{1}{2}$ times blacker than the darkest black of the matte print and that the waxed print has a blackness about 75 per cent greater than the unwaxed print. Furthermore, the waxed matte and the glossy prints both have greater contrast than the matte print, evidenced by the steepness of the curves in the straight portions. In addition, the waxed and the glossy prints both have longer scales of gradation than the matte by a factor of about 17 per cent.

With a vigorous long-scale negative there will be more detail in the shadows of a glossy print or a waxed surface than in those of a matte surface. This is true in spite of the greater contrast. If the differentiation of tone of the matte print is satisfactory, a negative must be less contrasty to give equal differentiation of tones on a waxed surface or a glossy paper. In addition the glossy print will reproduce greater subject brilliance because of the greater maximum black that can be attained in the glossy print.

At its maximum density the paper reflects about 1 per cent of the incident light, which corresponds to a reflection density of 2. Therefore the longest tone range possible is about 100 to 1.

Varieties of Printing Papers Available.—Beside varying in contrast, printing papers are made with various surface textures (smooth or matte, rough, glossy, canvas, etc.), on paper backing material of various tints or colors, of various weights (single or double weight, etc.) etc. These matters are treated more fully in the chapter on Photographic Materials.

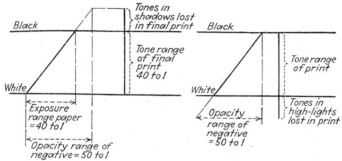

Fig. 3.—Loss of shadow or high-light tones caused by using paper with too short an exposure range for the negative.

Practical Considerations in Printing. *Selection of Paper.*—The printing paper must be selected, not only with regard to the contrast to fit the negative to be printed, or to produce the desired end result, but also with regard to the texture of the paper, its thickness, and its color. These are matters of opinion rather than matters of fact.

Brightness Range Encountered in Practice.—Fortunately the brightness range of the average outdoor or studio scene is such that ordinary negative materials will record it accurately. Mees[1] shows a photograph of a typical outdoor scene in which the brightness of a sunlit cloud was 4250 ft.-lamberts and the deepest shadow had a brightness of 162 ft.-lamberts. This represents a brightness range of 26 to 1. Scenes with brightness ranges of 100 to 1 do not reproduce well, nor do scenes of range of less than 10 reproduce well. It is seldom that brightness ranges greater than 20 or 30 to 1 will be encountered.

Most negative emulsions are capable of reproducing easily the ranges of brightness found in studio or outdoor subjects.

Effect of Using Improper Contrast Grade.—Suppose a subject has a brightness range of 50 to 1 and that it is printed on a paper with an exposure range of 40 to 1. The paper cannot reproduce the entire range of the subject. Suppose the paper is exposed to the negative (which has an opacity range of 50 to 1) in such manner that the high

[1] MEES, C. E. K., "Photography," Macmillan (1937).

lights produce a just perceptible deposit of silver.   The deep shadow will now be full black, but so will many tones which are merely approaching the shadow end of the subject brightness scale.   On the other hand suppose the paper is so exposed that the deepest shadows only are black.   Now the high lights will be white, but there will be many tones toward the high-light end of the subject scale which will also be white. Thus a portrait may show a totally blank white face—no half tones.

If, however, a subject with a range of only 40 is printed on a paper with a scale of 50, different results will occur.   If the paper is exposed so that the high lights produce a just perceptible blackening, the shadows will be gray and muddy because fifty times as much exposure is needed to make this paper black, while the subject produces an effect only forty times as great as that produced by the high-light portion of the negative.   If, on the other hand, the exposure is such that the shadows are black, then the brightest high lights will be darker than white, and the over-all effect will be a muddy and an unpleasant print.   Of course, it is possible to lose tones at both ends, as by using a hard negative with soft paper and placing it midway between white and black on the curve.   All tones will be gray.

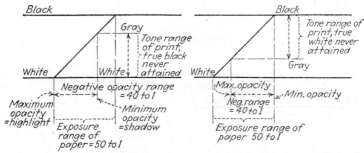

Fig. 4.—Production of weak, limited-tone-range prints by using paper with too long an exposure range for the negative.

It is possible to take advantage of the exposure scale of a paper in another way. If a "snappy" or brilliant print is desired from a negative correctly reproducing a fairly flat subject, then a contrast grade of paper may be employed.   On the other hand, it is possible to reduce the contrast of a subject, correctly reproduced in a negative, by printing that negative on a paper of less than normal contrast.   This has the effect of making more important the intermediate tones existing between the black and white limits of the original subject.   It is impossible, however, to put half tones into a silhouette.   If the original had no intermediate tones, such tones cannot be found on the negative and cannot be printed into the positive.

Methods of Matching Paper and Negative.—Photographers who do much work learn by experience how to select paper to fit negative.   But the casual printer does not acquire this necessary experience.   It is possible that the professional could turn out better prints if he had an accurate means of measuring the scale of his negative and thereby determining which grade of paper he should use.

By means of an exposure meter, or other form of photometer, the photographer can measure the transmission of light through the densest and the thinnest portions of his negative.   This gives an immediate index to the brightness (exposure) ratio that must be accommodated by the printing paper.   After measuring this range the decision can be made whether to use a hard or soft or a medium paper.   Suitable photometric devices are described on page 436.

Several devices are on the market which are useful in determining the exposure to give a certain negative when printing it on a certain paper.   These instruments

Fig. 5.—Effect of printing low-, normal-, and high-contrast negatives. Middle negative (left) and print (right) are normal. If the low-contrast negative were printed on hard paper and the high-contrast negative were printed on soft paper, the resultant prints would resemble closely the print made on medium paper from the normal negative. (*Courtesy of Agfa Ansco Corp.*)

measure the average or integrated amount of light that gets through the entire negative. They will not help the photographer determine the grade of paper to be used since they do not make it possible to measure small areas and thereby to determine opacity differences between the high-light and the shadow portions.

It may be said here, however, that a negative having high contrast should be printed on a paper having less than normal contrast, and conversely, a flat negative requires a more contrasty paper to produce the best results.

Practical Considerations in Negative and Positive Materials.—So far it has been assumed that emulsion characteristics were perfectly straight and of sufficient length to reproduce brightness ranges found in practice. Actual materials, however, are not ideal; the relation between opacity and exposure in negatives is not completely linear; at low values of exposure and at high values of exposure the curvature of the characteristic means that distortion will result if these "toe" and "shoulder" portions are used.

Curves are employed to represent the relation between exposure and opacity of photographic materials. In practice these relations are usually plotted as the logarithm of the exposure against the logarithm of the opacity (called density). There are two reasons for this procedure: (1) a longer range may be represented conveniently in a small space in logarithmic units, and (2) the response of the eye to a light stimulus is more nearly proportional to the logarithm of the stimulus than to the numerical value of the stimulus.

If a brightness ratio is to be reproduced which is so great that the curved "toe" and "shoulder" portions of the D-$\log_{10} E$ curve must be used, then the extreme high lights and the darkest shadows will not be truthfully translated into opacity ratios (or density differences). This is because of the curvature of the relation between exposure and opacity (or density). If the brightness range is small, it may be placed anywhere on the straight part of the curve with the knowledge that the opacity ratios (or density differences) will be proportional to brightness ratios if not exactly equal to them.

The slope of the straight-line part of the D-$\log_{10} E$ curve, when plotted as logarithm of exposure against density, is known as "gamma." It is actually equal to:

$$\gamma = \frac{\Delta D}{\Delta \log_{10} E} = \frac{D_2 - D_1}{\log_{10} \ (E_2/E_1)} \tag{1}$$

Gamma and contrast are often used as synonomous terms, although incorrectly. The contrast of a negative is the difference between the greatest and the least density, no matter whether these densities represent only the straight-line portion of the D-$\log_{10}E$ curve or not. Gamma pertains only to the straight portion of the curve. Since, however, most photographers assume they are working only on the straight portion, they use gamma and contrast indiscriminately.

If the gamma (slope of the straight part of the D-$\log_{10} E$ curve) of the negative is unity, the negative represents accurately the subject brightness values both in proportion and in actual opacity values. The negative may be printed on a paper with a gamma of unity. But if the negative gamma is higher than unity (say 1.2) then the negative must be printed on a paper with a gamma of less than unity (in this case 0.83) to make a print that is a true representation of the original. Mathematical proof of this practical point will be found in the chapter on Photographic Sensitometry. If the product of the slopes of the negative and paper curves is equal to 1, accurate reproduction is procured if we neglect the extreme shadows and extreme high lights.

With printing papers, the portion of the density-exposure characteristic that is actually straight may be quite restricted in length or may be nonexistent. So long as the curve has no pronounced curvature at either end or anywhere else, it is probable that very few, if any, persons will be able to detect that distortion has entered into the printing of a given negative. It is the aim of the paper manufacturers, however, to make printing materials that are as near technically perfect as possible and at the same time to make them practical to use.

The exposure ranges that are often cited as being about 5 to 1 for a contrast paper and about 50 to 1 for a soft paper are secured by measuring the exposure differences required to produce certain density differences. If a considerable portion of the toe region of the curve is taken into this calculation, the exposure range cited will be greater than if only the truly straight part of the characteristic is considered, as one may see from the curves in Figs. 7 and 8. These are characteristic of Defender *B* Velour

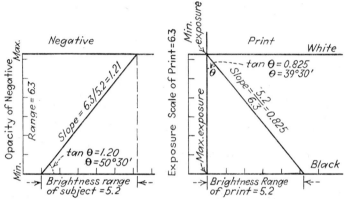

Fig. 6.—Theoretical curves relating brightness range of subject, opacity range of negative and brightness range of print. Here the product of negative and print gammas (1.21 × 0.825) equals unity; a requirement for correct tone reproduction.

Black (a projection paper) and of Apex (a Defender contact paper). Data for the following table were taken from these curves:

TABLE III.—CHARACTERISTICS OF PAPER

Paper—Apex

Grade	Exposure range	"Speed"	Gamma
00	17.0	390	1.25
11 soft	9.8	390	1.45
22	7.2	445	1.70
33 medium	5.2	710	2.02
44	3.2	850	2.80
55 hard	2.8	1150	3.30

Paper—Velour Black

	Exposure range	"Speed"	Gamma
11 soft	10.0	5.0	1.24
22 normal	5.5	7.1	1.88
33 medium	3.5	6.3	2.48
44 hard	2.7	14.3	3.20

The "speed" here is taken as the exposure in meter-candle-seconds required to produce a print density of 1.0. Thus the projection paper is seen to have a speed of about 100 times that of the contact paper (710 m.c.s. required to produce a density of 1.0 on the contact paper compared to 6.3 m.c.s. required for the projection paper; both grades being medium). The exposure range was estimated by considering the portion of the characteristic between a density 0.2 less than the maximum possible on the paper and 0.2 above the minimum measurable density. These exposure ranges would come more into line with the tables of such ranges already published if more of the toe region of the characteristic were used in making the range estimate. Gamma values were obtained in the customary manner, *viz.*, the ratio between the change in density to the change in the log exposure over the straight portion of the curve.

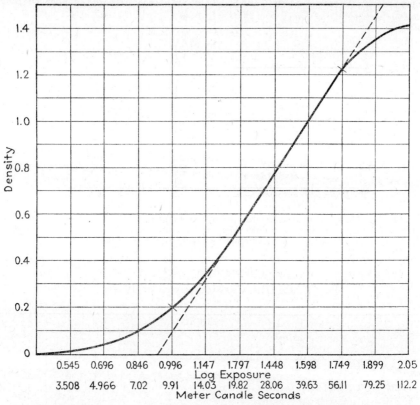

Fig. 7.—Points on D-$\log_{10} E$ curve used to calculate density range of paper.

It will be noted that these papers have definite straight portions to the characteristic, that the harder (more contrasty) papers have steeper characteristics, and that for these papers the exposure range is less than for the softer papers.

Effect of Curvature of Characteristic.—Since practical printing materials may have appreciable curvature in their D-$\log_{10} E$ characteristic, it is worth while to consider what happens when either the exposure has been incorrect so that the lower or upper bend is used or the brightness range of the subject is so great that both upper and lower curves must be used.

Suppose that the exposure has been insufficient to place the shadow portions of the subject up on the straight part of the curve. The high lights, however, are correctly exposed. The opacity ratios (density differences) in the high-light region will be directly proportional to the subject brightness ratios. But because of the curvature two shadow regions differing by, say 3 to 1 in brightness, will not produce opacity ratios of this value (when the characteristics of the printing material are such that $\gamma = 1$). They will produce less than a 3:1 ratio in opacity because over the curved region it requires more than a 3:1 exposure ratio to produce a 3:1 opacity ratio.

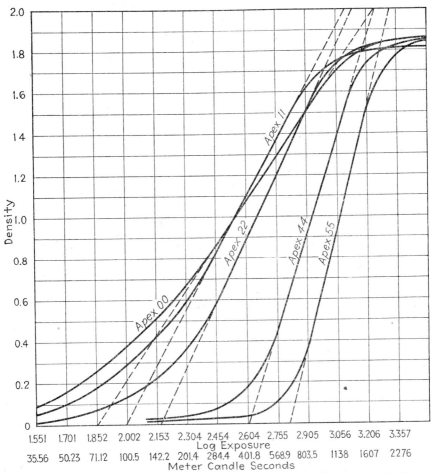

FIG. 84.—Contact-paper characteristics. Grade 00 is soft; 55 is extra contrast.

If, on the other hand, the shadows are exposed so that they lie on the straight part of the curve, the high lights may be overexposed, extending up beyond the straight portion of the H and D curve. Now they will be distorted since brightness ratio of 3:1 will not produce a 3:1 ratio in opacity; they will produce less than this variation. In this case the shadows of the negative (or print) will be correct and the high lights will be incorrect (blocked up).

In negative making, correct exposure is usually considered as that exposure which will get the shadows up on the straight portion of the curve. Then the straight part of the curve has sufficient length for the high lights not to reach the shoulder. But if appreciably greater exposure is given to the negative, the high lights may be blocked

up and will not be represented correctly.   In print making, correct exposure is usually
that exposure which will just slightly tint the paper in the strongest high lights.   Then
the shadows will usually be of the correct density if a paper of correct exposure range
has been chosen.

Because of the shortness of the straight-line portion of the paper characteristic
curve, it is often impossible to obtain perfect reproduction over the whole range of

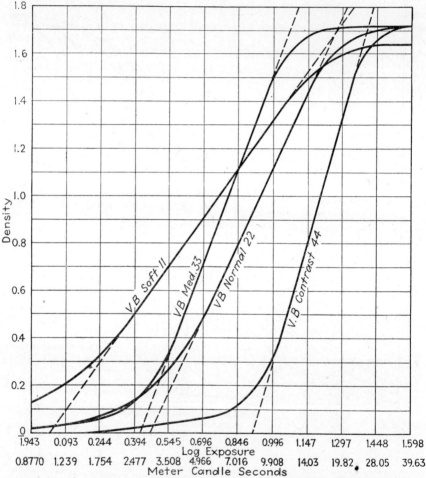

FIG. 8*B*.—Characteristics of Velour Black (projection) papers varying from soft to contrast
in grade.

tones.   If the extreme shadows are ignored, however, the exposure of the negative
can be so chosen that practically perfect reproduction is obtained, on the proper paper,
over the greater part of the tonal scale of the original subject.   It is also a fact that the
eye is not very critical to slight distortion of tone balances, while it is more sensitive
to fuzzy, out-of-focus effects and bad perspective.

Extreme high lights and shadows suffer from decreased contrast, however, because
of the curvature of the D-$\log_{10} E$ characteristic.

General Characteristics of Positive Printing Papers.—Under this heading in the chapter on Photographic Materials will be found a discussion of the various paper characteristics such as speed, color sensitivity, effect of development on contrast, image tone, sheen, texture, weight or thickness, etc.

Choice of Negative Contrast.—The question arises as to whether it is preferable to develop negatives to a low or a high gamma and then to use a paper of proper contrast to bring the final reproduction to the desired point, from the standpoint of true tone rendition. In general, it is preferable to develop the negative to a good contrast and then to use a soft grade of paper. In this manner better over-all rendition will be secured. The reason is the fact that there is less difference between the straight part and the toe and shoulder portions of a soft paper than of a hard paper.

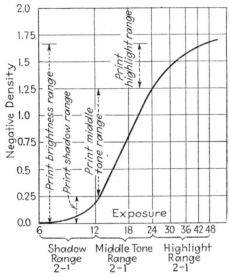

Fig. 9.—Compression of shadows and high lights by using curved parts of characteristic.

Negative opacity range 8-1   Print brightness range 52.5-1
Negative shadow range 2-1   Print shadow range 1.6-1
Negative medium tone range 2-1   Print medium tone range 11.0-1
Negative high-light range 2-1   Print high-light range 3.0-1

High Key. Low Key.—Prints are often labeled as "full scale," "soft," "low key," etc. The following table is taken from an article on print control, by Laurence Dutton, in *Miniature Camera Monthly:*

TABLE IV.—PRINT CHARACTERISTICS

Type of print desired	Type of negative needed	Paper	Printing directions
Full scale....................	Normal	Contrast equal to the negative	Minimum exposure and full development time
Soft........................	Soft	Less contrast than the negative	Adequate exposure and minimum development
Overscale..................	Hard	Greater contrast than the negative	Maximum exposure and development
Low key..................	Relatively soft	Soft	Expose for shadows
High key..................	Relatively soft	Soft	Expose for high lights

A very thorough and practical treatise on methods of printing on various papers, of methods of measuring the contrast of negatives, and of measuring the capabilities of printing papers will be found in Dutton's book, "Perfect Print Control," The Galleon Press, 1937.

Storage of Printing Papers.—Papers should be kept dry and free from chemical fumes, and from hypo dust. Preferably they should be stored in a cool place and under a certain amount of pressure to keep them flat. If they are in a moist warm atmosphere, they will mildew and stick together, being ruined for future use. Moisture seems to be able to penetrate numerous thicknesses of protective paper as well as the double envelopes in which most papers are now packed by the manufacturer. The only solution is to keep printing papers out of a humid hot atmosphere; or to place them in a simple drying closet which may be made by placing the paper in a box or cabinet in which an electric light bulb burns continuously. Of course, the paper must be protected from light if it is not to become fogged or exposed.

Contact Printing. *Comparasion of Contact and Projection Printing.*—The ultimate in sharpness of detail will only be secured by contact printing. When sharp negatives are enlarged a matter of two to four times this lack of definition is not noticeable, but in greater magnifications than these values the loss of sharpness is unavoidable. Therefore, for extreme detail as for engineering or scientific record prints or where reproduction by a photoengraving method is to be followed, the 8- by 10-in. contact print on glossy paper, well ferrotyped, cannot be equaled.

For portraits and pictorial subjects, however, there is often an advantage in a projection print which is not so sharp as a contact print. In projection it is possible to reduce still further the sharpness by the employment of diffusion attachments on the enlarger lens or by making the exposure onto the printing paper through silk or other diffusing material.

Only by projection may the final print be smaller or larger than the negative. For this reason, if a very large print is desired, it is practically impossible to get it in any other way than by projection. In commercial studios the 8- by 10-in. camera is almost the upper limit of size in general use. Of recent years there has been a remarkable trend toward smaller cameras, which are easier to operate, to move about, and which have lenses of greater depth of focus.

The miniature camera, with a lens of large aperture and short focal length has made it possible to make photographs with very great depth of focus and very short exposures. Negatives made in such cameras may be enlarged many times before grain inherent in negative emulsions becomes annoying and before the natural loss of definition with enlargement causes the print to suffer too much. Modern fine-grain materials processed according to fine-grain technique will yield enlargements of 10 diameters[1] before either grain or loss of detail becomes serious, and even greater enlargements are possible if the utmost in detail is not necessary.

There is little or no opportunity for dodging or holding back a portion of the negative in contact printing; in projection, dodging is very frequently employed. In this manner emphasis may be placed upon the part of the image that merits it; details not wanted may be subdued. The photographer is freed, somewhat, by this expedient from the vagaries of uneven lighting.

Negatives which are to be enlarged must be handled with great care. The commercial photographer, accustomed to making contact prints from an 8- by 10-in. negative must learn an entirely new technique if he hopes to turn out good prints from

---

[1] Two terms are used for indicating the magnitude of the enlargement: diameters and the general term magnification. Strictly, the latter term should indicate the enlargement in area. Practically, however, all enlargements are rated as the number of times any linear dimension is increased. Thus a 10 times (diameter) enlargement means that, for each inch of the negative along a side, the print will be 10 in.

miniature negatives. Every scratch, fingerprint, and speck of dust or lint is magnified with the image, and an invisible flaw becomes a ruinous blotch when magnified 20×. It is practically impossible to retouch miniature negatives; all handwork must be done on the final print.

One of the virtues of projection printing is the ability of the photographer to select a portion of a negative and to enlarge it to the desired degree. Often a negative looked at *in toto* will not reveal an excellent composition which becomes evident when only a portion is masked off and studied.

To sum up, for the utmost in detail and freedom from grain, make contact prints. For depth of focus, when the exposure must be short, for large prints, for dodging one portion of the negative at the expense of another, for reproducing only a portion of a negative, for soft effects, enlarge.

Contact-printing Equipment.—Gaslight or chloride paper used for contact printing may be processed safely in a room illuminated by ordinary incandescent lamps, provided a safe distance is maintained between lamp and paper. A better method is to use a yellow safe light to which the chloride paper is insensitive. The illumination on the printing table may be fairly high so long as it is of a color which will not fog the paper.

For the amateur a printing box is useful. This is simply a box with one or more bulbs (of 40 or 60 watts each) in it together with a small ruby lamp. A switch is connected with a hinged cover so that, when the exposure is to be made and the cover is pressed down, the exposing lamp is turned on and the ruby lamp is turned off. Between the exposing lamps and the negative is a diffusing ground glass. Some sort of reflector in the box aids in securing even illumination.

Printers for professional use are of the same general type but are more complex and are capable of accommodating larger negatives.

Making Contact Prints.—Contact printing involves these several steps:

1. Placing negative in printing machine or frame, emulsion side up.

2. Placing printing paper in contact with the negative, emulsion side down (the two emulsion surfaces are now in contact).

3. Turning on printing light, or if a printing frame and an external light source are used, bringing the frame near the exposing light.

4. Developing, rinsing, fixing, washing, drying, and mounting.

With a printing box or machine it is difficult to "dodge," *i.e.*, to expose one portion of the negative more or less than another part for the purpose of improving contrast of a particular portion or to even up the final brightness over the entire print. If a printing frame is used and the exposing light is fixed at a convenient distance from the frame, a piece of cardboard or other opaque material may be interposed between the light and the portion of the negative which is to be held back.

If a printing frame and an external source of light are used, it is wise to move the frame with respect to the lamp so that even exposure over the entire picture is secured. A simple light box can be made, however, which may consist of several incandescent bulbs of small size (perhaps, 25 watts) placed in the bottom. Between these lamps and the printing frame is a sheet of diffusing glass or paper.

A normal contact paper placed about 1 ft. from a 60-watt lamp will require 10 to 20 sec. exposure when printed from an average negative. It is wise to make a test of the exposure by using a small strip of the paper before exposing the entire sheet. This test strip is placed over a portion of the negative which has both high lights and shadows. The exposure should be such that after development the high lights show a just perceptible coloring compared to a sheet of unexposed paper.

It is good practice to arrange the printing light and the printing frame in such a manner that exposures of the order of 4 or 5 sec., minimum, are required. At one time it was thought that better contrast was obtained from flat negatives by printing them for a longer time at a greater distance from the light than customary. Nowadays the contrast is secured by using a harder paper. Standardized conditions of light sources and distance between light and paper are highly desirable.

Chloride papers are completely developed in about 45 sec. to 1 min. If the print becomes too dark in this time, it is overexposed. The image should show up in 10 to 15 sec.; if it flashes up a shorter exposure is required. The print should be left in the developer until the maximum blackness is attained.

Papers to Use for Certain Subjects.—Nearly all pictures will look well if printed on white stock; others look better if put on buff-colored, cream-colored, or other tinted papers. But egregious errors may be made by using the wrong paper for certain subjects. Portraits, interiors by artificial light, and some sunlight scenes may be printed on cream-, buff-, or ivory-tinted paper. Outdoor scenes such as beach and marine views and snow scenes do not look well on these papers. Moonlight scenes, as well as some snow and sand scenes look well if placed on paper which may be toned blue. Fire scenes may be toned red. In general, however, it is always safe to use a white paper.

For reproduction purposes, glossy prints are desired. In any case, if the finest detail and the greatest tone range is desired, glossy paper is preferred. Glossy paper seems to be the mode for amateur prints made by commercial finishing establishments. This style may change as has the style of using deckle edges and other out-of-the-ordinary fads. Rough papers are useful for broad effects of light and shadow but are not of much use if fine detail is to be preserved. All surfaces will take retouching with the spotting brush and spotting colors, and all but glossy and silk surfaces will take the spotting pencil.

Projection Printing. *The Projection Method.*—If the print is to be larger or smaller than the negative from which it is to be made, projection printing must be used. In this manner of printing, the image of the negative is projected upon the printing paper by means of an objective lens. The projection system may be especially constructed for enlarging purposes, or it may be a camera used backward, *i.e.*, the negative is placed in the rear of the camera and illuminated by a source of light. The image from the lens is then focused upon the sensitive paper.

Because of the loss of light in the projection system, papers adapted for contact printing require very long exposures. The projection papers, therefore, are much more sensitive than contact chlorides. There is no reason, however, aside from the longer exposures required (or the stronger source of light required), why contact-type papers should not be used for projection or why projection papers should not be used for contact printing. The bromide type of projection paper may be as much as 100 times as sensitive as the chlorides used for contact printing.

Projection Equipment.—In simplest terms the enlarging camera may consist of the light source, a holder for the negative, a lens for focusing the image on the paper to be exposed, some means for varying the lens-paper and negative-lens distances, and an easel upon which the sensitive paper is placed. More complicated equipment involves the use of several devices to adjust these necessary distances; some enlargers have these two distance controls mechanically coupled together so that one operation changes both lens-to-negative and lens-to-paper distances. These are known as automatic-focus enlargers.

The housing for the illuminant and the easel need not necessarily be attached to the focusing lens system. Consequently an ordinary camera may be used as an enlarger by attaching the camera to the lighting system so that the negative is held between glass plates (or in some other manner) and placed between the rear of the camera and the light house. The easel need not be on the same bench as the camera and light house.

Fixed-focus Enlarger.—If the photographer is content with a single degree of enlargement, he may use a fixed-focus enlarger. The maximum size of film that may be enlarged is controlled by the dimensions of the negative holder; the size of the largest sheet of paper upon which the image may be focused is controlled by the dimensions of the paper holder. Ordinarily these enlargers are used by amateurs who are accustomed to use a single size of negative and who are satisfied with a single size of paper, *e.g.*, 3¼ by 4¼ in. enlarged to post-card size or to 5 by 7 in. The lens is placed at the proper position between the negative and the paper and is sufficiently corrected for the purpose. After the negative and printing paper have been placed in their respective holders, the enlarger may be brought out of the darkroom and exposure may take place to the open sky or to some other source of illumination. The camera may be knockdown in style so that it may be packed out of the way when not in use or so that it may be readily transported; more modern fixed-focus enlargers contain a source of illumination.

Variable-focus Enlargers.—This type of equipment is much more versatile than the fixed-focus arrangement. With such an enlarger, any degree of magnification between the minimum and maximum possible with the physical equipment may be accomplished. In addition, if the lens may be placed far enough away from the negative and close enough to the easel, a print reduced in size from the negative may be secured.

Variable-focus enlargers may fall into one of two general classes depending upon the type of illumination. If a single source of light (usually a concentrated filament lamp or an arc) is used, a pair of plano-convex condensing lenses is employed to bring the light to a focus in the center of the objective (focusing) lens. This type of equipment is more economical of light, and it requires more adjustments than the type described below in which diffused lighting is used. Flaws and negative grain become more apparent in prints made from this type of equipment than is the case when using the second type.

The second general type of equipment utilizes one or more lamps, the illumination being broken up by diffusion plates (usually ground glass or opal glass) interposed between source and negative so that the diffusing medium becomes the source of light as far as the enlarging process is concerned. A diffusion system provides even illumination over the entire negative without any adjustments of lamp-to-negative distance; flaws and grain are minimized but much of the available light is wasted in the diffusion equipment. Prints made from diffusion-type enlarger will be less contrasty than those made from a condenser system.

Some enlargers, notably those used for enlarging miniature negatives, use a condenser lens to concentrate the beam and a diffuser to provide even illumination.

Present trends are toward the diffusion type of equipment.

In any variable-focus enlarger there are two adjustments necessary to get sharp focus of the image upon the printing paper: the lens-to-negative distance and the lens-to-paper distance. In addition to these adjustments a condenser system requires that the light-source-to-negative distance be accurately adjusted to get even illumination over the entire negative.

In operation the photographer places the negative in the holder and focuses the image to the required size upon the easel by adjusting the distances mentioned above. Then he may stop down the objective lens to the desired point, place the projection paper on the easel, and make the exposure. Proper exposure is controlled both by the diaphragm in the lens and by the time of exposure. Stopping down will tend to minimize effects of poor focusing, but it is always wise to effect the best possible focus before making the exposure.

If the light source requires adjustment, this is done after the desired magnification has been determined and before the negative is placed in the holder. The distance, light to negative holder, is varied until the easel is evenly covered with illumination.

If incorrectly placed, the light will cast upon the easel only a small circle of intense light; the rest of the negative will not be covered properly and the enlargement will show these light variations clearly.

If a negative is dense and it is difficult to get accurate focus, a useful expedient is to place in the negative holder a well-fogged negative on which fine scratches in the emulsion have been made. When these scratches are sharply defined on the easel, the test negative is in focus and may be replaced by the negative to be enlarged.

Equipment for working with miniature negatives will usually produce enlargements up to 15 or 20 diameters with the physical equipment built into the enlarger. If still greater magnifications are desired, some means must be found for increasing the distance from lens to paper. Usually, sufficient adjustment of the lens-to-negative distance is built into the enlarger so that its enlarging ability is beyond the limit set by the lens-to-paper distance. This is generally accomplished by placing the paper on the floor and by turning the camera so that the rays of light from the objective clear the table upon which the camera stands. With enlargers adapted for negatives of large size, *e.g.*, $3\frac{1}{4}$ by $4\frac{1}{4}$ in. and up, magnifications much greater than four or five diameters are not possible because of the considerable lens-to-easel distance required. The only solutions in this case are to use a lens of shorter focus or to use an accessory lens to reduce the focal length of the objective.

Enlargers for miniature negatives may use lenses of 50 to 100 mm. focal length.

Present-day equipment is constructed on the vertical plan, the camera extending up in the air, the easel being below it and horizontal. Vertical space is seldom at a premium in the darkroom, and a horizontal easel is much easier to work with.

Certain older equipment had other adjustments in addition to those mentioned. For example, the negative might be tilted, or swung about a vertical pivot through the center of the negative, or the negative might be raised or lowered so that one portion could be brought nearer the center of the rays from the light source. Modern equipment has few or none of these additional adjustments. If one edge of the easel is tilted with respect to the negative, certain correction in the lines of the negative may be effected. For example if the lines of a building converge because the camera has been tilted in making the original exposure, the easel may be tilted in the opposite direction. In general, however, modern enlarging practice has little need of these additional adjustments.

Most modern equipment includes a yellow or red filter which may be swung into the beam from the lens to make it possible to focus directly upon the sensitive paper. When the exposure is to be made, this filter is removed from the light beam.

Condenser Enlarger.—This type of equipment is useful when the utmost sharpness of detail is desired, or when the maximum use of the light source must be secured. Because of this sharpness of detail, flaws in negatives are not subdued at all in enlarging so that retouching on negatives to be projected must be much more carefully done than if the enlarged print is to be made by a diffusion system.

In condenser equipment, rays of light are scattered more in the heavier portions of the negative than in the less dense portions. The latter go straight through the negative and are collected by the projection lens. Some of the scattered rays, however, are not collected by the lens and do not reach the printing paper. For this reason, the contrast of prints made by a condenser system is greater than prints made by a diffusion system. This is known as the "Callier effect." Placing a simple diffusing medium between the light source and the negative will eliminate this effect, but the advantage of the condensing system is lost.

The details of a condenser system are shown in Fig. 10. Theoretically, if the illuminant is a true point source, the condenser lens brings the rays that pass through it to a focus in the center of the projection lens. If the lens is moved farther away from the negative to produce a smaller image, the light source must be moved closer to the negative to get even illumination. These adjustments must be made with considerable accuracy to secure good focus and even illumination. Practically, however, the light source is never an exact point source. Rays that illuminate the negative are both transmitted through the lens and scattered by the negative image and do not go through the lens.

In miniature enlarging equipment no attempt is made to simulate a point source. An opal-glass bulb is used which presents to the negative, through the condenser, a very large source of light. No attempt is made to adjust the distance from light to condenser. The only adjustments, therefore, are the lens-to-negative and lens-to-easel distances.

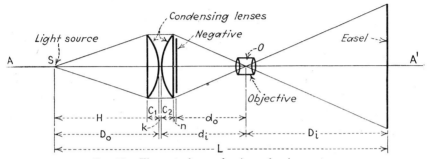

Fig. 10.—Element of a condensing enlarging system.

Condensing Lens.—The plano-convex lenses are mounted with the flat sides out, the inner surfaces touching or separated by a small distance. The equivalent focal length of the pair may be calculated from the formula

$$f = \frac{f_1 \times f_2}{f_1 + f_2 - d} \qquad (2)$$

where f = the combined focal length;
  f_1, f_2 = the focal lengths of individual lenses;
  d = the distance between lens centers.

In operating the enlarger, the distance D_i from the objective to the easel controls the size of the image. To bring the image into focus on the easel, the distance d_0 between objective and negative must be changed. These distances are related as follows:

$$D_i = fM + f \qquad (3)$$

$$d_0 = \left(\frac{f}{M}\right) + f \qquad (4)$$

where f = focal length of objective;
  M = magnification.

The condenser enlarger requires more space than the diffusing type because of the considerable distance between the light source and the condensers. Furthermore, unless objective and condenser are chosen carefully with respect to each other, the space required for the enlarger may become very great indeed. If the focal length of the condenser is less than that of the objective and if large values of magnification are to be used, the distance between objective and easel may be such that the enlarger cannot be accomodated within the darkroom. Thus, if a condenser with equivalent focal length of 6 in. is used with an objective of 12 in., a magnification of 10 diameters will require some 13 ft. for the distance between condenser and easel.

The focal lengths of the objective and the condensers should be of the same general dimension or, perhaps, the objective may be somewhat greater in focal length than the condenser.

An approximate expression for the distance between lens and easel is $(M + 1)f$, where M is the magnification and f is the focal length of the objective.

Degree of Enlargement.—With any enlarger the degree of enlargement increases as the distance between lens and easel increases. The formulas below relate the magnification and the distances between negative and lens and lens to easel. If f is the focal length of the projection lens, d_0 is the distance from negative to lens, and D_i is the distance from lens to paper, the sum of the reciprocals of these distances must equal the reciprocal of the focal length of the lens. Then the magnification is the ratio between the two distances,

$$\frac{1}{f} = \frac{1}{d_0} + \frac{1}{D_i} \qquad (5)$$

$$M = \frac{d_0}{D_i} \qquad (6)$$

For practical purposes, however, it is simpler to use a table like that shown on page 433, worked out from these relations.

Objective Lens.—The lens should be an anastigmat of flat field and fairly large aperture. It should be equipped with a diaphragm, but if considerable light is employed, this diaphragm should not be made of material that will easily warp from the resultant heat generated. Since the condenser concentrates the beam of light coming through the negative, the amount of light through the enlarger lens does not vary with the f-number in the same manner as in a camera. A lens stopped down to $f/8$ may pass as much light as one marked $f/4.5$ because of this concentration. Therefore one must make trial exposures each time the aperture or magnification is changed. If, however, exposures are not too short to be controlled at full aperature, there is no object in stopping down the lens.

The lens from any camera that will bring rays to a sharp focus may be used in an enlarger. A better lens, of course, will produce better definition, but many a good camera lens will make a good enlarger lens. Lenses especially made for enlarging work are often better corrected over a small angle than camera lenses. The lens must be capable of "covering" the desired negative.

Modern miniature enlargers are often designed so that the photographer can use a lens interchangeably for camera or for enlarger, thus saving himself the expense of owning two lenses.

Diffusion Enlargers.—In this equipment the light from the source is scattered through one or more diffusing mediums, which may be ground glass or flashed opal glass. Because of the scattering of the light, rays arrive at the negative from all angles with respect to the surface of the negative. The illuminated diffusing medium becomes the light source for the negative. Scratches and flaws are minimized.

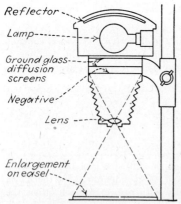

Reflector

Lamp

Ground glass diffusion screens

Negative

Lens

Enlargement on easel

Fig. 11.—Diffusion enlarger of the vertical type.

According to Tuttle (*Journal of the Optical Society of America*, October, 1934), the difference in contrast between complete diffusion obtained by heavy pot-opal glass and no diffusion amounted to about 3 to 1 when Eastman SuperSensitive Panchromatic film was used as the sensitive material.

TABLE V.—REDUCING AND ENLARGING TABLES

Focal length of lens used, inches	Reductions, size							
	Same	$\frac{1}{2}$	$\frac{1}{3}$	$\frac{1}{4}$	$\frac{1}{5}$	$\frac{1}{6}$	$\frac{1}{7}$	$\frac{1}{8}$
	Enlargements, size							
	Same	$2\times$	$3\times$	$4\times$	$5\times$	$6\times$	$7\times$	$8\times$
3	6	9	12	15	18	21	24	27
	6	$4\frac{1}{2}$	4	$3\frac{3}{4}$	$3\frac{3}{5}$	$3\frac{1}{2}$	$3\frac{3}{7}$	$3\frac{3}{8}$
$3\frac{1}{2}$	7	$10\frac{1}{2}$	14	$17\frac{1}{2}$	21	$24\frac{1}{2}$	28	$31\frac{1}{2}$
	7	$5\frac{1}{4}$	$4\frac{2}{3}$	$4\frac{3}{8}$	$4\frac{1}{5}$	$4\frac{1}{12}$	4	$3\frac{15}{16}$
4	8	12	16	20	24	28	32	36
	8	6	$5\frac{1}{3}$	5	$4\frac{4}{5}$	$4\frac{2}{3}$	$4\frac{3}{7}$	$4\frac{1}{2}$
$4\frac{1}{2}$	9	$13\frac{1}{2}$	18	$22\frac{1}{2}$	27	$31\frac{1}{2}$	36	$40\frac{1}{2}$
	9	$6\frac{3}{4}$	6	$5\frac{5}{8}$	$5\frac{2}{5}$	$5\frac{1}{4}$	$5\frac{1}{7}$	$5\frac{1}{16}$
5	10	15	20	25	30	35	40	45
	10	$7\frac{1}{2}$	$6\frac{2}{3}$	$6\frac{1}{4}$	6	$5\frac{5}{6}$	$5\frac{3}{7}$	$5\frac{5}{8}$
$5\frac{1}{2}$	11	$16\frac{1}{2}$	22	$27\frac{1}{2}$	33	$38\frac{1}{2}$	44	$49\frac{1}{2}$
	11	$8\frac{1}{4}$	$7\frac{1}{3}$	$6\frac{7}{8}$	$6\frac{3}{5}$	$6\frac{5}{12}$	$6\frac{2}{7}$	$6\frac{3}{16}$
6	12	18	24	30	36	42	48	54
	12	9	8	$7\frac{1}{2}$	$7\frac{1}{5}$	7	$6\frac{5}{7}$	$6\frac{3}{4}$
7	14	21	28	35	42	49	56	63
	14	$10\frac{1}{2}$	$9\frac{1}{3}$	$8\frac{3}{4}$	$8\frac{2}{5}$	$8\frac{1}{6}$	8	$7\frac{7}{8}$
8	16	24	32	40	48	56	64	72
	16	12	$10\frac{2}{3}$	10	$9\frac{3}{5}$	$9\frac{1}{3}$	$9\frac{1}{7}$	9
9	18	27	36	45	54	63	72	81
	18	$13\frac{1}{2}$	12	$11\frac{1}{4}$	$10\frac{4}{5}$	$10\frac{1}{2}$	$10\frac{3}{7}$	$10\frac{1}{8}$
10	20	30	40	50	60	70	80	90
	20	15	$13\frac{1}{2}$	$12\frac{1}{2}$	12	$11\frac{2}{3}$	$11\frac{3}{7}$	$11\frac{1}{4}$
11	22	33	44	55	66	77	88	99
	22	$16\frac{1}{2}$	$14\frac{2}{3}$	$13\frac{3}{4}$	$13\frac{1}{5}$	$12\frac{5}{6}$	$12\frac{2}{7}$	$12\frac{3}{8}$
12	24	36	48	60	72	84	96	108
	24	18	16	15	$14\frac{2}{5}$	14	$13\frac{5}{7}$	$13\frac{1}{2}$

Upper numbers of pairs are distances of lens from easel in enlarging or from lens to photo being reduced in copying. Lower numbers of pairs are distances from lens to negative being enlarged or camera extension for reduction. The cap end of lens should face bromide paper in enlarging and in reducing should face object being copied.

Diffusion enlargers are simpler to construct and to operate than condenser systems. The loss of light in the diffusion means may be considerable and may prolong exposures appreciably. In general the lack of light efficiency is not too important, because of the ease of supplying sufficient light to print in a reasonable time. In this case, however, care must be taken to dissipate the heat effectively.

Use of Camera as Enlarger.—If a camera has a removable back and if it has sufficient bellows extension to accommodate the range of magnification desired, it may be made into a successful enlarger. All that is necessary, in addition to the camera, for the negative to be enlarged is a source of even illumination and a holder. The light source may be made up of several low-wattage bulbs in a white wooden box, or a metal box painted with glossy white paint, of such dimensions that it fits over the rear of the camera. One or more plates of opal or ground glass may be interposed between the bulbs and the rear of the camera to secure even illumination. These diffusion mediums should be a short distance from the film to be enlarged so that the grain of the diffusion medium is not in focus at the same adjustment that brings the negative image into focus on the easel. Reflectors of any sort placed back of the bulbs will improve the light efficiency.

The film or plateholder may be simply two glass plates between which the negative is placed. Masks may be fixed, permanently, to the glass plates. A simple slot structure into which the assembly of glass plates and negative fits will enable the negative to be held parallel to the rear of the camera during focusing and exposure.

These homemade enlargers are usually horizontal, although it is not impossible to make a vertical system that is entirely satisfactory. The photographic journals have published many descriptions of such equipment. Several such articles are noted below.[1]

With four 40-watt bulbs and a single sheet of opal glass, exposures of the order of 10 sec. to several minutes may be required when enlarging 9- by 12-cm. negatives up to 8 by 10 in. with a 13.5 cm., $f/4.5$ lens.

One of the problems with homemade enlargers is to maintain the negative and the easel parallel to each other and perpendicular to a line through the center of the camera. Another problem is to get even illumination over the entire negative. If the negative is small, this is not so difficult, but in this case considerable degrees of magnification may be required, and then the proper mounting of camera, negative, and easel becomes different.

It is probably uneconomical to attempt the construction of a high-grade miniature enlarger at home. The precision of construction must be considerable if high-class enlargements are to be made.

Exposure Related to Magnification.—With diffusion enlargers the exposure required for any desired degree of enlargement when the correct exposure is known for some other degree of magnification is given by

$$E_2 = \frac{(M_2 + 1)^2 \times E_1}{(M_1 + 1)^2} \tag{7}$$

where E_1 and M_1 correspond to the known exposure time and magnification and M_2 and E_2 are for another degree of magnification.

To Measure Degree of Enlargement.—If two lines are scratched on a plate which has been thoroughly fogged and processed, the ratio of the distance between the lines projected on the easel to the actual distance on the negative will be a measure of the degree of enlargement. Thus, if the lines are 5 cm. apart on the final print and only 1 cm. apart on the negative, the image has been enlarged five times.

[1] Hibbs, Wyatt, A Horizontal Enlarging Outfit, *Am. Phot.*, July, 1935. This used four photofloods with a switch to reduce the voltage by a series connection for focusing. The camera was an Zeiss Ideal B.

Ramley, Edward J., A Reflected Light Source, for Photographic Enlarger, *Am. Phot.*, September, 1937.

Jardine, Donald C., A Home-made Vertical Projection Printer, *Camera*, February, 1936.

Sources of Illumination.—Present-day enlarging is done largely with incandescent lamps. At one time daylight was utilized, either by pointing the negative end of the enlarger to the sky or by directing skylight into the projection equipment by means of a mirror. Daylight is very seldom used, today, however.

The incandescent lamps may be of the ordinary house-lighting kind designed to have a normal life of 1000 hr.; they may be of the photoflood type which are operated at higher than normal temperatures so that the illumination is increased at the expense of decreased life; or ordinary electric lamps may be burned at a voltage slightly above normal so that they furnish more than their rated amount of light but less light than a photoflood lamp.

Mercury and other vapor lamps are occasionally recommended for printing. A vapor tube is much more efficient than an incandescent lamp. A given amount of power consumed will produce a greater quantity of light. The lamp will run cooler than the bulb type of illuminant, and there will, therefore, be less danger of harming a negative from excessive heat.

These vapor lamps, however, have certain disadvantages. They require time to heat up. They cannot be turned off and on like an incandescent lamp. When first turned on a mercury lamp is very rich in ultraviolet light, but after 10 or 20 min. the intensity of the ultraviolet decreases, and therefore the printing time varies as the tube warms up. To get even illumination special reflectors are needed, and somewhat heavy diffusion must often be used between light source and negative. The over-all efficiency, therefore, may be no higher than with an ordinary incandescent bulb.

Effect of Lamp Voltage upon Exposure.—Few photographers realize the close relation between light output of incandescent lamps and the voltage at which they are operated. Not only the luminous output, but its spectral distribution as well, is dependent upon the operating voltage. For example, a 1000-watt lamp will emit only 50 per cent of its rated output if its voltage is reduced by 16 per cent. If exposures are required that seem too long, the trouble may be due to reduced voltage on the light source. Printing papers are not sensitive to yellow light, and yet the output of an incandescent lamp becomes more and more yellow and less and less blue as the voltage is decreased from normal. A paper that requires 10 sec. exposure when exposed to a 115-volt incandescent lamp operating at normal voltage may require about 30 per cent more exposure if the lamp is operated at 110 volts.

Chlorobromide papers are somewhat more critical in this regard because their sensitivity is largely in the violet region of the spectrum. Enlarging lamps are available in voltages of 110, 115, and 120 volts and the photographer should use the lamp whose rated voltage is nearest his normal line voltage. Lamps operated at higher than rated voltage will permit shorter exposure times. The lamp life will be shortened, however.

Lamp voltage should be accurately regulated by means of resistance or by means of an autotransformer of the Variac type if exposures must be critically controlled. This will enable the separate exposures, as in color photography, to be made at the same voltage, and color balance in the final print will be more easily attained. The autotransformer is a means of raising or lowering the lamp voltage compared to the line voltage. A resistance will lower lamp voltage but cannot raise it above line voltage.

Exposure and Enlargement.—Although modern projection papers have certain latitude as regards correct exposure, it is advisable, always, to come as close as possible to the "best" exposure. Not only must the photographer determine the absolute value of the exposure, but he must determine the contrast grade of the printing paper he is to use. A negative of considerable contrast may require a paper of less than normal contrast. Negatives made in miniature cameras, for example, are usually developed to a contrast or gamma of less than unity so that the printing papers to be used with miniature camera negatives have a natural contrast somewhat greater than would be required for a "normal" (gamma equals unity) negative.

Furthermore the absolute value of the exposure is a function of the paper used (as some papers are more sensitive than others) and upon the degree of enlargement.

Test-strip Method of Determining Exposure.—If the photographer eliminates all variable factors in the process of development (by always developing completely), then the final result depends entirely upon choice of paper contrast and upon the exposure. To determine experimentally the correct exposure time a test strip of the paper to be used may be exposed to the focused image for a time judged to be correct. When developed, this print may be inspected carefully to determine if more, or less, exposure is desirable.

The portion of the image chosen for the test should be a high light, perhaps the brightest important portion of the image. Correct exposure will be that which will produce a just discernible density after development. If the contrast grade of paper chosen is correct, then the darkest shadow of the scene as represented by the negative will be the darkest attainable color in the print. If the contrast (density range) of the negative is greater than the printing paper will reproduce—this is frequently the case—the photographer must decide which end of the scale to sacrifice, *i.e.*, some of the high lights or some of the shadows.

The correct exposure will give a just perceptible deposit of silver in the brightest high light. If normal paper is being used and if the first exposure is too short, double it for the second test. For contrast grades of paper, increase the exposure about 30 per cent for the second test.

Exposure Meters.—Various means have been worked out for avoiding the test-strip method of determining correct exposures. If only the correct exposure is desired, any means of estimating the average transmission of light through the negative will aid in arriving at the exposure. But if the correct contrast grade of paper is to be determined, then the photographer must have means for measuring the transmission of the most and the least dense portions of the negative.

One means that has been developed utilizes the photoelectric type of exposure meter, so useful in estimating negative exposures.

An ordinary printing box or contact printer is used as the light source. It may be necessary to put a photoflood bulb in it to get sufficient light for measurement purposes. A mask is cut for the top of the contact printer. In this is cut a small hole, $\frac{1}{4}$ in. in diameter for example. Over this hole is placed the portion of the negative to be tested. The photoelectric exposure meter is then placed on top of the negative so that the light getting through the hole and the negative shines on a portion of the sensitive disk near the edge. A greater reading will be obtained in this way than if a spot near the center of the disk is chosen. The printing light is turned on, and a reading of the exposure meter is taken. Then a reading without the negative is taken. The ratio of the reading with negative to the reading without negative will give the transmission. If a reading of 250 is obtained without the negative and 25 with the negative, the opacity is 10 and the transmission is 0.1 or 10 per cent. Of course, the scale on the exposure meter must be calibrated in numbers which are proportional to the light intensity if this method is to be satisfactory.

To determine the grade of paper that should be used, it is necessary to make two measurements, one of the transmission (or opacity) through the densest portion of the high light desired to be correctly reproduced and one through the thinnest portion of the shadow that is to be correctly reproduced. The ratio of these two transmissions (or opacities) will give the exposure range required if the paper is to reproduce the desired range correctly. As an example, suppose that the thinnest portion of the negative represents and opacity of 4, and that the densest portion an opacity of 40. The ratio of these two quantities is 10. The printing paper, therefore, must be capable of reproducing an exposure range of 10 to 1 to reproduce accurately the opacity ratio in the negative which, it is assumed, accurately reproduces the brightness range of the original subject.

Many other schemes have been developed for measuring the transmission of light through a film in an endeavor to determine the opacity ratio or the density difference over the desired portions of the negative scale. These may employ various forms of comparison photometers; or they may permit direct measurement of the quantity of light transmitted through the film. In the simplest case, a source of light distinct from the enlarger illumination is varied, by an iris diaphragm in the lens, until the illumination on the easel through the negative just matches the illumination on the easel from the external source as determined from visual examination. Then by trial and error the exposure necessary to produce a good print on a certain grade of a certain kind of paper is determined. Once determined, this exposure will be the same under the same conditions. All that is necessary is to have sufficient adjustment of the illumination through the objective to cover all types of negatives that will be printed. The eye is surprisingly accurate in making illumination comparisons of this kind.[1]

A simple and inexpensive device of recent development is an adaptation of the well-known grease-spot photometer. A small battery-operated incandescent lamp illuminates one side of a semitransparent piece of material. The image from the enlarger is focused upon this screen, and the lamp current is adjusted by a rheostat until the screen illumination from the lamp and from the focused image have the same brightness as viewed by the photographer. The rheostat is calibrated in terms of exposure and contrast grades of modern papers.

Prints for Half-tone Engravings.—In the *Agfa Diamond*, for January and February, 1938, Lloyd Varden, speaking of prints for reproduction, states:

"In decreasing order of preference we might list print surfaces for reproduction purposes as follows:

"1. Black and white prints of uniform glossy or semiglossy surface.

"2. Semi-matte or smooth matte white surfaces.

"3. Rough or textured surfaces."

Now it is quite true, that among half-tone workers a preference is made for either glossy, ferrotyped or unferrotyped, or smooth semimatte papers. Glossy prints especially on paste-up jobs, create undesirable reflections, and for this reason are not so satisfactory for this work as semimatte surfaces. Especially contrasty negatives are best printed on semimatte or smooth matte surfaces, for the final reproduction is enhanced by the softening of contrast due to the matte paper. However, if a negative is of normal contrast, or of flat contrast, it is best printed on glossy paper, and for the latter instances, therefore, glossy surfaces cannot be surpassed. Art work, if necessary, usually calls for a surface other than glossy, but print retouching is by no means impossible on glossy prints. Under all circumstances, time permitting, the engraver should be consulted about the proper surface, for he might have very excellent suggestions to offer, and the photographer also has an opportunity to explain his reason for wanting to use a particular paper.

[1] The following bibliography will direct the reader to several sources of data on homemade photometers, etc., for this purpose. Especially, the reader should consult "Perfect Print Control," by Lawrence Dutton, Galleon, 1937.

COLT, RALPH S., Simple Method of Timing Enlargements, *Am. Phot.*, April, 1938.

BROCKMAN, FRANK G., Photoelectric Timing for Projection Printing, *Am. Phot.*, September, 1936. See also discussion of this paper by Ronald L. Ives, *Am. Phot.*, September, 1937.

WEILAND, W. F., Exposure in Projection Printing, *Am. Phot.*, July, 1936.

It has been a mistaken fancy among the photographic profession that engravers want contrasty prints. On the contrary, contrasty prints have black shadows and high lights of little gradation, which means that the engraver cannot possibly make a reproduction containing the detail which is more than likely in the negative. The engraver has little trouble in increasing the contrast of a print, but he cannot put in detail which does not exist. He wants prints that are *black and white*, but this does not mean contrasty. Prints of full scale, with plenty of detail and black and white tones are the most satisfactory prints for reproduction.

In ordinary half-tone reproduction black-and-white prints are most suitable. Whether the actual color of the black should be an olive tone or a blue-black tone is mostly a matter of preference on the part of the engraver. Generally speaking, though, a good blue-black or neutral black is preferred. Red proofs or sepia prints are not so good as black-and-white prints, but sepia prints are more satisfactory than red proofs. However, if red proofs or sepia prints must be submitted, the situation which demands it should be explained to the engraver in order that his full cooperation can be secured on the job. Monocolored prints of this type should never be placed on the same panel with black-and-white prints, and black-and-white prints in themselves should be of uniform tone.

The success of producing good half tones from photographs resolves itself, therefore, into correct selection of surface, color, and contrast. If that be done, the engraver will have little difficulty.

Printing Control Processes.—In this section are discussed several control methods frequently used in projection printing to obtain special effects.

Dodging, Masking in Projection.—Many times a negative will produce a better print if certain portions are exposed more or less than other portions, so that the final print has a more uniform density, or so that one portion is lighter or darker than the other portions. Local reduction and intensification (*q.v.*) may be employed. In the printing process certain control methods are available which may produce the desired result without making recourse to corrective processes.

If one portion of the negative is to receive less exposure in printing than other portions, the light from the enlarger is kept from exposing the paper in these portions by use of some opaque object, often the operator's hand. A portion of a print may be made completely black by illuminating it, while printing, with a small flash lamp or other source of illumination.

If one small portion of a negative is to be printed deeper than the remainder of the negative, a small hole may be cut in an opaque material and moved about in the light from the enlarger so that all portions except that which is to be dark receive less exposure than the selected portion. On the other hand, if one portion is to receive less exposure than the majority of the print, a small piece of opaque material of the proper shape and size may be placed in the beam from the enlarger and moved about so that a sharp edge between light and dark parts of the final print does not result. This opaque material may be moved by fixing to it a small wire handle.

If the dodging tool is made of red celluloid, the photographer may watch the entire image on the printing paper and thereby better perform the dodging, but the blue rays to which the paper is sensitive will be stopped by the dodging device.

Practice and trial and error are the only means of determining whether the proper amount of dodging has been secured.

White borders around prints are secured by masking the edges of the negative, or print, or both, so that these edges are not exposed. A sharper edge will be obtained if the mask is placed over the printing paper, rather than if it is placed only over the negative.

Black borders around prints are secured by trimming the negative so that only the picture area is left. The printing paper is somewhat larger than the image, and the negative is not masked. The edges of the paper which are fully exposed will become full black in the developer.

Diffusion.—Pictorial and portrait prints are frequently enhanced in appearance by printing the negative through some diffusion medium, such as a piece of thin silk, linen, etc. If the material is laid on the paper during the exposure, the texture of the material is impressed upon the final print. If the material is interposed between the printing paper and the lens of the enlarger and kept in motion during the exposure a general lack of definition or diffusion of the image results. The amount of diffusion depends upon the position of the diffusing medium with respect to the printing medium, upon its motion during exposure, upon the weave or mesh of the diffusing medium, etc. The desired result must be attained by trial and error.

"Printing-in" Clouds, Etc.—It is desirable, at times, to add clouds to the print made from a negative in which no clouds appear. This is typical of another control process in which experience is the best teacher; only trial and error will enable the photographer to determine best conditions for the printing-in procedure.

In general, adding clouds or other material without going to the intermediate negative process is carried out as follows: The picture should be fairly well divided between foreground and sky. Let us suppose that the foreground is printed first. In exposing the print, the sky is covered with an opaque mask so that no light gets to the sky portion. After the foreground exposure is complete, this portion is protected from further exposure, while the clouds from another negative, carefully placed in the enlarger or printing frame, are allowed to expose the sky portion of the print. Proper exposure of each portion to produce the desired density must be determined by experiment.

If the sky line is not straight or if trees or other objects protrude into the sky, the process is somewhat more intricate. If the protruding element will print quite dark it may be ignored because the cloud may then be exposed on top of the protruding object without showing owing to the greater density of the object. But, if the object will be light in density in the final print, perhaps of the same density as the clouds, then greater care must be taken. An outline of the method is as follows:

First project on the easel the lower, or cloudless, part of the picture. Make exposure tests until the desired print density is secured. Make note of this exposure. Now project the cloud negative on the easel and determine proper exposure time. Finally make the foreground exposure by cutting up the preliminary cloud print so that only the clouds remain. Remove the protruding objects from this cloud print, and hold this print, more or less cut to the shape of the cloud outline, so the sky portion of the final print is held back in exposure.

Now trim the test print made from the foreground negative, leaving in the protruding objects, and expose the upper or sky part of the final print.

All this sounds easier than it is in practice. It is difficult to avoid line of demarkation between sky and foreground. One should learn the procedure by using negatives in which the sky line is fairly straight and in which there are no protruding objects, proceeding then to more complicated subjects. The negatives which are easiest to use are those in which clouds do not go clear to the horizon but leave a short gap between cloud and horizon. This gap may be used to bridge over the region between tree tops and the point where the clouds are to appear in the final picture.

True photo montages are made in this manner, although several negatives may be made to produce the final print. Accurate and careful work is necessary to determine the printing time of each negative so that violent clashes in print density do not occur;

so that all parts of the paper, except that which is being exposed at the moment, are protected from exposure; so that the exact position of each portion is determined and under control.

Many so-called montages are merely "paste ups" in which portions of several or many prints are cut to shape and pasted together to form some sort of pattern. The true montage is much more difficult to do. Often two negatives are printed so that the print from one overlaps that of the other. There are other modifications.

Correction of Distortion.—By tilting the easel upon which the printing paper is placed for exposure, certain distortion occurring in making the negative may be corrected. Conversely, distortion may be produced by tilting the easel when printing from a normal negative. If the camera has been pointed upward when making a photograph of a tall building, the lines of the building will converge toward the top. If, now, the easel is so tilted that the lines of the image tend to diverge toward the top, the lines of the building in the print may be parallel and therefore neither converge or diverge.

If much correction is to be performed in this manner, the fact that one portion of the paper is further distant from the lens than another must be taken into account, and the nearer portion should be given slightly less exposure.

By distorting the shape of the printing paper, as by holding the edges, or the center away from the easel, queer distortions of various sorts may be effected.

Processing Prints.—Development serves the same purpose in making positive prints as in making negatives. The exposed silver halide must be converted to metallic silver; then the unexposed silver must be disposed of so that the print will be permanent. Developing formulas recommended by the manufacturers for use with their papers may be depended upon to give excellent results. For consistent results the processing conditions (temperature, dilution of stock solution, age of developer) must be carefully controlled.

Positive prints are usually developed at 70°F. and the temperature of the conventional developers should not be allowed to vary more than a few degrees from this temperature. Developer should be freshly made; exposure conditions should be standardized.

Theories of development will be found in the chapters on Development. In this chapter only the more practical aspects of developing procedure will be discussed.

Contrast Control.—The contrast of a paper print depends largely upon the grade of the paper that is employed. It also depends to some extent upon the conditions of processing. This is particularly true of bromide papers. For highest contrast the paper must be adequately exposed and fully developed. If, for any reason, a print having less contrast is desired, the print may be removed from the developer before the full density in the shadows has been attained.

Prints taken from the developer before a minimum developing time (1½ to 3 min. for projection papers) will lack contrast, lack detail in the shadows, and will be poor in tone. Overexposure and underdevelopment produce flat prints of poor color. Underexposure or overdevelopment is likely to produce fogged prints in which detail and contrast are lacking.

Exposure Latitude.—At one time it was felt that a desirable paper was one which had a soft gradation (low gamma) with short development and a steep gradation (high gamma) with a longer development. Such a paper would have the characteristics of a negative emulsion, gamma increasing with increasing development time. Such a paper had limited exposure latitude, for the same character of print, but gave a supposed increase in latitude for taking care of negatives of varying degrees of contrast. Such a latitude was at the expense of print color.

Nowadays the photographer controls print contrast by the use of a particular contrast grade of paper. Figure 12 shows the characteristics of a modern printing paper (Velour Black), indicating that print character will be the same for varying degrees of development time.. Thus a longer development (short of fog) will produce the same gamma as a shorter or normal development time. Such parallelism of the characteristics for varying development time indicates a desirable quality. The photographer has a certain latitude in making exposures.

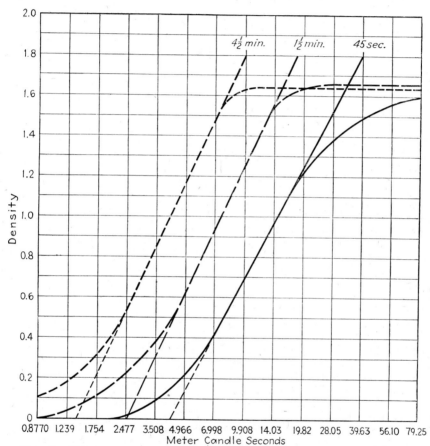

FIG. 12.—Effect of varying development time of a modern projection paper. Note that the contrast of the final print is the same whether developed for 1½ or 4½ min. Because the curves are displaced, a variation in developing time may be used to provide a certain degree of latitude in exposure.

Tone Control.—By varying the development technique of chlorobromide papers, considerable variation in tone may be effected. Silver particles, when small, exhibit color. The first particles developed are these small colored particles; longer development produces larger and blacker grains. The final color depends upon the proportion of the colored grains to the larger black grains. This proportion is controlled by the amount of potassium bromide used in the developer and by the time the print is left in the developer.

An idea of the color changes that may be effected may be obtained from Table VI below, taken from Ilford's Manual. It is applied to Ilford Chlorona paper which is a typical chlorobromide.

DEVELOPER FORMULA FOR ILFORD CHLORONA PAPER

Glycine	60	gr.	3.4	g.
Hydroquinone	60	gr.	3.4	g.
Sodium sulphite	2½	oz.	62.5	g.
Sodium carbonate	4	oz.	100	
Potassium bromide	6	gr.	0.35	g.
Water, up to	20	oz.	500	cc.

TABLE VI.—COLOR CONTROL TABLE FOR ABOVE DEVELOPER

Color	Exposure	Developer dilution	Potassium bromide, 10 per cent, per oz.		Developer time, min.
Warm—black	Normal	Full strength	None		1½
Sepia	2 times	5 times	20 minims	1 cc.	5
Warm sepia	3	10	60	3	10
Red brown	4	15	100	5	15
Red	5	20	120	6	20

To secure "warm" tones, *i.e.*, black mixed with brown, the amount of bromide is increased and the exposure is increased. If the exposure is not increased, the final print color will be the same as if the print had been developed in the solution with less bromide, but it will take longer for the final color to be attained.

Slow papers will respond more readily to changes of potassium bromide than the faster papers. Changes of tone should be effected by varying the amount of bromide plus the variations in exposure time, rather than in merely varying the time in the normal developer solution for various exposures. Increased exposure and under-development in a normal developer will produce warm tones, but the shadow detail will be poor, the shadows will not be black, and the print will not be uniformly colored.

Modifications in Development.—Although the formulas recommended by the manu-facturers are to be followed wherever possible, the following effects of changing formulas are to be noted in case unusual conditions are met.

Increasing metol and decreasing hydroquinone makes softer prints. Reversing these changes produces greater contrast and brilliance.

Additional carbonate in the developer increases developing action and yields black tones without an olive cast. Less carbonate gives softer results and slows up developing.

To increase contrast, increase hydroquinone and carbonate. For less contrast, double usual amount of metol, halve the hydroquinone, and halve the carbonate.

Increase bromide to slow development, to decrease fog, to clear high lights, to add warmth of tone.

Typical Print Developers.—The chapters on Development contain numerous developing formulas for papers. The formulas on page 443, however, are those sug-gested by manufacturers whose papers are widely used in this country.

Inspection during Development.—Under a red- or yellow-printing safe light, it is often difficult to judge print color correctly. Prints appear darker under the safe light than in white light. It is wise, therefore, to fix a test print and to inspect it by white light to determine if it is satisfactory. Another expedient is to use a green safe light (Wratten Series OA). Under this light the prints will appear more like they will under white light. (For safe light for certain papers, see chapter on Darkrooms and Dark-room Practice.)

TABLE VII.—DEFENDER FORMULAS

	Artura Iris	Apex. *a*	Apex. *b*	Velour Black. *c*	Velour Black. *d*	Veltura
Hot water, oz...............	16	32	32	40	40	16
Metol, gr.................	22	15	14	15	20	22
Sodium sulphite (dry), oz.....	¾	½	192 gr.	½	½	¾
Hydroquinone, gr...........	90	60	52	60	60	90
Sodium carbonate (dry), oz...	½	¾	365 gr.	½	¾	½
Potassium bromide, gr.......	10	9	4	25–60	20	10
Cold water to make..........	32	....	.....	....	....	32
Dilution..................	1–1	....	1–2	....	....	1–1
Temperature, °F............	65°	70	65–70	70	70	70
Developing time, sec........	45–60	45–60	45–60	1½–4 min.	....	1½ min.

a. Normal
b. Photo finishing.
c. Use for Apex portraits.
d. Fast development.

TABLE VIII.—EASTMAN PAPER DEVELOPERS

	Chlorobromide olive tones		General purpose	Photo finishing
	D-52	D-74	D-72	D-73
Water (125°F.), oz..........................	16	16	16	16
Elon, gr..................................	22	12	45	40
Sodium sulphite.............................	¾ oz.	350 gr.	1–½ oz.	1 oz., 140 gr.
Hydroquinone, gr..........................	90	64	175	155
Sodium carbonate...........................	½ oz.	175 gr.	2–¼ oz.	2–½ oz.
Potassium bromide, gr.......................	....	32	27	12
Water, oz.................................	32	32	32	32
Dilution..................................	*a*	*b*	*c*	*d*
Athenon..................................	....	64		

a. Dilute 1 to 1.   To each 32-oz. dilute developer add ½ oz. of 10 per cent potassium bromide.
b. Dilute 1 to 1.   Develop 1 to ½ min.
c. Dilute 1 to 2 for chloride; 1 to 4 for bromide.
d. Dilute 1 to 2.

TABLE IX.—AGFA DEVELOPERS

	N-103	120 (B-20)	125 (B-5)	135 (W-5)
Metol........................	51 gr.	¼ oz. 70 gr.	45 gr.	24 gr.
Sodium sulphite (anhydrous)......	1¾ oz. 50 gr.	1 oz. 88 gr.	1½	¾ oz., 20 gr.
Hydroquinone.................	¼ oz. 55 gr.	....	¼ oz. 65 gr.	96 gr.
Sodium carbonate (monohydrated)	2½ oz. 35 gr.	1 oz. 88 gr.	2¼ oz.	¾ oz., 20 gr.
Potassium bromide.............	18 gr.	27 gr.	30 gr.	40 gr.
Water.......................	32 oz.	32 oz.	32 oz.	32 oz.
Dilution....................	1–1*a* 1–4*b*	1–2	1–4	1–1
Temperature.................	70	70	70	70°F.
Developing time.............	1 min.*a* 1½–2*b*	1½–3*b* min.	1½–3*b* min.	1½–2*b* min.

a Convira.
b Brovira.

When working with prints which are to have one of the warm colors, the correct tone is still more difficult to estimate under safe-light conditions. Therefore a small bulb, of perhaps 5 cp., may be used to make a quick inspection to see if the desired color has been attained.

It must be remembered that color, density, and contrast are determined by the developer formula and its age and temperature.

Prints often change color in the fixing bath because, before fixation, print color is controlled by the combination of black silver and of unexposed, undeveloped silver halide which is light yellow. Upon fixation the unexposed emulsion disappears and the shadows of the print will be blacker than before immersion in the fixing bath.

Short Stop, Fixing, and Washing.[1]—After the print is thoroughly developed, it may be placed in the fixing bath, then washed and dried. An acid rinse bath may be used between the developer and the fixer to stop development and to insure that the print will have uniform color. The acid rinse neutralizes the alkalinity of the developer and prevents the acidity of the fixer from being neutralized. It prolongs the life of the fixing bath. Prints may be kept in the rinse bath until all are ready, and then all put through the fixing bath at once.

Prints should be left in a fresh fixing bath for about 15 min. It is most important that their position should be changed frequently. Prints matted together and left stagnant in the bath will lack permanence. Best results are secured by the use of two baths, one partially exhausted for preliminary fixing, and one made up fresh for final fixation.

The acid rinse between developer and fixer will aid materially in prolonging the usefulness of the fixing bath. For example, the Eastman Kodak F-1 fixing solution will treat 120, 8- by 10-in. prints per gallon when the SB-1 rinse is used; but only half this number without the stop bath.

Washing is equally as important as any part of the printing process. The general tendency to throw the prints in a tray or stagnant pool of water and to stir them up occasionally is not satisfactory. Prints should be run through numerous changes of water, and the order of prints from top to bottom of the pile should be changed occasionally. Prints on heavy supports require longer washing periods than single-weight papers.

SHORT STOP (EASTMAN SB-1)

Water..	32 oz.	1 l.
Acetic acid (28 per cent)...	1½ oz.	48 cc.

This is sufficient for 100, 3¼ by 5½-in. prints.

ACID HARDENING FIXING BATH
(Eastman F-1 and Defender 2-F)

Water..	64 oz.	2 l.
Hypo...	16 oz.	480 g.
When completely dissolved add		
Water (about 125° F.) (52° C.).................................	5 oz.	160 cc.
Sodium Sulphite (desiccated)...................................	1 oz.	30 g.
Acetic Acid (28 per cent pure)[1].............................	3 oz.	96 cc.
Potassium Alum...	1 oz.	30 g.

[1] To make 28 per cent acetic acid from glacial acetic acid, dilute 3 parts glacial acid with 8 parts water.

To mix the hardener, dissolve the chemicals in the order given. The sulphite should be dissolved completely before adding the acetic acid. After the sulphite-acid solution has been mixed thoroughly, add the potassium alum with constant stirring. Cool the hardener, and add it slowly to the cool hypo solution while stirring the latter rapidly.

[1] See aso Chapter on Fixing, Washing, and Drying.

When a number of prints are fixed at one time, they must be separated occasionally to insure even fixing, and in hot weather they must not be left in the solution for a longer time than is necessary to fix them, as a warm bath may turn them brown. At all times have plenty of solution, preparing and using fresh bath frequently. The above fixing solution, prepared as described, will fix approximately 275, $3\frac{1}{4}$- by $5\frac{1}{2}$-in. prints or the equivalent in larger sizes if an acid short stop (SB-1) is used, or about 220, $3\frac{1}{4}$- by $5\frac{1}{2}$-in. prints if only a water rinse is used.

Prints may be dried in several ways. Mechanical devices are available which act fairly quickly and produce prints that lie flat when dry. These machines consist usually of rolls of some absorbent material, such as blotting paper, between which the prints are placed. Then hot air is blown through the assembly, or the entire stack of paper, and the blotter is heated by electricity.

Prints may be laid on top of cheesecloth frames after they have been squeezed free from the surface water. Alternately, the wet prints may be wiped off and then placed in a stack of blotters under weight. Prints dried in this manner will tend to curl because of the unequal contraction of the gelatin surface and the paper support.

Immersing prints in a glycerin solution before drying (or after the dried prints have curled) will aid in keeping them flat. Prints that have curled may be straightened by moistening the backs and immediately putting them between blotters and under weight or in a mechanical press.

Greater details on fixing, washing, and drying will be found in Chap. XIII.

Mounting.—Prints may be mounted with several kinds of adhesive (pastes, etc.,) but most photographers have standardized upon dry mounting tissue. This is a semitransparent tissue which is impregnated with substances which melt easily and firmly cement together the print and its mount. For satisfactory results, large prints practically require a mounting press, with heat applied electrically, but even an 11- by 14-in. print may be mounted on a salon-size card (16 by 20 in.) by means of a flatiron.

Mounting tissue a bit larger than the print is attached to the back of the print at several places by using the tip of the iron or a special tool provided for the purpose. Then print and tissue are trimmed. Next the print and tissue are carefully placed in position upon the mount. With the tip of the iron, or with the tool, the tissue is cemented to the mount at several places by lifting up a corner of the print giving access to the tissue. Finally the print is placed in the mounting press or is gone over with the flatiron so that it is firmly fixed to its mount. If the flatiron is used, it is wise to cover the face of the print with a sheet of protective paper.

Correct temperature is important. If the iron is too hot, the tissue will adhere to the mount but not to the print; and if not hot enough the tissue will stick to the print but not to the mount. It is possible to scorch the print so that it will turn brown or yellowish. A good working temperature is 140°F.

Color of Mount.—It is easy to spoil the appearance of an excellent print by the use of a mount of improper dimensions or of wrong color. There are few prints that do not look well on a light-colored mount (white or cream); there are many that will look bad on anything but a light mount. A light-colored mount is nearly always safe. If the mount has any appreciable color, it is likely that it will appear more important than the print.

Salons prefer 16- by 20-in. mounts; the picture should be placed so that there is a little more space between top of print and top of mount than there is between the sides of print and mount; there should be less space at the top than at the bottom. A small print may look best in a rather large mount.

Often a print which is light in general tone may be enhanced in appearance by mounting it first on a piece of black paper, so that about $\frac{1}{8}$ in. of the black projects beyond the limits of the print, thereby framing it. Then the print and its black frame are mounted on a light cardboard. A thin black line drawn about ⅛ in. from the edges of the print will often serve the same purpose.

Embossing Prints.—"Prints which have a die-sunk line embossed around the edge of the picture are attractive and easily made. Any double weight paper is suitable for embossing.

"The prints should have wide white margins; and standards of size should be adopted, as a mark and form must be made for each size. The embossed line for a print, say 6 by 9 in., on an 11- by 14-in. sheet of paper, should be about ⅜ in. from top and sides of the picture image and ⅝ in. from the bottom, making the embossing form 6¾ by 10 in. The form should be the same thickness as the print so an old print may be used for this purpose.

"Cut it 6¾ by 10 in. and then draw a line ⅜ in. from top and sides and ⅝ in. from the bottom, as shown in the diagram. Cut out the corners as indicated by dark triangles. These openings are to locate the corners of the print when adjusting the form.

"A square of plate glass with a light beneath makes an excellent embossing table. Place the form on the plate glass over the light. Place the print over the form, locating the corners of the picture in the triangular openings. Hold the print firmly and run a print embosser [available at photo supply stores] over the back, following the edge of the form. If the pressure of the embossing tool is even, the result is a distinct plate-sunk line that adds to the print's attractiveness.

Fig. 13.—Method of embossing mounts.

"Before prints are embossed, their backs should be moistened evenly to the edges with a solution of equal parts of wood alcohol and water. They should then be placed between blotters under pressure. If not allowed to become bone-dry, the prints will lie flat and emboss without cracking." (Eastman Kodak Co.)

Paper Negatives.—Exhibition prints are frequently made by the "paper negative" process.[1] This consists in making a positive print from the original negative, making an intermediate negative from this positive, and making the final positive from this negative. The advantages of the method over straight negative-to-positive printing are as follows: (1) Local work may be performed on both the first positive and the intermediate negative; (2) certain objects may be added to or subtracted from the print that either do not exist on the original negative or which, if they do exist, detract from its composition or are otherwise objectionable; (3) the intermediate negative may be larger than the original negative. Therefore a large contact-paper print may be made on paper so slow that a projection print from the original, and smaller, negative would be impractical. (4) The texture of the paper on which the intermediate negative is made may appear in the final print.

The process is as follows:

1. Make negative on paper, either from a positive print or direct in the camera.
2. Make corrections on this negative.
3. Make final print from this negative.

Or as follows:

1. Make positive on paper or film from negative, by contact or by projection.

[1] So-called because the "intermediate negative" is usually made on a paper rather than on a film.

2. Make corrections on this positive.

3. Make paper negative from this positive, and make corrections on this positive.

4. Make final positive print from this negative.

Direct Paper Negative.—In this case paper instead of film is loaded and exposed in the camera. A fast single-weight matte or glossy paper may be used. Naturally the exposure will be longer than if a film negative is to be made. Experiment will determine the correct exposure, which, for bromide paper will be about twenty times as long as is required for average speed film. A soft working developer is recommended.

The exposure should be ample to register details in the shadows; development may be a bit longer than for normal print development. The negative should look somewhat overdeveloped. The negative should be fixed and dried carefully so that no creases appear. A trial print may be made from this negative, to determine what is to be touched up on the negative.

Paper Positive.—By contact or by projection a print is made from the desired negative on a semigloss or glossy single-weight paper. The print should be the size of the final print. If the exposure is made through the paper support, the grain of the paper will be minimized in the final print. This intermediate print may look blotched by reflected light, but when viewed by transmitted light, the mottle of the paper support is not nearly so evident.

The positive should be overexposed somewhat and must be fully developed. From this positive the paper negative is made by contact. The final positive print is made by contact with the paper negative.

Handwork may be carried out on both the paper positive and the paper negative made from it. If something is to be added to the final print which does not exist in the original negative, it must be sketched in on the positive with soft pencil or with retouching material worked on with a chamois.

Film Positive.—In this case the positive is made by projection or by contact on a film. A matte-back film is preferred because the retouching may be made on the back. Exposure must be full, but development should be shortened to keep contrast down. Dust specks and other flaws must be kept to a minimum if the positive is to be enlarged in making the intermediate negative.

Intermediate Negative.—This negative may be made on ordinary printing papers or, better, on the translucent papers now available, such as Eastman Translite or Defender Adlux. These papers have emulsions on both sides. The negative must be fully exposed but somewhat underdeveloped to bring out high-light detail and to keep shadow density down. For Translite, as an example, the negative should be developed about 45 sec. or 1 min.

Paper fiber does not show on this negative when it is viewed by transmitted light. As the light passes through the paper stock and exposes the back emulsion, the paper fibers tend to cancel their images on the back emulsion. The paper should be laid down on black paper when making the exposure.

The enlarged paper negative, when made on the semitransparent materials mentioned above, offers excellent opportunity for handwork with lead pencil, charcoal pencil, or chamois stump dipped in powdered charcoal or lead pencil dust. The negative should not be oiled when making the final positive print.

Photo Murals.—Murals are enlargements of considerable size which are usually made in sections and mounted on the wall from which they are to be viewed. Printing paper is available 42 in. wide by 10 ft. long so that fairly large sections may be made at one time, provided one has the equipment in which to develop, fix, and wash the individual strips.

Techniques differ among the individual mural experts. One professional photographer, who has made many of the best known murals, uses a 4- by 5-in. negative as the original. This is projected to make a glossy 11- by 14-in. print. This print is spotted and is rephotographed on an 11- by 14-in. plate. The final "blow up" is made from this plate. The final sections are 40 in. wide and are developed in D-72, diluted 1 to 6 and kept at constant temperature. The prints are then mounted on three-ply wood.

If the mural is to be made up of portions of several unrelated pictures cut at odd dimensions and sizes, the problem is largely artistic and not photographic.

Murals are often made up of distinct portions of several prints assembled into a pattern which may be regular, as rectangular, or it may be irregular, the individual portions which make up the whole being in assorted sizes and shapes.

Given a job of this kind the photographer often finds that he has thrust upon him prints of varying color, varying tone range, varying degrees of gloss, varying size. They may be the only prints available and the negatives may be unobtainable.

The dimensions of the finished mural are known. The photographs are, therefore, to be made into a design in miniature. The scale may be an inch to the foot or any other convenient reduction. The photographer's or artist's design will be ultimately copied on film and then projected into the final dimensions. If the original layout is large enough to require more than one negative, there must be natural places where one negative may stop and another one take up the design. There must be a line of cleavage which by design is invisible but nevertheless there.

Parts of the prints that are to be cut away are outlined with a razor blade, and the actual cutting only goes through the emulsion or at least not very deep into the paper itself. Then the print is torn so that the paper support tears away beneath the image and leaves the latter very thin. This edge may then be laid down on the adjacent print and fixed in place. The better artists do not use an airbrush or other means of obliterating the edge because of the difficulty in preventing the material from getting under the feather edge (which may be thinned with sandpapering on the back of the print) and from being more apparent than before the brush was used.

The final design is photographed and projected upon mural paper in strips of the proper dimension. These strips are processed like any other photographic paper except that large tanks or trays are necessary.

Transparent murals or mosaics may be printed upon paper which has an emulsion on both sides such as Adlux, Translite, etc. Murals may be tinted or actually painted in transparent oils. This coloring is done after the mural is on the wall, and the actual coloring is a job for an artist, not a photographer.

Enlarged Negatives by Reversal.—Where retouching must be done on miniature negatives, the following method of making enlarged negatives is useful (see "Leica Manual," 1st ed., p. 133.) The negative is projected upon process film or upon an ortho film of somewhat softer gradation. Develop the film, wash, fix, and bleach it in potassium permanganate to which has been added silver nitrate; clear in sodium bisulphite, wash, and give second exposure. Then develop; again fix, wash, and dry. Retouching can now take place upon this enlarged negative which may be used for contact printing, or which may be projected so that a larger print may be secured.

Photographic Sketching.—A combination of photographic processes and of drawing makes it possible to produce very creditable sketches which resemble freehand drawings.

In one method, the negative is projected upon a sheet of white drawing paper where the image is a negative. If the white lines of the image as projected are gone over with a crayon or a soft pencil until all such white lines have been covered, a positive sketch will have been made of the image on the negative. Now the drawn print is photographed to the final size desired and photoprints are made from this negative.

In another method, a positive print is gone over with waterproof India ink. In this case the black lines are covered. Judgment must be exercised as to the strokes used, *viz.*, crosshatching, curves, etc. With a little practice the results are unusual and distinctive. Then the print is bleached so that the photographic image disappears leaving only the hand-drawn sketch.

A satisfactory bleach for disposing of the silver image is

Water...	$3\frac{1}{2}$	oz.
Potassium permanganate..	3	gr.
Sulphuric acid...	1	dram

This will leave a discolored print. To remove the permanganate stain immerse the print in a bath made up of 50 to 100 gr. of sodium bisulphite in 4 oz. of water. This will leave a perfectly clean white print on which remain only the India ink lines. Additional lines may be added to this print if desired.

Since the India ink must be placed over the black lines of the original print, it is sometimes difficult to tell when all the necessary lines have been covered, or to judge how well the work has progressed. The solution to this difficulty is to place the black lines on a negative print. In this case the ink is placed upon the white lines of the negative.[1]

Lantern Slides.—Lantern slides are made on glass plates coated with an emulsion somewhat similar to that used for making positives. Standard sizes are $3\frac{1}{4}$ by 4 in. and $3\frac{1}{4}$ by $3\frac{1}{4}$ in. Several degrees of contrast are available. Eastman provides soft, medium and contrast. The first two may be developed under a Wratten safe light Series O or OA for contrast and medium plates; Series 1 safe light must be used for soft plates which are more sensitive.

Any negative that will make a good print will make a good slide. The slides may be printed by projection or by contact. Blemishes must be kept to a minimum because of their subsequent enlargement when the slides are projected. The Eastman plates vary in sensitivity as follows: contrast plates require about three times the exposure required for medium, and medium about seven times as much exposure as soft.

Exposure.—Using a 25-watt frosted lamp at a distance of about 6 ft. between light and printing frame, the exposure required for an average negative on medium plates is about 5 sec. It is advisable at first to make use of the test-strip method of determining correct exposure. Cover two-thirds of the slide with an opaque cardboard and give an exposure of 40 sec.; uncover part of the slide so that only one-third is now covered, and give an exposure of 8 sec. Finally uncover the entire slide and give an exposure of 2 sec. Now the slide will have portions exposed for 2, 10, and 50 sec. In varying exposures, double or halve them, as smaller exposure changes will make so little difference the operator will not learn much. To make positive from miniature frames, use the positive stock film, print by contact; for 10 sec., 6 in. from a 10 cp. lamp is a good trial exposure. Use weak developer.

Development.—Slides may be developed in D-72 (see developers for paper, above). Develop in a white tray and judge development as one would a printing paper. When development is complete, the highest light should show appreciable color. Dilute D-72 and develop as follows: soft plate, dilute 1 to 4, develop 2 to 3 min. at 70°F.; medium plate, dilute 1 to 2, develop 1 to 2 min. at 70°F.; contrast plate, dilute 1 to 1, develop 3 to 5 min. at 70°F.

---

[1] There are several other modifications of the photo-sketching process. A good survey of this process will be found in Some Suggestions on Photo Sketching, by E. A. Yunker, *Am. Phot.*, December, 1935, p. 746.

The plates should be rinsed in a short-stop bath and then fixed in any good hardening fixing bath. They should be washed 20 min.

Mounting.—The slides should be varnished to protect them and prevent absorption of moisture in damp weather, which causes "dewing" or condensation of moisture on the cover glass when it is heated by the lantern. Special varnish for this purpose may be purchased from the supply houses.

The shape of the mask should usually be rectangular. Oval or round masks are seldom necessary or desirable. The standard size mask opening for motion-picture theaters is 3 by 2½ in. The mask, which may be cut from black paper or purchased ready to use, is placed on the emulsion side of the slide.

After masking, the slide is bound in contact with a thin cover glass which is placed on the emulsion side. A white spot or label should be placed on the lower left-hand corner when holding the slide in the hand so that the image appears on the screen properly. This label not only identifies the slide but is useful to the projection-machine operator in inserting the slide in the machine properly.

Cover glasses for slides 2 in. square are now available for Kodachrome and other positives made with cameras using 35-mm. film. These slides are mounted and bound in the same manner as the larger slides. Cellulose or Scotch tape may be used to bind up the positive with its cover glass.

Direct Positive Paper.—This paper is used for making negatives which, by the reversal process, are changed into positive prints. Correct exposure for the negative determines the quality of the print, therefore a fixed light source and a definite exposure are required. Underexposure will produce a dark picture, while overexposure produces pictures which are too light.

The reversal process includes exposure, development of the negative, bleaching the negative, clearing, reexposure, development of the positive, fixing. Fixing is not essential, but it gives the print a slightly increased brilliance. Fixed prints should be washed for 10 min. in running water. If not fixed, prints should be washed for 4 or 5 min. The Eastman direct positive emulsion is coated on a waterproof support which permits rapid drying. An inexpensive electric hair dryer can be used effectively to facilitate drying. The Series 2 Wratten safe light should be used for workroom illumination.

A satisfactory division of time in the different solutions is as follows: developing, 45 sec. to 1 min.; bleaching, 30 sec.; clearing, 30 sec.; developing or redeveloping, 30 sec.; fixing, 30 sec. It is necessary to wash the prints thoroughly in running water for at least 15 sec. between the different solutions. When the solution D-88 is used for developing a black-and-white positive, it is necessary to expose the paper to artificial light directly after clearing. If convenient, the white light may be turned on as soon as the prints are placed in the clearing bath.

DEVELOPER (D-88)

Water (about 125° F.) (52° C.)	96 oz.	3	l.
Sodium sulphite (desiccated)	6½ oz.	195	g.
Hydroquinone	3¼ oz.	97.5 g.	
Boric acid (crystals)	¾ oz.	22.5 g.	
Potassium bromide	150 gr.	10.5 g.	
Sodium hydroxide (caustic soda)	3¼ oz.	97.5 g.	
Water to make	1 gal.	4	l.

The caustic soda should be dissolved in a small volume of water, in a separate container, and added to the solution which has been made by dissolving the chemicals in the order given. Water should then be added to make 1 gal. (4 l.). When dissolving the caustic soda, stir constantly so that the heat generated will not cause the solution to boil with explosive violence and spatter the hot caustic on the hand and face, which would produce serious burns. Use the developer full strength at a temperature of 70°F. (21°C.).

Use a crystalline boric acid as specified. Powdered boric acid dissolves with difficulty.

BLEACHING SOLUTION

Water	1	gal.	4.0 l.
Potassium bichromate	1¼	oz.	37.5 g.
Sulphuric acid (c.p.)	1½	fl. oz.	48.0 cc.

Use full strength at 65 to 70°F. (18 to 21°C.). For more rapid bleaching, the amounts of acid and bichromate may be increased.

CLEARING SOLUTION

Sodium sulphite (desiccated)	12 oz.	360 g.
Water	1 gal.	4 l.

Use full strength at 65 to 70°F. (18 to 21°C.).

Printing-out Paper.—At one time the photographer's best medium was P O P, printing-out paper, in which the image is visible after exposure and before development. Proofs of negatives were often submitted on paper of this type because the prints would fade if exposed to the light and so the person photographed could not retain the proof print with any degree of satisfaction. He was forced to let the photographer make a print with a more permanent image. For rendition of fine detail, a glossy P O P paper is superior to more modern developing-out papers and for reproduction by means of half-tone engravings, P O P is still recommended.

P O P is very slow compared to present-day printing papers. It is exposed to the negative by direct daylight or very strong artificial light. It may be handled in a well-lighted room. The negative should be of average contrast. Flat negatives will produce weak and flat prints. Prints should be exposed somewhat longer than appearances would dictate as determined by inspection during the exposure. Some color is lost in subsequent processing. The parts which are to be pure white in the final print should show some slight color in the correctly exposed print.

After exposure, the prints should be washed thoroughly, *i.e.*, until the wash water no longer shows any milkiness. Five or six complete changes of water are required.

Toning Bath.—Innumerable baths may be used to tone P O P. In some there is a combination of the toning and fixing processes. The following formulas are a few examples of those which have been recommended.

If the toning and fixing are to be distinct baths, the following method is recommended by Ilford.

Two stock solutions are necessary for making up the working toning bath.

SULPHOCYANIDE SOLUTION A

Ammonium sulphocyanide	200 gr.	12 g.
Water	20 oz.	500 cc.

GOLD SOLUTION B

Gold chloride	15 gr.	1 g.
Water	20 oz.	500 cc.

For use, take 2 oz. each of A and B and add to 20 oz. water (50 to 400 cc. water). Add the gold solution slowly and shake well.

After about 5 or 10 min. in this bath, prints begin to lose their characteristic red color and take on their final purplish color. After toning, the prints should be thoroughly washed, then immersed in hypo, 3 to 20 oz. water (75 g. to 500 cc. water), and moved about for 10 min. The fixer should be used but once. Finally the prints must be thoroughly washed, Ilford recommending 2 hr.

Combined Toning and Fixing.—Use of a combined bath saves time, but at the expense of less permanency of the image

COMBINED TONER AND FIXER

Hypo...	6 oz.	150 g.
Sodium chloride..	20 gr.	1 g.
Lead nitrate (or lead acetate)...........................	20 gr.	1 g.
Gold chloride..	4 gr.	0.2 g.
Water to make...	20 oz.	500 cc.

Prints may be immersed in this solution without the preliminary washing. Toning is complete in about 6 min.

Papers are available (Seltona and Enitone of Ilford) which contain the gold chloride in the emulsion. After exposure, these papers are placed in a hypo solution in which they are rendered permanent.

Bibliography

GIBBS, C. W.: Paper Negatives, *Am. Phot.*, October, 1934, p. 591.

WOODLEY, A. J.: Composite Pictures, *Am. Phot.*, November, 1934, p. 678.

SPICER, DON R.: Dry Mounting, *Am. Phot.*, December, 1934, p. 760.

MOUAT, L. W.: An Exposure Calculator (for printing), *Am. Phot.*, January, 1935, p. 34.

OSTERNDORFF, E. R.: Photo Sketching, *Camera*, December, 1935, p. 391.

YUNKER, E. A.: Photo Sketching, *Am. Phot.*, December, 1935, p. 74.

CASSIDY, E. H.: The Psychological Point of View, *Am. Phot.*, February, 1936, p. 102.

COLE, P. J.: Meter Measurement of Enlarging Exposure, *Camera*, May, 1936, p. 316.

BENEDICT, H. C.: Condenser Enlarger, *Camera Craft*, June, 1936, p. 275.

YOUNG, L. H.: Relation between Condenser and Objective in Enlarger, *Am. Phot.*, June, 1936, p. 358.

WEILAND, W. F.: Exposure in Projection Printing, *Am. Phot.*, July, 1936, p. 420.

BROCKMAN, F. G.: Photoelectric Timing in Projection Printing, *Am. Phot.*, September, 1936, p. 604.

RUSSELL, GRANT: A Comparison of Print Developers, *Am. Phot.*, November, 1936, p. 718.

HUFF, M. O.: Gaseous Discharge Tubes for Enlarging and Printing MO, *Camera*, December, 1936, p. 362.

KORTH, FRED G.: Making Photomontages in the Enlarger, *Am. Phot.*, January, 1937.

PIKE, H. W.: Miniature Lantern Slides, *Am. Phot.*, June, 1937, p. 398.

HOPKINSON, R. G.: New Approach to the Problem of Tone Reproduction, *Phot. J.*, September, 1937, p. 542.

Dubbing in Clouds, *Agfa Diamond*, September–October, 1937, p. 5.

TUTTLE, CLIFTON: Photoelectric Photometry in Printing Amateur Negatives, *J. Franklin Inst.*, September, 1937, pp. 315–331.

———: Devices for the Photoelectric Control of Exposure in Printing, *J. Franklin Inst.*, November, 1937, pp. 615–631.

MORSE, R. S.: Black and White Prints from Kodachrome, *Am. Phot.*, January, 1938, p. 1.

SANIAL, A. J.: Making Lantern Slides, *Am. Phot.*, January, 1938, p. 4.

MOWBRAY, G. M.: A Novel Dodging Device, *Camera*, February, 1938, p. 91.

Home Sensitized Prints and Iron Salts, *Photo Art Monthly*, April, 1938.

COLT, R. S.: Simple Method of Timing Enlargements, *Am. Phot.*, April, 1938, p. 244.

CARSON, KENNETH: Paper Negatives, *Defender Trade Bull.*, March-June, 1938.

HERBERT, JR., W. A.: Hints on Mounting Salon Photographs, *Camera*, June, 1938, p. 386.

———: Simplicity of Paper Negatives, *Camera*, June, 1938, p. 375.

HEYSER, C. A.: Drawings and Etchings from Photographs, *Am. Phot.*, June, 1938, p. 414.

DESME, R. G. J.: Print Quality and Development, *Am. Phot.*, July, 1938, p. 460.

WELLER, JR., H.: Print Reversal, *Camera*, August, 1938, p. 102.

NORGREN, C. A.: Photo-Etching, *Am. Phot.*, September, 1938, p. 640.

DONALDSON, E. W.: Etchcraft for the Beginner, *Am. Phot.*, September, 1938, p. 642.

GREENSLADE, T. B.: Photographic Murals, *Am. Phot.*, September, 1938, p. 654.

BOALS, R. B.: Amateur Slide Making, *Am. Phot.*, October, 1938, p. 685.

Printing in Clouds, *Photo Art Monthly*, October–November, 1938.

WESTERMAN, A. W.: An Efficient Print Washer, *Am. Phot.*, November, 1938, p. 800.

GREENLEAF, A. R.: Simplified Print Developers, *Am. Phot.*, November, 1938, p. 810.

DUTTON, LAWRENCE: Types of Photographic Papers, *Am. Phot.*, December, 1938, p. 872.

Mounting and Embossing, *Photo Art Monthly*, December, 1938, p. 596.

CHAPTER XV

TONING

By Donald Burchan and Ira Current

One of the fundamental, and ofttimes little understood, characteristics of a photographic print is the color or tone which makes up its image. In the ordinary black-and-white print this tone is very subtle, and the presence of color is often unnoticed. This tone or color is fundamentally determined by the emulsion characteristics of the paper and is controlled, within limits, by the nature of the developer used and the amount of its dilution. The usual color range is from a cold blue-black to a warm brown, although it is also possible to obtain tones up to red by direct development.

While this method is rather involved and requires careful attention to details of exposure and development, it has, we believe, a definite place in a discussion of toning methods. The careful technique that is required is such that probably only the advanced worker may be sufficiently recompensed to reward his patience and perseverance; however, by toning processes in which the silver image is actually changed to another compound having the color desired, it is possible to produce, easily and uniformly, brown, red, blue, and green tones, as well as many of their intermediate shades.

By the use of toning processes the photographer can produce pictures which are more effective because of their tone or color. For instance, some snowscapes are much enhanced when the photographic image has been rendered in a brilliant blue or a fireside picture more appealing in a reddish brown. The possibilities are unlimited as one becomes familiar with the colors that the different methods are capable of producing.

As different kinds of paper react differently to most toning processes, a short explanation of these papers and their behavior will be given before proceeding with the various toning processes. Bromide papers as a class do not produce a wide variety of good tones. They tend to the cold browns and purples. It is better whenever possible to choose papers of the chlorobromide or chloride group. The chlorobromides are the so-called slow enlarging papers, while the chloride papers are used only for contact printing because of their slow speed. As all leading manufacturers have papers of these two groups in a variety of surfaces, it is possible for the most exacting worker to find the surface which will satisfy his particular demands. After he has made his choice of paper, it would be well for the beginner to experiment in its manipulation, following suggestions of the manufacturer. It is only by mastering the art of making good black-and-white prints that success can be obtained in toning. This point cannot be stressed too much for many of the troubles experienced in toning can usually be traced directly to a faulty original print.

Toning, as it is generally spoken of, involves a chemical conversion of the silver image of the "developed print" into one or more insoluble substances having various colors, for example, brown silver sulphide, or colored compounds of such metals as copper, uranium, iron, etc. But it is also possible to obtain colored metallic silver images, as we have suggested, by modification of development.

Toning by Direct Development.—When developers of a special composition are used and the developing time is shortened or the solution diluted, a coloring of the image is noticed; this usually is brownish. Here again some papers have properties which yield themselves to these modifications of development more than others. These are the chlorobromide papers that yield warm olive tones even in ordinary developers, and some of the chloride papers. Most chloride papers, especially those used for commercial and photo-finishing purposes, are blue-black in tone when developed in the recommended formulas. Bromide papers, as a rule, are not readily adaptable to toning by direct development.

The reducing agents used in a developing formula and their proportions to one another play an important part in the determination of the final color of a print. It must be remembered that an agent such as hydroquinone has a tendency, when used without any other agents, to yield warm tones, especially in the presence of fairly large quantities of potassium bromide. Metol, on the other hand, besides having soft-gradation-producing characteristics, generally makes the tones of prints black or blue-black.

In most photofinishing establishments contact prints with a blue-black tone are desired, and these result from using a developer having a high energy factor, *i.e.*, one having a large proportion of alkali or energizer and properly balanced amounts of metol and hydroquinone. Such a developer is of the following composition and may be used for contact and bromide papers when cold blue-black tones are desired.

STOCK SOLUTION (AGFA 103)

Hot water (125°F. or 52°C.)	750	cc.	24	oz.
Metol	3.5 g.		50	gr.
Sodium sulphite (anhydrous)	45	g.	1½	oz.
Hydroquinone	11.5 g.		¼	oz., 55 gr.
Sodium carbonate (monohydrated)	78	g.	2½	oz., 35 gr.
Potassium bromide	1.2 g.		18	grains
Water to make	1	l.	32	oz.

Dilute 1 part stock solution with 2 parts water.
Chloride papers: Normal development time, 1 min. at 70°F. (21°C.).
Bromide papers: Normal development time, 1½ to 2 min. at 70°F. (21°C.).

A chlorobromide paper when developed in such a formula will have a tendency to produce rich blacks, although the medium tones will be more olive in color, especially if through use the developer has been allowed to accumulate an amount of bromide. By reducing the amount of metol in such a formula, the warm-toned results will be even more pronounced. If the solution is diluted in order to control the rate of development, still warmer tones will result.

There are other reducing agents, which, when used in the developing formulas in the proper proportions, will yield tones even more brilliant in color than those obtained from the methods outlined above. Examples of these reducing agents are Adurol and glycine.

Adurol will produce tones which range from a rich brown-black to brilliant reds when the dilution of the developer is very great; the exposure time has been increased enough to compensate for this dilution, and increasing amounts of potassium bromide have been added. The formulas on page 455 were developed by Ilford Limited of London and published in their "Manual of Photography." The table of exposure time, dilution, etc., has been changed slightly to meet the requirements of American papers.

These formulas used as mixed, without any dilution, will produce warm black-toned prints. By diluting the solution, increasing the exposure, adding a certain amount of a 10 per cent solution of potassium bromide, and prolonging the developing time, we may change this tone from warm black to reddish brown. While different papers may not all work the same, the difference in result will not be very great. With a few experiments in exposure and developing time, it is possible to arrive at the tone desired.

ADUROL FORMULA

Adurol	6.8 g.	97	gr.
Hydroquinone	6.8 g.	97	gr.
Sodium sulphite (anhydrous)	62.4 g.	2	oz., 85 gr.
Sodium carbonate (monohydrated)	54.4 g.	1¾	oz., 60 gr.
Potassium bromide	0.7 g.	11	gr.
Water	1000 cc.	32	oz.

TABLE I.—DILUTION, EXPOSURE TIME, ETC., FOR THE ADUROL FORMULA

Dilution	Addition of 10 per cent solution of potassium bromide to 1000 cc. developer, cc.	Relative exposure time	Approximate developer time, min.	Tones formed
1:0	0	1	1½	Warm black
1:10	40	4– 5	9	Warm sepia
1:15	120	6– 8	14	Red-brown sepia
1:30	240	9–15	30	Bright red

If the Adurol in the above formula is replaced by glycine and the amount of sodium carbonate increased, we get a similar range of tones.

GLYCINE FORMULA

Glycine	6.8 g.	97 gr.	
Hydroquinone	6.8 g.	97 gr.	
Sodium sulphite (anhydrous)	62.4 g.	2 oz. 85 gr.	
Sodium carbonate (monohydrated)	88.4 g.	3 oz. 50 gr.	
Potassium bromide	0.7 g.	11 gr.	
Water	1000 cc.	32 oz.	

TABLE II.—DILUTION, EXPOSURE TIME, ETC., FOR THE GLYCINE FORMULA

Dilution	Addition of 10 per cent solution of potassium bromide to 1000 cc. developer, cc.	Relative exposure time	Approximate developer time min.	Tones formed
1:0	0	1	1½	Black
1:2	20	1½ to 2½	3 to 6	Engraving black to warm black
1:4	40	2 to 4	5 to 15	Warm black to sepia
1:8	80	4 to 8	12 to 30	Sepia to red-brown

As tones produced by direct development are not always those that may be desired and because the results are not always easily reproduced, except through very strict attention to small details, methods which convert the silver image to some other compound possessing the color desired are used. The simplest of these methods are those known as sulphide toners.

Sulphide Toning Processes.—The sulphide processes produce sepia tones by converting the silver image into insoluble silver sulphide. Prints toned by these methods are permanent and will keep their tones indefinitely without fading. Such toners are easy to use, are economical, and can be depended upon to duplicate values fairly well.

The success of these methods depends upon the character of the original black-and-white print. As a general rule maximum exposure and full development produce prints which will tone well by these processes. Underexposure and overdevelopment and the reverse, *viz.*, overexposure and underdevelopment should be avoided in all instances. A few trial prints made on the paper selected with varying times of exposure and development, but all approximately the same density, will easily establish the correct procedure. Fresh solutions should always be used and care taken that they are not overworked. The temperature of the developer should be kept as near 70°F. as possible. Bromide in the developer used for the black-and-white prints has quite an influence on the final results; *i.e.*, slightly increasing the bromide content, will yield somewhat warmer tones in the final print tone.

The sulphide processes may be divided into two classifications.

1. Direct sulphide process in which the silver image is changed directly to silver sulphide with no intermediate steps.

2. Indirect sulphide process in which the silver image is first changed to an insoluble silver salt or a mixture of silver and mercury salts which are then changed to the sulphides of these metals.

Direct Sepia Process.—The three most commonly used direct processes are hypo alum, hypo-alum gold chloride and "liver of sulphur." As all these direct methods have hypo as one of their ingredients, it is not necessary to wash the prints after fixing, but they may be transferred directly to the toning bath.

The chief disadvantage of these methods is that the solution must be used hot (approximately 120°F.), and it is necessary to have some method of keeping this temperature fairly constant. It takes from 15 to 60 min. to tone prints at this temperature, depending on the kind of paper used. Toning in a cold solution would require about 10 to 12 hr. Some photographers leave prints in these mixtures overnight, but this is not good procedure and should be avoided. Another caution that is very important is to use these toners in a separate room or at least at a distance from any sensitized materials, such as paper or film, for direct sepia toners give off sulphur fumes when heated which are destructive to sensitized materials. Good ventilation is absolutely necessary. Abrupt changes of temperature should be avoided, prints should be allowed to cool after being removed from the toning bath and before washing. If this is not done, frilling and blistering will result. Prints should be sponged off carefully after removal from the toning baths, to remove sediment; allowed to cool; and then washed in cold running water for 15 to 20 min.

Hypo-alum Sepia Method.—Two common photographic chemicals are used in this formula, *viz.*, hypo and potassium alum. When alum, which is acid, is added to a solution of hypo (sodium thiosulphate), free sulphur is precipitated. This precipitated sulphur, when combined with the silver image of the print during toning, forms brown silver sulphide.

A silver "ripener" which retards the bleaching action due to the hypo must also be added to the solution. Chloride, bromide, or iodide are used for this purpose. If six or eight waste prints are at hand, it is possible by toning these prints to dispense with the ripener, as the silver salts supplied by these prints will serve the same purpose. The bath may be used indefinitely or until it is so reduced by evaporation that it is necessary to replenish it, when a fresh solution must be added.

Very definite instructions are given as to how these ingredients should be combined in the bath, and any deviation from this order will result in failure. It is equally important to keep the solution at the temperature given, as too hot a bath will cause blistering and frilling, and a cold bath not only slows up the toning action but tends to produce cold purplish tones. Prints should be agitated constantly while toning to prevent them from sticking together and toning unevenly.

As this method does not work progressively but carries the toning to completion and then stops, the prints should be left in long enough to insure complete toning.

Hypo-alum Toner

This toner is recommended for beautiful reddish-brown tones.

Solution A

Water	2350 cc.	80 oz.
Hypo	450 g.	16 oz.

Solution B

Water	30 cc.	1 oz.
Silver nitrate	1¼ g.	20 gr.

Solution C

Water	30 cc.	1 oz.
Potassium iodide	2½ g.	40 gr.

Add solution *B* to solution *A*. Then add solution *C* to the mixture. Finally add 105 g. (3½ oz.) of potassium alum to this solution, and heat the entire bath to the boiling point, or until sulphurization takes place (indicated by a milky appearance of the solution). Tone prints 20 to 60 min. in this bath at 110 to 125°F. (43 to 52°C.). Agitate prints occasionally until toning is complete.

Hypo-alum Gold Sepia Method.—A toner which yields even more beautiful sepias than the hypo-alum is made by adding a soluble gold salt to a solution which is made up of hypo-alum and a ripener. Gold chloride or gold sodium chloride is used. When the print is placed in this gold solution, the silver will replace the metal in solution, and the gold will be deposited in place of the silver. It is necessary for a good tone that this gold deposit be rapid. This bath must be kept alkaline, a condition which is accomplished by the addition of sodium phosphate. A definite test for this alkalinity is the use of red litmus paper which turns blue in an alkaline solution.

Hypo-alum Gold Toner

Solution A

(1)	Boiling water (distilled)	4000 cc.	128 oz.
	Hypo	450 g.	16 oz.
	Alum potassium	56 g.	2 oz.

Boil the above 2 or 3 min., allow it to cool and then add

Sodium phosphate	56 g.	2 oz.

Test the resulting solution with red litmus paper. If the litmus paper does not turn blue within 1 min., heat bath again, and add sodium phosphate in 2-oz. (56-g.) quantities until the bath has become slightly alkaline. Then dissolve

(2)	Silver nitrate	4 g.	60 gr.
	Water	30 cc.	1 oz.
	Potassium bromide	8 g.	120 gr.
	Water	30 cc.	1 oz.

Separate solutions are made of the silver and bromide, each dissolved in 1 oz. (30 cc.) of water. The bromide solution is poured into the silver solution. The resulting mixture, precipitate and all, is then added to the hypo-alum bath after the latter has thoroughly cooled.

SOLUTION *B*

Gold chloride	1 g.	15 gr.
Water	15 cc.	1 oz.

To use add 1 dram (3.7 cc.) of gold solution (solution *B*) to each 16 oz. (500 cc.) of hypo-alum bath (solution *A*), tone at 90 to 110°F.—not more than 110°F. Prints should be examined as the toning proceeds and removed when the desired tone is reached.

This toning bath as mixed will tone approximately 150 4- by 6-in. prints. When used up to this point, it should be discarded and a new bath mixed.

Prints should be agitated during toning to insure even toning. After toning is completed they should be carefully sponged to remove any surface sediment, fixed again in the regular acid hypo fixing solution for about 5 min., washed and dried in the usual manner.

Liver-of-sulphur Sepia Method.—This is an easy economical method of sepia toning giving results which are comparable to the hypo-alum process on some papers. As results vary with different papers, it would be well to test this method thoroughly before adopting it.

Liver of sulphur is a mixture of potassium sulphide along with other compounds such as sulphates, carbonates, hypo, etc. The actual toning agent is not known, but it is thought that the sulphur acts on the silver image forming silver sulphide as in the other sulphide toners. It is well to get liver of sulphur from a reputable chemical concern, as most of it is impure and not fit for photographic use. It is necessary in this process to be sure the prints are well hardened, as liver of sulphur in a hot solution has quite a softening effect on the emulsion.

LIVER-OF-SULPHUR SEPIA METHOD

Liver of sulphur	30 gr.
Water	40 oz.

Use at 80°F.

Indirect Sepia Process.—This process is used extensively for sepia prints because of its simplicity and economy and because the solutions are used at room temperature. Two solutions are necessary: (1) the "bleach," so called because the image disappears; and (2) a weak solution of sodium sulphide which changes the bleached image into brown silver sulphide, as in the direct toning processes. It is very important that the black-and-white print be thoroughly washed, as silver bromide, which is first formed in the bleaching operation, is soluble in hypo; so part or all of the image may be dissolved if the print has not been washed in running water for at least 20 to 30 min. This precaution should be especially noted, for the cause of about 50 per cent of all the troubles experienced with this process is due to prints that are not washed thoroughly. Clean enameled trays without any chipped or broken places in the enamel should be used, for contamination by iron rust will cause blue spots on the finished print. These blue spots may also be caused by iron rust from the water, and where this occurs the water should be filtered through several thicknesses of flannel or felt, which may be placed directly over the water taps.

Bleach prints in solution 1 until the image is converted to a very light brown.

BLEACH FOR SULPHIDE REDEVELOPMENT
SOLUTION 1

Potassium ferricyanide solution (10 per cent)	500 cc.	17½ fl. oz.
Potassium bromide solution (10 per cent)	100 cc.	3½ fl. oz.
Sodium carbonate solution (10 per cent)	200 cc.	7 fl. oz.
Water	200 cc.	7 fl. oz.

Wash prints for about 5 min., and redevelop in the following solution:

Sulphide Redeveloping Solution
Stock Solution

Sodium sulphide	45 g.	1½ oz.
Water to make	500 cc.	16 oz.

For use, dilute 1 part stock solution with 8 parts water.

After using this toner it is advisable to harden the prints. To do this mix the following hardener:

Hot water (125°F. or 52°C.)	150 cc.	5 oz.
Sodium sulphite, anhydrous	15 g.	½ oz.
Acetic acid (28 per cent)	45 cc.	1½ oz.
Potassium alum	15 g.	½ oz.

After removing prints from sulphide redeveloper solution wash for 2 or 3 min. and place in the above hardener bath for 5 min. Then wash thoroughly for 30 min. This hardener solution has no effect on either the color or gradation of the print.

Mercury Sulphide Sepia Toner.—The four sepia toners just described depend on the formation of one compound, silver sulphide, which, although it allows some altering of the shade of brown by means of the nature of the original print image and by the bleaching methods used, is essentially a compound with a limited range of colors. By producing a combined silver sulphide and mercury sulphide image, the range of tones available is lengthened. The addition of mercury sulphide to the image is accomplished by adding mercuric chloride to the bleaching bath. The compound formed in the bleaching is then a combination of a silver and a mercury salt. Upon subsequent development with sodium sulphide, silver sulphide and mercury sulphide are formed. By varying the amounts of mercuric chloride in the original bleach, the color of the final print image is easily controlled; the larger the amount of mercury used, the blacker or colder the image. The gelatin on the print has quite a strong affinity for the mercury, and for this reason, after bleaching, the prints are bathed in several changes of dilute hydrochloric acid to remove any mercury which is in combination with the gelatin. The mercury which is combined with the silver image is not affected by this treatment, so there is no loss in the richness of the image. Mercury sulphide is a compound just as stable as silver sulphide, so there need be no fear of impermanence in images made of mercury sulphide. The prints should be slightly lighter than for the other processes as mercury produces some intensification in the toned print.

Wash print well, eliminating all hypo.

Bleach in bath made as follows:

Mercury Sulphide Toner
Solution A

Potassium ferricyanide	30 g.	1 oz.
Potassium bromide	45 g.	1½ oz.
Water to make	266 cc.	9 oz.

Solution B

Mercuric chloride	4 g.	60 gr.
Potassium bromide	4 g.	60 gr.
Water to make	150 cc.	5 oz.

For use:

Engraving black—1 part *A*, 3 parts *B*, 16 parts water
Warm black—1 part *A*, 1 part *B*, 16 parts water
Cold sepia—1 part *A*, ½ part *B*, 12 parts water
Normal sepia—1 part *A* only, 12 parts water. (None of *B* added.)

After the prints are completely bleached, they are washed first and then rinsed in three baths of 1 per cent hydrochloric acid. The prints are then washed again and toned in the following solution:

STOCK SOLUTION

Sodium sulphide	45 g.	1½ oz.	
Water to make	500 cc.	16 oz.	

For use, dilute 1 part stock solution with 8 parts water.

Potassium Permanganate Sulphide Method.—Another bleach for sulphide toning consists in using potassium permanganate instead of potassium ferricyanide. This has one particular advantage over the ferricyanide bleach, inasmuch as any traces of hypo left in the print before toning will be destroyed by the permanganate and have no effect on the final image. A stain is formed when the image is bleached, but this will disappear in redevelopment. Wash print well and bleach in the following solution.

SOLUTION A

Potassium permanganate	2.5 g.	40 gr.	
Water	590 cc.	20 cc.	

SOLUTION B

Hydrochloric acid (c.p.) (36 per cent)	80 cc.	2¾ oz.	
Water to make	590 cc.	20 oz.	

To use take 1 part solution *A*, 1 part solution *B*, plus 6 parts water. Wash well and tone in sulphide solution.

SULPHIDE REDEVELOPING SOLUTION
STOCK SOLUTION

Sodium sulphide	45 g.	1½ oz.	
Water to make	500 cc.	16 oz.	

For use, dilute 1 part stock solution with 8 parts water. Wash prints for 15 min. after toning.

Intermediate Redevelopment Sepia Method.—The above bleach bath lends itself well to control of the resulting image by means of intermediate development of the print with a dilute developer after bleaching and before toning. The developer acts on the bleached silver compound forming a partial black metallic silver image. The remaining undeveloped silver compound, when treated with sodium sulphide in the toning bath, forms silver sulphide. Thus a combined image of black metallic silver and brown silver sulphide is formed, and the resulting degree of blackness depends on the proportion of metallic silver that makes up the final image. Procedure for this method is as follows: Bleach print according to instructions given for the permanganate sulphide method. After washing well, partially develop the print in a 1 to 2 dilution of the developer for blue-black tones given in the beginning of this chapter. Time the length of development and then tone in the regular sulphide toner given above. A few experiments will determine the length of intermediate development necessary to secure the desired tone.

The permanganate bleach will react on both the silver sulphide and silver image, so that, if the desired tone is not obtained with the first trial, the toned image may be bleached and retoned. Sometimes it is desirable to restore a toned print to its original black state: this may be accomplished by bleaching in a permanganate bath and redeveloping completely in a normal developer.

Engraving Black from a Silver Sulphide Print.—It is possible to intensify or darken sulphide-toned prints by means of lead compounds. The lead combines with some of the silver sulphide forming lead sulphide, which is black. The darkening is accomplished by treating the sulphide-toned print with a solution of lead acetate. Prints should be treated in the following solution until the desired intensity of tone has been reached.

ENGRAVING BLACK SOLUTION

Water	1000 cc.	32	oz.
Hypo	20 g.	¾	oz.
Lead acetate	5 g.	80	gr.

The action of this solution proceeds rather slowly and for a normal change in tone ½ to 1 hr. is required.

Red Tones from Sulphide-toned Print.—Silver sulphide images may be readily changed to brilliant and charming red tones by treatment with a gold chloride ammonium sulphocyanate bath. The prints, which have already been toned by one of the sulphide processes, are immersed in the following bath until the tone has changed to red. They are then fixed for several minutes in the regular acid fixing bath and washed and dried in the usual manner.

Tone directly in:

Water	500 cc.	16	oz.
Ammonium thiocyanate	50 g.	1¾	oz.
1 per cent gold chloride	30 cc.	1	oz.

With the above solution very deep-blue tones may be obtained by using ordinary black-and-white prints. The prints should be made in the ordinary manner, fixed and washed thoroughly and then toned in the above solution. After toning they should be fixed again for several minutes, washed and dried.

Sepia Tones on Bromide Papers.—The fact has been emphasized that bromide papers, as a class, do not tone so well as chlorobromide or chloride paper. There is a formula, however, which will produce tones from cold brown through red-brown on bromide papers.

The thoroughly washed black-and-white print is first bleached and then redeveloped, the tone being controlled by the amount of sodium carbonate added to the redeveloping solution. The table following the formula will give the amounts necessary for certain tones. Here, again, not all papers will react the same, but by increasing or decreasing the amount of the sodium carbonate, the desired tone may be achieved. The formula without any sodium carbonate will produce brilliant red tones. By increasing this carbonate in the redeveloping solution, we may achieve many different shades of red-brown, sepia, and cold brown. Only two additions of carbonate are given in the table, but experimentation will yield the desired tones on any bromide paper.

Bleach the well-washed print in the following solution:

Potassium ferricyanide (10 per cent)	500 cc.	16 oz.
Potassium bromide (10 per cent)	100 cc.	3 oz.
Sodium carbonate (10 per cent)	200 cc.	6 oz.
Water	200 cc.	6 oz.

Wash and tone in the following solution:

Sodium sulphantimoniate (thioantiminate)	10 g.	¼ oz., 45 gr.
Sodium carbonate solution (10 per cent)	30 cc.	1 oz.
Potassium bromide solution (10 per cent)	160 cc.	5½ oz.
Water	810 cc.	26 oz.

Warm brown tones	Add 30 cc. 10 per cent solution sodium carbonate
Sepia tones	Add 100 cc. 10 per cent solution sodium carbonate

For colder tones increase the carbonate **30 cc.** at a time until the desired tone is reached.

Ferrocyanide Toners.—Ferrocyanide compounds of other metals than silver have various and brilliant colors and may be substituted for the silver image. Iron compounds are blue; uranium, brownish red and brown; copper, red, etc.

Ordinarily the silver image is first converted into silver ferrocyanide, and this is subsequently converted into the desired metallic compound by direct replacement of the silver by the metal of the ferrocyanide compounds. Usually other organic constituents are added to the formula to restrain the action of the toners, to prevent stains, etc. Most toning formulas of this class are similar in their reactions, although some of the single solution formulas form the silver ferrocyanide and the metallic ferrocyanide in one operation. Others involve two operations, first the conversion of the black silver image into silver ferrocyanide and subsequently the replacement of the silver in the silver ferrocyanide by the suitable metal higher in the electromotive series. The formulas we give may be considered representative of this type of toner.

Toners of this class are more susceptible to troubles caused by impurities and by deviations from recommended procedures than any of the others and therefore require considerably more care in their use. Also many of these metallic ferrocyanide compounds are soluble in even mild alkalies, and therefore water which is slightly alkaline when used in washing might remove some of the image. The use of these toners generally requires considerable care and experimentation in order to produce the desired results.

Copper Toner.—This toner hesitates for a moment, then a distinct toning action is noticed which proceeds quite rapidly at first. The tone goes from a cold brown, toward red, during which time a double tone, brown and red, is formed. After this the toning is progressive to red. The success in obtaining the desired tone by this method rests in the control of the time of toning and being able to judge just when the desired tone is reached. When using a toner of this type, it is wise to make several prints, toning them for different lengths of time with constant temperature, so that when the prints are dried one has several different tones from which to select. By this time method one may duplicate tones when prints in quantity are being processed. Toning solutions are as follows:

SOLUTION A

Copper sulphate (cupric)..	4 g.	60 gr.
Potassium citrate...	16 g.	240 gr.
Water to make..	600 cc.	20 oz.

SOLUTION B

Potassium ferricyanide.......................................	3.5 g.	50 gr.
Potassium citrate...	16 g.	240 gr.
Water to make...	600 cc.	20 oz.

To use, mix equal parts of *A* and *B* and tone the black-and-white print in this solution.

Iron Toner.—The following toner will produce blue tones.

Iron and ammonium citrate (ferric) (10 per cent)..................	60 cc.	2 oz.
Potassium ferricyanide (10 per cent)...........................	60 cc.	2 oz.
Acetic acid (10 per cent).....................................	600 cc.	20 oz.

Wash in pure water, but not too long, as blue color is soluble in water even slightly alkaline. Variations in brilliance of tone may be obtained by rinsing prints in a one-half per cent solution of borax which produces softer blue-gray tones depending upon length of treatment.

Uranium Toner.—Uranium toner yields shades from black through brown to a yellowish red. While this toner, in some instances and for certain effects gives satisfactory tones, the writers have never had very good results with it. It is included here for those workers who seek the unusual and bizarre.

Prints should be toned in the following solution after being thoroughly washed.

Bleach completely in

SOLUTION A

Potassium ferricyanide.	2.5 g.	38 gr.
Glacial acetic acid.	5.5 cc.	96 minims
Water.	250 cc.,	9 oz.

Wash well and tone in

SOLUTION B

Uranium nitrate.	2.5 g.	38 gr.
Water.	240 cc.	8 oz.

Wash well in water free from alkali.

Green Tones.—By a combination of iron ferrocyanide and silver sulphide green tones may be obtained. For this method the following stock solutions are required.

For green tones:

SOLUTION A

Potassium ferricyanide (red prussiate of potash).	5	g.	77	gr.
Ammonia.	1	cc.	5	drops
Water to make.	100	cc.	3½	oz.

SOLUTION B

Iron and ammonium citrate ferric.	2.2 g.		33	gr.
Hydrochloric acid (concentrated).	5	cc.	80	minims
Water to make.	100	cc.	3½	oz.

SOLUTION C

Sodium sulphide (pure crystal).	1	g.	15	gr.
Water.	100	cc.	3½	oz.
Hydrochloric acid (concentrated).	5	cc.	80	minims

In toning the following procedure should be followed: The thoroughly washed print is completely bleached in solution *A*. After washing has removed all the stain, print is immersed in solution *B* for about 5 min. Again the print is washed and then placed in solution *C* for about 5 min. Print should be washed again after removing from this solution and dried in the usual manner.

Dye Toning.—It is possible to replace the normal silver photographic image with one consisting primarily of a colored dye. In such a process the metallic silver is first converted into a mordant, such as silver ferrocyanide, which has the ability to attract and hold many basic dyes. The following mordanting bath is one recommended by Dr. B. T. J. Glover., in his book, "Lantern Slides," and although it is intended for lantern slides and film positives it may be used in some instances for paper prints.

MORDANTING BATH. STOCK SOLUTION

Uranium nitrate.	8 g.	70 gr.
Oxalic acid.	4 g.	35 gr.
Potassium ferricyanide.	4 g.	35 gr.
Water to.	1 l.	20 oz.

The chemicals are each dissolved separately in 5 oz. of water, and the solutions added together in the following order: oxalic acid, uranium nitrate, potassium ferricyanide, and finally water to make the required quantity. The solution when properly compounded should be of a pale-yellow color; and because of its light sensitivity should be stored in the dark. For use, 1 part of this stock solution is diluted with 4 parts of water.

The positive after fixing and washing is placed in the mordanting bath until the black silver image has been converted to a light-brown color. It is then washed to remove the yellow stain and transferred directly to the following "dye" solution:

Dye	0.2 g.	3 gr.
Acetic acid (10 per cent)	5 cc.	75 minims
Water	1 l.	35 oz.

The dye is dissolved in hot water and filtered. The acid is then added, together with cold water to make up the required bulk. The positives are left in the dye solution until the desired tone is obtained and then washed until the excess dye is removed from the lighter areas of the picture.

A partial list of basic dyes suitable for dye toning is the following:

Rhodamine G	Red
Auramine	Orange
Chrysoidine	Yellow
Malachite Green	Green
Methylene Blue	Blue
Methyl Violet	Violet

When working with paper prints, the dye is usually held by the fibers and baryta coat of the paper base to quite a great extent, but sometimes a large part of this excess dyeing may be removed by washing with water. Finally, any objectionable coloring of the whites or high lights may be removed from the dried print by immersing in the following clearing solution for from 1 to 2 min.:

Potassium permanganate	4 g.	3½ gr.
Sulphuric acid	1½ cc.	20 minims
Water to	1 l.	20 oz.

Another mordanting bath is one which is described in the *British Journal and Almanac* for 1927:

Copper sulphate	40 g.	350 gr.
Tribasic potassium citrate	60 g.	524 gr.
Glacial acetic acid	30 g.	262 gr.
Potassium or ammonium sulphocyanide	20 g.	175 gr.
Water	1 l.	20 oz.

The print is mordanted for from 1 to 15 min., washed for about 30 min., laid out on a sheet of glass and surface dried. A 10 per cent solution of the dyes or mixture of dyes, and 1 per cent acetic acid is then applied with a tuft of cotton or flat brush.

Crabtree and Ives have described a method of dye toning with a single solution, which, although intended for toning motion-picture films, may also be used with a certain measure of success on some papers. Here the dye is mixed with the mordanting solution in a concentration of from 0.02 per cent to 0.04 per cent, and sometimes higher, depending on the kind of dye used. The combined mordanting and dye formulas follows:

Dye (to make a final concentration of 0.02 to 0.04 per cent depending on the kind of dye)	X g.	X gr.
Acetone	100 cc.	3½ oz.
Potassium ferricyanide	1 g.	15 gr.
Acetic acid (glacial)	5 cc.	75 minims
Water to make	1 l.	32 oz.

The dye should be dissolved completely in a small volume of hot water, and added, with stirring, to the acetone. This mixture is then immediately diluted to about three-fourths the final volume with cold water. The potassium ferricyanide is dissolved in a small volume of water, and the acetic acid added. This mixture is added to the dye solution with constant stirring, and the whole diluted to the final volume for use.

Some experimental work will have to be done in order to determine the proper concentration of dye in the solution before serious work is attempted. As a rule various dyes may be mixed to obtain almost any color desired; although some dyes have a tendency to precipitate out in the presence of one another.

There are several points which have been mentioned in this chapter that are important enough to be repeated. As the original black-and-white print plays such an important part in the final toned print, it is necessary that the art of producing good prints be mastered before venturing into the field of toning.

After selecting the papers to be used, it is good practice to follow carefully the manufacturer's directions as to developers, developing time, and general procedure. These recommendations are based on the results of long and painstaking research and constitute the best methods available for the particular paper.

All photographic processes, including toning, are chemical by nature; therefore, neatness, cleanliness, and accuracy are necessary at all times. Clean, orderly workrooms, clean utensils, care and accuracy in mixing all solutions, and a rigid adherence to all instructions are a requisite for satisfactory results.

The photographer who likes to experiment will find that these formulas provide a basis for many interesting trials. Many interesting and unusual results may be obtained which will compensate for the time and trouble. However, if we may be allowed to repeat, master the fundamentals first.

Bibliography

Periodicals:

POWER, H. D'ARCY: Chemical Control and Modification of Bromide Prints, *Am. Ann. Phot.*, **23**, 93 (1909).

ZERBE, WILLIAM H.: Even Toning with the Cold Hypo Alum Bath, *Am. Ann. Phot.*, **33**, 122–123 (1919).

DE SAULLES, R. H.: Green Tones on Bromide Paper, *Brit. J. Phot.*, **70**, 705 (1923).

LUMIÈRE, A., L. LUMIÈRE, and SEYEWETZ, A.: Discoloration of the Whites in Sepia Toning, *Brit. J. Phot.*, **70**, 732–733 (1923).

SHAW, W. B.: An Improved Method of Nitro-sulphide Toning, *Brit. J. Phot.*, **70**, 759–760 (1923).

UNDERBERG, G.: Experiments in Sulphur Toning, *Brit. J. Phot.*, **71**, 50–52 (1924).

SEYEWETZ, A.: A Review of Dye Toning Processes, *Brit. J. Phot.*, **71**, 611–614 (1924).

FORMSTECHER, F.: The Principles of Toning with the Noble Metals, *Camera*, **3**, 100–103 (1924).

WALL, E. J.: Sulphide Toning I and II, *Am. Phot.*, **21**, 620–628 (1927); **22**, 22–34 (1928).

CRABTREE, J. I., and IVES, C. E.: Dye Toning with Single Solutions, *Am. Phot.*, **22**, 656–665 (1928).

STEIGMANN, A.: Toning and Intensification of Selenium Toned Prints and Negatives, *Phot. Ind.*, **26**, 902 (1928).

WIEGLEB, P.: Methods of Sulphite Toning, *Brit. J. Phot.*, **76**, 344, 363, 375 (1929).

MILBAUER, J.: Selenium Toning, *Phot. Korr.*, **65**, 10, 45 (1929).

JARMAN, A. J.: Improving the Color of Prints by Toning with Gold, *Am. Phot.*, **24**, 584 (1930).

BENNETT, HENRY W.: Uniformity in Sulphide Toning, *Am. Phot.*, **26**, 132–138 (1932).

JELLEY, EDWIN E.: Cause of Yellowness in Sepia Toning, *Phot. J.*, **72**, 480–485 (1932).

NIETZ, H.: Paper, Developer and Bleach in Sulphide Toning, *Brit. J. Phot.*, **79**, 486 (1932).

HOUBEN, L.: Uses of Thiourea in Photography, *Photo Rev.*, **45**, 179–180, 199–200 (1933).

MORRIS, O. J.: Stains in Sulphide Toning, *Brit. J. Phot.*, **80**, 127–128 (1935).

BACKSTROM, HELMER, and ARTHUR BOSTROM: The Influence of the Bleaching Bath on the Colour Obtained in the Indirect Sulphide Toning Process, *Phot. J.*, **76**, 607 (1936).

BASSETT, IVOR: Print Toning with Potassium Ethyl Xanthate, *Camera* (*Phila.*), **54**, 217–226 (1937).

NICKOLAUS, J. M.: Toning Film by Machine Methods, *J. Soc. Motion Picture Engrs.*, **29**, 65–67 (1937).

FASSBENDER, ADOLPH: Blue Toning, *Am. Phot.*, **32**, 638 (1938).

WADDELL, J. H.: Toning Prints and Transparencies, *Photo Technique*, **1**, 35, (1939).

Books:

FRAPRIE, FRANK R.: "How to Make Prints in Color," Am. Photographic Pub. (1921).

BLUMANN, SIGISMUND: Toning, "Photographic Handbook," pp. 75–89, Photo-Art Publisher, (1935).

"Ilford Manual," pp. 234–244, Ilford, Ltd. Toning.

"Tinting and Toning of Eastman Positive Motion Picture Film," Eastman Kodak Company.

GLOVER, DR. B. T. J.: "Lantern Slides," British Periodicals, Ltd.

WHEELER, CAPT. OWEN: "Photographic Printing Processes," Am. Phot. Publ. Co.

British Journal & Almanac.

CHAPTER XVI

SPECIAL PRINTING PROCESSES

By Paul L. Anderson

Carbon Printing. *Theory.*—Carbon printing depends on the fact that, if a colloid substance, such as gelatin or gum arabic, is sensitized with any one of several chromium salts and is exposed to light, the salt breaks down, giving off nascent oxygen, this nascent oxygen rendering the colloid more or less insoluble, in proportion to the amount of light action. In practice, the colloid used in carbon work is gelatin, and the "tissue" as purchased consists of a moderately heavy backing paper or support, one side of this carrying a layer of gelatin with which some earth pigment such as lampblack, burnt umber, etc., has been incorporated. This tissue is sold insensitive and is sensitized and dried in the dark just before use. It is then printed under a negative and developed in warm water, when the soluble portions of the gelatin wash off, taking their quota of pigment with them and leaving behind the insoluble portions, which with their pigment adhere to the paper, thus giving the print.

Advantages.—The prints are absolutely permanent, as is the case with platinum.

Any one of about 20 different colors may be used.

Practically any support may be used. This includes not only various papers but also glass, ivory, porcelain, celluloid, etc. Very beautiful miniature portraits are sometimes produced by carbon printing on ivory.

Modifications of total contrast are very easily made.

Local modifications of values may be made to a slight extent.

Multiple printing is very easy, not only in one color, but in various combinations of colors. Some very beautiful special effects may be attained in this manner.

Carbon has a very long scale of gradation, and gives exceedingly rich blacks, fully equal to those given by platinum.

Disadvantages.—It is almost impossible, except in very special cases, to avoid the luster of the gelatin emulsion, particularly in the shadows. This may be an advantage, since it adds to the richness of the deeper tones, but it interferes with our enjoyment of the texture of the support.

Like platinum, carbon requires a strong light for printing, therefore it cannot be be used for enlarging, except with very special apparatus; it is strictly a contact process.

The technique is slightly more difficult than that of platinum, though no more so than that of gaslight or bromide printing.

It is not easy to handle carbon in either very dry or very damp weather; a humidity of 65 to 70 per cent is desirable. Still, by proper precautions, this difficulty may be overcome.

It is extremely difficult to secure absolutely pure high lights, without recourse to brush development. This disadvantage, though, is of minor importance, since almost pure lights may readily be obtained, and it is seldom that absolute purity is desirable.

The Negative.—Carbon being a long-scale medium, if its full possibilities are to be exhausted, the negative must be rather stronger than for bromide or gaslight paper;

466

about the same quality is desirable as in the case of platinum printing. It is, of course, not necessary to exhaust the scale of the paper; medium or low-keyed prints may be made as well as with any other medium, though when a very high key is required, carbon is not so satisfactory as platinum.

Since the print is not developed on the original backing paper but must be transferred to some other support for development, it follows that, if the picture is to be the right way around, it must be printed from the back of the negative, or a reversed negative must be made. In pictorial work it is usually satisfactory to print from the back of the negative, for, whether the negative is on film or on glass, there will be little or no perceptible diffusion if a concentrated source of light is used and the printing frame is not moved during exposure. If, however, the negative is to be on a glass plate, a diffused source of light is used, the picture must be the right way around, and the utmost in fine detail is required—all of which is a rather unusual combination of circumstances—then a reversed negative must be made, or double transfer must be resorted to.

The Tissue.—"Tissue" is rather a misnomer, since the combination of backing paper and gelatin emulsion is rather heavy. The tissue is sold insensitive, in cut sheets 8 by 10 in. or in rolls 30 in. by 12 ft. It should be stored in a cool dry place, in which case it will keep indefinitely before sensitizing; if it is allowed to remain moist for any length of time, bacteria may grow in the gelatin, and the prints, on development, will show irregular blank patches.

A roll of thoroughly dry tissue is very intractable and very brittle; it is almost impossible to unroll and cut it without cracking the gelatin. It may be rendered more flexible by allowing it to stand for a few hours in a damp atmosphere or, in emergency, by steaming it slightly over a teakettle, when it can be easily handled and cut. The roll should then be permitted to dry out again, and the cut pieces should be stored under moderate pressure and allowed to become thoroughly dry before sensitizing.

The various colors of tissue differ to a considerable extent in their working characteristics, as regards not only printing speed but also scale of gradation. One of the pleasantest for general use is the Ivory Black, which is a pure translucent black of very long scale; being translucent, it takes a tone from the transfer paper, so that a print in this tissue on a white paper is a pure black, whereas on a toned paper it will have a very pleasing warmth of color even in the deep shadows. Since the gelatin of this particular tissue is heavily loaded with pigment, it is possible to make prints in a high, or even a medium, key which are free from luster even in the shadows.

Transfer Paper.—When the carbon tissue is printed, it is the layer of gelatin which is next the negative that is first insolubilized. Therefore, if it were developed directly on the backing paper, only those portions which had been printed clear through the gelatin would adhere to the support, the other areas washing off, and we should have merely a silhouette of the deep shadows. For this reason, it is necessary to transfer the layer of gelatin to another support, strip off the backing paper, and develop the gradations from the back of the layer of gelatin.

About 15 different transfer papers of various textures and colors are commercially available, or a transfer paper may easily be made by fixing out a sheet of bromide or chloride paper without exposure to light, using plain (not acid) hypo, and washing as usual. If this is done, care must be taken to choose a bromide paper which is suitable for bromoil work, many of the commercial silver papers having a protective super-coating of hard gelatin to which the carbon tissue will not adhere.

In general, the writer prefers to make his own transfer paper, which is readily done, as follows:

SOLUTION *A*

Water, cool	350	cc.	12 oz.
Gelatin	12.0 g.		180 gr.

Cooking gelatin may be used, but Nelson's No. 1 Hard is preferable. Allow the gelatin to soak until it is thoroughly swollen, then melt in a double boiler.

SOLUTION *B*

Water, hot	60	cc.	2 oz.
Chrome alum	2.5 g.		36 gr.

Pour *B* into *A* slowly, with constant stirring. The solution must be used hot.

It is most convenient to prepare the paper in large sheets, later cutting it to size. Pin a sheet down on a flat surface, wet a small sponge in water as hot as the hand can bear, squeeze it out, and take up with it a small amount of the hot gelatin solution. Rub this over the surface of the paper, scrubbing it well into the pores, then hang the paper up to dry. Do the same with several other sheets, giving each one a second coat as soon as the first is dry. It is impossible to say definitely how many applications will be necessary; a very rough paper, such as a Whatman Cold Pressed Rough, or a very soft paper, may require as many as five; on the other hand, a hard or a smooth paper may not need more than two; only experience can tell the precise amount of gelatin necessary.

When dry, the transfer paper may be cut to size and stored; the chrome alum renders it less liable to the attacks of bacteria than is the tissue. It should be cut rather larger than the print is to be, say 9 by 11 or 10 by 12 for an 8- by 10-in. print, and it is well to mark the back with pencil, since the coated side cannot be distinguished from the uncoated when it is wet.

Sensitizing.—Many different formulas have been suggested for sensitizing the tissue, the best with which the writer is acquainted being the following, which was suggested and worked out by Kirtland Flynn and A. K. Aster, members of the Orange Camera Club.

Water, distilled	1000.0 cc		30 oz.
Potassium chromate	30.0 g.		440 gr.
Citric acid as much as suffices to neutralize the solution (about 22 gr.) will be required.			

This sensitizer gives a film which behaves very nicely during development, and appears to hold gradation in the high lights better than any other that has yet been worked out.

The sensitizer keeps indefinitely and may be used repeatedly if stored in a brown bottle or otherwise kept from the light and if filtered back into the bottle after use. Sensitizing may be done in an ordinary room, since the tissue is not sensitive to light until dry. The sensitizer should be used at a temperature between 65 and 70°F.; it can be used warmer, but if it is too warm the gelatin may be softened excessively.

To sensitize, pour the solution to a depth of ¾ in. or more into a clean tray, take the carbon tissue by the edges and immerse it, face up, in the solution. The tissue will tend to curl, coated side in, and should be pressed down under the surface. After about a minute it will lie flat, when it should be turned over, and any adhering bubbles should be brushed from the back. Any bubbles which may have adhered to the coated side should, of course, be broken by a light touch of the finger as soon as they appear. The tissue is now turned face up, and the tray is rocked, keeping the tissue under the surface of the solution, until a total time of 2½ min. from the first immersion has elapsed. It is then lifted by two corners, drained for a few seconds, and laid face down on a clean sheet of glass, being lightly squeegeed on the back to remove the excess of sensitizer, when it is stripped off and hung up in the dark to dry.

An alternative method of drying, which takes somewhat longer but gives better results, is to squeegee the tissue on a ferrotype plate and to allow it to dry there The ferrotype plate should first be thoroughly cleaned with water and a mild soap, such as Castile, then dried, and powdered with talcum, which is well rubbed over the surface and dusted off with a clean cloth. It should not be waxed in the usual manner employed when squeegeeing glossy prints, for the carbon tissue may then refuse to adhere to the transfer paper. Care should be taken to squeegee out all air bubbles which may be trapped under the tissue, but the squeegeeing should not be heavy. Drying may be hastened by the draft from an electric fan, and, when it is complete, the tissue will snap off the ferrotype plate. This gives a more satisfactory working surface than drying freely in the air.

The squeegee used in this and subsequent operations should be of the scraper, not the roller, type. An automobile windshield-wiper blade is too soft, and the ordinary photographic scraper squeegee is too hard; a satisfactory article is that sold in hardware and housefurnishing stores for cleaning windows.

All squeegeeing should be done from the middle toward the ends of the print; the squeegee must not be scrubbed back and forth.

Printing.—The sensitiveness of the different tissues varies somewhat, the blacks and blues printing in general a little faster than the browns and reds; further, the sensitiveness varies to some extent with the moisture content, a tissue which is bone dry printing faster than one which is not absolutely desiccated. In general, the Ivory Black tissue, when fully dry, prints a trifle faster than a silver printing-out paper, so if a print is made, proof deep, from the negative which is to be printed and the carbon tissue is printed for three-quarters of the time required for this proof, the result will be about right; further, there is considerable latitude in development, so the printing need not be meticulously exact.

Printing should preferably take place as soon as the tissue is dry, as the gelatin tends to become insoluble even without exposure to light. If printing is to be postponed for any reason, the dry tissue should be stored in a lighttight receptacle which contains also a small quantity of calcium chloride to keep the air dry; even with this precaution, the tissue will probably not remain in good condition for more than 2 or 3 days.

When printing, it is necessary to have a "safe edge;" *i.e.*, a border of at least $\frac{1}{4}$ in. and preferably $\frac{1}{2}$ in. wide all around the tissue must be protected from light, or frilling will take place during development. Therefore the tissue should be cut 1 in. larger each way than the negative, which latter should be masked with opaque paper. Also it is advisable to have a freshly cut edge on the tissue; hence this latter should be trimmed to size immediately before printing.

Transferring should take place immediately after printing, since with any bichromated colloid there is a "continuing action," *i.e.*, the printing, once started, takes place even after the tissue is removed from the light. If for any reason transferring cannot be done at once, this continuing action may be slightly retarded by keeping the print under heavy pressure and may be entirely arrested by washing the print thoroughly in cold water to remove the sensitizer. If this washing is done, the print may be dried in the light and may then be transferred and developed at a future time, even weeks later.

Transferring.—The transfer paper should be soaked for a time in cold water to soften the gelatin; with an ordinarily smooth paper, 15 min. will be enough, whereas a very rough one may require $\frac{1}{2}$ hr. When both transfer paper and print are ready, the latter is immersed, face up, in a tray of cold water and pressed down under the surface. It will at first tend to curl up, face inward, gradually flattening out as it absorbs water. Slightly before it is flat, it should be placed face to face with the transfer paper, the two being lifted together from the water and placed on a horizontal sheet of glass, the tissue uppermost.   The two are then held together by pressure of the fingers at one end, while with the other hand they are squeegeed together.   This squeegeeing is not difficult, but there is a slight knack to it, and it should be done in a certain definite way.   The squeegee should start a little beyond the middle of the paper, the first few strokes being light, merely to expel the water and any possible air bubbles between the gelatin surfaces.   Then, the tissue being held down at the other end, the squeegeeing is repeated in the other direction.   All water and air bubbles having been driven out by this light squeegeeing, the squeegee is then applied more heavily, to press the transfer paper and the tissue into firm contact.   This part of the operation should be very strongly done—though not enough so as to tear the tissue—and should be continued until the backing paper begins to rub up in tiny rolls.

When squeegeeing is completed, a piece of lintless blotter is placed on the print, another sheet of glass is laid on this, and rather heavy pressure is placed on the whole. With moderately smooth papers a weight of 15 or 20 lb. is sufficient; with the very rough surfaces of transfer paper, it may be necessary to use a copying press.   Some workers prefer to use waxed paper instead of blotting paper, but the writer feels that if the combination dries out somewhat better adhesion is secured.   The print should remain under pressure for from 15 min. to 1 hr., the longer time being for the very rough papers; probably 20 to 30 min. is a good average time.   It is then removed from between the sheets of glass and is developed.

Development.—A tray a size larger than the transfer paper is filled to a depth of 1 in. or so with water at about 95°F., and the transfer paper with its adhering tissue is lifted from the glass, taking care not to bend it to any great extent and is slid gently into the water, the tray being then rocked almost continuously.   Air bubbles will appear in great number on the back of the tissue, and these should be lightly brushed off.   The temperature of the water is gradually raised a few degrees, either over a gas stove or an electric plate or by the addition of a little hot water, until at about 100 to 105°F. —the exact point depending on various circumstances—the pigmented gelatin will be seen oozing out from under the edges of the backing paper.   This oozing should be allowed to continue for 1 or 2 min., when one corner of the backing paper is lifted by means of a fingernail and an attempt is made to strip it off.   If it is ready to release, it will come away from the transfer paper very readily; if it resists, the corner should be pressed down very lightly and the temperature of the water raised 2 or 3 degrees, when, after a minute or so, another attempt may be made.   When the backing paper releases easily, it may be stripped off, keeping the entire combination under water and using a smooth uninterrupted pull.   Resistance to stripping comes from one of three causes: (1) the water is not warm enough, (2) the print is seriously overtimed, or (3) the print has been allowed to dry out too much under pressure.   If more than an extremely slight amount of force is used in stripping, frilling or tearing of the print is very likely to result; the backing paper should release with the very slightest effort. An indication of the correctness of printing time and of transferring may, perhaps, be found at this point, since with an average negative, if the work has been properly done, the backing paper will probably show a more or less distinct negative image. The pigmented gelatin remaining on the transfer paper will be soft and smudgy, giving little or no indication of an image.

The backing paper is thrown away, and development of the print proceeds.   The easiest way to do this is to grasp one corner of the transfer paper and jiggle it back and forth under the surface of the water, raising it from time to time for the dissolved gelatin to drain off.   This operation is continued until all or nearly all the surplus gelatin and pigment have been washed off; quite possibly it will be necessary to raise the temperature of the developing water a few degrees in order to reach the desired result. The print will dry slightly darker than it appears when wet, and allowance should be made for this, the print being developed until it seems slightly lighter than the finished result is to be.

When the print has reached the proper stage of development, the warm water is emptied from the tray, the print is rinsed in three or four changes of cold water to set the gelatin and prevent running of the pigment, and it is then hung up to dry. When dry, the print may have a slight yellowish tone from the trifle of sensitizer still remaining in the gelatin. This may be removed by soaking the print for a few minutes in a 5 per cent solution of alum, a 5 per cent solution of sodium bisulphite, or a 5 per cent solution of potassium metabisulphite, with subsequent washing. There does not seem to be much choice among these three agents; the last is possibly the most effective, although it is commonly advised to use alum, on the ground that it tends to harden the gelatin, but there seems little point in this, since the dried gelatin of the finished print is very hard and resistant in any case. It is not absolutely imperative to dry the print before clearing, but it is advisable to do so since, if this is done, blisters and frilling are less likely to result.

There is considerable latitude in the development of a carbon print. One which is badly undertimed is hopeless, but if the undertiming is not serious, the print may often be saved by keeping the developing water relatively cool. On the other hand, an overtimed print may be developed at a temperature a good deal higher than 105°F., the ordinary practical limit in this respect being about 120°F. The writer has at times used the developing water as warm as 160°F., but this is very likely to cause blisters and frilling. If raising the temperature of the water to 120°F. does not produce the desired result, it should be reduced to about 105°F., and a trifle of any alkali should be dissolved in the water. This is rather drastic treatment and is very likely to cause blisters or frilling or even a complete eating away of the gelatin in the high lights; hence it should be done very cautiously, and the print should be promptly rinsed in cold water when the desired result has been attained. The addition of 1 level teaspoonful of anhydrous sodium carbonate, or an equivalent amount of any other alkali, to 2 qt. of water will have a marked effect.

Local development may be used to a slight extent. This is done by brushing gently over the portions of the print which are to be raised in key, using a wet tuft of loosely packed cotton or a soft camel's-hair brush. This work must be done very cautiously, for the gelatin is likely to tear, there being more danger of this in the high lights than in the shadows. Pouring water slightly warmer than the developing water over the portions which are to be lightened is at times effective, as is also spraying water from an atomizer or a spray bottle.

When the fully developed print is dry, it is finished and may then be mounted in any desired manner.

Spotting.—It is ordinarily advised to save the backing paper, soften the pigmented gelatin which remains thereon (using warm water for the purpose), and do any necessary spotting with this pigment (applying it with a pointed brush). The writer finds this to be rather unhandy and, except in the case of definitely colored prints, such as reds and greens, unnecessary. An ordinary carbon spotting pencil, sharpened to a needle point on sandpaper, will take care of any black or brown prints satisfactorily.

Multiple Printing.—Additional contrast may be secured with a soft negative or additional richness and shadow depth with either a soft or a normal negative by multiple printing. It is usual, though not imperative, to print first for the high lights, adding one or more lighter printings for the shadows. When this is done, it is neither necessary nor advisable to clear the print until after the last printing has been added since the additional printings, being lighter than the first, will be developed in cooler water. If the first printing has been dried before adding the subsequent ones, its gelatin will be amply hard to withstand the later processing. If, however, the first printing has been light and the later ones are to be heavy, it is well to bathe the first one 5 min. in a 5 per cent alum bath before proceeding with the further printings. In this case the print must be thoroughly washed, for the alum remaining in the gelatin will damage the subsequent prints.

In multiple printing, the first print is used precisely as the transfer paper was for the first printing, the additional prints being transferred to it and developed on it exactly as has been described. It is, however, necessary to adopt some means for registering the several printings with one another, and this is most easily done as follows:

The mask for the negative is made, in the case of a film, of thin brown pressboard, and the negative is attached to it by a touch of Duco cement at one end; it should not be fastened down all around, or it will certainly buckle during printing. If a glass negative is used, the mask is made of cardboard of the same thickness as the negative, or slightly less, and a hole is cut in it so that the negative fits snugly in this hole. Four register marks are made on this mask, as indicated in Fig. 1, and when the

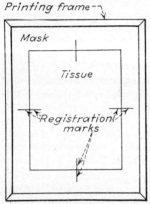

FIG. 1.—Mask with registration marks for negatives.

carbon tissue is placed in the frame for printing, four corresponding marks are made on it with a sharp pencil. Then, after the print has been squeegeed to the transfer paper and just before development, four marks are made on the face of the transfer paper, corresponding to the marks on the backing paper. Development then proceeds in the usual manner. The carbon tissue for the second printing is cut the same size as that for the first, and when it is placed in contract with the negative in the frame, four marks are made on it, corresponding to those on the mask. When squeegeeing this second print to the transfer paper on which the first printing has already been developed, these marks are placed in register with the marks on the transfer paper. By this means, any number of printings may be applied, with the assurance that all will register with one another. It will very possibly be found that the transfer paper will change slightly in size with processing, but the difference is not likely to be great, and since by the method indicated it will be split both ways, any failure in precision is not likely to be troublesome. In general, it is possible to work by this method within ½ mm., a difference which is not important except in three-color work.

This method has been used to produce prints in color, the worker masking out certain areas in the various printings, so as to obtain, say, a sunset sky in red with the landscape in green, or a still life of a rose with the flower red and the foliage green. Inasmuch as the colors obtainable are rather definite and lacking in delicacy, the results of this procedure are almost sure to be harsh and unpleasant; those that the writer has seen were without exception very painful. But by using various harmonizing colors, allowing the later printings to take a tone from the earlier ones, results may be obtained which are similar, though far superior, to those obtained by the toning of bromide prints. Thus the writer has made a very delightful portrait by using a first printing of Red Chalk, printed rather deep and transferred to a buff transfer paper, with five subsequent very light printings of Ivory Black. The final print ranged from a buff in the extreme high lights to an exceedingly rich warm black in the shadows. Of course, for this purpose a very soft negative was used. In general, when multiple printing is used, its value lies in the great richness of the shadows, a richness and transparency akin to that which the painter secures by repeated over-paintings of a transparent color.

Double Transfer.—This method is used in three-color work or when the print must be the right way around and must possess very fine detail. It is not, in general, useful to the pictorial worker, since it not only introduces an extra—and rather delicate—operation, but limits the choice of transfer paper to a comparatively smooth surface.

To make prints by double transfer, secure a sheet or several sheets of the temporary support, which is sold by the dealers in carbon materials, together with a bottle of waxing solution and several sheets of double transfer paper. The temporary support is carefully cleaned with warm water, dried, given a coat of the waxing solution, and then lightly polished with a tuft of cotton. The print is transferred to this and developed on it as described above. When this operation is completed, the well-soaked double transfer paper is squeegeed to the print and allowed to remain under pressure, between blotters, for a few minutes. It is then stripped off the temporary support and allowed to dry in the usual manner.

Prints on Ivory.—Carbon prints may be made on ivory, porcelain, celluloid, and other materials, using the single transfer method. The support to be used may be coated with the gelatin-chrome alum solution, described above, by dipping and should then be dried in a dust-free atmosphere. The subsequent operations are as already described.

Transparencies.—Very fine transparencies for the making of enlarged negatives may be made by carbon printing, the great advantage of this method being that the gradations of the original negative are faithfully reproduced with no danger of loss through incorrectly estimating the exposure and development, as often happens when making such transparencies on dry plates or films.

Instead of transfer paper, a piece of ground glass, which has been well washed with soap and water and thoroughly rinsed, is used. All the operations are as already described, except that the tissue should be printed about four times as long as for a print on paper. The tissue is transferred to the ground side of the glass, which needs no special preparation. A special transparency tissue is sold for this purpose, but the writer prefers to use the regular Ivory Black. If a slight grain in the large negative is not objectionable, the transparency may be used as soon as it is dry, but if grain must be avoided, the transparency should be flowed with some ordinary negative varnish, which will eliminate the grain of the ground glass.

Miscellaneous Notes.—Frilling of the print during development may be caused by (1) no safe edge, (2) failure to use a freshly cut edge on the carbon tissue, (3) excessively hot water used at first in developing, (4) stripping before the gelatin has been sufficiently softened, (5) an alkaline sensitizer, (6) the use of excessively hot water for developing, (7) development forced with excessive alkali in the developing water, (8) excessive soaking of the print before squeegeeing to the transfer paper, (9) insufficient pressure during squeegeeing, (10) failure to allow the print to remain long enough in contact with the transfer paper before development. Blisters may result from (3), (4), (5), (6), or (7) or from allowing air bubbles to remain between the print and the transfer paper, when squeegeeing. Frilling or blisters may also result from the use of insufficient gelatin on the transfer paper or from the use of an excessively hard gelatin such as that on a supercoated bromide paper, but in this case the failure is more likely to be a definite tearing away of the print in large areas than a true frilling or blistering. It should be noted that the failure due to an excessively alkaline sensitizer or to the use of excessive alkali in the developing water is more likely to be a breaking down of the gradations in the high lights—a sort of corrosion of the thinner portions of the print—than an actual frilling or blistering. Handling the dry carbon tissue—either sensitive or not—with greasy fingers may cause blisters, though it is more apt to result in white finger marks in the finished print.

The sensitizer may be either *slightly* alkaline or *slightly* acid, but the best results are secured when it is as nearly neutral as possible.

More or less contrast may be secured by varying the strength of the sensitizer, a strong solution producing a faster printing and softer working tissue, whereas a weaker sensitizer gives a slower printing and stronger working tissue. The same result may be secured by varying the time of immersion in the sensitizing bath, though the writer prefers to accomplish this by varying the concentration of the bath rather than by varying the time. The possible limits of concentration, beyond which it is not safe to go, are $\frac{1}{2}$ per cent for a weak bath, and 6 per cent for a strong bath.

A carbon print, when dry, may often be waxed and polished to advantage, as described in the section on Platinum Printing (see page 478) and here the damage to the surface texture is less than with platinum since the carbon print already has a gelatin surface which masks the texture of the support.

From the description given of the process, with the list of possible failures, it may seem that carbon printing is a very complicated and difficult operation, but this is by no means the case. If ordinary care is used, none of the possible failures is likely to occur, and with a little practice the entire operation may be carried through rapidly and successfully. As an illustration of this, the writer has known a man who did carbon printing for a professional studio, many years ago, when carbon was in vogue for portraits. This man, working alone for a 10-hr. day, was required, as his regular day's work, to sensitize, print, transfer, and develop 200 carbon prints a day—which would seem to be enough to satisfy almost any amateur.

Carbro Printing.—The word "carbro" is a combination of the first syllables of "carbon" and "bromide," and the process is so named because it is a method whereby a true carbon print can be made from a bromide print, without the use of light. In practice, the sensitized carbon tissue, instead of being dried and printed under a negative, is squeegeed into contact with a bromide print while still wet, the gelatin becoming insoluble not through the action of light on the sensitizer but through the chemical reaction between the sensitizer and the silver of the bromide print. Stripping and development follow in much the same manner as with carbon, the final result being an actual carbon print, exactly as in the previously described process.

Advantages.—The advantages of carbro are the same as those of carbon, with the additional ones that no very strong printing light is required, that enlargements can be made without making an enlarged negative, and that multiple prints can be made without the need for registration.

Disadvantages.—The disadvantages and possible failures are those of carbon, plus the fact that carbro is decidedly more temperamental than carbon, demanding a closer adjustment of the controlling factors if success is to result.

The Bromide Print.—There are two methods of working carbro, the transfer and the nontransfer methods. In the former the sensitized carbon tissue is left in contact with the bromide print long enough for insolubility to take place, being then stripped off and squeegeed to a piece of transfer paper, where it is developed. In the non-transfer method, the sensitized carbon tissue is developed directly on the bromide print, which then acts as the final support for the picture.

If the transfer method is employed, almost any bromide, chlorobromide, or chloride paper can be used, but if the nontransfer method is preferred, care must be taken that the original silver print is made on a paper having a soft gelatin. Most of the American enlarging papers are hardened in manufacture, and some have a protective supercoating of hardened gelatin; such papers cannot be used for non-transfer carbro, since it is almost, if not quite, impossible to soften this hard gelatin sufficiently to let the gelatin of the carbon tissue adhere to it.   However, any paper which is satisfactory for bromoil will work well with nontransfer carbro, and there are several English papers of this sort.   Kodak Royal Bromide is excellent for the purpose, and in this country, the Defender Photo Supply Company will furnish, on order, several grades of Velour Black which are specially manufactured for bromoil use.   Doubtless there are many other papers which will give good results with carbro.   An experienced worker can tell whether or not any particular paper will be satisfactory by soaking it for $\frac{1}{2}$ hr. or so in cold water, then judging the degree of swelling of the gelatin by feeling it between finger and thumb.

The bromide print should be completely developed as is done with one which is to be toned by the bleaching and sulphiding process, *i.e.*, development should be continued for at least 2 min. after the print has ceased to gain strength.   It should be printed a trifle darker than would be the'case with an ordinary bromide print since it is easier to retain gradation in the high lights of the carbro print if this is done.   It should be fixed in plain, not acid, hypo, and it should not be hardened in any way whatever.   If the bromide print is *slightly* blocked up in the shadows, this does no harm, since the carbro print will bring out detail which is not visible in the darker parts of the bromide.   Any ordinary developer may be used.

Care must be taken that the bromide print is entirely free from hypo since, if any remains, it will combine with the potassium ferricyanide in the sensitizer to form Farmer's reducer, which will dissolve the silver image, causing pale, or even completely blank, spots in the carbro print.   Potassium permanganate must not be used as a hypo eliminator; the only safe procedure is thorough washing with plain water.

Solutions Required.—Two solutions are necessary, the sensitizer and the control bath.   The sensitizer is made up as follows:

Water, distilled	1000.0 cc.	20 oz.
Potassium bichromate	12.0 g.	110 gr.
Potassium ferricyanide	12.0 g.	110 gr.
Potassium bromide	12.0 g.	110 gr.

Note that potassium ferricyanide, not ferrocyanide, is used.   This sensitizer will keep indefinitely if protected from strong light and may be used repeatedly, merely adding to the bulk from time to time, as required.

The control bath is made up as follows:

Formaldehyde (40 per cent)	650.0 cc.	22 oz.
Acetic acid (glacial)	30.0 g.	1 oz.
Hydrochloric acid (c.p.)	30.0 g.	1 oz.
Water, distilled	45.0 g.	$1\frac{1}{2}$ oz.

This forms a stock solution.   Probably, after a few days, and especially if the solution is exposed to light, a white precipitate will settle in the bottle.   This may be filtered off, or it may simply be ignored, provided care is taken to decant the clear solution and to avoid getting any of the precipitate into the working bath.   This stock solution keeps indefinitely.

For use, take

Stock solution	30.0 cc.	1 oz.
Water	1000.0 cc.	32 oz.

This dilute control bath changes in strength as successive prints are treated in it, therefore it should not be used for more than half a dozen or so and should not be kept but should be thrown away when used.

Sensitizing.—The carbon tissue is sensitized exactly as described in the section on Carbon Printing, except that the time of immersion should be 3 instead of $2\frac{1}{2}$ min.

At the expiration of the 3 min., the tissue is lifted from the sensitizer, is drained for 15 sec., and is then placed in the control bath.

Use of the Control Bath.—The control bath governs the depth of color in the final print; a long immersion results in a soft high-keyed carbro, whereas shorter immersion gives a stronger, deeper print. Thus it is possible to secure very widely varying results from any given bromide print; there is doubtless a limit to the control which is possible by this means, but the writer has secured a carbro which was hardly more than a ghost of a print from a decidedly heavy bromide and a strong carbro from a very weak silver print. Hence the time of immersion in the control bath may vary between 5 and 90 sec.; probably a satisfactory time for average results will be in the neighborhood of 15 or 20 sec.

When the tissue has had the proper time in the control bath, it is lifted out and, without draining, is squeegeed down on the bromide print.

Squeegeeing.—The bromide print should have been soaked for from 15 min. to ½ hr. in water at room temperature, as described for the transfer paper in the section on Carbon Printing. It is then laid face up on a sheet of glass, the sensitized and controlled tissue is laid on it, and the two are squeegeed together as in carbon printing.

A caution is necessary at this point. The tissue must be carefully lowered on the bromide print and must be held firmly in place while squeegeeing goes on; it must not slip. Slight slipping does no harm in carbon printing, but in carbro, since insolubilization begins as soon as the tissue and the bromide print are in contact, any slipping inevitably means a double image in the final print.

If the transfer method is to be used, squeegeeing should not be so firm or so long continued as in carbon work; it is merely necessary to secure definite contact between the tissue and the bromide. If the nontransfer method is preferred, then squeegeeing should be as firm as in carbon work.

When squeegeeing is completed, the bromide print, with its adhering carbon tissue, is placed under pressure and left for at least 15 min. At this point there is a slight difference of opinion among carbro workers as to whether waxed paper or blotting paper should be placed over the adhering print; the writer's preference is to use waxed paper and light pressure in the transfer method and blotting paper with heavy pressure if nontransfer is being used.

Transfer Method.—At the expiration of 15 min. or so (slightly longer will do no harm), the carbon tissue is peeled from the bromide print and is squeegeed down on a piece of previously soaked single transfer paper. Here it is left under pressure, then stripped and developed as in carbon printing. If a hard-surfaced bromide paper has been used and squeegeeing has not been excessive, the tissue will peel from the bromide print with only a moderate use of force; if it does not strip easily, soaking in cold water may loosen it, but care should be taken not to use violence enough to cause tearing.

If the carbon tissue, after stripping from the bromide print, is immediately squeegeed to the transfer paper, as is usually recommended, it will very likely fail to adhere properly, so that the gelatin will frill or even tear badly when the backing paper is stripped off for development. This trouble may be entirely avoided if, instead of being transferred at once, the carbon tissue is rinsed in several changes of water to remove the sensitizer, is then dried, and when dry is transferred as described for single transfer in the section on carbon printing.

When the transfer method is used it will very likely be found that there is a slight loss in print quality; some of the more delicate gradations are not rendered so beautifully as in the nontransfer method. For this reason, as well as on account of its greater ease and certainty, the writer prefers to work by the nontransfer process whenever it is at all possible to do so.

Nontransfer Method.—In this method, the bromide print and its adhering carbon tissue are treated exactly as described for stripping and development in carbon work. If, however, the work has been properly done, the carbon tissue will strip and develop somewhat more freely than in carbon work and will be a trifle more delicate and liable to injury. Therefore this part of the work should be carried out rather carefully, the worker feeling his way more slowly and gradually than in carbon.

Large Prints.—Carbon tissue larger than about 11 by 14 in. is not easy to handle by the above method, and in this case the sensitizing and control baths may be combined in the following proportions:

Water	15 oz.
Sensitizer	16 oz.
Stock control bath	¼ oz.

Sensitize for 2½ min., then proceed with squeegeeing and subsequent operations in the usual manner. This combined bath should be mixed immediately before use, and should not be kept over, as it decomposes in the course of a few hours, even without use.

Hard Water.—In localities where the tap water contains a large proportion of dissolved calcium or magnesium salts, it will probably be found that the carbro prints show a decided erosion or breaking down in the high lights. It is sometimes recommended, in order to avoid this trouble, that the bromide prints receive 5 min. in a 3 per cent hydrochloric acid bath, followed by not less than 10 min. or more than 40 min. washing in running water, this treatment to follow the washing after fixing or to precede the soaking for squeegeeing. The writer has not found this technique to be invariably successful, and he prefers, where the local water is hard, to process the bromide prints and the carbon tissue *throughout,* up to the point of developing the carbro, in distilled water.

When distilled water is used, or where the local water is exceptionally soft, it will probably be necessary either to shorten the time in the control bath or to use this bath more dilute; the latter method is preferable since it can be more accurately adjusted. Thus the writer finds that, when processing with distilled water throughout, he obtains normal results with 20 sec. in a bath made up of

Water	1000.0 cc.	64 oz.
Stock solution	15.0 cc.	1 oz.

Obviously, this is a matter which each worker must adjust for himself.

Safe Edge.—In carbro, as in carbon, it is desirable to have a freshly cut edge on the carbon tissue, and it is imperative to use a safe edge. This safe edge may be attained by simply allowing the carbon tissue to extend over the print by ½ in. or so all around, in which case waxed paper should be placed under the bromide print, before squeegeeing, so that the carbon tissue will not be squeegeed to the glass at any point. The writer feels it preferable, however, to make the bromide on a large sheet of paper, masking the paper so as to get 1 in. or so of clear margin all around the print. The tissue should then be cut to such a size that its edge comes between the printed portion and the edge of the bromide paper. Thus, for an 8 by 10-in. carbro, he would use 11- by 14-in. paper and cut the carbon tissue to about 9 by 11 in.

Aftertreatment of Bromide Print.—The effect of the sensitizer on the silver image is to bleach it out, precisely as in the case of toning by means of bleaching and sulphiding. The carbro print having been developed, it follows that there are several ways in which the bromide print may be treated.

If the transfer method is used, the bromide print, after thorough washing, may be redeveloped in any ordinary developer and used for the production of other carbros, exactly as at first. It should be noted, though, that this bleaching and redeveloping has a slight intensifying action on the bromide print, and allowance for this should be made in the use of the control bath. Owing to mechanical causes, the limit to this use is about six carbros to each bromide.

If the nontransfer method is used, there are three possible courses.

1. The residual silver image may be completely removed with Farmer's reducer. In this case the final result is a pure carbon print.

2. The residual silver image may be redeveloped with sodium or barium sulphide (not sulphite) to a brown, in which case the result is a brown image underlying the pigment image of the carbon and adding strength as well as a warm color to it. Barium sulphide is preferable to the sodium salt, as it gives a cooler, richer brown, but, if it is used, care must be taken to swab off the scum that settles on the face of the print and to give a final rinse after this is done. If the silver image is thus redeveloped to a brown under a carbon image in Ivory Black, the whole being on a buff stock, the richness and color of the result are very desirable in the case of portraits with a dark background or in the case of sunny landscapes.

3. The residual silver image may be redeveloped to a black, using any ordinary developer, and may then be left that way or may be made the basis for multiple printing.

Whichever one of these final treatments is selected, the carbro print should always be dried before the aftertreatment since, if this is done, there is less danger of blisters and frilling.

Multiple Prints.—The making of multiple prints by nontransfer carbro is exceedingly simple and easy. The bromide print is redeveloped to a black with any ordinary developer; it is well washed and dried; and a second printing of carbon is placed on the first, using the bromide-carbon print exactly as the original bromide was used. Obviously, there is no need of any special registration, since this is automatically taken care of by the bromide print, *i.e.*, by the silver image which reacts with the sensitizer to insolubilize the gelatin of the carbon tissue. It is, of course, apparent that, provided there is no slipping during squeegeeing, registration will be perfect even though the bromide print may not have shrunk back to its original size. In the writer's opinion, the chief merit of carbro lies in the extreme ease with which the great richness of multiple carbon prints may be attained in large sizes.

Prints in Colors.—It is possible with carbro to produce prints in arbitrary combinations of colors. Thus, if a landscape is to be printed and it is desired to have the foreground in green and the sky in blue, the foreground in the bromide print is bleached out, using an ordinary ferricyanide-bromide bleacher, and applying it with a brush. Then a carbro print is made from this semibleached bromide, using a blue tissue when only the sky is printed. Then the bromide is redeveloped to a black, and the sky is bleached out, after which the foreground is used as a basis for a green carbro. In general, however, the results of this technique are extremely unsatisfactory, being harsh and unconvincing. However, it is often the case that multiple prints in different colors are very pleasing, if the colors are so chosen that they harmonize, the various colors being used merely to modify the tone of earlier or later printings, as was suggested for carbon work.

Platinum Printing.—At the time of writing, there is no commercial platinum paper on the market, but the operation of preparing homemade sensitized material, together with the subsequent printing and processing, is so extremely simple and easy as to be well within the capability of even the least experienced amateur. The results obtained are in many respects so far superior to those given by any other photographic printing medium as amply to repay the slight effort involved.

Advantages.—The prints are absolutely permanent. If properly developed, cleared, and washed and if made on a good grade of linen paper, platinum prints will remain in new condition unless the paper support is destroyed mechanically or by fire.

Variations in total contrast are very easily obtained. Almost any degree of contrast may be secured by altering the composition of the sensitizer, and still further variations are possible through varying the constitution of the developer.

Almost any paper support may be used. This makes possible the use of very beautiful charcoal and drawing papers, as well as of vellums and tissues, so that widely varying effects may be obtained by this means.

A range of colors from cold and neutral black through gradually increasing warmth of brown, even to sepia and red, is easily secured by slight changes in the developer. Further, these colors do not involve any loss of permanence, as is often the case in the toning of silver papers.

Platinum gives a very long scale of gradations and renders the delicate tones of the negative better than any other medium.

There is no gelatin emulsion, therefore the image does not interfere with the spectator's appreciation of the texture of the support. This is a characteristic which is highly esteemed by those artists to whom fine print quality is of importance.

Platinum is by far the easiest photographic printing process, so far as technique is concerned; it is vastly easier to make a good platinum print than it is to make a bromide enlargement or a gaslight print.

Disadvantages.—It is rather expensive. At the current prices for chemicals, an 8- by 10-in. print costs about 40 cts to make, and an 11 by 14 in. about double that. Against this, however, must be set the fact that the cost of developer is practically nil, the cost of clearing baths very slight, and there is no reason whatever for failures. With a little care, the worker can count on complete success in this work. Of course, to those workers who wish a few fine prints rather than many mediocre ones, this matter of cost has little importance; one good platinum print is more to be desired than a thousand ordinary bromides or chlorobromides.

Internal modifications of values are not easily made. In this respect Fresson, gum, and bromoil are superior to platinum, for, although it is possible to modify values by brush development of the print with a developer diluted with glycerin, the results are not usually very satisfactory; good prints have been made with this technique, it is true, but in general they are likely to look more like wash drawings than like photographs.

Platinum is definitely a contact process. Enlargements have been made on platinum paper, but only with very special apparatus, and as a rule it is necessary, if a large print is desired, to make an enlarged negative. This is due to the relative slowness of printing, and as a corollary it follows that for contact printing a strong light is required. This involves the use of sunlight, a carbon arc, a mercury-vapor lamp, or a sunlight lamp of the type supplied for therapeutic use. Any one of these is satisfactory; probably the best is the mercury-vapor lamp, and next to it the carbon arc. Sunlight is, of course, the cheapest, as well as the most variable.

The Negative.—It is commonly said that platinum requires a strong negative, but this is by no means the case; exquisite prints in either high, medium, or low key may be made from soft negatives, and the possibilities of variation are such that excellent results may be obtained from any negative of reasonable quality. It is, however, true that platinum has such a long scale of gradation that to exhaust its possibilities a rather contrasty negative is needed, and it is further true that for average results with an average sensitizer the negative should be somewhat stronger than for average results with a medium grade of chloride paper. Still, practically any quality of print can be obtained from any quality of negative.

It should be noted, though, that for a given degree of contrast a finer print will be secured from a thin negative than from a dense one, *i.e.*, if we have two negatives of the same contrast, one of them thin and the other dense, the former will give the sweeter print. This is by no means true of platinum alone but holds good with most printing mediums.

The Paper.—Practically any paper which is neither too absorbent nor too highly sized can be used. Satisfactory results have been obtained on Whatman Cold Pressed drawing papers, on Strathmore, Michallet, and Lalanne charcoal papers, on Strathmore Alexandra Japan Vellum, on the Shidzuoka Vellum of the Japan Paper Company, and on various linen letter and typewriter papers.

To determine whether or not any given paper will work well, pin a piece of it about 8 by 10 in. on a table, pour on it ¾ dram of water, and brush this water back and forth with the sensitizing brush. If the paper is surface dry, or nearly so, in less than 30 sec., it is too soft and should be sized (see page 483, under Multiple Printing) before use; if it is still wet after 2 or 3 min. of brushing, it is too hard, and should be rejected.

It should be noted that different qualities of paper give very different contrasts. This will be discussed later, under Increased Contrast, page 482.

Sensitizing Brush.—This should preferably be a flat Japanese paintbrush, as sold in various Japanese art stores. The advantages of this type are that the bristles are short and are set in a thin row, causing little waste of sensitizer, and that no metal is used in its construction. Three inches is a convenient width for prints up to 16 by 20 in.

If such a brush is not readily obtainable, a painter's graining brush may be used, though if this is bound with metal, some steps should be taken to protect the sensitizer from contact with the metal ferrule. This may be done by diluting Duco cement with a mixture of acetone and alcohol and introducing a small quantity of the dilute cement among the hairs, at their base. Capillary attraction will spread it, forming a base past which the sensitizing solution will not go. It will also shorten the effective flexible length of the hairs, but this does no harm, since the hairs in such a brush are longer than necessary.

The Solutions.—Make up three solutions, as follows:

SOLUTION I

Water (distilled), warm	55.0 cc.	2 oz.
Ferric oxalate	15.0 g.	240 gr.
Oxalic acid	1.0 g.	16 gr.

SOLUTION II

Water (distilled), warm	55.0 cc.	2 oz.
Ferric oxalate	15.0 g.	240 gr.
Oxalic acid	1.0 g.	16 gr.
Potassium chlorate	0.3 g.	4 gr.

SOLUTION III

Water (distilled), warm	65 c.c.	2⅜ oz.
Potassium chloroplatinite	13.0 g.	219 gr. (equals ½ oz. avoir.)

Note that ferric, not ferrous, oxalate is used. This should be in the form of dry bright-green scales. If the scales have a brownish tinge or show any tendency to stick together, the sample is stale and should be rejected; this chemical must be perfectly fresh. Note also that potassium chloroplatinite, not chloroplatinate, must be used. This has the form of bright ruby-red crystals, the chloroplatinate being yellow. No trouble is likely to be caused by the other chemicals, provided reasonably pure samples are obtained.

These solutions are the basic ones from which the actual sensitizer is made, and they should be protected from strong light. A convenient plan for storing and handling them is to keep the solutions in three properly labeled brown-glass 2-oz. dropping bottles, with a medicine dropper in each. These droppers should be of the guaranteed type, giving drops of equal size. If a single dropper is used for all three solutions, it should be well rinsed in distilled water before going from one solution to the next.

The sensitizing solution is made up as follows:

For very soft prints:
Solution I.. 22 drops
Solution II... 0 drops
Solution III.. 24 drops
For moderately soft prints:
Solution I.. 18 drops
Solution II... 4 drops
Solution III.. 24 drops
For average prints:
Solution I.. 14 drops
Solution II... 8 drops
Solution III.. 24 drops
For strong prints:
Solution I.. 10 drops
Solution II... 12 drops
Solution III.. 24 drops
For very strong prints
Solution I.. 0 drops
Solution II... 22 drops
Solution III.. 24 drops

Note that in each of the solutions the amount of III is always 24 drops; that the sum of I and II is always 22 drops; and that increasing the proportion of II with respect to I increases contrast.

The required number of drops may be measured into a small graduate; a very slight amount of shaking will mix the solutions sufficiently. The amount given—46 drops—is a satisfactory quantity for an 8- by 10-in. sheet of average paper; a very rough paper, such as Whatman Rough, may need perhaps 50 per cent more by volume.

Sensitizing.—The paper to be sensitized should be cut slightly larger than the negative that is to be printed—say, 10 by 12 in. for an 8- by 10-in. negative—and should be pinned down on a smooth board. Guide lines may be drawn in pencil on it, to indicate the exact area which is to be sensitized, but it is well to sensitize a slightly larger area than that of the negative, so that the excess may be used as test slips in printing. It is the writer's practice to sensitize an area 8 by 12 in. for an 8- by 10-in. negative, this giving two test strips 2 by 4 in.

The brush is wetted under a faucet of cold water and is shaken out slightly. The sensitizer is then poured in a pool on the paper and is spread back and forth over the paper with the brush. It is not necessary to work very rapidly, nor is it necessary to be meticulous in spreading the solution evenly, as is the case in gum printing. In platinum work the printing goes just as far as the light action calls for, and if there is enough sensitizer in any area to take care of this light action, a satisfactory print will result even though the paper may be very unevenly sensitized. However, it is well to spread the solution as uniformly as is convenient.

Brushing is continued until the paper begins to be surface dry, when the paper is hung up in the dark for drying to be completed. Temperature and humidity in the drying room should be such that the paper is bone dry in from 10 to 20 min., but if these conditions are not obtainable, drying may be completed over a gas stove or an electric plate. If this is done, care must be taken to see that the sensitizer is not scorched. This will occur long before the paper itself shows any signs of scorching and will result in uneven and irremovable areas of excessive darkness in the print; further, this scorching of the sensitizer is not apparent until after the print is developed.

The sensitizing may be carried out in an ordinary room or by the light of a 100-watt Mazda lamp, since the paper is only slightly sensitive while wet.

Brush and graduate should be well washed under the faucet immediately on completion of sensitizing.

Printing.—As has been said, a strong light is required for printing, and, as with any paper, the time will depend on the density of the negative and on the character of the result desired. It is the writer's practice to make negatives somewhat softer than the average, and in unobstructed July sunlight or 15 in. from a 110-volt 15-amp. twin carbon arc, using White Flame carbons, the printing time ranges between 2 and 5 min., with the sensitizer for average results. The printing time will vary slightly with the different sensitizers, those for stronger prints requiring somewhat more time and those for soft prints a little less. If the carbon-arc lamp is used, White Flame carbons are preferable to the Panchromatic.

When printed, the image will appear brownish yellow on a yellow ground, but it is not distinct enough to serve as a guide to timing, and test strips should be printed and developed before printing the full sheet.

Developing.—The developer is made up as follows:

Water, warm	1500.0 cc.	48 oz.
Potassium oxalate	500.0 g.	1 lb.

In some localities, where the water is very hard, it may be advisable to make this up with distilled water, but as a rule this is not necessary.

The developer is ordinarily used at room temperature, *i.e.*, from 65 to 80°F., moderate variations in temperature having little effect on the results. A tray a size larger than the print should be used, the developer being poured into this to a depth of ½ in. or so and the print being slid in face up, so that the developer covers the print with an even sweep. If there is any stoppage so that the print is not evenly covered, development marks may occur at normal temperatures and are certain to result when the developer is used warm.

Development should take place immediately after printing since, although there is no continuing action as there is with bichromated colloid processes, the paper is very hygroscopic, and if it absorbs moisture from the air, the print will have degraded high lights.

At normal temperature, development will require 3 or 4 min. and should be continued until it has gone as far as it will. In the case of an overprinted print, it is sometimes possible to save it by withdrawing it before development is complete, but this is uncertain and should not be depended upon. An undertimed print cannot be forced after development has begun, though if underprinting is discovered before development, the print can sometimes be saved by warming the developer.

Clearing.—The clearing bath is

Water	2000.0 cc.	60 oz.
Hydrochloric acid (c.p.)	35.0 cc.	1 oz.

The print should be given three successive baths of the above strength, after which it is washed in running water (or in half a dozen changes) for a few minutes and is hung up to dry. Clearing must be thorough, to remove all the iron salts from the paper, or the print will gradually darken on exposure to light.

Increased Contrast.—If sufficient contrast cannot be obtained by varying the sensitizing solution, as given above, still further contrast may be obtained by printing to normal depth but in a very weak light, so that a long time is required. If still more is desired, it may be secured by overprinting and by adding a small amount of potassium bichromate to the developer. It is impossible to give precise instructions as to the quantity of this chemical to use since this depends on the balance between printing time and contrast desired.   However, a lump the size of a large pea in 32 oz. of developer will have a marked effect, and even greater amounts may be used.   If this modification is carried too far, the prints will have a granular appearance.

With any given sensitizer, the use of a hard-surfaced paper gives more contrast than a softer, *i.e.*, a more absorbent, one.   This is due apparently to the fact that the harder paper requires longer printing in order to keep the sensitizer on the paper in the lighter areas, and while this longer printing is taking place, the shadows, of course, gain in depth.   This fact may be used to advantage when printing from a soft negative and should, of course, be allowed for in any case when adapting the sensitizer to the negative and to the desired result.

Decreased Contrast.—If the prints have too much contrast even when the softest working sensitizer is used, softer effects may be obtained by the addition of a very small amount of hydrochloric acid to the developer.   Again, it is impossible to say precisely how much to use, but a perceptible effect will result if a finger is dipped into the 1 to 60 clearing bath, and the adhering acid is stirred into the tray of developer.

Another method for diminishing contrast is to print lightly and heat the developer, though here also the balance must be determined by circumstances.   In extreme cases, the writer has developed prints at 200°F., but this is rarely necessary, about 150°F. being the ordinary limit.   It should be noted that a warm developer not only cuts down contrast, but also gives warmer tones in the finished print.

Colder Tones.—Blue-black tones may be secured by using a developer made up as follows:

Water, warm	1000.0 cc.	48 oz.
Potassium oxalate	180.0 g.	9 oz.
Monobasic potassium phosphate	60.0 g.	3 oz.

This must be used cool, *i.e.*, not above 70°F.

Warmer Tones.—A warm black or even a brown tone may be obtained by using a hot developer, as described above.   If still more warmth is required, it may be obtained with normal printing time by the addition of mercuric (not mercurous) chloride to the developer.   The amount to use must be decided by the worker, but 60 gr. per 32 oz. (4 g. per liter) of developer will have a decided effect.   It should be noted that mercuric chloride (which is also known as bichloride of mercury and as corrosive sublimate) is a dangerous poison and should be handled carefully.

Multiple Printing.—If, through the softness of the negative or because of incorrect choice of a sensitizing mixture, the print lacks the desired contrast when finished, more strength may be given it by sensitizing and printing a second time.   The sensitizing may be carried out exactly as at first, and printing may, of course, be either full or partial; *i.e.*, a comparatively light printing may be given, merely to add weight to the shadows, or the second sensitizing may be printed to the same depth as the first, when all the gradations will have a weight equal to the original added to them.

No special method of registration is needed as with multiple printing in carbon and gum.   The sensitized print is simply placed on the negative in the printing frame and moved about with the fingers until it is in register, this point being clearly visible if the negative and print are viewed by strongly concentrated transmitted light.   It may be that the first processing has caused the print to shrink so that perfect registration cannot be obtained; in this case the worker must use his own judgment as to whether to split the difference through the entire print or to register certain portions—say, the eyes in a portrait—and let the rest of the picture be out of register.   In any case, the difference is not likely to be great enough to be objectionable for pictorial work.

It will very likely be found that the first processing has removed the size from the paper to such an extent that it must be resized before the second sensitizer is applied; also, some papers will require sizing before the first sensitizing. The operation of sizing may be carried out as follows:

Sizing.—Make up the following solutions:

SOLUTION A

Water, cool	350.0 cc.	12 oz.
Gelatin	12.0 g.	180 gr.

Cooking gelatin is perfectly satisfactory. Allow the gelatin to soak until well swollen, then melt in a double boiler.

SOLUTION B

Water, hot	60.0 cc	2 oz.
Chrome alum	2.5 g.	36 gr.

Pour *B* into *A* while both are hot, stirring constantly. Pour the hot solution into a tray, and immerse the print or paper in it, allowing it to remain until well soaked, then hang it up to dry. There will undoubtedly be bubbles on the surface of the paper, but these may be removed by drawing the paper over the edge of the tray when taking it from the size or by wiping the surface with a glass stirring rod or a soft automobile windshield-wiper blade.

It may be found that this gives a heavier sizing than is desired, in which case the size may be diluted with hot water to the desired point. The size should be kept warm when in use, and after sizing one batch of paper or prints, it should be thrown away, as it does not work well if allowed to cool.

Brush Development.—If local modification of values is desired, the only way it can be attained is by brush development with glycerin. The materials required are: two or three soft camel's-hair brushes of different sizes; a supply—16 oz. or so—of glycerin; a sheet of glass somewhat larger than the print; developer; three small receptacles, such as 1- or 2-oz. graduates; and a plentiful supply of clean hard-surfaced blotters. The print should be timed much more fully than normal. A layer of glycerin having been placed on the glass, the print is plastered down on this. A rather thick coat of glycerin is then painted over the surface of the print; the graduates are filled—one with clear developer, one with a mixture of equal parts of developer and glycerin, and one with clear glycerin. The various areas of the print are then developed by brushing one or another of the solutions over the surface, as required, and blotting freely from time to time. The function of the glycerin is to retard development and give opportunity for what local bringing up of values may be desired. When the operation has gone to the desired point, the print is cleared and washed as usual, the final operation being generally to place the finished print face down in the ash can. It will be apparent that the desirability of the results depends almost entirely on the worker's manual dexterity and his appreciation of the tonal relationships necessary to produce a satisfactory picture, this latter point being one in which most amateur photographers (and professionals also) are notably weak. However, it must be admitted that very fine pictures have been produced by this method.

Gum Platinum.—If it is desired to increase the depth and richness of the shadows in a platinum print, the finished print may be given a coating of a gum-pigment mixture, as described in the section on Gum Printing. This gum coating is printed and developed in the usual manner. This treatment often adds tremendously to the appearance of the final print, though it destroys the characteristic surface texture of the platinum paper. It is almost invariably necessary to size the paper before applying the gum coating, and it will probably be found that a more dilute size than that recommended under Multiple Printing is desirable. This, however, each worker must decide for himself. It should be noted that gum-platinum printing is much easier than straight gum printing; it is usually possible to get the same richness and depth of tone with one printing of platinum and one of gum as with six or seven printings of gum alone.

Miscellaneous Notes.—Having no gelatin emulsion, platinum prints have no tendency to curl; once flattened, they remain flat.

With most papers, the surface has much more tendency to rub, especially when wet, than is the case with bromide or gaslight papers. Therefore platinum prints should never be processed in bulk, and they should be handled with some care. Damp or dirty fingers placed on the surface of the paper at any time between sensitizing and development will be almost certain to leave marks.

Platinum paper is very hygroscopic and, if allowed to become damp, will give fogged or degraded prints. Therefore it should be sensitized immediately before use and developed as soon as printed. If it is to be kept for any length of time, it should be stored in an airtight receptacle with a small amount of calcium chloride, which, being even more hygroscopic than the paper, acts as a preservative. Even so, the length of time which the paper can be kept without fogging is about 3 months. Old or fogged paper can often be salvaged by the use of a small amount of potassium bichromate in the developer, as described under Increased Contrast.

Sometimes, through improper choice of paper or of sensitizing formula, the dry print may have a dull, sunken look in the shadows; this occasionally results also from letting the print soak too long in the developer or the clearing baths. In such a case, the brilliant appearance of the wet print may be restored by simonizing, either Simoniz wax or Old English Floor Wax being used; the former gives the print a slightly greenish tone, the latter being a pure yellow. The wax is brushed as evenly as convenient over the surface of the dry print and is then polished with a rather stiff scrubbing brush, such as a nail brush or a vegetable brush. This polish, of course, destroys the characteristic surface texture of the paper, and if this is not desirable, a marked lightening of the shadows may be obtained by applying the wax as described, then melting it into the paper over a gas flame or an electric plate, taking care not to set the turpentine in the wax afire. The polishing should not be omitted, or the wax will probably go into the paper unevenly, causing streaks. The yellow tone thus obtained is often very valuable in the case of portraits or sunlit landscapes. It should be noted that this waxing operation tends to make the print more brittle, so a waxed print must be handled rather more carefully than an unwaxed one.

Various methods of toning platinum prints to red, blue, green, and other colors have been suggested. Since these depend chiefly on the use of salts of iron or uranium, they impair the permanence of the prints and are not recommended. Von Hübl has shown that the warmth of tone secured by the use of mercuric chloride does not depend on the addition of any other substance to the platinum image but is solely a question of the grain size of the deposited metal. Therefore a properly cleared and washed print is as permanent if developed with mercury as if processed for a pure black.

Unless working on a very large scale, it is not worth while to salvage the platinum from the clearing baths and the trimmings of paper. However, the developer should never be thrown away; age does not impair its working qualities, and an older developer will contain a considerable quantity of platinum as well as of iron. This forms a sludge at the bottom of the bottle, and for use the clear solution is poured off. A certain amount of the solution, of course, adheres to the prints, so that the total bulk must be kept up by the occasional addition of new solution, but the main body of solution should never be thrown out; the developer which the writer is now using dates back at least 25 years and is giving perfect results.

If potassium bichromate is used in the developer, this chemical is used up and must be renewed from time to time. This is not the case with the bichloride of mercury, which never loses its effect.

Trays and graduates should be kept scrupulously clean, or the prints may show white spots. If enameled trays are used, care should be taken to avoid those which are chipped or cracked, as the presence of iron in the developer may cause blue spots in the prints.

Gum Printing.—The printing process which is variously known as the gum process, the gum-pigment process, and the gum-bichromate process is the most flexible and at the same time one of the most beautiful of all photographic printing mediums. It is commonly believed that it is a difficult process to use, but this is by no means the case. The trouble lies in the facts that it is extremely flexible and that the average amateur approaches it in a hit-or-miss fashion, so that he becomes confused among the great number of variables inherent in the medium. But if anyone will systematize his work, operating along definite lines and varying one element at a time, he will find that the process, though somewhat laborious, offers no difficulties of any consequence and that the beauty of its results well repays the necessary effort.

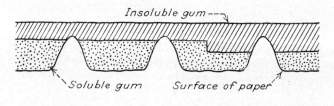

Fig. 2.—Diagram showing cross section of paper used in gum printing.

Gum is analogous to carbon and Fresson in that it depends on the insolubilization by light of a pigmented bichromated colloid film produced by light, but it differs from these processes in that the colloid used is gum arabic and that development is effected simply by floating the printed paper face down on cold water. Also the paper is not a commercial article but must be coated by the worker himself. There is still a further difference, which has a profound influence on the results and which is illustrated in the accompanying sketch. In this sketch it is seen that the outer portion, or layer, of the gum film becomes insoluble first, when printed under a negative, and that this insoluble layer adheres to the high points of the paper, allowing the soluble gum and pigment to seep out through it. When the fully developed print is dried, this insoluble layer retracts into the hollows of the paper, thus adhering to the latter wherever the gum has been insolubilized. From this it follows that the gum-pigment emulsion must be spread very thinly on the paper, or the soluble gum will not seep out through the overlying insoluble layer but rather will tear it off, causing flaking of the print. From this thinness of the emulsion it follows that single gum is a very short-scale process and does not give rich blacks. If rich black are to be secured, it is necessary to resort to multiple printing, from three to five coatings and printings being required for a very deep black. If a long scale is desired, from five to eight printings will be demanded. It is this need for multiple printing which makes the process laborious, but on the other hand it offers an exceedingly valuable means of control, as by this method it is possible to render the gradations of a negative which is far too strong for any other printing process and it is also possible to emphasize any desired set of tones, either high, middle, or low, by varying the manner of coating and the time of printing.

Advantages.—If the paper and the pigments are correctly chosen, the prints are absolutely permanent.

Almost any color or texture of support may be used.

Almost any color or combination of colors of pigment may be used.

Modifications of total contrast are very easily made.

It is extremely easy to make modifications of local values.

Multiple gum printing offers a longer scale of gradation than any other printing medium.

Extremely rich blacks may readily be obtained.

It is commonly believed that gum printing is suitable only when very broad effects are desired, but this is far from true. By the proper selection of paper as fine detail may be obtained as on a medium rough bromide or chloride paper, though not so fine as on a glossy or semimatte surface.

Gum is the cheapest of all printing mediums.

Disadvantages.—Like most of the quality mediums, gum is suitable only for contact printing, as it requires almost as strong a light as carbon or platinum. Hence it follows that for large prints, an enlarged negative is required.

It is somewhat laborious to handle.

We will now consider the actual working of the process.

The Negative.—The ideal negative for gum printing is one which has so short a scale of gradation that it can be fully rendered in one printing of gum. Additional printings are used merely to add weight and contrast. However, this is by no means imperative. By multiple printing and varying the times of exposure so as to register successively the high lights, half tones, and shadows, it is possible to render satisfactorily a negative of practically any degree of contrast. In fact in this respect multiple gum is far more flexible than any other printing medium.

As is the case with other printing mediums, for a given degree of contrast a thin negative is preferable to a dense one. This holds good with gum to an even greater degree than with platinum, carbon, or Fresson, so on all accounts it is desirable that a negative which is to be used for gum printing have full exposure and brief development.

The Paper.—This must be a stock which will stand prolonged soaking in cold water, and it must have a slight tooth or grain. As may be inferred from the sketch and from the accompanying remarks, it is practically impossible to make a gum print on a very smooth surface, since the insoluble layer of gum must have slight irregularities to which it can adhere. A print on a perfectly smooth paper will be merely a silhouette, only those portions of the film adhering which have been printed clear through the emulsion. A print on a smooth surface can, it is true, be made by stippling the gum emulsion while it is still tacky, in the process of coating the paper, but the results are not satisfactory. It is not necessary, however, to use a very rough paper; the texture of the ordinary sketch pads which are sold in art stores is rough enough. If desired, for broad effects, almost any degree of roughness is admissible; the writer has made excellent prints on Whatman Cold Pressed Rough, though such exceedingly rough papers are seldom suitable for prints smaller than 11 by 14 in. In general, the writer prefers Whatman Cold Pressed Medium or Michallet Charcoal for prints 11 by 14 or 8 by 10 in. and for smaller ones either Michallet Charcoal, Strathmore Charcoal, or some of the ordinary drawing papers which are sold for use by artists and draftsmen.

In the interests of permanence, the paper chosen should be a good linen stock.

The Brushes.—Two will be required, a flat, soft paintbrush about 3 in. wide, set in rubber, for coating; and a flat badger blender about 5 or 6 in. wide for blending. This latter brush is rather expensive, costing about $5 or $6, but it lasts indefinitely; the writer has been using his present one for about 27 years. As there is considerable drag on the hairs in the blending process, it is advisable to reinforce the setting of the blender, using a thinned Duco cement in the manner described in the section on Platinum Printing.

The brushes should be thoroughly washed in cold water as soon as the coating operation is completed, for, if the coating mixture is allowed to dry in them and is exposed to light, it will be impossible to remove it.   They should be hung up to dry, bristles down, so that they may keep their shape.

The Pigments.—These must be either water-color paints or dry-powder colors, the former being preferable; oil colors will not do, and though some authors recommended tempera colors, the present writer has not found them satisfactory.   They must be the so-called "earth pigments," such as lampblack, Ivory Black, burnt umber, burnt siena, Venetian red, Prussian blue, cobalt blue, cadmium orange, cadmium yellow, etc.; the aniline colors will not do.   It is better to buy a good grade of water-color tubes; the powder colors are much cheaper, but they must be ground for use, and the time thus consumed amounts to more than the money saved.

It is immaterial what manufacturer of colors is favored; the pigments of Talens & Son, Winsor & Newton, Devoe & Reynolds, or, in fact, any standard maker can be relied on; the writer prefers those of Talens, but this is partly the result of habit and partly because that firm puts up an excellent black, known as Photo Engraver's Black, which is much cheaper than the ordinary water colors.   The selection of colors given above will be ample for any ordinary use; as a matter of fact, three or four tubes are plenty to start with—say, Ivory Black for a neutral black and burnt umber or Venetian red to warm it up, with cobalt blue for cool blacks.

Whatever make of pigments is used, the same one should be adhered to throughout, since the pigment will be measured by the number of inches squeezed from the tube, and the apertures of the tubes vary with different makers.

The Gum Solution.—This is a fairly thick solution of gum arabic in water, and, as different samples of gum vary, it is well to use that of one single maker; even so, there will be some variation between lots.   It should be granular, not in the form of tears or powdered, as the first is easiest to dissolve.   The writer favors McKesson & Robbins Gum Acacia No. 1 Granular, but this again is a matter of habit; an equivalent article from any good maker will be satisfactory.

Some preservative will be necessary, for, although a sour gum solution works as well as a fresh one, it works differently, and the progressive souring will throw the worker's calculations out.   Formaldehyde and carbolic acid are unsuitable for this purpose, and, though oil of cloves is sometimes recommended, the writer prefers bichloride of mercury, which, as noted in the section on Platinum Printing, is a dangerous poison and should be used with care.   It is, however, an efficient preservative; the writer has known a gum solution so treated to remain perfectly fresh for 18 years.

The formula which is preferred by the writer, and on which subsequent formulas will be based, is as follows:

Water	1000.0 cc.	32 oz.
Gum arabic (granular)	500.0 g.	1 lb.
Mercuric chloride	6.0 g.	90 gr.

The gum is most conveniently dissolved by rubbing it up in a mortar, a little at a time, with portions of the water.   The preservative may be rubbed in at any stage of the proceedings but should be thoroughly stirred through the final solution.   This manner of dissolving the gum is tedious but is more satisfactory than the method sometimes recommended, of putting the gum into a bag and suspending it in the water; if the latter plan is used, the gum coagulates into a mass which requires a very long time to go into solution.

It is advisable to store the gum solution in a wide-mouthed screw-cap bottle or, if the bottle has been ground with reasonable accuracy, merely to lay a piece of glass over the top, to prevent evaporation. The neck of the bottle should be wiped each time that any of the solution is poured out, to avoid cementing the cap fast.

The Sensitizer.—The sensitizer commonly recommended is potassium bichromate, but the writer prefers sodium bichromate, as it is far more soluble than the potassium salt, wherefore a given amount of a saturated solution contains much more of the sensitizing agent and gives a much more rapidly printing film. The formula follows:

Water, warm	500.0 cc.	16 oz.
Sodium bichromate (technical)	500.0 g.	1 lb.

Filter, and store in a brown bottle. This will keep indefinitely if not exposed to strong light. It is approximately a saturated solution.

Sizing.—If it is found necessary to size the paper, this may be done by the method which is used for making single transfer paper for carbon printing and is described in the section on that subject. One, or at most two, applications will be sufficient.

Coating Mixture.—As the longest scale of gradation is secured when the coating mixture contains the largest possible amount of pigment and as a long scale is usually desired, it follows that the coating mixture should hold as much of the pigment as can satisfactorily be used. But for every paper, every pigment, and every gum solution there is a maximum relation of pigment to gum which can be used without staining the paper—or rather, to be precise, there are two such maxima, one for automatic development, the other for brush development. The method of determining these maxima is as follows:

Squeeze into a small mortar an inch length of the pigment, and rub this up with ½ dram of the gum solution. With a fine brush dipped into the mixture, make a small mark on the paper which is to be used, and opposite this mark, pencil "1 in. to ½ dram." Add ½ dram of gum solution to the mixture, rub it up well, and make another mark, labeling this "1 in. to 1 dram." Add another ½ dram of the gum solution, and label the resulting mark "1 in. to 1½ drams." Continue thus until a series of marks extending to "1 in. to 10 drams" is reached. Then allow these gum-pigment marks to dry thoroughly, and let the paper float face down in a tray of water at room temperature for ½ hr. On inspection it will be found that some of the marks have entirely disappeared, while others remain visible. Suppose, for example, that the last visible mark is opposite the notation "1 in. to 4½ drams"; then it is known that, if pure whites are to be secured with automatic development, the maximum proportion of pigment to gum solution in the coating mixture must be 1 in. to 5 drams. Now with a soft camel's-hair brush, brush over the remaining marks, when it will be found that others will disappear. As an example, suppose that the last one visible after this brushing is opposite the label "1 in. to 2 drams"; then it is known that, if brush development is to be used and pure whites are to be obtained, the maximum allowable proportion of pigment to gum is 1 in. to 2½ drams. If a note is made of these proportions, it will be possible at any future time to predict accurately the maximum gum-pigment relationship for that pigment and that paper. This should be done for the various pigments which are to be used and for the various papers. A table can then be drawn up giving the sundry relationships at a glance, thus avoiding the "by-guess-and-by-gosh" method so common in gum printing.

This method serves also to indicate the possible maximum when two or more pigments are mixed to secure variations in color. Thus, if it has been determined that a certain black requires 5 drams of gum solution to 1 in. of pigment for automatic development and burnt umber requires 4 drams to 1 in., then, if it is desired to mix these pigments in the proportion of 2 to 1, it follows that the worker will use 1 in. of the black, ½ in. of the burnt umber, and 7 drams of the gum solution.

Note that no sensitizer is used in these determinations.

It may seem that this method of determination involves a great deal of work, but actually the labor is not excessive, and, if the experiments indicated are carried out and the suggested table is drawn up, a vast amount of effort and disappointment will in the long run be saved.

The complete mixture must be dilute enough to spread to a sufficient, but not excessive, thickness on the paper. Only the worker's own experience can indicate this characteristic, as it varies with different samples of gum arabic and with different papers, a rough paper admitting of thicker coating than a smooth one. If the coating is too thin, an excessive number of printings will be required to secure depth and scale; if it is too thick, it will flake off instead of developing smoothly. A suggested formula which the writer has used successfully with Whatman Cold Pressed Medium follows. It must be borne in mind, however, that this is no more than a suggestion, put forward as a basis for the reader's own experiments.

Talens Photo Engraver's Black	25.0 mm.	1 in.
Gum solution	15.0 cc.	4 drams
Sensitizer	35.0 cc.	10 drams

The pigment is squeezed from the tube into a mortar, is well rubbed up with the gum, and the sensitizer is added and stirred in. The mixture is then ready to be spread on the paper.

Coating the Paper.—This operation is like driving a golf ball or sawing a board, in that it can be described and instructions can be given for doing it, but only experience makes it possible for the worker to accomplish it properly; a certain manual deftness or knack is required, and this comes only with practice.

The paper, which should be cut 2 in. or so larger all around than the finished print, is to be is pinned face up on a smooth board, using—most conveniently—pushpins at the four corners. The coating brush is dipped into the mixture, it is lightly pressed out against the side of the mortar, and the mixture is brushed rapidly back and forth over the paper until the surface is well coated. Then the blending brush is taken up and is drawn lightly but rapidly back and forth over the paper, both crosswise and up and down. It will be found that the brush marks left in coating are smoothed out, eventually disappearing altogether as the gum sets. As the gum sets, the action of the blender becomes gradually lighter and more of a whipping than of a dragging motion, and it should be stopped at just the right point. If it is arrested too soon, the gum will run together in tiny puddles, and if it is continued too long, the coating will be streaked. A slight puddling or streaking does no harm, since it tends to blend out to smoothness while the paper is hanging up to dry.

If several sheets of paper are coated at one time, it will probably be found that the blender becomes clogged with the mixture; it should then be well rinsed in running water and dried by rolling the handle rapidly between the palms of the hands, when its use may be continued at once.

The commonest fault in coating gum paper is that the beginner tries to get the coating mixture on too thick. The coated paper should not look black but should be of a light greenish gray.

If the blending has been carried on too long or if the paper buckles so that it is difficult to blend evenly, a uniform coating may be obtained by using the blender with a stippling action. This renders the coating spotty, but most of the spots will blend out as the paper dries, and the others will disappear during development.

All the above operations can be carried out in an ordinary room, since the coating is not sensitive to light until dry; but the coated paper should be dried in the dark. In proper conditions of heat and humidity, drying will not take more than a few minutes, but it may be hastened by an electric fan or over a gas stove, taking care to avoid scorching.

The paper should be printed as soon as it is dry, since it keeps in good condition for not more than a few hours at most.

Printing.—It is, of course, impossible to say definitely how long a time the printing will take, but as compared to other quality mediums, gum is fairly rapid. As an example, the average printing time for one of the writer's negatives, printing in unobstructed July sunlight for the high lights, will be from 2 to 3 min., and for the half tones and shadows it will range from 2 min. to 20 sec.

Development.—Development should take place as soon as printing is completed, on account of the continuing action which occurs in gum as in other colloid-bichromate mediums and which cannot here be arrested by washing the print in cold water, as with carbon and Fresson, as the gum is soluble in water at any temperature.

To develop, the print is washed in several changes of cool water, to remove most of the sensitizer, and is then turned face down and allowed to float on $\frac{1}{2}$ to 1 in. of water in the tray. It may be lifted and drained from time to time, to follow the progress of development. The stage of development is noted by watching the water that drains from one corner back into the tray; this water will be seen to carry with it more or less pigment, the amount of color gradually diminishing as development proceeds. If the printing has been correctly timed, $\frac{1}{2}$ hr. will find the print developed to the proper point, which will be indicated partly by the general appearance and partly by the fact that the drainings will be practically free from pigment. It is not necessary that they carry absolutely no pigment whatever, but only a trifling amount should be seen running off the print. Here again, experience is the only precise guide. Obviously, if the print is too light at the end of $\frac{1}{2}$ hr., it is underprinted, and if it is still too dark, printing has been excessive. In neither case is it necessary to throw the print away; an undertimed print should be developed as far as it will go and made the basis for a multiple print, and one which is overtimed can be forced by the use of warm water—up to 212°F.—or by the use of a small amount of alkali in the developing water, as described in the section on Carbon Printing. In the case of gum, however, the addition of alkali has little effect at normal temperatures; it is most effective when the water is warm. In any case it should be used very cautiously, as an excess causes the same trouble as in carbon, *viz.*, a complete washing out of the lighter gradations, and perhaps flaking of the film.

The colloid film of a gum print is much softer and less likely to tear than that of either a carbon or a Fresson print, consequently much more local development may be indulged in than with either of the other processes. In fact, the possible modifications are so great that there is a serious temptation to overdo them, producing a result which, even though it may not be obviously scratched up in imitation of a charcoal or pencil drawing—as far too many gum prints are—still is evidently false in its values. This is a danger which should be guarded against. As in any medium, only such local modifications as are definitely necessary should be made; the temptation to play with the print should be sternly resisted.

Since the purpose in local modification is to remove the softened gum from the paper, many ways of doing this will suggest themselves. Water from a hose may be allowed to run on the spot which is to be lightened; if the hose is held at such a height that the water falls in drops, the effect will be greater than that of a continuous stream. A spray from an atomizer may be used, or a jet from a washing bottle, or, if this is not sufficient, a soft camel's-hair brush. It is not generally advisable to use a stiff brush, since this tends to leave a scratchy appearance. Whatever method of local modification is used, the effect will be less obvious—and less likely to be unpleasant—if the work is done under water.

When local development is planned, it is best to use a gum-pigment mixture which will give a slight staining with automatic development. To print slightly deeper than normal, allow the development to go as far as it will automatically and do the brush-work on the pigment stain.

When development is complete, the print is hung up to dry. It will probably have a slight amount of sensitizer stain, which may be removed by a few minutes' immersion in a 5 per cent solution of potassium metabisulphite, followed by several rinsings in clear water. Sodium bisulphite or ordinary alum may be used, but the potassium salt seems to be rather more effective than either of these. It is commonly advised to use alum, on the ground that it hardens the film, but the writer has not found this to be at all necessary; the printed and developed film, after drying, is hard enough to stand almost any amount of rough handling. Clearing should not take place until after the print has been dried, or, in the case of a multiple print, until after the last printing has been dried.

Multiple Printing.—One reason that so many beginners in gum work get into trouble is that they expect the first printing from the negative to look like a print and try to make it do so. It should not; it should look like a very sick imitation of a print—pale, washed out, very likely no more than a flat tone in the shadows, and in general thoroughly unsatisfactory. It is astonishing to an inexperienced worker to see how the print assumes vigor and character with the addition of subsequent printings.

If the negative is soft enough so that its entire range of gradations is rendered in one printing of gum, then when the print has been developed and dried it may be coated a second time and printed again, for the same printing time, and developed as at first. Thus the second and subsequent printings are used merely to add depth and contrast. It is much more likely, however, that the scale of the negative will be too great to render in one printing of gum, in which case the shadows—perhaps even the half tones—of the first printing will be merely a flat tone and must be brought out by the later printings. The coating mixture may, perhaps, be the same as for the first printing but the printing time less, *e.g.*, if the negative requires three printings to render its full scale, the first one may be timed for 4 min., the second for two, and the third for one, each printing being developed fully. Some workers have been known to use 16 or 17 printings, and the writer knows of one who went to 25, but this is sheer frivolity. Using a well-sized paper, which permits the use of a fairly large amount of pigment, the utmost richness and depth of blacks can be got in five printings, and the scale of practically any negative can be rendered in six or eight printings.

It will be apparent that very great variations in coating and printing are possible in order to secure various effects. Thus a long scale may be secured with little depth of shadow by using a relatively small amount of pigment in the coating mixture; or the shadows may be emphasized by using light doses of pigment for the high-light and half-tone printings, with a heavy amount, printed lightly, for the shadows. Each worker will think up these variations for himself, but it cannot be too strongly urged that he keep a record of what he has done in each case. If he fails to do this he will not know where he is; he will be unable either to duplicate or to predict results, and he is likely to abandon gum printing under the impression that it is too difficult. As a matter of fact, gum printing is not at all difficult, but it does demand care and accuracy. Given these and a moderate amount of experience, gum printing will be found not only much easier than bromoil or even than plain bromide enlarging, but far more satisfactory in its results.

General Remarks.—Registration in multiple gum has been the subject of many inventions; the simplest and best method is that recommended for multiple printing in carbon, *viz.*, the use of a mask around the negative, of a printing paper larger than the negative but smaller than the mask, and four registration marks on mask and paper.

A very beautiful effect, which is particularly delightful in the treatment of sunlit water, a sunny landscape, or any subject in which a vibrating, shimmering effect of light is desired may be secured by very slight underprinting, by very slight underdevelopment, and by drying the print in a horizontal position on a sheet of glass or other flat level surface. In this case the gum and pigment run slightly, giving a peculiar blurring of the outlines which is not obtained in any other way or in any other medium. This is a very difficult effect to obtain, since it demands the most exact timing throughout, but if secured, it has a remarkable charm.

One of the finest characteristics of multiple gum lies in the extreme richness and depth of the blacks obtainable, a quality in which gum rivals multiple carbon. This effect, in both mediums, is due to the fact that we are looking through, rather than at, successive layers of pigment suspended in a transparent medium, and, as in carbon, the effect may be enhanced in a gum print by waxing and polishing.

In conclusion: work systematically; keep a record of all you do; do not expect to get a good picture with one printing; and do not overdo your local modifications. If these recommendations are followed, success will result.

Fresson Printing.—Fresson is, in effect, a revival of the Artigue process, which was more or less used some 25 or 30 years ago, and like carbon and gum it depends on the fact that a colloid film, when sensitized with a chromic salt and exposed to light, becomes more or less insoluble in water.

The paper supplied for this process consists of a sheet of paper carrying a basic layer of some hard colloid—presumably either gelatin or glue—which has a high melting point. Over this is laid a stratum of softer colloid—probably gelatin—which melts at about 96°F. and which carries a relatively heavy content of pigment. The paper is supplied insensitive and is sensitized just before use by immersion in a solution of potassium bichromate, being afterward dried and printed under a negative. At this point the process diverges from both gum and carbon, since, instead of being developed by floating on cold water, as with gum, or by washing with hot water, as with carbon, the printed paper is soaked for a short time in tepid water, is then laid face up on a slanting surface, and is developed by pouring over it a soup of boxwood sawdust in water.

Advantages.—The process has a long scale of gradation, gives very rich blacks, and has a beautiful absolutely matte surface closely resembling that of platinum.

The prints are absolutely permanent.

The paper may be obtained in several different colors, and on several different supports.

Modifications of total contrast are very easily made.

It is extremely easy to make modifications of local values.

The process is very easy to work, requiring but little technical skill. Also there is great latitude in handling.

Disadvantages.—Fresson is a contact-printing process, requiring a very strong light, and it is practically impossible to use it for enlarging.

It is somewhat laborious to work, requiring a good deal of time for development if the best expression of the process is to be obtained.

The surface of the paper, both before and after printing, is very delicate and easily marred, so finished prints must be handled carefully.

The Paper.—As has been said, this is bought insensitive and, if stored in a cool dry place, will keep almost indefinitely, though the colloid gradually hardens with time, requiring slightly warmer water for processing. It is advisable to store it flat, under light pressure, to minimize its tendency to curl. The paper may be obtained in black, dark brown, sepia, blue-green, green-blue, and red and on either a white or cream support, which last may be either smooth or slightly rough.

As the emulsion is very delicate and as the warmth of the fingers is sufficient to melt the colloid, it is advisable to handle the paper only by the edges; therefore it should be purchased and used a size larger than the print is to be *i.e.*, 5 by 7 in. for a 4- by 5-in. print, or 11 by 14 in. for an 8- by 10-in. print. If larger prints are wanted, it is best to get the full-size sheet, approximately 23 by 35 in. and cut it to size.

The Sawdust.—This is a special boxwood sawdust, put up by the manufacturers of the paper and sold in packages of the proper amount to make 5 or 6 qt. of the soup. The exact amount of water is not important; the soup should be thin enough to pour readily but not so thin as to be ineffective, and within these wide limits the strength does not greatly matter.

The sawdust may be used repeatedly—almost indefinitely, in fact—and does not lose its effectiveness. It is simply allowed to dry between the occasions of use, being mixed again with water when desired. It is sometimes stated that a preservative should be used in the soup to prevent putrefaction of the gelatin which is washed off the prints; but the writer has not found this to be at all necessary, having used the same batch of sawdust for more than 4 years with no trouble whatever. It is true that the gelatin forms a hard crust over the sawdust as the water evaporates, but this does no harm, being readily soaked soft again.

The Sensitizer.—This is normally a 1 per cent solution of potassium bichromate, made up as follows:

Water...	1000.0 cc.	30 oz.
Potassium bichromate....................................	10.0 g.	144 gr.

This keeps indefinitely if protected from light and may be used repeatedly.

Different strengths of sensitizer may be used for different purposes, as will be discussed under Variations in Contrast.

Sensitizing.—The potassium bichromate solution is poured into a clean tray to a depth of ½ in. or more, and the sheet of Fresson paper is slid into it, the edges being pressed down as they curl up, any adhering air bubbles being broken by a light touch of the fingertip or of a soft brush, and the tray being rocked. At the expiration of 4 min. from the first immersion, the paper is lifted from the sensitizer and is hung up to dry in the dark; clips are used at the corners. It is advisable to hang it cornerwise, so that the sensitizer will drain from one corner.

Sensitizing may be done in any ordinary room, as the paper is not sensitive until dry; it should, however, be dried in the dark, since when dry it is slightly more sensitive than a printing-out paper.

The sensitized paper will dry, in proper conditions of humidity, in a very short time—drying may be hastened by an electric fan—and the paper should be used as soon as possible, since when dry it tends to become insoluble without exposure to light. Even if kept in a sealed tin with preservative, as is done with platinum paper, it will not keep in good condition for more than a few days.

The sensitizer should be used at a temperature of between 65 and 75°F.; if too warm, it will soften the gelatin of the paper excessively.

If the paper is allowed to become bone dry while hanging up, it will curl very badly. It is therefore advisable to take it down when it is dry enough not to stick to anything and then to finish drying under light pressure. This is not, however, absolutely necessary, as with care, the paper can be handled even when badly curled.

Printing.—This requires a strong light, such as is used for platinum or carbon, and no precise directions can be given as to time, as this varies with the negative, the color of the tissue, the possible moisture content of the colloid film, and the effect desired. Generally speaking, the cooler colors print more rapidly than the warm ones, and a bone-dry paper will print more rapidly than one which is faintly damp. Using the black paper, working with it bone dry, and working for normal results, the writer makes a test on P O P, then prints the Fresson for about three-quarters of this proofing time.

Developing.—The print should be developed immediately after taking from the printing frame, since there is the same continuing action with Fresson that there is with carbon and gum.

To develop, the print is immersed for 4 min. in water at room temperature, then for 1 min. in water at 88°F. It is then laid face up on a smooth slanting surface, and the sawdust soup is poured repeatedly over it. A convenient arrangement for this apparatus was designed and made of sheet zinc by W. G. Houskeeper. It consists of a semicylindrical trough about 18 in. long and 5 in. in diameter, supporting a sheet of zinc which has had the edges bent up so that the soup will not run off them. The trough has feet to keep it upright, the sheet has a lip which projects slightly over the edge of the trough, and the upper end of the sheet is supported by a piece of 2- by 4-in. wood. An enameled cup from the 5-and-10-cent store is used for pouring. The exact angle of the support is of no great consequence. So long as there is slant enough for the soup to run off freely, it is all right—an angle of 30° with the horizontal is satisfactory.

Development is continued until it has reached the proper point, when the print is rinsed in cold water to remove any adhering bits of sawdust and to set the gelatin. It is then hung up to dry; no further fixing or washing is necessary. The print will dry somewhat darker than it appears while wet—this darkening is more apparent in the shadows than in the high lights, so development should be continued until the print seems a little lighter than it should be when finished.

If for any reason it is not desired to develop the print at once, the continuing action may be arrested by washing the undeveloped print in six or more changes of water to remove the sensitizer. It may then be dried and developed in the usual manner at any subsequent time.

Unless printing has been so deep as to require the use of water at 96°F., it will probably be found that the margins of the print, even though masked in printing, will not develop clear but will retain more or less of the pigmented gelatin. Apparently a slight amount of light action is necessary if absolutely pure whites are to be secured. This residual tint is often very pleasing but may be removed with a brush if it is not desired.

For any given temperature of the soaking water, the print will develop to a certain depth, after which continued pouring of the soup has no effect. If it does not develop far enough after soaking at 88°F., the print may be placed for 1 min. into water at a slightly higher temperature, after which development is resumed in the usual manner. It is not advisable, however, to go above 94 to 96°F., since at this temperature the pigmented film will probably strip entirely from the paper, and even if it does not do this, the high lights of the picture will probably flake off, leaving blank spaces. If 96°F. will not bring the print up to the proper point, it is seriously overprinted and should usually be thrown away, though it may sometimes by salvaged by brushing with a soft brush. This treatment, however, is likely to result in unsightly scratches on the surface of the print.

Variations in Contrast.—For normal sensitizing, the softest contrast is obtained when the paper is printed to such a depth that it will develop satisfactorily after 1 min. of soaking at 88°F. Deeper printing, up to double the normal time, with the use of a warmer soaking water, up to 96°F., gives marked increase of contrast; this latter technique tends to give a grainy texture to the print which may be undesirable.

If this method of control is not desired, greater contrast may be obtained by the use of a weaker sensitizer, say ½ or ¼ of 1 per cent, together with a correspondingly longer printing time—two or four times normal—and a soaking water at the standard temperature of 88°F. Overprinting and a warmer water may also be used in conjunction with the weaker sensitizing.

If softer prints than normal are wanted, the sensitizer may be used stronger than 1 per cent, with correspondingly shorter printing. It is not advisable, however, to attempt to use the sensitizer stronger than 5 per cent at most, since above this concentration it will tend to strip the emulsion from the paper.

Local Modifications.—It is extremely easy to make local modifications of values. Extra weight may be given to an area by avoiding it in pouring the soup, or by tilting the support at such an angle that the soup does not run over the portion which is to be left dark. Broad areas may be lightened by pouring the soup from a greater height, so that it strikes the print with more violence in some places than in others; this technique, however, is likely to result in a grainy appearance in the finished print. Still greater lightening may be secured by the use of a soft brush, though this must be applied carefully, a little at a time, if scratches and brush marks are to be avoided. It is best to rinse the print free of sawdust, place it in a tray of cool water, and work under the surface of the water. However, it is sometimes necessary, in order to secure the maximum effect, to work in the air. However, by working carefully, it is possible to carry this local modification very far indeed without it becoming apparent; in this respect, Fresson is far more flexible than carbon, and almost as much so as gum.

Javelle Water.—It is sometimes recommended that the Fresson paper be greatly overprinted and given a preliminary soaking in a dilute Javelle water before development. The writer has found this technique to be altogether unsatisfactory; the great desirability of Fresson lies in the extremely delicate manner in which it renders the gradations of the negative, together with the beauty of surface of the finished print, but the treatment with Javelle water increases contrast, loses the finer gradations, and gives a coarse and grainy texture to the surface. The result is quite foreign to the best expression possible with the medium.

Final Remarks.—If the print is too dark when dry, it may be soaked until limp in cool water, placed for 1 min. in water 2 or 3° warmer than was used in the original development, and then developed still further with the sawdust. This treatment may be repeated several times and does no harm.

It is ordinarily recommended that Fresson prints be spotted by softening an unsensitized piece of the paper in warm water and using the pigmented gelatin thus loosened, applying it with a brush. This is necessary when large areas are to be spotted, especially if they are in the darker portions of the print, as any great amount of penciling will leave a shiny mark. But for small spotting the writer prefers to use a carbon spotting pencil (sharpened to a needle point on sandpaper) and stippling rather than stroking, 'this being much easier than the brush method.

If for any reason the finished Fresson seems too dull and heavy, it may be given the brilliant appearance of a wet print by waxing, as described in the section on Platinum Printing, though this, of course, destroys the inherent beauty of the matte surface.

If greater strength or richness is desired in a somewhat weak Fresson, this may be secured by coating the finished print with a gum-pigment mixture, printing and developing as described in the section on Gum Printing. Both waxing and the addition of a printing of gum are more satisfactory on the rough Fresson paper than on the smooth.

At its best, Fresson may fairly be considered a worthy rival of platinum, its long scale of gradation, rich blacks, and matte surface giving it a good claim in this respect.

It does not, it is true, admit of the use of the more beautiful paper supports, but on the other hand it is far more flexible than platinum in the matter of local modifications. The finest expression of the process is secured by printing as lightly as possible, using relatively cool water for soaking—sometimes as low as 86 or even 84°F.—and developing slowly and gently, pouring the sawdust easily and lightly with no violence whatever. This technique means slow development—the writer not infrequently spends an hour or more in developing an 8- by 10-in. print—but the result amply repays the trouble involved if the worker cares for exquisite print quality.

Oil and Bromoil Printing and Transfer.—Oil printing depends on two facts: (1) when a bichromated gelatin film is exposed to light, it becomes more or less tanned in proportion to the amount of light action; and (2) if this film is soaked in water, it absorbs water and becomes repellent to an oily ink in inverse proportion to the amount of light action. In bromoil—which is an outgrowth of oil, exactly as carbro is an outgrowth of carbon—the tanning action takes place as a result of the chemical reaction between a special sensitizer (ordinarily called the "bleacher") and the silver image of a bromide print or enlargement. After the sensitizing, drying, and printing in the case of oil or the bleaching, fixing, and washing in the case of bromoil, the print is soaked until the gelatin is properly swelled; it is then surface-dried. A suitable ink is dabbed on with a special brush until a sufficient amount has adhered to the print to give the desired image, when the print is pinned up to dry and may be considered finished. Or, if desired, the print, may be placed in contact with a piece of plain paper while the ink is still soft, and may be run through a press similar to an etching press, in which case the ink is transferred to the plain paper, giving an effect quite different from that of the original print. After such transferring, the print may be soaked and inked a second, third, or fourth time, or even oftener, and these inkings may either be transferred to different pieces of paper or may be transferred to the first one, thus producing a multiple print. Since there is great latitude not only in the matter of the original oil or bromide print but also in the matters of soaking, choice of inks, and manner of applying the ink, the oil and bromoil processes are exceedingly flexible, almost equaling multiple gum in this respect.

As will be seen from the above, the oil process is a contact medium requiring a strong light for printing, whereas the bromoil process makes it possible to produce large prints without the need for an enlarged negative. Other than this, they are practically if not entirely identical in the results obtainable. It is true that one author claims that bromoil gives a longer scale of gradation than oil, but the present writer has not found this to be the case and believes that the error is due to the fact that the special paper which is supplied for oil printing is thinly coated with gelatin. If a sheet of bromide paper of a type suitable for bromoil is fixed without exposure to light, washed, sensitized, printed, and soaked, it gives as long a scale as though it were used by the bromoil process.

Advantages.—If the proper paper and inks are used, the prints are absolutely permanent.

The process is extremely flexible, in respect to both modifications of total contrast and local modifications of values.

A very beautiful quality of richness and depth in the shadows is possible.

By varying the thickness of the ink, the mode of handling the brush, or both, very delightful variations in texture may be secured. This characteristic is even more apparent when transfer is used, since a final support of almost any desired character may be used.

Very wide variations in color are possible through choice of inks.

Multiple prints are readily made by transfer, this making possible still greater modifications of total contrast and of local values.

Disadvantages.—As has been said, oil is a contact process, demanding an enlarged negative if large prints are to be made.

It is somewhat laborious.

It does not render the delicate gradations of the negative as finely as do some other mediums; for this reason, it is not so well adapted to sunny snow scenes, high-keyed portraits, and the like, as platinum, carbon, gum, or Fresson, but is at its best when broader effects are desired.

The advantages and disadvantages of bromoil are the same as those of oil, with the following exceptions: (1) large prints can be made without the use of an enlarged negative and (2) it is a much more tricky and temperamental process. The first argument, however, is scarcely a valid one, since fully as much labor and skill are required to make a bromoil print as to make an enlarged negative and a platinum print.

The Paper.—This should be a bromide paper having a soft gelatin emulsion, without a supercoat of gelatin. The same paper should be used for both oil and bromoil, since the best oil paper results from fixing, without exposure to light, a sheet of heavily coated bromide paper. This fixing should be done in plain, not acid, hypo, since it is necessary to avoid any hardening of the gelatin.

Suitable surfaces of Velour Black will be supplied by the Defender Photo Supply Company, of Rochester, N. Y., provided that the order specifies "for bromoil," and the Kodak Royal Bromide, obtainable from the Medo Photo Supply Corporation, 15 West 47th St., New York City, can be recommended when a buff stock is desired. There are numerous other good bromoil papers, most of them, however, originating in England, where the process is more popular than it is in this country.

Whatever paper is used, it should be as fresh as possible.

The Negative.—For either oil or bromoil, the negative should be soft and well graded, since it is very easy to secure any desired degree of contrast, and a relatively soft original print will render the gradations better than a stronger one. The best type of negative for either process is one which will give a moderately soft enlargement on an ordinary medium-contrast chlorobromide paper. As in other printing processes, a thin negative is preferable to a dense one, for a given degree of contrast.

Sensitizing for Oil.—Having been fixed, washed, and dried, the paper is sensitized by 3-min. immersion in a solution of potassium bichromate and is hung up to dry in the dark. Sensitizing may take place in any ordinary room, since the paper is not sensitive to light until dry.

The normal strength of sensitizer, for average results, is a $2\frac{1}{2}$ per cent solution, but it may range in strength from $\frac{1}{2}$ of 1 per cent to 5 per cent, the stronger solution giving a quicker printing film and less contrast.

Printing for Oil.—For either oil or bromoil, the paper should be masked so as to give a blank margin at least $\frac{1}{2}$ in. wide—and 1 in. is better—all around the picture.

Sensitized oil paper should be printed as soon as dry, since it does not keep well. If this is not possible, it should be stored in a sealed airtight box, with calcium chloride as a desiccator. Even so, it will not keep in good condition for more than a very few days.

Printing is carried out by sunlight, carbon arc, or mercury-vapor arc and should be continued until gradation is clearly visible in the high lights. The print has much the appearance of an undeveloped platinum print, though somewhat deeper; in each case, the image shows as a yellowish brown on a yellow ground.

After exposure, the print should be washed immediately in water at approximately room temperature until the free sensitizer is completely washed out, when it may be either soaked in warmer water (if necessary) and inked at once or allowed to dry and soaked and inked at some future time. It is not well, however, to postpone the soaking and inking for more than a week or so, since with time the gelatin tends to become hard and resistant to swelling.

Printing for Bromoil.—Printing may be either by contact or by enlarging, though, if the former is used, there is no gain over oil and there is the additional—and sometimes tricky—operation of bleaching. To be satisfactory for bromoil, the enlargement should be distinctly on the soft side; there should be no very deep shadows, since if these are present it will be difficult to hold up shadow detail in inking; and the lights should be a trifle darker than they would be for the ideal bromide print. If this quality is maintained, inking will be much easier than otherwise, and, though it is desirable to adjust the negative so that the ideal print quality is maintained with normal treatment, this is not absolutely imperative. If the negative is slightly too strong, a satisfactorily soft bromide print may often be secured by giving two or three times normal exposure, diluting the developer to about a quarter of normal strength, and removing the print from the developer when the lights have reached the proper depth. This technique is a "touch-and-go" sort of performance, since the tray must be rocked *constantly* if uneven development is to be avoided. The print must be snatched at exactly the right point—a trifle before it reaches the desired depth—and it must be promptly and evenly immersed in the hypo, where it is rocked for ½ min. or so after immersion. Still, this plan is often useful, especially since it is not at all necessary, with bromoil, that the print be developed to infinity, as is required when toning by the bleaching and sulphiding process is contemplated.

Almost any developer which is suitable for bromide paper can be used, though it is generally best to employ Amidol, since this, working without alkali, has little or no chemical effect on the gelatin.

Many bromoil workers favor a stop bath between development and fixing, giving the print ½ min. or so in

Water	1000.0 cc.	32	oz.
Acetic acid (28 per cent)	45.0 cc.	1½	oz.

or (which is the same thing)

Water	1000.0 cc.	32	oz.
Acetic acid (glacial)	12.0 cc.	3	drams

The present writer, however, prefers to put the print directly from the developer into the hypo, a technique which demands clean trays, clean hands, and prompt working if stains and uneven development are to be avoided, but which, in his opinion, gives a print which is more easily inked than if the intermediate acid bath is used.

Fixing must be done in a 25 per cent solution of *plain* hypo, since any hardening of the gelatin must be avoided. Washing after fixing must be thorough, since if any trace of hypo remains in the emulsion it may react with the chemicals of the bleacher, causing uneven tanning of the gelatin.

Bleaching.—Bleaching may take place immediately after washing, or the print may be dried and then bleached at some future time. It is not well to postpone the bleaching too long, or the gelatin may tend to harden spontaneously. If a dried print is to be bleached, it should first be soaked in water until thoroughly limp.

It is not possible to give a general formula for the bleacher, since this varies with different papers, with different inks, with the temperature of the soaking water, with the worker's style, and with the results desired. Each bromoil worker, therefore, must try different techniques until he finds that which is most satisfactory.

A technique of bleaching which is recommended by John Kiem, of the Orange Camera Club, for Defender Velour Black, is as follows:

Water	1000.0 cc.	20 oz.
Copper sulphate	10.5 g.	96 gr.
Potassium bromide	10.5 g.	96 gr.
Potassium bichromate	2.0 g.	18 gr.
Hydrochloric acid (c.p.)	10.0 g.	10 drops

Bleach, wash well, and fix in

Water	1000.0 cc.	20 oz.
Hypo	95.0 g.	2 oz.

Wash well, and dry. Resoak for inking.

The formula which is recommended for Kodak Royal Bromide is as follows:

Water	1000.0 cc.	20 oz.
Copper sulphate	10.0 g.	90 gr.
Potassium bromide	7.0 g.	65 gr.
Chromic acid	0.3 g.	3 gr.

Bleach, wash well, fix, and dry as above. Resoak for inking.

The writer has found both of these formulas to work well, but there are many others from which to choose.

The print should be bleached until all the characteristic black image has been converted to a yellowish brown strongly resembling that of an undeveloped platinum print or that of a newly printed oil paper. There will be a residual image, which may darken later, with exposure to light, and the second fixing recommended above is to remove this image, thus preventing future deterioration of the print.

Some workers advise giving the bleached, fixed, and washed print 5 min. in a 3 per cent solution of sulphuric acid (c.p.) which tends to soften the gelatin and make it easier to secure the proper relief for inking. This solution may be used warm (up to 110°F.), in which case the effect is still greater. A higher degree of softening of the gelatin, with consequently greater relief, may be obtained by using the bleacher warm rather than cold.

It is generally advised to dry the bleached print and resoak before inking, some workers even going so far as to state boldly that this is imperative. Such, however, is by no means the case; the writer has frequently made thoroughly satisfactory bromoil prints by inking immediately after the second fixing and washing. The difference of opinion hinges on the fact that the gelatin, by drying, acquires a greater power of *differential* swelling, thus increasing the scale of gradation which it is possible to secure in inking. But if high-keyed or other short-scale prints are desired, it may often be preferable to swell and ink directly after the second fixing and washing, rather than to dry and resoak. This is a point for individual judgment in each case.

Soaking.—Here again, no definite instructions can be given, since the degree of swelling required varies with the paper, the ink, and the result which is to be obtained. The temperature of the soaking water may vary from 65 to 150°F. (though it is not usually safe to go above 110°F.) and the time from 5 min. to 1 hr. Generally speaking, brief soaking in warm water tends to give more contrast than prolonged soaking at a lower temperature, and the longer the soaking at any given temperature, the greater the relief obtained with consequently greater resistance to the ink. Only experience furnishes a satisfactory guide on this point, though some indication may be got from feeling the clear margin of the print, which should be definitely slippery when rubbed between finger and thumb; if, however, the gelatin breaks down under this treatment, the water has been too hot, and the print must generally be thrown away.

In connection with the matter of soaking, the following point should be noted.

Other things being equal, the temperature of the soaking water controls the degree of swelling of the gelatin and consequently its resistance to the ink, *i.e.*, warm water produces greater swelling than cool. In some cases, it may not be feasible to complete inking at one sitting, in which case the print may be dried and resoaked for further inking. But a print cannot be swelled to a lesser degree the second time than was done at first; *i.e.*, if the first soaking water was used at 100°F., for example, and after drying the print is resoaked at 70°F., the second swelling will be as great as the first one. On the other hand, if the second swelling is done at 110°F., a greater relief will be obtained than at first, and any subsequent soaking at a lower temperature will produce the same relief as though done at 110°F. This is an important point to bear in mind, since obviously it furnishes an additional means of control and at the same time limits, to some extent, the possible variations in the matter of inking.

The Brushes.—Special brushes are required for the inking operation, these being made either of polecat or fitch hair or of hog bristles. The last is used chiefly for broad effects or for the first application of ink, the others for finer work or for smoothing out the rather coarse texture given by the bristle brush. It is advisable to have several brushes of different sizes, ranging from ½ to 1½ in. diameter, for different purposes; and they should be of the type in which the hairs are cut slanting and are domed, the square-cut brushes being less flexible in use and more likely to tear the gelatin.

The brushes must be thoroughly cleaned after use; the ink should not be allowed to dry in them. There are two ways of cleaning them. The method preferred by most workers is to wash them with gasoline or carbon tetrachloride (which is sold under the trade names of Carbona and Energine Non-inflammable Cleaning Fluid, as well as sundry others). The writer prefers to wash his brushes with Castile soap and water, for two reasons: (1) he feels that this is less likely to take the spring out of the hairs (this is a debatable point) and (2) frequent applications of water tend to keep the setting of the hairs more fully swelled, so that the brush is less likely to shed. It is true, however, that a brush cleaned with gasoline or carbon tetrachloride can be used again sooner than one washed in soap and water, since the latter usually takes several days to dry satisfactorily.

The brushes should be kept in cones of stout paper to preserve their shape and should be hung up, bristles down, when not in use, though this last is not imperative.

The Inks.—These are oily inks, much stiffer than ordinary printer's ink, and are sold especially for oil and bromoil work. The two best known are the Drem and the Sinclair, the former having a wax base, the latter an oil base. There does not seem to be any choice between them, so far as results are concerned; which to use is a question of individual preference.

Another ink which works as well as those mentioned (though differently) and is vastly cheaper than either of them is that sold by the makers of printer's inks under the name of Stiff Litho Ink. This is somewhat softer than the bromoil inks and requires greater swelling of the gelatin, but, if properly handled, it gives results equal in quality to the more expensive article. This matter of cost, however, is not important unless much work is to be done, since a 50-ct. tube of bromoil ink will give a great many prints, only a very small quantity being required for one inking.

The inks may be obtained in a number of different colors, though, as in gum printing, the rational worker will confine himself to neutral, warm, and cool blacks and various browns. Sinclair makes two warm-black inks, known, respectively, as Encre Machine and Encre Taille Douce, the latter being a relatively thin ink which may either be used alone or may be mixed with stiffer inks to thin them down for special purposes.

It is well to have some thinner available, but there is no need to buy the special bromoil thinner. A small bottle of linseed or olive oil is perfectly satisfactory, the amount taken up on a broom straw or a large pin being usually enough to add when the ink must be thinned.

Inking.—When the print has been swelled to the proper point, three or four lintless blotters, somewhat larger than the print, are dipped into water, drained, and laid on a sheet of glass or other smooth, approximately level surface. The print is then taken from the soaking water, drained, and laid face up on them. The purpose of this blotter pad is not, as most workers believe, to keep the print from drying out during inking; it has, indeed, little or no effect on the rate of drying of the gelatin, being used simply to furnish a soft support, so that the gelatin is less likely to be torn by the repeated impact of the brush.

The print is then surface-dried. This may be done by dabbing with a piece of chamois skin (or the soft-tanned leather which is sold under this name in the 5-and-10-cent stores) or with a wadded-up piece of soft well-washed linen or cotton cloth. Some writers on the subject say that it is imperative to surface-dry the print by dabbing and that it must never be wiped, but this is by no means true. A perfectly satisfactory way to dry it, which is much quicker than dabbing, is to wipe it lightly but firmly with a soft automobile windshield-wiper blade.

A small amount of the ink is then squeezed from the tube to a sheet of glass or other nonabsorbent surface (a dinner plate or the back of an old 8- by 10-in. glass negative is excellent) and is spread out thin with a palette knife. A quantity the size of a small pea will ink several 8- by 10-in. prints. The brush is pressed rather firmly into this film and is dabbed several times on a clean area of the glass to spread the ink evenly among the hairs. It is then applied to the print. If the preliminary work has been correctly done, it will be found that the ink adheres to the gelatin in proportion to the degree of tanning of the film, *i.e.*, it takes most freely in the shadows, less freely in the half tones, and least of all in the lights, thus with repeated application gradually building up the picture. But this building up must be slow and gradual; an attempt to work the print up rapidly is almost certain to defeat itself, except when done by a very experienced worker.

Up to this point the operations have been more or less mechanical, but this is where the fun begins.

There are almost as many different techniques of inking as there are bromoil workers. One man prefers to use a thin ink and to work rapidly; another uses a stiff ink, working slowly. One man inks the print all over, building up contrast by going over and over the entire surface; another inks up a small area to its final point, then passes on to another. The writer generally spends from $\frac{1}{2}$ to 1 hr. in inking a $6\frac{1}{2}$- by $8\frac{1}{2}$-in. print, but he knows a man who habitually inks a 10- by 12-in. print in 10 min. It depends on the worker's preference and on the results that he desires. In general, the writer feels that the best results are obtained through relatively slow inking, and he prefers to ink a landscape or similar subject all over at first, gradually building up the contrasts, but to ink the face of a portrait fully, working up the background and surroundings afterward. This, though, is a matter for each worker to decide for himself.

There are certain fundamental points to be remembered, as follows:

If the ink, at first application, shows a tendency to take on the clear margin of the print, the print has not been swelled enough for that particular ink, though a stiffer one may work all right.

If, later, the ink shows a marked tendency to take on the margin before the inking is completed, the print is drying out too rapidly.

The brush should not be held vertically over the print but at an angle of about 60°.

A slow, dabbing, legato brush action puts ink on the print. A staccato motion (called "hopping") takes ink off the print. This hopping is a trick of the hand which must be acquired by practice, but it can best be described as throwing the brush lightly at the print and catching it on the rebound.

There are wire holders sold for hopping, the idea being that by placing the brush at the end of a long wire, and, gripping the other end, a slight vibrating motion of the hand will produce the desired bouncing action of the brush. These should be carefully avoided, as they are by no means easy to handle, and have a marked inclination to cause tearing of the gelatin.

If the ink does not take sufficiently to give the desired depth, it may be thinned down with a trifle—and a very small trifle—of oil. On the other hand, if it takes too freely, it may be wiped off with a wet cloth and a stiffer ink used or the print swelled at a higher temperature.

A thin ink can be applied over a stiffer one; a stiff ink cannot be applied over a thinner one, unless the latter has been allowed to dry thoroughly.

If the print dries out too rapidly to finish it at one sitting, it may be allowed to dry completely, being subsequently resoaked and the inking being resumed. If this is done, it is well to allow time enough for not merely the gelatin but the ink to dry thoroughly, since, if the print is soaked again while the ink is soft, the latter is apt to run or smudge.

It is extremely difficult to work fast enough so that the gelatin will not dry out excessively if the work is done in the ordinary artificially heated house; a humidity of at least 65 per cent is desirable in the workroom, and even higher than this is better.

If a small amount of ink remains on the margins of the print when inking is completed, this may be cleaned off by wrapping a soft cloth around the finger, dipping it into water, and wiping firmly.

When the print is finished, it should be pinned up to dry in a vertical position, to minimize the settling of dust on the surface, and it is well to pin it by all four corners, to minimize its tendency to curl.

The worker must carefully avoid getting any water on the brush during inking, as this will cause white spots in the print. White spots may also result from tearing of the gelatin, if this has been excessively softened or if the brush is used too violently.

If the brush becomes clogged with ink during inking, so that the ink is deposited in black specks, it must be laid aside and a clean one taken up.

The brush should never be carried directly from the original pool of ink to the print, but should always be dabbed out on the area reserved for that purpose.

There is one caution which should be written in large letters and hung on the wall of every bromoil worker's workroom: "don't overdo." The flexibility of the medium is so great and the opportunities for personal expression are so wide that the temptation to play with the print overcomes a great many users of the process. Further, comparatively few photographers have studied nature with sufficient attention and thoroughness to know definitely how things look, the result of these two facts being that painfully false values are more often found in bromoil than in any other printing medium. This does not mean that the photographer should confine himself to the true values of nature, any more than the writer of fiction should confine himself to fact. Exaggeration is legitimate—in fact, necessary—in any art medium whatever, but the productions of the bromoil worker, like those of the fiction writer, should be convincing. They need not be true, but they must imperatively seem true. It is therefore necessary for the bromoil worker, more than for the user of any other medium except gum, to know how things should look, so that when he falsifies he may do it convincingly.

Degreasing.—Also called "defatting." The final appearance of an oil or a bromoil print shows a lustrous quality of surface, this characteristic being, of course, greater in a print which has rich, deep, blacks than in a higher keyed one. This luster may or may not be desirable; it adds richness to the shadows, but in some cases the dead matte quality of a platinum or Fresson print may seem preferable. When this matte surface is desired, it can be secured by allowing the print to dry until the ink is thoroughly hard, then rocking it for a few minutes in a tray of benzol (also called "benzene," but *not* "benzine," which has a different chemical composition). This benzol removes the oily or waxy base, leaving a pure matte surface which is very beautiful and which may be worked on to advantage with a carbon spotting pencil or—to lighten desired areas—with a soft pencil eraser. If the benzol is applied before the ink is hard, some or all of the ink will be removed, and the print will be ruined.

Transferring.—The advantages of transferring are that almost any texture of paper can be used for the final support; that multiple prints are readily made, thus permitting the emphasizing of desired areas or the combination of various colors; and that the final result has a fine matte quality of surface which is quite unlike that of the oil or bromoil print, even though the latter may have been degreased. So far as textural appearance is concerned, a bromoil transfer has the beautiful quality of a platinum print, though, of course, it lacks the exquisite delicacy of gradation of the latter.

Complete instructions for the transfer process would require more space than can be given here; workers who are interested in this medium are therefore referred to "Bromoil Printing and Transfer," by Emil Mayer, obtainable from The American Photographic Publishing Company, 353 Newbury Street, Boston, Mass. This is an admirable and very complete book, but it must not be received as absolute gospel, since it contains a few statements which are, to say the least, highly debatable; however, it may in general be relied upon.

In transferring, the bromoil print, as soon as it is fully inked, is placed in contact with a sheet of plain paper and is run through a suitable press, the ink which is on the bromoil thus being transferred to the plain paper. To secure the best results, the bromoil should be so strongly swelled by the use of warm water for soaking as to require a decidedly soft ink; the stiffer the ink, the less readily will it transfer. The bromoil print should be so inked as to have clean high lights (unless these are, for artistic reasons, to be veiled in the final result), and the shadows should be somewhat more heavily inked than they would be if transferring were not to be used; the ink usually transfers more completely in the high lights than in the shadows, therefore allowance must be made for this fact when inking.

Generally speaking, the most suitable paper is one which is tough but has a soft, moderately absorbent surface. One which is too highly surfaced may be rendered suitable by dipping it into water, placing it between lintless blotters, running it through the press, then transferring while it is still damp. If the paper is too absorbent, it should be given a coat of size made by mixing 60 gr. of laundry starch with 4 oz. of water and boiling, with constant stirring, until it is clear. The various charcoal and drawing papers can generally be used without any preparation.

There are two types of bromoil transfer press. In the first, the print and transfer paper are passed together between two rolls, one of which is operated by a crank, the other by the friction between it and the pack. In the second type, the print and paper are laid on a flat bed and passed under a roll, this roll being geared to the bed. The first type has the advantage that the regulation of pressure (an important point in transfer work) is accomplished by means of a setscrew that bears on the frame carrying the upper roller, whereas in the second type the necessary variations in pressure are secured by increasing or decreasing the number of blotters or of felt blankets in the pack, a much less convenient method. On the other hand, the second type of press eliminates the chance of the print "creeping" on the transfer paper, a circumstance which is often very troublesome when making multiple prints. There is also a variant of the first type, having the same advantages and disadvantages, in which the pack is laid on a flat bed and passed under a roll, the bed moving freely on rollers but being operated by friction alone. Which type of press is chosen is largely a matter of personal preference; in the writer's opinion, the first type is the better for single transfers, the second when multiple prints are to be made.

To transfer, two or three pieces of lintless blotter are laid on a sheet of pressboard, a ferrotype plate, or—in the case of a flat-bed press—on the bed. The transfer paper is then laid on these blotters and the inked print, face down, on the paper. One or two lintless blotters are laid on the print and over these, if necessary, one or more felt blankets such as are used by etching printers. This pack is then run through the press, using comparatively light pressure; it is not necessary or advisable to use so much pressure that great muscular effort is required to turn the crank. The high lights of the print will transfer most readily, and the print may be lifted at one end— taking care that it does not shift on the transfer paper—to see whether or not the shadows have transferred satisfactorily. It will probably be found that they have not, in which case the pressure may be slightly increased and the pack run through the press again. If the inking, the transfer paper, and the pressure are properly adjusted, a satisfactory transfer should be obtained this time, but if not, the operation may be repeated. Too much pressure, however, will probably cause the gelatin of the print to adhere to the transfer paper in the high lights, resulting in its tearing loose from the support. If sufficient depth is not readily obtained in the shadows, it is usually better to reink the bromoil and make a multiple transfer, rather than to try to transfer all the ink of the shadows by heavy pressure.

After transferring, the bromide print may be stripped away from the transfer paper, resoaked, and reinked, either for another transfer or for the purpose of adding another printing to the first transfer. Register marks should, of course, be made on the back of the bromoil and on the face of the transfer paper before the first transferring if multiple printing is contemplated. The possible number of printings to be had from one bromide print depends on the roughness or gentleness of the handling which it receives and varies widely—from, say, 5 to 25. The variation is purely mechanical and does not depend on any chemical action whatever.

After the transfer is perfectly dry, it may be worked on with pencil, stump, or a soft pencil eraser, to practically an unlimited extent.

In conclusion, we may say that the chief merits of oil and bromoil printing and of transfer lie in the extreme richness and depth of the shadows which may be obtained by this process and in the great flexibility of the medium. Its chief fault lies in the fact that it is not a truly photographic process. By this last, the writer does not mean to imply any objection to manual control of results in photography; he has no fault to find with such control, provided it is properly done. But the essential merit of photography, the characteristic in which it surpasses all other graphic mediums whatever, is the unrivaled delicacy with which it represents the gradations of light on surfaces, and this is precisely the point in which oil and bromoil and transfer are inferior to other photographic printing mediums. This, however, is a matter for individual choice; after all, the great desideratum is, not the production of a photograph, but the production of a picture, and each worker will select the medium which best expresses the idea that he has in mind, making use at times of the delicacy and precision of platinum and at other times and for other purposes employing the breadth of expression and the control of bromoil.

Bibliography

Sawyer: Gum, *Am. Phot.*, February, 1933, p. 82.

Hanson, R. E.: Landscape—Bromoil Printing, *Am. Phot.*, May, 1933, p. 257.

Lewis, C. E.: Simple Bromoil, *Am. Phot.*, February, 1934, p. 125.

Anderson, Paul L.: The Gum-pigment Process, *Camera*, April-September inclusive, 1935.

English, F. L.: Bromoil on Enlarging Paper, *Am. Phot.*, May, 1935, p. 290.

————: Bromoil on Ordinary Enlarging Paper, *Am. Phot.*, May, 1935, p. 290.

BAUXBAUM, E. C.: Carbro, A Neglected Pictorial Process, *Am. Phot.*, June, 1935, p. 366.

ANDERSON, PAUL L.: The Fresson Process, *Am. Phot.*, October, 1935, p. 597.

MORTENSEN, WILLIAM: Bromoil Transfer Factors in Inking, *Camera Craft*, June, 1936, p. 261.

Gum Bichromate, *Photo Art Monthly*, August, 1937, p. 394.

ANDERSON, PAUL L.: Hand-sensitized Platinum Paper, *Am. Phot.*, October, 1937, p. 685.

————: Hand-sensitized Palladium Paper, *Am. Phot.*, July, 1938, p. 457.

FLEMING, WILLIAM D.: Home Manufacture of Materials for Carbon Printing, *Am. Phot.*, August, 1938, p. 570.

PARTRINGTON, CHARLES H.: Bromoils and Transfers, *Defender Trade Bull.*, September, 1938.

HAMMOND, ARTHUR: Bromoil Printing for the Professional, *Defender Trade Bull.*, reprint.

MAYER, DR. EMIL: Bromoil Printing and Transfer, Am. Photographer's Pub.

CHAPTER XVII

DEFECTS IN NEGATIVES AND PRINTS

By Beverly Dudley

DEFECTS IN NEGATIVES

In the ideal case, defects in negatives do not occur; in practice defects of one kind or another occur with sufficient frequency that the perfect negative is somewhat of a rarity. It is seldom that the fault can be laid to the photosensitive materials. In nearly every case the defects could have been avoided by cleanliness and complete and proper attention to details in the exposing, developing, fixing, washing, and drying of the negative. The best assurance that perfect negatives will be obtained therefore is to take all precautions toward the prevention of occurrence of possible defects.

But even under the best of conditions, blemishes of one kind or another will occur, and, when they do, a corrective or remedial measure is desired so that the film or plate may be made to produce a satisfactory print. The prevention of defects in negatives and the correction of these defects so as to produce satisfactory prints are, consequently, two separate and distinct problems so far as the technique of manipulating negatives is concerned. It is not always possible to find a remedy for certain types of defects or blemishes in negatives, however, so that prevention of the cause of the defect is the only true "remedy." But whether or not a defective negative can be corrected through remedial measures, it is desirable to know the visual and photographic characteristics of the defect and the actual or probable cause, after which the method of prevention and remedy can often be determined. This chapter deals with such matters.

To make this chapter as useful as possible the various defects which may occur in negatives are classified into eleven groups depending (usually) upon the visual appearance of the defects as seen by transmitted or reflected light.[1] The 11 groups into which the defects are somewhat arbitrarily classified are:

Blotches, lines, and streaks (page 508)
Blurred negatives (page 512)
Distorted images (page 514)
Fogged negatives (page 517)
Incorrect contrast (page 520)
Incorrect density (page 522)
Markings and spots (page 523)
Mechanical or physical defects (page 529)
Scum, slime, and deposits (page 532)
Stains and discolorations (page 534)
Uneveness (page 537)

By determining into which of these 11 groups the defect falls and then further following up the individual listings given under this grouping, information on a specific defect may be obtained quickly.

[1] See also Defects in Development, p. 361.

Blotches, Lines, and Streaks

Here are listed those defects of negatives which appear on the film or plate as white, gray, or black (but otherwise usually uncolored) blotches, lines, and streaks. Blotches are considered to be usually irregular in shape and larger than those defects which might be classified as spots, which are treated elsewhere. The edges of lines are usually sharply defined; in the case of blotches and streaks, the edges may be sharply defined or not.

Abrasion Lines and Scratches.

1A. Distinguishing Characteristic.—Fine dark lines on the negative, frequently straight; often appearing in multiple in which case they are usually parallel.

2A. Cause.—Scratches caused by improper handling of the negative prior to development. Such lines are often caused by dirt or grit abrading the emulsion. Such grit may come from the interior of the camera, especially if a camera with large bellows is employed, from the tables or other apparatus in the darkroom, or even from unfiltered sources of water used for processing. (a) If the lines are parallel to the long side of the film, they may easily have been caused by dust, dirt, grit, or even small burs of metal in the roll film camera or in the film pack. Occasionally such lines may be caused by scratching the surface of the negative with the dark slide of the plate or film holder. (b) If the lines are at some random angle with respect to the edges of the negative or if they are not straight, they may have been caused prior to development or in the early stages of development by abrasion of one negative with another or with a gritty surface such as the darkroom table or developing tray.

3A. Prevention.—Absolute cleanliness is the best safeguard against such defects. Films or plates should be loaded into their holders shortly before being used, and should be inserted in the camera just before being exposed. The camera bellows should be cleaned periodically. Processing tanks and trays should be wiped free from dust and grit, and the water and other processing solutions should be filtered to free them from foreign matter. Boxes containing unexposed negatives should be stored on end to prevent pressure on top from bringing the emulsion into contact with other surfaces which might scratch.

4A. Remedy.—Scratches are difficult to remedy, especially if they occur on miniature negatives from which fairly large enlargements are to be made. Careful retouching may help in both contact and projection printing. The effects of scratches may sometimes be minimized or eliminated in projection printing by dipping the negative in glycerin after which it is placed between two sheets of glass before being placed in the enlarger. Air bubbles must, of course, be removed.

1B. Distinguishing Characteristic.—Fine, light lines on the negative, frequently straight; often appearing in multiple in which case they are usually parallel.

2B. Cause.—Abrasion subsequent to fixing, usually occurring after the negative is dried. In motion-picture and other miniature roll films, "cinching," *i.e.*, winding the film tighter when in roll form, especially where grit is present, is a frequent source of trouble.

3B. Prevention.—Cleanliness and proper handling of developed film is the best safeguard. Processed plates and negatives should be stored in a manner as to protect them from scratches. Glazine or cellophane envelopes are especially suitable for storing negatives. Roll film should be stored in dust-free boxes, should be handled as little as possible, and should never be "cinched." Motion-picture film should be reeled moderately tight with uniform pull during winding and should be stored in dust-free containers. It likewise should not be "cinched."

4B. Remedy.—(See 4A above.)

Branched Lines with Black Spots.—(See Static Markings, page 511.)
Brush Marks.

1. *Distinguishing Characteristic.*—Streaks and blotches resembling brush marks.

2. *Cause.*—Incorrectly compounded or exhausted developing solutions are the most probable causes for such streaks.

3. *Prevention.*—Use of correctly compounded developing solutions of full concentration for the negative being processed. Prepared developers are available which, when dissolved in the proper amount of water will give solutions of the proper strength and compounding. Certain developers for tray development are not recommended by the manufacturers for tank development when diluted.

4. *Remedy.*—Probably none other than retouching the negative or print.

Dark or Black Streaks or Blotches.

Streaks and blotches occur in several different forms, so that it is not possible to identify the cause of the defect quite so readily as in the case of certain other defects of negatives. For this reason, means for the prevention of the defect sometimes may be difficult to determine. The streaks and blotches may take various shapes, may be sharply defined with sharp edges, or may be poorly defined with edges of varying gradation.

1*A*. *Distinguishing Characteristic.*—Dark or black streaks or blotches, usually with shaded edges.

2*A*. *Cause.*—Uneven development which may be due to: (*a*) failure to immerse a portion of the film during development; (*b*) protection of a portion of the negative against development by intimate contact with another negative or the surface of the developing tank or tray; (*c*) failure to provide relative motion between negative, solution, and developing tray or tank.

3*A*. *Prevention.*—Immerse negative quickly and completely in developing solution. During the first few minutes of development, maintain relative motion between negative and developing solution by agitating solution, moving the negative in the solution, or rocking or tilting the developing tray or tank.

4*A*. *Remedy.*—Local intensification of the less dense portions of the negative may be employed to assist in bringing the negative to its proper and uniform density.

1*B*. *Distinguishing Characteristic.*—Irregular dark blotch, resembling splashed or spattered liquid.

2*B*. *Cause.*—Developer splashed on negative prior to development. The action of this splash of developing solution for a longer time than developer acting on the rest of the negative produces a darker spot, otherwise uncolored if nonstaining developer is used.

3*B*. *Prevention.*—Cleanliness and careful habits in developing. Do not permit negatives to lie around the darkroom, especially if unprotected.

4*B*. *Remedy.*—Local reduction may sometimes be used to advantage in this case (see chapter on Intensification and Reduction).

1*C*. *Distinguishing Characteristic.*—Dark or opaque streaks or blotches.

2*C*. *Cause.*—Dirty developing tray or tank or, perhaps, the use of fixing tray or tank for developing.

3*C*. *Prevention.*—Cleanliness and systematic habits in developing. Where a single tank is used for carrying out all processing of the negative, it may be advisable to run clear water through the tank between processing solutions. For single-tank processing, special care should be given to the matter of thoroughly cleaning the tank and plate or film supports after each use.

4*C*. *Remedy.*—Probably none, other than local reduction.

1*D. Distinguishing Characteristic.*—Dark or opaque streaks, often reasonably straight, with fairly sharp edges; sometimes accompanied by general fogging of the negative.

2*D. Cause.*—Light striking and fogging the plate or film. (*a*) If the edges of the negative are clear (transparent), fogging is indicated as having taken place within the camera. (*b*) If the entire negative is fogged, fogging may have taken place in the darkroom, while loading the negative material into the camera, or at any other point at which the entire negative may have been exposed to radiations. (*c*) Certain resinous woods, varnishes, composition slides, etc., have also been known to produce irregular streaks or blotches or fog.

3*D. Prevention.*—Determination of the cause of the streaks or fog will usually suggest suitable remedy. (*a*) Pinholes in the camera bellows, old and faulty film or plateholders, and improper insertion of the slide in the plateholder are frequently responsible for this type of defect. The slide should not be inserted in the film holder by one corner, as this opens the velvet light trap and permits fogging. The entire edge of the slide should be inserted all at once. (*b*) Handle negatives, especially the sensitive panchromatic emulsions, in complete darkness or in a safe light which has been proved to be safe for the type of emulsions used. Use changing bag, if necessary, when loading negatives into their holders. Exclude all light (and other radiations such as X ray, ultraviolet, infrared, and undue heat) from the darkroom during processing. (*c*) Airing the camera, plateholder, or other offending and fog-producing apparatus in fresh air and exposing it to sunlight has sometimes been found helpful. Painting the interior of the metal and wood parts of the camera with a weak solution of bichloride of platinum is also useful. Change from composition to metal plate slides is advantageous in some cases.

4*D. Remedy.*—General and local reduction may have some remedial effects.

Dark Straight Lines.

1. *Distinguishing Characteristics.*—Dark straight lines, starting from one edge of dark portions of the negative (high lights) and running in one direction in a straight line away from the high light.

2. *Cause.*—Insufficient agitation of the developing solution, permitting silver to be deposited on the emulsion below the point where the greatest deposit of silver occurs —the high lights. In motion-picture development, or in other processes in which the film is continuously moved through the developing solution in a steady continuous motion, this defect is caused by the fact that the first part of the film is acted upon by fresh developer; later portions are acted on by more or less exhausted developer.

3. *Prevention.*—Agitation of the developing solution, or of the negative in the developer.

4. *Remedy.*—Local reduction of the negative, if carefully carried out, may help.

Fan-shaped Lines.—(See Static Markings, page 511.)
Forked Lines Resembling Lightning.—(See Static Markings, page 511.)
Light or Transparent Streaks or Blotches.

As in the case of dark streaks or blotches, those which are transparent or lighter than the mean density of the negative may have various shapes and may have poorly or sharply defined edges.

1*A. Distinguishing Characteristics.*—Light streak, sharply defined or moderately defined at edges.

2*A. Cause.*—Obstruction before the lens or in the camera between lens and negative which did not permit light to act on the negative. The more sharply defined the streak is, the more likely it is that the obstruction was close to the negative.

3*A*. *Prevention.*—Determining and removing the cause of light obstruction. A common source of trouble by beginners in photography is that of placing their fingers in front of the lens, thereby obstructing light from part of the desired image. Improperly folded bellows may sometimes cut off light from edges of negative.

4*A*. *Remedy.*—None.

1*B*. *Distinguishing Characteristic.*—Irregular streaks.

2*B*. *Cause.*—Prevention of uniform development of the negative. Sometimes this may be caused by oil or grease from the fingers which prevents action by the developer. If the negative is washed in water before developing, especially in cold water, certain areas which are resistant to the action of the developer may be produced in the washing.

3*B*. *Prevention.*—If due to oil or grease, cleanliness and systematic habits in processing will prevent recurrences of this defect. If due to washing prior to development (such washing is of much assistance in preventing the formation of air bells during development), the wash water should be at the same temperature as the other processing solutions, preferably between 60 and 70°F.

4*B*. *Remedy.*—Probably none if due to grease. If due to resistant areas set up by wash water, local intensification may be useful.

1*C*. *Distinguishing Characteristics.*—Light area on negative appearing as (*a*) a smudge or (*b*) generally approximately circular with irregular, sharply defined edges.

2*C*. *Cause.*—Sodium thiosulphite coming in contact with negative before development. In (*a*) the hypo is transferred to the negative by hypo-stained fingers, whereas in (*b*) the hypo appears to have been splashed on the negative.

3*C*. *Prevention.*—Cleanliness and careful habits in developing. Do not permit unprotected negatives to lie around the darkroom where they may be subjected to contamination.

4*C*. *Remedy.*—Local intensification may sometimes be found useful.

Static Lines and Markings.

1. *Distinguishing Characteristics.*—Dark spots with diffused edges singly or in combination with thin, dark, irregular, forked or branched wavy lines. Static markings have been classified by Crabtree and Ives as follows: (*a*) small black spots with diffused edges similar to certain types of moisture spots or spots caused by chemical dust; (*b*) black spots with radiating branches; (*c*) treelike markings; (*d*) fan-shaped markings; and (*e*) combinations of dots, branches, and fans.

2. *Cause.*—These marks are caused by static electrical charges accumulating on the negative. The charges may accumulate within the camera, during processing, or in handling the dry film. In the case of rolled motion-picture film, reeling or unreeling the film during cold, dry weather may produce appreciable static. A common source of camera static is that in which the negatives in film packs or roll films slide over a velvet protected corner or through a light trap.

3. *Prevention.*—Camera static may be prevented by removing all sources of friction between the film and the camera and by making all parts of the camera of electrically conducting material so far as this is possible. Winding the roll film slowly, or pulling through an exposed film in film packs very slowly, will help diminish the formation of static charges on the film. Since static is most easily formed with dry substances, rehumidifying the film, especially if motion-picture reel, will tend to diminish formation of static. Conducting the combustion products of an alcohol lamp into the camera chamber is also given as a method of prevention by Crabtree and Ives. In the case of motion-picture processing, static produced in the laboratory processing may be discharged by passing the film through tinsel or tin foil playing over both surfaces

of the film, the tinsel being grounded.   In this case care should be taken to see that scratches are not produced by this process.

  4. *Remedy.*—None.

Treelike Lines.—(See Static Lines and Markings, above.)

BLURRED NEGATIVES

In the majority of cases, blurred negatives are the result of improper technique in the focusing or taking of the picture, of excess relative motion between the subject and camera for the shutter speed used, unsteadiness in holding the camera, etc., rather than defects in the negative per se as a result of processing.

Blurred Negatives.

  1*A. Distinguishing Characteristic.*—Part of image blurred; objects nearer or farther than main point of interest may be sharp, or not.

  2*A. Cause.*—(*a*) Camera not correctly focused or (*b*) too great an aperture and consequently too small depth of focus for the purpose.

  3*A. Prevention.*—(*a*) Proper focusing of camera, making sure that the image of the principal part of the picture is in sharpest focus.   With many small hand cameras and especially box cameras no focusing is possible, and in this case proper results can be obtained only with the subject not too close to the camera.   With many hand cameras, focusing is accomplished by turning the front element of the lens system or by increasing the distance between lens and negative with slide or rack and pinion arrangement. In such cases suitable distance markings are given on the lens mount or on a scale attached to the camera bed, dependence being placed on the judgment of the photographer to estimate distances correctly.   For such cases, a distance meter may be useful.   If a ground-glass back is provided, still subjects may be focused by means of this back; distances for moving subjects will have to be estimated.   Graflex and reflex cameras are usually provided with a focusing arrangement which permits the photographer to view the subject and make focusing adjustments at least up to the time of making the picture.   Many high-grade miniature cameras are provided with an optical distance meter which is also coupled to the lens system, so that setting the range finder automatically focuses the camera lens.   (*b*) Insufficient depth of focus may be prevented by using a smaller aperture or *f*-stop or, if perspective considerations permit, this result may be minimized by using a lens of shorter focal length.

  4*A. Remedy.*—None.

  1*B. Distinguishing Characteristic.*—Image completely blurred, although properly focused.

  2*B. Cause.*—Camera was moved during the exposure.

  3*B. Prevention.*—Hold camera steady during exposure.   If the camera is held in the hands, an exposure of about $\frac{1}{25}$ sec. is the longest that many people can make without running the risk of blurring.   For exposures longer than this, a tripod support for the camera will be found useful or even necessary.

  4*B. Remedy.*—None.

  1*C. Distinguishing Characteristic.*—Background blurred, but image of moving object in foreground reasonably sharp.

  2*C. Cause.*—In order to obtain sharp image of moving object, camera has been moved to follow it.   The background has been sacrificed to obtain sharp image of moving object.   Such results are often obtained in photographing fast-moving objects.

  3*C. Prevention.*—This type of blur may be eliminated or at least minimized by (*a*) photographing the moving object from a greater distance so that the relative motion is less apparent, (*b*) photographing the subject so as to obtain a more nearly "head on" view, (c) using a shorter exposure so as better to arrest the relative motion. In the latter case a larger aperture or a faster emulsion may be required to obtain the proper exposure with the shorter shutter speed.

4C. *Remedy.*—None.

1D. *Distinguishing Characteristic.*—Some planes of the image in sharp focus; other planes out of focus.

2D. *Cause.*—Insufficient depth of focus.

3D. *Prevention.*—Depth of focus may be increased by using a smaller aperture in taking the picture. For a given aperture, greater depth of focus will be obtained with a lens of short focal length rather than one of long focal length, but perspective considerations must be taken into account in selecting a lens of proper focal length.

4D. *Remedy.*—None.

1E. *Distinguishing Characteristic.*—Image generally indistinct.

2E. *Cause.*—A negative lacking in sparkle, snap, or contrast may be due to (a) a dirty lens in the camera, (b) flat lighting or lack of contrast in the original subject, (c) insufficient contrast due to insufficient development, or (d), although relatively rare, fog or moisture condensing on the lens of the camera. This latter condition is especially prevalent if the lens is suddenly removed from a cold dry atmosphere to a warm moist atmosphere, in which case moisture condenses on the lens until the lens reaches temperature equilibrium with its surroundings.

3E. *Prevention.*—(a) Cleanliness is the only answer here. The lens should be kept clean. Dust should be removed with a camel's-hair brush. A dirty lens may be cleaned with soft lens tissue, after the lens has been breathed upon so as to condense moisture upon it. Water, alcohol, or other liquids should not be used, nor should linty or coarse cloth be used in wiping the lens. (b) Flat lighting or lack of contrast in the original subject often cannot be prevented, especially when making outdoor pictures on cloudy days. (c) Contrast can be increased (up to its limiting value) only by proper exposure and development. Contrast depends upon the exposure range, but for flat subjects with little contrast the apparent contrast may be increased by fairly long development of the negative and then printing on a contrasty grade of paper. (d) Do not subject the lens to sudden changes in temperature or humidity. If this cannot be avoided, allow the lens to reach equilibrium conditions with its surrounding atmosphere before making exposures.

4E. *Remedy.*—Printing a flat negative on a contrasty grade of printing paper is perhaps the best remedy for improving contrast. No remedy for other causes.

1F. *Distinguishing Characteristic.*—Parts of film out of focus or indistinct, with remainder of film satisfactorily sharp. Sometimes the images may also be somewhat wavy.

2F. *Cause.*—Film was buckled in film holder during exposure; not perfectly flat.

3F. *Prevention.*—Maintaining the film at uniform temperature, allowing film to reach equilibrium temperature with its surroundings before taking picture if it has been subjected to sudden temperature changes, and loading the film in its holder just prior to exposure are useful in minimizing this type of defect. Buckling of film occurs much more frequently with large than with small negatives. The film holders should be inspected to see that they hold the film properly flat. In extreme cases, it may be necessary to use plates rather than film.

4F. *Remedy.*—None, although retouching may be used in many cases to counteract the undesired fuzziness due to buckling.

Multiple Images.

1. *Distinguishing Characteristic.*—Multiple images appearing superimposed on the same negative.

2. *Cause.*—Exposure of the same film more than once.

3. *Prevention.*—Certain modern miniature cameras cannot be operated until the roll film has been wound so as to have a new frame in place. Thus, double exposure is automatically prevented. For other roll-film cameras, turn the roll film until a new (unexposed) portion of the film is in place immediately after each exposure. For film-pack cameras, pull the exposed negative after each exposure to the back of the pack with the paper tab provided for that purpose. For plate cameras, remove exposed plates from the cameras immediately after exposure, and mark the holders to indicate plate has been exposed.

4. *Remedy.*—None.

DISTORTED IMAGES ON NEGATIVES

Distorted images on negatives, like blurred negatives, are to be regarded more correctly, as a general rule, as being due to defects in the manufacture, application, or use of the optical system of the camera rather than negative defects per se. The discussion of distorted images included here is intended as an aid to the photographer in perfecting his technique and in locating possible trouble in or improper use of his equipment.

Distortion Due to Buckling of Negative.

1. *Distinguishing Characteristic.*—Part of negative out of focus and fuzzy, although remainder of negative may be quite satisfactory.

2. *Cause.*—Buckling of film in the plateholder before or during exposure.

3. *Prevention.*—Care in inserting film in film holder and making sure that the film is held perfectly flat; inserting film in camera just prior to exposure; maintaining film at constant temperature and humidity are effective aids in minimizing buckling. Buckling is greater with large film than with small films. In extreme cases, plates rather than films may be required.

4. *Remedy.*—None, aside from retouching negative.

Distortions Due to Camera Adjustments.

1. *Distinguishing Characteristic.*—There are several possible distinguishing characteristics for distortions due to camera adjustments or misadjustments. The most common and most important of these include: (a) too much of subject included in the picture; (b) insufficient amount of subject included in the picture with, perhaps, part of desired subject not included; (c) improper perspective; (d) vertical lines converging; (e) too much or too little foreground included; (f) slight lateral distortion.

2. *Cause.*—Generally the defects mentioned above are caused by improperly using the camera adjustments, or may result because the camera is not provided with adjustments, which are required for the type of work being undertaken and which would enable the photographer to prevent these distortions. More specifically, the causes may be given, respectively, as follows: (a) If the perspective is satisfactory but the image is too small, the difficulty was that the camera was too far removed from the desired subject. If the perspective is bad, this may mean that a lens of too short focal length or too wide an angle of view was used. Bad perspective may also be due to viewing the picture from incorrect distance, when either a contact print or an enlargement is made. (b) This defect may be the reverse of (a) or may be due to improperly aiming the camera at the desired subject. If the image is of proper perspective and size but the subject is not entirely included in the picture, faulty aiming of the camera is indicated. While such results can always be avoided with view cameras, cameras provided with precise view finders corrected for parallax, and single-lens reflex cameras, results of the type mentioned are not infrequently encountered with less expensive

cameras having view finders at the edge of the camera and which are not corrected for parallax. The condition will be most aggravated in photographing subjects near the camera. If the perspective is poor, a lens of too long a focal length may have been used for the conditions under which the print is to be viewed. If the perspective is correct but the full subject is not included in the picture, the camera was placed too close to the subject. The matter of perspective depends not only on the focal length of the lens used, but also on the degree of enlargement and the normal viewing distance of the print. (c) Improper perspective may be due to using lens of improper focal length, improperly viewing the picture, or enlarging the picture so that when viewed in the normal manner it does not present proper perspective. (d) Convergence of vertical lines is often caused by pointing the camera up at an angle in order to include the top of the desired subject. This type of distortion is frequently encountered in architectural photography where its effects are also most objectionable. (e) Too much foreground results from pointing the camera down or, more usually, by not properly raising the rising and falling front. Too little foreground results from the reverse condition. (f) Lateral distortion, especially objectionable in portraiture, often results from attempting to photograph a long object at an oblique angle. Relatively few view cameras are provided with lateral swing backs, use of which would prevent this defect.

3. *Prevention.*—(a) Bringing the camera closer to the subject and using lens of proper focal length will assist in preventing these distortions. The focal length of the lens should be approximately equal to the diagonal of the negative for good perspective. (b) Faulty pointing of the camera may be prevented by using a ground-glass back for focusing. For the case of small cameras provided with a reflecting view finder or wire iconoscope having no provision for correcting parallax, it is frequently possible to obtain better results by focusing as well as possible with the view finder and then correcting for parallax by turning the camera slightly about a vertical axis through the lens. Some experience is required to obtain the proper degree of shift, although judgment of the proper shift is aided by sighting along the camera as close as possible along the optical axis. A lens of shorter focal length or of wider angle will also allow more of the subject to be included on the negative, although perspective considerations must be given attention. Otherwise the camera should be removed farther from the subject. (c) For prevention of incorrect perspective, see pages 26 and 94. (d) Convergence of vertical lines can be prevented by making use of the swing back. Swinging front, and rising front, if these adjustments are provided on the camera. The back of the camera (or more strictly, the plane of the negative) should always be vertical when making architectural photographs, to prevent distortions. The reason for this is one of convention and in having become accustomed to artists' drawings, rather than one of intrinsic correctness. It is also preferable that the axis of the lens be horizontal when normal architectural subjects are photographed. The tops of tall buildings may then be included by raising the rising front, and if this adjustment is insufficient, by tilting the bed of the camera upward to further raise the lens with respect to the negative. (e) By raising the rising front, less foreground is included; by lowering the front, more foreground may be included. (f) Lateral distortion may be prevented or minimized by making use of the vertical tilt back, if the camera is provided with this adjustment.

4. *Remedy.*—In general, there is no remedy for negatives containing the distortion defects enumerated above, except retouching of the negative, or making a new photograph under more desirable and correct conditions. In certain cases some forms of distortion may be corrected or minimized in projection printing by tilting the bed of the enlarger to compensate for distortion in the print. But while satisfactory in some cases, such corrective measures are inferior to the results which might be obtained from a negative originally without distortion.

Distortion Due to Film Shrinkage.

1. *Distinguishing Characteristics.*—Shrinkage of film so that negative is not a properly scaled image of the subject.

2. *Cause.*—Swelling, expanding, and contraction of gelatin.

3. *Prevention.*—Some swelling of the gelatin always takes place when it is wet. Distortions to film expansion or contraction can be minimized by processing in solutions, all of which are at the same temperature. In copying or process work where slight distortions due to shrinkage are most serious, plates will be found preferable to film.

4. *Remedy.*—None.

Distortion Due to Improper Monochromatic Rendition of Color.

1. *Distinguishing Characteristic.*—In monochromatic photography, the brightness of the gray image on the negative is not inversely proportional to the brilliance of the colored image as evaluated by the human eye. This is sometimes difficult to determine in the negative but is usually apparent in a print, since the monochromatic rendition of colors does not bear a close direct relation to the visual brilliance of the corresponding part of the subject.

2. *Cause.*—This defect may be due to any one or more of the following causes: (a) use of orthonon (noncolor sensitive) or orthochromatic materials, which are deficient in sensitivity for some regions of the visible spectrum; (b) failure to use proper light filters, or failure to use any filters whatsoever; (c) use of light source having such spectral-energy distribution as to produce incorrect or undesired results with the type of negative emulsion and filter employed. For a more complete discussion of this subject, see chapter on Light Filters, page 312.

3. *Prevention.*—The proper use of the correct type of negative emulsion, filter, and light source to give the desired result.

4. *Remedy.*—None, aside from retouching the negative or prints made from it.

Distortions Due to Lenses.

1. *Distinguishing Characteristic.*—When the distortions of an image on the negative are due to distortions produced by the lens system, a wide variety of distinguishing characteristics may be observed, depending upon the lens defect, or the improper use and application of the optical system of the camera. The most common distinguishing characteristics (although hardly common even in inexpensive cameras of good manufacture) are (a) same image does not appear identical when taken under conditions identical in all respects except that the lens (and consequently the camera) is rotated 90° about its central or optical axis; (b) colored images are lacking in detail and sharpness and are difficult to focus sharply on ground glass, although sharp focusing may be obtained with monochromatic subjects; (c) images are curved, so as to give effect of barrel or pincushion distortion which is especially objectionable when photographing architectural subjects or copying line drawings; (d) distortion of bright point into a pear-shaped image; (e) center of picture in focus, but outer edge out of focus, or vice versa; (f) image cannot be sharply focused under any conditions with either colored or monochromatic subject, and consequently fuzzy and unsharp negatives result; (g) unequal illumination of field; (h) negative shows image in a circle, usually with diffused edges.

2. *Cause.*—These distortions are due, respectively, to: (a) astigmatism, (b) chromatic aberrations, (c) curvilinear distortion, (d) coma, (e) curvature of field, (f) spherical aberrations or perhaps scratches in the lens, (g) probably due to lens

being off center from center of camera, and (*h*) using lens which will not cover the entire negative area.

3. *Prevention.*—Since these defects are inherent in the lens system itself, there is usually nothing that the photographer can do which will prevent or correct these distortions without changing his lens system. Every lens contains some defects and distortions although in most cameras these have been reduced to the point where they are of no consequence for the ordinary run of work. In certain classes of work, where high precision, sharp definition, and absolute freedom from distortion are required, the best possible lenses will be required. Under (*g*) the photographer may be able to align the lens and camera so as to produce even illumination if the defect is caused simply by improper alignment. In (*h*) the difficulty may be due to use of a lens of insufficient covering power for the plate or film used, rather than an inherent lens defect. Replacing by lens of greater covering power, or using a smaller plate which the lens will cover, will correct this trouble.

4. *Remedy.*—The remedy for a defective optical system in a camera consists in obtaining another but satisfactory lens system, or returning the defective lens to the manufacturer for whatever grinding, polishing, or other corrections may be required. Items (*g*) and (*h*) may be corrected by the photographer as enumerated under Prevention.

Fogged Negatives

Fog may be defined as a uniform darkening of the negative due to a deposit of silver which does not form a part of the image and which may partially or completely obliterate the image. Fog tends to increase the density and decrease the contrast of the negative. Fog may be general, in which case the entire negative is more or less uniformly darkened, or it may be local, in which case only a part of the negative is darker than it should be.

Aerial Fog.

1. *Distinguishing Characteristic.*—General veiling of the negative or portions of the negative exposed to air during development.

2. *Cause.*—Exposure to air during development. The tendency toward aerial fog is especially marked with certain freshly prepared developers or by developers containing formaldehyde. Aerial fog is produced only with hydroquinone under ordinary processing conditions, but developers such as pyro, glycine, and para-aminophenol produce aerial fog in the presence of traces of copper or tin salts. Even slight traces of salts of copper produce decided aerial fog. Fogging increases as the proportion of alkali and hydroquinine is increased in metal-hydroquinine developers. It is especially bad in some methods of processing motion-picture film.

3. *Prevention.*—Aerial fog may be reduced by the use of desensitizers, by the addition of sulphite or bromide to the developer, or by the use of partially oxidized developers. Under ordinary conditions, the addition of 2 parts of pinakrytol green per 1,000,000 parts of developer will prevent aerial fog. A predevelopment bath of 1 part of pinakryptol green to 25,000 parts of water is also effective in preventing aerial fog.

4. *Remedy.*—Sometimes reduction may be resorted to, but frequently there is no remedy.

Dichroic Fog.

1. *Distinguishing Characteristic.*—Two-color fog which appears as green or reddish-green sheen by reflected light and red by transmitted light.

2. *Cause.*—This type of fog is produced by a deposit of finely divided particles of silver, the size of the particles determining the color as seen by transmitted light. I

may, therefore, be produced wherever free silver is encountered such as in the developing or fixing baths. In development, dichroic fog is formed in the presence of some silver bromide solvent such as ammonia, an excess of sulphite or alkali, or hypo. Thus, in single-tank processing, residue of hypo in the tank may produce dichroic fog the next time development is done. If the fixing bath is not acid, or if it is exhausted or contains an excess of dissolved silver, dichroic fog may be produced in the fixing process.

3. *Prevention.*—Dichroic fog may be prevented from being produced in the developer by adding lead acetate to the developer or cleaning the processing system with a hot sodium hypochlorite solution. This procedure prevents the formation of sulphide accumulations. The addition of 1.5 g. of potassium iodide per liter of developer will tend to decrease formation of fog by converting dissolved silver bromide into relatively insoluble silver iodide. In the fixing bath, dichroic fog may be prevented by maintaining the bath at its normal acidity and by using an intermediate bath of clear water between developing and fixing so as to diminish the amount of developer carried over into the hypo. Hardening the gelatin before development also tends to reduce tendency for the formation of dichroic fog.

4. *Remedy.*—Dichroic fog may be removed by rinsing the negative in a solution of 0.5 gr. of potassium permanganate ($KMnO_4$) to each ounce of water until the fog has disappeared. The brown stain of manganese oxide which forms during this rinse may be removed by washing the negative in a 5 per cent solution of potassium metabisulphite or of sodium bisulphite.

Chemical Fog.—(See Development Fog.)
Development Fog.

1. *Distinguishing Characteristic.*—General or local veiling of image due to deposit of silver on the negative.

2. *Cause.*—Practically all fogging troubles not directly caused by light are grouped together under the general classification of chemical fog or development fog. Development fog may result from any number of factors (some of which are treated separately in this section) and includes certain types of fog which are likewise treated elsewhere in this section. Thus development or chemical fog may be due to (a) the nature of the negative emulsion, (b) the factory processing of the emulsion (emulsion fog), (c) the age and past history of the negative, (d) the nature of the developer, (e) impurities in the developer, (f) the time of development processing, (g) the temperature of development processing, (h) the presence of metallic salts in the developer, (i) the presence of sodium sulphide in the developer, (j) the general processing during development which may give rise to aerial fog, or (k) the nature and intensity of the darkroom illumination, for example.

3. *Prevention.*—The manner of preventing the various types of development or chemical fog depends upon the specific cause of the fog. According to the classification given above, the following preventive measures have been found useful.

a. The amount of fogging of a negative is proportional to the speed of the negative or its sensitivity to light. Consequently, most difficulty from fogging may usually be expected from fast panchromatic emulsions, with minimum fogging resulting when slow noncolor-sensitive emulsions are used. Some fog always occurs, although under proper conditions this may usually be neglected for practical purposes.

b. Emulsion fog results from the presence of developable grains of silver halide in the unexposed portions of the emulsion. Emulsion fog is usually greater in fast emulsions than in slow emulsions and may be produced in the process of manufacture by contact with fogging materials or by deterioration with age.

c. During storage, emulsions may show a tendency to fog. This tendency is aggravated in the presence of moisture and heat and in the presence of such gases and vapors as hydrogen sulphide, coal gas, and fumes of turpentine and benzol. Consequently, preventive measures should be those which will protect the stored negative material from exposure to chemicals, gases, fumes, light, undue heat, and other radiations. Keep on hand only such material as will meet normal demands for negative material.

d. When properly used, none of the common developers produce sufficient fog to be serious in practical photography, except possibly in certain kinds of scientific work. Fresh and properly compounded developers are the best preventive against fog produced by the developer itself. The developer should be free from impurities, especially those of metallic salts, and should be used at the normal recommended temperature. This will ordinarily be between 60 and 70°F.

e. Impurities in the developer may produce appreciable fogging. Excess of sulphite or the presence of metallic salts in the developer or the metals themselves are a relatively common source of fog. The only preventive is to use properly compounded developers of chemical purity and to ascertain that impurities do not contaminate the developing solution. Traces of metals or metallic salts may easily come from metallic developing tanks.

f. The amount of fog is roughly proportional to the time of development, so that, so far as fog is concerned, it is inadvisable to prolong development beyond the normal time recommended by the manufacturer of the photosensitive material.

g. Development, as practically all chemical reactions, proceeds at a more rapid rate at high than at low temperatures. Consequently the tendency toward fog increases as the temperature of the developer is increased. For normal processing, the usual recommendation of manufacturers is that the developer temperature should not exceed 70°F. or 21°C.

h. The presence of metallic salts or of metals in the developers is to be avoided.

i. The presence of excess sulphite in the developer should be avoided.

j. Since aerial fog results from exposure of the wet negative to the air during development, this type of fog may be reduced or eliminated by keeping the negative material completely submerged in solution during development.

k. Too intense a darkroom light or the wrong type of safe-light filter for the type of emulsion being processed may result in light fog or in partial or complete reversal of the image during development. The darkroom safe light should (1) pass only those wavelengths for which the negative is insensitive or (2), in the case of panchromatic emulsions, should transmit freely only in the region for which the human eye is most sensitive at low light intensities. The recommendations of the manufacturer may be taken for the type of safe-light filter to use with a given emulsion. Manufacturer's recommendations concerning the amount of light to use may be taken as a general guide, but practical tests will indicate whether or not any particular situation produces fogging.

Generally speaking, development or chemical fog may be eliminated or minimized by (1) using fresh, pure, and properly compounded developers, (2) developing for the correct time and at the correct temperature, (3) keeping the negative completely submerged in developer, (4) developing in absolute darkness or with a safe light which has been proved satisfactory.

4. *Remedy.*—General reduction of the negative may sometimes be helpful.

Emulsion Fog.

1. *Distinguishing Characteristic.*—General veil of fog on negative not accounted for by light or chemical fog.

2. *Cause.*—Presence of developable grains of silver halide in the unexposed portions of the negative. Probably due to (*a*) contact of negative with fogging materials, (*b*) deterioration of negative material with age, or (*c*) as a result of manufacturing operations.

3. *Prevention.*—(*a*) Store so as to be free from light, undue heat, or other radiations or from gases and fumes. (*b*) Use materials within the expiration date established by the manufacturer. Store in cool, dry atmosphere. (*c*) There is no remedy in this case, although the amount of emulsion fog due to manufacturing processes should never be appreciable with products made by a reliable concern.

Light Fog.

General fog may be produced by light as well as by chemical action. Light fog is the more common type of fog, especially if a properly compounded, fresh developer of chemical purity is used,

1. *Distinguishing Characteristics.*—General fog or darkening of the negative; also local fog which may appear as streaks, often with straight edges.

2. *Cause.*—In general light fog is caused by light striking the negative prior to fixation in the hypo bath. The manner in which the light may strike the photosensitive material varies considerably, but among the possibilities may be mentioned: (*a*) fog produced within the camera due to imperfect, old, or loose construction which permits passage of light through various parts or through joints; (*b*) by the improper use of camera equipment, such as inserting the slide of the plateholder by one corner instead of by the entire edge; (*c*) use of camera and accessory fittings not intended to be used together, such as incorrectly fitting plateholders; (*d*) loading or unloading the photosensitive material in light which is too strong; (*e*) by using too strong a safe light in the darkroom or a safe light with filter unsuited for the emulsion or by permitting the negative to be exposed too long to the darkroom lamp; (*f*) by chemical emanations from the finish of camera parts.

3. *Prevention.*—In general, the best prevention for light fog is to handle and process the photosensitive material in sufficiently subdued light (or in the case of panchromatic emulsions, in complete darkness), so that light radiations can produce no fog. Preventive measures for items (*a*) to (*e*) above will suggest themselves when the true cause of the fog has been determined. In the case of (*f*), exposure of camera parts to strong sunlight and painting interior of the camera parts with a weak solution of potassium permanganate have been found helpful.

4. *Remedy.*—Reduction may sometimes be useful in remedying general fog.

Local Fog.

1. *Distinguishing Characteristic.*—Fog or uniform darkening of parts of the negative in a manner having no relation to the photographed image.

2. *Cause.*—Same as Light Fog (see above).

3. *Prevention.*—Same as Light Fog; see above. A frequent cause for local light fog is pinholes in the bellows of the camera. In this case, the pinholes may be detected by placing a lighted electric lamp inside the bellows, and watching for the spots of light in a darkened room. The pinholes may be repaired by cementing a piece of thin black opaque leather or cloth over the hole.

4. *Remedy.*—Local reduction of the more dense portions of the negative may sometimes be helpful.

INCORRECT CONTRAST

It is sometimes difficult for the beginner to distinguish between incorrect density and incorrect contrast in negatives, especially since a given negative may possess both defects simultaneously. For this reason it is suggested that the section following, *i.e.*, Incorrect Density, be read in conjunction with this one if any doubt exists as to the proper interpretation of density and contrast. It is also suggested that reference be made to the chapter on Photographic Sensitometry, where the matter of proper exposure and rendition of tones in negatives is taken up in some detail.

Incorrect contrast is usually caused by incorrect development if it may be assumed that the original subject had satisfactory contrast and was correctly lighted.

Contrasty Negatives.

1*A*. *Distinguishing Characteristic.*—Shadows lack detail and other tones are too contrasty.

2*A*. *Cause.*—Underexposure and overdevelopment. Overdevelopment may have been caused by using too strong a developer, developing too long a time, or developing at too high a temperature.

3*A*. *Prevention.*—Give longer exposure and less development. Use developer of proper strength at proper temperature for proper time.

4*A*. *Remedy.*—Excessive contrast can be corrected by printing on a soft-grade or flat printing paper. No remedy for lack of detail in shadows.

1*B*. *Distinguishing Characteristic.*—Detail in all tones, but all tones too contrasty.

2*B*. *Cause.*—Proper exposure but overdevelopment.

3*B*. *Prevention.*—Develop for proper time and at proper temperature.

4*B*. *Remedy.*—Printing on soft grade of paper will correct contrast. Since the negative is correctly exposed, full correction can be made in printing.

1*C*. *Distinguishing Characteristic.*—High lights lack detail; other tones too contrasty.

2*C*. *Cause.*—Overexposure and overdevelopment.

3*C*. *Prevention.*—Less exposure and less development.

4*C*. *Remedy.*—Printing on soft grade of paper will correct for excessive contrast. No remedy for loss of detail in high lights.

Drying Down.

1. *Distinguishing Characteristic.*—Negative appears properly exposed and developed when wet, but contrasty and overexposed in the high lights after being dried.

2. *Cause.*—Slow drying of negative at high temperature and high humidity.

3. *Prevention.*—The temperature at which drying takes place should usually not exceed 95°F. unless the negative is hardened. Best drying is obtained with the relative humidity between 40 and 70 per cent.

4. *Remedy.*—Contrast may be lessened in printing by printing on a soft or flat paper. No remedy if high-light detail is lacking because of overexposure.

Flat Negatives.

1*A*. *Distinguishing Characteristic.*—Shadows lack detail and the other tones are too flat and lacking in contrast.

2*A*. *Cause.*—Underexposure as indicated by lack of shadow detail; underdevelopment as indicated by lack of contrast.

3*A*. *Prevention.*—Proper exposure and proper development. A good exposure meter will assist in properly determining exposure. The recommendations of the film manufacturer should be followed in developing, both as to time and to temperature.

4*A*. *Remedy.*—Density may be increased by intensifying, although lack of shadow detail cannot be corrected. The best corrective measure is to make a print on contrasty paper, although shadow detail will still be lacking.

1*B*. *Distinguishing Characteristic.*—Detail in all tones, but all tones too flat.

2B. Cause.—Proper exposure, but insufficient development. Developer too cold; insufficient developing time.

3B. Prevention.—Develop at time and temperature recommended by the manufacturer.

4B. Remedy.—This condition may be remedied in the final print by printing on a contrasty grade of paper.

1C. Distinguishing Characteristic.—High lights lack detail, and all tones are too flat.

2C. Cause.—Overexposure and underdevelopment.

3C. Prevention.—Correct exposure and development. Give less exposure. Develop for a longer time or at higher temperature. Make sure the developer is not exhausted.

4C. Remedy.—Printing on contrasty paper will remedy lack of contrast in the negative, but lack of detail in high lights cannot be corrected.

Reversal of Image.

1. *Distinguishing Characteristic.*—All or part of the negative shows positive rather than negative image when viewed by transmitted light. The type of image seen by reflected light cannot be considered as giving true indication.

2. *Cause.*—Reversal image may be due to excessive exposure or, more usually, to light fog of the negative during development. In the latter case the image which first develops serves as a negative for the exposure from the darkroom illumination during development. Thus the already developed image is impressed on the silver grains in a lower layer of the emulsion, so that a positive image results. Reversal of image due to operation on the negative slope of the H and D curve requires excessive exposure time in most cases but can be obtained for exposures of reasonable time when photographing the sun or other bright bodies.

3. *Prevention.*—Sufficiently subdued darkroom illumination and protection of negative from exposure during development, or manipulation of entire photographic processes in complete darkness. Reversal of image due to overexposure is sufficiently difficult to produce that any reasonable exposure will prevent this occurrence.

4. *Remedy.*—None.

Incorrect Density

As incorrect density and incorrect contrast are frequently present simultaneously in the same negative, it is suggested that this section be read in connection with the previous section on Incorrect Contrast if any doubt exists as to proper interpretation of characteristics of the negative.

Dense Negatives.

1A. Distinguishing Characteristic.—Negative generally dense, with detail lacking in high lights; other tones too flat.

2A. Cause.—Overexposure and underdevelopment.

3A. Prevention.—Less exposure and greater development.

4A. Remedy.—Print on contrasty grade of printing paper. Dense negative will require relatively long printing time. No remedy for lack of detail in high lights.

1B. Distinguishing Characteristic.—Negative dense. High lights lack detail; other tones correctly rendered.

2B. Cause.—Overexposure but correct development.

3B. Prevention.—Less exposure.

4B. Remedy.—Print on normal grade of paper. No remedy for lack of high-light detail.

1*C. Distinguishing Characteristic.*—Negative dense with detail lacking in the high lights; other tones too contrasty.

2*C. Cause.*—Overexposure and overdevelopment.

3*C. Prevention.*—Less exposure and shorter development, or development at lower temperature.

4*C. Remedy.*—Print on soft grade of paper. Dense negative will require relatively long printing time. Printing time may be reduced by reducing negative. No remedy for lack of high-light detail.

Thin Negatives.

1*A. Distinguishing Characteristic.*—Negative fairly transparent without much deposit of silver. Shadows lack detail; other tones too flat.

2*A. Cause.*—Underexposure and underdevelopment.

3*A. Prevention.*—Greater exposure and development.

4*A. Remedy.*—Thin negatives will require short printing time, which may be increased by intensifying negatives. Print on contrasty paper. No remedy for lack of detail in shadows.

1*B. Distinguishing Characteristic.*—Negative thin and lacking in shadow detail; other tones correctly rendered.

2*B. Cause.*—Underexposure and correct development.

3*B. Prevention.*—Increased exposure.

4*B. Remedy.*—Print on normal grade of paper. No remedy for lack of shadow detail.

1*C. Distinguishing Characteristic.*—Negative thin and lacking in shadow detail; other tones too contrasty.

2*C. Cause.*—Underexposure and overdevelopment.

3*C. Prevention.*—Greater exposure and less development.

4*C. Remedy.*—Print on soft or flat grade of printing paper. No remedy for lack of detail in shadows.

Uneven Density.

1. *Distinguishing Characteristic.*—Streak or area of incorrect density.

2. *Cause.*—Uneven development or uneven fixing.

3. *Prevention.*—Immerse entire film rapidly and completely in developer and agitate solution during development. Kept negative moving with respect to both solution and tray or tank by shaking or tilting tank or tray. If due to incomplete or uneven fixing, refixing to completion will prevent uneven density.

4. *Remedy.*—If due to uneven development, local intensification may be of some help. If due to uneven fixing, refixing to completion will sometimes help.

MARKINGS AND SPOTS

Air Bells or Gas Bells.

1. *Distinguishing Characteristic.*—Round transparent spots with well-defined edges. Occasionally in motion-picture processing the spots may be elliptical rather than round.

2. *Cause.*—Formation of air or gas bells on the emulsion side of negative during processing which prevents the solution from acting upon the emulsion. (*a*) A light or transparent spot indicates the formation of the air bell during development. (*b*) A dark or opaque spot indicates formation of bubble during fixing. (*c*) A spot which appears as a brown or yellow-brown discoloration upon aging indicates the formation of air bubbles during washing, but this is infrequent as negatives are usually agitated

during washing sufficiently well as to prevent formation of air bells. Shaded edges which may be fuzzy rather than sharp indicate that the size of the air bell changed during processing.

3. *Prevention.*—Sufficient agitation of the negative in the processing solutions is a general preventive for the formation of air or gas bells. Bubbles may also be eliminated by brushing the surface of the negative with a soft camel's-hair brush during processing. Formation of air bells during development may often be eliminated by rinsing the negative in clear water prior to development.

4. *Remedy.*—Local reduction or intensification may be effective, although retouching will probably be required.

Bare Spots.

1. *Distinguishing Characteristic.*—Spot of bare glass or film free from emulsion.

2. *Cause.*—Defect in manufacture. Occurs very infrequently, especially with negative materials manufactured by reliable concerns.

3. *Prevention.*—None, so far as photographer is concerned.

4. *Remedy.*—None, except possibly retouching. Manufacturers will usually replace defective materials.

Black Spots.

1. *Distinguishing Characteristic.*—Dark or opaque spots of various shapes, usually sharply defined at the edges.

2. *Cause.*—Foreign matter imbedded in the emulsion during fixing, developing, washing, or drying.

3. *Prevention.*—Keep negative free from contamination of dust, lint, and other particles. See that all solid particles are dissolved before using solutions. Filter all solutions if necessary.

4. *Remedy.*—Retouching.

Brown Spots.

1. *Distinguishing Characteristic.*—Brown spots, usually sharply defined, irregular, and often small.

2. *Cause.*—Dry particles of developing agents settling on dry negative before processing.

3. *Prevention.*—Cleanliness in processing. Avoid mixing chemicals where they may come into contact with photosensitive materials.

4. *Remedy.*—Sometimes such spots may be removed by hardening the film in a 10 per cent solution of formalin for several minutes to prevent swelling and frilling, after which the film is washed in water. The film is then bleached in a solution of equal parts of (*a*) 5 g. of potassium permanganate per liter of water, and (*b*) 75 g. of sodium chloride (common table salt) and 15 cc. of sulphuric acid per liter of solution. The solutes (*a*) and (*b*) must be thoroughly dissolved before the solutions are combined. After bleaching for 3 or 4 min., the brown stain of potassium permanganate is removed by immersing the negative in a 5 per cent solution of sodium bisulphite. The negative should then be rinsed in water and developed in strong light with a nonstaining developer, such as metol-hydroquinone.

Cinch Marks.

1. *Distinguishing Characteristic.*—Fine transparent parallel scratches on emulsion.

2. *Cause.*—From the friction produced when adjacent layers of film in a roll slide past one another. They are frequently produced when attempts are made to tighten a loosely wound roll by pulling on the free end.

3. *Prevention.*—Cinch marks can be prevented only by proper and careful handling of rolled films. Loosely wound rolls should not be tightened except by complete rewinding onto a new spool or reel.

4. *Remedy.*—None.

Cloudy or Wavy Appearance.

1. *Distinguishing Characteristics.*—Cloudy or wavy appearance of negative; uneven density.

2. *Cause.*—Insufficient developer to cover the negative or failure to agitate the negative in the developer, resulting in uneven development.

3. *Prevention.*—Use sufficient developer to completely cover negative. Immerse negative quickly and completely in solution, and agitate solution during development.

4. *Remedy.*—Local intensification or dodging in printing may help in certain cases.

Drop Marks.

1. *Distinguishing Characteristics.*—(*a*) Spots with gray halos. (*b*) Dark-gray spots with small white centers. (*c*) Hazy white spots. (*d*) Spots with dark narrow outlines.

2. *Cause.*—These marks are due to water marks on the film during the drying process. (*a*) This type of spot is most commonly formed by drops of water on the base side of the film, although in some cases the water mark may have been on the emulsion side. (*b*) This type of spot often occurs when a large spot of water is left on the film which is subjected to rapid drying at high temperatures. (*c*) Sometimes hazy white spots occur if processing has been carried on at temperatures well above 70°F. or when the film is dried rapidly at high temperatures even though all excess moisture has been removed. (*d*) Spots having the same density as the rest of the film but with a dark outline at the edge of the drop are caused by large drops of water on the emulsion side of the negative.

3. *Prevention.*—Careful and systematic habits in processing will guard against such spots. The negative should be protected from splashing solutions. Squeegeeing to remove surplus and excess surface moisture or removing this water by blotting the surface with lintless cloth or a sponge before drying is also effective.

4. *Remedy.*—In some cases it may be possible to eliminate water-drop marks by rinsing the negative in water and redrying under proper drying conditions. Water marks on base side of film sometimes may be removed by breathing upon the film and then wiping it with a clean soft cloth.

Dust Marks.

1. *Distinguishing Characteristic.*—Dust or lint imbedded in film.

2. *Cause.*—Drying in dust- or lint-laden atmosphere.

3. *Prevention.*—Drying under properly controlled conditions. Removal of surface moisture and drying negatives in dustproof frames covered with closely woven fine-mesh cloth which has been starched or glazed will help to prevent dust reaching the negative.

4. *Remedy.*—Frequently none. Sometimes washing and drying a second time under proper conditions may be useful.

Halation.

1. *Distinguishing Characteristic.*—Dark band, circle, or area surrounding high lights and frequently suggestive of double image.

2. *Cause.*—Halation is due to the reflections which occur from the back of the negative support when brightly lighted objects, such as street lamps in night street

scenes, are photographed. The condition is usually worse with plates than with film negatives, because the greater thickness of plates produces a larger area of halation.

3. *Prevention.*—The use of films or plates having light-absorbing or "antihalation" backing will usually prevent halation. Films usually produce less objectionable halation than plates. In processing films or plates likely to show halation, give full exposure and full development. The developer should contain initially a small amount of accelerator, and the amount of accelerator should be increased in small amounts, gradually, as development proceeds.

4. *Remedy.*—Local reduction or retouching may help sometimes.

Fading.

1. *Distinguishing Characteristic.*—Brown, yellow, or sepia tones in the negative, appearing some time after processing.

2. *Cause.*—Incomplete fixation, or, more usually, incomplete washing after fixing. Use of old or exhausted fixing bath containing excess of silver. Insufficient agitation when first immersing films in fixing solution. Tendency to stain increases with old fixing baths which have become neutral or alkaline rather than acid and with strongly alkaline developing baths.

3. *Prevention.*—Complete fixing and washing. A rule which is often followed is to fix the negative twice as long as the time required for the white opalescence to disappear completely. Wash until all traces of hypo are removed. Make sure that the fixing bath is acid.

4. *Remedy.*—No remedy is available which is entirely satisfactory in all cases although printing or copying the negative through a yellow filter has sometimes proved quite successful. These yellow silver stains sometimes may be eliminated by removing hypo by washing thoroughly in water, and dissolving sodium thiosulphite with a 1 per cent solution of potassium cyanide in which the negative is washed. Potassium cyanide is a deadly *poison* and gives off poisonous fumes of hydrocyanic acid. Extreme care should be taken to keep this solution from the mouth and to prevent breathing cyanide fumes. The operation with potassium cyanide should be carried out in a well-ventilated room. The film should be removed from this bath as soon as signs of reduction of the image appear and should be washed thoroughly in clear water.

Finger Marks.

1. *Distinguishing Characteristic.*—Finger marks, frequently showing Bertillion fingerprint lines.

2. *Cause.*—Impressing moist, wet, dirty, or greasy fingers on the wet or dry negative. Damage is most easily done when the negative is wet, especially if the finger print is made on the emulsion side of the negative. (a) Marks showing the lines of the fingers are most frequently caused by handling the dry negative with dirty, moist, or greasy fingers. (b) If the dark marks show merely an outline of the finger, the probable cause is that of handling the negative with wet or greasy hands. (c) If the finger marks are dark, contamination of the fingers with developer is indicated. (d) If the finger marks are light or semitransparent, contamination of the fingers with hypo is indicated.

3. *Prevention.*—Cleanliness and care are the best preventatives, as these defects are due only to lack of cleanliness.

4. *Remedy.*—Grease fingerprints impressed on a dry negative may frequently be removed by wiping negative with lens tissue or soft lintless cloth dampened with carbon tetrachloride. No remedy for other causes.

Irregularly Shaped Spots.

1. *Distinguishing Characteristic.*—Spots of irregular shape; often along the edge of the negative but rarely uniformly over the entire negative.

2. *Cause.*—Exhausted developer.

3. *Prevention.*—Use of fresh and properly compounded developer.

4. *Remedy.*—None.

Microscopic Spots.

1. *Distinguishing Characteristic.*—Small, light, or transparent spots, irregular in shape and small or microscopic in size.

2. *Cause.*—Dust deposited on the negative.

3. *Prevention.*—Keep negative free from dust, in the camera as well as in the darkroom. Keep camera bellows clean by brushing dust out regularly. In the darkroom keep negative protected until ready for processing. Dust may be removed from the dry negative by playing a camel's-hair brush over the negative.

4. *Remedy.*—Careful spotting or retouching.

Mottled Appearance.

1. *Distinguishing Characteristic.*—Mottled appearance of part or all of image.

2. *Cause.*—Probably due to (a) lack of agitation during development, (b) absorption of moisture by the film before development, (c) use of old film, or (d) possibly oil spots.

3. *Prevention.*—(a) Keep developing solution agitated. (b) Store unused negatives in cool dry atmosphere until ready for use. (c) Use films before date of expiration of manufacturer's guarantee.

4. *Remedy.*—None.

Oil Spots.

1. *Distinguishing Characteristic.*—(a) Chain of small gray areas. (b) Irregular light-gray areas. (c) Mottled areas. (d) Black spots. (e) Black spots with white centers. (f) Stippled streamline effects.

2. *Cause.*—Oil on the surface of the negatives. The fine small areas are due to thin spray of fine oil drops; the larger areas are due to oil spread over negative.

3. *Prevention.*—Keeping oil from contact with negative. Ordinarily this is not difficult, and oil spots are probably most frequent in machine processing of motion-picture film. In this case, proper design and use of processing equipment will do much to reduce to a minimum damage from oil spots.

4. *Remedy.*—No remedy if processing is begun before detection of oil spots. If oil marks are discovered prior to development or other processing, they may be removed by (a) emulsification of the oil with sodium carbonate solution previous to development or (b) dissolving the oil through the use of carbon tetrachloride or benzene, after which the negative should be squeegeed and dried thoroughly before developing.

Opaque or Semiopaque Spots.

1. *Distinguishing Characteristic.*—Small, irregularly shaped dark or black spots.

2. *Cause.*—Most commonly caused by undissolved particles in the developer, but may be result of iron in solution in the wash water.

3. *Prevention.*—All chemicals should be thoroughly dissolved before solutions are used. When two solutions are used, the constituents of each should be thoroughly dissolved before the solutions are mixed. Filtering solutions is also helpful.

4. *Remedy.*—None.

Purple Spots.

1. *Distinguishing Characteristic.*—Purple spots on negative.
2. *Cause.*—Dry particles of the developer settling on negative.
3. *Prevention.*—Keep negative protected from chemicals. Do not mix chemicals in same room in which processing is being done.
4. *Remedy.*—See remedy for Brown Spots, page 524, for remedy which is useful in some instances.

Rack Marks.

1. *Distinguishing Characteristic.*—Single, or double line markings which may sometimes be mottled; marks uniformly spaced.
2. *Cause.*—Drying roll film on wooden or metal racks. The marks are produced where the rack touched the film and prevented free circulation of solutions. Most frequent in motion-picture processing.
3. *Prevention.*—In motion-picture processing, continuous machine rather than rack processing will prevent these marks. If rack processing is used, some means of shifting or rolling the film on the racks so that the same portion of film is not always adjacent to the racks during processing will help prevent rack marks.
4. *Remedy.*—None.

Small Circular Spots.

1. *Distinguishing Characteristic.*—Small, circular, light or transparent spots.
2. *Cause.*—Air in water used for making or diluting developer, or excessive agitation during development.
3. *Prevention.*—Use of distilled or boiled water free from air. If this is not possible, let water stand for at least an hour before using it to make up solutions. If due to excessive agitation, less vigorous agitation is required.
4. *Remedy.*—Possibly local intensification.

Small Circular Spots with Shaded Edges.

1. *Distinguishing Characteristic.*—Small, circular, transparent spots with shaded edges.
2. *Cause.*—Air bells or bubbles forming on negative during development.
3. *Prevention.*—Removing of air bells by wetting the negative completely prior to development. Agitate negative in developer to prevent formation of bubbles, or brush over the surface with soft camel's-hair brush. Agitate developer.
4. *Remedy.*—None.

Spots of Irregular Shape.

1. *Distinguishing Characteristic.*—Light or transparent spots of irregular shape, usually distributed along one side of negative and less frequently over entire negative.
2. *Cause.*—Exhausted or improperly compounded developer.
3. *Prevention.*—Use of fresh or correctly compounded developer.
4. *Remedy.*—Retouching.

Transparent Spots.

1. *Distinguishing Characteristic.*—Light or transparent spots indicating a deficiency of silver deposit.
2. *Cause.*—Such spots may be caused by: (*a*) dust or dirt on film during exposure or development; (*b*) air bells (*q.v.*); (*c*) air in water making up developing solution;

(*d*) chemical or other dust floating on surface of developer; or (*e*) a solvent of free silver acting on the negative after development.

3. *Prevention.*—(*a*) See Microscopic Spots, page 527. (*b*) See Air Bells, page 523. (*c*) See Small Circular Spots, page 528. (*d*) Make sure that developer is free from undissolved particles or other foreign matter. Particles which have gathered on the top as scum may be removed by means of a wire frame covered with cheesecloth or by patting the top of the solution with an absorbent cloth. Filtering the solutions is also helpful. (*e*) Cleanliness and protection of the negative from chemicals other than those intended to act upon it will prevent the last-mentioned defect.

4. *Remedy.*—None.

Yellow Spots.

1. *Distinguishing Characteristic.*—Yellow spots, circular in shape, with fairly sharply defined edges.

2. *Cause.*—Air bells or bubbles in the fixing bath.

3. *Prevention.*—Agitate negative and developing solution. Remove air bells by brushing the surface of the negative with soft brush during fixing.

4. *Remedy.*—If observed after negative has just been fixed, they may be removed by brushing off air bells and refixing.

Water Spots.—(See Drop Marks, page 525.)

MECHANICAL DEFECTS AND INJURIES

Under this heading are listed those defects and injuries in which the negative fails to meet the normal mechanical or physical requirements or in which the negative is mechanically damaged. These defects may be in addition to other defects which are given in this chapter.

Blisters.

1. *Distinguishing Characteristic.*—Emulsion raised from the gelatin, when the negative is wet with an appearance similar to blisters of the flesh. After the negative has dried, blisters appear as small craterlike depressions in the emulsion.

2. *Cause.*—Blisters are caused by gas pockets forming between the emulsion and the film support due to loosening of the gelatin as a result of (*a*) permitting wash water to fall directly on the emulsion side of the negative; (*b*) processing solutions too warm; (*c*) developing or fixing bath too concentrated; or (*d*) insufficient rinsing of the negative after developing, especially if this is followed by placing negative in a strongly acid fixing bath. The blisters are produced by the formation of carbon dioxide gas during processing especially at relatively high temperature when the gelatin is too soft to withstand the disruptive effect of the gas. Carbon dioxide is evolved when the sodium carbonate of the developer is neutralized by the acid in the fixing bath. Tendency toward the formation of blisters is increased during hot weather, when the processing solutions are too warm, and when the film is not sufficiently hardened.

3. *Prevention.*—(*a*) Do not permit wash water to fall directly on negative with appreciable force. (*b*) Solutions should not normally be at a temperature exceeding 70°F. unless the negative is hardened and tropical development is being used. (*c*) Using solutions at their normal concentration and temperature will help prevent formation of blisters. (*d*) Washing the negative in clear water between developing and fixing will remove most of the developer so that the tendency toward the formation of carbon dioxide is diminished when the negative is placed in the fixing bath.

Hardening the negative prior to processing will also help prevent formation of blisters, especially in hot weather. Replacing carbonate in the developer by a noncarbon dioxide forming substance, such as borate or phosphate is another way of avoiding blisters.

4. *Remedy.*—None.

Brittleness.

1. *Distinguishing Characteristic.*—Film is too brittle and dry.

2. *Cause.*—Brittleness is usually the result of (*a*) drying the film too completely or in an abnormally dry atmosphere, (*b*) the use of hardening stop baths, or (*c*) excess hardener in the fixing bath.

3. *Prevention.*—To maintain its pliability, film must contain a certain amount of natural moisture, which can be provided by maintaining the film in an atmosphere of 70 per cent relative humidity. The relative humidity of the atmosphere during the drying of the film should be between 40 and 70 per cent.

4. *Remedy.*—Brittleness can be remedied by submitting the films to storage in an atmosphere of 40 to 70 per cent relative humidity, as in humidifying tanks.

Buckle.

1. *Distinguishing Characteristic.*—Waviness in the center or along the edges of the film.

2. *Cause.*—Buckle is due to nonuniform expansion or contraction of the negative. Buckle is commonly produced by (*a*) drying the film in an atmosphere of high humidity, (*b*) forced drying at high temperature, or (*c*) drying in atmosphere of too low humidity.

3. *Prevention.*—Buckle can usually be prevented by proper drying conditions. For proper drying the relative humidity should be between 40 and 70 per cent and the temperature should not exceed 90°F.

4. *Remedy.*—Buckled film frequently may be improved by soaking in water and drying in a properly conditioned atmosphere. Buckled motion-picture film may often be freed from buckle by winding the film on a dry reel and placing it in a relatively humid atmosphere.

Creeping.

1. *Distinguishing Characteristic.*—Creeping or movement of emulsion on its supporting surface.

2. *Cause.*—Insufficient ventilation and high temperature during drying.

3. *Prevention.*—Proper drying conditions.

4. *Remedy.*—None.

Curled Negatives.

1. *Distinguishing Characteristic.*—Negatives not flat but curled. In extreme cases they may be curled up into a tube.

2. *Cause.*—Difference in contraction or expansion coefficient between that of the emulsion and that of the gelatin support. Since the emulsion contracts more than the gelatin, the film curls with the emulsion on the concave or inside surface.

3. *Prevention.*—Modern films are so made that excessive curling is largely eliminated. Drying negatives with clips or weights attached to the bottom edge will keep the negatives straight during drying and will help prevent curling. Storing dry film flat tends to keep it so, whereas storing films in rolls tends to aggravate curling.

4. *Remedy.*—After films are thoroughly dry, they may frequently be relieved from curling by placing them between sheets of clean white paper and applying pressure as by placing them between the leaves of large books. Another method, which may be used if care is taken, is to press the film between two sheets of clean white paper

with a warm (not hot) flatiron. For negatives badly curled, soak in water and dry with weights as described above.

Frilling or Softening.

1. *Distinguishing Characteristic.*—Emulsion at edges of negative loosened from its support. Edges of negative may be corrugated.

2. *Cause.*—Frilling may occur as a result of: (*a*) using solutions which are too warm; (*b*) insufficient hardening of the emulsion; (*c*) exhausted fixing bath; (*d*) fixing bath containing insufficient hardener; (*e*) too strong a fixing bath; (*f*) excessive washing, especially in warm water; or (*g*) careless handling.

3. *Prevention.*—The manner of prevention depends upon the contributing causes. (*a*) Keep processing solutions between 60 and 70°F. During the summer it may be necessary to immerse tanks in cold water solution to which ice may be added. Ice should never be added to the processing solutions, as this dilutes them and may introduce undesirable contaminations. (*b*) The negatives may be hardened before processing in a 10 per cent solution of formalin. Contributing causes (*c*), (*d*), and (*e*) are the result of improperly prepared or improperly used fixing baths and may be eliminated by using properly prepared fixing baths at temperatures between 60 and 70°F. (*f*) Ordinarily, excessive washing is not harmful if the temperature is 70°F. or less. (*g*) Proper handling technique, involving care and cleanliness, is essential in all photographic operations.

4. *Remedy.*—None.

Lint or Dust Particles.

1. *Distinguishing Characteristic.*—Lint or dust particles adhering to the surface of the negative.

2. *Cause.*—Drying the negative in dust- or lint-laden atmosphere. The emulsion gets tacky during drying, and at this stage particles floating in the air may easily adhere to the negative, especially if this is a film.

3. *Prevention.*—Clean atmosphere during drying is the best preventive, although much can be done to prevent this defect by removing the surface water from the negative before hanging it up to dry. A lintless cloth or blotter or a viscose sponge should be used for this purpose. The film should be blotted or patted rather than rubbed with absorbent, as scratches may occur in the latter case.

4. *Remedy.*—Frequently there is no remedy for the removal of dust or lint particles, and these will show up as white spots on the finished print. The situation is especially serious in the case of miniature negatives from which enlarged prints are made. Sometimes improvement can be made by rewashing the negative in plain water and redrying in a clean atmosphere.

Pit Marks.

1. *Distinguishing Characteristic.*—Fine holes or pits in the emulsion.

2. *Cause.*—(*a*) Excessive amount of alum in the fixing bath. (*b*) Precipitate of sulphur from the fixing bath present when the negatives are fixed in tray or tank. (*c*) Too rapid drying of the negative.

3. *Prevention.*—The prevention becomes obvious when the cause is definitely determined.

4. *Remedy.*—Retouching of negative or print.

Reticulation.

1. *Distinguishing Characteristic.*—Emulsion wrinkled and indented, having the appearance of leatherlike grain.

2. *Cause.*—Subjecting the gelatin to sudden strains through sudden changes in temperature. The strain may be produced by transferring the film from one solution to another at appreciable temperature difference. This condition is especially serious when the solutions are warm, as in this case the gelatin swells and is then more likely to contract unevenly.

3. *Prevention.*—Keep solutions between 60 and 70°F. Whenever possible, all processing solutions should be at the same temperature within this limit. This may be accomplished by storing the solutions side by side so that they may be exposed to the same temperature variations. If it is necessary to cool solutions, all the solutions required may be cooled simultaneously in the same water bath, which should be agitated for best results.

4. *Remedy.*—Reticulation may sometimes be removed by placing the negative in a 10 per cent solution of formaldehyde for a few minutes and drying quickly at elevated temperatures. This procedure is not recommended except as a last resort.

White Transparent Spots.

1. *Distinguishing Characteristic.*—Transparent spots, marks, or scratches on the negative from which the emulsion has been removed.

2. *Cause.*—Removal of emulsion from the support during processing, caused by gouging the emulsion with the fingernail, edge of film, or other relatively hard substance. This difficulty tends to increase when processing at elevated temperatures when the emulsion is soft and swollen.

3. *Prevention.*—Carefulness in processing, maintaining processing solutions below 70°F., and hardening the film before processing will all help to prevent and minimize such gouge marks.

4. *Remedy.*—None, except retouching negative or print.

SCUM, SLIME, AND DEPOSITS

Crystalline Surface.

1. *Distinguishing Characteristic.*—Surface of emulsion takes on a crystalline appearance similar to frosted windowpane or some forms of "crackle" enameling.

2. *Cause.*—From crystallization of hypo remaining in the film after incomplete washing.

3. *Prevention.*—Complete washing of the negative after fixing.

4. *Remedy.*—The crystals of sodium thiosulphate are soluble in water, so the negative may be freed from these crystals by rewashing completely.

Greenish-white Scum.

1. *Distinguishing Characteristic.*—Greenish-white scum deposited upon the surface of the negative.

2. *Cause.*—Precipitate of chromium hydroxide or of basic chromium sulphite deposited on the negative when chrome alum stop or fixing baths are used.

3. *Prevention.*—Use developer containing as little alkali as possible. If necessary, acidify developer at intervals. Formation of scum may also be prevented by agitating the negative thoroughly while immersed in the stop or fixing bath.

4. *Remedy.*—The scum may be removed while the negative is still wet, by means of moist lintless cloth, paper, or cotton. Difficult or impossible to remove after negative is dry.

Scum.

1. *Distinguishing Characteristic.*—Deposit of scum on film.

2. *Cause.*—A deposit of scum on film occurs as a result of the accumulation of solid matter floating on the surface of the processing solutions. It may be picked up when

the film is first immersed in the solution or when the negative is withdrawn from the solution. The scum may be composed of oil, grease, insoluble particles of the processing solution, oxidization products of the developer or other processing solutions, etc. A frequent cause of scum on negatives is the precipitation of hardener in the fixing bath by excess developer carried over by the negative.

3. *Prevention.*—The formation of scum may be prevented by washing the processing equipment with a hot solution of sodium hypochlorite. Scum may be removed from the surface of the solution by a skimming device consisting of a wire framework over which fine-mesh cloth has been stretched. "Patting" of the surface of the solution with a blotter or cloth is also effective in removing surface scum.

4. *Remedy.*—The remedy for scum, if any, will depend upon the nature of the scum deposit. Oil and grease may be removed with carbon tetrachloride. Alcohol is a solvent for some waxes and resins but should not be used on acetate films. The use of a scum-resistant hardening fixing bath, such as the Eastman F5 or F10 will help if the scum is due to precipitation of hardener in the fixing bath.

Silvery Deposit.

1. *Distinguishing Characteristic.*—A silvery deposit or scum on the surface of the negative.

2. *Cause.*—Such a deposit may be (*a*) silver sulphide formed by the interaction of hydrogen sulphide of the air with silver salts of the developer, the silver sulphide resulting from the sodium sulphite of the emulsion or (*b*) metallic silver precipitated during development as a fine colloid and settling on the film.

3. *Prevention.*—(*a*) The formation of silver sulphide may be prevented by scouring the processing equipment with a hot solution of sodium hypochlorite. (*b*) The silver is probably caused to precipitate owing to the presence of a silver solvent, such as hypo. The preventive measure is therefore to scrub the developing tanks thoroughly to free them from hypo. Agitation of negatives during development aids in preventing formation of silver deposit.

4. *Remedy.*—The deposit of metallic silver can be removed by rubbing it off the film if this is done before the film has dried.

Slime.

1. *Distinguishing Characteristic.*—Deposit of slime on negative.

2. *Cause.*—The slime formed on the walls of tanks containing running water may become loose and deposit on the film.

3. *Prevention.*—Slime may be prevented by cleaning the tanks periodically, especially if they are made of wood, and sterilizing with a solution of sodium hypochlorite.

4. *Remedy.*—If discovered while the negative is still wet, the slime may usually be washed off with clear water.

White Deposit Covering Negative.

1. *Distinguishing Characteristic.*—White granular deposit on negative.

2. *Cause.*—Sulphur deposited on the surface of the negative during fixing when an improperly compounded or exhausted fixing bath is used. The deposit may also result from incomplete washing.

3. *Prevention.*—Properly compounded, fresh fixing bath, and complete washing.

4. *Remedy.*—None.

White Opalescent Deposit on Film.

1. *Distinguishing Characteristic.*—White opalescent deposit on film or plate.

2. *Cause.*—Often caused by use of undiluted alcohol and too high temperatures in quick drying. This causes excessive desiccation of gelatin producing opalescence.

3. *Prevention.*—For drying negatives quickly using alcohol bath, the alcohol should be diluted slightly with water. Ten parts of alcohol to one part of water is approximately correct. The temperature of the drying air should not exceed 95°F.

4. *Remedy.*—The white opalescence may be removed by soaking the film in water and redrying slowly.

STAINS AND DISCOLORATIONS

Aluminum Sulphite Stains.

1. *Distinguishing Characteristic.*—White powdery stains on negative.

2. *Cause.*—Aluminum sulphite stains caused by an insufficiently acid fixing bath as a result of using an exhausted or incorrectly compounded fixing bath. When sodium sulphite, as from the developer, is added to a fixing bath containing alum, the acid fixing bath is neutralized, and ultimately a white precipitate of aluminum sulphite is formed which turns the bath milky white and settles as a white sludge.

3. *Prevention.*—Avoid a developer containing excessive alkali. Between development and fixing, the negative may be washed in clear water or in an acid stop bath. If an acid stop bath is used, care must be taken to see that the acid carried over into the fixing bath is not sufficient to cause sulphurization of the fixing solution.

4. *Remedy.*—Aluminum sulphite stains may be removed by hardening the negative in an alkaline formalin solution. The negative should then be washed for several minutes in a 5 per cent solution of sodium carbonate, after which the negative should be washed thoroughly in clear water.

Blue-green Stain.

1. *Distinguishing Characteristic.*—Blue-green stain after fixing.

2. *Cause.*—Frequently caused by using chrome-alum fixing bath at elevated temperatures.

3. *Prevention.*—Maintaining fixing bath at temperatures not exceeding 70°F.

4. *Remedy.*—None.

Blue Stains.

1. *Distinguishing Characteristic.*—Blue stains covering part or all of negative.

2. *Cause.*—Usually due to presence of iron in the processing solutions, but is sometimes due to the presence of amidol.

3. *Prevention.*—In making up solutions, use iron-free water.

4. *Remedy.*—If stains are due to iron, they may be removed as indicated under Developer Stains, page 535. If due to Amidol, they may be removed by immersing the negative in a 10 per cent solution of sodium bicarbonate, washing, and drying.

Brown Areas.

1. *Distinguishing Characteristic.*—Brown areas on negative often occurring as scum deposit on the surface.

2. *Cause.*—Probably from scum of oxidized developer or deposits of silver sulphide in the developing or fixing baths.

3. *Prevention.*—Use of fresh and properly compounded processing solutions.

4. *Remedy.*—(See under Developer Stains, page 535.)

Colored Areas.—(See Dye Stains, page 535.)
Colored Negatives.

1. *Distinguishing Characteristic.*—General, over-all stain on negative, usually yellow, brown, or sepia.

2. *Cause.*—Stains produced during development (see Developer Stains).

3. *Prevention.*—(See Developer Stains.)

4. *Remedy.*—(See Developer Stains.)

Developer Stains.

1. *Distinguishing Characteristic.*—Local or general staining of the negative. Developer stains are usually yellow, brown, or sepia, although the color depends upon the developer used. May be produced either in developing or fixing bath.

2. *Cause.*—Developer stains may be caused by: (*a*) alkaline or old fixing bath, (*b*) old or discolored developer, or (*c*) developer containing impure or insufficient sulphite. Certain developers, such as pyro, for instance, are much more likely to stain the negative than other developers. If the stain is general and uniform, the contrast may be altered, and the printing time may be increased without other undesirable effects being present.

3. *Prevention.*—The use of fresh and properly compounded processing solutions is essential. Care should be taken to see that the developer contains the proper amount of sulphite. Nonstaining developers, such as metol-hydroquinone, may also be used. Increasing the amount of sulphite in the developer will help prevent stains.

4. *Remedy.*—Harden the negative in a solution of 10 cc. of formalin and 5 g. of sodium carbonate per liter of solution, and wash in clear water for 5 min. Bleach in equal parts of: (*a*) 5.3 g. of potassium permanganate per liter, and (*b*) 75 g. of sodium chloride and 16 cc. of sulphuric acid per liter, making sure that all particles are thoroughly dissolved before the two solutions are mixed. Bleaching should be completed in about 4 min. The brown stain which is produced may be removed by immersing the negative in a 1 per cent solution of sodium bisulphite. The negative should then be rinsed well and developed in strong light with a nonstaining developer. Local yellow stains may be handled by making a new negative or a print from the stained negative through the use of a strong yellow filter.

Dye Stains.

1. *Distinguishing Characteristic.*—Areas of negative that are colored red, green, or other color, especially at the edges where developer may not have reached negative completely, as in tank development.

2. *Cause.*—These stains are those of the sensitizing dyes used in the manufacture of some orthochromatic and panchromatic films. The stains are due to incomplete removal of these dyes because the developer and fixing bath are kept from free circulating contact with the back of the negative. The effects are often observed in tank development where the film has been inserted in a holder or frame which prevents free circulation at the edges of the negative.

3. *Prevention.*—Thorough agitation of the negative during development.

4. *Remedy.*—These dye stains are soluble in water and consequently may be removed subsequent to fixing by immersing in clear water until the stains have disappeared.

Fading.

1. *Distinguishing Characteristic.*—Brown or yellow stains on parts of the negative, or covering the entire negative, apparent some time after fixing.

2. *Cause.*—Incomplete fixing or, more usually, incomplete washing.

3. *Prevention.*—Complete fixing and washing.

4. *Remedy.*—(See remedy for removal of Developer Stains, above.)

Green Dichroic Stain.

1. *Distinguishing Characteristic.*—Green metallic sheen by reflected light and red or pinkish color by transmitted light.

2. *Cause.*—(See Dichroic Fog, page 517).

3. *Prevention.*—(See Dichroic Fog, page 517).

4. *Remedy.*—(See Dichroic Fog, page 517; also see page 165, Motion-picture Laboratory Practice 1936.)

Green Stain.

1. *Distinguishing Characteristic.*—Negative has appearance of being dyed green: occurs in stop bath.

2. *Cause.*—Stain appearing in stop bath is a function of the relative amounts of carbonate and sulphite in the developer and the concentration of the chrome alum in the stop bath, and it increases with increasing temperature of solution.

3. *Prevention.*—Properly compounded and fresh processing solutions maintained at a temperature not exceeding 70°F.

4. *Remedy.*—Usually this green stain can be removed by immersing the film in a 5 per cent solution of potassium hydroxide or 5 per cent solution of potassium citrate. This treatment destroys the hardening properties of film negatives.

Purple Stain.

1. *Distinguishing Characteristic.*—Purple discoloration on negative.

2. *Cause.*—(a) Purple stains may be due to presence of iron in the water used in making up processing solutions. (b) This stain occurs frequently in the fixing bath if negatives stick together so that complete fixing cannot be accomplished. The stain occurs where the negatives make contact, because of the continuance of developing action in the fixing bath.

3. *Prevention.*—(a) Use of distilled or at least filtered water for making up processing solutions will assist in removing iron particles. (b) Agitation of negatives in fixing solution.

4. *Remedy.* (See remedy under Blue Stains, page 534.)

Silvery-white Opalescence.—(See Yellowish-white Opalescence, below.)
Stains from Ferricyanide.

1. *Distinguishing Characteristic.*—Green or blue discoloration.

2. *Cause.*—Sometimes caused when ferricyanide reducer is employed.

3. *Prevention.*—Do not use ferricyanide reducers.

4. *Remedy.*—Immerse negative, until stain is removed, in a solution of 6 cc. of nitric acid and 6 g. of alum per liter of solution. Wash in clear water and dry.

Yellowish-white Opalescence.

1. *Distinguishing Characteristic.*—Yellowish white or silvery white opalescence on part or all of the emulsion, suggestive of opal.

2. *Cause.*—This opalescence may be due to: (a) incomplete fixing; (b) use of alcohol to hasten drying; (c) drying rapidly in warm air; (d) excessively high temperature of fixing bath; or (e) presence of colloidal sulphur in improperly compounded fixing bath containing excess acid.

3. *Prevention.*—(a) Complete fixing with properly compounded, fresh fixing bath. (b) When alcohol is used to hasten drying, it should be diluted with water to give a solution having 80 per cent alcohol. (c) Dry negative less rapidly in atmosphere of from 40 to 70 per cent humidity and at a temperature not exceeding 90°F. (d) The

temperature of the fixing bath should be between 60 and 70°F. (*e*) Properly compounded fixing baths will prevent formation of colloidal sulphur.

4. *Remedy.*—(*a*) If the opalescence is discovered while the negative is still wet, it may be removed by immersing the negative in the fixing bath until opalescence has completely disappeared. (*b*) Wash negative in clear water and dry slowly. If negative was incompletely fixed or incompletely washed, this treatment is not effective. (*c*) Wash negative in clear water and dry slowly at temperature not above 90°F. and preferably with atmosphere of 40 to 70 per cent humidity. (*d*) and (*e*) The stain or opalescence of free sulphur on the negative may be removed by hardening the film in a 5 per cent solution of formalin and by washing well with clear water. The negative should then be washed in a 10 per cent solution of sodium sulphite at 100 to 110°F. Obviously with such high temperatures, extreme care will be required in order not to damage the negative in other respects.

Yellow Stains.

1. *Distinguishing Characteristic.*—Portions or all of negative colored yellow.

2. *Cause.*—Yellow stains are frequent sources of trouble and may be caused by a number of factors, among them being: (*a*) weak, exhausted, or improperly compounded fixing bath; (*b*) exhausted or oxidized developing solution; (*c*) failure to rinse negatives between developing and fixing, either with clear water or stop bath; (*d*) uncleanliness in developing or impurities in the developer; (*e*) hypo or fixing bath in the developer; (*f*) insufficient washing; (*g*) too much carbonate in the developing solution; and (*h*) leaving negative incompletely covered in the fixing bath.

3. *Prevention.*—When the most probable cause of the stain has been determined, the preventive action will usually become apparent.

4. *Remedy.*—Most of these stains can be removed by the methods suggested for Developer Stains, page 535.

Unevenness

Directional Effects.

1. *Distinguishing Characteristic.*—Developed image appears to have "tail."

2. *Cause.*—Directional effect of developer which enables image to be built up more rapidly at one portion of the negative than at other. Also due to fresh developer working on first part of moving film during processing and partially exhausted developer acting on later portions of film. Especially noticeable in certain types of motion-picture processing.

3. *Prevention.*—Thorough agitation of solution during development so that the developer at the surface of the negative is changed uniformly and rapidly during processing.

4. *Remedy.*—None.

Uneven Development.

1. *Distinguishing Characteristic.*—Streaks or areas of density different from the normal density of the remaining portion of the negative.

2. *Cause.*—Failure to immerse the negative entirely and completely in the developing bath, or permitting two or more negatives to come in contact in the developer for appreciable time.

3. *Prevention.*—The negatives should be immersed quickly and uniformly in the developer and should be agitated during development, so that the solution may work uniformly and completely over the entire surface of the negative.

4. *Remedy.*—Local intensification may sometimes be employed to bring up the density of the areas protected during development.

Uneven Emulsion.

1. *Distinguishing Characteristic.*—Variations in thickness of emulsion.

2. *Cause.*—Faulty manufacture and inadequate manufacturing inspection.

3. *Prevention.*—None, except that such instances, which are fortunately rare, are even more so with the products of reliable manufacturers.

4. *Remedy.*—None. If the defective material is returned to the manufacturer with a complete statement of all conditions, replacements may be made.

Uneven Fixing.

1. *Distinguishing Characteristic.*—Variations in density in areas of the negative not related to the image produced on the negative.

2. *Cause.*—Improper or incomplete immersion of the negative in the fixing bath. The same result is obtained by allowing two or more negatives to come into contact for prolonged periods in the fixing bath.

3. *Prevention.*—This defect may be prevented by separating the negatives in the fixing bath, agitating the negatives and solution, and completely and entirely immersing the negatives in the fixing bath.

4. *Remedy.*—None.

DEFECTS IN PRINTS

This section deals with defects in prints made by contact or projection printing on bromide or chloride papers. No consideration is given to defects due to coloring, toning, retouching, or other aftertreatments; other methods of producing prints, such as printing with salts of other metals, bichromated colloids, the gum bichromate process, oil processes, etc., are not considered here. For details on printing methods other than those using silver halide salts, reference should be made to the appropriate section of the book dealing with these other printing processes.

Defects in negatives may show up as defects in prints. In this section it is assumed that the negative is free from defects and hence that the defects actually occurring are those due only to the printing process.

BLOTCHES, LINES, AND STREAKS

Abrasion Marks or Streaks.

1. *Distinguishing Characteristic.*—Surface of paper abraded or scratched, often resulting in fine scratches, especially when glossy-surfaced paper is used.

2. *Cause.*—Scratching, abrading, or friction on the emulsion side of the paper.

3. *Prevention.*—Store paper so that it stands vertically and is free from applied pressure on its faces. Handle carefully. Make sure that processing solutions are free from grit, undissolved matter, or foreign particles.

4. *Remedy.*—Sometimes these abrasion marks may be removed by adding $\frac{1}{8}$ gr. potassium iodide to each ounce of developing solution.

BLURRED PRINTS

Bad Definition in Spots.

1. *Distinguishing Characteristic.*—Spots of print blurred, as if out of focus.

2. *Cause.*—Imperfect contact between negative and paper in contact printing, so that those portions of the negative which are slightly removed from the surface of the print do not print sharply.

3. *Prevention.*—Make sure that the printing device presses the printing paper into firm contact with the negative during contact printing. Frequently the difficulty is due to worn padding on the pressure top of the printer or loosening of the pressure

springs of the printer. In the case of printers with pneumatic pressure plates, the difficulty may usually be prevented by keeping the pressure pad fully inflated.

4. *Remedy.*—Retouching.

Blurred Print.

1. *Distinguishing Characteristic.*—Print generally blurred and lacking in sharpness, although negative is satisfactorily sharp.

2. *Cause.*—(*a*) In contact printing, this lack of sharpness may be due to printing with the emulsion side of the negative away from the emulsion side of the print. This is definitely the cause if the picture is reversed left to right. (*b*) In enlargement printing, the difficulty is probably due to relative motion between the negative and the print during printing or to an unsteady and perhaps vibrating enlarger.

3. *Prevention.*—(*a*) The emulsion side of the print and the emulsion side of the negative must always be kept in contact during printing. (*b*) Solidity of the enlarger is the only prevention for blurred prints in enlarging which are caused in the manner suggested above. Mechanical adjustments, repairs, or reinforcements of parts may be required. Vibration may sometimes be prevented by mounting the enlarger on a resilient support, as rubber pads, or suspension from springs.

4. *Remedy.*—None.

Fog

Fog.

1. *Distinguishing Characteristic.*—(*a*) General gray cast over entire print, especially noticeable in parts which should be white. (*b*) Gray or granular appearance of print.

2. *Cause.*—Fog of printing paper which may be due to (*a*) light-struck paper; (*b*) use of too strong a safe light, safe light too close to printing paper, safe light acting on printing paper for too long a time, or safe light with improper filter; (*c*) forced development so that silver halides not acted upon by light are reduced; (*d*) improperly compounded or impure developer.

3. *Prevention.*—(*a*) Protect printing paper by keeping it in black lighttight envelopes, boxes, or drawers when not in use. Do not permit paper to lie around in the darkroom unless protected from the safe light. (*b*) Test safe light to ascertain that light is not too intense and that the safe-light filter used is suitable for use with the printing paper. Do not expose printing paper to safe light longer than necessary. (*c*) Develop printing paper in accordance with directions provided by manufacturer. Avoid forcing development. (*d*) Use properly compounded developers made up with fresh pure chemicals. Do not use exhausted, old, or deteriorated developer. Use developer recommended by the manufacturer of the printing paper, and develop according to manufacturer's directions.

4. *Remedy.*—Make new print.

Incorrect Contrast

Contrasty Prints.

1. *Distinguishing Characteristic.*—Prints have excessive contrast, or are lacking in detail, so that they present a "soot and whitewash" effect. Detail may be lacking in both high lights and dark tones.

2. *Cause.*—Use of too contrasty a printing paper for the range of densities in the negative.

3. *Prevention.*—Use a less contrasty printing paper. Such papers are also known as soft or flat papers.

4. *Remedy.*—Make a new print.

Flat Prints.

1. *Distinguishing Characteristic.*—Prints lack contrast; dark parts too light, light parts too dark, or both.

2. *Cause.*—Use of improper grade of printing paper for the range of densities in the negative.

3. *Prevention.* Use a printing paper suited for flat negatives, *i.e.*, one having greater contrast. Contrasty printing papers are also known as "hard" papers.

4. *Remedy.*—Make a new print.

INCORRECT DENSITY

Prints too Dark.

1*A*. *Distinguishing Characteristic.*—Print generally too dark. High lights (dense portions of the negatives) lacking in detail. (*a*) Other tones too flat. (*b*) Other tones correctly rendered. (*c*) Other tones too contrasty.

2*A*. *Cause.*—Overexposure. In (*a*) and (*c*) incorrect printing paper for the range of densities in the negative has been used.

3*A*. *Prevention.*—Less exposure in printing. In (*a*) a more contrasty grade of paper should be used. In (*b*) the grade of contrast of the printing paper is correct. In (*c*) a less contrasty grade of printing paper should be employed.

4*A*. *Remedy.*—When defects of this type occur in prints, it is usually cheaper, quicker, and generally more satisfactory to make another print than to attempt remedial measures.

1*B*. *Distinguishing Characteristic.*—Prints generally too dark, with granular gray appearance over entire print.

2*B*. *Cause.*—Overexposure and overdevelopment. In addition, a grade of printing paper unsuited for the range of densities in the negative may have been used (see items above).

3*B*. *Prevention.*—Proper exposure and correct development according to the recommendations of the manufacturer.

4*B*. *Remedy.*—Make a new print.

1*C*. *Distinguishing Characteristic.*—Prints generally too dark.

2*C*. *Cause.*—Too strong a developer or too little bromide in the developer, causing development to progress too rapidly.

3*C*. *Prevention.*—Properly compounded developer, made with fresh pure ingredients.

4*C*. Remedy.—Make new print.

Prints Too Light.

1*A*. *Distinguishing Characteristic.*—Prints generally too light so that there is a deficiency of silver on the print. Shadows lack detail. (*a*) Other tones too flat. (*b*) Other tones correctly rendered. (*c*) Other tones too contrasty.

2*A*. *Cause.*—Underexposure. In (*a*) and (*c*) incorrect printing paper for the range of densities in the negative has been used.

3*A*. *Prevention.*—Greater exposure in printing. In (*a*) a more contrasty grade of paper should be used. In (*b*) the grade of contrast of the printing paper is correct. In (*c*) a less contrasty grade of printing paper should be used.

4*A*. *Remedy.*—Make a new print with greater time of exposure.

1*B*. *Distinguishing Characteristic.*—Print generally too light; detail only in the dark parts of print (light parts of negative).

2*B*. *Cause.*—Underdevelopment.

3B. Prevention.—Proper development. Increase time of development. If the developer is exhausted, replace with new developing solution.

4B. Remedy.—Make a new print.

1C. Distinguishing Characteristic.—Print generally too light (too weak) when washed and dried, although satisfactory after developing. Delicate shading and detail destroyed; print lacking in snap.

2C. Cause.—Bleaching of print in strong fixing bath, or too long in fixing bath.

3C. Prevention.—Proper fixing of prints.

4C. Remedy.—Since loss of fine detail and gradations is due to the strong fixing bath attacking and partially reducing the metallic silver, it may sometimes be possible to remedy this defect by putting the print through a bath of a reducing agent, such as a developer, and following this with subsequent fixing and washing. Usually it is more desirable to make a new print.

MARKS AND SPOTS

Air Bells.

1. *Distinguishing Characteristic.*—Round spots with shaded but fairly well defined edges. The spots may be (*a*) lighter or (*b*) darker than the rest of the print. (*c*) Spots which show up as discoloration upon aging.

2. *Cause.*—The spots are due to air bells adhering to the print during the processing, and hence preventing the processing solutions from reaching the print. (*a*) If the spots are lighter than the rest of the print, the air bells (bubbles) were formed during development so that the developer could not act on the print where the bubbles formed. (*b*) If the spots are darker than the rest of the print or are discolored, the bubbles have formed in the fixing bath. (*c*) Spots which show up discolored after some time are due to formation of air bells in the washing operation, so that hypo was not entirely removed.

3. *Prevention.*—Immerse the print quickly in the various solutions, agitating it in solution so that air bells may be prevented from forming. Brushing the surface of the print with a camel's-hair brush or soft cloth or chamois is helpful in removing bubbles.

4. *Remedy.*—Local retouching will be required.

Brown Spots.

1. *Distinguishing Characteristic.*—(*a*) Brown-red stains, usually small, well defined, and of irregular shape, although sometimes covering a large area somewhat uniformly. (*b*) Brown stains or smudge covering part or all of the print.

2. *Cause.*—The red-brown stains in (*a*) are caused by particles of rust being deposited upon the print from oxidized iron processing utensils, such as tanks or trays, hanging clips, ferrotype plates, etc. They may also be caused by the deposit of chemical particles or dust on emulsion of the print. (*b*) Brown smudges, marks, or spots, are probably caused by exhausted or oxidized developer.

3. *Prevention.*—(*a*) When the brown spots are due to rust, the rusted utensil should either be discarded or should be cleaned by removing the rust and lacquering or enameling to prevent further rusting. Spots which are due to loose particles of chemicals may be prevented by mixing chemicals in a room separate from that used for processing prints (or films), and by keeping the printing paper protected in its black envelope, cardboard box, or in a drawer until ready for use. (*b*) Brown spots due to exhausted or oxidized developer may be prevented by using properly compounded developer made from pure fresh chemicals.

4. *Remedy.*—In some instances it may be possible to wash off rust particles, thereby ridding the print of stains. Usually, however, it is best to make a new print.

Fading.

1. *Distinguishing Characteristic.*—Fading upon aging of the print, especially when accompanied by yellow or brown discoloration.

2. *Cause.*—Incomplete fixing or washing of the print.

3. *Prevention.*—Proper fixing and washing.

4. *Remedy.*—None.

Finger Marks.

1. *Distinguishing Characteristic.*—Imprint of fingers on the print, the finger marks being (*a*) lighter or (*b*) darker than the rest of the print or (*c*) showing up upon aging as a discoloration.

2. *Cause.*—Impressing the fingers on the emulsion side of the print, especially when the print is wet with processing solution. (*a*) If the finger marks are lighter than the rest of the print, grease from the fingers may have been deposited on the print prior to development. White fingerprints may also be due to touching the print with hypo-contaminated fingers. (*b*) If the fingerprints are darker than the rest of the print, grease from the fingers may have been deposited prior to development but after fixing. (*c*) The appearance of finger marks, upon aging, as a discoloration indicates inadequate washing, which may be due to grease preventing full action of the wash water in removing hypo.

3. *Prevention.*—Cleanliness in handling prints. Wearing rubber gloves or rubber finger tips will prevent grease from fingers from reaching the print and, since the rubber is smooth and nonabsorbent, will assist in keeping the hands clean.

4. *Remedy.*—Make a new print.

Freaks. Uneven Marks and Spots.

1. *Distinguishing Characteristic.*—Uneven marks and spots, sometimes appearing as if deposit of oil or grease has been made on the print.

2. *Cause.*—(*a*) This may be due to uneven development, (*b*) a weak developing solution, or (*c*) an actual deposit of oil or grease.

3. *Prevention.*—Causes (*a*) and (*b*) may be prevented by proper development. The developer should be properly compounded from pure and fresh materials. The print should be immersed quickly and thoroughly in the developer and should be agitated in solution so that even development, without the formation of air bells, may result. In case (*c*) cleanliness is the only preventative.

4. *Remedy.*—None; make new print.

Greenish-brown Spots.

1. *Distinguishing Characteristic.*—Greenish-brown spots on print.

2. *Cause.*—These spots may be caused by (*a*) excessive amount of potassium bromide in developer, (*b*) exhausted or old developer, or (*c*) overexposure.

3. *Prevention.*—In (*a*) and (*b*), the defect may be prevented by using fresh and properly prepared developers and by discarding exhausted or oxidized solutions. In (*c*), correct exposure is the preventive.

4. *Remedy.*—Make new print.

White Spots on the Print.

1. *Distinguishing Characteristic.*—(*a*) Small irregular white spots with sharply defined edges. (*b*) Round white spots with fairly well-defined edges.

2. *Cause.*—(*a*) These spots are often caused by dust or dirt either on the negative itself or upon the glass top plate of the printer. If the particles of foreign matter are on the emulsion side of the negative, they will produce sharp images on the print,

whereas if they are on the plain side of the negative or upon the glass plate of the printer, the images will be less sharply defined.   (b) Formation of an air bell on the print during development prevents the developing solution from acting on the spot covered by the bubble, so that no development takes place and a white spot results.

3. *Prevention.*—(a) Cleanliness is the only preventive where spots are due to dust, lint, dirt, or other foreign matter.   (b) See Air Bells, page 541.

4. *Remedy.*—Careful spotting and retouching will be required.

MECHANICAL DEFECTS

Curling of Prints.

1. *Distinguishing Characteristic.*—Prints curled upon drying.

2. *Cause.*—The emulsion contracts to a greater extent than the paper backing on prints, so that, upon drying, prints tend to curl with the emulsion on the concave side.

3. *Prevention.*—Curling may be prevented by washing the print in a bath consisting of from 1 to 2 parts of glycerin in 10 parts of water.   The print should be washed in this bath for 5 min. (or until the back paper support is thoroughly saturated with the solution), after which the print may be dried in the usual manner without further washing.   The prints may also be dried flat by laying them (emulsion side down) on the drying stretcher and sponging the back paper slightly with alcohol or water.   With this method, the total time required for drying will be increased, but the prints will dry much flatter than with ordinary drying.

4. *Remedy.*—Prints may be straightened by drawing the print, emulsion side out, over a smooth, rounded corner of a drawing board, table, or similar surface in such a way as to impart concavity to the back of the print.   While this method is quite satisfactory, care should be exercised.   Care is especially necessary with prints having a glossy surface, as the surface of the prints may be cracked.

Frilling.

1. *Distinguishing Characteristic.*—Emulsion separating from the paper backing.

2. *Cause.*—(a) Processing solutions too warm.   (b) Careless handling of print.

3. *Prevention.*—(a) All solutions should be between 60 and 70°F., and all solutions should, preferably, be at the same temperature.   They may be brought to the same temperature by setting them in a water bath for a length of time sufficient to have all solutions reach equilibrium.   (b) Care in handling prints is the only prevention in this case.

4. *Remedy.*—None.

Spotty Glazing.

1. *Distinguishing Characteristic.*—Surface of print not uniformly glossy.

2. *Cause.*—Imperfect or improper ferrotype glazing due to (a) imperfect contact between ferrotype plate and print, (b) improperly prepared surface of ferrotype tin, or (c) failure to squeegee the print on the ferrotype tins.

3. *Prevention.*—(See chapter on Washing, Fixing, and Drying for proper method of ferrotyping.)

4. *Remedy.*—Sometimes spotty glazing may be remedied by soaking the print in water and again drying on the ferrotype plate.

White Deposit on Print.

1. *Distinguishing Characteristic.*—White deposit covering emulsion side of print.

2. *Cause.*—Use of exhausted or incorrectly mixed fixing bath; impurities in fixing bath.   White precipitate in bath deposits on print.

3. *Prevention.*—Properly prepared fixing bath made with fresh pure chemicals. Swab print before washing, but after fixing.

4. *Remedy.*—The deposit may sometimes be removed by soaking the print in water, removing the white or milky deposit, and washing in fresh water, after which it is dried in the usual manner.

STAINS, DISCOLORATIONS, AND IMPROPER TONE REPRODUCTION

Gray or Granular Appearance.

1. *Distinguishing Characteristic.*—Gray or granular appearance of the print, especially at the edges.

2. *Cause.*—Among the causes may be listed: (a) use of old printing paper; (b) underexposure and forced development, (c) printing paper kept in moist atmosphere, (d) insufficient amount of potassium bromide in the developer, (e) light fog.

3. *Prevention.*—When the true source of the gray or granular appearance is determined, the preventive measures will suggest themselves.

4. *Remedy.*—None.

Gray or Lead-colored Print.

1. *Distinguishing Characteristic.*—Gray or lead-colored instead of white high lights in print.

2. *Cause.*—(See Gray or Granular Appearance.)

3. *Prevention.*—(See Gray or Granular Appearance.)

4. *Remedy.*—(See Gray or Granular Appearance.)

Green, Contrasty Prints.

1. *Distinguishing Characteristic.*—Prints are too contrasty and have green appearance.

2. *Cause.*—(a) Underexposure and overdevelopment. (b) Excess bromide in developer.

3. *Prevention.*—(a) Correct exposure and correct development. (b) Properly compounded developer, made from fresh pure chemicals.

4. *Remedy.*—None; make new print.

Purple Discoloration.

1. *Distinguishing Characteristic.*—Print contains purple discoloration.

2. *Cause.*—Improper fixing in which the developer is permitted to act on the print during fixing.

3. *Prevention.*—Immerse print quickly and entirely in fixing solution, agitating it while in solution. Do not permit print to float on surface of fixing solution.

4. *Remedy.*—Make new print.

Tones in Print Are Muddy.

1. *Distinguishing Characteristic.*—Prints have muddy appearance.

2. *Cause.*—Muddy tones in a print may be due to (a) overexposure and over-development, (b) excess potassium bromide in developer, (c) exposure of printing paper to dampness, (d) exposure of paper to chemcal fumes.

3. *Prevention.*—When the real cause for the muddy tones has been determined, the necessary preventive measures required will be self-evident.

4. *Remedy.*—Make new print.

Yellow Stains.

1. *Distinguishing Characteristic.*—Yellow stains on portions of print.

2. *Cause.*—Yellow stains are a fairly frequent source of difficulty and may be due to a number of causes, among them: (*a*) exhausted fixing bath which permits development to proceed, (*b*) forced development, (*c*) weak or exhausted developer, (*d*) hypo carried into the developer, (*e*) failure to rinse prints between developing and fixing baths, (*f*) uncleanliness or impurities in development, (*g*) incomplete washing of the print after fixing, (*h*) exposure of print to light after development but before fixing has been completed, (*i*) prolonged exposure of paper to moist salty atmosphere.

3. *Prevention.*—The preventive measure which will be required will suggest itself when the true cause of the yellow stains has been discovered.

4. *Remedy.*—Make new print.

UNEVENNESS

Small Black Spots.

1. *Distinguishing Characteristic.*—Small black spots, usually circular, on the print.

2. *Cause.*—Print made from negative which has unretouched pinholes.

3. *Prevention.*—Printing from perfect or retouched negative.

4. *Remedy.*—The black spots in the print may be bleached out by applying a small amount of tincture of iodine, applied with a fine brush or sharpened stick of wood, after which the print is washed in hypo. The black spot is changed to a white spot which may be retouched in the usual manner with a spotting brush (see *Camera*, December, 1937, p. 404).

Uneven Development.

1. *Distinguishing Characteristic.*—Streaks of varying density in the print, sometimes accompanied by yellow discoloration.

2. *Cause.*—Uneven development.

3. *Prevention.*—Immerse print in properly prepared, full-strength developer quickly and thoroughly, agitating it during the first few seconds. The print should be thoroughly immersed in developer solution, it should not be permitted to float on top of the solution, and the tank or tray should be rocked.

4. *Remedy.*—Local intensification may be used to build up the less dense portions of the negative.

Uneven Fixing.

1. *Distinguishing Characteristic.*—Uneven density in print, which bears no relation to image.

2. *Cause.*—Uneven fixing. More specifically the cause may be due to (*a*) air bells forming on print (see Air Bells); (*b*) failure to agitate print sufficiently well in fixing bath; (*c*) prints sticking together during fixing, so that protected areas do not become fixed.

3. *Prevention.*—Immerse print quickly and thoroughly in fixing bath. Agitate print during fixing.

4. *Remedy.*—Make new print.

Bibliography

Periodicals:

CRABTREE, J. I., and G. E. MATTHEWS: Study of Markings on Motion Picture Film Produced by Drops of Water, Condensed Water Vapor, and Abnormal Drying Conditions, *Trans. Soc. Motion Picture Engrs.*, **7,** 29 (1923).

————, and M. L. DUNDON: Investigations on Photographic Developers; Sulphide Fog by Bacteria in Motion Picture Developers, *Trans. Soc. Motion Picture Engrs.*, **8,** 28 (1924).

————, and ————: Static Markings on Motion Picture Films, *Trans. Soc. Motion Picture Engrs.*, **9,** 67 (1925).

————, and ————: Rack Marks and Air Bell Markings in Motion Picture Film, *Trans. Soc. Motion Picture Engrs.*, **9,** 95 (1925).

HICKMAN, K. C. D.: Washing Motion Picture Film, *Trans. Soc. Motion Picture Engrs.*, **9,** 365 (1925).

CRABTREE, J. I., and M. L. DUNDON: Staining Properties of Motion Picture Developers, *Trans. Soc. Motion Picture Engrs.*, **10,** 108 (1926).

DUNDON, M. L., and J. I. CRABTREE: Investigations on Photographic Developers, *Trans. Soc. Motion Picture Engrs.*, **10,** 111 (1926).

CRABTREE, J. I.: Graininess of Motion Picture Film, *Trans. Soc. Motion Picture Engrs.*, **11,** 77 (1927).

————, and H. O. CARLTON: Cleaning Liquids for Motion Picture Film, *Trans. Soc. Motion Picture Engrs.*, **11,** 227 (1927).

MATTHEWS, G. E., and J. I. CRABTREE: Oil Spots on Motion Picture Film, *Trans. Soc. Motion Picture Engrs.*, **11,** 728 (1927).

DUNDON, M. L., and J. I. CRABTREE: Fogging Properties of Developers, *J. Soc. Motion Picture Engrs.*, **12,** 1096 (1928).

CARLTON, H. C., and J. I. CRABTREE: Some Properties of Fine Grain Developers for Motion Picture Film, *Trans. Soc. Motion Picture Engrs.*, **13,** 406 (1929).

ROSS, J. F., and J. I. CRABTREE: Fogging Properties of Developing Solutions Stored in Contact with Various Metals and Alloys, *Am. Phot.*, **13,** 254 (1929).

DUNDON, M. L., G. H., BROWN, and J. G. CAPSTAFF: A Quick Test for Determining the Degree of Exhaustion of Developers, *J. Soc. Motion Picture Engrs.*, **15,** 389 (1930).

CRABTREE, J. I., and J. F. ROSS: Method of Testing for the Presence of Sodium Thiosulphite in Motion Picture Films, *J. Soc. Motion Picture Engrs.*, **15,** 419 (1930).

————, G. E. MATHEWS, and J. F. ROSS: Materials for the Construction of Motion Picture Processing Apparatus, *J. Soc. Motion Picture Engrs.*, **16,** 330 (1931).

————, and ————: Effect of Water Supply in Processing Motion Picture Films, *J. Soc. Motion Picture Engrs.*, **16,** 347 (1931).

IVES, C. E., A. J. MILLER, and J. I. CRABTREE: Improvements in Motion Picture Laboratory Practice, *J. Soc. Motion Picture Engrs.*, **17,** 26 (1931).

CRABTREE, J. I.: Directional Effects in Film Processing, *J. Soc. Motion Picture Engrs.*, **18,** 207 (1932).

————, and J. H. WADDELL: Directional Effects in Sound Film Processing, *J. Soc. Motion Picture Engrs.*, **18,** 207 (1932).

WHITE, D. R.: Drying Conditions and Photographic Density, *J. Soc. Motion Picture Engrs.*, **18,** 340 (1932).

CRABTREE, J. I., and H. D. RUSSELL: Reducing Action of Fixing Baths on the Silver Image, *J. Soc. Motion Picture Engrs.*, **18,** 371 (1932).

————, and J. H. WADDELL: Directional Effects in Sound Film Processing, *J. Soc. Motion Picture Engrs.*, **18,** 351 (1933).

JONES, L. A., and J. H. WEBB: Reciprocity Law Failures in Photographic Exposure, *J. Soc. Motion Picture Engrs.*, **19,** 142 (1934).

SHEPPARD, S. E.: Uniformity in Photographic Sensitometry, *J. Soc. Motion Picture Engrs.*, **20,** 512 (1935).

PARKER, H., and J. I. CRABTREE: Rapid Processing Methods, *J. Soc. Motion Picture Engrs.*, **21,** 406 (1936).

Books:

NEBLETTE, C. B.: "Photography Principles and Practice," Van Nostrand.
"Motion Picture Laboratory Practice," Eastman Kodak Co.
"Elementary Photographic Chemistry," Eastman Kodak Co.
"Commercial Photofinishing," Eastman Kodak Co.

CHAPTER XVIII

INTENSIFICATION AND REDUCTION

By Beverly Dudley

The ideal situation to be striven for in the technique of the photographic process is to produce negatives and prints that are free from blemishes and in which the opacities of a portion of the image are properly related to the visual brightness of the corresponding areas of the original subject. When the negative or print departs from these ideal—or other desired—conditions, corrective processes may sometimes be employed to advantage. Among the most important corrective processes may be listed intensification and reduction which are chemical in their characteristics. Physical or mechanical corrective processes, such as retouching, spotting, and the various control methods which may be used in printing will not be discussed in this chapter. The chemical corrective processes may be applied either to the negative or to the print. Usually, however, it is more satisfactory to make a new print than to attempt to correct for certain defects, so that intensification and reduction are used on prints relatively infrequently. Consequently, the majority of the material in this chapter refers primarily to intensification and reduction of negative materials.

INTENSIFICATION

Intensification is the photographic process by which the density and contrast of the silver image are increased. Intensification may be necessary or advisable for several reasons: (1) The negative may be underexposed and so thin that the printing time to obtain the desired result may be inconveniently short. (2) The negative may be underdeveloped and therefore lacking in contrast, in which case intensification may be used to increase contrast. (3) Portions of the negative may be so thin that the resultant print is dark and lacking in detail. In this last case, local intensification of the negative may be quite helpful.

In a negative, intensification may be effected by any chemical or dye process which decreases the transmission of light through the negative. Because such light-absorbing substances may not be neutral, i.e., gray, in color and because the sensitivity characteristics of the human eye differ from those of the photographic paper upon which the negative is to be printed, the visual effect of intensification may differ from the photographic effect. Consequently, it is not always possible to determine the degree of photographic intensification from visual examination or measurements made on an intensified negative. In positive prints, intensification may be effected by any chemical process which increases the visual density of the deposit of silver on the paper, but where prints are concerned, it is highly desirable that the intensification produce a neutral rather than a colored effect.

Classification of Intensifiers.—Intensifiers may be classified according to the three common methods by which intensification may be accomplished:

1. A new film or deposit of silver may be added to that already existing on the negative or print. The silver intensifiers are the only ones producing intensification of neutral color. They have the further advantage in producing a permanent effect.

2. The original silver deposit may be treated with substances which will unite with the metallic silver so as to produce a combined deposit of greater density than that provided by the metallic silver grains alone. Chromium, mercury, lead, copper, and other metals may be used to combine with the original silver. While some of these methods produce an appreciable increase in density, the intensified image may not be neutral in tone.

3. The color of the original deposit may be altered to provide greater opacity to the passage of light through the negative. In such cases the visual and photographic intensification may be quite different, so that visual inspection does not give a good indication of the photographic effect which this type of intensification produces. This is especially true where the color of the intensified negative is yellow, for a yellow stain has relatively high absorption in the blue end of the spectrum to which printing materials are most sensitive.

Instead of classifying the intensification process, as we have done, according to its *modus operandi*, a classification based on the visual and photographic effects is sometimes employed. According to this classification there are three types of intensification:

1. Intensification methods giving both visual and photographic intensification. This is the most common and useful class of intensifiers.

2. Methods giving photographic intensification but visual reduction.

3. Methods giving visual intensification with photographic reduction obtained only when intensifiers having a bleaching effect are employed with negatives which were originally considerably colored or stained.

Considerations in Intensification.—The characteristics of intensifiers as they affect the original negative should be considered in selecting an intensifier for any particular purpose. Permanence of the intensified image is important when prints are to be made over a long period of time from the same negative. Another factor of considerable importance, especially in scientific work, is preservation of gradation of the original image.

Since the desired degree of intensification may not be obtained with a single treatment, it is important to determine whether or not the particular method chosen permits repeated intensification by successive treatments. The color of the intensified image may also have important practical consequences, for it may be extremely difficult to determine by visual inspection the extent of photographic intensification when the intensified image is colored. Thus colored images which result from the use of such intensifiers as uranium and the copper-tin mercuric iodide intensifier followed by Schlippe's salt or an alkaline developer may produce considerably greater photographic intensification than might be judged from visual inspection.

Excessive intensification may have been attained in the intensification process. In such cases it is advantageous to know the conditions under which the intensified image may be reduced.

The important characteristics of the more useful intensifiers are given in Table I. For details on other intensifiers, or for additional data not given here, the reader is referred to more complete articles given in the bibliography.

Sensitometry of Intensification.—The quantitative measurement of the intensification which is possible through the use of various intensifying agents may be determined and expressed in much the same manner as the sensitometric characteristics of photographic materials.[1]

In determining the characteristics of intensifiers, a strip of film is given a series of known, graded or stepped exposures and is then developed, washed, fixed, and dried in

---

[1] Suitable methods for determining sensitometric characteristics have been given in the chapter on Photographic Sensitometry.

TABLE I.—CHARACTERISTICS OF SOME COMMON INTENSIFIERS

Intensifier	Degree of intensification (first bath)	Color of intensified image	Permanence	Effects of successive treatments	Reduction of image	Remarks
Chromium	Moderate. 40% increase in density	Slight. Color depends on nature of redeveloper, and becomes more pronounced with successive treatments	Permanent	Intensification can be increased by repeated bleaching and redevelopment. More than two treatments usually impractical	Can be reduced by dilute HCl or H_2SO_4 solution. Film must be hardened with formalin prior to acid treatment	Reliable. May be used repeatedly
Mercury (Monckhoven's)	High. 80-100% increase in density	Slightly brown when developed in MQ developer	Permanent with ferrous oxalate developer. May not be permanent with other developers	Successive treatments not recommended if permanence is required	Reduction possible by treating with 5% hypo solution. Density reduced to original value with 5-min. treatment	Suitable where high contrast is required. Not subject to as easy control as chromium intensifier
Silver (physical)	Density increases with time of treatment as follows: 25% in 10 min. 50% in 20 min. 56% in 30 min.	None (neutral)	Permanent	High degree of intensification is possible with successive redevelopment	Farmer's or Belitzski's reducer suggested. These do not affect the contrast	Easy to control. Only intensifier giving neutral images
Uranium	Very high. 200% increase in density	Red to brown, depending on the developer	Only moderately permanent	Seldom necessary	....	Suitable for very thin negatives not made usable by other means

the usual manner. The density of the various steps is then measured, and the densities are plotted against the corresponding exposure in the form of the usual D-$\log_{10} E$ characteristic. Such a curve gives the sensitometric characteristics of the test film under the specified processing conditions.

The test strip is then processed in the intensifying bath, according to the conditions required for the particular intensifier in question. After the strip has been dried, the

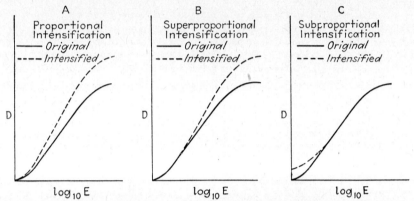

Fig. 1.—Characteristic curves of intensified materials for various types of intensifiers.

densities of the various steps are again measured and plotted as a second D-$\log_{10} E$ curve. We thus have two density determinations for various exposed portions of the test strip; one made before and one made after intensification. The characteristics of the intensifier in altering the original density of the unintensified test strip may

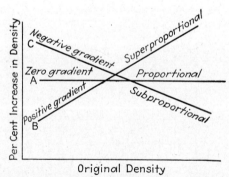

Fig. 2.—The characteristics of various types of intensifiers, plotted against the density of the unintensified material. This type of curve shows the same characteristics as Fig. 1, although in a different form.

then be interpreted from such a graphical plot. Figure 1 illustrates the D-$\log_{10} E$ characteristics of a test strip without intensification, as well as for three idealized types of intensifiers. In curve A, represented by a proportional intensifier, all the densities of the original negative are increased in the intensification process by the same per cent. In curve B, the higher densities are increased a relatively greater amount than the lower densities, whereas in curve C the lower densities receive greater intensification than the higher densities. The desired characteristic of practically all intensifiers is that given by curve A, and most intensifiers have, at least approximately, this general characteristic of proportionality.

As shown in Fig. 2, another method of showing the characteristics of intensifiers is to plot the percentage increase in density due to intensification as ordinates against the original density of the test strip as abscissas. The curves of Fig. 2 correspond to similarly lettered curves of Fig. 1. The curves of Figs. 1 and 2 are idealized for the purpose of illustration, and do not represent the measured characteristics of any particular intensifying agent.

According to whether the slope of the curve of Fig. 2 is positive, zero, or negative, intensifiers have been classified as positive-gradient, proportional, and negative-gradient intensifiers, respectively. According to the published work of Nietz and Huse,[1] and Crabtree and Muehler,[2] the following classification of intensifiers with examples of each type, is permissible:

1. Proportional or zero-gradient intensifiers
    Chromium intensifier
    Mercury intensifier (Monckhoven's intensifier)
    Silver intensifier
2. Positive-gradient intensifiers
    Copper-tin
3. Negative-gradient intensifiers
    Mercuric iodide and Schlippe's salts
    Mercuric iodide and paraminophenol
    Bichromate and hydrochloric acid and Amidol

Because all densities are increased by the same per cent in proportional intensifiers, such intensifiers have the effect of increasing the γ of the developed film. The effect is much the same as if the negative had been developed for a longer time or at a higher temperature since the contrast is increased. Because of their desirable characteristics and their extensive use, only proportional intensifiers will be discussed in this chapter. For details of the other types of intensifiers, reference should be made to the paper by Nietz and Huse.

Intensifiers. *Chromium Intensifier*—Intensification with chromium is a favorite method for moderate degree of intensification and lends itself to various control methods, depending upon the composition of the bleaching bath.

In chromium intensification, the original silver image is bleached in a solution of potassium bichromate and hydrochloric acid or hydrobromic acid or, alternatively, a solution of chromic acid and sodium chloride. The bleaching process is then followed by redevelopment in any ordinary developer and by washing.

Although the exact proportions of the various constituents may be varied over rather wide limits, a suitable bleaching bath may be made as follows:

Potassium bichromate	8 g.	1 oz.
Hydrochloric acid	6 cc.	¾ oz.
Water	1 l.	1 gal.

Research by Carnegie and Piper[3] has indicated that the degree of intensification depends upon the concentration of the constituents, especially that of the acid. By

[1] Nietz and Huse, *Phot. J.*, **58**, 81 (1918); *J. Franklin Inst.*, March, 1918; *Brit. J. Phot.*, **65**, 179, 191 (1918).

[2] Crabtree, J. I., and L. E. Muehler, Reducing and Intensifying Solutions for Motion Picture Film, *J. Soc. Motion. Picture Engrs.*, **17** (No. 6), 1001–1053 (1931).

[3] Carnegie, D. J., and C. W. Piper, Intensification and Redevelopment, *Am. Phot.*, **40**, 336, 1904.

varying the concentration, various degrees of intensification are possible. The greatest intensification is produced with relatively small amounts of acid (2 cc. per l.) and bichromate (10 g. per l.), whereas the degree of intensification decreases as these concentrations are increased. The quantity of acid cannot be increased indefinitely, as the rate of bleaching slows down. The maximum concentration recommended by Carnegie and Piper was 20 g. bichromate per liter and 40 cc. acid per liter. The formula given on p. 551 is that recommended by Crabtree and Muehler[1] and gives an increase of 40 per cent in density for a single treatment when redeveloped in D-72 developer. The intensification can be increased and greater speed of bleaching results if 5 g. potassium bromide is added to each liter of solution. If desired, the solutions can be made up for storage with ten times the concentration given above and may be diluted 10 to 1 for use as required.

Bleaching will require about ½ to 3 min. Incomplete bleaching results in relatively greater intensification of the lower densities compared with the higher. After bleaching, the negative is washed in running water until all trace of bichromate has been removed. The negative is then redeveloped in a nonstaining developer. Since the sulphite may result in reduction of lower densities, the developer is preferably one in which the sodium sulphite concentration is low. Suitable developers include those composed of Amidol, metol-hydroquinone, metol, or paraminophenol. See chapter on Developers and Theory of Development. A suitable developer is the Eastman D-72, which is prepared as follows:

Hot water (approximately 125°)	500	cc.	64 oz.
Metol (Elon)	3.1 g.		180 gr.
Sodium sulphite (desiccated)	45	g.	6 oz.
Hydroquinone	12.5 g.		1 oz. 260 gr.
Sodium carbonate (desiccated)	67.5 g.		9 oz.
Potassium bromide	1.9 g.		¼ oz.
Water to make	1	l.	1 gal.

Develop from 3 to 10 min. (depending upon degree of intensification desired) at 65 to 70°F. Rinse the negative and immerse in fixing bath for 5 min., wash thoroughly, and then dry.

The intensification process may be repeated, if desired, although the degree of intensification decreases with each treatment as the number of treatments is increased.

Mercury Intensifier.—Intensification with mercury is accomplished by depositing metallic mercury or one of its compounds on the silver image. This is accomplished by first bleaching the silver image in mercuric chloride or mercuric bromide to produce silver mercurous chloride. The compound thus produced is reduced, in the process of development, to silver and mercury compounds or mercury and compounds of silver and mercury, according to the character of the redeveloper.

A suitable bleach consists of

Potassium bromide	22.5 g.	3 oz.
Mercuric chloride[1]	22.5 g.	3 oz.
Water to make	1	l.	1 gal.

[1] Mercuric chloride is extremely poisonous and should be handled accordingly.

It is essential that negatives be free from hypo before bleaching, or local stains may result. The negative is bleached until the image is white. After bleaching, wash the negative in running water for 5 to 10 min., and redevelop.

Several suitable redeveloping solutions are possible, but the silver cyanide redeveloper (forming with the above bleach what is known as Monckhoven's intensifier) is one of the most suitable and best known. Monckhoven's intensifier results in a high degree of intensification, although reduction occurs for the very low densities.

This intensifier is consequently well suited to black-and-white line work, or where high contrast is desired. The silver cyanide redeveloper consists of

Sodium or potassium cyanide (poison)	15 g.	2 oz.
Silver nitrate	22.5 g.	3 oz.
Water to make	1 l.	1 gal.

The cyanide and silver nitrate should be dissolved separately, and the latter added to the former until a permanent precipitate is just formed. After the mixture has stood about an hour, it should be filtered and is then ready for use. After redeveloping, the negative is washed and dried. The intensified images are not entirely permanent.

Silver or Physical Intensifiers.—Intensification with silver, sometimes called "physical intensification," produces a permanent image of neutral color. The degree of intensification may be easily controlled by varying the duration of the intensification bath or through the use of successive treatments. Silver intensification is accomplished by immersing the negative in an acid solution of silver nitrate which contains a reducing agent such as metol. In this solution silver is precipitated in colloidal form upon the original silver image. This colloidal silver deposits differentially on the silver image substantially in proportion to the amount of silver in the original image. Consequently all densities are increased to the same extent, and true proportional intensification results. Furthermore a permanent image of neutral color is obtained, since the products of the intensification are the same as those of the original image.

The following silver intensifier, taken from Crabtree and Muehler[1] is more stable and satisfactory than those previously recommended:

SOLUTION 1

Silver nitrate	60 g.	2	oz.
Water to make	1 l.	32	oz.

SOLUTION 2

Sodium sulphite (desiccated)	60 g.	2	oz.
Water to make	1 l.	32	oz.

SOLUTION 3

Sodium thiosulphate crystals	105 g.	3.5	oz.
Water to make	1 l.	32	oz.

SOLUTION 4

Sodium sulphite (desiccated)	15 g.	219	gr.
Elon (metol)	24 g.	351	gr.
Water to make	3 l.	96	oz.

To prepare the intensifier, add one part of solution 1 slowly to one part of solution 2, obtaining a thorough mixture by stirring or shaking. A white precipitate will form which is dissolved by the addition of one part of solution 3. The resulting solution should be permitted to stand until clear, after which three parts of solution 4 should be added, with constant stirring. The film should be treated immediately in this solution. This mixed solution is stable for about 30 to 45 min. at 70°F.

The degree of intensification obtained depends upon the length of time the film is immersed in the solution, but because the solution is not stable for a much longer time, this should not exceed 25 min. After intensification, the film should be immersed and agitated in a plain 30 per cent hypo bath for 2 min. It should then be washed thoroughly. Since it has been found that hypo baths have some reducing action on the silver image, the film should not be left in the hypo bath too long.

A 50 per cent increase in density can be obtained by immersing the film in the silver intensifier for 10 min., but a much higher degree of intensification may be obtained through the use of successive treatments.

[1] *Ibid.*

Reduction of the intensified image may be accomplished by the use of such subtractive reducers as Farmer's and Belitzski's reducers. These reducers do not affect the contrast of the intensified image. Suitable formulas giving proportional reduction with the silver image have not been developed to date, so that the desired contrast will have to be determined in the intensification process.

Uranium Intensifier.—Uranium intensification produces an extremely high degree of intensification[1] primarily because of the color of its image, which varies from reddish brown to bright red. A disadvantage of uranium intensification is that the photographic intensification is considerably greater than visual intensification, so that the desired effect may be difficult to judge. Moreover, the intensified image is not completely permanent. Because of the high intensification produced, the method is suitable for use with very thin negatives where other intensification methods might be unsuitable, or it may be used as a local intensifier.

A suitable uranium intensifier may be made with the following two solutions:

SOLUTION 1

Potassium ferricyanide	50 g.	384 gr.
Water	1 l.	16 oz.

SOLUTION 2

Uranium nitrate	50 g.	384 gr.
Potassium bromide	20 g.	154 gr.
Water	1 l.	16 oz.

Immerse the negative in solution 1 until bleached, then wash thoroughly in water. Immerse in solution 2 until no further action takes place, and wash in a dilute bath of acetic acid. Finally wash in plain water, and dry.

Because of the change in color produced, uranium intensification is sometimes considered as a toning process.

REDUCTION

Photographic reduction is the process by which the effective density of the photographic deposit is diminished. Reduction of the photographic image may be desirable for several reasons: (1) It may be desired to diminish the average density of the negative so that the printing time may be reduced; (2) reduction may be used to increase or decrease the contrast; (3) traces of fog may be removed by reduction; (4) effects of overexposure or overdevelopment of a positive image may be modified by reduction.

The process of reduction consists in dissolving away some of the silver deposit of the image. Depending upon the differential action of the reducing agent on the density of the original silver image, the effect of photographic reduction varies with the type of reducer employed. This gives rise to the following convenient classification of photographic reducers:

Types of Reducers.—Subtractive reducers are those which remove an equal amount of silver from all parts of the image or from all densities. Through their use the general or mean density of the negative is diminished but the density range (and consequently the contrast) is usually increased. Subtractive reducers are used mainly to improve overexposed negatives and positives, or for the removal of fog. Subtractive reducers are also known as "cutting" or "surface cutting" reducers.

Proportional reducers are those which remove the silver deposit in proportion to the amount originally present in the image. Thus, all densities are reduced by the same percentage, and contrast is decreased. Proportional reducers are used mainly to reduce excessive density and contrast due to overdevelopment.

Superproportional reducers remove a greater percentage of silver from the high densities than from the low. Accordingly the decrease in density due to reduction is

[1] NIETZ and HUSE, *Phot. J.*, **58**, 81 (1918); *J. Franklin Inst.*, **185** (No. 2), 231 (1918).

proportional to the amount of silver originally present in the image. Such a reducer decreases the contrast and is used chiefly for the reduction of overdeveloped negatives of contrasty subjects.

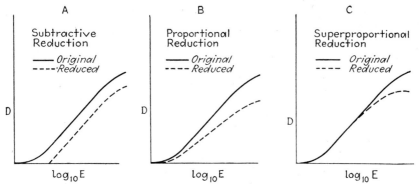

Fig. 3.—Characteristic curves of original and reduced photographic materials for various types of reducers.

Sensitometry of Reducers.—The characteristics of reducing agents may be determined in exactly the same manner as the characteristics of intensifiers are determined, and the results may be plotted in the same form. Figure 3 shows the D-$\log_{10} E$ characteristics of an assumed photographic material, together with hypothetical characteristics of the three idealized types of reducers. Figure 4 shows the characteristics of reducers plotted in such a way that their classification is somewhat more readily recognized. In Fig. 3, curve A represents the subtractive reducer, curve B the proportional reducer, and curve C the superproportional or "flattening" reducer. These three types of reducers, as may be seen from Fig. 4, may be labeled as positive-gradient,

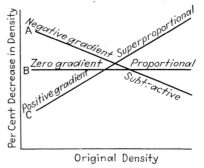

Fig. 4.—The characteristics of various types of reducers, expressed in percentage change of the original density.

zero-gradient, and negative-gradient reducers, corresponding, respectively, to superproportional, proportional, and subproportional reducers of Fig. 3.

According to this classification, the following three types of reducers together with representative formulas are permissible:

1. Superproportional or positive-gradient reducers
    Farmer's reducer
    Haddon's reducer
    Iodine-cyanide reducer
    Ferricyanide and cyanide reducer
    Modified Belitzski reducer
    Potassium permanganate reducer
    Bichromate reducer
    Ceric ammonium nitrate reducer
    Ceric ammonium sulphate reducer
    Ferricyanide and ammonium sulphocyanide

      Iodide-hypo reducer

      Copper reducer

  2. Proportional or zero-gradient reducers

      Ferrocyanide-hypo

      Permanganate in acid state

      Quinone

      Quinone sulphonates } with sulphuric acid

      Deck ammonium persulphate

      Ferric salts

  3. Subproportional or negative-gradient reducers

      Alkaline persulphate (ammonium persulphate)

      Persulphate reducer

      Bensoquinone

      Erdmann's salt

      Potassium permanganate with ammonium sulphocyanide

The literature on photographic reducers is so voluminous that no attempt will be made to describe more than the most common and satisfactory reducers in general use. For additional information, the reader is referred to the references given in the bibliography.

Subtractive Reducers. *Farmer's Reducer.*—A popular reducer introduced by Howard Farmer consists of a mixture of potassium ferricyanide and sodium thiosulphate. In this reducer, the silver image is attacked and oxidized by the ferrocyanide, and silver ferrocyanide is formed. Since this silver ferrocyanide is soluble in hypo, the silver removed from the negative goes into solution.

Farmer's reducer is used as a single solution reducer, although it is made up in two stock solutions since the mixture does not keep well. A satisfactory formula is

Solution 1

Potassium ferricyanide	37.5 g.	1¼	oz.
Water to make	500 cc.	16	oz.

Solution 2

Sodium thiosulphate (hypo)	480 g.	16	oz.
Water to make	2 l.	64	oz.

For use, 30 cc. (1 oz.) of solution 1 and 120 cc. (4 oz.) of solution 2 are diluted with water to make 1 l. (32 oz.) of reducing solution. The negative is immersed in this working solution until the desired reduction is obtained, after which the negative is washed and dried. The reducing action continues slightly after the film is removed from the reducing solution, so that it is well to remove the negative to the wash bath just before the desired reduction is obtained. The action may best be carried out in a shallow white tray which facilitates easy inspection of the degree of reduction taking place. The mixed solution does not keep well, and if sufficient reduction is not obtained after about 5 min., the film should be transferred to a fresh bath until the desired result is obtained.

While classed as a subtractive or cutting reducer, the effect produced by this reducer depends to a large degree upon the nature of the reducing solution and the image which is being reduced. Crabtree and Muehler have found that a two-solution reducer is more satisfactory and permits greater control than the single-solution Farmer's reducer. A vigorously acting formula such as one containing 1 per cent of potassium ferricyanide and 10 per cent sodium thiosulphate, produces almost purely subtractive reduction of the silver image. The color of the reduced image may be slightly brown, but this is ordinarily not objectionable.

Farmer's double-solution reducer is made up as two stock solutions, according to the formula:

SOLUTION 1

Potassium ferricyanide	7.5 g.	1 oz.
Water to make	1 l.	1 gal.

SOLUTION 2

Sodium thiosulphate (hypo)	200 g.	1 lb. 11 oz.
Water to make	1 l.	1 gal.

The negatives are agitated in solution 1 for from 1 to 4 min. (depending upon the reduction desired) at 65 to 70°F. The film is then immersed in solution 2 for 5 min., after which it is washed thoroughly. If more reduction is desired, the process may be repeated.

Haddon's Reducer.—A single solution made of ferricyanide and ammonium sulphocyanide, formulated by Haddon, is of the subtractive type but has the advantage that the solution is stable. The reducing solution is made as follows:

Potassium ferricyanide	5 g.	22 gr.
Ammonium sulphocyanide	10 g.	44 gr.
Water to make	1 l.	10 oz.

The negative is immersed in this solution until the desired reduction is obtained, after which the film is washed in running water and dried. With this reducer, there is a tendency for a slight white deposit to form on the film. The deposit is soluble in sodium thiosulphate as well as in sodium cyanide and may be removed by immersing the negative in hypo. A small quantity of sodium cyanide may be added to the reducer to prevent formation of this deposit.

Iodine-cyanide Reducer.—A subtractive reducer which removes a slightly greater quantity of silver from the denser portion than from the lower densities may be made of a dilute solution of sodium or potassium cyanide with a small amount of iodine. A suitable formula is

Sodium cyanide (poison)	5 g.	22 gr.
Iodine crystals	1 g.	4.5 gr.
Water to make	1 l.	10 oz.

The solution is highly unstable and must therefore be prepared immediately before use. Approximately 30 per cent reduction in density may be obtained in 10 min. After suitable reduction has been obtained, wash in clear water, and dry.

Ferricyanide and Cyanide Reducer.—A solution of potassium ferricyanide and sodium cyanide forms a stable reducer of the subtractive type. Its disadvantages are that it is highly poisonous and softens the gelatin, so that preliminary hardening in a formalin bath (see Chapter on Fixing, Washing, and Drying) is necessary. A suitable formula is:

Potassium ferricyanide	2.5 g.	10.5 gr.
Sodium cyanide	2.5 g.	10.5 gr.
Water to make	1 l.	10 oz.

By doubling the concentration of the ingredients, a more rapid rate of reduction is obtainable. After the desired reduction, wash the negative in water, and dry.

Modified Belitzski's Reducer.—This reducer partakes of the characteristics of both subtractive and proportional reducers. It reduces the slope of the D-$\log_{10} E$ curve of the photographic material, although a greater proportion of silver is removed from the lower than from the higher densities. The solution keeps from 3 to 5 days. The modification recommended by Crabtree and Muehler is

Ferric chloride (crystals)	25 g.	3⅓ oz.
Potassium citrate	75 g.	10 oz.
Sodium sulphite (desiccated)	30 g.	4 oz.
Citric acid	20 g.	2⅓ oz.
Sodium thiosulphate crystals	200 g.	1 lb. 11 oz.
Water to make	1 l.	1 gal.

Potassium Permanganate Reducer.—A dilute solution of potassium permanganate acidified with sulphuric acid may be classified as a subtractive reducer, although like the modified Belitzski's reducer, it shows characteristics intermediate between subtractive and proportional reducers. The solution is not stable in contact with the air for more than a few hours when a single-solution reducer is used. Accordingly the reducer may be made up in two stock solutions as follows:

SOLUTION 1

Potassium permanganate	1.0 g.	1¾ oz.
Water to make	0.5 l.	32 oz.

SOLUTION 2

Sulphuric acid (concentrated)	5.0 cc.	1 oz.
Water to make	0.5 l.	32 oz.

The working solution is made up of one part of each of the stock solutions.

After the desired reduction has been obtained, the film should be immersed in a 1 per cent solution of sodium bisulphite for several minutes, or in an acid fixing bath, and should then be rewashed. This reducer has the characteristics of a subtractive reducer, but by decreasing the amount of sulphuric acid or by using a weak acid, such as acetic acid, the reducer is more nearly proportional in its characteristics.

Proportional Reducers. *Krauss' Ferric Ammonium Sulphate Reducer.*—A reducer having little or no action on low values of density but appreciable action on densities greater than about 0.5 may be made of ferric ammonium sulphate in acid solution. The formula, originally suggested by Krauss, but modified by Crabtree and Muehler is

Ferric ammonium sulphate	15 g.	0.5 oz.
Sulphuric acid (concentrated)	10 cc.	0.3 oz.
Water to make	1 l.	32 oz.

In order that stains may not result, it is essential that the film to be reduced be freed of hypo and silver salts and that the film be not permitted to come into contact with the air during reduction. A disadvantage of this reducer is that it softens the gelatin during treatment, so that prehardening in a formalin bath is desirable.

The film is immersed in the above solution until the desired reduction is obtained, but this should not exceed about 8 min., as otherwise the low values of densities are reduced and the property of proportional reduction is no longer maintained. Treatment for 6 min. gives about 30 per cent reduction in density.

Nietz and Huse Reducer.—Subtractive and superproportional reducers may be combined to produce a proportional reducer. Such a proportional reducer may be made by combining potassium permanganate and ammonium persulphate reducers.

The following, worked out by Nietz and Huse, is a satisfactory formula for proportional reduction:

SOLUTION 1

Potassium permanganate	0.25 g.	38.0 gr.
Sulphuric acid (10 per cent)	15 cc.	0.25 oz.
Distilled water to make	1 l.	35 oz.

SOLUTION 2

Ammonium persulphate	25 g.	0.75 oz.
Distilled water to make	1 l.	35 oz.

For use one part of solution 1 is added to three parts of solution 2. The keeping properties of the combined solutions is very poor so the solutions should be mixed immediately before use. After reduction, which requires from 1 to 3 min., the negative should be immersed in a 1 per cent solution of potassium metabisulphite. This bath will remove the stains produced by the manganese salts precipitated in the gelatin.

Superproportional Reducers.—Only a few substances produce superproportional reducers, and of these the alkaline persulphates (usually ammonium) alone are of practical utility. As photographic reducing agents, the persulphate reducers are erratic in their behavior. Since they act more rapidly as reduction proceeds, negatives reduced in persulphate reducers should be watched carefully in order that reduction is not carried beyond the desired degree. The reducing action may be halted by placing the negative in an acid fixing bath. A suitable formula is

Water..	500 cc.	5 oz.
Ammonium persulphate................................	60 g.	262 gr.
Sulphuric acid (concentrated).........................	3 cc.	15 minims
Water to make......................................	1 l.	10 oz.

Because of the erratic behavior of persulphate reducers, it is best to make up this solution just prior to use. The quantity of acid controls the rate of reduction.

When the desired degree of reduction is attained, immerse the film in an acid fixing bath for several minutes and then wash in clear water. If the action of this reducer is too vigorous, the rate of reduction may be decreased by further dilution.

Harmonizing.—A corrective treatment which stands midway between intensification and reduction is the process commonly known as "harmonizing." Essentially this process carries out intensification of shadow detail without affecting the high lights or reduces the high lights without altering the shadows or lower densities. This method is useful in treating highly contrasty negatives or negatives which have been underexposed and overdeveloped.

The negative is first bleached in a solution consisting of

Potassium bichromate...	8 g.	1	oz.
Hydrochloric acid (concentrated)...............................	6 cc.	0.75	oz.
Potassium bromide..	5 g.	0.6	oz.
Water to make..	1 l.	1	gal.

When the negative has been completely bleached, it is redeveloped in a dilute developer composed of the following:

Elon (metol)...	2 g.	$\frac{1}{4}$	oz.
Sodium sulphite (desiccated)...................................	10 g.	$1\frac{1}{4}$	oz.
Sodium carbonate (desiccated).................................	10 g.	$1\frac{1}{4}$	oz.
Water to make..	1 l.	1	gal.

Redevelopment of from 1 to 2 min. results in superproportional reduction of the higher densities, but proportional intensification of the low values of density. After bleaching, the negative is immersed in an acid fixing bath for 5 min., washed in clear water, and dried.

Local Intensification and Reduction.—So far consideration has been given only to general intensification and reduction of the entire negative. In some cases, however, it may be desired to intensify or reduce portions of the negative without affecting other portions. Treatment of a portion of the negative is called "local intensification" or "local reduction," and this may be highly useful in bringing out certain shadow details or in reducing the density of a high light.

Local intensification or reduction may be carried out by applying the proper solution directly to the negative by means of a soft camel's-hair brush. If fairly large areas must be treated, tufts of absorbent cotton saturated with the solution may be preferred to the use of a soft brush. If the negative has been dried, it should be soaked in clear water for 10 or 20 min. before attempting to apply the solution. The negative should be moist for this afterwork, but should not contain too much water. Best results are usually obtained when the surface moisture has been removed by means of lintless blotters or sponges.

If care is taken with this method, few difficulties will be encountered. In order that the desired intensification may be obtained, it is preferable to choose an intensifier which does not stain appreciably. It may be desirable to dilute the intensifying or reducing solutions to prevent too rapid action and to keep the treatment completely under control. The main difficulty with this method of correction, especially for the inexperienced, is one of keeping the applied solutions from spreading to undesired portions of the negative. This difficulty may be reduced to a minimum by working over small areas and by removing the surface water from the negative.

Yellow or orange dyes or well-diluted water colors may be applied to portions of the negative for local tone lightening. These colors should be applied with a moist, rather than wet, brush, and only a small amount of coloring should be added at a time. The surplus water should be removed as soon as the desired area has been treated. Through the use of successive applications, the density may be built up to the desired amount. A disadvantage of this system is that it is difficult to determine, by visual inspection, the degree of photographic intensification which has been obtained.

Intensification may also be carried out by darkening the negative with lead or lithographic pencils, although this process is, perhaps, more properly to be regarded as one of retouching than of intensification.

A simple method of intensification which does not involve treatment of the particular negative may be effected by making a duplicate negative with a higher scale of density than the original. Intensification may be carried out in the making of the positive from the original negative and again when making the final negative.

The use of a duplicate negative, having a lower contrast than the original, may also be used for reduction.

A simple method of reduction consists of removing some of the silver through the use of an abrasive reducing paste applied to the image on the negative or through the application of an abrasive pencil or rubber eraser.

The contrast of a negative may be reduced by practically any desired degree by printing from a negative a positive transparency, and binding this positive mask with the negative. The mask may be made on sensitive material on a slow film or plate and may have low or high contrast, according to the degree of masking required.

Bibliography

Periodicals:

HADDON, A.: Potassium Ferricyanide and Ammonium Sulphocyanide Reducer, *Brit. J. Phot.*, **39,** 49, 60 (1892).
PIPER, C. W., and D. J. CARNEGIE: Intensification and Redevelopment, *Amateur Phot.*, **40,** 336 (1904).
HUSE, K., and A. H. NIETZ: Proportional Reducers, *Brit. J. Phot.*, **63,** 580 (1916).
NIETZ, A. H., and K. HUSE: The Sensitometry of Photographic Intensification, *J. Franklin Inst.*, **185,** 389 (1918).
KRAUSS, H.: Reduction of Photographic Plates with Ferric Ammonium Sulphate, *Z. wiss. Phot.*, **18,** 192 (1919).
BUNEL, L. J.: Harmonizing Negatives by Intensification with Chromium, *Brit. J. Phot.*, **70,** 625 (1923).
CRABTREE, J. I., and L. E. MUEHLER: Reducing and Intensifying Solutions for Motion Picture Film, *J. Soc. Motion Picture Engrs.*, **17** (No. 6), 1001–1053 (1931).

Books:

WALL, E. J.: "Intensification and Reduction," Am. Photographic Pub.
"The Tinting and Toning of Eastman Positive Motion Picture Film," Eastman Kodak Co.

CHAPTER XIX

DARKROOMS AND DARKROOM PRACTICE

By Keith Henney

General Characteristics of Darkrooms.—The darkroom is the photographer's laboratory and as such deserves special consideration with regard to (1) size, (2) layout and location of apparatus, (3) location, (4) lighting, (5) ventilation, (6) treatment of walls and ceiling, (7) temperature, humidity, and dust, and (8) water supply and drain.

Size.—The dimensions of the darkroom will depend on the space that is available, on the nature of the work to be done, or on the financial or mechanical ability of the photographer to make his laboratory exactly what he wants it to be.

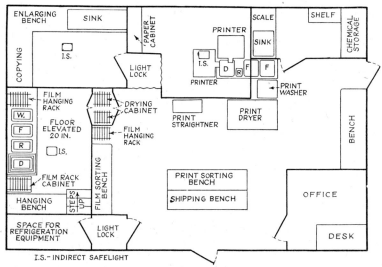

Fig. 1.—Layout of darkroom for photofinishing plant.

Although it is probable that no darkroom was ever too large, a rambling place with apparatus at opposite ends of the room is more tiring and time consuming to work in than a small but well-arranged room. Many amateurs accomplish remarkable work in small closets, in the bathroom or kitchenette of a small apartment, or in a corner of the basement. These workshops must be considered as distinct handicaps to the serious worker, although, perforce nothing much can be done about it. Photography with the miniature camera, of course, requires much less space than work with large plates or films.

A large commercial studio may have several darkrooms, or several divisions of a main laboratory. A small darkroom (loading room) is frequently placed next to the exposing studio or gallery so that plateholders may be handed to the cameraman through some sort of lighttight cabinet. This loading room need not be large, but it should not be a part of the place where negatives are developed or printed, if this

561

separation is possible. Neither should the loading room be part of a room where chemicals are stored or are mixed.

Whenever possible, a room at least 10 by 10 ft. should be available, even for amateur activities.

Layout.—If a single room must suffice for all operations, it must be carefully planned and arranged. The layout should be flexible, however, since no one can tell in advance of having worked in the darkroom exactly how and where the several pieces of equipment should be situated. After the room has been in service for a time, the photographer may wish to reorganize it so that he may work with greater ease and efficiency.

Sufficient space, and proper arrangement, are vitally necessary to the photographer who will make color prints. More equipment and more chemicals will be needed. Every facility must be provided the worker so that he does not waste material.

A dry place to load film or plateholders is essential. It should be as far from the sink as possible so that no drop of water or chemical can fall upon and ruin an important negative. Chemicals should not be stored, weighed, or mixed in the processing room. Dry specks of chemical are sure to fall upon the workbench, later to be blown into the air and perhaps to settle on a wet film or plate.

If possible, sensitive materials should be stored somewhere else than in the processing room. Because the processing room tends to be humid, plates, films, and papers tend to deteriorate unless pains are taken to keep them free from moisture. The layout should be such that an easy flow of work can take place.

Placement of the Darkroom.—Because of the quantities of liquid exposed to the air in the processing room, this room tends to be damp. If, at the same time, it is cooler than the surrounding rooms, moisture will condense from water-laden air entering from warmer rooms. For this reason the basement is a poor place for a darkroom. The surrounding earth keeps the room cool in summer, and it is then that most trouble is had with humidity. Wooden apparatus is likely to swell and stick, metal parts to oxidize, and sensitive materials to mildew.

The operator of a commercial studio has greater choice of a proper place than has the amateur and can locate the processing rooms on the first or other floors above the level of the ground.

The attic is hot in summer and cold in winter and may be far from sources of water or from drainage.

The first or second floor of the house is the ideal place for the amateur's darkroom. Here the workroom is easily heated, drainage is simple, and water can usually be had without too much trouble. Wherever placed, the darkroom must be above the drain pipes for the house. Otherwise trouble may be experienced in disposing of waste liquids (see Water and Drain, page 564).

Lighting.—It is a mistake to paint the darkroom walls and ceiling or benches in dark colors. A light green or buff color will be easy on the eyes and under safe-light illumination will enable one's work to be viewed much easier than if the walls and ceiling are black. Under ordinary illumination (not safe light) the photographer should have as much light as he can conveniently get into the room. Prints should be viewed by illumination by which they will finally be judged. A print that is to be looked at in daylight, should be criticized by the photographer in that light, or as near as he can attain it, before it is termed finished or ready to be released. Several hundred watts of incandescent "daylight" illumination are not too much, particularly if color printing is part of the photographer's work.[1]

In the darkroom there should be numerous outlets for electricity. More outlets should be installed than seem necessary. All will be used at some time or other. A

[1] Recent introduction of fluorescent lamps has provided the photographer with an excellent source of illumination which is very efficient and which has characteristics approaching daylight.

consistent scheme of switching should be employed, *e.g.*, snap switches for safe lights, push switches for general illumination.   Then in the dark, there is little chance of turning on the wrong lights.   A still safer system is to make it necessary to insert a key into the switch that controls the general illumination; but the trouble with this is that the key may be lost, unless it is permanently attached to the switch in some manner.   A foot switch controlling a light used for inspecting a print, frees both hands for rocking a tray, etc.,

Special paints are available for darkroom use.   For use on trays, benches, sinks, etc., these paints should be acid and alkali resistant, and light in color.   Kodacoat of Eastman Kodak, Larkaloid of Larkin Co., Tornesite of May Products Co., and Pliolite of Pratt and Lambert are recommended.   It seems to be extremely difficult to get a paint which certain developing agents will not stain, but frequent painting will assure that benches, etc., are kept clean and in good condition.

Ceilings and the upper parts of the walls may be painted with a light buff or green.   Equipped with an indirect illumination scheme, the light-colored ceiling will contribute to general illumination which will be much better than that secured by directly illuminating the object to be inspected by rays from the safe light.   Lower parts of walls, likely to be touched with wet hands, may be painted a darker color and with a paint which may be more stain resistant.

Ventilation.—It is highly important that those who work in a processing room be provided with a copious supply of fresh air and that stale and noxious air be constantly withdrawn from the room.   Since the room must be absolutely dark at times, this ventilation problem is serious in the small darkroom, although the commercial establishments have the funds and facilities for doing a thorough job of ventilation.   If a vent is cut at the top and at the bottom of the walls of the darkroom and if these vents are properly light-trapped, a circulation of air will take place, the warmer air at the top leaving through the upper vent, and the cooler air coming in at the bottom.   If sufficient circulation does not take place naturally, a fan may be installed to force air out of the room.

Eastman Kodak Co. and others provide simple blowers which may be installed in the wall and which provide a constant and sufficient change of air for darkrooms of various sizes.   Clerc cites a French law requiring 10 cu. meters of fresh air for each person working in the laboratory, the air to be completely changed at reasonable intervals.

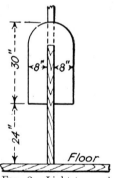

FIG. 2.—Light-trapped ventilator.

Temperature and Humidity.—The darkroom should be maintained at a temperature of 65 to 70°.   The latter is a comfortable working temperature, and any temperature within this range is satisfactory for processing of all kinds.   It is difficult, however, to maintain a darkroom at a constant and desirable temperature without special efforts, which are usually beyond the means of any but the larger establishments. If the darkroom temperature is outside the range 65 to 70°, the photographer is distinctly handicapped in doing consistently good work because he must engage in a constant struggle to maintain his solutions above or below the ambient temperature. Developers for paper prints should not vary much from 70° for best results; films and plates will develop to different contrasts unless the temperature (and strength) of the developer is always the same.   This is particularly important to the worker in color photography who is faced with the problem of making three negatives with exactly the same contrast: virtually an impossible task if the developer cools or heats up during the development period.

It is easier to warm the darkroom than to cool it. Warm air may be taken from surrounding rooms; or electric, gas, or hot-water heaters may be utilized. Open flame is dangerous particularly if much nitrate film is used. It must be remembered that warm air and water rises and that, if the darkroom is on the same level as the furnace or heat supply, it may be difficult to force heat into the room.

Refrigerating systems are available for the commercial plants. The best commercial plants are not only heated but air conditioned. Suitable equipment is described by Crabtree and Matthews.[1]

If miniature camera negatives are to be processed or if color photography is to be done, certain other requirements must be met. Miniature negatives are frequently enlarged as much as ten to twenty times or even greater. The slightest flaw on the negative, such as scratches, dust spots, or finger marks, are enlarged to the same extent as the desired image and often form the practical limit of successful enlargement. Negatives marred by scratches or with dust or lint will produce prints which may require considerable time and labor in spotting.

It is necessary, therefore, that the darkroom worker who is responsible for miniature film processing take extreme precautions to deliver clean negatives to the printer; the printer also must work in a clean and not too dry atmosphere. Greatest trouble in enlarging miniature negatives occurs on cool dry days when it may become practically impossible to place the negative in the enlarger without getting it covered with dust or lint floating about in the air.

Air coming into the miniature processing room should be cleaned if possible, and if the room itself can be maintained slightly humid, dust troubles will be lessened.

Certain color processes may require rooms of given temperature range and of given humidity. These requirements practically force the photographer to install air-conditioning equipment.

Water and Drain.—Hot and cold running water are essential. Hot water is necessary for carbro and wash-off color printing and for certain print toning operations. It is useful in maintaining solutions at temperatures above the ambient. Cold water, of course, is absolutely essential.

There must be a drain to the sink. This makes it necessary for the darkroom to be above the level of the drain pipes in the building, or it will be necessary to provide a separate drain for waste water and solutions. One expedient is to place a large metal tank, *e.g.*, an oil barrel, in the ground below the darkroom level. If the tank is equipped with pipes or vents running into the surrounding earth—from which there must be good drainage—it will serve as an adequate disposal arrangement. Such a waste disposal device may be against the sanitary laws of the community, however.[2]

Several faucets should be provided, or other arrangements should be made so that the water may be utilized at various positions. Most city water is dirty and is contaminated with organic matter and iron rust from pipes. The water, therefore, should be filtered before mixing solutions or washing films. This can be done by tying several layers of cheesecloth over the end of a hose attached to the faucet; or by running the water through felt. Commercial filters for this purpose are available.

It will be an advantage if the floor is smoothly cemented, sloping to a drain in the center. Over the cement may be placed boards which may be removed occasionally

---

[1] "Photographic Chemicals and Solutions," Am. Photographic Pub. (1939). A considerable quantity of valuable data will be found in "Motion Picture Laboratory Practice," Eastman Kodak Co. (1936).

[2] The author has used a 50-gal. tank of this type in a small color laboratory for over a year. The quantity of waste water at any one time is not very great and on Long Island, where the darkroom is located, the soil is sand and glaciated gravel having good drainage. It is necessary to have an air vent in such a tank, however, or water will not run into it.

for the purpose of flushing the cement with a hose. The wooden overcovering will be easier to stand and to walk upon than cement. There is the additional advantage that beakers or graduates will not break so easily if dropped upon wood as if dropped upon cement. Linoleum too is easier to stand and walk upon than cement. A layer of air between the cement and the wooden decking will keep the feet warmer if the darkroom tends to be cold.

Darkroom Equipment. *Safe Lights.*—There is no truly "safe" light. Lights in the darkroom are only relatively safe. The commercial devices known as safe lights are safe in that materials viewed under them do not fog provided they are not held too close to the source of illumination nor for too long a period. The "safeness" of such sources of illumination depends upon their intensity and upon the color of light emitted. Ordinary blue-sensitive films or papers may be viewed under a generous amount of red or orange illumination; the more sensitive materials, however, must be handled with greater caution. They must not be exposed to red or orange light for too long a period. The more sensitive the material, the less exposure to the safe light will be required to produce fog.

Orthochromatic materials should be processed under a red light which is quite dim if the materials are highly sensitive (fast films or plates). Panchromatic materials

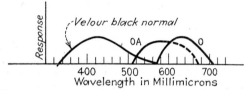

Fig. 3.—Transmission characteristic of OA and O filters and response of Velour Black paper.

are sensitive to all colors and must be processed in darkness or with the aid of a very dim green light. The reason for choosing green lies in the fact that the eye is more sensitive to green than to red and that this difference in favor of green increases as the intensity of illumination is decreased. Orthochromatic films are very sensitive to green, but not to red, and for this reason a panchromatic green safe light should not be used in processing orthochromatic materials.

If a 25-watt lamp is used in a Wratten safe light or a 10-watt lamp in an Eastman safe light, no fog should be produced on the material for which the safe-light filter is designed, provided the material is exposed no closer than 3 ft. for a period of 30 sec.

Red bulbs, which are cheaper than safe-light filters, are rarely safe. They must be used with considerable caution to avoid fogged film or paper.

An electric coil heater emitting very little light will fog bromide paper if held too close to a tray in which the paper is being developed.

The criterion of the best safe light for a given sensitive material involves the spectral sensitivity of the material, the spectral transmission of the safe light, and the physiological characteristics of the eye. The following data taken from the *Defender Trade Bulletin*, September–October, 1938, are concerned with Defender Velour Black, a projection paper.

The question may be asked, which is better for this paper, a Wratten OA (greenish yellow) or a Wratten O (bright orange), with lamps of equal wattage behind them. The series O is much brighter than the OA and produces more fog. If, however, the distances are adjusted so that equal illumination is secured on the paper, the OA is less safe. This may be proved from the spectral characteristics of the safe light and the paper. Note that in the OA the far red is eliminated but that the O safe light transmits in this region.

Physiologically there is an advantage in the OA even if it is adjusted, by distance, so that it gives less illumination on the paper. Contrasts appear greater in red light than in yellow or green. The apparent contrast of a print under the yellow-green light of the OA is more nearly the contrast under daylight than if the series O is used.

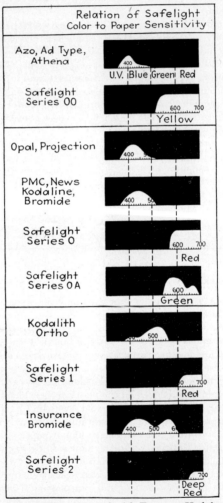

Fig. 4.—Safe lights to be used with Eastman Kodak papers.

Therefore, with Velour Black, or any projection paper which has any sensitivity in the red, *e.g.*, chlorobromides, it is better to work in the yellow-green light of the Wratten OA safe light, even if the illumination is less than with the series O.

Trays and Tanks.—Trays are universally employed for developing prints and are very often used for processing negative materials. Trays may be made of steel which has been enameled, or of stainless steel, hard rubber, glass or pyrex. In emergencies kitchen dishes may be employed. If need arises for a tray of special size or dimensions, it may be made of wood (or heavy cardboard) coated with a thick layer

TABLE I.—SAFE LIGHTS

Agfa No.	Wratten Series	Color	Use
105	OO	Yellow	Contract printing papers
104	O	Orange	Enlarging papers, lantern slides
	OA	Yellow-green	Same as O; better for judging contrast
	1	Red	Ordinary films and plates
107	2	Dark red	Orthochromatic materials
108	3	Dark green	Panchromatic materials (slow)

of wax, or given several coats of corrosion-resistant paint, each coat being dried thoroughly before the next one is applied.

Enameled trays will chip if dropped on a hard surface; glass and hard rubber trays will break if similarly dropped. On the other hand, acid does not attack hard rubber or glass trays while it will attack enameled metal trays if a slight break in the surface material occurs. Enamel will be stained by certain developing solutions or by dyes used in mordanting prints. These stains may be removed, however (see page 568 for tray-cleaning solutions).

When any appreciable number of films or plates are to be processed, tanks of the appropriate size are usually employed. These may be made of metal or nonmetallic materials. Slots are placed along the side into which the plates slide, or the materials are placed in hangers which are large enough not to slip into the solution when laid across the top of the tank. In the average laboratory it is probable that solutions kept in tanks will be allowed to become exhausted more often than if tray processing is done, because of the bother of cleaning the tanks and mixing up new solutions.

Obviously the size of trays or tanks will depend upon the size of materials to be processed. Two sizes of tray will suffice for general amateur work, a set of small ones for negatives, up to 5 by 7 in. and a set of large trays for 11- by 14-in. prints. A tray for an 11- by 14-in. print must have an inside dimension that is larger than 11 by 14 if it is to be used successfully. The following table will indicate the dimensions that have been found useful for making prints of various sizes.

TABLE II.—PRINT AND TRAY SIZES

Over-all Tray Size, In.	Negative or Print Size, In.
4⅝ × 6⅝	4 × 6
5¼ × 7⅜	5 × 7
7¼ × 9½	7 × 9
8¾ × 10⅝	8 × 10
10¾ × 12¾	10 × 12
12⅛ × 15⅛	11 × 14

Tanks for use with miniature films (35 mm., etc.) differ in construction, naturally, from flat tanks used for cut films or plates. They are of two general types. In one the film is threaded into slots in a composition (hard rubber, bakelite, etc.) molded form. This operation must be done in the darkroom. The reel is then placed in the tank, a lighttight lid is affixed after which the tank may be taken out into ordinary daylight. In the other type the film is placed on an "apron" made of celluloid, soft rubber, or other material which fits into the tank. A metal tank will change temperature in accordance with the ambient, so that greater care must be exercised in maintaining its temperature while processing is taking place. The bakelite tanks do not transmit temperature changes so easily, and, if the solution is placed in the tank at the proper temperature, it will remain so for a reasonable period.   Rubber or bakelite tanks will break; metal tanks will dent if dropped on a hard surface.

Certain small metal tanks for plates or films have tight-fitting covers, rubber gasketed, so that the tank may be inverted during development insuring that the solution is properly agitated.   They may be fitted with spigots and filling spouts so that only the loading need be done in the darkroom.

Large tanks for photofinishing and motion-picture processing are best purchased from manufacturers specializing in this type of equipment.   They may be made of wood, steel covered with thin soft rubber, earthenware, etc.

Tray Cleaners.—Trays frequently become discolored from silver and dye or from the oxidation products of developers.   Two formulas for tray cleaners are given below.

TRAY CLEANER (EASTMAN TC-1)

Water	32 oz.	1 l.
Potassium bichromate	3 oz.	90 g.
Sulphuric acid (pure concentrated)	3 fl. oz.	96 cc.

SILVER-STAIN REMOVER (EASTMAN TC-2)

Water	32 oz.	1 l.
Potassium permanganate	73 gr.	5 g.
Sulphuric acid (pure concentrated)	2½ drams	10 cc.

Add the acid slowly to the solution while stirring the solution rapidly.

Pour the solution into tray and swish around so that all tray parts are covered. Then rinse and use the following:

CLEARING SOLUTION

Water	32 oz.	1 l.
Sodium bisulphite	145 gr.	10 g.

Wash trays well after applying the clearing solution.   Acid dyes as used in imbibition color printing may be removed from trays by the use of ammonia.

Sinks.—The sink is a most important part of the darkroom equipment.   It should be centrally located so that no unnecessary steps must be taken to get to it from any part of the darkroom.   It must be large enough to accommodate the largest trays in the laboratory.   It should be so constructed that a portion of it may be blocked off with a weir which divides the sink into two portions, one containing the drain and the other either without a drain or fixed with a good stopper.   In this manner, water at the proper temperature may be used in one portion while access to the drain is available in the other portion.

Sink materials may be wood, properly treated, stoneware, lead-lined wood, or porcelain.   Wooden sinks are not expensive to make.   Cypress or maple may be used.   Individual pieces of the wood should be tongued and grooved and then held together with strong bolts or braces.   The inner surfaces which come into contact with liquids should be given several coats of a corrosion-resistant paint before being used.   Each coat must be allowed to dry thoroughly before the next is applied.   If the paint is light in color, it will probably stain, but will reflect light from the overhead illumination and contribute to the general illumination.

A rack should be arranged to be moved about over the top of the sink so that trays may be placed upon it with the certainty that liquid slopping out will fall into the sink and be disposed of through the drain.   Shelves back of the sink should be deep enough so that bottles cannot fall off into the sink or into trays of solution.

Another useful adjunct to the sink is a float in which trays may be placed and supported in a water bath of a required temperature.   Such a float may be made of wood in which a rectangular space has been cut of such a size that the overhang on the tray top will prevent the tray from falling through into the sink.   If, then, one portion of the sink is filled with water at some desired temperature, while the weir blocks off the remainder of the sink (the portion containing the drain) the tray of solution may be floated in the larger body of water while the drain is available for waste disposal.

Stone or earthenware sinks should be covered with a material which is softer than the sink itself so that beakers or other glassware dropped on it will not break. Rubber mats, floor mats, or door mats may be used; linoleum or asbestos is satisfactory.

Thermometers, and Weighing Scales.—Metric system weights are to be preferred, although avoirdupois weights are satisfactory. Most formulas are now written in both systems. In a small studio a maximum weight of $3\frac{1}{2}$ oz. (100 g.) will probably be encountered and so the smallest studio scales may be employed. Scales for larger laboratories must, naturally, weigh greater quantities of material. Scales capable of measuring up to 25 lb. may be placed upon a shelf or table; scales for greater quantities exist in the form of platform scales.

The pans of a laboratory scales should not be permitted to touch any of the chemicals; a piece of paper should be placed upon the weighing pan and counterbalanced by a similar piece on the other pan. If the scales are kept in a damp darkroom, the wooden base may swell, the metal parts tarnish or become covered with verdigris, and the bearings may become so dirty that accurate weighing is difficult. This is another reason why the weighing of chemicals and the compounding of formulas should not be done in the processing room itself.

It does not matter much whether thermometers are calibrated in Fahrenheit or centigrade. Probably most American and English workers are more familiar with Fahrenheit and have a better idea of the variation caused by 1° difference in temperature in this system than centigrade. Metal thermometers have a bad habit of tarnishing so that the calibration is hard to see; they also peel off in thin layers of oxide. Glass thermometers which are also used as stirring rods frequently lose the paint in which the calibrations are marked, making it most difficult to read the temperature scale in the semilight of the darkroom.

The Weston type of thermometer consisting of a long thin metal rod with a dial-type indicator at the top does not seem to corrode; the action is remarkably fast, and the dial is easy to read. It is inclined to be top heavy, however, and, when placed in a tray which is rocked or tilted, has a tendency to roll around and get in the way or to roll out and break. The "crystal" glass cover over the dial is heavy but it will break.

Darkroom Practice. *Flow of Work.*—If the darkroom is properly arranged, work done there will flow easily from one stage to another. For example, sensitive paper should not have to be moved over a tray of developer to be placed in a printer or under an enlarger. In a photofinishing establishment this even and easy flow of work is very important so that operators do not get in each other's way. Operations which may be carried out in full illumination should be excluded from the processing laboratory if possible, so that full advantage of better working conditions (better visibility etc.) can be utilized.

If the photographer works out a standardized method of procedure, he will find that he will have less waste and that his work will be less tiring. Thus developing, rinsing, fixing, washing may proceed from left to right (or vice versa), and this should be standardized no matter whether it is films that are being developed in absolute darkness or whether prints are being processed under appreciable illumination.

Maintenance of Temperature.—If the darkroom is warmer or cooler than the desired solution temperature, the photographer must take steps to overcome the progressive change in solution temperature. The simplest method is to float a tray containing the solution in a larger tray filled with water of the required temperature. By means of a mixing faucet in which cold and hot water may be brought to the desired temperature, the water in the larger tray may be held continuously at the required temperature above or below ambient.

If cold water is not available in the summer, or warm water in the winter, recourse must be had to ice, or to water heaters. Ice should not be placed in the solution itself because it will dilute the solution as it melts. It must be realized that it will be difficult to maintain a tray or tank of developer at a desired temperature by the use of ice packed around the solution, and that only a cooling effect may be secured. The temperature of melting ice is 32°F., and a tray floated on melting ice will tend to attain this temperature.

To heat trays or tanks of solution, electricity may be used. A tray may be placed over a metal-topped box (or a portion of the workbench with a cut-away portion over which is placed a metal plate or sheet). In the box, or below the cut-away portion of the bench, may be placed electric lamps which are turned off or on as the conditions require. They may be controlled automatically by means of a thermostat placed in the solution to be maintained at a given temperature. Cheap bimetallic strips can be purchased and often serve very well for this temperature-maintenance purpose.

It is easier to heat than to cool a solution. Therefore it is a good plan to surround a tray with melting ice which is raised in temperature by electricity. (See data on floats in paragraph on Sinks above.)

Timing Photographic Processes.—Many timing devices, mostly clocks, are on the market. Equipped with a large second hand, they enable the photographer to time accurately any process not taking place in absolute darkness. Some timers are equipped with an alarm which warns the worker when a certain time has elapsed. These are especially useful when the worker is processing panchromatic materials in darkness.

If exposures of only a few seconds are required to be made in darkness, *e.g.*, in making color-separation negatives from color transparencies, a useful device is one which automatically turns off the exposing light at the end of a certain period. These devices may be based on one of several principles.

A synchronous motor may revolve a contactor through a series of cog wheels. In general illumination the contacts may be moved to such a position that the exposure will take place for a certain number of seconds; then the sensitive material is placed in position in darkness, and a switch is thrown which will start the motor and at the same time turn on the exposing lamp. When the motor has rotated the contact wheel a certain number of degrees, contact with the light source is broken, and the exposure is ended.

Other devices are electronic in nature, using vacuum tubes. In this case the fundamental principle is the charge and discharge of a condenser which is in the grid circuit of the tube. The rate at which a condenser charges (or discharges) is a function of the resistance in series or in parallel with it. A certain combination of resistance and capacity may be chosen which will keep the grid of the tube overbiased for a certain period of time. At the end of this time the charge in the condenser is dissipated, and the grid draws current which is reflected in a current in the plate circuit of the tube. In this circuit is an electrical relay whose contacts control the illumination by which the exposure is made. These electronic devices may be made to hold a circuit closed (or open) from a fraction of a second up to 1 min. or more. In general they are less stable and accurate over a period of time than a purely mechanical contactor timer as represented by a synchronous motor.

The cheaper synchronous-motor units have a tendency to stall. A loud buzz indicates that the motor has stopped (or a relay in the unit has struck or is chattering), with the result that the exposing light does not turn off.

Accuracy in Compounding Solutions.—Errors or inaccuracies in making solutions should not be greater than a few per cent. If the photographer wishes to convert a formula written in metric units to avoirdupois, he will often "round off" the quantities to get convenient values. Care must be taken in this rounding off to see that cumulative errors are not caused. For example, the ratio between metol and hydroquinone in any MQ developer is important. In rounding off, if one uses a figure 3 per cent low for metol and 3 per cent high for hydroquinone, the total error is 6 per cent, which is about the limit that should be tolerated. Similar difficulties may arise in changing the ratio between carbonate and sulphite in a solution.

The following table will be useful in converting formulas from metric to avoirdupois and vice versa. Other conversion factors and tables will be found in Appendix *A*.

TABLE III.—AVOIRDUPOIS TO METRIC WEIGHT

Pounds	Ounces	Grains	Grams	Kilograms
1	16	7,000	453.6	0.4536
0.0625	1	437.5	28.35	0.02835
0.002205	0.03527	15.43	1	0.001
2.205	35.27	15,430	1000	1

In converting United States liquid to metric measure, remember that 1 gal. is equal to 4 qt. or 8 pt. or 3.785 l.; that 1 oz. is 8 drams or 30 cc. (29.57 cc. actually); that 1 qt. is approximately 1 l. (actually 946.3 cc.).

English formulas are frequently worked out for 40 oz. rather than in units of 16 oz. (United States pints) or quarts. This is because 1 qt. in the British imperial liquid measure is equal to 40 British fluid ounces. Therefore, to convert a 40-oz. solution to a 32-oz. solution, multiply all ingredients in the 40-oz. formula by 0.8. Conversely, to make up a 40-oz. solution from a 32 oz. formula, multiply the 32-oz. values by 1.25.

Bibliography

Periodicals:

JOURDAN, ALBERT: Metol Poisoning, *Am. Phot.*, July, 1935, p. 397.
DIEFFENBACH, A. M.: Cooling Bath for Hot Weather Development, *Am. Phot.*, July, 1935, p. 435.
SNODGRASS, L. L.: Is Photography Your Hobby? (Darkrooms for the Amateur), *Am. Home*, May, 1936.
FINK, D. G.: For Photographers Only (Description of an Electronic Darkroom Timer), *Electronics*, June, 1937.
HERTZBERG, ROBERT: An Efficient Ventilator, *Camera*, July, 1937, p. 20.
LOOTENS, C. L.: Modern Motion Pictures Laboratory, *J. Soc. Motion Picture Engrs.*, April, 1938, p. 363.
SMITH, H. A.: Stainless Steel and Its Application to Photographic Processing Equipment, *J. Soc. Motion Picture Engrs.*, April, 1938, p. 410.

Books:

"Supplies for the Graphic Arts," Eastman Kodak Co.
"Commercial Photo Finishing," Eastman Kodak Co.
"Fundamentals of Radiography," Eastman Kodak Co.
"Motion Picture Laboratory Practice," Eastman Kodak Co.

CHAPTER XX

STEREOSCOPIC PHOTOGRAPHY

By Vannevar Bush and John T. Rule

General Stereoscopic Theory. *Types of Vision.*—Monocular vision consists in the reception on a surface (the retina) of a single two-dimensional image, which has been projected through the crystalline lens of one eye from a scene in space, and the resultant interpretation by the brain of this image.

Except for the lack of color and the presence of the texture of the film, such an image is closely reproduced on the film of a single-lens camera making black-and-white pictures. The resultant print when properly viewed reproduces an image on the retina similar to that which it would have received had the eye occupied the position of the camera lens when the picture was taken. From this two-dimensional image the brain infers the original three-dimensional space scene.

Binocular vision consists in the reception on the two retinas of two images of a single scene in space and the resultant fusion and interpretation by the brain of these images. Since the position of the two eyes is not the same, different portions of objects are visible and near objects obscure different areas of far objects. Thus the two retinal images are not identical. The brain fuses these two different two-dimensional images and interprets them as a single three-dimensional space scene in which depth appears to exist as a definite reality.

If two photographs are taken from the positions occupied by the two eyes and the resultant prints are properly viewed—the left eye viewing only the print taken from the left and the right eye only that taken from the right—two retinal images are produced which correspond to those which would have been formed had the eyes occupied the positions of the camera lenses. With proper viewing aids the resultant fusion and interpretation is substantially the same as that of binocular vision including the sense of the reality of depth. This reproduction of the effect of binocular vision by the use of two two-dimensional images is "stereoscopic vision."

Factors Influencing Judgment of Depth.—For the purposes of this chapter the word "depth" is always used to mean distance away from the eyes.

The important factors which contribute to depth judgment in monocular vision are perspective, light and shade, apparent size of known objects, obscuring of remoter objects by nearer ones, decreasing sharpness of detail with distance, and motion of foreground objects against background objects.

All the factors entering into depth judgment in monocular vision are equally operative in binocular vision. In addition, without evaluating their importance here, the following factors are present:

1. *Two Views.*—As stated above the two views of binocular vision are different. This difference is a major factor in the resultant depth effect. The physiology of the resultant fusion and interpretation are not well understood.

2. *Convergence.*—In looking at a point in space, an angle is formed by the two rays from the point to the eyes. The eyeballs turn inward until the axis of each is coincident with its entering ray. This "angle of convergence" grows larger as the point approaches. It always has a fixed value for any fixed position of the point with respect to a given position of a pair of eyes.

3. *Accommodation.*—In viewing space the accommodation or focusing of the eyes varies with the distance to the object and consequently gives some indication of depth. Change in accommodation involves a change of shape of the eye lenses, whereas change in convergence involves a change in direction of the eye axes.

All the factors, except that of motion, entering into depth judgment in monocular vision are equally operative in stereoscopic vision. In addition the following factors are present:

1. The presence of two views is the same as in binocular vision.

2. The theory of convergence is the same as in binocular vision. However, the two rays of light to the two eyes do not originate from a point in space but from the two views of the point on the stereograph. Thus the actual convergence may differ from that of the original space scene by varying separation between the two views or by the use of various stereoscopes.

3. Accommodation in stereoscopic vision is fixed either at the distance from the plate to the eyes or at infinity by the proper use of lenses. This is an important fundamental difference between binocular and stereoscopic vision.

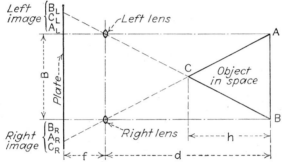

Fig. 1.—Diagram of three-dimensional object for which conditions of stereoscopic vision are derived.

4. The presence of a fixed plane as represented by the location of the print or transparency.

5. The presence of a definite visible limit to the edges of the two views acting as an enclosing frame which restricts the sense of size and depth.

Apparent Location and Size of Stereoscopic Images.—Geometrically, convergence gives an accurate method of determining the distance of any point from the two eyes. Consequently it should give the brain a perfect depth-sensing device.

The following formulas are derived from the geometry of convergence. It should be clearly understood that they are based upon the fundamental premise that the apparent location of the stereographic image of a point can be obtained by projected rays from the eyes through the respective stereographic views of the point, the image being located at the intersection of the rays. In other words they are based on the assumption that the convergence of the lines of sight is an absolute determinant of the location of the image.

It can be stated definitely, however, that *the absolute convergence of a single point never determines its apparent depth in a stereoscopic image.* Its relative convergence with other points is used by the brain to locate it with regard to those points after the general position of the image is fixed.

Thus the formulas do not accurately indicate the absolute apparent location or size of a stereoscopic image in space as seen through a stereoscope. They do determine the mechanical conditions under which stereoscopic viewing should take place and the relative positions of points in the image. They also give an accurate method of determining the actual location of points in space from stereographs of them.

Figure 1* represents a plan view of a pyramid ABC photographed by the double-lens camera focused on the plane AB, with sufficient depth of field to include the entire object. The images of A, for instance, are at A_L and A_R, respectively, for the left and right lenses. This figure is used because of its simplicity. Any other figure would lead to the same formulas.

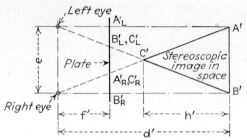

FIG. 2.—Conditions existing when viewing object by means of a stereoscope.

Figure 2 represents the conditions which exist when the resultant plates are transposed and enlarged m times and viewed as a stereograph. $A'B'C'$ is the resultant stereographic image in space as fused from the two halves of the stereograph—$A'_R B'_R C'_R$ and $A'_L B'_L C'_L$.

The following formulas can be derived from Figs. 1 and 2:

$$\frac{d}{d'} = \frac{mf}{f'}\frac{B}{e} \tag{1}$$

$$\frac{AB}{A'B'} = \frac{h}{h'}\frac{mf}{f'} \tag{2}$$

An orthostereoscopic view is one in which the resultant image is of exactly the same size and shape and has the same location with respect to the observer's eyes as the original space scene.

Formulas (1) and (2) indicate that the following conditions are necessary to obtain an orthostereoscopic view:

1. Without enlargement, f must equal f'. With enlargement, mf must equal f'; *i.e.*, the distance from the eyes to the plate, in viewing, must equal the distance from the lens to the plate, in taking, multiplied by the enlargement of the plates.

It is illuminating to state this thus: the angle subtended by the object at the camera must equal the angle subtended by the print at the eye.

2. B must equal e; *i.e.*, the photographic base—the distance between camera lenses for the two views—must equal the interocular distance.

The above mathematical treatment covers the basic features of the theory of convergence. A complete mathematical analysis with especial reference to the conditions necessary for obtaining orthostereoscopic views may be found in an article entitled Orthostereoscopy, by Henry Kurtz, in the October, 1937, issue of the *Journal of the Optical Society of America*.

Effect of Other Depth Factors.—The absolute location and size of a stereoscopic image depend upon the degree to which the various depth factors listed above are present, upon the particular method of viewing, and, being partly subjective, upon the individual observer. No rigid rules for locating such images can be laid down. Consequently the subject must be discussed in general terms. It is assumed in the

* After Hardy and Perrin.

following discussion that mechanical conditions for orthostereoscopic viewing, such as proper focal lengths and bases, have been achieved.

First consider the effects of viewing stereographs without a stereoscope. It is well to restate that in such viewing absolute convergence is not of importance. In viewing the stereograph of Fig. 2, for instance, the resultant image would not seem to be of exactly the indicated size and shape and would not be located at the indicated distance d' from the eyes.

A possible reason for this can be seen if it is remembered that in binocular vision there is a fixed tie between accommodation and convergence. Thus in looking at a point 2 ft. away the eyes are focused for 2 ft. and the axes of the eyeballs intersect at 2 ft. Regardless of the distance of the fixation point, nearly the same angle of convergence always goes with any given focus, only varying slightly for objects not directly in front of the observer. Both change together as objects of different depth are viewed.

In stereoscopic vision this established tie is broken. The two views of the point on the stereograph determine the convergence. This convergence changes with changes of separation between different points on the two views. However, the accommodation remains constant, *i.e.*, the focus of the eyes is either fixed for the distance from the eyes to the stereograph or by a distance dictated by the lenses of the stereoscope—usually infinity. This split of the accommodation-convergence habit is the outstanding difference between binocular and stereoscopic vision. Since the eyes are presented with a situation foreign to binocular vision, the psychological interpretation tends to differ from that of binocular vision.

In very simple stereographs containing only separate points and lines[1] and viewed without a stereoscope, the resultant interpretation tends to place one prominent point or plane of the picture—called the "fixation" point or plane—in or near the plane of the plate. Thus one point is approximately determined from the accommodation. The depth of the rest of the points of the picture are interpreted from this point in accordance with both the relative convergence with this point and the other depth factors relating the points and objects to each other.

This accounts for the fact that a change in the separation of the two views of the stereograph causes no perceptible change in the position or size of the resultant image. Regardless of what this separation may be, so long as fusion is maintained, the eyes "draw the views together" until the fixation point appears in the proper plane. The relative convergence of various points remains the same in any case.

The location of the final image differs for different observers. The resultant effect, however, is that the image is drawn forward from where it should be on convergence principles and is smaller with a proportionally greater decrease in the depth than in the other dimensions.

As the views are made more complex by the use of planes which obscure each other, perspective elements, and objects of known size, these added factors tend to dominate the interpretation of the size and location of the image, while accommodation and convergence become of increasingly less importance. The use of relative convergence becomes so bound up with perspective elements that its effect cannot be separated from them.

Regardless of the degree to which other depth factors are present, the tendency to fix one point in the plane of the plate never entirely disappears, with the result that the stereographic image, without the use of a stereoscope, always appears smaller and less deep than the natural object.

When a stereoscope is used for viewing, a change in separation of the two views still causes no change in the resultant image. The accommodation, if proper focal

[1] FRENCH, J. W., *Trans. Optical Soc.* (*London*), vol. 24.
TRUMP, R. J., *Trans. Optical Soc.* (*London*), vol. 25.

lengths are maintained, is generally fixed at infinity. Consequently both absolute convergence and accommodation are of little importance.

Eliminating these factors, each of the other depth factors has its own tendency as follows:

All the normal factors of monocular vision, perspective, known size of objects, etc., tend to make the resultant image of the proper size and at its proper location in space.

Relative convergence tends to place the parts of the image in their proper relation to one another according to the final location of the image as a whole.

The tendency to find a fixation point in the plane of the plate is the greater the more obvious the texture or grain of the plate.

The enclosing frame around the fused image tends to make any point near the edge appear to lie in the plane of this plate. A stereoscope scene may appear quite natural as a whole. Yet if successive points near the edges are fixed, they will all appear to lie in or near the plane of the frame, regardless of the fact that they are obviously in different planes in the whole view.

The enclosing frame is supplied either by the edge of the plate around the stereograph or by the restricting parts of the stereoscope. Since the eyes normally see over an angle of about 120° each, a camera capable of covering a field of 120° would be necessary to eliminate this frame. A stereoscope would then be necessary which would permit both eyes to cover this range such as a mirror stereoscope where the mirrors superimpose the views. In a lens stereoscope the right eye cannot be permitted to see the left view and vice versa. The usual camera and the usual lens stereoscope both permit angles of less than 60°. Consequently the enclosing frame is always present in one form or another.

The total resultant image is a compromise on the part of the eyes and brain between these various factors. It is more perfect when the factors which place it correctly are more obvious and the factors which draw it forward and decrease its size are more nearly eliminated.

In normal photographic work the depth of any object in the scene is not exactly known to the observer. Consequently he has no means of judging the accuracy of the location and size of the stereoscopic image of it. So long as the illusion of reality is maintained the tendency is to accept the image as correct.

From the above discussion the photographer should remember:

1. Extremely simple objects which primarily must depend on convergence to give depth judgment will tend to appear smaller, nearer, and somewhat distorted. If the accurate judgment of the size and shape of rather uniform objects, such as cubes or geometrical figures, is desired, other elements should be added to the picture which will aid in this judgment.

2. Scenic views appear quite natural though they have a tendency to be cramped. As more elements are added which normally aid depth perception in monocular vision, the scene will more closely approach its true size and shape in space.

3. Every effort should be made to eliminate print or plate textures and the obviousness of the enclosing frame.

4. No absolute criteria for depth judgment exists; consequently the experience and capabilities of the photographer will inevitably play a large part in determining the degree to which the illusion of reality is approached.

It must be realized that the entire discussion of depth judgment in stereographs is put forth only tentatively in the absence of a more exact knowledge of the subject. The sense of depth in a stereograph is so striking that no great sensibility to its variability has yet been developed. As stereographs become more common the interpretation of their realistic and artistic effects will become more acute. The field offers an enormous opportunity for research on the part of the photographer.

Limits of Stereoscopic Vision.—Binocular vision and consequently stereoscopic vision occurs only within relatively near distances. The maximum distance depends upon the minimum relative convergence that the eye is able to detect. This distance differs considerably with different individuals.

Helmholtz considered the minimum difference in convergence angle that could be resolved to be 1 min. of arc. Later experiments show the average value to be in the neighborhood of 20 sec. of arc, possibly less.

Given two points at the same distance from the eyes, d_1. They appear to be equidistant. If one point then recedes from the eyes while the other remains stationary, the eyes are not capable of detecting that a difference in distance exists until the convergence angle for the receding point has diminished 20 sec. of arc. Calling the difference between the two distances D and the distance to the far point d_2, there is, for any value of d_1, a minimum value of D for which the difference in convergence angle becomes 20 sec. of arc.

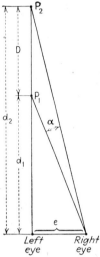

This can be very closely determined from the formula:

$$D = \frac{\alpha d_1{}^2}{e - \alpha d_1} \qquad (3)$$

where e = interocular distance;

α = difference in convergence angle between d_1 and d_2 expressed in radians (1 rad. = 57.3°).

Fig. 3.—Diagram from which the data of Table I was calculated.

Using 2.5 in. for e and 20 sec. of arc for α, the following table gives the separation away from the eyes that two objects must have if a stereograph of them taken with a 2.5-in. base is to show any depth. These are only approximate values that will give the photographer some idea of the sort of depth effects he may expect with various spacing of objects. The things to be noticed are the rapidity with which D must be increased beyond 100 ft. and the fact that binocular vision disappears entirely near 2000 ft.

TABLE I.—CONDITIONS FOR BINOCULAR VISION

If d_1 Equals	D Must Equal or Exceed, Ft.
10 inches	0.005
2 ft	0.002
5 ft	0.01
10 ft	0.05
25 ft	0.3
100 ft	5.0
200 ft	20
500 ft	160
1000 ft	925
2000 ft	∞

The limit of stereoscopic vision on the near side is generally considered to be the minimum distance for clear focusing by the eyes. A minimum value of 15 in. is recommended.

Stereography with a Single Camera or with Two Single Cameras. *With Single Camera.*—Stereographs of motionless scenes may be made with any single camera. It is important to remember, however, that in stereographs sharpness of detail over the whole scene is more important than in ordinary photographs, as blurred details greatly detract from the depth effect and the illusion of reality that a sharp stereograph gives.

As short-focal-length lenses have more depth of focus and the distance beyond which everything is in focus is less than in lenses of long focal length, shorter focal lengths are preferable for stereoscopic work. Several methods of making stereographs with a single camera are possible.

Camera May Be Shifted between Exposures.—If the distance to the object is small, the camera should be pointed at the same spot near the center of the object in both views. If the distance to the object is greater than 6 ft. a simple lateral displacement is all that is required.

The distance between the two positions of the lens should be about $2\frac{1}{2}$ in. unless a hyperstereoscopic effect is desired.

The lens must be at the same distance from the object in both views.

The camera should be at the same elevation and level in both views.

The stops and lighting conditions should remain the same.

Many devices can be made to aid in shifting the camera (see "Stereoscopic Photography," A. W. Judge). For cameras with flat bases, such as the box types, a tray may be constructed, the width of the tray being equal to the width of the camera plus the interocular distance. It is then necessary only to push the camera against the opposite ends for the two views.

A rigid frame may be built around the camera which slides in another frame and locks in the proper positions.

Some manufacturers (Leica, Rolleiflex) furnish devices for this purpose. In general these are constructed to fit between the tripod and the camera. They either swing or slide the camera the requisite distance. Leica[1] furnishes a Stereo Slide Bar which permits the camera to be locked in any position up to a separation of 15 cm., thus permitting the taking of hyperstereoscopic views up to that maximum base.

The Object May Be Shifted the Interocular Distance.—The object must be against a plain background with no other objects in the view unless such objects are also shifted.

The shift must be level and perpendicular to the axis of the camera.

The object should not be much closer than 6 ft. from the camera. At shorter distances the camera should preferably point to a spot between the two positions of the object.

The light should preferably be uniform, not from a concentrated source.

The stops and the lighting conditions must remain the same.

This is a convenient method for photographing small objects that are easily shifted on a table.

The Object May Be Rotated.—This is a more accurate method than shifting the object particularly for short distances between the object and the camera.

The object should be against a plain background. If it is not or if other objects not rotated around the same center also are in the view, the background and these objects will show no relief in the stereograph.

The proper angle of rotation for orthostereoscopic views can be calculated from the formula:

$$\alpha = 2 \sin^{-1}\left(\frac{1.25}{d}\right) \tag{4}$$

A greater rotation gives a hyperstereoscopic effect.

A simpler method of rotation is to pick out or mark two points on the object in line with the lens of the camera and the center of the object. Then rotate the object until a line through these same points passes $2\frac{1}{2}$ in. to the right or left of the lens.

[1] See Leica Manual.

All the above methods demand that the scene be motionless for the time required to change the film or plate and to reset the camera or object.

Use of Stereoadapter.—By the use of a stereoadapter a stereograph with a single-lens camera and a single exposure can be obtained. This permits moving objects to be photographed.

Such adapters consist of arrangements of mirrors or prisms designed to bring the two views into the left and right halves of the lens, respectively. Figure 4 shows the simplest arrangement of mirrors for accomplishing this purpose.

A distinct advantage of such adapters lies in the fact that the refraction through the lens reverses the views so that they appear in proper position upon the negative and do not have to be transposed.

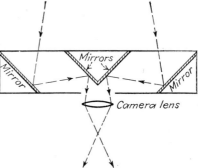

Leica manufactures a stereoadapter, called a Stereoly, using prisms. The device fits in front of the lens. It divides the standard 36- by 24-mm. picture into two of 18 by 24 mm. A special viewer for rolls of films of this type is also furnished.

The use of a stereoadapter involves a great reduction in the amount of light reaching the film. Splitting the lens cuts the intensity to one-half, while the absorption of prisms or mirrors further reduces it. Consequently longer exposures are necessary.

Fig. 4.—Simple arrangement of using two sets of mirrors to provide stereoscopic effects with a single-lens camera.

The camera should be of such a type that the film used in it can be divided into two areas which are approximately square.

Stereographs with Two Cameras.—If cameras are small, two may be clamped together so that the lenses are separated by $2\frac{1}{2}$ in. or slightly more. This means that the plates must not be larger than $2\frac{1}{2}$ in. in width. If the separation between lenses is greater than $2\frac{1}{2}$ in., a hyperstereoscopic effect results.

Care must be taken that the following conditions are fulfilled:

The lenses must be well matched. The manufacturer should be willing to do this when the cameras are purchased.

The line between lens centers must be level with the resultant base of the combined cameras.

Indicated equal shutter speeds and diaphragm openings must be in reality equal. In cheap cameras there may be considerable variation in shutter speeds causing a difference in exposure times.

The shutters must work simultaneously. Leverages or connecting bars must be designed for this purpose for the particular cameras to be used.

With inexpensive cameras this affords a very cheap and satisfactory method of making stereographs. The beginner who cares to experiment with stereoscopic possibilities will do well to start in this manner.

Double-lens Cameras.—A stereoscopic camera with two matched lenses separated by the interocular distance permits the taking of stereographs of any type of scene in exactly the same manner that ordinary photographs are taken. As long as the shutters, focusing devices, and diaphragm openings are each linked together and each set by one adjustment, the operation is no different from that of the usual camera.

Most stereoscopic cameras are fitted with lens caps so that one lens may be covered if it is desired to take single pictures or hyperstereographs. In the latter case the right lens is covered for the right view while the left lens is covered for the left view. The camera is shifted the desired distance between views. This eliminates the necessity for transposing the plates.

As it is desirable that a stereograph be level, the more expensive cameras are fitted with levels and the lenses are held in a sliding front which permits of a small vertical displacement for centering objects slightly above or below the level of the lenses.

A list of the chief types of camera on the market follows. The list is not complete but gives an idea of the field.

Eho. An inexpensive box-type camera. $2\frac{1}{4}$- by $3\frac{1}{4}$-in. roll film. $f/11$ lenses. Fixed focus. Time and single-speed shutter. Direct-vision wire view finder. Sands, Hunter & Co., London. (Price about $15 in England.)

The Puck. Similar to the Eho. Central brilliant-type view finder. Messrs. Thornton Pickard, London.

Heidoscope. A high grade, precision camera. Plate changing box for twelve plates. Two sizes:

45 by 107 mm. Zeiss Tessar lenses $f/4.5$. Focal length, 5.5 cm. Zeiss anastigmat view-finder lens $f/3.2$ centrally located. Variable-speed shutter. Variable focus. Lens caps. Spirit level. (Price about $270 in England.)

60 by 130 mm. Zeiss Tessar lenses $f/4.5$. Focal length, 7.5 cm. Zeiss anastigmat view-finder lenses $f/4.2$. Other features the same as above. R. F. Hunter Ltd., London. (Price about $290 in England.)

Rolleidoscope. The 60 by 130 Heidoscope made for roll films. (Price about $260 in England.)

Voigtlander. 45- by 107-mm. plate changing box for 12 plates. $f/4.5$ lenses. Focal length, 6 cm. Variable-speed, Compur sector shutters to $\frac{1}{250}$ sec. Variable focus. Lens caps. Spirit level. (Price about $270.)

Ica Plaskop. An inexpensive camera. 45 by 107 mm. six individual plateholders. Ica Novar anastigmat $f/6.8$ lenses. 6-cm. focal length. Time- and single-speed shutters. Direct-vision wire view finder.

Ica polyskop. 45 by 107 mm. Plate-changing box. Zeiss Tessar lenses $f/4.5$. Compur sector shutters to $\frac{1}{250}$ sec. Direct-vision view finder. Variable focus.

Ica Minimum Palmos. 60 by 130 mm. Folding-bellows type. Zeiss Tessar lenses $f/4.5$. Focal-plane shutter to $\frac{1}{1000}$ sec.

Verascope. Numerous types. 45 by 107 mm. and 60 by 130 mm. All have plate-changing box. Standard, and roll-film adaptors, optional. Lenses $f/6.3$ on cheapest type; $f/4.5$ on others. Central view-finder lens. Variable speed shutters. Manufacturer—J. Richard, Paris. Agent—R. J. Fitzsimons, 75 Fifth Ave., N. Y.

Other sizes and types of camera, many having been made to order, many of discontinued makes, can be obtained secondhand by watching photographic periodicals.

Viewing Instruments. *Viewing without Aid.*—The viewing of stereographs without the aid of some form of viewing instrument always causes eyestrain. With considerable practice it can be done with a fair amount of ease but is certainly never to be recommended as a common practice. The judgment of depth by this means is never accurate. This was discussed on page 572.

If it is desired to experiment with this form of viewing, a piece of cardboard or other flat shield should be placed normal to the two views and between them to render them mutually exclusive to the two eyes. Without this shield three views will be seen of which the center one will be the stereoscopic image.

In this form of viewing the two views will seem to draw together until they are superimposed. It is helpful to fix on some prominent feature and draw this feature together before attempting to focus the eyes. Once the views are together, an effort is required to bring them into focus. This focus cannot be held more than a few seconds without considerable strain.

It is also possible to fuse stereographs by looking at them cross-eyed. This produces a small image in front of the plate which is psuedoscopic—reversed in depth. This method can be employed on stereographs before they are cut apart and transposed, in which case they will not be psuedoscopic.

Lens Stereoscopes.—The usual type of stereoscope for general work is the lens stereoscope. The purpose of the lenses is primarily to relax the accommodation. In split-lens stereoscopes the views are also partially drawn together by refraction.

The lenses thus serve to keep the eyes focused on infinity which is approximated in normal vision by all objects more than a few feet away. Thus the normal accommodation-convergence ratio is not too seriously violated as it is when the eyes are forced to remain focused at the distance of the plate.

Full-lens Type.—In stereoscopes of short focal length, full lenses are usually used separated by 2½ in. They are available as box or as folding types.

The box type is used for transparencies. It is a simple box with a ground-glass screen in one end and the lenses mounted in the other end. The lenses are usually fitted with a rack-and-pinion focusing device much after the manner of a pair of opera glasses. The plate is inserted through a slot in front of the glass screen. The latter serves to diffuse the light over the entire scene. The instrument must be pointed at a satisfactory light source unless it is fitted with a light in back of the glass screen.

The folding type is convenient for carrying in the pocket for use with prints. It consists of a collapsible metal framework containing the lenses and a rack for the plate. These may be constructed of two pieces which slide in each other in order to permit focusing; or they may be of one piece with a fixed focus.

The value of this type of stereoscope is that it can be made very cheaply and is of a convenient size for carrying. However, the cheaper forms lack rigidity and easily get out of alignment.

Spectacle Type.—Pairs of lenses much like a pair of spectacles are also obtainable. These require that the plate be held in the hand and moved until fusion is made. This requires a certain amount of practice. This type is very convenient for use with books in which stereographs are published.

The Camera as a Stereoscope.—For theoretically perfect orthostereoscopic viewing the stereograph should be viewed with the pair of lenses with which the pictures were taken. Some cameras on the market are so constructed that they may also be used as viewers. However any pair of lenses of the same focal length and a comfortable diameter will give excellent results.

Split-lens Type.—The common hand type, or Brewster stereoscope, the American parlor stereoscope, is of the split-lens type. This system is shown in Fig. 5. The single lens is split vertically through the center and the two halves are mounted with the optical centers out. These centers are separated somewhat in excess of the interocular distance. (Keystone telebinocular, 95 mm.) This allows wider separation of the prints and consequently larger prints may be used without overlapping.

The alteration of depth of the objects in the stereograph in this type of stereoscope when used with a camera of interocular separation is not detectable in the ordinary photograph. It need only be given serious consideration in technical work where the accurate judgment of depth relative to width and height is of importance. In such cases the use of a camera of lens separation equal to the distance between optical centers in the stereoscope eliminates the distortion though the image is theoretically nearer and smaller on hyperstereoscopic principles.

In general this type of stereoscope has a longer focal length than the full-lens type. The difficulty here is that the focal length is usually longer than that of most cameras. On the other hand the splitting of the lens allows of a larger and consequently flatter full lens. This reduces both chromatic and spherical aberration.

Stereoscopes for Roll Films.—Small full-lens type stereoscopes are also made for use with standard-size motion-picture films. The Tru-View Co., Rockford, Ill., manufactures one of these in America. The prints are small, so that it is possible to interlock them. The first and fourth, third and sixth, fifth and eighth, seventh and tenth, etc., views being paired. The second view is a blank never appearing before either lens. A roll of films is fed through a vertical slot at the right side of the viewer. A lever shifts the films the requisite distance. The stereoscope is of the box type with a fixed focus. The films are positive transparencies.

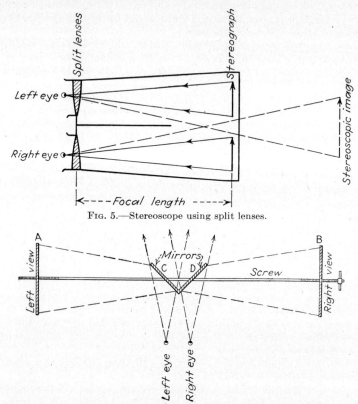

Fig. 5.—Stereoscope using split lenses.

Fig. 6.—Mirror stereoscope, as originally used by Wheatstone.

Leica also manufactures a stereoscope of this type already mentioned under stereoadaptors.

Lens-type stereoscopes should be fitted with side shields to eliminate stray light around the eyes, a shield between the two views to render them mutually exclusive, and a sliding plateholder or lens adjuster for focusing. If for use with transparencies, they should completely exclude all light except that coming through the ground glass.

Mirror Stereoscopes.—There are many types of mirror stereoscopes possible. In all of them the two views are superimposed by reflection.

The original mirror stereoscope was that of Wheatstone shown in Fig. 6.

The two prints are mounted facing each other at *A* and *B* and are reflected into the eyes from the mirrors *C* and *D*. The prints may be moved together or apart by means of the screw.

As but a single reflection occurs, the resultant view is reversed from the right to the left. Printing, for instance, reads backward. This can be remedied by having the prints reversed from the negatives.

Polished metal or front-silvered mirrors should be used as a faint second image is received off the front surface of ordinary mirrors.

A refinement and extension of this type is used extensively for viewing X-ray stereographs. Transparencies are used and placed in the machine reversed.

The most common form of mirror stereoscope is of the double-reflection type shown in Fig. 7. It is extensively used in aerial photography work. The path of the light is as shown in the figure. The double reflection eliminates the reversal effect of the original Wheatstone stereoscope.

It is possible to design this stereoscope for prints of any size. Prints of varying size may be used in any given machine, provided focal lengths are approximately correct. The use of large prints has the advantage of minimizing the obviousness of the print texture with relation to the picture.

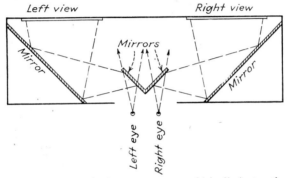

Fig. 7.—Double-reflection type of mirror stereoscope which eliminates the reversal effect of the Wheatstone type.

The total distance that the light travels from the print to the eye corresponds to the focal length of the instrument. As this is quite large in comparison to lens stereoscopes, considerable enlargment should be made of views taken with ordinary cameras. This can successfully be done as the problem of overlapping does not present itself.

For observing aerial photographs the machine is usually placed so that the observer looks down on the prints. Such views usually have only a portion of their areas in common. These are adjusted by eye until they fuse.

A single large metal plate polished on both sides may be used as a single mirror stereoscope. The plate is placed between the eyes and normal to them. The eyes look into the plate at the reflections of the prints. Here the prints are reversed from right to left due to the single reflection.

Many other types of mirror stereoscopes are possible. Unusual designs are occasionally resorted to for some technical purpose. For general purposes the double-reflecting type is undoubtedly the most satisfactory.

Anaglyphs.—An anaglyph is a stereograph in which the two views are respectively printed in complimentary colors. Red and green have been universally used for this purpose. Since a picture of one pure color disappears when viewed through a glass of the same color and is most visible, appearing black, through a complimentary color, the views can be rendered mutually exclusive by a pair of spectacles of the same colors. Thus, if the right view is red, the right spectacle must be green. The light spaces in the scene appear in both views but, being complimentary colors, fuse as white.

The advantages of this system are (1) the two views may be superimposed, thus allowing prints of any size to be used; (2) the space is only one-half that used for the same size in other systems; (3) the spectacles may be simple cellophane masks and consequently flat and very cheap.

These facts make the system the best for publication work. Numerous magazines have published anaglyphs inserting masks in each copy of the issue. The system has been, and is, extensively used in aerial photography publications.

The disadvantages of the system are (1) the difficulty of getting proper dyes, (2) the great absorption of light through the masks, (3) the inherent impossibility of making colored stereographs, (4) the green and red colors do not fuse into white around the edges of objects against a light background, but (5) leave an edge of color over that part of the background which is obscured by a foreground object in one of the views but not in the other.

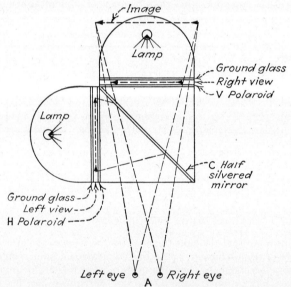

Fig. 8.—Stereo viewing device using polarizing plates. It is necessary for the observer to wear polarizing glasses to obtain the fusion of images.

Negatives used for anaglyphs should be very sharp for satisfactory fusing. Stopping down the lens aperture is consequently recommended when making negatives for this purpose.

In viewing an anaglyph the plane of the paper is usually obvious. The best impression is received if the scene seems to stand out from the paper rather than recede into it. This is achieved by printing so that correspondingly distant points in the two views are coincident in the superposition. If foreground points are coincident, the scene will recede into the paper.

Polaroid System.—A very convenient, recently developed form of viewer involves the use of Polaroid, a material which polarizes light. This viewer is shown in Fig. 8.

The H and V are sheets of Polaroid mounted at right angles to each other. They polarize the light from the two lamps horizontally and vertically, respectively. The transparencies representing the right and left views are inserted between the ground glass and the Polaroid. The sheet C which makes 45° angles with the Polaroid sheets is a half-silvered mirror which transmits one-half the incident light and reflects one-half. Thus an observer at A receives the reflected one-half of the horizontally polarized light and the refracted one-half of the vertically polarized light.

If the observer wears a pair of Polaroid spectacles in which the right glass is polarized vertically and the left glass horizontally, the views are rendered mutually exclusive and a stereoscopic fusion results.

Theoretically there is only one possible position in which the observer may place his eyes and see the views orthostereoscopically. This can be approximately found by moving the head back and forth until the view appears most natural. However, where the accurate judgment of depth is not of great importance there is a considerable area within which a normal scenic view of objects or persons appears quite natural. This area is large enough for six or more persons to view the scene at the same time. The size of the area depends upon the size and the correct viewing distance of the plates. The larger these are, the larger the area and the more persons who can view the stereograph.

As a device for showing stereographs to small groups of people, this system is unequaled by any other unless projection is resorted to, as it enables more than one person to view at the same time.

A further advantage is that Polaroid offers the possibility of making stereographs in color in which the illusion of reality is very startling.

The only objection to the system is that the resultant view being enclosed in a visible box tends to seem restricted in size to the size of the box. At the present time it is fairly expensive.

Processing, Mounting, and Viewing Stereographs. *Developing and Printing.*— The photographic processes of developing and printing stereographs are exactly the same as for ordinary photographic work. In developing negatives the photographer should aim at sharp detail, low contrast, and lack of graininess. All these are particularly important in stereographs of small size where the magnification of the stereoscope is large. The elimination of graininess is particularly important in view of the effect of the presence of the plane of the plate on the location of the image.

For transparencies either glass plates or films may be used. The problem is exactly the same as that of making lantern slides.

Methods of obtaining the desired results with respect to detail, contrast, and graininess are discussed elsewhere in the volume and need not be duplicated here.

Reversal of Views.—In taking stereographs with a double-lens camera, the two views must be transposed—interchanged, the right view being put on the left and vice versa—before viewing. The reason for this can best be understood by remembering that the negative in the camera has the image on it upside down and reversed from right to left. The stereograph consequently has two upside-down views side by side. If the plate is rotated through 180°, the two views come right side up and correct from left to right, but the view taken by the right lens is now on the left and vice versa. Consequently either the negative or the resultant positive must be cut apart and remounted.

If prints or negatives are separated and it is desired to determine which is for the right eye and which for the left, this can almost always be done by inspection as follows:

Pick a sharp point or vertical line in the foreground which appears quite close to some sharp feature of the background. The horizontal distance between these two will differ in the two views, the difference being greater when the difference in depth is greater. *The view in which the foreground point is farthest to the right with respect to the background is the left-eye view.*

Many of the methods for making stereographs are primarily for use with cameras already on hand or readily available. Since the stereoscope should have the same focal length as the camera, either a stereoscope must be obtained of approximately equal focal length or, if the stereoscope has a greater focal length than the camera (generally the case), the resultant prints should be enlarged.

Reference to formula (1) shows that, if the stereoscope has a focal length m times that of the camera, the print must be enlarged m times for orthostereoscopic viewing. As an example, the most common American hand stereoscope has a focal length of 20 cm. With this instrument and a camera of 6 cm. focal length, the prints should be enlarged $3\frac{1}{3}$ times.

As the centers of the prints should remain a distance apart equal to or less than the distance between the optical centers of the stereoscope, any considerable enlargement will cause the prints to overlap necessitating trimming. If a portion is trimmed off one print, the corresponding portion must be trimmed off the other. Since the left and right sides must be trimmed off the right and left views, respectively, both sides must be trimmed off both views. If this is to be done, the photographer must remember when taking the picture that objects near the edge of the finder may be out of the final stereograph.

To avoid overlapping much smaller enlargements than are theoretically called for can be used for general work. Though the resultant depth will be exaggerated this may add to the effectiveness of the stereograph rather than detract from it.

A compromise is usually the best answer. It is recommended that the prints be enlarged to the point where overlapping begins, taking into consideration the possible maximum separation of the prints. The result can then be viewed in the stereoscope to determine if the scene is objectionably distorted.

Alignment of Prints. Horizontal Separation between Prints.—On convergence principles the distance between the two views of an infinitely distant point on the plates should be equal to the distance between the lenses of the camera and of the stereoscope. This can easily be done by picking some sharp point in the background of one view and measuring the required distance in the proper direction for the same point in the other view.

Mounting should be done by measurement whenever possible. However, the distance between prints can be considerably lessened without any effect on the resultant image. With split-lens stereoscopes it is customary to mount the prints with less separation.

Thus it is possible for the photographer to mount the prints arbitrarily at a chosen distance less than the theoretical distance or by adjustment while viewing them in the stereoscope. If the latter method is used and the photographer has a greater than average interocular distance, he should be careful to place the prints somewhat closer together than his maximum fusion distance.

Vertical Alignment.—A line drawn between the two views of any point must be parallel to the line between optical centers, *i.e.*, parallel to the line through the eyes.

The eyes actually allow a small amount of vertical variation between the two views. The physiological reasons for this are not clearly understood.

The best way of achieving proper alignment is to place a straightedge over the center of the two prints parallel to the lower edge of the mounting card. Then adjust the prints so that the straightedge intersects the same points on each. This assures both vertical and rotational alignment. The center of the card and the center of the prints should be used, as this insures the prints being in the center of the viewing area with a consequent minimum of aberration.

Proper alignment may be obtained by observation through the stereoscope. The breakdown of fusion as the prints get out of alignment is quite sharp. One print can be placed in the center of its viewing area and the other moved until it is in the center of the fusion area.

If the latter method is used, care should be taken that the rotational alignment is correct. One central point of both prints may be in vertical alignment, while one print is slightly rotated with respect to the other. The eyes will allow an appreciable rotation accompanied by a twisting distortion of the image without breaking fusion. This can be avoided by watching the outside edges of the image, where fusion breaks down with the least rotation while the center of the image remains fused.

If possible, prints taken with a double-lens camera should not be cut apart until ready for mounting as the distance between the views and the vertical alignment of the prints is perfect in the uncut prints. By aligning corresponding points on the prints, parallel to the base of the mounting card, with the prints centrally located, the four corners of each view may be marked on the card. The prints can then be cut apart and each mounted in the space formerly occupied by the other.

Alignment of Transparencies.—Transparencies are made with exactly the same materials of which lantern slides are made. They may be made by printing directly from the uncut negative as follows: Place the left half of the transparency plate in contact with the right half of the negative being sure that the edges are parallel. Shield the halves not in contact and expose. Place the right half of the transparency in contact with the left half of the negative. Shield the halves not in contact and expose.

A simple frame can be made for this purpose composed of three sections each the size of one view. The two end sections are shielded and the center one is open. The negative and the transparency plate occupy two sections each, overlapping in the center section. After exposure they are shifted to opposite ends and exposed again. Zeiss manufactures such a frame.

The value of this method is that, once the frame is properly constructed, the alignment and spacing of the resultant transparency is automatically correct.

Alignment for Mirror Stereoscopes.—In mirror stereoscopes where large separate prints are used, the prints can be cut to fit against stops in the stereoscope or they can be aligned by observation. The latter requires a little knowledge on the part of the observer of how to move the prints.

Correct Viewing.—The prints or transparencies being properly mounted must still be properly inserted in the stereoscope and the latter held level. In showing stereographs to persons unfamiliar with them, fusion is frequently not achieved, either because the slide is not level in the stereoscope or because the stereoscope is not held level with the eyes. Both of these should be checked for persons having difficulty with fusion.

Adjustment of Stereoscope.—The viewing of stereographs after they have been properly placed in the stereoscope is quite simple. Most lens-type stereographs have focusing devices. It will be found easier to achieve fusion and involves less eyestrain if the carriage or the lenses are brought forward to the proper position rather than started forward and moved back.

In mirror-type stereoscopes no focusing occurs. Views set in a particular position may be made to fuse by changing the distance of the eyes from the mirrors.

An effort should be made to obtain an even illumination over both views whether prints or transparencies are used. The degree to which illumination may differ and satisfactory fusion occur is certainly considerable. However, uneven illumination makes the initial fusion a great deal more difficult and certainly detracts from the resultant effect.

Stereoscopes for both prints and transparencies can be equipped with a light mounted in such a way as to give an even illumination.

When a light is used on prints care must be taken to avoid glare. As a glossy print makes a more satisfactory background than a dull one, this glare can be considerable. It is sometimes eliminated by warping the prints into a slight curve.

Transparencies vs. Prints.—The question of the use of transparencies as opposed to prints is largely a matter of personal preference.

The light effect of transparencies gives a much greater illusion of the actual existence of light-filled space. They also have a brilliance which cannot be obtained with prints. Furthermore they permit the use of color in the same way that it is used in colored films. For these reasons they are generally considered to be superior.

On the other hand prints are much easier to handle and not so susceptible to damage. They are much easier to view as individual photographs. They require less light intensity and can usually be viewed in any position without searching for a source of light, up to which they can be held. A number may be viewed, as single photographs, at once for purposes of selection. For these reasons they usually give greater satisfaction to the beginner.

Hyperstereoscopy.—If the separation between camera lenses is increased beyond the interocular distance the two resultant photographs of any object will be the same as could have been taken, using the interocular distance, of an exactly similar object both smaller and nearer the camera.

On convergence principles if the base is increased m times the object will appear $1/m$ the distance and $1/m$ the size. Thus, if the base is doubled, the resultant object should appear as a "reduced model" of half the size at half the distance.

Since the ability to detect depth is much greater at greater convergences (see Table I) the objects in this "reduced model" will appear to stand out from their backgrounds much more obviously than in an orthostereoscopic view. The perception of depth is consequently enhanced.

As the base increases, the convergence angle consistent with a reduced model interpretation becomes greater and soon passes beyond any value natural to binocular vision or stereoscopic viewing. Certainly at some point the eyes cease interpreting the image as a reduced model and begin interpreting it as a similar object of increased depth. This exaggeration of depth then increases as the base is further increased.

The entire phenomenon of the interpretation of hyperstereoscopic images needs more thorough investigation before more exact statements can be made concerning it.

In aerial photography it is usually assumed that the most natural relief, or the nearest approach to a properly shaped image, is obtained when the two views of a point on the ground appear the interocular distance apart in relative position on the two plates. The base for this most natural relief can be calculated from the formula

$$B = \frac{ed}{f} \tag{5}$$

where B = distance between exposures in feet;

e = interocular distance in inches;

d = height of camera above ground in feet;

f = focal length of camera in inches.

If the base as obtained from this formula is exceeded, the resultant stereoscopic image is certainly exaggerated in depth. By this means low buildings can be made to appear as skyscrapers and normally imperceptible details of relief can be made apparent.

The hyperstereoscopic effect, if judiciously used, can add greatly to a stereograph's effectiveness by its strong emphasis of the depth quality. It is best used on mountain or landscape views which have few foreground objects.

From considerations of the limits of stereoscopic vision, objects over 2000 ft. away must be photographed with an increased base if any stereoscopic effect is to be obtained. The photographer need not expect any pronounced binocular effect of depth on objects over 1000 ft. unless he uses an increased base.

Projection Systems. *Fundamental Problems.*—The projection of stereographs involves certain problems not present in individual viewing. These are:

1. The projected stereograph must be viewable from a number of different positions. This presents two major problems: that of keeping the stereographs at equal distances from the eyes and that of distortion due to oblique viewing.

If the projected stereographs are large and side by side they will be at different distances from the eyes of all observers, except those near the normal to the center of the screen. This difference in size increases as the observer moves farther to the side or nearer to the screen. If fusion can still be maintained, the question of eyestrain arises.

This difficulty cannot be cured by devices involving mirrors, prisms, or lenses at the eye unless each observer has a device suited to his particular position. It is completely cured by systems which permit the superposition of the two views. Anaglyphs and the polaroid system are of this type.

The problem of distortion is much the same as that in a motion-picture theater complicated and emphasized by the presence of depth. Theoretically there is but one correct viewing point. From this point there is an increase of depth as the observer moves back and a decrease as he moves forward. In addition, as he moves to the side, the scene appears narrower and twisted, objects on the near side of the screen moving toward the observer with respect to objects on the far side.

Such distortions are, in general scenes, not too annoying. In the event of three-dimensional movies on a large scale, theaters may be made somewhat narrower than is now the custom.

2. The stereographs must be made mutually exclusive to the eyes of a number of individuals. This necessitates some form of stereoscope or spectacles at the eye of every observer. This introduces the problem of expense, and, as a commercial proposition, the overcoming of the slight annoyance entailed.

The only possibility of separating the stereograms for every observer at the screen rather than at the eyes seems to lie in the Ives' system (see page 590) in which other difficulties are almost insuperable.

3. The increased difficulty of getting the proper separation between views. This problem does not arise if the system permits superposition on the screen. If views are placed side by side, one above the other, or in any other position, mirrors or prisms must be used at the eyes to effect fusion.

4. If motion pictures are contemplated, the additional problems of synchronization of shutters and films presents itself together with the doubling of a number of expenses.

No detailed discussion of the above problems or of the following systems is given, as the field is still in the laboratory stage.

The anaglyph system is the same as that discussed on page 583. Its advantages and disadvantages are the same as set forth there. Its chief advantages for projection work lie in the ability to superimpose the views and in its cheapness. Its chief disadvantages lie in the loss of light due to the colors employed and its inadaptability to color work.

In anaglyphic movies the edges of color around moving objects against a light field causes an annoying flashing of color. However, anaglyphic movies have been successfully shown as a novelty in American and Continental theaters.

The Polaroid system is the same as that discussed on page 584. The two views are projected through Polaroid and superimposed on the screen. The advantages of the system lie in the possibility of superposition and of using color. On the other hand powerful light sources are needed owing to the cutting out of a large portion of the light in polarizing. This demands that an adequate system of cooling the bulbs be devised. The Polaroid Corp. is rapidly conquering the difficulties in this system.

Ives' System.—Figure 9a represents a scene in space photographed by a battery of cameras. Figure 9b represents the scene replaced by a screen which has the characteristic of reflecting all incident light in a horizontal plane directly back upon itself

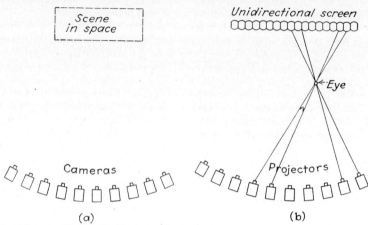

Fig. 9.—Diagram illustrating the steoescopic system devised by H. E. Ives of the Bell. Telephone Laboratories.

while diffusing it vertically. The cameras are replaced by projectors projecting the respective pictures.

It will be seen that the eye located anywhere in view of the screen sees a vertical strip of the projected view from each camera. The eye, being below the direct rays from the projector, does not interfere. It thus builds up from the various strips the complete image of the original scene as it appeared from its location. Since each eye does this for itself, the two images are different and mutually exclusive. Consequently a stereoscopic image results.

A screen having the necessary characteristics can be made from vertical transparent rods ground cylindrically on the front and rear surfaces with the rear surface painted with a white diffusing paint.

This is the method of H. E. Ives.

Such a system would be perfect if the number of cameras approached infinity and the width of the screen rods approached zero. As the number of cameras decrease and the width of the rods increases, the resultant image becomes more obviously a series of vertical strips.

Fig. 10.—Stereoscope viewing device designed for educational purposes.

The system has been demonstrated experimentally. Obviously it is enormously expensive and commercially entirely impractical. It is of interest as being the only projection system which can be viewed by a number of persons without any device at the eyes.

Full technical information is obtainable in the *Journal of the Optical Society of America*, vol. 21, pp. 109–118; or Bell Telephone System, *Technical Publications*, Monograph B-550.

Distortions and Aberrations.—Any change in shape of a stereoscopic image from the original scene should be classified as a distortion. For purposes of convenience changes in size have also been included in the following discussion. Certain of the

TABLE II.—DISTORTIONS AND ABERRATIONS IN STEREOPHOTOGRAPHY
Distortions in Stereoscopic Images

Cause	Effect on						
	Shape of image			Size of image		Dist. of image from eyes	
	Unchanged	Decreased in depth	Increased in depth	Smaller	Larger	Decreased	Increased
$f_S > f_C$			√				√
$f_S < f_C$		√				√	
$d_S > f_S$			√				√
$d_S < f_S$		√				√	
$M_S > M_C$			√				√
$M_S < M_C$		√				√	
$e < B_C$	√			√		√	
$e > B_C$	√				√		√
$e < B_S$	√			√		√	
$e > B_S$	√				√		√
Prints reduced			√				√
Prints enlarged		√				√	

Subscripts: S refers to stereoscope; C refers to camera.
f = focal length;
d = distance of plate from lenses;
M = magnification of lenses;
B = distance between optical centers of lenses;
e = interocular distance.

elements causing these have been discussed on page 573 under Location and Size of Images and on page 588 under Hyperstereoscopy. These will not be discussed again here.

Other distortions arise from many causes when the conditions for orthostereoscopy are not fulfilled. As the actual image formation is a composite of a number of variables, the distortions listed in Table II and the subsequent discussion are the tendencies set up by the conditions which cause them. These must be weighted against the other factors present.

Improper mounting may cause distortions:

If both views are rotated around their individual centers in the same direction the entire scene is twisted in that direction. This is liable to occur if mounting is done by eye, for, if the first print is not level, the second will be rotated to obtain fusion.

If the views are rotated in opposite directions, say the bottoms separated and the tops brought together, then the bottom area will recede and become smaller while the top area approaches and becomes larger.

If the stereograph is improperly placed in the stereoscope, the following distortions may occur: If it is tipped forward or backward from the vertical, the image loses height while the approaching portion comes nearer.

If the stereograph is not parallel to the line between the lens centers while fusion is maintained, the image is twisted in the same direction while losing width.

An occasional individual has no capacity for stereoscopic vision. The chief reasons for this are the habit of depending on a master eye or the fact that one eye is considerably weaker than the other. No accurate figures are available, although the number of such individuals is said to be in the neighborhood of 8 per cent of the population.

With lens-type stereoscopes chromatic aberration occurs. In full-lens stereoscopes in which the eyes are centered on the optical centers, white areas to the left of center appear blue on the left side and red on the right. Areas to the left of center appear the reverse.

In split-lens stereoscopes white areas in the left-side view appear blue on the right and red on the left. White areas in the right-side view appear the reverse. In the fused image these somewhat cancel each other though a band of color remains.

These effects are never bothersome, the edges of color generally being very fine and only detectable if attention is directed to them. Such aberration can be corrected by the use of crown and flint glass in the stereoscope. In general the expense of doing this is greater than warranted.

The presence of residual color in anaglyphs was mentioned under that subject.

If the lenses of the stereoscope are exact duplicates of those of the camera, no spherical aberration will occur. If the curvature of the lenses is different or if mirror stereoscopes are used, such aberration does occur. It is exactly the same problem as is present with an ordinary single-lens camera and need not be discussed here.

Miscellaneous Applications. *Astronomy.*— Stereography has certain limited uses in astronomy. All these are based on motion of the astronomical body with respect to the earth.

Fig. 11.—Graflex camera fitted with two lenses for stereoscopic photography.

Stereographs may be made of the moon, owing to its librations. These slight oscillations are the same as a rotation of the moon. Consequently two views taken at opposite ends of a libration cycle will show a stereoscopic effect.

Stereographs may be made of astronomical bodies which move appreciably against the background of the stars. This is done by photographing them twice so that they appear shifted against the background. Aside from the fact that the object photographed, a comet or a planet, does stand out from the background in a stereoscopic manner such stereographs have no technical value whatever, as the resultant depth is a completely false one. The object shows no depth within itself.

Cloud stereographs can be made in the same manner, provided there is some lateral motion of the clouds without an accompanying change of shape. The farther the clouds move between views the nearer the earth they will appear.

The possibility of applying stereography to other astronomical phenomena are extremely limited. They certainly are restricted to the solar system. The maximum possible base is twice the distance of the earth from the sun or 186,000,000 miles. From formula (3) this means that a star would have to be within ½ light year of the sun to show any relief against an infinitely distant background. The nearest star is greatly in excess of this distance. This shift is, of course, used to measure the distance of near stars, as a much smaller angle can be measured than the eye can detect in a stereograph.

Wide-angle System.—The angle of view of a normal eye runs to 120° or more. The average stereoscopic camera covers an angle in the neighborhood of 60°. This imposes a restriction on stereographs which detracts from their reality.

A lens system is available which satisfactorily increases this angle up to 90°. The system is practically free from chromatic aberration and is corrected for distortion. It involves two lenses as shown in Fig. 12. Complete technical information on this system can be found in L. E. W. von Albada, A Wide Angle Stereoscope and a Wide Angle View Finder, *Trans. Optical Soc. (London)*, vol. 25, no. 5; and in A. W. Judge, "Stereoscopic Photography."

Fig. 12.— Diagram of wide-angle lens system for stereoscopes.

Pseudoscopic Views.—If the two views of a stereograph are transposed so that the right eye sees the left view and vice versa, a pseudoscopic view results.

If the stereograph is of separated objects the order of depth of these objects is reversed, *i.e.*, the background objects appear in the foreground and vice versa.

If the stereograph is of a simple geometric figure or of such a nature that the solidity of the object can be reversed without destroying its meaning, such reversal will occur. Thus a pseudoscopic stereograph of the pyramid in Fig. 1 would appear to be a pyramid with the base in the foreground and the apex in the background.

In normal scenes including persons, buildings, or landscapes, the pseudoscopic stereograph leads only to confusion as the depth factors indicating the true scene are opposed to the pseudoscopic factor. Confusion and loss of depth are the result.

Bibliography

The literature of stereography is extremely limited. The following list contains the most important works on the subject:

Periodicals:

WHEATSTONE, CHARLES: Contributions to the Physiology of Vision, *Phil. Trans. (London)*, (1838).
FRENCH, J. W.: Stereoscopy Re-stated, *Trans. Optical Soc. (London)*, vol. 24 (1922–1923).
ALBADA, L. E. W. VON: A Wide Angle Stereoscope and a Wide Angle View Finder, *Trans. Optical Soc. (London)*, vol. 25 (1923–1924).
TRUMP, R. W.: Binocular Vision and Stereoscopic Sense. *Trans. Optical Soc. (London)*, vol. 25 (1923–1924).
KURTZ, HENRY: Orthostereoscopy, *J. Optical Soc. Am.*, October, 1937.

Much of the literature has been in the form of short articles. Some of these have appeared in the following journals:

Philosophical Magazine.
Photo Miniature.
American Photography.
British Journal of Photography.

Transactions Optical Society of London.
Technology Review.
Journal of The Optical Society of America.

Books:

BREWSTER, DAVID: "The Stereoscope, Its History, Uses and Construction" (1858).
CAZES, L.: "Stéréoscope de precision, theory et practique," Paris (1895).
ROTHWELL, C. F.: "The Elements of Stereoscopic Photography," London (1896).
DROUIN, F.: "The Stereoscope and Stereoscopic Photography," London (1897).
PULFRICH, C.: "Neue stereoskopische Methoden und Apparate für die zweckeder Astronomie, Topographie und Metronomie," Berlin (1903).
HARTIG, TH.: "Das Stereoscop." Leipzig (1907).
PULFRICH, C.: "Stereoskopische Sehen und Messen," Jena (1911).
JUDGE, A. W.: "Stereoscopic Photography," Am. Photographic Pub. (1935).
ROHR, MONTZ VON: "Die Binokularen Instrumente," Berlin.

CHAPTER XXI

PHOTOGRAPHY BY ULTRAVIOLET AND INFRARED

By Walter Clark

The visible spectrum, ranging from wavelengths 3900 to 7600 Å., covers a very small portion of the known spectrum of radiation which extends from the short cosmic rays to the long waves of radio. The invisible wavelength region shorter than 3900 Å. constitutes the ultraviolet, which may be considered to have its short wavelength limit at 136 Å. It merges into the X rays and is customarily divided at about 2000 Å. into two parts known as the far and near ultraviolet, the latter being the region which borders on the visible spectrum. The invisible portion of the spectrum which is an extension of the visible into longer wavelengths is known as the infrared. As the infrared wavelengths become longer, they constitute the heat rays, and these merge into the long Hertzian or radio waves.

The first invisible part of the spectrum to be discovered was the infrared, by Sir William Herschel in 1800. Herschel passed a thermometer through the spectrum of the sun and found that the temperatures recorded were higher beyond the red than in the visible region. The ultraviolet was discovered shortly after the infrared by Ritter and Wollaston, who showed that the blackening action of sunlight on silver chloride occurred readily in the part of the spectrum beyond the visible limit in the violet. All salts of silver—in particular the chloride, bromide, and iodobromide used in photographic papers, plates, and films—are sensitive to ultraviolet radiation. There is also sensitivity in the visible violet and blue and, in the case of the bromide and iodobromide of negative materials, in the blue-green. In order to extend the response to the remainder of the visible green, the red, and the infrared, it is necessary to resort to sensitizing by means of dyes. Commercial photographic plates and films are available which permit photography of the whole spectrum from about 2000 Å. in the ultraviolet to beyond 13,000 Å. in the infrared. They provide the physicist and astronomer with their most convenient means of recording spectra over this region, and have many other special applications in the fields of science and technology.

ULTRAVIOLET PHOTOGRAPHY

Although all normal photographic plates and films are sensitive to radiation in the near ultraviolet, at a wavelength of about 2500 Å. the gelatin of the emulsion begins to absorb the rays, and at 2000 Å. this absorption is so great that plates and films will no longer respond. This wavelength, therefore, represents the shortest which can be recorded on commercial plates and films unless special conditions are employed. If it is desired to photograph by wavelengths shorter than 2000 Å., it is necessary to use plates having very little gelatin, such as the so-called "Schumann plates," or to treat normal plates with a substance which fluoresces in the short wavelength radiation, emitting light of longer wavelengths to which the plate is readily sensitive. If the camera is fitted with lenses of quartz instead of glass, wavelengths down to 1850 Å. are passed to the plate, provided they do not have to travel through a long path of air, the oxygen of which begins to exert a strong absorption at about 2000 Å. Optical glass, such as is normally used in camera lenses, absorbs the ultraviolet strongly at wavelengths shorter than about 3300 to 3500 Å., the actual limit depending on the nature of the glass. For photography in the region from this point to 2000 Å. it is necessary to use quartz lenses.

There are two distinctly different ways of using ultraviolet radiation for taking photographs. The first of these, called the "reflected ultraviolet method," is strictly analogous to ordinary photographic methods, whereby the photograph is taken by the light which is reflected from the subject. In the case of ultraviolet photography by this method, the source of radiation, or the camera, is provided with filters which transmit only the invisible ultraviolet and allow no visible light to pass. The second method, known as the "fluorescent light method," depends on the ability of ultraviolet to induce visible fluorescence in some materials. The ultraviolet is absorbed by the material, and energy is reemitted in the form of visible light. The wavelength of the fluorescent light is always longer than that of the ultraviolet which excited it, and its color may range from violet to red according to the nature of the material. In addition to the fluorescent radiation there is always present some ultraviolet which is reflected directly by the object. This reflected ultraviolet is invisible, but it is much more effective photographically than the fluorescent light. In the fluorescent-light method it is desired to make the exposure by the fluorescence alone, and it is therefore necessary to prevent the reflected ultraviolet from reaching the lens of the camera. This is achieved by placing over the lens a filter which absorbs all the ultraviolet but which allows the visible light to pass freely. Although the reflected ultraviolet method is very frequently used, the fluorescence method is the more important. There is no general rule, however, by which the appropriate method can be chosen. If it is required to show detail which can be seen by the fluorescent light, it can be photographed by the fluorescent-light method. If detail is not shown in this manner, it may be possible to reveal it by reflected ultraviolet photography, but only experiment will tell. The reflected ultraviolet method is the quicker of the two, and, if convenient, it should be tried first.

Sources of Ultraviolet. *Sunlight.*—Ultraviolet is present in the radiation from the sun but to an extent of less than 5 per cent, as compared with 41 to 45 per cent in the visible and from 50 to 58 per cent in the infrared. No radiation of wavelength shorter than 2900 Å. reaches the earth from the sun, and the actual threshold varies with the atmospheric conditions and the elevation of the sun. Some ultraviolet photographs have been made out of doors using sunlight as the source, and some of the planets have been photographed by the ultraviolet in the sunlight which they reflect. Means have been proposed for using the sun as a source of ultraviolet for photography indoors, but they are inefficient, and in general the sun can be eliminated as a source for general ultraviolet photography.

Incandescent Tungsten-filament Electric Lamps.—The amount of ultraviolet energy in the radiation from the normal type of electric lamp is so small that the lamps are not suitable sources. By using overvolted lamps the ultraviolet intensity is increased but not sufficiently to make the lamps of importance for general use.

Carbon-arc Lamps.—The carbon arcs provide the highest temperatures available in artificial light sources, and together with the sun they are the sources most used for ultraviolet therapy. By introducing metal salts into the cores of the carbons, manufacturers have been able to increase the emission of radiation in various parts of the spectrum, including the ultraviolet. Such carbons are made for therapeutic purposes, an example being the National Carbon Company's Therapeutic "C" carbons. Most carbon arcs, including the Sunshine, Sun, High Intensity, and White Flame arcs, have a strong emission at about 3900 Å. They are suitable sources of near ultraviolet insofar as energy is concerned, but they have certain disadvantages which include disintegration of the carbons, inconvenience due to heat, and need for attention during operation. If a studio is equipped with them, however, they might well be used. Enclosed metallic arcs, such as the Pointolite and Tungsarc lamps do not have sufficient energy in the ultraviolet to be of general use.

Gaseous-discharge Lamps.—The gaseous-discharge lamps, particularly the mercury arcs, provide the most convenient sources for ultraviolet photography. The earliest form was the Cooper-Hewitt mercury-vapor lamp, which consists of an evacuated glass tube containing mercury and two metal electrodes connected to a source of electric supply. An arc discharge is caused to pass between the electrodes by tilting the tube to make and break a conducting link of mercury or by applying a high potential across the electrodes. The light from the tube consists of the emission spectrum of mercury vapor. The strongest line in the near ultraviolet, and the one most useful photographically, is that at 3650 Å. Improvements in the lamp consisted in introducing a considerable pressure of mercury vapor and introducing rare gases into low-pressure mercury tubes, provided with electrodes of oxides of the rare earths and heated by a tungsten filament. A very efficient type is the high-pressure mercury lamp in which oxide-coated electrodes are used and the mercury is at a relatively high pressure, the amount present being limited so that it is all vaporized before the normal operating temperature is reached. The most recent types consist of a short narrow-bore quartz capillary tube, and they operate at mercury-vapor pressures up to 40 atm. in the open air and several hundred atmospheres when water-cooled. These capillary lamps emit energy of very high intensity, but there is a strong background of continuous spectrum in addition to the mercury lines. In addition to ordinary glass, mercury lamps are made of glass having transmission farther in the ultraviolet, such as Corning Corex A, Corex D, and Pyrex. For the highest ultraviolet emission, quartz tubes are used instead of glass. The lamps are of various shapes, mainly long straight tubes and tubes bent into U or M form, and are manufactured by the General Electric Vapor Lamp Co., Hoboken, N. J., and the Hanovia Chemical and Mfg. Co., Newark, N. J. Most of these lamps are designed for general studio illumination, laboratory work, and as light sources for enlargers. They can obviously be readily adapted for copying by ultraviolet. In order to ensure the maximum of convenience for this type of work, L. Bendikson, of the Huntington Library, San Marino, Calif., designed a quartz mercury-vapor lamp in the form of a spiral, which could be placed in a metal reflector round the camera lens. The sun lamps S-1 and S-2, made by the General Electric Co., may be classed as mercury-arc lamps, although some light is emitted from incandescent tungsten electrodes. There are two electrodes bridged by a filament in an evacuated bulb containing mercury. When a voltage is applied to the filament through an appropriate transformer, an arc forms in the mercury vapor between the electrodes. There is high energy emission at the 3650 Å. line and a strong continuous spectrum due to the filament. The bulb is of ultraviolet-transmitting Corex glass, and the lamp may be used for ultraviolet photography if steps are taken to filter out the visible spectrum. The lamps are not so efficient as the other mercury-discharge lamps for photographic purposes.

Other Sources.—There are many other sources which have a strong emission in the ultraviolet. They include metallic arcs, such as those with electrodes of iron, electric sparks, and Geissler tubes. They are of great importance for spectrography but are not convenient for general ultraviolet photography.

Filters.—Filters for ultraviolet photography are of two kinds: (1) those which transmit the ultraviolet and absorb visible light, and (2) those which absorb the ultraviolet and transmit visible light. In photography, filters of the first kind are used over the source, or over the lens, by reflected ultraviolet. They generally consist of a special glass containing nickel oxide and are of a very deep purple or opaque appearance. Those in most common use are the Wratten No. 18A filter, which is usually employed in the form of optically worked sheets over the lens, and the Corning glass Violet Ultra No. 586, which is available in the form of molded and polished squares for use over the source and which can be optically worked for use over the lens. Some other Corning glasses are suitable provided a certain amount of transmission in the red can be tolerated. They are the glasses: Heat Resisting Red Purple Ultra No. 587; Red Purple Ultra No. 597; Red Ultra No. 584; and Red Purple Corex A No. 986. An ultraviolet-transmitting glass made in England by Chance Bros. and Co., Ltd., is known as No. 14 Ultraviolet, while the Jena Glass Works of Schott und Gen, in Germany, make similar glasses known as UG1, UG2, and UG4. All these filters transmit a relatively narrow band of ultraviolet, extending roughly from 3000 to 4000 Å., with a maximum at about 3600 Å. They are therefore very suited for isolating the 3650 Å. line of the mercury spectrum. The General Electric Vapor Lamp Co. manufactures Cooper-Hewitt lamps in which the tube is made of a visually opaque, ultraviolet-transmitting glass known as Nico. Many other filters transmitting ultraviolet and absorbing visible light have been described, but in general they are not so convenient or efficient as the glass filters. Perhaps the most interesting is a plate of quartz or ultraviolet-transmitting glass coated with silver, which has a transmission band at 3200 Å.

Filters of the second kind, absorbing ultraviolet radiation, and transmitting the visible freely, are used in fluorescent light photography on the lens of the camera. The most used of these is the Wratten No. 2A filter, which absorbs all radiation of wavelength shorter than 4100 Å., and transmits the visible fully. The Wratten No. 2 Aesculine filter absorbs below 3900 Å. but is fluorescent, and the No. 2A is to be preferred. Many types of liquid filter have been proposed for this purpose, but some of those which are often recommended are not very efficient absorbers. A layer of a solution of cerium ammonium nitrate, 1 cm. thick and containing sulphuric acid to dissolve the salt in a concentration of 0.1 per cent, absorbs below 3750 Å. and in 1 per cent concentration absorbs below 4600 Å. A layer of triphenylmethane solution (0.5 g. in 75 cc. cf ethyl alcohol) 1 cm. thick, a filter often recommended, is not satisfactory since it transmits freely above 3000 Å.

Cameras.—Any camera employed for normal photography is satisfactory for use in the ultraviolet by either method. For the fluorescent-light method the normal lens may be used, as the photograph is made by visible light. The ordinary lens can also be employed for the reflected ultraviolet-light method, provided it transmits the wavelengths it is desired to record. For wavelengths shorter than about 3500 Å. it is necessary to use a quartz lens, and, if records are required below 2000 Å., the lens must be made of fluorite. However, photography in this short-wavelength region is only possible if the air is evacuated from the camera and if plates containing little gelatin are used. It falls, therefore, outside the sphere of operation of the ordinary photographer and is chiefly of interest to the physicist recording spectra. The focus of a lens in the ultraviolet is not quite the same as in the visible region, but little difficulty is encountered on this score if a small aperture is used.

Photographic Plates and Films.—All plates and films are sensitive in the near ultraviolet to about 2000 Å., although on account of the absorption by the gelatin their sensitivity begins to fall off at 2800 Å. and is noticeably reduced at 2500 Å. In the region from 2500 to 3900 Å., however, and in the visible region, normal photographic materials may be used. The plate or film selected will depend on the speed and contrast desired, the choice being made in the same manner as for photography by visible light, except that it should be borne in mind that the contrast in the ultraviolet is lower than in the visible, and plates and films of high contrast are preferred. For photography by the reflected ultraviolet method the highest sensitivity is given by the noncolor-sensitized plates which have the highest speed to visible blue light, such as the Eastman 40. If contrast is desired and some sensitivity can be sacrificed, plates of the type of the Eastman 33 and Eastman Process and films like Eastman Commercial and Eastman Process will be satisfactory. For fluorescent-light photography it is necessary to use materials which are sensitive throughout the visible spectrum. All panchromatic plates and films will be suitable, although usually fair contrast is desired, and a material of the type of the Wratten Panchromatic Process or Wratten M plate will be selected.

Methods of Ultraviolet Photography. *Reflected-ultraviolet Method.*—The subject to be photographed is irradiated with ultraviolet from one or two sources and is placed at the appropriate distance to give the evenness of illumination desired. To prevent visible light from reaching the plate in the camera, an ultraviolet transmitting filter

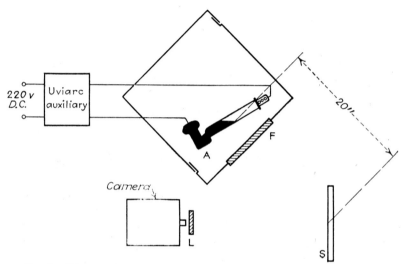

Fig. 1.—Diagram showing illuminant for reflected ultraviolet photography.
A—G. E 220-volt Horizontal Uviarc burner
S—Subject
F—Ultraviolet transmitting filter, Corning "Ultra" glass, No. 586
L—Ultraviolet absorbing filter, for photography of fluorescent effects, Wratten No. 2A
Exposure on Wratten Process Panchromatic Plates
With filter L about 20 min. at *f*/4.5.
Without filter L about 1 min. at *f*/16.

must be used over the source or lens. In the former case the mercury-vapor lamp, or other source, should be placed in a ventilated reflector which is completely covered with a filter, such as the Corning Violet Ultra No. 586, and the operations must take place in a totally darkened room. If the filter (Wratten No. 18A) is used on the lens, the room may be lightened. There is a convenience in applying the filter to the source rather than to the lens, since the same lighting unit can then be used for the fluorescent-light method as well. If the arrangement shown in Fig. 1 is used, employing a single General Electric Uviarc 220-volt horizontal burner with a Corning No. 586 filter over the lamp and placing the lamp at 20 in. from the subject to be copied, the required exposure will be of the order of 1 min. at *f*/16 on the Wratten Panchromatic Process plate.

Fluorescent-light Method.—The same arrangement of the lights can be used as in the previous method, but it is essential that the ultraviolet transmitting filter be used in front of them. A filter must be used on the lens to absorb the reflected-ultraviolet and transmit the visible fluorescence radiation freely. The arrangement shown in Fig. 1 is satisfactory, using a single Uviarc burner in conjunction with the Corning No. 586 filter and the Wratten No. 2A filter on the lens. In the conditions depicted, the exposure will be of the order of 20 min. at $f/4.5$, using the Wratten Panchromatic Process plate.

Applications of Ultraviolet Photography. *Criminology.*—The use of ultraviolet photography in detecting alterations in documents, in the examination of watermarks and postage stamps, and in revealing invisible writing will be dealt with in the section on Documentary Photography. One of the most important applications of ultraviolet documentary photography in the field of criminology is in the detection of forgery. Forged bank notes have been detected by the fluorescence of the papers but particularly by that of the printing inks, which may be of a different nature and so fluoresce differently. Alterations in the inks of written or typewritten documents may be detected by the fluorescence method, although it is not always reliable for identifying a particular ink. Writing may be deciphered on stained and worn documents and specific inks detected on used blotting paper if they have characteristic fluorescence. Textile fibers, dyes, stains, and markings may be compared by their fluorescence. Stains of blood, urine, seminal fluid, and manure on clothes or other objects, and vegetable particles, organic chemicals, pigments, grains of mineral origin, and other clues have been identified or differentiated by fluorescence photography. Fingerprints cannot usually be identified directly, but they are revealed quite clearly if dusted with a fluorescent powder, such as anthracene, before photographing. The method shows some promise for the detection of drugs, etc., in body fluids. Adhesives and sealing wax which may appear identical to the eye may show differing fluorescence, so that tampering with letters and packages may be detectable. Its importance in the determination of the authenticity of works of art will be treated in a later section.

Documentary Photography.—One of the most important applications of ultraviolet photography is in the examination of documents, particularly those which have been altered by age, or wear, chemical or mechanical erasure, substitution, and overwriting, and in the detection of secret writing. The fluorescence method is the more useful because paper, parchment, pigments, etc., fluoresce when irradiated with ultraviolet. The extent of the fluorescence varies with the nature of the material and the treatment which it has undergone. One of the earliest and most successful applications of the method was in the deciphering of the original writing on palimpsests. These are manuscripts, usually on vellum, from which the original writing has been mechanically erased by fine pumice, in order that the clear surfaces so obtained may be used again by another scribe. Invisible traces of ink or pigment left embedded in the vellum may fluoresce to a less or greater extent than the vellum itself. Usually it is less, and if a fluorescent-light ultraviolet photograph is made, the original writing will be revealed in the negative as lighter than the background. The method may be applied to other documents in which erasures have left invisible traces of the original writing. Erasures due to wear may be photographed in the same manner.

Chemical erasures may often be successfully revealed by the fluorescent-light method. Ink eradicators are frequently used by forgers to remove original writing for which other writing or typewriting is substituted. By visible light the rewriting alone is usually seen, while ultraviolet photography will often disclose the original writing. In many cases it provides the only reliable test. Secret writing by so-called "invisible inks" may be similarly revealed. In general, where the paper has been chemically treated locally for any purpose, it is probable that the areas of change can be shown by fluorescence photography. Examples are the removal of foxing marks, collectors' markings, names, dates, and invisible marks due to presence of saliva, milk, soap, urine, etc. Papers themselves fluoresce differently in the ultraviolet, according to the nature of the pulp, the sizing and other treatment of the paper, the age, and the kind of pigment or dye added to color it. Paper deliberately stained or dyed to represent another in color may be detected by the ultraviolet if the dyes fluoresce differently.

Watermarks have been studied by the ultraviolet in order to distinguish between genuine and false ones. Artificial watermarks produced by the application of an oil or a wax generally fluoresce brightly. Others may be produced by impression with a

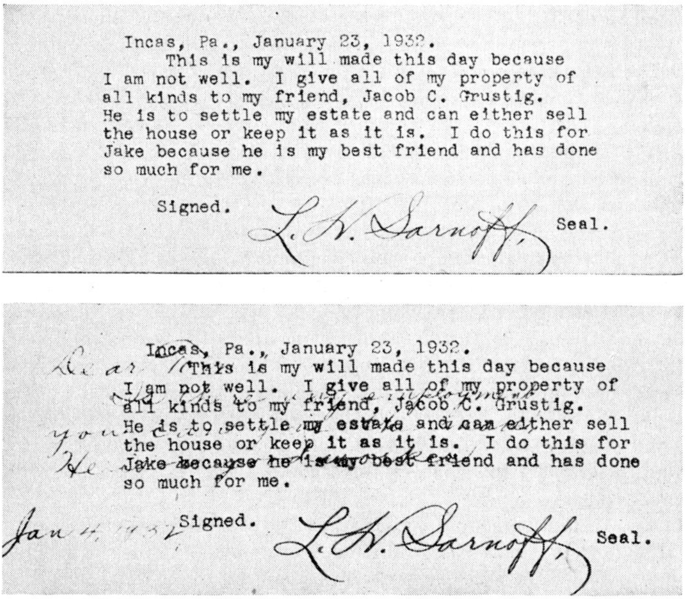

Fig. 2.—Photographs showing detail which may be obtained through ultraviolet photography. The top photograph shows a copy of a letter made with ordinary photographic methods. The bottom illustrations shows additional detail made visible through ultraviolet photography.

rubber roller before the paper is dried. This renders parts of the paper thin by compression, although the fibers are more densely packed in these parts. In a genuine watermark the wet fibers are pushed aside, in making the paper, by the wire design, so that the mark is actually thinner than the surrounding paper. Although it is not possible to distinguish between these two types of watermark directly by fluorescent photography, they can be identified after application of a sizing test solution which consists of water or an oil containing a fluorescent material. The solution will penetrate a genuine watermark more quickly than the surrounding paper, so that it will fluoresce before the paper. In an artificial watermark made by compression, the rates of penetration are the same, so that the watermark will not be distinguished by fluorescence.

Postage stamps may be examined by the ultraviolet, and eradicated cancellations, repairs to the paper, changes in the dye or pigment, or false watermarks detected. Sealing wax varies markedly in its fluorescence according to its origin, color, age, and the method of manufacture, so that fraudulent seals can often be detected, especially if a genuine seal is available for comparison.   Adhesives and binding materials may be identified or compared by the fluorescence method.

Works of Art.—Ultraviolet photography is an important instrument for the determination of the authenticity of works of art and for the detection of repairs, overpaintings, and forged signatures.   In the field of sculpture, marble, alabaster, limestone, sandstone, and granite can be examined by ultraviolet fluorescence to determine the origin of the stone, its age, and the presence of restorations and reworking.   Precious and semiprecious stones can sometimes be distinguished from paste stones and artificial pearls from the natural variety.   Old ivory can be distinguished from the more recent material and from bone and the artificially aged material from that colored naturally.   The method has also been successfully applied to the examination of textiles and ceramics, glass, enamels, prints and drawings, and particularly paintings.   In this case it is used in conjunction with chemical analysis and photography by X rays and the infrared.   Restorations may be distinguished by the difference in fluorescence between old and new paints and by changes in the fluorescence of the varnish if the restoration is made over the varnish.   Sometimes a varnish will fluoresce to such an extent as to mask the fluorescence of the underlying pigments, and allowance must be made for this.   The use of the method in the examination of palimpsests and other documents has been described in the preceding section.

Other Applications.—It is impossible to enumerate all the uses to which ultraviolet photography can be put, and the interested reader should consult the works listed at the end of this chapter, particularly "Fluorescence Analysis in Ultra-violet Light," by Radley and Grant.   Important applications are in the field of photomicrography, particularly photographing by the 3650 Å. line of the mercury spectrum, which results in increased resolving power over that obtainable by visible light.   Fluorescence photography can also be satisfactorily carried out through the microscope.   These subjects and the very important physical applications in spectrography and astronomy are beyond the scope of this chapter, but there is a very extensive literature devoted to them.

Warning.—Attention should be drawn to the ease with which wrong conclusions can be drawn from ultraviolet and fluorescence photographs.   The photographer will require considerable experience before he can use the method reliably, but when once this has been acquired, the method is an extremely important one.   It should be remembered that many dyes are bleached by exposure to ultraviolet radiation and that it is much used for artificially aging materials.   Caution should, therefore, be used in its employment.

INFRARED PHOTOGRAPHY

Infrared photography is by no means a new subject, since methods of making photographic plates responding to the infrared were known to scientists during the last century.   The subject assumed a new interest, however, in 1931 when infrared sensitive plates began to be made which could be used with the ease of ordinary plates and films.   Within a few years it became possible to record the spectrum out to beyond 13,000 Å. in the infrared, and many discoveries of great importance to physics and astronomy resulted.   At the same time the subject grew to be of great importance in other fields of science, technology, medical and aerial photography, long-distance photography, criminology and documentary photography, cinematography, and the commercial and amateur spheres.

The usefulness of infrared photography is due to the discovery of classes of dyes by addition of which photographic emulsions could be made to respond readily to wavelengths longer than those which could be recorded on panchromatic materials.   The dyes belong to the classes known to the organic chemist as the cyanines, the most important for recording the longer wavelengths being the carbocyanines and the di-, tri-, tetra-, and pentacarbocyanines. By proper selection of the sensitizing dyes during the manufacture of the emulsions, it is possible to make plates and films which respond to bands of wavelengths from the visible red to the infrared beyond 13,000 Å. Those which sensitize in the longer wavelength regions are mainly of interest for scientific purposes, while those which permit photography in the region from 7000 to 9000 Å. are most used for general applications.

There is no fundamental difference between the practice of infrared photography and that in which visible light is used. Any photographer equipped for work with panchromatic plates and films can make infrared photographs with no extra expenditure other than that necessary to purchase the proper kinds of plates and films and a filter for use on the camera lens. The light sources commonly found in photographic studios for ordinary practice happen to be the most suited for infrared photography. Some precautions necessary in handling infrared materials differ slightly from those necessary in common practice, but they present no difficulties and will be mentioned in the following text. The value of photography by infrared lies in the fact that the radiations are very often transmitted and reflected by materials to an extent which bears no relation to the way in which they behave toward visible light. Generally they penetrate more freely.

Sources of Infrared.—All sources which depend on incandescence for the production of light emit infrared radiation freely. They include sunlight, arcs, electric-filament lamps, oil lamps, gas burners, candles, and other sources which rely on a material being raised to a high temperature. They are not all equally efficient, however, and the discussion here will be limited to those which might be of value. In addition to the incandescent sources, there are some gaseous-discharge lamps which produce spectra containing lines in the infrared, but they are little used in practice.

Sunlight.—About one-half of the energy in sunlight lies in the infrared, and the sun is therefore a very satisfactory source. It cannot be conveniently used in the studio, but it is the natural source for outdoor photography and permits very important work to be done in the infrared. There is much variation in the intensity and quality of the sunlight which reaches the surface of the earth, and it is necessary for the photographer to adapt his exposure to meet the changing conditions. The chief causes of the variation are changes in the amount of heat energy radiated from the sun; variations in the distance of the earth from the sun; variations in the amount of water vapor, dust, etc., in the atmosphere of the earth; the zenith distance of the sun; and the altitude of the photographic station above sea level. In a clear atmosphere at sea level at midday in midsummer, about one-third of the energy from the sun is in the part of the infrared which can be photographed. This figure can be considered as a maximum and will be decreased as the factors above mentioned come into play. There is no strict relationship between the intensity of infrared and of visible light from the sun, a fact which makes ordinary exposure meters unreliable for estimating infrared exposures. The intensity of infrared in sunlight is much higher than that in any other source.

Incandescent-filament Electric Lamps.—The earlier types of electric lamp consisted of filaments of carbon or metals, particularly tungsten, in an evacuated glass bulb. Later lamps have filaments made exclusively of tungsten wire and contain an inert gas, usually a mixture of 80 per cent of argon and 20 per cent of nitrogen, and the filament is in the form of a coil. The gas-filled coiled-filament lamp is very much more efficient than the older types of vacuum lamp. For general infrared photography it is not necessary to use more of the spectrum than the region from about 7000 to 10,000 Å. It is desirable, therefore, to select sources of infrared which have as great as possible a

proportion of their energy in this region.   It so happens that the types of incandescent
tungsten-filament electric lamps most used for illumination and for photography by
visible light possess this characteristic.   The wavelength of maximum energy and the
actual amount of energy in the infrared varies with the kind of lamp.   For lamps
used for general lighting, the maximum ranges in position from 9500 to 10,500 Å.   In
the case of lamps for special purposes it may be at still shorter wavelengths.   For
instance it is at 8000 to 8500 Å. for the photoflood types of lamp, and at 9000 Å. for
the 500-watt projection lamps.   In general, the higher the wattage of the lamp, the
greater is the energy at the maximum.   It will be clear that any of the higher wattage
lamps and those of the overvolted photoflood types will be suitable for infrared photography.   Those in common use are the studio types of lamp, the 500-watt projector
lamps, and photofloods.   Since carbon-filament lamps and certain types of electric
radiant heaters have been much recommended for infrared therapeutical treatment, it
has often been supposed that they would be very suitable as sources for infrared
photography.   They are not nearly so useful as the common incandescent tungsten-
filament lamps, however, because they emit very inefficiently in the spectral region in
which photographic plates can be sensitized.

Carbon-arc Lamps.—The spectrum of the radiation from the carbon arcs consists
of a continuous background extending from the visible far into the infrared, and on
this are superposed lines and bands caused by the arc vapors.   By modifying the
composition of the carbons, it is possible to modify the characteristics of the radiation
so that the spectrum consists mainly of lines.   In the plain carbon arcs the chief source
of the radiation is the electrically positive carbon, while, in the case of those arcs using
carbons which are cored or impregnated with salts to give the flame arcs, the chief
source is the luminous flame between the electrodes.   The carbon arcs provide the
highest available artificial temperatures, and they are very suitable sources for the
infrared.   As was mentioned in the section on Ultraviolet Photography, the inclusion
of certain metals in the cores produces arcs having a very strong emission in the ultraviolet.   The carbons may be similarly modified, by incorporation of other metal salts,
to give high emission in the red and infrared.   All carbon arcs may be used for infrared
photography, the most suitable being those with carbons of the following types:
National Carbon Co. Sunshine and Motion Picture Studio carbons; White Flame arc
carbons; Low Intensity Projector arc carbons; Suprex positive carbons; High Intensity
Projector carbons; High Intensity Sun Arc carbons.   The Pointolite and Tungsarc
lamps are convenient sources of infrared of moderate efficiency.

Gaseous-discharge Lamps.—The mercury-vapor lamps, described under Ultraviolet
Photography, are not very useful sources for general infrared photography.   The
greatest emissions in the photographic infrared are at the 10,140 and 11,289 Å. lines.
This is at too long a wavelength for general purposes, although, for cases where it might
be desired to work at these wavelengths, the mercury arcs would be very suitable.
None of the other gaseous-discharge lamps are of importance for practical infrared
photography.

Photoflash Lamps.—The photoflash lamp emits its maximum energy at about
9000 Å.; it is a very good source of infrared radiation and is very convenient.

Special applications of infrared photography will be surveyed in a later section
of this chapter.   At the risk of anticipating this somewhat, we shall include here a
table of the sources most useful for a variety of purposes of infrared photography.

Filters.—Infrared plates and films are sensitive to the ultraviolet, to the violet
and blue, to part of the green, and to a particular region in the infrared.   To confine
the exposures to the infrared, it is therefore necessary to use a filter which does not
transmit the shorter wavelengths to which the material responds.   The filters are
made of dyed sheets of gelatin used alone or cemented in glass, or of plates of glass

TABLE I.—SOURCES OF INFRARED FOR VARIOUS PURPOSES

General Infrared Photography:
  Sunlight
  Tungsten-filament lamps of high efficiency
  Studio- and projector-type lamps
  General-purpose lamps of 500 watts and higher
  Carbon arcs: flame, neutral-cored, and plain arcs and all types of studio and projection arcs
  Photoflash lamps
Cinematography:
  Sunlight
  All types of tungsten-filament lamps used for studio illumination
Medical Photography:
  All the sources grouped under General Infrared Photography
Photomicrography:
  Tungsten-filament lamps used in normal photomicrography, especially the ribbon-filament lamps
  Carbon arcs and enclosed metallic arcs, such as the Pointolite and Tungsarc lamps
  Mercury-capillary lamps
Documentary, Graphic Arts, Criminology, Scientific Record:
  All the sources grouped under General Infrared Photography
Photography in Total Darkness:
  The artificial light sources given under General Infrared Photography, especially the tungsten-filament lamps and photoflash lamps

which is itself colored. The filters most useful for general infrared work are red in color, and if it is desired to confine the exposure to the invisible infrared when the plate or film has some sensitivity in the deep visible red, the filters must be opaque. Filters may be characterized by the wavelength below which they absorb radiation and above which they transmit it. They must also be sharp cutting, *i.e.*, the transition from absorption to transmission must cover as short a range of wavelengths as possible. The following table shows filters commercially available which are suitable for infrared photography, as well as the wavelengths at which they cut. The filter selected for a particular purpose will be chosen according to the minimum wavelength it is desired

TABLE II.—FILTERS FOR INFRARED PHOTOGRAPHY

Manufacturer	Name of filter	Wavelength beyond which filter transmits, Å.
Eastman Kodak Co.	Wratten No. 25	6000
	" " 29	6200
	" " 70	6700
	" " 89	6800
	" " 89A	7000
	" " 88	7200
	" " 88A	7400
	" " 87	7700
	Special, Batch 5233	About 9200
Corning Glass Works	No. 243	6300
	No. G986A, 3.2 mm. (also transmits ultra-violet)	7100
	No. 255, 3.5 mm.	8000
	No. 254, 2mm.	8600
Schott und Gen. Jena	RG1, 2mm.	6000
	RG2, 2mm.	6300
	RG5, 2mm.	6700
	RG8, 2mm.	7000
	RG7, 2mm.	About 9000

to record, bearing in mind the region of the spectrum to which the plate or film responds.

All filters absorb some radiation to which plates and film respond, so that it is necessary to give longer exposures than would be necessary without the filter. The factor by which the exposure must be multiplied is known as the "filter factor." It has no significance in infrared photography, because infrared plates and films are not used without a filter. It is customary, therefore, merely to denote the time of exposure required for a certain subject under definite conditions when used with a particular filter. Since there is usually a gap in the spectral sensitivity of infrared materials from the middle of the green to at least as far as the middle of the red, all filters having their transmission threshold in this region will require the same exposure. On the other hand, if the filter absorbs some of the infrared to which the plate or film responds, extra exposure will be required. For instance, with the Eastman Infrared Sensitive plate, the exposures will be identical through the Wratten filters Nos. 25 and 29, whereas through the No. 87 filter, twice this exposure will be necessary.

Cameras.—There is no difference in principle between cameras used for normal photography and those for the infrared. There are, however, a few precautions which must be observed. The bellows, the shutter blades, and the dark slides must be opaque to infrared; otherwise fogging of the plate will occur. Bellows used on most modern cameras are quite satisfactory, particularly if they are made of leather or artificial leather containing black-carbon pigment and backed by a sheet of black cloth. Certain kinds of hard rubber and wood are very transparent to the infrared and must be avoided in plateholders and shutter blades. Some manufacturers test the hard rubber of their dark slides for opacity to the infrared. Those made by the Eastman Kodak Co. and the Folmer Graflex Corp. carry five dots embossed on the metal tops if they have been tested for safety in the infrared. Metal is quite safe.

Photographic lenses made for good quality photography with panchromatic materials are designed so that their focus is the same for light in the violet and yellow. Other wavelengths are not in the same focus, but achromatizing for these two gives quite satisfactory results for white light and modern plates and films. The position of correct focus changes rapidly as the wavelengths increase into the infrared, so that it is sometimes necessary to make a correction of focus if sharp pictures are to be obtained. Lenses differ very markedly in their infrared focus, and it is not possible to give a general rule as to the change in bellows extension which must be made after focusing visually on the ground glass or by scale. In all cases where a correction is required, the lens must be racked out for a distance slightly longer than that necessary for good panchromatic focus. This is equivalent to focusing on a nearer object. One recommendation has been to increase the bellows extension by $\frac{1}{200\text{th}}$ of the focal length of the lens, but this rule is by no means general. For Tessars of $f/4.5$ and $f/3.5$ and of moderate focal length, Zeiss recommends an extension of 3 per cent of the focal length. Leitz lenses of the Elmar series should be set at a scale reading of 100 ft. in order to focus distant objects by infrared. The Hektor series requires somewhat less compensation. The Summar lens is provided with a special index mark on the mount for focusing by infrared. The Ross $f/4$ Wide Angle Xpres lens is specially corrected for the infrared, and the following Cooke lenses are corrected for coincidence of focal planes of 7500 Å. and white light: 6 in., $f/2.5$; $9\frac{1}{2}$ in., $f/2.5$; $6\frac{1}{4}$ in., $f/3.5$; $8\frac{1}{4}$ in., $f/4.5$; $10\frac{1}{2}$ in., $f/4.5$; 25 in., $f/4.5$; 13 in., $f/6.3$. The Kodak Anastigmats, of aperture $f/4.5$ and of focal lengths shorter than 10 in., and the $f/7.7$ Anastigmat are generally satisfactory. In the case of lenses of short focal length used at small relative aperture, the correction is so small that it can be neglected. Long-focus lenses may require a correction. If there is doubt as to the correction to be applied, the lens can be calibrated by making a series of photographs at slightly different settings of the lens, starting with the position of correct visual focus. The lens mount or focusing scale can then be marked at the position corresponding to the sharpest negative of the series. Much help is obtained if the picture is focused with a red filter on the lens. This reduces the brightness of the image, however, so that focusing should be done at full aperture, after which the lens may be stopped down to the opening desired. Apochromatic lenses are generally in correct focus in the near infrared.

Photographic Plates and Films.—Infrared plates and films are made by treating noncolor-sensitized emulsions with dyes which confer sensitivity in the desired region of the infrared. Many of these dyes are available, so that plates may be obtained sensitive in relatively narrow regions in the infrared out to beyond 13,000 Å. Most of the plates sensitive to the longer wavelengths are very slow and suited only for spectrographic work. For general infrared photography, those sensitized between 7000 and 9000 Å. are most useful and of highest speed. The selection of the material will depend on the purpose in mind, being made according to the requirements of speed, contrast, and region of sensitivity. For aerial and snapshot photography and

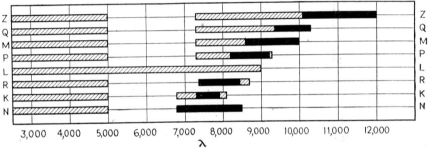

Fig. 3.—Spectral response of Eastman Spectroscopic plates. The cross-hatch areas show regions of good sensitivity, whereas the black areas show regions of maximum sensitivity.

cinematography, materials of high speed are available. On the other hand, for photoengraving and other purposes where contrast rather than speed is the requirement, materials corresponding to the process type of plate are made. For scientific and special purposes the Eastman Kodak Co. manufactures six types of emulsion, differing in contrast, speed, and resolving power; these types are sensitized in eight different regions of the infrared. They are known as Eastman Spectroscopic plates, and the spectral regions to which they respond are shown in the chart in Fig. 3. The letters at the sides of the chart indicate the class of sensitizing, the shaded areas represent the spectral regions of total sensitivity, and the black areas show the region for which the sensitizings are particularly valuable. The following is a list of the infrared plates and films available in the United States for general purposes:

Plates:
    Eastman Infra-red Sensitive Plates
    Eastman Infra-red Process Plates
Films for miniature cameras:
    Agfa Infra-red Film (Agfa Ansco)
    Kodak Infra-red Film, Type IR-135
Films for motion-picture photography:
    Agfa Infra-red Film Series 158
    Agfa Infra-red Film Type B, Series 159
    Eastman Infra-red Sensitive Motion Picture Negative Film

Films for Aerial Photography:
Agfa Infra-red Aero Film
Eastman Infra-red Aero Film

All the foregoing materials are sensitive in the near infrared in a band somewhere between 6500 and 8500 Å. They have the general characteristics of fast negative emulsions with the exception of the Eastman Infra-red Process plate, which is a process-type material.

Methods of Infrared Photography.—For general infrared *landscape photography* a plate camera or a miniature camera using 35-mm. film is used with the Wratten No. 25 or a similar filter on the lens. The plates or films sensitive in the region between 6500 and 8500 Å. are the most satisfactory. Correction for infrared focus should be made if necessary. Exposure meters which measure visible light are not reliable, and the manufacturer's exposure guides should be used. Typical exposure for a sunlit open landscape in summer is ½₅ sec. at f/5.6 through the Wratten No. 25 filter using the Eastman Infra-red Sensitive plate or Kodak Infra-red film type

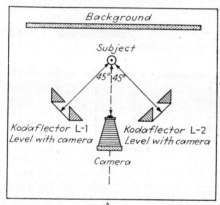 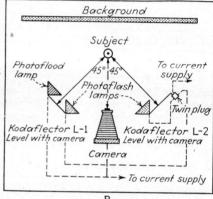

Fig. 4.—Typical arrangement of lights for infrared photography. The diagram at *A* shows the use of photoflood lamps, whereas *B* shows a method of using photoflash lamps.

IR-135. In practice it appears that on dull days the increase in exposure for infrared materials is about double that which would be required for panchromatic plates and films.

For *photography indoors* using artificial light, two arrangements are possible. In one case, the lights are used open, with a filter on the lens of the camera. In the other, it is desired to make pictures in total darkness, and in this case filters must be used over the lamps to absorb all visible light and to transmit the infrared freely; no filter is necessary on the lens. For infrared portraits in the lighted studio, the normal studio lamps are employed, but the lighting should be rather flat, because it is rarely required to produce modeling in the subject, but merely differences in reflection and transmission of the skin. This is particularly so with medical subjects. In infrared copying of documents and photography of general objects, the normal arrangement of flat lighting is used. Typical arrangements of the lights are shown in Fig. 4. In arrangement *A* two pairs of photoflood lamps or 500-watt projector type lamps are used in reflectors arranged symmetrically to the subject at 45°. If a single photoflash lamp is employed, it should be placed as near the camera axis as possible. Better results are obtained by using two photoflash lamps as shown in arrangement *B*. They are fired simultaneously by an appropriate switch wired to the two lamps. A single photoflood or other lamp is used for focusing and composition and is wired into the circuit as shown in the diagram. The following table gives exposure data for (*a*) the Eastman Infra-red Sensitive plate, the Eastman Clinical Camera (with $f/7.7$ lens), and the Kodak Recomar "33" (with $f/4.5$ lens); the Wratten No. 87 filter over the lens; photoflood or photoflash lamps in Kodaflectors; development for 5 min. in the Eastman D-19b or the Eastman X-ray developer at full strength at 65°F. (*b*) the Kodak Retina I and Retina II using Kodak Infra-red Film, Type IR-135; the Wratten No. 87 filter over the lens; photoflood or photoflash lamps in Kodaflectors; development for 12 to 15 minutes in Kodak fine-grain developer DK-20 at 65°F.; if D-76 developer is used, one-half the indicated exposures should be given and the film developed for 10 to 15 min. at 65°F. If the Wratten No. 25 filter is used instead of the No. 87, one-half the exposures indicated may be given.

TABLE III.—EXPOSURE DATA FOR INFRARED MATERIALS

a. Exposure Data for Infrared Photography with Eastman Clinical Camera and Kodak Recomar "33"

Scale-setting Eastman Clinical Camera	Subject-film distance Kodak Recomar "33," in.	No. 1 photoflood lamps			No. 10 photoflash lamps	
		Light distances, in.	Aperture	Time, sec.	Light distances, in.	Aperture
1	22	36	$f/11$	1	48	$f/16$
$3/4$	24	36	$f/11$	1	48	$f/16$
$1/2$	28	36	$f/11$	1	48	$f/16$
$1/4$	44	60	$f/8$	1	48	$f/16$

b. Exposure Data for Infrared Photography: Kodak Retina I and Kodak Retina II

Focus-scale setting		Supplementary lens		Subject-lens distance		Area of subject in picture		No. 1 photoflood lamps			No. 11 photoflash lamps	
Kodak Retina		Kodak Retina		Kodak Retina		Kodak Retina	Kodak Retina	Light distances, in.	Aperture	Time, sec.	Light distances, in.	Aperture
I, ft.	II, ft.	I	II	I, in.	II, in.	I, in.	II, in.					
$3\frac{1}{2}$	$3\frac{1}{2}$	A & B	C	$11\frac{1}{4}$	$12\frac{3}{8}$	$5\frac{1}{8}\times7\frac{3}{4}$	$5\frac{5}{8}\times8\frac{9}{16}$	48	$f/16$	1	60	$f/16$
13	7	A & B	C	14	$14\frac{1}{8}$	$6\frac{5}{8}\times9\frac{15}{16}$	$6\frac{5}{8}\times9\frac{15}{16}$	48	$f/16$	1	60	$f/16$
4	4	A	A	22	22	$10\frac{1}{8}\times15\frac{1}{4}$	$10\frac{1}{8}\times15\frac{1}{4}$	48	$f/16$	1	60	$f/16$
$3\frac{1}{2}$	$3\frac{1}{2}$	None	None	42	42	$19\frac{3}{4}\times29\frac{5}{8}$	$19\frac{3}{4}\times29\frac{5}{8}$	48	$f/16$	1	60	$f/16$

If pictures are to be made in *total darkness*, the Wratten No. 87 filter should be used over the light sources, arranged in a holder that will prevent white-light leakage. The Wratten No. 87 filter is specially made for this purpose in sizes 10 by 12 in. and 8 by 10 in. in the same form as safe lights. Using two pairs of photoflood lamps in reflectors, and the Eastman Infra-red Sensitive plate, the exposure will be of the order of 1 sec. at $f/4.5$ if the lamp units are about 6 ft. from the subject. The filaments of the lamps will just be visible to the subject as a deep red if he looks straight toward them, although the onlookers will normally see no light.   Complete darkness for all concerned can be attained by using indirect illumination, the lamps being arranged in reflectors pointed toward the ceiling and covered with sheets of the No. 87 filter.   Exposures in this case will naturally be longer and must be determined by trial. In cinematography by infrared using 35-mm. Agfa Infra-red Film Type B, or Eastman Infra-red Sensitive Motion Picture film, using a 180° shutter and 24 frames per second, an aperture of about $f/4.5$ will be required outdoors in bright sunlight.

Infrared materials should be handled and developed in total darkness or by the light of special green safe lights.   The green safe lights made for use with panchromatic materials are quite unsuited, because they transmit infrared freely.   No special methods of development are necessary.   The manufacturers' instructions should be followed.

Applications of Infrared Photography. *Aerial and Long-distance Landscape Photography.*—The most important application of infrared photography is in the photography of landscapes from the ground or air.   Its particular usefulness lies in the ability of the infrared to penetrate atmospheric haze more readily than does visible light, so that improved rendering of distant detail is attained.   Haze scatters violet and blue light, and so blurs distant detail when it is photographed on ordinary noncolor-sensitive plates and films.   As the wavelengths become longer, the scattering becomes less, so that improved penetration of haze results if panchromatic plates and films are used in conjunction with a yellow, or particularly a red, filter.   With the longer wavelengths of infrared and a filter to absorb the shorter wavelengths, still greater penetration is effected.   By using the infrared, therefore, it is possible to photograph over longer distances than are attainable with panchromatic materials, and in the case of aerial photography, where haze normally seriously decreases the rendering of detail on the ground, the infrared offers a special advantage.   In refutation of claims made by overenthusiastic newspaper correspondents and inventors, it should be clearly stated that it is not possible to penetrate dense fog by infrared photography.   The ability of the infrared to penetrate an atmospheric suspension such as haze, smoke, and fog increases as the sizes of the suspended particles decrease or as the wavelength of the infrared increases.   The sizes of the particles of dust, water vapor, etc., which form haze are small enough to permit penetration by infrared of the wavelengths which can be photographed.   On the other hand, the droplets of water present in mists, fog, and clouds are so large that they are impenetrable by the photographic infrared.   It can be stated as a general rule that the less the visibility through the atmosphere, the less is the chance of increasing it by infrared photography. In the case of a fog which presents a danger to safe navigation at sea or to safe landing of aircraft, infrared photography offers no advantages over the eye.   On the other hand, however, haze which limits visibility to a few miles can be further penetrated by the infrared, so that photography with these longer wavelengths can be of special benefit in photographic survey from the ground and the air, in reconnaissance, and so on.

In addition to showing detail at greater distances through haze than is attainable by normal photography, the infrared landscape photograph has other particular characteristics, which may or may not be an advantage.   Grass and the leaves of deciduous (hardwood) trees are rendered very light, somewhat as if they were covered with snow.   This is because the chlorophyll which imparts the green color is very transparent in the near infrared, so that the rays can pass through it to the tissues of the leaves, which reflect it back again.   They thus photograph as if they were light in color, whereas in normal photographs they appear dark owing to the absorption of visible light by the chlorophyll.   Coniferous (softwood) trees usually reproduce darker than the hardwoods, and dead trees can also be distinguished by their darker rendering. These facts make infrared photography of interest to the forest surveyor. The sky is rendered as very dark, because blue skylight is relatively devoid of infrared. Clouds appear white, because they reflect sunlight which contains infrared. Shadows are very dark, especially if the sky is clear and the only light in them comes from the blue sky. Water generally reproduces as black. Buildings will be reproduced in tones which depend on the manner in which their materials of construction reflect the infrared, and soil and rock may also appear in tones which are different from their visual appearance. These effects all assist in determining the characteristic appearance of infrared landscape photographs. They may be attractive to the pictorial and commercial photographer and may offer advantages or otherwise to the surveyor whose prime interest is in rendering and identifying detail.

Criminology.—In the field of criminology, infrared photography has found many applications which include the following: detection and deciphering of erasures and forgeries; deciphering of charred documents, or those which have become illegible as the result of age or abuse; differentiation between inks, dyes, and pigments which are visually identical; distinguishing between cloths which are visually identical but dyed with different dyes; detection of stains and irregularities in cloth; examination of cloth, fibers and hair which are dyed too darkly to be easy of study by visible light; study of fingerprints; examination of the contents of sealed envelopes; detection of certain kinds of secret writing; detection and demonstration of blood stains on cloth; determination of carbon monoxide impregnation of victims of gas poisoning; photography in the dark. All these applications rely on the fact that the reflection and transmission of infrared by materials is frequently very different from the behavior to visible light. Straightforward infrared photographic methods are used, due regard being paid to the region of spectral sensitivity and the contrast desired.

Documentary Photography.—Some of the most elegant uses of infrared photography are to be found in the field of the examination of documents. The most important application is in the deciphering of writing made illegible by charring, deterioration as a result of age or the accumulation of dirt, obliteration by application of ink as by a censor or forger, invisible inks, and deliberate chemical bleaching or mechanical erasure and subsequent overwriting. In these fields, the infrared method forms a valuable adjunct to ultraviolet photography. Inks, pigments, and other materials which may appear identical to the eye are frequently rendered quite differently in an infrared photograph. If an ink transparent to the infrared is applied over one opaque to it, the underlying ink will show up in an infrared photograph. The original writing on charred documents may be revealed, although success will depend on the degree of charring of the paper. Writing which has been mechanically erased may be revealed by virtue of traces of carbon or other pigment left embedded in the paper fibers. Chemically bleached writing is often deciphered if the product resulting from the reaction of the bleach with the ink absorbs infrared radiation more fully than the surrounding paper. Dyes and pigments visually identical can be distinguished if they differ in their transparency to the infrared.

Medical Infrared Photography.—Infrared photography shows promise of being a valuable means of diagnosis. By the use of infrared-sensitive plates and films it is possible to make pictures showing the superficial veins, some of which are not discernible either visually or in ordinary photographs. Distinct changes from the normal venous pattern have been recorded in connection with several diseases: axillary thrombosis, cirrhosis, and some tumors, for instance, show a marked disturbance of the adjacent venous circulation. On the basis of this, it has been suggested that in surgery for carcinoma of the breast, an infrared photograph made before the operation might reveal very useful information. Changes in the superficial venous pattern of the thorax and abdomen during pregnancy can be shown distinctly, and there is a marked difference in the appearance of infrared photographs of primipara and multipara. In dermatology, infrared photography may be useful in various ways. In cases of eczema, the exterior eczematic appearance does not show in the infrared photograph, while the underlying varicose veins which usually accompany this condition are rendered clearly. In lupus cases under treatment by ultraviolet radiation, the whole of the lesion is covered by a scab, and it is impossible to see how the clearance is progressing. The infrared rays penetrate the scab, however, and present a clear picture of the healed areas. In ophthalmology, photographs of the iris of the eye by infrared present detail which escapes ordinary photographic materials. Dark-brown pigmented irides appear lighter in tone than blue pigmented irides, and the deeply pigmented trabeculae register lighter than the rest of the iris. If atrophy has

Fig. 5A.—Photograph made on ordinary plates with general illumination.

begun in the iris, resulting in the destruction of the pigment and replacement by grayish-white tissue, the infrared photograph will show this region of atrophy as darker than the normal tissue of the iris would appear. Abnormalities of the margin of the pupil, not readily visible in black-and-white or color photographs, are clearly recorded by the infrared technique. Since infrared penetrates turbid mediums better than does visible light, it can be used to photograph the iris through a cornea which is so opaque that visual examination is impossible. Infrared photography is of value in the examination of gross specimens, particularly in the case of injected specimens for checking the completeness of the injection without clearing. Since most tissues transmit infrared more readily than visible light, infrared photomicrographs of deeply pigmented tissues and relatively thick histological specimens, such as celloidin and frozen sections, frequently show details which are not discernible in those made by visible light.

Photography in the Dark.—Since infrared radiation is invisible, it is possible to make photographs in total darkness. Although the ultraviolet is also invisible, it is not satisfactory for dark photographs, because it induces visible fluorescence in many common materials. Infrared photographs can be made in the dark by using radiators which emit only infrared and no visible light or, preferably, by powerful sources of light from which the visible radiations are absorbed by filters which permit the infrared to pass freely. These photographs are primarily of interest for amusement, although the attempt has been made to use them in the detection of criminals at work and in the observation of spiritualist seances. Of more interest are the photographs of hot bodies made in total darkness by the infrared radiation which they emit. By using infrared plates it is possible to obtain an idea of the distribution of temperature over heated materials, such as electric heaters, hot metal ingots, radio tubes, and cylinder heads and exhaust manifolds of internal-combustion engines.

Portraiture.—Infrared portraits can readily be made in the manner described in the section on Methods of Infrared Photography. They are, however, of little interest except for amusement and medical purposes. They differ entirely from those made by visible light. The flesh has a white translucent appearance, the lips are light, the eyes dark, all lines in the face are strongly emphasized, and the beard appears as if it

Fig. 5*B*.—Infrared photograph of the same subject made on infrared plates using heat of the flatirons as the only source of "illumination."

were a stubbly growth, even on a clean-shaven face. The skin of negroes is reproduced light in tone.

Scientific and Technical Applications.—Infrared photography has proved of importance in many fields of investigation, and its value is increasing as it becomes more applied. It is not possible to mention more than a few special uses in this chapter, but the imaginative photographer should have no difficulty in widening its field. Useful references will be found in the attached bibliography. In plant pathology the infrared has provided a valuable means of studying and diagnosing plant diseases in which there is change in the pigment or cellular material. Different kinds of wood show marked variation in their transparency to the infrared, and photographs have shown that the infrared may be of much value in coal petrology and other fields of paleobotany. In the textile industry infrared photography has been successfully applied to the detection of irregularities in the dyeing and weaving of cloth and damage to the fibers, particularly where the material is dyed in such a manner as to render visual observation difficult. The graphic-arts industry has used infrared-sensitive plates to differentiate between light and dark blues in multicolor printing and in preparing the negative of the black printing plate from originals prepared in specially selected colors. In the field of technology other applications are in the study of the interiors of furnaces while they are operating, the detection of carbonaceous matter in lubricating oils which have been used in internal-combustion engines, and the study of the porosity of tin plate.   Infrared photography has proved of enormous value in astronomy and spectrography.   Hundreds of new lines have been recorded in the spectra of the elements, and much has been learned of the composition of the stars and of the atmospheres of the planets.   Photographs have been made through the haze of nebulae, showing up stars normally invisible behind them, and large numbers of new stars have been discovered by the infrared radiation which they emit.   It has been found that the night sky is relatively much stronger in radiation of wavelength 8500 Å. than in the violet and blue parts of the spectrum.   In photomicrography much use has been made of the infrared in the fields of entomology, cytology, histology, embryology, and botany.   In general, photomicrographs of deeply pigmented tissues and the thicker microscopic sections and specimens show details of internal structure when made by infrared which are not visible in ordinary photomicrographs.

Special-effects Photography.—The dark skies, black shadows, and light grass and trees, characteristic of outdoor infrared photographs, give them the appearance of having been made by moonlight.   Advantage is taken of this in the motion-picture industry to make imitation moonlight photographs by operating in bright sunlight. The method is superior to the use of underexposure of sunlit subjects, which has sometimes been proposed, and it has the advantages of not requiring the transportation of lighting equipment outdoors at nighttime and of imposing no abnormal demands on the players.   Moonlight itself cannot be used because it would require exposures which are unattainable in motion-picture practice.

Works of Art.—Infrared photography has taken its place with chemical study and X-ray and ultraviolet photography as an important means of determining the authenticity of paintings.   Pigments vary in the way in which they transmit and reflect the infrared, even if they appear identical in color.   Infrared photography can, therefore, sometimes be of use in detecting the presence of overpainting and other alterations and in distinguishing between an original and a later copy.   Important factors are the varnish and medium, which differ in their infrared transparency according to their nature and age.   Paintings which have so deteriorated due to darkening of the varnish that detail can scarcely be seen may be revealed by infrared photography.   Similarly, photographs, daguerreotypes, engravings, drawings, maps, and other such documents which have become badly discolored or faded by age or misuse have been successfully photographed by infrared.

Bibliography

Ultraviolet

Periodicals:

BENDIKSON, L.: A New Type of an Ultra-violet Light Source for Documentary Photography, *Library J.*, **59,** 690–692 (1934).

——: A Cycle of Ultra-violet Light Sources for Various Uses, *Library J.* **61,** 16–17 (1936).

BUTTOLPH, L. J.: Uviarc Lamps and the Ultra-violet, General Electric Vapor Lamp Co., Hoboken, N. J., Engineering Dept. *Bull.* 105*B.*

General Electric Vapor Lamp Co.   Various publications on Cooper-Hewitt lamps.

Books:

RORIMER, J. J.: "Ultra-violet Rays and Their Use in the Examination of Works of Art," Metropolitan Museum of Art, New York (1931).

RADLEY, J. A., and GRANT, J.: "Fluorescence Analysis in Ultra-violet Light," 2d ed., Chapman (1935).

GRANT, J.: "Books and Documents.   Dating, Permanence and Preservation," Grafton & Co. (1937).

BECK, H.: "Photographie des Unsichtbaren," Photokino-Verlag, Berlin (1936).

"Ultra-violet Photography."   Eastman Kodak Co.   Pamphlet, revised frequently.

Infrared

Periodicals:

CLARK, W.: Seeing the Invisible, *Science Monthly*, **41,** 481–489 (1935).
————: Photography of the Infra-Red, *Am. Ann. Phot.*, **51,** 13–22 (1937).

Books:

HELWICH, O.: "Die Infrarot-Fotografie," W. Heering-Verlag, Halle (1934).
ISERT, G.: "Infrarotphotographie," 2d ed. Photokino-Verlag, Berlin (1934).
RAWLING, S. O.: "Infra-red Photography," 2d ed. Blackie & Son, Ltd., (1935).
BECK, H.: "Photographie des Unsichtbaren," Photokino-Verlag, Berlin (1936).
HELWICH, O.: "Practical Infra-red Photography" (translated from the German by J. L. Baring), British Periodicals, Ltd. (1936).
"Photographic Plates for Use in Spectroscopy and Astronomy," 3d ed. Eastman Kodak Co. (1937).
"Infra-red Photography with Kodak materials," p. 5, Eastman Kodak Co. (1937).
MORGAN, W. D., and H. M. LESTER: "Leica Manual," 3d ed., Morgan and Lester (1938).
CLARK, W.: "Photography by Infrared. Its Principles and Applications," Chapman (1939).

CHAPTER XXII

COLOR PHOTOGRAPHY

By Olindo O. Ceccarini

Introduction.—It might be safely said that color photography began with the formulation of the wave theory of light by Wünsch and Young and the theoretical work of Helmholtz and Maxwell.

White light can be decomposed into a very large number of colored radiations, and the colors constituting the visible spectrum range from violet to deep red.

The three colors particularly striking to the human eye are blue, green, and red. Maxwell demonstrated that a mixture of blue, green, and red lights in a suitable proportion produced the physiological sensation of white light.

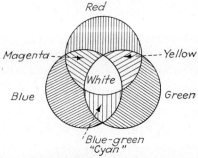

Fig. 1.—Diagram showing effect of mixing lights of "primary colors."

Mixture of Colored Lights.—In mixing colored lights the luminosity of the mixture is greater than the luminosity of each color alone. Taking, for instance, blue and green lights, it is possible to obtain all the possible shades from the pure blue to the pure green by suitable variations of the individual components. The diagram of Fig. 1 represents the colors to be obtained by mixing lights of the "primary colors," blue, green, and red, taken two by two and all three together in proportions suitable to produce white light.

Yellow is evidently produced by the addition of red and green primary lights, and, since it does not contain blue, it is called its "complementary," or "minus blue."

In a similar manner the addition of blue and green lights gives blue-green (also known as "cyan"). Cyan is evidently "complementary" to red, or "minus red."

Red and blue lights produce "magenta" which is "complementary" to green, or "minus green."

Pigments.—The behavior of a mixture of colored pigments is entirely different from that of the mixture of colored lights. For instance, a yellow pigment spread evenly on a sheet of white paper, if observed with a spectroscope, shows practically complete absence of blue light. The conclusion is therefore that the yellow "absorbs" or "subtracts" blue from the white light reflected by the paper. If now a magenta pigment is added on the yellow, the resultant color will be a deep red, for both blue and green colors have been subtracted from the light of the paper. Adding now a cyan pigment to the two already existing the result will be "black" or the complete absence of color.

The diagram of mixture of pigments is given in Fig. 2.

The photographic analysis of a color object is carried out with filters of primary colors, while the synthesis can be performed by mixture of lights also of primary colors giving rise to the so-called "additive process" or by mixture of pigments in complementary colors by means of the so-called "subtractive process."

616

The additive process finds its application in the making of color transparencies. It is also used sometimes for the projection of motion pictures in natural colors.

The subtractive process can be used for transparencies and for motion pictures in natural colors the same as the additive process. It is in addition the only successful process which permits obtaining natural-color prints on paper to be viewed by reflected light. From this particular standpoint the subtractive process is by far the most important of all the photographic color processes as yet evolved.

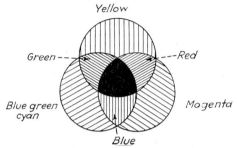

Fig. 2.—Diagram showing mixing of pigments.

Description and working instructions of the various subtractive and additive color processes practiced today will be given in the order of their importance.

Color-separation Negatives.—The production of color-separation negatives from the original subject represents the first step in any color process. Three exposures are necessary behind red, green, and blue filters, respectively.

An exception to this rule is in the case of the so-called "color screen plates" or films by the additive method in which the original negative, containing the three-color-

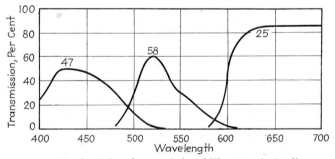

Fig. 3.—Transmission characteristics of Wratten tricolor filters.

filter elements in mosaic form, is converted by chemical reversal to the final positive. These color screen plates and films will be described later.

The three primary-color filters necessary for making the three-color-separation negatives must respond to certain definite requirements. Each filter must cover a convenient section of the visible spectrum and must overlap into the region of the adjacent filter by a moderate amount. The characteristics of these filters have been extensively debated, but the recent investigations of D. A. Spencer[1] have proved conclusively that the present commercial standard filters, of which the Wratten three-color filters are typical examples, represent the best possible compromise

[1] SPENCER, D. A., *Phot. J.*, July, 1935, p. 377; *Penrose Ann.*, 1938.

when the characteristics of three-color printing pigments and inks are taken into consideration.

The characteristic transmission curves of the Wratten three-color filters Nos. 25, 47, and 58 are given in Fig. 3.

The presence of a color filter in the path of the light reduces the total amount of light reaching the photographic emulsion and therefore a longer exposure is necessary.

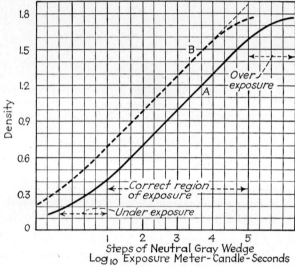

FIG. 4.—Typical characteristic curves of panchromatic emulsions. Curve *B* represents the characteristic of the film when exposed through a green filter.

This increase in exposure is called the "filter factor," and it is ordinarily given by the manufacturer of the photographic material. In the case of three-color filters the factor pertaining to each filter is of such value as to permit obtaining the same general results when all three negatives are developed all together for the same length of time. For accurate results color-separation negatives should be developed to the same contrast, which, as we shall see immediately, requires different developing times.

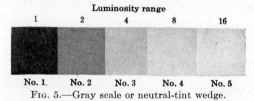

FIG. 5.—Gray scale or neutral-tint wedge.

Therefore a slight readjustment of the filter factor is desirable for color-separation negatives to be correctly processed.

A typical characteristic curve of a panchromatic emulsion is given in Fig. 4.

The curve is subdivided into three well-known regions: underexposure, the useful region, and the region of overexposure.

The necessity of correct exposure in color photography will be immediately evident from the following considerations.

Let it be assumed that a neutral-tint wedge, Fig. 5, is placed alongside the subject.

The various grey tints range from almost total black to almost the pure white of the paper. A successful three-color process should permit a faithful reproduction of the above wedge by means of the complementary printing pigments, yellow, magenta, and cyan, taken in the correct amount and superimposed one on the other. If we refer again to Fig. 4, it will be noticed that the light range represented by the straight-line proportion of the curve (useful range) for this particular emulsion is just about 16 to 1 (density 0.4 to 1.6 or transmission 50 to 2.5 per cent). This is also the luminosity range chosen for the gray wedge as indicated by the figures above each square.

In order to faithfully reproduce these luminosities in the negative, it is necessary to choose such an exposure as to give, upon correct development to gamma of unity, a density of 0.4 to correspond to step 1 and so on to density 1.6 for step 5. If the exposure factor for each one of the three-color filters is correctly chosen and the three negatives are developed to exactly the same gamma, the three wedges will appear identical and will have the same densities by actual measurement. Under these conditions each successive step of the wedge from light to dark in the negative represents the same increment of density, or the light transmission of each step is one-half that of the previous step.

Now let it be assumed that one of the negatives (the green-filter negative, for instance) has been exposed twice as much as the others. In this negative the density and transmission of the various steps will be as given in Table I (dotted curve of Fig. 4):

TABLE I.—DENSITY AND TRANSMISSION OF A TYPICAL SENSITOMETRIC STRIP

Step, number	Density	Transmission, per cent
1	0.7	20
2	1.0	10
3	1.3	5
4	1.6	2.5
5	1.75	1.78

It is evident that in this case the ratio between steps is constant except for the last step, which should have had a density of 1.9 instead of 1.75. When printing these negatives, it is necessary to print the green-separation negative twice as long as the other two. This procedure, however, will give three prints in which steps 1 to 4 are correspondingly the same, but step 5 will be heavier in the case of the green-separation negative as compared with step No. 5 of the blue and red separation. After the three positives are converted to the three complementary colors and superimposed, it will be found that steps 1 to 4 are of neutral gray, corresponding to the original; but step No. 5 will appear reddish, being deficient in yellow and cyan.

If the range of luminosity of the wedge had been 8 to 1, the reproduction would have been correct all the way through in spite of the overexposure of the green-separation negative. The same applies to the case of underexposure of some of the color-separation negatives.

Illumination of the Subject.—The considerations pertaining to the luminosity range of the gray wedge apply equally well to the range between the high lights and the shadows of the subject.

While extreme range between light and shadows should be avoided for the reason just discussed, altogether too much stress has been placed in the past on the desirability of flat lighting.

The fallacy of a totally flat light can be best seen by an extremely elementary example. Assume a red cube placed on a white cardboard. The camera lens looks at the cube at 45°. If the cube is illuminated by a uniform light all around, the finished picture will appear as in Fig. 6 which, although it shows a red object on a white background, does not give the faintest indication of the actual shape of the red object. Illuminate now the red cube with a single light source at an oblique angle. The results will now be as in Fig. 7.

Evidently proper lighting is giving perspective, and it shows correctly the geometrical shape of the object. Color in this case adds the additional information of a red cube onto a white background.

To be of real practical value, color photography must be made to extend the scope of black-and-white photography.

Since the filter factors vary considerably with the type of light, it is not permissible to mix lights of different types. If it is necessary to diffuse the source of light, this should be done with wire gauze or any diffusing device which does not introduce any change in the color value of the light. For the same reasons discolored reflectors should also be avoided.

The light source should also be steady. Daylight, incandescent, and photoflood are all equally satisfactory. Each type obviously requires different filter factors.

Fig. 6.—Cube illuminated by flat lighting fails to show tone gradations.

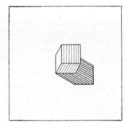

Fig. 7.—Cube lighted obliquely. Several tones are present.

The best method of measurement consists in reading with a photometer the light reflected by a white card placed directly over the high lights of the subject. This exposure should be slightly below the overexposure mark. Exposure meters, such as Weston, carry this information.

Flash bulbs also can be used satisfactorily, but great experience is necessary. It is advisable to arrange the lighting and composition first by means of incandescent bulbs placed in proximity with flash bulbs. Just before the firing of the flashes the incandescent lights can be turned off.

It is not always possible to identify the three color-separation negatives and in order to avoid errors three patches of colors corresponding to three filters or, if desired, to three complementary printing colors should be placed along side the neutral-gray wedge.

When the gray wedge and color patches are properly illuminated to correspond approximately to the high light of the subject, they will serve several purposes; *i.e.*, identification of the negatives, measurement of contrast, and measurement of printing ratio. The identification of the negatives can be obtained also by suitable marks along the edges of the holders or of the filters in close contact with the emulsion, and the contrast of development can be assured by standardizing time and temperature. However, the possibility of being able to measure the printing ratio is a convenience which must not be underestimated if one wishes to avoid disappointments and waste of time and material.

Sensitive Material.—Panchromatic films and plates sensitive to all colors are ordinarily used for obtaining color-separation negatives in connection with the three primary-color-separation filters—red, green, and blue.

It is possible to deviate from this rule by using an ordinary plate or film sensitive to the blue end of the spectrum only for the blue-separation negative without blue filter. This type of material approaches very closely the characteristic of the standard blue filter.

For the green-separation negative it is possible to use an orthochromatic emulsion which is sensitive to blue and green in connection with a yellow filter or the standard green-separation filter.

For the red the usual panchromatic emulsion and red filter is always used, as an emulsion sensitized for red only to be used with either a yellow or the standard red filter is not easily obtainable.

The combination of ordinary emulsion for the blue, orthochromatic emulsion for the green, and panchromatic emulsion for the red can be obtained assembled as a unit under the commercial name of Tripac. Put up in this form the ordinary and orthochromatic emulsions are placed face to face, and the panchromatic emulsion is placed behind.

Fig. 8.—Photometric wedge for emulsion tests.

The ordinary or blue-sensitive emulsion carries a yellow dye which prevents the blue light from penetrating into the following two emulsions. The orthochromatic negatives carry on their backs a layer of gelatin containing a red dye acting as filter for the back emulsion.

The tripack can be exposed in any ordinary camera provided with a suitable holder for maintaining the three emulsions in good contact. It has many disadvantages, however. It is slow as compared with other arrangements. The green-separation negative which prints magenta is slightly diffused owing to the light scattered by the front emulsion, and the red negative or cyan printer, which should contribute most to the definition, is decidedly diffused. The tripack represents solely a compromise. Other combinations involving the use of tripack and bipack will be described in connection with various types of color cameras.

Negative Development.—The development of color-separation negatives should be carefully standardized and a developer which can be discarded immediately after use is much preferred over others which allow repeated use. Very satisfactory types of developers for this purpose are the three-solution pyro developer, the two-solution pyro developer, and the three-solution metol-pyro developer. Eastman formulas Nos. D1, D21, and D7 are typical.

A standard temperature for the developer should be decided upon and maintained to assure uniform results.

In order to determine the correct time of development, a photometric wedge (Fig. 8) and a densitometer (Fig. 9) are necessary.

The following is the usual procedure: An incandescent light source over which can be placed in succession the three standard color-separation filters should be arranged conveniently in the darkroom. Five pieces of the negative material to be tested should be exposed, each for the same length of time, in contact with the photometric wedge with the red filter in front of the light source. A similar number of exposures are to be made with the green and with the blue filter, allowing, of course, for the proper filter factor. When all the exposures are complete, each group can be put away temporarily in a lightproof box while preparing for development. Of course, the negatives of each group must be properly identified with respect to the other groups.

The rate of development is materially affected, not only by the composition and temperature of the developer, but also by the agitation during development. Furthermore, a moderate amount of agitation is necessary in order to prevent irregularities and streaks around areas of heavy exposure. The most satisfactory method is to use

FIG. 9.—Densitometer for measuring the transmission density of films or the reflection density of prints.

a tank appreciably larger than for ordinary black-and-white negatives. With 5- by 7-in. negatives, for instance, the 1-gal. hard rubber tank with the regular No. 4 Eastman developing hangers is very convenient. Use it for only six negatives at a time with the standard pyro ABC developer made up as recommended, *i.e.*, 9 oz. each of A, B, and C and water to make up 1 gal. at a temperature of 68°F. The six negatives, which are first loaded in the hangers, are immersed all together in the developer, pulled out of the developer, reimmersed all together twice, and then pushed all together toward one end of the tank. Then *one by one* the negatives are slid toward the opposite end of the tank and so on back and forth until the time of development is up. During these back and forth movements, the negatives should always be maintained, fully immersed in the developer. At the completion of development the negatives are lifted out all together, given a brief rinse, and then immersed in the fixing bath.

For carrying out the development test with the negatives exposed behind the photometric wedge described, the following is a convenient procedure: The developer is carefully compounded and its temperature adjusted to 68°F. Three tanks containing developer, rinse water, and hypo are placed alongside each other with the developer at the left. The exposures made with the red filter are loaded in the hangers, they are placed in the developer, and agitation is started in the manner just described. At the end of 6 min. the first negative at the right is removed, rinsed for an

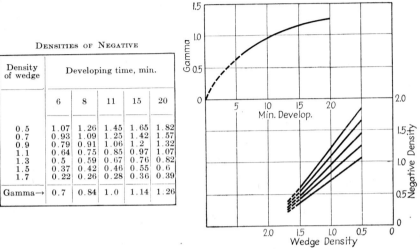

DENSITIES OF NEGATIVE

Density of wedge	Developing time, min.				
	6	8	11	15	20
0.5	1.07	1.26	1.45	1.65	1.82
0.7	0.93	1.09	1.25	1.42	1.57
0.9	0.79	0.91	1.06	1.2	1.32
1.1	0.64	0.75	0.85	0.97	1.07
1.3	0.5	0.59	0.67	0.76	0.82
1.5	0.37	0.42	0.46	0.55	0.6
1.7	0.22	0.26	0.28	0.36	0.39
Gamma→	0.7	0.84	1.0	1.14	1.26

FIG. 10.—Characteristics of panchromatic material exposed through red filter.

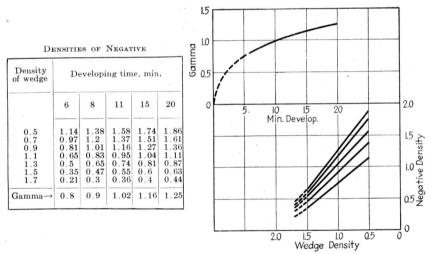

DENSITIES OF NEGATIVE

Density of wedge	Developing time, min.				
	6	8	11	15	20
0.5	1.14	1.38	1.58	1.74	1.86
0.7	0.97	1.2	1.37	1.51	1.61
0.9	0.81	1.01	1.16	1.27	1.36
1.1	0.65	0.83	0.95	1.04	1.11
1.3	0.5	0.65	0.74	0.81	0.87
1.5	0.35	0.47	0.55	0.6	0.63
1.7	0.21	0.3	0.36	0.4	0.44
Gamma→	0.8	0.9	1.02	1.16	1.25

FIG. 11.—Characteristics of panchromatic material exposed through green filter.

instant, and then placed in the fixing bath. In the meantime the agitation and development of the remaining negatives continues in the normal way. At the end of 8 min. the second negative at the right is removed from the developer, rinsed, and placed in the fixing bath. This procedure is followed till the last negative is removed from the developer at the end of 20 min. In this manner the red negatives are developed for 6, 8, 11, 15, and 20 min.

The negatives exposed behind the green and blue filters are developed in exactly identical manner with the developer renewed each time.

When all the negatives are dry, they can be measured in the densitometer and the values thus obtained plotted on cross-section paper with the density of the wedge on the horizontal axis and the density of the negative on the vertical axis.

Three families of curves are thus obtained, one for each filter. The value of gamma or contrast for each curve is the ratio of the intercept on the horizontal axis to the intercept on the vertical axis by the straight line passing through the straight section of the curve and prolonged to meet the horizontal and the vertical axis.

Figures 10, 11, and 12 are typical tests conducted on Dupont panchromatic films.

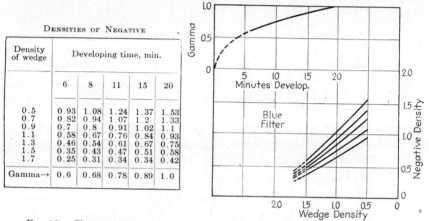

DENSITIES OF NEGATIVE

Density of wedge	Developing time, min.				
	6	8	11	15	20
0.5	0.93	1.08	1.24	1.37	1.53
0.7	0.82	0.94	1.07	1.2	1.33
0.9	0.7	0.8	0.91	1.02	1.1
1.1	0.58	0.67	0.76	0.84	0.93
1.3	0.46	0.54	0.61	0.67	0.75
1.5	0.35	0.43	0.47	0.51	0.58
1.7	0.25	0.31	0.34	0.34	0.42
Gamma→	0.6	0.68	0.78	0.89	1.0

Fig. 12.—Characteristics of panchromatic material exposed through blue filters.

It is obvious from the time-gamma curve that in order to obtain a gamma equal to 1 with the Wratten three-color filters and ABC pyro developer at 68°F., the red-, green-, and blue-separation negatives must be developed 11, 11, and 20 min., respectively.

The blue-filter negative of a given panchromatic emulsion usually requires a longer development time to build up the same gamma as the other two negatives. This phenomenon can be partially explained by the fact that blue light penetrates less into the depth of the emulsion as compared with light of longer wave length.[1]

In color photography the most satisfactory type of negative is one which gives a good print on a normal type of bromide paper. This corresponds to approximately unity gamma, and such value should be adopted as standard with great advantage.

Cameras and Equipment for Exposing Three-color Separation Negatives.—Before entering into discussion of color printing processes it will be convenient to review the type of cameras and various equipment for exposing three-color-separation negatives. The types of cameras here described are those in which each color-separation negative sees the total cone of light emerging from the lens.

These types are therefore free from the so-called "parallax" error which occurs when each color-separation negative covers only a zone of the exit pupil of a lens. Cameras with parallax errors are also defective from the standpoint of even distribution of light throughout the area of negative.

[1] An exception to this rule is the new Ilford Trichrome plate which builds up the same gamma irrespective of the filter. Therefore three color-separation negatives made with this type of plate are developed for the same length of time.

The color-separation negatives of still-life subjects indoors can be made by successive exposures with an ordinary camera rigidly mounted to preclude any chance of movement while changing negative holders and color filters. The filters can be slipped onto the lens in the usual manner. Care must be taken that the three film or plateholders register correctly.

Several devices to shorten the total time required for the triple exposure have been invented, among which outstanding is the repeating back by Miethe.

Colour Photographs, Ltd., London, has introduced the fully automatic repeating back, in which the sliding of the plateholder and the operation of the shutter is accomplished automatically in accordance with a predetermined setting.

A repeating back in its simplest form is obtainable from the Autotype Company, London. The three-color-separation filters of a repeating back are placed immediately in front of each negative.

The most satisfactory method of obtaining color-separation negatives by simultaneous exposure is by subdividing the light emitted from the lens by means of partial reflecting mirrors.

Single-mirror Camera.—The simplest form of camera designed on this principle is the one involving the use of a single partial reflecting mirror and shown schematically in Fig. 13. To obtain three-color-separation negatives with this type of camera, it is necessary to expose two of the negatives in bipack arrangement. The location of the bipack in the camera depends entirely on the nature of the partial mirror. The following important points must be carefully considered in designing the camera:

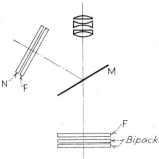

Fig. 13.—Diagram illustrating optical system of single-mirror camera.

1. The commercial bipack available today is composed of an orthochromatic emulsion in front and a panchromatic emulsion in the back. The two emulsions are facing each other, but the front emulsion has an additional layer of gelatin carrying a reddish filter dye. If the bipack is exposed through a magenta or minus green filter (Wratten No. 32), it yields a blue-sensation negative (front emulsion) and a red-sensation negative (back emulsion). If, on the other hand, the bipack is exposed through a yellow filter (Wratten K3) it yields the green-sensation negative (front emulsion) and red-sensation negative (back emulsion). Under this condition the sensitivity of the red negative overlaps somewhat too much into the green.

In any case the red negative, which gives a positive in blue-green or cyan color, is decidedly diffused due to the separating layer of gelatin carrying the red filter and the light-scattering effect of the front emulsion. The blue-green color of the positive print is the most important color for assuring the definition of the whole picture, and therefore the use of the standard bipack for this type of camera should be avoided if possible.

2. The commercial tripack can be split up for use with the single-mirror camera in two parts by removing the back emulsion to be exposed separately. The two front emulsions exposed as bipack, but without any filter, yield a sharp blue-sensation negative (front emulsion) and a very slightly diffused green-separation negative (second emulsion). Since a yellow filtering dye is incorporated in the first emulsion without any extra layer of gelatin, the contact between the two front emulsions is much closer than in the case of the standard bipack, and the resulting green-separation negative is sufficiently sharp for all practical purposes.

3. In case of a partial mirror made of plain white glass aluminized and camera balanced for incandescent and photoflood light, the mirror must be metal coated to a ratio of reflected to transmitted light of 3:1. By making the reflected beam the greater of the two, the secondary image created by the back surface of the mirror is not sufficiently strong to record. With this arrangement the two front emulsions of the tripack are exposed at right angles in the reflected beam without filter, and the third or back emulsion of the tripack in the transmitted beam through the standard red filter (Wratten No. 25). The ground glass for focusing can be placed in the reflected beam. The glass mirror, of course, must be optically flat but not too thick, otherwise the distortion caused by the refraction of the glass might become too great. A moderate amount of distortion can be compensated by tilting the plateholder carrying the red negative.

4. To avoid the refraction error and the presence of any secondary image, the partial mirror can be made of extremely thin transparent material, such as collodion, stretched on an optically flat frame. This transparent film can be also coated with a thin deposit of evaporated gold or aluminum to the desired reflection-transmission ratio. In this case it is immaterial as to which of the two beams is the greater. Obviously the bipack will be exposed in the path of the stronger beam. The idea of using pellicular mirrors for color cameras is quite old (see L. Geisler, U. S. Pat. 1060444, Apr. 29, 1913). Geisler also suggested coloring the thin transparent mirrors for the purpose of using them for filters as well.

When the reflected beam of a pellicular mirror is much lower than the transmitted beam, then the angle of the mirror with respect to the optical axis should be preferably less than 45° unless a very long focal-length lens is used, otherwise there is a danger of uneven distribution of light throughout the area of the reflected beam. This becomes immediately evident from Fig. 13.

The angles of the boundary rays in Fig.

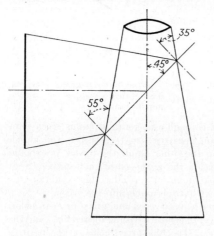

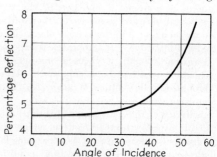

Fig. 14.—Uneven angle of reflection of boundary rays for mirror placed at 45°.

Fig. 15.—Reflection coefficient of a glass surface in air as function of angle of incidence. Index of glass = 1.55.

14 are, respectively, 35° and 55°. The coefficient of reflection for a pellicular surface having an index of reflection of 1.55 would be 5 and 9.5 per cent, respectively, for the surface without any metallic coating. The unevenness of illumination is therefore quite apparent. This unevenness, however, decreases materially as the thickness of the metallic coating increases.

The construction of this type of camera is quite simple as the only necessary requirement is to maintain the length of the optical paths identical with respect to both beams.

Double-mirror Camera.—The most satisfactory type of camera for three-color-separation negatives is the double-mirror type. The mirrors in this camera can be arranged in various manners, each of which offers its own advantages and disadvantages. In Figs. 16 to 21 are shown the arrangements most commonly used.

For convenience of reference the three partial beams are indicated throughout as No. 1 for the first reflection, No. 2 for the second reflection, and No. 3 for the beam straight through.

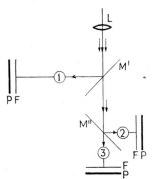

FIG. 16.—Optical system of two-mirror camera with mirrors at right angles.

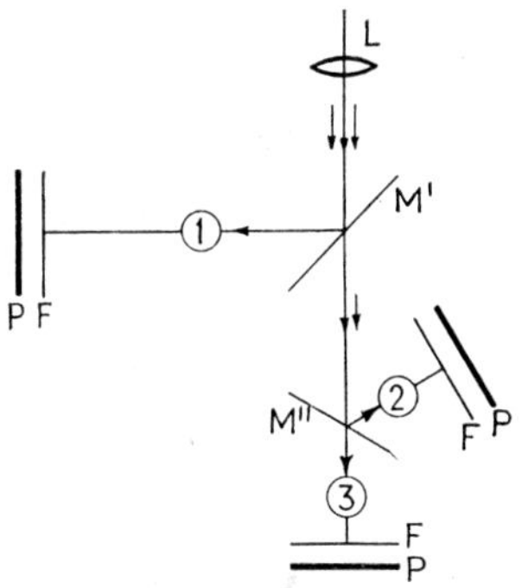

FIG. 17.—Optical system of two-mirror camera in which first mirror is at 45° angle and second at smaller angle to incident light.

There is indeed very little difference between the various arrangements and each one can be properly set up to give satisfactory performance, provided that the necessary precautions are taken in carrying out each design. In addition it might be said that in general the weak points of one particular arrangement are not necessarily shared by the others.

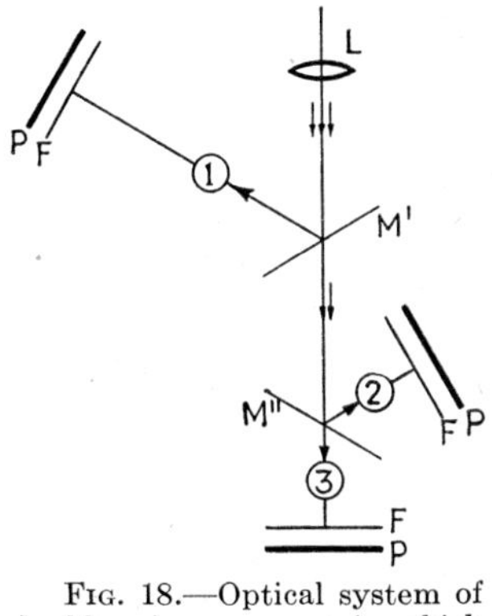

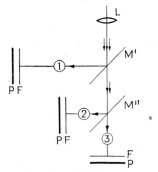

FIG. 18.—Optical system of double-mirror camera in which both mirrors are at angles smaller than 45° to the incident light.

FIG. 19.—Optical system of double-mirror camera in which both mirrors are parallel and at 45° to the incident beam.

The following general remarks apply to all the various arrangements:

1. Partial mirrors of plain white optical glass should have the reflected beam greater than, or at least equal to the transmitted beam. This is necessary to reduce the secondary image to a negligible quantity unless the back surface is evaporated with a transparent substance of refractive index lower than that of the glass itself, or unless the surface of the glass is chemically treated to reduce its index in contact

with air.　Colored glasses are in general more satisfactory but are more expensive and
the sequence of the color filters becomes fixed once and for all.　It is also obvious that
with plain white glass the three light beams cannot be of equal magnitude, but No. 1
beam is the strongest and No. 3 the weakest.　This arrangement is satisfactory when
designing a color camera balanced to incandescent light.　The angular position of both

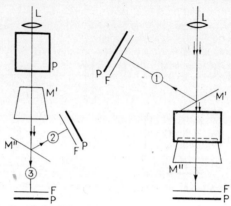

Fɪɢ. 20.—Optical system of double-mirror camera when the mirrors are not on the same
vertical plane and are at an angle less than 45°.

mirrors can be then less than 45° for evenness of light distribution as previously
explained.

2. Pellicular mirrors permit any desired ratio between reflected and transmitted
light.　The straight through or No. 3 beam is generally preferred strongest.　This,
however, demands that greater attention be given to the question of evenness of light
distribution.　Furthermore, the light scattered by the surface of the filters interposed

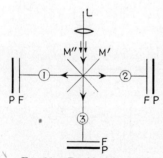

Fɪɢ. 21.—Double-mirror color
camera with mirrors crossed at
45°.

in the path of beams 1 and 3 is directed toward
negative 2 with the result of a very slight fog
appearing in negative 2, particularly with extremely
intense light and short exposure.　This results in an
apparently lower gamma which is in general not serious but should be avoided.　The effect of scattered
light is materially reduced by making the reflection
of the second mirror greater than its transmission
or by adopting the arrangement of Fig. 20.　The
arrangement of Fig. 19 is also free from this defect,
but greater emphasis must be given to the problem
of evenness of light distribution, unless the lens is
of exceptionally long focus.　In general the disposition of Fig. 20 can be considered as the most satisfactory with any type of mirrors.

In considering the subject of scattered light and the path which it follows it is
solely necessary to compute its amount, which ordinarily is of the order of $4\frac{1}{2}$ per cent
of the incident light for normal incidence, and to consider that the partial mirrors
behave in identical fashion with respect to the light which arrives from the lens or
from a different point within the camera.

In order to achieve the greatest possible speed, the first mirror is sometimes made
only very lightly coated, and the negative material facing beam 1 is a plain blue-
sensitive emulsion of very high speed exposed without blue filter.　Beam 2 from the

second mirror, also lightly coated, faces a very fast orthochromatic emulsion with a yellow filter, and the major amount of the light in beam 3 faces a fast panchromatic emulsion with the standard red filter. Other alternative variations are also possible, but all these special arrangements seem to be hardly justified in view of extremely fast panchromatic emulsions available today.[1]

Whatever the type or combination of negative material used, a careful study of its development characteristics must be made or obtained from the manufacturer in order to standardize the various processing operations.

Color-printing Methods for Prints on Paper.—Of the many color-printing processes developed, only those of practical value and in actual use today will be considered. Their description follows in the order of their practical importance. These processes are

Carbro

Imbibition—Eastman wash-off relief and Pinatype

Dyebro (Combination of Carbro and imbibition)

Chemical toning—Chromatone

Gelatin relief with color pigment in suspension—Duxochrome

Dye toning by the mordant process.

The Carbro Process. *Outline.*—Bromide prints by contact or enlargement are made from each color-separation negative. Carbon tissues containing soluble gelatin with colored pigments in suspension are sensitized in suitable solutions and then squeegeed onto the appropriate bromide. During the time of contact, the sensitizing chemicals of the tissues react with the silver image of the bromide, and a partial insolubilization of the gelatin of the tissue takes place in a manner proportional to the quantity of the silver of the image of the bromide. After several minutes of contact, the tissues are stripped from the bromides and transferred onto temporary supports. After another brief lapse of time, the temporary supports with the adhering tissues are placed in hot water in which the gelatin of the tissue, in still soluble condition, washes away, leaving a colored image in relief adhering to the temporary support. The three color images in relief are then finally transferred in register onto a final support.

Measurement of the Negatives.—After the three color-separation negatives have been exposed and developed, they must be measured to determine the correct printing ratio. This is done by measurement of the densities of the various steps of the neutral-gray wedge of each negative. The results of measurement should be entered in a notebook in tabulated form somewhat as in Table II.

The density of all the steps of the gray wedge need to be measured only when checking the correctness of development. For the purpose of determining the printing ratio it is only necessary to measure the densest step of the wedge in each negative.[2] Another important measurement, particularly in portraits, is the density of the forehead (F.H.). This measurement is used to compute the basic exposure for the blue bromide. In addition an empirical factor based on the measurement of the forehead density in the three negatives can be readily deducted, and this information will be found useful at other times when for some reasons the gray wedge is omitted. The measurements of the forehead are of value only in case of female studies. Great

---

[1] The effective speed to daylight of a panchromatic film in a double-mirror camera might range from Weston 3 to about Weston 12. This last value can be realized only with extremely fast emulsions such as Eastman Super-Panchro-Press with No. 25 filter for the red negative and Eastman Super-Ortho-Press with the K3 and No. 47 filters for the green and blue negative respectively.

[2] Theoretically this would be correct only for properly exposed negatives. Departure from true color balance, however, is mostly noticeable in the light tones of a finished print, and, therefore, it is desirable to adjust the color balance with respect to the densest step of the wedge. In case of portraits it is best to compute the printing ratio from the step of the wedge which most nearly matches the density of the forehead of the red filter negative.

TABLE II.—MEASUREMENTS ON COLOR-SEPARATION NEGATIVES

Printing color	Step	Density	Transmission, per cent	Ratio	Factor[1]	Printing exposure and remarks
Blue (red filter)	1	1.3	5	1	×1	1 = 12 sec. at $f/8$; 3 × magnification;
	2					paper Illingworth normal; developed
	3					1½ min. in Amidol
	4					
	5					
	F.H.					
Magenta (green filter)	1	1.2	6.3	0.8	×1.6	1.28 = 15½ sec. "
	2					
	3					
	4					
	5					
	F.H.					
Yellow (blue filter)	1	1.39	4.1	1.22	×1.2	1.47 = 18 sec. " Results O.K.
	2					
	3					
	4					
	5					
	F.H.					

[1] The meaning of this factor will be explained later.

attention, however, must be paid to the measurement of exactly the same spot in the three negatives.

To illustrate the use of this information the portrait of a young woman will be chosen as subject. The densitometric measurements are given in Table II. Here the transmission values of the No. 1 step in the three negatives are 5, 6.3, and 4.1 per cent, respectively. Taking the ratio of the magenta and yellow with respect to the blue-green, it is found that the magenta bromide should receive 0.8 and the yellow 1.22 times the exposure of the blue-green.

The correct exposure of the blue-green is found empirically, and it depends obviously on the type of enlarger and on the intensity of its light source. It depends also on the aperture of the lens diaphragm and the degree of enlargement.

With an enlarger having a diffused light source, a scale of magnification will be found very valuable.

A very valuable adjunct to the darkroom is the Kodak enlargement exposure calculator (correct only for enlargers having a diffused light source).[1]

With the above equipment it is solely necessary to determine once and for all the exposure necessary to produce the faintest silver deposit on the blue-green bromide, which corresponds to the maximum density of the red-filter negative. The information thus obtained can be jotted down and kept for future information. For instance:

Red-filter negative maximum density, 1.3; transmission, 5 per cent; exposure, 12 sec., $f/8$; magnification, 3×; Paper, Illingworth normal; development, 1½ min. in Amidol.

The printing time of another set of color-separation negatives of which the red-filter negative has a maximum density of say 1.6 (transmission 2.52 per cent) can be

[1] This calculator is based on the formula:

$$K(m + 1)^2 = E$$

where E is the resulting exposure,
m is the scale of magnification or reduction,
K is a consant determined for $m = 1$.

obtained at once by taking the ratio of the standard reference transmission above (5 per cent) to 2.52. This gives $5/2.52 = 2$ approximately. The blue-green bromide for this new set should therefore be exposed $12 \times 2 = 24$ sec., approximately, at $f/8$ and $3\times$ magnification. Its correct exposure for different values of lens stop and different magnifications can be derived quickly from the enlargement exposure calculator.[1]

The saving of time and material and the uniformity of results which can be realized by a systematic procedure must not be underestimated.

Carbro Solutions.—The carbro solutions for sensitizing the carbon tissues consist of a bleaching agent as potassium ferricyanide with potassium bromide as accelerator, and hardening agents as potassium dichromate with chromic acid for controlling the contrast.

Alternative solutions consist of potassium ferricyanide, potassium bromide, and potassium dichromate as bleaching and hardening agents and glacial acetic acid and hydrochloric acid as controlling agents.

Potassium chrome alum or formaldehyde are added in small quantities to the above solutions for the purpose of producing a slight superficial tanning in order to preserve the high lights.

TYPICAL STOCK SOLUTIONS
(Type I Solutions Using Chromic Acid)
STOCK SOLUTION A

Potassium ferricyanide	1 oz.	50 g.
Potassium bromide	1 oz.	50 g.
Water (distilled) to	10 oz.	500 cc.

STOCK SOLUTION B

Potassium dichromate (c.p.)	180 gr.	18 g.
Chromic acid	40 gr.	4 g.
Chrome alum	100 gr.	10 g.
Water (distilled) to	10 oz.	450 cc.

WORKING BATH 1

Stock solution A	1 part
Water	4 parts

WORKING BATH 2

Stock solution B	1 part
Water	4 parts

Each color tissue is immersed in working bath 1 for 3 min., drained for 10 or 15 sec. or squeegeed gently face down on a clean piece of plate glass to remove the surplus of bleaching solution, and then immersed in working bath 2 for a time which might vary from 15 to 40 sec. depending on the type of bromide paper used and on the degree of contrast desired.

After removal from bath 2, each tissue is squeegeed on its appropriate bromide and left in contact with it for 10 or 15 min.

The precautions to be followed in sensitizing and the method of squeegeeing, etc., will be considered later.

With Type II solutions also each color tissue is immersed in working bath 1 for 3 min., drained for 10 or 15 sec., and then immersed in working bath 2 for a time which might vary from 15 to 40 sec. depending on the type of bromide and degree of contrast required.

It has been often recommended, particularly with tissues which had too great a tendency to frill, to reduce the time of immersion in the No. 1 bath down to 2 min.,

---

[1] A photoelectric exposure meter with a full scale sensitivity of 7.5 ft.-candles can be obtained from the General Electric Co. on special order and at a price slightly higher than the standard model. The shape and sensitivity of this meter are such as to permit any kind of measurements of the light from enlargers. Its indications are, of course, equally correct with diffused- and condenser-type light sources.

particularly during hot weather. Too short immersion, however, prevents even absorption of chemicals throughout the full depth of the gelatin layer, and this ordinarily results in large irregular color patches particularly noticeable in the blue-green image. These irregularities are readily avoided by treating the tissues in the first bath for a full 3-min. period.

Type II Solutions (Using Acetic and Hydrochloric Acid)
Stock Solution A

Potassium dichromate	1 oz.	28 g.
Potassium ferricyanide	1 oz.	28 g.
Potassium bromide	1 oz.	28 g.
Water (distilled) to	20 oz.	566 cc.

Stock Solution B

Glacial acetic acid	1 oz.	35 cc.
Hydrochloric acid (c.p.)	1 oz.	35 cc.
Formaldehyde	22 oz.	770 cc.
Water (distilled)	1½ oz.	50 cc.

Working Bath 1

Stock solution A	1 part
Water	3 parts

Working Bath 2

Stock solution B	1 part
Water	32 parts

While it is comparatively simple to carry through small carbro prints by the two-solution method, it becomes decidedly awkward when prints larger than 8 by 10 in. are to be handled.

Since the single-bath method in which the controlling chemicals are mixed with the bleaching and hardening agents has all the conceivable advantages with adequate control, it will be described in detail.

The manner of handling carbon tissues applies naturally to both methods.

Carbro Solutions for Single-bath Method
Type I Solutions (Autotype)
Stock Solution A

Potassium bromide	1 oz.	28 g.
Potassium ferricyanide	1 oz.	28 g.
Potassium dichromate	1 oz.	28 g.
Water (distilled) to	20 oz.	566 cc.

Stock Solution B

Chromic acid	150 gr.	9.7 g.
Chrome alum	300 gr.	19.4 g.
Water (distilled) to	20 oz.	566 cc.

Working Bath

Stock solution A	1 part
Stock solution B	1 part
Water	3 parts

Type II Solutions
Stock Solution A

Potassium bromide	1 oz.	28 g.
Potassium ferricyanide	1 oz.	28 g.
Potassium dichromate	½ oz.	14 g.
Water (distilled) to	20 oz.	566 cc.

Stock Solution B

Glacial acetic acid	1 dram	3.5 cc.
Hydrochloric acid (c.p.)	1 dram	3.5 cc.
Formaldehyde (40 per cent)	10 drams	35 cc.
Water	12 drams	42 cc.

For convenience of accurate measurement the stock solution B could be made up in one-third the normal strength or

STOCK SOLUTION *BB*

Stock solution *B*.. 1 part
Water (distilled).. 2 parts

WORKING BATH

Water.. 20½ oz.
Stock solution *A*... 3 oz.
Stock solution *BB*.. 11 dram

The above Type II single-bath formula and the compounding of the working bath have been highly recommended in the past by outstanding color workers. With this proportion of chemicals, however, the deep shadows of the image in the bromide do not completely bleach out, and there is danger of losing proportionality. On the basis of very careful investigations it has been found desirable to increase the amount of bleaching chemicals in the working bath.

The following is a very dependable working bath:

WORKING SOLUTION M1

Water.. 19¾ oz.
Stock solution *A*... 4 oz.
Stock solution *BB*.. 11¼ dram

With the single-bath method, irrespective of the type of solution adopted, each tissue should be immersed in water for 3 min., drained for 15 or 20 sec., and then immersed in the carbro solution for about 45 sec.; after this it is squeegeed onto the appropriate bromide without draining and left in contact for 10 or 15 min.

The single-bath method with the Type II solution is to be preferred over any other because, although not as critical as the double-bath method, it offers nevertheless an appreciable amount of control, by increasing or decreasing the length of time of immersion in the carbro bath. The preliminary water bath for 3 min. must not be reduced, otherwise irregularities might result.

It is important also to note that the contrast increases with successive tissues owing to the fact that the consumption of acid is greater than that of bleaching chemicals.

This effect could be made use of by treating the tissues in the sequence: magenta, yellow, and blue-green because, as it will be seen shortly, the magenta tissue should be the least contrasty of all.

Greater flexibility of control, however, can be best obtained by mixing up the carbro solution in sufficiently large quantity, dividing it in three parts and using one part for each tissue.

A convenient amount for an 11- by 14-in. set would be (Type II)

WORKING SOLUTION M2

Water.. 59 oz.
Stock solution *A*... 12 oz.
Stock solution *BB*.. 4½ oz.

For use take approximately 25 oz. for each tissue. For larger or smaller tissues the quantity of solution should be proportional to the ratio of the tissue area as compared with the 11- by 14-in. set.

Since the area of an 11- by 14-in. tissue is 154 sq. in., an 8- by 10-in. tissue measuring 80 sq. in. would require $154/80 = 1.93$ less solution or $25/1.93 = 13$ oz.; hence a total quantity of 39 oz. of working bath should be made up if dealing with an 8- by 10-in. set.

If the above quantity is considered too large for 11- by 14-in. tissues, a total amount of 45 oz. of working bath can be made up using 15 oz. for each tissue.

It must be pointed out, however, that a smaller quantity of solution for a given area increases the contrast, and therefore the stock solution *BB* must be slightly increased.

For a 45-oz. total solution a suitable compounding would be

$$
M3 \begin{cases} \text{Water} \dots\dots\dots\dots\dots\dots\dots\dots\dots\dots\dots\dots\dots\dots\dots\dots\dots & 34\frac{1}{2} \text{ oz.} \\ \text{Stock solution } A \dots\dots\dots\dots\dots\dots\dots\dots\dots\dots\dots\dots & 7 \text{ oz.} \\ \text{Stock solution } BB \dots\dots\dots\dots\dots\dots\dots\dots\dots\dots\dots & 3\frac{1}{2} \text{ oz.} \end{cases}
$$

Use 15 oz. for each tissue.

It is not advisable to decrease the quantity of solution below 15 oz. for each tissue.

It is a well-known fact that the color contrast of a blue pigment (spectral reflecting power) is much less than that of a magenta and yellow pigment.

This difficulty is greatly accentuated when copying a color print. The Eastman Kodak Co. has lately advocated an automatic masking method in making paper prints from original Kodachrome slides. But even when working from color-separation negatives made directly from the original subject a vast improvement in general color balance can be secured by chemically reducing the contrast of the magenta and yellow tissues with respect to the blue. This procedure, however, necessitates considerable increase in the exposure of the bromides for the magenta and yellow tissues and a subsequently longer immersion in the carbro solution.

It is necessary to emphasize strongly at this time that the color contrast of the tissues and the exposure of the bromides, although related to one another, are two entirely different things. For instance if the three tissues are processed in strictly identical manner and the bromides are so exposed as to give correct balance in the high lights, then the shadows will tend toward orange. If now the contrast of the magenta and yellow tissue is decreased to match the contrast of the blue without any change in the exposure of the magenta and yellow bromide, the result will be a preponderance of blue both in the high lights and in the shadows.

With a correct set of negatives developed to gamma of unity and printed on an Illingworth de luxe bromide paper, normal grade, and developed in Amidol, correct color contrast will be obtained by sensitizing the blue tissue for 45 sec., the magenta for $1\frac{1}{2}$ min., and the yellow for $1\frac{1}{4}$ min. in the Type II single-bath method just described. This applies equally well to M2 and M3 formulas.

With the above treatment of the tissues it will be necessary to expose the bromide for the magenta tissue 1.6 times and the bromide for the yellow tissue 1.2 times the exposure of the bromide for the blue tissue.

A slight variation in this factor might be found necessary with different stocks of tissue. The above figures, however, will be found sufficiently accurate to start with.

This is the factor appearing in column 5 of Table II.

As the carbon tissues are removed from the carbro solution, they must be brought into intimate contact with the corresponding bromide. It is necessary that each soaked bromide be held in readiness by placing it face up on a piece of plate glass and covered with an even pool of water. At the expiration of the time of sensitizing, the tissue is withdrawn and, without draining, brought down face to face on the bromide. The thin pool of water prevents intimate contact and allows time for squeegeeing. The tissue and bromide are held together by steady pressure with the left-hand fingers along the safe edge at the extreme left, and a flat rubber squeegee held with the right hand moved across the sandwich from left to right with a steady, gentle, but quite firm stroke. The next stroke of the squeegee is taken in the opposite direction by holding it with the left hand and holding down the tissue and bromide with the fingers of the right hand along the safe edge at the extreme right.

Four strokes of the squeegee, two in each direction, will be found ample.

It is extremely important to avoid any movement of the tissue when once in contact with the bromide as the chemical action begins at once and any movement would give rise to a double image and spoil the results.

The three tissues are handled in succession in a similar manner.

The actual operation of squeegeeing the tissues on the appropriate bromides is very critical and the chances of spoiling the results are altogether too many. Although the correct technique can be satisfactorily mastered, the serious color worker is advised to resort to the use of an automatic mechanical squeegee which can be readily put together without any difficulty.

Figure 22 represents a schematic plan of the automatic squeegeer which consists of a usual photowringer mounted horizontally under a table top with the top cut out and beveled as shown. The two rollers should be geared to prevent slipping.

An apron made from two pieces of matte celluloid (0.010 in. thick) and hinged together with a strip of Kodatape will be found indispensable. Three aprons should be provided, one for each tissue.

The various operations leading up to a carbro print are listed as follows in a systematic manner:

1. Negatives are measured and printing exposure decided upon. A test exposure for the blue-green bromide (red-filter negative) can be made if desired. Information thus obtained should be entered in the notebook: Exposure, lens stop, magnification, type of bromide paper, developer, and time of development.

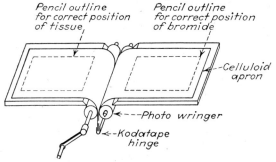

Fig. 22.—Wringer for placing bromide and carbro tissue in contact.

2. Bromides are exposed and developed in succession (large quantity of developer to avoid irregularities or a fresh moderate quantity of developer prepared in advance for each bromide, making sure that the temperature remains sufficiently constant). The bromide paper recommended is the Illingworth de luxe bromide, normal grade, special for carbro, with grain cut in the same direction. Defender Velour Black C (double weight) or N (single weight) special for carbro are also satisfactory.

The developer recommended is Amidol compounded as follows:

Water.. 1000 cc
Sodium sulphite (dry).. 25 g.
Amidol... 5 g.
Potassium bromide (10 per cent)..................................... 4 cc.

Develop for $1\frac{1}{2}$ to 2 min. —temperature 68°F.

3. Fixing of bromides should be done in plain hypo for about 15 min. (water, 32 oz.; hypo crystals, 4 oz.). A stop bath or an acid in the hypo should be avoided, as it will affect the action of the carbro solutions unless the washing operation is carried out for a very long time.

4. The bromides should be washed in running water for 15 to 20 min. A large tray and a siphon will be found very convenient for the purpose. (The Eastman Automatic Tray Syphon is a good typical example.)

5. While the bromides are washing, the celluloid temporary supports must be prepared by treating the surface with waxing solution. A suitable waxing solution can be made up by taking 1 g. of Autotype trichrome waxing compound, breaking it up in very small pieces and letting it dissolve in 500 cc. of benzine (cleaner's benzine) or in 500 cc. of benzol. One gram of pure beeswax dissolved in 500 cc. of benzine or benzol will be found equally satisfactory. Benzol is to be preferred in any case. This waxing solution must be prepared well in advance as the wax dissolves very slowly. A small tuft of cotton is soaked with the waxing solution and used to go over the entire surface of each celluloid. The evaporation of the solvent will take place very quickly particularly if benzol is used. As soon as dry, the celluloids will be immersed in a water bath containing a small amount of chrome alum; a teaspoonful of chrome alum in 2 gal. of water is satisfactory. When immersed, the celluloid should be given a lateral shaking and left to settle on the bottom of the tray until ready to be used. It is generally agreed that the most convenient thickness for the celluloids is 0.020 in. Thinner celluloids are difficult to handle and thicker ones resist too much the bending force of the transfer paper during the drying stage. Furthermore, the celluloids should be matte on one side, and this is the surface to be waxed and used to carry the colored image. It will be found that the colored image on a matte celluloid surface is more resistant to abrasions which readily occur when superimposing the celluloids with the dried colored images in order to judge the color balance.

The weak chrome-alum bath for the celluloids is very desirable. By means of it the waxed surface of the celluloid becomes completely wet, and this condition is necessary to produce intimate contact between the tissue and the waxed surface, thus permitting complete avoidance of air bells and any tendency to frill during hot-water development.

6. To avoid any deleterious effect from wash water, the bromides should be placed at the completion of wash, in a tray containing 1000 cc. of water and 4 cc. of glacial acetic acid. The tray should be rocked and moved about to insure uniform action for 4 min. The three bromides can be treated in this acid bath all together. At the expiration of 4 min. the bromides are washed again in running water for another 4 min., after which, pending the preparation of the tissues, they are placed in a tray containing a small quantity of water.

7. The carbro solution is prepared as outlined above, divided in three parts and each amount located conveniently at hand. The two trays for the preliminary water bath and for the carbro solution are placed next to each other. It is assumed that the three tissues are already cut to size with the grain in the same direction. Since the bromides have a white safe margin, the tissues can be of the same outside dimensions as the bromides.

8. The first celluloid apron is inserted in the automatic squeegee, as indicated in Fig. 22, and opened up. A few drops of water should be sprinkled on its surface. This water is necessary to decrease the adhesion of both the bromides and the tissues with the celluloid apron, otherwise creases might result while passing through the squeegee. This is not necessary for double-weight bromide paper (Defender C) but is absolutely necessary for single-weight bromide paper and for the tissue.

9. A stop watch or a timing clock hung in a visible place is started, and the following operations are carried out in accordance with the time schedule as indicated below:

Time Schedule for Carbro Process

0	Blue tissue is placed in the tray of water, face up, and forced under.
30 sec.	Tissue turned face down in water and forced under, holding it down with left hand; each corner of tissue can be folded slightly back to help uncurling.

1 min.	Tissue is turned face up again and forced under water by rocking the tray. The tissue, being now quite limp, will remain under water with gentle rocking.
2 min. 15 sec.	The blue bromide is now removed, without draining, from water in which it was placed after the final wash, is placed on the apron in coincidence with the pencil outline, as indicated on Fig. 22, and is left in this condition.
2 min. 55 sec.	The blue tissue is now removed from water and held in a vertical position to permit draining for 15 sec.
3 min. 10 sec.	Blue tissue is placed, face up, on bottom of adjacent tray.
3 min. 15 sec.	First part of carbro solution poured onto it and tray quickly rocked to insure even flowing of solution over entire surface of tissue. The tray is kept rocking to insure that tissue is always covered with solution.
3 min. 52 sec.	The tissue is removed from the carbro solution and, without draining, placed on the apron at the opposite side of the bromide and in coincidence of the pencil lines, as indicated also on Fig. 22.
4 min.	Tissue and bromide are rolled into contact through the squeegee and the apron with the sandwich inside removed from the chute at the lower side of the automatic squeegee. The apron is gently lifted to avoid separating the bromide from the tissue; the sandwich is completely peeled off the apron and placed on a clean blotter; and the surface moisture is gently blotted off with another clean blotter, after which the bromide and its adherent tissue are placed away, preferably on a clean blotter, until ready to be stripped apart.
	The used apron is now wiped off with a clean rag and hung up to dry in a convenient corner. The second dry apron is inserted in the automatic squeegee, opened, and a few drops of water sprinkled onto it in the same manner as was done for the first apron. The carbro tray is next emptied in preparation for the second quantity of fresh solution.
6 min.	The red tissue is now placed in the tray of water face up and handled in the same manner as the blue tissue.
6 min. 30 sec.	Red tissue turned face down in water and corners gently bent back to help flattening.
7 min.	Red tissue turned face up and kept under water by rocking tray.
8 min. 15 sec.	Red bromide placed on the celluloid apron.
8 min. 55 sec.	Red tissue lifted out of water and drained for 15 min.
9 min. 10 sec.	Red tissue placed face up on bottom of tray.
9 min. 15 sec.	Second portion of carbro solution poured over red tissue and tray rocked quickly and continuously to insure even flow of carbro solution over the full area of tissue.
10 min. 37 sec.	Red tissue removed from solution and without draining placed on apron.
10 min. 45 sec.	Red tissue rolled into contact with bromide.
	Sandwich is removed from within the apron surface, moisture blotted off and placed away to allow chemical action.
	Apron wiped off and put away. Third apron placed in the automatic squeegee and sprinkled with water.
	Second part of used carbro solution thrown away.
12 min.	Yellow tissue is immersed in water bath face up and forced under water.
12 min. 30 sec.	Yellow tissue turned face down and again treated in same way as previous tissues.
13 min.	Tissue turned face up in water and kept immersed by rocking tray.
14 min. 15 sec.	Yellow bromide placed on celluloid apron.
14 min. 55 sec.	Yellow tissue removed from water and drained for 15 sec.
15 min. 10 sec.	Yellow tissue placed face up on bottom of tray.
15 min. 15 sec.	Third part of carbro solution poured onto yellow tissue and tray rocked.
16 min. 22 sec.	Yellow tissue is removed from solution and, without draining, placed on apron.
16 min. 30 sec.	Yellow tissue and bromide are rolled into contact in automatic squeegee. The sandwich is removed from within the apron, surplus moisture blotted off and put away.
	The used-up carbro solution is now thrown away and a plate of glass prepared for squeegeeing the tissues on the celluloids. This operation is best done by placing the glass on a wood rack in the sink. A very convenient arrangement is to place the glass plate on two small wood blocks within a large tray for the purpose of collecting the water thrown off during the squeegeeing operation.
18 min.	A piece of celluloid temporary support is removed from the dilute alum bath and rinsed, the surplus moisture from its back removed by sliding it on a piece of blotter and placing on top of the prepared glass with the waxed surface (which is now completely wet) face up. If too much moisture is left on the back of the celluloid, it will not adhere sufficiently to the glass surface, and it will slide during the squeegeeing operation. The blue tissue is stripped by a steady pull from its bromide, passed face down in cold-water bath, and, without draining, placed face down on the celluloid support.
	A piece of thin Kodaloid (0.005 in. thick) is now laid on the tissue to prevent it being damaged with the flat squeegee and the whole thing firmly squeegeed back and forth

with firm hand to expel the moisture from between the tissue and the celluloid. Eight or ten strokes will be sufficient and the celluloid support with its adherent tissue placed under moderate pressure (four pieces of plate glass) between blotting paper until the next celluloid and tissue are ready to take its place.

24 min. The next celluloid support is removed from the alum bath, handled in the same manner as the first one, and placed on the piece of plate glass. The red tissue is now stripped from its bromide, dipped in water, squeegeed and placed under pressure with its celluloid in place of the blue sandwich, which is now laid out in the open, after carefully wiping off any trace of moisture along the edge of the tissue.

30 min. The third celluloid and yellow tissues are handled in the same manner as the two previous ones. Hot-water bath at about 105°F. is now prepared.

36 min. The third celluloid with its yellow tissue is removed from under pressure and laid out in the open.

The blue tissue on its celluloid support is now placed in the hot-water bath and after about 1½ min. the paper backing is stripped off by pulling gently from two opposite corners.

The blue image is now fully developed by lateral shaking of the celluloid under water. This operation will take about 2 min. to fully develop (a condition which can be readily judged).

The celluloid with its blue image is passed in cold water and rinsed until no appreciable amount of blue color runs off, after which it is hung up to dry.

42 min. The red image is now developed in hot water, rinsed in cold water, and hung up to dry.

48 min. The yellow image is finally developed in hot water, rinsed in cold water, and put to dry.

The three colored images, when dry, are to be assembled together in correct register upon a final paper support. This assembling operation can be carried out in two ways: by single- and by double-transfer method.

Single Transfer.—Decision as to which method is to be followed must be made before printing the bromides because with the single-transfer method the bromides must be printed from reversed negatives, otherwise the final image will be laterally reversed with respect to the original subject.

With the single-transfer method the yellow image must be transferred first to the final paper, then follows the magenta, and finally the blue-green image uppermost.

For final support a fixed-out bromide paper or the regular transfer paper which is available commercially could be used.

The final paper should be soaked in cold water for at least ½ hr., and, when ready to make the first transfer, the celluloid carrying the yellow image should be also immersed in the cold water for a few minutes and the two lifted out together, avoiding air bells between them. A moderate squeegeeing with the flat squeegee is desirable, after which the sandwich can be hung up to dry. When completely dry, the celluloid will automatically detach itself leaving the yellow image on the final paper. A slight amount of wax always transfers with the image, and it must be carefully removed before proceeding with the next transfer. This is best done by going over the yellow image with a tuft of cotton dipped in rectified spirit of turpentine. The turpentine is allowed to remain for a minute or so. Another tuft of cotton is now soaked in benzine and applied gently to the yellow image, after which the benzine and turpentine together are cleaned off with a piece of dry cheesecloth. The cleaning of the print by means of benzine should be repeated three or four times and each time cleaned off with cheesecloth. Finally the surface of the print should be gone over with a large piece of clean cotton flannel.

The final support with its yellow image should now be placed again in cold water or better still in a tray containing a weak solution of gelatin (1 oz. of Nelson's gelatin No. 1 dissolved in 32 oz. of water). The gelatin solution is highly desirable to permit intimate adhesions between the yellow image and the magenta image which has to follow. The celluloid bearing the magenta image is also placed in cold water and finally passed into the gelatin solution and placed in approximate registration with the yellow image. The two are withdrawn together and laid on a sheet of plate glass with the paper support uppermost. The flat squeegee can be applied gently to the sandwich to remove the excess of gelatin solution, after which the sandwich can be reversed right side up and a final registration carried out by gently sliding the celluloid. When a satisfactory registration is accomplished, the sandwich can be hung up to dry. Occasionally it may be necessary to bend the celluloid to secure accurate registration, particularly after the paper support with the yellow image has been soaked too long in the water. This, however, should not be necessary if the soaking of the paper support is not carried out beyond $1\frac{1}{2}$ min.

Instead of a flat squeegee the surplus gelatin solution can be forced out by applying a dry cloth over the back of the paper support. When dry and the celluloid is detached leaving the red and yellow images together, the image surface is again cleaned free of wax in the same manner as before and the blue-green image transfer carried out in exactly the same manner.

Double Transfer.—The double-transfer method has many points of advantage, and it is highly recommended in preference to the single-transfer method. It is very difficult to register the red to the yellow image, particularly if the transfer has to be carried out with incandescent light, for the yellow image is almost invisible with artificial light. With the double-transfer method, however, the blue-green image is first transferred to a temporary support which consists of soluble gelatin on a thin paper base. With a soluble temporary support it is not necessary to use the gelatin solution as recommended for the single-transfer method. The removal of the wax after each transfer should be carried out in the same way as previously described. The sequence of transfer with the double-transfer method is blue-green image first, then the magenta image, and finally the yellow image on top. It will be found very easy to register the yellow image by this method. The wax must be again removed from the yellow surface after the three transfers are complete.

The temporary soluble support with the complete color image is now placed again in cold water and brought into contact with the final paper support which could be also a fixed-out bromide paper or regular single-transfer paper available commercially. The two are squeegeed together with a flat squeegee and placed under pressure between blotting papers for 15 or 20 min. The sandwich is finally placed into hot water at 100°F., and after 1 or 2 min. the paper backing of the temporary soluble support can be readily stripped, leaving the complete image on the final support. The soluble gelatin left by the temporary support can be gently washed off, and the complete picture is put away to dry.

By the double-transfer method it is possible to trim the temporary support, with the color image on it, down to the exact size of the latter, but if this procedure is followed it is necessary to allow the soluble support to remain in contact with the final paper until completely dry. When this is done, the stripping of the paper support in hot water should be preceded by a bath in cold water for 10 or 15 min. Unless this precaution of drying the sandwich first is taken, there is a danger of the image frilling and becoming damaged because of lack of the safe margin which was removed by the trimming operation.

With the double-transfer method the bromides must be printed right side up.

Concluding Remarks.—In carrying out a carbro process great care must be exercised to avoid contamination with the usual darkroom chemicals. Developing chemicals have a tendency to bleach the blue tissue, and therefore if small circular white spots occur in a blue tissue, these can invariably be ascribed to traces of developer. These spots ordinarily disappear in a span of 24 hr. Their disappearance, however, can be expedited by treating gently the finished color picture, locally, with a weak solution of hydrochloric or acetic acid.

There is no satisfactory way of reducing the strength of the blue image of a carbro print. The magenta, however, can be reduced by treating the full print in a weak solution of potassium permanganate rendered slightly acid with a trace of hydrochloric acid or sulphuric acid. When sufficiently reduced, the action can be stopped at once by immersion in a weak solution of sodium bisulphite followed by a slight wash.

The yellow image can be reduced by treating the complete image in a weak solution of plain hypo, again followed by careful washing.

It is not recommended, however, to resort to such chemical reduction of the magenta and yellow images because the over-all contrast is invariably disturbed. These reducing agents have an even effect throughout the image and therefore can be classified among the so-called "cutting" reducers, the sole purpose of which is to increase the contrast.

Small traces of bichromate always remain in suspension in the colored images and a partial insolubilization of the soluble temporary support might take place if the transfers are carried out in strong daylight or sunlight. Insolubilization might also occur if the last transfer onto the final support is delayed too long (over 30 hr.). A safe rule is therefore to avoid too strong daylight and sunlight and to carry through the various transfers within a span of a few hours.

When properly carried out the carbro process permits results of great beauty and naturalness not readily achieved by other processes.

The room temperature for the carbro process is not critical. A comfortable value of 65 to 70°F. will be found to be best.

Eastman Wash-off Relief.—The Eastman wash-off relief method represents a typical imbibition process.

Outline.—Prints in natural color can be made by transfer of water-soluble dyes by means of images produced in relief on celluloid film. This process is based on the property of the silver, forming the photographic image, to render the surrounding gelatin insoluble when the development is carried out in a tanning developer or by a subsequent treatment of the image with suitable bleaching chemicals. The Eastman wash-off relief is typical among the processes of this type. The positive prints from corresponding color-separation negatives are made on a special film carrying a silver emulsion made with highly soluble gelatin. The exposure of the film must be made through the celluloid base. The development of the positive film is carried out in a normal positive developer, after which the films can be given a brief wash and passed to the bleaching bath without intermediate fixing.

Exposure and Development of the Positives.—The wash-off relief films are printed by contact or projection from the appropriate color-separation negatives. The exposures should be such as to give a faint silver deposit in the highest lights of the subject.

The wash-off relief positives may be developed in Eastman developer DK-50 for about 5 min. at 70°F. Developers DK-11 and D-76 may also be used. The three films can be developed simultaneously in a tank suspended in the usual film-developing hangers. Development can be also carried out in trays, treating such film individually in a fresh quantity of developer with uniform rocking.

The operations of washing, bleaching, and developing of the reliefs in hot water could be made to follow the development without the intermediate fixing. This requires, however, that these various operations be carried through in yellow light. It might be preferable, however, to rinse briefly the wash-off relief films after the development and then place them to fix in the nonhardening fixing-bath formula F-24. Following this they can be washed for 5 min. in running water.

Bleaching.—The bleaching of the silver image of the film is carried through in a bleaching solution (R-10a) diluted as indicated. The three films can be placed all together in a tank if suspended in the usual hangers.

If trays are used, however, each film must be placed separately in a fresh bleaching solution. The quantity of working bleach solution recommended is 8 oz. for an 8- by 10-in. tray. The three films must be evenly rocked during the bleaching operation to avoid streaky effects. The bleaching solution should be discarded immediately after use.

Hot-water Development.—The bleached films should now be placed in a tank of hot water at 110°F. and the hangers lifted out of the tank and replaced in it about every 10 sec. This is to allow the melted emulsion to be drained away from the films. In carrying out this operation, the greatest possible attention must be paid to prevent the films from rubbing against each other as the relief image at this time is extremely delicate. It is advisable to change into a clean tank of hot water again at 110°F. after 1 min., continuing the agitation. After about 3 min., the film should be given another rise in clean hot water; it can then be passed again into the fixing-bath formula F-5. One minute in a fixing bath will be sufficient, after which the films can be put to wash for about 5 min. in cold running water. If the hot-water development of the films is carried out in trays, each film must be handled separately and the hot water changed two or three times, but in any case the hot water should never be poured over the film. Three of four changes of hot water for each tray will be sufficient, after which the films will be passed into a fixing bath and washed.

A faint trace of brown image remains in the relief film after treatment in a fixing bath. This can be completely disregarded when the relief images are used to print by dye transfer on paper. When making transparencies, however, it might be further desirable to remove such a residual image by treating in a permanganate reducer formula (R-2), followed by fixation in formula F-5 and additional wash.

It is advisable to dry the relief images before staining in the appropriate dye baths.

Treatment in the Dye Solutions.—The three dye solutions are made up in accordance with the instructions attached to each dye container, and in order to increase the keeping qualities of the dye it is advisable to add 5 cc. of formalin to each 500 cc. of dye solution. Each dye has placed in it a certain amount of 5 per cent acetic acid, the amount controlling the amount of dye taken up by the matrix. Thus the color contrast may be controlled. The amounts of acid are of the order of 5 to 20 cc.

It is also best to filter the dye solution through rapid filtering paper before use.

Each relief film is now put in its appropriate dye bath for about 30 minutes at 68°F. and the tray occasionally rocked. The dyed relief films, when removed from the dye baths, should be rinsed in two changes of $\frac{1}{2}$ per cent solution of acetic acid and distilled water. After this rinsing the three films can be placed in a tray containing $\frac{1}{2}$ per cent of acetic acid until ready for the dye transfer.

At this stage, the three stained reliefs can be superimposed to judge the color balance—this is best done on the bottom of a white porcelain tray—and examined in strong white light, after which they can be returned to the tray containing $\frac{1}{2}$ per cent solution of acetic acid or dried, the transfer process taking place at another time.

Preparation of a Transfer Paper.—The transfer of the dyes can be made on any ordinary type of bromide paper fixed in a fresh fixing bath (formula F-24) or the especially prepared paper called imbibition paper.

The paper must be first prepared by treating it for 5 min. in a mordanting solution (formula M-1). This treatment should be followed by a wash for 5 min. in running water and then by a treatment, also for 5 min., in a buffer solution consisting of a 5 per cent solution of sodium acetate. Finally the paper should be washed again for another 5 min.

Several papers can be treated at the same time and put away to dry for future use. A transfer paper, which has been previously treated and dried, should be given a preliminary soaking in plain water for at least 5 min. and then placed, gelatin side up, on a sheet of plate glass. It is preferable to place over the paper a piece of a damp blotter to maintain the paper in a moistened condition throughout the various transfers.

The magenta-dyed relief is removed from the acidulated water bath and placed image face down on the prepared paper. Holding one edge of the film with fingers to prevent sliding, the surplus water and air bubbles are expelled by going over the film with a flat squeegee a few times in both directions with increasing pressure. The contact between the relief film and the transfer paper must be intimate. The sandwich can now be covered with another sheet of plate glass and allowed to remain in this manner for a time which might vary from 10 to 30 min., depending on the strength of the relief image.

The transfer of the dye can be expedited by increasing the pressure and keeping the sandwich warm. This can readily be done by placing some additional weight over the plate glass and covering with towels dampened in hot water.

The relief film should be left in contact with the transfer paper long enough to allow a complete transfer of the dye. When this is accomplished, the film is peeled off the transfer paper and put away to dry or replaced in a magenta dye tray if additional prints are to be made. Without giving the transfer paper a chance to dry, a thin sheet of Kodaloid or celluloid should be dampened and placed directly over the transfer paper. On top of the Kodaloid place the second relief film stained in the blue-green dye.

The Kodaloid sheet should not be placed entirely over the magenta image, but a small safe margin at the extreme left should be left exposed to permit holding down in contact the blue-green relief and the transfer paper, still permitting the Kodaloid sheet to be pulled off when the right registration is accomplished. In this manner the registration can be carried out with plenty of time without any danger of the blue-green dye transferring out of the register and blurring the results. When one is satisfied with the registration, the blue-green relief should be clamped down on the extreme left edge with fingers and then the right-hand edge bent back to allow the removal of the Kodaloid sheet, after which the blue-green relief is allowed to fall down in contact with the transfer paper. The surplus water and any air bubbles are squeegeed off rapidly with increasing pressure, as was done with the first transfer.

The time of transfer for the blue-green image is about 10 to 30 min., depending on the pressure applied and the temperature.

The transfer of the yellow dye is accomplished in identical manner, although the time required for the yellow transfer is appreciably less than for the other two colors. When the yellow relief is removed from the transfer paper, the final color print should be dried quickly to preserve the sharpness of the image.

The following formulas for the developing of the relief images, the bleaching and the fixing bath are those recommended by the Eastman Kodak Co. and it is advisable to follow them very closely.

DEVELOPER (FORMULA DK-50)

Water (about 125°F.) (52°C.)	64 oz.	2 l.
Elon	145 gr.	10 g.
Sodium sulphite (desiccated)	4 oz.	120 g.
Hydroquinone	145 gr.	10 g.
Kodalk	1 oz. 145 gr.	40 g.
Potassium bromide	29 gr.	2 g.
Cold water to make	1 gal.	4 l.

Without dilution, develop 5 min. at 65°.

Wash-off Relief Bleaching Solution (Formula R-10)
Stock Solution A

Water..	16	oz.	500 cc.
Ammonium bichromate.........................	290	gr.	20 g.
Sulphuric acid (c.p.) (E. K. Co.)............	4	cc.	4 cc.
Water to make...............................	32	oz.	1 l.

Stock Solution B

Sodium chloride (table salt).................	1½	oz.	45 g.
Water to make...............................	32	oz.	1 l.

For use, take one part of *A*, one part of *B* and six parts of water.

Nonhardening Fixing Bath (Formula F-24)

Water (about 125°F.) (52°C.).................	16	oz.	500 cc.
Hypo..	8	oz.	240 g.
Sodium sulphite (desiccated).................	145	gr.	10 g.
Sodium bisulphite...........................	365	gr.	25 g.
Water to make...............................	32	oz.	1 l.

Acid Hardening Fixing Bath (Formula F-5)

Water (about 125°F.) (52°C.).................	80	oz.	2.5 l.
Hypo..	2	lb.	960.0 g.
Sodium sulphite desiccated..................	2	oz.	60.0 g.
Acetic acid (28%)...........................	6	oz.	190.0 cc.
Boric acid, crystals........................	1	oz.	30.0 g.
Potassium alum..............................	2	oz.	60.0 g.
Cold water to make..........................	1	gal.	4.0 l.

Table of Dilutions of Acetic Acid

Concentration, per cent	Amount	
	Glacial acetic acid	28 per cent commercial acetic acid
⅒	1 cc. diluted to 1 l., or ¼ fluid dram diluted to 32 oz.	3.6 cc. diluted to 1 l., or 1 fluid dram diluted to 32 oz.
½	5 cc. diluted to 1 l., or 1¼ fluid drams diluted to 32 oz.	18 cc. diluted to 1 l., or 5 fluid drams diluted to 32 oz.
5	50 cc. diluted to 1 l., or 13 fluid drams diluted to 32 oz.	180 cc. diluted to 1 l., or 5¾ fl. oz. diluted to 32 oz.

Aluminum Sulphate Solution for Mordanting Paper (Formula M-1)
Solution A

Aluminum sulphate..........................	6¾	oz.	200 g.
Water to make..............................	32	oz.	1 l.

Solution B

Sodium carbonate (desiccated)..............	1 oz. 145	gr.	40 g.
Water to make..............................	16	oz.	500 cc.

Add *B* slowly to *A*, stirring well during the addition. A white precipitate is at first formed, but this dissolves upon stirring. If a trace should remain, it can be filtered out with a rapid filter paper.

5 Per Cent Sodium Acetate Solution

Dissolve sodium acetate (anhydrous)........................	50 g. in 950 cc. water.
Or dissolve sodium acetate (anhydrous)....................	1⅔ oz. in 32 oz. water.

Pinatype Process.—Gelatin has the property of absorbing some type of dyes in a manner inversely proportional to its degree of hardness. This property can be utilized for the purpose of transferring coloring dyes instead of producing the wash-off relief image as described before. A process based on this principle was introduced commercially several years ago under the trade name of Pinatype. Material for this process is obtainable from the Agfa-Ansco Company.

Plates coated with gelatin and suitable as matrices for Pinatype-dye transfer are available commercially, although the usual diapositive plates fixed in plain hypo can be equally satisfactory.

The usual procedure is to sensitize the plates for 3 or 4 min. in a solution of 2 or 3 per cent of potassium bichromate and to allow them to dry in the dark. Although the plates are not sensitive until dry, the sensitizing should be carried out in subdued daylight or under incandescent light. The plates so prepared should be utilized within 24 hr.

The matrices must be printed from positives, and it is therefore necessary to first print the negatives either by contact or by enlargement on positive plates or films of the final size.

The necessity of preparing first positive transparencies constitutes an additional step in disfavor of this process. However, this particular step can be utilized to compensate for exposure irregularities of the original negatives. The printing of the bichromated plates must be made by contact with the positive transparencies in a printing frame by means of sunlight or arc light. Since the image on the bichromated gelatin is only slightly visible, it is best to place behind it, in a printing frame, a piece of printing-out or proof paper to act as a photometer. The correct degree of printing must be determined empirically and judged completely by the image on the printing-out paper. After printing, the bichromated plates are to be freed of the bichromate by washing in running water for 10 or 15 min. As the sensitivity to light ceases immediately when the plates are immersed in the water, the washing can be carried out under ordinary light.

The Pinatype printing plates must be carefully identified by suitable markings, or they could be slightly stained in the appropriate dyes to avoid any later mix-up. It is best to let them dry completely before the final staining. The dye solutions are made up in a concentration in accordance with instructions of the manufacturer. The order of transfer to the final paper can be the same as with the Eastman wash-off relief, *viz.*, red, blue and yellow or blue, yellow and red or blue, red and yellow. It is best, of course, not to transfer the yellow first, as otherwise the registration becomes too difficult. The insertion of a thin Kodaloid sheet between the matrix and a final paper for the purpose of obtaining correct registration will be found of great advantage.

The time required for staining the matrix the first time will be about 15 min. each, after which each matrix must be well washed until no appreciable color is given off. The type of paper and its preparation for final transfer can be as described under Eastman wash-off relief.

An alternative method consists in utilizing the positive transparencies as matrices. With this method the positive transparencies fixed in plain hypo and well washed are sensitized for 3 or 4 min. in a bath consisting of

Ammonium bichromate	12½	g.
Water	1000	cc.
Ammonia	25	cc.

The sensitized transparencies should then be put to dry in the dark and, when dry, exposed to sunlight or arc light with the glass or celluloid sides toward the light source. The amount of exposure to the light in this case also can be controlled by placing behind each diapositive a sheet of printing-out paper. The diapositives must be then washed for 10 or 15 min. to completely remove any trace of bichromate, after which they can be stained immediately in the appropriate dyes or allowed to dry as before. If it is considered desirable to remove the silver image before staining with dye, this can be readily carried out with regular Farmer's reducer.

The advantages to be derived by using the positive transparencies for dye printing are as follows: Since the exposure to the light has taken place through the back, the degree of relief is extremely small and the successive stainings take place in a much more uniform manner, as compared with the previous method. The contact with the final paper is a good deal more intimate and the delicate details are retained a great deal more faithfully than with the straight Pinatype method.

With both methods, however, positive films can be used to advantage in place of glass plates, as the squeegeeing operation can be carried out much more easily.

Dyebro Process.—Relief images on thin celluloid supports can be produced also by the carbro method. The only deviations from the standard carbro method are as follows: Instead of trichrome tissues, an appropriate gray tissue with very slight coloration is being used. All the various operations, however, are strictly identical to the previously described carbro process. After being made insoluble in contact with bromide papers, the tissues are transferred to the celluloids, without any waxing, and developed in hot water as usual.

The staining of these reliefs, the final transfer paper, and the method of dye transfer is strictly identical with the Eastman wash-off relief. The carbro reliefs on the thin, transparent celluloids should be given an additional final hardening in a 5 per cent solution of formaldehyde, before staining, to increase their durability.

Chemical Toning Processes.—A positive silver image can be converted into a colored image by replacing the silver of the image by means of metallic compounds. Methods for producing satisfactory blue and yellow tones have long been known, but a satisfactory magenta image by chemical toning has been made available only recently by Defender and the complete process marketed under the trade name Chromatone.

By this process, prints from the three color-separation negatives are made on a special paper from which the image can be stripped and transferred in register to a final support. The emulsion of the printing paper is carried by an extremely thin collodion sheet which detaches from the paper base during the washing operation.

Three developers are recommended for use with the Chromatone printing paper, depending on the nature of the original three color-separation negatives.

STANDARD FORMULA 1—FOR PRINTS FROM NORMAL NEGATIVES

Water	40	oz.	2000	cc.
Metol	51	gr.		1.5 g.
Sodium sulphite (dry)	0.5	oz.		22.5 g.
Hydroquinone	60	gr.		6.5 g.
Sodium carbonate (dry)	0.5	oz.		22.5 g.
Potassium bromide	25	gr.		2.7 g.

Development: 1½ min. at 70°F.

FORMULA 2—FOR GOOD PRINTS FROM HARD NEGATIVES

Water			32 oz.	1000 cc.
Metol			44 gr.	3 g.
Sodium sulphite (dry)	1 oz.	88 gr.		36 g.
Sodium carbonate (dry)			263 gr.	18 g.
Potassium bromide			58 gr.	4 g.

For use, one part stock solution, three parts water, and develop 3 to 4 min. at 70°F.

Formula 3—Vigorous Developer for Good Prints from Soft Negatives
Solution A

Water...	32	oz.	1000 cc.
Hydroquinone.......................................	1.5	oz.	45 g.
Sodium sulphite (dry)...............................	1	oz.	30 g.
Sulphuric acid......................................	60	minims	4 cc.

Solution B

Water...	32	oz.	1000 cc.
Sodium carbonate (dry)..............................	4	oz.	130 g.
Potassium bromide...................................	120	gr.	8 g.
Sodium sulphite (dry)...............................	3	oz.	90 g.

Use equal parts of solutions *A* and *B* and develop 5 min. at 70°F.

Assuming that the negatives are carefully balanced or that a satisfactory measurement of the factor of the three negatives has been determined with a densitometer, an additional factor with respect to the three chromatic colors is necessary. A satisfactory print from the green-filter negative is first obtained. The exposure necessary for the print from the red-filter negative must be increased 10 per cent and the exposure of the print from the blue-filter negative by 25 per cent over the exposure given to the green-filter negative. After development with the appropriate developer, the three positives are fixed in an acid fixing bath. The Eastman F-5 fixing-bath formula is satisfactory for this purpose. The washing of the positive prints must be carried out for at least 15 min. in running water to make sure that every trace of hypo has been removed, otherwise the subsequent chemical operation might be badly affected. The manufacturers of the Chromatone material recommend the following thiocyanate fixing bath whenever speed is necessary, as even a trace of this chemical does not interfere with the toning solutions if the washing is not carried out fully:

Water...	1000 cc.
Potassium thiocyanate...............................	100 g.
Potassium alum.....................................	50 g.
Glacial acetic acid..................................	25 cc.

During the process of washing, the collodion emulsion ordinarily detaches from the paper base, and it must be carefully handled to avoid tearing.

Before proceeding with the toning operations, the following miscellaneous solutions must be made up:

Solution A—Dilute Hydrochloric Acid

Hydrochloric acid (c.p.).............................	16	oz.	500 cc.
Distilled water.....................................	48	oz.	1500 cc.

Solution B—Standard Hypo Solution

Granular or rice hypo...............................	2¼	oz.	70 g.
Distilled water.....................................	32	oz.	1000 cc.

Wherever the text refers to *standard hypo solution* this is the formula that must be used. A bath containing acid or alum will bring complete failure.

Solution C—Standard Ferricyanide Solution

Potassium ferricyanide..............................	½	oz.	11 g.
Distilled water.....................................	4	oz.	100 cc.

Working Solutions for Chromatone Color Prints
(Sufficient Quantity for Toning 5- by 7-In. Prints)
Red and Blue Toner A Working Solution

Water...	1	oz.	25 cc.
Red and blue toner *A*..............................	1	oz.	25 cc.
Standard ferricyanide solution......................	1½ drams		5 cc.

This solution does not keep well when mixed, and only sufficient should be prepared for prints in process.

Yellow toner A—No. 1	1 oz.	25 cc.
Yellow toner A—No. 2	1 oz.	25 cc.
Standard ferricyanide solution	1½ drams	5 cc.

Add No. 1 to No. 2, stirring gently until any precipitate that may appear is completely dissolved.

This solution does not keep well when mixed, and only sufficient should be prepared for prints in process.

Toning the Red and Blue Prints.—The stripped-off black-and-white positive prints, intended for the red and blue images, are placed together in one tray, and the red and blue working solution (red and blue toner *A*), made up as outlined above, is added. This preliminary *A* toning is actually a bleaching process. Care should be taken that the films are thoroughly saturated with the solution. It is advisable to turn them over repeatedly and to rock the tray to remove any air bubbles.

A swab of absorbent cotton or a wide rubber-set varnish brush is very useful to prevent all kinds of smear marks and uneven toning. The brush or swab should be used almost continuously and must not be transferred from one solution to another. The swabs can be thrown away after use and the brush thoroughly washed before reuse. This practice is valuable in the first toning stages of all three colors.

Swab the back to remove adherent back coating which may cause fading by contamination.

Keep the toning solutions cool. Their temperatures should not exceed 70°F. With higher temperatures, loss of high lights may occur.

Immersion in the *A* solution should be continued for at least 15 min. and, in any case, until all the black silver is removed. When a print is thoroughly toned, it will appear as a light greenish-brown image. It is then placed in running water and thoroughly washed for about 10 min. As an alternative the print may be washed in five complete changes of water in a tray. The washing operation after toning is of the greatest importance and must not be slighted.

It is also very essential that the hands be kept clean at all times in order not to contaminate one solution by transferring another solution to it.

After this washing, the red image is placed in the red toner *B* and allowed to tone for about 10 min. (the toning proceeds to completion in this time; a little longer time in the bath will do no harm). The solution is then poured off for use a second time, and the print is immersed for 3 min. in a standard hypo solution. It is now washed for about 15 min. in running water or in five or six complete changes of water. It is then ready for assembling.

Similarly the blue image is placed in the blue toner *B* and allowed to remain about 10 min., after which the toner is poured off for use a second time and the print is immersed in a tray of weak hydrochloric acid solution for about 1 min.: Use one part dilute solution with two parts water. The print is thoroughly washed in running water for about 10 min. or in five complete changes of water, after which it is placed in a tray containing standard hypo solution, made up as directed, until greenish tones have changed to blue. It is then washed for about 20 min. or in six complete changes of water. It is then ready for assembling.

Toning the Yellow Image.—The yellow toning solution (yellow toner *A*) is supplied in two solutions and must be made ready for use as described. The print to be toned yellow is immersed in this solution for about 10 min. This work may be carried on simultaneously with the blue and red toning operations, separate trays being used.

After about 15 min. the solution is poured off into a graduate, and 10 cc. (3 drams) standard hypo solution is added to every 50 cc. (2 oz.) working solution, and thoroughly mixed. Next wash the print for 1 min. in running water, or in one complete change of water, return it to the tray and pour the solution back on the print. The operation should be done quickly, and the tray should be vigorously rocked for about 1 min. to prevent any streaking of the yellow image. If some degree of streaking is apparent at this point and is not too pronounced, it may be ignored. If care is taken, however, no difficulty will be experienced. The print is now allowed to remain in the solution for about 3 min., after which the solution is discarded, the print is washed for 1 or 2 min. in clear water, and then it is immersed for about 1 min. in a solution made up of one part standard hypo solution and three parts water. Do not keep the print longer than 1 min. in this solution, as the image at this stage is slightly soluble in hypo and high-light detail may be lost thereby. Wash the film immediately for not less than 20 min. in running water or in five or six complete changes of water in a tray.

The yellow image, after thorough washing, is immersed for about 2 min. in the yellow toner B, and then washed in running water for about 20 min. or in six complete changes of water in a tray. It is then ready for assembling.

Assembling the Three-color Print.—The third step in making color prints by the Chromatone process is assembling the finished photograph.

The three-color images are now registered on a gelatin-coated paper (Chromatone backing paper) which has been previously soaked thoroughly in water. Lay the backing paper, gelatin side up, on a clean ferrotype tin, clean glass or Masonite tempered hard board, or on any flat waterproof surface. The yellow image is placed first on the paper and squeegeed firmly into place, emulsion side down, and allowed to remain for a few minutes to prevent sliding while registering. The red image is then placed on top of the yellow, pushed carefully into register, squeegeed lightly, the register checked, adjusted if necessary, and the red image squeegeed firmly into place. If at this point the two images do not appear exactly in register, the red sheet may be peeled off carefully, remoistened, and registered again. It will be found easier to register the red and yellow images if they are viewed through a light-blue filter.

The blue image is then superimposed upon the other two, precisely as described above, completing the color print; all prints emulsion side down.

The collodion support of the emulsion, although extremely thin and transparent, is to some extent objectionable, not only because it reduces the brilliancy of the final image, but also because it tends to curl inward in drying and prevents the prints laying absolutely flat. This difficulty can be avoided by removing the collodion support after each transfer by dissolving it with acetone. This is best done by allowing each transfer to practically dry before removing the collodion in order to avoid any damage to the gelatin emulsion. If the removal of the collodion is decided upon, it is advisable to use a weak gelatin solution between transfers to produce a more complete adhesion of the partial images.

With this process, as well as with the others so far described, short cuts are not advisable and instructions issued by the manufacturers of the materials are usually published after careful studies and should therefore be scrupulously adhered to in order to avoid waste and disappointments.

Since variations are introduced from time to time in the quality of the material, it is advisable to request up to date information from the manufacturers.

Gelatin Relief with Color Pigment in Suspension. *Duxochrome.*—Several years ago H. J. C. Deeks introduced a process for color prints on paper consisting of silver bromide emulsions coated on thin celluloids from which the emulsion could be stripped at a later stage. The emulsion carried in suspension, the appropriate color pigments and three different emulsions were supplied, each one with the corresponding complementary colors—yellow, blue-green, and magenta. The printing exposure for each emulsion was determined by comparison with a standard bromide paper. The exposure, of course, was made through the celluloid support and the development was carried out with a tanning developer such as

Water	1000	cc.
Metol	1.5	g.
Hydroquinone	1.5	g.
Sodium sulphite (dry)	2	g.
Sodium carbonate (dry)	17.5	g.
Potassium bromide	1.5	g.

or

Water	1000	cc.
Hydroquinone	4	g.
Sodium sulphite (dry)	2	g.
Sodium carbonate (dry)	15.5	g.
Potassium bromide	1	g.

or

Water	1000	cc.
Pyrocatechin	2	g.
Sodium sulphite (dry)	2	g.
Sodium hydroxide	1.5	g.
Potassium bromide	1	g.

or

Water	1000	cc.
Pyrogallol	2	g.
Sodium sulphite (dry)	16	g.
Sodium carbonate (dry)	8	g.
Potassium bromide	0.5	g.

These developers do not keep because of the small quantity of sulphite and should therefore be made up just before use.

Immediately after development and without fixing, the silver images were passed into a bath of hot water in which the emulsion, not affected by the tanning action of the developer, washed away, leaving the colored image in relief. The black silver image was subsequently removed by any of the well-known reducers. The color images were later transferred and registered on a final support in the order—yellow, magenta, and blue-green.

Although remarkably beautiful results were obtained from this process, it did not meet with any degree of success for reasons not attributable to the process itself.

Recently a very similar process has originated in Germany and is being marketed throughout the world under the trade name Duxochrome.

The Duxochrome color films are obtainable in packages containing an equal amount of the three colors. The speed of Duxochrome film is approximately that of an ordinary bromide paper. Exposure for this film also must be made through the celluloid support, and the magenta and yellow emulsions require appreciably longer exposure than the blue. The ratio of exposure is, roughly; blue, 1; magenta, 2; yellow, 3. The developer recommended is the one supplied by the manufacturer of the color film and is put up in two separate packages to make up stock solutions A and B.

The processing of Duxochrome film is best carried out by first preparing the various solutions necessary in a stock form from which the working solutions can be quickly prepared by simple dilution. The following stock solutions are necessary:

Stock solution A and B are made up in accordance with directions in the container.

STOCK SOLUTION *C*

Potassium metabisulphite	12 oz.
Plain water (warm)	24 oz.

STOCK SOLUTION *D*

Potassium ferricyanide	1 oz.
Plain water (warm)	36 oz.

STOCK SOLUTION *E*

Glacial acetic acid	4 oz.
Plain water (warm)	24 oz.
Copper sulphate (c.p.)	3 oz.

STOCK SOLUTION *F*

Ammonium chloride	12 oz.
Plain water (warm)	24 oz.

STOCK SOLUTION *H*

Hypo crystals	16 oz.
Warm water to make	32 oz.

The working developer is made up by taking

Stock solution *A*	2 parts
Stock solution *B*	2 parts
Distilled water	20 parts

Satisfactory results could be obtained also by using the tanning developer formulas given above.

The time of development with the Duxochrome developer is of the order of 4 min. at 70°F. when prints are made from normal negatives obtained directly from the original subject and processed to about gamma of unity or slightly less. When, however, the printing is made from color-separation negatives of Kodachrome or Dufay films, the required development time of the positive might be appreciably shorter since the original color transparency is ordinarily very contrasty. The correct time of development must be ascertained in such cases by trial.

When dealing with very thin negatives an increase of contrast can be obtained by increasing the strength of the developer such as, for instance,

Stock solutions *A*	3 parts
Stock solutions *B*	3 parts
Water	20 parts

In addition the time of development can also be appreciably increased.

It is imperative that the Duxochrome developer be made up with distilled water. The development of the three-color films must be carried out with as much uniformity as possible, either by developing the three films all together with a fair amount of uniform agitation or by developing each film individually in fresh developer for the same length of time and same agitation.

The degree of development cannot be judged by the appearance of the image as in the case of bromide papers because the exposure was made through the celluloid support. Furthermore, under the darkroom safe light the images would appear appreciably different because of the color pigments in the emulsion.

Following development, the color films should be quickly passed, without rinsing, into a stop bath as follows:

Stock solution *F*	2 oz.
Stock solution *H*	2 oz.
Water	32 oz.

The films can remain in this bath for only a few seconds, after which they should be transferred to the fixing bath made up as follows:

Stock solution *H*	4 oz.
Stock solution *C*	½ oz.
Water	4 oz.

The time of fixing is about 10 min., and the films should be moved about occasionally. The following operations can be now carried out in full daylight:

After fixing, the color films should be washed in running water for about 3 min.

The next operation is the removal of the emulsion which has not been affected by the developer. This is obtained by immersing the color films in a tray of hot water, at about 125°F., to which a few drops of glacial acetic acid have been added.

It is not advisable to treat the three films all together because of the danger of damaging the delicate relief image by sliding one over another. The development of each film in hot water can be carried out in succession or in separate trays. Each film should be given a few rinses in hot clean water until no appreciable trace of color drains out.

The bleaching of the silver image is next carried out in a solution made up as follows:

Stock solution *H*	2 oz.
Stock solution *D*	2 oz.
Water	8 oz.

The bleaching time is about 5 min., or it should be continued until every trace of black silver has disappeared.

Following the bleach, the image should be given a wash of 5 or 10 min. in running water.

At this stage both the yellow and magenta images can be put away to dry. The blue-green image, however, should be given a 3-min. treatment in a solution made up as follows:

Stock solution *E*	1 oz.
Water	8 oz.

Then it should be briefly rinsed in cold water, after which it can be also put away to dry.

A certain amount of correction to improve the color balance can be carried out before the emulsions are dry. For this purpose it is best to superimpose the three wet images together on the bottom of a white enameled tray to judge the over-all balance. In case of a predominance of one color that particular film can be further treated in hot water until reduced sufficiently. It is best, however, to avoid this partial correction as much as possible.

The assembly of the three colored images on the final paper is carried out in the following manner: The yellow film and a piece of final paper of the correct size are immersed in cold water for about 5 min. The two are withdrawn together carefully, avoiding air bells, and squeegeed with a flat squeegee to remove the excess water. Then the two are placed between blotting paper under a heavy pressure, such as a letterpress. After about 10 min. the sandwich is removed from under pressure and placed to dry in a warm stream of air. When completely dry, the celluloid support will readily detach, leaving the yellow image on the final paper.

The blue film is now soaked in cold water for about 5 min., after which the paper carrying the yellow image is also passed into cold water for exactly 1 min. and the two brought into contact and removed together from water, carefully avoiding air bells. The two are squeegeed lightly together, carefully expelling any air bubbles which might exist, and the correct registration is assured by sliding the film gently. Again the sandwich is placed between blotting paper and under pressure for another 10 min. The drying is then done by gentle heat.

The red image is finally transferred to the other two in the same manner.

The surface of the finished colored print will assume a semimatte effect if soaked for several minutes in warm water and allowed to dry in cool air.

The Duxochrome process lends itself to the making of color transparencies.

The material for this process is marketed in the United States under the trade name of Colorstil by Ruthenberg Color Photography Company, Hollywood, Calif.

Color Prints by Dye-mordanting Process.—There are metallic compounds which have a strong affinity for basic dyes. This property has been made use of for producing color prints on paper as well as transparencies, although the process lends itself much more readily for the making of color transparencies.

Copper mordant is very probably the most satisfactory, and it is the one used extensively by Uvachrome. A satisfactory formula is one published by Namias[1] and modified by Christensen in 1925. This can be made up in stock solution as follows:

STOCK SOLUTION *A*

Sodium citrate	37.5	g.
Copper sulphate (c.p.)	3.4	g.
Water	1000	cc.

STOCK SOLUTION *B*

Potassium ferricyanide	4	g.
Water	40	cc.

For use:

Stock solution *A*	130	cc.
Stock solution *B*	5	cc.

The printing is best made on positive films and the image should be decidedly on the thin side when viewed by transmitted light. With a little experience, the strength of images can be readily determined.

A satisfactory developer for a positive film is as follows:

Pyrocatechin	10	g.
Sodium sulphite	25	g.
Potassium carbonate	25	g.
Potassium bromide	0.5	g.
Water	500	cc.

For use:

Stock solution	1	part
Water	7	parts

Develop films until the right contrast is obtained.

The fixing of the positive films can be carried out in an ordinary acid fixing bath following by a washing for about 20 min. The positives are bleached in the mordant bath made up as given above. Although the bleaching can be completed in about 4 or 5 min., the action should be allowed to continue for 8 or 10 min. to make sure that every trace of silver has been converted.

The positives should be washed again for about 15 min., after which each positive will be passed into appropriate dye solution. Dyes satisfactory for this process are the following:

FOR BLUE

Methylene blue H.G.G.	1.4	g.
Glacial acetic acid	6	cc.
Water	1125	cc.

FOR MAGENTA

Pyronin red G (300 per cent)	8	g.
Glacial acetic acid	12	cc.
Water	1125	cc.

FOR YELLOW

Theoflavin yellow	6	g.
Glacial acetic acid	12	cc.
Water	1125	cc.

[1] NAMIAS, R., La fotographia a colori, 5th ed., II Progresso Fotografico (1930).

The positive film should be left in a dye bath for approximately 10 min. Following a brief rinse, it can be passed into a clearing bath for about 2 min. and finally washed in several changes of water for about 10 min. It is not advisable to wash the positive in running water. The clearing bath is made up as follows:

Hypo	50 g.
Sodium chloride	25 g.
Water	500 cc.

The assembly of the color positives on a final paper support can be carried out as follows: A gelatin-coated paper, which could be an ordinary fixed-out bromide of smooth surface, is first thoroughly soaked in water and finally passed into a tray containing a weak gelatin solution such as:

Nelson gelatin	1 oz.
Water	32 oz.

The celluloid containing the blue image is also passed into the tray of gelatin and brought into contact with the bromide paper, emulsion to emulsion, and the two withdrawn, avoiding air bells. The two are now thoroughly squeegeed together to expel any adhering air bells and the surplus gelatin. Following this, the two can be placed under pressure for a few minutes and then allowed to dry in open air.

When completely dry, the celluloid backing of the blue image must be removed by treating it with acetone. This operation is not difficult as it is only necessary to moisten the celluloid backing with acetone, after which the celluloid can be readily scraped off. After wiping the surface off two or three times with a rag soaked in acetone, the surface is ready for transfer of the second image, which may be either the yellow or the red. Transfer of the yellow and red should also be done in a solution of gelatin to assure perfect adhesion between images.

This process appears complicated, but beautiful results can readily be obtained. It must be born in mind, however, that basic dyes are not so fast to light as acid dyes and therefore prints made with basic dyes should not be unduly exposed to direct sunlight.

Color Transparencies.—Color transparencies to be viewed by transmitted light or suitable for projection can be obtained by any of the processes so far described. It is important to note, however, that not only must the positive images be printed stronger but the contrast also must be practically doubled as compared with the paper prints. This becomes immediately obvious by considering the fact that in the case of the paper print the light is absorbed by the color layer in passing through, and absorbed again when reflected back by the paper base. In this manner the density of the image has a double effect.

Within moderate values of densities the contrast of the photographic image to be viewed by reflected light is approximately twice as much when compared with transmitted light.

Since the color pictures to be viewed as transparencies are ordinarily mounted between glasses, it is often very convenient to develop one color image to one glass and another one to another glass to be mounted face to face with the first one. The third image on a thin celluloid base can then be mounted in register in between.

If the transparencies are made entirely by the carbro process, the intermediate step of developing the color tissues on a transparent celluloid base for two of the images can be omitted by developing them directly on the final glass plates, which must naturally have a gelatin coating for best results. The third color, preferably the yellow, will be developed on the celluloid support as usual and finally transferred to one or the other of the two images developed on glass. Since the two glass plates will be ultimately bound together, emulsion to emulsion, one of the two images developed on glass must be reversed with respect to the other.

It is recommended that for the yellow image a specially transparent yellow tissue be used instead of the standard yellow ordinarily employed for paper prints.

Other alternative arrangements suggest themselves. For instance, the blue-green image could be obtained by iron toning, and the magenta and yellow either by dye transfer or by the carbro method. A suitable formula for producing very acceptable blue-green images by an iron toning is the following:

Ammonium persulphate	1	g.
Ferric alum (ferric ammonium sulphate)	2.5	g.
Oxalic acid	6	g.
Potassium ferricyanide	2	g.
Ammonium alum	10	g.
Hydrochloric acid (10 per cent)	2	cc.
Water to make	2000	cc.

The method of compounding this bath is rather important. Each chemical should be dissolved separately in a small quantity of warm water, allowing it to cool and then filtering it into a tank in the order given above—with the water added to make the required volume. A properly compounded bath should be pale yellow and perfectly clear. The ordinary toning time is about 10 min. Since this toning bath has a strong intensifying action, the original positive must be rather thin.

It is not, in general, recommended, however, to make transparencies by combining various processes because it is usually difficult to obtain an over-all satisfactory contrast except by very careful study of the chemical action of each method employed.

Additive Processes.—The additive process which permits color reproductions to be obtained by the addition of color lights has found extensive applications for color transparencies. As far as the color prints on paper are concerned, however, it has not met with any degree of success, although several attempts have been made from time to time.

The chief drawback of any additive process is the great waste of light encountered in viewing the final color image. This point becomes immediately apparent if we consider the additive synthesis obtained by means of three black-and-white positives made from the original three color-separation negatives, these positives being projected by illuminating each one of them with light of the proper color.

When a single source of light is available, it simply means that the source of light must be split up in three components and into each component the appropriate projection filter introduced. If it is assumed, for instance, that each filter will transmit only one-third of the white light directed on it, then the total light available on the screen will be approximately one-third of the light from the original source. In practice this efficiency is never reached, and ordinarily the total amount of light available will be nearer to one-fourth of the total light emitted by the source or even less.

Although theoretically both additive and subtractive processes are strictly identical, in practice the additive process is capable of permitting far more faithful results than the subtractive process if the waste of light is not taken into consideration. This, however, is not always the case, particularly in connection with motion pictures where the amount of light available must be utilized with the greatest possible efficiency. In such case the tendency is to reach a compromise between quality of results and efficiency. This is done by utilizing very diluted projection filters and very thin positives. When a suitable compromise is reached, it is ordinarily found that the results are very comparable with the subtractive process or not as good. Since mechanical difficulties are introduced by the requirement imposed by the additive process of having to split up the light source, this process is invariably thrown into discard.

In the case of single transparencies to be viewed visually, the so-called "screen plates" and films in which the three-color filters are incorporated with the emulsion in a regular or irregular pattern, a fairly high degree of success has been achieved. In this class can be listed the Lumière Autochrome plate and Filmcolor, and the Agfa color plate. These three types carry the color filter elements coated on the support in irregular mixture of very small transparent elements, stained with the three primary colors. On this color screen layer, there is a protective coating and then the panchromatic emulsion. The exposure of these plates or films is made through the supports.

The processing of screen plates or film is very simple and consists in first developing the original exposure, and then, without fixing, the developed silver image is removed by a suitable bleach. The balance of emulsion, which was not affected by the first development, is exposed again to a white light and redeveloped, resulting in a final positive image.

The reversal process, in order to be satisfactory, requires that the original exposure be kept within fairly narrow limits in order to leave sufficient emulsion to later produce the positive image. The development also must be carefully carried out as very little latitude is permissible.

The manufacturers of these materials issue complete instructions to be found included in each package, and it is strongly recommended that these instructions be carefully followed.

In order to permit an exposure under different light conditions, suitable compensating filters are necessary; these filters can be obtained commercially from the manufacturers. To assure correct results, compensating filters appropriate to each light source must be used in accordance with the manufacturer's instructions.

Agfa Screen Plate.—The following instructions in condensed form cover the processing of the Agfa color plate, and for additional informations the reader should refer to the instructions supplied with the negative material.

FIRST DEVELOPER

Water	1000	cc.
Metol	3.25	g.
Sodium sulphite (dry)	25	g.
Hydroquinone	1	g.
Potassium bromide	1.5	g.
Ammonia (spec. gr. 1.91)	7.5	cc.

For a correctly exposed plate, the normal time of development will be approximately 3 min. at 65°F. About 2 oz. of the above developer will be necessary to develop a 3¼- by 4¼-in. plate. For larger plates the quantity of developer should be increased in proportion. This developer can be used also for second development, but, as it loses strength by the evaporation of ammonia, it should be discarded after the second development.

When the first development is complete, the plate should be rinsed for about 1 min. in a large tray of water, or running water if it is conveniently at hand, and then immersed in the reversing bath made up as follows:

Water	900	cc.
Potassium bichromate	50.6	g.
Sulphuric acid (c.p.)	110	cc.

This is a stock solution; for use take 1 part solution to 10 parts water.

A few seconds after the plate has been immersed in the reversing solution, the white light can be turned on and the processing continued under normal white light. The reversal will be complete in about 2 or 3 min.; the plate should be washed in running water for another 2 or 3 min. and then immersed again in the developer and left there until the remaining emulsion is completely blackened. The plate should now be given a final wash in running water and placed to dry.

Varnishing the emulsion of the plate with a 3 per cent solution of gum dammar in benzol is recommended. The varnishing should be done by pouring a small quantity in one corner and then gradually tilting the plate to allow the varnish to flow throughout the surface, after which the surplus varnish can be drained back into the bottle.

The brilliancy of a color plate can be increased by intensification, and for this purpose the Agfa mercury intensifier put up for the purpose will be found very convenient. Intensification, of course, should be done before varnishing the emulsion of the plate.

If the original exposure of a color plate has been too great, the final result will be a thin positive after the reversal, and conversely, if not enough exposure was given originally, the final positive will be very dark. In the previous case some correction can be obtained by the intensification method already described, while in the latter case, some kind of compromise could be obtained by reducing chemically the final positive. In general, however, the reduction of the color plate does not lead to successful results, and it is best to control the original exposure by correctly measuring the light value by means of an exposure meter.

Lumière Autochrome Plates and Filmcolor.—The Lumière Autochrome plates and Filmcolor can be processed in the same type of developer and reversal bath as recommended for the Agfa color plate.

The manufacturers, however, recommend the following developer as the most suitable:

Distilled water	1000 cc.
Metoquinone (quinomet)	15 g.
Sodium sulphite (dry)	100 g.
Ammonia (sp. gr. 22° Baumé)	32 cc.
Potassium bromide	16 g.

For second development it is recommended to use an Amidol developer of the following composition:

Water	50 cc.
Sodium sulphite (dry)	1500 g.
Amidol (Dinol)	2½ g.

Intensification can be carried out with mercury intensifier. The Lumière Autochrome plate also can be varnished with gum dammar as described previously, although this is not necessary with color film.

It is possible to make color-separation negatives from Agfa color plates as well as from Lumière color plates and film, and for the purpose very sharp filters should be used. The most suitable are the Wratten filter Nos. 29, 61, and 50. In general, however, the results obtainable by using color screen plates and film as originals do not approach in the least the results obtainable by making color-separation negatives directly from the original subject.

Dufaycolor Film.—Of late Dufaycolor film has come into prominent use. This film is made up essentially in the same manner as the Lumière Filmcolor with the exception of the color-filter elements which consist of a geometric pattern of small squares of the three primary colors, upon which is the regular panchromatic emulsion.

In the same way as the color-screen material previously described, the Dufaycolor film requires special compensating filters when the exposure is made with various light sources. The processing also is carried out in an essentially similar manner: *i.e.*, first development, followed by a bleach, and a second development.

For the Dufaycolor film the following method of processing is recommended:

Water	100 cc.
Metol	1 g.
Sodium sulphite (dry)	50 g.
Hydroquinone	8 g.
Sodium carbonate (dry)	35 g.
Potassium bromide	5 g.
Potassium thiocyanate	9 g.

The time of development may vary from 4 to 6 min., according to the amount of exposure, at about 68°F.

After a brief rinse in water, the Dufaycolor film is passed into a bleaching bath made up as follows:

Water	1000 cc.
Potassium bichromate	5 g.
Sulphuric acid (commercial grade of sp. gr. 1.87)	10 cc.

The bleaching will be completed in about 4 min., after which the film can be given a brief wash for about 2 min. and then immersed in a clear bath composed of

Sodium bisulphite	25 g.
Water	1000 cc.

This immersion lasts for about 2 min.; the film is again washed for 2 or 3 min. The purpose of the clearing bath is to remove any yellow stain of potassium bichromate.

After the film has been immersed in the bleaching solution, the white light can be turned on and the bleaching completed in diffused white light.

For second development any MQ developer can be used, the following being recommended:

Water	1000 cc.
Metol	1 g.
Sodium sulphite (dry)	50 g.
Hydroquinone	5 g.
Sodium carbonate (dry)	20 g.
Potassium bromide	1 g.

The bleaching of the film can be carried out with a solution of potassium permanganate instead of bichromate. The following is a suitable solution:

Water	1000 cc.
Potassium permanganate	3 g.
Sulphuric acid (specific gravity 1.87)	10 cc.

The bleaching in permanganate, however, must be preceded by a brief treatment in the following hardening bath to avoid frilling:

Water	1000 cc.
Formalin (40%)	28 cc.
Sodium hydroxide	1.5 g.
Sodium sulphate	150 g.

The exposure to light after bleaching can be done with incandescent light instead of diffuse daylight. One minute of exposure at a distance of 12 in. from a 100-watt lamp will be found sufficient.

The exposure to white light can be omitted if the second developer is replaced by the following chemical reversal bath:

Water	1000 cc.
Sodium hydrosulphite	14 g.
Sodium bisulphite	10 g.

One minute of treatment will be sufficient. This bath does not keep and it must be made up just before use.

Following the second development or reversal the film must be again washed for 2 or 3 min. and fixed in a hardening bath made up as follows:

Water	1000 cc.
Hypo	360 g.
Potassium metabisulphite	12 g.

Dissolve separately:

Water	1000 cc.
Chrome alum	10 g.

This should be added to the first solution. Fixing should be followed by a final wash for about 15 min.

Dufaycolor film also can be intensified and reduced. The following mercury intensifier is recommended:

Water	1000 cc.
Mercury bichloride	65 g.
Ammonium chloride	50 g.

The film should be left in this bath until entirely white. This requires 3 or 4 min., followed by washing in running water for about 15 min., after which the emulsion should be blackened in a solution as follows:

Water	1000 cc.
Sodium sulphite (dry)	50 g.

The action of the sodium sulphite can be stopped when the right degree of intensification has been obtained.

A suitable reducing formula for Dufaycolor film follows:

SOLUTION *A*

Water	1000 cc.
Potassium ferricyanide	40 g.

SOLUTION *B*

Water	1000 cc.
Hypo	200 g.

For use take equal parts of *A* and *B* and dilute with 10 parts of water. After sufficient reduction, the films should be thoroughly washed in running water.

Although it is satisfactory to intensify the Dufaycolor film to increase the brilliancy, the reduction is not recommended, and it is best to calculate the original exposure correctly by means of an exposure meter.

To make color-separation negatives from Dufaycolor film for color prints on paper by any of the subtractive processes previously described, sharp cutoff filters must be used. The filters recommended for this purpose are the Dufay separation filters, although satisfactory results can be obtained by using for the red the Wratten 25 plus 33; for the green Wratten 52 plus 58; for the blue Wratten 34 plus 47.

Very satisfactory duplication of Agfa color plates, Lumière Autochrome plates and films, and Dufaycolor films cannot be made. When an original subject is to be photographed with the idea in view of making several duplicate color transparencies, it is best to resort to another color process which permits any number of duplicates to be obtained.   This is the Finlay color process.

Finlay Process.—The Finlay color process is identical with the previously described screen color plates with the exception that the color-screen elements are independent of the panchromatic negative emulsion and are carried to a separate glass plate (taking screen) where the color elements are disposed in geometrical pattern in small squares similar to the Dufaycolor film.   The usual procedure is to place the color-taking screen in contact with the plate carrying a panchromatic emulsion and expose the two together in an ordinary camera with the glass side of the taking screen toward the lens.   The contact between the taking screen and the panchromatic emulsion must be fairly good, otherwise diffusion and poor color results will be obtained.

Suitable panchromatic plates for the above purpose are manufactured by Ilford in England and by Eastman in the United States; they are marketed as a special Finlay-Ilford panchromatic plate and Finlay-Eastman panchromatic plate.   Suitable compensating filters for different types of lights are also available with this process.

After exposure, the panchromatic plate is removed from contact with the color-taking screen and developed in the usual manner.   When examined with a magnifying glass, the developed negative plate shows an image broken up into very small squares very similar to the usual photomechanical process screen used for half-tone printing in book illustrations.

If now a positive transparency plate is placed in contact with the negative and printed under artificial light in intimate contact in a printing frame, the positive image that is obtained will also have the image broken up into minute squares, just as the original.

To reproduce the original colors, the positive plate is now placed in intimate contact with a positive viewing screen of very much similar composition to the original color-taking screen and having color elements of exactly the same size as the original color-taking screen.

The operation of registering the positive plate with the positive viewing screen requires a little experience, but it represents no great difficulties.   When satisfactory registration has been obtained, as depicted by natural colors showing up satisfactorily by transmitted light, the two are permanently bound together.

It is obvious that any number of positive prints can be obtained in this way from the original negative on ordinary positive plates, each of which can be assembled together with its own viewing screen, assuring identical results.

There are certain definite advantages with the Finlay color process as compared with the other additive process already described.   These advantages consist mainly in the facts that the negative emulsion is a standard panchromatic emulsion of very high gradation and an appreciable latitude of exposure is permissible since one is not concerned with the amount of emulsion left unexposed, this balance of emulsion not being used to reproduce a positive by reversal methods.

For the purpose of color reproduction on paper, color-separation negatives from the Finlay color transparency can be made up also by rephotographing the transparency through sharp separation filters such as the Wratten Nos. 29, 50, and 61. However, the most satisfactory method consists in utilizing a special blocking-out screen manufactured exclusively for the purpose of photomechanical reproduction, without any additional use of color-separation filters.   Two of these block-out filters are available.   One of the screens is used for both the red and the blue printer and the other for the yellow printer.

Because of better emulsion qualities permitted with the Finlay color process and the use of block-out screens, color reproduction on paper from this process can be obtained of a quality superior to that of the other screen plates and film on the market.

The only disadvantage of the Finlay process is in the fact that the individual color elements are fairly coarse, equivalent to about a 175-line half-tone screen.

With the Dufaycolor film, Lumière Autochrome plate and Filmcolor and the Agfa color plate, a slight degree of enlargement in reproduction is permissible before the broken-up structure of the image begins to show up. With the Finlay process, however, this is not permissible as the 175-line half-tone dot formation is just small enough to be invisible when viewed at normal distance, but any slight enlargement would show up the screen immediately.

The processing of both the negative and positive plates for the Finlay process is best carried out in the developers recommended by both the Eastman and Ilford companies for their negative and positive material.

Color Cinematography.—The successful production of color transparencies by both the additive and subtractive processes has led to a great variety of attempts to apply these processes to motion-picture photography. The degree of success along this line of activity has been rather limited.

While the additive process is in itself the simplest, from the laboratory standpoint, since the film does not need to be colored, it is nevertheless the least successful from the standpoint of photographic and projection requirements. The reason lies with the difficulty of producing three separate images side by side through the same optical system free of parallax, which is unavoidable in multiple optical combinations. Similar optical systems must be also employed in projection, which means low light efficiency caused by the necessity of splitting up the total light source into three different components, each of which must be intercepted by the necessary primary filter.

The various optical systems schemed out for the additive synthesis do not lend themselves readily to the projection of ordinary black and white. This means that the optical system must be changed during the transition period from color-additive projection to standard black-and-white projection. As a matter of fact successful optical systems which permit obtaining simultaneously three sharp images without parallax and within the narrow space demanded by the internal arrangement of a motion-picture camera, and also suitable for projection are not available as yet. Other systems which involve running both the camera and projector at a double or triple speed by arranging the three-color-separation negatives and positives one after the other, are not practical, because they demand duplicate apparatus in theaters, unless such color systems could be universally adopted and made to supplant completely black-and-white projection.

Possibly the attempt nearest to success has been by means of the Dufaycolor film, which can be exposed through the ordinary camera and projected through the standard projector, except that in this case also, an adequate amount of light on the screen can only be obtained by both powerful arc lights and extremely thin positive films. Within this class can also be included the lenticular type of film, based on the Keller-Dorian and Berthon patents, with the exception that this film needs an additional projection filter, which, of course, could be easily swung in position in front of the projection lens when required.

Most successful have been subtractive processes in which the color positive is produced either by dye transfer or by combination of chemical toning, dye toning, and dye transfer.

The Technicolor process,[1] which really is the only one being used to any great extent today, is based solely on the dye-transfer method by means of wash-off relief matrices. The three-color separation negatives of Technicolor are produced by a

[1] BALL, I. A., The Technicolor Process, *J. Soc. Motion Picture Engrs.*, August, 1935, No. 2, p. 127.

combination of a bipack and a third separate film. The light beam emitted from the lens is split up by a glass cube made up of two right-angled prisms cemented along the hypotenuse, this being slightly coated with a reflecting metal, such as gold or silver, to a definite reflection-transmission ratio. The lenses of a Technicolor camera are specially designed to work in connection with the prism block. ˙ The fact that the dyes have a slight tendency to wander and the difficulty of transferring three-dye images in absolute register by automatic means tend to make any process of this type not quite so critically sharp as black and white. In addition, one of the negatives is in itself slightly diffused, being the back negative of the bipack.

Motion-picture film in color, by the combination of dye mordant and dye transfer, is ordinarily carried out by using a positive film coated with emulsion on both sides with the two most important colors, magenta and blue-green, printed back to back. These two-color images are produced by first treating the silver images with a mordant, such as copper or iodine, then floating each side on the appropriate basic dye bath. The third color, yellow, is obtained by transferring a yellow dye to one side or the other, by means of a wash-off relief matrix, in substantially the same way as is done with Technicolor. Color-positive films by the Brewster and Cinecolor processes are somewhat along these lines.

The positive blue image can also be produced by strictly chemical toning, such as iron toning described before; the magenta can be produced by dye mordant, and the yellow by dye transfer.

Presumably, the magenta and blue-green images on the double-coated stock could also be produced by means of the Chromatone toning process, by first bleaching the complete film in the red and blue Chromatone toner *A*, and then floating each side onto the appropriate *B* toner. In this case also the yellow would have to be applied by transfer.

Color images produced by chemical toning or by dye mordant are usually sharper than images produced by dye transfer. However, the problem of correctly printing the partial images in exact register is common to both methods.

Very promising are the new tripack subtractive films issued by Eastman Kodak, under the trade name Kodachrome, and by Agfa, under the name new Agfacolor. The three emulsions in these tripacks cannot be separated.

The colors in a Kodachrome tripack are introduced in each layer after development by very elaborate and carefully controlled operations. The new Agfa color film, on the contrary, has embodied in each layer the nondiffusing color formers. When the film is developed in a coupler developer, these color formers combine with the oxidation products of development to form insoluble dyes. The new Agfacolor is obtainable in both the reversal and negative-positive form. With the reversal type the coupler developer is used only during the second development, while with the negative-positive type the colors in a negative are produced during the first development, and the negative is subsequently fixed and cleared of the silver image. The positive is produced by printing this negative on a similar film, which is again submitted to the action of a coupler developer followed by fixing and removal of the silver image as done with the negative.

The new Agfacolor will probably be available in the future for making color prints on paper, as well as color motion pictures. Little is known at this time about the stability of the colors produced by this chemical method.

The complicated manufacturing process of both the Kodachrome and new Agfacolor might render these films too expensive for color-positive motion-picture releases at the present time. It is therefore very likely that the immediate use of these films will be for the purpose of replacing the multiple negatives in the present motion-picture camera, thus permitting greater speed and economy of light. The release positive prints might then be made by dye transfer or a combination of dye transfer and toning.

Another interesting process for making motion-picture prints in color is the so-called Gaspar color. With this process a special triple-layer positive film carries the corresponding dyes, which are destroyed afterward in a bleach bath and, to a degree, controlled by the density of the silver image.

Bibliography

Periodicals:

MATTHEWS, GLENN E.: Processes of Photography in Natural Colors, *J. Soc. Motion Picture Engrs.*, **15,** 188–219 (1931). This article contains a large list of references.

DUBRAY, J. A.: The Morgane Color Process, *J. Soc. Motion Picture Engrs.*, **20,** 403 (1933).

SPENCER, D. A.: *Phot. J.*, July, 1935, p. 377; *Penrose Ann.* (1938).

MANNES, L. D., and L. GODOWSKY: The Kodachrome Process, *J. Soc. Motion Picture Engrs.*, **24,** 65 (1935).

BALL, I. A.: The Technicolor Process, *J. Soc. Motion Picture Engrs.*, **24,** 127 (1935).

HAMLIN, L.: Composition of Baths for Color Sensitizing by Bathing, *Am. Phot.*, December, 1935, p. 784.

STRONG, J.: On a Method of Decreasing the Reflection from Non-metallic Substances, *J. Optical Soc. Am.*, **26,** 73 (1936).

RENWICK, F. E.: *Phot. J.*, January, 1937.

BAUMBACH, H. L.: New Metallic Toners for Three Color Photography, *Camera*, January, 1937, p. 21.

CAPSTAFF, J. G., O. E. MILLER, and L. S. WILDER: Projection of Lenticular Color Films, *J. Soc. Motion Picture Engrs.*, **28,** 123 (1937).

HARRISON, G. B.: Negative-positive Processing of Dufaycolor, *Phot. J.*, April, 1937, p. 250.

HARDY, A. C.: Theory of Three Color Photography, *J. Soc. Motion Picture Engrs.*, **29,** 227 (1937); **31,** 331 (1938).

FORREST, J. L., and F. M. WING: New Agfacolor Process, *J. Soc. Motion Picture Engrs.*, **29,** 248 (1937).

CECCARINI, O. O.: Color Stills, *J. Soc. Motion Picture Engrs.*, **29,** 397 (1937).

HARRISON, G. B.: Theory of Additive Three-color Photography, *Phot. J.*, December, 1937, p. 706.

Colour Photographs, Ltd.: Color Separation Negatives, *Brit. J. Almanac*, 1938, p. 385.

MORSE, R. S.: Black and White Prints from Kodachrome, *Am. Phot.*, January, 1938, p. 1.

MACADAM, D. L.: Fundamentals of Color Measurement, *J. Soc. Motion Picture Engrs.*, **31,** 343 (1938).

TRITTON, F. J.: Survey of Photographic Masking Methods for Three and Four Color Printing, *Phot. J.*, December, 1938, p. 732.

Books:

HÜBL, A. VON: "Three Color Photography," A. W. Penrose & Co., London (1915).

WALL, E. J.: "History of Three Color Photography," Am. Photographic Pub. (1925).

————: "Practical Color Photography," 2nd ed., Am. Photographic Pub. (1928).

NAMIAS, R.: La fotographia a colori, 5th ed., Il progresso Fotografia, Milan (1930).

WHEELER, O.: "Color Photography," Pitman (1935).

NEWENS, F. R.: "The Technic of Three Color Photography," Blackie & Sons, Ltd. (1936).

DUNN, C. E.: "Natural Color Processes," Am. Photographic Pub. (1936).

"The Chromotone Process," 5th ed., Defender Photo Supply Co. (1937).

SPENCER, D. A.: "Colour Photography in Practice," Pitman (1938).

HENNEY, KEITH: "Color Photography for the Amateur," McGraw (1938).

"Wratten Light Filters," Eastman Kodak Co. (1938).

CURTIS, T. S.: "Curtis Dufaycolor Printing System," T. S. Curtis Laboratories, Huntington Park, Calif.

"Modern Masking Method of Correct Color Reproduction," Eastman Kodak Co.

POTTER, R. S.: "Methods of Making Three Color Separation Negatives," Defender Photo Supply Co.

"Handbook of Physics and Chemistry," 12th ed., Chemical Rubber Pub. Co.

"Trichrome Printing by the Autotype Carbro Process," The Autotype Co., Ltd., London, and George Murphy, Inc., New York.

"Color Printing with Eastman Wash-off Relief Film," Eastman Kodak Co.

"Printing and Toning of Eastman Positive Motion Picture Film," Eastman Kodak Co.

"Practical Color Photography with Finlay Natural Color Process," Finlay Photographic Processes, Ltd.

"The Dufaycolor Manual," Dufaycolor. Inc., New York.

CHAPTER XXIII

MOTION-PICTURE PHOTOGRAPHY

By Carl Dreher

Introduction.—This chapter is limited to a description of black-and-white professional motion-picture photography as practiced in the United States. Aside from some design differences the same principles govern the art abroad, and since American practice is generally regarded as occupying a leading place, it has not been judged necessary to include data on such national peculiarities as exist.

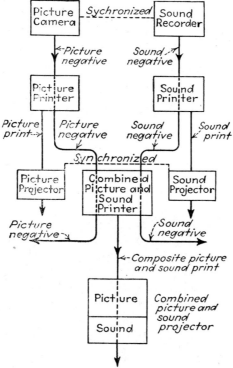

Fig. 1.—Correlation of picture and sound.

Another limitation excludes the treatment of sound recording by photographic methods, but as by far the greater part of professional motion-picture footage is now associated with sound tracks, the correlation of action and sound records will be briefly described here. In some cases, as in certain types of newsreel work and the production of sound pictures in locations where portability of equipment is essential, sound and scene are simultaneously recorded on one film, but the usual practice, illustrated in the block diagram of Fig. 1, involves separate, synchronously operated equipments for recording picture and sound, resulting in two negatives, from which separate prints, known as "dailies" or "rushes," are made for studio viewing and editing purposes. These dual prints are run on synchronized picture and sound projectors. For exhibition, however, the sound and picture negatives are printed on a single

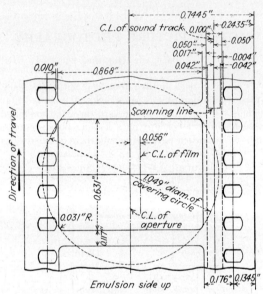

Fig. 2.—Standard film dimensions. (*Courtesy of Academy of Motion Picture Arts and Sciences.*)

film, known as a "composite" or "movietone" print, and shown by means of a combined picture and sound projector.

The standard dimensions of a composite 35-mm. print of this type appear in Fig. 2. The camera aperture dimensions, it will be noted, are 0.868 by 0.631 in. The projector aperture is sufficiently smaller (0.825 by 0.600 in.) to prevent showing the frame lines in projection. The latter dimensions therefore represent the working area of the camera field or that portion of the photographed scene which will be shown in

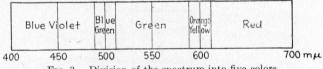

Fig. 3.—Division of the spectrum into five colors.

the theater. The 4:3 ratio of frame width to height has been found to be satisfactory from an aesthetic standpoint.

In theater projectors the picture head is located above the sound head, hence, for synchronism, the sound must lead the picture by an appropriate distance along the film, which has been fixed at 18 frames. This displacement is effected in the printing operation.

Since sound is recorded at a standard speed of 90 ft. per min., corresponding to 24 frames per second, both photography and theater projection must adhere to the same speed. Higher or lower speeds may be employed in photography, as for slow-motion effects or to give the effect of accelerated movement in chases, etc., but in either case sound cannot be synchronously recorded; hence the track must later be adjusted to the picture. Silent pictures were usually photographed at 16 frames per second, but markedly superior rendition of motion is secured at the present standard of 24 frames.

Films and Film Characteristics.—Before proceeding with a discussion of motion-picture films and their characteristics it is well to have in mind the division of the visible spectrum into five color areas, as shown in Fig. 3. The numbers at the bottom of the diagram represent wavelengths in millimicrons (one millimicron equals one-millionth of a millimeter, or 10 Ångstrom units). For a practical understanding of the spectrographic aspects of the subject the reader will frequently find it necessary to correlate the data presented, both here and in later sections of this chapter, with the color divisions of Fig. 3.

Negative Films.—The types of negative films now used in 35-mm. motion-picture photography are developments from older and simpler forms. Referring to the wedge

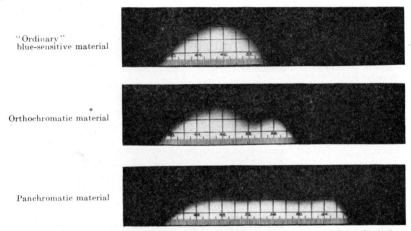

"Ordinary"
blue-sensitive material

Orthochromatic material

Panchromatic material

Fig. 4.—Spectral sensitivity of three types of photographic material for daylight.

spectrograms[1] of Fig. 4, the top one represents an "ordinary" gelatin-silver bromide emulsion, with sensitivity at a maximum in the blue region and extending on either side into the violet and the blue-green. By the addition of sensitizing dyes it became possible to extend the photographic response into the green and yellow, giving the somewhat optimistically named "orthochromatic" type of emulsion shown in the center spectrogram. The latter material would obviously render the various hues of a scene in a more nearly correct gray scale than the "ordinary" emulsion. Ortho-chromatic materials were generally used in motion-picture photography until about 1927, when the admixture of other dyes resulted in red sensitivity, theretofore lacking. This produced what is known as "panchromatic" film, which, as shown in the bottom spectrogram of Fig. 4, is sensitive throughout the visible spectrum.

More recently the principal advances in negative film materials have been in the direction of a marked increase in speed and a reduction in graininess. Since 1933 the speed of negative materials has been increased fully fourfold, thus tending to relieve the cameraman of the fear of underexposure, giving better detail in the shadows, and affording the laboratories greater development latitude. At the same time camera-

[1] While wedge spectrograms do not give absolute values of spectral sensitivity, they are useful for purposes of qualitative comparison.

men have been enabled to reduce lighting or to stop down lenses and improve depth of focus—an opportunity of which not all have taken advantage.

Reduction in grain size has entailed the use of appropriate developers, especially those of the borax type. As will appear in later sections of this chapter, improvements in lighting and chemical treatment have accompanied improvements in sensitive mate-

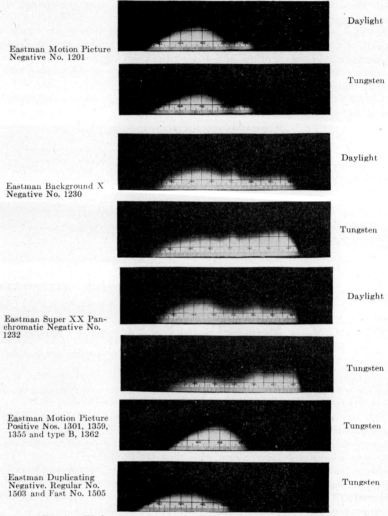

Fig. 5.—Wedge spectrograms for Eastman motion-picture films.

rials throughout motion-picture history, and if further progress is brought about in materials, it will no doubt be reflected in the associated fields of exposure and processing.

A discussion of motion-picture-film characteristics will have only academic interest unless it deals with actual materials available in the market. For this reason raw stocks supplied by the Eastman Kodak Co., the Agfa Ansco Corp., and the DuPont Film Manufacturing Corp. will be named and described on the basis of data on

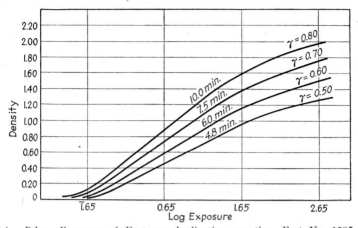

Fig. 6*A*.—*D*-log₁₀ *E* curves of Eastman duplicating negative, Fast No. 1505 (ortho-chromatic).

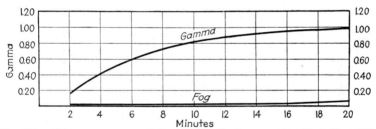

Fig. 6*B*.—Time-gamma curve of Eastman duplicating negative, Fast, No. 1505.

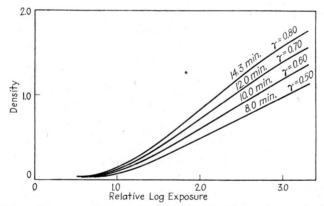

Fig. 7.—*D*-log₁₀ *E* curves of Eastman Background X Panchromatic negative No. 1230.

typical films. In addition to spectrographic information these data include—for each film—Hurter-Driffield curves of density against the logarithm of the exposure and curves showing the variation of gamma with development time.

The wedge spectrograms for Eastman motion-picture negative films, together with certain positive films to be described later, are found in Fig. 5. Except in the case of duplicating negative and all positive films, which are úsed only with artificial light, the

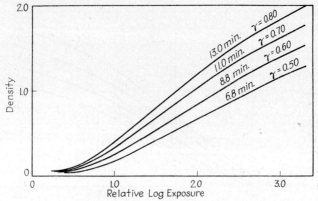

Fig. 7*A*.—*D*-log$_{10}$ *E* curves of Eastman Plus X Panchromatic negative No. 1231.

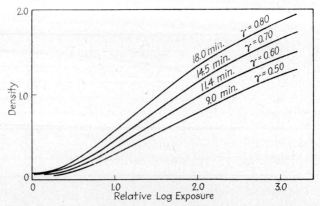

Fig. 7*B*.—*D*-log$_{10}$ *E* curves of Eastman Super XX Panchromatic negative No. 1232.

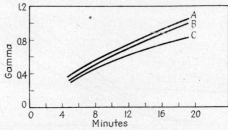

Fig. 8.—Time-gamma curves of Eastman Panchromatic negatives. *A*, Plus X No. 1231; *B*, Background X No. 1230; *C*, Super XX No. 1232.

wedge spectrograms for both daylight and tungsten exposure are given, the latter being affected by the greater proportion of red and yellow light. For the duplicating and positive materials, since they are required to reproduce only half tones, the color sensitivity is confined to a relatively narrow band.

The *D*-log *E* and time-gamma curves for the Eastman negative stocks are given in Figs. 6 through 10. Each figure contains two graphs: the *D*-log₁₀ *E* characteristics

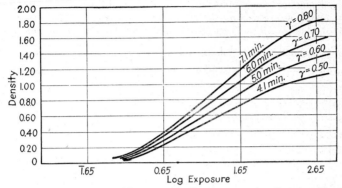

Fig. 9*A*.—*D*-log₁₀ *E* curves of Eastman duplicating negative, Regular, No. 1503.

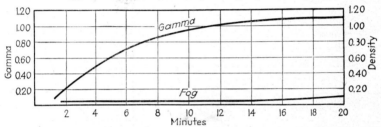

Fig. 9*B*.—Time-gamma curve of Eastman duplicating negative, Regular, No. 1503.

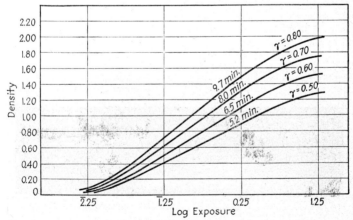

Fig. 10*A*.—*D*-log₁₀ *E* curves of Eastman motion-picture negative, No. 1201 (ortho-chromatic).

and the time-gamma curve. In all cases development was in an Elon-hydroquinone-borax developer (Formula D-76), the composition of which is given under Laboratory Practice in this chapter.[1]

[1] Since the time of development for a given gamma is influenced by such factors as temperature and degree of agitation, all time-gamma curves shown are accurate only for the conditions under which they were made and would vary somewhat in other laboratories.

The Agfa Ansco Corp. likewise supplies a full line of motion-picture films, including panchromatic, fine-grain background, title, and infrared negatives, and a positive raw stock of standard characteristics. To avoid additional duplication, only the two most important Agfa films are illustrated (Figs. 16 and 17). These are fast, fine-grain, double-coated panchromatic negatives, Nos. 153 and 356. A slower

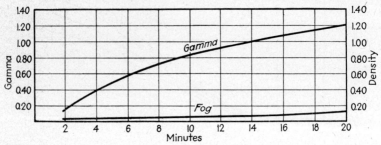

FIG. 10B.—Time-gamma curve of Eastman motion-picture negative No. 1201 (ortho-chromatic).

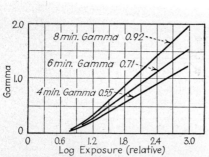

FIG. 11A.—D-log₁₀ E curves of DuPont type 112 negative (orthochromatic).

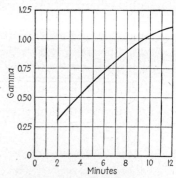

FIG. 11B.—Time-gamma curve of DuPont type 112 negative (ortho-chromatic).

FIG. 11C.—Spectrogram of DuPont type 112 orthochromatic negative (daylight).

panchromatic negative, Superpan No. 154, is not shown, but is included with 153 and 356 in a table of filter factors for Agfa negatives. (See Exterior Photography and Filters, below.)

The characteristics of the corresponding films supplied by DuPont are shown in Figs. 11 through 14. In these figures, however, the wedge spectrograms accompany the graphs. Development of these films took place in the ND-2 developer, the composition of which is given in Laboratory Practice.

The data for the above films are in general self-explanatory in the light of what has been said previously about ordinary, orthochromatic, and panchromatic emulsions. The special-purpose emulsions, however, require additional comment. These comprise the duplicating negatives (Eastman 1503 and 1505; DuPont 107) and the background negative (Eastman 1230).

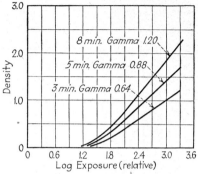

FIG. 12A.—D-$\log_{10} E$ curves of DuPont panchromatic negative No. 116.

The latter is used in making "keys" or "plates" for process photography (see Process Photography). Usually these represent outdoor scenes, such as streets with traffic or bodies of water, which are rear-projected on a translucent screen and rephotographed in combination with foreground action. For such a purpose it is desirable to utilize a negative having about the same color characteristics and latitude as standard negative, but of extremely fine grain, since graininess is one of the principal obstacles to effective use of process backgrounds. The fineness of grain is secured at some sacrifice of speed. The contrast of back-

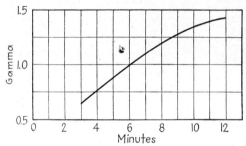

FIG. 12B.—Time-gamma curve of DuPont panchromatic negative No. 116.

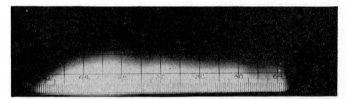

FIG. 12C.—Spectrogram of DuPont panchromatic negative No. 116 (daylight).

FIG. 12D.—Spectrogram of DuPont panchromatic negative No. 116 (tungsten).

ground negative is high enough to compensate for losses and stray-light interference in projection. The background negative being developed for the same time as standard negative, a higher gamma results, and the background print, when developed to the regular positive gamma, provides the higher contrast desired.

Duplicate negatives are made for protection against loss of the original negative or excessive wear on it, for release printing in foreign countries, for optical printer treat-

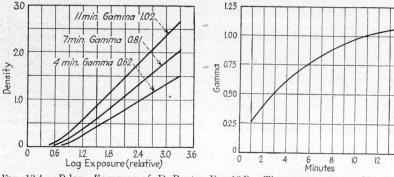

FIG. 13A.—D-$\log_{10} E$ curves of DuPont Superior panchromatic negative No. 100.

FIG. 13B.—Time-gamma curve of DuPont Superior panchromatic negative No. 100.

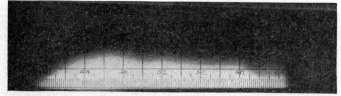

FIG. 13C.—Spectrogram of DuPont Superior panchromatic negative No. 100 (daylight).

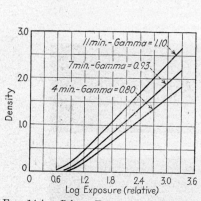

FIG. 14A.—D-$\log_{10} E$ curves of DuPont duplicating negative, type 107.

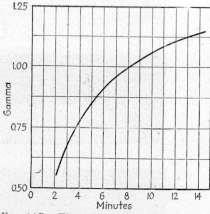

FIG. 14B.—Time-gamma curve of DuPont duplicating negative, type 107.

ment, etc. The procedure involves printing a master positive on special stock, from which the new negative, likewise on special stock, is made. The approved duplicating technique involves operating at a relatively low negative gamma (0.5 to 0.6) and a high positive gamma (1.8 to 2.0) to avoid excessive negative grain. (The negative material is susceptible to grain with higher gammas, while the positive grain remains rela-

Fig. 14C.—Spectrogram of DuPont duplicating negative, type 107 (tungsten).

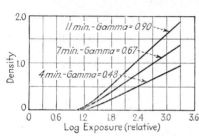

Fig. 15A.—*D*-log$_{10}$ *E* curves of DuPont infrared negative, type 105.

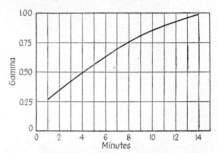

Fig. 15B.—Time-gamma curve of DuPont infrared negative, type 105.

Fig. 15C.—Spectrogram of DuPont infrared negative, type 105 (daylight).

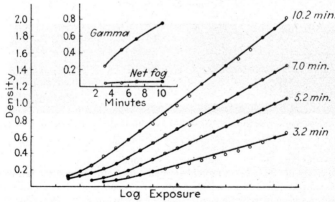

Fig. 16A.—*D*-log$_{10}$ *E* and time-gamma curves of Agfa Supreme panchromatic negative No. 153.

tively constant.)   The negative-duplicating emulsion contains a yellow dye, which dissolves in development, to increase resolving power by controlling light scattering, extending latitude, and holding down maximum contrast.   Like the background negative, the duplicating negative must be of extremely low grain.   The speed is sufficient for optical printing, in which the light reaching the unexposed film may be considerably less than in contact printing.

By reason of refinements in materials and processing, the quality of release prints from duped negatives has been raised to a point where it is often indistinguishable from

Fig. 16*B*.—Spectrogram of Agfa Supreme panchromatic negative No. 153 (tungsten).

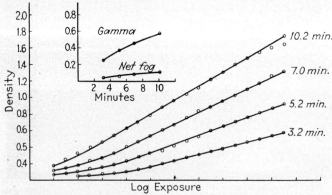

Fig. 17*A*.—*D*-$\log_{10} E$ and time-gamma curves of Agfa Ultra-speed panchromatic negative No. 356.

Fig. 17*B*.—Spectrogram for Agfa Ultra-speed panchromatic negative No. 356 (tungsten).

that of prints taken off original negatives, in spite of the fact that the duped negative accumulates the defects of three different processings.

Another type of negative differing markedly from panchromatic is the infrared sensitized form, the processing and spectral characteristics of which are given in Fig. 17.   The composition of the emulsion, it will be noted from the spectrogram, is such that the film is blind in the green-yellow region, the response being confined to the red and infrared and, at the other extreme, the blue.   Such emulsions are useful in penetrating haze, but, more frequently in cinematography, they are employed to secure night effects in the daytime. It is only necessary to use a light-red or orange filter to hold back the blue radiation from the sky, which then photographs dark; while green

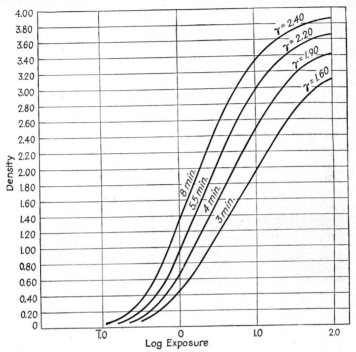

FIG. 18A.—D-log₁₀ E curves of Eastman positive film, No. 1301.

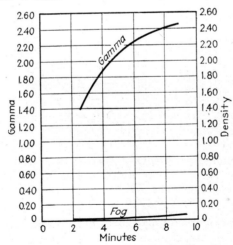

FIG. 18B.—Time-gamma curve of Eastman positive film, No. 1301.

foliage, reflecting red and infrared to a considerable extent, appears as though bathed in moonlight. The speed of the latest infrared emulsions is not markedly less than that of standard negative nor is the contrast much higher.

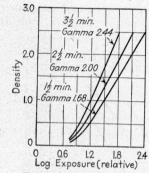

FIG. 19A.—D-log₁₀ E curves of DuPont positive film, No. 213.

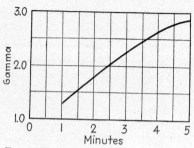

FIG. 19B.—Time-gamma curve of DuPont positive film, No. 213.

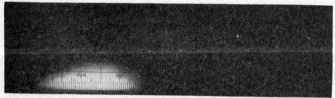

FIG. 19C.—Spectrogram of DuPont positive film No. 213 (tungsten).

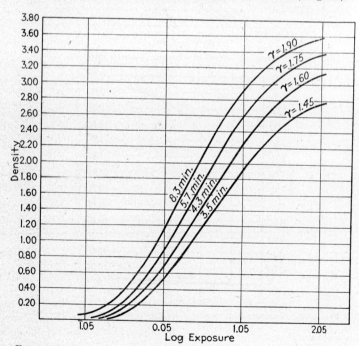

FIG. 20A.—D-log₁₀ E curves of Eastman duplicating positive No. 1355.

Modern motion-picture negative film is generally manufactured with a gray backing or base to reduce halation. The principal cause of this defect, which manifests itself by halos surrounding bright lights in the scene, is reflection of light from the base back into the coating. While films having a thin base are less liable to this trouble

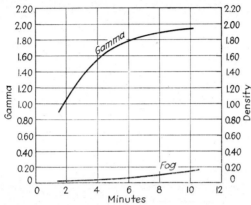

Fig. 20*B*.—Time-gamma curve of Eastman duplicating positive, No. 1355.

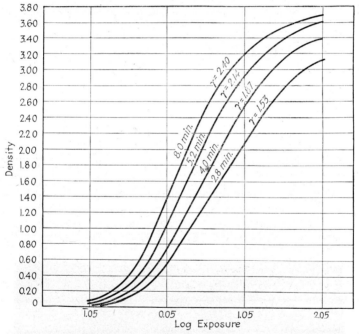

Fig. 20*C*.—*D*-log₁₀ *E* curves of Eastman duplicating positive No. 1362.

than plates for a given size of image, the motion-picture frame size is so small that the effect is disturbing with a clear base. The gray base provides an effective remedy. Sometimes this preventive layer is interposed between the base and the emulsion. In either case it merely requires an increase of 1 to 1.5 points in printing.

Positive Films.—Release prints are made with relatively slow-speed high-contrast fine-grain noncolor-sensitive emulsions. The spectral characteristic of the Eastman 1301 type has already been shown in Fig. 5. The D-$\log_{10} E$ curves and the time-

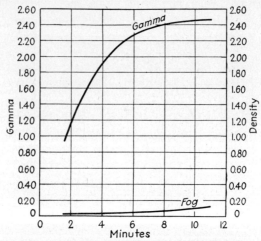

Fig. 20*D*.—Time-gamma curve of Eastman duplicating positive No. 1362.

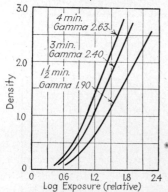

Fig. 21*A*.—D-$\log_{10} E$ curves of DuPont duplicating positive No. 204.

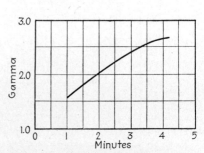

Fig. 21*B*. Time-gamma curve of DuPont duplicating positive No. 204.

Fig. 22*A*.—Spectrogram of DuPont duplicating positive No. 204 (tungsten).

gamma curve are illustrated herewith in Fig. 18, and the same characteristics for the corresponding DuPont positive, together with a wedge spectrogram, appear in Fig. 19. The former were obtained with the D-16 developer, the latter with the PD-2 developer, the composition of both of these positive developers being given in Laboratory Practice.

Duplicating positives for master prints, like the duplicating negatives previously described, are characterized by high resolving power, fine grain, and wide latitude.

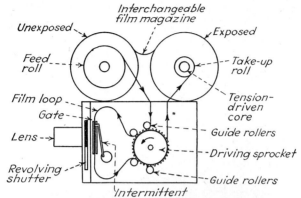

Fig. 22B.—Schematic diagram of camera mechanism.

Fig. 23.—Mechanism of Bell & Howell camera.

Eastman provides two types, the characteristics of which appear in Fig. 20. The former (No. 1355) begins to flatten out at a gamma of about 1.7, while the latter (No. 1362), which does not reach the same point until a gamma of about 2.4 is reached, is suitable for use at very high gammas. DuPont also provides a high-gamma duplicating positive (No. 204), shown in Fig. 21. Duplicating positives are usually distinguished by a lavender base.

Cameras and Their Operation.—A motion-picture camera is essentially a mechanism for driving film intermittently and exposing successive frames while the film is at rest. Its basic elements are shown schematically in Fig. 22. An unexposed roll of negative is carried on a freely revolving core on one side (left) of a film magazine.

Fig. 24*A*.—Detail of camera parts (shutter, sprocket, gear train).

Fig. 24*B*.—Detail of camera parts (film movement mechanism).

The usual amount of film in such a feed roll is 1000 ft., although 400-ft. magazines are also furnished. The film is pulled down through a light trap by a sprocket wheel and its associated guide rollers, whence, in the form of a loop, it is carried to and held flat in a gate behind the lens. Returning to the other side of the sprocket wheel, it is finally wound on the take-up roll (right), the core of which is tension driven, so that as the diameter of the roll increases the rotational speed is proportionately diminished.

The motion of the film is continuous from the feed magazine to the sprocket wheel and remains continuous on the wheel and later between the wheel and the take-up

Fig. 25.—External view of camera, right (operating) side.

Fig. 26.—External view of camera, left side.

roll, but in the gate it must be driven intermittently so that it may be at rest during the periods of exposure. The intermittent mechanism is shown schematically as a claw actuated by a cam. The alternation of movement and rest requires a revolving shutter, shown between the lens and the gate, to cut off the light during the period of motion and admit it again during the "dwell time" when the film is at rest and exposed to the light.　As pictured in the diagram, the shutter is cutting off the light, its opaque sector being between the lens and the film.

The sprocket, the intermittent mechanism, and the take-up are driven through suitable gears by a motor, usually of the synchronous a.-c. type to permit interlocking with the sound recorder and the accurate maintenance of synchronism at the required 90-in. per min. speed.

The operating elements of the camera being understood, reference to Fig. 23 will identify the principal parts of an actual professional camera.　This happens to be a Bell and Howell model, this company and the Mitchell Camera Corporation being the principal manufacturers of such equipment in the United States.　The lens mount and

Fig. 27.—External view of Twentieth Century-Fox silent camera.

motor are absent from the photograph, a hand crank being in place of the latter.　The shutter assembly is at the extreme left, the gate, the intermittent mechanism, and the driving sprocket with the various guide rollers being shown successively to the right. The magazine is mounted above.　The path of the film may readily be followed.

In Fig. 24 parts of the camera mechanism are shown in more detail—these include the shutter, some of the gearing, the sprocket, and the intermittent.　It may be mentioned at this point that, partly owing to the requirements of process photography, modern cameras are built with pilot-pin registration movements which keep the film accurately registered even at speeds up to 128 pictures per second.

Figure 25 shows the camera complete, with magazine, motor, and lens mount, in an external view from the operating side.　The take-up belt shows in this figure. From this view it is clear that there is much more to a professional motion-picture camera than the basic parts so far described.　Instead of a single lens, four lenses are mounted on a turret (right) in order to be easily interchangeable.　A footage counter will be noted at the left of the crank.　Exposure being controlled both by the aperture of the lens and the adjustment of the shutter opening (0 to 170° in the model shown), a dial and control handle are provided for the latter. Dissolves and fades may be made in the camera manually or automatically, the light being cut off or increased by variation in the angular opening of the shutter. These operations are more commonly done in the optical printer (see Process Photography). The prismatic magnifier used for focusing is just in back of the slot provided for focusing vignettes, and above the latter there is an exposure indicator plate. In focusing it is also possible to use an attachment, not shown in Fig. 25, whereby the film is used as a focusing screen, the image being viewed from the back by transmitted light.

On the left side of the camera (Fig. 26) the view finder is mounted. This is equipped with mattes corresponding to the various lenses commonly used, defining the field for each lens. This photograph also shows a combination sunshade, matte box, gauze carrier for diffusing purposes, filter carrier, vignette holder, and an iris for irising in or out on any desired part of the picture.

An interesting camera of recent design is the Twentieth Century silent model shown in Fig. 27, developed at the Twentieth Century-Fox Film studio in Hollywood. To date this appears to be the only camera of domestic origin which may be used on sound stages under normal conditions without some form of "blimp" or sound-insulating covering. The mechanism has been silenced to a degree where the cylindrical housing itself provides sufficient insulation. The motor of this camera drives direct to the shutter. The speed with which the film is moved from frame to frame has been reduced by about 20 per cent, the acceleration is uniform, and the dwell time is so long that a 200° shutter opening may be employed. At the moment of engagement and disengagement the take-down pins have no vertical movement and go straight in and

FIG. 28.—Hand camera (*Bell & Howell*).

out of the perforations. All parts are sealed against dirt, sand, and water. The lens-focusing scale is uniform for any focal-length lens, and by means of a special optical design incorporating automatic correction for focus and parallax, the view-finder image always conforms to the image on the film.

In newsreel work small portable 35-mm. silent cameras are often used. These may be mounted on a tripod, as shown in Fig. 28, or held in the hands. Some types have a single lens, usually of 50-mm. size and speed $f/2.5$; others carry a three-lens turret. They are driven by a hand crank, spring motor, or, less often, by an electric motor.

Motion-picture lenses are usually of large aperture, ranging to a maximum of $f/1.3$ in some sizes. The most frequently used focal lengths are between 25 mm. (1 in.) to 100 mm. (4 in.), although sizes up to 200 mm. are often kept on hand. The bulk of the work is usually done with 40-, 50-, and 75-mm. lenses of about $f/2.0$ speed.

Advances in motion-picture lens design have followed progress in the manufacture of film. As long as motion-picture films were sensitive mainly in the blue region, lenses were generally constructed to accurate focus for the blue F and yellow D Fraunhofer lines. As the spectral range of the film was extended, it became common practice to bring the blue G and red C lines to the focal plane. Other correction requirements have likewise become more critical.

The so-called "zoom" lens is peculiar to motion-picture photography. It is used to give the effect of a moving shot with a stationary camera, by varying the focal length and the magnification during the shot. This is accomplished by rotating a crank coupled with a dial indicating the focal length and magnification. In the Cooke type of zoom lens the range of focal lengths is 40 to 120 mm. at apertures of $f/8$ and $f/5.6$. At larger apertures the range is reduced.

Motion-picture cameras are usually mounted on rigid tripods, but for moving shots a variety of types of "dollies" are employed. One form, known by the trade name Rotambulator, is shown in Fig. 29 with camera and operator in place. The principal

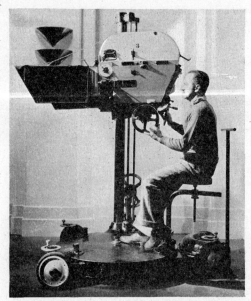

Fig. 29.—Camera dolly (rotambulator).

requisites of a good dolly are ease, speed, and quietness of movement. The type illustrated may be fixed in position by lifting the platform off the wheels, the platform may be rotated for "panning," and the camera table may be moved horizontally and tilted; convenient controls are provided for all these operations.

For three-dimensional movement over wide ranges, camera cranes are utilized. Some of these are large, elaborate structures carrying two or three men in addition to the camera, with equivalent counterweighting to ensure fast and safe operation.

A common pattern of shooting, derived from experience, is to start with a long or full shot, cut to a medium shot, and then to a close-up, in this way establishing the scene and the characters and proceeding naturally to an intimate vantage point. Or, depending on the script, the opposite order may be appropriate in some cases.

The angles and inclusion of field in motion-picture photography vary so widely that all one can say is that anything is possible and almost everything has been tried, sometimes with results scarcely repaying the effort. A number of years ago there was a restless striving, more on the part of directors than cameramen, for grotesque angles, distorted perspective, and a constantly moving camera. In time this urge corrected its own excesses. It is now a generally recognized rule that, while cinematography should not become a traditional or conventional art, anything bizarre that is done with the camera should first of all be dramatically purposeful. Movement of the camera, for example, should not call attention to itself, but to a significant action on the screen. In itself it does not speed up the tempo of a photoplay, and it may detract

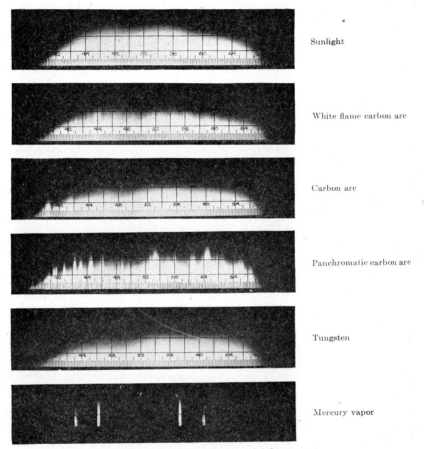

Sunlight

White flame carbon arc

Carbon arc

Panchromatic carbon arc

Tungsten

Mercury vapor

Fig. 30.—Wedge spectrograms of light sources.

from it. The sole purpose of all the elaborate equipment and technique of cinematography is to tell a story pictorially and dramatically.

Lighting.—Until 1914 the sun was the only practical illuminant for motion-picture production. Studios, when not open to the elements, were built with glass roofs and walls, cloth diffusing curtains and metal reflectors being used to control the light, after a fashion, as the sun traversed its path or the weather changed.

When artificial lighting was introduced, it was at first only with the idea of supplementing daylight, later, of replacing daylight with the same flat, uniform illumination. The lighting units were arc lamps, similar to those used in street lighting, hung overhead and equipped with hoods to reflect the light downward. Mercury-vapor tubes, adapted from industrial lighting service, were also used. As a rule the lamps were fixed in position, and the sets were built to conform to the lighting installations, in contrast to the modern practice of adjusting the lighting to the sets.

At this time arc and mercury-vapor lamps were not only the sole types available in the sizes required, but with the "ordinary" and orthochromatic emulsions of the period they were the most suitable from the standpoint of quality of light. The wedge spectrograms of Fig. 30 show the spectral characteristics of sunlight and of the five principal electrical illuminants. The peculiarity of gaseous-conductor lamps is that their spectrum consists of a few bright lines, which, especially in the blue and violet, are adapted to exposures on blue-sensitive emulsions. This is likewise true of sunlight and of carbon arcs, which closely resemble sunlight in that they contain fairly equal proportions of blue, green, and red. Incandescent lamps, being richer in the red-yellow region, did not become a serious factor in motion-picture lighting until after panchromatic-sensitive materials were introduced. The general adoption of incandescent lighting at this point was greatly accelerated by the requirements of sound, for the arc lamps of 1928 were by no means as quiet as the types available today.

Spotlighting lamps of the condensing-lens type were first adapted for motion-picture service from the theater stage. The parabolic-mirror spotlight originated in lighthouse and military searchlight service. A spotlight is distinguished from a floodlight by its sharply concentrated beam and directivity, but at the beginning these qualities were used in motion-picture lighting principally to project light into deep sets where the overhead units left shadows. Modeling, the purposeful creation of high lights and shadows by means of spotlights, did not come until years later.

Light sources vary in intensity as well as in spectral and directional properties. Mercury arcs of the Cooper-Hewitt type, as used in early motion-picture practice, gave a feeble light of the order of 15 foot-candles per sq. in. This degree of brightness was increased in the quartz mercury arc to 500 to 1000 foot-candles per sq. in. The tungsten-filament lamp is capable of 10,000 foot-candles, while the carbon arc yields as much as 100,000 foot-candles per sq. in. in the positive crater. At present there is some speculation relative to the possibilities of water-cooled high-pressure vapor-type lamps, but the commercial sources remain the incandescent lamp and the carbon arc.

The basic characteristics of a good lamp for motion-picture photography may be summarized as follows:

1. Electrical efficiency, *i.e.*, relatively high ratio of emitted light to power input.
2. Spectral characteristics matching those of the film being exposed.
3. Accurately adjustable directivity and beam width, without dark centers, hot rings, hot spots, or other nonuniformities, whether in the form of shadows of the lamp mechanism or optical aberrations.
4. Freedom from "spill light" or random radiation outside the useful beam.

Factors 3 and 4 are correlated somewhat with 1, in that electrical and optical efficiency are of equal importance in making a sufficient level of illumination available in the places where it is needed.

In respect to factor 1, even the best modern light sources are only relatively efficient. For example, incandescent lamps are burned at 21 lumens per watt or at 33 lumens per watt. (The latter figure entails operating the bulb at a temperature of about 3380°K. by overvoltaging, *i.e.*, burning 90- or 105-volt filaments at 115 volts, the voltage prevailing on motion-picture sets. This necessarily shortens the life of the filament but gives a whiter light at greater efficiency.) At 21 lumens per watt the efficiency of the lamp (light output/electrical input) is about 11 per cent. At 33 lumens per watt the efficiency is about 17 per cent. The arc lamp, operating at 45 lumens per watt, has an efficiency approximating 23 per cent. Of the total energy *radiated* by lighting units, only about a fourth in the case of high-temperature incandescent lamps and a third in the case of carbon arcs are in the 340 to 700 mμ photographic band, the rest being radiant heat in the infrared 700 to 5000 mμ region.[1]

In respect to factor 2, the spectral characteristics given in Fig. 30 may be modified by filtering at the lamp. For example, in the case of high-intensity arcs, if it is desired to simulate daylight more closely, the excess blue and violet radiation may be held back with light straw-colored or amber filters. Conversely, the tungsten lamp may be brought closer to daylight color balance by means of blue filtering.

The discussion of factors 3 and 4 entails a description of actual types of lamps used in the studios, prefaced by a further consideration of the two basic methods of lighting.[2] The traditional division, as we have already seen, is between general lighting

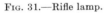
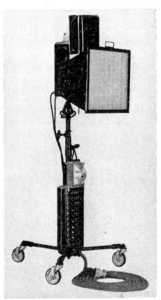

FIG. 31.—Rifle lamp.   FIG. 32.—Side-arc.

over the entire set, at an average illumination of 200 to 400 foot-candles, and specialized lighting by means of concentrated beams, variously known as "modeling," "spot," "personal," and "effect lighting." The latter produce high lights in a scene already illuminated to the foundation intensity of 200 to 400 foot-candles; these high lights may be about 400 to 9000 foot-candles. All these figures are merely estimates since cameramen differ widely in their lighting pecularities, and a "heavy lighter" may habitually work with intensities two times or more as great as a "low-key lighter." Moreover, while the distinction between modeling and general lighting is valid and useful, there is no hard-and-fast division nor is the classification of equipment for one purpose or the other always rigid. While modeling units are normally employed for specific lighting in narrow beams (10 to 20°), most types are capable of being flooded out to angles between 20 and 45°. The angle of demarcation between spotlighting and floodlighting is generally accepted as 20°.

[1] These figures are taken from R. E. Farnham, Lighting Requirements of the Three-color Technicolor Process, *Am. Cinematographer*, July, 1936.

[2] In this, as in some other portions of this section, principal reliance has been placed on the reports of the Studio Lighting Committee of the Society of Motion Picture Engineers, especially the report published in the January, 1937, issue of *J. Soc. Motion Picture Engrs.*

Since general lighting does not present problems of great complexity, in practice it is usually relegated to the "gaffer" or head electrician of the producing unit. Spotlighting, on the contrary, being a means of imparting depth and character, is the responsibility of the cameraman.

Typical general lighting units are shown in Figs. 31, 32, and 33.[1] The first shows a so-called "rifle" lamp, usually mounting a 1000- or 1500-watt incandescent lamp horizontally in a deep metallic reflecting cup with a spirally corrugated surface. This and the "side-arc" of Fig. 32 are usually arranged in rows along the camera lines or in other positions about the set. The "scoop" shown in Fig. 33 is an overhead general lighting unit. It is an arc type; both the scoop and the side-arc generally incor-

Fig. 33.—Overhead scoop.

porate twin 40-amp. flame arcs. Other types of general lighting equipment include multiple-lamp overhead "strips" of five or more 500- or 1000-watt bulbs. In addition small auxiliary lamps are often positioned behind portions of the set, as in back of doorframes, and 250- to 500-watt bulbs are used in visible lighting fixtures to give the impression that the illumination comes from these sources.

The design of modeling units is, as would be expected, more complicated than that of floodlighting units. The principal types are the condensing-lens spotlight, the parabolic-reflector spotlight, and combination forms employing both a reflector and a condensing lens. The simple condensing-lens spotlight is characterized by even distribution of light within the beam and a sufficient spread, but the intensity is limited by the fact that the lens collects only the light from the forward portion of the globe, and lens-transmission losses are high owing to the required thickness of the

---

[1] The lighting units illustrated in this section and the distibution curves accompanying them were furnished by Mole-Richardson, Inc.

lens, which must resist considerable heat, and to its long focal length. The reflecting spotlight is efficient with a sharply concentrated beam, but as the beam is widened, it

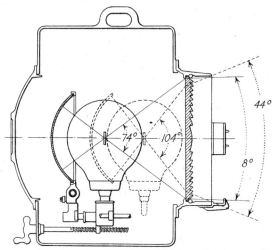

Fig. 34.—Schematic drawing of "Solarspot" incandescent, showing angular light collection.

becomes a ring of intense light surrounding a shadowed center, necessitating diffusion and overlapping of a number of beams to build up the required intensity over a suffi-cient area. This type of lamp is normally used with a "spill ring" to reduce forward radiation from the source in directions other than that parallel to the axis of the beam. The spill ring is merely a spiral of sheet metal, positioned with its axis coinciding with the beam axis, so that from the front of the unit the spiral is seen edgewise and stary light is trapped by the turns.

A widely used spherical mirror-condensing lens type of spotlight is shown schematically in Fig. 34. The lens, constructed of heat-resisting glass, is of the Fresnel or echelon type—a compound lens present-ing a corrugated surface, built up of a succession of fitted annular lenses about a central lens, all having a common focus. It is the equivalent of a plano-convex condensing lens of short focal length and large aperture but considerably thinner and more efficient. This lens is used in conjunction with a spherical mirror, which collects rear light, with both incandescent and arc sources. An incan-descent lamp type is illustrated in the photograph of Fig. 35, and Fig. 36 shows the light distribution at various spot and flood divergences. In Fig. 37 a high-intensity arc with its associated resistor is shown; its distribution curves appear in Fig. 38.

Fig. 35.—5,000-watt incandes-cent lamp.

In both types the lamp house may be lifted from the pedestal and mounted on an elevated parallel or catwalk; in the case of arcs the resistance unit is also detachable.

The mechanism of a high-intensity arc is portrayed in the photograph of Fig. 39. The angle between the positive (horizontal) and negative electrodes is 127°. The

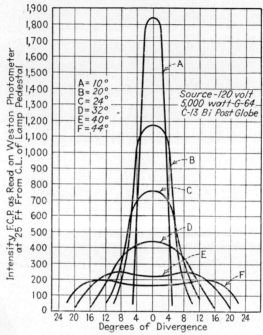

Fig. 36.—Light-distribution diagram of 5,000-watt incandescent.

lamp is struck manually to minimize chipping of the rim of the positive crater. The positive electrode rotates at a speed of 14 r.p.m., maintaining a symmetrical crater or, in the event of damage, restoring symmetry quickly. Both electrodes are fed forward by

TABLE I.—CHARACTERISTICS OF TYPICAL SPOTLIGHTS

Spot	Arc current, amp.	Incandescent lamps power, kw.
36-in. reflector....................................	150	10
24-in. reflector....................................	150	5
18-in. reflector....................................	150	2
	120	
	80	
Lens, large.......................................	150	10
	120	
Lens, medium.....................................	50	5
		2
Baby...	...	1.0
		0.5
		0.1
"Lupe" lights....................................	...	1.0

TABLE II.—SCOPE OF LIGHTING

	Close-up		Small room, 20 × 20 ft.		Medium size, 50 × 50 ft.		Large size, over 50 × 50 ft.	
	Min.	Max.	Min.	Max.	Min.	Max.	Min.	Max.
General lighting:								
Broadsides, side-arcs, rifles............	2	2	4	8	10	20	20	40
Overhead scoops.....................	—	—	2	3	5	10	12	30
Overhead strips or domes............	1	1	2	3	2	4	8	12
Modeling lighting:								
36-in. or 24-in. reflectors.............	—	—	1	2	2	8	4	16
18-in. reflectors....................	1	2	4	6	6	12	10	20
Lens spots, large....................	—	1	—	1	2	8	4	16
Lens spots, medium.................	1	2	2	6	4	8	12	24
Lens spots, small...................	1	1	2	4	2	4	2	8

motor continuously while burning, and they may also be adjusted manually. The motors have grease-packed reduction gears; most of the shafts and other rotating members are mounted upon ball bearings and are designed for quiet operation on sound stages. If it is necessary to position a lamp less than 6 ft. from a microphone, the motor may be stopped.

The Studio Lighting Committee lists the modeling units in their usual sizes[1] in Table I.

FIG. 37.—High-intensity arc.

In a typical interior set most of the lighting equipment is likely to be found on platforms suspended above the back line and side lines of the set. This overhead arrangement comprises both general lighting and modeling lamps, the latter including "back-lighting" units which, directed diagonally downward from the rear of the set, high-light the heads and shoulders of the principal actors.

Other lighting units may be disposed on the stage floor in two rows just off the camera line on either side. For follow-up or dolly shots one or several small lamps are frequently mounted on the dolly to maintain constant illumination on the players' faces during the entire maneuver. In order to clear the stage for moving shots, the tendency is to suspend as much of the lighting equipment overhead as possible.

The total amount of light required increases with the size of the set and the scope of the shot, being least for close-ups. The table above gives an idea of the ordinary limits of lighting equipment in current studio practice.

Diffusion or "silking"—the interposition of a thin scrim between the light source and the scene—is intended to scatter the rays and hence lessen glare and reflection. It is properly employed to avoid harsh lighting and secure softness of outline, but it should not be carried to the point of fuzziness.

---

[1] This table has been slightly modified to conform to later practice.

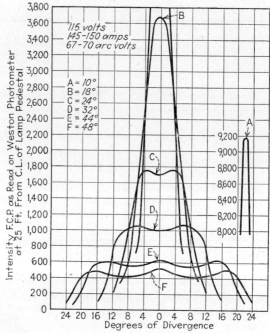

Fig. 38.—Light-distribution diagram of high-intensity arc.

Fig. 39.—Mechanism of high-intensity arc.

The present trend in motion-picture lighting is to subordinate general lighting to modeling, even to the extent of eliminating the former entirely.[1] This is an outgrowth of increases in lens speed from maximum values of from $f/4.5$ to $f/2.0$ and beyond, emulsions having an H and D speed of less than 400 to speeds of 1000, while shutter openings have increased from 90 to 120° to 180 and even 200°, and finally the improvements in lighting equipment of recent years. In consequence, it is now felt by many cinematographers that the conception of general flat lighting as the basis of photography is outdated and that convenience and quality are both served by dispensing with it in favor of spotlighting alone. With this technique the spot lamps are confined to the light platforms above the set and occasionally supplemented with a few floor lamps or a lamp mounted on the camera dolly. The shadows are lighted first to the requisite exposure level, after which the middle tones and high lights are built up. While the scene is being photographed dimmers are used to raise or lower individual lighting units for special effects, *e.g.*, to delineate the features of an actor during an important speech, but these changes are made unobtrusively to avoid distracting the attention of the audience. It is argued that this method not only takes maximum advantage of the close relationship between lighting and composition, but enables the discerning cameraman to exploit the photographic potentialities of a script, both in respect to the decorative utilization of the sets and the personal lighting of the actors, to the highest degree.

Many cameramen achieve their effects with only a rudimentary understanding of the principles of optics, chemistry, and scientific photography. The present tendency, however, is toward a more precise handling of the factors involved. For several years after the introduction of convenient direct-reading photometers or exposure meters, few cameramen could be persuaded to take an interest in their use. Now, however, it has become fairly general practice to employ meters, especially of the photronic type, to read light intensities in foot-candles in various parts of the set, so that more uniform results may be achieved, often more quickly and at less expense. This practice has been fostered by Technicolor, whose cameramen are obliged to keep a record of photometric readings of the intensity and direction of light, a procedure which, according to one color cinematographer, has been of great service in matching outdoor long shots of actors with close-ups later made indoors.

The photometer is used, not only to determine general exposure, but to balance lights on the set. For the latter purpose the light received at the camera is too heterogeneous, hence the instrument should be read in positions close to the people and such parts of the set as are photographically important, the lights being adjusted accordingly.

Exterior Photography and Filters.—Lighting is the foundation of composition and the basic factor in every photographic operation. In studio photography lighting is under the cameraman's control, whereas in outdoor photography, while he sometimes has a measure of control, through the use of reflectors and booster lights, over foreground illumination, he must constantly adapt himself to natural conditions. In this endeavor the cameraman frequently resorts to the use of filters for such purposes as penetrating haze, modifying contrast, enhancing cloud effects, holding down the brilliancy of the sky, and, as already recounted under Films and Film Characteristics, securing special effects such as simulating night scenes in daylight.

The wider application of filters in outdoor photography has been rendered possible by the greatly increased color range and speed of modern emulsions. Except for very special conditions filters are not needed nor used in studio photography.

[1] GAUDIO, A., A New Viewpoint on the Lighting of Motion Pictures, *J. Soc. Motion Picture Engrs.*, August, 1937.

The filters usually employed are of the Wratten type put out by the Eastman Kodak Co. Since more than 100 different forms are available, a comprehensive treatment is impracticable here, but a few examples will be cited, together with sufficient theory to make these instances intelligible.[1]

In Fig. 40, top, the reader will note a wedge spectrogram of Eastman panchromatic negative film as already described under Films and Film Characteristics, taking in the full band from about 400 to about 670 mμ. The effect of a typical filter, the light yellow Wratten No. 3 (Aero 1), used with daylight illumination, is shown in the bottom spectrogram. The longer wavelengths are unaffected, but the

Wedge spectrogram of film without filter (daylight)

Spectrophotometric absorption curve of No. 3 filter

Wedge spectrogram of film with filter (daylight)

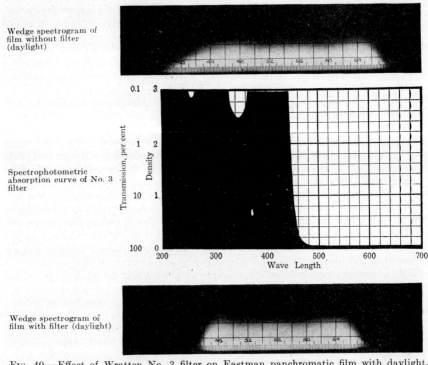

FIG. 40.—Effect of Wratten No. 3 filter on Eastman panchromatic film with daylight.

shorter wavelengths are cut off in the neighborhood of 450 mμ. The spectrophotometric absorption diagram in the center shows how the filter produces this effect. The white area of such a diagram is read downward logarithmically in transmission percentage, while, conversely, absorption is read upward logarithmically in the black area. Black represents the absorption of the filter, while white shows its transmission. Ignoring the slight transmission in the ultraviolet, we note that this filter cuts out the ultraviolet, violet, and a portion of the blue up to 450 mμ, and passes the rest of the visible spectrum. Hence this filter would be used whenever suppression of the short-wave side of the total band is desired.

Since the function of the filter is, by absorption, to prevent a portion of the light from reaching the film, it necessitates an increase in exposure corresponding to the degree of absorption. The number of times the exposure must be increased with a

[1] For full data on specific filters see "Wratten Light Filters," published by the Eastman Kodak Co.

given filter is the filter factor. It is the inverse of the percentage of light transmitted by the filter; thus if 80 per cent of the incident light is absorbed and 20 per cent transmitted, the filter factor equals 5.0. This multiplier, however, is not to be regarded as a constant of the filter, for obviously it depends also on the spectral sensitivity of the film and the spectral composition of the light. Specifying a filter factor is meaningless unless these two elements are defined. For example, the No. 3 filter described would have a much higher filter factor with a blue-sensitive emulsion than with a panchromatic emulsion, the sensitivity of which extends into the region where the filter has no absorption. Likewise for light in which blue-violet predominates the filter factor would be higher than for tungsten illumination rich in yellow, orange, and red. This particular filter has a low multiplying factor (1.25) for light of normal daylight quality and a panchromatic material, *i.e.*, it may be used under these conditions practically without increase in exposure.

Figure 41 shows the effect under the same conditions of four widely used filters, in the following order from top to bottom: Nos. 5, 15(G), 23A, and 72. The absorption increases in the same order. For purposes of comparison these four filters and the No. 3 are listed in Table III.

Filter factors for three panchromatic negatives furnished by the Agfa Ansco Corporation are given in Table IV, which has been compiled by the manufacturer of these films.

Fig. 41.—Effect of Wratten filters on spectral response of Eastman panchromatic film with daylight source of illumination. 1, 5 filter; 2, 15(G) filter; 3, 23A filter; 4, 72 filter.

In general, a color filter which transmits light of a given color will lighten that color on the print, while a filter which absorbs light of a given color will darken that color. Consequently the following effects are typical:

Red filters tend to lighten reds markedly, also to lighten orange and yellow, to darken blues strongly, and to leave green unchanged.

Yellow filters tend to lighten yellows most, to lighten orange and green to a lesser degree, to darken blues, and to leave reds unchanged.

Green filters tend to lighten greens and yellows, to darken red, and to leave blue and orange unchanged.

The filter factor and the increased exposure required necessarily increase with depth of color, since the darker the filter the more light is lost.

Among the applications of filters itemized at the beginning of this section, the elimination of haze sometimes assumes importance, particularly in aerial cinematography. Haze and mist are caused by suspended water and dust particles scattering the violet and ultraviolet rays of the sun. The film being sensitive to these short wavelengths, a veiling of the distant portions of the landscape results, unless measures are taken to prevent the fogging light from reaching the film. Strong yellow filters

TABLE III.—FILTER DATA

Filter number	Color	Filter factor (daylight and panchromatic negative)	Transmits above, mμ	Purpose
3	Light yellow	1.25	450	Slight correction
5	Deeper yellow	1.5	480	Considerable darkening of blue sky
15(G)	Strong yellow	3.0	520	Further darkening of sky, bringing out clouds, darkening water, increasing contrast
23A	Light red	4.0	560	Darkening sky with little effect on foreground, securing miscellaneous scenic effects
72	Red	Requires full aperture, f/2.3–f/3.5	590	Night effects in daylight

TABLE IV.—EXPOSURE MULTIPLYING FACTORS FOR WRATTEN FILTERS IN
NORMAL DAYLIGHT
(Agfa Ansco Film)

Filter use	Ultra Speed 356	Superpan 154	Supreme 153
Aero No. 1	1.5	1.5	1.5
Aero No. 2	2.0	2.0	2.0
3N5	4.0	4.0	4.0
5N5	6.0	5.0	6.0
K-1	1.8	1.6	1.8
K-1½	2.0	1.8	2.0
K-2	2.0	1.9	2.0
Minus blue	2.5	2.5	2.5
G	2.5	3.0	3.0
23A	3.5	4.0	4.0
25A	5.0	5.5	6.0
B	9.0	7.0	9.0
C	10.0	7.0	8.0
C5	6.0	6.0	5.5
F	7.0	7.0	8.0
N.D. .25	1.8	1.8	1.8
N.D. .50	3.1	3.1	3.1
N.D. .75	5.6	5.6	5.6
N.D. 1.00	10.0	10.0	10.0
72	20.0	20.0	30.0

are most effective for this purpose; for overcoming light haze the filter may be proportionately lighter. The use of infrared-sensitive emulsions to penetrate fog is a special application, the film itself in this case discriminating in favor of the longer less-scattered wavelengths.

The combination of infrared emulsions and light-red or orange filters, referred to in Films and Film Characteristics as a means of getting night effects in daylight, requires no marked change in photographic technique, except that it is desirable to eliminate red in settings. To this end one Hollywood studio repainted its "Brownstone Street" a bluish gray, equally suitable for day shooting and infrared night scenes.

Standard negative with heavy filtering will also produce night effects in daylight, but because of the high exposures required, this method is inferior to the infrared system.

In marine photography, water reflecting blue sky may be darkened by the use of yellow or even red filters, without much modification of the foreground.

Polarizing Screens.—Polarizing screens take advantage, not of color differentiation, like filters, but of the fact that light is a form of transverse oscillation, which may be limited to a definite direction. Most light is heterogeneously polarized, *i.e.*, the oscillation occurs in every direction at right angles to the ray. But light passing through a prism, or reflected from certain mirrorlike surfaces, tends to be plane polarized, and by interposing a polarizing screen such light may be reduced in effect or eliminated. The screen, when placed over a lens and appropriately orientated, dis-

Fig. 42.—Developing machine.

criminates against polarized reflections which may be masking detail or otherwise interfering with the effect sought. It may also be used to change contrast. An increase in exposure of four times is usually entailed in such applications.

Laboratory Practice.—For all practical purposes a discussion of present-day motion-picture laboratory methods may be confined to machine development and sensitometric standardization as applied to the large-scale operations which machine processing has rendered possible. A machine of this type, shown in compact form in the photograph of Fig. 42, is one in which exposed film is unreeled and drawn continuously through the developing solution at a speed (for 35-mm. film) in the neighborhood of 100 ft. per min. for negative and 120 ft. per min. for positive, either by motor-driven sprockets or by a friction drive; then it is rinsed, fixed, and washed in successive containers; and finally it is dried and spooled at the output end of the mechanism. The time and degree of development may be varied by changes in the length of the path traveled, by changes in the speed of travel, or both.

The primary control instruments of laboratory processing are the sensitometer and the densitometer, which are described elsewhere in this volume.   The usual form of sensitometer available in motion-picture laboratories operates on the time-scale principle and utilizes a calibrated light source to impress on a strip of film a graduated series of exposures, in exposure times multiplied successively by $\sqrt{2}$ (1.414), so that 21 steps will produce an over-all range of exposures of 1024 to 1.   The density of the sections of such a record may be determined in two ways: (1) on a direct-reading densitometer of the optical comparison type, in which a single source furnishes light for the area under measurement and the comparison beam; or (2) on an electric densitometer, in which a modulated light source excites a constant type of photocell feeding a constant-gain amplifier which actuates an indicating instrument of the rectifier type through a calibrated attenuator.   In this case the attenuator setting required to give a reference reading is a measure of the density.   Both types of densitometer in their conventional forms read diffuse density in the range 0 to 3.

The reader is assumed to be familiar with the theory of H and D and time-gamma curves.   The distinction between gamma and contrast, however, may well be reiterated in this section.   Gamma affects contrast but is not its sole determinant.   Contrast depends on the range of light intensities in the scene, as well as on gamma regarded as a function of the emulsion, the developing solution, and the time of development.   Contrast therefore is the broader term; it has to do with a photographic result, a mingling of high lights and shadows affecting the eye.   Picture negatives of the same scene on the same material, developed to the same gamma, will still show varying contrast if the conditions of illumination under which they were exposed were different.   It follows that a sensitometric strip merely gives information on the degree of development, the gamma, and not on the contrast of variously exposed negatives going through the same bath in the same time.

There are two methods of motion-picture laboratory operation in common use, known respectively as the "time-and-temperature" or "constant-time" system, and the "test" system.   The time-and-temperature system is based on the maintenance of a constant laboratory condition to which the cameraman is expected to adjust his exposures.   The chemical formula of the solution, the temperature, the time of development, the turbulency, and consequently the gamma are assumed to be fixed within permissible limits of tolerance.   The cameraman relies on his negative going through the same bath each day at the same footage speed; consequently the only variations in the product should be those which he purposely aims for in lighting and exposure. The method is essentially a scientific one, based on the same premises as other applications of technology in mass production, and it offers similar advantages of impersonal operation, standardized procedure, and rationalization.   At the same time it should not interfere with any artistry of which the cameraman is capable, since he is free to move the camera, to shoot from any angle with any filters and lenses he may choose, and to dispose his lights as he sees fit.

The test system, as the name implies, involves the exposure of test strips 5 to 15 ft. in length at the end of each scene, all conditions remaining the same as during the takes.   These test strips are furnished to the laboratory and developed in 2- or 3-ft. sections at the time which has been found to give the desired results for the run of normally exposed negative.   A visual inspection is made of each developed strip by a timer or supervisor.   If the strip is correctly developed the takes go through at the normal footage speed.   If it appears that a higher or lower speed would be desirable, or, in the case of seriously under- or overexposed negative, necessary, appropriate adjustments are made.   What usually happens is that the bulk of the day's footage goes through at the normal speed, but a few scenes may deviate, sometimes by several minutes' development more or less.

An obvious advantage of the test system is that it affords a degree of protection to the studio and the cameraman against mistakes in exposure. It is certainly to be preferred in those cases where the cameraman has been "fighting light" outdoors late in the afternoon—perhaps shooting under protest—to get the requisite number of scenes for the day. It also permits over- and underdevelopment of negative as a means of securing uniformity in printing, but at the expense of quality—a dubious advantage. The disadvantages are the extra handling to which the negative is subjected in rewinding to detach and segregate the tests; the possibility of misjudgment by the timer; the possibility of conflict between the cameraman and the laboratory over questions of timing; and the tendency of some cameramen to rely on the laboratory to save them from the consequences of their under- and overtimings, to the ultimate deterioration of their work.

Whatever method is used, sensitometric control is required to keep the solutions constant, since variations in the "soup," whether erratic or gradual, are as little desired in laboratories employing the test system as in those which adhere to the constant-time system. When a new developer is mixed, it is necessary to determine the footage speed and development time which, for normally exposed negative, will yield the desired gamma. This involves varying the speed in the neighborhood of the normal speed, developing a number of sensitometric strips on the same photosensitive material as the negative which is to be developed, and from the resulting data constructing a short time-gamma curve from which the time and footage speed corresponding to the desired gamma may be read off. If the constant-time system is in use, all the negative then goes through at this speed, but every hour or half-hour the constancy of the conditions must be rechecked by the same procedure, a single strip being usually sufficient. Unless the original test is duplicated for both density and gamma, adjustments in the developing solution are required. Aside from variations in the agitation and temperature, which are unlikely in modern laboratories, an important variable is the chemical change in the developer as it acts on large quantities of film. It is necessary to replenish or "boost" it periodically, and the proper amount to be added is indicated by the tests, although usually it is quite accurately known from experience. New developer may be added manually or, preferably, by the drip method of constant admixture.

By the control methods described, the average negative gamma varies among motion-picture laboratories between 0.60 and 0.75, with an average of 0.67. The gamma is normally controlled to ± 0.03.

Another application of sensitometric control which requires mention is in connection with new emulsion numbers of raw stock, which must be correlated with the outgoing emulsion number. This is particularly important in connection with positive stock in order to ensure uniformity in release prints. The procedure is to select a number of rolls of the old and the new coatings, and to make from two to five sensitometric strips from each. Lengths of both emulsions are then printed on a master printer, maintained with special care mechanically, electrically, and optically as a reference machine. A selected picture negative is used as a standard for this printing. The prints on all the samples are made at the printer step which was correct for the old emulsion, and the sensitometric strips and prints are developed together under the preexisting conditions. The step densities are then read on the densitometer and plotted, whereupon any required change in printer point to compensate for the change from the old to the new emulsion becomes apparent.

Prints for studio use are a relatively small part of the work of the laboratory's printing department, in comparison with release printing, which usually requires several hundred copies of each feature in the form of composite prints. Modern printers operate at speeds of about 180 ft. per minute. A typical picture printer is shown in Fig. 43. This is a contact printer, *i.e.*, a printer in which the negative and positive pass through the same gate together. Contact printers are of two kinds: step printers and continuous printers. The step printer resembles the camera and the picture projector in that the two films are carried past the printing aperture and the positive is exposed through the negative frame by frame, a shutter being used to cut off the light while movement is taking place. The exposure is controlled by variation of the light. This type of printer has a straight gate. In the continuous printer, as the name indicates, the movement of the two films past the aperture is uniform. Exposure may be varied by changing the width of the aperture or the intensity of the light, the latter being more common. To reduce slippage between the two films, the gate of the continuous printer is curved. The picture may be printed on either type, but sound records can be printed only on a continuous printer. In making

Fig. 43.—Picture printer.

composite prints sound and picture may be printed consecutively, the picture being masked while sound is being printed, and vice versa. However, combined sound and picture printers are now in extensive use for making composite prints; these have twin mechanisms and optical systems to permit the positive film to be exposed successively to sound and picture in one operation, the light being adjusted in each case to the proper intensity. This adjustment is usually made automatically by electromagnetic control devices actuated by notches in the edge of the film or by traveling mattes in the shape of auxiliary films.

In the development of prints a constant gamma is maintained much as in the case of negative. Sensitometric strips exposed on positive stock are developed at regular intervals in each positive developing machine, and the time of development adjusted accordingly. The positive bath must be replenished in the same manner as the negative bath.

Printing exposure is in steps, one step, or point, being equivalent to 0.05 log E. In the better maintained laboratories, the positive gamma is maintained to within ± 0.05, or one-half a printer point. Positive gammas vary between 1.8 and 2.3, occasionally going higher. The average value is 2.10. The laboratory may vary the positive gamma to smooth out screen contrast where the gamma of the negative is too high or too low.

The product of the negative gamma and the positive gamma is called the "over-all" or "reproduction" gamma; its importance is that it expresses the ratio of the brightness differences of the positive in relation to those of the subject. Owing to the presence of stray light, both in photography and projection, there is a tendency for the picture on the screen to have less contrast than the subject, unless the loss is compensated for by making the over-all gamma greater than unity. Accordingly it is common laboratory practice to work to over-all gammas not lower than 1.2.

While most of the secondary features of development and laboratory operation must necessarily be passed over here, one point in developing-machine design deserves mention: the problem of overcoming directional effects in development. As the film is fed through the machine, the products of development (mainly oxides and bromide salts) tend to diffuse from areas of greater exposure into adjacent areas, in a direction counter to the direction of travel. The effect is to reduce the density of areas adjacent to and following regions of high exposure; thus a sensitometric strip passed through the machine with the light end leading will evidence a different characteristic than with the dense end leading.

In order to overcome this distortion, methods of turbulation and agitation have been devised to prevent the deposition of the development products which cause the trouble. The developer may, for example, be forced through nozzles beneath the surface of the fluid, and the resulting jets agitate the developer sufficiently to minimize such irregularities.

It has already been remarked that improvements in emulsions and lighting are closely correlated with improvements in development and other phases of laboratory operation. These relationships are illustrated by the work which has been done on developers in recent years. The primary ingredients of a developer are the reducing agent; an accelerator, which is usually an alkali; and a preservative, generally sodium sulphite. With orthochromatic film a very active developer, of the type now termed "dynamite soup," was necessarily used, since the film was slow and the light sources inefficient. The strong alkaline accelerator tended to cause grain clumping in development. As emulsions improved it became desirable to devise a more restrained developer of the borax type, such as is now in general use. This utilizes a weaker alkali, borax (sodium tetraborate), in combination with an excess of sodium sulphite, which has a solvent action on silver halides as well as preservative properties against aerial oxidation. Slower developers of this type afford a much finer grain characteristic.

The following are the compositions of the widely used negative and positive developers mentioned in Films and Film Characteristics:

Negative Developers
Formula D-76

Elon	2	g.
Hydroquinone	5	g.
Sodium sulphite (desiccated)	100	g.
Borax (granular)	2	g.
Water to make	1	l.

Formula ND-2

Rhodol (metol or Elon)	2.5	g.
Hydroquinone	3	g.
Sodium sulphite (anhydrous)	75	g.
Borax	5	g.
Water to make	1	l.

Positive Developers
Formula D-16

Water	750.0	cc.
Elon	0.31	g.
Sodium sulphite (desiccated)	39.6	g.
Hydroquinone	6.0	g.
Sodium carbonate (desiccated)	18.7	g.
Potassium bromide	0.86	g.
Citric acid	0.68	g.
Potassium metabisulphite	1.5	g.
Cold water to make	1.0	l.

The chemicals in the D-16 formula are to be dissolved in the above order. The replenisher differs somewhat from the composition of the original mixture, principally in that it contains twice as much sodium carbonate and half again as much hydroquinone.

Formula PD-2

Water	975.0	cc.
Rhodol (metol or Elon)	1.7	g.
Sodium sulphite (anhydrous)	67.5	g.
Hydroquinone	8.5	g.
Sodium carbonate (monohydrated)	26.0	g.
Potassium bromide	0.75	g.
Final volume	1.0	l.

Numerous other phases of motion-picture laboratory practice are outside the scope of this chapter. These include preferred layouts for laboratory buildings; fixing, washing, and drying; reduction and intensification; reclamation of silver from exhausted solutions; printer maintenance; storage of film; preservative treatment of finished prints; inspection, etc. For material on these subjects the reader is referred to the bibliography at the end of the chapter and especially to the Report of the Committee on Laboratory Practice of the Society of Motion Picture Engineers, and the Eastman book on "Motion Picture Laboratory Practice."

Process Photography.—The term "process photography" includes a variety of special effects, such as the making of dissolves, fades, and wipes, as well as more complex forms of scene-to-scene transitions of the montage type; the making of titles; reduction of 35-mm. films to substandard sizes; the improvement of faulty negatives by optical methods; providing backgrounds for studio production; trick shots of all kinds, usually involving matting, multiple exposure, etc.; combinations of photographs of real people and animals with photographs of cartoons or puppets; combinations of photographs of scenic paintings with photographs of real people, animals, and sets; and combinations involving the use of miniature models. Some of these effects may be secured in a standard motion-picture camera, either by itself or equipped with simple accessories like bipack magazines, but the majority require special apparatus, such as animation stands, optical printers, rear-projection equipment, etc. Moreover, the technique of process photography is so involved that normally it cannot be applied readily to day-by-day production activities and is better left for "aftertreatment," which affords the additional advantage of allowing preliminary editing of the picture before final decisions are made on what effects are to be employed and where they shall be inserted.

Composite photography as a means of supplying backgrounds has greatly extended the range of dramatic production and at the same time reduced expense, since it is usually cheaper to bring a scene to the studio photographically instead of transporting cast, company, and equipment to a distant location. It makes possible effects which could not be secured without prohibitive difficulty or danger in the field. Actually at the present time the only method in extensive commercial use is the rear-projection system, but of the numerous earlier techniques one, the color-separation or Pomeroy-Dunning system, deserves a brief treatment for its historical importance and because it is a classic illustration of photographic ingenuity.

Figure 44 is a schematic diagram of this method. It is desired to superimpose the foreground action of the two men on a previously photographed background scene. A dye-image transparency is printed from the background negative, and, as indicated in the figure, this "key" or "plate" is threaded through a special camera in front of and in contact with an unexposed negative. The most common color for the transparency is orange or yellow. The foreground action is lighted from above in the same color. Obviously, then, the foreground action will photograph through the transparency and form a latent image on the negative.

A plain backdrop is suspended behind the action and strongly illuminated with white light. The color of the backdrop bears a minus relation to the color of the transparency and the foreground light; thus for a yellow transparency the backdrop

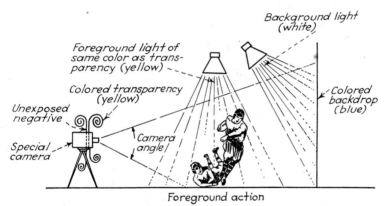

FIG. 44.—Composite photography by color-separation method.

will be the complementary blue. The blue light reflected from the backdrop, entering the lens of the camera, acts as a printing light for the transparency; where the transparency is a dense yellow, no blue rays will penetrate to the negative; where the transparency is light and the foreground action does not block the reflected blue of the backdrop, an image of the background will be formed on the negative. Thus a composite negative of the foreground action and the background scene will result.

The principal disadvantage of the Pomeroy-Dunning system is that the background is invisible while the composite photograph is being made, which may be a serious drawback whenever the foreground action must be synchronized with movement in the background, such as moving traffic. This defect is overcome by the rear-projection method of composite photography, shown in Fig. 45. Here the key print is projected from a special projector to the rear side of a translucent sanded-glass or cellulose screen. Sufficient light is used to permit rephotographing by a camera, which is driven synchronously and phased with the projector. The camera and projector motors are of the interlocked type, operating from a common source of alternating current, and by reason of the phasing the projected picture is at rest while the camera shutter is open. (Hence the projector requires no shutter.) The foreground action is lighted in the usual way. The main requirement for satisfactory results is a steady high-quality contrasty background negative (see Films and Film

Characteristics) and accurately registered prints free from excessive grain, dirt, scratches, etc., which would tend to show up in the final picture.

The principal implement of aftertreatment is the optical printer, shown schematically in Fig. 46. The printer head on the right is essentially a lensless projector equipped with a 500- or 1000-watt light source, providing uniform, diffused illumination at high intensity. It is usually a rebuilt motion-picture camera fitted with a registration or pilot-pin movement and mounted on a lathe bed opposite the photographing camera on the left, which is likewise equipped with a registration movement. Camera and

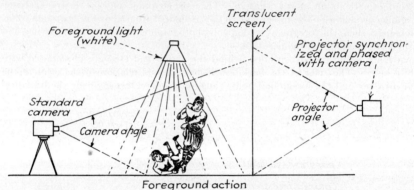

Fig. 45.—Composite photography by rear-projection method.

printer head are driven in exact synchronism from a common shaft. While the image in the printer head is moving, the camera shutter is closed; exposure occurs while both films are stationary. The lens shown between the camera and the projector is designed for unit magnification; it may be an ordinary camera lens stopped down to $f/8$ or $f/11$, although lenses especially corrected for photographing at short distances are preferred. Exposure may be controlled by altering the intensity of the printer light, the lens aperture, the shutter opening, or, in special cases, the speed of printing. The speed depends mainly on the work being done, 40 ft. per min. being about the maximum and

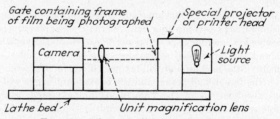

Fig. 46.—Schematic diagram of optical printer.

18 ft. per min. an average figure in practice. Provision is made for driving each unit forward or backward, mechanically or by hand, at the same or different speeds. With differential operation two or more camera exposures may be made of each image frame, slowing down the action, or one exposure may be made of every alternate or third image frame, speeding up the action. Rewinding is usually done at 90 ft. per min. Both the camera and projector may be moved laterally or vertically as well as along the lathe bed, or in place of the lateral and vertical movement of these units, the lens may be moved to adjust the picture. Special movements, such as rocking the camera during operation, may be employed to simulate the rolling of a boat, etc.

A fade is made in an optical printer by placing a master print in the projector and copying it on a new or duplicate negative, frame by frame. At the desired point the operator starts to close the camera shutter and continues to close it at a rate determined by the length of the fade. To fade in, the process is reversed. For a dissolve, where the outgoing and incoming scenes overlap, a double exposure is required, the dupe negative being exposed first to the scene fading out and then to the scene fading in, so that the two superimpose. (A fade, in which the screen goes black, denotes a considerable length of time; a dissolve indicates a briefer interval.) Instead of cross fading for dissolves, "wipes" may be used, a moving edge or outline, in a variety of shapes, obliterating one scene and bringing in the next. This may be accomplished in the optical printer by means of a moving shutter geared to the driving mechanism.

More complex composite effects are often managed in the optical printer by means of masks, stationary or traveling. A stationary matte or mask is one which blocks out the same portion of one of the components of a composite scene; it is simply an opaque material appropriately cut and inserted in a slot in front of the unexposed negative. When the area to be blocked out shifts in size or position, a traveling matte of film must be made, usually by intensification, and threaded appropriately with the print which is to be masked. The desired action then prints through the transparent portion of the mask. In this way montage effects or other composites of several films may be made, and the method also lends itself to trick effects of various kinds. Often multiple masking and multiple printing are required to give the desired illusion.

A detailed description of trick photography is not within the scope of this discussion, but one elementary illustration may be given. Let us assume that it is desired to show an actor working with a lion in a cage, the lion or the actor being of a disposition which precludes any actual fraternization between them. The scene may be photographed with the man at one side of the cage going through the appropriate action in the absence of the lion; the man then withdraws and the lion, persuaded by suitable means to remain on the opposite side of the cage, performs his role and is photographed. It is then a simple matter to combine the desired halves of the two negatives in the optical printer, matting off the undesired halves in turn and producing a dupe negative which shows the actor and the lion apparently occupying the cage together. The same effect could, of course, be obtained by matting and double exposure in the original photography, with the camera kept in the same position throughout, but it is generally preferable from the standpoint of both time and quality to resort to the optical printer.

As in composite photography, in optical printing everything depends on accurate registration, clean prints on stock of appropriate characteristics, and good laboratory procedure. In addition, it is necessary to take into account the fact that optical printing tends to introduce a change in contrast which is not encountered in contact printing. This is particularly the case with specular illumination, where the light is dispersed by the reduced silver in the print to an extent depending on the density, so that there is slight dispersion in the high lights and heavy dispersion in the shadows. In contact printing the dispersed light still reaches the new negative, so that the effect is of no great practical consequence, but in optical printing the dispersed light is lost before it reaches the lens, causing a loss of exposure in the shadows. Thus the contrast is in effect increased—doubled in some cases. The remedy is to use softer prints and to develop the negative to a lower gamma if necessary.

An animation or title stand used in cartoon and title work comprises a camera arranged to photograph film, title cards, drawings on celluloid, etc., by either transmitted or reflected light. The material to be photographed is mounted on an easel, which is generally positioned in the horizontal plane below the camera, the latter shooting down along a vertical optical axis. The camera may be driven at a wide range of speeds.   Many of the operations described in connection with the optical printer, such as the making of wipes and special transitions, may be conveniently performed on such a stand.   Effects titles, in which action or scenery appears behind title lettering, are made by a process of double-negative exposure from a title positive and a scenic or action positive, the former having previously been prepared by exposing film to a title card.   The more intricate title and transition effects are made on the optical printer rather than on title cameras.

Various types of effect shots involve paintings or miniatures.   For example, a painting on glass, in correct perspective size, may be interposed between the lens of an ordinary camera and a set.   Solid miniatures are commonly used, not only to save expense, but to show scenes of destruction—train wrecks, bombing of towns, etc.—which could not be filmed in actuality.   The correlations between the size of a miniature, the speed with which action takes place in or around it, the angles of photography, etc., are mathematically and experimentally determined and, when properly carried out, convey a convincing illusion of reality.

Sometimes three-dimensional "miniatures" are themselves of considerable size and cost.   One miniature of the city of London occupied a medium-sized dirigible hangar used as a stage.   In a recent marine film miniature frigates 18 ft. long, complete with cannon, 16-ft. masts, etc., were used for battle scenes, at a cost stated to be about 1 per cent of that of full-sized vessels.   Long- or medium-shot pictures of these miniatures were intercut with close-up action filmed on part of the main deck of a ship built to full size on a stage, where rear projection supplied sea, sky, and land backgrounds.

Miniature rear-projection screens are sometimes built into three-dimensional miniatures, the edges of the screens being camouflaged so that the action which takes place on them will merge photographically with the rest of the scene.   There is no limit to the combinations which may be devised or to the cinematic effects which ingenuity may produce by such methods.

Bibliography

Periodicals:

DUNNING, CARROLL H.: Dunning Process and Process Backgrounds, *J. Soc. Motion Picture Engrs.*, November, 1931.
WALKER, VERN: Special Process Technic, *J. Soc. Motion Picture Engrs.*, May, 1932.
LEAHY: Time-and-Temperature vs. the Test System for Development of Motion Picture Negative, *J. Soc. Motion Picture Engrs.*, May, 1932.
HUSE: Sensitometric Control in the Processing of Motion Picture Film in Hollywood, *J. Soc. Motion Picture Engrs.*, July, 1933.
Report on Progress in Setting Up Laboratory Controls to Improve Release Print Quality, *Acad. Motion Picture Arts Sciences, Research Council Tech. Bull.*, July 27, 1935.
MEYER: Sensitometric Studies of Processing Conditions for Motion Picture Films, *J. Soc. Motion Picture Engrs.*, September, 1935.
DUNN, LYNN: Optical Printing and Technic, *J. Soc. Motion Picture Engrs.*, January, 1936.
STROHM, WALTER: Progress in Lighting Means Economy, *Am. Cinematographer*, January, 1936.
JACKMAN, F.: Process Shot Economics Made "Captain Blood" Possible, *Am. Cinematographer*, February, 1936.
Report of Committee on Laboratory Practice, *J. Soc. Motion Picture Engrs.*, April, 1936.
HUSE: The Characteristics of Eastman Motion Picture Films, *Am. Cinematographer*, May, 1936.
MEYER: Describing Agfa's Infra Red Film, *Am. Cinematographer*, May, 1936.
FARNHAM, R. E.: Lighting Requirements of the Three-color Technicolor Process, *Am. Cinematographer*, July, 1936.
GREEN, HOWARD: Matching Technicolor Exteriors with Artificial Sunlight, *Am. Cinematographer*, October, 1936.
GOOD, FRANK B.: Using the Photometer to Balance Set Lighting, *Am. Cinematographer*, November, 1936.
DE MILLE, CECIL: A Director Looks at Process Shots, *Am. Cinematographer*, November, 1936.

Technical Progress of the Industry during 1936, *Am. Cinematographer*, December, 1936.

Report of the Studio Lighting Committee, *J. Soc. Motion Picture Engrs.*, January, 1937.

BUTTOLPH, L. J.: Mercury Arcs of Increased Brightness and Efficiency, *J. Soc. Motion Picture Engrs.*, January, 1937.

RICHARDSON, E. C.: Recent Developments in High-intensity Arc Spotlamps for Motion Picture Production, *J. Soc. Motion Picture Engrs.*, February, 1937.

NORLING, J. A.: Trick and Process Cinematography, *J. Soc. Motion Picture Engrs.*, February, 1937.

LINDSAY and WOLFE: A Wide-Range, Linear Scale Photoelectric Cell Densitometer, *J. Soc. Motion Picture Engrs.*, June, 1937.

GAUDIO, A.: A New Viewpoint on the Lighting of Motion Pictures, *J. Soc. Motion Picture Engrs.*, August, 1937.

RICHARDSON, E. C.: Recent Developments in Motion Picture Set Lighting, *J. Soc. Motion Picture Engrs.*

JACKMAN, F. W.: The Evolution of Special-effects Cinematography from an Engineering Viewpoint, *J. Soc. Motion Picture Engrs.*, September, 1937.

IVES-CRABTREE: Two New Films for Duplicating Work, *J. Soc. Motion Picture Engrs.*, September. 1937.

HOUGH-LEAHY: Infra-red Negative as Applied to Special Effects Photography, *J. Soc. Motion Picture Engrs.*, September, 1937.

Book:

"Motion Picture Laboratory Practice and Characteristics of Eastman Motion Picture Films," Eastman Kodak Co.

CHAPTER XXIV

AERIAL PHOTOGRAPHY

By Leon T. Eliel

Introduction.—There are two possible objectives in taking aerial photographs: (1) to produce a picture; (2) to make a map.

We draw a clear line of distinction between the use of this material for picture and for map purposes. The picture is a product which is to be looked at, to be used for its artistic and visual value and for its commercial applications where nothing but the photographic impression is required.

Maps compiled from aerial photography may also have photographic or visual value, but they are primarily maps made to scale for technical uses.

Two kinds of aerial photographs are taken to be used for such visual information as can be derived from them. The most commonly used is the oblique photograph, which is so termed because the camera axis is held obliquely at the time of exposure (Fig. 1). Most aerial photographs which are used for illustrative purposes are of this type.

The second type of aerial photograph used for visual purposes is the vertical photograph (Fig. 2). This photograph approaches being a map, although, because of various inherent defects and distortions, it cannot be considered as a map until it has been processed for this purpose.

Oblique photographs have a variety of uses including advertising; progress pictures; reports; collateral information to illustrate maps; recording emergencies such as floods, earthquakes, etc.; city planning uses for zoning, building counts, rate litigation, etc.; and a variety of other subjects.

Vertical photographs are extensively used for geological study, timber cruising, city planning, and right-of-way work. The most extensive recent use has been on the part of the Agricultural Adjustment Administration of the United States Department of Agriculture for checking contract compliance on the part of farmers operating under AAA benefits.

These vertical photographs are suitable for viewing stereoscopically in relief and, when properly handled in conjunction with certain measurements made on the ground, can render information of reasonable accuracy.

Maps compiled from aerial photographs may be of a number of kinds:

1. Photographic mosaic maps
2. Line maps:
    a. Planimetric maps (Fig. 3, page 710) (showing detail projected on one plane)
    b. Contour maps (Fig. 4, page 711) (showing elevations in addition to planimetric detail)

Details of most of the applications broadly noted above will be enlarged upon later in this article. With the general scope of aerial photography thus in mind, we can now proceed with some detailed considerations of the technique involved.

Requirements of Aerial Photography. *Airplane.*—For oblique photography, almost any kind of an airplane that is big enough to carry a pilot, a photographer, and

708

FIG. 1.—Typical oblique aerial photograph.

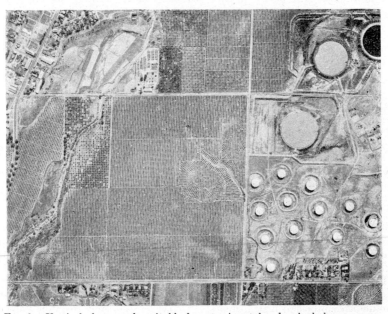

FIG. 2.—Vertical photograph, suitable for mapping, taken by single-lens camera.

a camera is suitable. The airplane should be chosen, however, with the following thoughts in mind. It must have a suitable window which can be opened to permit securing of the photograph without having any of the airplane structure, such as the wing tip and the tail, show in the picture. The airplane should be one which can fly reasonably slowly. The pilot and the photographer should be within speaking range of each other, as the closest kind of cooperation is essential to success.

The selection of an airplane for vertical photography is more complicated (Fig. 5). In the first place, the airplane must have a floor structure through which an adequate

Fig. 3.—Planimetric map which may be compiled from aerial photographs.

camera hole and window for the pilot may be cut. The airplane should carry an adequate gasoline supply and it should have sufficient horsepower to take its full load of crew, photographic equipment, and gasoline to comparatively high altitudes. Most vertical photography these days is being done at an elevation of about 15,000 ft. above sea level, although it is frequently necessary for the airplane to go as high as 25,000 ft. This airplane must be reasonably fast in order to combat the high wind velocities that are often encountered at high altitudes. It must be reasonably free from vibration, which might be imparted to the camera. Furthermore, it is desirable to select an airplane affording the pilot maximum visibility, forward, down, and to the side. For this reason, an airplane with a single seat in the pilot's compartment and a narrow

Fig. 4.—Contour maps of this type may be made from aerial photographs.

Fig. 5.—Type of airplane suitable for aerial photography.

fuselage is preferable to one with side by side arrangement, as in the latter case the pilot has difficulty in seeing downward on the far side of the ship and usually has to move back and forth from one seat to the other. Stability is another essential characteristic of the mapping airplane, as instability results in nonuniformity of overlap, badly tilted pictures, and furthermore keeps the pilot so busy in attempting to maintain an even keel that his efforts toward precision navigation are seriously impaired. The mapping airplane, in addition to the usual instruments, needs to have an exceptionally good compass, which is free from lag and undue oscillation. A sensitive-type altimeter is also important because the ordinary type of airplane altimeter has so much lag that the elevation can change appreciably before the altimeter is affected. Another instrument which is important is a strut thermometer giving the temperature of the outside air. This is essential in making corrections to the altimeter reading.

Fig. 6.—Nine-lens camera for making aerial photographs, mounted in floor of plane. Note oxygen arrangement.

Camera.—A great variety of camera equipment is employed in the various phases of aerial photography and aerial mapping. One particular company engaged in this type of work utilizes 15 different kinds of cameras, each for a different purpose.

For oblique photography, the camera question is comparatively simple. Acceptable obliques have been secured by homemade cameras and modified standard cameras, although a regular aerial camera is desirable. Factors to be taken into consideration in selecting a camera for oblique photography are

1. Focal length. The focal length should be as long as practical. A compromise must be effected between the long focal length which is desirable and weight and mobility. The camera must be light enough so that a man can easily handle it, point it, and move quickly with the camera in his hands from one subject to another. The most satisfactory all-round focal length for oblique photography is 12 in. This lens is generally used on a 7- by 9-in. photograph.

2. Speed. Lenses for oblique photography should have a speed of $f/4.5$ or faster.

3. Filters. The lens should be equipped with a bayonet type of filter, so that filters may be switched in the air as different conditions of haze, visibility, and light are encountered.

4. Exposure. Oblique photographs are generally exposed at $\frac{1}{150}$ sec. or faster.

The camera should be equipped with a couple of solid grips for holding and pointing it, with a trigger which is convenient to be operated while holding the camera by the grips. It should have a single-winding action, which changes the film and resets the shutter in one operation. An ordinary negative glass finder with peep sight is quite satisfactory.

The camera requirements for vertical photography are much more complex. In common use today are focal lengths ranging from 2 to 24 in. Cameras vary in construction from conventional single-lens instruments to nine-lens instruments. Various manufacturers supply aerial cameras either with or without interchangeable magazines and the cameras are classified as precision or nonprecision, depending upon whether they are suitable for merely taking vertical aerial photographs or whether they are calibrated instruments supplying pictures which may be made into contour maps.

A whole chapter could easily be devoted to a discussion of aerial cameras suitable for vertical photography. The following characteristics are common to all such aerial cameras:

1. The camera must be suitable for suspending in a vertical mount, taking a picture through the floor of the airplane.

2. The mount must be of the gimbal type or equivalent, permitting the leveling of the camera in flight.

3. The camera must have level bubbles.

4. Provision must be made for crabbing of the camera, to take care of conditions when the airplane is moving over the ground in a different direction from which it is headed owing to cross winds.

5. The camera must be of fixed infinity focus.

6. The shutter should have a speed range of from $\frac{1}{50}$ to $\frac{1}{150}$ sec. The shutter should have a diaphragm which may be stopped down to as much as $f/20$.

7. The camera must have a release trigger which can be operated from the back of the camera, as the lens is generally not accessible.

8. The winding mechanism must simultaneously change the film and cock the shutter.

9. The capacity of the film chamber should be at least 100 exposures and preferably 250.

10. The camera must be equipped with a view finder suitable for measuring progressive overlap of the pictures, or else an auxiliary instrument for this purpose must be available.

11. It is desirable to have a camera in which focal lengths are interchangeable.

12. The focal plane of the camera must hold the film exactly flat at the instant of exposure either by placing it against a glass plate or by air pressure or suction.

13. In the focal plane of the camera collimation marks must be provided which show in each photograph enabling the recovery of the principal point of the picture.

14. The camera must be made free from static discharge on the film.

15. All camera controls must be large and easily handled so that the operator, even though wearing heavy gloves, can adjust it quickly.

For oblique photography, either a between-the-lens or a focal-plane shutter is suitable. For vertical photography, when pictures are to be used for compilation of precise maps, only a between-the-lens type of shutter should be employed.

With the above general specifications for the aerial camera, a choice must be made between narrow-angle and wide-angle single-lens instruments; or multilens instruments.

When large-scale detailed pictures are desired, such as would be most suitable for city-planning work, a long-focus narrow-angle lens should be used. This permits the securing of pictures of the same scale at a higher altitude and minimizes distortions, which will be discussed later. At the other extreme of single-lens camera utility, we find a wide-angle lens of around 6-in. focal length covering a 9- by 9-in. picture. Such a camera would be used in small-scale mapping in order to cut down the number of pictures and the amount of flying and is particularly valuable in mapping high ground, such as the Rocky Mountain section, where it is not possible for the airplane to ascend high enough to utilize longer focal lengths of cameras. For some uses, such as military and very low coast reconnaisance surveys, multiple-lens cameras are used. Multiple-lens cameras also have advantages in contour mapping under some conditions.   These cameras may cover a very wide angle, so that the terrain photographed in a single composite exposure may have dimensions four or five times greater than the airplane altitude.   While such pictures are usually inferior in photographic quality to single-lens pictures, they have speed and economy on their side and are quite extensively used throughout the world.

Personnel.—There are fewer really competent photographic mapping pilots than in almost any imaginable type of occupation.   Out of 25 pilots who would be rated as excellent, by all the ordinary criteria, only one on an average will develop into an excellent pilot for aerial photography.   While practice will improve the performance of almost any pilot to a certain degree, the main qualification seems to be something instinctive over which a man has little control.   It has been found that a great many pilots can successfully map over so-called "sectionized country," *i.e.*, country like the middle west where the roads and fences all run true north and south or east and west. These serve as a guide and greatly simplify the problem of the pilot.   The moment the pilot starts over unsectionized country, particularly if he does not have good maps available, he is in trouble.   Very little can be said, in an article of this kind, which will help the pilot; the difficulties are being enumerated merely as a warning to inexperienced people who may underestimate the difficulties encountered in this phase of aerial surveying.

The aerial photographer should be familiar with general photography and should be at home in the air.   He must be able to estimate accurately his light conditions and must be experienced in determining the proper time interval between exposures and in turning the camera for the proper angle of crab.

Organizing the Photographic Mission.—In approaching an aerial-mapping project, a proper choice of airplanes and cameras must first be made.   In addition to the airplane qualifications listed heretofore, the airplane should have a capacity to maintain an altitude considerably higher than the altitude at which it is going to be called upon to work.   Otherwise it will prove unstable.

Similarly, a suitable camera should be selected, and the question as to whether a manually operated or an automatic camera is to be used may depend upon the availability of equipment and the extent of the project.   While manually operated cameras are thoroughly practical, experience has proved that automatic cameras, which run continuously at any desired interval, leave the operator more time to level the camera and correct the crab.

Weather study is of primary importance in planning the photographic mission. Within the United States weather averages will run all the way from less than one mapping day per month, at certain seasons of the year, to as high as 25 days per month. Obviously, this is the most important cost factor.   Weather information can generally be secured from the nearest U. S. Weather Bureau Office, and nation-wide weather averages, as they pertain to aerial mapping, are available through studies which have been made by the Soil Conservation Service and the Agricultural Adjustment Administration in the U. S. Department of Agriculture.

In selecting the base from which the airplane is to operate, the following factors are important:

1. Communications.   It is essential to get the exposed film quickly to the laboratory so that it may be checked, to avoid recurrence of any trouble.

2. Choice of airport.   The airport should be preferably close enough to the area to be mapped so that the area may be reached during the period the airplane is climbing.   Otherwise flying time is wasted each time the airplane goes out and comes back.   If possible an airport should be selected at which United States weather reports are available.

3. Hangar and service facilities. It is desirable but not necessary to select a base where the airplane can be kept in a hangar, and it is, of course, essential to determine that an adequate supply of suitable grades of gasoline and oil are available. Airplanes left on an open field should be staked down, and a watchman should be on duty with the ship.

Considerable study should be made of the type of terrain which is to be mapped. There is some choice in the film which is to be used, and this will depend upon the characteristics of the terrain and the camera. The film base may be either standard or topographic low-shrink base, depending on the purpose of the photography. Ordinarily three filters are carried on mapping projects, *viz.*, A1, A2, and Minus Blue.

If the flying is to be done at an elevation of 12,000 ft. or higher, the crew will perform much more efficiently if supplied with auxiliary oxygen. One suitable form of oxygen is a mixture of 95 per cent of oxygen and 5 per cent carbon dioxide, which is available at any oxygen house. The tank should be equipped with a metering device so that the flow of oxygen can be regulated, and tubes should be made available for both the pilot and photographer with ordinary pipe stems at the end of the tubes. There are many other methods of supplying oxygen, and the above is merely one which is in very general use. If a considerable amount of flying is to be done above 16,000 ft., the oxygen is absolutely essential. Mapping above 25,000 ft. should not be attempted because the reduction of pressure at these altitudes is apt to seriously impair the health of the operators.

Flying for Oblique Pictures.—Before starting off to take oblique pictures, the pilot should familiarize himself with the prevailing altitude requirements of the Department of Commerce and local ordinances such as are in effect in many communities. Before an oblique flight is attempted, a careful analysis of the subject to be photographed should be made. Buildings, for example, having east exposures should be shot in the morning, south exposures at midday, west exposures in the afternoon, and north exposures preferably in the summer season early in the day.

The composition of the picture must be given a proper amount of thought. For example, most pictures are more pleasing if taken at a fairly flat angle. Thus, if the city ordinances require that an altitude of 1500 ft. be maintained and if it is decided that a suitable angle is 45° from the horizontal, the nearest that the airplane can get to the subject is the hypothenuse of a triangle which is 1500 ft. on each side, which is about 2200 ft. away. The size of the image can now be determined. The scale of the image is arrived at by the following formula: $S = D/f$. This means the scale equals the distance away D, divided by the focal length f. Thus, if a 12-in. focal length is to be used at a distance of 2200 ft., we have:

$$S = {}^{2200}\!/_{12} = 183 \text{ ft. per in.} \tag{1}$$

In other words, an object on the ground which is 183 ft. long, at right angles to the lens axis, will appear 1 in. long in the photograph. Consequently, a fairly large building under these conditions is going to occupy only a small fraction of the total picture. Thought should be given as to the composition of the rest of the picture, *i.e.*, how much skyline to include, etc. It is customary when taking a small object like a building to subsequently enlarge that section of the picture which contains the building. Conversely, the aerial photographer is frequently called upon to photograph subjects which are so extensive that when the picture is taken from a distance great enough to include the entire subject, the detail becomes disappointingly small. Thus, for example, if pictures are required of a section of a city with one mile in the foreground, the picture may be so taken that the mile occupies 6 in. of image. Thus the scale of the foreground of the picture will be

$$ {}^{5280}\!/_{6} = 880 \text{ ft. per in.} \tag{2}$$

In this picture, a building which is 88 ft. across will have an image size of only $\frac{1}{10}$ in. This question of scale and coverage must be settled in every instance by a study of the purposes for which the picture is intended. Oftentimes, it is not possible to get a satisfactory amount of detail of a large tract all in one picture. In such a case, a series of pictures must be taken, perhaps some from close up and others of a general nature. It should be kept in mind that an overlapping series of oblique pictures can not be mosaiced into a unitary picture.

After all the details of the flight have been planned, it is the pilot's duty to get the airplane to the proper place and at the proper altitude. Oblique pictures should not be shot with the camera axis pointing at right angles to the airplane because at this angle the speed of the airplane is almost certain to result in blurring. The airplane should be maneuvered so that the camera can be pointed as far toward the tail of the ship as possible without actually photographing the tail. As the pilot approaches the point at which the photograph is to be taken, he will throttle back the ship so as to minimize engine vibration, pull the nose of his ship up so as to slow down the speed, and when he gets to the point of exposure which he has probably been approaching at right angles to the direction from which the photograph is to be taken, he should turn the ship slowly away from the object, giving the photographer a chance to shoot toward the tail when the desired position is reached.

The photographer will find that it takes a considerable amount of practice to handle a full-sized aerial-mapping camera. Owing to vibration imparted from the airplane and angular movements due to not holding the camera steady, a fairly large percentage of blurs appear in the work of beginners. Many oblique photographers support the camera with a sling of rubber shock cord while others employ the practice of holding the camera entirely clear of the airplane structure, pulling it back snugly against their chest at the instant of exposure.

If the aerial photographer is adept at his work, he will be able to take about three pictures, each time the airplane passes the subject, one slightly before the desired position, one right at it, and one slightly after. With a suitable camera the photographer should be able to take about one picture every 6 sec.

Flying for Vertical Photographs.—Planning the flight for vertical-map photography is of the utmost importance. First, the best suitable map of the area should be secured. In most of the developed parts of the United States, the maps published by the U. S. Geological Survey are available at stationery stores and afford the best type of information for a flight map. If the flight is of an area of which no suitable maps exist, it is necessary to have a person who knows the boundaries to be mapped fly along in the airplane and point them out or else the corners must be marked on the ground. This may be accomplished by marking the corners with long strips of cheap white cloth, in the shape of an L, the apex being at the corners of the property.

In most instances, U. S. Geological Survey maps will be available. On this map the boundaries of the property should be indicated by lines drawn in colored pencil. All lines on the flight map should be heavy so as to be seen at a glance by the pilot. After the boundaries are plotted, the direction of flight lines must be determined. If the terrain is flat and if there is no good reason for flying in some other direction, it is customary to fly north and south lines. If, on the other hand, the area is of a long, narrow valley running in some other direction, the most economical flight arrangement is to have the flight lines parallel to the length of the job.

If the terrain is mountainous, the preparation of the flight map becomes more complicated. In order to secure pictures at the desired scale, the area is frequently zoned according to ground elevation. In other words, an attempt is made to have the airplane fly as nearly as possible at a constant altitude above the various zones of ground elevation. In this case, the flight lines should preferably be parallel to the general trend of the topography. This means they should be parallel to the main rivers and drainage. In order to determine the altitude A above ground to fly, the following formula may be used: $S = A/f$. This formula is practically the same in its fundamental conception as the one used under the oblique section of this article. For example, if a scale S is desired of 1 in. = 1500 ft. and if the camera to be employed is of $8\frac{1}{4}$ in. focal length f, the altitude may be determined as follows:

$$1500 \text{ ft.} = \frac{A}{8\frac{1}{4}} \tag{3}$$

$$1500 \text{ ft.} \times 8\frac{1}{4} = A \tag{4}$$

$$A = 12,375 \text{ ft.} \tag{5}$$

A factor which may confuse the beginner is that there are two methods of expressing scale. A scale may be expressed, for example, as 1 in. = 1000 ft. Another way of expressing the same scale is 1:12,000 or 1/12,000. A scale stated in either of the latter two ways may be reduced to feet per inch by dividing by 12. For example, to determine the number of feet per inch when the scale is given as 1/20,000, divide 20,000 by 12, giving an answer of 1 in. = 1667 ft.

In estimating the cost of a photographic flight, it is, of course, necessary to determine the number of exposures and the amount of flying that will be involved. This will depend upon the specifications as to scale, progressive overlap (which means the amount that each picture must overlap the next consecutive picture), and strip overlap (which means the amount that each strip of pictures must overlap the adjacent strip of pictures). The specifications in most common use today call for a scale of $\frac{1}{20,000}$ (1 in. = 1667 ft.) ± 5 per cent, with the pictures taken so as to have 60 per cent progressive overlap and 30 per cent strip overlap.

If the strips must overlap 30 per cent and if the pictures are 9 in. wide, 30 per cent of each picture, or 2.7 in., should overlap. This leaves a net width for a 9-in. picture of 6.3 in. This 6.3 in. at a scale of 1667 ft. to the inch gives a distance of very close to 10,500 ft. as the separation between flight strips.

If the specification further requires that the progressive overlap be 60 per cent and if the size of the negatives is 7 in. in the direction of flight, then the overlap of each picture will be 60 per cent of 7 in., or 4.2 in. Therefore, one picture must be taken for each 7 in. minus 4.2 in., or 2.8 in. At 1667 ft. per in., a picture will thus have to be taken every 4670 ft., approximately.

We can now determine the number of pictures required to cover the area. By laying the strips that the airplane will fly off on our map with a separation of 10,500 ft. and measuring the length of each strip and dividing this distance by 4670, we can determine the number of pictures required for each strip and by adding up the sum of the strips, the total theoretical number of pictures for the area is determined. It should be kept in mind that specifications usually require that the pictures cover a certain amount beyond the actual boundaries of the area. It is the most common practice to specify that at least 25 per cent of the width of the pictures must cover outside the side boundaries of the job and that at least two picture centers must fall beyond the boundary at the ends of each strip. Experienced organizations mapping a large area generally take 25 per cent more pictures than the theoretical number. In mountainous country the theoretical number is frequently increased by 50 per cent in practice. Inexperienced personnel may shoot several times the theoretical number.

In determining the number of pictures which will be required to cover a given area, variations in the elevations of the ground must be taken into consideration. If the variations in ground elevation are not sufficient to require that the area be broken down into elevation zones, the elevation at which the airplane will fly is generally calculated from the mean elevation of the ground, in which case the overlap, both progressive and strip, must be calculated for the maximum elevation of the ground (Fig. 7). Thus, if the desired scale is 1 in. = 1500 ft. and the theoretical airplane altitude is 12,375 ft. above a mean ground elevation of 800 ft. above sea level, the airplane must fly at an elevation of 13,175 ft. above sea level. Now, if there are hills going up to an elevation of 1300 ft. above sea level, the scale for the flight should be figured as follows: 13,175 ft. − 1300 ft. = 11,875 ft.

With a focal length of $8\frac{1}{4}$ in., this gives a scale of approximately 1 in. = 1440 ft., rather than the theoretical scale of 1 in. = 1500 ft. The scale of 1 in. = 1440 ft. must

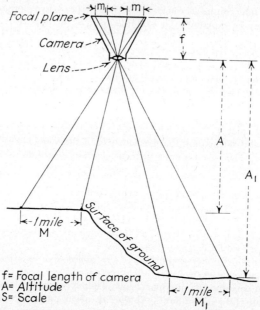

f = Focal length of camera
A = Altitude
S = Scale

Fig. 7.—If the plane does not fly over level ground, the scale of the photograph will not be uniform, and corrections will be required.

be used in laying out the separation between strips and determining the progressive overlap of the pictures.

After the flight has been planned and the flight map prepared, flying may be undertaken. The pilot should so plan his period of climbing that he is over the area to be mapped as much as possible. During this time he should study the area in relation to the map, locating the boundaries so that when the mapping actually starts, he will have these boundaries firmly in mind. He should also pick out prominent topographic features lying in the prolongation of the boundary, marking the beginning and ending of the strips. He will frequently find that there is nothing exactly under him by means of which to determine the boundary, and he will often be dependent upon aligning himself in between the two distant objects. As the airplane approaches the mapping altitude, the outside temperature should be noted. This temperature should normally decrease approximately 3°F., or 2°C., for each 1000 ft. of increased elevation. If the air temperature varies considerably from this theoretical gradient, the altimeter will be considerably in error. For example, suppose the pilot takes off with a ground temperature of +20°C. and flies to an indicated altitude of 15,000 ft. If upon reaching this altitude the temperature has dropped only to +10°C., the altimeter will read 15,000 ft. when the true altitude is about 15,500 ft. Great variations in the temperature gradient do not frequently occur but are present often enough to justify the exercise of considerable caution. This is particularly true when flying over hot desert regions or under conditions of extreme winter cold. The following empirical formula may be employed for approximate corrections. If the quantity in the bracket comes out minus, the altitude is too high, descend; if plus, ascend. The correction is given by:

$$ C = \frac{A}{500} \left[30 - \frac{A}{500} - T_g - T_a \right] \text{ft.} $$

where A = indicated altitude from altimeter;

T_g = temperature on the ground one hour after sunrise, plus 2°C. for each 1000 ft. of ground elevation above sea level;

T_a = temperature aloft (Centigrade, outside of cabin in free air).

If quantity in bracket comes out +, ascend.

If quantity in bracket comes out −, descend.

Example:

A = 15,000 ft., flying field at sea level

T_g = +30°C.

T_a = +10°C.

$$ C = \frac{15,000}{500} \left[30 - \frac{15,000}{500} - 30 - 10 \right] $$

$$ = 30 \, [30 - 30 - 30 - 10] $$

$$ = 30 \, (-40) $$

C = −1200 ft. (minus sign, you are too high, go down)

Upon reaching the desired altitude, the pilot should trim ship and start down the course at a constant air speed following landmarks or in accordance with the compass reading. In the beginning of this strip, he should line up at some distance ahead two easily recognized landmarks which can be used as sights for checking drift. If there is a cross wind, he will note almost immediately that he is drifting off this imaginary line, and he should at once commence to crab the ship into the wind experimentally until he finds the desired amount of crab to carry him along the predetermined course. Having determined the proper amount of crab, he should continue along this course while the photographer turns his view finder the correct amount to compensate for the crab of the airplane and makes the necessary time studies (if he is going to operate by time) to determine the interval between exposures. When the photographer has completed his determinations, the pilot should turn around and backtrack on the course following the same procedure in order to determine the time interval on the back course. As soon as the photographer has completed his studies on the back course, they are ready to start mapping. The pilot should settle down on the course 2 or 3 miles outside the boundary, and the photographer should get settled in a comfortable position from which he should move as little as possible, as his movement will affect the trim of the ship. There is some difference of opinion as to whether the pilot should instruct the photographer as to when to start photography, or vice versa.

Most operators consider that the pilot, who has the more comprehensive view, is in a better position to determine this than the photographer, whose head is down looking through the view finder.

As the flight proceeds down the strip, the photographer should watch through his view finder to pick up any variations in drift. Frequently he is able to detect this before the pilot is and should have a signal by means of which he can notify the pilot in case the crab changes abruptly. The photographer must also watch the level bubbles on his camera, must frequently check the time interval if he is shooting by stop watch, or must constantly watch his finder, if he is shooting in accordance with the image travel between two predetermined lines on his finder.

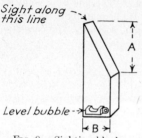

Fig. 8.—Sighting block.

Previous to the flight, the pilot should arrange a sight by means of which he can determine where the center line of the next adjacent strip may fall. One simple way of arranging this is to cut out a wooden block with a straight side which can be placed against the window of the ship (provided the window is vertical) with one edge of the block angling away from the window along which he can sight (Fig. 8). This overlap block can be laid out as follows:

If a picture 9 in. wide is to overlap the picture of the adjacent strip by 30 per cent, we previously determined that the strip spacing is 6.3 in. at the scale of the picture. Assume now that a camera of 8.25-in. focal length is being used, then 8.25 divided by 6.2 equals the proportion of the base to the altitude of the triangle along which the pilot will sight. In the illustration (Fig. 8) a simple form of block is shown in which *A* represents the focal length and *B* represents the strip separation.

The pilot should endeavor to line up sights on the airplane itself, so that he does not have to use the block continuously. For example, he may possibly be able to sight across the window sill to a certain point on the tire or the wheel. He will find it helpful if he frequently makes this sight, as he goes down a strip and remembers these points as the center line of the next adjacent strip. Such a procedure will prove almost indispensable in determining the amount to move over at the end of the strip, unless he is so fortunate as to have country with an abundance of detail and excellent maps so that he may select the starting point of each strip by comparing the map with the ground.

The work should be planned so that, insofar as possible, it is not necessary to change rolls of film in the middle of a strip. It is usually economical to change rolls of film at the end of the strip, even though 10 or 15 exposures may be wasted. The value of this wasted film is usually less than the cost of operating the airplane while the pilot circles around waiting for the photographer to change the film. Furthermore, there is always a strong possibility that the pilot will not be able to pick up the same line with sufficient precision to give an acceptable connection.

Laboratory Operations. *Developing the Film.*—Many different formulas are used in the development of film, depending upon the operator, type of country, and the purpose for which the film is to be used. In country which is tremendously contrasty, such as alternate green fields and very light-colored soil, a soft developer, such as a borax, is preferable. On the other hand, if the country has a monotonous character, such as desert or timber, the film should be developed with a maximum of contrast, such as can be obtained with a pyro developer.

Making the Prints.—In making the prints from the film negatives, it is advisable to have available the full range of contrast in contact papers, as frequently films in the same flight will give the best results on widely varying contrasts of paper.

Pictures which are to be used purely for visual observation, such as obliques, or pictures which are to be reproduced by half-tone cut should be ferrotyped. Prints for all other purposes should not be ferrotyped as this process distorts the image.

Prints which are to be used for any sort of precision work should be made on one of the several types of low-shrink paper, such as Air Map Special or Positype. If the prints are not to be used for the utmost precision, ordinary grades of contact paper may be used.

Prints which are put through a drum drier are appreciably distorted. For precision work, prints should be dried face down on cloth in the ordinary atmosphere of the room without the use of an electric fan.

Indexing.—There are a variety of ways of indexing an aerial survey. Sometimes the area covered by each photographic print is drafted on a map such as a U. S. Geological Survey map, but the preferred way with most customers is to assemble a set of contact prints in their proper relationship and either draft thereon large numbers or paste stick-up numbers on the prints and copy the assembly on a large negative.

Prior to the making of any prints, the question of numbering the negatives should be considered. A number which shows in the photographic image detracts from the artistic value of an oblique picture, so that for this type of negative it is most desirable to number the film in the margin and write this number on the back of the print at the time of printing. It is advantageous to have the number show on the face of prints which are to be used for various mapping purposes, and most vertical negatives are numbered with celluloid ink either freehand in a corner on the celluloid side of the film or are stamped on with a numbering machine.

Many contracts require that the final prints bear consecutive numbers. This requires that the film immediately upon development be assigned temporary numbers which are written in the corner of the film with an ink that can be washed off. After all the flights have been completed, rejected film is eliminated and the final index map compiled and numbered. A list can now be prepared by which the temporary numbers may be removed from the film and replaced with the permanent numbers.

Compilation of Maps.—Everything pertaining to an aerial survey should be planned with the ultimate purpose for which the survey is made in mind. If the pictures are purely for pictorial purposes, the matter of a small amount of lens distortion is generally negligible. If, on the other hand, the pictures are to be used for the making of precise mosaics or are for the purpose of determining land area or if they are to be ultimately used in the compilation of planimetric or contour maps, the characteristics of the lens become of paramount importance. For precision work a lens which is substantially distortion free must be used. For this purpose the symmetrical type of lens is generally suitable. If the operator proposes to use any lens which has not been especially designed for aerial photography, he will be wise to send the lens to the National Bureau of Standards, Washington, D. C., to have its characteristics determined.

It should be kept in mind that, while the definition of a lens can be improved by stopping it down, its distortion characteristics remain substantially the same at all stops.

Lenses for oblique purposes may have an absolute distortion of image of as much as 0.05 in. without seriously impairing the appearance of the picture. At the other extreme of precision, a lens which is to be used for contour mapping should ordinarily have no distortion greater than 0.0005 focal length.

All precision mapping by aerial photography is contingent upon the picture having been taken with the lens axis vertical. Any departure from a vertical lens axis is known as tilt. Actually the term vertical picture is generally used, whereas geometrically the important factor is that the focal plane be horizontal.   If the focal plane is truly horizontal, the resulting picture, if taken through a distortion-free lens, is a true conic projection of the ground.   When the focal plane departs from the horizontal, a perspective picture is secured in which lines which are parallel on the ground will converge on the photograph.   If the tilt is slight (less than 2°), the resulting errors are fairly negligible from the standpoint of most map uses.   If the tilt, however, is greater than this amount, the pictures must be rectified before they may be considered for the basis of map compilation (Fig. 9).

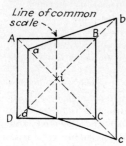

Fig. 9A.—Tilt of camera results in photographing a trapezoidal instead of a rectangular area.

For the purpose of correcting tilt, a rectifying camera is employed in which the negative and easel are inclined into conjugate focal planes to compensate for the tilt. Rectification is too complicated to more than mention in this article.   Details are fully available at any good library (Fig. 10).

A factor which is even more difficult to handle than tilt from the standpoint of map compilation is the variation in scale due to irregularity of the surface of the earth.   If, for example, a truly vertical picture is taken of flat but uniformly sloping ground, a picture will be secured with characteristics very similar to a tilted picture.   Such a picture may be substantially corrected in the rectifying camera.

When the surface of the earth is irregular such as in mountainous country, the problem of compilation of a precise map becomes much more difficult.   In such a

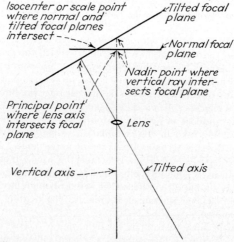

Fig. 9B.—Diagram illustrating the line of sight and plane of film when camera is level and when camera is tilted.

case there are no large uniform slope areas, and in order to achieve a precise result, elaborate methods or machines must be used.

Differences in elevation of the ground result in radial displacements on the photograph.   If, for example, a tall telegraph pole falls exactly in the center of the picture (Pole 1, T_1B_1, Fig. 11), the top of the pole will appear exactly superimposed over its base (t_1b_1).   If the same telegraph pole is photographed any place else in the picture other than in the exact center (Pole 2, T_2B_2), it will appear as a radial image with the top displaced radially outward from the base of the pole (t_2b_2). Thus it will be seen that a vertical photograph of rough terrain is a completely distorted image, with each point being out of position along the radial line passing through that point by an amount which is the result of the height of the object and its distance away from the center of the picture. The radial-displacement formula is fundamental in aerial photography and follows:

$$\frac{R_1}{R_2} = \frac{E_1}{E_2} \qquad (6)$$

This means that the true radial distance R_1 is to the displaced radial distance R_2 as the theoretical altitude of the airplane above datum E_1 is to the actual elevation of the airplane above the particular picture point E_2.

Another way of expressing this situation is as follows:

$$\Delta S = \frac{\Delta E}{f} \qquad (7)$$

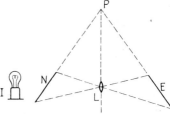

FIG. 10.—Rectification of photograph exposed with lens axis tilted from the vertical or of sloping ground is effected in a rectifying camera. *I*, source of illumination; *N*, negative; *L*, lens; *E*, easel; *P*, point at which plane of negative and lens must intersect to effect perfect rectification.

which means the difference in scale ΔS, equals the difference in elevation divided by the focal length f. Thus, if there is a difference in elevation of 1000 ft. between the

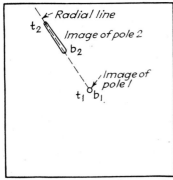

FIG. 11*A*.—Image of two poles (exaggerated) as seen by the camera lens. The pole 1 at t_1b_1 is on the optical axis, whereas pole 2 is not.

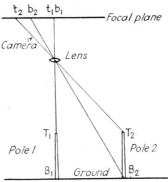

FIG. 11*B*.—Elevation view of camera photographing an object on optical axis, and another object removed from the axis.

top of a hill and the datum scale of the flight and if the camera used for photography has a focal length of 10 in., we have:

$$\Delta S = \frac{1000}{10} = 100 \text{ ft. per in.} \qquad (8)$$

The scale of the picture at the top of this hill will be 100 ft. per in. larger than the datum scale of the picture. Carrying this a step further, if the desired scale of the flight is 1 in. = 1000 ft., the airplane will be flying at $1000 \times 10 = 10{,}000$ ft. above the datum plane. If, while flying at this elevation, a mountain is photographed which rises 1000 ft. above the mean datum plane, the scale of the picture at the top of this mountain will be 1 in. = 900 ft.

By the use of the last formula, a picture may be taken into the field and the scale determined at a given ground elevation. Then, if the field operator wishes to know the scale of the picture at some other elevation, he uses the difference in the elevation and the focal length in this formula, which gives him the desired scale of the picture at the new ground elevation.

It should be kept in mind that this difference in scale results in a radial displacement of the image. Based upon this fundamental geometric relationship, methods have been derived for map assembly which are known by the general classification of "radial control."

Compiling the Mosaic Map.—Rough mosaic maps to give approximate picture information only are frequently assembled with complete disregard of the radial displacements described in the last section. A map so assembled may be a reasonably good general picture, but, in putting it together, sections of country will be entirely lost where the ground is higher than datum and double images of terrain will occur where the ground is lower than datum. In other words, on the high ground where the scale of the picture is too large, the image on two adjacent pictures is too large to fit and some must be cut away and entirely sacrificed in joining the pictures up. Where the ground is too low, the images are small and fail to meet, with the result that at the juncture double images will appear. Thus, if two prints were being joined in a rough mosaic and the pictures contained sloping ground, part of which was above datum and part below datum, the two pictures would join up perfectly at the datum elevation. Above the datum elevation, part of the image would be lost, the amount lost increasing as the elevation of the ground becomes higher. Below datum, double images would appear, getting farther and farther apart as the ground elevation decreases. Under these circumstances, a skillful mosaicer can make a reasonably acceptable picture by carefully choosing the places to cut the pictures together where the loss of image or double image is not going to be apparent. However, the user should be warned that maps compiled by this method are highly inaccurate whether the error can be easily seen or not.

For many purposes these rough mosaics, in spite of their errors, are good enough. One satisfactory way of assembling such a rough mosaic is to take a good base map, such as a U. S. Geological Survey sheet, enlarge this to the scale at which the mosaic is to be assembled and paste this enlarged bromide print of the Geological Survey map on a piece of composition board. Then the pictures, comprising the mosaic, can be pasted down in their approximate positions by making the major detail of the pictures match to the Geological Survey map. This method may be quite successful if the differences in the elevation of the ground are slight and if the flying has been skillfully done and a uniform altitude maintained.

In laying a precise mosaic, the first essential is adequate control. This control may be the U. S. Geological Survey map enlarged to scale as outlined in the previous paragraph. Frequently, however, such maps are not available, or if available were made many years ago, when the art of topographic mapping had not progressed to a point where the resulting maps were accurate.

If the operator is so fortunate as to have a modern Geological Survey map available, he may approach the problem of making a precision map by measuring the distance between identifiable objects on the U. S. Geological Survey map and comparing this measurement with the corresponding objects on the contact print. A ratio can thereby be established for the enlargement or reduction of the contact print to fit the particular points measured on the Geological Survey map. The print which is made to such data is known as a ratio print; it may be pasted down over the

Geological Survey map and will be accurate between the points from which the measurement was made. This method of map making may be carried to considerable elaboration if the use to which it is being put justifies. For example, from the contours on the Geological Survey map, the picture may be broken down into small parts, each to be considered as a uniformly sloping plane. One print may then be calculated for each such small part of a negative and made in a rectifying camera. From each of the several prints representing a small part of the one negative, the part for which the print is designed can be cut out and pasted in its proper position. In this way, the large errors are reduced to many small errors, all of which may be brought within the tolerance of a specification by proper care.

Another method by which precise mosaics are made on the basis of available contour maps is called "pyramiding." By this method, the contours are transferred from the Geological Survey map to the print, and depending upon the precision called for in the specification, a separate print is made from the same negative for each zone of elevation. If the map is to be very precise, one print may be made for every 100 ft.

If the specifications give greater tolerances, a print may be made for every 500 ft. or every 1000 ft. These varying prints are then trimmed in accordance with the contour line representing the elevation for which the print was designed, and the prints are built up one on top of the other with their centers superimposed, with the largest ratio print on the bottom and the smallest one on the top. This is a very tedious and very expensive method of mosaic compilation but has been frequently used where the resulting precision justified the cost.

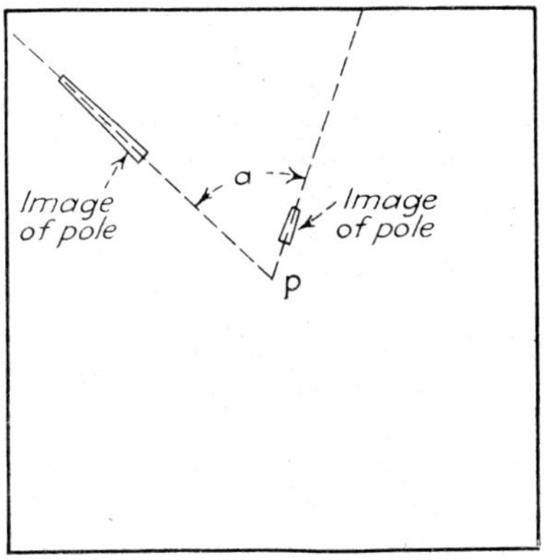

By far the most common practice for the assembly of precise mosaics is by the radial-control method. We learned earlier that differences in elevation resulted in a radial displacement of image. Thus, regardless of

FIG. 12.—Diagram illustrating that the image will lie along a radial line drawn from the optical axis.

variation in elevation, the image will lie some place along the radial which passes through the position for the true point. In other words, the angle between the radials passing through any two images is constant regardless of the elevation (Fig. 12). Utilizing the constancy of this central angle, we can now visualize radial control as building up a net of graphic triangulation.

Preparatory to making a radial-control layout, the boards upon which the mosaic is to be assembled must have the known control plotted thereon.

If the mosaic is of a large area, a "projection" must be laid out upon the mosaic board. This projection generally constitutes drawing latitude and longitude lines in their proper positions which take into consideration the fact that the curved surface of the earth is to be compiled into a flat map. Thus on the polyconic projection, which is the most usual form of aerial-map assembly, lines of latitude which run true north and south on the surface of the earth will converge toward the north on the projection.

Tables and instructions for laying out projections of this nature may be secured from the U. S. Coast and Geodetic Survey or the U. S. Geological Survey at Washington, D. C.

With the projection now plotted upon our mosaic board, we must next plot the known control points. Perhaps these are points which have been established by the government, which in many parts of the country has a very complete system of control already established. This control system will have been put in either by the Coast and Geodetic Survey or the Geological Survey; by one of the other federal agencies, such as the Forest Service; or possibly by a state, local, or commercial organization. In any event, this existing control will probably be available to the map compiler in the form of a description of the control point with information as to how to reach it and the coordinates, *i.e.*, the latitude and longitude of the point.

It will now be necessary to take the contact prints to the ground, follow the published description of how to reach the point, and then identify this point upon the photograph. The control point on the ground will be marked, perhaps, by a concrete monument, by a brass cap cemented in the rock, or in the case of less permanent surveys by a stake driven into the ground, none of which will show on the photograph. Nearby, however, will always be identifiable objects, such as a tree, fence corner, a house, a bend in a stream or some other feature from which a measurement can be made to the control station. Then the position of this station can be pricked on the picture, circled, and annotated for future reference.

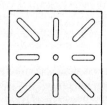

Fig. 13*A*.— Points marked on photograph for purposes of aligning individual prints for making a mosaic.

Fig. 13*B*.—Slotted templet for radial control assembly.

After all the control points have been identified upon the pictures, the assembly of the mosaic may be started. On each photograph at least eight points, disposed as indicated in Fig. 13, should be selected. These same points should be identified in the overlapping section of the adjacent picture. Occasionally a point will fall on as many as six separate pictures. It must be precisely pricked and circled on every picture. When at least eight such points have been selected for every picture in the area, radial lines should be drawn through the points extending perhaps an inch on both sides of the point.

Next the radial-control assembly may proceed by any of three methods:

1. Graphic method.
2. Transparent-templet method.
3. Slotted-templet method.

In all three methods, the fundamental principle is identical, the main differences between them being in the ease of adjustment, time consumed, and ultimate quality of the result.

Perhaps the easiest method to understand is the slotted-templet method, which will be described in full. The operator who does not have slotted-templet equipment available will be able to accomplish the same result by more tedious means by either of the other two methods, which will be briefly described hereinafter.

The picture with the points which are to be used for the radial control, pricked, is placed over a piece of thin cardboard, which should be the same size as the picture, and the points which are pricked on the picture should be pricked through to the cardboard. In addition to this, the center point of the picture, which is indicated by most aerial cameras, should also be pricked through to the cardboard. The cardboard templet is then given a number to correspond to the picture, and a hole, perhaps $\frac{1}{8}$ in. in diameter, is punched at the center of the templet. Radial slots are punched centering at each radial point which has been pricked to the cardboard.

Amongst the eight points which have been pricked on each picture, it is, of course, essential to prick all the control points which have been identified in the field, as these are the key points upon which the entire construction depends. At the time these control points are pricked through from the picture to the cardboard templet, the name or designation of the control point should be written on the cardboard control templet for future use. This designation should be written in such a position on the templet that it will not be cut away when the control point is punched. Posts with a flat base and a neck of just the diameter of the slot in the templets are now nailed down to the mosaic board over the plotted position of each known control point. To begin with, a group of templets is selected representing a strip of pictures on which two known control points separated by a number of pictures appear. The templet on which the first control point appears is now laid down on the mosaic board with the slot which represents that point placed over the post. Additional posts are now placed in all the other slots on this templet. The next templet in series is now picked up and laid over the first templet which may be accomplished by sliding the posts in the first templet back and forth in their slots until they fit the slots of the second templet. Now in the second templet, posts are placed through all the remaining slots and the third templet is placed over these latter posts in the same manner. This process is continued through the series of prints until the templet is reached in which a slot has been cut representing the next control point. It will probably be found that the assembly of templets is either too long or too short to permit the slot representing this control point to be placed over the post which is nailed to the mosaic board at this control point. However, the entire assembly of templets is flexible and may be lengthened or contracted like an accordian. If the string of templets is lengthened, all the posts riding in the slots are spread out; if the string of templets is shortened, all the posts will move inward, automatically assuming a disposition proportional to the distance between the control points. Thus, by lengthening or shortening the string of templets, it may be adjusted so that the proper slot may now be placed over the post representing the second control point. We have now established the scale of assembly, and every post is in the correct scale position for the point it represents. The balance of the templets in each strip—strip by strip—may be buttoned to their respective posts until the entire area is covered.

The posts have a vertical hole in them, and the next step is to drive a pin, fastening each post to the mosaic board. Now the templets may be lifted off, one by one and as each templet is removed from its posts, the post which passed through the center hole of that templet is numbered on the board to correspond to the negative and templet number (which are, of course, identical). After the templets are removed, the posts are pulled from the board one by one, and the small hole which is left by the pin which secured the post in position is circled. This hole represents the correct position for each image point which was represented by a slot and a post.

We now have a pattern laid out on our mosaic board with the center and at least eight outlying points established for each print which is to go into the mosaic. Measurements may now be compared between these points and the corresponding image points on the pricked set of contact prints and a ratio factor calculated for the enlargement or reduction of the print or any part thereof. In more elaborate mosaics these measurements are used as the basis for determining the angle of tilt by which the entire print or parts thereof are to be corrected in the rectifying camera.

The result is, of course, that the ratio print made from the comparative measurements between the mosaic board points and the points on the contact print will fit the mosaic board and permit the assembly of a precise map.

The first method listed above was the graphic method of radial control. This method utilizes the radial lines which were first drawn on the print. Instead of buttoning the print templets together as was done in the slotted templet method, the graphic method traces the radial lines from each print on a piece of tracing cloth and causes the successive radial lines to intersect as nearly as possible at a point. This method is tedious because, after the first run of radial prints between the two known control points, it is usually found that the scale selected for the control plot is too large or too small. A correction factor must then be established between the first two prints of the run, and the whole run must be duplicated perhaps two or three times until by trial and error the proper scale is found.

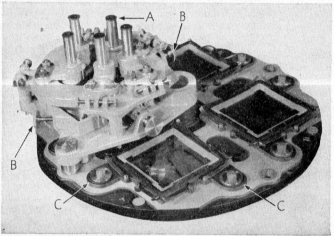

Fig. 14.—Fairchild four-couple transformer jig set over plateholders. *A*, five microscopes so set as to correspond to the five index marks of the four-couple camera; *B*, adjustment screws used to bring plates into proper position under the microscope; *C*, clamping down nuts to hold the plates securely in position after adjustment.

The second method of radial control which was enumerated is the transparent-templet method. In this method, a celluloid templet is traced from the contact print, *i.e.*, the center and the radial lines are traced from the contact print. The method differs from method 1 in that the celluloid templets are laid down one over another and the radial lines so adjusted that they intersect at a point. Then when the second control point is reached, if the scale is too large or too small, each templet is moved a little closer or a little farther from its adjacent templets so that the scale is adjusted.

A simpler method of mosaic assembly, which has proved satisfactory, particularly in regions of very moderate relief, is known as the print-to-print ratio method. This method is based on the geometrical principle that regardless of displacement due to difference in elevation, the distance of an image when measured perpendicularly to the line joining the centers of two adjacent prints is the same on both prints (disregarding lens distortion and tilt). The purpose of this method is to compensate for variations in the airplane altitude. If the airplane altitude changes between one picture and the next, a direct ratio may be derived by making measurements perpendicular to the center line and to common images on the adjacent prints. When the ratio from print to print is thus established and recorded, an over-all measurement is made between two known control points. A factor is then worked out for the enlargement or reduction of the entire strip of pictures to get the correct over-all distance with corrections, print to print, according to the perpendicular measurements. This method breaks down badly with tilted pictures or in case of much change in the elevation of the ground. Its principal advantage is its simplicity of use. The results derived from the use of this method do not compare in precision with the radial-control method, but the method is cheaper and faster and requires less experience to operate.

Contour Mapping.—Compilation of contour maps for aerial photography is the most advanced and precise stage of the art. The aerial camera which is employed must be a precision instrument, equipped with a lens which is sensibly free from distortion. The lens must be very carefully mounted in the camera in accordance with

Fig. 15.—Standard single-lens camera installation. Photographer is looking into view finder between his knees. On the side of the cabin is the intervalometer for automatic camera operation.

the manufacturer's data. It is desirable to have the lens mounted by the manufacturer in a barrel, which is installed in the camera intact. This will insure that the internal principal ray is a continuation of the external principal ray or at least as close to this condition as the manufacturer with his factory facilities can produce. The focal plane of this camera must be exactly perpendicular to the lens axis and the collimation marks in the focal plane must precisely indicate the intersection of the principal ray with the focal plane. Everything about the camera must fit rigidly, so that, in case of disassembly or reassembly, parts will fall back precisely in the same position. Interchangeable magazines are not tolerable in a precision camera unless the magazine is doweled to the camera body and provided with elaborate provisions for maintaining the focal plane constantly in its required position. This camera must, of course, be equipped with a between-the-lens type of shutter and pictures should be exposed at $\frac{1}{150}$ sec. or faster to get the maximum of sharpness.

Fig. 16.—The stereoplanigraph for drawing planimetric or contour maps from aerial photographs.

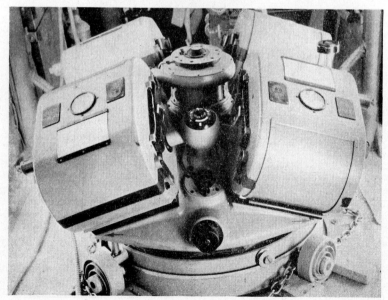

Fig. 17.—Four-lens aerial camera.

Flying for the ultimate purpose of compiling contour maps must be done with the utmost precision. The flying pattern is fundamental in the ultimate economy of the job, as costs are a direct function of the number of pictures involved.

Film which is to be used for contour plotting must be handled with special care in development. The emulsion should not be swabbed with cotton, as this introduces the danger of slightly moving small sections of the emulsion which may not be firmly adhered to the base. This film should be dried slowly in a room where comparatively high humidity prevails, and the film should be supported hanging free from a wire with at least one support for each foot of film.

Most contour maps are plotted from glass diapositives which should be made from the film either during the period of the first 48 hr. after development or after 3 weeks have elapsed. Between these periods most types of film are at maximum

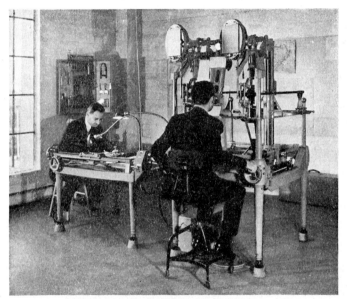

Fig. 18.—The aerocartograph is one of the older types of machines for plotting contours from aerial photographs.

instability. The film itself, which is used for the original pictures, must be of the low-shrink base type, which has been subjected to special conditioning to minimize nonuniform shrinkage and expansion.

A number of different methods are available for producing contour maps from aerial photographs. The methods are all based upon the principle of stereoscopic vision or the somewhat equivalent flicker method. Precision contour maps can be plotted from these aerial photographs only by highly trained experts using elaborate equipment, such as the stereoplanigraph, aerocartograph, or multiplex.

Bibliography

Perodicals:

Map Compilation from Aerial Photographs, Topographic Instructions of the *U. S. Geol. Survey, Bull.* 788, Appendix F, 1928.

ACKLAND, F. W.: Use of Aerial Photographs for Mapping, *Canadian Topographical Survey, Bull.* 62, 1932.

Air Corps Aerial Photography, *War Dept., Training Manual* 2170–6.

Books:

McKINLEY, A. C.: "Applied Aerial Photography," Wiley (1929).

HOTINE, M.: "Surveying from Air Photographs," Richard R. Smith (1931).

GRUBER, O. VON: "Photogrammetry" (collected papers), Chapman (1932).

"Multiple Lens Aerial Cameras in Mapping," Fairchild Aerial Camera Corp. (1933).

JUDGE, A. W.: Stereoscopic Aerial Photography, from "Stereoscopic Photography," Chap. 20. Am. Photographic Pub. (1935).

SHARP, H. O.: "Photogrammetry," Rensselear Union Book Committee, Troy, N. Y. (1936).

CHURCH, EARL: "Analytical Computations in Aerial Photogrammetry," Edwards Bros. Inc. (1936).

WINCHESTER and WILLIS: "Aerial Photography," Chapman.

REEVES, D. M.: "Aerial Photographs," Ronald.

Aerial Photographic Mapping Training Regulations, p. 190–227, U. S. Army, Superintendent of Documents, Washington, D. C.

TALLEY, B. B.: "Engineering Applications of Aerial and Terrestrial Photogrammetry," Pitman (1938).

CHAPTER XXV

ASTRONOMICAL PHOTOGRAPHY

By Harlan True Stetson

Fundamental Problems.—It is probably a fair estimate that 90 per cent of the observational material gathered in the modern astronomical observatory is obtained by means of photography. In a few specialized fields of astronomy, such as the determination of fundamental positions of certain standard stars by means of the meridian circle or transit, and more especially the physical observations of the surface details of the planets or the measurement of the close double stars, the human eye still seems to have the advantage over photography. Considerable experimenting, however, has been done in recent years in applying the photographic plate and also the photoelectric cell to instruments where times of transits of stars are desired. In the determination of latitude, results obtained with a photographic zenith tube have already shown an increase in precision over visual observations made with a zenith telescope.

The advantages of photography as applied to astronomy are twofold:

1. A permanent and unbiased record is obtained reproducing the exact conditions of any astronomical event for investigation or study, and for reference at any subsequent date. Mistakes or errors in the measurement of the photograph may be easily rechecked, but a mistake or error in the record of a visual observation can seldom if ever be examined by an exact duplicate of the original observation.

2. The effect of starlight on the photographic film is cumulative. The longer the exposure, the greater is the amount of silver in the emulsion reduced. Experiments with the human eye indicate that in about $\frac{1}{5}$ sec. or less the retina will record all that the eye sees. Further exposure results in fatigue rather than enhancement of vision. In the case of the photographic plate, however, prolonged exposure may be used with given optical equipment to obtain images of celestial objects too faint to be recorded with the telescope when the eye alone is used as the detector.

Another advantage of the application of photography to the field of astronomy is that the relative positions of a large number of stars representing the whole field of the photographic plate can be recorded at one and the same time. For determination of position as well as the recording of the relative brightness of stars, the photographic plate is a mass-production affair as compared with the highly individualized work of the visual observer where the entire attention must be given to one celestial object at a time.

Photography of celestial bodies entails certain unique problems, foremost of which is some form of automatic mechanism that will keep the camera or photographic telescope constantly directed to the object being photographed while the latter apparently drifts across the sky as a result of the diurnal rotation of the earth on its axis. No wholly automatic device has yet been invented that will succeed completely in accomplishing the purpose, though experiments are now being conducted with this end in mind. The human eye and hand are still necessary adjuncts in the control of the direction finder if a star is to imprint an unblurred image on the photographic plate during a prolonged exposure.

Unlike terrestrial photography, the source of light from celestial objects is outside the atmosphere of the earth and is bent or refracted upon entering it at an oblique angle. Since the observer is constantly changing his position with respect to the direction of a star on account of the motion of the earth, refraction is a variable quantity and is particularly mischievous in dislocating the line of direction of objects in the sky near the horizon. Were it possible, therefore, to effect a mechanical drive which with unfailing uniformity would offset the motion of the earth, refraction alone would necessitate continual "guiding" for a photographic plate with respect to the star. Moreover, since the usual optical equipment for astronomical photography employs an optical system of great focal length compared with the usual camera, small irregular movements of star images are brought about through the turbulence of the atmosphere through which we view them.

It may be pertinent to remark that the so-called "image" of the star obtained on the photographic plate is not in a strict sense an image of the star. All stars except the sun are but luminous points of light at such great distances from us that no telescope yet made or that we may hope to make could ever resolve their size or shape. The so-called image obtained on the photographic plate is therefore but a cluster of silver grains reduced by the feeble light falling in a restricted location on the emulsion. In general, the center of this cluster of silver grains will correspond to the mean position of the light beam producing the reduction. Furthermore, since the star is sensibly a point source, a diffraction pattern results, and the photographic "image" of the star becomes therefore the impression gained through the integration of the effect of light diffracted through the circular aperture of the telescope.

There are many problems peculiar to astronomical photography when we consider the interpretation of the photographic record. If it is the position of the stellar images with which we are concerned, a question of distortion of the film immediately enters as a source of error. Furthermore, the degree of flatness of the field and its rectilinear character are important factors in correcting for distortion of the scale on the plate, a distortion which would depend upon the distance of the image from the optical center or axis. Either of these problems enters when we come to the interpretation of the amount of silver reduction as an indication of the relative light-giving power or magnitude of the star represented. While the technique of handling plates, making exposures, or developing is much the same in astronomical photography as in any other field to which photographic processes may be applied, certain factors such as the effect of temperature and moisture and a variation in the sensitivity of the emulsion become of serious consequence, when the plates are used for quantitative results, if the exposure has been prolonged. These problems will receive detailed attention in subsequent paragraphs.

Instrumental Equipment.—With celestial photography the "camera" is generally a telescope of recognized form in which the eyepiece, which would be used for visual observations, is replaced by a convenient receptacle for carrying the plateholder that contains the photographic emulsion. Telescopes may be divided into two major classifications: (1) the refracting type in which an achromatic lens at the upper end of the tube gathers the light and forms the image on the photographic plate; (2) the reflecting type where a concave mirror at the lower end of the tube does the work of a lens as the objective and brings the light to a focus on the plate at the upper end of the tube.

Refracting and Reflecting Telescopes.—The simplest practical form of telescope lens is a doublet, consisting of a double convex element of crown glass paired with a concave lens of flint glass. In the more common form the crown lens is placed at the upper end of the tube and is backed by the flint lens, whose negative curvature may be made to conform to the curvature of the rear side of the crown disk. In astronomical technology the word "doublet," however, is not generally used for such a single combination of a pair of lenses. The word "doublet" is reserved for a combination of two achromatic lenses spaced some distance apart, as in the older type of portrait lens, thus giving a relatively large field for the focal length. In the conventional type of telescope constructed for visual observations of celestial objects, the lens is made achromatic for wavelengths in the neighborhood of the D lines of sodium, which is the part of the spectrum to which the eye is most sensitive. If the telescope lens is specially made for photographic work, it is achromatized for a region in the neighborhood of 4500 Å. The telescope with such an objective, however, is practically useless for visual observations since the color dispersion in the region of 5900 Å is too great to produce a sharp focus. The so-called "visual lens" may be utilized for photography, however, if a color "screen" or suitable filter is employed. As a filter should be selected which will best transmit the flat part of the color curve of the telescope lens, an orthochromatic plate or one that is yellow sensitive must be employed since the yellow region of the spectrum alone will be available for photographic action.

The Thaw telescope at the Allegheny Observatory is equipped with an achromatic objective specifically designed for photographic light and has proved very effective for astronomical photography where a great focal length is desired, as in determination of star positions for "parallax" and "proper motion."

In the reflecting type of telescope a mirror is employed which forms the image of the celestial object by reflected light, the curvature of the mirror being figured in the form of a parabaloid so that parallel light will be brought to a single focus. The reflecting telescope or the reflector has the distinct advantage in astronomical photography of providing a perfect achromatic optical system. Since the image is formed by a reflection from a silvered or aluminized surface and not by light transmitted through glass, no dispersion of light results. Another great advantage of the reflector is that it is possible to construct a reflecting surface of far greater diameter than is the case when clear glass disks must be provided for a system dependent upon transmitted light.

The present practice of depositing a reflecting surface of aluminum by evaporation in a vacuum chamber in place of the chemical deposition of silver has brought about marked improvement in the use of the reflector in astronomy. The aluminum coating not only has the advantage of greater resistance to tarnish on exposure to air but at the same time has a higher coefficient of reflectivity at the violet end of the spectrum, to which the ordinary photographic plate is most sensitive.

It is of astronomical interest to note that the reflecting telescope invented by Sir Isaac Newton came into being as the antidote for the dispersional lens system. With the development of the achromatic lens, refractors rivaled reflectors since the question of the deterioration of the reflecting surface did not enter. In the latter part of the nineteenth century when photography seriously began to replace visual observations, the merits of the reflector were rediscovered, and our largest astronomical instruments today are of the reflecting type. The 100-in. Hooker telescope of the Mount Wilson Observatory of the Carnegie Institution of Washington is, and will probably remain, the largest telescope in the world until the completion of the 200-in. reflector provided for Mount Palomar.

One serious disadvantage of the reflector is the comparatively limited region of the field that is sufficiently flat to be utilized in astronomical study. The adjunct of a 1:1 power lens system to flatten the field of the reflector is a recent development to offset this difficulty. Since in astronomical photography one is usually concerned with the obtaining of records of the faintest objects that may be recorded, the large light-gathering power of a great reflector, together with its perfect achromatism, renders this form of telescope for the photography of nebulae the instrument par excellence.

Whether the refractor or the reflector is employed for photography, the fundamental requisite is a stable mounting so designed and mechanized as to make possible the continued registration of a given star field on the emulsion of the plate, in spite of the diurnal motion of the sky.

Mechanical Aids for "Following."—Since in all latitudes except at the equator and the poles, the diurnal motion of a celestial object has both a vertical and horizontal component, the only practical mounting for celestial photography is the so-called "equatorial" form. In the equatorial mounting of a telescope, the principal axis, known as the polar axis, is fixed so that it is with high accuracy parallel to the direction of the axis of the earth at any given observing station. The polar axis of the telescope mounting, therefore, will be directed to the true pole of the sky about which all the stars appear to revolve. If a motor or clockwork with suitable gearing engages with this axis, it will be so rated that the telescope will make one complete revolution about this axis in the course of one sidereal day. The sidereal day is the period of the rotation of the earth with respect to a fixed star and is shorter than the ordinary solar day by 3 min. 56 sec.

In order that the celestial camera or telescope may be directed to any part of the sky, it must be possible to turn the instrument about an axis at right angles to the polar axis. This second axis gives a movement of the telescope tube north and south along the great circle, passing through the celestial poles. Since the stellar coordinate representing the angle of departure of a star from the celestial equator is known as declination, the axis which provides for the motion of the telescope in declination is known as the "declination" axis. When the telescope has once been directed to the object in the sky to be photographed, it will be firmly clamped in declination. If the image is then centered on the plate and the driving clock of the telescope is allowed to turn the polar axis, the object will continue to maintain its approximate position with respect to the center of the plate.

For exposures of but a few minutes on bright star fields when the focal length of the telescope is comparatively short, the instrument may be left to itself to record the photography of the star field. The instrument in this sense is practically automatic. Such self-operating instruments have been in nightly use as "patrol" cameras at Harvard and elsewhere.

For prolonged exposure with instruments of large focal length, some auxiliary guiding device is necessary to compensate for irregularities in the clockwork and for the variations in refraction and atmospheric disturbances encountered by the starlight in reaching the plate. Such auxiliary "guiding" may be performed by utilizing a visual telescope of the same or greater focal length made integral with the mounting of the photographic telescope. This auxiliary telescope provided with a pair of "cross wires" or intersecting spider threads at the focus of the eyepiece may be utilized for detecting the slightest trace of movement of the star from the central position in the field. Mechanical slow motions attached to the axes of the telescope and under manual or electrical control may be used for keeping the star image in exact agreement with the intersection of the cross wires. A satisfactory continued registration of the star image in the field of such a "finder" will result in perfect registration of the image on the photographic plate.

In the employment of large instruments with very limited fields, one often needs a guiding telescope of as large an aperture as the photographic one if faint stars are to be employed for guiding purposes. The cost of such double construction, to say nothing of the added mechanical difficulties involved, necessitates the employment of some alternative mechanism. Hence came the development of the double-slide plateholder.

The Double-slide Plateholder.—In the double-slide plateholder, no attempt is made to introduce small compensating movements about the polar and declination axes of the instrument, but the plateholder is moved slightly east and west or north and south by means of micrometer screws provided in the mechanism to which the plateholder itself is immediately attached. A small eyepiece or sometimes two eye-pieces sliding in ways on the border of the telescopic field and outside the dimensions of the photographic plate itself may serve for "finding" a suitable guiding star. The eye-piece will contain the conventional cross wires upon which a star image, obviously not the one being photographed, may be located. In the double-slide-plateholder method the main lens or mirror which is used in photography becomes also the objective for forming the image of the guiding star. The cross wires of the eyepiece in any guiding mechanism are provided with some form of faint illumination, so that the observer may see both the cross wires and the image of the guiding star simultaneously. The double-slide plateholder has the advantage over the guiding telescope or auxiliary finder in that in the case of the large instruments the entire mass of the telescope tube does not have to be moved to follow the capricious waves of starlight introduced through atmospheric disturbances. While the photographic plate is being exposed, the observer will keep his eye constantly on the star in the guiding eyepiece and a hand on each of two micrometer screws. A skilled

Fig. 1.—The double-slide plate-holder designed by the author for the Perkins Observatory. Here small, specially constructed electric motors provide for moving the micrometer screws by remote control.

observer may succeed in making several small movements with the micrometer screws of this mechanism each second as he observes the guiding star, constantly readjusting the plateholder to maintain the star at the intersection of the "wires."

Lenses Used in Astronomical Photography.—The variety of problems encountered in astronomy entail the employment of a wide variety of optical equipment. Contrary to popular opinion, much serious astronomical work not only can be done with modest optical equipment but often can be performed more efficiently and with a higher degree of satisfaction than with the use of large telescopes whose operations are restricted to special problems.

Bruce Doublet.—The introduction of the portrait lens into astronomy for the photography of star fields covering several square degrees of the sky was largely due to the genius of the late Edward Emerson Barnard, for many years astronomer at the Yerkes Observatory. Barnard's early training involved an apprenticeship in a commercial photography studio. Early in his career of astronomy he experimented with portrait lenses attached to conventional telescope mountings. The excellent results obtained in photographing sections of the Milky Way led to a specially designed doublet with a unique mounting for photographing a complete map of the Milky Way. The resulting instrument, named for the donor who contributed funds to the Yerkes Observatory for its construction, became known as the Bruce telescope.

It has become a standard pattern for an astronomical photographic doublet for many years. The design of the Bruce telescope comprised actually three telescopes on a single mounting—two photographic objectives, one of 10 in. in diameter and the other of 6 in. in diameter, and a visual telescope, of appropriate focal length.   Each of the photographic telescopes had as its lens system two pairs of achromatic lenses separated by an appropriate distance.   The relatively large ratio of aperture to focal length, $f/5$, made the equipment particularly fast.   The photographs of star clouds

and comets and the exquisite atlas of the Milky Way which were obtained as the result of many years' work won for Barnard the medal of the Royal Astronomical Society of Great Britain. Success with the Bruce doublet resulted in the introduction of similar equipment in many other observatories.

The short-focus doublet in a variety of sizes has proved an invaluable tool for mapping the entire sky.   The "Harvard Sky" maps cover the entire heavens on 55 plates showing stars to about the twelfth magnitude.   Another extensive star map is comprised in the Franklin Adams charts which cover the entire heavens to stars of about the sixteenth magnitude.   The Franklin Adams charts were made with cameras of 6- and 10-in. apertures and yield a scale of approximately $1° = 15$ mm.

An astrographic chart of the entire heavens together with a catalogue giving the positions of stars measured from photographic plates was undertaken about 1900 with the cooperation of observatories in all parts of the world.   The project is under the auspices of the International Astronomical Union and has been about half completed.   The instrumental equipment of the observatories cooperating has been standardized.

FIG. 2.—Ten-in. Bruce telescope, designed and constructed by the Warner Swasey Company, Cleveland.

The objectives of the telescopes have an aperture of 344 mm. and a focal length of 3.44 m.   Each plate covers an area of the sky approximately 2° square.   As the lenses of the astrographic telescopes, however, comprise only two-element objectives, the 2° square field shows rather poor images at the periphery.

Choice of Aperture.—The choice of aperture of a photographic telescope will depend upon the length of time of the exposure that one may profitably allot to obtain the registration of star images of a given degree of brightness.   The scale of brightness of stars in common use in astronomy is designated as a "scale of magnitude."   Stars just visible to the naked eye fall generally in the classification of sixth magnitude stars. Stars of the fifth magnitude are approximately 2.5 times brighter, whereas a star of the seventh magnitude is 2.5 times fainter than one of the sixth magnitude.   The law representing the ratio in brightness of a star of a given magnitude M_1 to that of magnitude M_2 is given by the following:

$$\log \frac{b_1}{b_2} = 0.4(M_2 - M_1) \tag{1}$$

The limiting magnitude found on star charts of the Franklin Adams series is about 16.   With prolonged exposure of the largest telescope equipment, it has been possible to photograph stars to about the twenty-first magnitude.   Generally a photographic telescope is operated at full aperture since an astronomer desires all the light obtainable from a relatively faint source. Occasionally a diaphragm is used to stop down the aperture for the sake of sharpening the focus near the periphery of the field, thus increasing the effective area which may be satisfactorily utilized on a plate of a given size.

Focal Ratio and Scale.—The focal length of lenses employed in astronomical photography will be governed by the desired scale in the photographs to be obtained, and by considerations depending upon the faintness of the objects to be photographed. The speed of astronomical cameras or telescopes used for astronomical photography varies inversely as the squares of their focal ratios when faint extended areas like nebulae or comets are concerned. For stars yielding substantially point images, the speed has been found to vary more nearly as the inverse first power of the focal ratio.

In determining the relation of focal length to plate scale, it is convenient to remember that there are 3438' in 1 rad. A telescope whose focal length is 3.438 m. will yield a photograph of a given region of the sky in which the angular unit dimension of 1' of arc will be represented by 1 mm. on the photographic plate. Hence the relation:

$$F = 3438s \qquad (2)$$

where F is the focal length in mm. and s is the scale in mm. per 1' of arc.

Some of the problems involving the measurement of small angular dimensions are (1) measuring the distances between the components of double stars; (2) the small annular drift of positions in stars, known as "proper motion"; and (3) the seasonal variation in the position of a star known as "parallax." Here telescopes of a focal length of 15 ft. and up are desirable to produce the requisite scale on the plates used. Among the large telescopes in use for parallax programs in which the distance of the nearer stars is determined from angular displacements of 0.01'' or more is that of the Yerkes Observatory of the University of Chicago, situated at Williams Bay, Wis. The aperture of the Yerkes lens is 40 in., and its focal length is approximately 65 ft.

For the scale of the plate to yield 0.1 mm. per 1'' of arc a total length of 20.63 m. (20626 mm.) is required. Here, from Eq. (2)

$$s = \frac{20.63}{3438} = 6.0 \text{ mm. per } 1' \qquad (3)$$

If the position of the star on such a plate can be measured with a microscopic comparator to the precision of 0.001 mm., the position of the star may be determined to within 0.01'' which is about the order of accuracy obtainable in parallax determinations.

The value of the reflector for positional work in astronomy is seriously handicapped by the very limited field of the instrument. Distortion due to coma and spherical aberration of a parabolic reflector become serious as we proceed away from the optical axis of the mirror. For the purpose of producing a flat field over a considerable area two devices have been perfected for use in connection with the reflector.

Ross Corrector.—One of these is the Ross corrector of practically zero power which usually consists of a doublet, one element of which is convex and the other concave. The lens is placed somewhat inside the focal plane of the reflector and is so figured as to reduce the coma formed in the images, which increases as the distance along the radius from the center of the field increases. The specification of the lens must be suited to each particular instrument employed. F. E. Ross of the Yerkes Observatory has designed several such lenses. The one for the 100-in. telescope at Mount Wilson has three separate elements. The reduction of coma is made possible at the sacrifice of a certain amount of astigmatism but the increase in the usable field of the reflector resulting has added materially to the service which reflectors of large aperture may render.

Schmidt Camera.—A very novel type of astronomical camera was announced in 1932 by Bernhard Schmidt of the Hamburg-Bergedorf Observatory. The Schmidt camera is an ingenious combination of a spherical mirror with a thin lens of peculiar curvature which is placed at the center of curvature of the mirror. The lens eliminates the spherical aberration introduced by the mirror and makes possible a construction of a camera of extremely short focal length and wide aperture ratio.

Perhaps the most notable of Schmidt cameras was that recently installed at Mount Palomar in California which is the site for the projected 200-in. reflector. In this particular telescope the spherical mirror is of 24-in. aperture and the correcting lens 18 in. in diameter. Since the lens is at the center of curvature of the mirror, it

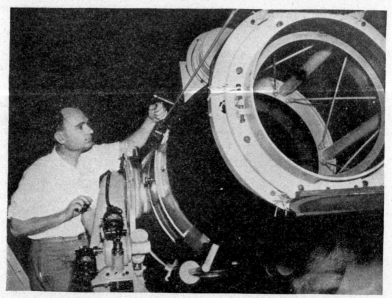

Fig. 3.—Eighteen-in. Schmidt telescope on Palomar Mountain, Calif.

occupies a place at the upper end of the tube of the camera. The plate is placed at the focus of the mirror, halfway between the surface of the mirror and the thin lens. The mirror is necessarily made larger than the lens so that the 18-in. beam of light from the stars off the axis may be fully reflected from the surface of the mirror. The Schmidt arrangement, therefore, makes possible a much wider effective field than can be obtained from either a mirror or a lens alone and has the advantage of permitting a focal ratio in this instance of $f/2$. It was with this instrument that the two notable supernovae of 1937 were discovered by Zwicky.

The ingenuity of design of the Schmidt arrangement makes possible a focal ratio of even $f/1$. Such a camera of only 4-in. focal length has been constructed for the Ladd Observatory of Brown University under the direction of C. H. Smiley. Mention should here be made of a 48-in. Schmidt camera which is now being planned for the Mount Palomar Observatory.

While the Schmidt arrangement has the great advantage of large aperture and exceptional speed, it is not without some disadvantages. The extremely short focal length necessitates a removal of a large amount of glass near the center of the spherical mirror, thus adding to the difficulties of grinding. Furthermore, a lens to introduce the minimum amount of chromatic aberration entails a complicated figure which is somewhat convergent in the center, becoming divergent toward the edge. The field of the camera is of high curvature and requires the molding of plates or films to conform with the curved field. In spite of these difficulties, no other camera has been constructed combining high speed with the wide field obtainable in the Schmidt arrangement.

Auxiliary Equipment.—A photographic plate is the logical medium for spectroscopic work in astronomy, hence various forms of spectrographs are employed in connection with the telescope for the analysis of starlight. As the user of this handbook is hardly likely to enter the highly specialized field of astronomical spectroscopy unless he be professionally employed at an observatory, a general description of spectroscopic instruments as an illustration of the adaptation of photography to astrophysics will suffice.

Stellar Spectrographs.—The simplest form of stellar spectrograph and one widely used where small-scale spectra of large numbers of stars are required, such as for general classification purposes, is the so-called "objective prism." The objective prism as the term implies is a prism of glass, preferably of an ultraviolet-transmitting quality, that is placed immediately in front of the objective of the telescope or astronomical camera, thus dispersing starlight from each star in the field of the telescope.

Since each star is essentially a point source of light, the image of the star photographed will be drawn out into lines with interruptions corresponding to the wave lengths represented by the absorption frequencies of the stellar atmosphere. In order to give an appreciable breadth to the spectra, the base of the prism may be oriented parallel to one axis of the telescope and a slow motion imparted about the other axis, thus drawing the slender spectrum into suitable breadth for examination purposes. The interruptions in the slender spectra, therefore, broaden out into lines or bands characteristic of the appearance of a spectrogram made with the ordinary laboratory slit spectroscope.

For telescopes of comparatively great focal length a relatively small angle, *e.g.*, 5 to 10°, for the dispersion prism may be adopted and yet render a sufficient length of spectrum for classification purposes. To take advantage of the full amount of the beam of starlight falling on a telescope of given aperture, it is obviously necessary that the aperture of the prism should be as large as that of the telescope. The great advantage of the objective prism is that it uses the full amount of starlight available and at the same time records large numbers of spectra on a single plate.

When photographing stars with the objective prism, the telescope, of course, cannot be pointed in the direction in which stars are seen, but allowance has to be made for the angle of refraction through the particular prism employed. This entails some slight inconvenience in directing the telescope to the sky as compared with the employment of the more conventional slit spectrograph where the telescope is directed immediately to the star, the light of which falls on the slit as would be the case of any light source utilized in laboratory apparatus.

For a study of stellar spectra of larger dispersion and greater resolution than can be photographed by the objective prism, the slit spectrograph must be employed. This form of apparatus obviously is necessary for determining shifts in wavelengths of stars introduced by velocity along the line of sight. Utilizing Doppler's principle, radial velocities of approach and recession for many thousands of objects in the sky have now been determined at the major observatories. A slit spectrograph for astronomical work differs little in form from that of a standardized laboratory instrument, except for the criterion of design necessitated by the optical system of the telescope and the introduction of mechanical devices which will render convenient its attachment to the telescope.

On account of the wide ranges of temperature encountered in the dome of an observatory which, of course, is open to out-of-door conditions, the optical parts of the spectrograph must be housed in a constant temperature case thermostatically controlled. In guiding the telescope for spectroscopic work, a guiding eyepiece is provided to enable the observer to be certain that the stellar image falls on the slit continuously. The guiding arrangement usually embodies a series of right-angle prisms through which, by total internal reflection, light from the star image on the slit is brought to a convenient observing point.

For purposes of determining line shifts, means must be provided for comparing the wavelengths of lines in the spectrum of a star with laboratory standards of line positions. To accomplish this, some auxiliary apparatus is needed for imposing a comparison spectrum on the same plate with the spectrum of the star. This is usually performed by the use of a spark gap or vacuum tube near the slit end of the spectroscope, light from which may be brought into the spectrograph by means of an auxiliary reflecting prism. By means of a suitable slit diaphragm the comparison spectrum is photographed on portions of the plate not occupied by the spectrum of the star. By making exposures for the comparison spectrum, both before and after the exposure has been made on a star, a check is assured on the requisite registration. If, through accident or change in flexure, the spectrum is disturbed during the process of exposure, the second comparison exposure obviously will not register coincident with the comparison spectrum made on the first exposure. For the interpretation of the line shift on spectrograms, recourse is made to the comparator or micrometer microscope.

Details of the design of stellar spectrographs for the Mount Wilson, Yerkes, and Dominion Astrophysical observatories have been printed in their publications and serve as technical descriptions of this form of instrument. A recent modification has been introduced at the Yerkes and Perkins observatories where the spectrographs are of the autocollimating type. In this form a single lens is used both for the collimator and the camera of the instrument. In the case of the brighter stars the grating may be utilized, producing a normal spectrum of relatively high dispersion.

The Spectroheliograph.—The spectroheliograph is an interesting adaptation of the spectrograph for the purpose of photographing the entire image of the sun in the light of specific emissions from the lines of known elements in the sun. This was originally designed by Hale in this country and by Deslandres abroad. The spectroheliograph utilizes the principle of a grating spectroscope by means of which the absorption line of a single element in the sun may be isolated, such as the Hα line of hydrogen. The camera consists of an arrangement by means of which a moving plate follows an imposed motion of the image of the sun across the primary slit of the spectrograph. The resulting photograph consists essentially of a series of adjacent laminations, each of which gives a representation of the proportion of the image of the sun covered by the slit in the moment of exposure of each lamination and in the light of the chosen wavelength only. Since the plate moves with the same speed as does the solar image across the primary slit, each elemental line section of the disk of the sun occupies a fresh position on the photographic emulsion. If the apparatus is performing smoothly, the integrated image of the sun appears continuous, rendering beautiful details of hydrogen clouds or flocculi that may be in evidence at the moment of exposure. It is with the spectroheliograph that a continuous watch is now kept of eruptions of hydrogen and calcium on the face of the sun, which in many instances coincide with disturbances in the ionosphere of the earth, causing fade-outs in radio reception.

The adaptation of the spectroheliograph to motion-picture photography has been accomplished by McMath and Hulbert of the McMath-Hulbert Observatory of the

University of Michigan. Such a device is called a "spectroheliokinematograph." At the present date (1939) a new tower telescope with spectroheliographic and spectroheliokinematographic equipment has been constructed at the site of the McMath-Hulbert Observatory at Lake Angelus, Mich. By means of motor-driven mirrors, sunlight is brought through the top of the tower vertically downward to the slit of the spectrograph in the observing room. The spectrograph itself is contained in a well extending below ground to a depth of 31 ft., thus insuring convenient temperature control. A 6-in. grating of 15,240 lines to the inch is used for the formation of the spectrum. The motion-picture camera is a modification of the Bell and Howell Superspeed check-pawl mechanism such as has been made only on order for the large picture producers. Synchronous motors insure uniform motion, both for the film and for the motion of the slit with respect to the image of the sun. An excellent brochure on the design and detailed construction of the equipment is contained in *Publications of the Observatory of the University of Michigan,* Vol. 7. The most remarkable motion pictures of solar eruptions ever yet recorded have already resulted from the ingenuity and skill of the McMath-Hulbert observers. From the point of view of science, this is perhaps one of the most remarkable adaptations of photography of modern times.

In addition to the photography of the solar prominences and flocculi with the spectroheliokinematograph, mention should be made of the very successful work of the McMath-Hulbert Observatory in producing motion pictures of the moon showing its rotation, the rising and setting of the sun, and conspicuous lunar craters and mountains. Motion-picture photography of this observatory has also included probably the finest record of a total eclipse of the sun yet recorded on motion-picture film.

Heliostat, Siderostat, and Coelostat.—In many problems of astronomical photography involving heavy apparatus of a complex nature such as a spectrograph or a spectroheliograph, it is often desirable to have the telescope fixed in either a horizontal or vertical direction. Under such circumstances, an auxiliary mirror driven by clockwork, or a synchronous motor, reflects light from the celestial objects into the lens system. One type of instrument used for reflecting light from the sun or star in a constant direction is called a "heliostat" or sometimes a "siderostat." This consists of an optical-plane mirror mounted on a polar axis turned by the driving mechanisms. The mirror is also pivoted along a diameter at right angles to the polar axis, so that it may have a supplementary motion in declination to reach the sun or star on either side of the celestial equator. A great disadvantage of this single mirror heliostat is that the field of view rotates in the telescope as the mirror is driven by clockwork about the polar axis. To obviate this difficulty, the coelostat has been devised. In the coelostat a second mirror is placed south of and above the level of the primary mirror from which the beam of light is first reflected. By the use of this second mirror the light beam received from the moving mirror can be sent in any convenient direction, irrespective of the position of the sun or the celestial object. However, on account of the changing declination of the sun and the wide difference in declination of the star, it is necessary to mount the secondary mirror on a carriage capable of longitudinal motion in two directions. Or, as is sometimes the case, the primary mirror of the heliostat may be mounted on the carriage providing longitudinal motion east and west, while the secondary mirror may be moved along a track north and south. The adjustment of the carriages on the track provide for reaching light from the sun or stars in almost any position of the sky and directing it along the axis of the telescope to be placed in either a vertical or horizontal position.

This combination of two mirrors, which comprises the coelostat, has the advantage that the field does not rotate with the turning of the main mirror about the polar axis if the latter has been adequately adjusted parallel to the axis of the earth for the station of observation. It may be remembered that in the case of the coelostat, a clock or a motor moves the main mirror at a rate of one complete rotation about the polar axis in 48 hr., not once in 24 hr. as is the case of the directly mounted telescope. The explanation is, of course, that the motion of the beam of light reflected from a moving surface is displaced by twice the angle at which the reflecting surface is displaced in the unit of time.

Photographic Plates and Stellar Spectra.—In commercial photography at the present time, photographic emulsions are largely used on celluloid films. The celluloid film has the advantage of lightness in weight, small storage space, and freedom from breakage. In astronomical work, glass, however, is still extensively used for supporting the photographic emulsion. The chief reason for this is the need for making accurate measurements between positions of stars recorded on the plate and for determining with high precision the wavelengths of lines in stellar spectra. For qualitative work to some extent, celluloid film may be employed for astronomical purposes where the question of expansion or shrinkage of the emulsion with moisture or temperature is not sufficiently serious to promote observable distortion. One good example of the use of celluloid film in astronomy is in connection with motion-picture photography of solar prominences and flocculi with the spectroheliokinematograph described in an earlier section.

As much of the observing, however, is astrometrical in nature, the celestial photographer must make provision for adequate storage of glass plates. As each glass plate is essentially an astronomical record of some portion of the sky at a given instant, a collection of such plates forms a veritable photographic library to which references may be later made in case of the appearance of new stars or the discovery of comets, meteors, or minor planets whose earlier history may have escaped attention at the time of the original exposure. The most extensive photographic library of the sky exists at the Harvard College Observatory which now comprises some 400,000 plates.

Speed vs. Grain.—There are two important requisites in the selection of plates for astronomical purposes: (1) speed and (2) grain. Since exposures upon faint celestial objects are necessarily long, often entailing the entire period of darkness in a single night, it is desirable that the emulsion selected should be as fast as is possibly consistent with quality and with size of grain. Some rapid plates that have been developed have poor keeping qualities and contain many blemishes, which, while not a serious handicap in commercial photography, render the plates prohibitive for scientific use, since blemishes and unequal sensitivity may cause false deductions when astronomical objects are examined. In general a fast plate is of coarse grain impeding the detailed recording of celestial objects requiring the highest possible resolution. Furthermore, since stellar images are at best but a small aggregation of reduced silver grains and since the distances between many pairs of images on a photographic plate are often to be measured with the micrometer microscope, a plate of coarse grain introduces difficulties for the measurer in endeavoring to bisect the image of the star with the spider thread of a micrometer microscope. For many purposes, therefore, a relatively slow plate of fine grain is preferable, even though it may add materially to the patience required of the observer by increasing the exposure time at the telescope.

The question of the building up of the photographic image under the action of light and the law of increasing density with illumination and exposure time, commonly known as the "reciprocity law," have been adequately described elsewhere in this handbook. The response of different emulsions to light for a given exposure depends not only on intensity and exposure time but quite as much upon the spectral distribution by wavelengths. The emulsions, therefore, must be selected with a view to color response to which they are most sensitive. The accompanying chart represents the wavelength response of some typical emulsions produced by the Eastman Kodak Co. for astronomical and spectroscopic work. At the lower end of the diagram it will be observed that the O emulsion is responsive to wavelengths between 2500 and 5000 Å. At the extreme upper right of the diagram the emulsion is particularly responsive to wavelengths of 10,000 to 12,000 Å.

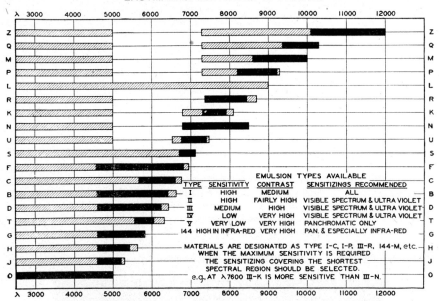

Fig. 4.—Sensitivity of Eastman materials for spectroscopic use. Black portions show wavelengths for which plate is most sensitive. Shaded areas indicate wavelengths of good sensitivity.

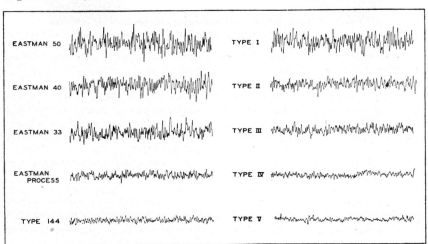

Fig. 5.—Microdensitometer tracings showing the graininess of materials.

The relative graininess of several standard plates manufactured by the Eastman Kodak Co. may be illustrated from microphotometer tracings of regions which have been uniformly blackened. The illustration herewith reprinted by the courtesy of the Eastman Kodak Co. shows these tracings for their plates as follows:

TABLE I.—RESOLVING POWER TO WHITE LIGHT

Material	R. P.	Material	R. P.
Eastman 50	38	Type I	45
Eastman 40	40	Type II	50
Eastman 33	60	Type III	70
Eastman Process	80	Type IV	85
		Type 144	80
		Type V	160

The column marked R. P. opposite the types of emulsions gives the corresponding resolving power which may be defined as the number of lines (black and white of equal width) per millimeter on the plate that may be fully resolved into separate entities. The list is arranged in order of decreasing sensitivity in each of the two listings.

Color Curves.—The selection of plates for photography with refracting telescopes requires that a plate be employed with spectral sensitivity specially suited to the region for which the lens of the refractor has its best field if star images of good definition are to result. This presupposes a knowledge of the color curve of the lens. The color curve of the lens may be determined by finding the exact focus of a star for specified wavelengths as will be explained in a later section.

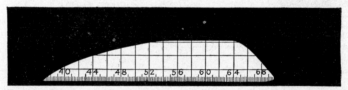

FIG. 6.—Color-sensitivity curve for emulsion *B.* (*Eastman Kodak Co.*)

For most visual refractors the flattest part of the color curve is in the neighborhood of 5600 Å. For photography with such a telescope, plates particularly sensitive to this region should therefore be selected, such as the panchromatic plate of Class B or Class C sensitizing. To prevent blurring of the stellar image by out-of-focus rays of shorter or longer wave lengths, a yellow filter should be used in front of the emulsion, such as the Wratten filter No. 12 which has been adopted by most of the major observatories. The color curve of the panchromatic emulsion B represented above shows fairly uniform sensitivity from wavelengths 5200 to 6400 Å.

The reflecting telescope has, of course, a great advantage in that there is very little spectral selectivity in the reflection of light from a silvered or aluminized surface, at least throughout the spectral region transmitted by the atmosphere of the earth. In astronomical work involving investigations of colors of stars, a variety of plate emulsions may be utilized by the same instrument in conjunction with appropriate filters. This, of course, cannot be so effectively done with the refracting type of instrument on account of the strong color characteristics of the lens.

The existence of dark stars whose radiations are too far in the infrared to make an impression on the ordinary plate have been recently found by Hetzler of the Yerkes Observatory through the use of supersensitive panchromatic emulsions. Often the sensitivity of these emulsions may be materially increased by hypersensitizing with ammonia just prior to exposure. The procedure recommended is to bathe the plate for 1 min. in a 4 per cent solution of 28 per cent ammonia. To avoid fogging, the temperature should be maintained below 55°F. and the plate dried as rapidly as possible immediately afterward. In the use of a fan, care should be exercised to see that the air is dust free, such as will be the case if the procedure is carried out in a suitably constructed drying box. If plates so hypersensitized are not used with reasonable promptness after the hypersensitizing process, they should be kept in a refrigerator until used. On account of their low humidity, mechanically cooled refrigerators are to be preferred to those employing natural ice. The refrigerated plate should be brought to normal temperature 24 hr. before use to prevent the condensation of moisture upon the emulsion during exposure.

Exposures.—Except in the case of photography of the sun, moon, and planets, exposures in celestial photography may vary over a range extending from a few minutes to many hours, depending upon the faintness of the object photographed. There is an old adage current in the early days of photography, "Expose for the shadows; the high lights will take care of themselves." This may be paraphrased for the celestial photographer, "Expose for the faintest stars desired, and let the brightest take care of themselves." The exposure time, therefore, for a celestial photographer depends entirely upon the equipment available, speed of the plate, and the magnitude of the faintest stars which it is desirable to record.

For the faintest extra-galactic nebulae on which theories of the expanding universe depend, the largest telescopes available necessitate exposures equivalent to several nights of observations.

When an exposure of greater length than the duration of darkness in a single night is needed, the slide of the plateholder is closed, the plateholder, however, being left in place, and the instrument undisturbed until the following night. At the beginning of the next period of darkness, the telescope is again directed to the region in question. The same guiding star is brought exactly to the same intersection of the cross wires in the guiding eyepiece. Then the slide of the plateholder is withdrawn and exposure continued. This procedure is not at all uncommon in the case of photographing spectra of faint objects.

In the case of direct photography, there is a certain amount of illumination of the night sky which introduces a slight fogging of the background of the plate. To prolong the exposure so that this fog obliterates the faintest star images recordable is obviously futile. Hence for a given type of emulsion and a given form of telescope, the light of the night sky usually sets a limit to the maximum practical exposure period.

If groups of brighter stars only are desirable, exposure may be restricted to as short an interval as will produce a measurable image of the given stars. The smaller and better defined the star image becomes, the more satisfactory the result. When the plate is exposed for stars of faint magnitude, the stars of the second and first magnitude will be grossly overexposed, producing a large blotch on the plate which will often obscure faint stars in the immediate vicinity of the brighter ones. Often a rotating sector is employed during the exposure to cut down the light of an interfering bright star.

It is appropriate to mention here the marked characteristics on the image of brighter stars found on the images of the photographic plate taken with a reflector as compared with a refractor. In the case of a reflector, the brighter images are characterized by a diffraction pattern which tends to produce a square image, often taking the form of a Greek cross, as the exposure is prolonged. The square image and the cross in the case of the reflector are due to the diffraction pattern of light produced as the result of the finlike supports at the upper end of the tube of the reflector that hold the auxiliary mirror in the axis of the telescope. For stars not overexposed, this characteristic seldom appears and the round images can scarcely be distinguished from those taken with the refractor or lens camera.

Determination of Focus.—Unlike the sun, moon, planets and an occasional comet, the images of stars on photographic plates give no delineation of the object photographed since even the largest stars at the distances encountered in astronomical photography have an angular diameter far below the resolving powers of either the telescope or the photographic plate. The star images obtained vary in size depending upon the brightness of the star photographed. Each image, of course, represents the reduction of a substantial number of silver grains acted upon by the light forming the diffraction image of the source. As the exposure is prolonged, the area of reduction of the silver grains spreads more or less uniformly in all directions, thus enlarging the latent image. In order to produce images of the faintest stars, it is necessary that the plate be in the exact focus of the lens or mirror employed. The focus for stellar work may be determined either by (1) trial and error or (2) calculation from extra-focal images.

In the trial-and-error method a series of exposures of a few seconds are made on a bright star, starting with the plate well within the known focus of the objective or mirror, and making successive exposures after changing the focal setting by 1 or 2 mm. until the final exposure is made with the plate well outside the known focus. By turning one of the micrometer screws of the plate carrier between each exposure, a suitable separation of the multiple images can be secured.

After the plate has been developed, a series of star images will be observed of varying size, depending upon the distance of the plate from the focus at the time of each exposure. If the focal settings for the exposures have been appropriate, there will appear two or three of the smallest images of about the same size. By interpolation, therefore, the focal setting for the smallest image or position of sharpest focus is thus determined.

It is important to record the temperature of the air surrounding the camera, for, owing to the expansion and contraction of the telescope with temperature, the focus thus determined will not be correct for any other operating temperature. If care is taken to provide a series of focal settings for widely different thermometer readings, a curve may be drawn for a given instrument which thereafter will show the proper setting of the plate for any

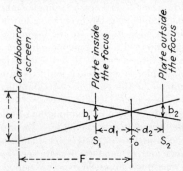

Fig. 7.—Diagram showing method of determining focal length of telescope by extra focus method.

temperature encountered under working conditions. It is obvious that a calibrated scale of some sort should be provided, along with an appropriate index attached to the plateholder to indicate relative settings of the plate with respect to the optical system of the instrument.

It is often desirable to determine the photographic focus of a given telescope or astronomical camera by calculation from the results of two exposures, one of which is made well inside the focal plane and the other of which is made well outside the focal plane.

In determining the focus by the extra-focal method, a cardboard diaphragm is placed in front of the lens or mirror with two openings at the extremities of a diameter. In the case of a lens of 10-in. aperture the openings in the cardboard screen may be cleanly cut round holes of about 1 cm. in diameter. Punches such as are used for cutting wads for gun cartridges or those used by sailmakers for punching holes in canvas to receive grommets serve as excellent tools for the purpose.

If a represents the distance between the two openings in the cardboard screen and b_1 and b_2 represent the corresponding distances between the images formed on the plate taken inside and outside the focal plane at distance d_1 and d_2 from the focal plane, then the following proportion holds:

$$\frac{b_1}{b_2} = \frac{d_1}{d_2} = \frac{a}{F} \tag{4}$$

where F is the distance of the desired focus from the lens or cardboard screen.

In general it is inconvenient to determine by measurement d_1 and d_2 since the position of the focus is itself unknown. If, however, the attached scale reads continuously with increasing numbers from a point inside the focus to points outside the focus, if s_1 and s_2, respectively, represent the scale readings of the index for the positions of the plateholder to which the two exposures are made, and if f_0 equals the scale setting for the focal point, we observe that

$$s_2 - s_1 = d_1 + d_2 \tag{5}$$

From the geometry of the situation

$$\frac{b_1}{a} = \frac{f_0 - s_1}{F} \tag{6}$$

and similarly

$$\frac{b_2}{a} = \frac{s_2 - f_0}{F} \tag{7}$$

Eliminating both a and F from these equations and solving for f_0, we find

$$f_0 = \frac{s_2 b_1 + s_1 b_2}{b_1 + b_2} \tag{8}$$

This gives very simply by calculation the scale setting of the plate for the focal point f_0.

This method has the advantage, in that less labor is entailed in making the series of determinations of the focus for changes in temperatures. It will be observed that neither a, the distance between the apertures in the cardboard screen, nor F, the exact distance to the focal point from the lens, enters into the final result. If the precise focal length of the lens or mirror is desired, *e.g.*, to determine the scale of the plate, this may be found from the expression

$$F = \frac{a}{b_1}(f_0 - s_1) = \frac{a}{b_2}(s_2 - f_0) \tag{9}$$

where a is known from measurements.

It is often desirable, instead of using cardboard diaphragms with a single pair of apertures connected by a diameter, to employ a screen containing two pairs of apertures arranged along diameters at right angles to each other. If the focal setting is different as determined from these separate pairs of apertures, some astigmatism is present in the optical system. A cardboard screen containing multiple holes arranged at different radii from the geometrical center of the lens and in different position angles is frequently employed in observatories for determining the optical quality of the lens or mirror by actually calculating the focus for the objective for different zones and in different planes distributed around the optical axis in position angle.

If a prism is placed to intercept two converging pencils of light from the two-aperture screen, curved spectra of a star will be photographed. By measuring the distances b_1 and b_2 between the components of each pair of spectra at the positions of known wavelengths of the spectrum, *e.g.*, the principal absorption lines of hydrogen, an accurate determination of the color curve of a lens may be made. A graph of the results gives at once the relationship between the focal setting and the wavelengths of the light passing through the lens.

Measurements of the Photographic Plate in Astronomy.—The principal uses of astronomical photographs may be divided roughly into two categories—qualitative and quantitative. In the first category, astronomical photographs may be used for the discovery of new stars, the so-called "novae," comets, and asteroids. Here the important element is the existence of plates taken at different dates or times. The use of a "blink" comparator, whereby it is possible for the eye to scan rapidly the objects first on one plate and then on the other, facilitates very quickly the discovery of an object which exists at a certain date that was not visible at a different epoch. Similarly variations in the brightness of stars known as "variable" stars may be readily detected since the size of the photographic image diminishes with a diminution in the brightness of the variable in question. Large numbers of stars of varying brightness have been found in this way, and a considerable number of planetoids have been added to the asteroid group as a result of their presence being caught on photographic plates taken at various epochs. Many new stars and comets have likewise been found by the sudden impression they have made on the photographic record of a given night. These qualitative uses of the photographic plate continue to form a major feature in the program of many leading observatories.

The more precise use of the photographic plate involves the determination of the exact positions of the star images on the plate and determination of the relative brightness of the objects involved from the apparent size and brightness of the stellar images represented. The branch of astronomy which has to do with the calculations of the exact positions of the stars from their photographic records is known as photographic "astrometry," whereas the field of investigation involved in determining the brightness of the stars from the appearance of their photographic images comprises the branch of astronomy known as photographic "photometry."

Astrometry.—In utilizing the photographic plate for determining accurately the positions of the stars represented upon it, use is made of a precision comparator, or measuring machine. This machine constructed in various forms usually consists of a carriage to which the negative is attached and which is capable of movement by micrometer screws in two directions at right angles to each other. It is of paramount importance that the lead screws of the measuring machine should be of the highest possible precision if great accuracy is to be expected in the results of plate measurements. A microscope provides for a suitable magnification for the photographic images, each of which is bisected by the cross wire in the eyepiece of the microscope while the scale readings of the micrometer screws are set down in turn. It is considered good practice to make from three to five settings upon each star image in turn, always approaching the star image with the cross wire moving in the same direction to avoid backlash. After readings have been made on all the desired objects, the plate is then usually reversed 180° on the carriage for a complementary series of measurements.

The results of the two series are then averaged together for the *x* and *y* coordinates of each object referred to a hypothetical origin. The reduction of these *x* and *y* linear measurements to the astronomical coordinates, "right ascension" and "declination," involve fundamental equations in spherical astronomy, corrections to the curvature of the field of the telescope, and corrections to the adopted scale value of the instrument involved. These considerations are beyond the scope of this chapter.

Distortion.—The interpretation of the positions of stars determined from photographic plates raises the question of possible distortion that may be introduced through the contraction or shrinkage of the photographic gelatin emulsion during the process of development and drying. Extensive investigations have been made to determine the degree of uncertainty which may be introduced on this account through the use of the photographic film in astronomical astrometry. Schlesinger in 1906 concluded from extensive investigation that the amount of error of measurement in photographic plates which could be attributed to distortion were in general of the order of about $+0.009$ mm. (average mean error). The corresponding mean error in the observer's bisection of a star image was calculated to be ± 0.0020 mm.

The subject of film distortion has also been investigated by S. Albrecht, Perrine, Ross, and others. All conclude that the amount of error likely to be introduced by distortion on the photographic film mounted on glass is small compared with errors of bisection of the image by the measurer. It is, perhaps, worth mention that a series of tests by F. E. Ross in 1912 gave for the probable error of the measured distance of air-dried plates $+0.0020$ mm., while the probable error of a measured distance on alcohol-dried plates was ± 0.0012 mm. It would appear that uniformity of drying, a feat which is accomplished very effectively by immersion of the plate in alcohol, is an important factor in keeping film distortion to a minimum. This has been established at least for plates of small dimensions, such as the 27 by 37 mm., used in the investigation by Ross.

Photographic Photometry.—From the introduction of the dry plate into astronomy it was early sensed that the size of the stellar image upon the plate might be taken as an index of the brightness or magnitude of the star. In the year 1857 Bond of the Harvard Observatory demonstrated an empirical relation between the exposure time t and the diameter y of the photographic image which he represented by the equation

$$P + Q = y^2 \tag{10}$$

In the formula P and Q are constants of the plate used. Later investigations by Charlier showed that a close agreement between stellar magnitudes and measured diameters followed if the relationship were expressed logarithmically by the equation

$$m = a - b \log_{10} d \tag{11}$$

where m is the magnitude and d the diameter of the stellar image, a and b being plate constants.

At the Royal Observatory in Greenwich a similar expression involving a square root relationship was found to be applicable to a wider range of conditions as regards plates and instruments than could be satisfied by the logarithmic expression. Accordingly the following form, well known in many observatories, has found wide acceptance:

$$m = a - b\sqrt{d} \tag{12}$$

In utilizing this formula for the calculation of magnitudes of stars from their photographic images, some instrument of precision such as the micrometer microscope is utilized in measuring the value of d, the diameter of the stellar image. The quantities a and b are constants of the plate which may easily be determined from simultaneous equations when two or more stars of known magnitude m are photographed.

Since the photographic image of the star at best shows no well-defined periphery, the principal source of error in measuring is the uncertainty of locating the extremities of the diameter to be measured. It is customary in measurement to measure two diameters at right angles to each other and to take the mean. This is particularly necessary if through poor guiding or optical difficulties the images are at all elongated. Experience shows that even the same eye may pass different judgments on large and small images in the same field. The fact that different observers using the same method will show reasonably good agreement indicates at least the degree of reliability of the results obtained in this way. The process is at best tedious and time consuming so that other methods for calculation of magnitudes from stellar images on photographic plates are employed where a large amount of material needs to be studied. One of these is the scale method, long in use at the Harvard College Observatory.

In this method a scale of varying stellar images is obtained by making multiple exposures at intervals on a single star. By increasing the time of successive exposures in a definite ratio, a series of images varying in size by more or less constant steps may be made. Such a series of images forms a scale plate. By comparing the images on this transparent scale plate with the images of stars of known magnitude on the photographic plate under investigation, it is possible to calibrate this arbitrary scale in terms of magnitudes. With the constants thus determined for the scale plate, visual comparisons are made between the scale plate and stars whose magnitude it is desired to determine. If for example a star image of unknown magnitude is found to fall midway between two images of the scale plate which have been calibrated as 4.2 and 4.8 magnitudes, respectively, the magnitude of the star represented by the image under observation will be designated as 4.5. Such a method has the advantage of rapidity of operation and is effective where estimates of a tenth of a magnitude gives the requisite precision.

Another method extensively used in observatories is that of extra-focal images. In this extra-focal method the plate is purposely placed either inside or outside the focus of the telescope. In this position the converging pencils of light rays from the star are intercepted so that a circular disk of more or less uniform blackening is obtained for each star. If the position of the plate is sufficiently far removed from the focus, all these circular disks will be of the same diameter but will vary in their degree of blackening, depending on the brightness of the star for a given exposure. The degree of blackening of the several images is measured by some form of densitometer in which a calibrated photographic wedge such as is used in the Hartmann microphotometer is frequently employed.

In 1916 the author published an account of an apparatus and method for determining stellar magnitudes from photographic plates, utilizing a thermocouple in conjunction with a light source and galvanometer. The apparatus thus devised was called a "thermoelectric photometer" and was found to be useful not only for measuring the density of the extra-focal images but, through the provision of suitable diaphragms, for the determination of magnitudes from focal images. The thermoelectric photometer has the advantage over visual densitometers in that no auxiliary photographic wedge is necessary. Furthermore a physical method of measurement eliminates eye fatigue and the personal equation involved where visual estimates must be made.

Various adaptations of the thermopile and photoelectric cell have since been made in several forms of densitometers for measuring the blackening of appreciable areas. The advantage of the thermoelectric photometer, herein described in its original form, lies in the fact that it is equally adaptable to the measurement of focal images of stars that vary very widely in size, the apparatus effectively integrating or practically counting the total number of silver grains reduced by a given amount of starlight with a given amount of exposure.

The apparatus consists essentially of a light source consisting of an incandescent lamp fed by constant voltage whose highly condensed filament is projected to the stage of the instrument completely covering a small pinhole diaphragm that may be varied from 0.1 to 1 mm. in size. The diaphragm occupies a position in the center of the observing stage of the instrument. By a suitable optical system an image of the illuminated diaphragm is projected on the surface of the thermocouple in electrical connection with a sensitive galvanometer. A long-focus microscope is used for viewing the small diaphragm at stage center. The photographic plate is placed film down in physical contact with the diaphragm, and the plate is so moved that a star image is adjacent to the diaphragm. Radiation passing from the light source through the diaphragm to the thermocouple produces a given deflection D on the galvanometer. The plate is then moved until the star image to be measured is seen to be central within the diaphragm. The deposit of silver grains in the photographed image will then obstruct a given amount of energy from the cone of light passing into the diaphragm to the thermopile, producing a new galvanometer deflection D'. The relationship holding between the magnitude of the stars and the galvanometer deflections has been found to be

$$m = \alpha - \beta\delta^{\frac{1}{4}} \tag{13}$$

where α and β = plate constants;

δ = the proportional fall in the galvanometer deflection represented by the ratio;

$$\delta = \frac{D - D'}{D} \tag{14}$$

Where δ has been determined for two or more stars of known magnitude appearing on a given plate, the quantities α and β may be at once evaluated. The value of the galvanometer deflection D for a given reading will depend, of course, upon the transparencies of the plate film, the thickness of the glass, the voltage of the source, and the resistance of the thermopile-galvanometer circuit.

Since in the reduction, however, only the ratio $(D - D')/D$ is involved, it will be noted that any change in D due to a change in intensity of the light source or transparency of the film will not affect the result, provided the conditions remain constant through the measurement of D and D' for a given star. Since it is found that variations exist in the transparency of the glass and film over different parts of a plate, it is necessary that measurement through the unexposed portion of the film be taken in the immediate neighborhood of the star for the background readings D. In practice two readings are customarily made on the star image and three readings made on the background immediately adjacent, the respective means being taken for reduction to magnitude. Instruments of the above design have been in use at Harvard, at the Case School of Applied Science, at the Steward Observatory of the University of Arizona, at Perkins Observatory, and the Argentine National Observatories.

A modification of the thermoelectric photometer by Schilt has been in use at Yale, Columbia, and elsewhere. In the Schilt instrument mechanical movements of the plate in rectangular coordinates have been provided with appropriate scales for recording the approximate positions of the stars measured. In the Schilt instrument the plate is held in a vertical plane, whereas in the author's design the plate is allowed to occupy a horizontal position.

Visual Magnitudes and Color Index.—Since the ordinary photographic plate is in general much more sensitive to the blue and violet end of the spectrum, high-temperature stars whose emission is strong in the region of short wavelengths will produce larger and blacker images on the photographic negative than yellow or red stars that to the eye give the impression of equal brightness. Magnitudes of stars therefore determined from the photographic plate will differ considerably from magnitudes of the same stars made with a visual photometer, on account of the large differences in color. Such magnitudes are therefore referred to as photographic magnitudes as distinguished from visual or photometric magnitudes. The photographic plate, however, with an auxiliary yellow filter such as the Eastman Minus Blue may be used to record magnitudes on a visual scale by the photographic process. When the yellow color screen is used, plates sensitive to yellow light, often referred to as orthochromatic plates, are employed. Stellar magnitudes on such a visual scale determined from orthochromatic plates with yellow filters are termed "photovisual" magnitudes.

If one compares photovisual magnitudes with the ordinary photographic magnitudes determined from the usual blue-sensitive plate, the difference is connotated "color index." This quantity is obviously an index of the color of a yellow or red star as compared to a white or blue star. Sometimes a red filter is employed in conjunction with a panchromatic plate in determining the degree of redness a star possesses. A careful comparison of color indices with respect to spectral types of stars yields a rather close correlation, so that stars of such faint magnitudes that a spectroscopic analysis is impossible may roughly betray the type of spectrum from a determination of the color index alone. From the color index the black-body temperature of the stellar surface may likewise be inferred. By the use of plates especially sensitized for the infrared, such as the Eastman M or P, Hetzler of the Yerkes Observatory has been able to photograph dull-red stars not previously rendered visible.

Precautions.—Since photographic photometry is in a sense a quantitative process, certain precautions should be mentioned in the use of star images for photometric purposes.

When focal images of stars are used, stars off the optical axis will produce images that increase in diameter as the distance from the optical center increases. This is due to the fact that the field of any telescope has a certain amount of curvature, and unless, as is done in some instances, provision is made for curving the plate to the known curvature of the field of the lens or mirror, images of stars off the optical axis will be slightly extra focal; hence they are somewhat enlarged.

It is possible to make a magnitude correction for this off-the-axis effect. To do this, the driving clock of the telescope may be stopped just as a bright star is coming into the field of the plate and exposure made. For a bright star a few seconds suffice to gain an impressionable image. After a few moments wait, a second exposure is made, and this process repeated until the star has passed over the entire plate due to the diurnal motion of the sky. If the telescope has been properly focused, the images of the stars at the axis will be true focal images and therefore appear to be of smaller dimensions than the outlying images. By any one of the various means of measurements previously mentioned, the magnitude differences of each of the off-axis images may be determined and plotted against the linear distance of each image from the plate center. From these data a correction curve can be drawn from which a magnitude correction may be deduced to reduce any determined magnitude of a star off the axis to the photographic magnitude which it would have if it had been exposed in the position of the optical axis itself.

In developing plates that are to be used for photometric measurements, relatively weak solutions are employed for a developer, and a development time of 5 min. is desirable. Care should be taken to see that the plate is completely covered with the developer and the tray rocked manually or mechanically throughout development. This insures uniformity in the chemical treatment of the emulsion and also tends to reduce to a minimum the difficulties attributable to the so-called Eberhard effect.

Eberhard Effect.—The Eberhard effect is particularly conspicuous on plates which have been overdeveloped, especially where there is considerable sky fogging in the background. It is noticeable as an aureole or light ring immediately surrounding the stellar image. Its appearance is explained by assuming a slight dilution of the developer in the immediate neighborhood of the star image where reduction of the silver grains draws most heavily upon the constituents of the developing agent. Rocking of the tray during development reduces the trouble to a minimum, as in so doing a fresh supply of developer is constantly brought into the region of each star image reduced. The Eberhard effect when present is particularly troublesome in making "background" readings in the thermoelectric method of measuring a photographic plate, and presents similar difficulty whenever measured diameters are involved.

If photographic magnitudes determined from one plate are to be compared with similar measurements on control plates, it is essential that both plates be developed together in the same tray and likewise receive the same treatment in fixing, washing, and drying.

There are certain characteristics of the photographic plate which the celestial photographer should constantly keep in mind. Some of these greatly affect the sensitivity of the emulsion.

Experience shows that the sensitivity of photographic plates gradually deteriorates with storage. After development this can be noted qualitatively by a certain degree of fogginess, especially near the edges of the plate. If there is a long delay between exposure and development, this change in sensitivity is well marked. Dark areas tend to become darker and light areas fainter with delay between exposure and development. One might say that the contrast is materially increased by delaying the development. In celestial photography, however, this means that faint stars or other celestial objects which might have been near the threshold value of the plate and therefore just detectable upon immediate development may be lost if the time between exposure and development is unduly prolonged. King states that on such plates as he has tested a 15 per cent change has been noted after a month's delay. In one case, where an interval of 9 months elapsed between exposure and development, a change of 80 per cent was noted. In terms of stellar magnitudes, differences as great as a half a magnitude have been found in results, depending upon whether the magnitude scale was based on the brighter or the fainter images on the plate concerned.

Another element affecting the sensitivity of the plate is the amount of humidity present during exposure. Even a small amount of moisture decreases the sensitiveness of a photographic plate seriously. When making exposures for photometric purposes, if comparisons are to be made with a standard light or a comparison star, it is desirable that a control exposure be made both at the beginning and at the end of any series of exposures for photometric purposes. Almost as important as the degree of humidity is the air temperature to which the plate is exposed. With the lowering of the temperature, a plate will in general show fainter stars for a given exposure time. If a series of exposures is made to determine the variation of brightness of a variable star and the temperature is falling, an allowance must be made for this change in temperature during the series of exposures. Usually this is done by comparing the images of other stars in the field whose light is regarded as constant. It is always desirable that plates taken from the darkroom should be in the plateholder and exposed to the temperature of the telescope several hours before the exposure is actually to be made.

Spectrographic Measurements.—The problem of measuring spectrograms in astronomical work is not very different from that of measuring spectrographic plates from laboratory sources. The determination of line positions on a linear scale is made with a suitable comparator. The reduction of scale ratings to wavelengths in the case of prism spectra is usually effected by the use of the well-known Cornu-Hartmann formula

$$\lambda = \lambda_0 - \frac{bs}{s + a} \qquad (15)$$

in which s is the measured distance from the line of reference, while λ, a, and b are constants whose value must be determined from simultaneous equations covering at least three known wavelength measurements.

The problem of determining the abundance of elements from the intensities of the lines in stellar spectra now forms an important study in astrophysics. The theory of ionization phenomena and the method of measuring line contours by means of tracings made with a suitable microphotometer is similar to the problem of the physicist working in a laboratory in spectroscopy. The wide variations in stellar spectra with the varying densities of stellar atmospheres, together with their temperatures, afford intriguing problems for the astronomical spectroscopist.

A problem of astronomical spectroscopy not frequently encountered in ordinary laboratory technique is that of the determination of the radial velocities of stars and nebulae from the displacement of lines in the spectra of celestial objects from their normal standard positions. If Dopper's principle is utilized, the velocity may be determined from the formula

$$v = \frac{c\delta\lambda}{\lambda} \tag{16}$$

where $\delta\lambda$ = the changed wavelength due to the approach or recession of the object under observation;

λ = the standard wavelength of the known line;

c = the velocity of light;

v = the radial velocity or velocity in the line of sight.

The quantity v obviously is plus if $\delta\lambda$ is plus, *i.e.*, if there is an increase in wavelength in the star line from that of the normal position. Similarly v will be minus if the wavelength decreases. In the first instance the celestial object is receding from the earth and in the second instance approaching the earth at the time the spectrogram was made.

Since in general the radial velocity of the star will be desired with respect to the sun, corrections must be made for the orbital motion of the earth and, for greater accuracy, corrections for the movement of the observer on account of the rotation of the earth. A third correction, depending upon the small amount of motion of the earth about the center of gravity of the earth-moon system, must be made for still greater refinement. The reduction of observations involving such corrections and the detailed procedures employed at various observatories are beyond the scope of this handbook. The reader is referred to Campbell's "Stellar Motions," André's "Astronomie Stellaire," and similar works.

Caution sometimes has to be used in interpreting apparent plate velocities for actual velocities of the celestial objects themselves in the line of sight. Pressure and relativity effects also serve to displace lines from their normal positions. It is perhaps patent here to remark the question of the theory of the expanding universe rests upon interpreting plate velocities of the extra-galactic nebulae in terms of the Doppler effect alone. Should there occur reasons for believing in a change of frequency of light through astronomical distances and large units of time, doubt would at once be cast upon the validity of interpreting plate velocities as actual velocities in the line of sight.

Experiments made by McCuskey at the Harvard Observatory hold considerable promise for utilization of objective prism plates for the measurement of radial velocities. Such a method has the advantage of collecting a large amount of data from many stars on a single photograph without recourse to the refinements of the more complicated temperature-controlled stellar spectrograph.

Astronomical Photography Applied to Special Objects.—Much of what has previously been written in this section concerns chiefly stellar photography. For photography of the sun, moon, and planets some special methods of exposure and procedure are necessary. Likewise, the photography of comets and of meteors requires special technique. The application of photography on occasions of total solar eclipses presents again unique problems deserving special consideration.

Photography of the Sun.—Photographs of the sun may be taken satisfactorily with almost any telescope, provided the light is sufficiently diminished and the exposure sufficiently short. In solar photography it is desirable to use a diaphragm over the objective with an aperture which will provide a focal ratio in the neighborhood of from $f/50$ to $f/100$, the smaller ratio being used in the case of telescopes of large aperture. For making the exposure, a focal-plane shutter capable of rendering an exposure of $\frac{1}{1000}$ sec. is desirable. Care must be taken in case of larger focal ratios that a black curtain shutter is not unduly exposed to the image of the sun, as it may be burned through the excessive heat. For this reason use is sometimes made of a metal shutter carrying a narrow slit that may be passed rapidly in front of the plate. The author has found a very serviceable solar camera can be made by utilizing the back of an old Graflex. The back must be provided with a suitable adapter for attaching to the eye end of the telescope. The curtain shutter is set for time exposure with the full aperture open to the ground-glass screen for focusing the image of the sun; the plate-holder is then inserted, the curtain screen reset for exposure, the slide drawn, and the exposure quickly made. As soon as the exposure is made, the telescope is directed away from the sun. In this mode of operation there is little danger from the heat on the curtain shutter. In the case of a visual refractor a color filter must, of course, be employed.

In professional equipment for solar photography at observatories specializing in this work, the telescope may be permanently fixed in a horizontal or vertical position and light from the sun fed to the objective from a heliostat or coelostat. In the case of the heliotelescope the entire building housing the lens and plate forms in itself a darkroom and replaces the more conventional telescope tube. A coelostat is placed in the open under separate shelter, light from which passes through a circular window in the observing house to the telescope objective.

At the Mount Wilson Observatory near Pasadena, Calif., and the McMath-Hulbert Observatory at Lake Angelus, Mich., a vertical form of telescope is employed for solar work. The telescope tube is held in a vertical position by suitable supports to a surrounding tower. At the top of the tower is the coelostat, easily protected from the weather by a dome. The movements of the dome and of the coelostat itself are effected by the use of motors with remote control at the ground end. An observing shelter completely enclosed is constructed at the ground end of the telescope tube. The solar image is formed directly on the plate which reposes in a horizontal position. Because of the form of structure employed in the vertical telescope, such an instrument is frequently called a "tower telescope" or "solar tower."

A tower telescope has an advantage over the horizontal telescope in that the atmospheric disturbances in the case of the vertical tube are less disastrous than is the case in the horizontal telescope where heated strata of air near the ground are constantly rising across the optical path. Since at best, in photographing the sun, a large amount of heat from the ground and surrounding objects creates a turbulence of air through which the light waves pass, it has been found in some localities that the best hours of the day for solar photography are in the early morning before the air and ground have become highly heated.

Because of the value of a knowledge of the number and distribution of spots on the surface of the sun, a group of observatories throughout the world are now cooperating in securing daily photographs of the sun, the results of which are forwarded in this country to the U. S. Naval Observatory in Washington which publishes monthly a summary of solar data.

Photography of the Moon.—While the moon is a very much smaller body than the earth, its proximity to our planet renders it a disk of approximately the same diameter as the sun in the sky. The solar camera forms, therefore, a useful piece of apparatus for lunar photography, the only difference in operation being in the length of the exposure. Under similar conditions, an exposure of the moon should be in the neighborhood of ⅕ sec. as compared with exposures of the sun of 1/1,000 sec. or less, depending upon the filter and focal ratio. The large amount of detail on the lunar surface, including mountain ranges and craters, together with the ever constant change in the illumination as the sun rises and sets over the principal lunar features, presents a fascination to the amateur photographer who has a telescope that may be adapted to the purpose.

If two exposures on the moon are made with the moon at the same phase, but separated approximately one month apart in time, it will be found in general that the features in the second photograph occupy slightly different positions in regard to the lunar disk than in the first photograph taken. This is due to the fact that the lunar axis is tipped slightly toward the earth and also on account of the fact that, while the moon rotates uniformly on its axis in a period of one month, thereby always presenting its same face to the earth, its slightly eccentric orbit causes it to travel at a nonuniform motion. The apparent displacements of certain lunar features, therefore, with respect to the disk for the reasons mentioned, are called "librations." If the two photographs taken at intervals of one month at corresponding phases of the moon are mounted together and viewed with a stereoscope, a beautiful stereoscopic effect results from these librations, the moon presenting in the stereoscope a very real spherical form. For one who is interested in lunar photography detailed maps of the lunar surface have been published and may be obtained from book sellers and scientific supply houses.

Photography of Comets.—The appearance of a comet in the sky affords unusual opportunity for the celestial photographer. Great detail may be obtained from cometary photographs that cannot be observed by the naked eye. The principal trick in photographing a comet is to have an auxiliary guiding telescope attached to the photographic telescope so that the head or nucleus of the cometary object may be set on the cross wires of the guiding eyepiece and kept in position by means of the slow motions provided through the entire exposure. This is necessary since a comet is a relatively swift-moving object among the stars.

The driving clock of the telescope can be expected to follow only the general diurnal motion of the sky as the stars move from east to west. As the observer must make the photographic plate register constantly with the comet itself, star images on the plate after development will be found to take the form of streaks or trails rather than round images. The length of the streak or trail will obviously increase with the length of the exposure, and the general direction of these star trails will represent the motion of the comet among the stars while the object is being photographed. The exposure time will depend entirely upon the brightness of the object and the amount of detail desired. It may extend from a few minutes to several hours. The development of the first trial plate will give an index as to the requisite exposure time to bring out features that may be desired.

Photography of Meteors.—The photography of meteors or shooting stars requires cameras of relatively short focus. Since the appearance of a meteor is in a large sense accidental and there is no way of determining with any accuracy the precise point in the sky at which meteors appear, an astronomer frequently employs a battery of cameras of wide-angle lenses pointed in different directions, so that a large area of the sky can be covered. On the occasion of anticipated meteoric showers, such as the Perseids which occur during the month of August or the Leoneids which appear in the middle of November, the cameras may be pointed in the general direction of the so-called "meteor radiant," the constellation of Perseus for the August meteoric shower and the Sickle in the constellation of Leo for the November meteors. The battery of cameras is easily attached to an axis which will be driven by clockwork so that the stars in the region being photographed will appear as point images and afford a background for determining positions of the meteor trails as they may occur. The flash of a meteor across the field of view will leave its impression as a streak on the photographic plate. Frequently such a streak will be of nonuniform brightness, depending upon sporadic changes in the brightness of the meteor itself.

Photography is the one exact means for determining with accuracy the positions of meteor trails from different points of observation. A comparison of plates simultaneously exposed at two stations a few miles apart makes possible the determination of the altitude above the earth at which the meteor first became visible and also frequently the altitude at which the meteor vanished. The mathematical calculation of the altitude of meteor trails from such photographic observations is beyond the scope of this book, and the reader is referred to the more extended treatises on this branch of the subject.

Photography of the Planets.—Photography of the planets, with the possible exception of Jupiter and Saturn is rather beyond the scope of the amateur. In planetary photography an auxiliary enlarging lens is employed in the optical axis of the telescope objective and somewhat inside the focal plane. Because of the variation in "seeing" conditions and the necessity for satisfactory moments when the atmosphere is particularly tranquil, an auxiliary visual telescope is a prerequisite to planetary photography. A shutter which may be quickly operated by a bulb or finger release is also essential. The double-slide plateholder is a convenience in planetary photography for moving the plate between exposures. Since at best a planetary image is exceedingly small, multiple exposures may be made on a single plate, the images being duly separated by appropriate movements of the double-slide plate carriage between exposures. The observer, who is scrutinizing the planet through the visual telescope, awaits the supreme moment which is well known to all seasoned observers. At such times planetary detail may be caught at its best during the few brief seconds when atmospheric disturbances are at a minimum. At this moment the shutter is released for appropriate exposure but is instantly closed if the planetary image becomes blurred through atmospheric turbulence. Extraordinarily good photographs of Jupiter, Saturn, and Mars under favorable conditions have been taken at the Lick and Lowell Observatories. The Lick Observatory located on Mount Hamilton, Calif., and the Lowell Observatory at Flagstaff, Ariz., are particularly well favored climatically for planetary photography.

Various filters are frequently employed to bring out planetary details. Photographs of Mars made in blue and red light on plates sensitive to these colors invariably show wide differences in the characteristics. It appears that with blue-sensitive plates light is reflected or scattered chiefly from the atmosphere surrounding the planet, giving a somewhat diffuse image. In the case of photography with red light, the filtered rays are those that have penetrated more extensively the atmosphere of the planet and are reflected more completely from the surface of the planet, rendering visible a large amount of surface detail that it is not possible to photograph in the use of ordinary plates which are blue sensitive. For further details on planetary photography, the reader is referred to publications on these subjects issued by the Lick Observatory of Mount Hamilton, Calif., and the Lowell Observatory of Flagstaff, Ariz. A good photographic image of any of the planets will stand enlargment from the original negative several times. By repeated copying, contrast may also be enhanced.

Eclipse Photography.—One of the primary objects in expeditions to observe total eclipses of the sun is the photography of the solar corona, that gaseous appendage to the sun which is visible only when the brilliant disk of the sun itself is hidden by the dark disk of the moon that completely covers it during the moments of total eclipse. A total eclipse of the sun may last from a fraction of a second to a period of 7 min. 40 sec. Exposures on the corona are usually made with lenses of great focal length to obtain images of requisite size to show the desired details. Suitable exposure times will vary from 1 sec. to ½ min. or more. Usually a series of plates will be taken with varying exposures. The short exposures are necessary to gain detail of the structure of the corona near the edge of the sun. The longer exposures will reveal the outlying stretches or extremities of the corona, but the inner parts on the resulting negative will be greatly overexposed. By suitable local reduction of the negative, however, it is often possible to get a fair representation of the entire structure of the corona from the edge of the sun to the outlying rims. A plate locally reduced, however, loses much of its scientific value since the relative blackening of the various parts of the corona in the untouched negative provide an index of the relative brightness of the emission of the light from the various regions. In preparing the plates for eclipse photography, it is quite necessary that the plate be backed with any one of a number of suitable backings to prevent halation, or double-coated nonhalation plates should be employed.

Lenses up to 40-ft. focal length are frequently transported to all parts of the world on eclipse expeditions. Since it is possible to calculate in advance the exact place which the sun will occupy in the sky during the moments of eclipse, temporary structures can be built for supporting such lenses and the elaborate equatorial mounting of the telescope dispensed with. In the case of the cameras of great focal length, usually no attempt is made to move the lens during the period of exposures, but the plateholder itself is mounted on a carriage, and clockwork is provided for moving the same laterally at right angles to the optical axis in order to follow the small shift in the image of the sun during the exposure, thus facilitating very greatly the mechanical arrangements involved. In the case of a total solar eclipse lasting 4 min., the movement of the solar image during this interval for a lens of 40-ft. focus will be approximately 8.4 in. This gives an idea of the amount of movement of the plate required for an eclipse of average duration. The necessity for providing motions of the plate during even a single exposure becomes apparent when we see that in this instance the solar image would be displaced by ½ in. during even the relatively brief exposure of 15 sec. Photographs of eclipses with ordinary cameras having no guiding mechanism have been satisfactorily made by giving very brief exposures in cases where the lenses used are of but a few inches focal length. Such photographs, however, can scarcely be said to have much professional or scientific value.

The application of motion-picture photography to the registration of eclipse phenomena, however, has come to occupy an important part in connection with eclipse expeditions. With the best of lenses of 20-in. focal length, an image of the sun of satisfactory size can be secured on the ordinary 35-mm. film. The complete registration of both the total and partial phases of the eclipse forms an important record of sky conditions, transparency, passing of clouds, etc. It is often of considerable value afterward in checking visual impressions. During the partial phase it is necessary that the smallest stop possible be employed, together with a dense red filter, in order to diminish sufficiently the direct rays of the sun to prevent overexposure. At the moment of complete obscuration of the solar disk by the encroaching moon, the filter must be removed, and the stop opened widely in order to obtain the requisite amount of exposure for the corona itself. At the first indication of the reappearance of the disk of the sun, the aperture is again reduced and the filter restored while the motion-picture camera continues to record the second partial phase.

Since the total duration of eclipse phenomena including both partial phases will last for something like 4 hr., it is obviously a waste of time and film to photograph the partial phase continuously in the kinematograph. A single exposure with the motion-picture camera made at ½- or ¼-min. intervals is entirely sufficient in the partial phase. An exposure once in 8 sec. has also been frequently used. In any of these procedures an abundant amount of film will result for educational or entertainment purposes in depicting the progress of the phenomenon. It is necessary, of course, if satisfactory registration is to be obtained, that the motion-picture camera be fixed to an equatorial mounting driven by clockwork to follow the movement of the sun during the interval. A guiding telescope for checking the registration continuously is also desirable. It is hardly necessary to remark that the guiding telescope should be provided with a dense dark glass in front of the eyepiece for the proper protection of the eyes of the observer.

Bibliography

STETSON, H. T.: On an Apparatus and Method for Thermoelectric Measurements for Photographic Photometry, *Astrophys. J.*, **43** (Nos. 4 and 5) (1916).
————: Investigations of Plate Errors with the Thermo-electric Photometer, *Astrophys. J.*, **58** (No. 1) (1923).
KING, E. S.: "A Manual of Celestial Photography," Eastern Science Supply Company (1931).
————: Standard Tests of Photographic Photometry, *Harvard Observatory Ann.*, **59**.
ROSS, F. E.: "Physics of the Developed Photographic Image," Eastman Monograph 5.

CHAPTER XXVI

HIGH-SPEED PHOTOGRAPHY

By Harold E. Edgerton

High-speed photography is defined for this section as applying to single-exposure cameras that take photographs in less than 1/10,000 sec. and to motion-picture cameras that operate at speeds in excess of 300 frames per second. These limitations are purposely set to exclude cameras of the moving-shutter type, such as the Compur and focal-plane types, and high-speed motion-picture cameras of the intermittent-motion types—all of which are discussed elsewhere in this book.

By the use of high-speed photography an observer is able to obtain a picture or a series of pictures which accurately record an action as a function of time, permitting a detailed study which cannot be made otherwise. The pictures in a series may be analyzed frame by frame, or they may be projected on the screen in ultra-slow motion, enabling the eye to see vagrant actions that would not otherwise be seen. Furthermore, since the film records the position of objects as a function of time, velocity and acceleration can be calculated. Speed photography has proved its worth in scientific and industrial research and is destined to an important future in photography in all fields of endeavor.

Single-exposure High-speed Cameras.—In this classification are grouped cameras capable of taking single photographs in less than 10^{-4} sec. Both mechanical and photographic factors make difficult, if not impossible, a camera of any of the usual types for very short exposures, and therefore they are not considered here. The cameras described are of the type that rely upon an electrically controlled flash of light for both the required very high intensity of illumination and for the short duration of exposure time. The most satisfactory electrical arrangement consists of a spark in air or in a gas-filled discharge tube through which the energy stored in a condenser is discharged at the desired instant. With this method the exposure time is determined entirely by the duration of the flash of light and not by any mechanical shutter. It should be mentioned that this camera may require a darkened room to prevent exposure due to the ordinary light, though in many cases the shutter setting, the lens aperture, and the type of film are such as to give no appreciable exposure with the average level of illumination.

In general there are two methods of lighting: (1) silhouette and (2) the usual reflected-light type. The silhouette method takes several forms, each requiring a point source of light for best results. In some cases an open spark is satisfactory. The dimensions of the spark can be restricted mechanically by causing the spark to occur in a small hole in an insulator. Figure 1 illustrates several methods of silhouette photography, and it is to be noted that all use a point source of light—a spark in air. The upper sketch shows the simplest method of silhouette photography and one that produces excellent results. It is to be noted that no lens is used, as the image is a true shadow of the subject. Therefore the size of the film must be comparable to the size of the subject. A second limitation to this method is the requirement of a darkened room so that the ordinary light will not fog the film. In some cases this is inconvenient, since considerable time is usually required to uncover a large sheet of film or sensitive paper. A modification of the method is to substitute a ground glass for the film and then photograph the image from the back with an ordinary camera.

The second method illustrated in Fig. 1 uses a large condensing lens (not necessarily of high optical quality) between the subject and the light source. Adjustments are made so that the image of the light source appears on the film as a circle large enough to cover the film. The camera lens is then focused on the subject (using reflected light), and a shadow of the subject appears on the film, reduced in size optically as in ordinary photographic procedure. The aperture is very small, since it is determined by the dimensions of the light source, and therefore the depth of focus is

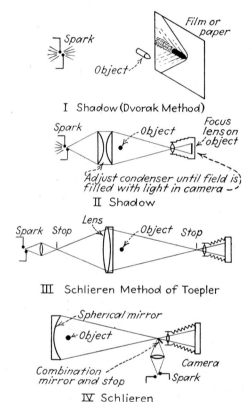

I Shadow (Dvorak Method)

II Shadow

III Schlieren Method of Toepler

IV Schlieren

Fig. 1.—Diagram illustrating various methods of making high-speed silhouette photographs.

great. Two advantages result from the use of this arrangement, *viz.*, (1) the effective use of the light, since a large cone of light is collected; and (2) the ability to change the image size on the film. However, the field is restricted to the diameter of the condensing lens. This method is useful for taking high-speed motion pictures on continuously moving film with stroboscopic light.

The last two arrangements of Fig. 1 illustrate methods of the "Schlieren" type of silhouette photography. The upper diagram shows the use of a lens, and the lower, of a mirror. In both most of the light is cut off by stops, and variation of the refractive index of the material in the field of view deflects the light rays passing through the affected region slightly, so that they clear or strike the stop and thereby either increase or decrease the amount of light reaching the film at the corresponding image points. In this way variations in density in a volume of gas, such as those produced by sound waves, and thermal disturbances, may be observed and photographed.

An optically perfect lens or mirror is required for Schlieren photography in order to obtain a uniformly illuminated field. In fact, the arrangement is exactly the same as the test used for the final polishing of optical surfaces.

The size of field is naturally limited to the size of the lens or mirror. Since corrected lenses of large diameter are very expensive or not obtainable, mirrors are more commonly used. The references show numerous different optical arrangements.

Shadow photography is often of great advantage in many practical problems because the amount of light required is small compared with that needed for reflected-light photography. Furthermore, a sharp image is obtained which is useful for measurement. The waves in air, such as are caused by bullets, may be recorded by the silhouette methods, especially the Schlieren method, which can be made very sensitive. In fact the Schlieren arrangement can be made sufficiently sensitive to observe heat waves rising from one's hand, because of the fact that the index of refraction of air

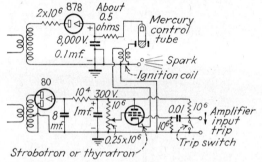

Fig. 2.—Electrical circuit for making silhouette photographs.

changes with temperature. The principal disadvantages of the silhouette method are that only an outline is obtained and that with some kinds of shadow photography the experiment must be performed in a darkened room.

The electrical circuit of a typical arrangement for taking silhouette photographs is shown as Fig. 2. The various circuit elements are labeled in the figures. Many other circuits are described in the references, which should be consulted for further details.

Since the light from the sparks in air and from most of the other gaseous-discharge sources is largely in the blue end of the spectrum, the less sensitive films or papers—such as the process or positive types—are often satisfactory.

The duration of the flash which determines the exposure time for silhouette photographs depends upon the electrical arrangement and also upon the afterglow in the gas. The duration is dependent on the natural frequency of the discharge circuit, which in turn increases with the size of the condenser and the inductance resulting from the connecting wires and the internal inductance of the condenser. Furthermore, discharges in circuits of this type usually oscillate a great many cycles—sometimes as many as 10 or more. For this reason sufficient resistance is often added to damp critically the oscillations. This resistance decreases the duration of the flash but at the same time reduces the quantity of light by from five- to tenfold, which is a serious disadvantage. The mercury-control tube shown in Fig. 2 has the advantage of tending to prevent the reversal of current, as well as serving as a switch for starting the spark gap at the required instant. The ignition coil starts conduction in the mercury-control tube and simultaneously causes the spark gap to break down. The effective exposure time for silhouette spark photographs may easily be made as short as 10^{-6} sec. and, under favorable conditions, may be as short as 10^{-7} sec.

Reflected-light Spark Photography.—Reflected-light photography, with illumination from sparks or from gas-filled tubes, produces photographs similar to those obtained with ordinary lighting and camera technique, except that since the exposure time is not limited by a mechanical shutter, it may be made extremely short. The electrical circuit for producing the short condenser discharges through the lamps is similar in operation to that used for silhouette photography. However, with reflected-light illumination it is not necessary to have a point source of light; in fact, it is usually better to have a light source of large area to give a better distribution of illumination. Reflected-light photography usually requires considerably more energy because the light is not so effectively used. Therefore the energy-storage capacity of the condensers must be larger than is required for silhouette photography. A typical circuit is shown in Fig. 3 with the details explained in the caption. This equipment will give sufficient illumination for photographing an area approximately 6 ft. square, using an $f/8$ stop, orthochromatic film, and an effective exposure of about $1/50,000$ sec.

The effective exposure time for reflected-light photographs is longer than for silhouette photographs, principally because the energy required is much larger. How-

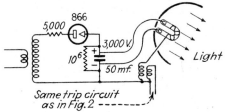

Fig. 3.—Diagram of electrical circuit for making high-speed photographs by reflected light.

ever, a very short flash is seldom necessary, and except for certain ballistic problems a flash duration of less than $1/50,000$ sec. is entirely adequate and easily obtained. Reflected-light photographs of small areas can be taken with an exposure time of 10^{-6} sec. if circuit conditions are adjusted properly and if the afterglow in the gas is extinguished.

Correct timing of the flash of light is often the most important part of any particular problem. For example, to obtain a photograph of a golf ball compressed with a driver requires that the flash of light be timed to about $1/10,000$ sec.; otherwise the photograph will be taken either before the ball is hit, or after it has left the club. The simplest method of timing is to arrange the switch marked "trip" (Figs. 2 and 3) so that contact is made at the desired instant. In the case of the golf ball two small wires can be arranged behind the ball so that the club will knock them together at the desired part of the swing. A series of photographs with different positions of the trip wires shows successive stages of the action, if the action can be repeated. Other methods of tripping can be used, such as the interruption of a beam of light to a photocell or the use of a microphone to pick up a sound impulse. A time delay can be introduced electrically to delay the flash of light by a known interval of time after the signal is received.

Single-flash high-speed photography is much more convenient to use than high-speed motion-picture photography, since the apparatus required is much simpler and since standard cameras and lens equipment can be used. Any camera is capable of taking photographs with effective exposures of 10^{-5} to 10^{-6} sec., simply by using a source of light actuated by a condenser discharge. While only one photograph at a time can be taken by this method, in contrast to a large number by the high-speed motion-picture camera, many practical problems can be solved by this method, particularly if the action of the subject can be repeated.

High-speed Motion-picture Cameras.—Motion pictures taken at high speed and subsequently shown at ordinary projection speeds have the effect of slowing fast motions so that the eye can see what is going on. Naturally the faster the action that is being photographed, the faster the camera must be driven. It seems impractical, because of mechanical limitations, to drive the usual intermittent types of motion-picture cameras at speeds in excess of about ten times normal. Practically all cameras operating above this speed depart from the intermittent-motion mecha-

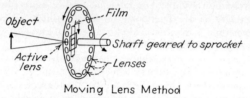

Moving Lens Method

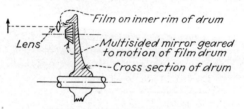

Moving Mirror Method

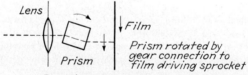

Rotating Plane Prism Method

Fig. 4.—Diagram showing various possible optical systems for use in high-speed motion-picture cameras.

nism and use instead a continuously moving-film mechanism. Although the film moves continuously during the exposure, the image cast by the lens on the film must either move with the film or the film must not move an appreciable distance during the exposure time. The first requirement is met by the use of a moving optical system to keep the image stationary with respect to the moving film during the exposure time; and the second, by the use of intermittent illumination (stroboscopic light) for exposing the photographs, each flash of light lasting such a short time that sharp images are obtained although the film is moving. The moving-optical-system method is especially well adapted to the study of subjects which emit their own light, common examples of which are the burning of vapors, the action of explosives, the motions of an electric arc, the reactions in a photoflash lamp, and the behavior of the cathode spot in a mercury-arc tube.

There are three general types of the moving-optical-system camera: (1) those using rotating lenses or slits, (2) those using rotating mirrors, and (3) those using rotating prisms. Some of these are illustrated in Fig. 4. A comprehensive treatment of these and other moving-optical systems as applied to projectors has been made by Tuttle and Reed.

The rotating-prism type is available from the Eastman Kodak Co., Rochester, N. Y. The Carl Zeiss Company, Jena, Germany, manufactures a camera in the second classification. Cameras of the moving-lens type are made by the Allgemeine Elektrische Gesellschaft, Berlin, Germany, and by the Merlin and Gevin Company, Grenoble, France.

In high-speed cameras employing stroboscopic light, the film is moved past the lens at a constant speed; and each time the film has moved the distance occupied by one frame, the subject is illuminated by a short intense flash of light. The time at which the flash occurs is in some cases controlled by a contact disk rigidly attached to the film-driving mechanism and properly spaced so that the motion-picture film is properly framed for projection in standard equipment. Normal illumination such as that encountered indoors is insufficient to fog the film in a stroboscopic-light camera because the film passes the lens so rapidly. A stroboscopic-light camera is manufactured by the General Radio Company, Cambridge, Mass.

When motion pictures are taken at high speed with either type of camera,[1] the film must move rapidly, and one of the important problems in the design is to make the film travel at the requisite speed without vibrating, fluttering, or breaking. The rapidly moving film must be guided properly, but the friction in sliding contacts may generate enough heat to ignite it. Static charges of electricity resulting from the friction must also be avoided, as they cause dendriform exposures on the film. Further than simply traveling smoothly at a high speed, it is important that the film accelerate rapidly so that it will attain the proper speed before much of it has passed through the camera. The acceleration must be uniform as well as rapid, as sudden jerks are likely to break the film.

TABLE I.—SPEED OF FILM IN TERMS OF FRAME HEIGHT AND RATE OF EXPOSURE

Frame height, in.	Exposures per second							
	500	1000	2000	4000	8000	16,000	32,000	64,000
	Film velocity, ft. per sec.							
0.75[a]	31.25	62.5	125.0	250	500	1000	2000	4000
0.30[b]	12.50	25.0	50.0	100	200	400	800	1600
0.15	6.25	12.5	25.0	50	100	200	400	800
0.075	3.175	6.25	12.5	25	50	100	200	400

[a] Standard 35-mm. frame height.
[b] Standard 16-mm. frame height.

The height of the frame, as well as the rate of making exposures, is a factor influencing the film speed, since it is not necessary for the film to move as rapidly for a small frame as for a large one. Most of the very high-speed pictures are small in size, in some cases so minute as to be of little use in presenting detail even after enlargement. Conversely, if the film speed is increased in order to produce larger pictures, the camera becomes so bulky that it is no longer portable, and the subjects must be brought to

[1] Possible exceptions are those high-speed cameras employing stationary film and a large number of lenses or a number of spark sources of light.

the camera—a serious limitation to its usefulness. Table I shows the speed of the film in feet per second as a function of the height of the frame and the number of exposures per second.

When film speeds higher than about 150 or 200 ft. per sec. are desired, a short strip of film is usually placed on the periphery of a drum. The length of film that can be used is limited to the circumference of the drum, but very high film velocities can be attained in this way more easily than with a long strip. There are no acceleration problems, since the film may be brought up to speed as slowly as desired. Cameras of this type require a shutter that remains open during one revolution only, to prevent multiple exposure of the film.

Still another method employs a stationary film over which the beam of light is rapidly thrown by means of a rapidly rotating mirror.

The electric spark in air produced by the discharge of an electrical condenser through an air gap has been extensively used as a source of stroboscopic light. The duration of the flash can be made as short as 1/100,000 sec., or less. A spark gap, however, presents serious problems when it is desired to produce enough light to illuminate an area several feet square 1000 or more times a second, because of the great power required and the difficulty of controlling it. Although a spark is not an efficient source of light, it is sufficient for some purposes, such as silhouette photography. The light is highly concentrated, having a high intrinsic brilliancy which permits the use of reflectors and condensing lenses.

The discharge of electrical condensers through gas-filled tubes, such as the argon-filled tube of Fig. 3, provides an efficient source of intermittent light for taking high-speed motion pictures. In service the lamp is connected to a condenser and is made to flash at the desired instant by suddenly charging an external grid to a high potential. Naturally the circuit must be capable of recharging the condenser in time for the next flash, and this becomes increasingly difficult as the frequency of exposure or the power used per flash is increased. Difficulty is sometimes encountered because of the tendency of the tube to hold into a steady glow or to fail to deionize, *i.e.*, to trip by itself as the voltage builds up across the condenser. A mercury-control tube of the type shown in Fig. 2 can be used to advantage to overcome these limitations.

Bibliography

Periodicals:

ABRAHAM, H., E. BLOCH, and L. BLOCH: Ultra-rapid Kinematograph, *Compt. rend.*, **169**, 217 (1919).

LEGG, J. W.: The Polar, Multi-exposure, High Speed Camera, *Elec. J.*, **16**, 509–512 (1919).

CONNELL, W. H.: The Heape and Crylls Machine for High-speed Photography, *J. Sci. Instruments*, **4**, 82–87 (1926).

JENKINS, C. F.: The Chronoteine Camera, *J. Soc. Automotive Engrs.*, **22**, 200–202 (1928); *Trans. Soc. Motion Picture Engrs.*, No. 25, p. 25 (1926).

SUHARA, T.: New High Speed Kinematographic Camera, *Proc. Imp. Acad. (Tokyo)*, **5**, 334–337, 1929.

CRANZ, C., and H. SCHARDIN: Kinematographie auf ruhendem Film und mit extrem hoher Bildfrequenz, *Z. Physik*, **56**, 147 (1929). Contains a short bibliography.

SUHARA, T.: New Ultra-Speed Kinematographic Camera, Aeronaut. Research Inst., *Tokyo Imp. Univ. Rept.* **60**, 187–194 (1930).

ENDE, W.: Theorie des Thunschen Zeitdehners und ihre Anwendung in der Aufnahmepraxis, *Z. tech. Physik*, **11**, 394 (1930); *A E G Zeitdehner*, *A E G Mitt.*, November (1933).

HARVEY, E. N., and A. L. LOOMIS: High Speed Photomicrography of Living Cells Subjected to Supersonic Vibrations, *J. Gen. Physiol.*, **15**, 147–153 (1931).

ROTHROCK, A. M.: The N.A.C.A. Apparatus for Studying the Formation and Combustion of Fuel Sprays and the Results from Preliminary Tests, *Nat. Advisory Comm. Aeronaut. Tech. Rept.* 429 (1932).

TUTTLE, F. E., and C. D. REED: The Problem of Motion Picture Projection from Continuously-Moving Film, *J. Optical Soc. Am.*, **22**, (No. 2), 39 (1932). Also in *J. Soc. Motion Picture Engrs.*, **20**, 3 (1933).

TUTTLE, F. E.: A Nonintermittent High-Speed 16-mm Camera, *J. Soc. Motion Picture Engrs.*, **21**, 474 (1933).

SCHARDIN, H.: Das Toeplersche Schlierenverfahren, *Z. Ver. deut. Ing.* **367,** August (1934).   Contains a very comprehensive bibliography.

SEQUIN, A.: Les appareils stroborama et leurs applications, *Bull. soc. franç. élec.*, **4,** 405 (1934).

SUITS, C. G.: Notes on High Intensity Sound Waves, *Gen. Elec. Rev.*, No. 39, 430 (1936).

EDGERTON, H. E., K. J. GERMESHAUSEN, and H. E. GRIER: High-Speed Photographic Methods of Measurement, *J. Applied Phys.*, **8** (No. 1) (1937).

BEAMS, J. W.: High Rotational Speeds, *J. Applied Phys.*, **8** (No. 12), **795** (1937).

SCHARDIN, H., and W. STRUTH: Neuere Ergebnisse der Funkenkinematographie, *Z. tech. Physik*, **11,** 474 (1937).

HERRIOTT, W.: High-speed Motion Picture Photography Applied to the Design of Telephone Apparatus, *J. Soc. Motion Picture Engrs.*, **30,** 30 (1938).

————: High Speed Motion Picture Photography, *Bell System Tech. J.*, **17** (No. 3), 393–405 (1938).

TAYLOR, H. G., and J. M. WALDRAM: Improvements in the Schlieren Method, *J. Sci. Instruments*, **10** (No. 12), p. 378, 1932.

QUAYLE, PHILIP P.: Spark Photography and its Application to Some Problems in Ballistics, *Nat. Bur. Standards (U.S.), Sci. Papers* 508.

Books:

WORTHINGTON, A. M.: "A Study of Splashes," Longmans (1908).

CRANZ, C.: "Lehrbuch der ballistik," Vol. 3, Chap. 8, Springer, (1926).

CHAPTER XXVII

PHOTOMICROGRAPHY AND TECHNICAL MICROSCOPY

By Francis F. Lucas

Principles of Photomicrography. *Introduction.*—Technical microscopy and photomicrography are widely employed in science and industry. The microscope produces an image which the eye can see; photomicrography is the art of recording the image photographically so that a permanent record is available for reference and study. At its best the microscope will reveal on the photographic plate details of structure which the eye fails to observe.

Metallography, or that particular branch of it which relates to the microstructure of metals, has grown in the life span of those now living to be one of the most important single control methods of the metal industry. In the paint, pigment, and color industries, improved methods of producing fine pigments have taxed the powers of visible-light microscopes, and to photograph clearly very small pigments, the ultraviolet microscope is the last resort. In the medical and biological sciences the microscope fills an important place. With recent developments in ultraviolet microscopy the resolving powers available for biological investigations have been more than doubled. Since selective absorption to ultraviolet light is manifested by many cells, it is now possible to photograph living cells at extremely high magnifications. By means of the ultraviolet microscope photographs may be taken on optical planes spaced $\frac{1}{4}\mu$ apart, making it possible to photograph a single living cell, though microscopic in size, on many different planes from the top to the bottom of the cell. The same technique may also be applied to many problems of industrial microscopy.

Improvements in resolving powers have made it possible to photograph details of structure which measure but 200 atom diameters across. Vision has been pushed downward into the range of colloidal matter so that by ultraviolet microscopy and refined methods of ultramicroscopy the behavior of colloidal dispersions may be studied to better advantage.

The aim in photomicrography should be a faithful reproduction of the image. The image should be in exact focus. Out-of-focus effects may result in misleading conclusions. No one should ever attempt to interpret details in terms of structure or composition when the particular details are not in exact focus. Halos, shadows, flares, and other abnormal effects of lighting, photography, or microscopy have no place in scientific or industrial photomicrography. When photographing a preparation which consists of particles of matter differing in size or when the detail is not all confined to a single focal plane, it is obvious that some of the detail will be above or below the focal plane and therefore out of focus. Such conditions are encountered frequently. The photographic results are of value only as they relate to the details which are in focus in the photomicrograph.

Principles, Technique, and Optics of Photomicrography.—This section treats of principles, technique, optics, light, and materials. It omits, intentionally, descriptive matter of apparatus, information about which is liberally distributed by manufacturers.

The design trend of scientific apparatus is being changed from time to time. This has resulted in the gradual evolution of better apparatus which is more stable, is made of better materials, possesses better mechanical and optical features, can be operated more easily, and is readily and conveniently altered to suit a wide diversity in work. Research laboratories are having little difficulty with the present inverted-type microscope whereas older apparatus was a constant source of trouble, largely because the assembly was flexible on an optical bench and was not easily aligned and coordinated. The older equipment also had mechanical weaknesses which tended to introduce optical misalignment often difficult to recognize and rectify.

By photomicrography is meant the adaptation of photography to microscopy or the art of photographing a magnified image. The scope of the art embraces the reproduction of images ranging from actual size to magnifications of several thousand times. Low-power photomicrography may be considered as treating with magnitudes from about 1 to 30 diameters, medium-power work with magnifications from about 30 to 500 diameters, and high-power photomicrography generally includes all magnifications in excess of about 500 diameters. The apparatus used in each case is different, and the preparation of the material and its treatment also differ. For low-power work the microscope is often dispensed with entirely, the lens being secured directly to the camera; in other cases the microscope serves only as a support for a specialized camera lens. In the treatment of most transparent mounts an illuminating device termed a "substage condenser" is necessary, the microscope then forms a very necessary adjunct to low-power photomicrography.

Medium-power photomicrography always requires a microscope, and because rigidity in mounting and accuracy in adjustment are necessary, an optical bench is desirable on which the microscope and a suitable illuminating train are mounted.

For high-power photomicrography great attention is given to the mechanical and the optical design of the apparatus. It is extremely important to prevent shocks, vibrations, and extraneous disturbances from reaching the optical bench or camera. It is also important that the apparatus and the camera vibrate or move as a unit and that vibrations are not introduced, through use of the apparatus, which will result in a slight change in focus of the microscope objective. The operations of removing a focusing screen and substituting a plateholder can introduce sufficient shock to throw the image completely out of focus unless the mechanical design has been carefully worked out. For high-power photomicrography only the best optical systems should be employed. A skilled technician may produce remarkable medium-power results with quite ordinary apparatus but in high-power photomicrography nothing can make up for the actual shortcomings of an objective.

Optical System of Microscopes.—The optical system of the compound microscope is shown diagrammatically in Fig. 1. In the diagram three parallel pencils of light are shown reflected upward into the condenser which illuminates a transparent object placed in position on the microscope stage. As shown, the objective would form an inverted real image of the object O_1 at O_2 but the rays are intercepted by the lower lens of the eyepiece before the real image is formed. The lower eyepiece lens in combination with the upper eyepiece lens forms a magnified virtual image O_4 of the real image O_2. There are two magnifications of the object, and the resulting final magnification is the product of the magnifying powers of the objective and the eyepiece.

It should be noted that the objective produces an enlarged image of the object and that the eyepiece further magnifies this image; from this it is evident that if detail is lacking or if the image is not a good likeness of the object, the eyepiece will not make up for the shortcomings of the objective. The objective then becomes the most important part of the microscope. No one objective will serve all purposes because of the limited range throughout which each particular objective is most useful; hence it is desirable to have a representative group of objectives available so that an objective may be selected to suit the specimen and the requirements of the work.

Classes of Objectives.—Objectives are divided into four general classes: achromatic, semiapochromatic, apochromatic, and monochromatic. These objectives do not consist of single lenses but are composed of two or more lenses very accurately centered and permanently mounted in a metal holder. The component parts of the lens system are selected so as to correct or compensate certain errors which are always characteristic of a simple lens. The value of the objective depends on the degree to which these

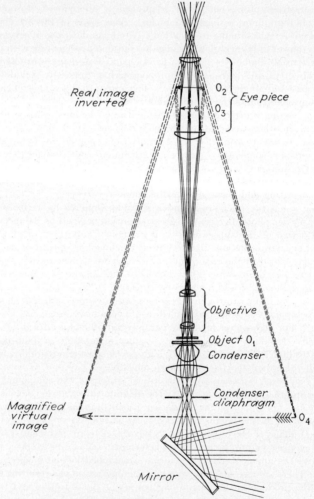

Fig. 1.—Optical system of compound microscope.

imperfections have been overcome. The difference in quality between the first three classes of objectives is primarily a matter of the degree to which corrections for chromatic and spherical aberrations have been applied. The achromatic objectives are intended primarily for visual observations and the principal optical defects are corrected or approximately so for the yellow-green of the visible spectrum since the eye can see best with light of this color. In these objectives the correction becomes less and less complete toward the extremes of the visible spectrum, and there are also residual imperfections in the fusion of the rays. The apochromatic objectives represent the highest order of correction, and the semiapochromats are about intermediate in the quality of correction.

Objectives are listed according to their optical characteristics such as primary magnification, numerical aperture, focal lengths, and whether "dry" or "immersion." The term dry signifies that the objective, when properly used, is separated from the specimen by a stratum of air. In the case of immersion objectives some one fluid for which medium the objective has been computed, such as water, glycerin, cedarwood oil, etc., is used to connect the front lens of the objective with the specimen.

Resolving Power.—The ability of an objective to resolve detail is dependent, theoretically, upon the numerical aperture of the objective and the wavelength of light used.

The relation is expressed numerically by the equation

$$n = \frac{2 \text{ N.A.}}{\lambda} \tag{1}$$

and shows that, if the numerical aperture N.A. of the objective is increased or if the wavelength λ of the light is decreased, the number of lines n capable of being resolved will be increased.

This theoretical resolving ability might well be termed "potential resolving ability"; the ability to resolve is inherent in the lens but whether it is achieved in practice is quite another matter. In theory two things are of interest: numerical aperture and wavelength of light.

The fundamental difference between a dry objective and an immersion objective is one of resolving power. An immersion objective has greater light-gathering power than a dry lens of corresponding focal length. This light-gathering power is expressed by the numerical aperture.

The present commercial limit for numerical aperture is 1.40 for the best apochromatic objectives. Objectives of 1.60 N.A. are available for metallurgical work.

The apochromats of 1.40 N.A. have a primary magnification of about ninety times so that they not only possess the ability to resolve but also the ability to magnify greatly. The full magnifying power of the optical combination is secured almost irrespective of all other conditions. The specimen may be well prepared or very poorly prepared; the illumination may be critical, or it may be very poorly arranged; the operator may be skillful or unskillful; and many other combinations may occur short of total disruption which will not alter the magnification but which will impair very seriously, if not wholly ruin, definition and consequently the resolving ability of the combination.

Numerical Aperture.—Figure 2 shows the conditions prevailing in a metallurgical microscope where light is directed by suitable means to the prepared surface of the specimen from which it is reflected. Two rays, such as rays 1 and 2 leaving the object at the same angle, will behave quite differently. Ray 2 is refracted by the immersion oil or bent inward. Ray 1, which is pictured to show the conditions without immersion oil, just enters the front lens of the objective. Other rays leaving at a greater angle than ray 2 will also be bent inward, and some extreme ray, such as ray 3, will just enter the front lens of the objective.

Figure 3 illustrates numerical aperture when the specimen is viewed by transmitted light. In this case the specimen is mounted on a glass slide, which is placed on the stage of the microscope and is illuminated through the substage condenser. For purpose of illustration the right half of the front lens of the objective is assumed to be that of a dry lens and the left half that of an immersion objective. Thus an immersion objective has greater light-gathering power than a dry objective. This light-gathering power or numerical aperture supplies a measure for several essential qualities of an objective. Abbe, who first defined the conditions, expressed the relationship by the formula

$$\text{N.A.} = n \sin U \tag{2}$$

where n is the refractive index of the medium contained between the specimen and the front lens of the objective and U the semiapertural angle of the system.

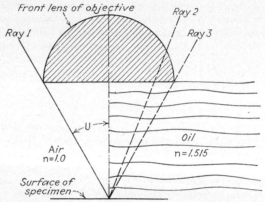

FIG. 2.—Optical conditions prevailing in metallographic microscope.

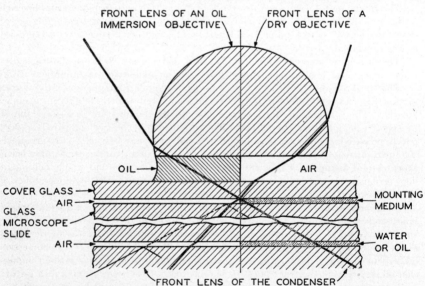

FIG. 3.—Comparison of paths of light rays for oil immersion and dry objectives.

The resolving power of the objective is directly proportional to the numerical aperture, and the brightness of the image to the square of the numerical aperture. As the numerical aperture increases, the depth of penetration, *i.e.*, the power of the objective to resolve detail simultaneously at different depths or distances from the objective, and the flatness of the field both decrease.

Figure 4 shows the relationship of theoretical resolving power, numerical aperture, and dominant wavelength of light for immersion objectives having numerical apertures ranging from 1.25 to 1.60. The equation expressing theoretical resolving power is based on the assumption that the detail being resolved consists of equally spaced lines, in other words, a very fine ruling or grating.

The designation "lines-per-inch," as a measure for resolution, is not a very fortunate one because few specimens exhibit a uniform arrangement and spacing of detail. Perhaps the nearest approach is in the age-hardening (or softening) phenomenon of metals in which a hard constituent is precipitated from the matrix in a very fine particle size—so fine that we must see millions of particles only as a cloud. These particles under suitable treatment may be induced to coalesce and to grow in size so that they may easily be recognized at low powers as single particles. The utmost in resolving power is required to reveal the smaller particles.

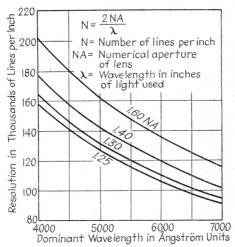

Fig. 4.—Relationship of theoretical resolving power, numerical aperture, and dominant wavelength of light.

Color Correction of Objectives.—The numerical aperture of an objective does not disclose information concerning the chromatic or spherical corrections which have been applied to the objective. The value of an objective also depends on the degree to which aberrations inherent in a simple lens have been corrected.

In the achromatic objectives the correction is least perfect of all, and in the apochromatic objectives the correction is of the highest order. The semiapochromatic objectives, as their name implies, occupy a position about intermediate. All lens systems have some imperfections, in the fusion of the rays.

The achromat is an objective which is designed for visual work. It is corrected to work at its best with the particular color of light which is most effective to the eye, *viz.*, the yellow-green. This color is referred to as the preferred color.

The achromats are corrected chromatically for two colors and spherically for one color. As the extremes of the visible spectrum are approached, the fusion of the rays becomes less and less complete. When an achromat objective is properly corrected, residual colors of the secondary spectrum remain.

Apochromatic objectives are corrected chromatically for three colors and spherically for two, and the fusion of the rays is more nearly perfect. The colors of the secondary spectrum are eliminated altogether in a good objective, and only a faint tertiary spectrum remains as residual color. Objects are rendered in their natural colors with apochromatic objectives.

The correction of semiapochromatic objectives is better throughout than that of the achromatic objectives. The residual color of the secondary spectrum, which is always characteristic of the achromatic and semiapochromatic objectives, makes it necessary to use a filter which will exclude all secondary images when photographing with these objectives.

Tests with the Apertometer.—The numerical aperture of an objective may be determined in several ways; one of the most convenient is by means of the Abbe apertometer, Figs. 5 and 6. This instrument consists of a semicylindrical plate of optical glass with two scales engraved on its upper surface. A revolving arm, bearing a target with cross lines, revolves in close contact with the cylindrical wall of the plate. Near the middle of the straightedge of the plate is a circular disk of silver which has a small slit. An auxiliary objective is screwed into the thread at the lower end of the microscope drawtube.

Fig. 5.—Abbe apertometer assembled for use.

In operation, the plate is placed upon the stage of the microscope, and the objective, the aperture of which is to be measured, is focused on the small slit in the circular disk of silver, using any convenient eyepiece. Illumination of the slit is secured by directing diffused light toward the cylindrical wall of the plate. After the objective has been focused, the drawtube of the microscope is carefully removed and the auxiliary objective screwed into position. The drawtube is then replaced and a Huyghenian eyepiece is inserted. The drawtube now becomes an auxiliary microscope for viewing the back lens of the objective. The cross lines of the target are sharply focused by sliding the drawtube in or out within its collar. Measurements are made by displacing the target along the periphery of the plate until the cross lines just touch the boundary of the circle of light.

Figure 7A is a diagram illustrating what one sees through the microscope when focused on the silver slit of the apertometer. Figure 7B illustrates how the back lens of the objective appears when looking through the auxiliary microscope. The target should be displaced both to the right and to the left, and the mean of the readings of the outer peripheral scale gives the value of the numerical aperture of the objective under test. The mean of the readings of the inner scale gives the values of the apertures in terms of the air angles.

Testing Objectives with the Abbe Test Plate.—For the purpose of testing the correction of microscope objectives for spherical and chromatic aberrations, we may use a prepared test object of maximum contrast. It takes the form of a crude ruling or grating and is known as the Abbe test plate. The test plate is a means for testing and studying some characteristics of objectives.

It consists of several sets of parallel lines ruled across a thin film of silver deposited upon a cover glass. The cover glass is a long narrow strip of glass worked optically plane on either side and in such a way that the strip tapers gradually in thickness from about 0.1 mm. at one end to about 0.2 mm. at the other end. The cover glass with the film side down is permanently mounted on a microscope slide on which is engraved a scale indicating, by increments of 0.01 mm., the thickness of the cover glass from one end to the other.

The ruled lines are usually designated as the "white spaces" and the undisturbed silver film between adjacent ruled lines as the "black spaces." The silver film is not

FIG. 6.—Photograph showing the various parts of Abbe apertometer.

totally opaque but is sufficiently transparent to reveal the silver grains. The ruled lines have jagged edges which form a delicate test object for high-power objectives.

To test objectives, a microscope should be used which is fitted with the usual sub-stage illuminating apparatus, in order to provide for a rapid transition from axial to oblique illumination.

The quality of the image at the center of the field and the changes which occur when the illumination is changed from axial to oblique are carefully observed. The

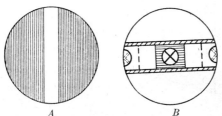

A   B

FIG. 7.—Testing numerical aperture of objectives with Abbe apertometer. *A* shows silver slit of apertometer as viewed through microscope. *B* shows the back lens of an objective as viewed through the auxiliary microscope. Cross hairs are displaced to right and left. The mean of the readings is the numerical aperture of the objective.

performance of an objective is judged by the way in which the sharp edges of the rulings and the silver grains themselves are defined and also by the color and width of the color fringes which border the edges of the black spaces.

Figure 8 illustrates diagrammatically the appearance of color fringes as seen with a test plate and a semiapochromatic objective when using axial light. If the objective is pushed within the focus, the edges appear violet, and if the objective is drawn without the focus, the color fringes change to apple green. This is known as "symmetrical" coloring because both edges of the black spaces are colored the same.

The cause of these color fringes is made clear in Fig. 9, which illustrates in an exaggerated way the formation of the images with a semiapochromatic objective when using white light and axial illumination of the test plate. In this diagram, the colors are indicated separately instead of blended.

When the objective is lowered, the yellow-green fringe first appears, and, if the objective is lowered still further, the orange-blue and the red-violet combinations successively appear. It is evident that, if the objective is pushed within the focus, blue-violet fringes should appear bordering the black spaces of the test plate, or, if the objective is pulled without the focus, the fringes should appear yellow-green.

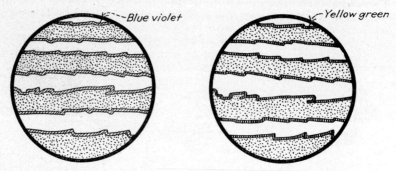

Objective within the Focus   *Objective without the focus*

Fig. 8.—Diagram of color fringes as seen with test plate and a semiapochromatic objective when using axial light.

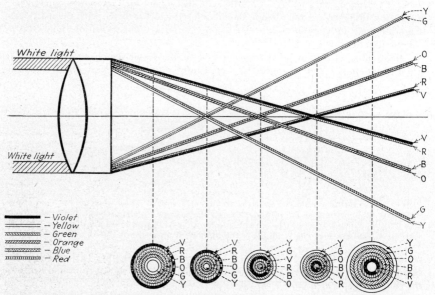

Fig. 9.—Diagram illustrating the formation of color fringes with semiapochromatic objective and white-light axial illumination of test plate.

When oblique light is used with the test plate and a semiapochromatic objective, the upper borders of the black spaces are fringed with apple-green color and the lower borders with violet, as illustrated diagrammatically in Fig. 10. If the light is directed from a diametrically opposite direction, the order of colors will be reversed, the apple green appearing where formerly the violet appeared and vice versa. The same color arrangement persists regardless of whether the objective is pushed within or pulled without the focus. The coloring is now termed nonsymmetrical because the edges are not colored the same.

The reasons for this nonsymmetrical coloring with oblique light are illustrated in Fig. 11. Light enters from the lower third of the substage condenser and illuminates the white space of the test plate A^1-A^2. At A^1 the image is really in the apple green, but, unless very closely observed, this color is lost because of the brilliancy of the white space. The orange-blue (omitted to simplify the diagram) and the blue-violet appear as passing through the black space and have been so represented in the diagram. At A^2 just the opposite conditions obtain. The orange-blue and the blue-violet are lost and the yellow-green appears to come through the black space. No matter whether the objective is raised or lowered, the same color relationship persists.

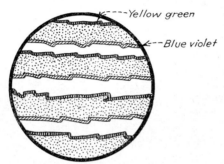

Whether the objective is within or
without the focus the coloring
remains the same

FIG. 10.—Coloring of borders of subject when oblique light is used with test plate and semiapochromatic objective.

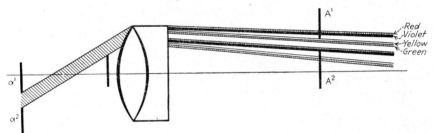

FIG. 11.—Diagram illustrating nonsymmetrical coloring of the type shown in Fig. 10.

Cleaning Objectives and Oculars.—Objectives must be clean if they are to perform at their best. After an immersion objective is used, the immersion fluid should be wiped from the front lens with a fresh piece of lens paper moistened with pure benzene. It may be necessary to use several pieces of lens paper and repeat the operation until the lens and its mount are clean, bright, and dry. The objective should then be stored in its case. When handling objectives, the fingers should be confined to the knurled collar, and they should not come in contact with the front and back lenses.

To care properly for objectives and oculars simple appliances are useful. A supply of very clean fine-grade absorbent cotton should be stored dust free in a covered glass vessel. Tufts of this cotton are twisted securely about the ends of wooden applicators. Care should be exercised to see that the end of the stick is deeply buried in the cotton. This cotton swab is then moistened in benzene and the lens surfaces gently and carefully wiped. Several different swabs should be used in succession, especially if any immersion fluid has dried on the lens mounts or surfaces. All of this must be removed. The lens surfaces are inspected with magnifiers. Finally a small hand syringe is used to blow loose dust particles and cotton linters from the lens surfaces.

Microscopy of Metals. *Development of Metallography.*—Metallography is that branch of science which deals with the anatomy of metals and teaches how the structure changes under the influence of mechanical and thermal treatments. It is the means by which good, poor, or indifferent physical properties are explained on the basis of structure. With control of structure comes control of physical properties.

Two decades ago optical systems were available which theory indicated were capable of resolving some 140,000 lines per inch, and others could be developed with considerably greater resolving powers. Yet photomicrographs of metal structures

Fig. 12.—Precision high-power metallographic apparatus.

were at low magnifications, and the lens systems employed had low resolving powers. Immersion objectives of high numerical aperture probably were seldom utilized, and, if so, the resulting photomicrographs were of doubtful scientific or industrial value. Such interest as they attracted was due more to the large magnification employed rather than to any real information disclosed by the photographs. High-magnification images were not crisp or brilliant but were the exact opposite. Resolution probably was of the order of a few thousand lines per inch. The best optical systems were not used to their full potential resolving ability, and except in rare cases it appears likely that objectives of 1.40 N.A. were not employed in the microscopy of metals.

The preparation of metal specimens was crude and in the course of evolutionary development. Better and more uniformly graded abrasives were needed to replace the ones which had been adopted from the metal-polishing and buffing trades. Specimens were left in a scratched and pitted condition, and, when subsequently etched, any fine details which existed in the structure were not developed and were oftentimes obliterated.

The development of high-power metallography led to the utilization of the full potential resolving ability of existing optical systems. In order to make use of this resolving power, it was necessary to learn how to prepare metal specimens to better advantage for microscopic examination.

The trend in the design of metallographic apparatus has been entirely toward the inverted type of microscope. Many faults of the early inverted microscope have been overcome. These instruments are more convenient to use than any other type, and they are more compact so that the illuminating train, microscope, and camera can be rigidly mounted as a unit and insulated by spring suspensions, or otherwise, from outside disturbances. A great deal of care and attention has been devoted by the manufacturers to the optical and mechanical design of the apparatus. It has been made largely foolproof, so that the average worker of limited experience can achieve remarkable results. Twenty years ago magnifications of $100\times$ to $500\times$ were the rule with an occasional photograph at $1000\times$, but common practice today has increased magnifications to $3000\times$ with good definition and a high order of resolution.

The optical systems of higher numerical aperture are coming into common use, and with increase in numerical aperture of objectives more skill and experience are required on the part of the user. The monobromnaphthalene objective of 1.60 N.A. is now available for metallographic work but because of certain inherent characteristics of this lens it is used only with considerable difficulty.

Preparation of Specimens.—The preparation of specimens for metallographic examination is a laborious and somewhat tedious job but can be systematized so as to take from the task much of the drudgery. The vast majority of specimens are alloys, which usually have more than one phase present. Most specimens contain solid nonmetallic inclusions. Some specimens are cold-worked in whole or in part, and some contain fractures, cracks, or discontinuities which it is desired to study. Some specimens are hard and some are so soft that any attempt to polish a surface results in a myriad of scratches which are difficult to remove. When etched deeply enough to get below the scratches, these soft specimens generally have their fine details of structure and often the coarser ones obliterated by the very operation which was intended to disclose them. When more than one constituent is present in a specimen, differences in solubility of the constituents are disclosed by etching and, if care and understanding are not exercised, misleading conclusions are apt to occur. The use of oblique illumination, dark field, or polarized light cannot compensate for faulty workmanship in the preparation of a metallographic specimen. The detail must be developed in the specimen, and then the order of resolving power and magnification in the optical system must be sufficient to reveal the detail clearly. Since photography in the final analysis is rendering in black and white the contrasts and gradations in tone and color value which exist in the object, it follows that, if one is to achieve crisp, brilliant images photographically, the subject must have extremely well-developed detail, otherwise we could not photograph it at all at very high magnifications.

Soft metals such as lead cable-sheath alloys, precious metals, aluminum, etc., can best be prepared by cutting a specimen with a very rugged microtome. A very satisfactory one is the Jung wood-sectioning microtome. The feed of this instrument can be set for any thickness of section from 2 to 50 μ. The specimen is first roughly cut to a flat surface by setting the feed to cut off slices about 10μ thick. This thickness is gradually reduced to the minimum cut of 2 μ. The sections or slices are not used in the subsequent metallographic examination. After the block or specimen has been removed from the microtome, the cut surface is etched without any further treatment.

It is obvious that the serrations in the knife edge produce scratches in the face of the specimen and that any section cut from the specimen will have scratches on the upper face due to the previous cut of the knife and on the lower face due to the cut just completed. By decreasing the thickness of the sections, a point will be reached when a complete section is no longer secured but only fragments of a section, *i.e.*, the scratches on top and bottom have so little material in between that the section crumbles. It has been found that, when the microtome cuts complete sections 2μ in thickness, the surface of the specimen will be satisfactory to etch for metallographic examination. If it is necessary to set the microtome at 4μ to cut sections, it indicates that the knife is not well honed or stropped. These specimens will not etch free of scratches when viewed under the microscope. Even a well cut and etched specimen often presents to the unaided eye the appearance of slight furrows or undulations in the prepared surface, but these imperfections disappear and are not troublesome under the microscope. From the standpoint of what can be seen with the microscope there is no comparison between the old polishing technique as used for lead specimens, for example, and the newer method of microtome preparation. Moreover a specimen may be prepared in 2 or 3 min. by the sectioning method while the old method not uncommonly required several hours work to prepare a single specimen. The improved means of preparation makes it possible to study the structural effects of small quantities of alloying elements, incipient fusion, cold-working, aging phenomena, etc.

Hard specimens such as iron and steel are gradually brought to a plane smooth surface free from scratches, pits, and other polishing imperfections by a sequence of grinding and polishing operations.

Large specimens are more difficult to prepare and require a much longer time in preparation than small specimens. The ideal specimen is one about ¾ or 1 in. in diameter and not more than ½ in. in height. If the specimen is much higher than this, difficulty will be encountered in maintaining a flat surface. For smaller specimens the height should be proportionately less. Specimens much smaller than ½ in. in diameter are difficult to hold in the fingers, and it will be found advantageous to mount small specimens and irregularly shaped ones in a plastic molding medium such as bakelite. If the edge of the specimen is to be examined, it is always advisable to mount the specimen either by molding it in a compound or clamping it between metal blocks.

Surface Preparation.—The first step in the preparation of the surface is to grind one face of the specimen flat. A bench grinder may be used for the purpose, and it is desirable in many cases to keep the specimen cool by directing a stream of cold water against the wheel. For general work an Aloxite Brand—60 grit—Grade J Bond 3-ft. wheel measuring 8 by 1 in. and revolving at about 3400 r.p.m. in a vertical plane is recommended. Grinding wheels should not be used if their surfaces are clogged or scored. The edges of the specimen should be beveled slightly on the grinding wheel. If this is not done, the paper work to follow will produce on the specimen a sharp knifelike edge which is liable to catch and tear the lap cloths used in subsequent polishing operations.

After grinding on the wheel the specimen is ground by hand on various abrasive papers. Aloxite papers are recommended for the purpose, starting with No. 240 and grinding in turn on Nos. 280, 320, and 400. The papers are placed on a bench plate or other smooth hard surface such as a piece of plate glass. The specimen is then held firmly in the fingers and pushed back and forth slowly under pressure the entire length of the paper. The direction of grinding on the No. 240 paper should be across the previous wheel scratches, and this grinding operation should be continued until the wheel scratches are completely removed. On each succeeding paper a new set of uniform scratches is established across the preceding scratches until the latter are completely replaced by finer ones. From the 400 paper, the specimen goes to a horizontal lap wheel covered with broadcloth and charged with 600 alundum powder where the polishing continues until the scratches are removed. Final polishing is carried out on another lap wheel covered with a very fine broadcloth and charged with a magnesium oxide paste. The paste is made by mixing magnesium oxide with water or with a mixture of water and glycerin. Magnesium oxide forms carbonates readily when in contact with air and water, and because of the difficulty encountered in securing uniformly good powder it is advisable to prepare the powder by air floatation.

It is not within the scope of these brief notes to give complete details for preparing specimens, but the successful photography of the specimen depends to a large extent on the care with which the surface has been prepared. For that reason it has been deemed advisable to give some indication of recommended procedure. More detailed

Fig. 13.—Bench and horizontal laps for polishing metal specimens.

accounts and modifications of the procedure will be found in the literature, to which reference should be made.

The Ultraviolet Microscope. *Development of the Ultraviolet Microscope.*—About 1900 Köhler of the Zeiss Works developed a microscope which had about twice the resolving power of other systems. Its superior resolving power was due to the use of ultraviolet light. Prior to that time only visible light had been employed to illuminate microscopic preparations. To take advantage of the greater resolving power through the use of shorter wavelengths, Köhler devised an apparatus which operated at a wavelength of 2750 Å. Since glass is opaque to wavelengths in this region of the spectrum, all optical parts were made of quartz. The system is monochromatic because optical materials of suitable refractive and dispersive powers are not available with which to achromatize objectives for a range of wavelengths in the ultraviolet region. Chromatic aberrations are eliminated by confining the system to a single wavelength of light. Spherical aberrations are corrected by virtue of the curves to which the lens elements are ground. Monochromatic light is secured by means of a suitable monochromator.

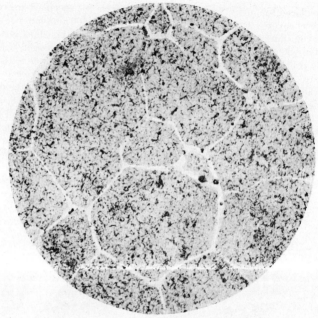

Fig. 14A.—Structure of lead-antimony cable sheath which has seen long service. Note the widened grain boundaries and mottled grain. (Magnification, 200 ×.)

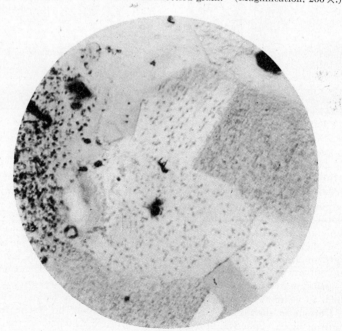

Fig. 14B.—Same as Fig. 14A but at a magnification of 2450 × to reveal details of intergranular structure.

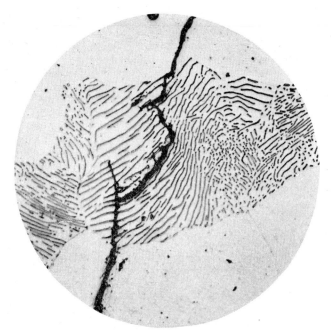

FIG. 15*A*.—Internal stress raisers in cast iron due to fatigue.   Minute serrations in the walls of graphite flakes and the very small tips of the flakes are internal stress raisers of major importance.   The path of a fatigue crack is generally from one such structural detail to another.   (Magnification 1000 ×.)

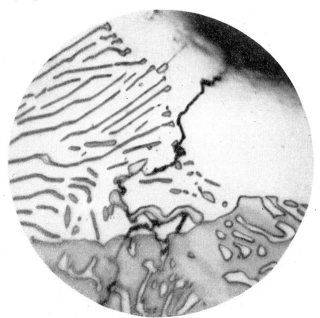

FIG. 15*B*.—Internal stress raiser in cast iron. This is the same as Fig. 15*A* but at a magnification of 3700 ×.

To visualize the image, a fluorescent screen is employed. This takes the form of a uranium glass wedge on which the image is received. The image is viewed by a small magnifier and is focused in the ordinary way by racking the tube of the microscope upward and downward. In principle this seems rather simple, but in practice it did not work out very well because operators had difficulty in coordinating a system with light which could not be seen. In the first place, the intensity of the light is low, and the image is very small on the uranium glass wedge. Fluorescence in uranium glass is not a surface effect entirely, and this made it difficult to focus the instrument.

Beck and Barnard of London attempted to get around the focusing trouble by means of an interferometer focusing arrangement which they incorporated in an ultraviolet microscope of their design. Köhler in recent years has developed a more powerful light source and has improved the searcher eyepiece or focusing device, but in principle and in application it is essentially the same as the original. The fact remains that the original apparatus, as available in 1900, was a workable precision system although its successful use was delayed a quarter of a century.

More powerful illumination for inert material such as finely divided mineral matter, for opaque metallurgical specimens, or for preparations which are quite absorbent at 2750 Å. unquestionably would be of great benefit. However, organic and living material especially may be affected by exposure to a stronger source of energy. This is something which will have to be determined but the indications are that, while many living cells may be photographed successfully with the present intensity of light, there is no assurance that disintegration may not occur if the intensity of the light source is much increased.

In this country Bausch & Lomb have developed a simple ultraviolet system on an entirely different system. They have corrected objectives for two wavelengths, one in the visible region of the spectrum and one in the near ultraviolet. The preparation is focused in the visible light and photographed in the ultraviolet. The source of illumination is a mercury-vapor lamp, and separation of wavelengths is accomplished by filters. Since the wavelength used in the ultraviolet is the 3650 Å line, optical glass may be employed instead of quartz.

The Köhler system, of which the Beck system is essentially but a modification, is without doubt the most powerful microscope ever devised. Its highest power objective has a numerical aperture of 1.25, but owing to the short wavelength of light used its effectiveness is equivalent to an objective with a numerical aperture of at least 2.50 when used with visible blue light. However, for many purposes this system has advantages over those using visible light which scarcely can be reckoned in terms of numerical aperture.

The ultraviolet microscope was intended originally for biological research, but inability to use it successfully all but caused its complete abandonment. About 1925 it was redesigned as a metallurgical microscope and was provided with a quartz plate vertical illuminator. At best these illuminators are not efficient, and with the rather weak source of ultraviolet light available it was practically impossible to do much with the instrument in the field of metallography. The metal specimens absorbed practically all the light and thus very seriously complicated the problems of focusing and photography.

A great deal of experimental work was done with the equipment in an attempt to improve conditions but without much avail. It was discovered, however, that the system had inappreciable depth of focus, and it was reasoned that, if a transparent biological specimen or one approximately so was substituted for the opaque metallurgical specimen, the ultraviolet light could be transmitted through the specimen from below in the usual way and that it should then be possible to photograph the specimen on successive planes. By spacing the planes from top to bottom of the specimen slightly more than the depth of penetration of the system, optical sectioning was obtained.

In developing the art of optical sectioning, experimental malignant tumor material was used. At first this material was fixed and stained, but soon it was discovered that staining of tissues was unnecessary and that better results were secured with unstained material. Differentiation of structure resulted by selective absorption of the ultra-violet light. The fact that organic material manifested selective absorption paved the way to the study of living material and the elimination of changes in the specimen

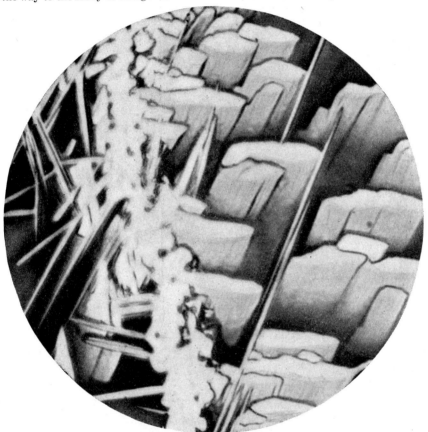

Fig. 16.—A three-dimensional picture of manganese steel, water toughened and drawn at 750°C. (Magnification, 3500 ×.)

(artifacts) incident to fixation, staining, and mounting. Thus it became possible to photograph living cells in isotonic salt solutions most of which readily transmit ultra-violet light. Further experimental work demonstrated that most living cells were not affected by light of wavelength of 2750 or 2573 Å. of intensity and duration of exposure ordinarily required in ultraviolet microscopy. The rule, however, is not universal in its application, as some few living organisms are almost immediately disintegrated and others soon shrivel and die. Most cells are immune to long exposures at 2750 and 2573 Å., but at shorter wavelengths such as those of the 2300 Å group and for still shorter wavelengths, the lethal action is very rapid.

Thus it became possible to photograph most living material at very high powers (1200 to 3600 diameters), to take optical sections on planes spread $\frac{1}{4}\ \mu$ apart, and to avoid many of the artifacts which have perplexed cytologists. Cytological studies soon demonstrated that some of the details of structure attributed to cells on the basis of fixed and stained material did not appear to be present in the living cell. As a tool for biological research the ultraviolet microscope offers far-reaching possibilities, notwithstanding the fact that a more precise technique is required than for the visible-light microscope.

In science and industry it has much to offer. High resolving power and the characteristic crisp, brilliant images obtained make it possible to photograph very

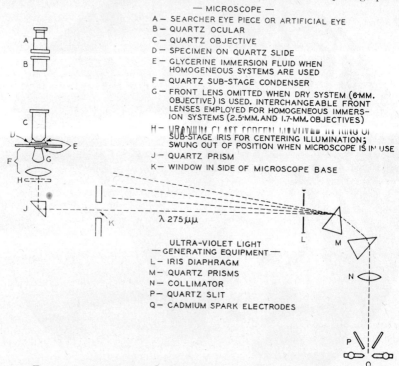

— MICROSCOPE —

A — SEARCHER EYE PIECE OR ARTIFICIAL EYE
B — QUARTZ OCULAR
C — QUARTZ OBJECTIVE
D — SPECIMEN ON QUARTZ SLIDE
E — GLYCERINE IMMERSION FLUID WHEN HOMOGENEOUS SYSTEMS ARE USED
F — QUARTZ SUB-STAGE CONDENSER
G — FRONT LENS OMITTED WHEN DRY SYSTEM (6-MM. OBJECTIVE) IS USED. INTERCHANGEABLE FRONT LENSES EMPLOYED FOR HOMOGENEOUS IMMERS-ION SYSTEMS (2.5-MM. AND I.7-MM. OBJECTIVES)
H — URANIUM GLASS SCREEN MOUNTED IN RING OF SUB-STAGE IRIS FOR CENTERING ILLUMINATION; SWUNG OUT OF POSITION WHEN MICROSCOPE IS IN USE
J — QUARTZ PRISM
K — WINDOW IN SIDE OF MICROSCOPE BASE

$\lambda\ 275\ \mu\mu$

ULTRA-VIOLET LIGHT
— GENERATING EQUIPMENT —
L — IRIS DIAPHRAGM
M — QUARTZ PRISMS
N — COLLIMATOR
P — QUARTZ SLIT
Q — CADMIUM SPARK ELECTRODES

Fig. 17.—Diagram illustrating optical system of ultraviolet microscope.

small particles such as pigments, fillers, etc. Organic compounds such as soaps, oils, fats, waxes, etc., can be studied in the same manner as tissue preparation. Problems in catalysis, adsorption, filtration, etc., are open to study as never before, and the deposition of metallic salts and compounds can be traced and detected oftentimes to far better advantage than by any other means. In a system in which two or more phases are present, selective absorption differentiates the phases and enables one to trace their origin or history through manufacturing or production cycles. Under favorable conditions particles of matter which measure only a few hundred atom diameters across can be clearly photographed. When absorption is strong, resolution can be extended downward to about 200 atom diameters. In the colloidal state of matter the ultraviolet microscope has provided the means to secure real images, not diffraction effects of the submicrons. Photographs of these bodies may be analyzed mathematically as one might the photograph of coarse pigments and fillers. From the photographs, distribution curves may be plotted on the basis of particle diameters in fractions of a micron or in small units of mass. In some cases it is surprising how little the older visual-light microscopes have revealed in comparison to the wealth of detail developed with the high power of the ultraviolet microscope.

Optical System.—The optical diagram of the ultraviolet microscope as arranged for transmitted-light is shown in Fig. 17. The microscope parts are at the left and the light-generating parts at the right. The system is designed to operate on wavelength of 2750 Å. (cadmium, 2748) from a high-tension spark generated across cadmium electrodes. The light is spectroscopically decomposed into the slit images of the light source. The slit images are not monochromatic in the strict sense of the word, but each slit image is composed of a small group of lines which the monochromator fails to separate as individuals. For practical purposes, however, the slit images of the 2750 and 2573 Å. groups are monochromatic. Each group contains a strong line and one or more weak lines.

The slit images have been analyzed and their true spectroscopic nature determined. Spectroscopic data are given in Table I. The image is photographed with the strong line, before the weaker lines register. Some workers have used a strong magnesium group at 2800 Å. because of its greater brilliancy, but the resulting photographic image suffers since a separate image is obtained from each of the strong lines in the group. Photographic negatives taken with this group lack the crispness and brilliancy which are characteristic of the cadmium groups at 2750 and 2573 Å. While the optical system is corrected for 2750 Å., experience shows that it may be used with equal facility with light at 2573 Å. At the lower powers quite good photographs can be secured with the magnesium group at 2800 Å., or the cadmium group at 2300 Å., but at high powers and when the utmost in resolving power is required, it is necessary to employ monochromatic light or its practical equivalent. For some purposes differentiation in structure through selective absorption of the ultraviolet light is more important than high resolving power, and in such cases the illumination can be adjusted to

TABLE I.—WAVELENGTHS USED WITH ULTRAVIOLET MICROSCOPE

Electrode metal	Slit image wave-length group in mμ	Wavelengths comprising the slit image in mμ	Spark-intensity rating from Kayser's tables
Cadmium....................	2750	2707	2
		2734	2
		2748	10
		2764	3
		2775	3
Cadmium....................	2573	2552	2
		2573	10
Cadmium....................	2300	2306	3
		2312	10
		2321	7
		2329	6
Cadmium....................	2265	2265	10
		2288	10
Cadmium....................	2194	2194	4
Cadmium....................	2144	2144	6
Zinc........................	2138	2138	2
Zinc........................	2100	2100	8
		2102	6
		2104	5

meet the circumstances, due allowances being made in the interpretation of results for the falling off in the quality of the image. Similarly, to study the effects of various wavelengths in the ultraviolet region on living cells and organisms, the slit image may be altered and the effects observed visually in the searcher eyepiece or recorded photographically. For such work the lower powers of the system should be used to simplify the procedure. Perhaps the best practice is to photograph the field with a wavelength of 2750 Å., then irradiate it with some other wavelength, and again photo-

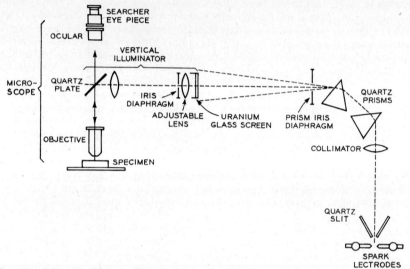

Fig. 18.—Schematic diagram for optical system for working in the ultraviolet range when using reflected light.

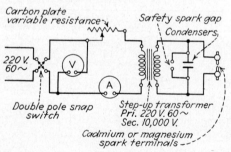

Fig. 19.—Diagram showing electrical system for ultraviolet illumination.

graph it with 2750 Å. This has the advantage of yielding good photographic images but the disadvantage of having to refocus the substage condenser and illuminating system for each change in wavelength. It must be remembered that, if the illumination is not properly focused, the intensity of the ultraviolet light on the specimen per unit of area is greatly reduced. When observing the lethal or stimulating effects of a given wavelength, the results will mean little unless the illumination is properly focused and centered.

The optical system of the microscope as arranged for opaque objects is shown in Fig. 18. The only difference in this assembly from that for transmitted light is the elimination of the substage apparatus and the addition of vertical illumination.

Electrical System.—The details of the electrical system are shown in Fig. 19. The assembly of the apparatus as illustrated in Fig. 20 has been arranged to protect the user against accidental electric shock and from exposure to short-wavelength ultraviolet light. These short waves have an injurious effect on the skin, producing premature aging and small tumorous growths. If the spark-generating apparatus is not

FIG. 20.—The ultraviolet microscope.

shielded, long-continued exposure may result in serious injury to the operator. The hands especially are exposed to the radiations when adjusting the spark, and some frequent adjustment is required; the spark source is covered with a housing. A flexible shaft provides a means for controlling the electrode. The housing must be ventilated by an exhaust fan to prevent the fumes generated by the spark from contaminating the atmosphere within and absorbing the ultraviolet light.

TABLE II.—MONOCHROMATIC OBJECTIVES CORRECTED FOR $\lambda = 275$ Mμ AND 160-MM TUBE LENGTH

System	Focal length f, mm.	N.A.	Relative resolving power
Dry...	16	0.20	0.40
Dry...	6	0.35	0.70
Glycerin...	2.5	0.85	1.70
Immersion...	1.7	1.25	2.50

Tables II and III contain data on the monochromatic objectives and the quartz oculars. Table IV gives the magnifications which result from various optical combinations and optical camera lengths. The optical camera length is the distance in centimeters from the top of the ocular to the plane of the photographic plate.

TABLE III.—QUARTZ EYEPIECES

Descriptive no.	Magnification	Focus, mm.
5	5	36
7	7	26
10	10	18
14	14	13
20	20	9

TABLE IV.—MAGNIFICATIONS AND OPTICAL CAMERA LENGTH FOR THE MONOCHROMATS AND THE QUARTZ EYEPIECES AT 160-MM. TUBE LENGTH AND $\lambda = 275$ Mμ

Objectives		Eyepieces				
		5	7	10	14	20
16 mm. N.A. = 0.20	Magnifications	75	100	150	200	300
	Optical camera lengths	27.5 cm.	26.5 cm.	27.5 cm.	26.5 cm.	27.5 cm.
6 mm. N.A. = 0.35	Magnifications	200	300	450	600	900
	Optical camera lengths	24 cm.	25.5 cm.	27 cm.	25.5 cm.	27 cm.
	Magnifications	250	400	500	800	1000
	Optical camera lengths	30 cm.	34 cm.	30 cm.	34 cm.	30 cm.
2.5 mm. N.A. = 0.85	Magnifications	500	700	1000	1400	2000
	Optical camera lengths	26.5 cm.	26.5 cm.	26.5 cm.	26.5 cm.	26.5 cm.
	Magnifications	600	800	1200	1600	2400
	Optical camera lengths	31.5 cm.	30 cm.	31.5 cm.	30 cm.	31.5 cm.
1.7 mm. N.A. = 1.25	Magnifications	700	1000	1500	2000	3000
	Optical camera lengths	24 cm.	24.5 cm.	26 cm.	24.5 cm.	26 cm.
	Magnifications	900	1300	1800	2500	3600
	Optical camera lengths	31 cm.	32 cm.	31 cm.	31 cm.	31 cm.

Mounted on the rear of the spark-generating stand is a mercury-vapor lamp in a suitable metal housing. A flask in front of an opening in the housing contains a green-filter solution. The flask and the filter solution concentrate the light of the mercury-vapor lamp on a small mirror which may be swung against the prism face and thus reflect the light into the microscope for preliminary adjustment and focus of the microscope.

Operation of Apparatus.—The objectives are provided with centering mounts which first of all should be carefully adjusted so that, when the illumination is centered for one objective, it will be practically centered for all objectives. The centering of the objectives maintains the same field of view when objectives are changed.

For preliminary adjustment a 20× achromat objective and a 5× Huyghens glass ocular are fitted to the microscope. The substage condenser, with front lens removed and with the condenser adjusted centrally in its centering mount, is inserted in the substage holding ring. Light from the mercury-vapor lamp is then reflected into the base of the microscope. A suitable specimen is placed on the microscope stage and the microscope focused in the usual way. The condenser is focused to bring the field-of-view diaphragm into focus. When the diaphragm is partly closed, the bright circular area should be centered by turning the microscope prism and by adjusting the leveling screws of the optical bench of the spark-generating apparatus. The uranium glass disk is now substituted in place of the substage condenser; the reflecting mirror in front of the prism is swung out of position; and the mercury-vapor lamp is extinguished.

Fig. 21.—Ultraviolet microscope fitted with graduated half circle, graduated slider. and the aluminum pointer attached to the slow-motion thumb-screw. In this particular assembly, 1° on the protractor corresponds to a change in focal planes of $\frac{1}{4}$ μ. A sensitivity of $\frac{1}{2}°$ in adjustment may easily be attained. By means of a different slow-motion mechanism a spacing in focal planes of about $\frac{1}{16}$ μ may be secured, although a spacing of $\frac{1}{4}$ μ seems adequate for most work.

The spark is generated with cadmium electrodes and the 2750 Å slit image sharply focused on the uranium glass disk, as indicated by a small circle marked on the disk. The spark is now turned off and a low-power quartz objective and quartz ocular of 5× or 10× power substituted for the glass optical parts. The mercury-vapor lamp is again used as the illuminant. The specimen, mounted on a quartz slide and covered with a quartz slip, is placed on the stage and focused with the visible light. The apparatus is now ready for final adjustment with the ultraviolet light. The searcher eyepiece is swung around into position over the ocular. This searcher eyepiece consists of a uranium glass wedge on the surface of which are ruled two cross lines. This is the surface on which the image fluoresces, and the image is observed by a small adjustable magnifier which forms part of the searcher eyepiece. The image, as it appears on the uranium glass wedge, is very small and so must be enlarged by the magnifier to make even the gross details of structure visible. The magnifier is focused on the cross rulings, and the microscope is focused in the usual way, which brings into focus the fluorescent image.

The focal plane is different for each wavelength. The microscope was focused with

FIG. 22.—Diagram showing method of optical sectioning with the ultraviolet microscope.

visible light since, to enter the focal plane in the ultraviolet, the tube of the microscope must be racked downward and, to focus the illumination as indicated by the field-of-view diaphragm, the condenser must be racked upward. The bright central area as seen in the searcher eyepiece will not be exactly centered but should be made so by adjustment of the centering condenser mount. When the image is in focus in the searcher eyepiece, it will also be in focus approximately 30 cm. above. The camera is swung around into this position and a photograph taken.

Optical sections are taken by changing the focal adjustment mechanically by very small increments. This technique requires precision slow-motion adjustment of the

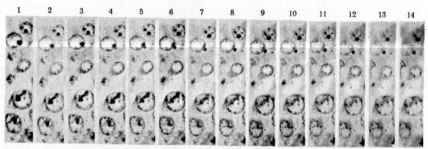

FIG. 23.—Optical sections of fixed but unstained mouse-tumor specimen, photographed on planes spaced ¼ μ apart.

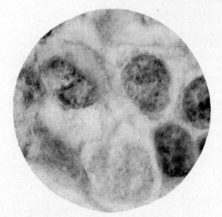

FIG. 24A.—A fixed specimen of tumor material photographed by ultraviolet light. (Magnification 1500 ×.)

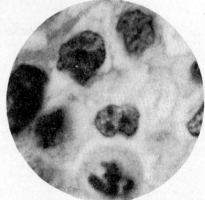

FIG. 24B.—A fixed specimen of tumor material photographed by visual light methods. (Magnification 1000 ×.)

microscope and accurate adjustment of all mechanical features of the microscope. The slow-motion drum requires some amplification. A simple arrangement consists of an aluminum counterbalanced pointer attached to the slow-motion screw and a semicircular scale mounted on the microscope stand. This scale has a slider with four 4° divisions. Each 1° is made to equal $\frac{1}{4}$ μ change in focus. The first division of the slider is set to the pointer at the starting position. The slider is a convenient means to show the starting position and the number of exposures in the photographic sequence. This arrangement is shown in Fig. 21. A modification of the same idea provides an extension of the slow-motion drum which terminates in a larger drum divided into microns and these subdivided into quarters.

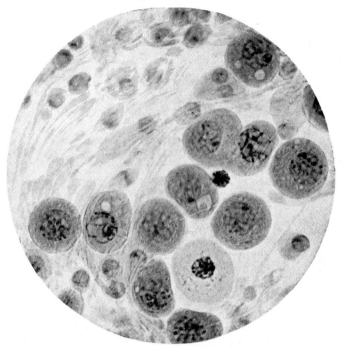

Fig. 25.—Living sperm cells of the grasshopper. (Magnification 500 ×.)

Photographic Materials for Ultraviolet Microscopy.—The most suitable plates for use at 2750 and 2573 Å. are the process-type plates. Plates which can be recommended are the Eastman Process, Eastman Contrast Process, and Hammer Process. Used with a contrast developer such as the Eastman D-19,[1] they give excellent results. When absorption in the specimen is not very strong, the Eastman Contrast plates are recommended. For the wavelengths between 2500 and 1900 Å. special ultraviolet-sensitive plates are required as the ordinary plates are insensitive at these wavelengths.

[1] EASTMAN D-19 CONTRAST DEVELOPER FOR METALLOGRAPHIC PHOTOGRAPHY

STOCK SOLUTION

Water (about 125°F.)	64 oz.	2.0 l.
Metal (Elon)	128 gr.	8.8 g.
Sodium sulphite (desiccated)	12 oz. 360 gr.	384.0 g
Hydroquinone	1 oz. 75 gr.	35.2 g
Sodium carbonate (desiccated)	6 oz. 180 gr.	192.0 g.
Potassium bromide	300 gr.	20.0 g.
Cold water to make	1 gal.	4.0 l.

Use without dilution. Develops 3 to 6 min. in a tray at 65°F. according to the contrast desired.

These special ultraviolet-sensitive plates are now available through the Eastman Kodak Co.

Gelatin absorbs light in the ultraviolet region of the spectrum, and the absorption becomes strong for wavelengths below 2800 Å. Practically all the light is absorbed below 2000 Å. even by very thin layers of gelatin. Shumann plates which contain only a small trace of gelatin or none at all have been extensively used for ultraviolet photography, but these plates were handmade and quite expensive. Another method also used to increase the sensitivity in the ultraviolet consists in dissolving the gelatin of an ordinary plate. A method which has been successfully applied by Lyman and others consists in bathing the plate with some fluorescent material, such as mineral oil, which transforms the short wavelengths into longer ones capable of penetrating the gelatin and thus exposing the plate. Burroughs, of the Eastman Laboratories, found in his researches on the fluorescent properties of a large number of organic substances that the ethyl carboxylic ester of dihydro-credladine was particularly satisfactory as an ultraviolet-sensitizing medium for ordinary plates. This substance is insoluble in water but can be dissolved in certain organic substances. When a plate is bathed in a solution of it and allowed to dry, the surface of the plate is covered with a microcrystalline deposit which fluoresces strongly under ultraviolet light. The fluorescent materials after exposure of the plate can be removed by washing the plate with acetone before development or, if desired, by brushing the plate with a camel's-hair brush as soon as it is in the developer. The crystals loosen and are thus brushed off. The sensitized plates are supplied ready for use, or the material may be secured with which to sensitize plates.

Plates, plateholders, and camera of the ultraviolet microscope must be clean and free of dust, otherwise speckled plates arising from dust or paper fibers on the plate surface will be sure to result. Some plates are not carefully wrapped, and during manufacture, shipment, and handling the sensitized surfaces seem to collect a great deal of dust particles which are difficult to remove completely. For ordinary photographic work the dust, lint, particles of glass, etc., which lodge on the plate surfaces may be brushed or wiped off reasonably well. When the plate is used for ultra-

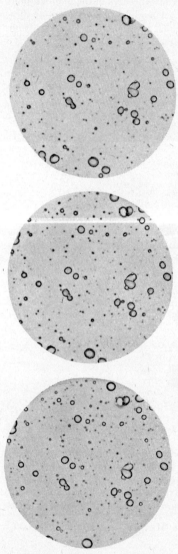

Fig. 26.—Rubber latex particles clearly resolved by means of ultraviolet light. Optical sections spaced ¼ micron apart. (Magnification 1800×.)

violet microscopy, every little particle completely blocks out the ultraviolet light and, of course, shows up as an unexposed spot on the developed negative. Dust particles are not easy to remove, presumably because they become electrified by brushing and merely move about. However, by carefully brushing the plates in one direction with a camel's-hair brush, they can be made dustfree. It is best to avoid the use of all plates which are poorly packed.

Preparation of Specimens.—For ultraviolet microscopy specimens are prepared somewhat differently than for visible-light systems. Since ordinary glass is wholly opaque to ultraviolet light of short wavelengths, special quartz slides and cover slips must be used. Some of the special ultraviolet-transmitting glasses may serve but these lack the full transmitting qualities of quartz and consequently reduce the efficiency, lengthen the exposure, and make the problem of focusing more difficult. Slides and cover slips of these materials are relatively cheap compared with quartz slides and covers, but, since the latter may be cleaned and used repeatedly, there is little point in working with the glass slides. The quartz slides measure 26 by 30 mm., and the cover slips are 12 mm. in diameter. The slides are placed in a small metal holder of the same size as an ordinary glass slide, and thus are convenient to handle.

Usually, for examination with visible-light microscopes, tissue is fixed, sectioned, stained, and mounted on glass slides. Many of the biological fixatives contain substances which are totally opaque to ultraviolet light or by combination with the tissue render the latter opaque. Other fixatives, such as formaldehyde, are satisfactory, but they often have serious limitations for cytological studies. Practically all common stains absorb ultraviolet light. Differentiation of structure will result through selective absorption of the ultraviolet light.

For ultraviolet microscopy of tissue the best practice, as previously pointed out, is to use living material mounted in a suitable isotonic salt solution. The cover slip is sealed with a mixture of vaseline and olive oil applied by a small camel's-hair brush while revolving the slide on a turn table. This sealing medium has no effect on the preparation, whereas lacquer and other similar mediums may infiltrate the mounting medium and have harmful effects.

Other mounting mediums, such as glycerin, mineral oil, olive oil, castor oil, water, and some of the synthetic resins and gums, may be used for special purposes with technological preparations. Most of the natural gums, balsams, etc., are opaque to ultraviolet light and therefore not suitable for use.

Bibliography

Periodicals:

Köhler, A.: Microphotographic Examinations with Ultraviolet Light, *Z. Wis. Mikroskopie,* **21,** 129–165 and 273–304 (1904).

Köhler, A., and M. Von Rohr: A Microphotographic Arrangement for Ultraviolet Light, *Zeit. Instrumentenk.* **24,** 341 (1904).

Lucas, F. F.: Photomicrography and Technical Microscopy, *Bell System Tech. J.,* **3** (No. 1) (1924).

———: High Power Metallography, *J. Franklin Inst.,* **201,** February (1926).

———: An Introduction to Ultra Violet Metallography, *Mining and Met.,* June (1926).

———: Microtome Methods for the Preparation of Soft Metals for Microscopic Examination, *Mining and Met.,* February (1927).

———: Observations on the Microstructure of the Path of Fatigue Failure in Specimen of Armco Iron, *Trans. Am. Soc. Steel Treating,* **11,** April (1927).

———: A Résumé of the Development and Application of High Power Metallography and the Ultra Violet Microscope, *Proc. Intern. Congr. Testing Materials* (Amsterdam, Holland), September (1927).

———: Photomicrography and Its Application to Mechanical Engineering, *Mech. Eng.,* **50,** March (1928).

———: Further Observations on the Microstructure of Martensite, *Trans. Am. Soc. Steel Treating,* **15,** February (1929).

———: Structure and Nature of Troostite, *Bell System Tech. J.,* **9,** January (1930); also in *Proc. World Eng. Congr. Tokyo.*

———: The Architecture of Living Cells, *Proc. Nat. Acad. Sci. U. S.,* **16,** September (1930).

———: On the Art of Metallography, *Mining and Met.,* May (1931).

—— and Mary B. Stark: A Study of Living Sperm Cells of Certain Grasshoppers by Means of the Ultra Violet Microscope, *J. Morphol.*, **52** (No. 1), September (1931).

——: Advances in Microscopy, *Proc. Intern. Congr. Testing Materials* (Zurich, Switzerland), September (1931).

——: On the Design and Construction of a Precision High Power Metallographic Apparatus, *Trans. Am. Soc. Steel Treating*, **21**, December (1933).

Köhler, A.: Some Innovations in the Field of Photomicrography with Ultraviolet Light, *Naturwissenschaften*, **21**, 165–173 (1933).

Lucas, F. F.: Nodular Troostite, *Metal Progress*, February (1935).

——: Late Developments in Microscopy, *J. Franklin Inst.*, **217**, June (1935).

——: On the Preparation of Iron and Steel Specimens for Microscopic Investigations, *Trans. Am. Soc. Metals*, **24** (1936).

——: On the Resolving Powers of the Infinity Objective of N.A. 1.40 and N.A. 1.60 used with a Precision High Power Metallographic Apparatus, *Anniversary Vol. Sci. Repts. Tôkyô Imp. Univ.*, Series 1; dedicated to Dr. Honda (1936).

——: How Flaws Occur in Metals, *Nat. Safety News*, February (1937).

——: Progress in Microscopy, *Proc. Intern. Congr. Testing Materials* (*London*) (1937).

——: Ultra Violet Microscopy of Hevea Rubber Latex, *Ind. Eng. Chem.*, **30**, February (1938).

Stern, H. S.: Inexpensive Photomicrography, *Am. Phot.*, 618, October (1934).

Pratt, J. G.: Photomicrography of Opaque Objects, *Am. Phot.*, 348, June (1936).

Weiland, W. F.: Photomicrography as Applied to Metals, *Camera*, 1, January (1937).

Wilman, C. W.: Notes on Low-power Stereoscopic Photomicrography, *Phot. J.*, 491, August (1937).

Warner, E. E.: Extension Tubes for Macro-photographs, *Camera*, 242, October (1937).

McKay, H. C.: Photomicrography for Everyone, *Am. Phot.*, 786, November (1937).

Pittock, F. J.: Techniques in a Biological Laboratory, *Phot. J.*, 218, April (1938).

Dent, R. V.: Photographic Illustration of Medical Subjects, *Phot. J.*, 197 (April 1938).

Books:

Hall, W. T., and R. S. Williams: "Chemical and Metallographic Examination of Iron, Steel and Brass," McGraw (1931).

Bentley, W. A., and W. J. Humphries: "Snow Crystals," McGraw (1931).

Sauveur, A.: "The Metallography and Heat Treatment of Iron and Steel," McGraw (1935).

Williams, R. S., and V. O. Homerburg: "Principles of Metallography," McGraw (1939).

CHAPTER XXVIII

GEOLOGIC PHOTOGRAPHY

By Robert F. Collins

Ability to photograph geologic phenomena clinically in the field is a rare and valuable attribute. Equipment and procedure are simple and attainable by the average amateur and when employed they assure superior results. For outdoor work in geologic photography there are three axioms:

1. Work in the field, not the darkroom.
2. Stop down and use a tripod.
3. Use a sunshade.

The importance of following these three rules cannot be overemphasized; they hold true regardless of the film, lens, and shutter used.

Photographic Field Equipment.—Equipment for field photography must be adequate and practical. Five items are fundamental and should be assembled in a kit which can and will be carried by the owner in the field at all times: camera, tripod, sunshade, exposure meter, and filter kit. Pictures are not obtained by equipment left in the car.

The camera may be of any sturdy type, not prefocused, equipped with an anastigmat lens. A focusing back is not essential and action shots are never taken; hence box reflexes are unnecessary, and fast shutters a luxury. On the contrary, shutter speeds from $\frac{1}{10}$ to 2 sec. are most useful. Size of negative today is not of prime importance, anything from 35 mm. to $3\frac{1}{4}$ by $4\frac{1}{4}$ in. is satisfactory and practical. Larger cameras, of course, yield very fine results, but their bulk and weight are entirely unnecessary; the 5- by 7-in. ones are absurd for field photography. Fast lenses are not required, except for some color work; an $f/7.7$ or $f/6.3$ is entirely adequate. The lens, however, should be of the very best correction for flare, coma, and spherical and chromatic aberration; the ultimate limit of needle-sharpness will naturally be determined by lens refinement. Fortunately nearly all modern high-quality speed anastigmats are satisfactory for field photography if stopped down.

A tripod which will support the camera firmly is essential. Slightly oversize good-quality telescoping metal tripods will usually hold the camera satisfactorily in various wind conditions. Bulky and heavy tripods, in spite of their greater stability, are impractical for the field geologist; they are too much to carry. A valuable procedure, in addition to shortening the tripod legs when a field photograph must be taken in a stiff breeze, is to suspend a 4- or 5-lb. rock close under the tripod head. Finally, use the tripod on every shot, even if there is an $f/1.5$ lens on the camera.

A sunshade should be used at all times. Direct sun rays are only one danger; bright sky light, water surface reflections, and snow glare are others. Use a sunshade for every exposure, and for peace of mind use a good one and a big one.

A photoelectric exposure meter should be carried and used. In spite of the latitude of modern film, an exposure that is correct pays dividends later. For color work, a photoelectric meter is a necessity.

Filters, selected according to the owner's experience, should be part of the field kit. K2, K3, infrared, and panchromatic green should be ample for black-and-white work.

Close-up Technique.—Geologic field photography is of two types: (1) close-ups to show details of fossils, joints, and rock texture; and (2) land-surface views to record a sweep of country. Details of field procedure are given below:

Close-ups are taken with tripod, sunshade, small stop, and panchromatic film, usually at a distance of 6 ft. or less. Focusing should be done with a ground-glass back, steel tape, or accurate range finder. Filters are rarely needed, and many times orthochromatic film will be satisfactory.

Needle-sharpness and depth of focus are desiderata. Best results are obtained by using a small stop and avoiding sunlit surfaces if possible. Apertures of $f/32$ or smaller are advisable except in a strong wind. Shadow contrast is usually desirable only when illustrating surface texture of rock.

Relative scale must be indicated by including some readily recognizable article in the picture, such as hammer, knife, compass, watch, or coin. Do not depend upon vegetation to give scale when photographing rock exposures close up; a clear record of scale on the negative is superior to any statement in type. For scientific work, people in geologic photographs are generally unsatisfactory and should not be used. Human interest is not desired and is distracting, if only because clothing styles change within the useful lifetime of a scientific negative.

View Technique.—Land-surface views are scientific landscape photographs made to record geologic features over large areas. They are among the most difficult negatives that the geologist is required to make. The following points should be observed:

Sharpness and clarity are of first importance. In spite of the temptation of a fast lens and a distant view, always stop down and use tripod, sunshade, and exposure meter. This procedure cannot be overemphasized.

Filters should be used judiciously. If there is absolutely no haze, a filter will not improve the scientific value of the negative. Usually there is some haze in the distance, however, and filters should be selected according to the owner's experience. The best technique for really distant views is infrared photography. Prints from infrared negatives of distant topography are unequaled in sharpness and detail; the false color values rendered are seldom of any hindrance to the geologist.

Correct perspective and advantageous viewpoint are essential. An assortment of lenses, including a wide angle and telephoto, are valuable and usable additions to the field geologist's photographic kit; unfortunately the investment is frequently prohibitive. Telephoto lenses require exact focusing and absolutely rigid support, and with most cameras such a lens calls for a heavier tripod than would be employed otherwise. Excellent land-surface views are obtainable, however, with standard lenses judiciously employed.

Position of the camera and of the sun are important considerations in photographing distant geologic subjects. An elevated camera position is usually chosen, if available, to minimize the immediate foreground and increase the field of view. Shots against the sun are avoided, although much of the resulting flare effect can be eliminated by the use of a polarizing screen. Shadow development should be considered where erosional forms are being photographed; registering the shadow relief produced by a low-angled late-afternoon sun will mean the difference between success and failure in many cases. Under noonday sun even areas of high relief usually photograph with unwanted flatness. It should be noted that the desired type of shadow contrast cannot be produced by darkroom manipulation; like portrait lighting, it must be registered on the original negative.

Although the scientist professes abhorrence of art in his publications, it behooves the physiographic photographer to employ such artistic instincts as he may possess. A strictly technical photograph of a land surface will be looked at and remembered longer if its sky has clouds. Again, a pine bough framing an unused corner of the film will add depth of perspective to distant valley and mountain. Finally, in framing the finished print under the enlarger, regard for the rules of pictorial composition and rhythm will yield subtle but sure results. This is not to advocate soft-focus effects, bromoils, or pebble-surfaced paper; the scientist's medium is the needle-sharp ferrotype print from which he should and must not swerve. Nevertheless artistic principles are as much needed in scientific photography as a good voice in a scientific lecturer; there is no merit in nasality nor in poor pictorial composition.

Color photography is not yet practical for the field geologist. The exposure technique and equipment are simple enough, but the limited advantage of colored field photographs as scientific data does not compensate for their high cost and relatively narrow range of usefulness. Furthermore there is comparatively little need for color representation in geologic field photography.

Darkroom procedure is standard. Tank development with suitable developers and projection printing on glossy paper are recommended. The procedure should be worked out carefully and standardized, both for efficiency and to justify the care exercised in making the field exposure. Projection printing is strongly urged not only because it eliminates the need for large negatives but especially because it permits a careful selection of the most desirable area of the original film.

Recording field data and filing negatives are necessary practices. The geologist's notebook will receive the geologic data for each picture; for photographic data a printed form, similar to Fig. 1, which can be filled in largely by check marks, is recommended for its completeness and convenience. Negative filing systems are legion and subject to strong personal preferences; the essential thing is that some adequate system of filing be employed.

Geologic Laboratory Photography.—Photographic technique employed in geologic laboratories is exacting and varied and differs markedly from geologic field photographic technique in that conditions are controllable.

Serial No.					
Film Positive			Panchromatic		
Orthochromatic			Super-panchro.		
Sun Intense	Bright	Hazy	Dull		VeryDull
Object in Full sun, near glare			Camera points		
Full sun					
Shade, open sky					
Shade no open sky					
Heavy shade					
Interior					
Distance			Hour		
Tripod	yes	no	Filter	I	II III
Stop			Time		
Auxiliary lens	1	2 3	Sun shade	yes	no
Main lens	35mm. f/3.5	50mm. f/2.5	50mm. f/3.5	90mm. f/4.0	135mm. f/4.5
Date			Field No.		
Remarks					

Fig. 1.—Printed form which is useful in quickly checking data taken in the field.

controllable. Aside from routine work, such as copying and lantern-slide making, geologic laboratory photography falls into two main groups: (1) thin-section photography through the petrographic microscope, and (2) photography of objects possessing surface relief.

Equipment.—The camera should be a well-constructed "view type" plate camera, from a 3¼- by 4¼-in. to a 5- by 7-in. in size, according to the user's preference. A removable lens board, a rising front, a revolving back, and ground-glass focusing are essential. For indoor work, when weight and portability are not of prime importance but accuracy is, glass photographic plates will furnish a higher percentage of perfect negatives than any type of film; the cost per unit area is no higher, and breakage of plates troubles only clumsy workers. Plate size will vary with personal preference and with the demands of the work. A convenient device is to employ a 5- by 7-in. camera and plateholders equipped with insert frames to hold 4- by 5-in. plates when desired. Interchangeable lenses are a necessity; the removable lens board is more convenient than a threaded flange and, for megascopic work, possesses sufficient accuracy.   For fine microscopic work an accurately threaded metal flange should be employed as the lens mount.   (The writer does not advocate the laboratory use of ultra-small cameras because the purchase price and operational effort, if expended on standard-size equipment will yield better results.   Obviously portability and even low operational expense are not of prime importance in the laboratory.)

Lenses should be of the highest possible quality; a rapid rectilinear, stopped down, will not equal a good anastigmat, even in copying.   In scientific laboratory photography the quality standards are properly set so high that only the best lenses available should be considered.   One other generalization is possible: one lens will not be sufficient.   A geologic photographic laboratory should possess objectives of the Micro-Tessar or Micro-Summar class for photographing opaque relief objects of almost microscopic size, and well-corrected anastigmats of 4- and 8-in. focal length for routine megascopic work.   Obviously the size and relief of the specimen, together with the desired image size, will determine the proper lens and in many cases will allow little leeway.   Shutters cease to be important in most geologic laboratory photography.   Usually shutters are unnecessary, although for shorter exposures than 1 sec. a between-the-lens shutter will be required.   Focal-plane shutters are unnecessary and unwise because of vibration.   A lens shade is a valuable accessory.

Camera supports should be of generous proportions and good design.   A solid-leg wooden tripod with revolving and tilting head is the best general support commercially available for megascopic work; its size should be adequate for the camera employed. Provision against slippage of the tripod feet should be made, such as soft rubber tips or a light chain loop placed around the feet.   When makeshift supports are employed occasionally for megascopic work, it is imperative that the assembly of camera and support be solid and vibration be eliminated.   Positive connection of parts by screws, thumb nuts, or C clamps is necessary, and the insertion of a vibration trap, beneath the camera, consisting of sponge rubber mat or four tennis balls, will improve long-exposure negatives.

Object supports are a great convenience in megascopic work and frequently are necessities.   Small- and medium-sized specimens are supported adequately by a piece of plasticene modeling clay covered with wax paper to protect the back of the specimen; large rocks may be held for photographing by blocking up with wood or lead blocks.   Control of background is best gained by employing a deep box of sufficient size, lined with black flannel or velvet.   The specimen should be supported in the plane of the open top on glass or a stiff pillar from the box bottom; for white backgrounds a glass-topped box, covered with smooth tracing cloth (or ground glass) and lighted evenly from inside, is used to support the specimen.

Illumination is best provided by strong—500 watt or more—prefocused-type incandescent lamps, mounted in parabolic reflectors and held by metal floor stands whose arms permit three-way adjustment.   At least three units, consisting of lamps, reflector, and floor stand, should be provided.   Heavy ring stands may be substituted for floor stands in table-top work.   Photoflood bulbs are less satisfactory, although cheaper, for permanent equipment, because of their short life and rapid change in the quantity and spectrum of their emissions.

The microscope and accessories employed in thin-section technique should be the best quality petrographic microscope obtainable.   Especial attention should be given the objectives used for photographic work; they should be apochromatic if possible. Accessories in keeping with the microscope need no further comment, except for the camera itself.   For any small amount of work a temporary setup of view camera may prove satisfactory.   A lighttight sleeve around the ocular tube, convenience in focusing and changing plates, and absolute rigidity are essential.   For any considerable amount of thin-section photography it is advisable to purchase a standard photomicrographic camera.

Thin-section Technique.—Photography of rock and mineral material in thin section may be done with either unpolarized incident or reflected light, or with polarized light between crossed Nicol prisms or polaroid plates. When using thin sections with unpolarized light, the photographic problem is to secure correct definition and adequate contrast of grain boundaries and microscopic structure. Definition is obtained by routine focusing of an adequately equipped microscope and in extreme cases by employing monochromatic light and suitable filters; contrast is obtained largely by altering the illumination intensity and angle of incidence until the desired results show on the focusing panel. Many workers prefer a clear-glass focusing panel to ground glass, because the critical focus point is sharper. The practice of cementing a thin cover glass on a ground-glass plate to secure a clear spot is not recommended because the focal plane is shifted thereby.

Photomicrographs made through crossed Nicol prisms should be exposed on panchromatic plates to gain correct color rendering. Here apochromatic objectives and oculars are desirable for the best work since they bring nearly all wavelengths into focus on a single plane. More light is required when working with crossed Nicols, although the usual laboratory microscope lamp will generally prove strong enough. Very dense, deeply colored sections may require a stronger source such as a laboratory arc illuminator.

Relief-object Technique.—When photographing geologic specimens, other than thin sections, more or less surface relief is present and must be photographed sharply. This involves mastery of two details: securing depth of focus, and control of lighting. For megascopic negatives sufficient depth of focus is usually attained with a small diaphragm opening. With small relief objects, whether photographed through a compound microscope or through the Micro-Tessar or Micro-Summar lens in a view-type camera, the securing of sufficient depth of focus is often the most serious problem. The two approaches are through stopping down the objective and guarding against vibration during the lengthened exposure and, secondly, employing lenses with as short a focal length as possible. When the resulting negative is of the very highest quality, it is possible to obtain some additional magnification by ordinary darkroom enlargement without loss of definition, this method, however, is not a substitute for lens quality and skill in making the original negative.

Illumination of relief objects evolves into a trial-and-error technique employing the few comparatively simple devices mentioned above, *i.e.*, shadow contrast is secured by low-angle illumination and detail in shadows by a somewhat weaker high-angle light. Methodical experiments leading to a standardized technique for a given laboratory is the best solution of the lighting problem. Among special devices which will be useful at times are the time-tested ammonium chloride coating blown on fossils when a matte white surface will show detail better; the ingenious use of water for "painting" outlines of obscure details such as footprints and plant impressions; and the cloth or tissue paper "tent" separating the light sources from the camera lens and object when it is necessary to prevent point reflections from crystal faces or highly polished surfaces into the camera. Polaroid screens are valuable for the latter purpose also.

Color Technique.—Natural-color photographs in the geologic laboratory are valuable chiefly for recording details of minerals and petrographic thin sections between crossed Nicol prisms. The indoor technique resembles that of field color photography, except for the use of artificial light and accompanying filters, and follows standard indoor color procedure. Except for lantern-slide illustrations for mineralogy and petrography, color photography does not appear to be practical or necessary for indoor geologic photography.

CHAPTER XXIX

SPECTROSCOPIC PHOTOGRAPHY

By G. R. Harrison

The Spectrograph.—Any device for separating a beam of light into its component wavelengths or colors is called a "spectroscope," and any spectroscope which is provided with a camera for photographing the spectrum which it produces is called a "spectrograph." The light to be analyzed is sent into the spectrograph through a slit, and a suitable optical system produces an image of this slit for each wavelength present in the light beam. These slit images are called "spectrum lines," and taken together they form a "line spectrum," while a plate or film on which they have been photographed is called a "spectrogram." Light from certain sources like the incan-

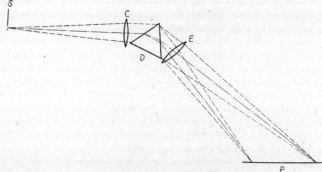

Fig. 1.—Component parts of spectrograph, consisting of slit *S*, condensing lens *C*, dispersing prism *D*, camera lens *E*, and photographic plate *P*.

descent lamp contain waves whose lengths vary continuously over a wide range, and the resulting slit images merge together, forming a continuous spectrum.

The usual component parts of a spectrograph (Fig. 1) are the slit *S*, a collimating lens *C* or mirror to make parallel the rays of light from the slit, a dispersing element *D* which may be a prism or a diffraction grating, and a special type of camera. This camera usually contains one or more lenses *E* which, though uncorrected for chromatic aberration, have been specially figured for sharpness of focus and flatness of field and which are set to focus on the plate *P* the parallel bundles of light which come from the dispersing element. The position of a spectrum line on the spectrogram gives a measure of the wavelength of the light producing it, while the density of the image of the line, when measured under controlled conditions, can be used to determine the intensity of the light which produced it.

Choice of Spectrograph.—In selecting a spectrograph, the important properties to be considered are the range of wavelengths over which it can be used, its dispersion, its resolving power, and its speed, as determined by the brightness of the spectrum which it produces. Secondary characteristics, such as the variation of dispersion

804

with wavelength, the amount of scattered light, and the sizes and shapes of the spectrum lines produced, are sometimes of importance.

In choosing a spectrograph for any problem one should first determine whether a prism or a grating instrument will be most suitable. The advantages of prism instruments are their high light-gathering power (which results in greater intensity of the spectrum and hence in shorter exposures when it is to be photographed), their ruggedness and permanence, and the fact that they can readily be made to give stigmatic spectra. They suffer from the disadvantage that their dispersion changes markedly with wavelength (although much less with frequency), and they can, of course, be used only in regions of the spectrum to which their optical parts are transparent. Their fundamental dispersion and resolving power are usually smaller than those which can readily be obtained with diffraction gratings. Prisms are very widely used in portable instruments, for studying comparatively simple spectra, and for any purpose for which relatively great light-gathering power is required.

The diffraction grating is coming more widely into use even where only low resolving power and dispersion are needed, and since it is unrivaled for obtaining high values of these quantities, it seems destined to play a much larger part in the development of spectroscopy in the future than it has in the past. It can be used in such a way as to produce an almost normal spectrum, in which the dispersion is nearly uniform over the length of a spectrum plate, and it requires a minimum of adjustment.

A further advantage of the grating is that it can be used in the reflecting concave form (page 813) without any transparent optical parts; consequently a single instrument can be used over the entire photographic range. Grating spectroscopes can be obtained having a resolving power as high as 400,000 and with dispersions of as much as 0.1 Å. per mm. Their chief disadvantage is that most gratings throw the light not into one spectrum but into several, and since usually only one of these is wanted at a time, much of the light may be wasted.

Spectral Range.—Spectrum photography in the infrared is commonly limited to the range 12,000 to 7500 Å., in the visible it covers the entire range 7500 to 4000 Å., and in the ultraviolet it goes from 4000 to 1000 Å., although these limits are somewhat arbitrary.

Prisms have limited transparency, and several must be provided to cover the different ranges. Flint glass, quartz, and rock-salt prisms are most frequently used for the infrared, glass prisms of various sorts for the visible, and quartz or rock-salt prisms for the ultraviolet down to 2000 Å. Below this wavelength only fluorite or lithium fluoride optical parts can be used. Fluorite is transparent to about 1250 Å., while lithium fluoride which will transmit to 1050 Å. can occasionally be produced. No suitable material has yet been found which is transparent to shorter wavelengths and only the concave grating spectrograph can be used in this region. For wavelengths shorter than about 2000 Å. all light paths must be in vacuum (except that dry nitrogen, hydrogen, and helium can be used in parts of these regions) since the air begins to absorb at this wavelength.

The most common practice is to use glass optical parts in prism instruments designed for the visible and photographic infrared and crystal quartz optical parts for those photographing that part of the ultraviolet to which air is transparent.

Dispersion.—The dispersion of a spectrograph can be measured as angular or as linear dispersion. The angular dispersion $d\theta/d\lambda$, the change in angle with wavelength of the light emerging from the prism, is fundamental and depends on the dispersing element. The linear dispersion is of more practical interest, as it gives the actual separation of two close lines on a spectrogram. In common practice the spectral range covered by 1 mm. of plate is used to measure the dispersion; thus 30 Å. per mm. is a low dispersion, while 1 Å. per mm. is a relatively high value. The linear dispersion obtained with a given angular dispersion can be varied by changing the focal length of the camera lens. It depends also on the inclination of the focal curve to the optic axis of the camera.

The dispersion of prism spectrographs is nonuniform, depending as it does on the variation of the refractive index of the prism material with wavelength, and may vary tenfold along one short spectrogram. Prisms deviate the short waves more than the longer, and the dispersion increases as the wavelength decreases.

Resolving Power.—The ability of a spectrograph to separate close-lying lines is measured by its resolving power. Resolving power P is defined as $\lambda/d\lambda$, $d\lambda$ being the wavelength difference between two lines which the instrument can just resolve at wavelength λ. If unresolved, the two lines will appear as one.

Most spectrographs have theoretical resolving-power values lying between 2000 and 200,000, the lower value being typical for a small prism instrument and the higher for a large diffraction grating. The theoretical limiting resolving power of a given spectrograph increases as the linear aperture of its camera lens is increased (if this is kept filled with light) and as the angular dispersion of its prism or grating is increased. By using good optical parts it is possible to approach the theoretical resolving power very closely.

Dispersion and resolving power are closely related but are two distinct properties of a spectrograph and should not be confused. Increased linear dispersion may separate the centers of two close spectrum lines more widely, but since, if unaccompanied by an increase in resolution or of angular dispersion, it results merely in increased magnification, the lines are no more clearly resolved than before.

The ability of a spectrograph to resolve two close lines may be reduced by its auxiliary parts. When properly designed, a spectrograph will be provided with a camera of such focal length that the resolving power $\lambda/d\lambda$ of the instrument will match, through the linear dispersion $d\lambda/dl$, the resolving power λ/dl of the photographic materials used to record the spectrum, unless some other consideration such as speed intervenes.

Speed.—The efficiency of a spectrograph is commonly defined as its speed times the purity of the spectrum it produces. Speed depends on the intensity of the transmitted light, which will in turn depend on the fraction of incident intensity of each wavelength which penetrates the instrument, and on the numerical aperture of the camera lens. The total light flux which can be obtained from any spectrograph, assuming that a light source of the extent required to fill the slit used is available, is limited by the size of slit which can be used with a given purity of spectrum. This means that the larger a spectrograph is made, if its proportions are kept the same, the more light flux can be sent through it. With a given spectrograph, shortening the focal length of the camera lens will increase the light intensity, the spectrum lines being correspondingly reduced in size.

Most prism spectrographs operate at numerical apertures of from $f/12$ to $f/24$, while grating instruments may have apertures as low as $f/70$. Exposure times required may range from a few seconds to several hours, depending on the speed of the instrument and of the photographic materials used and the intensity and energy distribution of the source being photographed.

The Slit.—Since spectrum lines are merely images of the slit, this slit is one of the most important parts of a spectrograph. It should be carefully made and adjusted, with its edges kept clean and smooth. The opening of the slit should be variable in width, preferably between 1 and 0.002 mm. The slit jaws are usually drawn apart by a calibrated screw acting in opposition to a spring which tends to move the jaws together. A typical slit is shown in Fig. 2.

In order that the space between the jaws shall form a suitable line, it is necessary that their edges be accurately straight and that they be mounted with their edges truly parallel and with their front faces lying in the same plane. The jaws are usually beveled, and placed with the beveled side turned away from the entering beam, so that light reflected from them will not enter the spectrograph.

Slits in which only one jaw is movable are cheaper than the symmetrically opening type but have the disadvantage that the center of the spectrum line produced with them moves when the slit width is changed. The best adjustable slits are made to close at the ends only, so that their sharp jaws will not be marred by careless operaton of the screw. The jaws should be made of some hard and durable material, such as stainless steel, which can be ground to a sharp edge and polished.

Simple slits can be made by coating a plate of quartz or other transparent material with a thin opaque coating of metal or lacquer and by engraving lines of the desired widths in this. Slits of several widths can thus be provided, the proper one being set into the slit holder as needed. For certain purposes such slits are more useful than the adjustable type, since a definite slit width can be reproduced more accurately than by setting a screw in which backlash and zero position may change.

The slit is usually mounted in a drawtube in such a way that it can be moved into or out of the spectroscope for focusing purposes, or rotated about a horizontal axis so that it can be brought accurately parallel to the faces of the dispersing element.

Fig. 2.—Typical slit of spectrograph. The width of the slit may be varied by the knurled knob and scale in the lower left-hand corner of this illustration.

The slit should be provided with diaphragms by means of which its length or the parts of it being used can be varied.

With stigmatic spectrographs (see page 810) an almost closed slit may cause horizontal streaks to appear in the spectrum, due to dust particles which close the slit entirely in spots. Such a slit should be cleaned by opening it and carefully stroking its edges in one direction with a freshly sharpened stick of soft wood.

The Camera.—In spectrographs, provision is made for holding a photographic plate or film so that the spectrum is in focus throughout all parts which are simultaneously recorded. A criterion which distinguishes a good spectrograph from a poor one is that, while both may give sharp lines in certain spectral regions, it will be found impossible to get all parts of the spectrum into good focus at once in the poor instrument.

The plate must be bent to fit the focal curve, and it is desirable to keep this curvature as small as possible. The plate or film is held in a plateholder which is provided with templates to bend it to the proper curvature, this plateholder, in portable instruments, being provided with a dark slide. The plateholder is in turn carried in a mounting which usually has provision for moving the plateholder vertically so that a number of different spectra can be photographed on the same plate.

On account of the nonuniform dispersion of prism instruments, they are frequently provided with wavelength scales, which can be impressed on the spectrogram by swinging the engraved transparent scale up into position before the plate and making a brief exposure to a small incandescent lamp provided for the purpose in the spectrograph.

Prisms.—Dispersing prisms are almost always cut with 60° refracting angles. This angle is a compromise between smaller angles which give less dispersion and larger angles which require more material, produce a greater loss of light by reflection, and give a decreased aperture.

A dispersing prism should be used in such a way that the ray of mean wavelength passes through it at the angle of minimum deviation, this ray then passing through the prism parallel to its base. Under these conditions the effective free aperture of the prism is a maximum, and the light loss by reflection is a minimum. The resolving power of a prism is proportional to the difference in thickness between the prism base and its refracting edge. The exact calculation for the resolving power of a prism as used in a given spectroscope is exceedingly complex since it depends on many factors, including the method of illumination of the slit.

A prism is usually shaped so that it will transmit a beam of circular cross section falling on its front face at the proper angle for minimum deviation. This condition leads to a standard set of dimension ratios for any material, the length of a face being for most substances roughly 1.6 times the height. For good definition the prism height should be at least three times as great as the maximum length of slit which is to be used with it, and preferably the ratio should be even greater. Spectrum lines produced with prisms are curved, and definition may be lost when the prism slit-height ratio is too small.

Prisms made of crystalline quartz show double refraction, and produce doubled spectra even when cut with their optic axis parallel to the crystalline axis. Cornu showed how to overcome this defect by making a 60° prism of two 30° prisms in optical contact, one of left-handed and the other of right-handed quartz, the second thus serving to offset the optical rotation produced by the first. When a reflection prism is used, only one type of quartz is required, since the beam passes through it both ways.

Gratings.—Diffraction gratings consist essentially of a large number (sometimes as many as 180,000) of close equidistant slits, which are usually made by ruling lines with a diamond on a smooth surface. The greater the number of these slits, the greater the resolving power of the grating. Light which falls on a grating is thrown into several orders of spectra, and the resolving power P of the grating is given by the formula $P = nm$, where n is the total number of lines on the grating and m is the order being considered. Theoretically, resolving powers of 500,000 can be realized in the higher orders of some gratings which have been produced, but actually values of P greater than 300,000 are seldom found.

The angular dispersion of a grating depends on the distance between successive rulings (the grating space d) and can be derived by differentiating the grating formula $m\lambda = d (\sin \theta \pm \sin i)$ where θ is the angle of emergence, i is the angle of incidence, and m is the order. The dispersion can also be written $d\theta/d\lambda = A/nm$, where A is the linear aperture of the grating.

Small gratings are sometimes ruled on glass, successive lines being ruled as closely as 500 per inch for a very coarse grating or 15,000 per inch for a fine grating of high dispersion. Glass gratings can be used only in the visible and infrared regions to which the glass is transparent, and require collimator and camera lenses to make the light parallel and refocus to it. For larger instruments and for those suited to all spectrum regions, gratings are commonly ruled on highly polished reflecting surfaces, either plane or concave. Gratings up to 7 in. in diameter have been successfully ruled with 20,000 and even 30,000 lines per inch.

The fact that a grating throws the light which falls on it into a number of orders naturally results in a loss of light in any one spectrum, but this loss can be reduced somewhat by shaping the point of the ruling diamond so that more light will be thrown to one side than the other. When very high resolving power is desired, a grating can sometimes be found in which most of the energy is thrown into the higher orders, and it is desirable, if possible, to have most of the light in the orders on one side. In general, if a grating shows high intensity in one order in a given direction, all other orders lying in that same direction will tend to be strong. Thus a grating which is found to give high intensity on one side in the second-order green (5500 Å.) may be expected to be bright also for the infrared near 11,000 Å. in the first order, though other factors may prevent this.

In selecting a grating, it should be tested for brightness in the various orders and for resolving power, line shape, amount of scattered light, and intensity of ghost lines. Ghosts are false lines produced by regularities in some irregularity of ruling of the grating. In a good grating the intensity of a ghost line should be less than 0.1 per cent that of the real line corresponding to it. Lyman ghosts are very objectionable, but fortunately these have been successfully eliminated in the better ruling engines. Rowland ghosts occur near the lines which produce them and hence can readily be

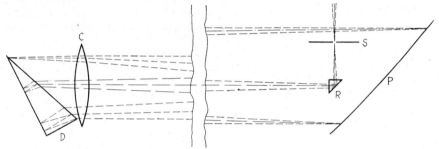

Fig. 3.—Diagram illustrating the principle of the Littrow mounting.

identified. While these can usually be kept to less than $\frac{1}{1000}$ the intensity of the parent line, a grating which has Rowland ghosts of $\frac{1}{100}$ the parent line may still be usable for many purposes. Lyman ghosts can be tested for by illuminating the grating strongly with collimated light from a slit, behind which is placed a powerful mercury arc, and by looking into the grating near the central image or elsewhere where no spectrum lines should be visible. If colored lines are seen, they may be Lyman ghosts, and the grating should be carefully tested photographically.

Gratings should be kept free from dust, which can be removed by gently stroking with a soft camel's-hair brush. When dirty, gratings should be cleaned by light and careful rubbing in the direction of the rulings with a piece of clean cotton moistened with absolute alcohol and dipped in very fine precipitated chalk or tin oxide. Great care must be taken not to scratch the grating. A portion of the unruled surface should be rubbed gently before the rulings are touched to make sure that no gritty particles are on the cotton. Fingerprints should not be produced on the grating face, and acid or other fumes which tarnish the surface should be carefully avoided.

Mountings.—The device of autocollimation developed by Littrow is widely used with either prisms or plane gratings, when it is desired to obtain high linear dispersion by the use of a camera lens of long focus. The principle of the method is illustrated in Fig. 3. The diverging beam from the slit *S* is made parallel by the collimator *C* and enters the dispersing system *D*, which in the case illustrated is a half prism with a mirror coating on its back face. The light is reflected from this mirror, passes back through the prism, and retraverses the collimator, which behaves now as a camera lens and brings the spectrum to a focus on P.

Two defects keep the Littrow mounting from displacing all other types of prism mounting to the extent that its simplicity and compactness would lead one to expect. The proximity of slit and plateholder requires the introduction of a reflecting prism or other device to separate the incoming and outgoing beams, and the reflection and scattering of light from the front face of the collimator directly back to the photographic plate may cause objectionable fogging which is hard to eliminate. This can often be decreased either by tipping the lens slightly, which will introduce a certain amount of astigmatism but throws the reflected light above the plate, or by introducing stops and diaphragms at strategic points. In any event the inside of the case surrounding a Littrow mount should be thoroughly blackened and numerous baffles should be used to cut down stray light.

To locate the cause of plate fogging, when this is found to occur with a Littrow mounting, the slit may be widened to its fullest extent with a high-intensity incandescent lamp placed in front of it. On looking at the collimator lens through the horizontal slot which admits light to the cassette, the location of any bright points of light should be noted, and these should be eliminated by some means which will cut off as little as possible of the main beams of light. In order to carry out this operation successfully, it is sometimes necessary to eliminate as much as one-fourth of the lens aperture with diaphragms. In attacking stray light a polished reflecting surface which directs an unwanted beam of light into a dark pocket is often more satisfactory than a rough blackened surface which may scatter some of the radiation falling on it.

In one widely used and excellent type of Littrow instrument having quartz or glass optical parts, the length of the case is over 7 ft., but as the optical system may be considered as having been folded together in the middle by use of the autocollimation principle, the dispersion obtained is equivalent to that furnished by an instrument twice as long.

The prism and lens are mounted on a carriage which moves along a slide, their positions on this being determined by means of a scale and index. The prism can be rotated to throw various regions of the spectrum on a 4- by 10-in. plate, which is held in a cassette-plateholder combination which in turn can be rotated to bring it into coincidence with the focal curve for any spectral region between 2000 and 8000 Å.

Plane-reflection gratings are almost always mounted in the Littrow manner. A grating so arranged has the advantage over a concave grating in the Eagle mounting (page 813) of giving stigmatic images, with a resulting increase in brightness and resolution in the higher orders. A lens carefully corrected for chromatic aberration must be used in all orders except the first, however, for otherwise the various overlapping orders will not be brought to a focus on the same curve.

Stigmatic and Astigmatic Spectrographs.—A camera lens or mirror, unless especially designed, produces a true image of an object only when image and object are close to the optic axis. As the beam angle departs more and more from the optic axis, greater amounts of astigmatism are introduced, the rays being brought to one line focus at a certain distance and to a second line focus perpendicular to the first at a greater distance. In common types of prism spectrographs the astigmatism can usually be neglected, as extremely fine focus is needed only in the horizontal direction to resolve close spectrum lines and a focus only one-tenth as sharp will serve in the vertical direction.

The spectrum lines produced by a concave grating as ordinarily used are astigmatic images of the slit, each illuminated point of this slit being imaged as a vertical line in the Rowland circle. No decrease in the purity of the spectrum results so long as the slit is accurately parallel to the rulings of the grating and if neither the slit nor the astigmatic images are curved. With most gratings a slight line curvature does exist, and it is advisable to keep the illuminated portion of the slit as short as possible when high resolving power is required. However, since each astigmatic line image has a central portion of uniform intensity whose brightness depends on the length of the illuminated slit, astigmatism may cause a serious decrease of intensity. Stigmatic spectrographs have the advantage that with them small right-angled prisms and Hartmann diaphragms can be used at the slit for introducing comparison spectra, rotating sector disks or step diaphragms can be used at the slit for photographic photometry, and Fabry-Perot or other interferometers can be crossed with them. Also, if the source is imaged on the slit, variations in intensity along the lines produced may give useful information as to the points of origin of the lines in the source. These considerations make especially useful the stigmatic mounting of the concave grating, devised by Wadsworth and realized by Meggers and Burns.

Astigmatism is occasionally useful, as with certain types of intensity measurements where uniform spectrum lines are desirable and for producing spectrograms which are neat in appearance. Also it is possible in certain cases to utilize the separation of the horizontal and vertical focal curves to image slit and photometric device on a single plate simultaneously.

Commercial Spectrographs.—Most spectrographs manufactured commercially are enclosed, portable units, varying in length from 18 in. to 8 ft. In the smaller instruments no adjustments of the prism or camera are necessary, since the entire transmitted spectrum can be obtained at a single setting. In larger instruments, where the whole spectrum cannot be recorded at once on a plate of reasonable size, some provision must be made for turning the prism and changing the focal distance of the lenses and the tilt of the plate when various regions of the spectrum are to be photographed.

The greatest number of spectrographs of any one type manufactured are those which contain quartz optical parts. These can be obtained in three or more standard sizes, the small and medium models being of fixed focus.

The small quartz spectrograph usually covers the range 8000 to 1850 Å., with a spectrum length of about 85 mm. This type finds its greatest usefulness at wave-lengths shorter than 2500 Å., where its relatively great light transmission and high aperture aid in rapid photography of a difficult region where absorption and lack of plate sensitivity conspire to reduce the intensity of the recorded spectrum. It can be obtained fitted with a transparent wavelength scale, and a fluorescent screen can be used to make the ultraviolet spectrum visible and thus to aid in the preliminary focusing adjustments.

Until recently the most commonly used spectrograph was the medium-sized quartz instrument, manufactured by a number of firms. Lenses of about 600-mm. focus and 50-mm. diameter are used, giving a spectrum from 2100 to 8000 Å. about 200-mm. long. The prism, of the Cornu type, may be about 40-mm. high by 65-mm. length of face. A standard 4-by 10-in. photographic plate is ordinarily used. This is the largest standard size of quartz instrument which will give the entire ultraviolet region in air at a single setting of the prism and camera.

The medium-sized instrument can be obtained with or without a transparent scale of wavelengths. The variation of dispersion with wavelength is well illustrated by the scale shown in Fig. 4.

Fig. 4.—Scale of wavelengths for prism-type spectroscope. The variation of dispersion with wavelength is indicated by nonuniformity of the scale calibration.

Typical spectrograms taken with the instrument depicted in Fig. 5 are shown in Fig. 6. The numerical aperture, $f/12$, is sufficient to give short exposures with most ordinary arc and spark sources, and the resolution and dispersion in the ultraviolet are ample for simple spectra, and for absorption spectrophotometry of solutions.

In purchasing any fixed-focus instrument care should be taken to see that the manufacturer has provided sufficient rigidity to the adjustment of prism and lenses so that they will not readily get out of focus when once adjusted, and that the cassette and plateholder are constructed so they will not warp. Manufacturers should be asked to submit sample spectrograms taken on the instrument to be purchased and are usually very willing to do so.

Where higher dispersion is needed than the medium-sized quartz instrument will supply, recourse is usually had to the Littrow type of mounting (see page 810) in order to save space and improve rigidity. The large quartz Littrow is now the most widely used of all spectrographs, being especially suited to spectroscopic analysis of materials.

Almost any quartz spectrograph can be obtained with glass optical parts which will render it suitable for use in the visible region. While quartz is also transparent in this region, its dispersion is so low as to make quartz spectrographs almost valueless

FIG. 5.—Bausch and Lomb medium quartz spectrograph.

at wavelengths longer than about 5200 Å., beyond which, also, the ordinary photographic plate becomes insensitive and special plates must be used.

The dispersive properties of even heavy flint glass are not so great as is desirable, and several prisms are sometimes used in train to increase dispersion and resolving power in the visible region. In general the concave diffraction grating, with its uniform dispersion, usefulness for all wavelengths, and simplicity of adjustment, is to be preferred to prism spectrographs when high resolution and dispersion are important.

While grating spectrographs can be obtained from certain manufacturers, satisfactory gratings are so difficult to obtain that the grating spectrograph is not standard. The great usefulness of the grating in the past has come largely from its high dispersion and resolving power, and since gratings of 6-in. aperture or over are not unusual, while prisms of over 2-in. aperture are rare, grating spectrographs ordinarily have three or more times the focal length of prism instruments. On account of their size, large grating instruments ordinarily are assembled by their user and operated uncovered in a darkened room, though standard commercial models in the smaller sizes are appearing on the market.

TABLE I.—MOUNTINGS AND THEIR CHARACTERISTICS

Rowland..........	Spectrum of uniform dispersion; simple to change region
Abney...........	Same as Rowland, but source and slit move while grating and camera are fixed
Eagle...........	Long and narrow, relatively low astigmatism, reaches higher orders
Paschen..........	Broad spectral coverage with single exposure
Wadsworth.......	Stigmatic, and of high light-gathering power; best for most purposes of applied spectroscopy

Concave Grating Mountings.—If a diffraction grating be ruled on a concave spherical mirror, no collimator or camera lenses are required, for light sent through a slit placed anywhere on a circle whose diameter equals the radius of curvature of the mirror and passes through the mirror will be brought to focus on this circle as a spectrum. The focal curve is known as the "Rowland circle." Since so many possible relative dispositions of slit, grating, and camera are possible, numerous special mountings have been designed for special purposes.

Table I gives the advantages of the standard mountings for concave gratings.

Small commercial concave-grating spectrographs, which are of necessity portable, ordinarily use the Eagle or in some cases the Rowland mounting. When one is faced with the necessity of choosing the most suitable mounting for a large grating, the first consideration must be that of the space available. Where only a long narrow corridor or a small vertical shaft can be used, the Eagle mounting is useful. The cross section of its containing box is conditioned only by the length of spectrum which it is desired to photograph at one setting, and by the baffles needed to cut down stray light.

If a room of medium size (say 12 by 15 ft.) is available, a 21-ft. grating in the Wadsworth mounting will probably be found more useful than a shorter focus grating in any other mounting. This is because the grating of longer radius will cost no more than a shorter one for the same area of ruling, and the advantages of a stigmatic mounting are obtained, while the grating can always be used at its full dispersion in another mounting.

The Paschen mounting is so much more flexible than others that its use is advantageous in many cases where sufficient space is available. For a 21-ft. grating the room should be at least 25 by 15 ft. for a half circle or 30 by 25 ft. for a full circle, with a separate room to serve as a source room, the slit being mounted on a pier and let through the partition between the two rooms. Detailed directions for adjusting gratings in the Rowland and Abney mountings will be found in Kayser's "Handbuch der Spektroskopie," while the original article by Eagle should be consulted in connection with his mounting.

When the camera of a grating spectrograph has been placed in approximately the proper position, it is clamped in the position of best focus by viewing the spectrum lines produced on a piece of white paper or a fluorescent screen when a broad

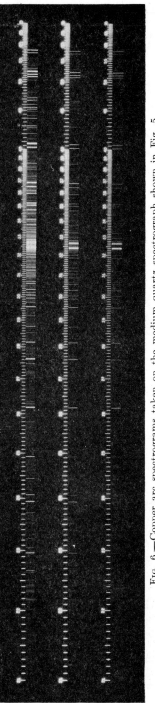

Fig. 6.—Copper arc spectrograms taken on the medium quartz spectrograph shown in Fig. 5.

slit is used.   In this way the focal curve can be located within 1 in. or less either way.   An eyepiece can be used in the visible region to approximate still more closely to the focal curve, the slit being greatly narrowed for this purpose.   The remainder of the focusing process must be carried out photographically.

A number of small brackets are hung on the camera, each holding a small piece of photographic plate inclined at an angle of 45° to the vertical, the center of each plate lying in the focal plane of the camera, as in Fig. 7.   Photographs are taken with these inclined plates distributed at intervals, and the spot of best focus is marked

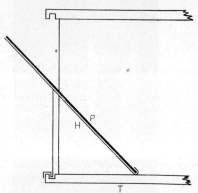

on each plate.   The camera is then moved to the position corresponding to best focus and inclined test plates are taken again but at intermediate points.   This process is repeated until the whole of the camera is in satisfactory focus.

Illumination of the Spectrograph.—Various methods are available for directing into the spectrograph the light to be studied, that most commonly used being one in which an image of the source is focused on the slit by means of a double-convex lens.   Either one of the two conjugate foci of this lens can be used, the first giving a diminished and the second an enlarged image.   The latter is generally to be preferred when the source is of small extent, provided the angular aperture of the lens is sufficient to fill the collimator of the spectrograph with light under these conditions.   This is illustrated in Fig. 8, from which it will be seen that use of an extra-large collecting lens L_3 is of no value if it more than fills the angular aperture of the spectrograph collimator.

FIG. 7.—Use of inclined photographic plate for determining position of best focus.

In certain cases one can place the source directly in front of the slit in such a way that the spectrograph is filled with light.   Under such circumstances, as in a third method (Fig. 9) in which a lens is placed directly in front of the slit in such a way as to throw an image of the source on the collimator lens, unless the slit is narrow the lens may not be filled with coherent radiation, and a loss in resolving power may result.

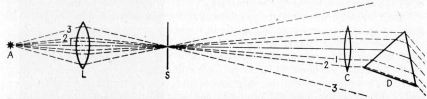

FIG. 8.—Diagram illustrating illumination of spectrograph.   The light source A, and lens L, illuminate the slit S, the collimating lens C, and the dispersing element D.

At a certain optimum slit width, given approximately by the formula $W/\lambda = \text{N.A.}$, where W is the slit width, λ is the wavelength of the light considered, and N.A. is the numerical aperture of the collimator, the line intensity reaches a maximum, though the intensity of the continuous spectrum continues to increase as the slit is widened. For this reason a narrow slit may help to reduce continuous background relative to the line spectrum.

In considering the efficiency of any method of spectrograph illumination, it should be kept in mind that so long as the entrance slit and the collimator lens or other internal limiting aperture remain constant in area and filled with light of each wavelength considered, nothing done outside the spectrograph will increase the illumination which passes through it from a given source. With certain types of source it may be difficult to fulfill these conditions, in which case auxiliary focusing apparatus is desirable. But the method, frequently suggested by the beginner, of using a collecting lens of very short focus and high aperture, produces no increase in intensity.

Certain manufacturers provide optical benches attached to their spectrographs to aid in alignment of light sources. In lining up an optical bench or a source-lens combination, the lens should first be removed and the light from the unaided source be allowed to fall on the widened spectroscope slit. The cover of the spectroscope, if this be enclosed, should then be removed and a white card held directly behind the collimator lens. The source may be shifted until the small spot of light coming through the slit is centered in the collimator both horizontally and vertically. The collector lens should then be placed in position to focus the source on the slit, if this type of illumination is desired, and the collimator should now be found filled with light when the slit is narrowed to any desired extent. If the light beam falling on the collimator more than fills this, the collecting lens should be stopped down or a lens of different

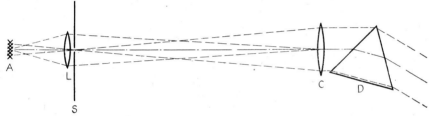

Fɪɢ. 9.—Illumination of spectrograph.

focal length should be used, since overfilling the collimator may give rise to undesirable scattered light inside the spectrograph.

The collecting lens should, needless to say, be transparent to the entire spectrum region transmitted by the spectrograph with which it is to be used, but need not be of high quality. Ordinary spherical lenses of spectacle quality will usually serve, though when the maximum intensity at all wavelengths is needed it is desirable to use a lens free from chromatic aberration. In using uncorrected quartz lenses, it should be kept in mind that the focal length for the ultraviolet rays is much shorter than that for the visible, so focusing should be done with a fluorescent screen or by deliberately bringing the source closer to the lens so as to throw the visible beam somewhat out of focus.

A concave mirror can be used instead of a lens for focusing light on the slit, though usually with some loss in intensity and with difficulties due to astigmatism substituted for those arising from chromatic aberration. Glass mirrors covered with a thin coating of aluminum have high reflecting power throughout the visible and ultraviolet regions.

Adjustment and Focusing of Spectrographs.—Commercial spectrographs of fixed focus are usually shipped with their optical parts in adjustment, and instruments with variable setting are provided either with calibrated controls or a table of scale settings. Occasionally mechanical or optical parts are moved in shipment and readjustment may be necessary.

After unpacking, the cover of the instrument should be removed and the optical surfaces of prisms and lenses wiped clean with a soft piece of cloth, or with Japanese rice paper or the lens paper sold by optical manufacturers. The faces of diffraction gratings should not be cleaned with a cloth unless glass enclosed, but they should be carefully stroked, parallel to the rulings, with a very soft camel's-hair brush. The slit should be cleaned with a freshly sharpened stick of soft wood and should be set at a moderately narrow adjustment; its parallelism to the vertical edge of the prism or grating should be checked.

A test photograph should be taken using a mercury or iron arc, or some other source having a profusion of fine lines. If satisfactory spectrograms are obtained, the lines being sharp and straight, in good focus, and the spectrogram clean and free from fogging and scattered light, no further adjustment is necessary.

When a spectrograph does not function satisfactorily the following procedure will be found useful. After the slit has been checked for parallelism to the dispersing edge, it is widened to perhaps 0.5 mm. Light from a high-power mercury arc is sent through it, and with dispersing element and camera lens removed, the slit-collimator distance is adjusted until light of the wavelengths in a median spectral region is made into a parallel beam as shown by focusing on a distant screen or wall. The prism is then replaced and turned until the beam containing the same central wavelength is found to be bent least, as shown by the fact that its diffuse image caught on a white card (or fluorescent screen for the ultraviolet) moves first in one direction and then back as the prism is rotated continuously forward. After this position of minimum deviation for the central wavelength has been found, the prism is moved sideways, if necessary, so that the collimated beam is centered on it, and is clamped in position. The camera lens is then adjusted in the beam so that it is filled with light of all desired wavelengths, and the camera-plate distance and plate tilt are adjusted to bring the spectrum into good focus on a viewing screen held in the plateholder.

The final focusing adjustment can best be carried out photographically. Once prism and camera lens are set, it may be found most convenient to make fine adjustments by slightly altering the slit-collimator distance and the plate tilt. Using a narrow slit, a series of photographs is taken moving the collimator (or slit) by $\frac{1}{2}$-mm. steps, and the position of best focus is marked by dots for a number of uniformly spaced lines. When these dots are in a horizontal line, the collimator lens need merely be set in the position indicated as best; when the line they form is straight but inclined, the plateholder angle must be changed. When they lie on a curved line the plate curvature must also be changed to compensate, though manufacturers usually provide holders of the proper curvature for their instruments, of course, and a setting of the lenses and prisms can often be found after a number of combinations have been tried, which will suit the curvature furnished. The inclined-plate technique described on page 814 for focusing large gratings can often be used to advantage with smaller spectrographs also.

Comparison Spectra.—For many purposes it is desirable to impress several spectra on a plate without moving that plate, for even if the plateholder moves in carefully made vertical ways, some measurable lateral displacement is sure to result. With stigmatic instruments a 45° reflecting comparison prism can be moved into position over a portion of the slit and used to throw in a beam of light from a second source. Or a Hartmann diaphragm can be used to cover parts of the slit during one exposure and to uncover these parts for others. This type of diaphragm, illustrated in Fig. 10 together with a standard fishtail diaphragm used for varying the slit length, is designed to be slipped into place over the spectrograph slit in the ways usually found provided for this purpose.

With astigmatic instruments it is necessary either to use some type of diaphragm at the position of the external vertical focus or to place occulting diaphragms in front of the plate. These should be as close to the plate as convenient, to provide sharp boundaries between contiguous spectra.

When diaphragms are used at or before the slit, one should remember that the lower part of a spectrum line corresponds to the upper part of the slit and vice versa, since a spectrograph produces inverted real images of its slit.

Identification of Spectrum Lines.—A spectrum line is best identified by its wavelength, which can be deduced from its position in the spectrum and under proper conditions can be determined to one part in several million. Most wavelength determinations are made photographically and involve first the determination of the relation between the wavelengths λ of known lines and the distances *l* of these lines from some fixed point on the plate. This relation, when plotted graphically, gives the dispersion curve of the plate, which is seldom a straight line. The dispersion curve can be plotted graphically or determined mathematically without plotting, and from it the wavelengths of unknown lines can be deduced by interpolation of their observed positions.

Wavelengths can be determined from theoretical dispersion formulas, but so many easily identifiable lines have now been precisely measured that these formulas are seldom used except in special cases.

Standards of Wavelength.—The international angstrom unit is defined as a length equal to the wavelength of a certain red line in the cadmium spectrum divided by 6438.4696. In other words, this red line, the so-called "primary standard" of wave-

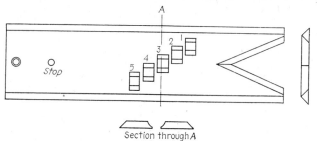

Fig. 10.—Diaphragms for shortening the lengths of spectrum lines in making wavelength determinations.

length, has by definition the length 6438.4696 Å. A number of "secondary standards" have been measured in terms of this line by means of interferometers. Wavelengths of the secondary standards are given in the *Transactions of the International Astronomical Union*, **3**, 86 (1928); and International Critical Tables, Vol. 5, p. 275.

The secondary standards are somewhat far apart in the spectrum for convenient use, and to fill the gaps between them, "tertiary standards" have been carefully measured by means of gratings and interferometers. These "working standards" of wavelength, as adopted by the International Astronomical Union, are given in the International Critical Tables, Vol. 5, p. 275.

Wavelength Tables.—For routine spectrographic work sufficiently precise wavelength values can be obtained from the "Handbuch der Spectroskopie," by H. Kayser, an encyclopedic work of eight volumes in German which lists more than 120,000 lines. More convenient is the shorter list of "Tabelle der Hauptlinien der Elemente," by Kayser, which gives wavelengths for approximately 19,000 of the more important spectral lines of the elements, and the M.I.T. wavelength tables which list wavelengths and intensities for the 110,000 most important lines between 10,000 and 2,000 Å. Wavelengths determined before 1911 are usually on the old Rowland scale which has been superseded by the International Scale, and require corrections varying between 0.12 Å at 2950 Å and 0.28 Å at 7700 Å.

Wavelength Determinations.—When an unknown spectrum is photographed, provision should be made to photograph a known spectrum and a spectrum containing standard lines on the same plate, care being taken to allow no sideways displacement of the plate between exposures.   Even the racking of a plate from one position to another will involve some sidewise displacement, and the two spectra should be taken with no intervening motion of the plate when precision is required.   Diaphragms may be inserted to shorten the lengths of some of the lines, as in Fig. 10, so that lines of the two spectra can be separated readily.

The positions of the lines are usually determined with a wavelength comparator, which consists of a carriage to which the plate can be clamped, an observing microscope provided with a cross hair, and a precision screw which moves the plate (or less conveniently, the microscope itself).   Comparators can seldom be read more precisely than to ∓ 0.001 mm., which is sufficient for most spectrograms.   Care should be taken to avoid undue magnification in the comparator eyepiece, as unless the spectrum

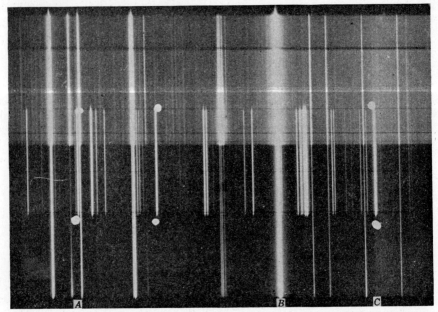

Fig. 11.—Identification of unknown spectrum wavelength by means of known spectrum.

lines are extremely sharp, they can be set most accurately on the cross hair when magnifications of from 5 to 15 diameters are used.   In some comparators the spectrum is projected on a screen for measurement.

For routine identification of lines precision to 0.01 mm. often suffices, in which case a simple plate magnifier with engraved scale will serve.   These can be obtained with scales 20 mm. long, engraved with 0.1-mm. divisions which can be estimated to 0.01 mm.

Knowing the wavelength of any one line, the distance to an unknown line can be measured with the eyepiece or comparator.   Multiplying this distance by the approximate dispersion of the plate at that point gives the wavelength of the unknown line. For example, in Fig. 11 line A was identified as 3542.079 of iron.   The distance to line B was measured as 9.972 mm.   The dispersion between lines A and C was $3542.079 - 3521.264(20.815\text{Å}.)$, divided by 14.820 mm. or 1.403 Å. per mm.   Multiplying the distance AB by 1.403, we obtain 14.006 Å. from A to B, which subtracted from 3542.079 Å. for A gives 3528.073 Å. for the wavelength of B.

This method is called "linear interpolation," and, while it always involves some error, this error can be made negligible by choosing known lines lying so close together that the dispersion of the spectrograph varies but slightly between them.

Simplified Line Identification.—Most spectrum lines have been observed and measured many times, and many can be identified from their appearance or the patterns they form with other lines. Unknown lines can often be identified by merely comparing them directly with spectra of known elements photographed on the same or a similar plate. It is often convenient with a newly acquired spectrograph to photograph the arc and spark spectra of a number of the more common elements which can be obtained comparatively pure, the resulting plates being marked and kept to aid in identifying unknown lines. These plates can be laid directly over later plates taken with the same instrument, so that corresponding lines appear in juxtaposition. Atlases of spectral lines can be used similarly, though less directly because usually their dispersion scale is different.

To aid in identifying wavelength positions approximately, a simple well-known spectrum such as that of mercury or of copper may conveniently be impressed on each plate taken. The iron spectrum should then be impressed on the plate also, to give more precise locations of desired lines.

Light Sources for Emission Spectroscopy.—The source most commonly used for producing line spectra is the electric arc in air, preferably run on 220 volts d.c. with a

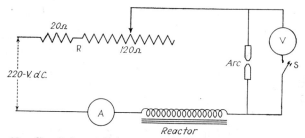

Fig. 12.—Circuit for arc light source suitable for use in spectroscopy.

current of from 2 to 10 amp. The circuit used is shown in Fig. 12. A rheostat R capable of carrying 10 amp., whose resistance can be varied from 20 to 120 ohms, is kept in series with the arc, together with an ammeter A and a stabilizing reactance made by winding a few hundred turns of wire on an iron core. A voltmeter V may be provided to read the voltage across the arc terminals, but this should not be connected except when being read, as when the arc goes out a high voltage may be built up across its terminals. The series reactance helps keep the arc burning steadily, and use of 220 volts d.c. instead of 110 volts also gives greater steadiness.

The arc may be burned between pure graphite electrodes, the lower electrode being cupped to receive small samples of the material whose spectrum lines are to be studied. Or the electrodes themselves may be formed from the material to be studied. Metals, ashes, or liquids may be burned in the cup, and even slags and glasses can be thus handled. When the material is a poor conductor, it is desirable to mix with it some conducting material such as ammonium sulphate, which emits few spectrum lines in the visible or ultraviolet regions, and to moisten the mass with pure dilute hydrochloric acid.

The condensed electric spark, connected as shown in Fig. 13, is used almost as much as the arc as a spectrum source. Most of the spectrum lines which appear in the arc also appear in the spark, and in addition new lines, usually produced by atoms from which one or more electrons have been removed, also appear. Strong fuzzy lines due to air are frequently seen in spark spectrograms; these can usually be diminished in strength or eliminated entirely by inserting a coil of a few dozen turns of wire, with iron core, as shown in Fig. 13.   The number of turns should be adjusted so that the air lines are reduced as much as possible without too greatly reducing the intensities of the lines which are being studied.

Advantages of the arc compared to the spark are that it is safer electrically, is more intense, is usually quieter, produces no air lines, and shows greater variation between lines so that they can be identified more readily by their appearance.   Advantages

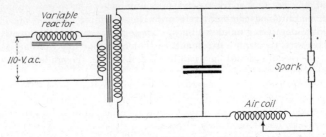

Fig. 13.—Electrical circuit of spark light source for use in spectroscopy.

of the spark are that it burns less material, needs less attention, brings out some lines not found in the arc, and produces fewer band lines.   The cyanogen bands are particularly annoying in the violet and near ultraviolet regions when a graphite arc is burned in air.   Burning metallic material in the arc weakens these bands.   They produce a strong violet light in the arc, and by carefully watching it and refilling with material when this color appears, the intensity of the bands can be reduced.

There is no royal rule as to when an arc is to be preferred to a spark, or vice versa. Most spectroscopists keep both available and use whichever is best for the problem

Fig. 14.—Spark *A* and arc *B* spectrograms made under identical conditions.

in hand.   Figure 14 shows spectrograms taken under identical circumstances of the same material, *A* being a spark exposure, and *B* an arc exposure.

High-frequency arcs, high-voltage arcs, vacuum arcs and sparks, electrodeless discharges, and numerous other light sources are often found useful for spectroscopic purposes and will be found described in the literature.

Light Sources for Absorption Spectroscopy.—When transparent liquids or solids are studied by absorption spectrophotometry, new absorption bands can be located most readily if light producing a continuous spectrum is sent through the absorbing material.   The most convenient source for this purpose between 10,000 and 4000 Å. is a straight-filament incandescent lamp, while between 6000 and 2000 Å. a high-voltage discharge through hydrogen gas in a quartz tube is useful.   A high-tension spark discharge under distilled water between tungsten or aluminum electrodes, or electrodes of almost any other metal, gives a useful continuous background throughout the entire spectrum, though this is usually crossed with occasional emission or absorption lines. A condensed spark in air between cadmium electrodes can be made to give a heavy continuous background in the ultraviolet region, though crossed with a number of emission lines. Exploded wires probably give the most intense continuous background, but, compared to the other methods listed, these are difficult to control and inconvenient to use.

When extinction coefficients are to be measured, especially in the ultraviolet region, a rich line spectrum can be used conveniently for background, since measurements must be made at known wavelengths and these need not be continuously spread. A spark between tungsten-steel electrodes is commonly used for this purpose. Uranium electrodes are also useful—in fact, any hard metal with numerous lines in the ultraviolet will serve for this purpose. A spark source is commonly used with the Hilger Spekker Photometer and with rotating-sector disk photometers, which are commonly used for ultraviolet absorption spectrophotometry.

Bibliography

Periodicals:

LITTROW, O.: *Am. J. Sci.*, **35**, 413 (1862).
ROWLAND, H. A.: On Concave Gratings for Optical Purposes, *Am. J. Sci.*, **26** (No. 3), 87–98 (1883); *Phil. Mag.*, **16** (No. 5), 197–210 (1883).
ABNEY, W.: *Phil. Trans.*, **177**, 457 (1886).
AMES,: *Phil. Mag.*, **5**, 369 (1889).
WADSWORTH, F. L. O.: *Phil. Mag.*, **38**, 137 (1894).
————: *Astrophys. J.*, **2**, 370 (1895); **3**, 46 (1896).
LYMAN, T.: False Spectra with the Rowland Grating, *Phys. Rev.*, **12**, 1–13 (1901).
EAGLE, A.: On a New Mounting for Concave Gratings, *Astrophys. J.*, **31**, 12 (1910).
CORNU, A.: *J. phys.*, **4**, 261 (1914).
ANDERSON, J. A.: *Astrophys. J.*, **51**, 37 (1920).
MEGGERS, W. F., and K. BURNS: *Natl. Bur. Standards, Sci. Papers*, **18**, 185 (1922).
SAWYER, R. A. and A. L. BECKER: *Astrophys. J.*, **57**, 98 (1923).
WOOD, R. W.: *Phil. Mag.*, **48**, 497 (1924).
FRERICHS, R.: Intensity Measurements of Multiplets, *Ann. Physik*, **81**, 807–845 (1926).
HARRISON, G. R.: *Phys. Rev.*, **24**, 466–477 (1926).
HARRISON, G. R.: Instruments and Methods Used for Measuring Spectral Light Intensities by Photography, *J. Optical Soc. Am.*, **19**, 5 (1929).
KISTIAKOWSKY, O. B.: High Power Source of Continuous Ultraviolet Spectrum, *Rev. Sci. Instruments*, **2**, 549 (1931).
DIEKE, G. H.: Astigmatism of the Concave Grating, *J. Optical Soc. Am.*, **23**, 274 (1933).

Books:

"The Physical Papers of H. A. Rowland," Johns Hopkins (1902).
KAYSER, H.: "Tabelle der Hauptlinien der Linienspektra Aller Elemente," Springer (1926).
BALY, E. C. C.: "Spectroscopy," Longmans (1929).
HARDY, A. C., and F. H. PERRIN: "The Principles of Optics," McGraw (1932).
HARNWELL, G. P., and J. J. LIVINGOOD: "Experimental Atomic Physics," McGraw (1933).
WOOD, R. W.: "Physical Optics," 3d ed., Macmillan (1934).
KAYSER, H., *et al.*: "Handbuch der Spectroskopie," S. Hirzel, Leipzig (1910–1934).
JENKINS, F. A., and H. E. WHITE: "Fundamentals of Physical Optics," McGraw (1937).
FORSYTHE, W. E., *et al.*: "Measurement of Radiant Energy," McGraw (1937).
LYMAN, T.: "Spectroscopy of the Extreme Ultraviolet," Longmans.

CHAPTER XXX

RADIOGRAPHY

By ROBERT C. WOODS

Introduction.—The shadow picture resulting when X rays pass through an object and fall upon a sensitive photographic film is known as a "radiograph." The process of taking such a picture is called "radiography," and the apparatus used is a "radiographic machine." While these terms are most commonly used, others may be correctly substituted, such as skiagraph for radiograph or roentgen ray for X ray.

Radiography may be roughly divided into three classifications: (1) clinical, (2) industrial, and (3) diffraction. The purpose of clinical radiography is to study the outline of the human frame with all its surrounding tissues so as to locate accurately the site of possible disease, injury, or foreign body. Industrial radiography provides a nondestructive test for studying the internal structure of industrial materials with the purpose of discovering subsurface defects. While diffraction methods are not generally classed under radiography, a literal interpretation of the word "radiograph" requires the inclusion of diffraction patterns, since they are also shadowgraphs produced by X rays. Diffraction pictures are used as a method to disclose the crystalline, molecular, or atomic structure of almost any material and are invaluable in many ways to industry, medicine, and pure research.

Characteristics of X Rays.—The principal characteristics of X rays may be summarized as follows: X rays are produced in special types of vacuum tubes by the impact of electrons on a target of hard metal, the rays being emitted in straight lines from the target where they originate. The number of rays produced is proportional to the current passing through the tube, whereas their penetrating power depends upon the voltage at which the tube is operated. X rays are a form of electromagnetic energy and travel with a velocity approaching 186,000 miles per second. X rays behave sometimes as waves and sometimes as discrete particles, in common with other forms of electromagnetic radiations. The X-ray spectrum has a mean wavelength which depends upon the voltage at which this tube is operated. The rays are incapable of producing visual sensation unaided, but their presence may be indicated visually through the use of fluorescent screens which emit visible light when acted upon by X rays. The rays are capable of penetrating substances which are opaque to visible light but are attenuated more or less in passing through solid materials, the amount of attenuation depending upon the thickness of the object and its atomic structure.

X-ray Photography.—It has been found that X rays have the very important property of producing a latent image on photographically sensitive materials, and this property is made use of in radiography. It enables the X-ray worker to record on film facts about the internal condition of closed structures which would normally be invisible. This effect depends on the fact that wherever X rays strike a gelatin emulsion of silver bromide, the silver salt is reduced to a black metallic condition. For all practical purposes this reduction is proportional to the intensity of the incident radiation. The photographic effect is also approximately inversely proportional to the square of the distance between the target of the X-ray tube and the sensitive film.

X-ray film emulsion, while it follows the same principle as that of photographic film, is slightly different both as to chemical and physical characteristics, being more sensitive to X rays. Even so, less than 1 per cent of X-ray energy is absorbed by such an emulsion, and the remaining 99 per cent passes through without performing any useful work. To utilize some of the wasted 99 per cent energy, screens coated with some salt like calcium tungstate are placed in direct contact with the double-sensitized film surfaces. These screens, under X-ray bombardment, fluoresce, *i.e.*, absorb X rays and emit visible light. Thus the X-ray effect on film emulsion is increased many times by the addition of visible light from the screens. This not only reduces exposure time but makes practical the radiography of several thicknesses.

The grain size of fluorescent coatings on screens is larger than that of film emulsions, and the result is some loss of fine detail in the finished radiograph. The best picture will be made without screens, but many times the use of screens is imperative, and so they may be classed as a necessary evil.

X-ray Protection.—X rays have a deleterious effect on the human system and every possible precaution should be taken by the operator of an X-ray machine to avoid repeated personal exposure. Before engaging in X-ray work of any kind, it is essential to make a thorough study of X-ray protection under all conditions which might arise. Those technicians who are unequipped with electroscopes or other instruments for detecting stray radiation should carry out the dental film test while at their work. This consists in attaching a silver coin to the front of a dental packet loaded with photographic film and carrying it, coin outward, in the vest or watch pocket. If, after several days of X-ray work, the film is developed and shows an image of the coin, it indicates the operator is being exposed to X-rays and should immediately take steps to obtain better shielding. Too much emphasis cannot be laid on this phase of the work, for serious illness, and even death, can ensue from small X-ray doses constantly taken.

X-ray Equipment.—No attempt will be made to describe in detail the various possible electrical circuits which are capable of producing X rays. For this information, reference may be made to any of several excellent books on the subject. At the same time, a brief mention of the fundamentals may not be amiss.

X rays are produced by the impact of electrons on a target of solid hard metal, which is usually tungsten. In modern practice, X rays are produced in a vacuum tube containing a heated filament and the anode or target. The filament is heated to incandescence by means of a transformer operating from the 110-volt line and supplying suitable filament voltage and current to the tube. When the filament becomes incandescent, the thermal energy is sufficient to liberate a source of free electrons which are capable of traveling through the vacuous space within the tube. In order that these electrons may travel through the tube rather than cluster around the filament from which they are emitted, it is necessary to accelerate them in a direction toward the target. Since the electrons are negatively charged particles of electricity, they may be made to move in the direction of the target by applying a voltage between the filament and target such that the target is at a positive potential with respect to that of the filament.

In impinging upon the target, the electrons give up the kinetic energy which was imparted to them by virture of the positive charge on the target, and in so doing they produce those radiations known as X rays. The penetrating power of the X rays depends upon the potential difference between the filament and target. The number of rays depends upon the number of available electrons *i.e.*, the current through the tube, and this in turn depends upon the temperature of the filament which is regulated by the filament voltage and current. Thus, by controlling the filament temperature and the filament-target voltage, the operating characteristics of the tube may be determined at will. The voltage between the filament and target (sometimes called the "cathode" and "anode," respectively) may be as high as 1,000,000 volts, although ordinarily voltages of from 30,000 to 200,000 volts (30 to 200 kilovolts) are used. The current through the tube is commonly between about 10 and 100 ma. (0.010 to 0.100 amp.).

The point at which the beam of electrons emitted from the filament strikes the target is known as the focal spot. This spot should be as small as possible in order that the tube may simulate as much as possible a point source, and thereby produce radiographs which are as sharp as possible. If this focal point is unduly large, the resulting radiographs will be less sharply defined.

Factors in Making Radiographs.—In addition to as small a focal spot as is possible, there are other conditions which contribute to correct radiographic images. The distance between the anode and the object being radiographed should be as great as is practical. While a distance of 25 in. from anode to film may be satisfactory for radiography of the extremities, with thicker parts it is usually necessary to increase this distance.

The film should be as close to the object as possible. Distance between object and film allows the rays to spread to such an extent before reaching the film that haziness occurs.

The film should not deviate too far from perpendicularity to the line of the principal rays; otherwise serious distortion will result.

In the radiography of thick objects, scattered rays form the greater part of the radiation passing to the film. Any effective method of preventing this scattered radiation from reaching the film produces a marked improvement in the quality of the image.

In the medical field the most effective way to reduce scattered rays from the object is through the use of a Potter-Bucky diaphragm. This apparatus is a moving grid interposed between the part to be taken and the film. The grid is composed of a series of lead strips held in place by intervening wood strips. The lead strips are so tilted that the plane of each is in line with the tube focal spot; these strips have the function of absorbing the scattered rays which come from the part radiographed, so the larger image portion is formed by primary rays from the tube focal spot.

The grid can be flat or curved, but, to eliminate direct shadows of the lead strips, it must be attached to some mechanism for moving it between object and film while an exposure is being made; such a device is generally incorporated as part of the diaphragm.

For correct use of the Bucky diaphragm, the anode-film distance must be at least 25 in. or more, dependent upon its design, and it must be placed so the primary X-ray beam will pass directly through the spaces between the lead strips. Longitudinal shifts are permissible, but lateral shifts should not be extended more than 1 or 2 in. from the grid center.

Medical Radiography.—It is almost impossible to condense into table form all the variable factors which affect the taking of a clinical radiograph. Added to the large number of X-ray tubes with different ratings, there is the variation in calibration of machines and difference in size of patients, as well as the preference of the attending physician in matters of film density, contrast, etc. Nor is it practical for a technician to learn the correct position for the patient in various pictures except through actual observation. As an example of the variation in X-ray tube ratings and their effect on technique, an instance may be cited. The General Electric X-ray Co. recommends the following factors for radiography of the kidney with two of their tubes: With one tube the exposure is given as 100 ma. at 50 kilovolts for 2 sec. at a distance of 36 in., while with another the technique is 60 ma. at 56 kilovolts for 2 sec. at 30 in. Also the technician or doctor in charge of the X-ray department may find that some other combination of factors produces a radiograph more to their liking. The operative-technique chart with accompanying remarks shows the procedure for one particular model X-ray unit and tube.

A rough beginning for techniques with other apparatus may be obtained from this chart (Table I) as follows: Take the product of current (milliamperes, ma.) multiplied by the time, which will give milliampere-seconds, and then adhere to the other factors shown. For instance, in this chart, radiography of the gall bladder calls for 60 ma. at 56 kilovolts for 2 sec. at 30 in. distance. If it is desired to make this radiograph with an outfit that will not run so high as 60 ma. for 2 sec., the first step is to determine the current-time factor, which in this case is 60 times 2, or 120 ma.-sec. If another machine will operate at 30 ma. for 4 sec. at 56 kilovolts, the resulting film should be about the same using a 30-in. distance. In any event, use of similar total milliampere-seconds, with other factors as shown, will serve as a starting point for development of a satisfactory technique.

Exposure times for areas subject to movement should be as short as possible. A heart which completes its diastole and systole 80 times a minute performs one of these functions in about 0.3 sec. Therefore, to avoid blurring, a heart picture must be taken in as small a fraction of a second as possible. Also to be considered is the fact that each heart beat displaces various surrounding tissues, *e.g.*, the lung.

Clinical Interpretation.—Correct interpretation of clinical radiographs depends almost entirely on experience under some efficient diagnostician. No amount of study can take the place of actual viewing of films. Film diagnosis is not part of an X-ray technician's work and under no condition should the technician attempt to give such information to a patient without the consent of the radiologist in charge. Infraction of this rule may lead to serious consequences.

Industrial Radiography.—While the application of X rays in industry for determination of flaws and internal defects in industrial materials is a more recent development than that of medical radiographic diagnosis, it has progressed so rapidly in the past few years that the value of this inspection method is no longer questioned. Industrial radiography is the only nondestructive test now known for the actual visualization of subsurface conditions. X-ray examination of welds, castings, molds, radio tubes, and countless other manufactured articles is now a routine occurrence in numerous plants throughout the world. As in medicine, the basis of industrial radiography is the differential absorption of X rays by matter of varying densities. In radiography of an object containing areas which, intentionally or not, differ in density from surrounding material, those areas will register on a film providing they are not too small. In general, defects $1\frac{1}{2}$ to 2 per cent of the total thickness of the object under inspection can be detected, and in special instances flaws as small as 1 per cent can be demonstrated. If, for example, in a sample of carbon steel the carbon has precipitated in one section, that area will be of lower density than the surrounding steel and allow X rays to pass more freely. The result will be a dark spot on the film signifying increased exposure. Any section of increased density will absorb X rays more readily and record a lighter area on the film. When handled correctly, areas of increased and decreased density may be registered on a film in faithful reproduction of the original as to size and shape. Ordinary radiographic technique does not magnify or enlarge any objects or their defects on the final film.

Industrial X-ray Apparatus.—Industrial X-ray apparatus operates on the same principle as medical radiographic machines, but whereas clinical equipment only occasionally exceeds a rating of 100,000 volts, industrial work often requires a 200,000-volt technique and in some instances industrial apparatus can be run as high as 400000, volts.

TABLE I.—OPERATIVE TECHNIQUE CHART[1]
Extremities

Region	Kv.	Ma.	Time, sec.	Dist., in.	Screens
Hand	44	10	5	30	No
	40	75	$\frac{1}{10}$	36	Yes
Wrist	48	10	5	30	No
	44	75	$\frac{1}{10}$	36	Yes
Wrist	56	10	5	30	No
	52	75	$\frac{1}{10}$	36	Yes
Elbow	60	10	5	30	No
	57	75	$\frac{1}{10}$	36	Yes
Elbow	63	10	5	30	No
	59	75	$\frac{1}{10}$	36	Yes
Shoulder*	45	10	5	30	Yes
	65	75	$\frac{1}{10}$	36	Yes
Foot	50	10	5	30	No
	46	75	$\frac{1}{10}$	36	Yes
Foot	53	10	5	30	No
	50	75	$\frac{1}{10}$	36	Yes
Ankle	63	10	5	30	No
	59	75	$\frac{1}{10}$	36	Yes
Ankle	59	10	5	30	No
	54	75	$\frac{1}{10}$	36	Yes
Knee	42	10	5	30	Yes
	62	75	$\frac{1}{10}$	36	Yes
Knee	39	10	5	30	Yes
	59	75	$\frac{1}{10}$	36	Yes

Head

Region	Kv.	Ma.	Time, sec.	Dist., in.	Bucky	Screens
Skull	70	10	5	25	Yes	Yes
	52	50	2	30C	No	Yes
Skull*	65	10	5	30	Yes	Yes
	44	50	2	30	No	Yes
Occipital	70	10	5	25	Yes	Yes
	52	50	2	30C	No	Yes
Frontal sinus*	70	10	5	25C	Yes	Yes
	54	50	2	30C	No	Yes
Maxillary sinus*	74	10	5	25C	Yes	Yes
	59	50	2	30C	No	Yes
Ethmoid sinus*	70	10	5	25C	Yes	Yes
	54	50	2	30C	No	Yes
Sphenoid sinus*	74	10	5	25C	Yes	Yes
	59	50	2	30C	No	Yes
Sinuses*	50	10	5	25C	Yes	Yes
	38	50	2	30C	No	Yes
Mastoid*	65	10	5	25C	Yes	Yes
	50	50	2	30C	No	Yes
Mastoid*	54	10	5	25C	Yes	Yes
	44	50	2	30C	No	Yes
Jaw*	53	10	5	25C	Yes	Yes
	40	50	2	30C	No	Yes

C = Use of cone or cylinder recommended.

TABLE I.—OPERATIVE TECHNIQUE CHART.[1]—(*Continued*)
Trunk

Region	Kv.	Ma.	Time, sec.	Dist., in.	Bucky	Screens
Cervical spine*............	63	10	5	36	Yes	Yes
Cervical spine*............	62	75	½	72	No	Yes
Dorsal spine...............	64	10	20	30	Yes	Yes
Dorsal spine**.............	70	10	5	30	Yes	Yes
Lumbar spine..............	59	10	20	30	Yes	Yes
Lumbar spine..............	77	10	30	30	Yes	Yes
Pelvis....................	56	10	20	30	Yes	Yes
Sternum*.................	70	10	5	30	Yes	Yes
Sternum*.................	63	10	5	30	Yes	Yes
Ribs*....................	70	10	1	30	Yes	Yes
Ribs*....................	58	60	3	30	Yes	Yes
Ribs*....................	75	10	1	30	Yes	Yes

Organs

Region	Kv.	Ma.	Time, sec.	Dist., in.	Bucky	Screens
Chest**...................	68	75	$\frac{1}{10}$	72	No	Yes
Chest**...................	68	75	$\frac{3}{10}$	72	No	Yes
Chest**...................	68	75	$\frac{2}{10}$	48	No	Yes
Heart**..................	68	75	$\frac{1}{10}$	72	No	Yes
Kidney*..................	56	60	2	30	Yes	Yes
Urinary bladder*..........	56	60	2	30	Yes	Yes
Gall bladder*.............	56	60	2	30	Yes	Yes
Stomach*.................	73	60	½	25	Yes	Yes
Stomach*.................	78	60	½	25	Yes	Yes
Stomach*.................	78	60	1	25	Yes	Yes
Colon*...................	68	60	1	30	Yes	Yes
Fetus*...................	76	60	2	30	Yes	Yes

Infants

Region	Kv.	Ma.	Time, sec.	Dist., in.	Bucky	Screens
Wrist....................	40	75	$\frac{1}{20}$	36	No	Yes
Elbow...................	44	75	$\frac{1}{20}$	36	No	Yes
Shoulder.................	48	75	$\frac{1}{20}$	36	No	Yes
Ankle...................	44	75	$\frac{1}{20}$	36	No	Yes
Knee....................	46	75	$\frac{1}{20}$	36	No	Yes
Trunk...................	50	75	$\frac{1}{10}$	36	No	Yes
Chest...................	46	75	$\frac{1}{20}$	36	No	Yes
Skull....................	44	75	$\frac{1}{10}$	30	No	Yes
Sinuses	48	75	$\frac{1}{10}$	30C	No	Yes
Mastoid.................	44	75	$\frac{1}{20}$	25C	No	Yes

[1] 1937 General Electric X-Ray Corp.

"This chart is based upon an adult of average size.

"In this chart, all milliampere values over 10 ma. are for use with the large focal spot.

"The Kv. values given in the chart are to be used simply as a starting point or guide.

"For regions such as sinuses, gall bladder, etc., with or without the Potter-Bucky Diaphragm, the smallest cone available should be used to cover the desired area—particularly for heavy parts without the Potter-Bucky Diaphragm.

"The distance as given on the chart in those instances where a cone or cylinder is recommended,

Industrial X-ray Technique.—In making an industrial radiograph the factors to be considered are (1) thickness and composition of object under examination, and (2) size and shape of the object. There are, naturally, many other influencing factors, but they are mostly small mechanical problems which vary from one piece of work to another and can be solved with a little ingenuity.

1. Thickness and composition of the object determine the voltage, current, and time to be used in making an exposure. In the majority of cases voltage and time are the only factors changed, and the current remains at some predetermined setting; say 5 ma. Many curves have been published to give the proper settings for penetration of "steel," but they are notably unreliable and inaccurate. "Steel" has become a loose, generic term which no longer denotes any specific metal with fixed chemical and metallurgical properties, and it covers a wide range of alloys. Variations in metal densities, atomic properties, X-ray machine calibration, development technique, etc., involve such large exposure differences that it is far better for each individual operator to establish his own exposure charts by the trial-and-error method. After a number of exposures on different alloys, the technician will develop a sense of exposure technique which can then be enhanced by reference to a table of element and alloy densities.

TABLE II.—SPECIFIC GRAVITY OF METALS ENCOUNTERED IN RADIOGRAPHY

Metal	Specific Gravity
Iron (99.94 Fe)	7.86
Iron, cast (94 Fe, 3.5 C, 2.5 Si)	7.00
Stainless steels (90 Fe, 8 Cr, 0.4 Mn, 0.1 C)	7.75
Alleghany metal (Fe, 18 Cr, 8 Ni, Mn, Si, C)	7.86–7.95
Copper (99.9 Cu)	8.50
Brass, ordinary (67 Cu, 33 Zn)	8.40
Aluminum (99.2 Al)	2.71
Nickel (99.5 Ni)	8.86
Nichrome (80 Ni, 20 Cr)	8.50
Monel metal (60 Ni, 33 Cu, 6.5 Fe)	8.90
Lead (93 Pb, 7 Sb)	11.00
Gold, standard Gt. Br. (92 Au, 8 Cu)	17.17
Platinum (90 Pt, 10 Ir)	21.61
Tungsten	14.00

A few of the metals frequently encountered in industrial X-ray work are given in Table II with their composition and specific gravities. The higher the relative gravities are, the higher the X-ray voltage must be to penetrate the metal. Gravities

---

depends on the type of cone available. In any instance, the best results will be obtained when the smallest possible cone is used, according to the area to be covered.

"The procedure changes with the size of cone used. The smaller the cone, the greater the energy required, and the larger the cone the less energy required. However, the improved contrast made possible by the smaller cone, despite the increase in energy necessary, makes its use advisable whenever possible, either with or without the Bucky diaphragm.

"To change the radiographic density for any area, the best results will be obtained if only one factor at a time is changed. The two factors which may be considered variable are voltage and exposure time. Of these two, voltage is the variable factor of preference.

"To change a Potter-Bucky procedure to one without the diaphragm, either deduct approximately 15 kv. or use ¼ the exposure time as given on the chart for Potter-Bucky work. To reverse the procedure, either add 15 kv.p. or use 4 times the exposure time.

"Immobilization of the part should always be provided when practical; sand bags for such parts as extremities, and immobilizing bands for the skull, pelvis, spine, etc.; cones or cylinders for sinuses.

"½ mm. to 1 mm. of aluminum should be used as a filter, with the following exceptions: soft tissue technic in extremity work; radiography without screens; chest.

"For children from 5 to 12 years of age, either a reduction in penetration of approximately 10 kv.p., or ½ the exposure time given on the chart, should be made.

"One star * indicates that the patient should stop breathing.

"Two stars ** indicate that the patient should take a full breath and hold it."

which differ only slightly may be radiographed satisfactorily by changing the time and keeping the voltage constant. By establishing exposure values for a few different metals, by studying the effect of composition on density, and by becoming familiar with various settings on his own X-ray machine, the operator will soon be able to make a good radiograph of almost any object with one trial exposure.

This table shows why lead is used as a shield against X rays. Only gold, platinum, and tungsten are greater X-ray absorbers and the last three are expensive whereas lead is cheap.

2. Size and shape of the object examined are important and are frequently such that they provide the major problem of the work. It is desirable to place the film in its holder as near as possible to the area where defects are likely to occur, and to avoid, in the case of complicated castings and machine parts, interposition of irrelevant sections between film and X-ray tube. Ideal radiographic conditions are those which allow the X-ray beam to pass from the target through the area to be inspected and thence, without interruption, to a film placed perpendicular to the line of the main beam (Fig. 1).

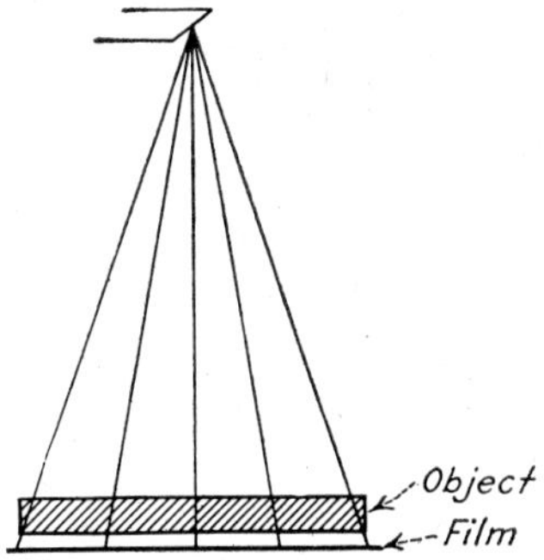

Although this condition is often unattainable, the nearest possible approach should be made. In some cases it is better to place the film other than perpendicularly, to avoid overlapping of undesired shadows on the film (Fig. 2).

Fig. 1.—Diagram illustrating operation of X-ray photography. A source of electrons striking the target produces waves which spread out as indicated by the diverging lines. These waves pass through the object to be radiographed, where they are partially absorbed, and thence to the film where a permanent record is produced.

In the case of curved surfaces care should be taken to center the target and film, and the distance should be such as to permit the whole film to be exposed. Some allowance must also be made for the fact that the ends of the film are farther from the target than the center because of their curvature (Fig. 3).

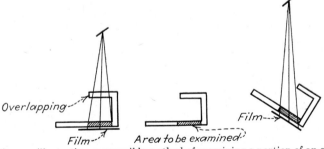

FIG. 2.—Diagram illustrating one possible method of examining a portion of an object having sections which ordinarily would provide some shielding of X rays.

This distance defect may be overcome either by increasing the target-film distance or by shortening the X-ray film. In the first the exposure time is increased to compensate for the distance, and in the second instance more pictures must be made to cover the total area, so that conditions prevailing at the time must decide which is the better course.

In cases where the entire film is not covered by the object some provision must be made to keep scattered radiation from "creeping" in around the edges and utterly ruining the radiograph. In most instances shielding with lead blocks or formed lead sheets will be sufficient, but on oddly shaped objects it is often necessary to resort to a more plastic type of shielding material. There are a number of these on the market, none of which is entirely satisfactory. Were it not for its tendency to amalgamate with some metals and penetrate the crystalline interstices of others, mercury would be an ideal shield where a liquid is needed of high atomic weight. Even so, it has been used on occasion and gives a fine radiograph free from all scattering fog. Various lead salts in solution have been used as has the finely powdered red oxide of lead made into a paste with different oils.

These various shielding materials may also be used as filler where on the same film it is necessary to penetrate two different thicknesses. In some cases, correct exposure for one part will result in a high overexposure of a thinner part. The thinner part is then built up to the same density as the thicker portion.

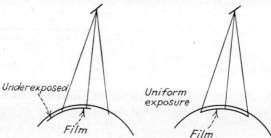

Fig. 3.—For best results in examining curved objects, the film should be symmetrically placed with respect to the source of radiation as shown at the right.

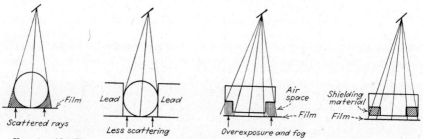

Fig. 4.—Shielding by means of lead blocks will assist in reducing scattered radiation.

With small, easily penetrated objects fluorescent screens are not needed. However, beginning with ¼ in. of steel or its equivalent, exposure times are so prolonged or such a high voltage is necessary that too much time is used for each picture or the final film loses detail due to excessive penetration. At this point it is advisable to resort to use of fluorescent screens, one on each side of the film in a lighttight holder. Care must be taken not to bend the screens for their fluorescent coating is easily cracked, thus introducing errors into the radiograph. A slight curvature is permissible, but where more than this is required to place the screen against the area to be inspected, it is wisest to keep the film flat even if the resulting picture loses something in quality. Where the film holder can be placed against the weld or casting, many simple methods will come to mind for holding it in place and for keeping good contact between screens and film. For example, while examining welding in a large tank, the film may be held against the inner surface by use of a flexible wooden pole slightly longer than the internal diameter of the tank.

Industrial Radiographic Interpretation.—In the interpretation of industrial radiographs, as in medical work, there can be no substitute for experience and observation. It is necessary for the operator to be more or less familiar with industrial processes such as welding, casting, molding, etc., and he should have at least a working knowledge of the fundamentals of metallography. For the beginner a fairly safe rule is as follows: if on the radiographic film of a weld, casting, mold, plate, or other supposedly

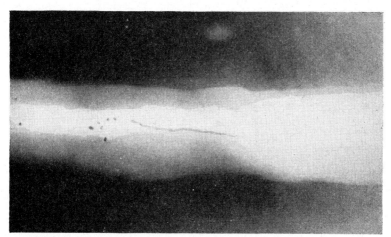

Fig. 5.—Radiograph of welded steel plates showing gas pockets and cracks of faulty weld.

homogeneous material, one or more dark spots or lines appear in an otherwise even field, these areas represent defects.

Example: Fig. 5 is an actual radiograph of two steel plates which have been placed edge to edge and welded together. The dark areas are the plain steel and the light center strip is the weld material which is denser than the surrounding metal. Within this center strip numerous spots and one or more dark lines appear. The spots are small gas pockets while the lines are cracks. This is a faulty weld and, if subjected to

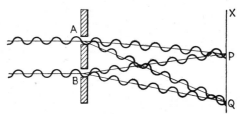

Fig. 6.—Diagram illustrating diffraction of X rays.

high pressures or excessive strain, is likely to fail. This film is fairly representative of the general run of industrial radiographs, the interpretation of which depends on a knowledge of the relative densities involved in the object being inspected.

X-ray Diffraction.—Although X-ray diffraction is not usually classed under radiography, a strict interpretation of the word radiograph would require the inclusion of this application of X rays. A simple explanation of this phenomenon is as follows:

Reference to Fig. 6 shows that a single light beam L divided at pinholes A and B will produce alternate light and dark areas on surface X—points like P, equidistant from A and B will be brightly illuminated by reinforcing similar-phased waves, but points like Q, unequally distant from A and B, will be unlighted due to the arrival there of canceling, out-of-phase waves.

Such reinforcements and cancellations due to single-wavelength light traveling different distances can also be caused by reflecting a beam from surfaces at varying distances. Thus in a system of parallel mirrors a, b, and c, as in Fig. 7, which reflect light of wavelength λ, all waves starting from line $AA'A''$ and ending at X will not have

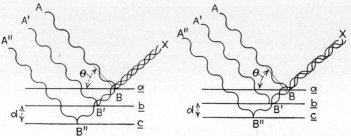

Fig. 7.—Diffraction reinforcements (right) and cancellations (left) of X rays caused by crystal structure.

covered the same distance. If the angle at which the light strikes a mirror is θ and d is the distance between planes, then route $A'B'X$ is longer than route ABX by twice the distance times the sine of angle θ. Therefore, although all waves starting from $AA'A''$ are in phase, they will be in phase on arrival at X only when the distance-difference between them $(2d \sin \theta) = \lambda$, or 2λ, or 3λ, or . . . $n\lambda$. A graphic means of illustrating X-ray diffraction by a single crystal is the combination of Figs. 6 and 7 into

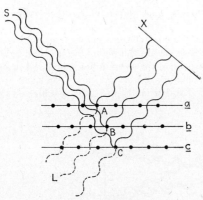

the crystal atom of Fig. 8, a three-dimensional affair with many planes at different angles. A monochromatic X-ray beam, S is reflected from the atom sheets a, b, and c (which compose the crystal) on surface X. As in Fig. 7, those sheets so spaced that X rays are reflected at some whole wavelength distance ahead or behind other rays make a diffraction pattern characteristic of the crystalline. The result is as though the energy beam had come from L (see also Fig. 6) and had been diffracted from pinholes at A, B, and C.

Fig. 8.—Reflections of diffracted X-ray beam coming from S behave as though they came from L and passed through apertures A, B, and C.

Various diffraction methods are used widely in industrial processes to reveal facts about the internal structure of material which could be disclosed in no other way. Analysis of crystal structure in all different types of metals and alloys is a particularly fertile field. This application is also bringing to light fundamental facts in biology, in medicine, and in research into the structure of the atom and its energy relations.

Although widespread application of diffraction methods is relatively new, it is proving a remarkable instrument wherever investigation takes place into the essential processes of nature.

Radiographic Darkroom.—The principles involved in processing X-ray films are the same as in any other photographic procedure, and the ordinary photographic darkroom may be used for X-ray film work. There are, however, certain differences between the two. Developing and fixing solutions made specifically for X-ray films should always be used. The usual process of developing, fixing, and washing is followed, but the times used are different. When the processing factors are correct and the radiographs are found to lack density, it can be assumed that underexposure has taken place, and when the radiographs are too dense, overexposure is indicated. Any change in exposure time should be an increase or decrease of the original factor by about 35 per cent.

After a certain number of films have passed through the solutions, it will be found necessary to add 1 min. to the development time to obtain the desired density. This time, in turn, will have to be augmented by another minute at a later date. While no formula can be given for change of development time, in general, after 100 films 14 by 17 in. have been processed, the development should be raised to 6 min. Smaller

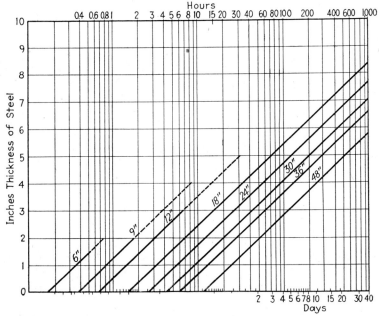

Fig. 9.—Gamma-ray exposure chart for steel of various thickness.

films take correspondingly less life from the solutions, and one 14- by 17-in. film can safely be made to equal three 8- by 10-in. films, two 10 by 12 in., or one 11 by 14 in. plus one 8 by 10 in. Likewise, after fifty 14- by 17-in. films, or equivalent, have been processed, it is wise to increase the time to 7 min. At the end of another fifty units, the solution has about reached the limit of its efficiency and introduction of new solutions should be considered. The life of solutions varies so that the above recommendation should be viewed more as a rough guide than as an absolute formula.

In actual use the tank system, where proper temperature can be controlled by regulating the flowing water around the tanks, is the most efficient system of processing. Here the technique is merely to place the exposed film on a hanger which can be conveniently immersed in developer, rinse water, fixer, and wash water for the predetermined intervals; the hanger should be held flat throughout the procedure. The tray system may be used if a tank installation is not available, although more care must be taken not to scratch or otherwise damage the surface of the film.

Radium Radiography.—In recent years the use of gamma rays from radium as a means of visualizing subsurface faults has received increasing attention in cases where the examined material is too thick to be conveniently penetrated with X rays. Gamma rays are similar in nature to X rays but are of much shorter wavelength than the X rays used in general practice and are therefore able to pass through substances opaque to the X ray. Figure 9 shows a gamma-ray exposure chart for steel.

The apparatus necessary for gamma radiography is extremely simple and does not require the space, trouble, or attention encountered in X radiography. A small capsule container of radioactive material is held rigidly in front of the specimen to be inspected and X-ray films in holders are fastened to the back of the specimen. After the required time has passed, radium and films are removed. It will be found on development of the film that the gamma rays passing through the specimen have recorded, as with the X ray, conditions existing within the sample.

The exposure chart given is applicable for practically any type of steel because gamma radiography errors in exposure time generally amount to a small fraction of the total.

Bibliography

Books:

" X-ray Laboratory Manual," Eastman Kodak Co.
"Handbook of Physics and Chemistry," Chemical Rubber Pub.
GEZELIUS, R. A., and C. W. BRIGGS: "Radium for Industrial Radiography," Radium Chemical Co.
COMPTON and ALLISON: "X-ray in Theory and Experiment," Van Nostrand.
CLARK, G. L.: "Applied X-rays," McGraw.
TERRILL, H. M., and C. T. UREY: "X-ray Technology," Van Nostrand.
POULLIN, V. E.: "Engineering Radiography," G. Bell.

Periodicals:

WOODS, R. C.: Industrial X-ray Practice, *Electronics*, February, 1936.
————: Radium Inspection of Metal Structures, *Iron Age*, July 16, 1936.
————: Details of Industrial X-ray Apparatus, *Iron Age*, Oct. 16, 1936.
X-ray Protection, *Nat. Bur. Standards, Handbook* 15.

APPENDIX A

TABLES OF CONVERSION FACTORS

COMPILED BY BEVERLY DUDLEY

TABLE I.—AVOIRDUPOIS WEIGHT—FOR GENERAL COMMODITIES

Multiply → By / To obtain ↓		Metric				United States and English			
		Milli-grams	Deci-grams	Grams	Kilo-grams	Grains	Drams	Ounces	Pounds
		mg.		g.	kg.	gr.		oz.	lb.
Milligrams	mg.	1	100	1,000	10^6	64.80	3887.93	28,350	453,600
Decigrams		0.01	1	10	10,000	0.6480	38.879	283.5	4,536
Grams	g.	0.001	0.1	1	1,000	0.06480	3.8879	28.35	453.6
Kilograms	kg.	0.000001	0.0001	0.001	1	6.480×10^{-5}	0.003888	0.02835	0.4536
Grains	gr.	0.01543	1.543	15.43	15,430	1	27.34	437.5	7,000
Drams		5.643×10^{-4}	0.05643	0.5643	564.3	0.01667	1	7.292	116.7
Ounces	oz.	3.527×10^{-5}	3.527×10^{-3}	0.03527	35.27	0.002286	0.1371	1	16
Pounds	lb.	2.205×10^{-6}	2.205×10^{-4}	0.002205	2.205	1.429×10^{-4}	0.008571	0.0625	1

TABLE II.—TROY WEIGHT—FOR GEMS AND PRECIOUS METALS

Multiply → By / To Obtain ↓		Metric				United States and English			
		Milli-grams	Deci-grams	Grams	Kilo-grams	Grains	Drams	Ounces	Pounds
		mg.		g.	kg.	gr.		oz.	lb.
Milligrams	mg.	1	100	1,000	10^6	64.80	1,555	31,100	373,200
Decigrams		0.01	1	10	10,000	0.6480	15.55	311.0	3,732
Grams	g.	0.001	0.1	1	1,000	0.06480	1.555	31.10	373.2
Kilograms	kg.	0.000001	0.0001	0.001	1	6.480×10^{-5}	0.001555	0.0311	0.3732
Grains	gr.	0.01543	1.543	15.43	15,430	1	24	480	5,760
Drams		6.430×10^{-4}	0.0643	0.6430	643.0	0.04167	1	20	240
Ounces	oz.	3.215×10^{-4}	0.00325	0.03215	32.15	2.083×10^{-3}	0.05	1	12
Pounds	lb.	2.679×10^{-6}	0.0002679	0.002679	2.679	1.736×10^{-4}	0.004167	0.08333	1

TABLE III.—GENERAL LIQUID MEASURE

Multiply → By / To Obtain ↓	Metric		United States			
	Milli-liters	Liters	Gills	Pints	Quarts	Gallons
	ml.	l.		pt.	qt.	gal.
Milliliters ml.	1	1,000	118.3	473.2	946.4	3,785
Liters l.	0.001	1	0.1183	0.4732	0.9464	3.785
Gills	0.008453	8.453	1	4	8	32
Pints pt.	0.002113	2.113	0.25	1	2	8
Quarts qt.	0.001057	1.057	0.125	0.5	1	4
Gallons gal.	0.0002642	0.2642	0.03125	0.125	0.25	1

TABLE IV.—APOTHECARIES LIQUID MEASURE

Multiply → By / To Obtain ↓	Metric			United States		
	Milli-liters	Centi-liters	Liters	Minims	Fluid drams	Fluid ounces
	ml.		l.			oz.
Milliliters ml.	1	10	1,000	6.161×10^{-2}	3.697	29.57
Centiliters	0.10	1	100	6.161×10^{-3}	0.3697	2.957
Liters l.	0.001	0.01	1	6.161×10^{-5}	0.003697	0.02957
Minims	16.23	162.3	16,230	1	0.01667	0.002083
Fl. drams	0.2705	2.705	270.5	60	1	0.1250
Fl. ounces oz.	0.003382	0.3382	33.82	480	8	1

TABLE V.—LENGTH

Multiply → By / To Obtain ↓	Metric				United States and English			
	Milli-meters	Centi-meters	Deci-meters	Meters	Inches	Feet	Yards	Rods
	mm.	cm.		m.	in.	ft.	yd.	
Millimeters mm.	1	10	100	1,000	25.40	304.8	914.4	5029
Centimeters cm.	0.10	1	10	100	2.540	30.48	91.44	502.9
Decimeters	0.01	0.1	1	10	0.2540	3.048	9.144	50.29
Meters m.	0.001	0.01	0.1	1	0.02540	0.3048	0.9144	5.029
Inches in.	0.03937	0.3937	3.937	39.37	1	12	36	198
Feet ft.	0.003281	0.03281	0.3281	3.281	0.08333	1	3	16.5
Yards yd.	0.001094	0.01094	0.1094	1.094	0.02778	0.3333	1	5.5
Rods	0.0001988	0.001988	0.01988	0.1988	0.005050	0.06060	0.1818	1

TABLE VI.—TEMPERATURE

Fahrenheit	Centigrade	Reaumur	Kelvin or absolute
°F.	°C.	°R.	°K. or °A.
0.0	− 17.8	−14.2	255.2
5.0	− 15.0	−12.0	258.0
10.0	− 12.2	− 9.8	260.8
14.0	− 10.0	− 8.0	263.0
15.0	− 9.4	− 7.6	263.6
20.0	− 6.7	− 5.3	266.3
23.0	− 5.0	− 4.0	268.0
25.0	− 3.9	− 3.1	269.1
30.0	− 1.1	− 0.9	271.9
32.0	0.0	0.0	273.0
35.0	+ 1.7	+ 1.3	274.7
40.0	4.4	3.6	277.4
41.0	5.0	4.0	278.0
45.0	7.2	5.8	280.2
50.0	10.0	8.0	283.0
51.0	10.6	8.4	283.6
51.8	11.0	8.8	284.0
52.0	11.1	8.9	284.1
53.0	11.7	9.3	284.7
53.6	12.0	9.6	285.0
54.0	12.2	9.8	285.2
55.0	12.8	10.2	285.8
55.4	13.0	10.4	286.0
56.0	13.3	10.7	286.3
57.0	13.9	11.1	286.9
57.2	14.0	11.2	287.0
58.0	14.4	11.6	287.4
59.0	15.0	12.0	288.0
60.0	15.6	12.4	288.6
60.8	16.0	12.8	289.0
61.0	16.1	12.9	289.1
62.0	16.7	13.3	289.7
62.6	17.0	13.6	290.0
63.0	17.2	13.8	290.2
64.0	17.8	14.2	290.8
64.4	18.0	14.4	291.0
65.0	18.3	14.7	291.3
66.0	18.9	15.1	291.9
66.2	19.0	15.2	292.0
67.0	19.4	15.6	292.4
68.0	20.0	16.0	293.0
69.0	20.6	16.4	293.6
70.0	21.1	16.9	294.1
71.0	21.7	17.3	294.7
71.6	22.0	17.6	295.0
72.0	22.2	17.8	295.2
73.0	22.8	18.2	295.8
73.4	23.0	18.4	296.0
74.0	23.3	18.7	296.3
75.0	23.9	19.1	296.9
76.0	24.4	19.6	297.4
77.0	25.0	20.0	298.0
78.0	25.6	20.4	298.6
79.0	26.1	20.9	299.1
80.0	26.7	21.3	299.7
85.0	29.4	23.6	302.4

TABLE VI.—TEMPERATURE.—(*Continued*)

Fahrenhe it °F.	Centigrade °C.	Reaumur °R.	Kelvin or absolute °K. or °A.
86.0	30.0	24.0	303.0
90.0	32.2	25.8	305.2
95.0	35.0	28.0	308.0
100.0	37.8	30.2	310.8
104.0	40.0	32.0	313.0
105.0	40.6	32.4	313.6
110.0	43.3	34.7	316.3
113.0	45.0	36.0	318.0
115.0	56.1	36.9	319.1
120.0	48.9	39.1	321.9
122.0	50.0	40.0	323.0
125.0	51.7	41.3	324.7
130.0	54.4	43.6	327.4
131.0	55.0	44.0	328.0
135.0	57.2	45.8	330.2
140.0	60.0	48.0	333.0
145.0	62.8	50.2	335.8
149.0	65.0	52.0	338.0
150.0	65.6	52.4	338.6
155.0	68.3	54.6	341.3
158.0	70.0	56.0	343.0
160.0	71.1	56.9	344.1
165.0	73.9	59.1	346.9
167.0	75.0	60.0	348.0
170.0	76.7	61.3	349.7
175.0	79.4	63.5	352.4
176.0	80.0	64.0	353.0
180.0	82.2	65.8	355.2
185.0	85.0	68.0	358.0
190.0	87.8	70.2	360.8
194.0	90.0	72.0	363.0
195.0	90.6	72.4	363.6
200.0	93.3	74.7	366.3
203.0	95.0	76.0	368.0
205.0	96.1	76.9	369.1
210.0	98.9	79.1	371.3
+212.0	+100.0	+80.0	+373.0

APPENDIX B

APPROXIMATE RELATIVE VALUES FOR SPECIFYING SPEED OF PHOTO-GRAPHIC MATERIALS

A	B	C	D	E	F	G	H	I	J	K	L
Relative speed	Weston	American and British H & D (K = 10)	Continental H & D	Watkins	Wynne	Burroughs Wellcome	American Scheiner	Continental Scheiner	Eder-Hecht	DIN	Ilford
1.00	0.23	5.8	27	10.5	F/21	2.83	1.00	6.00	42.5		
1.25	0.29	7.2	34	13.2	F/23.4	2.24	1.9	6.9	45.0		
1.60	0.37	9.3	44	17.0	F/26.5	1.75	2.9	7.9	47.4		
2.00	0.46	11.6	55	20.5	F/29.5	1.38	3.8	8.8	50.0		
2.50	0.58	14.5	69	26.4	F/33.0	1.10	4.8	9.8	52.0		
3.00	0.69	17.0	83	30.8	F/36.2	0.925	5.5	10.5	54.0		
4.00	0.93	23	111	42.4	F/41.9	0.880	6.7	11.7	57.0		
5.00	1.16	29	135	53.0	F/47.0	0.550	7.6	12.6	59.5	0/10	
6.40	1.48	37	173	68.0	F/53.0	0.425	8.6	13.6	62.0	1/10	
8.00	1.85	46	215	85.0	F/59.3	0.338	9.6	14.5	64.0	2/10	
10.00	2.33	58	270	106	F/66.0	0.270	10.5	15.4	67.0	3/10	
12.5	2.90	72	336	133	F/74.0	0.215	11.4	16.4	69.4	4/10	
16.0	3.70	93	430	171	F/84	0.170	12.4	17.4	72.0	5/10	A
20.0	4.65	116	535	214	F/94	0.135	13.3	18.3	74.0	6/10	
25.0	5.80	145	670	268	F/105	0.108	14.2	19.2	76.5	7/10	B
30.0	6.90	174	810	320	F/115	0.090	15.0	20.0	78.5	8/10	
40.0	9.30	232	1,080	425	F/133	0.068	16.2	21.2	81.5	9/10	
50.0	11.6	290	1,350	535	F/148	0.054	17.1	22.1	83.8	10/10	C
64.0	14.8	371	1,730	685	F/167	0.043	18.1	23.2	86.5	11/10	
80.0	18.5	464	2,170	860	F/187	0.034	19.0	24.1	88.0	12/10	
100.00	23.3	580	2,700	1,070	F/209	0.028	20.0	25.0	92.0	13/10	
125	29.0	725	3,400	1,350	F/234	0.022	20.9	26.0	93.6	14/10	D
160	37.0	930	4,400	1,730	F/265	0.018	22.0	27.0	96.1	15/10	
200	46.5	1,160	5,500	2,170	F/295	0.014	22.9	27.9	98.5	16/10	E
250	58.0	1,450	6,900	2,720	F/330	0.011	23.8	28.8	101.0	17/10	
300	69.0	1,740	8,300	3,300	F/362	0.0092	24.6	29.6	103.0	18/10	
400	93	2,320	11,200	4,400	F/420	0.0088	25.8	30.7	106.0	19/10	
500	116	2,900	14,000	5,500	F/470	0.0055	26.7	31.7	108.0	20/10	F
640	148	3,710	18,000	7,100	F/530	0.00425	27.7	32.7	110.8	21/10	
800	186	4,640	22,500	9,000	F/595	0.00338	28.6	33.6	113.0	22/10	
1,000	232	5,800	28,500	10,700	F/665	0.00370	29.5	34.6	115.5	23/10	

NOTE: It is not possible to make exact comparisons between the various systems of rating speeds, and therefore the above table should be considered only as approximations. The data for the above table were obtained from several sources as listed below. In a few of the columns the values were extended in order to have a more complete set of data.

Recent film speeds published by the Eastman Kodak Co. [see "The Problem of Film Speeds" by Walter Clark, *Photo Technique*, **1**, 12 (1939)] indicate that the Kodak speeds are, numerically, about four or five times the speed as given by the Weston rating. However, the available data are not regarded as being sufficiently complete to warrant listing Kodak film speeds in this tabulation.

A, C, E, F, H, and J. JONES, L. A., "Photographic Sensitometry."

B. Compiled by A. T. Williams.

G. "Wellcome Handbook and Diary" (common fractions have been converted to decimals).

D and I. Values in columns D and I are representative of the continental ratings, which are always higher than the American ratings. The Scheiner ratings usually are from 3 to 6 units higher than the equivalent American speeds. The values given are from Turner, *Brit. J. Phot.*, July 8, 1938.

K. "Handbook of Physics and Chemistry," 21st ed.

L. TURNER, *Brit. J. Phot.*, July 8, 1938.

APPENDIX C

DENSITY-OPACITY-TRANSMISSION CONVERSION FACTORS
COMPILED BY BEVERLY DUDLEY

Density	Opacity	% Transmission
0.00	1.000	100.00
0.01	1.023	97.72
0.02	1.047	95.50
0.03	1.072	93.33
0.04	1.095	91.20
0.05	1.122	89.13
0.06	1.148	87.10
0.07	1.175	85.11
0.08	1.202	83.18
0.09	1.230	81.28
0.10	1.259	79.43
0.11	1.288	77.62
0.12	1.318	75.86
0.13	1.349	74.13
0.14	1.380	72.44
0.15	1.413	70.79
0.16	1.445	69.18
0.17	1.479	67.61
0.18	1.514	66.07
0.19	1.549	64.57
0.20	1.585	63.10
0.21	1.622	61.66
0.22	1.660	60.26
0.23	1.698	58.88
0.24	1.738	57.54
0.25	1.778	56.23
0.26	1.820	54.95
0.27	1.862	53.70
0.28	1.905	52.48
0.29	1.950	51.29
0.30	1.995	50.12
0.31	2.042	48.98
0.32	2.089	47.86
0.33	2.138	46.77
0.34	2.188	45.71
0.35	2.239	44.67
0.36	2.291	43.65
0.37	2.344	42.66
0.38	2.399	41.69
0.39	2.455	40.74
0.40	2.512	39.81
0.41	2.570	38.90
0.42	2.630	38.02
0.43	2.692	37.15
0.44	2.754	36.31
0.45	2.818	35.48

DENSITY-OPACITY-TRANSMISSION CONVERSION FACTORS.—(*Continued*)

Density	Opacity	% Transmission
0.46	2.884	34.67
0.47	2.951	33.88
0.48	2.020	33.11
0.49	3.090	32.36
0.50	3.162	31.62
0.51	3.236	30.90
0.52	3.311	30.20
0.53	3.388	29.51
0.54	3.467	28.84
0.55	3.548	28.18
0.56	3.631	27.54
0.57	3.715	26.92
0.58	3.802	26.30
0.59	3.890	25.70
0.60	3.981	25.12
0.61	4.074	24.55
0.62	4.169	23.99
0.63	4.266	23.44
0.64	4.365	22.91
0.65	4.467	22.39
0.66	4.571	21.88
0.67	4.677	21.38
0.68	4.786	20.89
0.69	4.898	20.42
0.70	5.012	19.95
0.71	5.129	19.50
0.72	5.248	19.05
0.73	5.370	18.62
0.74	5.495	18.20
0.75	5.623	17.78
0.76	5.754	17.38
0.77	5.888	16.98
0.78	6.026	16.60
0.79	6.166	16.22
0.80	6.310	15.85
0.81	6.457	15.49
0.82	6.607	15.14
0.83	6.761	14.79
0.84	6.918	14.45
0.85	7.079	14.13
0.86	7.244	13.80
0.87	7.413	13.49
0.88	7.586	13.18
0.89	7.762	12.88
0.90	7.943	12.59
0.91	8.128	12.30
0.92	8.318	12.02
0.93	8.511	11.75
0.94	8.710	11.48
0.95	8.913	11.22
0.96	9.120	10.96
0.97	9.333	10.72
0.98	9.550	10.47
0.99	9.772	10.23
1.00	10.000	10.000
1.01	10.23	9.772
1.02	10.47	9.550

DENSITY-OPACITY-TRANSMISSION CONVERSION FACTORS.—*(Continued)*

Density	Opacity	% Transmission
1.03	10.72	9.333
1.04	10.95	9.120
1.05	11.22	8.913
1.06	11.48	8.710
1.07	11.75	8.511
1.08	12.02	8.318
1.09	12.30	8.128
1.10	12.59	7.943
1.11	12.88	7.762
1.12	13.18	7.586
1.13	13.49	7.413
1.14	13.80	7.244
1.15	14.13	7.079
1.16	14.45	6.918
1.17	14.79	6.761
1.18	15.14	6.607
1.19	15.49	6.457
1.20	15.85	6.310
1.21	16.22	6.165
1.22	16.60	6.026
1.23	16.98	5.888
1.24	17.38	5.754
1.25	17.78	5.623
1.26	18.20	5.495
1.27	18.62	5.370
1.28	19.05	5.248
1.29	19.50	5.129
1.30	19.95	5.012
1.31	20.42	4.898
1.32	20.89	4.786
1.33	21.38	4.677
1.34	21.88	4.571
1.35	22.39	4.467
1.36	22.91	4.365
1.37	23.44	4.266
1.38	23.99	4.169
1.39	24.55	4.074
1.40	25.12	3.981
1.41	25.70	3.891
1.42	26.30	3.802
1.43	26.92	3.715
1.44	27.54	3.631
1.45	28.18	3.541
1.46	28.84	3.467
1.47	29.51	3.388
1.48	30.20	3.311
1.49	30.90	3.236
1.50	31.62	3.162
1.51	32.36	3.090
1.52	33.11	3.020
1.53	33.88	2.951
1.54	34.67	2.884
1.55	35.48	2.818
1.56	36.31	2.754
1.57	37.15	2.692
1.58	38.02	2.630
1.59	38.90	2.570

DENSITY-OPACITY-TRANSMISSION CONVERSION FACTORS.—(*Continued*)

Density	Opacity	% Transmission
1.60	39.81	2.512
1.61	40.74	2.455
1.62	41.69	2.399
1.63	42.66	2.344
1.64	43.65	2.291
1.65	44.67	2.239
1.66	45.71	2.188
1.67	46.77	2.138
1.68	47.86	2.089
1.69	48.98	2.042
1.70	50.12	1.995
1.71	51.29	1.950
1.72	52.48	1.905
1.73	53.70	1.862
1.74	54.95	1.820
1.75	56.23	1.778
1.76	57.54	1.738
1.77	58.88	1.698
1.78	60.26	1.660
1.79	61.66	1.622
1.80	63.10	1.585
1.81	64.57	1.549
1.82	66.07	1.514
1.83	67.61	1.479
1.84	69.18	1.445
1.85	70.79	1.413
1.86	72.44	1.380
1.87	74.13	1.349
1.88	75.86	1.318
1.89	77.62	1.288
1.90	79.43	1.259
1.91	81.28	1.230
1.92	83.18	1.202
1.93	85.11	1.175
1.94	87.10	1.148
1.95	89.13	1.122
1.96	91.20	1.096
1.97	93.33	1.072
1.98	95.50	1.047
1.99	97.72	1.023
2.00	100.00	1.000
2.01	102.3	0.9772
2.02	104.7	0.9550
2.03	107.2	0.9333
2.04	109.6	0.9120
2.05	112.2	0.8913
2.06	114.8	0.8710
2.07	117.5	0.8511
2.08	120.2	0.8313
2.09	123.0	0.8128
2.10	125.9	0.7943
2.11	128.8	0.7762
2.12	131.8	0.7586
2.13	134.9	0.7413
2.14	138.0	0.7244
2.15	141.3	0.7079
2.16	144.5	0.6918

DENSITY-OPACITY-TRANSMISSION CONVERSION FACTORS.—(*Continued*)

Density	Opacity	% Transmission
2.17	147.9	0.6761
2.18	151.4	0.6607
2.19	154.9	0.6457
2.20	158.5	0.6310
2.21	162.2	0.6166
2.22	166.0	0.6026
2.23	169.8	0.5888
2.24	173.8	0.5754
2.25	177.8	0.5623
2.26	182.0	0.5495
2.27	186.2	0.5370
2.28	190.5	0.5248
2.29	195.0	0.5129
2.30	199.5	0.5012
2.31	204.2	0.4898
2.32	208.9	0.4786
2.33	213.8	0.4677
2.34	218.8	0.4571
2.35	223.9	0.4467
2.36	229.1	0.4365
2.37	234.4	0.4266
2.38	239.9	0.4169
2.39	245.5	0.4074
2.40	251.2	0.3981
2.41	257.0	0.3890
2.42	263.0	0.3802
2.43	269.2	0.3715
2.44	275.4	0.3631
2.45	281.8	0.3548
2.46	288.4	0.3467
2.47	295.1	0.3388
2.48	302.0	0.3311
2.49	309.0	0.3236
2.50	316.2	0.3162
2.51	323.6	0.3090
2.52	331.1	0.3020
2.53	338.8	0.2951
2.54	346.7	0.2884
2.55	354.8	0.2818
2.56	363.1	0.2754
2.57	371.5	0.2692
2.58	380.2	0.2630
2.59	389.0	0.2540
2.60	398.1	0.2512
2.61	407.4	0.2455
2.62	416.9	0.2399
2.63	426.6	0.2344
2.64	436.5	0.2291
2.65	446.7	0.2239
2.66	457.1	0.2188
2.67	467.7	0.2138
2.68	478.6	0.2089
2.69	489.8	0.2042
2.70	501.2	0.1995
2.71	512.9	0.1950
2.72	524.8	0.1905
2.73	537.0	0.1862

DENSITY-OPACITY-TRANSMISSION CONVERSION FACTORS.—*(Continued)*

Density	Opacity	% Transmission
2.74	549.5	0.1820
2.75	562.3	0.1778
2.76	575.4	0.1738
2.77	588.8	0.1698
2.78	602.6	0.1660
2.79	616.6	0.1622
2.80	631.0	0.1585
2.81	645.7	0.1549
2.82	660.7	0.1514
2.83	676.1	0.1479
2.84	691.8	0.1445
2.85	707.9	0.1413
2.86	724.4	0.1380
2.87	741.3	0.1349
2.88	758.6	0.1318
2.89	776.2	0.1288
2.90	794.3	0.1259
2.91	812.8	0.1230
2.92	831.8	0.1202
2.93	851.1	0.1175
2.94	871.0	0.1148
2.95	891.3	0.1122
2.96	912.0	0.1096
2.97	933.3	0.1072
2.98	955.0	0.1047
2.99	977.2	0.1023
3.00	1000.0	0.100

NOTE:—The values of density, opacity, and transmission given in Appendix C are the values most commonly used in photography. The table may be easily extended for other values, which, however, are not frequently encountered. Every time another digit is added in the density column, the corresponding opacity is increased ten times its value by moving the decimal point one place to the right; the transmission is reduced to 10 % of its values by moving the decimal point one place to the left. Thus, density 0.3 has opacity of 1.995 and transmission of 0.5012, whereas density 1.3 has opacity of 19.95 and transmission of 0.05012.

APPENDIX D

FILTER FACTORS

TABLE I.—FILTER FACTORS FOR WRATTEN FILTERS AND EASTMAN FILMS

Filter	Ordinary		Ortho-chromatic		Pan A		Pan B		Pan C	
	Day	Tung	Day	Tung	Day	Tung	Day	Tung	Day	Tung
Aero 1	4	3	2	1.5	2	....	1.5	....	1.5	
Aero 2	18	14	2.5	2	2.5	....	2	....	2	
Kodak Color	8	5	2	1.5	2	1.5	1.5	1.5	1.5	1.5
K 1	4	3	2	1.5	2	1.5	1.5	1.5	1.5	1.5
K 1½	8	5	2	1.5	2	1.5	1.5	1.5	1.5	1.5
K2	12	9	2.5	2	2.5	2	2	1.5	2	1.5
K3	20	15	2.5	2	2.5	2	2	1.5	2	1.5
No. 12	....	....	3	2.5	3	2.5	2	1.5	2	1.5
G	....	....	5	3	4.5	3	3	2	2.5	2
B	....	....	8	4.5	12	9	6	6	7	6
A	....	....	....	....	8	4	4	4	4	2
C4	6	6	9	12	10	5	12	24	12	24
C5	2.5	2.5	3	3.5	3	5	5	10	5	10
E	....	....	...	....	7	3.5	5	3.5	3.5	2
F	....	....	...	....	12	5	15	8	8	4
L	....	....	...	....	20	30	24	40	24	40
N	....	....	...	....	14	10	7	7	9	8
X1	....	....	....	....	....	....	....	3	5	
X2	....	....	....	....	....	....	....	....	....	5

ORDINARY MATERIALS
Process films and plates
Commercial film
X-Ray film
Safety Positive film
Sound Recording film
Eastman 33 plates
Eastman 40 plates
Eastman Universal plates
Eastman Post Card plates
Eastman Lantern Slide plates

ORTHOCHROMATIC MATERIALS[1]
Super Speed Portrait Ortho (AH)
Ortho Press film
Verichrome
Wratten Metallographic plates
Polychrome plates
Ortho Press plates
Par Speed Portrait sheet film
Commercial Ortho sheet film
Super Ortho-Press sheet film
Commercial Ortho plates
S. C. Ortho plates
D. C. Ortho plates
Eastman 50 plates

PAN A
Commercial Panchromatic film
Process Panchromatic film
Recordak film

PAN B
Portrait Panchromatic film
Micro-file Panchromatic Safety film
Super XX 35-mm. and Bantam films
Panatomic X roll films and film packs
Panatomic X sheet film

Super XX Panchromatic sheet film
Super XX Panchromatic Negative 16-mm. Safety film
Wratten Tricolor Panchromatic plates
Wratten Panchromatic plates
Wratten Process Panchromatic plates
Wratten M plates
Wratten Contrast Thin Coated plates
Panatomic X
Plus X

PAN C
SS Pan sheet film
SS Pan Aero film
SS Pan Cine Negative film
Panatomic X Aero film
Super XX Panchromatic Aero film
Panatomic Bantam film
Super X Cine Negative Panchromatic film
Super XX Panchromatic roll films and film packs
Super Panchro-Press sheet film
Tri X Panchromatic sheet film
Cine Kodak 8 Panchromatic film
Cine Kodak Panchromatic Negative film
Cine-Kodak Safety film
Cine-Kodak Super X Panchromatic Safety film
Cine-Kodak Super XX Panchromatic Safety film
Cine-Kodak Eight Super X Panchromatic Safety film
Background Panchromatic Motion Pciture Negative film
Plus X Panchromatic Motion Picture Negative film
Super XX Panchromatic Motion Picture Negative film
Background Cine Negative Panchromatic
Fine Grain Duplicating Negative Panchromatic
Panchro Press film

[1] Filter factors for orthochromatic materials not listed will vary only slightly from those given for the above films and plates.

TABLE II.—FILTER FACTORS FOR LEITZ YELLOW AND GREEN FILTERS

The yellow filters serve to render correctly the colors in conjunction with the more or less sensitized film. For instance, they enable one to capture cloud effects when photographing landscapes. The filter factor for the exposure becomes less in proportion to the degree of sensitivity of the film.
The filter factors for the exposure are approximately as follows:

Type of film	Daylight										Artificial light					
	U.-V. Filter	Filter No. 0	Filter No. 1	Filter No. 2	Filter No. 3	Green filter	Orange-red filter	Red filt., light	Red filt., medium	Red filt., heavy	Filter No. 0	Filter No. 1	Filter No. 2	Filter No. 3	Orange-red filter	Green filter
Agfa:																
Plenachrome	2	2	3	6	8	6	2.8				1.4	1.6	2	2	2.5	2.5
Finopan	1.3	1.4	1.6	2	2	3	4				1.4	1.5	1.8	2	2.5	2.5
Supreme	1.2	1.5	1.8	2.2	2.2	3	2.8				1.2	1.3	1.5	1.8	2.5	6
Superpan Rev	1.2	1.5	1.8	2.2	2.8	5	2.8				1.2	1.4	1.4	1.6	2.8	3
Ultra-Speed Pan	1.3	1.4	1.6	2	2	3		16								
Infra Red								10	15	20						
DuPont:																
Micropan	1.5	1.5	1.7	2.5	3	3	5				1.3	1.5	1.7	2.5	3.5	2
Superior	1.5	1.5	1.7	2	3	4	4				1.3	1.5	1.8	2	3	3
Parpan	1.5	1.5	1.7	2	3	4	5				1.3		1.8	2	4	3
Infra-D								32	32	64						
E. Kodak:																
Panatomic X	1.5	1.5	1.5	2	3	3	4				1.5	1.5	1.5	2	3	2.5
Plus X	1.5	1.5	1.5	2	3	3	4	15			1.5	1.5	1.5	2	3	2.5
Super XX	1.5	1.5	1.5	2	3	3	4	15			1.5	1.5	1.5	2	3	2.5
Infra Red								20	30	30						
Gevaert:																
Panchromosa	2.8	2.1	2.3	2.9	3.2	2.9	6				1.3	1.6	1.5	2.7	4	1.8
Express Superchrome	1.8	2	3.3	6.5	8.5						1.8	2.1	3.5	4		
Microgram	2	2	2	2.9	3.2	2.9	6				1.3	1.6	1.5	2.7	4	1.8
Perutz:																
Neo-Persenso	2.2	1.9	2.7	4.1	5.5	3.2	6				1.5	2.1	2.3	3		
Perpantic	2	1.8	2.8	3.5	4	3.2	5				1.5	1.6	1.8	2.5	3	2.4
Peromnia	2.2	1.8	2.2	2.5	3.5	3.2	6				1.5	1.7	1.7	2.8	3.5	2.4
Pergrano	2.2	1.8	2.8	3	4	3.2					1.7	1.6		2.5	3	2.4
Mimosa Extrema	1.8	1.7	3.4	4.7	6	4.5						2.1	2.9	3		

The values have been computed by E. Leitz. The latitude between the figures given in the table is due to the various factors which affect the time of exposure, e.g., composition of the light, variations in the emulsion, mode of development, etc.
The figures given in the table under "Daylight" factors are correct for white light, e.g., blue sky with white clouds. The exposure should be increased by approximately one-half when the light is dark blue, e.g., in summer from about 11 A.M. to 2 P.M. (blue sky without any noteworthy clouds).

TABLE III.—Filter Factors for Zeiss Ikon and Carl Zeiss Filters[1]

Filter	Color	Agfa Ansco Corporation — Orthochromatic No. 1 (D / T)	No. 2 (D / T)	Panchromatic No. 3 (D / T)	No. 4 (D / T)	No. 5 (D / T)	No. 6 (D / T)	No. 7 (D / T)	No. 8 (D / T)	No. 9 (D / T)	Infra-red No. 10 (D / T)	Defender Photo Supply Co. — Orthochromatic No. 11 (D / T)	No. 12 (D / T)	Panchromatic No. 13 (D / T)
G-0	Ultra violet	1.4 / 1.4	1.4 / 1.4	1.4 / 1.2	1.4 / 1.2	1.4 / 1.2	1.4 / 1.2	1.4 / 1.2	1.4 / 1.2	1.4 / 1.2	…	1.5 / 1.2	1.0 / 1.0	1.1 / 1.0
G-1	Light yellow	2.0 / 1.6	2.0 / 1.8	1.6 / 1.4	1.6 / 1.4	1.6 / 1.4	1.6 / 1.4	1.8 / 1.6	1.6 / 1.4	1.4 / 1.4	…	2.0 / 1.3	3.0 / 2.0	1.5 / 1.5
G-2	Medium yellow	2.5 / 2.0		2.0 / 1.8	2.0 / 1.8	1.8 / 1.8	2.0 / 1.8	2.5 / 1.8	2.0 / 2.0	2.0 / 1.8	…	2.5 / 1.5	5.3 / 3.5	1.7 / 1.6
G-3	Dark yellow	4.0 / 2.5	16 / 8	2.5 / 2.0	2.5 / 2.0	2.5 / 2.0	2.5 / 2.0	3.0 / 2.4	3.0 / 2.4	2.5 / 2.5	…	4.5 / 2.0	30.0 / 15.0	2.6 / 1.8
G-4	Orange	12 / 8	64 / 32	2.5 / 2.4	2.5 / 2.4	2.6 / 2.4	2.5 / 2.4	3.0 / 3.0	3.0 / 3.0	3.0 / 3.0	…	8.5 / 2.0	125.0 / 35.0	3.3 / 2.0
B-40	Blue	2.0 / …	8 / 8	2.0 / 1.4	2.0 / 1.4	1.4 / 1.4	1.4 / 1.4	2.0 / 1.5	1.6 / 1.5	2.5 / 1.6	…	12.0 / 2.5	6.0 / 3.0	1.2 / 1.8
GR-55	Yellow green	3.0 / 3.0	8 / …	2.0 / 2.0	2.0 / 2.0	3.0 / 2.0	2.0 / 2.0	4.0 / 2.5	3.0 / 3.0	3.0 / 3.0	…	6.0 / 1.2	5.0 / 5.0	2.2 / 1.6
GR-50	Green	3.0 / 3.0	8 / 5	2.8 / 4	3.0 / 3.0	3 / 3	2.5 / 2	4.0 / 4	4.0 / 4	3.0 / 3.0	…	6.5 / 1.4	5.0 / …	2.2 / 2.2
R-10	Light red	…	…	…	6.0 / …	…	…	…	8 / …	…	*	… / 2.0	…	3.0 / 2.2
R-15	Medium red	…	…	…	…	…	…	…	…	…	*	…	…	25.0 / 13.0
R-20	Dark red	…	…	…	…	…	…	…	…	…	*	…	…	1500.0 / 800.0
R-30	Infra red	…	…	…	…	…	…	…	…	…	†	…	…	…
Zeiss L	Light yellow	1.6 / 1.4	4 / 4	1.6 / 1.4	1.6 / 1.4	1.6 / 1.6	1.4 / 1.4	1.8 / 1.6	1.6 / 1.6	1.6 / 1.4	…	4.5 / 1.7	17.0 / 7.0	2.2 / 1.2
Zeiss D	Dark yellow	2.5 / 2.0	…	2.0 / 2.0	2.0 / 1.8	3.0 / 1.8	1.8 / 1.8	2.5 / 1.8	2.0 / 1.8	3.0 / 3.0	…	5.5 / 2.0	37.0 / 9.0	2.7 / 1.5
Zeiss G	Green	4.0 / 3.0	…	3.0 / 3.0	3.0 / …	6 / 3	4.0 / 3	4.0 / 4	3.5 / 5	4.0 / 3.0	…	…	…	…
Zeiss R	Red	…	…	22 / 8	8 / 4	…	…	16 / 8	12 / 6	…	*	…	…	4.0 / …
Bernotar	Polarizer	4.0 / 4.0	4.0 / …	2.5 / 2.5	2.5 / 2.5	2.5 / …	2.5 / …	…	…	…	…	4.0 / 3.0	4.0 / 5.5	4.0 / 2.5

* The filters checked are suitable for infrared correction with Agfa-Ansco Infrared film, and all require exposure of 1/25 sec. f/3.5, bright sun.

† Use 50 times more exposure than for the R-10 filter.

[1] Zeiss Mag., June, 1937, partially revised to September, 1939.

AGFA ANSCO CORPORATION

No. 1. ORTHOCHROMATIC
Plenachrome Roll Film
Superplenachrome Pack & Roll Film
Finegrain Plenachrome
Supersensitive Plenachrome
Super Plenachrome Press
Commercial Ortho
No. 2. ORTHOCHROMATIC
Portrait Standard
No. 3. PANCHROMATIC
Superpan Supreme
No. 4. PANCHROMATIC
Finopan

No. 5. PANCHROMATIC
Ultra Speed Panchromatic
No. 6. PANCHROMATIC
Superpan Press
Triple S Panchromatic
No. 7. PANCHROMATIC
Commercial Panchromatic
No. 8. PANCHROMATIC
Superpan Portrait
No. 9. PANCHROMATIC
Supersensitive Panchromatic
No. 10. INFRA RED
Infra Red, Type A

DEFENDER PHOTO SUPPLY COMPANY

No. 11. ORTHOCHROMATIC
X-F Orthochromatic Film
No. 12. ORTHOCHROMATIC
Portrait HGS Film
Portrait Film

No. 13. PANCHROMATIC
X-F Panchromatic Film
Fine Grain Panchromatic Film
Panchromatic Process Film

DUPONT FILM MANUFACTURING CORPORATION

No. 14. PANCHROMATIC
35 mm Superior Film
No. 15. PANCHROMATIC
35 mm. Micropan Film
No. 16. INFRA RED
35 mm. Infra-red Film

TABLE III.—FILTER FACTORS FOR ZEISS IKON AND CARL ZEISS FILTERS.—(*Continued*)

Filter	Color	No. 14 D	No. 14 T	No. 15 D	No. 15 T	No. 16 D	No. 16 T	No. 17 D	No. 17 T	No. 18 D	No. 18 T	No. 19 D	No. 19 T	No. 20 D	No. 20 T	No. 21 D	No. 21 T	No. 22 D	No. 22 T	No. 23 D	No. 23 T	No. 24 D	No. 24 T
		\<Panchromatic (DuPont)\>				\<Infra red\>		\<Ordinary\>		\<Orthochromatic (Eastman Kodak)\>						\<Panchromatic (Eastman Kodak)\>						\<Infra red\>	
G-0	Ultra violet	1.0		1.5				5.0	4.0	2.0	1.5	2.0	1.5	2.0	1.5	1.5	1.5	1.5	1.5	1.5	1.5		
G-1	Light yellow	1.4	1.4	1.5	1.4			8.0	6.0	2.5	2.0	2.5	2.0	2.5	2.0	2.0	1.5	1.5	1.5	1.5	1.5		
G-2	Medium yellow	1.4	1.4	1.9	1.5			12.0	9.0	5.0	4.0	3.5	2.5	2.5	2.0	2.5	2.0	2.0	1.5	2.0	1.5		
G-3	Dark yellow	1.5	1.5	2.0	1.6	14		20.0	15.0	9.0	5.0	5.0	3.0	2.5	2.0	2.5	2.0	2.0	1.5	2.0	1.5		
G-4	Orange	2.1	1.6	2.9	1.9					20.0	10.0	9.0	7.0	4.0	2.5	4.0	2.5	2.5	2.0	2.0	2.0		
B-40	Blue							1.2	1.5	1.3	1.5	1.3	1.5	1.5	2.0	2.0	3.0	2.0	3.0	2.0	3.0		
GR-55	Yellow green	1.9	1.6	2.0	1.6					7.0	5.0	3.0	2.0	3.0	2.0	2.0	1.5	1.5	1.5	1.5	1.5		
GR-50	Green	2.1	2.0	2.9	2.4					8.0	5.0	6.0	4.0	6.0	4.0	6.0	4.0	3.5	3.0	5.0	4.0		
R-10	Light red	9.5	4.8	25.0	13.0	30										12.0	5.0	15.0	8.0	8.0	4.0	15	2.0
R-15	Medium red					30																15	2.0
R-20	Dark red					30																25	3.0
R-30	Infra red					2000																40	5.0
Zeiss L	Light yellow	1.4	1.4	2.0	1.6			8.0	5.0	4.0	3.0	3.0	2.0	2.0	1.5	2.0	1.5	1.5	1.5	1.5	1.5		
Zeiss D	Dark yellow	1.5	1.5	2.0	1.7					9.0	5.0	5.0	3.0	2.5	2.0	2.5	2.0	2.0	1.5	2.0	1.5		
Zeiss G																							
Zeiss R																							
Bernotar	Polarizer							4.0	3.5	3.0	3.0	3.0	2.5	2.5	2.5	2.5	2.5	2.5	2.0	2.5	2.0		

EASTMAN KODAK COMPANY

No. 17. ORDINARY MATERIALS

Process Plates and Films
Commercial Film
Motion Picture Positive Film
33 Plates
40 Plates
Universal Plates

No. 18. ORTHOCHROMATIC—Type A

Regular N. C. Film
Par Speed Portrait Film
Commercial Ortho Film
Polychrome Plate
Commercial Plates
S. C. Ortho Plates
D. C. Ortho Plates

No. 19. ORTHOCHROMATIC—Type B

Super Speed Portrait Film
50 Plates

No. 20. ORTHOCHROMATIC—Type C

Super Speed Portrait Ortho (AH)
Ortho Press Film and Plates
Verichrome

No. 21. PANCHROMATIC—Type A

Commercial Panchromatic Film
Process Panchromatic film
Cine Kodak Panchromatic Film

No. 22. PANCHROMATIC—Type B

Super Sensitive Panchromatic Roll Film
Portrait Panchromatic Film
Wratten Panchromatic Plates
Wratten Process Panchromatic Plates

No. 23. PANCHROMATIC—Type C

Super Sensitive Panchromatic Cut Film
Super Sensitive Panchromatic Aero Film
Super Sensitive Panchromatic Cine Negative Film
Super Sensitive Panchromatic Cine Kodak Film

Panatomic Roll Film
Panatomic Safety Cut Film
Panatomic Aero Film
Super X Cine Negative Panchromatic Film
Cine Kodak 8 Panchromatic Film
Cine Kodak Panchromatic Negative Film
Background Cine Negative Panchromatic
Panchro Press Film
Wratten Hypersensitive Panchromatic Plates

No. 24. INFRA RED

Cine Negative Pan K
Aero Pan K
Retain Pan K

APPENDIX E

WESTON FILM-SPEED RATINGS

The film-speed ratings given in this appendix are those compiled by the Weston Electrical Instrument Co. In conjunction with suitably calibrated exposure meters these ratings may be used to determine correct exposure. However, it should be recognized that processing conditions and errors in shutter speed or aperture may make it necessary to deviate from these speed ratings in order to obtain the best negatives. T indicates tentative value subject to further test.

FILM LISTING

The number given for each film in the listing on this sheet represents a group of three consecutive emulsion speeds. For the sake of simplicity, the group number listed is the mean value for the group, and is the rating to use for those who have had no previous experience with the film or who do not know what developer will be used.

The following table shows the group number and the three emulsion speeds that it represents.

Daylight

Speed Range	Group Number
160—200—250	200
80—100—125	100
40— 50— 64	50
20— 24— 32	24
10— 12— 16	12
5— 6— 8	6
2.5— 3— 4	3
1.2—1.5— 2	1.5

Tungsten

Speed Range	Group Number
100—125—160	125
50— 64— 80	64
24— 32— 40	32
12— 16— 20	16
6— 8— 10	8
3— 4— 5	4
1.5— 2—2.5	2

ROLLS AND PACKS

Daylight Group No.		Tungsten Group No.
	Agfa	
100	Superpan Press	64
50T	Super Plenachrome	32T
24	Finopan	16
24	Plenachrome	16
12	Standard	4
24	Superpan	16
	Eastman	
100	Super XX	64
24	Verichrome	16
24	Panatomic X	16
12	N. C.	4
	Gevaert	
24	Panchromosa	16
12	Express Superchrome	4

Miniature Camera Films

Daylight Group No.		Tungsten Group No.
	Agfa	
100	Ultra Speed Pan	64
50	Superpan Supreme	32
24	F. G. Plenachrome	8
24	Finopan	16
24	F. G. Rev. Superpan	16
	DuPont	
24	Superior	16
12	F. G. ParPan	8
6	Micropan	4
	Eastman	
100	Super XX	64
50	Plus X	32
24	Super X	16
24	Panatomic X	16
24	Panatomic	16
	Microfile	0.25
	Gevaert	
12	Express Superchrome	4
12	Panchromosa	8
12	Panchromosa Micrograin	4
	Perutz	
12	Peromnia	8
12	Neo Persenso	4
12	Perpantic	8
6	Pergrano	4

Portrait and Commercial

Daylight Group No.		Tungsten Group No.
	Agfa	
100	Triple S Pan	64
50	Isopan	32
24	S. S. Pan	16
24	Superpan Portrait	16
24	S. S. Plena	16
24	Commercial Pan	16
12	Portrait	8
12	Commercial Ortho	8
12	Commercial	4
	Defender	
24	X. F. Pan	16
24	X. F. Ortho	16
24	Portrait H. G. S.	16
24	Pentagon	16
24	F. G. Pan	16
24	Seed 27 Plate	8
12	Portrait	4
12	Commercial	8
12	Seed L Ortho Plate	8
12	Seed 26 X Plate	8
12	Seed L NH Plate	8
12	Stanley Reg. Plate	8
12	Stanley Ex. Imp. Plate	8
12	Standard Orthonon Plate	8
6	Seed 23 Plate	2
	Eastman	
100T	Tri-X Panchromatic	64T
100T	Ortho-X	64T
50T	Super XX	32T
24	S. S. Ortho port	16
24	S. S. Pan	16
24	Portrait Pan	16

Daylight Group No.		Tungsten Group No.
24	Commercial Pan	16
24	Par Speed Portrait	8
24	Panatomic X	16
12	Commercial Ortho	8
12	Commercial	4
Plates		
24	Polycrome Plate	8
50	W & W Tri Color Plate	32
24	50 Plate	16
24	40 Plate	8
24	D. C. Ortho Plate	8
24	S. C. Ortho Plate	8
24	33 Plate	4
24	Universal Plate	8
12	W & W Pan Plate	8
12	Postcard Plate	4
24	Commercial Plate	4
12	W & W M Plate	8
6	W & W Metallographic Plate	4
	Gevaert	
24	Studio High Speed	16
24	Superchrome	8
24	Ultra Panchro Plate	16
12	Studio Ultra Panchro	8
12	Commercial Ortho	8
12	Commercial	4
12	Sensima Ortho Plate	4
6	Super Chromosa Plate	4
	Hammer	
24	Tru Tone Pan	8
24	Portrait Ortho	4
24	Special Plates	8
24	Super Sensitive Ortho Plate	8
12	Commercial Pan	8
12	Medium Commercial Ortho	2
12	Medium Commercial	2
12	Commercial Pan Plate	4
12	Extra Fast Plate	4
12	Medium Commercial Ortho Plate	4
12	Medium Commercial Plate	2
6	Soft Gradation Pan Plate	2
3	Slow	1
3	Slow Ortho	1
3	Slow Plate	1
3	Slow Ortho Plate	1

PRESS FILMS
Agfa

100	Superpan Press	64
100	Super Plenachrome Press	32

Defender

50	X. F. Ortho Press	16
50	X. F. Pan Press	32

Eastman

100	Super Panchro Press	64
100	Super Ortho Press	32
50	Panchro Press	32
50	Ortho Press	16
50	Ortho Press Plate	16

Gevaert

24	Super Press Plate	16
24	Ultra Panchro Press	16

Daylight Group No.		Tungsten Group No.
	Hammer	
24	Super Ortho Press..	4
	PROCESS FILM	
3	Agfa Process...	2
3	Defender Process...	1
3	Defender Process Pan...	2
3	Eastman Process..	1
3	Eastman Process Pan..	1
1.5	Eastman Process Plates.......................................	0.5
3	Hammer Process..	1
3	Hammer Process Pan Plate.....................................	2

16 mm. M. P. FILM

Film for motion-picture cameras is processed by the manufacturer. Consequently, this film is rated in single numbers only.

Daylight Group No.		Tungsten Group No.
	Agfa	
100T	Triple S. Superpan Rev..	64T
24	Superpan Rev..	16
24	Hypan Rev..	16
16	Panchromatic Rev..	12
12	F. G. Plenachrome Rev.......................................	
64	Superpan Supreme Neg..	40
24	Finopan Neg...	16
	Du Pont	
32	Superior Pan Neg...	20
12	Regular Pan Neg...	8
	Eastman	
100	Super XX Pan Rev..	64
24	Super X Pan...	16
12	Cine' Kodak Safety...	8
100	*Measurement..	64

* For production study.

	Gevaert	
16	Ortho...	6
24	Panchro Super Rev...	16
12	F. G. Panchro Rev...	8

8 mm. M. P. FILM

8	Filmopan...	5
8	Keystone K-8..	5
	Eastman	
8	Cine' Kodak Reg. Pan..	5

RATINGS FOR COLOR FILMS

Since color film must be processed under carefully controlled conditions and, also, since exposure must be exact in order to obtain proper color rendition, color film is rated in single numbers only and not in blocks.

KODACHROME

	Daylight	Artificial
Roll Film		
8, 16, 35 mm. Regular...	8	3*
8, 16, 35 mm. Type A...	8*	12
Professional Film		
Daylight Type...	5	
Type B...	4†	6††

* With filter.
† Exposed through Wratten Filter No. 85B.
†† Used in Mazda only.

DUFAYCOLOR

Roll Film	Daylight	Artificial
Daylight (no filter)	8	
Daylight (with daylight green filter)	6	
Photoflood or Photoflash (1A filter)	...	3
Mazda (1B filter)	...	2

Above values include the filters recommended by the manufacturer.

TENTATIVE RATINGS FOR DUFAYCOLOR CUT FILMS

	Daylight	Artificial
Daylight (1D Filter)	6	
Daylight (3D Filter) in Photoflood	...	3
Daylight (4D Filter) in Mazda	...	3
Photoflood (1PF Filter)	4	
Photoflood (3PF Filter) in Photoflood	...	4
Photoflood (4PF Filter) in Mazda	...	2

DEFENDER

	Daylight	Artificial
Dupac	6	12
Tripac	1.5	3

AUTHOR INDEX

855

SUBJECT INDEX